EIGHTH EDITION

CRIMINAL JUSTICE IN AMERICA

George F. Cole
University of Connecticut

Christopher E. Smith
Michigan State University

Christina DeJong
Michigan State University

CENGAGE
Learning

Australia • Brazil • Mexico • Singapore • United Kingdom • United States

Criminal Justice in America, **Eighth Edition**
George F. Cole, Christopher E. Smith,
Christina DeJong

Product Director: Marta Lee-Perriard

Senior Product Manager: Carolyn Henderson
Meier

Senior Content Developer: Shelley Murphy

Product Assistant: Stephen Lagos

Media Developer: Ting Jian Yap

Senior Marketing Manager: Kara Kindstrom

Senior Content Project Manager: Christy Frame

Art Director: Brenda Carmichael,
Lumina Datamatics

Senior Manufacturing Planner: Judy Inouye

Production Service: Malvine Litten,
LEAP Publishing Services Inc.

Photo Development: Sarah Evertson

Photo Researcher: Priya Subbrayal,
Lumina Datamatics

Text Researcher: Nandhini Srinivasagopalan,
Lumina Datamatics

Copy Editor: Maggie Jarpay

Text and Cover Designer: Brenda Carmichael,
Lumina Datamatics

Cover Images: prison cell: bigjohn36/iStock
/Thinkstock; US Supreme Court building:
© Dave Newman/Shutterstock.com; police
badge: Tetra Images/Superstock;
eagle: Greg Newington/Peter Arnold
/Getty Images

Composition: Cenveo® Publisher Services

For product information and technology assistance, contact us at
Cengage Learning Customer & Sales Support, 1-800-354-9706.

For permission to use material from this text or product,
submit all requests online at **www.cengage.com/permissions.**
Further permissions questions can be e-mailed to
permissionrequest@cengage.com.

Library of Congress Control Number: 2014946325

ISBN: 978-1-305-26106-8

Cengage Learning
20 Channel Center Street
Boston, MA 02210
USA

Cengage Learning is a leading provider of customized learning solutions with office locations around the globe, including Singapore, the United Kingdom, Australia, Mexico, Brazil, and Japan. Locate your local office at:
www.cengage.com/global.

Cengage Learning products are represented in Canada by Nelson Education, Ltd.

To learn more about Cengage Learning Solutions, visit **www.cengage.com.**

Purchase any of our products at your local college store or at our preferred online store **www.cengagebrain.com.**

Unless otherwise noted, all content is © 2016 Cengage Learning.

Printed in the United States of America
Print Number: 01   Print Year: 2014

George F. Cole is Professor Emeritus of Political Science at the University of Connecticut. A specialist in the administration of criminal justice, he has published extensively on such topics as prosecution, courts, and corrections. George Cole is also coauthor with Christopher Smith and Christina DeJong of *The American System of Criminal Justice*, coauthor with Todd Clear and Michael Reisig of *American Corrections*, and coauthor with Marc Gertz and Amy Bunger of *The Criminal Justice System: Politics and Policies*. He developed and directed the graduate corrections program at the University of Connecticut and was a Fellow at the National Institute of Justice (1988). Among his other accomplishments, he has been granted two awards under the Fulbright-Hays Program to conduct criminal justice research in England and the former Yugoslavia. In 1995 he was named a Fellow of the Academy of Criminal Justice Sciences for distinguished teaching and research.

Trained as a lawyer and social scientist, **Christopher E. Smith**, J.D., Ph.D., is Professor of Criminal Justice at Michigan State University, where he teaches courses on criminal justice policy, courts, corrections, and law. He was named as the recipient of the "Outstanding Teaching Award" for the Michigan State University College of Social Science in 2012. In addition to writing more than 100 scholarly articles, he is the author of more than 20 books, including several other titles with Cengage: *Criminal Procedure*; *Law and Contemporary Corrections*; *Courts, Politics, and the Judicial Process*; *The Changing Supreme Court: Constitutional Rights and Liberties* with Thomas R. Hensley and Joyce A. Baugh; *Courts and Public Policy*; *Politics in Constitutional Law*; and *Courts and the Poor*.

Christina DeJong, Ph.D., is Associate Professor of Criminal Justice and Director of the Center for Integrative Studies in Social Science at Michigan State University. She earned her degrees at the University of Texas and the University of Maryland. At Michigan State, she is a noted researcher and award-winning teacher for a variety of criminology topics, including recidivism, violence against women, and police–community relations. She is the coauthor of *The Supreme Court, Crime, and the Ideal of Equal Justice*, and numerous articles in such journals as *Justice Quarterly*, *Criminology*, *Women and Criminal Justice*, and *Violence and Victims*.

BRIEF CONTENTS

FEATURES

CAREERS IN CRIMINAL JUSTICE

COMPARATIVE PERSPECTIVE

THE CRIMINAL JUSTICE PROCESS

CASES CITED

Criminal Justice in America, Eighth Edition, is designed for instructors seeking a textbook that provides students a thorough introduction to the dynamics of the American system of criminal justice without overwhelming them. The text is an offspring of *The American System of Criminal Justice*, which has been used by more than half a million students over the course of its 14 editions. But much has changed in the 30 years since the first edition of *The American System of Criminal Justice* was published. And that is exactly why we created *Criminal Justice in America*—a briefer, more applied, student-centered introduction to the American system of criminal justice. In creating this text, we did not merely drop a few chapters, combine others, and limit the graphic elements to reduce page count, however. We started from scratch. So while *Criminal Justice in America* relies on the research and conceptual framework of the larger text, it is not overly theoretical; throughout the book, examples from today's headlines are used to link the concepts and information to real-life criminal justice situations. And while the focus of *Criminal Justice in America* is just as interdisciplinary as the comprehensive book's focus is, it is less encyclopedic and benefits from added career-based material; international and comparative coverage; skill-building writing exercises; and up-to-the-minute coverage of technology, terrorism, homeland security, cyber crime, evidence-based practices, and other current topics.

The Approach of This Text

Three key assumptions about the nature of American criminal justice as a discipline and the way the introductory course should be taught run throughout the book.

1. *Criminal justice involves public policies* that are developed within the political framework of the democratic process.
2. *The concept of social system is an essential tool* for explaining and analyzing the way criminal justice is administered and practiced.
3. *American values provide the foundation on which criminal justice is based.*

With concerns about terrorism and civil liberties at the forefront of the national agenda, basic American values—individual liberty, equality, fairness, and the rule of law—need to be emphasized.

This book's approach has met with a high degree of acceptance and might be called the dominant paradigm in criminal justice education. Criminal justice is interdisciplinary, with criminology, sociology, law, history, psychology, and political science contributing to the field. The three themes of public policy, social system, and American values help place the research contributions of these disciplines in a context that allows students to better understand the dynamics of criminal justice.

Organization

The Eighth Edition is organized to introduce important fundamental concepts, use those concepts in presenting the important institutional segments of the justice system (police, courts, corrections), and then highlight important contemporary issues concerning reentry from prison, the use of technology, and juvenile justice. The organization of the book is designed to provide comprehensive coverage of the criminal justice system that follows an appropriate sequence, stimulates student interest, and illuminates contemporary issues and problems. The 15-chapter structure of the book creates an opportunity for instructors to move at a steady pace of approximately one chapter per week in the typical length of an academic semester.

Part One of the Eighth Edition presents three chapters that introduce core concepts of the criminal justice system, describe the nature and extent of crime, and supply a framework for understanding the role of law in defining crime and protecting individuals' rights.

Three chapters on police compose Part Two. Here the Eighth Edition builds upon the core concepts in Part One to describe and examine the history, functions, and organization of policing. One chapter examines contemporary issues affecting police, including choices about patrol strategies and delivery of services, the challenges of homeland security, and the increasing importance of private security. The legal issues surrounding police authority to conduct searches and question suspects are covered in a separate chapter. Part Two also examines issues concerning civic accountability and the abuse of police authority.

The focus of the chapters in Part Three is on the courts, plea bargaining, and adjudication. One chapter discusses the important roles of judges, prosecutors, and defense attorneys. Other chapters examine the bail process, plea bargaining, and trials. The final chapter in Part Three describes the sentencing process, including the forms and purposes of punishment.

Part Four concerns corrections and includes material on corrections history and prisoners' rights. One chapter covers detailed aspects of incarceration and prison society. A separate chapter presents probation and intermediate sanctions.

Part Five covers special issues in criminal justice, and the chapter on reentry and parole completes the community corrections coverage introduced in the final chapter of Part Four. Separate chapters examine the rapid changes in use of technology by all institutions within the criminal justice system. The final chapter examines juvenile justice and contemporary debates about appropriate punishment and treatment for youthful offenders.

New to the Eighth Edition

This edition encompasses important revisions in content and presentation. Users of the Eighth Edition will find many significant changes. In particular, we have expanded our coverage of evidence-based practices and policies to cover new developments and applications in policing, courts, and corrections. There are now Policy Debate features in every chapter that illuminate important contemporary issues and challenge students to analyze arguments on each side of these debates. Topically, there is new coverage of transnational crime, human trafficking, elderly crime victims, government surveillance, justice reinvestment, and lethal injection methods of execution. Amid significant budget cuts affecting criminal justice agencies at all levels of government, we have integrated discussions of the impacts of these budget reductions into topics concerning actors and agencies across the justice system. Throughout the book, we have increased our coverage of technology, homeland security, and cyber crime, reflecting the growing importance of these subjects in the study of criminal justice. In addition, new topics are covered in "Close Up," "The Policy Debate," and "Evidence-Based Practice and Policy" boxes that focus on such contemporary issues as research on police identification procedures, problem-solving courts, jury instructions, gun control policy, and privatization of prison health care. The remainder of this section outlines the major content changes in the book and then examines the elements in each chapter that are new to this Eighth Edition.

Enhanced Coverage

Expanded Coverage of Evidence-Based Practice and Policy   The Eighth Edition greatly expands coverage of evidence-based practices through box features in

most chapters. The most significant development affecting all segments of the criminal justice system is the new and ever-increasing focus on evidence-based policies and practices. The incorporation of research-driven decisions about policy and practice helps criminal justice officials to make the most effective use of their scarce and sometimes shrinking resources in addressing the important problems that they face. Evidence-based practices are often discussed primarily in terms of using police resources to combat crime (for example, targeting "hot spots" in the community and using new technology), but students need to be aware that evidence-based practices are also being used elsewhere in the system, such as prisons, probation, and reentry to help address the current goal of reducing expensive prison populations and more effectively placing offenders successfully in the community. For each feature, there is attention to students' need to recognize the challenges faced by criminal justice officials when trying to implement new evidence-based practices, especially when those practices are not consistent with the habits and beliefs of police officers, corrections officers, and others working directly in the field of criminal justice. Thus, each box feature asks the students to think about challenges faced by administrators in implementing evidence-based practices.

Expanded Coverage of Policy Debates Within Criminal Justice   Students can hone their analytical abilities by examining policy debates and evaluating competing arguments about important issues. The Eighth Edition expands the use of this pedagogical method and applies it to a policy debate within each chapter. The expanded coverage includes attention to the legalization of marijuana, the use of volunteers as law enforcement officers, the use of aerial drones by police agencies, judicially mandated prison reform, privatization of prison health care, and the use of individual body cameras by police officers.

Expanded Coverage of Technology and Cyber Crime   Rapidly expanding methods of cyber crime are imposing extraordinarily significant costs on governments, businesses, and individuals worldwide. To fully understand the ramifications of this misuse of technology, criminal justice students need to be aware of the challenges in addressing forms of criminal behavior that are continuously shifting and adapting with each technological innovation. In addition, law enforcement officials are incorporating new technologies to combat crime, including predictive software to guide deployment of officers, expanded technological capabilities in police vehicles, and gunshot detection technology.

Focus on the Effects of Budget Cuts on Criminal Justice Agencies   Integrated within the chapters are discussions and examples of the impact of budget cuts on police, courts, and corrections. Attention is directed toward police departments that must make difficult choices when personnel cutbacks reduce their ability to provide services. Similar issues affect other segments of the justice system as, for example, financial considerations drive efforts to reduce prison populations at a time when states are less able to fund beneficial reentry programs. By emphasizing the current budgetary environment, the material helps students to understand the connections between criminal justice agencies and broader government issues and to appreciate the specific problems currently facing police chiefs and other administrators who must make tough choices about how to use limited resources.

Chapter-by-Chapter Changes

- **Chapter 1,** "The Criminal Justice System," opens with a new vignette concerning the highly publicized trial and acquittal of George Zimmerman, the private citizen who followed and shot Trayvon Martin in the racially charged case that drew national attention. The case illustrates the various stages of the justice process. The chapter discusses the growing importance of evidence-based policies and practices. There is a new "Evidence-Based Practice and Policy" feature that examines drug policy and options for treatment and decriminalization. There is also a new "The Policy Debate" feature on federalism debates concerning whether drug policy should be controlled by the federal government or the individual states.

- **Chapter 2,** "Crime and Crime Causation," begins with a new vignette concerning the movie theater shooting in Florida when two patrons argued about the use of a cell phone in the theater prior to a movie. That crime is contrasted with the example of a woman arrested for identity theft and tax fraud to challenge students to consider the causes of crime and whether different kinds of causes may be at work for different crimes, situations, and offenders. The chapter contains new material on transnational crime, human trafficking, routine activities, explanations of crime, legalization of marijuana, and recent controversies about politically motivated crimes involving the unauthorized release of secret government documents.

- **Chapter 3,** "Criminal Justice and the Rule of Law," opens with a new vignette describing the use of the insanity defense by James Holmes, the shooter in the Colorado movie theater who killed 12 people and injured 70 others. Because the insanity defense was raised, the case illuminates issues of criminal responsibility and legal defense. New to this edition are other recent examples that illustrate various points of law, including a schizophrenic man's confession to a murder that he did not commit and Michael Dunn's self-defense claim in shooting Jordan Davis in a Florida parking lot after an argument over loud music. The chapter includes recent decisions by the U.S. Supreme Court, including two cases concerning defense attorneys' responsibilities in plea bargaining (*Missouri v. Frye*, 2012; *Lafler v. Cooper*, 2012). The chapter concludes with a new "Question of Ethics" that examines a warrantless police search when officers knocked on the door of an apartment upon smelling marijuana and then justified their uninvited entry with the claim that they thought the apartment's occupants might be destroying criminal evidence.

- **Chapter 4,** "Police," opens with a description of the events leading to the 2013 shooting deaths of two Santa Cruz, California, police officers. This vignette effectively illustrates the unexpected dangers that law enforcement officers face every day. The chapter contains new material on evidence-based policing and intelligence-led policing. Material on the use of volunteer law enforcement officers is presented in the new format of a "Policy Debate" feature. A new "Evidence-Based Practice and Policy" feature examines how research can develop practices to protect police officers' well-being. A new "Close Up" examines potential conflicts of interest when police officers earn outside income.

- **Chapter 5,** "Policing: Contemporary Issues and Challenges," presents a new opening vignette concerning the tragic mass shooting at the Newtown, Connecticut, elementary school. There is new material on such topics as racial disparities in police stops and government data collection as part of homeland security programs. The new "Evidence-Based Practice and Policy" feature examines the translation of research into practice for the use of police patrol in crime prevention. A new "Policy Debate" feature examines the use of aerial drones for domestic law enforcement purposes.

- **Chapter 6,** "Police and Law," opens with the facts underlying the Supreme Court's decision in *Florida v. Jardines* (2013) concerning a police officer's warrantless use of a drug-sniffing dog at the front door of a house. A new "Close Up" feature examines Supreme Court justices' divided opinions and reasoning in *Missouri v. McNeely* (2013), the case that limited police officers' authority to automatically obtain blood samples from suspected drunk drivers. A new "Evidence-Based Practice and Policy" feature examines social science studies concerning identification procedures, such as lineups, and new research-based methods for reducing the risks of mistaken identifications of criminal suspects. A new "Question of Ethics" feature examines reports about New York City police officers making false arrests in order to gain extra overtime pay. There is also new material on recent Supreme Court decisions: *Bailey v. United States*

(2013) concerning the detention of suspects while a home is searched, *Maryland v. King* (2013) concerning the acquisition of DNA samples from arrestees, *Florence v. Board of Chosen Freeholders* (2012) concerning strip searches of arrestees at jails, and *United States v. Jones* (2012) concerning warrantless use of a GPS tracking device on a drug suspect's vehicle.

- **Chapter 7,** "Courts and Adjudication," has a new opening vignette about the highly publicized case of Ariel Castro, the Cleveland man who kidnapped three women and held them as prisoners for a decade while he physically abused them. New material on problem-solving courts is presented in a new "Close Up" feature. Material on the accountability of prosecutors is presented in the format of a new "Policy Debate" feature. There is new material on the impact of budget cuts on indigent defense and court decisions concerning right to counsel. The new "Question of Ethics" feature concerns controversial statements made by judges in courtrooms, including the use of profanity and criticisms of lawyers for failing to donate money to judges' political campaigns.

- **Chapter 8,** "Pretrial Procedures, Plea Bargaining, and the Criminal Trial," uses an opening scenario that focuses on the 2013 trial of a University of Montana football star who was accused of rape. There is new material on bail and examples of bail bondsmen convicted of crimes for bribing justice system officials. A new "What Americans Think" feature shows the results of a 2013 public opinion poll concerning Americans' views about juries. A new "Policy Debate" feature examines whether peremptory challenges should be elimnnated from the jury selection process. Proposed reforms in the process for giving jury instructions at the close of trials are presented in a new "Evidence-Based Practice and Policy" feature. The new "Question of Ethics" feature highlights concerns about plea bargaining agreements, including provisions that bar defendants from later raising issues of prosecutorial misconduct and ineffective assistance of counsel by defense attorneys.

- **Chapter 9,** "Punishment and Sentencing," begins with a new opening vignette on the 2013 sentences imposed in the high-profile tax crime cases of singer Lauryn Hill and actor Stephen Baldwin. The significant differences in their sentences, as well as a comparison with the sentence imposed on movie star Wesley Snipes in an earlier tax case, serve to illuminate several issues about severity and fairness in sentencing. New material is presented concerning the contemporary issues with the drugs used for lethal injections as well as the latest cases of exonerations of wrongly convicted individuals. A new "What Americans Think" features a public opinion poll on Americans' views on capital punishment. The new "Evidence-Based Practice and Policy" feature examines issues concerning gun control laws. The new "Question of Ethics" feature concerns the 2014 probation sentence given to a wealthy teenager who killed four people while driving drunk.

- **Chapter 10,** "Corrections," There is new material on the racially discriminatory use of leased convict labor in American corrections history. A new "Evidence-Based Practice and Policy" feature examines the challenges of jail management. The new "Close Up" feature illuminates the Supreme Court's controversial decision in *Brown v. Plata* (2011) that mandated a reduction in state prison populations in order to address deficiencies in overcrowded prison facilities and services for medical care and mental illness treatment. The new "Policy Debate" feature explores controversies about the proper role of judges in examining prison problems and ordering remedies. The new "Question of Ethics" feature focuses on a judge's orders for specific drug-testing requirements for probationers when the jobs of his wife and son were both tied to the private, profit-seeking companies that handled the court-mandated drug testing. In addition, there is new material on prisoners' and detainees' rights concerning religion, searches, and grounds for lawsuits.

- **Chapter 11,** "Incarceration and Prison Society," begins with an illustrative comparison showing the similarities in the typical daily prison schedule at Alcatraz 50 years ago and a contemporary prison in North Carolina. There is new material on the recruitment and pay for corrections officers, including a comparison of salaries in Texas and California in 2014. A new "Policy Debate" examines the privatization of prison health care. New material presents a program in Illinois to foster connections between imprisoned mothers and their children. There is also new material about a 2014 proposal in New York to resume state funding for college courses in prison. A new "Question of Ethics" examines problems related to criminal activities by incarcerated offenders using cell phones that were smuggled into institutions by corrections officers.

- **Chapter 12,** "Probation and Intermediate Sanctions" presents a new opening vignette on the latest issues with probation compliance and sanctions concerning singer Chris Brown and actress Lindsay Lohan. There is new material on the federal Justice Reinvestment Initiative to encourage the use of money saved from reducing prison populations for reinvesting in community-based alternatives to prison. A new "What Americans Think" shows a 2014 public opinion survey on Americans' attitudes toward the punishment of nonviolent drug offenders. There is new material on several topics, including the philosophy of community justice programs and problems with the use of electronic monitoring of offenders. The new "Evidence-Based Practice and Policy" feature concerns probation and community corrections. The new "Policy Debate" feature illuminates conflicts and challenges in siting community corrections centers in the face of fears and opposition by residents of local neighborhoods.

- **Chapter 13,** "Reentry into the Community," opens with a vignette that highlights reentry programs in New Orleans and Anchorage. The chapter presents new information on U.S. Attorney General Eric Holder's effort to examine reentry issues as they affect a range of public policy issues beyond public safety. There is also new material on the impact of budget cuts on reentry programs as well discussion of the reemphasis on parole officer's "social worker" role to enhance parole success. There is new material on the trend toward the increasing frequency of granting parole while also reducing the frequency of parole revocations. The new "Evidence-Based Practice and Policy" feature focuses on suggestions by the Justice Policy Institute for approaches that states can use to enhance the effectiveness of parole and reentry.

- **Chapter 14,** "Technology and Criminal Justice," presents a new opening vignette concerning the use of technology to identify and apprehend the surviving suspect in the 2013 Boston Marathon bombing. There are numerous new examples of technology and crime: the 2014 security breach in Target stores' computer systems; the 2014 arrests of individuals in India, China, and Romania, as well as their American customers, through international law enforcement cooperation to stop an email hacking operation; the 2013 development of a new $100 bill to counteract counterfeiting efforts by the North Korean government and others; and the 2013 Supreme Court decision approving taking DNA samples from arrestees (*Maryland v. King,* 2013). The chapter contains new material on updated technology in police patrol vehicles, including 2014 examples from Wyoming and Tennessee. There is also new material on the use of predictive software by police for crime prevention efforts in deploying law enforcement resources. The new "Close Up" feature examines gunshot detection technology. The new "Policy Debate" feature concerns the use of individual body cameras by police officers, including individual officers' resistance to the impact of the surveillance technology on their daily activities.

- **Chapter 15,** "Juvenile Justice," provides a new opening vignette concerning the highly publicized Steubenville, Ohio, rape case that involved high school football players who circulated videos of the crime. The chapter contains new material on juvenile diversion programs in North Carolina and the holding of juveniles in the Baltimore City Detention Center. A new "What Americans Think" examines public attitude about sentences for homicide offenders. A new "Close Up" feature illustrates a teen court program as an alternative to the formal justice system process of criminal charges against juveniles. The new "Question of Ethics" feature discusses the use of pepper spray as a control mechanism in juvenile detention facilities in California.

Study and Review Aids

To help students identify and master core concepts, *Criminal Justice in America* provides several study and review aids in each chapter:

- *Chapter outlines* preview the structure of each chapter.
- *Opening vignettes* introduce the chapter topic with a high-interest, real-life case or illustrative discussion of a major policy issue, enhancing the book's relevancy for today's student.
- *Learning Objectives* highlight the chapter's key topics and themes and serve as a road map for readers.
- *Checkpoints* throughout each chapter allow students to test themselves on content and get immediate feedback to help them assess their understanding of concepts as they progress through the chapter.
- End-of-chapter *Summaries* and *Questions for Review* reinforce key concepts and provide further checks on learning.
- *Key Terms and Cases* are listed at the end of each chapter; these are defined throughout the text in the margins and included in the Glossary.

Promoting Understanding

Aided by the features just described, diligent students can master the essential content of the introductory course. While such mastery is no small achievement, most instructors aim higher. They want students to complete this course with the ability to take a more thoughtful and critical approach to issues of crime and justice. *Criminal Justice in America*, Eighth Edition, provides several features that help students learn how to think about the field.

- **Stop & Analyze** This feature follows each set of Checkpoint critical-thinking questions and asks students to concretely articulate arguments and analytical conclusions about issues relevant to the preceding section of the text.
- **Close Ups and Other Real-Life Examples** Understanding criminal justice in a purely theoretical way does not give students a balanced understanding of the field. The wealth of examples in this book shows how theory plays out in practice and what the human implications of policies and procedures are. In addition to the many illustrations in the text, the "Close Up" features in each chapter draw on newspaper articles, court decisions, first-person accounts, and other current sources.
- **A Question of Ethics: Think, Discuss, Write** In the criminal justice system, decisions must be made within the framework of law but also be consistent with the ethical norms of American society. At the end of each chapter, completely revamped boxes entitled "A Question of Ethics: Think, Discuss, Write" use actual news reports on the justice system to place students in the context of decision makers faced with a problem involving ethics. Students become aware of the many ethical dilemmas that criminal justice personnel must deal with and the types of questions they may have to answer if they assume a role in the system. Moreover, they are challenged to offer solutions that administrators might employ in using training, supervision, or other approaches to reduce behavior problems by justice system employees.
- **Evidence-Based Practice and Policy** The most significant and expanding development in criminal justice today is the effort to identify and implement policies and practices that are based on the results of high-quality research. These new boxed features throughout the book highlight the opportunities and challenges of applying evidence-based approaches to policing, courts, and corrections. Each feature challenges students to consider the impediments to implementation as practitioners may not wish to change their customary practices or they

may adhere to beliefs about effective policies that are not supported by research studies.

- **What Americans Think** Public opinion plays an important role in the policy-making process in a democracy. As such, we present the opinions of Americans on controversial criminal justice issues, as collected through surveys.

- **The Policy Debate** This edition includes boxes presenting important policy issues for student discussion and debate. In each, we describe an issue such as aggressive policing or the death penalty, outline its pros and cons, and then ask students to decide which policy they think the United States should adopt. Now this feature appears in each chapter in order to utilize this teaching tool to help develop students' critical-thinking skills.

- **Careers in Criminal Justice** The topical focus on career opportunities is primarily intended to help students think about the wide range of occupational possibilities in criminal justice. As they examine the qualifications and career path of an actual criminal justice professional, students gain insights about who plays what role in the criminal justice system. Each professional featured provides an insightful comment on the challenges of his or her particular occupation.

- **Criminal Justice: Myth & Reality** Through the examination of widely held beliefs about criminal justice, students can look critically at the actual complexity or unexpected consequences of various policies and practices. By addressing viewpoints that many students themselves hold, students are encouraged to question assumptions and seek information before drawing conclusions.

- **Comparative Perspective** The globalization of crime and the need for international cooperation in criminal justice require that students be aware of criminal justice issues and institutions in other countries. Moreover, American students can gain additional perspective on their own system by contrasting the United States with other countries. The "Comparative Perspective" feature, included in each section of the text, presents such diverse topics as the role of the defense attorney in Russia, pretrial detention in the Philippines, and the use of day fines in Europe.

- **Inside the Criminal Justice System & Beyond** Many students have limited first-hand knowledge of what it is like to be "processed" by the criminal justice system. A hallmark of *Criminal Justice in America* is this essay by Chuck Terry that is presented on the book's companion website. Terry, a college professor and criminal justice scholar, served time in prison for drug offenses as a young man. Terry's moving story provides a rare insider's look at the steps in the criminal justice process.

Supplements

A number of supplements are provided by Cengage Learning to help instructors use *Criminal Justice in America* in their courses and to aid students in preparing for exams. Supplements are available to qualified adopters. Please consult your local sales representative for details.

To access additional course materials, please visit **www.cengagebrain.com**. At the CengageBrain.com home page, search for the ISBN of your title (from the back cover of your book), using the search box at the top of the page. This will take you to the product page where these resources can be found.

To get access, visit CengageBrain.com.

MindTap Criminal Justice **MindTap** from Cengage Learning represents a new approach to a highly personalized, online learning platform. A fully online learning solution, MindTap combines all of a student's learning tools—readings, multimedia, activities, and assessments into a singular Learning Path that guides the student through the curriculum. Instructors personalize the experience by customizing the presentation of these learning tools for their students, allowing instructors to seamlessly introduce their own content into the Learning Path via "apps" that integrate into the MindTap platform. Additionally, MindTap provides interoperability with major Learning Management Systems (LMS) via support for open industry standards and fosters partnerships with third-party educational application providers to provide a highly collaborative, engaging, and personalized learning experience.

Instructor's Resource Manual with Lesson Plans and Test Bank   Revised by Chuck Hantz of Des Moines Area Community College, the manual includes learning objectives, key terms, a detailed chapter outline, a chapter summary, lesson plans, discussion topics, student activities, "What If" scenarios, media tools, a sample syllabus, and an expanded test bank with 30 percent more questions than the prior edition. The learning objectives are correlated with the discussion topics, student activities, and media tools.

Each chapter of the test bank contains questions in multiple-choice, true/false, completion, essay, and new critical thinking formats, with a full answer key. The test bank is coded to the learning objectives that appear in the main text, and includes the section in the main text where the answers can be found. Finally, each question in the test bank has been carefully reviewed by experienced criminal justice instructors for quality, accuracy, and content coverage so instructors can be sure they are working with an assessment and grading resource of the highest caliber.

Cengage Learning Testing Powered by Cognero   This assessment software is a flexible, online system that allows you to import, edit, and manipulate test bank content from the *Criminal Justice in America* test bank or elsewhere, including your own favorite test questions; create multiple test versions in an instant; and deliver tests from your LMS, your classroom, or wherever you want.

PowerPoint® Lectures   Helping you make your lectures more engaging while effectively reaching your visually oriented students, these handy Microsoft PowerPoint® slides, developed by Diane Evett of Pensacola State College, outline the chapters of the main text in a classroom-ready presentation. The PowerPoint® slides are updated to reflect the content and organization of the new edition of the text, are tagged by chapter learning objective, and feature some additional examples and real-world cases for application and discussion.

A Group Effort

No one can be an expert on every aspect of the criminal justice system. Authors need help in covering new developments and ensuring that research findings are correctly interpreted. The many criminal justice students and instructors who have used previous editions of *Criminal Justice in America* have contributed abundantly to this edition. Their comments provided crucial practical feedback. Others gave us their comments personally when we lectured in criminal justice classes around the country.

Many others have helped us as well. Chief among them was Senior Product Manager Carolyn Henderson Meier, who is very supportive of our efforts. Senior Content Developer Shelley Murphy contributed invaluable ideas and tremendous organizational skills as we revised the book. The project has benefited much from the attention of Senior Content Project Manager Christy Frame. As copy editor, Maggie Jarpay made valuable contributions to improving the effectiveness of our presentation. Marianne Miller made useful suggestions in her role as proofreader. Malvine Litten's managerial skills helped to successfully oversee the project from manuscript submission to the bound book. Brenda Carmichael of Lumina Datamatics designed the interior of the book. Finally, the following individuals contributed valuable comments and suggestions for this edition:

Desire' J.M. Anastasia, Metropolitan State University of Denver
Andre L. Barnes, City College of San Francisco
Robert Barnes, SUNY Westchester Community College
Curt Blakely, Truman State University
Kristen K. Bowen, Florida A & M University
Kenton J. Burns, South Plains College
Mark A. Byington, Jefferson College
Brian E. Cranny, Greenville Technical College
Barbara A. Crowson, Norwich University
Anthony Dangelantonio, Keene State College
Melchor C. de Guzman, The College at Brockport, SUNY
Peter Fenton, Kennesaw State University
Colin P. Gallagher, Wichita Area Technical College
Brian J. Gorman, Towson University
Michele Grillo, Monmouth University
Brittany Hayes, John Jay College
John E. Hertel, St. Louis Community College
Carly Hilinski-Rosick, Grand Valley State University
Susan S. Hodge, University of North Carolina at Charlotte
Daniel L. Lawson, City College of San Francisco
John Mabry, University of Central Oklahoma
Tamara D. Madensen, University of Nevada, Las Vegas
Shana Mell, Virginia Commonwealth University
Eric Metchik, Salem State University
Nathan Moran, Midwestern State University
Barry "Lynn" Parker, Palo Alto College
Rebecca Pfeffer, University of Houston-Downtown
Melissa L. Ricketts, Shippensburg University of Pennsylvania
Marny Rivera, University of Alaska, Anchorage
Martin D. Schwartz, George Washington University
Patrick L. Shade, Edison Community College
Susan Thomas, University of Tennessee Chattanooga
Suzanne Youngblood, Lancaster Campus, Harrisburg Area Community College

Ultimately, however, the full responsibility for the book is ours alone. We hope you will benefit from it, and we welcome your comments.

George F. Cole   georgefrasercole@gmail.com

Christopher E. Smith   smithc28@msu.edu

Christina DeJong   dejongc@msu.edu

1 The Criminal Justice System

LEARNING OBJECTIVES

1. Name the goals of the criminal justice system.
2. Identify the different responsibilities of federal and state criminal justice operations.
3. Analyze criminal justice from a systems perspective.
4. Identify the authority and relationships of the main criminal justice agencies, and list the steps in the decision-making process for criminal cases.
5. Explain the criminal justice "wedding cake" concept as well as the due process and crime control models.
6. Name the possible causes of racial disparities in criminal justice.

The case captured the attention of the nation, bringing together debated issues about race, crime, gun rights, and self-defense. People across the country awaited the verdict as the six jurors in Seminole County, Florida, deliberated about the fate of George Zimmerman. The 28-year-old Zimmerman faced second-degree murder and manslaughter charges for the shooting death of 17-year-old Trayvon Martin, an African American high school student (CNN, 2012). On February 26, 2012, Martin was visiting the home of his father's fiancée in a gated community in Sanford, Florida. Martin decided to walk to a convenience store to buy some snacks. While walking back from the store holding a bag of Skittles candy and a can of iced tea, he noticed that Zimmerman was following him in a car. Martin called his girlfriend with his cell phone and told her that someone was following him. Zimmerman was a Neighborhood Watch volunteer who had called 911 to report seeing a suspicious person—Martin—walking through the gated community. Although he was told by the 911 dispatcher to wait for police to arrive, Zimmerman eventually exited the vehicle to follow Martin on foot. Zimmerman was armed with a gun. Martin was not armed at all (CNN, 2012).

On the rainy night in question, residents along the street heard an altercation and cries of "Help! Help!" that ended with the sound of a single gunshot. Zimmerman shot Martin at close range. He claimed that he acted in self-defense after Martin allegedly attacked him. Controversy swirled around the case. Had an overly eager, armed vigilante initiated a confrontation with a teenager solely based on the teen's skin color? Was Zimmerman truthful in describing what happened? Detectives questioned why Zimmerman said he was too afraid to roll down the window of his vehicle to tell Martin that he was a Neighborhood Watch volunteer yet later exited the vehicle to follow Martin on foot. Technicians who analyzed tapes from neighbors' 911 calls raised questions about whether it was Zimmerman's voice, rather than Martin's, yelling "Help!" as Zimmerman claimed (*New York Times*, 2012).

Although the local police initially seemed to accept Zimmerman's self-defense claim, eventually greater attention from the national news media, the state of Florida, and the U.S. Department of Justice led the governor to appoint a special prosecutor who decided to charge Zimmerman. In addition, the local police chief was fired. The circumstances leading to the charges against Zimmerman led to claims that the local police did not care about the death of a young African American man and counterclaims that pressure from civil rights activists and politicians had led to murder charges against a man who was merely defending himself.

After a three-week trial that received intensive national news coverage followed by more than 16 hours of deliberation by the jury, on July 13, 2013, the jury issued a "not guilty" verdict on the charge of second-degree murder and the lesser alternative charge of manslaughter (Alvarez & Buckley, 2013). The prosecution had failed to prove Zimmerman's guilt "beyond a reasonable doubt," the high standard of proof used in American criminal cases. The verdict divided the nation, with 38 percent believing Zimmerman to be guilty of criminal homicide and 41 percent agreeing with the jury. Divisions in public opinion by race and age were even greater, with a majority of African Americans and a near majority of all adults under age 30 believing that the jury reached the wrong decision (Swanson, 2013).

Was justice achieved in the Zimmerman case? Often we never know if the criminal justice system produced an accurate result. There were only two eyewitnesses to the fatal encounter, but only one of them—Zimmerman—lived to have his version of events presented to the jury. Some observers argue that the Zimmerman case shows that the American criminal justice system "works" because the system declined to impose severe punishment without clear proof that Zimmerman acted with criminal intent in shooting Martin. Others believe that the system "failed" because no one was punished when an unarmed young man who was minding his own business was fatally shot by an armed man who followed and confronted him without

any justification. What is your view of the George Zimmerman case?

The Zimmerman case was unusual because he faced the possibility of severe punishment and his case was decided by a full jury trial instead of a negotiated admission of guilt. The vast majority of criminal cases concern lesser offenses and are concluded prior to reaching the stage of a jury trial. Nonetheless, the case against George Zimmerman illustrates many elements of the criminal justice system. As this chapter will discuss, cases are processed through a series of steps in which justice system officials make decisions about whether a case will move forward or leave the system. In the Zimmerman case, police officers examined the location of the shooting for evidence and questioned Zimmerman and other witnesses. Prosecutors ultimately decided not to believe Zimmerman's version of events. If they had decided otherwise, then the case would not have gone forward.

Similarly, a prosecutor decided what charges to pursue, and the decisions that judges subsequently made kept Zimmerman in jail for part of the time that he awaited the start of the trial. The jurors' verdict depended on the arguments formulated and presented by the defense attorneys representing Zimmerman, so those attorneys used their discretion (a term we discuss later in this chapter) in developing the best strategy to defend him in court. The result was to argue that bloody scratches on Zimmerman's head and witnesses' testimony about seeing two people engaged in a fight provided a basis for Zimmerman's self-defense claim.

Ultimately, Zimmerman's fate rested on the discussions and final decisions of citizens drawn from the community to serve on the jury. Their decisions were based on their understanding of the witnesses' testimony and the arguments by the prosecutors and defense attorneys. So, in the end, the jurors' understanding of what they heard in court determined the outcome of the case.

Think about the key factors in the Zimmerman story: discretionary decisions by justice system officials; a sequence of steps; interactions among attorneys, prosecutors, judges, and jurors; and a long delay for the *defendant* (the person charged with a crime—in this case, Zimmerman) while waiting for the attorneys to prepare evidence and arguments for trial. These elements affect criminal cases throughout the United States and reflect many essential characteristics of the justice system.

In this chapter, we examine how American criminal justice operates as a system. Accordingly, we shall see how that system's processes are shaped by its goals, scarce resources, individual decision makers, and other factors that can lead to divergent treatment for similar criminal cases. In cases that appear to be very similar, one defendant may be convicted and another defendant may, like George Zimmerman, be set free. Why do similar cases produce different results? Differences in the effectiveness of police and prosecutors in gathering evidence and in the persuasiveness of defense attorneys' arguments can be major factors. Another factor may be the attitudes and values of the decision makers in a case. For example, prosecutors in different counties may have varying attitudes about whether to seek maximum punishments for drug crimes or youthful defendants. Also, some jurors may make very close examinations of evidence while others may be swayed by their own emotional reactions to the crime or to the defendant.

Differences in the treatment of suspects, defendants, and offenders also may sometimes be related to issues of race, ethnicity, and social class as these demographic factors interact with the criminal justice system's processes.

Anyone in the United States, including law-abiding college students, can be drawn into the criminal justice system in a variety of roles: victim, witness, juror, defendant. Thus, all Americans need to gain an understanding of the system, how it operates, and how it affects people's lives.

The Goals of Criminal Justice

The criminal justice system focuses on the investigation and punishment of people who commit **crimes** as well as efforts to protect the public by preventing others from doing the same. In a general sense, crimes are actions that violate laws defining which socially harmful behaviors will be subject to the government's power to impose punishments, including deprivation of liberty through imprisonment.

crimes Actions that violate laws defining which socially harmful behaviors will be subject to the government's power to impose punishments.

Why does the law label some types of behavior as criminal and not others? For example, why is it a crime to use marijuana when it is legal to drink alcohol, a substance that also has serious intoxicating, addictive, and harmful health effects? The criminal law is defined by elected representatives in state legislatures and Congress, who make choices about the behaviors that the government will punish. Some of these choices reflect broad agreement in society that certain actions, such as rape and murder, are so harmful that they must be punished. Such crimes have traditionally been called *mala in se*—wrong in themselves.

mala in se Offenses that are wrong by their very nature.

However, legislatures may decide that certain actions are criminal even though many people in society disagree about the harmfulness of those actions. These crimes are called *mala prohibita*—they are crimes because they are prohibited by the government and not because they are necessarily wrong in themselves. Everyone does not agree, for example, that gambling, prostitution, and drug use should be punished.

mala prohibita Offenses prohibited by law but not necessarily wrong in themselves.

The definition of *crimes* in criminal law is the starting point for the criminal justice system. A good way to begin our study of that system is to look at its goals. Although these goals may seem straightforward when expressed as ideas, defining what they mean in practice can be difficult.

In 1967 the U.S. President's Commission on Law Enforcement and Administration of Justice described the criminal justice system as the means that society uses to "enforce the standards of conduct necessary to protect individuals and the community" (U.S. President's Commission, 1967:7). This statement provides the basis for our discussion of the goals of the system. Although there is much debate about the purposes of criminal justice, most people agree that the system has three goals: (1) doing justice, (2) controlling crime, and (3) preventing crime.

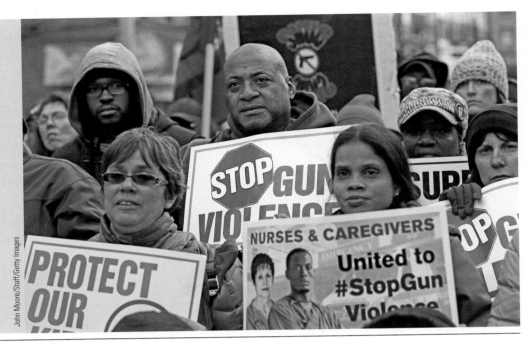

Periodically, people undertake public protests to call attention to social problems and crime in their communities. How can the interest and energy generated by such public events be translated into concrete actions to prevent crime?

John Moore/Staff/Getty Images

Doing Justice

Doing justice concerns fairness and equity in the treatment of people who are drawn into the criminal justice system. In the United States, doing justice forms the basis for the rules, procedures, and institutions of the criminal justice system. Without this primary goal, little difference would exist between the U.S. system and that of authoritarian countries where people lack legal rights.

Americans want to have fair laws, and they want to investigate, judge, and punish fairly. But more than that, doing justice also requires upholding the rights of individuals as well as punishing those who violate the law. Thus, the goal of doing justice embodies three principles: (1) offenders will be held fully accountable for their actions, (2) the rights of persons who have contact with the system will be protected, and (3) like offenses will be treated alike, and officials will take into account relevant differences among offenders and offenses (DiIulio, 1993:10).

Doing justice successfully is a tall order. We can easily identify situations in which criminal justice agencies and processes fall short of this ideal. But unlike in authoritarian political systems, in which criminal justice primarily serves the interests of those in power, people in democracies can try to improve the capacity of their institutions to do justice. Thus, however, imperfect they may be, American criminal justice institutions and processes can enjoy public support. In a democracy, a system that makes doing justice a key goal is viewed as legitimate and can therefore pursue the secondary goals of controlling and preventing crime.

Controlling Crime

The criminal justice system is designed to control crime by arresting, prosecuting, convicting, and punishing those who disobey the law. A major constraint on the system, however, is that efforts to control crime must be carried out within the framework of law. Thus, criminal law not only defines what is illegal but also outlines the rights of citizens and the procedures officials must use to achieve the system's goals. Police officers and prosecutors must follow the law when investigating crimes. They cannot use unrestrained methods of their own choosing in conducting searches and questioning suspects.

In every city and town, the goal of crime control is actively pursued: police officers walk a beat, patrol cars race down dark streets, lawyers speak before a judge, probation officers visit clients, and guards patrol the grounds of a prison. Taking action against wrongdoers helps control crime, but the system must also attempt to prevent crimes from happening.

Preventing Crime

Crime can be prevented in various ways, but perhaps most important is the deterrent effect of the actions of police, courts, and corrections. These actions not only punish those who violate the law but also provide examples that will likely keep others from committing wrongful acts. For example, a racing patrol car responding to a crime scene serves as a warning that law enforcement is at hand. Technological advances can deter crime as well, with new kinds of surveillance and searches, though sometimes at a cost to privacy and personal liberty.

Citizens do not have the authority to enforce the law; society has assigned that responsibility to the criminal justice system. Thus, citizens must rely on the police to stop criminals; they cannot take the law into their own hands. Still, they can and must be actively engaged in preventing crime by such commonsense measures as locking their homes and cars, installing alarm systems where appropriate, and refraining from walking in dangerous areas.

Advancing Goals: Evidence-Based Practices

Advancing the goals of criminal justice requires the development of specific policies to deal with a host of issues such as gun control, stalking, hate crimes, computer crime, child abuse, and global criminal organizations. Many of these issues are controversial. Policies concerning these and other issues must be hammered out in the political arenas of state legislatures and Congress. Any policy choice carries with it costs and consequences as well as potential benefits, yet predicting consequences can be difficult. In addition, legislators often enact laws based on their *beliefs* about the nature of a problem and the responses that will be effective in addressing the problem. These beliefs are not necessarily based on a thorough understanding of available research on the nature of problems in criminal justice. Similarly, police chiefs, prison wardens, and others who carry out laws and policies may rely on practices to which they have become accustomed rather than explore the full range of possible effective alternatives. Decision makers' reliance on unsupported beliefs or customary practices may result in missed opportunities to develop policies and practices that could have more effectively advanced desired goals.

One emerging trend in creating policies within criminal justice is the use of **evidence-based practices**. These are practices that have proven effective in research studies. Social scientists examine many aspects of criminal justice, including the causes of crime, the effectiveness of crime control strategies, and efficiency in police procedures, so as to discover which approaches are most useful and cost-effective in addressing problems. Research sometimes shows that certain approaches are unproven or ineffective. As described by Faye Taxman and Steven Belenko (2013:3), evidence-based practices are "practices that *should* be widely used because research indicates that they positively alter human behavior."

Legislators, police chiefs, prison wardens, and other decision makers are increasingly looking to scholars' research for guidance about which laws and policies to develop. However, even when evidence-based procedures are available, they are not always known or followed by decision makers. Legislators and other policymakers may resist adopting them because they conflict with their own strongly held beliefs or commitment to familiar, customary approaches. For an example, read the "Evidence-Based Practice and Policy" feature on a contemporary debate about drug policy that is influenced by evidence-based practices.

evidence-based practices
Policies developed through guidance from research studies that demonstrate which approaches are most useful and cost-effective for advancing desired goals.

Drug Policy

Research indicates that it is less expensive to provide drug-addicted offenders with treatment than it is to send them to prison. Moreover, although many people with substance abuse problems will eventually fall into their old ways, treatment provides a greater likelihood that they will not, and therefore will avoid committing new crimes. In one New York program, it cost only $32,000 to send drug-addicted offenders to a two-year residential treatment program that included job training whereas it would have cost taxpayers twice as much to send them to prison for the same time period. It is even less expensive for those offenders who pose no danger to society to live at home and attend outpatient treatment programs. Treatment programs inside prisons can also improve offenders' likelihood of avoiding drugs upon release, an important consideration as states speed up early releases in order to reduce the costs of imprisonment.

Thus, evidence-based policies should lead Americans to consider the question of whether it would be best to treat the use of addictive and intoxicating substances as a public health problem instead of a crime problem. Indeed, why is the use of such substances criminal while the consumption of alcoholic beverages is legal? Why not apply the education and treatment approaches used for nicotine addiction and alcoholism to marijuana and possibly to the addictive substances of cocaine, methamphetamine, heroin, and prescription painkillers?

Yet, as with other evidence-based approaches, there can be practical impediments to shifting criminal justice policies about substance abuse in an entirely new direction. Not only is it difficult to shift viewpoints about this behavior that has been perpetually and loudly condemned as "illegal" and "wrong" for many years, it is all the more difficult to change approaches when millions and millions of dollars have been spent on law enforcement efforts and correctional institutions to treat it.

In recent years, however, two factors have pushed legislators and other decision makers to reconsider American drug policy. First, the public's attitude toward marijuana is changing. In several states, voters have approved ballot issues that legalize the use of marijuana for medical purposes by people who have the approval of a doctor. In 2012 the voters in Colorado and Washington went a step farther and approved ballot issues that legalized individuals' possession and use of marijuana. These decisions may cause new problems as officials worry about such matters as driving under the influence of marijuana, medical harm to marijuana smokers' lungs, and a potential increase in marijuana use by young people. But despite these issues, the slow spread of decriminalization efforts through ballot issues approved by voters clearly indicates that the public is becoming less supportive of treating marijuana use as a crime issue.

Second, government budget cuts throughout the country have led officials to look for ways to send fewer people to prison and to reduce the sentence lengths that helped to dramatically expand the country's prison population in the last three decades. In 1980 there were 320,000 offenders serving sentences in American prisons. By 2011 that number had risen to more than 1.5 million despite the fact that crime rates fell steadily after 1992 (BJS, 2014). A tough-on-crime approach to sentencing led hundreds of thousands of additional offenders to be imprisoned. Many of these offenders were imprisoned on drug charges or for crimes such as thefts and robberies that were committed to support a drug habit. Imprisonment has been enormously expensive with respect to building and

☑CHECK POINT

1. **What is the difference between *mala in se* and *mala prohibita* crimes?**
   Legislatures define punishable, harmful behaviors that are wrongs in themselves, such as murder (*mala in se*), and other actions that they simply choose to prohibit as too harmful to be permitted (*mala prohibita*).

2. **What are the three goals of the criminal justice system?**
   Doing justice, controlling crime, preventing crime.

3. **What is meant by "evidence-based practices"?**
   The development of approaches to addressing problems in criminal justice and advancing the goals of criminal justice by using research studies to guide decisions about what will work effectively.

STOP&ANALYZE

What is the role of the individual citizen in crime prevention? List two things that you do right now that contribute to crime prevention. What are two additional things that you could easily incorporate into your daily life that would also contribute to crime prevention?

federalism A system of government in which power is divided between a central (national) government and regional (state) governments.

Criminal Justice in a Federal System

Criminal justice, like other aspects of American government, is based on the concept of **federalism**, in which power is divided between a central (national) government and regional (state) governments. States have a great deal of authority over staffing new prisons and supplying food, shelter, medical care, and supervision for hundreds of thousands of additional prisoners. This increase has also created huge costs for the spouses and children of prisoners because a parent and breadwinner can be sent away for years for committing the relatively minor crime of possession of illegal drugs.

These two influences will not necessarily lead to the legalization of drugs because the U.S. Department of Justice maintains that marijuana and other drugs remain illegal under federal law no matter what voters in any state decide. However, these factors have pushed officials to look at research studies in considering how to cut costs by using evidence-based practices.

We can look to additional research studies for guidance on dealing with risks that emerge from decriminalizing marijuana or making it easier to obtain, along with other substance abuse issues. For example, studies indicate that specific family counseling programs and school-based intervention programs can reduce alcohol and drug abuse by teenagers. Such early intervention programs may save society from long-term problems if these youths move away from a path that might have led them to engage in criminal acts that could eventually result in expensive periods of imprisonment.

Budgetary pressures and changes in public attitudes have combined to produce reconsideration of several aspects of drug policy, thereby creating an opportunity to seek guidance from evidence-based practices. However, it remains to be seen whether states will devote significant resources to prevention and treatment. Governments could save resources merely by reducing enforcement of marijuana laws, shortening prison sentences, and moving prisoners out through early release. But in the long run, more money might be saved through investments in research-based treatment programs that reduce the problem of drug abuse.

Implementing New Practices

Legislators face difficult choices when evidence-based practices clash with long-standing policies that may be firmly fixed in the minds of officials and the public. How many legislators would risk political backlash by advocating that the consumption of marijuana be decriminalized and that drug use be treated as a public health problem that requires an investment in rehabilitation rather than an emphasis on imprisonment? In addition, a shift to evidence-based policies may give rise to new, unanticipated problems, such as increased drug use or more robberies and thefts by drug users seeking to support their habits once the deterrent effect of criminal laws is removed.

Imagine that you are a legislator. Write a memo providing at least three arguments that present your position on whether the United States should treat substance abuse as a public health problem instead of a crime problem.

Researching the Internet

To listen to leading experts debate whether drugs should be legalized, go to http://www.npr.org/2012/11/15/165211562/should-we-legalize-drugs.

Sources: G.H. Brody et al., "Family Centered Program Deters Substance Use, Conduct Problems, and Depressive Symptoms in Black Adolescents," *Pediatrics* 129 (2012): 108–115; F. Bruni, "Colorado's Marijuana Muddle," *New York Times*, January 14, 2013, www.nytimes.com; D. McVay et al., *Treatment of Incarceration? National and State Findings on the Efficacy and Cost Savings of Drug Treatment versus Imprisonment* (Washington, DC: Justice Policy Center, 2004); F. S. Taxman and S. Belenko, *Implementing Evidence-Based Practices in Community Corrections and Addiction Treatment* (New York: Springer, 2013); K.C. Winters et al., "Brief Intervention for Drug-Abusing Adolescents in a School Setting: Outcomes and Mediating Factors," *Journal of Substance Abuse Treatment* 42 (2012): 279–288.

their own affairs, but the federal government handles matters of national concern. Because of federalism, no single level of government is solely responsible for the administration of criminal justice.

The U.S. government's structure was created in 1789 with the ratification of the U.S. Constitution. The Constitution gave the national government certain powers, including raising an army, coining money, and making treaties with foreign countries. But the states retained all other powers, including police power. No national police force with broad powers may be established in the United States.

The Constitution does not include criminal justice among the federal government's specific powers. Yet, the U.S. government is involved in criminal justice in many ways. For example, the Federal Bureau of Investigation (FBI) is a national law enforcement agency. Federal criminal cases are tried in U.S. district courts, which are federal courts, and there are federal prisons throughout the nation. Most criminal justice activity, however, occurs at the state level. The vast majority of crimes are defined by state laws rather than federal law. Thus, laws are enforced and offenders are brought to justice mainly in the states, counties, and cities. As a result, local traditions, values, and practices shape the way criminal justice agencies operate. For example, local leaders, whether members of the city council or influential citizens, can help set law enforcement priorities by putting pressure on the police. Will the city's police officers crack down on illegal gambling? Will juvenile offenders be

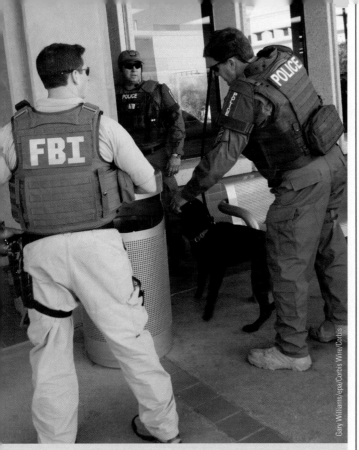

Federal law enforcement agencies bear special responsibility for certain crimes, such as antiterrorism investigations, bank robberies, and drug trafficking. Federal agencies also provide expert assistance for the investigation of crimes that rely on scientific evidence, such as arson. Also, local agencies may request assistance from federal experts. Would law enforcement nationwide be more effective if all police officers worked under a single federal agency rather than thousands of different state and local agencies?

turned over to their parents with stern warnings, or will they be sent to state institutions? The answers to these and other important questions vary from city to city.

Two Justice Systems

Both the national and state systems of criminal justice enforce laws, try criminal cases, and punish offenders, but their activities differ in scope and purpose. Although most crimes are defined by state laws, various national criminal laws have been enacted by Congress and are enforced by the FBI, the Drug Enforcement Administration, the Secret Service, and other federal agencies.

Except in the case of federal drug offenses, relatively few offenders break federal criminal laws compared with the large numbers who break state criminal laws. For example, only small numbers of people violate the federal laws against counterfeiting and espionage, whereas large numbers violate state laws against assault, larceny, and drunken driving. With respect to drug offenses, there are debates about whether federal or state laws should control decisions on the definitions of crimes and punishments. Read "The Policy Debate" feature about marijuana legalization to consider competing viewpoints on this controversial policy issue.

Expansion of Federal Involvement

Since the 1960s, the federal government has expanded its role in dealing with crime, a policy area that has traditionally been the responsibility of state and local governments. The report of the U.S. President's Commission on Law Enforcement and Administration of Justice (1967) emphasized the need for greater federal involvement in crime control at the local level and urged that federal grants be directed to the states to support criminal justice initiatives. Since then, Congress has allocated billions of dollars for crime control efforts and has passed legislation, national in scope, to deal with street crime, the "war on drugs," violent crime, terrorism, and juvenile delinquency.

Because many crimes span state borders, we no longer think of crime in general as being committed at a single location within a single state. For example, crime syndicates and gangs deal with drugs, pornography, and gambling on a national level. Thus, Congress expanded the powers of the FBI and other federal agencies to investigate criminal activities for which the states had formerly taken responsibility. As a national agency, the FBI can pursue criminal investigations across state borders better than any state agency can.

In addition, technology-based crimes, such as computer-fraud schemes and Internet-sourced child pornography, have also spurred new national laws from Congress and enforcement actions by federal agencies because these illegal activities can cross both state and international borders (Hermann, 2014). Moreover, federal officials have become increasingly active in pursuing arms dealers, narcotics traffickers, and terrorists who operate in other countries but whose harmful activities violate the laws of the United States. For example, Russian arms dealer Viktor Bout was arrested in Thailand and brought to the United States, as was reputed Jamaican drug kingpin Christopher Coke, who was brought to New York in 2010 to face trial (Weiser, 2011).

Disputes over jurisdiction may occur when an offense violates both state and federal laws. If the FBI and local agencies do not cooperate, they might each seek to

TABLE 1.1   Department of Homeland Security

Congress approved legislation to create a new federal agency dedicated to protecting the United States from terrorism. The legislation merges 22 agencies and nearly 170,000 government workers.

	Agencies Moved to the Department of Homeland Security	Previous Department or Agency
Border and Transportation Security	Immigration and Naturalization Service enforcement functions Transportation Security Administration Customs Service Federal Protective Services Animal and Plant Health Inspection Service (parts)	Justice Department Transportation Department Treasury Department General Services Administration Agriculture Department
Emergency Preparedness and Response	Federal Emergency Management Agency Chemical, biological, radiological and nuclear response units Nuclear Incident Response Teams National Domestic Preparedness Office Office of Domestic Preparedness Domestic Emergency Support Teams	(Independent Agency) Health and Human Services Department Energy Department FBI Justice Department (From various departments and agencies)
Science and Technology	Civilian biodefense research program Plum Island Animal Disease Center Lawrence Livermore National Laboratory (parts)	Health and Human Services Department Agriculture Department Energy Department
Information Analysis and Infrastructure Protection	National Communications System National Infrastructure Protection Center Critical Infrastructure Assurance Office National Infrastructure Simulation and Analysis Center Federal Computer Incident Response Center	Defense Department FBI Commerce Department Energy Department General Services Administration
Secret Service	Secret Service including presidential protection units	Treasury Department
Coast Guard	Coast Guard	Transportation Department

Source: *New York Times*, November 20, 2002, p. A12.

catch the same criminals, or one agency may miss an opportunity to make an arrest if information is not shared (Viser, 2013). These problems can have major implications if the agency that makes the arrest determines the court to which the case is brought. Usually, however, law enforcement officials at all levels of government seek to cooperate and to coordinate their efforts.

After the September 11, 2001, attacks on the World Trade Center and the Pentagon, the FBI and other federal law enforcement agencies focused their resources and efforts on investigating and preventing terrorist threats against the United States. As a result, the role of the FBI as a law enforcement agency has changed. One month after the attacks, 4,000 of the agency's 11,500 agents were dedicating their efforts to the aftermath of September 11. The FBI has continued to increase its attention to terrorism and cyber crimes in the subsequent years of the twenty-first century and thereby diminished its involvement in aspects of traditional law enforcement. In a 2013 speech, FBI Director James Comey emphasized that "counterterrorism remains our top priority" while also focusing attention on the FBI's increasing attention to cyber crimes (Comey, 2013).

The reorientation of the FBI's priorities is just one of many changes made in federal criminal justice agencies to address the issues of national security and terrorism. The most significant expansion of the federal government occurred with the creation of a new Department of Homeland Security (DHS) through the consolidation of border security, intelligence, and emergency-response agencies from other departments of government (see Table 1.1). Moreover, a new agency, the Transportation Security Administration (TSA), was created within DHS to assume responsibility for protecting travelers and interstate commerce by screening passengers and their luggage at airports throughout the country.

Which Level of Government Should Control Marijuana Policy?

In March 2013, the Maryland legislature's House of Delegates voted to create a medical marijuana program that would permit doctors to approve patients to ingest the long-illegal substance for pain relief. In the same month, the Maryland Senate voted to decriminalize the possession of less than 10 grams of marijuana, thus potentially moving toward permissible use of the substance even by those who do not suffer from painful medical conditions. When the proposal stalled, it was reintroduced in the House of Delegates in February 2014.

In taking these actions in each house of its legislature, Maryland moved a step closer to joining the 17 other states that have approved the use of medical marijuana, often through ballot issues endorsed by the states' voters. It also moved toward emulating the states of Washington and Colorado, where voters approved proposals to legalize the non-medical consumption of marijuana. Voters in a number of cities in recent years also approved measures to change possession of small amounts of marijuana from a criminal offense to a civil infraction warranting only a ticket and a fine.

These developments reflect changes in the public's attitude toward marijuana in many states. According to a Gallup Poll in October 2013, 58 percent of Americans believe that marijuana should be legal, a drastic change from just eight years earlier when only one-third of Americans endorsed that view. Because 67 percent of Americans between ages 18 and 29 believe that marijuana should be legal, it seems likely that public support for legalization will continue to grow as the older generation that is less supportive of legalization gradually dies off and the current younger generations become a larger proportion of the adult population.

Although the public has expressed clear support for either legalization of or access to medical marijuana in many states, the federal government continues to take a hard line on its production and use. In *Gonzales v. Raich* (2005), the U.S. Supreme Court endorsed the continuing authority of Congress to keep marijuana production criminalized and of the federal Drug Enforcement Administration to investigate and make arrests.

Under the Obama administration, the federal government has declined to prevent the introduction of legalized marijuana in Colorado and Washington. Indeed, the administration even issued new guidelines to reassure banks in Colorado that they would not face federal prosecution for providing financial services to legal marijuana businesses. Future presidential administrations may change directions and assert federal authority over the law governing marijuana. Such a change would create legal clashes with states' efforts to decriminalize private consumption of the intoxicant. However, a December 2012 national poll indicated that 64 percent of Americans want the federal government to stay out of marijuana policy in the states. Who should control marijuana policy—the federal government or the states? Here is a summary of key arguments for each side in the debate.

For Federal Control

- The U.S. Supreme Court has said that the U.S. Constitution and statutes enacted by Congress give the federal government control over marijuana policy, including the ability to override state laws by initiating arrests and prosecutions for activities that state laws say are legal.
- International drug trafficking gangs are deeply involved in smuggling, distributing, and selling marijuana. Only the federal government has the resources, expertise, and

---

Because both state and federal systems operate in the United States, criminal justice here is highly decentralized. As Figure 1.1 shows, almost two-thirds of all criminal justice employees work for local governments. The majority of workers in all of the subunits of the system—except corrections—are tied to local government. Likewise, the costs of criminal justice are distributed among federal, state, and local governments.

The nation's economic problems since 2007 have reduced government budgets for criminal justice in many cities, counties, and states. Federal agencies have been affected, too. When budget disagreements created a deadlock between Republicans and Democrats in Congress during 2013, automatic budget cuts were imposed through the federal government, resulting in a law enforcement hiring freeze, reduced training, and an inability to open new investigations by the FBI and other agencies (Horwitz, 2013). Indeed, as we shall see throughout the chapters of this book, budget problems during the last several years have forced criminal justice agencies at all levels of government to reduce law enforcement activities, release offenders early from prison, and take other measures to cope with a reduction in resources (Bluestein, 2011). These issues can have their greatest impact at the local level, especially when there are no longer enough police officers on duty to respond quickly to citizens' calls for assistance (LeDuff, 2011).

nationwide law enforcement coverage to combat these organized crime groups.

- Legalized marijuana in specific states will lead to increased flow of marijuana over state borders and into other states where it is not legal. The federal government has authority over crimes that cross state borders.
- Comprehensive policies concerning substance abuse issues can come only from Congress, an institution that represents the views and interests of the entire nation.

For State Control

- States control most of their own criminal laws and policies. There is no reason to regard marijuana laws as concerning a matter of special national significance or posing especially dangerous threats to the nation.
- The decriminalization and legalization of marijuana in various states reflect the will of the people through the democratic processes of statewide ballot issues or statutes created by the people's elected representatives.
- In a democracy, the people in a state are entitled to have laws that reflect their own political values and priorities. Unpopular laws should not be imposed on them by the federal government, especially laws that infringe on individuals' liberty to engage in private activities that are no more harmful than legal activities such as drinking alcohol.
- The federalism aspect of American government that includes authority for both state and federal governments is intended to permit states to experiment with policy reforms and innovations so that examples of policy change, such as legalization of marijuana, if successful, can provide ideas that other states may wish to copy.

What Should U.S. Policy Be?

The debates about marijuana laws include a variety of elements, including aspects of the human and financial costs of punishment, individual liberty, and the development of laws through democratic processes that reflect the will of the people. The United States has spent an enormous amount of money over the years on punishing people for marijuana possession, pursuing those who grow or import marijuana, and launching public relations campaigns to teach children to say "no" to drugs. Despite spending this money and threatening people with criminal punishments, many Americans continue to use marijuana and increasingly regard existing criminal laws as misguided and outdated. Do current trends in public opinion and changes in state laws indicate that the legalization of marijuana is inevitable? If so, should the federal government step back and permit states to move ahead with their own policy priorities and decisions on this issue?

Researching the Internet

For trends in public opinion concerning the legalization of marijuana, see http://www.gallup.com/poll/165539/first-time -americans-favor-legalizing-marijuana.aspx.

Analyzing the Issue

Imagine that you and your classmates are advisors to the president of the United States. You have been asked to present a complete set of arguments on both sides of the marijuana issue and then make a recommendation about what the president's position should be. Suppose the president expresses concern about the harm of marijuana to young people and the risk that increased availability will spread its use among high school students. He is tempted to use federal power to block legalization in the states but is unsure whether this is the best course of action. What arguments and recommendations will you and your classmates produce? What reasons will you give for your recommendations?

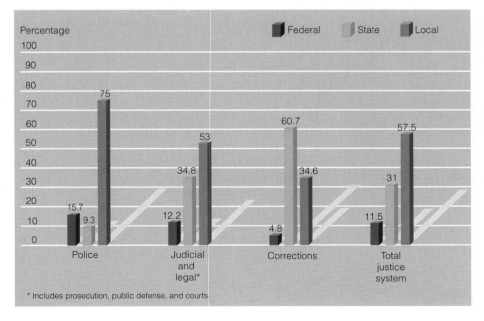

FIGURE 1.1

Percentage (Rounded) of Criminal Justice Employees at Each Level of Government The administration of criminal justice in the United States is very much a local affair, as these employment figures show. Only in corrections do states employ a greater percentage of workers than do cities and counties.

Source: T. Kyckelhahn and T. Martin, *Justice Expenditure and Employment Extracts, 2010— Preliminary.* Washington, DC: Bureau of Justice Statistics, July 1, 2013. NCJ 242544.

☑ **CHECK POINT**

4. **What is the key feature of federalism?**
   A division of power between a central (national) government and regional (state) governments.

5. **What powers does the national government have in the area of criminal justice?**
   Enforcement of federal criminal laws.

6. **What factors have caused the expansion of federal laws and involvement in criminal justice?**
   The expansion of criminal activities across state borders; efforts to combat terrorism, cyber attacks, and international criminal activities.

STOP&ANALYZE

Is there a risk that the American system of criminal justice is too fragmented because authority is divided among three levels of government? List three problems that can arise because the United States lacks a single, specific authority to be in charge of running criminal justice agencies throughout the nation.

Criminal Justice as a Social System

system A complex whole consisting of interdependent parts whose actions are directed toward goals and are influenced by the environment within which they function.

To achieve the goals of criminal justice, many kinds of organizations—police, prosecutors' offices, courts, corrections—have been formed. Each has its own functions and personnel. We might assume that criminal justice is an orderly process in which a variety of professionals act on each case on behalf of society. To know the complexities involved, however, we must look beyond the formal organizational structures. In doing so, we can use the concept of a **system**: a complex whole made up of interdependent parts whose actions are directed toward goals and influenced by the environment in which they function.

Each of the subsystems of the criminal justice system—police, courts, corrections—has its own goals and needs, but they are also interdependent. When one unit changes its policies, practices, or resources, other units will be affected. An increase in the number of people arrested by the police, for example, will affect not only the judicial subsystem but also the probation and correctional subsystems. For criminal justice to achieve its goals, each part must make its own contribution but also have some contact with at least one other part of the system.

exchange A mutual transfer of resources: a balance of benefits and deficits that flow from behavior based on decisions about the values and costs of alternatives.

Although criminal justice agencies and actors can be depicted as functioning as a system, this description should not be understood to imply that they always cooperate fully, operate smoothly, or achieve efficiency in undertaking their responsibilities. It is a human system, with flawed decisions, imperfect communication, and uneven distribution of resources. Yet, the various agencies and actors are connected to and dependent on each other in order to fulfill their assigned tasks.

In addition to understanding the nature of the criminal justice system and its subsystems, we also need to see how individual actors play their roles. This system is made up of a great many people doing specific jobs. Some, such as police officers and judges, are well known to the public. Others, such as bail bondsmen and probation officers, are less well known. A key concept here is **exchange**, meaning the mutual transfer of resources among individual actors, each of whom has goals that she or he cannot accomplish alone. Each needs to gain the cooperation and assistance of other individuals by helping them achieve their own goals. The concept of exchange allows interpersonal behavior to be seen as the result of individual decisions about the costs and benefits of different courses of action.

The system perspective emphasizes that criminal justice is made up of parts or subsystems, including police, courts, and corrections. Here, Judge Orlando Houston confers with prosecutors and defense attorneys during the Durham, North Carolina, trial of Michael Peterson, convicted of murdering his wife, Kathleen. How do decisions by actors at each stage in the process determine the fates of individuals such as Peterson?

FIGURE 1.2
Exchange Relationships between Prosecutors and Others The prosecutor's decisions are influenced by relationships with other agencies and members of the community.

Many kinds of exchange relationships exist in the criminal justice system, some more visible than others. Probably the most obvious example is the **plea bargain**, in which the defense attorney and the prosecutor reach an agreement: the defendant agrees to plead guilty in exchange for a reduction of charges or for a lighter sentence. As a result of this exchange, the prosecutor gains a quick, sure conviction; the defendant achieves a shorter sentence; and the defense attorney can move on to the next case. Thus, the cooperation underlying the exchange promotes the goals of each participant. See "A Question of Ethics" at the end of the chapter concerning the short jail sentence received by boxing champion Floyd Mayweather, Jr., and then consider whether prosecutors' use of discretion in plea bargaining should be guided by a concern for equal treatment of all similarly situated offenders.

The concept of exchange serves as a reminder that decisions are the products of interactions among individuals and that the subsystems of the criminal justice system are tied together by the actions of individual decision makers. Figure 1.2 presents selected exchange relationships between a prosecutor and other individuals and agencies involved in the criminal justice process.

plea bargain A defendant's plea of guilty to a criminal charge with the reasonable expectation of receiving some consideration from the state for doing so, usually a reduction of the charge. The defendant's ultimate goal is a penalty lighter than the one formally warranted by the charged offense.

☑ **CHECK POINT**

7. What is a system?
A complex whole made up of interdependent parts whose actions are directed toward goals and influenced by the environment within which they function.

8. What are the subsystems of the criminal justice system?
Police, courts, corrections.

9. What is one example of an exchange relationship?
Plea bargaining.

STOP&ANALYZE

Is plea bargaining beneficial for society, or does it inappropriately permit lawbreakers to escape appropriate punishment? Give two arguments favoring each side in this debate. Which side has the stronger arguments?

Characteristics of the Criminal Justice System

The workings of the criminal justice system have four major characteristics: (1) discretion, (2) resource dependence, (3) sequential tasks, and (4) filtering.

Discretion

All levels of the justice process reflect a high degree of **discretion**. This term refers to officials' freedom to act according to their own judgment and conscience

discretion The authority to make decisions without reference to specific rules or facts, using instead one's own judgment; allows for individualization and informality in the administration of justice.

TABLE 1.2 Who Exercises Discretion?

Discretion is exercised by various actors throughout the criminal justice system.

These Criminal Justice Officials . . .	Must Often Decide Whether or How to . . .
Police	Enforce specific laws Investigate specific crimes Search people, vicinities, buildings Arrest or detain people
Prosecutors	File charges or petitions for adjudication Seek indictments Drop cases Reduce charges
Judges or Magistrates	Set bail or conditions for release Accept pleas Determine delinquency Dismiss charges Impose sentences Revoke probation
Correctional Officials	Assign to [which] type of correctional facility Award privileges Punish for infractions of rules Determine date and conditions of parole Revoke parole

Source: Bureau of Justice Statistics, *Report to the Nation on Crime and Justice*, 2nd ed. (Washington, DC: U.S. Government Printing Office, 1988), 59.

(see Table 1.2). For example, police officers decide how to handle a crime situation, prosecutors decide which charges to file, judges decide how long a sentence will be, and parole boards decide when an offender may be released from prison.

The extent of such discretion may seem odd, given that the United States is ruled by law and has created procedures to ensure that decisions are made in accordance with law. However, instead of a mechanical system in which decisions are dominated by law, criminal justice is a system in which actors may take many factors into account and exercise many options as they dispose of a case.

Two arguments are often made to justify discretion in the criminal justice system. First, discretion is needed because the system lacks the resources to treat every case the same way. If every violation of the law were pursued from investigation through trial, the costs would be immense. Second, many officials believe that discretion permits them to achieve greater justice than rigid rules would produce.

Resource Dependence

Criminal justice agencies do not generate their own resources but depend on other agencies for funding. Therefore, actors in the system must cultivate and maintain good relations with those who allocate resources—that is, political decision makers such as legislators, mayors, and city council members. Some police departments gain revenue through traffic fines and property forfeitures, but these sources cannot sustain their budgets.

Because budget decisions are made by elected officials who seek to please the public, criminal justice officials must also maintain a positive image and good relations with voters. If the police have strong public support, for example, the mayor will be reluctant to reduce the law enforcement budget. Criminal justice officials also seek positive coverage from the news media. Because the media often provide a crucial link between government agencies and the public, criminal justice officials may announce notable achievements while trying to limit publicity about controversial cases and decisions. In the second decade of the twenty-first century, resource issues have become especially difficult and important for criminal justice officials because of widespread and deep budget cuts in many cities, counties, and states (Gest, 2013).

Sequential Tasks

Decisions in the criminal justice system are made in a specific sequence. The police must arrest a person before the case is passed to the prosecutor to determine if charges should be brought. The prosecutor's decisions influence the nature of the court's workload. The accumulated decisions of police, prosecutors, and courts determine the number of offenders sent to corrections agencies. The sequential nature of the system is key to the exchange relationships among the justice system's decision makers, who depend on one another to achieve their goals. In other words, the system is highly interdependent partially because it is sequential.

Filtering

We can see the criminal justice system as a **filtering process**. At each stage, some defendants are sent on to the next stage while others are either released or processed under changed conditions. As shown in Figure 1.3, people who have been arrested may be filtered out of the system at various points. Note that relatively few suspects are arrested in light of the number of crimes committed, and a portion of the arrestees will be released without being prosecuted or convicted.

CRIMINAL JUSTICE
MYTH&REALITY

COMMON BELIEF: The American criminal justice system is obviously not tough enough on criminal offenders, because so many of them go free and so few of them end up in prison.

- The filtering of people out of the justice system does not mean that the American system is not tough on offenders.
- In fact, the United States incarcerates more people and keeps them locked up for longer periods than do comparable democracies.
- The biggest challenge for police is gathering enough evidence to identify a suspect and justify making an arrest. This difficulty accounts for the largest gap between reported crimes and prosecutions.
- After a suspect is arrested, filtering occurs for a variety of reasons. Officials need proper evidence to prove guilt in order to move forward with cases. Sometimes the wrong person is arrested and further investigation leads to a release.
- The system also has limited resources. There are only so many police officers to investigate cases, prosecutors to prepare cases, courtrooms to process cases, and cells to hold detainees in jail and convicted offenders in prison.
- Thus, discretionary decisions must inevitably be made to use the system's limited resources to the greatest effect. Therefore, prosecutors focus their sustained attention on the most serious cases and consider ways to speed the processing of lesser cases and first offenders through plea bargaining.
- When prosecutors have sufficient evidence and therefore move forward with a prosecution, they see very high conviction rates.

Some go free because the police decide that a crime has not been committed or that the evidence is not sound. Or, in drug-related cases, the prosecutor may decide that justice would be better served by sending the suspect to a substance abuse clinic than by imposing imprisonment. Also, many defendants will plead guilty and receive lesser punishments, judges may dismiss charges against others, and juries may acquit a few defendants. Most of the offenders who are actually prosecuted for serious charges will be convicted, however. Thus, the criminal justice system is often described as a funnel—only a portion of the cases that enter the system result in conviction and punishment. Some people look at how few people end up in prison and conclude that the system is not tough enough on criminal offenders. Consider this idea as you read the "Criminal Justice: Myth & Reality" feature.

To summarize, the criminal justice system is composed of a set of interdependent parts (subsystems). This system has four key attributes: (1) discretion, (2) resource dependence, (3) sequential tasks, and (4) filtering. Using this framework, we look next at the operations of criminal justice agencies, and then examine the flow of cases through the system.

filtering process A screening operation; a process by which criminal justice officials screen out some cases while advancing others to the next level of decision making.

☑CHECK POINT

10. **What are the major characteristics of the criminal justice system?**

Discretion, resource dependence, sequential tasks, filtering.

STOP&ANALYZE

What is the most surprising aspect of Figure 1.3? Describe two aspects of the information presented in the figure that differ from your assumptions about the criminal justice system.

FIGURE 1.3

Criminal Justice as a Filtering Process Decisions at each point in the system result in some cases being dropped while others are passed to the next point. Are you surprised by the small portion of cases that remain?

Sources: Estimates calculated from Thomas H. Cohen and Tracey Kyckelhahn, "Felony Defendants in Large Urban Counties, 2006," Bureau of Justice Statistics *Bulletin*, May 2010, Figure 1; FBI, *Crime in the United States, 2009* [Uniform Crime Reports], Tables 25 and 28; Jennifer L. Truman and Michael R. Rand, "Criminal Victimization, 2009," Bureau of Justice Statistics *Bulletin*, October 2010, Tables 1 and 11.

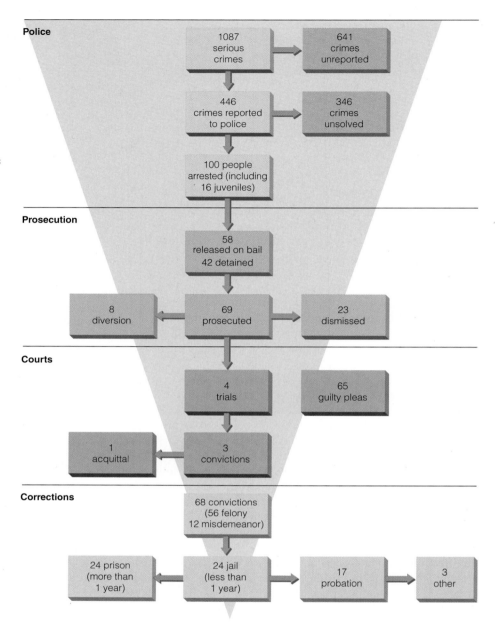

Operations of Criminal Justice Agencies

The criminal justice system has been formed to deal with people who are accused of violating the criminal law. Its subsystems consist of more than 60,000 public and private agencies with an annual budget of more than $250 billion and more than 2.5 million employees (Kyckelhahn & Martin, 2013). Here we review the main parts of the criminal justice system and their functions.

Police

We usually think of the police as being on the "front line" in controlling crime. The term *police*, however, does not refer to a single agency or type of agency, but to many agencies at each level of government. The complexity of the criminal justice system can be seen in the large number of organizations engaged in law enforcement. There are only 50 federal law enforcement agencies in the United States, whereas

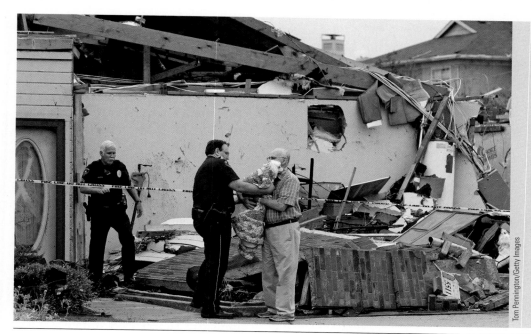

As part of law enforcement responsibilities, the police must deal with a wide range of witnesses and victims in emotionally charged situations. What skills and personal qualities are required to respond to emergencies? What skills do officers need to deal one to one with traumatized victims and witnesses?

Tom Pennington/Getty Images

17,985 state and local law enforcement agencies operate (Reaves, 2011). Fifty of these are state agencies. The remaining agencies are found in counties, cities, and towns, reflecting the fact that local governments dominate the police function. At the state and local levels, these agencies have more than 1 million full-time employees and a total annual budget that exceeds $80 billion (Reaves, 2011).

Police agencies have four major duties:

1. *Keeping the peace.* This broad and important mandate involves the protection of rights and persons in situations ranging from street-corner brawls to domestic quarrels.
2. *Apprehending violators and combating crime.* This is the task that the public most often associates with police work, although it accounts for only a small portion of police time and resources.
3. *Preventing crime.* By educating the public about the threat of crime and by reducing the number of situations in which crimes are likely to be committed, the police can lower the rate of crime.
4. *Providing social services.* Police officers recover stolen property, direct traffic, give emergency medical aid, help people who have locked themselves out of their homes, and provide other social services.

Courts

The United States has a **dual court system** that consists of a separate judicial system for each state in addition to a national system. Each system has its own series of courts; the U.S. Supreme Court is responsible for correcting certain errors made in all other court systems. Although the Supreme Court can review cases from both the state and federal courts, it will hear only cases involving federal law or constitutional rights. State supreme courts are the final authority for cases that solely concern issues of state law.

With a dual court system, laws may be interpreted differently in various states despite being worded similarly. To some extent, these variations in interpretation reflect different social and political conditions. The dominant values of citizens and judges often differ from one region to another. Differences in interpretation may also be due to attempts by state courts to solve similar problems by different means. For example, before the Supreme Court ruled that evidence the police obtained in illegal

dual court system A system consisting of a separate judicial system for each state in addition to a national system. Each case is tried in a court of the same jurisdiction as that of the law or laws broken.

Although prisons provide the most familiar image of corrections, two-thirds of offenders are actually in the community on probation, community-based sanctions, or parole. Do you ever notice the presence of convicted offenders serving their sentences in the community, or do they cause few problems that attract attention from the public?

ways should usually be excluded at trials, some states had already established rules barring the use of such evidence in their own courts.

Courts are responsible for **adjudication**—determining whether or not a defendant is guilty. In so doing, they must use fair procedures that will produce just, reliable decisions. Courts must also impose sentences that are appropriate to the behavior being punished. For example, in some cases involving drugs or juveniles, offenders may be sent to specialized courts that focus on those types of cases.

Corrections

On any given day, nearly 7 million American adults (1 of every 35) are under the supervision of state and federal corrections systems (L. Glaze & E. Herberman, 2013). There is no "typical" correctional agency or official. Instead, a variety of agencies and pro-

adjudication The process of determining whether the defendant is guilty.

grams are provided by private and public organizations—including federal, state, and local governments—and carried out in many different community and closed settings.

Although the average citizen may equate corrections with prisons, less than 30 percent of convicted offenders are in prisons and jails; the rest are being supervised in the community. Probation and parole have long been important aspects of corrections, as have community-based halfway houses, work release programs, and supervised activities.

The federal government, all the states, most counties, and all but the smallest cities engage in corrections. Nonprofit private organizations such as the Young Men's Christian Association (YMCA) have also contracted with governments to perform correctional services. And for-profit businesses have entered into contracts with governments to build and operate correctional institutions.

The police, courts, and corrections are the main agencies of criminal justice. Each is a part, or subsystem, of the criminal justice system. Each is linked to the other two subsystems, and the actions of each affect the others. These effects can be seen as we examine the flow of decision making within the criminal justice system.

☑ CHECK POINT

11. **What are the four main duties of police?**
    Keeping the peace, apprehending violators and combating crime, preventing crime, providing social services.

12. **What is a dual court system?**
    A separate judicial system for each state in addition to a national system.

13. **What are the major types of state and local correctional facilities and programs? What types of organizations operate them?**
    Prisons, jails, probation, parole, intermediate sanctions; public, nonprofit, and for-profit agencies carry out these programs.

STOP&ANALYZE

What kinds of problems can arise from having state and federal law enforcement agencies and courts operating in the same city? Briefly describe two difficulties that citizens may face because two justice systems exist in one location; then consider the same scenario and describe two problems that may arise for either police or prosecutors.

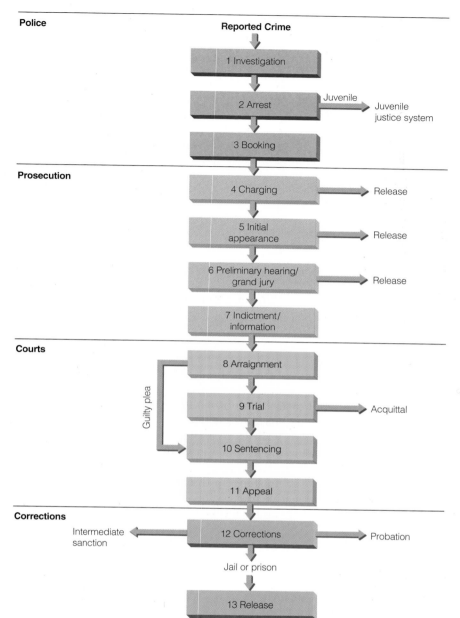

Police

Reported Crime

1 Investigation

2 Arrest → Juvenile → Juvenile justice system

3 Booking

Prosecution

4 Charging → Release

5 Initial appearance → Release

6 Preliminary hearing/ grand jury → Release

7 Indictment/ information

Courts

8 Arraignment

Guilty plea

9 Trial → Acquittal

10 Sentencing

11 Appeal

Corrections

Intermediate sanction ← 12 Corrections → Probation

Jail or prison

13 Release

FIGURE 1.4

The Flow of Decision Making in the Criminal Justice System Each agency is responsible for a part of the decision-making process. Thus, the police, prosecution, courts, and corrections are bound together through a series of exchange relationships.

The Flow of Decision Making in the Criminal Justice System

The processing of cases in the criminal justice system involves a series of decisions by police officers, prosecutors, judges, probation officers, wardens, and parole board members. At each stage in the process, they decide whether a case will move on to the next stage or be dropped from the system. Although the flowchart shown in Figure 1.4 appears streamlined, with cases entering at the top and moving swiftly toward the bottom, the actual route taken may be quite long and may involve many detours. At each step, officials have the discretion to decide what happens next. As a result, many cases are filtered out of the system, others are sent to the next decision maker, and still others are dealt with informally.

Moreover, the flowchart does not show the influences of social relations or of the political environment. In 2006 a retired FBI agent was charged with providing inside information to organized-crime figures so that informants could be murdered. It was then discovered that 30 years earlier, this agent had been caught illegally selling unlicensed handguns to undercover agents of the U.S. Bureau of Alcohol, Tobacco, and Firearms. If this FBI agent had been prosecuted for the handgun sales, his career in the FBI would have been over and he would never have achieved the high-level position that later allegedly allowed him to assist mobsters. However, according to one former federal prosecutor involved in the handgun case in 1976, a high official in the U.S. Justice Department used his discretion to drop the gun charges. According to the former prosecutor, the high official "expressed no other reason not to prosecute the guy except the guy was a cop—and he didn't want to embarrass the [FBI]" (Feuer, 2006). The flowchart does not take into account that someone in authority might exercise discretion unfairly in favor of certain people, such as those with wealth or political connections.

Social relations and official discretion can create specific situations that make potential prosecutions more difficult. For example, in 2004 Colorado prosecutors dropped rape charges against basketball star Kobe Bryant after the alleged victim changed her mind about her willingness to testify against him (T. R. Reid, 2004). Instead, the alleged victim reportedly accepted an undisclosed sum of money from Bryant to settle a lawsuit that she had filed against him (Sarche, 2005). The prosecutors chose not to pursue this case without the victim's cooperation. In other cases, though, prosecutors and judges have pressured witnesses to testify, even jailing some reluctant witnesses for contempt of court. In 2005, for example, a federal judge sent a news reporter to jail for initially failing to disclose sources concerning an investigation to identify the government officials who revealed the identity of a CIA officer.

Thus, it is important to recognize that political influence, personal relationships, and specific circumstances may affect how officials' decisions shape the paths and outcomes of individual cases. Might Kobe Bryant have been convicted of rape if prosecutors in Colorado had chosen to exert more pressure on the reluctant witness? Would the victim have been willing to testify if Bryant, a millionaire athlete, had not paid her the money she sought in her lawsuit against him? There is no way to know. Such factors may influence decisions in ways that are not reflected in a simple description of decision-making steps. In the next section, therefore, as we follow the 13 steps of the criminal justice process, bear in mind that the formal procedures do not hold in every case. Discretion, political pressure, and other factors can alter the outcome.

Steps in the Decision-Making Process

The criminal justice system consists of 13 steps that cover the stages of law enforcement, adjudication, and corrections. The system could be compared to a kind of assembly line, one where decisions are made about defendants. As these steps are described, recall the concepts discussed earlier: system, exchange, discretion, sequential tasks, and filtering. Be aware that the terms used for different stages in the process may differ from state to state and that the sequence of the steps differs in some parts of the country. In general, however, the flow of decision making follows this pattern:

arrest The physical taking of a person into custody on the grounds that there is reason to believe that he or she has committed a criminal offense. Police are limited to using only reasonable physical force in making an arrest. The purpose of the arrest is to hold the accused for a court proceeding.

1. *Investigation*. The process begins when the police believe that a crime has been committed. At this point, an investigation is begun. The police typically depend on a member of the community to report the offense. Except for traffic and public-order offenses, it is unusual for the police to observe illegal behavior themselves. Most crimes have already been committed and offenders have left the scene before the police arrive, placing the police at a disadvantage in quickly finding and arresting the offenders.
2. *Arrest*. If the police find enough evidence showing that a particular person has committed a crime, an arrest may be made. An **arrest** involves physically taking a person into custody pending a court proceeding. This action not only restricts the suspect's freedom but also is the first step toward prosecution.

Under some conditions, arrests may be made on the basis of a **warrant**—a court order issued by a judge authorizing police officers to take certain actions, such as arresting suspects or searching premises. In practice, most arrests are made without warrants. In some states, police officers may issue a summons or citation that orders a person to appear in court on a certain date. This avoids the need to hold the suspect physically until decisions are made about the case.

3. *Booking.* After an arrest, the suspect is usually transported to a police station for booking, in which a record is made of the arrest. When booked, the suspect may be fingerprinted, photographed, questioned, and placed in a lineup to be identified by the victim or witnesses. Before being questioned, all suspects in custody must also be warned that they have the right to counsel, that they may remain silent, and that any statement they make may be used against them later. Bail may be set so that the suspect learns what amount of money must be paid or what other conditions must be met to gain release from custody until the case is processed.

4. *Charging.* Prosecuting attorneys are the key link between the police and the courts. They must consider the facts of the case and decide whether there is reasonable cause to believe that an offense was committed and that the suspect committed the offense. The decision to charge is crucial because it sets in motion the adjudication of the case.

5. *Initial appearance.* Within a reasonable time after arrest, the suspect must be brought before a judge. At this point, suspects are given formal notice of the charge(s) for which they are being held, advised of their rights, and, if approved by the judge, given a chance to post bail. At this stage, the judge decides whether there is enough evidence to hold the suspect for further criminal processing. If enough evidence has not been produced, the judge will dismiss the case. The purpose of bail is to permit the accused to be released while awaiting trial and to ensure that she or he will show up in court at the appointed time. Bail requires the accused to provide or arrange a surety (or pledge), usually in the form of money or a bond. The amount of bail is based mainly on the judge's view of the seriousness of the crime and the defendant's prior criminal record. Suspects may also be released on their *own recognizance* (also known as *ROR*—"release on own recognizance")—a promise to appear in court at a later date without the posting of bail. In a few cases, bail may be denied and the accused held because he or she is viewed as a threat to the community.

6. *Preliminary hearing/grand jury.* After suspects have been arrested, booked, and brought to court to be informed of the charges against them and advised of their rights, a decision must be made as to whether there is enough evidence to proceed. The preliminary hearing, used in about half the states, allows a judge to decide whether there is probable cause to believe that a crime has been committed and that the accused person committed it. If the judge does not find probable cause, the case is dismissed. If there is enough evidence, the accused is bound over for arraignment on an **information**—a document charging a person with a specific crime.

   In the federal system and in some states, the prosecutor appears before a grand jury, which decides whether there is enough evidence to file an **indictment** or "true bill" charging the suspect with a specific crime. The preliminary hearing and grand jury are designed to prevent hasty and malicious prosecutions, to protect people from mistakenly being humiliated in public, and to decide whether there are grounds for prosecution.

7. *Indictment/information.* If the preliminary hearing leads to an information or the grand jury vote leads to an indictment, the prosecutor prepares the formal charging document and presents it to the court.

8. *Arraignment.* The accused person appears in court to hear the indictment or information read by a judge and to enter a plea. Accused persons may plead guilty or not guilty or, in some states, stand mute. If the accused pleads guilty, the judge must decide whether the plea is made voluntarily and whether the

warrant A court order authorizing police officers to take certain actions—for example, to arrest suspects or to search premises.

information A document charging an individual with a specific crime. It is prepared by a prosecuting attorney and presented to a court at a preliminary hearing.

indictment A document returned by a grand jury as a "true bill" charging an individual with a specific crime on the basis of a determination of probable cause as presented by a prosecuting attorney.

person has full knowledge of the consequences. When a guilty plea is accepted as "knowing" and voluntary, there is no need for a trial—the judge imposes a sentence, sometimes immediately for very minor offenses or at a later scheduled sentencing hearing for serious offenses.

Plea bargaining may take place at any time in the criminal justice process, but it is likely to be completed just before or soon after arraignment. Very few criminal cases proceed to trial. Most move from the entry of the guilty plea to the sentencing phase.

9. *Trial.* For the small percentage of defendants who plead not guilty, the right to a trial by an impartial jury is guaranteed by the Sixth Amendment if the charges are serious enough to warrant incarceration for more than six months. In many jurisdictions, lesser charges do not entail the right to a jury trial. Most trials are summary, or bench, trials; that is, they are conducted without a jury. Because the defendant pleads guilty in most criminal cases, typically fewer than 10 percent of cases go to trial and only about half of those are heard by juries. For example, among 33,000 felony defendants in the nation's 75 largest counties whose cases were concluded with either guilty pleas or trials in 2009, only 3 percent went through trials (Reaves, 2013). Whether a criminal trial is held before a judge alone or before a judge and jury, the procedures are similar and are set out by state law and U.S. Supreme Court rulings. A defendant shall be found guilty only if the evidence proves beyond a reasonable doubt that he or she committed the offense.

10. *Sentencing.* Judges are responsible for imposing sentences. The intent is to make the sentence suitable to the offender and to the offense within the limits set by the law. Although criminal codes place limits on sentences, the judge still typically has leeway. Among the judge's options are a suspended sentence, probation, imprisonment, or other sanctions such as fines and community service.

11. *Appeal.* Defendants who are found guilty may appeal convictions to a higher court. An appeal may be based on the claim that the trial court failed to follow the proper procedures or that constitutional rights were violated by the actions of police, prosecutors, defense attorneys, or judges. The number of appeals is small compared with the total number of convictions; further, in about 80 percent of appeals, trial judges and other officials are ruled to have acted properly. Even defendants who win appeals do not go free right away. Normally, the defendant is given a second trial, which may result in an acquittal, a second conviction, or a plea bargain to lesser charges.

12. *Corrections.* The court's sentence is carried out by the correctional subsystem. Probation, intermediate sanctions such as fines and community service, and incarceration are the corrections most often imposed. Probation allows offenders to serve their sentences in the community under supervision. Youthful offenders, first offenders, and those convicted of minor violations are most likely to be sentenced to probation rather than incarceration. The conditions of probation may require offenders to observe certain rules—to be employed, maintain an orderly life, or attend school—and to report to their supervising officer from time to time. If these requirements are not met, the judge may revoke the probation and impose a prison sentence.

Many new types of sanctions have been used in recent years. These intermediate sanctions are more restrictive than probation but less restrictive than incarceration. They include fines, intensive supervision probation, boot camp, home confinement, and community service.

Whatever the various reasons cited for having prisons, they exist mainly to separate criminals from the rest of society. Those convicted of misdemeanors usually serve their time in city or county jails, whereas felons serve time in state prisons. Isolation from the community is one of the most painful aspects of incarceration. Not only are letters and visits restricted, but supervision and censorship are ever present. Moreover, in order to maintain security, prison officials make unannounced searches of inmates and subject them to strict discipline.

13. *Release*. Release may occur when the offender has served the full sentence imposed by the court, but most offenders are returned to the community before that time, under the supervision of a parole officer. Parole continues for the duration of the sentence or for a period specified by law—unless it is revoked and the offender returned to prison because the parole conditions were not met or the parolee committed another crime.

To see the criminal justice process in action, read "The Criminal Justice Process" feature at the end of this chapter, which tells the story of Christopher Jones, who was arrested, charged, and convicted of serious crimes arising from the police investigation of a series of robberies.

The Criminal Justice Wedding Cake

Although the flowchart shown in Figure 1.4 is helpful, recall that not all cases are treated equally. The process applied to a given case, as well as its outcome, is shaped by many factors, including the importance of the case to decision makers, the seriousness of the charge, and the defendant's resources.

Some cases are highly visible, either because of the notoriety of the defendant or victim or because of the shocking nature of the crime. At the other extreme are "run-of-the-mill cases" involving minor charges and no media attention.

As shown in Figure 1.5, the criminal justice process can be compared to a wedding cake in the sense that different layers show how different cases receive different kinds of treatment in the justice process.

Layer 1 of the "cake" consists of "celebrated" cases that are highly unusual, receive much public attention, result in a jury trial, and often drag on through many appeals. These cases embody the ideal of an adversarial system of justice in which each side actively fights against the other, either because the defendant faces a stiff sentence or because the defendant has the financial resources to pay for a strong defense. The highly publicized 2014 trial and conviction of Michael Dunn, the man convicted in Jacksonville, Florida, after firing 10 shots into a vehicle occupied by four African American teenagers after arguing with them about how loud they were playing their music provides an example of a case in Layer 1 (Goldstein, 2014). Not all cases in Layer 1 receive national attention, however. From time to time, local crimes, especially cases of murder and rape, are treated in this way.

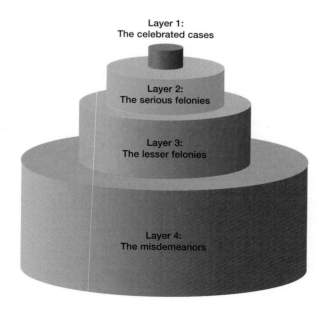

Layer 1:
The celebrated cases

Layer 2:
The serious felonies

Layer 3:
The lesser felonies

Layer 4:
The misdemeanors

FIGURE 1.5

The Criminal Justice Wedding Cake This figure shows that different cases are treated in different ways. Only a very few cases are played out as "high drama"; most are handled through plea bargaining and dismissals.

Source: Drawn from Samuel Walker, *Sense and Nonsense about Crime and Drugs*, 4th ed. (Belmont, CA: Wadsworth, 1998), 30–37.

In 2012 the federal government unsuccessfully sought to convict former presidential candidate John Edwards in a jury trial for improperly using campaign contributions to pay his mistress. The case had all of the earmarks of a Layer 1 case as the millionaire former U.S. senator refused to plead guilty and demanded a trial. Such cases embody the ideal of the due process model, with attorneys for each side battling in front of the jury. After a six-week trial, the jury found Edwards "not guilty" on one charge. Other charges were dropped by the prosecution when the jury could not agree on a decision. Should society devote enough resources to the justice system so that all defendants—rich and poor—can have Layer 1, adversarial trials?

AP Images/Chuck Burton

felonies Serious crimes usually carrying a penalty of death or of incarceration for more than one year.

misdemeanors Offenses less serious than felonies and usually punishable by incarceration of no more than one year in jail, probation, or intermediate sanctions.

These "Layer 1" cases serve as morality plays. The carefully crafted arguments of the prosecution and defense are seen as expressing key issues in our society or tragic flaws in individuals. Too often, however, the public concludes that all criminal cases follow the same pattern.

Layer 2 consists of **felonies** that are considered serious by officials. Here we see violent crimes committed by persons with long criminal records against victims unknown to them. Police and prosecutors speak of serious felonies as "heavy" cases that should result in "tough" sentences. In such cases, the defendant has little reason to plead guilty and the defense attorney must prepare for trial.

Layer 3 also consists of felonies, but the crimes and the offenders are seen as less important than those in Layer 2. The offenses may be the same as in Layer 2, but the offender may have no record, and the victim may have had a prior relationship with the accused, for example. The main goal of criminal justice officials is to dispose of such cases quickly. For this reason, many are filtered out of the system, often through plea bargaining.

Layer 4 is made up of **misdemeanors**. About 90 percent of all cases fall into this category. They concern such offenses as public drunkenness, shoplifting, prostitution, disturbing the peace, and traffic violations. Looked on as the "garbage" of the system, these cases are handled by the lower courts, where speed is essential. Prosecutors use their discretion to reduce charges or recommend probation as a way to encourage defendants to plead guilty quickly. Trials are rare; processes are informal; and fines, probation, or short jail sentences result.

The wedding cake model is a useful way of viewing the criminal justice system. Cases are not treated equally. Some are seen as very important; others, as merely part of a large caseload that must be processed. When one knows the nature of a case, one can predict fairly well how it will be handled and what its outcome will be.

TABLE 1.3 Due Process and Crime Control Models Compared

What other comparisons can be made between the two models?

	Goal	Value	Process	Major Decision Point	Basis of Decision Making
Due Process Model	Preserve individual liberties	Reliability	Adversarial	Courtroom	Law
Crime Control Model	Repress crime	Efficiency	Administrative	Police/pretrial processes	Discretion

Crime Control versus Due Process

Models are simplified representations that illustrate important aspects of a system. As we saw in discussing the wedding cake model, they permit generalized statements and comparisons even though no one model necessarily portrays precisely the complex reality of specific situations. We now look at two more models to expand our picture of how the criminal justice system really operates.

In one of the most important contributions to systematic thought about the administration of justice, Herbert Packer (1968) described two competing models of the administration of criminal justice: the **crime control model** and the **due process model**. These are opposing ways of looking at the goals and procedures of the criminal justice system. The crime control model is much like an assembly line, whereas the due process model is like an obstacle course.

In reality, no one official or agency functions according to one model or the other. Elements of both models are found throughout the system. However, the two models reveal key tensions within the criminal justice process, as well as the gap between how the system is described and the way most cases are actually processed. Table 1.3 presents the major elements of each model.

Crime Control: Order as a Value The crime control model assumes that every effort must be made to repress crime. It emphasizes efficiency and the capacity to catch, try, convict, and punish a high proportion of offenders; it also stresses speed and finality. This model places the goal of controlling crime uppermost, putting less emphasis on protecting individuals' rights. As Packer points out, in order to achieve liberty for all citizens, the crime control model calls for efficiency in screening suspects, determining guilt, and applying sanctions to the convicted. Because of high rates of crime and the limited resources of law enforcement, speed and finality are necessary. All these elements depend on informality, uniformity, and few challenges by defense attorneys or defendants.

In this model, police and prosecutors decide early on how likely it is that the suspect will be found guilty. If a case is unlikely to end in conviction, the prosecutor may drop the charges. At each stage, from arrest to preliminary hearing, arraignment, and trial, established procedures are used to determine whether the accused should be passed on to the next stage. Instead of stressing the combative aspects of the courtroom, this model promotes bargaining between the state and the accused. Nearly all cases are disposed of through such bargaining, and they typically end with the defendant pleading guilty. Packer's description of this model as an assembly-line process conveys the idea of quick, efficient decisions by actors at fixed stations that turn out the intended product—guilty pleas and closed cases.

Due Process: Law as a Value If the crime control model looks like an assembly line, the due process model looks more like an obstacle course. This model

crime control model A model of the criminal justice system that assumes freedom is so important that every effort must be made to repress crime; it emphasizes efficiency, speed, finality, and the capacity to apprehend, try, convict, and dispose of a high proportion of offenders.

due process model A model of the criminal justice system that assumes freedom is so important that every effort must be made to ensure that criminal justice decisions are based on reliable information; it emphasizes the adversarial process, the rights of defendants, and formal decision-making procedures.

assumes that freedom is so important that every effort must be made to ensure that criminal justice decisions are based on reliable information. It stresses the adversarial process, the rights of defendants, and formal decision-making procedures. For example, because people are poor observers of disturbing events, police and prosecutors may be wrong in presuming a defendant to be guilty. Thus, people should be labeled as criminals only on the basis of conclusive evidence—that is, the government must be forced to prove beyond a reasonable doubt that the defendant is guilty of the crime. Therefore, the process must give the defense every opportunity to show that the evidence is not conclusive, and the outcome must be decided by an impartial judge and jury. According to Packer, the assumption that the defendant is innocent until proved guilty has a far-reaching impact on the criminal justice system.

Prosecutors must prove their cases while obeying rules dealing with such matters as the admissibility of evidence and respect for defendants' constitutional rights. Forcing the state to prove its case in a trial protects citizens from wrongful convictions. Thus, the due process model emphasizes particular aspects of the goal of doing justice by protecting the rights of individuals and reserving punishment for those who unquestionably deserve it. These values are stressed even though some guilty defendants may go free because the evidence against them is not conclusive enough. By contrast, the crime control model values efficient case processing and punishment over the possibility that innocent people might be swept up in the process.

☑CHECK POINT

14. **What are the steps of the criminal justice process?**
    (1) Investigation, (2) arrest, (3) booking, (4) charging, (5) initial appearance, (6) preliminary hearing/grand jury, (7) indictment/information, (8) arraignment, (9) trial, (10) sentencing, (11) appeal, (12) corrections, (13) release.

15. **What is the purpose of the wedding cake model?**
    To show that not all cases are treated equally or processed in an identical fashion.

16. **What are the main features of the crime control model and the due process model?**
    Crime control: Every effort must be made to repress crime through efficiency, speed, and finality. Due process: Every effort must be made to ensure that criminal justice decisions are based on reliable information; it stresses the adversarial process, the rights of defendants, and formal decision-making procedures.

STOP&ANALYZE

Where in the wedding cake model is there a risk of incorrect or unjust outcomes? At the top—if effective defense lawyers persuade a judge or jury to acquit a guilty person? At the bottom—where quick administrative processing lacks the opportunity for defense attorneys to challenge the nature and quality of evidence? Make an argument for which layer of the wedding cake—and its related processes—carries the greatest risk of error.

Crime and Justice in a Multicultural Society

One of the most important American values is that of equal treatment. This value is prominently displayed in national documents such as the Declaration of Independence and the Fourteenth Amendment to the Constitution, which guarantees the right to "equal protection." Critics of the criminal justice system argue that this right is hampered by discretionary decisions and other factors that produce racial discrimination. Such discrimination calls into question the country's success in fulfilling the values that it claims to regard as supremely important. Consequently, it is instructive to look closely at whether or not discrimination exists in various criminal justice settings.

Disparity and Discrimination

African Americans, Hispanics, and other minorities are subjected to the criminal justice system at much higher rates than are the white majority (A. Baker, 2010; Carson & Golinelli, 2013; T. Cohen & Kyckelhahn, 2010; L. Glaze, 2011; Poston, 2011; Rainville & Smith, 2003; B. Reaves, 2006; B. Reaves, 2013; Spohn, 2011; Ulmer, Light, & Kramer, 2011). For example:

- African American men are sent to jails and prisons at a rate 6 times greater than that of whites. The incarceration rate for Hispanic men is nearly 3 times greater than that for whites. For women, the rates are 2.3 times greater (African Americans) and 1.3 times greater (Hispanics).

- In sentencing for federal crimes, African American male offenders on average received sentences more than 20 percent longer than those imposed on comparable white male offenders, and sentences for Hispanic men were nearly 7 percent longer.

- Studies of traffic stops regularly find that police stop and search African American and Hispanic drivers more frequently than white drivers, even though they are no more likely than whites to be found with weapons or drugs. In 2011 in Milwaukee, for example, African American drivers were 7 times more likely to be stopped and Hispanic drivers were 5 times more likely to be stopped. African American drivers were twice as likely to be searched.

- Forty-five percent of felony defendants in the 75 largest, most-populous counties were African American, although African Americans comprised only 14 percent of the population in those counties. Hispanics constituted 24 percent of felony defendants while comprising only 19 percent of the population.

- In the country's 75 most-populous counties, more than 55 percent of juvenile felony defendants were African Americans.

- A 2010 study in New York City concluded that African American and Hispanic pedestrians were 9 times more likely than whites to be stopped and searched by police, although they were less frequently found to be carrying illegal weapons and were no more likely than whites to be arrested.

The experiences of minority group members with the criminal justice system may contribute to differences in their views about the system's fulfillment of the goal of equal treatment (Lundman & Kaufman, 2003). Many young men, in particular, can describe multiple incidents when they were followed by officers, temporarily taken into custody, forced by police to hand over money and property, or subjected to physical force for no reason other than walking down the street (Peart, 2011; Brunson, 2007). See "What Americans Think" feature for more on this subject,

QUESTION: "I am going to read you a list of institutions in American society. Please tell me how much confidence you, yourself, have in each one."

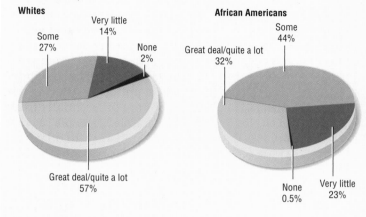

Confidence in the police

Whites
- Some 27%
- Very little 14%
- None 2%
- Great deal/quite a lot 57%

African Americans
- Some 44%
- Great deal/quite a lot 32%
- None 0.5%
- Very little 23%

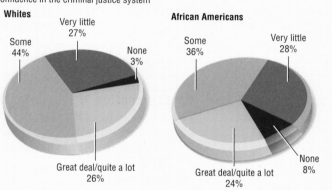

Confidence in the criminal justice system

Whites
- Some 44%
- Very little 27%
- None 3%
- Great deal/quite a lot 26%

African Americans
- Some 36%
- Very little 28%
- None 8%
- Great deal/quite a lot 24%

Note: Percentages do not sum to 100 due to rounding and omission of "Don't know" responses.

CRITICAL THINKING: Does it matter if different groups within society have different levels of confidence in the police and the criminal justice system? Make a list of three undesirable consequences that could emerge from these differences in opinions.

Source: Bureau of Justice Statistics, *Sourcebook of Criminal Justice Statistics* (2014), Tables 2.11.2012 and 2.12.2012.

and think about the impact on the criminal justice system, not just in respect to fairness, but also in relation to public cooperation with the police. An African American college student in New York City wrote the following after the fifth time he was searched for no reason and, in the last search, actually handcuffed while the officers took his keys and illegally entered his apartment: "The police should consider the consequences for a generation of young people who want nothing to do with them—distrust, alienation and more crime" (Peart, 2011).

A central question is whether racial and ethnic disparities like those just listed are the result of discrimination (S. Walker, Spohn, & DeLone, 2011). A **disparity** is simply a difference between groups. Such differences can often be explained by legitimate factors. For example, the fact that 18- to 24-year-old men are arrested out of proportion to their numbers in the general population is a disparity explained by the fact that this age group produces more crime. It is not thought to be the result of public policy of singling out young men for arrest. **Discrimination** occurs when groups are differentially treated without regard to their behavior or qualifications—for example, if people of color are routinely sentenced to prison regardless of their criminal history. In other words, a disparity could result from either fair or unfair practices.

Explaining Disparities

Racial disparities in criminal justice are often explained in one of three ways: (1) people of color commit more crimes; (2) the criminal justice system is racially biased, with the result that people of color are treated more harshly; and (3) the criminal justice system expresses the racial bias found in society as a whole. We consider each of these views in turn.

Explanation 1: People of Color Commit More Crimes Nobody denies that the proportion of minorities arrested and placed under correctional supervision (probation, jail, prison, parole) is greater than their proportion to the general population. However, people disagree over whether racial bias is responsible for the disparity.

disparity A difference between groups that may be explained either by legitimate factors or by discrimination.

discrimination Differential treatment of individuals or groups based on race, ethnicity, gender, sexual orientation, or economic status, instead of on their behavior or qualifications.

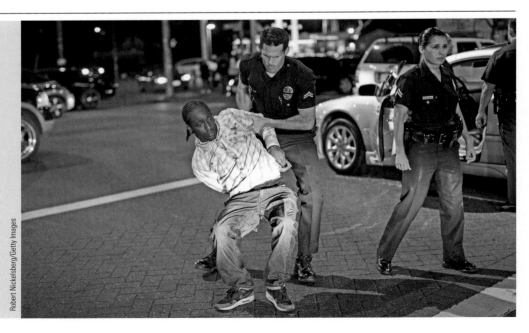

Many young African American and Hispanic men complain that police follow, stop, and search them without proper justification. In light of your own experience, do you see evidence that a person's race may play a role in arousing the suspicions of some police officers? What other factors may enhance police suspicions?

Robert Nickelsberg/Getty Images

Disparities in arrests and sentences might be due to legitimate factors. For example, prosecutors and judges are supposed to take into account differences between serious and petty offenses and between repeat and first-time offenders. It follows that more people of color will end up in the courts and prisons if they are more likely to commit a greater number of serious crimes and have more-serious prior records than do whites (S. Walker, Spohn, & DeLone, 2011).

But why would minorities commit more crimes? The most extreme argument is that they are more predisposed to criminality. This assumes that people of color are a "criminal class." Research-based evidence does not support this view. Behavior that violates criminal laws is prevalent throughout all segments of society. For example, police made more than 6.5 million arrests of *whites* in 2012, including more than 188,000 arrests for aggravated assault, nearly 35,000 arrests for robbery, and more than 4,000 arrests for murder and manslaughter (FBI, 2013). Moreover, there are similar rates of illegal drug and marijuana use for whites, African Americans, and Hispanics (U.S. Department of Health and Human Services, 2007). Indeed, self-report studies show that nearly every adult American has committed an act for which she or he could be jailed. However, most are never caught for such common acts as using drugs, falsifying business-expense reports, driving drunk, cheating on taxes, or inflicting violence on an intimate partner.

Many of these kinds of crimes are difficult to detect or are low priorities for law enforcement agencies. In other instances, affluent perpetrators are better positioned to gain dismissals because of their status within the community, social networks, or access to high-quality legal representation.

In evaluating theories about possible links between race and crime, we must be aware that many commentators may be focusing only on crimes that resulted in prosecutions. Such limitations can distort an accurate understanding of this important issue. Race itself is not a cause of criminal behavior. Instead, any apparent associations between crime and race relate only to subcategories of people within racial and ethnic groups, such as poor young men, as well as certain categories of crimes that are commonly investigated and prosecuted. Research links crime to social contexts, not to race (Bruce, 2003).

Crime problems evolve and change over time. Identity theft and computer crime, for example, cause economic losses in the billions of dollars, yet no one has claimed a link between these crimes and race. Even if we look at developments affecting only "street crimes," we can see that factors other than race appear to create the contexts for criminal behavior.

For example, one of the most significant crime problems to hit the United States at the dawn of the twenty-first century is the "meth crisis": the spread of highly addictive methamphetamine that can be "cooked" in homemade labs using over-the-counter medicines and readily available chemicals. Americans use this inexpensive, dangerous drug more often than crack cocaine or heroin. Yet, this drug's use has been most prevalent among poor whites in rural areas and has contributed to burglaries and robberies by white addicts seeking to support their drug habits (Harkin, 2005). Similarly, in 2014, the death of actor Phillip Seymour Hoffman generated news media attention to soaring rates for addiction and overdose deaths from heroin among white people in suburbs and small towns (Chen & Wilbur, 2014; Riddell, 2014). As with meth addiction, heroin use can lead to theft crimes and burglaries as addicts seek money to support their drug habits. Indeed, even the son of a U.S. senator was arrested for several thefts and car break-ins as he struggled with his heroin problem (Heil, 2014).

The link between crime and economic disadvantage is significant (Steffensmeier, Feldmeyer, Harris, & Ulmer, 2011; McNulty & Bellair, 2003). The meth crisis has spread among poor whites in rural areas and small towns. Other kinds of crime prevail among the poor in urban areas. Further, minority groups suffer greatly from poverty and unemployment. Less than 10 percent of whites live in poverty, compared with 27 percent of African Americans and 26 percent of Hispanics (U.S. Department of Health and Human Services, 2013). Unemployment rates are highest among people of color, and family income is lowest. In January 2014, white males over age 20 were unemployed at a rate of 5.4 percent, while the unemployment rate for African American men was 12 percent (Bureau of Labor Statistics, 2014a). The gap may actually be even larger if minorities are overrepresented among the half-million people classified as "discouraged workers" who are not counted in government unemployment statistics because they have given up trying to find a job.

If poor people seek to steal, it is likely to be through available means, whether burglaries at farmhouses or carjacking and shoplifting in urban areas. These sorts of crimes receive more attention from police than do crimes such as tax cheating, employee theft, and illegal stock transactions, which are associated with economic advantage. In light of the associations between race and poverty and between economic status and criminal opportunities, it is not surprising to find Native Americans, Hispanics, and African Americans to be overrepresented among perpetrators of certain categories of crimes, especially those that are the focus of police attention (Beckett, Nyrop, & Pfingst, 2006).

Explanation 2: The Criminal Justice System Is Racially Biased   Racial disparities may result if people who commit similar offenses are treated differently by decision makers in the criminal justice system because of their race or ethnicity. In this view, the fact that people of color are arrested more often than whites does not mean that they are more crime-prone. Critics point to *racial profiling*, as described in the Close Up box, as an example of what many people believe is a racially biased activity by police (K. Johnson, 2010). Evidence of its existence has led to new laws and policies that require police to keep records about their traffic–law enforcement patterns (Diedrich & Barton, 2013; Engel, Calnon, & Bernard, 2002).

Despite efforts to monitor and prevent such activities, evidence that some police officers use race as the basis for stopping, searching, and arresting individuals persists (Diedrich & Barton, 2013; Rojek, Alpert, & Decker, 2012; Alpert, 2007). Obviously, racial profiling activities—or the lack thereof—can vary from officer to officer and from police department to police department (Warren, Tomaskovic-Devey, Smith, Zingraff, & Mason, 2006). The recent studies showing that African American drivers are 7 times more likely than white drivers to be stopped in Milwaukee and African American pedestrians are 9 times more likely to be stopped and searched in New York City echo prior research that provides evidence of racial bias in many different states (Poston, 2011; A. Baker, 2010). For example, a 2005 study of Texas law enforcement agencies reported that the Houston Police Department searched 12 percent of African American drivers and 9 percent of Hispanic drivers stopped by its officers, but searched only 3.7 percent of white drivers who were pulled over (Steward & Totman, 2005). Finally, a nationwide study of traffic stops found that the odds of being searched were 50 percent higher for African American drivers and 42 percent higher for Hispanic drivers than for white drivers (Durose, Schmitt, & Langan, 2005; Engel & Calnon, 2004).

Is the criminal justice system racially biased? White Americans are less likely than African Americans to attribute the overrepresentation of minorities to biased decision making. A study published in 2008 found that 71 percent of African Americans believe that police bias is a "big reason" minorities are disproportionately convicted of crimes and imprisoned, but only 37 percent of whites share this view (Unnever, 2008). Yet, the arrest rate of minority citizens is greater than their offense rates justify. According to data from the Bureau of Justice Statistics, victims of aggravated assaults identified their assailants as African Americans in 24 percent of cases, yet African Americans made up 34 percent of suspects

Racial Profiling

Most people of all races and ethnic groups are never convicted of a crime, but stereotypes can work to brand all members of some groups with suspicion. These stereotypes are bad enough in the culture at large, but they also work their way into law enforcement through the use of criminal profiles, putting an undue burden on innocent members of these groups. Moreover, such actions produce stark collisions with important American values that we claim to hold dear, especially the values of equal treatment and fairness.

Many people of color, including well-known actors, prominent scholars, and successful doctors, can provide examples of being stopped and searched without justification. The evidence of profiling is not merely based on descriptions of specific incidents, however. Research has documented evidence of differential treatment. One study in Maryland found that African American motorists constituted 17 percent of the motorists and 17.5 percent of the speeders. But African American motorists were subjected to 77 percent of the automobile searches made by the police looking for contraband. And evidence of racial profiling in the criminal justice system is not limited to traffic enforcement. A study by the U.S. Government Accountability Office, the research agency that provides reports to Congress, discovered that African American women returning from abroad were 9 times as likely as white women to be subjected to X-ray searches at airports, even though white women were found to be carrying illegal contraband twice as often as African American women were.

Racial profiling is not limited to African Americans. Hispanics in many locations claim that they are targeted by police who assume that they are illegal immigrants or drug traffickers. Since the tragic hijackings on September 11, many Muslims, including people of Middle Eastern and Asian ancestry, claim that they are subjected to groundless suspicion and questioning by the police and airport security officials as part of the war on terrorism.

Determining when and how the police should use race to assess suspects and situations involves a complicated balancing of public safety and civil liberties. Law enforcement experts insist that effective police work depends on quick analysis and that skin color is one factor among many—like dress and demeanor—that officers must consider. But minority leaders say that racial profiling is based on the presumption that African Americans and Hispanics are linked to crime or that Arab Americans might be linked to terrorism. This has led to the humiliation and physical abuse of innocent citizens. As a result, some police agencies have attempted to develop specific policies to steer their officers away from improper use of race and ethnicity as factors in their decisions to make stops and conduct searches.

Researching the Internet

To see one public-interest legal group's reports on racial profiling throughout the United States at the ACLU website, visit https://www.aclu.org/.

For Critical Analysis

As you can see from this discussion, racial stereotypes held by law enforcement officers can contribute to stops and searches of specific people based on skin color or perceived ancestry. Is there any effective way to prevent criminal justice officials from using any degree of racial profiling? What impact does racial profiling have on people who believe that they have been subjected to it? Write a memo describing three steps you would take as a police chief to limit or stop racial profiling by your officers.

Sources: Drawn from Al Baker, "New York Police Release Data Showing Rise in Number of Stops on Streets," *New York Times*, May 12, 2012 (www.nytimes.com); Noah Kupferberg, "Transparency: A New Role for Police Consent Decrees," *Columbia Journal of Law and Social Problems* 42 (2008): 129–164; Ben Poston, "Racial Gap Found in Traffic Stops in Milwaukee," *Milwaukee Journal Sentinel*, December 3, 2011 (www.jsonline.com); Christopher Stone, "Race, Crime, and the Administration of Justice," *National Institute of Justice Journal* (April 1999): 24–32; U.S. General Accounting Office, *U.S. Customs Service: Better Targeting of Airline Passengers for Personal Searches Could Produce Better Results* (Washington, DC: U.S. Government Printing Office, March 2000); Benjamin Weiser and Joseph Goldstein, "Mayor Says New York City Will Settle Suits on Stop-and-Frisk Tactics," *New York Times*, January 30, 2014 (www.nytimes.com).

arrested for aggravated assault. African Americans were 57 percent of the arrested suspects for robbery, but only 42 percent of the reported suspects (Rand & Robinson, 2011). In sum, the odds of arrest are higher for African American suspects than for white suspects.

With respect to sentencing, research indicates that African American and Hispanic men are less likely than white men to receive the benefit of prosecutors' discretionary recommendations for charge reductions for federal weapons crimes and for lesser sentences in cocaine prosecutions (Shermer & Johnson, 2010; Hartley, Maddan, & Spohn, 2007). A similar finding of racial disparities emerged in a study of who benefits from Florida judges' discretionary authority to "withhold adjudication" for people sentenced to probation so that they can avoid having a felony record if they successfully complete the terms of their probation (Bontrager, Bales, & Chiricos, 2005). African Americans and Hispanics, especially young men, were less likely than whites to benefit from discretionary decisions and other factors so that, in the findings of a recent study, "young black and Hispanic males bear the disproportionate brunt of sentencing in the federal courts" (Doerner & Demuth, 2010:23).

Research findings indicating the existence of bias do not mean that every minority defendant is treated disadvantageously when compared with police treatment of white defendants. Instead, the existence, nature, and extent of discrimination can vary from community to community (Britt, 2000). Thus, racial discrimination may be limited to specific types of cases, circumstances, and defendants (S. Walker, Spohn, & DeLone, 2011).

Explanation 3: America Is a Racially Biased Society Some people claim that the criminal justice system is racially biased because it is embedded in a racially biased society. In fact, some accuse the system of being a tool of a racially biased society.

Evidence of racial bias exists in the way society asks the criminal justice system to operate. For example, even after Congress reduced the amount of crack cocaine needed for a specific mandatory sentence in 2010, federal sentencing guidelines still punish users of crack cocaine more harshly than they do users of powder cocaine, despite the drugs being virtually identical in their chemical composition and effect on users (Eckholm, 2010). The key difference is that whites tend to use powder, whereas people of color in the inner cities tend to use crack. Thus, the imposition of significantly harsher punishments for one form of the drug produces racial disparities in imprisonment rates. State and federal legislators pushed for lengthy prison sentences during the perceived "crack crisis" of the late twentieth century.

By contrast, government responses to the meth crisis of the early twenty-first century placed greater emphasis on prevention, such as limiting sales of over-the-counter medications used to manufacture meth, as well as treatment. For example, the state of Iowa's 2006 annual report entitled *Iowa's Drug Control Strategy* says, "More treatment and related resources need to be targeted to meth-addicted offenders . . . It is only by reducing the demand for meth and other drugs that we can hope to break the cycle of addiction" (Governor's Office on Drug Control Policy, 2006:8). Some observers suspect that the less punitive orientation toward meth offenders, who are predominantly white, may reflect race-based attitudes that perceive crack cocaine offenders, many of whom have been African American, as more dangerous and less worthy of rehabilitation (M. Alexander, 2011).

Other evidence of racial bias in American society shows up in the stereotyping of offenders. For example, African American and Hispanic professionals have been stopped for no legitimate reason and even falsely arrested when the police were looking for a person of color and these individuals happened to be perceived as "out of place." For example, television news host T. J. Holmes was stopped near his suburban Atlanta home by police officers who seemed uncomfortable when, upon recognizing him, could claim only that they stopped him to make sure he had insurance on his car (Roberts, 2012). Judge Claude Coleman was handcuffed and dragged through crowds of shoppers in Short Hills, New Jersey, while protesting his innocence; Princeton University philosopher Cornel West was stopped on false cocaine charges while driving across Massachusetts; and law student Brian Roberts was pulled over by the police as he drove in an affluent St. Louis neighborhood on his way to interview a judge for a class project (Tonry, 1995).

If people of color are overrepresented in the justice system because of racial bias in society, the solution may seem a bit daunting. Nobody knows how to quickly rid a society of biased policies, practices, and attitudes.

STOP&ANALYZE

If race is influential throughout the criminal justice system, what are three steps that might be taken to attempt to reduce disparities and biased decision making?

A QUESTION OF ETHICS

Think, Discuss, Write

In December 2011, boxing champion Floyd Mayweather, Jr., was sentenced to 90 days in jail in Las Vegas after pleading guilty to domestic violence charges. The charges had been reduced from more serious felony charges that could have produced a five-year prison sentence. By contrast, two weeks later, in Huntsville, Alabama, Toriano Nicolas Porter was sentenced to 20 years in prison after being convicted of domestic violence charges. The significant disparity in sentences may reflect the influence of several factors, including the system of federalism that permits states to impose their own punishments for crimes that would be treated more lightly elsewhere. A particularly powerful factor is the prosecutor's use of discretion in deciding what charges to file and whether or not to engage in plea bargaining. Porter's long sentence resulted from the Alabama prosecutor labeling him as a "habitual offender" due to two prior felony convictions. However, Mayweather also had several prior convictions for assault, yet Nevada and Michigan prosecutors permitted him to plead to lesser charges in each case. Is this justice? Were prosecutors influenced in their decisions by Mayweather's wealth and fame? Did Mayweather benefit from hiring expensive, prominent attorneys to defend him?

Discussion/Writing Assignment
Do prosecutors have an ethical obligation to treat people the same if they are facing similar charges, no matter who they are? Imagine that you are a newly elected county prosecutor. How would you instruct your assistant prosecutors to handle cases? Could you avoid being influenced by the desire to gain quick convictions through pleas in order to preserve the limited resources of your office—scarce resources that would otherwise be stretched through an increase in time-consuming trials? Write a memo providing instructions for the assistant prosecutors. Be sure to address any ethical issues that influence your position. In a second brief memo, describe how the criminal justice system and the processing of cases in your county would be affected by your instructions.

Sources: ESPN.com, "Floyd Mayweather Released from Jail," September 10, 2010 (www.espn.go.com); Brian Lawson, "Huntsville Man Sentenced to 20 Years Following Domestic Violence Conviction," *Huntsville Times*, January 6, 2012 (http://blog.al.com); Lance Pugmire, "Mayweather Gets 90-Day Jail Sentence," *Los Angeles Times*, December 22, 2011 (www.latimes.com).

① Name the goals of the criminal justice system.

- Criminal laws define punishable acts that are wrongs in themselves (*mala in se*) or acts that legislators believe deserve punishment (*mala prohibita*).
- The three goals of the criminal justice system are doing justice, controlling crime, and preventing crime.
- Doing justice forms the basis for the rules, procedures, and institutions of the criminal justice system.
- Controlling crime involves arresting, prosecuting, and punishing those who commit offenses.
- Preventing crime requires the efforts of citizens as well as justice system officials.
- Justice system officials increasingly rely on social science research in order to develop evidence-based policies that may increase their effectiveness in addressing problems and challenges.

② Identify the different responsibilities of federal and state criminal justice operations.

- Both the national and state systems of criminal justice enforce laws, try cases, and punish offenders.
- Federal officials enforce laws defined by Congress.
- Federal agencies have shifted greater attention to antiterrorist efforts since 9/11.
- Most criminal laws and criminal cases are under the authority of state criminal justice systems.

③ Analyze criminal justice from a systems perspective.

- Criminal justice is composed of many organizations that are interdependent and therefore interact as they seek to achieve their goals.
- The primary subsystems of criminal justice are police, courts, and corrections.
- The key characteristics of the criminal justice system are discretion, resource dependence, sequential tasks, and filtering.

④ Identify the authority and relationships of the main criminal justice agencies, and list the steps in the decision-making process for criminal cases.

- The processing of cases in the criminal justice system involves a series of decisions by police officers, prosecutors, judges, probation officers, wardens, and parole board members.
- The criminal justice system consists of 13 steps that cover the stages of law enforcement, adjudication, and corrections: (1) investigation, (2) arrest, (3) booking, (4) charging, (5) initial appearance, (6) preliminary hearing/grand jury, (7) indictment/information, (8) arraignment, (9) trial, (10) sentencing, (11) appeal, (12) corrections, (13) release.

⑤ Explain the criminal justice "wedding cake" concept as well as the due process and crime control models.

- The four-layered criminal justice wedding cake model shows that not all cases are treated equally.
- The small top of the wedding cake represents the relatively small number of very serious cases that are processed through trials.
- The lower, larger portions of the wedding cake represent the increasing frequency of plea bargaining for larger numbers of cases as one moves down toward less serious offenses.
- The crime control model and the due process model are two ways of looking at the goals and procedures of the criminal justice system.
- The due process model focuses on careful, reliable decisions and the protection of rights whereas the crime control model emphasizes efficient processing of cases in order to repress crime.

⑥ Name the possible causes of racial disparities in criminal justice.

- Analysts look to explain the disproportionate impact of the criminal justice system on minorities by examining the criminal behavior of different groups' members as well as how racial bias affects American society and the criminal justice system.
- Research does not support any theories about race causing criminal behavior.
- Evidence exists concerning differential treatment of members of various racial groups by criminal justice officials in some contexts.

Questions for Review

1. What are the goals of the criminal justice system?
2. What is a system? How is the administration of criminal justice a system?
3. Why is the criminal justice wedding cake model more realistic than a linear model depicting the criminal justice system?
4. What are the major elements of Packer's crime control model and due process model?
5. What evidence exists concerning the impact of the criminal justice system on members of racial minority groups?

Key Terms and Cases

adjudication (p. 20)

arrest (p. 22)

crime control model (p. 27)

crimes (p. 5)

discretion (p. 15)

discrimination (p. 30)

disparity (p. 30)

dual court system (p. 19)

due process model (p. 27)

evidence-based practices (p. 7)

exchange (p. 14)

federalism (p. 8)

felonies (p. 26)

filtering process (p. 17)

indictment (p. 23)

information (p. 23)

mala in se (p. 5)

mala prohibita (p. 5)

misdemeanors (p. 26)

plea bargain (p. 15)

system (p. 14)

warrant (p. 23)

In October 1998, police in Battle Creek, Michigan, investigated a string of six robberies that occurred in a 10-day period. People were assaulted during some of the robberies. One victim was beaten so badly with a power tool that he required extensive reconstructive surgery for his face and skull. The police received an anonymous tip on their Silent Observer hotline, which led them to put together a photo lineup—an array of photographs of local men who had criminal records. Based on the tip and photographs identified by the victims, the police began to search for two men who were well known to them, Christopher Jones and his cousin Fred Brown.

Arrest

Jones was a 31-year-old African American. A dozen years of struggling with cocaine addiction had cost him his marriage and several jobs. He had a criminal record stretching back several years, including attempted larceny and attempts at breaking and entering. Thus, he had a record of stealing to support his drug habit. He had spent time on probation and did a short stretch in a minimum-security prison and boot camp. But he had never been caught with drugs or been accused of an act of violence.

Fearing that Jones would be injured or killed by the police if he tried to run or resist arrest, his parents called the police and told them he was holed up in the bedroom of their home. As officers surrounded the house, the family opened the door and showed the officers the way to the bedroom. Jones surrendered peacefully and was led to the waiting police car in handcuffs.

At the police station, a detective with whom Jones was acquainted read him his *Miranda* rights and then informed him that he was looking at the possibility of a life sentence in prison unless he helped

the police by providing information about Brown. Jones said he did not want to talk to the police, and he asked for an attorney. The police thus ceased questioning Jones, and he was taken to the jail.

Booking

At the jail, Jones was strip-searched, given a bright orange jumpsuit to wear, and photographed and fingerprinted. He was told that he would be arraigned the next morning. That night he slept on the floor of the overcrowded *holding cell*—a large cell where people are placed immediately upon arrest.

Arraignment

The next morning, Jones was taken to a room for video arraignment. A two-way camera system permitted Jones to see the district courtroom in the neighboring courthouse. At the same time, the judge and others could view him on a television screen. The judge informed Jones that he was being charged with breaking and entering, armed robbery, and assault with intent to commit murder. The final charge alone could draw a life sentence.

Under Michigan law, these charges can be filed directly by the prosecutor without being presented to a grand jury for indictment, as is required in federal courts and some other states. The judge set bail at $200,000.

At a second video arraignment several days later, Jones was informed that he faced seven additional counts of assault with intent to commit murder, armed robbery, unarmed robbery, and home invasion for four other robberies. Bond was set at $200,000 for each alleged robbery. Thus, he faced 10 felony charges for the five robberies, and his total bail was $1 million.

Unable to make bail, Jones was held in the Calhoun County Jail to await his day in court. Eventually he would spend nine months in the jail before all of the charges against him were processed.

Defense Attorney

Under state court procedures, Jones was supposed to have a preliminary hearing within two weeks of his arraignment. At the preliminary hearing the district judge would determine whether enough evidence had been gathered to justify sending Jones's case up to the Calhoun County Circuit Court, which handled felony trials.

Jones received a letter informing him of the name of the private attorney appointed by the court to represent him, but he did not meet the attorney until he was taken to court for his preliminary hearing. Minutes before the hearing, the attorney, David Gilbert, introduced himself to Jones. Jones wanted to delay any preliminary hearing until a lineup could be held to test the victims' identifications of him as a robber. According to Jones, Gilbert said they must proceed with the preliminary hearing for the armed robbery case in which the victim was beaten with the power tool, because a witness had traveled from another state to testify. The testimony led the district judge to conclude that sufficient evidence existed to move that case to the circuit court on an armed robbery charge.

Lineup

Jones waited for weeks for the lineup to be scheduled. When he was taken to his rescheduled preliminary hearing, his attorney complained to the judge that the lineup had never been conducted. The judge ordered that the lineup be held as soon as possible.

At the lineup Jones and five other men stood in front of a one-way mirror. One by one, the victims of each of the six robberies looked at the men and attempted to determine if any were their assailant. At the end of each identification, one of the men was asked to step forward. Because he was asked to step forward only twice, Jones guessed that he was picked out by two of the victims.

Jones's defense attorney was unable to attend the lineup. Another attorney arrived and informed Jones that he would take Gilbert's place. Although Jones protested that the other men in the lineup were much shorter and older, he was disappointed that the substitute attorney was not more active in objecting that the other men looked too different from Jones to adequately test the victims' ability to make an accurate identification.

Preliminary Hearing

At the next preliminary hearing, the victims of the four additional robberies testified. Because they focused mainly on Brown as the perpetrator of the assaults and robberies, the defense attorney argued that many of the charges against Jones should be dropped. However, the judge determined that the victims' testimony provided enough evidence to send most of the charges against Jones to the circuit court.

Plea Bargaining

Jones waited for weeks in jail without hearing much from his attorney. Although he did not know it, the prosecutor was formulating a plea agreement and communicating to the defense attorney the terms under which some charges would be dropped in exchange for a guilty plea from Jones. A few minutes before a hearing on the proposed plea agreement, Gilbert told Jones that the prosecutor had offered to drop all of the other charges if Jones would plead guilty to one count of unarmed robbery for the incident in which the victim

was seriously injured by the power tool wielded by Brown and one count of home invasion for another robbery. Jones did not want to accept the deal, because he claimed he was not even present at the robbery for which he was being asked to plead guilty to home invasion. According to Jones, the attorney insisted that this was an excellent deal compared with all of the other charges that the prosecutor could pursue. Jones still resisted.

In the courtroom, Judge James Kingsley read aloud the offer, but Jones refused to enter a guilty plea. Like the defense attorney, the judge told Jones that this was a favorable offer compared with the other more serious charges that the prosecutor could still pursue. Jones again declined.

As he sat in the holding area outside the courtroom, Jones worried that he was making a mistake by turning down the plea offer. He wondered if he could end up with a life sentence if one of the victims identified him by mistake as having done a crime that was committed by Brown. When his attorney came to see him, he told Gilbert that he had changed his mind. They went right back into the courtroom and told the judge that he was ready to enter a guilty plea. As they prepared to plead guilty, the prosecutor said that as part of the agreement, Jones would be expected to provide information about the other robberies and to testify against Brown. The defense attorney protested that this was not part of the plea agreement. Jones told the judge that he could not provide information about the home invasion to which he was about to plead guilty because he was not present at that robbery and had no knowledge of what occurred. Judge Kingsley declared that he would not accept a guilty plea when the defendant claimed to have no knowledge of the crime.

After the hearing, discussions about a plea agreement were renewed. Jones agreed to take a polygraph test so that the prosecutor could find out which robberies he knew about. Jones hoped to show prosecutors that his involvement with Brown was limited, but no test was ever administered.

Scheduled Trial and Plea Agreement

Jones waited in jail for several more weeks. According to Jones, when Gilbert came to visit him, he was informed that the armed robbery trial was scheduled for the following day. In addition, the prosecutor's plea offer had changed. Brown had pleaded guilty to armed robbery and assault with intent less than murder and was facing a sentence of 25 to 50 years in prison. Because of Brown's guilty plea, the prosecutor no longer needed Jones as a witness against Brown. Thus, the prosecutor no longer offered robbery and home invasion pleas. He now wanted Jones to plead to the same charges as Brown in exchange for dropping the other pending charges. According to Jones, Gilbert claimed that the prosecutor would be very angry if he did not take the plea, and the attorney encouraged Jones to accept the plea by arguing that the prosecutor would otherwise pursue all of the other charges, which could bring a life sentence if Jones refused to plead guilty.

The next day, Jones was given his personal clothes to wear instead of the orange jail jumpsuit, because he was going to court for trial rather than a hearing. Prior to entering court the next day, Jones says Gilbert again encouraged him to accept the plea agreement in order to avoid a possible life sentence after trial. According to Jones, his attorney said that the guilty plea could be withdrawn if the probation office's sentencing recommendation was too high. Because he did not want to risk a life sentence and believed he could later withdraw the plea, Jones decided to accept the offer.

With his attorney's advice, he entered a plea of "no contest" to the two charges. A "no contest" plea is treated the same way as a guilty plea for punishment purposes.

Before taking the plea, Judge Kingsley informed Jones that by entering the plea, he would be waiving his right to a trial, including his right to question witnesses and to have the prosecutor prove his guilt beyond a reasonable doubt. Judge Kingsley then read the charges of armed robbery and assault with intent to do great bodily harm and asked, "What do you plead?"

continued

Jones replied, "No contest." Then the judge asked a series of questions.

Judge Kingsley: "Mr. Jones, has anyone promised you anything other than the plea bargain to get you to enter this plea?"

Jones: "No."

Judge Kingsley: "Has anyone threatened you or forced you or compelled you to enter the plea?"

Jones: "No."

Judge Kingsley: "Are you entering this plea of your own free will?"

Jones: "Yes."

The judge reminded Jones that there had been no final agreement on what the ultimate sentence would be and gave Jones one last opportunity to change his mind about pleading "no contest." Jones repeated his desire to enter the plea, so the plea was accepted.

Immediately after the hearing, Jones had second thoughts. According to Jones, "I was feeling uneasy about being pressured [by my attorney] to take the plea offer . . . [so I decided] to write to the judge and tell him about the pressures my attorney put upon me as well as [the attorney] telling me I had a right to withdraw my plea. So I wrote the judge that night." Jones knew he was guilty of stealing things in one robbery, but he had been unarmed.

When Gilbert learned that Jones had written the letter, he asked the judge to permit him to withdraw as Jones's attorney. Judge Kingsley initially refused. However, it became clear that the relationship between the lawyer and client had deteriorated when Jones spoke in open court, criticizing Gilbert, at his sentencing hearing. The judge decided to appoint a new defense attorney, Virginia Cairns, to handle sentencing at a rescheduled hearing.

Presentence Investigation
Probation officers are responsible for conducting presentence investigations, in which they review offenders' records and interview the offenders about their education, work history, drug use, and family background before making recommendations to the judge about an appropriate punishment. The presentence report

prepared by the probation office ultimately recommended 5 to 25 years for armed robbery and 4 to 7 years for assault.

Sentencing
Although arrested in October 1998, Jones was not sentenced until July 1999. At the hearing, Judge Kingsley asked Jones if he would like to make a statement. Jones faced the judge as he spoke, glancing at his family and at the victim when he referred to them.

First and foremost, I would like to say what happened to the victim was a tragedy. I showed great remorse for that. He is in my prayers along with his family. Even though, your Honor, I'm not making any excuses for what I'm saying here today, the injuries the victim sustained were not at the hands of myself nor did I actually rob this victim. I was present, your Honor, as I told you once before, yes, I was. And it's a wrong. Again I'm not making any kind of excuse whatsoever. . . .

Your Honor, I would just like to say that drugs has clouded my memory, and my choices in the past. I really made some wrong decisions. Only times I've gotten into trouble were because of my drug use. . . . One of the worst decisions I really made was my involvement of being around the codefendant Fred Brown. That bothers me to this day because actually we didn't even get along. Because of my drug use again I chose to be around him.

Jones also talked about his positive record as a high school student and athlete, his work with the jail minister, and his desire to talk to young people about his experiences to steer them away from drugs.

Attorney Cairns spoke next. She called the court's attention to several errors in the presentence report that recommended Jones serve 5–25 years for armed robbery and 4–7 years for assault. She emphasized letters of support from Jones's family, which she had encouraged them to write to the judge, describing his positive qualities and prospects for successful rehabilitation.

Next, the victim spoke about his injuries and how his $40,000 worth of medical bills had driven him to bankruptcy.

I went from having perfect vision to not being able to read out of my left eye. I got steel plates in my head. . . . They left me to die that morning. He took the keys to my car. . . . So today it's true, I don't think Mr. Jones should

be sentenced same as Brown. That's who I want—I want to see him sentenced to the maximum. He's the one that crushed my skull with a drill. But Jones did hit me several times while Mr. Brown held me there to begin with. It's true that I did hit him with a hammer to get them off me. But he still was there. He still had the chance of not leaving me without keys to my car so I could get to a hospital. He still had the choice to stop at least and phone on the way and say there's someone that could possibly be dead, but he didn't. . . . You don't treat a human being like that. And if you do you serve time and pretty much to the maximum. I don't ask the Court for twenty-five years. That's a pretty long time to serve. And I do ask the Court to look at fifteen to twenty. I'd be happy. Thank you.

Gary Brand, the assistant prosecutor, rose and recommended a 20-year sentence and noted that Jones should be responsible for $35,000 in restitution to the victim and to the state for the victim's medical expenses and lost income.

Judge Kingsley then addressed Jones. He acknowledged that Jones's drug problem had led to his criminal activity. He also noted that Jones's family support was much stronger than that of most defendants. He chastised Jones for falling into drugs when life was tougher after enjoying a successful high school career. Judge Kingsley then proceeded to announce his sentencing decision.

You are not in my view as culpable as Mr. Brown. I agree with [the victim] that you were there. When I read your letter, Mr. Jones, I was a bit disturbed by your unwillingness to confront the reality of where you found yourself with Mr. Brown. You were not a passive observer to everything that went on in my view. You were not as active a participant as Mr. Brown. . . . What I'm going to do, Mr. Jones, is as follows: Taking everything into consideration as it relates to the armed robbery count, it is the sentence of the Court that you spend a term of not less than twelve years nor more than twenty-five years with the Michigan Department of Corrections. I will give you credit for the [261 days] you have already served.

The judge also ordered payment of $35,000 in restitution as a condition of parole. He concluded the hearing by informing Jones of his right to file an application for a leave to appeal.

Prison

After spending a few more weeks in jail awaiting transfer, Christopher Jones was sent to the state correctional classification center at Jackson for evaluation to determine to which of Michigan's 40 prisons he would be sent.

Prison security classifications range from level I for minimum to level VI for "supermaximum," high security. Jones was initially assigned to a level IV prison. Because Jones was a high school graduate who had previously attended a community college, he was one of the most highly educated prisoners in his institution. After working as the head clerk of the prison library in one prison, he was transferred to another prison, where he earned a certificate in substance abuse counseling. He taught classes on substance abuse and addiction for other prisoners before he was transferred to several different lower-security institutions where he took classes, worked when prison jobs were available, and waited until he was eligible for parole.

Parole

After being incarcerated for more than nine and a half years, Jones came up for consideration for parole. He was interviewed by a parole board member through a closed-circuit television connection. The parole member had a favorable view of the record of Jones's behavior and self-improvement activities in prison. He warned Jones about the consequences if he were to resume taking drugs or commit any crimes after being released. Because Jones had suffered two heart attacks in prison, perhaps as the result of damage to his arteries from drug use, smoking, and other unhealthy habits prior to being incarcerated, Jones assured the parole board member: "Don't worry. I know that if I ever touch drugs again, it will kill me. And I don't want to die." Several months later, Jones received word that his parole had been granted, and he was released from prison after serving 10 years and 3 months of his 12-to-25-year sentence. He returned to his hometown facing the difficulties of finding a job in a depressed economy and attempting to reestablish relationships with his daughter and other family members.

A few months after his release, Jones was arrested and briefly placed in the county jail for violating his parole conditions by missing several appointments and drug tests with his parole officer. He was shaken by the thought of returning to prison. He became very conscientious about fulfilling his parole conditions. He volunteered to speak to churches and youth groups about the dangers of drugs, and even police officials began to invite him to speak to troubled youths. By the end of his two-year parole period, he was hired to work in a program for high school dropouts to help them earn their diploma and gain work skills. When that program lost its funding, he took community college courses and was hired by a different program as a counselor for ex-offenders who struggled with substance abuse problems and the challenges of reentering society successfully.

Researching the Internet

Examine closely the lineup procedure that was used to identify Jones as a suspect and then compare it with evidence-based lineup procedures later developed based on research about witnesses' perceptions and memories. Access the National Institute of Justice reports on lineup procedures at http://www.nij.gov/journals /258/Pages/police-lineups.aspx.

For Critical Analysis

Were any aspects of the processes and decisions in the Jones case unfair or improper? Did the outcome of the case achieve "justice"? List three possible issues concerning the processing of the case or the length and nature of the punishment. If you were the victim of the crime for which Jones was imprisoned, would you feel that justice had been achieved?

Sources: Calhoun County Circuit Court transcripts for plea hearing, May 20, 1999, and sentencing hearing, July 16, 1999; T. Christenson, "Two Charged in Violent Robberies," *Battle Creek Inquirer*, October 30, 1998, p. 1A; interview with Christopher Jones, St. Louis Correctional Facility, St. Louis, Michigan, October 19, 1999; letters to Christopher Smith from Christopher Jones, October and November 1999.

2 | Crime and Crime Causation

LEARNING OBJECTIVES

1 Categorize crimes by their type.

2 Describe the different methods of measuring crime.

3 Explain why some people are at higher risk of victimization than others.

4 Summarize the negative consequences of victimization.

5 Name the theories put forward to explain criminal behavior.

6 Explain why there are gender differences in crime.

On Monday, January 14, 2014, Chad Oulson and his wife sat in a theater in Wesley Chapel, Florida, waiting for a movie to begin. During the previews, Chad sent a text message to a daycare provider to check on his daughter. A retired police officer in the audience, Curtis Reeves, Jr., asked Chad to stop texting—when he did not, Reeves went to the manager of the theater to report him. After Reeves returned to his seat, the men got into an argument. Oulson reportedly threw a bag of popcorn at Reeves, and Oulson's wife pulled her husband back by placing her hand on his chest. Reeves took out a gun and shot Oulson in the chest. Oulson's wife was struck in the hand by a bullet (Lush, 2014).

Reeves later told detectives that he was afraid for his life and that he fired his gun in self-defense after being punched in the face by Oulson; however, video surveillance from the theater showed no physical contact between the two men, a fact substantiated by witnesses (Silman & Buie, 2014). Reeves was charged with murder and held without bail pending his trial.

Two hundred miles away in West Palm Beach, Florida, Tia Lashonda Miller sat in jail, awaiting trial for identity theft and tax fraud. She was accused of stealing over 700 identities in order to file false tax returns to pay her debts (Jacobson, 2014).

Reeves and Miller both allegedly committed acts that broke Florida law and caused harm to their victims and victims' families. Reeves's friends and family reported that he was a reputable police officer with a strong record and had never shot (or even assaulted) anyone before. Miller, on the other hand, had prior arrests for assault and credit card fraud over the preceding 14 years (Jacobson, 2014).

The shooting of Chad Oulson was highly publicized in national news reports due to the circumstances—a former police officer with no prior record of assaults shooting a man to death in an argument over a cell phone. What would lead Curtis Reeves to take such action? How might we explain his behavior? Who are the victims in this case besides Chad Oulson? He left behind a wife and young daughter—what emotional damage was inflicted on their family due to the actions of Curtis Reeves? How much financial harm did the Oulson family experience as a result of losing a father and husband? Was the movie theater harmed as a result of this event? Did the theater owners lose business? Was the reputation of their business damaged as a result of this crime? And if so, should society be concerned about whether a business or its owners experience harm as the result of a highly publicized crime?

Tia Miller's case produced little publicity outside her community. Miller did not physically harm anyone in her identify theft scheme. Yet, it is important to think about the impact of her action on victims. Some people presumably did not receive their tax refunds from the government, potentially resulting in the loss of hundreds or thousands of dollars. Is the U.S. government also a victim in this crime, and if so, how do we calculate the harm done to the government and the Internal Revenue Service? How might we explain Miller's behavior, particularly as compared with the actions of Reeves in using a handgun? Two different crimes. Two different motives. But were the crimes "caused" by specific factors that are common to all crimes? Or are there very different causes associated with very different crimes?

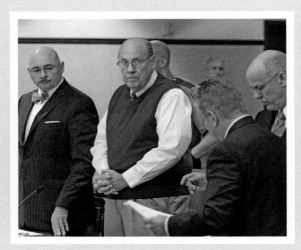

These are important questions to consider, because how we answer them will define the scope of the subject of criminal victimization. In other words, when we talk about the victimizing consequences of crime, should we talk only about the individuals most directly harmed by a crime, or should we also consider people who suffer less direct but equally real consequences? These questions actually have practical consequences under circumstances in which we speak of *victims' rights*, such as crime victims being entitled to compensation. But we need to define what we mean by "victim" before we can implement any such policies.

An additional important question looms in this and every other criminal case: why did the perpetrators do what they did? Criminal behavior is the main cause of criminal victimization. Scholars, policy makers, and the public have long pondered questions such as "What causes crime?" and "Why do criminal offenders cause harm to other human beings?" and "How do we define what 'harm' means in different circumstances?" These questions have significant implications for the subject of criminal victimization. Theories about crime causation often influence government policies for controlling and punishing violations of criminal laws.

In order to understand the criminal justice system, we must understand the nature of crime and recognize the range of people affected by it. Chapter 1 introduced you to decision makers in the system, such as police and prosecutors, as well as to the processes for handling criminal cases. Here you will consider other key individuals: criminal offenders and their victims. You will also examine the nature and extent of crime—the key elements that tell us how many offenders and victims will likely cause or be affected by crime in a given year.

Types of Crime

Crimes can be classified in various ways, as you will recall from the description in Chapter 1 of *mala in se* and *mala prohibita* crimes, as well as whether crimes are defined as felonies or misdemeanors. Crimes can also be categorized into seven types: visible crime, occupational crime, organized crime, transnational crime, victimless crime, political crime, and cyber crime. Each type has its own level of risk and reward, each arouses varying degrees of public disapproval, and each is committed by a certain kind of offender. New types of crime emerge as society changes. Cyber crime committed through the use of computers and the Internet is becoming a major global problem.

Visible Crime

Visible crime, often called "street crime" or "ordinary crime," ranges from shoplifting to homicide. For offenders, such crimes are the least profitable and, because they are visible, the hardest to hide. These are the acts that the public regards as the most "criminal." The majority of law enforcement resources are employed to deal with them. We can divide visible crimes into three categories: violent crimes, property crimes, and public-order crimes.

visible crime An offense against persons or property, committed primarily by members of the lower class. Often referred to as "street crime" or "ordinary crime," this type of offense is the one most upsetting to the public.

Violent Crimes   Acts against people in which death or physical injury results are *violent crimes*. These include criminal homicide, assault, rape, and robbery. The criminal justice system treats them as the most serious offenses and punishes them accordingly. Although the public is most fearful of violence by strangers, many of these offenses are committed by people who know their victim.

Property Crimes   *Property crimes* are acts that threaten property held by individuals or by the state. Many types of crimes fall under this category, including theft, larceny, shoplifting, embezzlement, and burglary. Some property offenders are amateurs who occasionally commit these crimes because of situational factors such as financial need or peer pressure. In contrast, professional criminals make a significant portion of their livelihood from committing property offenses.

Public-Order Crimes   Acts that threaten the general well-being of society and challenge accepted moral principles are defined as *public-order crimes*. They include public drunkenness, aggressive panhandling, vandalism, and disorderly conduct. Although the police tend to treat these behaviors as minor offenses, some scholars argue that stringent police enforcement of public-order crimes can result in significant reductions in violent crimes as well (Kane & Cronin, 2009).

Defining such behaviors as crimes, and enforcing laws against them, highlights the tensions between different interpretations of American values. Many people see such behavior as simply representing the liberty that adults enjoy in a free society to engage in offensive and self-destructive behavior that causes no concrete harm to other people. By contrast, other people see their own liberty limited by the need to be wary and fearful of actions by people who are drunk or out of control.

Those charged with visible crimes tend to be young men. Further, in many communities, members of minority groups tend to be overrepresented among those arrested and prosecuted for such offenses. Some argue that this is due to the class bias of a society that has singled out visible crimes for priority enforcement. They note that we do not focus as much police and prosecutorial attention on white-collar crimes, such as fraud and other acts committed by office workers and business owners, as we do on street crimes.

Occupational Crime

Occupational crimes are committed in the context of a legal business or profession. Often viewed as shrewd business practices rather than illegal acts, they are crimes that if "done right," are never discovered. Such crimes are often committed by respectable, well-to-do people taking advantage of opportunities arising from business dealings. Such crimes impose huge costs on society. Although there are no precise figures on the cost of occupational crime to American society, some researchers estimate that losses due to occupational crime may be significantly higher than losses attributable to street crime. Some estimates indicate that for every $1 lost in street crime, about $60 is lost as a result of occupational crime (Friedrichs, 2010).

occupational crimes Criminal offenses committed through opportunities created in a legal business or occupation.

Organized Crime

Rather than referring to criminal acts per se, the term **organized crime** refers to the framework within which such acts are committed. Organized crime "functions as

organized crime A framework for the perpetuation of criminal acts—usually in fields such as gambling, drugs, and prostitution—providing illegal services that are in great demand.

Organized crime has changed significantly from the stereotyped images of Italian American mobsters portrayed In the movies. These motorcycle gang members charged with crimes show that organized crime groups are not necessarily based on ethnicity. Why do you believe that people become involved in organized-crime groups?

AP Images/Steve K. Doi

a continuing enterprise that rationally works to make a profit through illicit activities and . . . ensures its existence through the use of threats or force, and through corruption of public officials" (Albanese, 2010:3). Those active in organized crime provide goods and services to millions of people. They engage in any activity that provides a minimum of risk and a maximum of profit. Thus, organized crime involves a network of activities, usually cutting across state and national borders, which range from legitimate businesses to shady deals with labor unions and the provision of "goods"—such as drugs, sex, and pornography—that cannot be obtained legally. In recent years, organized crime has been involved in new services such as commercial arson, illegal disposal of toxic wastes, and **money laundering**. Some crime syndicates have also acquired significant funds through illegal recycling operations (K. Coleman, 2011). Few members of organized crime are arrested and prosecuted.

Although the American public often associates organized crime with Italian Americans—and, in fact, the federal government indicted 73 members of the Genovese New York crime "family" in 2001 (Worth, 2001)—other ethnic groups have dominated at various times. Forty-five years ago, one scholar noted the strangeness of America's "ladder of social mobility," in which each new immigrant group uses organized crime as one of the first rungs of the climb (Bell, 1967:150). However, debate about this notion continues, because not all immigrant groups have engaged in organized crime (Kenney & Finckenauer, 1995), and some nonimmigrants have also become involved in these crime syndicates (Mallory, 2012).

Over the last few decades, law enforcement efforts have greatly weakened the Italian American Mafia. An aging leadership, lack of interest by younger family members, and pressures from new immigrant groups have contributed to its fall. However, other, somewhat similar groups have sprung up as the Italian American Mafia has declined. Organized crime has increased among "American" groups such as outlaw motorcycle groups and Hispanic and African American gangs.

money laundering Moving the proceeds of criminal activities through a maze of businesses, banks, and brokerage accounts so as to disguise their origin.

Drug dealing has brought Colombian and Mexican crime groups to U.S. shores, and groups led by Vietnamese, Chinese, and Japanese people have formed in California (Mallory, 2012).

Just as multinational corporations have emerged during the past 20 years, organized crime has also developed global networks. Increasingly transnational criminal groups "live and operate in a borderless world" (Zagaris, 1998:1402). In the aftermath of the events of September 11, American law enforcement and intelligence officials increased their efforts to monitor and thwart international organizations that seek to attack the United States and its citizens. Many of these organizations use criminal activities such as drug smuggling and stolen credit card numbers to fund their efforts. Others steal under the pretext of "terrorism" though not embracing the ideals of terrorist groups; rather, they are mostly interested in making money (Rosenthal, 2008). Policing organized crime on a global scale is a challenge for law enforcement, because the activities of these groups span different police jurisdictions. In addition, nongovernmental agencies must work with police in different countries to share information about organized crime groups that operate across borders (Harfield, 2008).

Transnational Crime

National borders define the boundaries of law enforcement agencies' authority and the definitions of particular crimes. Each country has its own police agencies that enforce its own laws. Borders do not, however, define or limit the nature of criminal activity (Bersin, 2012). The growth of global transportation systems, international trade, computerized financial transactions, and worldwide availability of information through the Internet has facilitated the expansion of the international economy. Simultaneously, these factors have provided the basis for **transnational crime**, a term that refers to crimes involving planning, execution, or victimization that crosses the borders of countries. Jay Albanese (2011) distinguishes profit-seeking transnational crimes from "international crimes," which are acts of terrorism, genocide, human rights abuses, or other crimes against humanity that violate international law. Transnational crimes, by contrast, involve theft, fraud, counterfeiting, smuggling, and other violations of individual countries' criminal laws that rely on transborder activities.

transnational crime Profit-seeking criminal activities that involve planning, execution, or victimization that crosses national borders.

Transnational crimes can be grouped into three categories (Albanese, 2011:3). The first category, provision of illicit goods, includes drug trafficking and moving stolen property, such as automobiles and artwork, from one country to another for sales that are difficult to trace back to the original theft (Alderman, 2012). It also includes the transportation and sale of counterfeit goods, such as prescription medications and designer clothing. The second category, provision of illegal services, includes human trafficking, such as transporting sex workers or undocumented immigrants illegally into a country (Shamir, 2012). This category also includes various cyber crimes that often involve fraudulent financial investments as well as child pornography. Bribery, extortion, and money laundering activities define the third category, called "infiltration of business or government" (Albanese, 2011).

Organized crime groups are involved in all of the foregoing transnational crimes. Individual lawbreakers can victimize people in other countries through Internet scams or the theft of financial information. However, most of the harm from transnational crimes comes from the activities of criminal formal organizations or, alternatively, criminal networks that connect individuals and organizations that undertake specific criminal acts together. According to the United Nations, annual proceeds from transnational organized crime activities amount to more than $870 billion annually, with drug trafficking producing the largest individual segment of that total amount (UNODC, 2011).

In addition to drug trafficking, governments and international organizations are especially concerned about human trafficking—sexual slavery and forced labor

Sex workers such as this prostitute provide a service that is in demand but illegal. Are these willing and private exchanges truly "victimless"? Why should this be considered a criminal activity?

(UNODC, 2011). These crimes occur when women and children are lured or transported across international borders and held as prisoners while being forced to sell their bodies in the sex trade for the benefit of their captors (Lehti & Aromaa, 2006). Human trafficking also occurs to obtain inexpensive laborers, who are held prisoner and forced to work under deplorable conditions (Feingold, 2005).

Law enforcement officials face huge challenges in attempting to combat transnational crime. Because American police agencies cannot operate in other countries without permission, they must depend on assistance from officials abroad. It can be difficult to coordinate efforts with agencies in other countries that operate under different laws and that have different priorities. There can also be problems if officials in some countries tolerate or protect transnational criminal organizations because of bribery and other forms of corruption. The United Nations Office on Drugs and Crime (UNODC) seeks to gather and disseminate information about transnational crime. Working with other organizations, it seeks to facilitate communication and cooperation between countries so that there is an ongoing framework for international coordination rather than repeated requests for assistance from one country to another in response to specific criminal acts.

Victimless Crimes

victimless crimes Offenses involving a willing and private exchange of illegal goods or services that are in strong demand. Participants do not feel they are being harmed, but these crimes are prosecuted on the grounds that society as a whole is being injured.

Victimless crimes involve a willing and private exchange of goods or services that are in strong demand but illegal—in other words, offenses against morality. Examples include prostitution, gambling, and drug sales and use. These crimes are called "victimless" because those involved do not feel that they are being harmed. Prosecution for these offenses is justified on the grounds that society as a whole is harmed because the moral fabric of the community is threatened. However, using the law to enforce moral standards is costly. The system is swamped by these cases, which often require the use of police informers and thus open the door for payoffs and other kinds of corruption.

The "war on drugs" is the most obvious example of policies against one type of victimless crime. Possession and sale of drugs—marijuana, heroin, cocaine, opium, amphetamines—have been illegal in the United States for over a hundred years. Especially during the past 40 years, all levels of government have applied extensive resources to enforce these laws and punish offenders. However, laws about drug use have been changing in some states, with medical marijuana now legally available in 20 states and the District of Columbia. As of January 1, 2014, the state of Colorado legalized the sale of marijuana (for recreational use), with the state recouping sales tax—some believe Colorado might collect over $100 million per year in taxes on the sale of the drug (Healy, 2014). The state of Washington also legalized personal use of marijuana. But despite changes to state laws, federal laws can emphasize different priorities. Even though possession of marijuana is still a federal crime, the U.S. Department of Justice has agreed not to challenge marijuana laws as long as they do not conflict with other priorities, such as convictions for selling marijuana to support terrorism (Johnson & Chebium, 2013).

The crime-fighting duties of police patrol officers typically focus on visible crimes and victimless crimes. But, as we shall see in later chapters, police officers also fulfill other functions, such as order maintenance and public service.

Political Crime

Political crime refers to criminal acts either by the government or against the government that are carried out for ideological purposes (F. E. Hagan, 1997:2). Political criminals believe they are following a morality that is above the law. Examples include James Kopp—arrested for murdering Dr. Barnett Slepian near Buffalo, New York, and for the murder of other doctors who performed abortions—and Eric Rudolph—convicted for the bombing of abortion clinics in Atlanta and Birmingham as well as for the pipe-bomb explosion at the Atlanta Olympics. Similarly, shocking acts of violence that are labeled as terrorism, such as the 1995 bombing of the federal building in Oklahoma City by Timothy McVeigh and the 2001 attacks on the World Trade Center and Pentagon, often spring from political motivations. Political crimes may also involve the release of classified documents, as when Edward Snowden and Chelsea Manning, both employees of the U.S. government, released classified documents in order to reveal government practices they felt were unethical or illegal.

In some authoritarian states, merely criticizing the government is a crime that can lead to prosecution and imprisonment. In Western democracies today, there are few actions deemed to be political crimes other than treason, which is rare. One rare example occurred in 2009 when a retired employee of the U.S. State Department and his wife were charged with being spies for Cuba. They reportedly stole government documents because of their ideological admiration for the Cuban government and hostile feelings toward the U.S. government, not because they were seeking financial payments from Cuba (G. Thompson, 2009). Many illegal acts, such as the World Trade Center and Oklahoma City bombings, can be traced to political motives, but they are usually prosecuted as visible crimes under laws against bombing, arson, and murder rather than as political crimes per se.

political crime An act, usually done for ideological purposes, that constitutes a threat against the state (such as treason, sedition, or espionage); also describes a criminal act by the state.

Cyber Crime

Cyber crimes involve the use of computers and the Internet to commit acts against people, property, public order, or morality. Thus, cyber criminals have learned "new ways to do old tricks." Some use computers to steal information, resources, or funds. In 2012, the federal government's Internet Crime Complaint Center (IC3) received 289,874 complaints about cyber crime, with most offenses related to fraudulent

cyber crimes Offenses that involve the use of one or more computers.

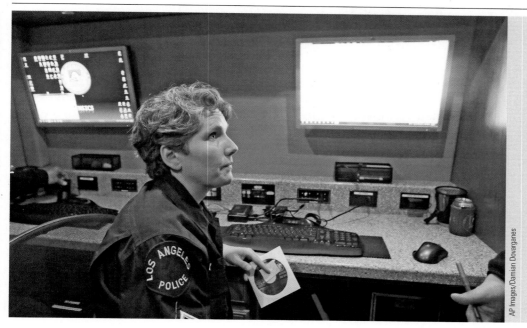

Los Angeles police officers check websites for child pornography. Cyber crime is a growing problem that costs American businesses and individuals millions of dollars each year. Law enforcement officials work diligently to keep up with the criminals' computer expertise, technology, and methods of deception. How can American police effectively combat the evolving and spreading threat of cyber crime, especially when so many cyber criminals are located in other countries?

online auto sales, email impersonation scams, and intimidation/extortion scams (Internet Crime Complaint Center, 2013). Other criminals use the Internet to disseminate child pornography, to advertise sexual services, or to stalk the unsuspecting. The more sophisticated "hackers" create and distribute viruses designed to destroy computer programs or to gain control of computers from unsuspecting individuals. Still others focus their attention on stealing funds or personal identities—in December 2013, the Target Corporation was infiltrated resulting in the theft of personal information and credit card numbers for 40 million customers (Hsu, Hamilton, & O'Brien, 2013). You will read more about cyber crime in the discussion of criminal justice and technology in Chapter 14.

Which of these main types of crime is of greatest concern to you? If you are like most people, it is visible crime. Thus, as a nation, we devote most of our criminal justice resources to dealing with such crimes. To develop policies to address these crimes, however, we need to know more about the amount of crime and all the types of crimes that occur in the United States. One of the most disturbing crimes, which has gained much attention lately, is victimization of the elderly; see the Close Up box for more.

☑CHECK POINT

1. **What are the seven main types of crime?**
   Visible crime, occupational crime, organized crime, transnational crime, victimless crimes, political crime, cyber crime.

2. **What is the function of organized crime?**
   Organized crime usually provides goods and services that are in high demand but are illegal.

3. **What is meant by the term *victimless crimes*?**
   These are crimes against morality in which the people involved do not believe that anyone has been victimized.

STOP&ANALYZE

Multiple states have legalized the use of medical marijuana in the past few years; however, marijuana is classified as a "Schedule I" narcotic. According to the U.S. Drug Enforcement Administration's (DEA) definition, this means "Substances in this schedule have a high potential for abuse, have no currently accepted medical use in treatment in the United States, and there is a lack of accepted safety for use of the drug or other substance under medical supervision." Given this classification, does it make sense for states to be allowed to make marijuana use legal for medicinal purposes? Alternatively, should marijuana be removed from the list of Schedule I drugs? Provide a brief argument for the option you think that policy makers should adopt as this issue develops.

How Much Crime Is There?

Many Americans believe that the crime rate is rising, even though it has generally declined since the 1980s. For example, the rate of violent crime decreased from 747.1 violent crimes per 100,000 people in 1993 to 386.9 violent crimes per 100,000 by 2012, including a 19 percent drop from 2006 to 2012 (FBI, 2013a: Table 1). According to the Bureau of Justice Statistics, "Rates of violent and property crime [measured by our survey] in 2009 were at the lowest overall levels recorded since 1973, the first year for which victimization estimates from the survey were produced" (Rand, 2010:1).

In December 2013, the FBI released preliminary crime statistics for the first half of 2013. The initial analysis showed a 5.4 percent decrease in violent crime. From January 2013 to June 2013, all types of violent crime decreased, with murder and aggravated assault down by about 7 percent (FBI, 2013b: Table 1). The largest decrease in violent crime occurred in the Midwest (7.4 percent), while the Northeast demonstrated the greatest decrease in homicide rates (14.0 percent) (FBI, 2013b: Table 2). Some scholars and law enforcement professionals were concerned when crime rates increased modestly in 2006 and 2007; however, the increase was small, and crime rates still remain low compared with the rates from two decades ago.

Much of the discussion in this section concerns national crime data and trends that affect the United States as a whole. Individual cities and their police

Victimization of the Elderly

Senior citizens have become attractive targets for scam artists looking to earn easy money and can also be subject to physical victimization by caretakers. As the number of elderly increases in the United States, due to the aging of the "baby boomer" generation, the greater the number of potential victims there are for scammers and abusers.

Many of these financial scams take advantage of older people in retirement, who may be on a fixed income and are seeking to increase their income through reverse mortgages and the like. In addition, elderly people tend to be at home more often than other people and are therefore more likely to be targeted in telemarketing scams and door-to-door sales. Finally, health care scams (selling cure-alls) prey on elderly people in poor health who may not be able to afford private health care.

In one type of scam, con artists target elderly people who have already been victims of crime. The offender approaches the victim, pretending to be a police officer investigating the crime. The "detective" tells the victim that the police department needs money from them to travel out of town to arrest a suspect, but police departments never make requests such as these.

The elderly are also frequent victims of physical abuse, typically perpetrated against them by caretakers—family members or nursing home staff. In Long Island, nine people were arrested for failing to respond to a medical alert alarm for two hours, when a temporary resident's ventilator became disconnected. The family was told she died of a heart attack. Severe crimes like this raise questions about the general level of attention given by staff to patients and about how many other elderly residents may have been neglected at a nursing home. The owner of this particular nursing home is also accused of stealing money from Medicaid, meant to help run the facility, for personal use. At other care facilities, elderly victims have been physically assaulted, and even raped. Abuse is more likely to occur against people who have physical or mental disabilities, who may be less likely to report such crimes to the police.

Some criminal justice agencies have created special task forces to investigate and prosecute crimes against the elderly. In California, the Los Angeles County District Attorney's Office provides special information to seniors to help them distinguish legitimate businesses from those peddling scams.

State legislatures have also been identifying gaps in their laws that may allow elder victimizers to escape punishment. Lawmakers in Iowa have created laws specifically designed to prosecute individuals who have power of attorney for elderly family members and use that power to steal funds from them. In Pennsylvania, laws are being passed that make it easier for elderly victims to sue those who have stolen from them in order to recoup some of their financial losses.

Thieves and abusers prey on the elderly due to their vulnerability and dependence on others. The trend toward increased attention by the criminal justice system and state legislatures may help reduce rates of financial theft and physical abuse of senior citizens in the United States.

Researching the Internet

To see the American Psychological Association's analysis of crimes against the elderly, visit the APA website at http://www.apa.org/pi/aging/resources/guides/elder-abuse.aspx.

For Critical Analysis

Should special punishments be leveled against offenders who target vulnerable groups such as the elderly? How can we better inform potential victims of the threats against them, particularly if this group is less likely to be engaged in technology and the Internet than younger people are?

Sources: Associated Press, "9 Arrested in L.I. Nursing Home Probe Following Patient's Death," CBS News, February 11, 2014 (http://newyork.cbslocal.com); CBSNewYork, "Aide Accused in Rape of Woman, 64, At Bronx Nursing Home," CBS News, February 18, 2014 (http://newyork.cbslocal.com); K. Brugger, "Better Protections for Vulnerable Victims," *Santa Barbara Independent*, February 27, 2014 (http://www.independent.com); Clay County (Florida) Sheriff's Office (http://www.claysheriff.com /CrimesAgainstElderly.asp); S. Tisinger, "Elder Abuse Bills 'Moving in the Right Direction,'" *The Muscatine Journal*, March 4, 2014 (http://muscatinejournal.com); Los Angeles County (California) District Attorney's Office (http://da.co.la.us/seniors/crimes.htm); National Center on Elder Abuse, U.S. Department of Health & Human Services (http://www.ncea.aoa.gov/); F. Sacco, "Proposed Bill Would Allow Elderly Victims of Fraud to Pursue Civil Action," *Observer-Reporter*, February 28, 2014 (http://www.observer-reporter.com).

departments, however, need to be keenly aware of patterns of crime within their own neighborhoods. By monitoring crime rates and trends, they can decide how to deploy their officers and what strategies to employ. Many cities employ their own crime analysts to help identify and track crime problems. As you read the "Careers in Criminal Justice" feature, consider whether you would like to develop the knowledge and skills necessary to become a crime analyst.

One of the frustrations in studying criminal justice is the lack of accurate means of knowing the amount of crime. Surveys reveal that much more crime occurs than is reported to the police. This is referred to as the **dark figure of crime**. Rape is an example of this type of crime.

dark figure of crime A metaphor that emphasizes the dangerous dimension of crimes that are never reported to the police.

FIGURE 2.1
Violent and Property Victimizations Reported to Police, 2010 Why are some crimes less likely to be reported to the police than others? What can be done to increase the likelihood that victims will report crimes to the police?

*Includes rape or sexual assault, robbery, and aggravated assault.

Source: Jennifer L. Truman, Lynn Langton, and Michael Planty, "Criminal Victimization, 2012," *Bureau of Justice Statistics Bulletin*, October 2013, Table 4.

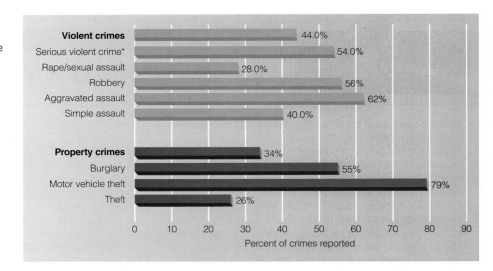

Most homicides and auto thefts are reported to the police. In the case of a homicide, a body must be accounted for, and insurance companies require a police report before they will pay for a stolen car. But large numbers of rape victims do not report the attack. Figure 2.1 shows the percentage of victimizations reported to the police according to type of violent or property crime.

Until 1972 the only crimes counted by government were those that were known to the police and that made their way into the Uniform Crime Reports (UCR) compiled by the Federal Bureau of Investigation (FBI). Since then, the Department of Justice has sponsored the National Crime Victimization Surveys (NCVS), which survey the public to find out how much victimization has occurred. One might hope that the data from these two sources would give us a clear picture of the amount of crime, crime trends, and characteristics of offenders. However, the picture is blurred, perhaps even distorted, because of differences in the way crime is measured by the UCR and the NCVS.

The Uniform Crime Reports (UCR)

Uniform Crime Reports (UCR) An annually published statistical summary of crimes reported to the police, based on voluntary reports to the FBI by local, state, and federal law enforcement agencies.

Issued each year by the FBI, the **Uniform Crime Reports (UCR)** publication is a statistical summary of crimes reported to the police. At the urging of the International Association of Chiefs of Police, Congress authorized this system in 1930 for compiling crime data (Rosen, 1995). The UCR data come from a voluntary national network of local, state, and federal law enforcement agencies policing 94.6 percent of the U.S. population (FBI, 2012b).

With the sharp drop in crime in recent years, new pressures have been placed on police executives to show that their cities are following the national trend. Some officials have even falsified their crime statistics as promotions, pay raises, and departmental budgets have become increasingly dependent on positive data. For example, an audit of police incident reports in Memphis in 2012 raised questions about whether the city's claims about reducing serious crimes were assisted by underreporting such crimes in official crime reports (Maki, 2012). In 2005 leaders of police unions in New York City alleged that officers were pressured to report felonies as misdemeanors in order to help the city show favorable results (Moses, 2005). The Detroit Police Department was accused of misclassifying and undercounting homicides. Newspaper reporters conducted their own count and alleged that the police undercount helped the city avoid acknowledging that it had the nation's worst homicide rate (LeDuff & Esparza, 2009). Because the FBI relies on reports from local police department to compile the UCR, its accuracy is compromised when agencies underreport crime.

CAREERS IN CRIMINAL JUSTICE

Crime Analyst
Mark Bridge, Crime Analyst, City of Frederick, Maryland

The primary responsibilities of the crime analyst's job include the following: conducting preliminary and advanced statistical analysis; compiling crime, arrest, and calls-for-service data; identifying trends and patterns in the data and generating maps, graphs, charts, and tables; briefing members of the command staff on crime patterns and intelligence matters; writing crime and intelligence analysis bulletins related to ongoing trends; making substantial contributions to the development and implementation of new analytical methods; and developing ways to collaborate with federal, state, and local agencies. Data used in crime analysis are derived from many resources, including record management systems (reports, incidents, arrests, and so forth), calls for service, field interviews, and probation and parole data.

A crime analyst must keep the police chief and shift commanders informed about trends in crime rates in various locations within a community. This allows those investing in law enforcement to see what they are getting for their dollar. It also allows for the budgeting and planning of future resources, such as the number of officers needed, which can be based on population growth,

Photo provided by Mark Bridge

calls for service, crime rates, and other factors. Tactical analysis enables patrol and special details to focus on areas where their efforts are most needed. By analyzing data, crime analysts can identify the peak days, times, and locations for crime problems within a community. Given a series of incidents that may involve the same suspect or suspects, the analyst can even use forecasting techniques based on data from previous crimes to project the most likely dates, times, and places of the next crime.

Mark Bridge earned an undergraduate degree and a master's degree in criminal justice. He studied statistics, research methods, theories of crime, policing, and the operations of the criminal justice system. Prior to becoming a crime analyst, he worked in state government analyzing operations of the court system.

The biggest challenge of being a crime analyst is turning raw data into timely and useful information. There are a lot of sources to obtain information from, and you, as the analyst, must decide what to use and how to use it.

The UCR uses standard definitions to ensure uniform data on the 29 types of crimes listed in Table 2.1. For 8 major crimes—Part I (Index Offenses)—the data show factors such as age, race, and number of reported crimes solved. For the other 21 crimes—Part II (Other Offenses)—the data are less complete.

The UCR provides a useful but incomplete picture of crime levels. Because it covers only reported crimes, these reports do not include data on crimes for which people failed to call the police. Also, the UCR does not measure occupational crimes and other offenses that are not included in the 29 types covered. And because reporting is voluntary, police departments may not take the time to make complete and careful reports.

In response to criticisms of the UCR, the FBI has made some changes in the program that are now being implemented nationwide. Some offenses have been redefined, and police agencies are being asked to report more details about crime events. Using the **National Incident-Based Reporting System (NIBRS)**, police agencies are to report all crimes committed during an incident, not just the most serious one, as well as all available data on offenders, victims, and the places where they interact. Whereas the UCR now counts incidents and arrests for the 8 index offenses and counts arrests for other crimes, the NIBRS provides detailed incident data on 46 offenses in 22 crime categories. The NIBRS distinguishes between attempted and completed crimes as well.

How is the NIBRS different from the UCR? In addition to including more types of crime than the UCR, NIBRS data are *disaggregated*—that is, rather than police departments reporting counts of crime to the FBI (as in the UCR), many jurisdictions now report information on individual crimes. Thanks to advances in technology and data transfer, police departments can now transfer data more easily than

National Incident-Based Reporting System (NIBRS)
A reporting system in which the police describe each offense in a crime incident, together with data describing the offender, victim, and property.

TABLE 2.1   Uniform Crime Report Offenses

The UCR presents data on 8 index offenses and 21 other crimes for which there is less information. A limitation of the UCR is that it tabulates only crimes that are reported to the police.

Part I (Index Offenses)	Part II (Other Offenses)
1. Criminal homicide	9. Other assaults
2. Forcible rape	10. Forgery and counterfeiting
3. Robbery	11. Fraud
4. Aggravated assault	12. Embezzlement
5. Burglary	13. Stolen property: Buying, receiving, possessing
6. Larceny/theft	14. Vandalism
7. Auto theft	15. Weapons (carrying, possessing, etc.)
8. Arson	16. Prostitution and commercialized vice
	17. Sex offenses
	18. Drug abuse violations
	19. Gambling
	20. Offenses against the family and children
	21. Driving under the influence
	22. Liquor laws
	23. Drunkenness
	24. Disorderly conduct
	25. Vagrancy
	26. All other offenses
	27. Suspicion
	28. Curfew and loitering laws (juvenile)
	29. Runaways (juvenile)

Source: Federal Bureau of Investigation, 2004, *Uniform Crime Reporting Handbook* (Washington, DC: U.S. Government Printing Office).

was possible when the UCR began collecting data from police departments in 1929. However, the reporting process is more difficult for NIBRS, and all agencies must adopt the same format for reporting data. These difficulties mean that not all states currently participate in the NIBRS system. As of February 2014, only 15 states reported NIBRS data for all of their jurisdictions (Arkansas, Delaware, Idaho, Iowa, Michigan, Montana, New Hampshire, North Dakota, Rhode Island, South Carolina, South Dakota, Tennessee, Vermont, Virginia, and West Virginia). The remaining states report at least some crime through NIBRS or are in training to do so in the near future (FBI, 2013b).

The National Crime Victimization Surveys (NCVS)

National Crime Victimization Surveys (NCVS) Interviews of samples of the U.S. population conducted by the Bureau of Justice Statistics to determine the number and types of criminal victimizations and thus the extent of unreported as well as reported crime.

As mentioned earlier, police agencies are aware that many crimes are not reported to them. In order to gain a better idea of the "dark figure of crime," the Census Bureau developed the **National Crime Victimization Surveys (NCVS)**. The NCVS is considered a "self-reported" measure of criminal behavior, because it uses survey research to ask people whether they've been victims of crime. Data have been gathered since 1972 on unreported as well as reported crimes. Interviews are conducted twice each year with a national probability sample of approximately 74,000 people in 41,000 households. The same people are interviewed twice a year for three years and asked if they have been victimized in the last six months (BJS, 2008).

Each person is asked a set of "screening" questions (for example, "Did anyone beat you up, attack you, or hit you with something such as a rock or a bottle?") to determine whether he or she has been victimized. The person is then asked questions designed to elicit specific facts about the event, the offender, and any financial losses or physical injuries caused by the crime.

Besides the household interviews, surveys are carried out in the nation's 26 largest cities; separate studies are done to find out about the victimization of businesses. These data allow us to estimate how many crimes have occurred, learn more about the offenders, and note demographic patterns. The results show that for the violent crimes measured (rape, robbery, assault, domestic violence), there were 6.8 million victimizations in 2012, which was down from 7.7 million in 2003 (Truman, Langton, & Planty, 2013). Interestingly, this number is much higher than the number of crimes actually reported to the police.

The NCVS data can also be used to track serial (or "repeat" victimizations). Those most likely to be repeated victims of crime tend to take actions involving more risks—such as going to bars or clubs, taking public transit, or "hanging out" where teenagers congregate—and they tend to live in neighborhoods characterized by greater levels of disorganization (Outlaw, Ruback, & Britt, 2002). Others have found that repeat sexual victimization is not affected by the same factors and that women who take actions to protect themselves from any sexual victimization avoid both initial victimization and repeated victimizations (Fisher, Daigle, & Cullen, 2010).

Although the NCVS provides a more complete picture of the nature and extent of crime than the UCR does, it too has flaws (J. P. Lynch & Addington, 2009). Because government employees administer the surveys, the people interviewed are unlikely to report crimes in which they or members of their family took part. They also may not want to admit that a family member engages in crime, or they may be too embarrassed to admit that they have allowed themselves to be victimized more than once. In addition, the survey covers a limited range of crimes, and the relatively small sample of interviewees may lead to erroneous conclusions about crime trends for an entire country of over 300 million people (Mosher, Miethe, & Phillips, 2002).

The NCVS data are also imperfect because they depend on the victim's *perception* of an event. The theft of a child's lunch money by a bully may be reported as a crime by one person but not mentioned by another. People may say that their property was stolen when in fact they lost it. Moreover, people's memories of dates may fade, and they may misreport the year in which a crime occurred even though they remember the event itself clearly. The Bureau of Justice Statistics routinely evaluates how the NCS collects data and sporadically makes changes in the NCVS to improve its accuracy and detail.

The next time you hear or read about crime rates, take into account the source of the data and its possible limitations. Table 2.2 compares the UCR and the NCVS.

Trends in Crime

Experts agree that, contrary to public opinion and the claims of politicians, crime rates have not been steadily rising. The NCVS show that the victimization rate has been dropping steadily over the past decade. From 2003 to 2012, some violent crimes decreased in number, such as simple assault (26.9 percent decrease) and domestic violence (15.0 percent decrease), while small increases were reported for rape (6.6 percent increase) and robbery (4.7 percent increase). Overall, victimizations decreased in most categories during this time period, with a total 10.9 percent decrease in total crimes reported (Truman et al., 2013). The UCR data show similar results, with steady decreases in both violent and property crime reported to the police since 1993 (FBI, 2013a: Table 1).

TABLE 2.2 The UCR and the NCVS

Compare the data sources. Remember that the UCR tabulates only crimes reported to the police, whereas the NCVS data are based on interviews with victims.

	UCR	NCVS
Offenses Measured	Homicide Rape Robbery (personal and commercial) Assault (aggravated) Burglary (commercial and household) Larceny (commercial and household) Motor vehicle theft Arson	Rape/sexual assault Robbery (personal) Assault (aggravated and simple) Household burglary Larceny (personal and household) Motor vehicle theft
Scope	Crimes reported to the police in most jurisdictions; in 2012, the data submitted represented 98.1% of the U.S. population.	Crimes both reported and not reported to police; all data are for the nation as a whole; some data are available for a few large geographic areas.
Collection Method	Police department reports to Federal Bureau of Investigation	Survey interviews: periodically measures the total number of crimes committed by asking a national sample of households about their experiences as victims of crime during a specific period. In 2012, 92,390 households were interviewed, representing 162,940 persons aged 12 or older.
Kinds of Information	In addition to offense counts, provides information on crime clearances, persons arrested, persons charged, law enforcement officers killed and assaulted, and characteristics of homicide victims	Provides details about victims (such as age, race, sex, education, income, and whether the victim and offender were related) and about crimes (such as time and place of occurrence, whether or not reported to police, use of weapons, occurrence of injury, and economic consequences)
Sponsor	Department of Justice's Federal Bureau of Investigation	Department of Justice's Bureau of Justice Statistics

Sources: Truman et al. (2013) and FBI (2013a).

Figure 2.2 displays four measures of violent crime, adjusted for changes made in the NCVS in 1992. The top two measures are based on the victimization survey; crimes recorded by the police and arrests are from the UCR and are presented below these. Remember that the differences in the trends indicated by the NCVS and the UCR are explained in part by the different data sources and different populations on which their tabulations are based.

What explains the drop in both violent and property crime well below the 1982 levels? Among the reasons given by analysts are the aging of the baby boom population, the increased use of security systems, aggressive police efforts to keep handguns off the streets, and the dramatic decline in the use of crack cocaine.

FIGURE 2.2
Four Measures of Serious Violent Crime Questions about homicides are not included in NCVS, so the data here include the assumption that the 14,827 homicides in 2012 were reported to the police.

Source: Jennifer L. Truman, Lynn Langton, and Michael Planty, "Criminal Victimization, 2012," *Bureau of Justice Statistics Bulletin*, October 2013; FBI, *Crime in the United States, 2012* [Uniform Crime Reports] (www.fbi.gov).

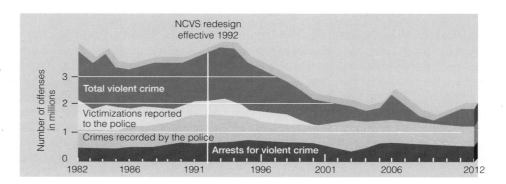

Other factors may include the booming economy of the 1990s and the quadrupling of the number of people incarcerated since 1970. Let us look more closely at how age distribution in the United States can be used to assess future crime levels.

Age Changes in the age makeup of the population are a key factor in the analysis of crime trends. It has long been known that men aged 16 to 24 are the most crime-prone group. The rise in crime in the 1970s has been blamed on the post–World War II baby boom. By the 1970s, the "boomers" had entered the high-risk crime group of 16- to 24-year-olds. They composed a much larger portion of the U.S. population than ever before, so between 40 and 50 percent of the total arrests during that decade could have been attributed to the growth in the total population and in the size of the crime-prone age group. Likewise, the decline in most crime rates that began during the 1980s has been attributed to the maturing of the post–World War II generation. During the 1990s, the 16- to 24-year age cohort was smaller than it had been at any time since the early 1960s, and many people believe that this contributed to the decline in crime.

In 1994 a small but influential group of criminologists predicted that by the year 2000, the number of young men in the 14- to 24-year-old cohort would greatly increase. It was argued that the decline in crime experienced in the 1990s was merely the "lull before the storm" (Steinberg, 1999:4WK). However, the predicted rise in violent crime has not occurred. In fact, after the homicide rate for young people peaked in 1993, it dropped to a new low in 2000 and continues to decline (Puzzanchera & Kang, 2011). The Office of Juvenile Justice and Delinquency Prevention found a 36 percent decrease in juvenile arrests for homicide between 2002 and 2011 (Puzzanchera, 2013).

There are many potential explanations for the continuing reductions in crime since the mid-1990s. Review the "The Policy Debate" feature to learn about the pros and cons of tough crime policy and whether this approach produced reductions in crime.

☑ **CHECK POINT**

4. **What are the two main sources of crime data?**
   Uniform Crime Reports; National Crime Victimization Surveys.

5. **What are key factors in crime trends?**
   Age cohorts and social conditions.

STOP&ANALYZE

The state of Florida has experienced a 33 percent drop in crime since 1999, and many in the private and public sectors are looking for an explanation (K. Stanley, 2011). Some criminologists are examining the relationship between economics and crime. While many believe that worsening economic conditions will lead to more crime (people stealing food, for example), the trends show that the opposite seems to happen. Why would worsening economic conditions actually *decrease* the crime rate?

Crime Victimization

Until the past few decades, researchers paid little attention to crime victims. The field of **victimology**, which emerged in the 1950s, focuses attention on four questions: (1) Who is victimized? (2) What is the impact of crime? (3) What happens to victims in the criminal justice system? (4) What role do victims play in causing the crimes they suffer?

Who Is Victimized?

Not everyone has an equal chance of being a crime victim. For example, people who are victimized by crime in one year are also more likely to be victimized by crime in a subsequent year (Menard, 2000). Research also shows that members of certain demographic groups are more likely to be victimized than others. Puzzling over this fact, victimologists have come up with several answers (Karmen, 2001:87). One explanation is that demographic factors (age, gender, income) affect

victimology A field of criminology that examines the role the victim plays in precipitating a criminal incident and also examines the impact of crimes on victims.

Have Tough Crime-Control Policies Caused a Decline in Crime?

There's good news, and there's bad news. The good news is that the amount of crime in the United States has been decreasing in recent years. Significant reductions have been seen in every type of violent and property crime, and virtually every demographic group has experienced drops in violent victimization.

Any reduction in crime is welcome, but the bad news is that experts do not agree on the causes for the decline in crime. Have the tough crime-control policies of the past 20 years really reduced crime? Or have crime rates lessened because of factors unrelated to anything police, prosecution, courts, and corrections have done?

Some experts point out that there are more police officers on the streets, sentences are longer, and the probability upon conviction of going to prison is greater. They say the police have been more aggressive in dealing with public-order offenses, the waiting period for handgun purchases has been effective, and more than a million Americans are already in prison and off the streets. In other words, the police and other agencies of criminal justice have made the difference.

Other experts question the impact of tough policies. They point out that the number of men in the crime-prone age group is relatively low compared with that age group's percentage of the national population from the 1960s to the 1980s. Many also say that the tough crime policies, instead of reducing crime, have devastated minority communities and diverted resources that could be used to deal with the poverty that underlies crime. They urge policies that "put *justice* back in criminal justice."

Although crime rates have been falling, fear of crime is rising. Some opinion surveys find that Americans rank crime among the nation's most prominent problems after the economy, wars, and terrorism. Arguably, crime should rank much lower, given the decrease in victimizations. Because views of crime are shaped more by television news than by statistics, Americans have an unrealistic picture of the crime problem. Grisly coverage of a murder scene on the evening news sticks in the mind in a way that the results of crime studies can never do.

Drugs and crime are perennially popular issues in U.S. politics. Legislators respond easily to pressures to "do something about crime." Who can argue with that? They usually act by coming up with new laws mandating stiffer sentences and allocating more money for police and corrections. But is this the best direction for public policy?

For Tough Crime Control

Supporters of tough crime-control policies say that crime, especially violent crime, is a serious problem. Even though rates have declined, they argue, violence is still many times higher here than in other developed democracies. We must continue to pursue criminals through strict law enforcement, aggressive prosecutions, and the sentencing of career criminals to long prison terms. They claim that taking the pressure off now will pave the way for problems in the future.

Here is a summary of the arguments for tough crime-control policies:

- The United States has a serious crime problem. Its laws must ensure that offenders receive strict and certain penalties.

lifestyle—people's routine activities, such as work, home life, and recreation. Lifestyles, in turn, affect people's exposure to dangerous places, times, and people (Varano, McCluskey, Patchin, & Bynum, 2004).

Routine activity explanations of crime posit that there are three factors that are important for explaining crime—specifically, that (1) likely offenders, (2) suitable targets, and (3) the absence of capable guardians converge to increase the likelihood of criminal behavior (Cohen & Felson, 1979). In other words, in order for a crime to occur, there must be people interested in committing crime, potential victims, and the lack of anyone "guarding" the victims. Thus, a man walking alone at night (having no guardian) who has just stopped at the ATM is a suitable target. All that is required is a likely offender looking to do harm.

Routine activity has been used to explain a number of different crimes, including cyber crimes—the presence of cyber criminals online combined with a suitable target (someone using an online credit card, for example) combined with lack of capable guardians (no antivirus software installed) can increase the odds of cyber crime (Holt & Bossler, 2009). In another example, the homeless are at extremely high risk for physical and sexual victimization (Tyler & Beal, 2010). Thus, differences in lifestyles lead to varying degrees of exposure to risks (R. F. Meier & Miethe, 1993:466). Considering this theoretical perspective, think of people whose lifestyle includes going to nightclubs in a "shady" part of town. Such people run the risk of being robbed if they walk alone through a dark high-crime area at two in the morning to their luxury car. By contrast, older individuals who watch television at night in their small-town home

- Crime is not caused by poverty, unemployment, and other socioeconomic factors. Instead, crime causes poverty.
- The expansion of the prison population has taken hardened criminals out of the community, thus contributing to the drop in crime.
- The police must have the resources and legal backing to pursue criminals.

Against Tough Crime Control

Opponents of the get-tough approach believe that better ways are available to deal with crime. They argue that crime is no more effectively controlled today than it was in the early 1970s and that in many respects the problem has worsened, especially in the poorest neighborhoods. Neither the war on crime nor the war on drugs has stopped the downward spiral of livability in these neighborhoods. Another price of the tough crime-control policies has been an erosion of civil rights and liberties—especially for racial and ethnic minorities. What is needed is an infusion of justice into the system.

Here is a summary of the arguments against tough crime-control policies:

- The get-tough policies have not significantly reduced crime.
- Resources should be diverted from the criminal justice system to get to the underlying causes of criminal behavior—poor housing, unemployment, and racial injustice.
- Tough incarceration policies have devastated poor communities. With large numbers of young men in prison, families live in poverty, and children grow up without guidance from their fathers and older brothers.
- Crime policies emphasizing community policing, alternatives to incarceration, and community assistance programs will do more to promote justice than will the failed get-tough policies of the past.

What Should U.S. Policy Be?

The justice system costs about $200 billion a year. Advocates of tough crime-control policies say that the high cost is worth the price and that the aggressive and punitive policies of the past two decades have worked to reduce crime. Opponents of these policies respond that the police, courts, and corrections have had little impact on crime. Other factors, such as the booming economy of the 1990s and the smaller number of men in the crime-prone age cohort, have been responsible for the reduction. The recession that began in 2008 has caused many government agencies to rethink their spending. Some have found new ways to increase efficiency, while others are considering combining police and fire services into one large agency.

Even though they are told that crime has gone down, Americans remain fearful. Their opinions translate into support for politicians who advocate the tough approach. No candidate for public office wants to be labeled "soft on crime." What would be the costs—economic and human—of continuing the get-tough policies?

Researching the Internet

To see a 2012 public opinion study about alternatives to imprisonment as a policy for addressing crime, go to http://www.pewstates.org/uploadedFiles/PCS_Assets/2012/PEW_NationalSurveyResearchPaper_FINAL.pdf.

For Critical Analysis

How can we determine which factors have caused the declines in crime rates? Are there ways to experiment with our public policies that might tell us the answer? Should the declining crime rates cause us to create any new policies, shift our allocation of resources, or give less attention to crime as a policy issue?

---

have a very low chance of being robbed. But these cases do not tell the entire story. What other factors make victims more vulnerable than nonvictims?

Women, Youths, Nonwhites The lifestyle-exposure model and survey data shed light on the links between personal characteristics and the chance that one will become a victim. Figure 2.3 shows the influence of gender, age, and race on the risk of being victimized by a violent crime such as rape, robbery, or assault. If we apply these findings to the lifestyle-exposure model, we might suggest that African American teenagers are most likely to be victimized because of where they live (urban, high-crime areas), how they may spend their leisure time (outside late at night), and the people with whom they may associate (violence-prone youths). Not surprisingly, juveniles who engage in a delinquent lifestyle are more likely to be victimized than those who do not (Melde, 2009). Lifestyle factors may also explain why elderly white men and women are least likely to be victimized by a violent crime. Perhaps it is because they do not go out at night, do not associate with people who are prone to crime, carry few valuables, and take precautions such as locking their doors. Thus, lifestyle choices directly affect the chances of victimization.

Race is a key factor in exposure to crime. African Americans are more likely than whites to be raped, robbed, and assaulted—the rate of violent crime victimization for whites is 25.2 per 1,000 people, compared with 34.2 per 1,000 for African Americans (Truman et al., 2012: Table 7). Although white Americans are fearful of being victimized by African American strangers (Skogan, 1995:59), most violent crime is intraracial.

FIGURE 2.3

Victimization Rates for Violent Crimes African American male youths generally have the highest victimization rates. Why are these young people more likely than other age, gender, and racial groups to be robbed or assaulted?

Note: Figures reflect average victimization rates for each demographic group for the time period 2003–2008. For specific demographic groups, data for an individual year would be excluded from the calculation of the average if there were fewer than 10 sample cases in the category.

Sources: Bureau of Justice Statistics, *Criminal Victimization in the United States, 2003—Statistical Tables* (July 2005), Table 10; Bureau of Justice Statistics, *Criminal Victimization in the United States, 2004—Statistical Tables* (June 2006), Table 10; Bureau of Justice Statistics, *Criminal Victimization in the United States, 2005—Statistical Tables* (December 2006), Table 10; Bureau of Justice Statistics, *Criminal Victimization in the United States, 2006—Statistical Tables* (August 2008), Table 10; Bureau of Justice Statistics, *Criminal Victimization in the United States, 2007—Statistical Tables* (February 2010), Table 10; M. R. Rand and J. E. Robinson, *Criminal Victimization in the United States, 2008—Statistical Tables* (May 2011), Table 10.

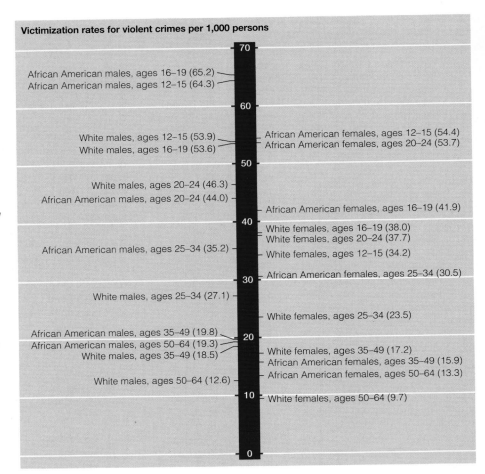

Victimization rates for violent crimes per 1,000 persons

African American males, ages 16–19 (65.2)
African American males, ages 12–15 (64.3)

White males, ages 12–15 (53.9)
White males, ages 16–19 (53.6)
African American females, ages 12–15 (54.4)
African American females, ages 20–24 (53.7)

White males, ages 20–24 (46.3)
African American males, ages 20–24 (44.0)
African American females, ages 16–19 (41.9)

White females, ages 16–19 (38.0)
White females, ages 20–24 (37.7)
White females, ages 12–15 (34.2)

African American males, ages 25–34 (35.2)
African American females, ages 25–34 (30.5)

White males, ages 25–34 (27.1)
White females, ages 25–34 (23.5)

African American males, ages 35–49 (19.8)
African American males, ages 50–64 (19.3)
White males, ages 35–49 (18.5)
White females, ages 35–49 (17.2)
African American females, ages 35–49 (15.9)
African American females, ages 50–64 (13.3)

White males, ages 50–64 (12.6)
White females, ages 50–64 (9.7)

For both white and black victims, about two-thirds of victims are of the same race as the attacker (Harrell, 2007). These numbers simply reflect that African Americans and whites often live in separate neighborhoods. Most of their daily contacts are with people who share their demographic characteristics. And, most importantly, African American neighborhoods are much more likely to experience what scholars call "high levels of socioeconomic disadvantage" with respect to unemployment, quality of schools, quality of housing, and other factors associated with income and wealth (Lauritsen & White, 2001). These factors are often associated with higher levels of street crime; other kinds of crime, such as occupational crime and computer crime, occur more frequently in other settings.

Low-Income City Dwellers Income is also closely linked to exposure to crime. Americans with incomes below $7,500 annually experienced a victimization rate of 44 violent crimes per 1,000 people. By contrast, those with incomes in excess of $75,000 experienced only 12.9 violent crimes per 1,000 people (BJS, 2010: Table 14). The reason is clear enough: economic factors largely determine where people live, work, and seek recreation. For low-income people, these choices are limited. Some have to live in crime-prone areas where housing is cheaper and they lack security devices for their homes, cannot avoid contact with people who are prone to crime, or cannot spend their leisure time in safe areas. Poor people and minorities have a greater risk of being victimized because they are likely to live in inner-city zones with high rates of street crime. People with higher incomes have more lifestyle-exposure choices open to them and can avoid risky situations (R. F. Meier & Miethe, 1993:468). Living in a city is, in fact, a key factor in victimization. For example, motor vehicle theft is much more common in urban areas (10.0 victimizations per 1,000 population) compared with rural areas, with 2.2 victimizations per 1,000 people (BJS, 2010: Table 18).

In the inner cities, where drug dealing and drug use pose significant and visible problems, murder rates are higher than elsewhere. Like their killers, most of the victims tend to be young African Americans. The national homicide-victimization rate among African American men aged 18 to 24 is 91 for every 100,000 of the same group, about eight times that for white men in the same age bracket (A. Cooper & Smith, 2011). But this does not tell the whole story, because homicide rates differ by city and state. In some cities and states, the gap between rates for African Americans and whites is even greater. Further, we cannot conclude that crime rates will be high in all poor urban areas. There is more crime in some poor areas than in others. Many factors besides poverty—such as the physical condition of the neighborhood, the residents' attitudes toward society and the law, the extent of opportunities for crime, and social control by families and government—can affect the crime rate of a given area.

Acquaintances and Strangers

The frightening image of crime in the minds of many Americans is the familiar scene played out in many movies and television shows in which a dangerous stranger grabs a victim on a dark street or breaks into a home at night. It is true that many crimes are committed by strangers against people they have never seen before. However, most Americans do not realize the extent to which violent crimes occur among acquaintances, friends, and even relatives. In 2009, for example, female victims of violent crimes were victimized by strangers in only 31 percent of those crimes; acquaintances, spouses, boyfriends, or relatives committed 68 percent of the violent crimes against female victims. Although only 45 percent of male victims suffered violent crimes at the hands of acquaintances and relatives, that figure still constitutes a significant percentage of violent crimes (Truman & Rand, 2010: Table 7). As you read the following "Criminal Justice: Myth & Reality," consider how you evaluate your risk of victimization in different situations.

According to the lifestyle-exposure model, demographic factors (age, gender, income) and exposure to dangerous places, times, and people influence the probability of being victimized. Based on this model, how would you assess your own risk of victimization?

The kind of crime a victim suffers tends to depend on whether strangers or nonstrangers are the perpetrators. Most robberies are committed by strangers, but sexual assault victims are more likely to be victimized by someone they know (Truman & Rand, 2010: Table 7). These differences reflect, in part, the contexts in which these crimes occur. In robberies, valuables are taken from an individual by force and then the robber typically runs away. Thus, the scenario fits situations in which the robber hopes to escape without being caught or identified. This result is much more difficult for a robber who is known to the victim. By contrast, sexual assaults often take place in isolated or private locations—people are most likely to place themselves in isolated or private locations, such as inside a house or apartment, with someone they know.

People may be reluctant to report crimes committed by relatives, such as the theft of their own valuables by a relative with a substance-abuse problem. They may be upset about losing their valuables, but they do not want to see their son, daughter, or cousin arrested and sent to prison. If the perpetrators of such crimes know that their relatives will not report them, they may feel encouraged to victimize these people further in order to support a drug habit. Thus, the prior relationships among people may facilitate some crimes and keep victims from seeking police assistance.

The lifestyle-exposure model helps us understand some of the factors that increase or decrease the risk of being victimized, but what is the impact of crime on the nation and on individuals? We turn to this question in the next section.

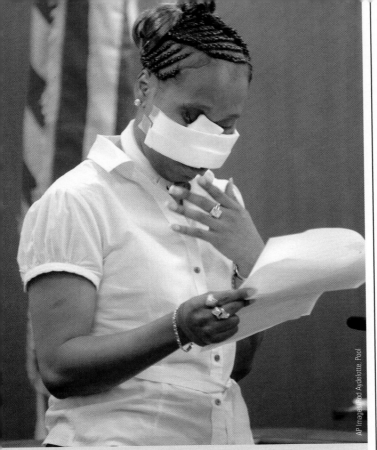

Although Americans often fear violent victimization at the hands of strangers, most violence against women is perpetrated by those with whom they are intimate—husbands, boyfriends, and former lovers. What policies could address this problem?

CRIMINAL JUSTICE
MYTH&REALITY

COMMON BELIEF: Women are more likely to be raped by a stranger than by someone they know.

- Most women take protective measures to avoid being attacked by strangers. They avoid walking alone at night, park their cars in well-lighted areas, or even carry weapons such as pepper spray.
- The "stranger-in-the-bushes" stereotype of rape certainly does occur, but women are significantly more likely to be raped by a friend or acquaintance than by a stranger.
- Approximately three-quarters of sexual assaults are perpetrated by someone the victim knows, whether an acquaintance, friend, or intimate partner (Truman, 2011).
- This misperception about the risk of sexual assault can lead women to take the wrong kinds of action to protect themselves from rape.
- For example, a college student drinking at a bar might fear walking alone at night and ask a male acquaintance from one of her classes to walk her home. While this action has reduced her risk of being raped by a stranger, it may actually increase her risk of victimization by placing her alone in the company of someone she does not know very well.

The Impact of Crime

Crime affects not only the victim but all members of society. We all pay for crime through higher taxes, higher prices, and fear. These factors impinge on key American values such as individual liberty and protection of private property and personal wealth.

Costs of Crime Crime has many kinds of costs: (1) the economic costs—lost property, lower productivity, and medical expenses; (2) the psychological and emotional costs—pain, trauma, and diminished quality of life; and (3) the costs of operating the criminal justice system.

The costs of economic losses from crime in 2008 were estimated at $17.4 billion (BJS, 2010: Table 82); however, this value only includes the property lost through events such as theft or vandalism. Costs associated with damaged or lost property, lost work time, and medical expenses increase that value significantly. In addition, the intangible costs (pain, trauma, lost quality of life) to victims are difficult to estimate accurately. Adding the costs of operating the criminal justice system each year increases the total economic loss of criminal victimization. In the United States in 2007, approximately $228 billion was paid for police, courts, and corrections (Kyckelhahn, 2011). One study estimates the total cost of *each* homicide to be about $8.9 million, after adding the costs to victims and the government (McCollister, French, & Fang, 2010).

Government costs also increased in the aftermath of the September 11 tragedy as more money was spent on airport security, border patrols, and counterterrorist activities. These figures do not include the costs to consumers stemming from occupational and organized crime. In 2012, complainants to the The Internet Crime Complaint Center reported total losses exceeding $525 million—an increase of 8.3 percent from those reported in 2011 (Internet Crime Complaint Center, 2013). It is difficult to estimate precise figures for economic losses, but clearly such losses are significant and appear to increase annually for crime such as Internet fraud and identity theft.

The costs of fighting crime came under increased scrutiny following the recession that began in late 2007. State agencies have begun to search for ways to save money, which frequently involve combining or sharing services with other agencies. In the state of Michigan, for example, several small police departments have been disbanded and local law enforcement is increasingly provided by larger neighboring police agencies. Such consolidation can increase response times, especially in rural areas. In other areas, 911 services are being shared by several agencies in an attempt to reduce operating budgets. Some areas are even taking the more drastic step of combining police and fire services into a single agency. Only time (and research) will determine if these cost-cutting measures will also result in significant reductions in crime.

Fear of Crime One impact of crime is fear. Fear limits freedom in that many people feel compelled to limit their activities to "safe" areas at "safe" times. Fear also creates anxieties that affect physiological and psychological well-being. Ironically, the very people who have the least chance of being victimized, such as women and the elderly, are often the most fearful (Miethe, 1995). Not all Americans experience the same fears, but some people do adjust their daily activities to prevent being victimized.

Since 1965, public-opinion polls have asked Americans whether they "feel more uneasy" or "fear to walk the streets at night." When people are afraid to walk near their homes, their freedom is severely limited. From 1972 to 1993, more than 40 percent of respondents indicated that fear of crime affected their nighttime activities in their neighborhoods. Coinciding with the declining crimes rates during the 1990s, the percentage of respondents who were fearful of walking near their homes dropped to 30 percent in 2001. However, as indicated in "What Americans Think," the percentage has remained around 37 percent since 2005—barely less than the percentages in some years with much higher national crime rates. Thus, a significant segment of the American public remains fearful despite the significant drop in crime rates over the past 20 years (Saad, 2010).

QUESTION: "Is there any area near where you live—that is, within a mile—where you would be afraid to walk alone at night?"

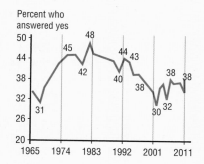

Percent who answered yes

CRITICAL THINKING: Should the government be more active in making the public aware about reduced crime rates and lessened risks of victimization? Alternatively, can increasing awareness about crime cause citizens to overreact to crime problems? In other words, might more information about crime lead to exaggerated fears rather than realistic ones?

Based on http://www.gallup.com/poll/144272/Nearly-Americans -Fear-Walking-Alone-Night.aspx.

Although crime rates are down, Americans' fears seem to exceed actual victimization risks. As we have seen, people do not have a clear picture of the true risk of crime in their lives. They gain perceptions about crime from conversations at their workplace and from politicians' statements and campaign promises. Their views about crime also seem to be shaped more by what they see on television than by reality (Chiricos, Padgett, & Gertz, 2000). Although less than 8 percent of victimizations involve violent crime, such crimes are the ones most frequently reported by the media.

The Experience of Victims in the Criminal Justice System

After a crime has occurred, the victim is often forgotten. Victims may have suffered physical, psychological, and economic losses, yet the criminal justice system focuses on finding and prosecuting the offender and often is not sensitive to the needs of victims. For example, defense attorneys may ask them hostile questions and attempt to paint them, rather than the defendant, as having caused the crime to occur. Similarly, whereas victims are a key source of evidence, the police and prosecutors may question them closely—and in a hostile fashion—to find out if they are telling the truth. Often the victim never hears the outcome of a case. Worse yet, sometimes a victim comes face-to-face with the assailant who is out on bail or on probation. This can be quite a shock, especially if the victim assumed that the offender was in prison.

Victims may be forced to miss work and lose pay in order to appear at judicial proceedings. They may be summoned to court again and again, only to learn that the arraignment or trial has been postponed. Any recovered property may be held by the court for months as the case winds its way through the system. In short, after cases have been completed, victims may feel that they have been victimized twice, once by the offender and once by the criminal justice system.

During the past three decades, justice agencies have become more sensitive to the interests of crime victims. This has happened partly because victims often are the only witnesses to the crime, so their help is needed. Many victims are not willing to provide such help if it involves economic and emotional costs. Some research indicates that victims are more likely to cooperate with the prosecutor if victim-assistance workers meet with them to provide comfort as well as information about how the court system operates (Dawson & Dinovitzer, 2001).

Various laws adopted in recent years provide funds to counsel victims and give financial compensation for injuries, although victims often do not receive enough timely information to take advantage of these programs (Sims, Yost, & Abbott, 2005). In addition, victims' rights statutes in many states permit crime victims to speak at sentencing and parole hearings and to receive information about any impending release of the offender who victimized them. The Justice for All Act passed by Congress in 2004 mandates such rights for victims in those criminal cases processed in the federal courts.

Victims' assistance laws raise questions about which individuals or family members can receive benefits as "victims" (Trulson, 2005). Questions about fairness may arise if some individuals receive different benefits than do others in this regard. Read "A Question of Ethics" at the end of the chapter to consider whether the families of crime victims in general are treated fairly compared with the families of 9/11 victims.

The Role of Victims in Crime

Victimologists study the role victims play in certain crimes. Researchers have found that many victims behave in ways that facilitate the acts committed against them. This does not mean that it is the victim's fault that the crime occurred. It means instead that the victim's behavior may have led to the crime through consent, provocation, enticement, risk taking, or carelessness with property.

What do studies tell us about these situations? First, some people do not take proper precautions to protect themselves. For example, they leave keys in their cars or fail to lock their doors and windows at night. They seem to lack the "common sense" of understanding the price of living safely in modern society. Second, some victims provoke or entice another person to commit a crime. Arguing with a stranger at a bar can lead to criminal assaults. Third, when the offender is known to the victim, the victim may be unwilling to help with the investigation and prosecution. These behaviors do not excuse criminal acts, but they do force us to think about other aspects of the crime situation.

☑ CHECK POINT

6. **What are the main elements of the lifestyle-exposure model?**
   Demographic characteristics, adaptations, lifestyle, associations, exposure.

7. **What are some of the impacts of crime?**
   Fear, financial costs, emotional costs, lifestyle restrictions.

8. **Why do some crime victims feel mistreated by the criminal justice system?**
   The system focuses on finding and punishing the offender; police and lawyers often question victims closely, in an unsympathetic manner; victims do not always receive assistance that covers their medical expenses and other losses.

STOP&ANALYZE

Fear of crime among Americans has remained relatively stable since the mid-1990s; however, during this period, the crime rate has decreased significantly. List two reasons that might explain this apparent "disconnect" between the perception of crime and the reality of crime. Why would the typical American fear crime at the same level when the United States has become safer over the last 20 years?

Causes of Crime

Whenever news of a crime hits the headlines, whether the crime is a grisly murder or a complex bank fraud, the first question is, "Why did he (or she) do it?" Do people commit crimes because they are poor, greedy, mentally ill, or just plain stupid? Do any of these explanations apply to the man who shot Chad Oulson, who was texting during movie previews? Would the same explanation be valid for Tia Miller, who stole the identities of over 700 people and defrauded the U.S. government?

Various theories about the root causes of criminal behavior have been developed, and scholarly research regularly tests these theories. Using the scientific method, criminologists generate hypotheses, collect data, and derive findings about which theories best explain criminal behavior. When substantiated, these theories can provide the basis for new public policies aimed at preventing crime.

Criminology is concerned mainly with learning about criminal behavior, the nature of offenders, and how crime can be prevented. Research focuses mainly on the offender. Fewer questions are asked about how factors such as the economy, government policy, family, and education affect crime (Messner & Rosenfeld, 1994:45–47). In this section, we look at the two major schools of criminological thought—classical and positivist. We will review biological, psychological, sociological, life course, and integrated theories of the causes of criminal behavior. We then take a look at women's criminal behavior and conclude with an overall assessment of the theories discussed in this section.

Classical and Positivist Theories

Two major schools of criminological thought are the classical and positivist schools. Each was pioneered by scholars who were influenced by the dominant intellectual ideas of their times.

The Classical School   Until the eighteenth century, most Europeans explained criminal behavior in supernatural terms. Those who did wrong were "possessed" by the devil. Some Christians believed that all humanity had fallen with Adam and had remained in a state of total depravity ever since. Indictments often began "[John Doe], not having the fear of God before his eyes but being moved and seduced by the instigation of the devil, did commit [a certain crime]." Before the eighteenth century, defendants had few rights. The accused had little chance to put forth a defense, confessions were obtained through torture, and the penalty for most offenses was physical punishment or death.

In 1764 Cesare Beccaria published *An Essay on Crimes and Punishment*. This was the first attempt to explain crime in secular, or worldly, terms, as opposed to religious terms. The book also pointed to injustices in the administration of criminal laws. Beccaria's ideas prompted reformers to try to make criminal law and procedures more rational and consistent. From this movement came **classical criminology**, whose main principles are as follows:

classical criminology
A school of criminology that views behavior as stemming from free will, demands responsibility and accountability of all perpetrators, and stresses the need for punishments severe enough to deter others.

1. Criminal behavior is rational, and most people have the potential to engage in such behavior.
2. People may choose to commit a crime after weighing the costs and benefits of their actions.
3. Fear of punishment is what keeps most people in check. Therefore, the severity, certainty, and speed of punishment affect the level of crime.
4. The punishment should fit the crime rather than the person who committed it.
5. The criminal justice system must be predictable, with laws and punishments known to the public.

Classical ideas declined in the nineteenth century, partly because of the rise of science and partly because its principles did not take into account differences among individuals or the way the crime was committed.

Neoclassical Criminology   After remaining dormant for almost a hundred years, classical ideas took on new life in the 1980s, when America became more conservative. Some scholars argue that crimes may result from the rational choice of people who have weighed the benefits to be gained from the crime against the costs of being caught and punished. But they also recognize that criminal law must take into account the differences among individuals. To a large extent, sentencing reform, criticisms of rehabilitation, and greater use of incarceration stem from a renewed interest in classical ideas. However, the positivist school of thought is what has dominated American criminology since the start of the twentieth century.

Positivist Criminology   By the middle of the nineteenth century, as the scientific method began to take hold, the ideas of the classical school seemed old-fashioned. Instead, **positivist criminology** used science to study the body, mind, and environment of the offender. Science could help reveal why offenders committed crimes and how they could be rehabilitated. Here are the key features of this approach:

1.   Human behavior is controlled by physical, mental, and social factors, not by free will.
2.   Criminals are different from noncriminals.
3.   Science can be used to discover the causes of crime and to treat deviants.

Understanding the main theories of crime causation is important because they affect how laws are enforced, guilt is determined, and crimes are punished. As we describe each of the theories, consider its implications for crime policies. For example, if biological theories are viewed as sound, then the authorities might try to identify potential offenders through genetic analysis and then segregate or supervise them. On the other hand, the acceptance of sociological theories might lead to efforts to end poverty, improve education, and provide job training.

Biological Explanations

The medical training of Cesare Lombroso (1835–1909) led him to suppose that physical traits distinguish criminals from law-abiding citizens. He believed that some people are at a more primitive state of evolution and hence are born criminal. These "throwbacks" have trouble adjusting to modern society. Lombroso's ideas can be summarized as follows (Lombroso, 1912/1968):

1.   Certain people are **criminogenic**—that is, they are born criminals.
2.   They have primitive physical traits such as strong canine teeth, huge jaws, and high cheekbones.
3.   These traits are acquired through heredity or through alcoholism, epilepsy, or syphilis.

Early biological studies traced the generations of specific families to count how many people in each violated criminal laws. These early studies may no longer seem credible to us, but they were taken seriously in their time and affected criminal justice for decades. For example, many states passed laws that required repeat offenders to be sterilized. It was assumed that crime could be controlled if criminal traits were not passed from parents to children. Not until 1942 did the U.S. Supreme Court declare required sterilization unconstitutional (*Skinner v. Oklahoma*).

Although **biological explanations** of crime were ignored or condemned as racist after World War II, they have attracted renewed interest. *Crime and Human Nature*, by James Q. Wilson and Richard Herrnstein (1985), reviews the research on this subject. Unlike the early positivists, the authors do not claim that any one factor explains criminality. Instead, they argue that biological factors predispose some individuals to commit crimes. Genetic makeup, body type, and IQ may outweigh social factors as predictors of criminality. The findings of research on nutrition, neurology, genetics, and endocrinology give some support to the view that these factors may contribute to violent behavior in some people (Brennan, Mednick, & Volavka, 1995:65). Other researchers have identified physiological factors associated with antisocial behavior, an association they see as a step toward considering a possible link between biology and crime (Cauffman, Steinberg, & Piquero, 2005).

These new findings have given biological explanations a renewed influence and have reduced the dominance of sociological and psychological explanations. Scientists are doing further research to see if they can identify biological factors that make some people prone to violence and criminality (Fishbein, 1990:27). For example, a single gene

positivist criminology A school of criminology that views behavior as stemming from social, biological, and psychological factors. It argues that punishment should be tailored to the individual needs of the offender.

criminogenic Having factors thought to bring about criminal behavior in an individual.

biological explanations Explanations of crime that emphasize physiological and neurological factors that may predispose a person to commit crimes.

can help predict which abused children are more likely to become violent or antisocial adults—abused children with this gene were twice as likely as other abused children to commit acts of violence (Hathaway, 2002). Other studies examine the role of nutrition, such as consumption of fish rich in omega-3 being associated with lower levels of hostility in young adults (Iribarren et al., 2004). Definitive research has revealed the impact of environmental lead, such as lead-based paint, on brain development and behavior (University of Pittsburgh Medical Center, 2005). Behavior may also be affected by head injuries, tumors in specific locations on the brain, and natural chemical imbalances within the body. These findings behind biology and behavior do not necessarily purport to seek a single explanation for crime. They merely demonstrate an increased recognition that biological factors influence certain kinds of behavior in some offenders.

Psychological Explanations

People have often viewed criminal behavior as being caused by a mental condition, a personality disturbance, or limited intellect. **Psychological explanations** of crime center on these ideas.

Sigmund Freud (1856–1939), now seen as one of the foremost thinkers of the twentieth century, proposed a psychoanalytic theory that crime is caused by unconscious forces and drives. Freud also claimed that early childhood experiences greatly affect personality development. Freud's followers expanded his theory, saying that the personality is made up of three parts: the id, ego, and superego. The id controls drives that are primarily sexual, the ego relates desires to behavior, and the superego (often referred to as the conscience) judges actions as either right or wrong. Psychoanalytic theory explains criminal behavior as resulting from either an undeveloped or an overdeveloped superego. For example, a person who commits a violent sex crime is thought to have an undeveloped superego, because the urges cannot be controlled. Alternatively, a person with an overdeveloped superego may suffer from guilt and anxiety. To reduce the guilt, the person may commit a crime, knowing that punishment will follow. To ensure punishment, the offender will unconsciously leave clues at the crime scene. Psychoanalysts say this occurred in the famous Loeb and Leopold murder of Bobby Franks in 1924 (Regoli & Hewitt, 1994).

Psychiatrists have linked criminal behavior to such concepts as innate impulses, psychic conflict, and repression of personality. Such explanations propose that crime is a behavior that stems from abnormal urges and desires. Although the psychological approach takes many different forms, all are based on the idea that early personality development is a key factor in later behavior. The terms *psychopath, sociopath*, and *antisocial personality* refer to a person who is unable to control impulses, cannot learn from experience, and does not feel emotions such as love. This kind of person is viewed as psychologically abnormal and may become a crazed killer or sex fiend.

Psychological theories have been widely criticized. Some critics point to the fact that it is hard to measure emotional factors and to identify people thought to be

In 2012, George Huguely, a former University of Virginia lacrosse player, was convicted of second-degree murder and sentenced to 23 years in prison in 2012 for the beating death of his ex-girlfriend, Yeardley Love, also a University of Virginia varsity athlete. Does criminological theory help us understand what motivated a privileged, prominent student-athlete to commit such an act?

psychological explanations
Explanations of crime that emphasize mental processes and behavior.

prone to crime. Others note the wide range of sometimes contradictory theories that take a psychological approach to crime.

Sociological Explanations

sociological explanations
Explanations of crime that emphasize as causes of criminal behavior the social conditions that bear on the individual.

In contrast to psychological approaches, **sociological explanations** focus on the way that belonging to social groups shapes people's behavior. Sociologists believe that criminality is not inborn but caused by external factors. Thus, sociological theories of crime assume that contact with the social world, as well as such factors as race, age, gender, and income, mold the offender's personality and actions.

In the 1920s, a group of researchers at the University of Chicago looked closely at aspects of urban life that seemed to be linked to crime: poverty, bad housing, broken families, and the problems faced by new immigrants. They found high levels of crime in those neighborhoods that had many opportunities for delinquent behavior and offered few legitimate means of earning a living.

From a sociological perspective, criminals are made, not born. Among the many theories stressing the influence of societal forces on criminal behavior, three types deserve special mention: social structure theories, social process theories, and critical theories.

social structure theories
Theories that blame crime on the existence of a powerless lower class that lives with poverty and deprivation and often turns to crime in response.

anomie A breakdown or disappearance of the rules of social behavior.

Social Structure Theories **Social structure theories** suggest that criminal behavior is related to social class. People in various social classes have quite different amounts of wealth, status, and power. Those in the lower class suffer from poverty, poor education, bad housing, and lack of political power. Therefore, members of the lower class, especially the younger members, are the most likely to engage in crime. Thus, crime is created by the structure of society.

In 1938 the sociologist Robert Merton, drawing from theories about the role of social change and urbanization on crime, concluded that social change often leads to a state of **anomie**, in which the rules or norms that guide behavior have weakened or disappeared. People may become anomic when the rules are unclear or they cannot achieve their goals. Under such conditions, antisocial or deviant behavior may result.

It is said, for example, that U.S. society highly values success but makes it impossible for some of its members to succeed. It follows that those who are caught in this trap may use crime as a way out. Theorists believe that this type of situation has led some ethnic groups into organized crime. Others argue that social disorganization brings about conditions in which, among other things, family structure breaks down, alcohol or drug abuse becomes more common, and criminal behavior increases. They assert that poverty must be ended and the social structure reformed if crime is to be reduced (R. J. Sampson & Wilson, 1995).

Contemporary theorists have drawn from social structure concepts and Merton's anomie theory to develop certain theories of crime causation. Prominent among modern approaches is the general theory of strain. According to this approach, negative relationships can lead to negative emotions. These emotions, particularly anger, are expressed through crime and delinquency. Strain is produced by the failure to achieve valued goals, which may particularly affect poor people in a society that values financial success. Strain is also produced by negative experiences, including unemployment, child abuse, criminal victimization, and family problems, which also tend to prevail in poor communities. Under this theory, those who cannot cope with negative experiences may be predisposed to criminal behavior (Liska & Messner, 1999:36–37).

As these ideas have become more refined, they have also been used to explain white-collar crime. To achieve even higher levels of success in a structure that values ever increasing wealth, individuals may break rules and violate laws in order to enhance their personal success. As with "street" crime, white-collar criminals may commit crimes due to economic strain, but they may also be influenced by a perceived inability to reach a particular social status or work-related strain. These strains, combined with other factors, can increase the likelihood that they will engage in white-collar crime (Agnew, Piquero, & Cullen, 2009).

Social Process Theories Despite such arguments, many criminologists believe that the social structure approach does not adequately explain criminality by middle-class and affluent people. More importantly, they fear that a focus on social structure erroneously emphasizes crime as primarily a problem of the poor. **Social process theories**, which date from the 1930s but did not gain recognition until the 1960s and 1970s, assume that any person, regardless of education, class, or upbringing, has the potential to become a criminal. However, some people are more likely to commit criminal acts because of the circumstances of their lives. Thus, these theories try to explain the processes by which certain people become criminals.

There are three main types of social process theories: learning theories, control theories, and labeling theories.

Learning theories hold that criminal activity is learned behavior. Through social relations, some people learn how to be a criminal and acquire the values associated with that way of life. This view assumes that people imitate and learn from one another. Thus, family members and peers are viewed as major influences on a person's development.

In 1939 Edwin Sutherland proposed a type of learning theory called the **theory of differential association**, which states that behavior is learned through interactions with others, especially family members (Sutherland, 1947). Therefore, criminal behavior is learned when a person encounters others who are favorably disposed toward crime rather than opposed to it. If a boy grows up in a family in which, say, an older brother is involved in crime, he is likely to learn criminal behavior. If people in the family, neighborhood, and gang believe that illegal activity is nothing to be ashamed of, this belief increases the chance that the young person will engage in crime.

Control theories hold that social links keep people in line with accepted norms (Gottfredson & Hirschi, 1990; Hirschi, 1969). In other words, all members of society have the potential to commit crime, but most are restrained by their ties to family, church, school, and peer groups. Thus, sensitivity to the opinion of others, commitment to a conventional lifestyle, and belief in the standards or values shared by friends all influence a person to abide by the law. A person who lacks one or more of these influences may be more likely to engage in crime.

Finally, **labeling theories** stress the social process through which certain acts and people are labeled as deviant. As Howard Becker noted, society creates deviance—and, hence, criminality—"by making the rules whose infraction constitutes deviance, and by applying those rules to particular people and labeling them outsiders" (1963:9). Decisions that result in the imposition of labels do not necessarily affect all individuals in the same way. Thus, researchers are exploring the association between labels and specific categories of people labeled as offenders (Chiricos, Barrick, Bales, & Bontrager, 2007).

According to labeling theories, social control agencies, such as the police, courts, and corrections, are created to label certain people as outside the normal, law-abiding community. When they have been labeled, those people come to believe that the label is true. They take on a deviant identity and start acting in deviant ways. Labeling theory suggests the justice system creates criminals by labeling people in order to serve its own bureaucratic and political ends. Those who support this view call for decriminalization of drug use, gambling, and prostitution.

Critical Theories In the mid-1960s, the reigning biological, psychological, and sociological explanations of criminal behavior were challenged by scholars who developed theories known as **critical criminology**. These theories assume that criminal law and the justice system are designed by those in power, whose purpose is to oppress those who are not in power (particularly the poor, women, and minorities). The powerful commit as many crimes as the less powerful, it is argued, but unempowered individuals are more likely to be caught and punished. Those in power use the law to impose their version of morality on society in order to protect their property and safety. They also use their power to change the definitions of crime to cover acts they view as threatening.

Several different theories can be said to fall under the umbrella of critical criminology. **Social conflict theories** posit that crime is the result of conflict within societies.

social process theories
Theories that see criminality as normal behavior in the sense that everyone has the potential to become a criminal, depending on (1) the influences that impel one toward or away from crime and (2) how one is regarded by others.

learning theories Theories that see criminal behavior as learned, just as legal behavior is learned.

theory of differential association The theory that people become criminals because they encounter more influences that view criminal behavior as normal and acceptable than they do influences that are hostile to criminal behavior.

control theories Theories holding that criminal behavior occurs when the bonds that tie an individual to society are broken or weakened.

labeling theories Theories emphasizing that the causes of criminal behavior are not found in the individual but in the social process that labels certain acts as deviant or criminal.

critical criminology Theories that assume criminal law and the criminal justice system are primarily a means of controlling the lower classes, women, and minorities.

social conflict theories
Theories that view crime as the result of conflict in society, such as conflict between economic classes caused by elites using law as a means to maintain power.

One type of social conflict theory has been proposed by critical, radical, or Marxist criminologists. It holds that the class structure causes certain groups to be labeled as deviant. In this view, "deviance is a status imputed to groups who share certain structural characteristics (e.g., powerlessness)" (Spitzer, 1975:639). Thus, the criminal law is aimed at the behavior of specific groups or classes. One result is that the poor are deeply hostile toward the social order, and this hostility is one factor in criminal behavior (Reiman & Leighton, 2012). Moreover, when the status quo is threatened, legal definitions of crime are changed in order to trap those who challenge the system. For example, vagrancy laws have been used to arrest labor union organizers, civil rights workers, and peace activists when those in power believed that their interests were threatened by these groups.

Feminist theories of crime are based on the idea that traditional theory centers on male criminality and ignores female offending. While this idea is adopted by all feminist theorists, some adopt less critical perspectives that integrate recognition of women's experiences into social process theories, psychological theories, and other existing approaches. Others, such as radical, Marxist, and socialist feminists, take a more critical view toward traditional, mainstream theories of crime. Recent feminist theorists underscore the need to integrate race and class issues with gender for a full understanding of crime (Burgess-Proctor, 2006).

Like other theories about the causes of criminal behavior, sociological theories have been criticized. Critics argue that these theories are imprecise, unsupported by evidence, and based on ideology. Even so, sociological theories have served as the basis for many attempts to prevent crime and rehabilitate offenders.

Life Course Theories

Life course theories seek to identify factors that shape criminal careers in order to explain when and why offenders begin to commit crimes and to see what factors lead individuals to stop their participation in crimes. Studies in this area often try to follow individuals from childhood through adulthood in order to identify the factors associated with beginning, avoiding, continuing, or ceasing criminal behavior. Criminal careers often begin at an early age; people who eventually become involved with crime often exhibit disruptive behavior, lack family support, and experiment with drinking and drugs as youths. Some theorists discuss *pathways* into crime, which may begin with minor habits of lying and stealing that lead to more serious offenses. However, pathways into crime are not identical for all kinds of offenders (S. R. Maxwell & Maxwell, 2000). For example, those youths who engage in bullying and fighting may begin a pathway toward different kinds of crimes than the crimes of those who start out using drugs.

As identified by life course theorists, the factors that can impact criminal careers overlap with factors discussed in psychological, social structure, and social process theories, such as unemployment, failure in school, impulsiveness, and unstable families. In other words, life course theorists' ideas about factors associated with criminal behavior are consistent with factors identified in other theories. However, these theorists study criminal behavior from a broader perspective.

The research of Robert Sampson and John Laub is among the most influential in examining the life course in relation to criminal careers (Laub & Sampson, 2003; Sampson & Laub, 1993). This study reanalyzed and built on the famous studies of Sheldon and Eleanor Glueck that followed the lives of 1,000 Boston-area boys from 1940 through the 1960s (Glueck & Glueck, 1950). Sampson and Laub gathered data on the same men in the 1990s, by which time the surviving "boys" from the original study were senior citizens.

Using their research, Sampson and Laub discuss informal and formal social controls over the life course. Unlike some researchers, who see youthful criminality as setting behavior patterns that continue into adulthood, Sampson and Laub emphasize *turning points* in life that move individuals away from criminal careers.

feminist theories Theories that criticize existing theories for ignoring or undervaluing women's experiences as offenders, victims, and people subjected to decision making by criminal justice officials. These theories seek to incorporate an understanding of differences between the experiences and treatment of men and women while also integrating consideration of other factors, such as race and social class.

life course theories Theories that identify factors affecting the start, duration, nature, and end of criminal behavior over the life of an offender.

For example, their study showed that military service, employment, and marriage served as particularly important factors leading away from criminal careers. By contrast, incarceration and alcohol abuse were associated with continued lawbreaking. Researchers have also sought to test other factors, such as the development of religiosity, but further studies are needed to see if such factors generate turning points away from crime (Giordano, Longmore, Schroder, & Seffrin, 2008).

Life course explanations do not seek to identify a single or primary factor as the cause of criminal behavior. Instead, they try to identify and evaluate the timing, interaction, and results of complex factors that affect people's lives.

Integrated Theories

As the number of theoretical perspectives has grown, researchers have called for the development of **integrated theories** drawn from different disciplines—that is, theories that merge several perspectives on crime. For example, in 1979 a group of researchers created a new theory from components of strain, social control, and social learning theories (D. S. Elliott, Ageton, & Cantor, 1979). From their data, they concluded that some juveniles enter delinquency through a combination of weak commitment to conventional norms (control theory) and vulnerability to delinquent peers (social learning theory). Others are more likely to become delinquent after forming strong commitments to conventional society (control theory), which are later weakened by their inability to achieve goals (strain theory). These weakened bonds lead to relationships with delinquent peers (social learning theory).

While the integration of theories makes sense, given the large array of factors that affect human behavior, there has been much debate about whether multiple theories can be integrated at all. For example, some theorists, such as Lombroso, postulate that humans are inherently criminal and that positive social forces are needed to keep people from offending, while other theorists believe that people are generally not prone to criminal behavior but that negative forces can lure them into committing crime (Henry & Lanier, 2006). These issues are currently being debated by modern criminologists in an attempt to construct valid, integrated theories of crime.

integrated theories Theories that combine differing theoretical perspectives into a larger model.

Women and Crime

As mentioned earlier in this section, theories about causes of crime are almost all based on observations of men. That women commit crime less often than do men (and that most criminologists have historically been male) helps explain this fact (D. Klein, 1973). Traditionally, many people assumed that most women, because of their nurturing and dependent nature, could not commit serious crimes. Those who did commit crimes were labeled as "bad" or "fallen" women. Much more than male criminals, then, female criminals were viewed as moral offenders.

Most traditional theories of crime cannot explain two important facts about gender and offending. First, a theory must explain why women are less likely to commit crime than are men (the "gender gap"). Women accounted for approximately 26 percent of all arrests in 2012, with men responsible for the remaining 74 percent (FBI, 2013a: Table 33). Second, a theory must explain why women commit different kinds of crime than do men—women are less likely to be arrested for violent crimes than are men, and women are more likely to be arrested for crimes such as embezzlement and prostitution (FBI, 2013a: Table 33).

Female suspects are less likely than male suspects to be arrested for any type of offense. In 2012, for example, 88 percent of arrested murder suspects and 87 percent of arrested robbery suspects were men. In addition, women are mostly likely to be arrested for larceny/theft than any other offense although they constituted only 43 percent of all arrestees for this offense (FBI, 2013a: Table 33).

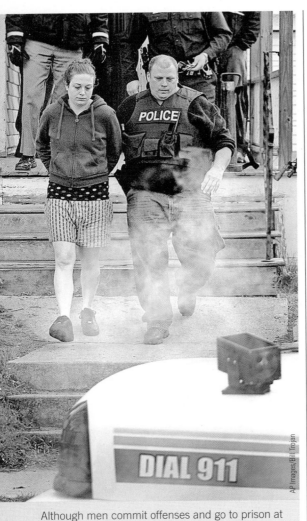

Although men commit offenses and go to prison at higher rates, there are concerns about increases in women's involvement in serious crimes. Should the government develop specific policies to attempt to steer young women away from crime and to provide special attention to women who are convicted of criminal offenses?

Two books published in 1975 attempted to explain these facts about female offending. Rita Simon's *Women and Crime* and Freda Adler's *Sisters in Crime* both hypothesized that women's liberation would result in increases in female offending. While Adler and Simon disagreed about how the *types* of crime committed by women would be affected by women's liberation, both predicted the gender gap would be reduced significantly. Although there are still significant differences in patterns of criminal behavior by men and women, these books helped alert scholars to societal changes that affect women's status, self-image, behavior, and opportunities to commit crimes.

Beginning in the 1990s, theorists recognized the importance of *social structure* in explaining female criminality. These theorists posit three things: that our society is structured in such a way as to create different opportunities for men and women in the workforce, that power differentials exist between men and women, and that important differences in sexuality shape the behavior of men and women (Messerschmidt, 1993).

Recent developments related to women and crime include life course theories, which focus on the paths taken by individuals through life and identify important turning points in people's lives. Recall that these "transitions" can affect individual behavior and lead people either to or away from criminal activity (Sampson & Laub, 1990). To explain gender and crime, feminist "pathways" researchers focus on the impact of critical life events, such as victimization, to determine why some women engage in criminal behavior. Research shows, for example, that many women working as prostitutes were sexually abused as children (Widom, 1995).

In recent years, scholars have pointed out the need to incorporate race and class into theories explaining female criminality. Known as "multiracial feminism," this perspective advocates not only the inclusion of race and class but also an awareness that opportunities and transitions are shaped by our race, class, gender, sexuality, and many other relevant factors (Burgess-Proctor, 2006). Other research indicates that although the gender gap is growing smaller, this is primarily due to a decrease in male offending rather than an increase in female offending (Lauritsen, Heimer, & Lynch, 2009).

Assessing Theories of Criminality

Scholars have presented evidence to support aspects of each theory of crime (see Table 2.3). This does not mean, however, that the strength of supporting evidence is the same for each theory. Also, some research may provide evidence for more than one theory. For example, research about the impact of neighborhoods may have implications for both social structure and social process theories (Kubrin & Stewart, 2006). When criminologists theorize that a recent rise in murders among young people in Boston is attributable, in part, to a "street culture" in which lethal violence is used to preserve reputations and respect (Llana, 2006), does that reflect social structure, social process, or some other theory? As yet, no theory is accurate enough to predict criminality or establish a specific cause for each offender's behavior.

The theories are limited in other ways as well. They tend to focus on visible crimes and the poor. They have less to say about upper-class or organized crime. Most of the theories also focus on male behavior. What is missing, and truly needed, is a theory that merges these disparate ideas about the causes of crime. Once we have a complete and testable account of what causes crime, we can develop better policies to deal with it.

TABLE 2.3 Major Theories of Criminality and Their Policy Implications

Scholars and the public support various types of policies. We know little about the real causes of crime, but note how many people think they have the answers!

Theory	Major Premise	Policy Implications	Policy Implementation
Biological	Genetic, biochemical, or neurological defects cause some people to commit crime.	Identification and treatment or control of persons with crime-producing biological factors; selective incapacitation; intensive supervision.	1. Use of drugs to inhibit biological urges of sex offenders. 2. Use of controlled diet to reduce levels of antisocial behavior caused by biochemical imbalances. 3. Identification of neurological defects through CAT scans. Use of drugs to suppress violent impulses. 4. Special education for those with learning disabilities.
Psychological	Personality and learning factors cause some people to commit crime.	Treatment of those with personality disorders to achieve mental health; employment of punishment for those whose illegal behavior stems from learned behavior so that they realize crime is not rewarded.	1. Psychotherapy and counseling to treat personality disorders. 2. Behavior modification strategies, such as electric shock and other negative impulses, to change learned behavior. 3. Counseling to enhance moral development. 4. Intensive individual and group therapies.
Social Structure	Crime is the result of underlying social conditions such as poverty, inequality, and unemployment.	Actions taken to reform social conditions that breed crime.	1. Education and job-training programs. 2. Urban redevelopment to improve housing, education, and health care. 3. Community development to provide economic opportunities.
Social Process	Crime is normal learned behavior and is subject to either social control or labeling effects.	Treatment of individuals in groups, with emphasis on building conventional bonds and avoiding stigmatization.	1. Youth programs that emphasize positive role models. 2. Community organizing to establish neighborhood institutions and bonds that emphasize following society's norms. 3. Programs designed to promote family stability.
Critical	Criminal definitions and punishments are used by some groups to control other groups.	Fundamental changes in the political and social systems to reduce class conflict.	1. Development of programs to remove injustice in society. 2. Provision of resources to assist women, minorities, and the poor in dealing with the criminal justice system and other government agencies. 3. Modification of criminal justice to deal similarly with crimes committed by upper-class members and crimes committed by lower-class members.
Life Course	Offenders have criminal careers that often begin with pathways into youth crime but can change and end through turning points in life.	Fostering of positive turning points such as marriage and stable employment.	1. Policies to reduce entry pathways associated with youth incarceration and substance abuse. 2. Policies to promote educational success, full employment, successful marriages, and stable families.

☑ CHECK POINT

9. What were the main assumptions of the classical school of criminology?
Criminal behavior is rational, and the fear of punishment keeps people from committing crimes.

10. What are the different kinds of sociological theories?
Social structure theories; social process theories; critical theories, including social conflict theory.

11. What are potential turning points for criminal careers in life course theories?
Military service, employment, marriage.

STOP&ANALYZE

The city of Los Angeles has instituted several social programs in an attempt to decrease gang violence. One of these programs, Summer Night Lights, keeps city parks open until midnight, providing meals, sporting events, and activities for local teens. Analysis has shown that gang violence is lower in L.A. neighborhoods with this program. Which theory might best explain this lower level of gang violence? Provide at least two reasons this theory accounts for the decrease.

Source: C. J. Lin, "Gang Violence Declines in Areas with Community Programs," *Daily News: Los Angeles*, January 10, 2012 (http://dailynews.com).

Think, Discuss, Write

Imagine the following scenarios: Two women—one in New York City and one in Chicago—arise early one morning to prepare to leave for their jobs at different insurance companies. As single parents, they both bear the responsibility of providing financial support as well as parental guidance to their children. After the Chicago woman parks in the underground garage next to her office building, an unfamiliar man sneaks up behind her, places a handgun against her face, and demands her purse and the keys to her car. Because she is startled and frightened, she drops her keys and reflexively bends to retrieve them. When she moves, the gun goes off and she is killed. In New York City, the woman is sitting at her desk in her office tower when suddenly her entire office suite bursts into flames in an explosion. She is killed instantly. The date is September 11, 2001. One woman has been killed in a parking garage in Chicago, and the other has died in the hijackers' attack on the World Trade Center in New York City.

In the aftermath of the September 11 tragedy, Congress enacted legislation to compensate victims with financial awards that exceed those of standard victim compensation programs and instead match the kinds of significant awards that someone might win in a wrongful death lawsuit. Thus, the family of the woman killed at the World Trade Center would be eligible for significant financial support from the federal government to replace the income that she would have provided for her family. According to information available in 2011, the average award to a family of someone killed at the World Trade Center was $2 million. By contrast, the family of the woman killed in the Chicago parking garage would be eligible for a maximum of only $27,000 under the Illinois Crime Victims Compensation Act. Both women were killed during sudden attacks by strangers. Both women left behind children who had relied on them for financial support as well as emotional support and parental guidance.

Discussion/Writing Assignment

Is it ethical for the federal government to provide financial support for one victim's family but not for the other? Are there any persuasive reasons to treat the two families differently? Imagine that you are the advisor to a commission that must propose a policy concerning compensation for future crime victims as well as future victims of terrorist attacks. Write a memo explaining how you would treat these two groups for purposes of government compensation. Be sure to explain the reasons for your recommendation.

Sources: Illinois Attorney General's Office, "Crime Victim Compensation: Frequently Asked Questions by Relatives of Deceased Victims" (http://www.illinoisattorneygeneral.gov/victims/CV_FAQ_RelativesDeceased_0809.pdf); Ray Salazar, "How Does a Chicago Public Schools Student Survive a Sibling's Violent Death—Twice?" *The White Rhino: A Chicago Latino English Teacher* (blog) *Chicago Now,* August 23, 2011 (www.chicagonow.com); Aaron Smith, "The 9/11 Fund: Putting a Price on Life," *CNN Money,* September 7, 2011 (http://money.cnn.com).

SUMMARY

❶ Categorize crimes by their type.
- There are seven broad categories of crime: visible crime, occupational crime, organized crime, transnational crime, victimless crime, political crime, and cyber crime.
- Each type of crime has its own level of risk and profitability, each arouses varying degrees of public disapproval, and each has its own group of offenders with their own characteristics.

❷ Describe the different methods of measuring crime.
- The amount of crime is difficult to measure. The National Incident-Based Reporting System (NIBRS), Uniform Crime Reports (UCR), and National Crime Victimization Surveys (NCVS) are the best sources of crime data.
- The complexity of crime statistics makes monitoring trends in crime a challenge.

- Crime rates are affected by changes in social conditions, including demographic trends and unemployment rates.

❸ Explain why some people are at higher risk of victimization than others.
- Young male residents of lower-income communities are among those most likely to be victimized by crime.
- A person's routine activities may increase the likelihood of victimization.
- Because of the connection between race and social status in the United States, African Americans are more frequently victimized by crime than are whites.
- A significant percentage of crimes, especially those against women, are committed by acquaintances and relatives of victims.

4 Summarize the negative consequences of victimization.

- Crime significantly affects all of society through financial and other costs.
- Financial costs from white-collar crime, employee theft, and fraud lead to huge financial losses for businesses.
- Medical costs, psychological effects, and insensitive treatment by justice system officials are among the burdens on individual crime victims.
- Fear of crime may make everyone in society feel less free to go certain places or live their daily lives comfortably.

5 Name the theories put forward to explain criminal behavior.

- The classical school of criminology emphasized reform—of criminal law, procedures, and punishments.
- The rise of science led to the positivist school, which viewed behavior as stemming from social, biological, and psychological factors.
- Positivist criminology has dominated the study of criminal behavior since the beginning of the twentieth century.
- Biological theories of crime claim that physiological and neurological factors may predispose a person to commit crimes.
- Psychological theories of crime propose that mental processes and behavior hold the key to understanding the causes of crime.

- Sociological theories of crime emphasize as causes of criminal behavior the social conditions that bear on the individual. Three types of sociological theory are social structure theories; social process theories; and critical theories, including social conflict theories.
- Feminist theories call attention to scholars' neglect of women's criminal behavior. Such theories often take a conflict perspective, but some feminist theorists may draw from other theoretical approaches in examining women and crime.
- Life course theories consider pathways into crime and turning points, such as marriage, employment, and military service, that move individuals away from criminal careers.
- Integrated theories combine components of theories from different disciplines. They attempt to provide a better explanation for crime than one single discipline can.

6 Explain why there are gender differences in crime.

- The criminality of women has only recently been studied. Some argue that as society increasingly treats women and men as equals, the number of crimes committed by women will increase.
- Theories of criminality are criticized for focusing too exclusively on lower-class and male perpetrators.

Questions for Review

1. What are the seven types of crimes?
2. What are the positive and negative attributes of the two major sources of crime data?
3. Who is most likely to be victimized by crime?
4. What are the costs of crime?
5. How does the criminal justice system treat victims?
6. What are the major theories of criminality?
7. What have scholars learned about the criminal behavior of women?

Key Terms and Cases

anomie (p. 68)

biological explanations (p. 66)

classical criminology (p. 65)

control theories (p. 69)

criminogenic (p. 66)

critical criminology (p. 69)

cyber crimes (p. 49)

dark figure of crime (p. 51)

feminist theories (p. 70)

integrated theories (p. 71)

labeling theories (p. 69)

learning theories (p. 69)

life course theories (p. 70)

money laundering (p. 46)

National Crime Victimization Surveys (NCVS) (p. 54)

National Incident-Based Reporting System (NIBRS) (p. 53)

occupational crimes (p. 45)

organized crime (p. 45)

political crime (p. 49)

positivist criminology (p. 66)

psychological explanations (p. 67)

social conflict theories (p. 69)

social process theories (p. 69)

social structure theories (p. 68)

sociological explanations (p. 68)

theory of differential association (p. 69)

transnational crime (p. 47)

Uniform Crime Reports (UCR) (p. 52)

victimless crimes (p. 48)

victimology (p. 57)

visible crime (p. 45)

3 | Criminal Justice and the Rule of Law

LEARNING OBJECTIVES

1 Identify the bases and sources of American criminal law.

2 Discuss how substantive criminal law defines a crime and the legal responsibility of the accused.

3 Describe how procedural criminal law defines the rights of the accused and the processes for dealing with a case.

4 Explain the U.S. Supreme Court's role in interpreting the criminal justice amendments to the Constitution.

With his hair dyed red like the screen villain "the Joker," 24-year-old James Holmes entered the movie theater in Aurora, Colorado, through the rear exit door that he had previously propped open. When he entered the midnight showing of the movie *Batman: The Dark Knight Rises* on July 20, 2102, many of those in the audience initially thought he was a live performer who was part of the show. He was dressed in dark, protective clothing, including a gas mask (Frosch & Johnson, 2012). However, when the former neuroscience graduate student pointed his guns at the audience and began to fire rapidly, it became very clear that a deadly mass murder had begun. When the shooting ended, 12 people were dead and more than 50 were wounded.

When police and emergency medical personnel rushed to the scene upon receiving the reports of a mass shooting, police officer James Oviatt noticed Holmes standing next to a car in the parking lot outside the theater. Officer Oviatt quickly realized that the young man was not a police officer—despite his helmet and gas mask—because Holmes was standing calmly and not rushing to provide aid to wounded movie patrons. During a preliminary court hearing for Holmes's murder case in 2013, Oviatt described Holmes as calm and matter-of-fact at the scene of the chaotic crime and said that he remained so even as he revealed to officers that he had also rigged his apartment with a web of explosives (Wian, Spellman, & Pearson, 2013).

Did mental problems lead Holmes to commit his murderous acts? He had been the patient of a university psychiatrist during his time as a graduate student at the University of Colorado–Denver (Wian et al., 2013). In June 2013 Judge Carlos Samour, Jr., the state district judge presiding over the case, ruled that Holmes's defense attorneys could file an insanity plea, meaning that they would argue in the 2014 trial that Holmes should be found "not guilty" by reason of insanity at the time of the crime (Spellman & Nottingham, 2013). Thus, under Colorado law, in order to seek a murder conviction and imposition of the death penalty, the prosecutor will bear the burden of proving that Holmes was not insane when he committed the crime (Spellman & Nottingham, 2013).

A criminal defendant's claim of insanity raises difficult questions for the justice system. Critics question whether such a defense should be available to permit people to avoid **legal responsibility** and punishment for their criminal acts. Should someone avoid imprisonment after committing the horrible acts for which Holmes was responsible? In light of the elaborate preparation that Holmes made before committing the crime, including dressing in protective clothing and wiring his apartment with explosive devices in an unsuccessful effort to harm the police who were sent there to conduct a search, can someone genuinely argue that he was insane? Without having any professional training in psychology or medicine, how does a judge, or in other cases, a jury, decide whether a defendant is legally insane? Yet, this is what our justice system asks these decision makers to determine. Psychological experts testify as witnesses for each side in such cases and typically provide opposing conclusions about whether or not a defendant was insane at the time of the crime. However, it is the jury or the judge, depending on the type of trial, who will

make the actual determination of whether the defendant was legally insane.

In this chapter, we shall examine the primary components of criminal law. *Substantive criminal law* is developed through statutes enacted by the American people's elected representatives in state legislatures and Congress. It addresses the specific acts for which people will be punished as well as the circumstances in which people may not be held fully responsible for their actions. We shall also introduce *procedural criminal law*, which defines the procedures used in legal processes and the rights possessed by criminal suspects and defendants. Even though Holmes clearly committed the mass killing, he was still entitled to a trial and representation by an attorney as he attempted to show why he should not be held fully responsible for his actions. The right to counsel and the right to a fair trial are two of the elements provided by procedural criminal law. The precise nature of individuals' rights under procedural criminal law is determined by judges' interpretations of the U.S. Constitution, state constitutions, and relevant statutes enacted by Congress and state legislatures.

Foundations of Criminal Law

legal responsibility
The accountability of an individual for a crime because of the perpetrator's characteristics and the circumstances of the illegal act.

Like most Americans, you are no doubt aware that law and legal procedures are key elements of the criminal justice system. Americans are fond of saying that "we have a government of laws, not of men (and women)." According to our American values, we do not have a system based on the decisions of a king or dictator. In the United States, even our most powerful leaders have to make decisions within limits imposed by law. The government can seek to punish only people who violate defined laws, and their guilt has to be determined through procedures established by law.

Laws tell citizens what they can and cannot do. Laws also tell government officials when they can seek to punish citizens for violations and how they must go about it. Government officials, including the president of the United States, who take actions according to their own preferences run the risk that judges will order them to take different actions that comply with the law. In 2004, for example, the U.S. Supreme Court ordered then-President George W. Bush's administration to permit a U.S. citizen being held as a suspected terrorist to meet with an attorney and have opportunities to make arguments in court (*Hamdi v. Rumsfeld*). Government officials are expected to follow and enforce the law. Thus, in a democracy, laws are major tools for preventing government officials from seizing too much power or using power improperly.

civil law Law regulating the relationships between or among individuals, usually involving property, contracts, or business disputes.

Criminal law is only one category of law. Peoples' lives and actions are also affected by **civil law**, which governs business deals, contracts, real estate, and the like.

State legislatures create criminal laws for their states, and Congress creates national criminal laws. These laws define acts that are illegal and specify punishments for each offense. Are there additional criminal laws that contemporary legislators should create for your state?

For example, if you damage other people's property or harm them in an accident, they may sue you to pay for the damage or harm. By contrast, the key feature of criminal law is the government's power to punish people for damage they have done to society.

One of the two categories of criminal law, **substantive criminal law**, defines actions that the government can punish. It also defines the punishments for such offenses. Often called the *penal code* (discussed further in the next section), substantive law answers the question "What is illegal?" Elected officials in Congress, state legislatures, and city councils write the substantive criminal laws. These legislators decide which kinds of behaviors are so harmful that they deserve to be punished. They also decide whether the punishment should be imprisonment, a fine, probation, or another kind of punishment. When questions arise about the meaning of substantive criminal laws, judges interpret the laws by seeking to fulfill the legislators' intentions.

By contrast, **procedural criminal law** defines the rules that govern how the laws will be enforced. It protects the constitutional rights of defendants and provides the rules that officials must follow in all areas of the criminal justice system. Many aspects of procedural criminal law are defined by legislatures, such as how bail will be set and which kind of preliminary hearing will take place before a trial. However, the U.S. Supreme Court and state supreme courts also play a key role in defining procedural criminal law. These courts define the meaning of constitutional rights in the U.S. Constitution and in state constitutions. Their interpretations of constitutional provisions create rules on issues such as when and how police officers can question suspects and when defendants can receive advice from their attorneys.

substantive criminal law
Law that defines acts that are subject to punishment and specifies the punishments for such offenses.

procedural criminal law
Law defining the procedures that criminal justice officials must follow in enforcement, adjudication, and corrections.

☑CHECK POINT

1. **What is contained in a state's penal code?**
   Penal codes contain substantive criminal law that defines crimes and also punishments for those crimes.

2. **What is the purpose of procedural criminal law?**
   Procedural criminal law specifies the defendant's rights and tells justice system officials how they can investigate and process cases.

STOP&ANALYZE

In 2011 the mayor of Baltimore proposed that the Maryland legislature enact a new law requiring a minimum 18-month prison sentence for anyone caught with an illegal, loaded firearm. Are legislators capable of predicting all the consequences of such a law? List three of your own predictions about the consequences of such a law. In light of your predictions, is the proposed law a good idea?

Substantive Criminal Law

Substantive criminal law defines acts that are subject to punishment and specifies the punishments. It is based on the doctrine that no one may be convicted of or punished for an offense unless the offense has been defined by the law. In short, people must know in advance what is required of them. Thus, no act can be regarded as illegal until it has been defined as punishable under the criminal law. While this sounds like a simple notion, the language of law is often confusing and ambiguous. As a result, judges must become involved in interpreting the law so that the meaning intended by the legislature can be understood.

Definitions and Classifications of Criminal Laws

felonies Serious crimes usually carrying a penalty of death or of incarceration for more than one year in prison.

In defining the behaviors deserving of punishment, legislatures also make decisions about the potential severity of punishments for various offenses. Typically, offenses are placed into specific categories according to the consequences that will follow. Crimes defined as **felonies** are those that can lead to incarceration for a year or more in state or federal prison as well as those subject to the death penalty. **Misdemeanors** are crimes for which the punishment may be a year or less in a county jail, but these are often punished with probation, fines, or community service instead. Some legislatures subdivide felonies and misdemeanors according to degrees of seriousness. For example, those crimes classified as third-degree felonies would lead to shorter sentences than the more serious crimes that are classified as first-degree felonies. Legislatures may also define a category of offenses as *petty offenses*, which are typically behaviors for which the punishment is only a small fine. Similarly, legislatures may define the most minor offenses as **civil infractions** that are punishable only by fines, do not make the violator subject to arrest, and do not produce any criminal record for the individual. For example, such actions as crossing a street against a traffic light ("jaywalking") or even possessing a small amount of marijuana for personal consumption can be defined as civil infractions if a legislature so chooses. Bear in mind that offenses within these classifications vary by state and that the terms used to define these classifications, such as "petty offenses," may also vary in their meaning in each jurisdiction.

Misdemeanors Offenses less serious than felonies and usually punishable by incarceration of no more than one year in jail or of probation or intermediate sanctions.

civil infractions Minor offenses that are typically punishable by small fines and produce no criminal record for the offender.

Legislatures do not necessarily define categories of crimes solely according to elected officials' ideal assessments of the seriousness of each offense. Due to budget crises affecting various states, several legislatures have redefined specific nonviolent felonies as misdemeanors in an effort to reduce the number of people sent to prison and thus lower the associated costs to the state. For example, Montana raised the threshold dollar amount for a charge of felony theft from $1,000 to $1,500 (K. Johnson, 2011). In 2014 the house of representatives in the state of Washington considered a proposal to change certain drug possession offenses from felonies to misdemeanors ("Under the Dome," 2014).

Legislatures do not act in isolation when developing definitions of crimes. Since the 1960s, they have been significantly influenced by the *Model Penal Code*. This suggested code came about when the American Law Institute, an organization of lawyers, judges, and law professors, produced model definitions of crimes to help states organize and standardize their many individual criminal statutes, which had developed over the course of the nation's first two centuries of existence. With guidance from legal scholars' commentaries explaining the reasons for the individual provisions within the *Model Penal Code*, as well as observation of actions and experiences in other states, many states revised their criminal statutes in the 1960s and 1970s (Robinson & Dubber, 2007).

Federal and state penal codes often define criminal acts somewhat differently. To find out how a state defines an offense, one must read its penal code; this will give a general idea of which acts are illegal. Then to understand the court's

TABLE 3.1   Definitions of Offenses in the Uniform Crime Reports (UCR) (Part I)

The exact descriptions of offenses differ from one state to another, but these UCR definitions provide a national standard that helps us distinguish among criminal acts.

1. **Criminal homicide:**

   a. Murder and nonnegligent manslaughter: the willful (nonnegligent) killing of one human being by another. Deaths caused by negligence, attempts to kill, assaults to kill, suicides, accidental deaths and justifiable homicides are excluded. Justifiable homicides are limited to (1) the killing of a felon by a law enforcement officer in the line of duty and (2) the killing of a felon by a private citizen.

   b. Manslaughter by negligence: the killing of another person through gross negligence. Excludes traffic fatalities. While manslaughter by negligence is a Part I crime, it is not included in the crime index.

2. **Forcible rape:**

   The penetration, no matter how slight, of the vagina or anus with any body part or object, or oral penetration by a sex organ of another person, without the consent of the victim.

3. **Robbery:**

   The taking or attempting to take anything of value from the care, custody, or control of a person or persons by force or threat of force of violence and/or by putting the victim in fear.

4. **Aggravated assault:**

   An unlawful attack by one person upon another for the purpose of inflicting severe or aggravated bodily injury. This type of assault usually is accompanied by the use of a weapon or by means likely to produce death or great bodily harm. Simple assaults are excluded.

5. **Burglary—breaking or entering:**

   The unlawful entry of a structure to commit a felony or a theft. Attempted forcible entry is included.

6. **Larceny/theft (except motor vehicle theft):**

   The unlawful taking, carrying, leading, or riding away of property from the possession or constructive possession of another. Examples are thefts of bicycles or automobile accessories, shoplifting, pocket picking, or the stealing of any property or article that is not taken by force and violence or by fraud. Attempted larcenies are included. Embezzlement, "con" games, forgery, worthless checks, and so on, are excluded.

7. **Motor vehicle theft:**

   The theft or attempted theft of a motor vehicle. A motor vehicle is self-propelled and runs on the surface and not on rails. Specifically excluded from this category are motorboats, construction equipment, airplanes, and farming equipment.

8. **Arson:**

   Any willful or malicious burning or attempt to burn, with or without intent to defraud, a dwelling house, a public building, a motor vehicle or an aircraft, the personal property of another, and so on.

Sources: Federal Bureau of Investigation, *Crime in the United States, 2012* (Washington, DC: U.S. Government Printing Office, 2013); Federal Bureau of Investigation, *Preliminary Semiannual Uniform Crime Report, January–June 2013* (Washington, DC: U.S. Government Printing Office, 2014) (http://www.fbi.gov).

interpretations of the code, one must analyze the judicial opinions that have sought to clarify the law.

The classification of criminal acts becomes complicated when statutes divide related acts, such as taking a person's life, into different offenses. For example, the definition of *criminal homicide* has been subdivided into degrees of murder and voluntary and involuntary manslaughter. In addition, some states have created new categories, such as reckless homicide, negligent homicide, and vehicular homicide. Each of these definitions involves slight variations in the action taken and the intention underlying the action. For example, did the individual plan in advance to kill someone, or was the death caused by the individual's careless action? Table 3.1 shows the definitions of offenses used in the Uniform Crime Reports (UCR), described in Chapter 2. The UCR is used as one means to track crime rates each year and is available on the FBI's website.

Beginning with the UCR issued in 2013, the FBI used a new, gender-neutral definition of forcible rape that focuses solely on sexual penetration without regard to whether the victim was female or male (U.S. Department of Justice, 2012). Under criminal homicide, there are important differences between intentional ("willful") homicides, which are labeled as murder and manslaughter deserving of severe punishment, and careless acts ("negligence") that lead to someone's death. These definitions are merely generic examples. Each state's actual statutes can have much more detailed wording to include various specific situations.

Criminal laws must be drafted carefully to define the specific actions and intentions that are regarded as deserving of punishment. Yet, judgments must still be made by prosecutors, judges, and juries about whether specific actions occurred and what state of mind or intentions motivated the action. In October 2011, for example, two 12-year-olds pushed a shopping cart off the fourth floor of a parking garage in New York City and it struck a pedestrian on the sidewalk below, leaving her unconscious and suffering with a life-threatening head injury (Robbins, 2011). If the victim had died, would this be have been considered a willful killing that should be classified as murder or manslaughter, or was this a careless act that should be classified as negligent homicide?

A close examination of statutes from different states helps to illuminate similarities and differences in statutes and to indicate legislatures' efforts to be precise in their definitions. Compare the statutes defining murder in Idaho and Delaware that follow. You will see that they both emphasize intentional killing as a fundamental characteristic of murder and that Idaho still uses the traditional phrase "malice aforethought" to mean specific intention. Look closely, however, and take note of the differences in the definitions and what the legislatures chose to emphasize in defining this crime for their states.

Idaho Statutes, Title 18, Chapter 40, 18–4001. Murder Defined.

Murder is the unlawful killing of a human being including, but not limited to, a human embryo or fetus, with malice aforethought or the intentional application of torture to a human being, which results in the death of a human being. Torture is the intentional infliction of extreme and prolonged pain with the intent to cause suffering. The death of a human being caused by such torture is murder irrespective of proof of specific intent to kill; torture causing death shall be deemed the equivalent of intent to kill.

As you examine the definition produced by the Idaho legislature, do you see any particular values or policy priorities reflected in the choice of language? Is it possible that highly publicized homicides that occurred in a certain manner may have influenced the legislature's emphasis and choice of words? Now examine the Delaware statute defining murder and ask yourself those same questions.

Delaware Statutes, Title 11, Chapter 5, section 636. Murder in the first degree; class A felony.

A person is guilty of murder in the first degree when:

(1) The person intentionally causes the death of another person; (2) While engaged in the commission of, or attempt to commit, or flight after committing or attempting to commit any felony, the person recklessly causes the death of another person; (3) The person intentionally causes another person to commit suicide by force or duress; (4) The person recklessly causes the death of a law-enforcement officer, corrections employee, fire fighter, paramedic, emergency medical technician, fire marshal or fire police officer while such officer is in the lawful performance of duties; (5) The person causes the death of another person by use of or detonation of any bomb or similar destructive device; (6) The person causes the death of another person in order to avoid or prevent the lawful arrest of any person, or in the course of and in furtherance of the commission or attempted commission of . . . escape after conviction.

Note that Delaware's legislature identified specific situations in which recklessly causing death would be punished as severely as intentionally causing the death of another person. Are there any homicide situations that would clearly be murder in one of these states but would be manslaughter or another lesser degree of homicide in the other state? The examples demonstrate the authority of legislatures in each state to develop the specific definitions of crimes for their own states, including emphasis on policy priorities that may not be evident in the statutes of other states.

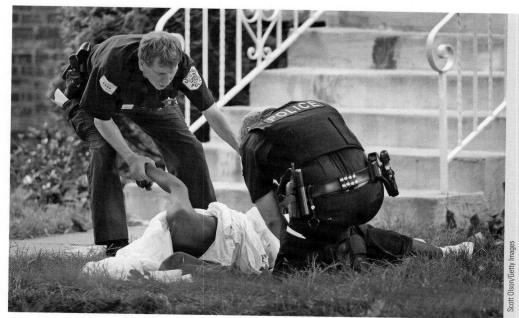

Police officers must carefully gather evidence at crime scenes in order to identify the proper suspect and then prove that the suspect actually committed the crime. They seek evidence relevant to each element in the definition of the specific law that was broken. Here officers gather evidence at a 2013 murder scene in Chicago. When suspects are arrested for this crime, what will the prosecutor need to prove in order to gain a murder conviction?

Scott Olson/Getty Images

Elements of a Crime

Legislatures define certain acts as crimes when they fulfill the seven principles under specific "attendant circumstances" while the offender has a certain state of mind. These three factors—the act, the attendant circumstances, and the state of mind or intent—are together called the *elements* of a crime. They can be seen in the following section from a state penal code:

> Section 3502. Burglary 1 Offense defined: A person is guilty of burglary if he enters a building or occupied structure, or separately secured or occupied portion thereof, with intent to commit a crime therein, unless the premises are at the time open to the public or the actor is licensed or privileged to enter.

The elements of burglary are, therefore, entering a building or occupied structure (the act) with the intent to commit a crime therein (state of mind) at a time when the premises are not open to the public and the actor is not invited or otherwise entitled to enter (attendant circumstances). For an act to be a burglary, all three elements must be present.

Although most definitions of crimes focus on specific acts that produce harm to persons or property, some crimes involve specific intentions and plans for harm even if those plans are never carried out. Obviously, planning is a form of action, but the action itself may never produce a specific harm. Yet, that can be the basis for a criminal conviction and punishment. Thus, the criminal law includes conspiracies and attempts, even when the lawbreaker does not complete the intended crime (Cahill, 2007a). These are called **inchoate** or **incomplete offenses**. For example, people can be prosecuted for planning to murder someone or hiring a "hit man" to kill someone. The potential for grave harm from such acts justifies the application of the government's power to punish.

inchoate or **incomplete offenses** Conduct that is criminal even though the harm that the law seeks to prevent has not been done but merely planned or attempted.

Seven Principles of Criminal Law

In analyzing the definitions of crimes and the elements necessary to lead to conviction and punishment, legal scholar Jerome Hall (1947) summarized the major principles of Western criminal law that must be present. To convict a defendant

FIGURE 3.1
**The Seven Principles
of Criminal Law**
These principles of Western law
provide the basis for defining
acts as criminal and the conditions required for successful
prosecution.

A crime is	
1 legally proscribed	(legality)
2 human conduct	(*actus reus*)
3 causative	(causation)
4 of a given harm	(harm)
5 which conduct coincides	(concurrence)
6 with a blameworthy frame of mind	(*mens rea*)
7 and is subject to punishment	(punishment)

of a crime, prosecutors must prove that all seven principles have been fulfilled (see Figure 3.1).

1. *Legality.* There must be a law that defines the specific action as a crime. Offensive and harmful behavior is not illegal unless it has been prohibited by law before it was committed. The U.S. Constitution forbids *ex post facto laws*, or laws written and applied "after the fact." Thus, when the legislature defines a new crime, people can be prosecuted only for violations that occur after the new law has been passed.

2. *Actus reus.* Criminal laws are aimed at human acts, including acts that a person failed to undertake. The U.S. Supreme Court has ruled that people may not be convicted of a crime simply because of their status. Under this *actus reus* requirement, for a crime to occur, there must be an act of either commission or omission by the accused. In *Robinson v. California* (1962), for example, the Supreme Court struck down a California law that made being addicted to drugs a crime. States can prosecute people for using, possessing, selling, or transporting drugs when they catch them performing these acts, but states cannot prosecute them for the mere status of being addicted to drugs.

3. *Causation.* For a crime to have been committed, there must be a causal relationship between an act and the harm suffered. In Ohio, for example, a prosecutor tried to convict a burglary suspect on a manslaughter charge when a victim, asleep in his house, was killed by a stray bullet as officers fired at the unarmed, fleeing suspect. The burglar was acquitted on the homicide charge because his actions in committing the burglary and running away from the police were not the direct cause of the victim's death (Bandy, 1991).

4. *Harm.* To be a crime, an act (or failure to act) must cause harm to some legally protected value. The harm can be to a person, property, or some other object that a legislature deems valuable enough to deserve protection through the government's power to punish. This principle is often questioned by those who feel that they are not committing a crime because they are causing harm only to themselves. Laws that require motorcyclists to wear helmets have been challenged on this ground. Such laws, however, have been written because legislatures see enough forms of harm to individuals and society from such actions to require protective laws. In our motorcycle example, these forms of harm would include not only injuries to helmetless riders but also tragedy and loss for families of injured cyclists, plus the medical costs imposed on society for head injuries that could have been prevented.

5. *Concurrence.* For an act to be considered a crime, the intent and the act must be present at the same time (J. Hall, 1947). Let us imagine that Joe is planning to murder his archenemy, Bill. He spends days planning how he will abduct Bill and carry out the murder. While driving home from work one day, Joe accidentally hits and kills a jogger who suddenly—and foolishly—runs across the busy street without looking. The jogger turns out to be Bill. Although Joe had planned to kill Bill, he is not guilty of murder, because the accidental killing was not connected to Joe's intent to carry out a killing.

6. *Mens rea*. The commission of an act is not a crime unless it is accompanied by a guilty state of mind. This concept is related to intent. It seeks to distinguish between harm-causing accidents, which generally are not subject to criminal punishment, and harm-causing crimes, in which some level of intent is present. As discussed previously, certain crimes require a specific level of intent; examples include first-degree murder, which is normally a planned, intentional killing, and larceny, which involves the intent to deprive an owner of his or her property permanently and unlawfully. Later in this chapter, we examine several defenses, such as necessity and insanity, that can be used to assert that a person did not have **mens rea**—"guilty mind," or blameworthy state of mind—and hence should not be held responsible for a criminal offense. The element of *mens rea* becomes problematic when there are questions about an offender's capacity to understand or plan harmful activities, as when the perpetrator is mentally ill or a child. The defense attorneys in James Holmes's murder case, described at the beginning of the chapter, sought to attack the *mens rea* element by claiming he was legally insane at the time that the crime was committed.

   Exceptions to the concept of *mens rea* are strict liability offenses involving health and safety, in which it is not necessary to show intent. Legislatures have criminalized certain kinds of offenses in order to protect the public. For example, a business owner may be held responsible for violations of a toxic-waste law whether or not the owner actually knew that his or her employees were dumping pollutants into a river. Other laws may apply strict liability to the sale of alcoholic beverages to minors. The purpose of such laws is to put pressure on business owners to make sure that their employees obey regulations designed to protect the health and safety of the public. Courts often limit the application of such laws to situations in which recklessness or indifference is present.

7. *Punishment*. There must be a provision in the law calling for punishment of those found guilty of violating the law. The punishment is enforced by the government and may carry with it social stigma, a criminal record, loss of freedom, and loss of rights.

> **mens rea** "Guilty mind," or blameworthy state of mind, necessary for legal responsibility for a criminal offense; criminal intent, as distinguished from innocent intent.

The seven principles of substantive criminal law allow authorities to define certain acts as being against the law and provide the accused with a basis for mounting a defense against the charges. During a criminal trial, defense attorneys will often try to show that one of the seven elements either is unproved or can be explained in a way that is acceptable under the law. Read the "Careers in Criminal Justice" box about Denver criminal defense attorney Abraham Hutt and consider the important role played by such attorneys in seeking to make sure that only truly guilty defendants are convicted and punished.

Defenses against Criminal Charges

Defendants' attorneys can use several defenses to seek to avoid criminal convictions in cases for which defendants actually committed the acts proscribed by criminal law. These defenses are traditionally divided into justifications and excuses (Samaha, 2011). *Justifications* focus on the act and whether the act was socially acceptable under the circumstances. Justifications are actions based on self-defense or necessity in which the individual reasonably felt obligated to cause harm, but the actions were those that are recognized and accepted by society as essential to the individual's self-preservation. *Excuses* focus on the actor and whether the actor fulfilled the elements required for being held responsible under a criminal statute. Excuses are defenses that under specific circumstances either eliminate (e.g., insanity) or diminish (e.g., intoxication) criminal responsibility because the individual did not possess the knowledge, state of mind, or intent required for a criminal conviction (Milhizer, 2004).

As indicated by these general descriptions of justifications and excuses in regard to the seven principles of criminal law, *mens rea* is crucial in establishing responsibility for the act. To obtain a conviction, the prosecution must show that

Criminal Defense Attorney

Abraham V. Hutt, Criminal Defense Attorney, Private Practice, Denver, Colorado

Defense attorneys must interview their clients and relevant witnesses when hired by a defendant or appointed by a court to handle criminal cases. These interviews might occur under difficult circumstances in jails or on street corners in tough neighborhoods. Defense attorneys must find all relevant evidence and evaluate that evidence in anticipation of how the prosecution will present its version of the case. They spend a significant amount of time in offices doing legal research, preparing legal documents, and reviewing legal papers. They also must appear in court to represent their clients at hearings where bail is set and judges consider whether there is sufficient evidence for a case to move forward. Defense attorneys discuss possible plea agreements with prosecutors. Occasionally, one of their cases will move through the entire justice process and become the subject of a trial. In the courtroom, defense attorneys present arguments and evidence to show the weaknesses in the prosecution's case. When a guilty verdict is issued, they may continue to represent their clients in the appeals process.

To become a lawyer in the United States, people must earn a four-year college degree in any subject before going to law school for three years of postgraduate study. Gaining admission to law school is a competitive process, so people interested in legal careers must work hard during college, earn good grades, and gain good scores on the Law School Admissions Test (LSAT). After graduating from law school, prospective lawyers must pass a state's bar exam in order to receive a license to practice law. Each state has its own bar exam, which typically lasts two days. A separate ethics exam may also be required. In most states, one day is devoted to a six-hour multiple-choice test on six subjects that are common to all states (contract, criminal, tort, evidence, property, and constitutional law). The other day involves six hours of essays on 12 or more subjects focused on state law, including business associations, taxation, and family law.

During college, Abraham Hutt spent two summers as an intern with the Colorado State Public Defender's Office,

Photo provided by Abraham V. Hutt

where he worked as an investigator interviewing witnesses and helping lawyers prepare to represent defendants who were too poor to hire their own attorneys. For one year after college, he worked as an investigator for a former public defender who became a private-practice attorney, representing criminal defendants who could afford to pay for legal representation. Hutt then went to law school for three years, passed the Colorado bar exam, and worked in a small law firm that specialized in criminal defense. Eventually, he started his own law firm that focused on criminal cases.

In preparing for a trial, a defense attorney is obligated to question the prosecutor's version of events and the truthfulness of any witness whose testimony is disputed by the accused. . . . Members of the public often erroneously believe that the defense attorney's goal is to prevent guilty people from receiving the punishment that they deserve. In fact, our adversarial justice system relies on defense attorneys to make sure that all mitigating information about the accused and his or her circumstances are made known to the prosecutor and the court and to require that prosecutors are actually able to prove that defendants are guilty beyond a reasonable doubt with lawfully obtained evidence. Our system is based on the principle that any person the government accuses of a crime is entitled to the assistance of a legal counselor and advocate who will stand up in that person's defense, no matter how harsh the accusations or how troubled the person's background. Without defense attorneys, the fundamental human dignity of many accused people would regularly be trampled by the system. . . . Similarly, without defense attorneys there would be no check or balance to the power of prosecutors and judges and no one to ensure that prosecutors follow the law and courts respect the constitutional rights of people drawn into the criminal justice process.

---

the offender not only committed the illegal act but also did so in a state of mind that makes it appropriate to hold her or him responsible for the act.

In 2011 two Indiana boys pleaded guilty in the shooting death of the older boy's stepfather. The 15-year-old received a 30-year prison sentence, and his 12-year-old accomplice was sentenced to 25 years (R. Green, 2011). In a case in Virginia in 2013, a teen was sentenced to 38 years in prison for a murder he committed when he was 15 years old (Adams, 2013). Were these youngsters old enough to plan their crimes and understand the consequences of their actions? Is a child capable of forming the same intent to commit a crime that an adult can form? The analysis of *mens rea* is difficult because the court must inquire into the defendant's mental state at the time the offense was committed. It is not easy to know what someone was thinking when he or she performed an act. Moreover, as discussed in the Close Up box,

Criminal Intent and the Appropriateness of Punishment

In 2009 an 18-year-old in Ohio was accused of beating his mother so badly that she died a few days later from internal injuries. Is this a clear-cut case of criminal responsibility? The suspect is an adult whose intentional violent actions caused a death. In this case, however, the suspect has autism. He has a limited ability to communicate, using specific words and phrases that only his mother understood. In his jail cell, the deputies positioned a television set just outside the bars and played recordings of *The Price Is Right* over and over again because watching his favorite show kept him calm. Friends and relatives were permitted to bring barbecue potato chips, McDonald's Happy Meals, and items from his bedroom at home as jail officials, lawyers, and judges tried to determine how best to detain him safely as judicial processes moved forward to decide whether he was competent to stand trial.

In Arizona in 2008, an eight-year-old boy shot his father and another man at point-blank range with a hunting rifle that his father had given him for his birthday. He stopped and reloaded as he shot each victim at least four times. He was charged with premeditated murder. Some news reports indicated that the boy was tired of being spanked by his father. Was this an intentional act of homicide? Apparently, yes. But should a child so young be held criminally responsible in the same manner as an adult?

In South Carolina, a 12-year-old boy walked into his grandparents' bedroom one night and killed them with two blasts of a shotgun as they slept. He was a troubled boy who lived with his grandparents because he had been abandoned by his mother and had serious conflicts with his father. At the time, he was taking an antidepressant medication prescribed by doctors—but one that cannot be prescribed for teenagers in some countries because it is known to affect thinking and behavior, and carries a risk of suicide. Could the medication have affected his thinking so that he actually did not have the requisite intent to commit the crime? Did he really know what he was doing that night?

While being questioned by police in Michigan in 2013, a man confessed to a killing after he was misidentified by a witness as being involved in the crime. While he was in jail, two psychiatrists diagnosed him as suffering from schizophrenia. Police soon discovered that he was innocent, and they arrested the actual shooter. However, the prosecutor expressed the intention of charging the schizophrenic man with a felony for giving a false confession to the police.

All four of these examples raise serious questions about how we evaluate *mens rea* and determine whether someone is capable of forming criminal intent. Advances in modern science affect such situations. For example, the development and use of new medications may lead to unintended consequences for people's clarity of thought and control over their actions. In addition, greater understanding of mental conditions and neuroscience—the science of the brain and thinking—may help us analyze the capabilities of people with specific medical conditions. Yet, there will always be difficult decisions to be made.

In Ohio a judge ordered the autistic homicide suspect be moved from the jail to a state residential facility for developmentally disabled people while the court system decided whether he should stand trial. The boy in Arizona was eventually permitted to plead guilty to one count of negligent homicide instead of facing trial on two counts of first-degree murder. He was ordered to remain under the custody and supervision of the state until age 18, with further determinations to be made about whether he should live in a juvenile detention facility, be sent to a treatment facility, be placed with foster parents, or be permitted to live with his mother. If he stayed out of trouble until age 18, his record would be expunged. By contrast, the South Carolina boy, Christopher Pittman, was unsuccessful in challenging the *mens rea* element of the crime by pointing to the effects of his medication. He was sentenced to 30 years in prison for murder. The U.S. Supreme Court declined to hear his appeal. In the Michigan case, the man was sent for an extended evaluation at the state mental hospital, and the prosecutor eventually decided not to pursue any criminal charges for the false confession.

Researching the Internet

To read about other cases that raise issues concerning *mens rea*, including cases that use the insanity defense, visit; http://www.apa.org/monitor/2013/02/jn.aspx.

For Critical Analysis

What rule could we formulate that would guide us in determining whether a person was capable of forming criminal intent and thus is deserving of punishment? Alternatively, how could we use a case-by-case approach effectively to analyze the capability of each defendant? Would we advance the goal of justice by thinking about appropriate treatment instead of punishment when such questions arise about a defendant? What would you decide about each of the four defendants profiled here? Write a memo detailing how each of the four defendants should have been punished and/or given treatment.

Sources: Akron Beacon Journal, "Son of Late KSU Professor Sent to State Facility," March 27, 2009 (http://www.ohio.com); Associated Press, "Autistic Murder Defendant Poses Challenges," March 19, 2009 (http://www.msnbc.com); articles from the *New York Times* (http://www.nytimes.com): S. Dewan and B. Meier, "Boy Who Took Antidepressants Is Convicted in Killings," February 15, 2005; J. Dougherty and A. O'Connor, "Prosecutors Say Boy Methodically Shot His Father," November 11, 2008; K. Grasha, "Mentally Ill Man Who Falsely Confessed Could Be Hospitalized Up to 15 Months," *Lansing State Journal,* February 20, 2014 (www.lansingstatejournal.com); S. Moore, "Boy, 9, Enters a Guilty Plea in 2 Killings in Arizona," February 20, 2009.

factors such as age, the effects of medications, and specific medical conditions can complicate the task of deciding whether someone acted with the intent necessary to deserve criminal punishment.

Although many defendants admit that they committed the harmful act, they may still plead not guilty. They may do so not only because they know that the state must prove them guilty but also because they—or their attorneys—believe that *mens rea* was not present. Accidents are the clearest examples of such situations: the defendant argues that it was an accident that the pedestrian suddenly crossed into the path of the car.

The absence of *mens rea*, as we have seen, does not guarantee a verdict of not guilty in every case. In most cases, however, it relieves defendants of responsibility for acts that would be labeled criminal if they had been intentional. Besides the defense of accidents, there are eight defenses based on lack of criminal intent: self-defense, necessity, duress (coercion), entrapment, infancy, mistake of fact, intoxication, and insanity. These defenses are often divided into two categories, as mentioned earlier: justifications and excuses.

Justification Defenses

Justification defenses focus on whether the individual's action was socially acceptable under the circumstances despite causing a harm that the criminal law would otherwise seek to prevent.

Self-Defense A person who feels that she or he is in immediate danger of being harmed by another person may ward off the attack in *self-defense*. The laws of most states also recognize the right to defend others from attack, to protect property, and to prevent a crime. For example, in August 2002, T. J. Duckett, an African American football player for the NFL's Seattle Seahawks, was attacked by three white men who also yelled racial slurs at him as he walked toward his car after a concert. After Duckett lost a tooth and suffered a cut that required four stitches when he was struck with a bottle in the surprise attack, the 250-pound running back defended himself. He knocked one attacker unconscious and caused a second attacker to be hospitalized with injuries. The third attacker ran away. The attackers received the most serious injuries, yet they faced criminal charges because Duckett was entitled to defend himself with reasonable force against an unprovoked criminal assault (Winkeljohn, 2002).

The level of force used in self-defense cannot exceed the person's reasonable perception of the threat (K. W. Simons, 2008). Thus, a person may be justified in shooting a robber who is holding a gun to her head and threatening to kill her, but homeowners generally are not justified in shooting an unarmed burglar who has left the house and is running across the lawn. In a Florida case in 2014, the jury did not accept a man's claim that he fired 10 shots into a fleeing vehicle, one of which killed a teenager, because he believed a shotgun had been pointed out the vehicle's window at him. Because no gun was found in the bullet-ridden vehicle, the jury presumably did not accept as reasonable the man's claim of a perceived threat. In addition, none of the witnesses to the event in a store parking lot saw a shotgun pointed from the shooting victim's vehicle (DeJohn, 2014). Moreover, the shooter's decision to fire additional bullets at the vehicle as it drove away led at least one juror to conclude that any perceived threat had ended before the final shots were fired (Kuruvilla, 2014).

Necessity Unlike self-defense, in which a defendant feels that he or she must harm an aggressor to ward off an attack, the *necessity* defense is used when people break the law in order to save themselves or prevent some greater harm. A person who speeds through a red light to get an injured child to the hospital or breaks into a building to seek refuge from a hurricane could claim to be violating the law out of necessity.

In 2011, for example, a man in San Francisco was acquitted on charges of illegally carrying a concealed weapon when the jury heard that he borrowed the handgun in order to retrieve his niece's baby food from a car while visiting a housing project in a high-crime neighborhood where he had previously been robbed ("Man Acquitted," 2011). The jury accepted the necessity of his conduct, which under other circumstances would have provided the basis for a criminal conviction.

In 2011 a three-judge panel in Connecticut found Stephen Morgan to be "not guilty by reason of insanity" for first-degree murder charges after he stalked and shot a female student in the Wesleyan University bookstore. The judges ordered that he be committed to a secure psychiatric facility. Should severe mental problems enable people who kill others to avoid prison sentences?

Excuse Defenses

Excuse defenses focus on the actor and whether she or he possessed the knowledge or intent needed for a criminal conviction.

Duress (Coercion) The defense of *duress* arises when someone commits a crime because he or she is coerced by another person. During a bank robbery, for instance, if an armed robber forces one of the bank's customers at gunpoint to drive the getaway car, the customer would be able to claim duress. However, courts generally are not willing to accept this defense if the person does not try to escape from the situation.

Entrapment *Entrapment* is a defense that can be used to show lack of intent. The law excuses a defendant when it is shown that government agents have induced the person to commit the offense. That does not mean the police may not use undercover agents to set a trap for criminals, nor does it mean the police may not provide ordinary opportunities for the commission of a crime. But the entrapment defense may be used when the police have acted so as to induce the criminal act.

During the twentieth century, the defense of entrapment evolved through a series of court decisions (Costinett, 2011). In earlier times, judges were less concerned with whether the police had baited a citizen into committing an illegal act and were more concerned with whether or not the citizen had taken the bait. Today when the police implant an idea for a crime in the mind of a person who then commits the offense, judges are more likely to consider entrapment claims.

Entrapment raises tough questions for judges, who must decide whether the police went too far toward making a crime occur that otherwise would not have happened (Carlon, 2007). The key question is the predisposition of the defendant. In 1992 the Supreme Court stressed that the prosecutor must show beyond a reasonable doubt that a defendant was predisposed to break the law before being approached by government agents. The Court's decision invalidated the conviction of a Nebraska farmer who purchased child pornography after receiving multiple solicitation letters from law enforcement officials pretending to be pen pals and bookstore operators (*United States v. Jacobson*).

entrapment The defense that the individual was induced by the police to commit the criminal act.

Infancy Anglo American law excuses criminal acts by children under age seven on the grounds of their *infancy* and lack of responsibility for their actions—in other words, *mens rea* is not present. Also called *immaturity*, this excuse is based on the recognition that young children do not yet have the capacity to think about and understand appropriate behavior and the consequences of their actions. Common law has presumed that children aged 7–14 are not liable for their criminal acts; however, prosecutors have on occasion been able to present evidence of a child's mental capacity to form *mens rea*. Juries can assume the presence of a guilty mind if it can be shown, for example, that the child hid evidence or tried to bribe a witness.

Of course, as a child grows older, the assumption of immaturity weakens. Since the development of juvenile courts in the 1890s, children generally have been tried using rules that are different from those applied to adults, but in some situations, they may be tried as adults—if, for example, they are repeat offenders or are charged with a particularly heinous crime. Because of the public's concerns about violent crimes by young people, in the 1990s, it became increasingly common to see prosecutors seek to hold children responsible for serious crimes in the same manner that adults are held responsible (Henning, 2013). As mentioned in the Close Up feature on page 87, in 2008 the U.S. Supreme Court declined to hear an appeal from Christopher Pittman, who as a 12-year-old had killed his grandparents, was tried as an adult, and was sentenced to 30 years.

Mistake of Fact   The courts have generally upheld the view that ignorance of the law is no excuse for committing an illegal act. But what if there is a *mistake of fact*? If an accused person has made a mistake on some crucial fact, that may serve as a defense (Christopher, 1994). For example, suppose some teenagers ask your permission to grow sunflowers in a vacant lot behind your home. You help them weed the garden and water the plants. Then it turns out that they are growing marijuana. You were not aware of this because you have no idea what a marijuana plant looks like. Should you be convicted for growing an illegal drug on your property? The answer depends on the specific degree of knowledge and intent that the prosecution must prove for that offense. The success of such a defense may also depend on the extent to which jurors understand and sympathize with your mistake.

For example, in 2008 a college professor attending a professional baseball game bought his seven-year-old son a bottle of "lemonade." Because he and his family seldom watch television, however, he had no idea that "hard lemonade" even existed. Thus, he made a mistake of fact by purchasing an alcoholic beverage for his underage son. When police officers spotted the child drinking the beverage, the boy was taken from the custody of his parents for a few days until officials decided that it was an unintentional mistake. If prosecutors had pursued criminal charges against the professor, his fate would have depended on whether the jury believed his claim of making an ignorant mistake of fact in purchasing the alcoholic "lemonade" for a child (Dickerson, 2008).

Intoxication   The law does not relieve an individual of responsibility for acts performed while voluntarily intoxicated. There are, however, cases in which *intoxication* can be used as a defense, as when a person has been tricked into consuming a substance without knowing that it may cause intoxication. Christopher Pittman's attorney attempted unsuccessfully to use this defense by arguing that the boy's prescribed antidepressant drugs caused his violent behavior. Some complex cases arise in which the defendant must be shown to have had a specific, rather than a general, intent to commit a crime. For example, people may claim that they were too drunk to realize that they had left a restaurant without paying the bill. Drunkenness can also be used as a mitigating factor to reduce the seriousness of a charge.

In 1996 the U.S. Supreme Court narrowly approved a Montana law that barred the use of evidence of intoxication even for defendants who claimed that their condition prevented them from forming the specific intent necessary to be guilty of a crime (*Montana v. Egelhoff*). Thus, states may enact laws that prevent the use of an intoxication defense.

Insanity   The defense of *insanity* has been a subject of heated debate. Four states—Idaho, Montana, Nevada, and Utah—no longer permit the insanity defense (Bennion, 2011). The public believes that many criminals "escape" punishment through the skillful use of psychiatric testimony. Yet, less than 1 percent of incarcerated offenders are held in mental hospitals because they were found "not guilty by reason of insanity." The insanity defense is rare and is generally used only in serious cases or where there is no other valid defense.

Over time, U.S. courts have used five tests of criminal responsibility involving insanity: the *M'Naghten* Rule, the Irresistible Impulse Test, the *Durham* Rule, the *Model Penal Code*'s Substantial Capacity Test, and the test defined in the federal Comprehensive Crime Control Act of 1984. These tests are summarized in

TABLE 3.2 Insanity Defense Standards

The standards for the insanity defense have evolved over time.

Test	Legal Standard Because of Mental Illness
M'Naghten (1843)	"Didn't know what he was doing or didn't know it was wrong."
Irresistible Impulse (1897)	"Could not control his conduct."
Durham (1954)	"The criminal act was caused by his mental illness."
Model Penal Code (1972)	"Lacks substantial capacity to appreciate the wrongfulness of his conduct or to control it."
Comprehensive Crime Control Act	"Lacks capacity to appreciate the wrongfulness of his conduct."

Source: National Institute of Justice, *Crime File*, "Insanity Defense," a film prepared by Norval Morris (Washington, DC: U.S. Government Printing Office, n.d.).

Table 3.2. One important feature of the insanity defense is the opportunity for state and federal laws to impose on defendants the burden of demonstrating their mental capacity. The prosecution bears the burden of proving the defendant's guilt beyond a reasonable doubt, but the Supreme Court has said laws "may place the burden of persuasion on a defendant to prove insanity as the applicable law defines it, whether by a preponderance of the evidence or to some more convincing degree" (*Clark v. Arizona*, 2006). Thus, if the defendant raises an insanity defense in a case, the law of that jurisdiction will dictate whether the defendant must present evidence to persuade the judge or jury about her or his insanity or whether the prosecutor must prove that the defendant did not fit the legal definition of insanity at the time of the crime.

M'Naghten Rule More than a dozen states use the *M'Naghten* Rule, which was developed in England in 1843. In that year, Daniel M'Naghten was acquitted of killing Edward Drummond, a man he had thought was Sir Robert Peel, the prime minister of Great Britain. M'Naghten claimed that he had been delusional at the time of the killing. The British court developed a standard for determining criminal responsibility known as the "right-from-wrong test." It asks whether "at the time of the committing of the act, the party accused was laboring under such a defect of reason, from disease of the mind, as not to know the nature and quality of the act he was doing, or if he did know it that he did not know he was doing what was wrong" (*M'Naghten's Case*, 1843).

Irresistible Impulse Test Four states supplemented the *M'Naghten* Rule with the Irresistible Impulse Test. Because psychiatrists argued that some people can feel compelled by their mental illness to commit criminal actions even though they recognize the wrongfulness of their conduct, the Irresistible Impulse Test was designed to bring the *M'Naghten* Rule in line with modern psychiatry. This test excuses defendants when a mental disease was controlling their behavior even though they knew that what they were doing was wrong. In James Holmes's case, discussed in the opening of the chapter, Colorado law required the prosecutor to persuade the court that, in accordance with the *M'Naghten* Rule and the Irresistible Impulse Test, Holmes knew what he was doing, knew it was wrong, and was able to control his own conduct (Spellman & Nottingham, 2013).

Durham Rule The *Durham* Rule, originally developed in New Hampshire in 1871, was adopted by the Circuit Court of Appeals for the District of Columbia in 1954 in the case of *Durham v. United States*. Under this rule, the accused is not criminally responsible "if an unlawful act is the product of mental disease or mental defect."

Model Penal Code's Substantial Capacity Test Arguing that the *Durham* Rule offered no useful definition of "mental disease or defect," the case of *United States v. Brawner* led the federal courts to overturn the *Durham* Rule in 1972 in favor of a modified version of a test proposed in the *Model Penal Code*. (As explained earlier, the *Model Penal Code* was developed by the American Bar Association as a model of what "should" be.) By 1982 all federal courts and about half of the state courts had adopted the *Model Penal Code*'s Substantial Capacity Test, which states that a person is not responsible for criminal conduct "if at the time of such conduct as a result of mental disease or defect he lacks substantial capacity either to appreciate the criminality [wrongfulness] of his conduct or to conform his conduct to the requirements of law." The Substantial Capacity Test broadens and modifies the *M'Naghten* and Irresistible Impulse rules. By stressing "substantial capacity," the test does not require that a defendant be unable to distinguish right from wrong.

Comprehensive Crime Control Act The Comprehensive Crime Control Act of 1984 changed the federal rules on the insanity defense by limiting it to those who are unable, as a result of severe mental disease or defect, to understand the nature or wrongfulness of their acts. This change means that the Irresistible Impulse Test cannot be used in the federal courts. It also shifts the burden of proof from the prosecutor to the defendant, who has to prove his or her insanity. Further, the act creates a new procedure whereby a person who is found not guilty only by reason of insanity must be committed to a mental hospital until she or he no longer poses a danger to society. These rules apply only in federal courts, but they are spreading to the states.

All of the insanity tests are difficult to apply. Moreover, deciding what to do with someone who has been found not guilty by reason of insanity poses significant difficulties. Another problem is that jurors' fears about seeing the offender turned loose might affect their decisions about whether the person was legally insane at the time of the crime.

John Hinckley's attempt to assassinate President Ronald Reagan in 1981 reopened the debate on the insanity defense. Television news footage showed that Hinckley had shot the president. Yet, with the help of psychiatrists, Hinckley's lawyers counteracted the prosecution's efforts to persuade the jury that Hinckley was sane. Hinckley did not go free, however. He has been confined to a mental hospital for more than 30 years, although doctors and a federal judge have approved opportunities for him to leave the hospital to visit his mother in recent years (Marimow, 2013). When Hinckley was acquitted, the public was outraged, and several states acted to limit or abolish the insanity defense. Twelve states introduced the defense of "guilty but mentally ill" (Klofas & Yandrasits, 1989). This defense allows a jury to find the accused guilty but requires that he or she be given psychiatric treatment while in prison (L. A. Callahan et al., 1992).

☑ CHECK POINT

3. What are the seven principles of criminal law?
Legality, *actus reus*, causation, harm, concurrence, *mens rea*, and punishment.

4. What are the defenses in substantive criminal law?
Self-defense, necessity, duress (coercion), entrapment, infancy, mistake of fact, intoxication, insanity.

5. What are the tests of criminal responsibility used for the insanity defense?
M'Naghten Rule (right-from-wrong test), Irresistible Impulse Test, *Durham* Rule, *Model Penal Code*, Comprehensive Crime Control Act.

STOP&ANALYZE

Look through the list of justification and excuse defenses, and choose one that is the *least* important or necessary. Make three arguments for abolishing that defense. What would be the risks and consequences of abolishing the defense? What is the strongest argument in favor of keeping it?

Procedural Criminal Law

Procedural law defines how the state must process cases. According to procedural due process, accused persons must be tried in accordance with legal procedures, which include providing the rights granted by the Constitution to criminal defendants. As we saw in Chapter 1, the due process model is based on the premise that freedom is so valuable that efforts must be made to prevent erroneous decisions that would deprive an innocent person of her or his freedom. But rights are not only intended to prevent the innocent from being wrongly convicted. They also seek to prevent unfair police and prosecution practices aimed at guilty people, such as conducting improper searches, using violence to pressure people to confess, and denying defendants a fair trial.

The importance of procedural law has been evident throughout U.S. history, which contains many examples of police officers and prosecutors harassing and victimizing those who lack political power, such as poor people, racial and ethnic minorities, and unpopular religious groups. The development of procedural safeguards through the decisions of the U.S. Supreme Court has helped protect citizens from such actions. In these decisions, the Supreme Court may favor guilty people by ordering new trials or may even release them from custody because of the weight it places on protecting procedural rights and preventing police misconduct.

Individual rights and the protection against improper deprivations of liberty represent central elements of American values. Americans expect that their rights will be protected. At the same time, however, the protection of rights for the criminally accused can clash with competing American values that emphasize the control of crime as an important component of protecting all citizens' freedom of movement and sense of security. Because the rules of procedural criminal law can sometimes lead to the release of guilty people, some observers regard them as weighted too heavily in favor of American values emphasizing individual rights rather than equally valid American values that emphasize the protection of the community.

Public opinion does not always support the decisions by the Supreme Court and other courts that uphold the rights of criminal defendants and convicted offenders. Many Americans would prefer if other goals for society, such as stopping crime and ensuring that guilty people are punished, took a higher priority over the protection of defendants' rights. Such opinions raise questions about Americans' commitment to the rights described in the Bill of Rights. Public opinion data indicate that most first-year college students believe that courts have placed too much emphasis on the rights of criminal defendants. This view, though reduced since 1998, remains stronger than in 1971. Although male and female students' support for rights differed in 1971, there is less difference between the two groups in later years (see "What Americans Think"). Do you agree that there are too many rights for defendants?

Unlike substantive criminal law, which is defined by legislatures through statutes, procedural criminal law is defined by courts through judicial rulings. Judges interpret the provisions of the U.S. Constitution and state constitutions, and those interpretations establish the procedures that government officials must follow. Because it has the authority to review cases from state supreme courts as well as

WHAT AMERICANS THINK

QUESTION: Percentage of first-year college students who agree with the statement "There is too much concern in the courts for the rights of criminals."

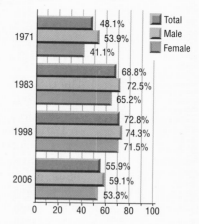

Year	Total	Male	Female
1971	48.1%	53.9%	41.1%
1983	68.8%	72.5%	65.2%
1998	72.8%	74.3%	71.5%
2006	55.9%	59.1%	53.3%

CRITICAL THINKING: Can you identify specific rights that give too much protection to criminal defendants? Would there be any risks from reducing the rights available in the criminal justice process?

Source: Bureau of Justice Statistics, *Sourcebook of Criminal Justice Statistics, 2014*, Table 2.92.2006.

from federal courts, the U.S. Supreme Court has played a major role in defining procedural criminal law. The Supreme Court's influence stems from its power to define the meaning of the U.S. Constitution, especially the Bill of Rights—the first 10 amendments to the Constitution, which list legal protections against actions of the government. Although public opinion may clash with Supreme Court rulings, the Supreme Court can make independent decisions because its appointed members cannot be removed from office by the voters but only through impeachment for misconduct.

The Bill of Rights and the Fourteenth Amendment

The U.S. Constitution contained few references to criminal justice when it was ratified in 1788 and 1789. Because many people were concerned that the document did not set forth the rights of individuals in enough detail, 10 amendments were added in 1791. These first 10 amendments are known as the **Bill of Rights**.

Bill of Rights The first 10 amendments added to the U.S. Constitution to provide specific rights for individuals, including criminal justice rights concerning searches, trials, and punishments.

American students typically gain exposure to the provisions of the Bill of Rights through required high school classes on civics and American government. Thus, many Americans know that rights concerning free speech and religion are contained in the First Amendment. Because of public debates about its meaning, many Americans also know that the Second Amendment contains the phrase "the right of the people to keep and bear arms, shall not be infringed." The details of the other numbered amendments are often not as familiar because they tend to receive less attention in politicians' speeches and news media articles. As described in "The Policy Debate" feature, the Second Amendment is one of several amendments in the Bill of Rights that has implications for criminal justice. However, the Second Amendment is not one of the four amendments that directly concern procedural criminal law. Instead, it is at the heart of debates about criminal justice policies that are shaped by judges' interpretations of the Constitution, scholars' studies of crime and violence, interest groups' beliefs about constitutional rights, and legislators' decisions about needed laws.

The first Congress debated and approved the Bill of Rights, the first 10 amendments to the U.S. Constitution. These amendments provided protections for suspects and defendants in the federal criminal justice process. Decisions by the U.S. Supreme Court later applied these protections to state court criminal cases, too. What might the American criminal justice system look like if it lacked the procedural rights provided by the Bill of Rights?

Library of Congress, Prints and Photographs Division

A. THOLEY, PINX.

JOHN ADAMS. MORRIS. HAMILTON. JEFFERSON.
LEADERS OF THE CONTINENTAL CONGRESS.

Should Ex-Felons' Gun-Ownership Rights Be Restored?

In 2010 more than 700,000 people were released from American prisons and returned to their home communities. The number of ex-felons gaining release is increasing as states seek ways to reduce the expense of imprisonment. It is much less expensive to have offenders under parole supervision in the community than it is to incarcerate them. These releases coincide with two developments. First, because of attention to voting rights for ex-offenders, there has been a political push to restore all constitutional rights for ex-offenders after they successfully complete their prison sentences and parole supervision within the community. Second, the U.S. Supreme Court issued decisions declaring that the Second Amendment grants to individuals the right to own handguns in their homes for personal protection (*District of Columbia v. Heller*, 2008) and that this Second Amendment right should limit gun regulations imposed by cities and states as well by as the federal government (*McDonald v. Chicago*, 2010). As a result, debates have emerged about whether gun-ownership rights should be restored for ex-felons. Proponents argue that ex-felons should have their gun rights restored, especially those who face daily dangers from living in high-crime neighborhoods and therefore need the necessary means to protect themselves and their families.

For Restoring Gun-Ownership Rights for Ex-Felons

Supporters of the restoration of gun-ownership rights focus on the fact that ex-offenders who have completed their punishment should be reintegrated into the community, recognized as equal citizens, and permitted to rebuild their lives with full citizenship rights.

The arguments for restoring gun-ownership rights are these:

- Ex-offenders have completed their punishment and need to be regarded as full and equal citizens in order to be reintegrated into the society.
- Many ex-offenders live in high-crime neighborhoods, and they need to be able to protect their homes and families.
- Gun ownership is a basic right guaranteed for all Americans by the Second Amendment.
- States that have enacted laws to expand opportunities for citizens to possess and carry guns have not experienced increases in crime rates as a result.

Against Restoring Gun-Ownership Rights for Ex-Felons

Opponents of restoration of gun-ownership rights raise concerns about permitting the possession of firearms for people whose past behavior demonstrated that they lacked self-control, acted in a violent manner, or otherwise failed to obey society's rules. As a result, there would be grave risks of additional shootings and homicides that might have been prevented by barring ex-felons from owning guns or by approving gun ownership on an individual case-by-case basis.

The arguments against permitting ex-felons to own guns are these:

- The Second Amendment does not guarantee gun rights for all Americans; the Supreme Court's decision specifically said, "nothing in our opinion should be taken to cast doubt on longstanding prohibitions on the possession of firearms by felons and the mentally ill."
- Congress and state legislatures can enact reasonable restrictions on gun ownership by specific categories of people as long as they do not prohibit handguns kept in the homes of people with established records of being law-abiding citizens.
- In states that require restoration of gun-ownership rights, there have been highly publicized shootings committed by mentally ill and otherwise troubled ex-felons.
- In addition to risks of shootings and homicides, gun ownership by ex-felons whose lives lack evidence of self-control, organizational skills, and concern for safety will also increase risks of gun accidents involving children, suicides, and the theft of unsecured firearms in burglaries and robberies.

What Should U.S. Policy Be?

What impact would the restoration of gun-ownership rights for ex-felons have on American society? Is it an essential element of reintegrating ex-offenders that all citizenship rights be restored? Would the availability of legal guns for ex-felons increase shootings, homicides, and other crimes and thereby harm society?

Researching the Internet

To read the Supreme Court's fundamental opinion on the definition of Second Amendment gun ownership rights, see *District of Columbia v. Heller* (2008) at http://www.law.cornell.edu/supct/pdf/07-290P.ZO.

For Critical Analysis

Are gun-ownership rights essential to ex-felons' successful reintegration into American society, to the restoration of their status as equal citizens, and to the protection of their families? Alternatively, is society subject to increased danger and harm when ex-felons can readily own guns? What policy do you see as best for the United States? Give three reasons for your conclusion about this issue.

Procedural criminal law is shaped by four specific amendments in the Bill of Rights, as well as by the Fourteenth Amendment, which was created in 1868 after the Civil War. The Fourth Amendment bars unreasonable searches and seizures. The Fifth Amendment outlines basic due process rights in criminal cases.

For example, consistent with the assumption that the state must prove the defendant's guilt, protection against **self-incrimination** means that persons cannot be forced to respond to questions whose answers may reveal that they have committed a crime. The protection against **double jeopardy** means that a person may be subjected to only one prosecution or punishment for a single offense within the same jurisdiction. The Sixth Amendment provides for the right to a speedy, fair, and public trial by an impartial jury, as well as the right to counsel. The Eighth Amendment bars excessive bail, excessive fines, and cruel and unusual punishments.

The texts of these four procedural criminal law amendments in the Bill of Rights are included here. Refer to these as you read the sections that follow. The first 10 amendments were ratified on December 15, 1791. The Fourteenth Amendment, which was ratified on July 28, 1868, also impacts procedural criminal law by providing rights to due process and equal protection of the laws. Unlike these four amendments that are primarily concerned with criminal justice, the Fourteenth Amendment also applies in a variety of other contexts, such as prohibiting racial discrimination in public schools and other government facilities and programs.

Fourth Amendment: The right of the people to be secure in their persons, houses, papers, and effects, against unreasonable searches and seizures, shall not be violated, and no Warrants shall issue, but upon probable cause, supported by Oath or affirmation, and particularly describing the place to be searched, and the persons or things to be seized.

Fifth Amendment: No person shall be held to answer for a capital or otherwise infamous crime, unless on a presentment or indictment of a Grand Jury, except in cases arising in the land or naval forces, or in the Militia, when in actual service in time of War or public danger; nor shall any person be subject for the same offence to be twice put in jeopardy of life or limb; nor shall be compelled in any criminal case to be a witness against himself, nor be deprived of life, liberty, or property, without due process of law; nor shall private property be taken for public use, without just compensation.

Sixth Amendment: In all criminal prosecutions, the accused shall enjoy the right to a speedy and public trial, by an impartial jury of the State and district wherein the crime shall have been committed, which district shall have been previously ascertained by law, and to be informed of the nature and cause of the accusation; to be confronted with the witnesses against him; to have compulsory process for obtaining witnesses in his favor, and to have the Assistance of Counsel for his defense.

Eighth Amendment: Excessive bail shall not be required, nor excessive fines imposed, nor cruel and unusual punishments inflicted.

For most of American history, the Bill of Rights did not apply to most criminal cases, because it was designed to protect people from abusive actions by the federal government. It did not seek to protect people from state and local officials, who handled nearly all criminal cases. This view was upheld by the U.S. Supreme Court in the 1833 case of *Barron v. Baltimore*. However, as we shall see shortly, this view gradually changed in the late nineteenth and early twentieth centuries.

The Fourteenth Amendment and Due Process

After the Civil War, three amendments were added to the Constitution. These amendments were designed to protect individuals' rights against infringement by state and local government officials. The Thirteenth Amendment abolished slavery, and the Fifteenth Amendment attempted to prohibit racial discrimination in voting; these amendments had little impact on criminal justice. However, the Fourteenth Amendment profoundly affected it by barring states from violating people's right to due process of law. Its key language says that "no State shall . . . deprive any person of life, liberty, or property, without due process of law; nor deny to any person within its jurisdiction the equal protection of the laws." These rights to due process and equal protection served as a basis for protecting individuals from abusive actions by local government officials. However, the terms *due process* and *equal protection* are so vague that it was left to the U.S. Supreme Court to decide if and how these new rights applied to the criminal justice process.

For example, in ***Powell v. Alabama* (1932)**, the Supreme Court ruled that the due process clause required states to provide attorneys for poor defendants facing the death penalty. This decision stemmed from a notorious case in Alabama in which nine African American men, known as the "Scottsboro boys," were quickly convicted and condemned to death for allegedly raping two white women—but one of the alleged victims later admitted that she had lied about the rape (Goodman, 1994).

In these early cases, the justices had not developed clear rules for deciding which specific rights applied to state and local officials as components of the due process clause of the Fourteenth Amendment. They operated on the assumption that procedures must meet a standard of **fundamental fairness**. In essence, the justices simply reacted against brutal situations that shocked their consciences. In doing so, they showed the importance of procedural criminal law in protecting individuals from abusive and unjust actions by government officials.

The Due Process Revolution

From the 1930s to the 1960s, the fundamental fairness doctrine was supported by a majority of the Supreme Court justices. It was applied on a case-by-case basis, not always consistently. After Earl Warren became chief justice in 1953, he led the Supreme Court in a revolution that changed the meaning and scope of constitutional rights. Instead of requiring state and local officials merely to uphold fundamental fairness, the Court began to require them to abide by the specific provisions of the Bill of Rights (Marceau, 2008). Through the process of **incorporation**, the Supreme Court during the Warren Court era declared that elements of the Fourth, Fifth, Sixth, Eighth, and other amendments were part of the due process clause of the Fourteenth Amendment. Previously, states could design their own procedures so long as those procedures passed the fundamental fairness test. Under Warren's leadership, however, the Supreme Court's new approach imposed detailed procedural standards on the police and courts.

As it applied more and more constitutional rights against the states, the Court made decisions that favored the interests of many criminal defendants. These defendants had their convictions overturned and received new trials because the Court believed that it was more important to protect the values underlying criminal procedure than single-mindedly to seek convictions of criminal offenders. In the eyes of many legal scholars, the Warren Court's decisions made criminal justice processes consistent with the American values of liberty, rights, and limited government authority.

To critics, however, these decisions made the community more vulnerable to crime and thereby harmed American values by diminishing the overall sense of liberty and security in society (Nowlin, 2012). Warren and the other justices were strongly criticized by politicians, police chiefs, and members of the public. These critics believed that the Warren Court was rewriting constitutional law in a manner that gave too many legal protections to criminals who harm society. In addition, Warren and his colleagues were criticized for ignoring established precedents that defined rights in a limited fashion.

From 1962 to 1972, the Supreme Court, under Chief Justices Earl Warren (1953–1969) and Warren Burger (1969–1986), applied most criminal justice rights in the U.S. Constitution against actions by state and local officials. By the end of this period, the process of incorporation was nearly complete. Criminal justice officials at all levels—federal, state, and local—were obligated to respect the constitutional rights of suspects and defendants.

***Powell v. Alabama* (1932)** Case deciding that an attorney must be provided to a poor defendant facing the death penalty.

fundamental fairness A legal doctrine supporting the idea that so long as a state's conduct maintains basic standards of fairness, the Constitution has not been violated.

incorporation The extension of the due process clause of the Fourteenth Amendment to make binding on state governments the rights guaranteed in the first 10 amendments to the U.S. Constitution (the Bill of Rights).

The Fourth Amendment: Protection against Unreasonable Searches and Seizures

The Fourth Amendment limits the ability of law enforcement officers to search a person or property in order to obtain evidence of criminal activity. It also limits the ability of the police to detain a person without proper justification (Taslitz, 2010). When police take an individual into custody or prevent an individual from leaving a location, such detentions are considered to be "seizures" under the Fourth Amendment. As we shall examine in greater detail in Chapter 6, the Fourth Amendment does not prevent the police from conducting searches or making arrests; it merely protects people's privacy by barring "unreasonable" searches and arrests. It is up to the Supreme Court to define the situations in which a search or seizure is reasonable or unreasonable.

The justices also face challenges in defining such words as *searches* and *seizures*. For example, in 2005 the Supreme Court ruled that no issues concerning Fourth Amendment rights arose when a K-9 officer had a trained police dog sniff the exterior of a vehicle that was stopped for a traffic violation (Lunney, 2009). The dog indicated to the officer that the car's trunk contained marijuana, and that discovery led to a criminal conviction. However, unlike a *search*, for which officers must have proper justifications, the use of the dog did not require any justification, because the dog's scent-based examination of the vehicle's exterior did not invade the driver's right to privacy (*Illinois v. Caballes*, 2005).

By contrast, in 2013 the Supreme Court said a search occurred and violated the rights of a homeowner when an unverified informant's tip led an officer to take a drug-sniffing dog to the front door of a house. The dog detected marijuana in the house, and the police obtained a warrant to do a search based on the dog's indication. However, because the officer lacked sufficient justification to bring the dog to the front door of the house, the homeowner's rights were violated by the improper search (*Florida v. Jardines*).

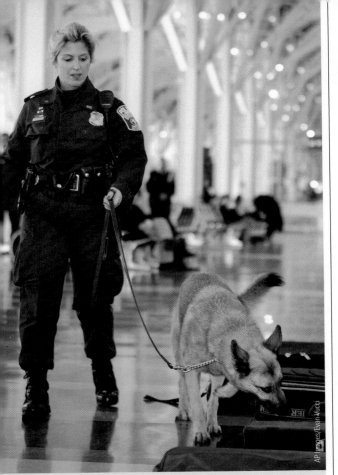

Police need to conduct searches and examine people's property as part of criminal investigations. They also need to search in order to prevent crimes by people who might conceal weapons, drugs, or other illegal items at airports, borders, nightclubs, and stadiums. All searches must either be done with warrants or be "reasonable" under judges' interpretations of the Fourth Amendment. Have you had your clothes or property examined by police or security guards? Is every examination of property a "search" under the Fourth Amendment? Is this dog "searching" the luggage?

The justices decided *Florida v. Jardines* (2013) by a five-to-four vote. Clearly the justices disagreed about whether the use of drug-sniffing dog at a house constituted a "search" under the Fourth Amendment. Because different Supreme Court justices do not always agree on the Constitution's meaning, the definitions of words such as "search," "seizure," and "unreasonable," and hence the rules for police searches, can change as the makeup of the Court changes (Soree, 2013).

Read "A Question of Ethics" at the end of the chapter to consider police officers' role in triggering behavior by the occupants of an apartment that the police then used to justify the warrantless search of the apartment. The example raises questions about whether police officers might have opportunities to act unethically in creating justifications for searches that otherwise would not be permitted.

The wording of the Fourth Amendment makes clear that the authors of the Bill of Rights did not believe that law enforcement officials should have the power to pursue criminals at all costs. The Fourth Amendment's protections apply both to suspects and to law-abiding citizens. Police officers are supposed to follow the rules for obtaining search warrants, and they are not permitted to conduct unreasonable searches even when trying to catch dangerous criminals. As we shall see in Chapter 6, improper searches that lead to the discovery of criminal evidence can lead judges to bar police and prosecutors from using that evidence to prove the suspect's guilt. Thus, police officers need to be knowledgeable about the rules for searches and seizures and to follow those rules carefully when conducting criminal investigations.

Police face challenges in attempting to respect Fourth Amendment rights while also actively seeking to prevent crimes and catch offenders. Officers may be tempted to go too far in investigating crimes without an adequate basis for suspicion and thereby violate Fourth Amendment rights. The discussion of racial profiling in Chapter 1 illustrates one aspect of the risk that officers will, by conducting stops and searches without an appropriate basis, use their authority in ways that collide with the Fourth Amendment (Harris, 2013).

The Fifth Amendment: Protection against Self-Incrimination and Double Jeopardy

The Fifth Amendment clearly states some key rights related to the investigation and prosecution of criminal suspects. For example, the protection against compelled *self-incrimination* seeks to prevent authorities from pressuring people into acting as witnesses against themselves. Presumably, this right also helps protect against torture or other rough treatment when police officers question criminal suspects. In Chapter 6, we shall discuss the Fifth Amendment rules that guide officers in questioning criminal suspects. Improper questioning can affect whether evidence obtained through that questioning can be used in court.

Because of the Fifth Amendment right that protects against *double jeopardy*, a person charged with a criminal act may be subjected to only one prosecution or punishment for that offense in the same jurisdiction. The purpose of the right is to prevent the government from trying someone over and over again until a conviction is obtained (Coffin, 2010). Generally, a person acquitted of a crime at trial cannot be tried again for that same crime.

As interpreted by the Supreme Court, however, the right against double jeopardy does not prevent a person from facing two trials or receiving two sanctions from the government for the same criminal acts (L. Griffin, 2010). Because a single criminal act may violate both state and federal laws, for example, a person may be tried in both courts. Consequently, when Los Angeles police officers were acquitted of assault charges in a state court after they had been videotaped beating motorist Rodney King, they were convicted in a federal court for violating King's civil rights. In yet another case, the Supreme Court permitted Alabama to pursue kidnapping and murder charges against a man who had already been convicted for the same murder in Georgia, because the victim was kidnapped in one state and killed in the other (*Heath v. Alabama*, 1985). Thus, the protection against double jeopardy does not prevent two different trials based on the same criminal acts as long as the trials are in different jurisdictions and based on different charges. In the preceding example, the violation of the Georgia murder law was a different charge than the violation of the Alabama murder law even though both charges concerned the same killing.

One of the rights in the Fifth Amendment, the entitlement to indictment by a grand jury before being prosecuted for a serious crime, applies only in federal courts. This is one of the few rights in the Bill of Rights that the Supreme Court has never applied to the states. A **grand jury** is a body of citizens drawn from the community to hear evidence from the prosecutor in order to determine whether there is a sufficient basis to move forward with a criminal prosecution (Washburn, 2008). Some states use grand juries by their own choice; they are not required to do so by the Fifth Amendment. Other states simply permit prosecutors to file charges directly against criminal suspects.

grand jury Body of citizens drawn from the community to hear evidence presented by the prosecutor in order to decide whether enough evidence exists to file charges against a defendant.

The Sixth Amendment: The Right to Counsel and a Fair Trial

The Sixth Amendment includes several provisions dealing with fairness in a criminal prosecution. These include the rights to counsel, to a speedy and public trial, and to an impartial jury.

The Right to Counsel Although the right to counsel in a criminal case had prevailed in federal courts since 1938, not until the Supreme Court's landmark decision in *Gideon v. Wainwright* (1963) was this requirement made binding on the states. Many states already provided attorneys, but in this ruling, the Court forced all of the states to meet Sixth Amendment standards. In previous cases, the Court, applying the doctrine of fundamental fairness, had ruled that states must provide poor people with counsel only when this was required by the special circumstances of the case. A defense attorney had to be provided when conviction could lead to the death penalty, when the issues were complex, or when a poor defendant was either very young or mentally handicapped.

Although the *Gideon* ruling directly affected only states that did not provide poor defendants with attorneys, it set in motion a series of cases that affected all the states by deciding how the right to counsel would be applied in various situations. Beginning in 1963, the Court extended the right to counsel to preliminary hearings, initial appeals, post-indictment identification lineups, and children in juvenile court proceedings. Later, however, the Burger Court declared that attorneys need not be provided for discretionary appeals or for trials in which the only punishment is a fine (*Ross v. Moffitt*, 1974; *Scott v. Illinois*, 1979). Even in recent years, the Supreme Court has continued to clarify the extent of the right to counsel (M. M. McCall, M. A. McCall, & Smith, 2013). In 2012, for example, the Court determined that defense attorneys must fulfill certain professional standards during the plea bargaining process by informing defendants of formal plea offers made by the prosecutor and by accurately providing advice on the consequences of turning down a plea offer (*Missouri v. Frye*, 2012; *Lafler v. Cooper*, 2012).

The Right to a Speedy and Public Trial The nation's founders were aware that in other countries, accused people might often languish in jail for a very long time awaiting trial and often were convicted in secret proceedings. At the time of the American Revolution, the right to a speedy and public trial was recognized in the common law and included in the constitutions of six of the original states. But the word *speedy* is vague, and the Supreme Court recognizes that the interest of quick processes may conflict with other interests of society (such as the need to collect evidence) as well as with interests of the defendant (such as the need for time to prepare a defense). These factors create challenges for the Supreme Court in cases that raise claims about violations of the right to a speedy trial.

The right to a public trial is intended to protect the accused against arbitrary conviction. The Constitution assumes that judges and juries will act in accordance with the law if they must listen to evidence and announce their decisions in public. Again, the Supreme Court has recognized that there may be cases in which the need for a public trial must be balanced against other concerns. For example, the right to a public trial does not mean that *all* members of the public have the right to attend the trial. The courtroom's seating capacity and the interests of a fair trial, free of outbursts from the audience, may be considered. In hearings on sex crimes when the victim or witness is a minor, courts have barred the public in order to spare the child embarrassment. In some states, trials have become even more public than the authors of the Sixth Amendment ever imagined, because court proceedings are televised—some are even carried on national cable systems through CNN.com/CRIME and truTV (formerly known as COURT-TV).

Gideon v. Wainwright (1963) Case deciding that indigent defendants have a right to counsel when charged with serious crimes for which they could face six or more months of incarceration.

The Right to an Impartial Jury The right to a jury trial was well established in the American colonies at the time of the Revolution. In their charters, most of the colonies guaranteed trial by jury, and it was referred to in the First Continental Congress's debates in 1774, the Declaration of Independence, the constitutions of the 13 original states, and the Sixth Amendment to the U.S. Constitution. Juries allow citizens to play a role in courts' decision making and to prevent prosecutions in cases in which there is not enough evidence. However, as discussed in "Criminal Justice: Myth & Reality," the right to trial by jury is not as widely available for criminal defendants as many Americans believe.

Several Supreme Court decisions have dealt with the composition of juries. The Court has held that the amendment requires selection procedures that create a jury pool made up of a cross section of the community (T. White & Baik, 2010). Most scholars believe that an impartial jury can best be achieved by drawing jurors at random from the broadest possible base (Vidmar & Hans, 2007). The jury is expected to represent the community, and the extent to which it does so is a central concern of jury administration. As you consider the importance of the Supreme Court's interpretations of the Sixth Amendment and other provisions of the Bill of Rights, read the "Comparative Perspective" on procedural criminal law in Russia to see a stark contrast in how the system in a country different from the United States processes criminal cases.

The Eighth Amendment: Protection against Excessive Bail, Excessive Fines, and Cruel and Unusual Punishments

CRIMINAL JUSTICE
MYTH&REALITY

COMMON BELIEF: Because the Sixth Amendment clearly says, "In all criminal prosecutions, the accused shall enjoy the right to a speedy and public trial, by an impartial jury, . . ." all criminal defendants who decline to plead guilty and choose to go to trial are entitled to a trial by jury.

- Despite the clear words of the Sixth Amendment, the U.S. Supreme Court has interpreted the constitutional right to trial by jury in a manner that limits the availability of jury trials.
- Although the justices did not specifically express concerns about the expense and time involved in jury trials, presumably such concerns were one unspoken aspect of their decision to limit the right to cases involving "serious" charges.
- In *Lewis v. United States* (1996), a majority of justices concluded that defendants charged with "petty" offenses, meaning those punishable by sentences of six months or less of jail time, are entitled only to a bench trial before a judge and not a jury trial under the Sixth Amendment.
- Ironically, someone charged with multiple petty offenses, if each offense led to a separate six-month sentence to be served consecutively, would still not have a right to trial by jury prior to being sent to prison for several years.
- According to the Supreme Court, the right to trial by jury is triggered by the definition of each charge as "serious" (more than six months of imprisonment) rather than by the total sentence that could occur upon conviction of multiple petty offenses.
- A postal worker charged with 20 separate petty offenses of "obstructing the mail" for stealing 20 letters from the post office could end up with a cumulative sentence of 10 years in prison, yet have not have a right to trial by jury (C. E. Smith, 2004).

Although it is the briefest of the criminal justice amendments, the Eighth Amendment deals with the rights of defendants during the pretrial (bail) and correctional (fines, punishment) phases of the criminal justice system.

Release on Bail The purpose of bail is to allow for the release of the accused while she or he is awaiting trial. The Eighth Amendment does not require that all defendants be released on bail, only that the amount of bail not be excessive. Many states do not allow bail for those charged with some offenses, such as murder, and there seem to be few limits on the bail amounts that can be required. In 1987 the Supreme Court, in *United States v. Salerno and Cafero*, upheld provisions of the Bail Reform Act of 1984 that allow federal judges to detain without bail suspects who are considered dangerous to the public.

Excessive Fines The Supreme Court ruled in 1993 that the forfeiture of property related to a criminal case can be analyzed for possible violation of the excessive fines clause (*Austin v. United States*). In 1998 the Court declared for the first time that forfeiture constituted an impermissible excessive fine. In that case, a man failed to comply with the federal law requiring that travelers report if they are taking $10,000 or more in cash outside the country (C. E. Smith, 1999). There is no law

Procedural Criminal Law in Russia

In the United States, the words in the Bill of Rights and the Fourteenth Amendment provide the basis for the procedural rights enjoyed by criminal defendants. Yet, these words alone do not provide the actual procedures and legal protections in the American criminal justice process. For example, the Sixth Amendment provision guaranteeing a right to counsel for criminal defendants does not, by itself, ensure that defense attorneys will represent those accused of crimes. The justices on the U.S. Supreme Court and other courts needed to interpret the right-to-counsel provision of the Sixth Amendment in order to determine when and how defense attorneys would take action in criminal cases. These judges issued decisions concerning such procedural criminal law even when those decisions were unpopular with the public and politicians, many of whom do not care to see criminal defendants protected by certain constitutional rights and procedures.

Russia adopted a new Code of Criminal Procedure in 2001 that guaranteed new rights for criminal defendants. Under that Russian code, prosecutors no longer had the power to order arrests and pretrial jailing of defendants. They also lost the power to make their own decisions about conducting searches and seizures. Instead, judges had to issue court orders for searches, arrests, and detentions. On the surface, these elements of their code provide protections for defendants, reduce the power of the state, and presumably reduce abusive practices and the harassment of innocent defendants. In reality, however, just as in the United States, the words in the code cannot readily change practices in the justice system.

In the American system, judges' efforts to be neutral and independent are an essential component of the constitutional rights' protections for defendants in procedural criminal law. By contrast, critics of the actual operations of the Russian system claim that many judges have never shifted their identity and actions away from their old role as members of the prosecution team under the communist system of the Soviet Union that governed Russia until the 1990s. Many of them apparently still worry about losing their jobs if they dare to disagree with the government and find defendants "not guilty." As a result, people charged with crimes in Russia generally assume that they will be convicted and punished no matter what the evidence is

because judges are not sufficiently neutral and independent to critically examine and reject the prosecution's claims. Indeed, more than 99 percent of prosecutions in Russia result in convictions.

Procedural criminal law is also affected by the very different roles played by defense attorneys in Russia. In the United States, as described in this chapter's "Careers in Criminal Justice" feature on page 86, defense attorneys are considered key protectors of constitutional rights by means of their role of investigating criminal cases and challenging the actions of prosecutors. In Russia, however, the defense attorney is not permitted to investigate the case but can only file objections to the findings of the official criminal investigator. The official investigator is a lawyer who is supposed to conduct an independent investigation but whose office is housed among the police and prosecutors. Russian judges' near universal support for the prosecution in criminal cases makes it unlikely that objections by the defense attorney will lead to a favorable outcome for any defendant.

For Critical Analysis

The example of Russia shows that constitutional rights and procedural criminal law depend as much on the professionalism and independence of decision makers in the justice system as on the actual words in laws such as the Bill of Rights. What suggestions could you make for increasing the independence of Russian judges and the independence of Russian defense attorneys? List two ideas. Bear in mind that the American system does not operate flawlessly. Can you also think of two ideas to improve the protection of constitutional rights or the processing of criminal cases in the United States?

Sources: David Greene, "In Russia, Defendants Find Justice Isn't Blind," January 26, 2011 (www.npr.org); Chad Oldfather, "Faculty Workshop on Criminal Procedure in Russia," *Marquette University Law School* (faculty blog), January 28, 2009 (www.law.marquette.edu/facultyblog/2009/01/28); Carl Schreck, "Russia's 99% Conviction Rate Thrown Into Question," *The National*, February 19, 2010 (www.thenational.ae); Olga B. Semukhina, "Russian Cultural Factors Related to Perceived Criminal Procedure Fairness: The Juxtaposition of Policy and Practice," Ph.D. dissertation, University of Central Florida, 2007.

against transporting any amount of cash. The law only concerns filing a report to the government concerning the transport of money. When one traveler at a Los Angeles airport failed to report the money detected in his suitcase by a cash-sniffing dog trained to identify people who might be transporting money for drug dealers, he was forced to forfeit all $357,000 that he carried in his luggage. Because there was no evidence that the money was obtained illegally and because the usual punishment for the offense would only be a fine of $5,000, a slim five-member majority on the Supreme Court ruled that the forfeiture of all the traveler's money constituted an excessive fine (*United States v. Bajakajian*, 1998). It remains to be seen whether any future Supreme Court decisions will address the "excessive fines" clause and

The Eighth Amendment protects offenders serving prison sentences. Under judges' interpretations of the Eighth Amendment, prisoners are entitled to food, shelter, sanitation facilities, and limited medical care. Is the maintenance of humane living conditions in prison an appropriate application of the protection against "cruel and unusual punishments"?

AP Images/Charlie Neibergall

thereby limit law enforcement agencies' practices in forcing criminal defendants to forfeit cash and property.

Cruel and Unusual Punishments   The nation's founders were concerned about the barbaric punishments that had been inflicted in seventeenth- and eighteenth-century Europe, where offenders were sometimes burned alive or stoned to death—hence the ban on "cruel and unusual punishments." The Warren Court set the standard for judging issues of cruel and unusual punishments in a case dealing with a former soldier who was deprived of U.S. citizenship for deserting his post during World War II (*Trop v. Dulles*, 1958). Chief Justice Earl Warren declared that judges must use the values of contemporary society to determine whether a specific punishment is cruel and unusual.

According to the test established by Justice Warren, punishments may be declared unconstitutional for being either disproportionate to the offense or comparable to a form of torture through the infliction of physical or psychological pain. In recent years, the Supreme Court has seldom regarded punishments other than the death penalty as disproportionate to any crime for which a legislature chooses to mandate it. The Court reinforced this view in 2003 by endorsing California's sentences of 25 years to life for offenders convicted of three felonies, even in a case when the third offense was merely shoplifting some children's videos from K-Mart (*Lockyer v. Andrade*, 2003). With respect to juvenile offenders, however, a majority of justices declared that life sentences without possibility of parole were unconstitutionally disproportionate for non-homicide offenses (*Graham v. Florida*, 2010). In 2012 the Supreme Court majority forbade the imposition of mandatory life without parole sentences for juveniles convicted of homicide offenses (*Miller v. Alabama*, 2012).

The Court's test has been used in death penalty cases, but the justices have strongly disagreed over the values of American society on this issue. These decisions in death penalty cases are extensively discussed in Chapter 9.

Since the 1950s, the rights of defendants in state criminal trials have greatly expanded. The Supreme Court has incorporated most portions of the Fourth, Fifth, Sixth, and Eighth Amendments. Figure 3.2 shows the amendments that protect defendants at various stages of the criminal justice process.

FIGURE 3.2
Protections of Constitutional Rights The Bill of Rights and the Fourteenth Amendment protect defendants during various phases of the criminal justice process.

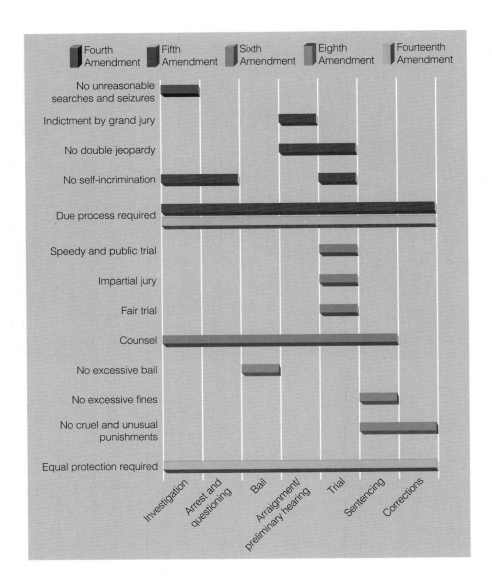

☑ CHECK POINT

6. **What is incorporation?**
   Taking a right from the Bill of Rights and applying it to protect individuals against actions by state and local officials through the inclusion of that right as a component of the due process clause of the Fourteenth Amendment.

7. **Which Supreme Court era made the most significant expansion in the definitions of constitutional rights for criminal defendants?**
   Warren Court era (1953–1969).

8. **What are the main criminal justice rights set forth in the Fourth, Fifth, Sixth, and Eighth Amendments?**
   Fourth: the protection against unreasonable searches and seizures; Fifth: the right against compelled self-incrimination and against double jeopardy (also the right to due process); Sixth: the right to counsel, to a speedy and fair trial, to a jury trial (also to confrontation and compulsory process); Eighth: the right to protection against excessive bail, excessive fines, and cruel and unusual punishments.

STOP&ANALYZE

If the phrase "cruel and unusual punishments" is to be interpreted according to contemporary values, what exactly does that mean? Consider the sentence of life in prison without possibility of parole for someone who drove the getaway car in a robbery in which the store owner was shot and killed by someone else involved in the robbery. Does that sentence violate the Eighth Amendment by being "cruel and unusual"? Make two arguments about whether that sentence violates contemporary values by being too severe and disproportionate to the driver's involvement in the crime.

Constitutional Rights and Criminal Justice Professionals

As a result of the Supreme Court's decisions, people in all states now enjoy the same minimum protections against illegal searches, improper police interrogations, and other violations of constitutional rights. In response to these decisions, police, prosecutors, and correctional officers have had to develop policies and guidelines to inform criminal justice professionals about what they are and are not permitted to do while investigating, prosecuting, and punishing criminal offenders.

If you were a police officer, prosecutor, or correctional officer, how would you feel about the Supreme Court's decisions defining rights that benefit criminal defendants? Although you would recognize the desirability of upholding constitutional rights in order to maintain democratic freedoms, you might also feel frustrated when court decisions limited your ability to conduct searches and question suspects. In addition, you would be concerned about whether the Supreme Court's decisions give you clear guidance about what to do. You would not want to make an unintentional error that prevents an offender from being properly convicted of a crime.

Many people question whether the Supreme Court has struck the proper balance between the protection of constitutional rights and the ability of criminal justice officials to punish offenders. Some people believe that criminal defendants' rights are too broad. Others believe that the Supreme Court favors law enforcement at the expense of constitutional rights. These debates are likely to continue even though the Supreme Court has moved consistently in one direction during the past two decades (C. E. Smith, DeJong, & McCall, 2011). In cases affecting criminal justice, the contemporary Supreme Court typically endorses the actions of police officers and prosecutors more frequently each year than it upholds constitutional rights' claims by suspects, defendants, and convicted offenders (M. M. McCall, M. A. McCall, & Smith, 2011).

In 2005 President George W. Bush appointed two new justices to the Supreme Court, Chief Justice John Roberts and Justice Samuel Alito. In their first terms on the Court, their decisions consistently reinforced the Court's support for broader police authority and more narrowly defined rights for criminal suspects and defendants (M. A. McCall, McCall, & Smith, 2008). In the aftermath of additional retirements from the Court, President Barack Obama subsequently had the opportunity to appoint Justices Sonia Sotomayor and Elena Kagan in 2009 and 2010, respectively. These justices were more supportive of rights for criminal defendants than were President Bush's appointees. Neither the Bush appointees nor the Obama appointees significantly altered the Court's patterns of decisions on constitutional rights because each new appointee replaced a justice with a similar orientation toward constitutional rights in criminal justice. For many issues, the Court remains deeply divided between those who seek to reduce the scope of constitutional rights in procedural criminal law and those who wish to retain the rights established during the Warren Court era and thereafter. If, however, one of the current justices retires and is replaced with a justice who has a very different viewpoint, the overall orientation of the Court may shift to strengthen one perspective or the other.

Among the justices on the Roberts Court (2005–current), several are older than 70 and presumably will not remain on the Court for many more years. Justice Ruth Bader Ginsburg turned 81 in 2014, and Justices Antonin Scalia and Anthony Kennedy celebrated their 78th birthdays in the same year. Justice Stephen Breyer celebrated his 76th birthday in 2014. The future of the Supreme Court will be significantly affected by the timing of their retirements and the outcome of the 2016 presidential election. If a Democratic candidate wins the election and, due to the timing of retirements, is able to successfully appoint a replacement for one of the Court's conservative members, the future Supreme Court may be more protective of constitutional rights in criminal justice. If a Republican candidate wins the presidential election and selects the replacement for a liberal justice, such as Ginsburg or Breyer, more Supreme Court decisions are likely to favor the powers of police and prosecutors while limiting the definition of constitutional rights.

Think, Discuss, Write

Police officers followed a drug suspect into an apartment building, but they were uncertain about which apartment he entered. They smelled the aroma of marijuana coming from one apartment. They pounded on the door and yelled, "Police, police, police." When they heard people moving around inside the apartment and decided that the sounds could be consistent with people acting to destroy evidence, they kicked open the door to the apartment and found marijuana and cocaine inside. The actual drug suspect whom they pursued into the building, however, was not in the apartment. He was subsequently found in a different apartment across the hall.

In its decision in the preceding case of *Kentucky v. King* (2011), the Supreme Court said that the police officers acted properly under the doctrine of "exigent circumstances," which permits searches without a warrant in urgent situations that pose a threat to public safety or the possibility that evidence will be destroyed. In dissent, Justice Ruth Bader Ginsburg argued that the police officers created the exigent circumstances themselves by pounding on the door and surprising the people inside the apartment. She argued that warrantless searches of people's homes based on exigent circumstances are justified only when the urgent threat to public safety or destruction of evidence exists independently of the police officers' own actions.

Does the Supreme Court's decision create a risk that police officers could go to a home that has aroused their curiosity, but one for which they have no concrete evidence of wrongdoing, and pound loudly on the door? If they hear people moving inside the dwelling, could they then enter based on the claim that they thought evidence was being destroyed? Could they walk down the hallway of an apartment building, pound on every door, and then use this justification to make a forcible entry into any apartment in which they heard people move about? If an unethical police officer used this tactic, what, if anything, would stop such invasions of people's homes?

Discussion/Writing Assignment

Write a memo as if you are a police chief who is very concerned about properly respecting people's Fourth Amendment rights. How would you train your officers to diminish the possibility that officers would simply knock on doors for no reason and then use any sounds inside the dwelling as an excuse to enter and search? Give two examples of what you would teach your officers. In addition, how would you monitor or supervise officers to make sure that they were not engaging in such actions without a proper basis? Give two examples of your approach to monitoring and supervision.

Source: George Dery, "Expedient Knocks and Cowering Citizens: The Supreme Court Enables Police to Manufacture Emergencies by Pounding on Doors at Will in *Kentucky v. King.*" *Berkeley Journal of Criminal Law* 17 (2012): 225–260.

SUMMARY

❶ Identify the bases and sources of American criminal law.

- Criminal law focuses on the prosecution and punishment of people who violate specific laws enacted by legislatures.
- Criminal law is divided into two parts: substantive law, which defines offenses and penalties, and procedural law, which defines individuals' rights and the processes that criminal justice officials must follow in handling cases.

❷ Discuss how substantive criminal law defines a crime and the legal responsibility of the accused.

- Substantive criminal law involves seven important elements that must exist and be demonstrated by the prosecution in order to obtain a conviction: legality, *actus reus*, causation, harm, concurrence, *mens rea*, and punishment.
- The *mens rea* element, concerning intent, or state of mind, can vary with different offenses, such as various degrees of murder.

- Criminal law provides opportunities to present several justification and excuse defenses, several of which focus on a lack of criminal intent: self-defense, necessity, duress (coercion), entrapment, infancy, mistake of fact, intoxication, and insanity.
- Standards for the insanity defense vary by jurisdiction, with various state and federal courts using several different tests: *M'Naghten* Rule, Irresistible Impulse Test, *Durham* Rule, *Model Penal Code*, and Comprehensive Crime Control Act.

❸ Describe how procedural criminal law defines the rights of the accused and the processes for dealing with a case.

- The provisions of the Bill of Rights were not made applicable to state and local officials by the U.S. Supreme Court until the mid-twentieth century, when the Court incorporated most of the Bill of Rights' specific provisions into the due process clause of the Fourteenth Amendment.

- The Fourth Amendment's prohibition on unreasonable searches and seizures seeks to impose limits on police authority to intrude on people's expectations of privacy with respect to their bodies, homes, and property.
- The Fifth Amendment provides protections against compelled self-incrimination and double jeopardy.
- The Sixth Amendment includes the right to counsel, the right to a speedy and public trial, and the right to an impartial jury.
- The Eighth Amendment includes protections against excessive bail, excessive fines, and cruel and unusual punishments. Supreme Court justices often disagree about whether certain sentences, including the death penalty, violate the prohibition on cruel and unusual punishments.
- The Fourteenth Amendment provides a right to due process of law as well as the right to equal protection of the laws.

④ **Explain the U.S. Supreme Court's role in interpreting the criminal justice amendments to the Constitution.**
- Changes in the Supreme Court's composition may affect decisions concerning specific legal issues. Such changes occur when presidents replace retiring justices with appointees who interpret constitutional rights in different ways than did prior justices.

Questions for Review

1. What are the two major divisions within criminal law?
2. What are the seven principles of criminal law theory?
3. What is meant by *mens rea*? Give examples of defenses that may be used by defendants in which they deny that *mens rea* existed when the crime was committed.
4. What is meant by the incorporation of rights into the Fourteenth Amendment of the U.S. Constitution?
5. What rights are contained in the Fourth Amendment?
6. What rights are contained in the Fifth Amendment?
7. What rights are contained in the Sixth Amendment?
8. What rights are contained in the Eighth Amendment?

Key Terms and Cases

Bill of Rights (p. 94)

civil infractions (p. 80)

civil law (p. 78)

double jeopardy (p. 96)

entrapment (p. 89)

felonies (p. 80)

fundamental fairness (p. 97)

grand jury (p. 99)

inchoate or incomplete offenses (p. 83)

incorporation (p. 97)

legal responsibility (p. 78)

mens rea (p. 85)

misdemeanors (p. 80)

procedural criminal law (p. 79)

self-incrimination (p. 96)

substantive criminal law (p. 79)

Barron v. Baltimore (1833) (p. 96)

Gideon v. Wainwright (1963) (p. 100)

Powell v. Alabama (1932) (p. 97)

4 Police

LEARNING OBJECTIVES

1. Describe how policing evolved in the United States.
2. Name the main types of law enforcement agencies.
3. Analyze the recruitment of police officers and how they learn their job.
4. Describe the elements of the police officer's "working personality."
5. List the functions of the police.
6. Describe the organization of the police.
7. Identify influences on police policy and styles of policing.

On February 26, 2013, in Santa Cruz, California, Detective Elizabeth Butler and Sergeant Loran Baker went to the home of Jeremy Goulet to arrest him for a sexual assault that occurred four days earlier. It is unknown whether the police officers knew that Goulet had served in both the U.S. Marine Corps and the U.S. Army before being given an "other than honorable" discharge in 2007 after being accused of raping two female officers. Goulet had also served two one-year jail sentences in Oregon on gun-related charges. He was released from jail in 2010 and subsequently moved to California, where he was jailed again and placed on probation for peering into houses (J. M. Brown, 2013).

Goulet spoke to the officers through a locked glass door, but he refused to come out of the house. He disappeared back into the dwelling, out of the officers' sight, so they walked around the building to identify the exits. Suddenly, Goulet emerged from a doorway and fired five shots in three seconds from a handgun that he owned. One shot hit Detective Butler and two shots hit Sergeant Baker, taking both officers to the ground (J. M. Brown, 2013). Goulet walked over to Baker and fired three more bullets into the officer at close range. He took Baker's handgun and used it to fire another shot into Butler. Both officers died at the scene of the shooting. Goulet drove away in the unmarked police car, taking with him both officers' guns as well as Baker's bullet-proof vest (Bigler, 2013).

Thirty minutes later, officers at the crime scene saw Goulet return and watch them from behind a fence. They attempted to persuade him to surrender. Instead, he ran down an alley and began firing at the officers. He fired a total of 15 shots. Four officers returned fire with 54 shots, striking Goulet numerous times and quickly causing his death (J. M. Brown, 2013).

The California police officers who were shot that day did not anticipate the lethal danger that they would face in carrying out a routine arrest. They apparently had no information suggesting that an armed man with military training would shoot at them. Of course, as veteran police officers, they were constantly aware of the possibility that their jobs might someday place them in extreme danger.

Despite such knowledge, officers place themselves in potential danger every day. When Goulet returned to the scene of the crime, their fellow officers bravely risked their lives in a gun battle, including one officer who was off-duty but rushed to the scene without being called after he heard reports about officers being shot J. M. (Brown, 2013).

Who would choose a career that might entail life-threatening danger? What attracts people to a public-service career that brings them into situations of conflict? Further,

how do the police, on an individual as well as an organizational level, carry out their duties in the face of such risks?

In this chapter, we examine several aspects of policing. A brief history of the police precedes discussion of the types of law enforcement agencies in the United States. We also examine the recruitment and training of contemporary police officers, the police subculture, and the functions, organization, and policies of policing.

The Development of Police in the United States

Law and order is not a new concept; it has been a subject of debate since the first police force was formed in London in 1829. Looking back even farther, we find that the Magna Carta of 1215 placed limits on constables and bailiffs. Reading between the lines of that historic document reveals that the modern problems of police abuse, maintenance of order, and the rule of law also existed in thirteenth-century England. Further, current remedies—recruiting better qualified people to serve as police, stiffening the penalties for official misconduct, creating a civilian board of control—were suggested even then to ensure that order was kept in accordance with the rule of law.

The English Roots of the American Police

The roots of American policing lie in the English legal tradition. Three major aspects of American policing evolved from that tradition: (1) limited authority, (2) local control, and (3) fragmented organization. Like the British police, but unlike police in continental Europe, the police in the United States have limited authority; their powers and duties are specifically defined by law. England, like the United States, has no national police force; instead, 43 regional authorities are headed by elected commissioners who appoint the chief constable. Above these local authorities is the home secretary of the national government, which provides funding and can intervene in cases of police corruption, mismanagement, and discipline. In the United States, policing is fragmented: there are many types of agencies—constable, county sheriff, city police, FBI—each with its own special jurisdiction and responsibilities.

Systems for protecting citizens and property existed before the thirteenth century. The **frankpledge** system required that groups of 10 families, called *tithings*, agree to uphold the law, keep order, and bring violators to a court. By custom, every male person above the age of 12 was part of the system. When a man became aware that a crime had occurred, he was obliged to raise a "hue and cry" and to join others

frankpledge A system in old English law in which members of a tithing (a group of 10 families) pledged to be responsible for keeping order and bringing violators of the law to court.

in his "tithing" to track down the offender. The tithing was fined if members did not perform their duties.

Over time, England developed a system in which individuals were chosen within each community to take charge of catching criminals. The Statute of Winchester, enacted in 1285, set up a parish constable system. Members of the community were still required to pursue criminals, just as they had been under the frankpledge system, but now a constable supervised those efforts. The constable was a man chosen from the parish to serve without pay as its law enforcement officer for one year. The constable had the power to call the entire community into action if a serious disturbance arose. Watchmen, who were appointed to help the constable, spent most of their time patrolling the town at night to ensure that "all's well" and to enforce the criminal law. They were also responsible for lighting street lamps and putting out fires.

Not until the eighteenth century did an organized police force evolve in England. With the growth of commerce and industry, cities expanded while farming declined as the main source of employment and the focus of community life. In the larger cities, these changes produced social disorder.

In the mid-eighteenth century, novelist Henry Fielding and his brother, Sir John Fielding, led efforts to improve law enforcement in London. They wrote newspaper articles to inform the public about crime, and they published flyers describing known offenders. After Henry Fielding became a magistrate in 1748, he organized a small group of "thief-takers" to pursue and arrest lawbreakers. The government was so impressed with Fielding's Bow Street Amateur Volunteer Force (known as the Bow Street Runners) that it paid the participants and attempted to form similar groups in other parts of London.

After Henry Fielding's death in 1754, these efforts declined. As time went by, however, many saw that the government needed to assert itself in enforcing laws and maintaining order. London, with its unruly mobs, had become an especially dangerous place. In the early 1800s, several attempts were made to create a centralized police force for London. While people saw the need for social order, some feared that a police force would threaten the freedom of citizens and lead to tyranny. Finally, in 1829 Sir Robert Peel, home secretary in the British Cabinet, pushed Parliament to pass the Metropolitan Police Act, which created the London police force.

This agency was organized like a military unit, with a thousand-man force commanded by two magistrates, later called "commissioners." The officers were called "bobbies" after Sir Robert Peel. In the British system, cabinet members who oversee government departments are chosen from the elected members of Parliament. Thus, because Peel supervised it, the first police force was under the control of democratically elected officials.

Under Peel's direction, the police had a four-part mandate:

1. To prevent crime without using repressive force and to avoid having to call on the military to control riots and other disturbances
2. To maintain public order by nonviolent means, using force only as a last resort to obtain compliance
3. To reduce conflict between the police and the public
4. To show efficiency through the absence of crime and disorder rather than through visible police actions (P. K. Manning, 1977)

In effect, this meant keeping a low profile while maintaining order. Because of fears that a national force would threaten civil liberties, political leaders made every effort to focus police activities at the local level. These concerns were transported to the United States.

Policing in the United States

As with other institutions and areas of public policy, the development of formal police organizations reflected the social conditions, politics, and problems of different eras of American history. The United States drew from England's experience but implemented policing in its own way.

The Colonial Era and the Early Republic

As settlers arrived in North America from Europe and eventually moved westward from the East Coast, they relied on each other for assistance and protection in all matters, from weather disasters to conflicts with Native Americans. They also needed to protect themselves and their neighbors from those who might cause harm through theft or other crimes.

Along the East Coast, the colonists drew from their experiences in England by adopting the English offices of constable, sheriff, and night watchman as the first positions with law enforcement responsibilities. Boston's **watch system** began before 1640. Such systems served to warn of dangers ranging from fires to crime. Each male citizen was required to be a member of the watch, but paid watchmen could be hired as replacements. Although the watch system originally operated at night, cities eventually began to have daytime watches, too. Over time, cities began to hire paid, uniformed watchmen to deal with public danger and crime (S. Walker, 1999).

In the South, **slave patrols** developed as organized forces to prevent slave revolts and to catch runaway slaves. These patrols had full power to break into the homes of slaves who were suspected of keeping arms, to physically punish those who did not obey their orders, and to arrest runaways and return them to their masters. Under the watch system in northern cities, watchmen reacted to calls for help. By contrast, the mobility of slave patrols positioned them to operate in a proactive manner by looking for African Americans whom whites feared would disrupt society, especially the economic system of slavery. Samuel Walker (1999) describes the slave patrols as a distinctly American form of law enforcement and the first modern police force in the United States.

Beginning in the 1830s and continuing periodically for several decades, many American cities experienced violent riots. Ethnic conflicts; election controversies; hostility toward free blacks and abolitionists; mob actions against banks during economic declines; and violence in settling questions of morality, such as the use of alcohol—all these factors contributed to fears that a stable democracy would not survive. The militia was called in to quell large-scale conflicts, because constables and watchmen proved ineffective in restoring order (Uchida, 2005). These disorders, along with perceptions of increased problems with serious crimes, helped push city governments to consider the creation of professional police forces.

American policing is often described in terms of three historical periods: the political era (1840–1920), the professional model era (1920–1970), and the community policing era (1970–present) (Kelling & Moore, 1988). This description has been criticized because it applies only to the urban areas of the Northeast and does not take into account the very different development of the police in rural areas of the South and West. Still, it remains a useful framework for exploring the organization of the police, the focus of police work, and the strategies employed by police (H. Williams & Murphy, 1990).

The Political Era: 1840–1920

The period from 1840 to 1920 is called the political era because of the close ties that were formed between the police and local political leaders at that time. In many cities, the police seemed to work for the mayor's political party rather than for the citizens. This relationship served both groups in that the political "machines" recruited and maintained the police while the police helped the machine leaders get out the vote for favored candidates. Ranks in the police force were often for sale to the highest bidder, and many officers took payoffs for not enforcing laws on drinking, gambling, and prostitution (S. Walker, 1999).

In the United States, as in England, the growth of cities led to pressures to modernize law enforcement. Around 1840 the large cities began to create police forces. In 1845 New York City established the first full-time, paid police force. Boston and Philadelphia were the first to add a daytime police force to supplement the night watchmen; other cities—Chicago, Cincinnati, New Orleans—quickly followed.

watch system Practice of assigning individuals to night observation duty to warn the public of fires and crime; first introduced to the American colonies in Boston and later evolved into a system of paid, uniformed police.

slave patrols Distinctively American form of law enforcement in southern states that sought to catch and control slaves through patrol groups that stopped and questioned African Americans on the roads and elsewhere in public places.

During the political era, the officer on a neighborhood beat dealt with crime and disorder as it arose. Police also performed various social services, such as providing beds and food for the homeless. Should today's police officers devote more time to providing social services for the public?

Joseph Byron/The Granger Collection

By 1850 most major cities had created police departments organized on the English model. A chief, appointed by the mayor and city council, headed each department. The city was divided into precincts, with full-time, paid patrolmen assigned to each. Early police forces sought to prevent crimes and keep order through the use of foot patrols. The officer on the beat dealt with crime, disorder, and other problems as they arose.

In addition to foot patrols, the police performed service functions such as caring for derelicts, operating soup kitchens, regulating public health, and handling medical and social emergencies. In cities across the country, the police provided beds and food for homeless people. In station houses, overnight "lodgers" might sleep on the floor or sometimes in clean bunkrooms (Monkkonen, 1981:127). The police became general public servants as well as crime control officers.

Police developed differently in the South because of the existence of slavery and the agrarian nature of that region. As noted previously, the first organized police agencies with full-time officers developed in cities with large numbers of slaves (Charleston, New Orleans, Richmond, and Savannah), where white owners feared slave uprisings (Rousey, 1984:41).

Westward expansion in the United States produced conditions quite different from those in either the urban East or the agricultural South. The frontier was settled before order could be established. Thus, those who wanted to maintain law and order often had to take matters into their own hands by forming vigilante groups.

One of the first official positions created in rural areas was that of **sheriff**. Although the sheriff had duties similar to those of the "shire reeves" of seventeenth-century England, the American sheriff was elected and had broad powers to enforce the law. As elected officers, therefore, sheriffs had close ties to local politics. They also depended on the men of the community for assistance. This is how the *posse comitatus* (Latin for "power of the county"), borrowed from fifteenth-century Europe, came into being. Local men above age 15 were required to respond to the sheriff's call for assistance, forming a body known as a posse.

After the Civil War, the federal government appointed **U.S. marshals** to help enforce the law in the western territories. Some of the best-known folk heroes of American policing were U.S. Marshals Wyatt Earp, Bat Masterson, and Wild Bill

sheriff Top law enforcement official in county government who was an exceptionally important police official during the country's westward expansion and continues to bear primary responsibility for many local jails.

U.S. marshals Federal law enforcement officials appointed to handle duties in western territories and today bear responsibility for providing federal court security and apprehending fugitives.

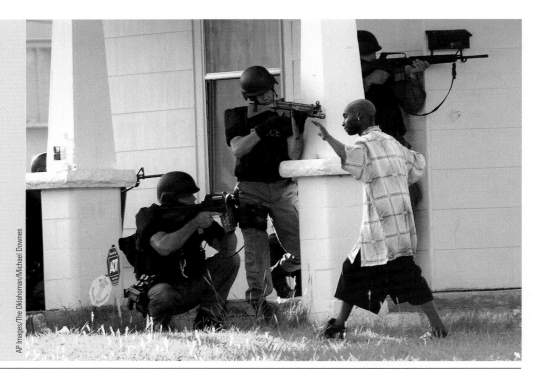

During the professional model era, the police saw themselves as crime fighters. Yet, many inner-city residents saw them as a well-armed, occupying force that did not support efforts to advance civil rights and racial equality. If you looked out your window and saw these heavily armed Oklahoma City SWAT team members in your neighborhood, would you have any concerns about how your neighbors might perceive the dress, demeanor, and actions of these officers? Might you have a different reaction if you lived in your city's poorest neighborhood?

AP Images/The Oklahoman/Michael Downes

Hickok, who tried to bring law and order to the "Wild West" (Calhoun, 1990). While some marshals did extensive law enforcement work, most had mainly judicial duties, such as keeping order in the courtroom and holding prisoners for trial.

During the early twentieth century, much of the United States became more urban. This change toward urbanization blurred some of the regional differences that had helped define policing in the past. Other changes in policing came about as a result of growing criticism of the influence of politics on the police, which led to reform efforts aimed at making police officers more professional and reducing their ties to local politics.

The Professional Model Era: 1920–1970   American policing was greatly influenced by the Progressive movement. The Progressives were mainly upper-middle-class, educated Americans with two goals: more efficient government and more government services to assist the less fortunate. A related goal was to reduce the influence of party politics and patronage (favoritism in handing out jobs) in government. The Progressives saw a need for professional law enforcement officials who would use modern technology to benefit the whole of society, not just local politicians.

The key to the Progressives' concept of professional law enforcement is found in their slogan, "The police have to get out of politics, and politics has to get out of the police." August Vollmer, the chief of police of Berkeley, California, from 1909 to 1932, was a leading advocate of professional policing. He initiated the use of motorcycle units, handwriting analysis, and fingerprinting. With other police reformers such as Leonhard Fuld, Raymond Fosdick, Bruce Smith, and O. W. Wilson, he urged that the police be made into a professional force, a nonpartisan agency of government committed to public service. This model of professional policing has six elements:

1. The force should stay out of politics.
2. Members should be well trained, well disciplined, and tightly organized.
3. Laws should be enforced equally.
4. The force should use new technology.
5. Personnel procedures should be based on merit.
6. The main task of the police should be fighting crime.

Refocusing attention on crime control and away from maintaining order probably did more than anything else to change the nature of American policing. The narrow focus on crime fighting broke many of the ties that the police had formed with the communities they served. By the end of World War I, police departments had greatly reduced their involvement in social services. Instead, for the most part, cops became crime fighters.

O. W. Wilson, a student of Vollmer, was another leading advocate of professionalism. He earned a degree in criminology at the University of California in 1924 and became the chief of police of Wichita, Kansas, in 1928. By reorganizing the department and fighting police corruption, he came to national attention. He promoted the use of motorized patrols, efficient radio communication, and rapid response. He believed that one-officer patrols were the best way to use personnel and that the two-way radio, which allowed for supervision by commanders, made officers more efficient (Reiss, 1992:51). He rotated assignments so that officers on patrol would not become too familiar with people in the community (and thus prone to corruption). In 1960 Wilson became the superintendent of the Chicago Police Department with a mandate to end corruption there.

The new emphasis on professionalism had also spurred the formation of the International Association of Chiefs of Police (IACP) in 1902 and the Fraternal Order of Police (FOP) in 1915. Both organizations promoted training standards, the use of new technologies, and a code of ethics. By the 1930s, the police were using new technologies and methods to combat serious crimes. Officers became more effective against crimes such as murder, rape, and robbery—an important factor in gaining citizen support.

In the 1960s, the civil rights and antiwar movements, urban riots, and rising crime rates challenged many of the assumptions of the professional model. In their attempts to maintain order during public demonstrations, police officers found themselves enforcing laws that tended to discriminate against African Americans and the poor. The number of low-income racial minorities living in the inner cities was growing, and the professional style kept the police isolated from the communities they served. In the eyes of many inner-city residents, the police were an occupying army keeping them at the bottom of society, not public servants helping all citizens. Concurrently, although the police continued to portray themselves as crime fighters, as crime rates rose, citizens became aware that the police often were not effective in this role.

The Community Policing Era: 1970–Present Beginning in the 1970s, calls were heard for a move away from the crime-fighting focus and toward greater emphasis on keeping order and providing services to the community. Research studies revealed the complex nature of police work and the extent to which day-to-day practices deviated from the professional ideal. The research also questioned the effectiveness of the police in catching and deterring criminals.

Three findings of this research are especially noteworthy:

1. Increasing the number of patrol officers in a neighborhood had little effect on the crime rate.
2. Rapid response to calls for service did not greatly increase the arrest rate.
3. Improving the percentage of crimes solved proved to be difficult.

Such findings undermined acceptance of the professional crime fighter model. Critics argued that the professional style isolated the police from the community and reduced their knowledge about the neighborhoods they served, especially when police patrolled in cars. Instead, it was argued, police should get out of their cars and spend more time meeting and helping residents. Reformers hoped that closer contact with citizens would not only permit the police to help them in new ways but also make citizens feel safer, knowing that the police were available and interested in their problems.

In a provocative article titled "Broken Windows: The Police and Neighborhood Safety," James Q. Wilson and George L. Kelling argued that policing should work

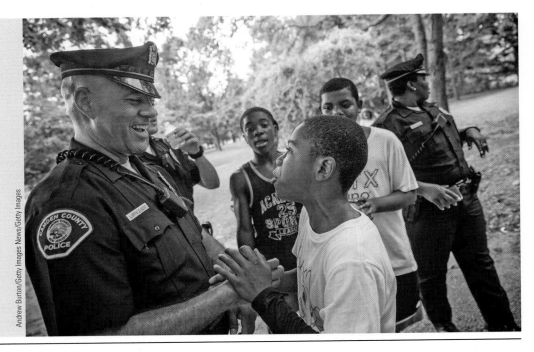

Community policing encourages personal contact between officers and citizens, especially interactions that facilitate citizens' cooperation with and support for the police. Is your own interest in criminal justice affected by your view of police officers and interactions with them?

Andrew Burton/Getty Images News/Getty Images

more on "little problems" such as maintaining order, providing services to those in need, and adopting strategies to reduce the fear of crime (1982:29). They based their approach on three assumptions:

1. Neighborhood disorder creates fear. Areas with street people, youth gangs, prostitution, and drunks are high-crime areas.
2. Just as broken windows are a signal that nobody cares and can lead to worse vandalism, untended disorderly behavior is a signal that the community does not care. This also leads to worse disorder and crime.
3. If the police are to deal with disorder and thus reduce fear and crime, they must rely on citizens for assistance.

community policing
Approach to policing that emphasizes close personal contact between police and citizens and the inclusion of citizens in efforts to solve problems, including vandalism, disorder, youth misbehavior, and crime.

problem-oriented policing
Community policing strategy that emphasizes solving problems of disorder in a neighborhood that may contribute to fear of crime and to crime itself.

Advocates of the community policing approach urge greater use of foot and bicycle patrols so that officers will become known to citizens, who in turn will cooperate with the police. They believe that through attention to little problems, the police may not only reduce disorder and fear but also improve public attitudes toward policing (Kelling, 1985).

Closely related to the community policing concept is **problem-oriented policing**. Herman Goldstein, the originator of this approach, argued that instead of focusing on crime and disorder, the police should identify the underlying causes of problems, such as noisy teenagers, battered spouses, and abandoned buildings used as drug houses. In doing so, they could reduce disorder and fear of crime (Goldstein, 1979). Closer contacts between the police and the community might then reduce the hostility that has developed between officers and residents in many urban neighborhoods (Sparrow, Moore, & Kennedy, 1990). Research indicates that problem-oriented policing can have positive effects on the problems of crime and disorder (D. Weiburd, Telep, Hinkle, & Eck., 2010).

In *Fixing Broken Windows*, written in response to the Wilson and Kelling article, George L. Kelling and Catherine Coles (1996) call for strategies to restore order and reduce crime in public spaces in U.S. communities. Many cities instructed police to pay greater attention to "quality-of-life crimes" by arresting subway fare-beaters; rousting loiterers and panhandlers from parks; and aggressively dealing with those who are obstructing sidewalks, harassing others, and soliciting. By handling these "little crimes," the police not only help restore order but also often prevent worse crimes. In New York, for example, searching fare-beaters often yielded weapons, questioning a street vendor selling hot merchandise led to a fence specializing in stolen weapons, and arresting a person for urinating in a park resulted in the discovery of a cache of weapons. This shift of emphasis therefore still retains police officers' crime fighter role.

The federal government created the Office of Community Oriented Policing Services, more commonly known as the "COPS Office," which provides grants for hiring new officers and developing community policing programs. Between 1995 and 2003, the COPS Office supplied nearly $7 billion to 13,000 state and local agencies to hire 118,000 new officers and implement training and other programs (Uchida, 2005). In 2009 the Obama administration provided $1 billion additional dollars to the COPS Office to fund the hiring of police officers around the nation as part of the stimulus program to revive the national economy (N. A. Lewis, 2009). For 2013 the COPS Hiring Program was given $127 million by Congress to help police departments hire new officers or rehire officers laid off through budget cuts. In addition, the agency's key priority areas were (1) assisting in hiring officers who would work with children in schools, (2) hiring military veterans to become police officers, and (3) helping police departments add additional officers to combat problems of gun violence in communities (COPS website, 2014).

In the 1980s, critics questioned whether the professional model really ever isolated police from community residents (S. Walker, 1984). Some wondered whether the opportunity to receive federal money and hire new officers led departments to use the language of community policing in portraying their activities even though they never fully adopted the new methods.

The Next Era: Homeland Security? Evidence-Based Policing?

Although many local police departments continue to emphasize community policy, after the 9/11 attacks, homeland security and antiterrorist efforts became two of the highest priorities for the federal government. As we shall see in Chapter 5, this event shifted the federal government's funding priorities for law enforcement and led to a reorganization of federal agencies. The shift also affected state and local police. According to Craig Uchida, "Priorities for training, equipment, strategies, and funding have transformed policing once again—this time focusing on homeland security" (2005:38). Federal money for state and local police agencies moved toward supplying emergency preparedness training, hazardous-materials gear, equipment for detecting bombs and other weapons of mass destruction, and the collection of intelligence data.

In public comments, a few police officials have referred to "terrorist-oriented policing," but how such a concept or emphasis would be defined at the local level is not clear (Kerlikowske, 2004). Some observers believe that a shift toward homeland security may appeal to traditionalists in law enforcement who prefer to see themselves as heroically catching "bad guys." Yet, a by-product of the increased emphasis on homeland security may be better coordinated services for society in non-crime-fighting situations such as public emergencies. For example, in 2007 Minneapolis police officials credited their training in a course on Integrated Emergency Management, conducted by the federal government, as one of the reasons they could respond so quickly and effectively when the I-35W bridge collapsed, killing 13 people, injuring 145 others, and forcing quick rescues of drivers in sinking vehicles that fell from the bridge and into the river below (Karnowski, 2008).

A factor in considering whether we have reached a new era in policing is that the emphasis on homeland security has grown in conjunction with the development of **intelligence-led policing**. The concept of intelligence in regard to policing means an emphasis on gathering, analyzing, and sharing information while incorporating those elements into community policing plans (M. Peterson, 2005). Intelligence-led policing is based on cooperation and coordination among law enforcement agencies

intelligence-led policing An approach to policing, in conjunction with concerns about homeland security, that emphasizes gathering and analyzing information to be shared among agencies in order to develop cooperative efforts to identify, prevent, and solve problems.

as well as between law enforcement officials and those in other sectors of government and business. Even though many police departments may not be directly affected by homeland security considerations in all of their daily operations, departments throughout the country have been affected by the spread of data analysis techniques. Departments analyze crime trends, locations of events, informants' tips, surveillance observations and tapes, and other sources of information in order to distribute personnel and take action to prevent crimes from occurring (Kirby, Quinn, & Keay, 2010).

As discussed in previous chapters, when data on problems in local communities are combined with social science research on "what works" in crime prevention and crime control, departments are attempting to incorporate the principles of evidence-based practices into policing. An awareness of evidence-based practices has become a major emphasis in policing and could develop in ways that will define the next era in policing. However, the dedicated use of evidence-based practices varies from department to department. Departments' ability to use evidence-based policing depends on both their resources and effectiveness in gathering and analyzing data about their communities as well as their openness and effectiveness in utilizing the results of scholars' research studies. Unfortunately, the contemporary era of budget cuts affecting personnel resources, training, and technology acquisition poses a significant barrier to the prospects of carrying out evidence-based policies and practices (Bueermann, 2012). It remains to be seen whether the establishment of priorities, the allocation of resources, and the implementation of practices will define a new era in policing.

Community policing will not disappear. Many police executives remain committed to its purposes and principles. However, budget issues may limit their ability to fulfill their ideal vision of policing. In addition, federal funding for local policing is more limited than in the past and currently reflects an emphasis on emergency preparedness and homeland security.

☑ CHECK POINT

1. **What three main features of American policing were inherited from England?**
   Limited authority, local control, organizational fragmentation.

2. **What are the historical periods of American policing?**
   Colonial era and early republic, political era, professional model era, community policing era.

3. **What were the major recommendations of the Progressive reformers?**
   The police should be removed from politics, police should be well trained, the law should be enforced equally, technology should be used, merit should be the basis of personnel procedures, and the crime-fighting role should be prominent.

STOP&ANALYZE

If you were a police chief in a city plagued by difficult crime problems, how might your distribution and use of police officers differ if you emphasized the crime fighter role instead of community policing? Would you do anything differently if you were equally committed to both goals?

Law Enforcement Agencies

As discussed in Chapter 1, the United States has a federal system of government with separate national and state structures, each with authority over certain functions. Police agencies at the national, state, county, and municipal levels are responsible for carrying out four functions: (1) enforcing the law, (2) maintaining order, (3) preventing crime, and (4) providing services to the community. They employ a total of more than 1 million sworn and unsworn personnel. Nearly 765,000 full-time sworn officers serve in state and local agencies, and an additional 120,000 sworn officers operate in federal agencies. Consider your own assumptions about the responsibilities of these agencies as you read the "Criminal Justice: Myth & Reality" feature.

Police agencies include the following (Reaves, 2012, 2011):

- 12,501 municipal police departments
- 3,063 sheriff's departments
- 50 state police departments
- 135 Native American tribal police agencies
- 30 federal agencies that employ 100 or more full-time officers authorized to carry firearms and make arrests

In addition, there are 1,733 special police agencies (jurisdictions limited to transit systems, parks, schools, and so on) as well as additional federal agencies with fewer than 100 officers each.

This list shows both the fragmentation and the local orientation of American police. Seventy percent of expenditures for policing occur at the local level. Each level of the system has different responsibilities, either for different kinds of crimes, such as the federal authority over counterfeiting, or for different geographic areas, such as state police authority over major highways. Local units generally exercise the broadest authority.

Federal Agencies

Federal law enforcement agencies are part of the executive branch of the national government. They investigate a specific set of crimes defined by Congress. Recent federal efforts against drug trafficking, organized crime, insider stock trading, and terrorism have attracted attention to these agencies even though they handle relatively few crimes and employ only 120,000 full-time officers authorized to make arrests.

The FBI   The Federal Bureau of Investigation (FBI) is an investigative agency within the U.S. Department of Justice (DOJ). It has the power to investigate all federal crimes not placed under the jurisdiction of other agencies. Established as the Bureau of Investigation in 1908, it came to national prominence under J. Edgar Hoover, its director from 1924 until his death in 1972. Hoover made major changes in the bureau (renamed the Federal Bureau of Investigation in 1935) to increase its professionalism. He sought to remove political factors from the selection of agents, established the national fingerprint filing system, and oversaw the development of the Uniform Crime Reporting (UCR) system (discussed in Chapters 2 and 3). Although Hoover has been criticized for many things, such as FBI spying on antiwar and civil rights activists during the 1960s, his role in improving police work and the FBI's effectiveness is widely recognized.

There are 13,913 **FBI special agents** and 22,231 support professionals (intelligence analysts, language translators, scientists, and computer experts) working out of 56 field offices and 381 additional satellite offices known as "resident agencies." The FBI (2013b) lists its priorities as follows:

1. Protect the United States from terrorist attack.
2. Protect the United States against foreign intelligence operations and espionage.
3. Protect the United States against cyber-based attacks and high-technology crimes.
4. Combat public corruption at all levels.
5. Protect civil rights.

CRIMINAL JUSTICE
MYTH&REALITY

COMMON BELIEF: The FBI is the most important law enforcement agency in the United States.

- The FBI handles many important responsibilities. However, it pursues only a limited number of crimes.
- As a federal agency, FBI agents are authorized to investigate federal crimes, including bank robbery, kidnapping, and a variety of terrorism and espionage matters.
- Whether or not the FBI is the "most important" agency is debatable, especially if one considers the impact of law enforcement on the daily lives of Americans.
- The vast majority of crimes are investigated by local police departments and county sheriff's departments. Officers from these departments also make the vast majority of arrests.
- When people experience medical emergencies, hear a window break during the night, or seek resolution of a dispute between neighbors, they call the local police. These are the kinds of police-related matters that most frequently affect the daily lives of Americans.
- Although local police officers do not receive the same attention from the news media as do special agents of the FBI, there are strong reasons to argue that local police are the most important law enforcement officials in terms of their daily impact on the quality of life and safety in neighborhoods and communities.

FBI special agents The sworn law enforcement officers in the FBI who conduct investigations and make arrests.

6. Combat transnational and national criminal organizations and enterprises.
7. Combat major white-collar crime.
8. Combat significant violent crime.
9. Support federal, state, county, municipal, and international partners.
10. Upgrade technology to successfully perform the FBI's mission.

As indicated by this list, the FBI has significant responsibilities for fighting terrorism and espionage against the United States. In addition, it continues its traditional mission of enforcing federal laws, such as those aimed at organized crime, corporate crime, corrupt government officials, and violators of civil rights laws. The bureau also provides valuable assistance to state and local law enforcement through its crime laboratory; training programs; and databases of fingerprints, stolen vehicles, and missing persons. With the growth of cyber crime, the FBI has become a leader in using technology to counteract crime as well as to prevent terrorism and espionage. The antiterrorist activities of the FBI will be discussed in greater detail in Chapter 5. In addition, Chapter 14 contains additional coverage of the FBI's role in fighting cyber crime.

Specialization in Federal Law Enforcement
The FBI is the federal government's general law enforcement agency. By contrast, other federal agencies enforce specific laws. Elsewhere within the Department of Justice is the semiautonomous Drug Enforcement Administration (DEA), which investigates the importation and sale of controlled drugs. The Internal Revenue Service (IRS) pursues violations of tax laws, and the Bureau of Alcohol, Tobacco, Firearms, and Explosives (ATF) deals with alcohol, tobacco, gun control, and bombings.

FBI evidence technicians helped local police gather evidence at a murder scene in California. As the FBI increasingly devotes attention to counterterrorism efforts, will local police departments be able to investigate complex crimes effectively despite less assistance from FBI experts?

The Department of Justice also contains the U.S. Marshals Service. Federal marshals provide security at courthouses, transport federal prisoners, protect witnesses, and pursue fugitives within the United States who are wanted for domestic criminal charges or who are sought by police officials in other countries. Because of the FBI's increased emphasis on terrorism, its agents are now less involved in the pursuit of fugitives. This has increased the U.S. marshals' responsibilities for those duties. For example, marshals apprehended more than 36,000 fugitives on federal warrants and assisted in the capture of 86,000 individuals wanted by local police departments in 2012 (U.S. Marshals Service, 2013).

Several federal law enforcement agencies were reorganized and relocated in conjunction with the creation of the Department of Homeland Security. These agencies include those responsible for Customs and Border Protection (formerly the separate agencies Customs Service and Border Patrol), the Secret Service, and the Transportation Security Administration. The Secret Service was created in 1865 to combat counterfeit currency. After the assassination of President William McKinley in 1901, it received the additional duty of providing security for the president of the United States, other high officials, and their families. The Secret Service has 3,200 special agents in Washington, D.C., and field offices throughout the United States. It also has 1,300 uniformed police officers who provide security at the White House, the vice president's residence, and foreign embassies in Washington.

Some other agencies of the executive branch, such as the National Parks Service, have police powers related to their specific duties. The park officers need to enforce law and maintain order to protect people and property at national parks. In addition, few people realize that some law enforcement officers investigate crimes while working in agencies with responsibility for policy issues that are not traditionally viewed as connected to the justice system. For example, special agents in the U.S. Department of Education investigate student loan fraud, and similar officers in the U.S. Department of Health and Human Services investigate fraud in Medicare and Medicaid programs.

State Agencies

Throughout the United States, the American reluctance to centralize police power has generally kept state police forces from replacing local ones. Each state has a police agency that patrols state highways; provides complete law enforcement services in rural areas; or, as in Hawaii, conducts statewide drug investigations and police services at state facilities and courts (Hawaii Department of Public Safety, 2012). All state forces regulate traffic on main highways, and two-thirds of the states have also given them general police powers. In only about a dozen populous states—such as Massachusetts, Michigan, New Jersey, New York, and Pennsylvania—can these forces perform law enforcement tasks across the state. For the most part, they operate only in areas where no other form of police protection exists or where local officers ask for their help. In many states, the crime lab is run by the state police as a means of assisting local law enforcement agencies.

County Agencies

Sheriffs are found in almost every one of the 3,063 U.S. counties except in Alaska and Connecticut. Sheriffs' departments employ 182,979 full-time sworn officers (Reaves, 2011). They are responsible for policing rural areas, but over time, especially in the Northeast, many of their criminal justice functions have been assumed by the state or local police. In parts of the South and West, however, the sheriff's department is a well-organized force. In more than 40 states, sheriffs are elected and hold the position of chief law enforcement officer in the county. Even when well organized, the sheriff's office may lack jurisdiction over cities and towns. In these situations, the sheriff and his or her deputies patrol unincorporated parts of the county or small towns that do not have police forces of their own.

In addition to performing law enforcement tasks, the sheriff often serves as an officer of the court; sheriffs may operate jails, serve court orders, and provide the bailiffs who maintain order in courtrooms.

Native American Tribal Police

Through treaties with the United States, Native American tribes are separate, sovereign nations and have a significant degree of legal autonomy. They have the power to enforce tribal criminal laws against everyone on their lands, including non-Native Americans (Mentzer, 1996). Traditionally, Native American reservations have been policed either by federal officers of the Bureau of Indian Affairs (BIA) or by their own tribal police. The Bureau of Justice Statistics identified 178 tribal law enforcement agencies with a total of nearly 3,000 full-time sworn officers (BJS, 2012). Police on some reservations face especially daunting problems due to high rates of unemployment, poverty, and crime (T. Williams, 2012).

Municipal Agencies

The police departments of cities and towns have general law enforcement authority. City police forces range in size from nearly 36,023 full-time sworn officers in the New

York City Police Department to fewer than 5 sworn officers in each of 5,400 small towns. Sworn personnel are officers with the power to make arrests. There are 461,063 full-time sworn municipal police officers nationwide (Reaves, 2011). Nearly three-quarters of municipal police departments employ fewer than 25 sworn officers. The five largest city police departments—New York City, Chicago, Los Angeles, Philadelphia, and Houston—together employ 15 percent of all local police officers (Reaves, 2011).

In a metropolitan area composed of a central city and many suburbs, policing is usually divided among agencies at all levels of government, giving rise to conflicts between jurisdictions that may interfere with efficient use of police resources. The city and each suburb buy their own equipment and deploy their officers without coordinating with those of nearby jurisdictions. In some areas with large populations, agreements have been made to enhance cooperation among jurisdictions.

Special Jurisdiction Agencies

More than 1,700 law enforcement agencies serve a special geographic jurisdiction. Among them are 508 four-year college and university police forces along with 253 additional two-year college police departments with sworn officers who can make arrests. These agencies employ approximately 57,000 sworn officers. More than 10,000 of these officers serve on college campuses (Reaves, 2011). Another large group of special jurisdiction agencies enforce laws as conservation officers and police in parks and recreation settings. For example, they may be responsible for law enforcement and safety in county parks, including the enforcement of laws for safe boating on lakes. These settings account for 14,571 sworn officers working for 246 agencies. In addition, there are 167 special jurisdiction agencies that enforce law and protect safety at specific mass transit systems, airports, bridges, tunnels, and ports. These agencies employ 11,508 sworn officers (Reaves, 2011). These agencies must coordinate and communicate with state and local officials and agencies that have general law enforcement responsibilities in the immediate vicinity. For example, if there is a major criminal event or large public disturbance on a college campus, state and local police are often called to provide assistance or special technical expertise for the campus police department.

☑CHECK POINT

4. **What is the jurisdiction of federal law enforcement agencies?**
   Enforcing the laws of the federal government.

5. **What are the functions of most state police agencies?**
   All state police agencies have traffic law enforcement responsibilities, and in two-thirds of the states, they exercise general police powers, especially in rural areas.

6. **Besides law enforcement, what functions do sheriffs perform?**
   Operate jails, move prisoners, and provide court bailiffs.

STOP&ANALYZE

What are the advantages and disadvantages of having a fragmented system of separate police agencies? List two advantages and two disadvantages.

Who Are the Police?

As they walk or drive on patrol, police officers never know what they might find around the next corner. What if they encounter an armed suspect who surprises them with gunfire as happened in the fatal California shooting described in the chapter opening? Who would want to face such risks? What motivates someone to choose such a career? These questions are important because they help determine which people will be granted the authority to carry firearms and make discretionary decisions about making arrests, conducting searches, and even ending the lives of other human beings by pulling the trigger during the stressful, fast-moving events that may confront police officers.

The police are no longer exclusively made up of white men. Women and minorities now represent an increasing portion of the force, especially in urban areas. Are women or minority group members visible among the police officers that you see where you live?

AP Images/Brennan Linsley

According to research, the biggest attractions of a career in policing are the opportunity to help people and job security. Other factors that attract people to a police career include the opportunity for excitement, a desire to fight crime, and job benefits such as early retirement (M. D. White, Cooper, Saunders, & Raganella, 2010; Raganella & White, 2004).

Because policing is such an important occupation, society would obviously benefit from recruiting its most thoughtful, athletic, and dedicated citizens as police officers. Happily, many such individuals are attracted to this field. Yet, many other people who would make fine law enforcement officers turn to other occupations because policing is such a difficult job. The modest salaries, significant job stress, and moments of danger involved in police work can deter some individuals from choosing this public-service occupation. As you read "Careers in Criminal Justice," consider whether you would want to be a police officer.

Recruitment

How can departments recruit well-rounded, dedicated public servants who will represent the diversity of contemporary America? Moreover, how can law enforcement agencies make sure that each individual is qualified to handle the wide array of responsibilities facing police officers? When considering applications, all agencies refer to a list of requirements regarding education, physical abilities, and background. Some federal agencies, including the FBI and Drug Enforcement Administration, seek additional skills such as expertise in computers and accounting or fluency in a foreign language. A typical list of basic requirements for a career in law enforcement includes the following (if you are interested in working for a particular agency, check for that agency's specific requirements):

- Be a U.S. citizen.
- Meet age requirements. The minimum age is normally 21, although some federal agencies place the minimum at 23. The maximum age for hiring in federal agencies ranges from 36 (FBI and DEA) to 39 (Border Patrol), depending on the agency.

Police Officer

Mary Peterson, Police Officer, Police Department, Glenview, Illinois

Police officers conduct preventive patrol in an assigned beat area and provide the initial response to requests for police service. Officers investigate complaints, enforce state laws and local ordinances, prepare necessary reports, participate in the prosecution of criminal cases, and provide many public-service activities. These responsibilities require a wide range of abilities, such as effective communication skills for interviewing witnesses and victims and physical skills for taking uncooperative arrestees into custody. Officers must be able to analyze situations quickly and accurately. They must also be able to function well during emergency situations.

Officer Peterson earned both undergraduate and graduate degrees in English. She worked in different jobs before

Photo provided by Mary Peterson

securing city government employment working in the office of a police chief. From her position, she received a close and accurate view of the working lives of police officers. She found herself attracted to the variety of responsibilities involved in this public-service career, as well as to the salary and pension benefits, including the possibility of early retirement. After undergoing the rigorous selection and training processes, she found that she really enjoyed "working the street."

The biggest challenge in police work is avoiding complacency. The major task of a genuine professional is to maintain officer survival skills learned early in training and initial experience while working in an atmosphere where those skills are not reinforced on a daily basis.

- Have a high school diploma. Increasingly, state and local agencies require some college coursework (for instance, a four-year college degree is required for some federal agencies such as the FBI and DEA).
- Possess a valid driver's license.
- Have a healthy weight in proportion to height, body frame, and age.
- Pass a medical health examination, including a hearing test—reliance on a hearing aid can result in disqualification.
- Be in excellent physical condition. Recruits are typically required to pass a physical fitness exam administered by the agency or as part of a certification program in a police-training academy. For example, the U.S. Border Patrol requires 20 push-ups in one minute, 25 sit-ups in one minute, 30 steps-per-minute up and down a one-foot step for 5 minutes, a 1.5-mile run in 13 minutes, a 220-yard dash in 46 seconds, and a timed obstacle course.
- Be able to lift and carry moderately heavy objects (45 to 60 pounds).
- Have vision correctable to 20/20 and uncorrected vision of at least 20/200; some agencies require normal color vision (the DEA, for example).
- Pass a background investigation, including a clean arrest record and credit check. Prior felony or serious misdemeanor convictions can disqualify an applicant, as can a misdemeanor conviction for domestic violence.
- Pass a polygraph examination (lie detector test).
- Take a urinalysis drug test. Often recruits are also required to respond to written or interview questions about any prior use of illegal drugs.
- Take a written test to demonstrate literacy, basic math skills, and reasoning ability. Knowledge of the law and other subjects is also sometimes tested.

In addition, agencies increasingly require recruits to undergo psychological evaluations because each officer will ultimately make important discretionary decisions, including those that determine life and death in stressful situations (Dantzker & McCoy, 2006).

Candidates for state and local enforcement positions must often obtain a certification for their state's law enforcement training agency, such as the Michigan

Commission on Law Enforcement Standards. Many small towns and counties cannot afford to send their officer-applicants to a police academy program for this certification. Thus, they advertise job vacancies with the requirement that applicants have already obtained **law enforcement certification** by attending a police academy, such as the 12- to 22-week non-degree classes offered through the criminal justice programs at many colleges.

Paying to attend police academy programs imposes an extra expense on many individuals who seek a career in law enforcement. However, some of these programs can fulfill several requirements for associate or bachelor's degrees in criminal justice, depending on the college offering the program. Larger cities are more likely either to pay for their selected candidates to attend a police academy or to run their own academies to train their new hires. State police agencies also typically run their own training academies for newly hired officers. The U.S. Marine Corps base at Quantico, Virginia, is home to the training academies for new special agents in the DEA (16-week program) and the FBI (17-week program). New agents in the U.S. Secret Service, the ATF, and other federal law enforcement agencies attend 11-week training academies at the primary Federal Law Enforcement Training Center (FLETC) in Glynco, Georgia. These agencies subsequently provide new agents with additional specialized training, sometimes at the other FLETC training centers in Artesia, New Mexico; Charleston, South Carolina; and Cheltenham, Maryland.

Which agencies are the most attractive to people seeking careers in law enforcement? According to the most recent federal government study, the average starting salary was $39,263 for local departments with collective bargaining (i.e., officers represented by unions or police officers' associations) but only $28,376 for departments without collective bargaining (Reaves, 2010). The foregoing figures are national averages, but salaries in different regions vary significantly. For example, starting salaries for new police officers in Seattle were more than $69,000 in 2014 with pay increases leading to salaries in excess of $90,000 after nine years of service (City of Seattle website, 2014). High salaries often exist in areas with a high cost of living, thus making the salaries less lucrative than they might appear. The variation in pay among local police agencies can create incentives for officers, especially in departments that pay lower salaries, to seek ways to supplement their income through off-duty work. Examine the Close Up feature on outside compensation for police, and consider whether you think such activities pose too many risks of problems.

Federal agencies, which offer higher salaries and better benefits than do many local departments, often attract large numbers of applicants. These positions also require higher levels of education and experience than do many local law enforcement agencies. Starting salaries for Border Patrol Agents are at least $38,619 per year while FBI special agents begin at $43,441. As described on the FBI website (FBI, 2014), agents may actually receive much higher pay if assigned to a city with a high cost of living:

> For example, a new Agent assigned to Washington, D.C., would make a base salary of $43,441 (GS-10, step 1 on the Law Enforcement Officers' salary table) + locality pay of $7,602 (based on Washington, D.C.'s locality adjustment of 17.5%) + availability pay of $12,761 (25% of base + locality) for a total salary of $63,804 their first year. If the new Special Agent qualified for the relocation bonus (e.g., moving from Atlanta to Washington, D.C.), they would also receive a one-time payment of approximately $22,000.

Federal agencies typically look for college graduates and often require special skills, such as foreign languages and knowledge of financial accounting, or graduate degrees. Most local law enforcement agencies, by contrast, require only a high school diploma, but they prefer to recruit new officers with at least some college education. In the largest cities, with populations greater than 500,000, about one-third of departments require at least some college and a small percentage require either a two-year or four-year degree (Reaves, 2010). Some departments will accept years of military service as a replacement for an equal number of years of college education. The percentage of state and local law enforcement agencies that

law enforcement certification Preservice training required for sworn officers in many states, which includes coursework on law, use of weapons, psychology, and police procedures. Police departments for state and large cities often run training programs called *police academies* for their own recruits.

Police and Outside Compensation

As an alternative to bullet-firing guns, Taser International manufactures and markets Tasers, a less lethal electroshock weapon for police. The company employs 263 police officers as part-time master instructors who train police departments in the use of the device. Tasers deliver a 50,000-volt shock that causes individuals to collapse in pain. Debate centers on whether the devices may inflict serious harm on some people, such as those with weak hearts. In Minneapolis an officer paid by Taser International to train officers in various departments was also involved in making the decision about whether to purchase Tasers for use in his own department. An officer in Arizona made a presentation to his city's council advocating the purchase of 300 Tasers. At the time, neither the council members nor his superiors knew that he had received stock options as a form of compensation by Taser International. In both cases, the officers resigned and went to work as sales managers for Taser International when their respective cities began conflict-of-interest investigations.

In another example in 2011, controversy erupted in New Orleans when it was revealed that senior police officers had created private companies to employ officers to review city traffic cameras and to supervise auto impound lots. Were these jobs that should have been done by on-duty officers as part of their salaried duties rather than a mechanism for officers to charge extra fees to the city for performing these duties? The mayor suspended two officers and initiated an investigation after newspapers began reporting the mechanisms through which New Orleans police earned extra income.

Researching the Internet

Go to the website of the International Association of Chiefs of Police (IACP), and examine the "Oath of Honor" for police officers. To link to this website, http://www.theiacp.org/What-is-the-Law-Enforcement-Oath-of-Honor.

For Critical Analysis

Should police departments prohibit all outside employment by their officers? Such a rule may prevent conflict-of-interest situations and risks of corruption, but would it also violate Americans' expectations about using their hard work and initiative to earn extra money during their off-duty hours? If you were a police chief, would you endorse such a rule? Why or why not? Write a memo giving three reasons for your decision.

Sources: Brendan McCarthy, "Biggest Earners in New Orleans Police Details Are Often High-Ranking Officers Overseeing the Jobs," *New Orleans Times-Picayune*, May 15, 2011 (www.nola.com); "Taser's Use of Police Officers Questioned," *Toledo Blade*, March 27, 2005 (http://www.toledoblade.com); Thor Valdmanis, "Taser Gave Four Officers Stock Options," *USA Today*, January 11, 2005 (http://www.usatoday.com).

required education beyond high school tripled between 1990 and 2007 and is likely to continue to increase over time (Reaves, 2010). See Table 4.1 for examples of educational requirements and starting salaries in various law enforcement agencies.

The Changing Profile of the Police

For most of the nation's history, almost all police officers were white men. Today, as illustrated in Figure 4.1, women and minorities represent a growing percentage of police departments in many areas. The Equal Employment Opportunity Act of 1972 bars state and local governments from discriminating in their hiring practices. Pressured by state and federal agencies as well as by lawsuits, most city police forces have mounted campaigns to recruit more minority and female officers (W. Jordan, Fridell, Faggianai, & Kubu, 2009). Since the 1970s, the percentage of minority group members and women working in policing has doubled. Approximately 25 percent of local police officers nationwide belong to minority groups. The percentage is even larger—40 percent—in police departments in cities with populations greater than 500,000 (Reaves, 2010).

Minority Police Officers Before the 1970s, many police departments did not hire nonwhites. As this practice declined, the makeup of police departments changed, especially in large cities. The fact that minority officers now constitute 40 percent of the officers in the nation's largest cities represents a dramatic change in staff composition over the past two decades. African Americans compose 12 percent of officers in local police departments. Latino officers constitute more than 10 percent

TABLE 4.1 **Educational Requirements and Starting Salaries in Law Enforcement Careers, 2014 (Selected Examples)**

Position	Agency	Education Required	Starting Salary
Local			
Police Officer	New York City Police Dept.	2 years college or 2 years military service	$44,744
Police Officer	Alamogordo, NM, Police Dept.	HS diploma	$32,619
Deputy Sheriff	St. Mary's County, MD, Sheriff's Dept.	HS diploma	$40,976
Deputy Sheriff	Oneida County, NY, Sheriff's Dept.	HS diploma	$34,638
State			
Trooper	Tennessee Highway Patrol	HS diploma	$35,580
Highway Patrol Officer	California Highway Patrol	HS diploma	$67,764
Federal (minimum salaries listed; higher salaries come with more education and skills)			
Special Agent	Drug Enforcement Administration	4-year college degree or substantial work experience	$49,746
Special Agent	U.S. Secret Service	4-year college degree or substantial work experience	$43,964

Source: Websites of individual law enforcement agencies.

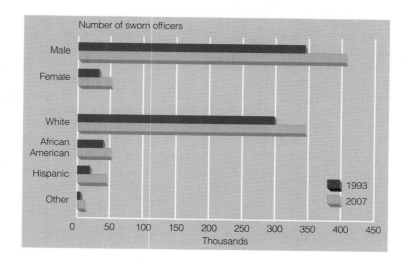

FIGURE 4.1
The Changing Profile of the American Police Officer Today about 1 in 10 local officers is female and 1 in 5 belongs to a racial or ethnic minority.

Sources: Brian A. Reaves, *Local Police Departments, 2007* (Washington, DC: Bureau of Justice Statistics, 2010); Brian A. Reaves, *Local Police Departments, 1993* (Washington, DC: Bureau of Justice Statistics, 1996).

of officers, and Asian, Pacific Islander, Native American, and multiracial officers are an additional 3 percent of local police forces nationally. For cities with populations in excess of 1 million residents, 23 percent of officers are Latino and nearly 18 percent are African American (Reaves, 2010).

As minority populations increase in some U.S. cities and as minorities more frequently gain election to local political offices, the makeup of their police forces reflects this trend, too. The extent to which the police reflect the racial composition of a city is believed to affect police–community relations and thus the quality of law enforcement (Cochran & Warren, 2012).

Women on the Force   Women have been police officers since 1905, when Lola Baldwin became an officer in Portland, Oregon. Prior to that time, many cities had "police matrons" to assist in handling women and children in jails, but these police matrons did not have the power to arrest or engage in investigative and patrol activities (Horne, 2006). After Baldwin became the trailblazing first officer, the number of women officers remained small for most of the twentieth century because of the prevailing belief that policing was "men's work." This attitude changed as the result of federal and state laws against employment discrimination as well as court decisions enforcing those laws. Court decisions opened up police work for women by prohibiting job assignments by gender; changing minimum height, weight, and physical fitness requirements; and insisting that departments develop job classification and promotion criteria that were nondiscriminatory (Kruger, 2007).

The percentage of female officers rose from 1.5 percent of sworn officers in 1970 to nearly 12 percent in 2007 (Reaves, 2010). Interestingly, the larger the department, the higher the proportion of women as sworn officers. In cities of more than 1 million inhabitants, women make up nearly 18 percent of officers, but in cities with fewer than 10,000 residents, women make up less than 8 percent of officers (Reaves, 2010). Yet, in large police agencies, women hold less than 10 percent of the supervisory positions, and women hold only 7 percent of the top command spots (rank of captain or higher) (Horne, 2006).

Many male officers were upset by the entry of women into what they viewed as a male world. They complained that if their patrol partner was a woman, they could not be sure of her ability to provide necessary physical help in times of danger. Although some male police officers may still question whether women can handle dangerous situations and physical confrontations, most policewomen have easily met the expectations of their superiors. Studies done by the Police Foundation and other researchers have found that, in general, male and female officers perform in similar ways.

Research has also found that most citizens have positive things to say about the work of policewomen (Haba, R. Sarver, Dobbs, & M. Sarver, 2009; Worden, 1993). Moreover, some researchers believe that women have generally superior performance in avoiding excessive use of force (Rabe-Hemp, 2008) and in interviewing crime victims, especially in cases of sexual assault and domestic violence (Prussel & Lonsway, 2001). Rape victims sometimes specifically request to be interviewed by a female officer, so gender diversity on a police force may be valuable in investigating specific types of crimes or dealing with certain kinds of victims and witnesses (J. Jordan, 2002). Despite these findings, women still face challenges when entering police work (Hassell & Brandl, 2009). Cultural expectations of women often conflict with ideas about the proper behavior of officers (Morash & Haarr, 2012).

In a few cities such as Atlanta, Portland, Boston, and Detroit, a small number of women have risen to the top ranks of police departments. Elsewhere, employment discrimination lawsuits have helped open promotional opportunities for women. In many other departments, however, few women have gained supervisory jobs. Thus, male administrators are usually the ones who must identify and combat any remaining barriers to the recruitment, retention, and promotion of female officers (Archbold & Hassell, 2009; V. B. Lord & Friday, 2003).

Training

The performance of the police is not based solely on the types of people recruited; it is also shaped by their training. As mentioned previously, aspiring officers may have to pay for their own police academy training if they are not hired by departments that pay for or provide the training. Police academy training courses range from two-week sessions that stress the handling of weapons to academic four-month programs followed by fieldwork. Recruits hear lectures on social relations, receive foreign-language training, and learn emergency medical treatment.

Formal training is needed to gain an understanding of legal rules, weapons use, and other aspects of the job. However, the police officer's job also demands social skills that cannot be learned from a lecture or a book. Much of the most important training of police officers takes place during a probationary period when new officers work with and learn from experienced ones. When new officers finish their classroom training and arrive for their first day of patrol duty, experienced officers may say, "Now, I want you to forget all that stuff you learned at the academy. You really learn your job on the streets." Many departments require newcomers to ride with an experienced training officer for a certain number of weeks or months before they can patrol on their own.

The process of socialization—in which members learn the symbols, beliefs, and values of a group or subculture—includes learning the informal rather than the rulebook ways of law enforcement. New officers must learn how to look "productive," how to take shortcuts in filling out forms, how to keep themselves safe in dangerous situations, and how to analyze conflicts so as to maintain order; they also must learn a host of other bits of wisdom, norms, and folklore that define the subculture of a particular department. Recruits learn that loyalty to other officers, esprit de corps, and respect for police authority are highly valued.

In police work—perhaps more than many other types of groups—the success of the group depends on the cooperation of its members. All patrol officers are under direct supervision, and their performance is measured by their contribution to the group's work. Besides supervisors, the officers' colleagues also evaluate and influence them. Officers within a department may develop strong, shared views on the best way to "handle" various situations. How officers use their personal skills and judgment can mean the difference between defusing a conflict or making it worse so that it endangers citizens and other officers. In tackling their "impossible mandate," new recruits must learn the ways of the world from the other officers, who depend on them and on whom they depend.

socialization The process by which the rules, symbols, and values of a group or subculture are learned by its members.

☑ CHECK POINT

7. **What are the main requirements for becoming a police officer?**
   High school diploma, good physical condition, absence of a criminal record.

8. **How has the profile of American police officers changed?**
   Better educated; more female and minority officers.

9. **Where does socialization to police work take place?**
   On the job.

STOP&ANALYZE

Why might it be important for police department personnel to reflect the racial and ethnic composition of the community that they serve? List three potential benefits of a diverse police force.

The Police Subculture

A **subculture** is made up of the symbols, beliefs, values, and attitudes shared by members of a subgroup within the larger society. The subculture of the police helps define the "cop's world" and each officer's role in it. Like the subculture of any occupational group that sees itself as distinct, police develop shared values that affect their view of human behavior and their role in society. As we just saw, the recruit learns the norms and values of the police subculture through a process of socialization (Oberfield, 2012). This begins at the training academy but really takes hold on the job through interactions with experienced officers. The characteristics of a subculture are not static, though; they change as new members join the group and as the surrounding environment changes. For example, the composition of the police has changed dramatically during the past 30 years in terms of race, gender, and education. We should thus expect officers with varied life experiences and perspectives to bring different attitudes and cultural values to the police subculture (Paoline, 2003).

There are four key issues in our understanding of the police subculture: the concept of the "working personality" (discussed next), the role of police morality, the isolation of the police, and the stress involved in police work.

subculture The symbols, beliefs, values, and attitudes shared by members of a subgroup of the larger society.

The Working Personality

Social scientists have demonstrated that there is a relationship between one's occupational environment and the way one interprets events. The police subculture produces a **working personality**—that is, a set of emotional and behavioral characteristics developed by members of an occupational group in response to the work situation and environmental influences. The working personality of the police thus influences the way officers view and interpret their occupational world.

Two elements of police work define the working personality of the police: (1) the threat of danger and (2) the need to establish and maintain one's authority (Skolnick, 1966:44).

working personality A set of emotional and behavioral characteristics developed by members of an occupational group in response to the work situation and environmental influences.

Danger Because they often face dangerous situations, officers are keenly aware of clues in people's behavior and body language or in specific situations that indicate that violence and law-breaking may be imminent. As they patrol the streets, they notice things that seem amiss—a broken window, a person hiding something under a coat—anything that looks suspicious. As sworn officers, they are never off duty—and because they are known to be officers, they may be called on at any time, day or night, by neighbors or other acquaintances who need their help.

Throughout the socialization process, experienced officers warn recruits to be suspicious and cautious. Rookies are told about officers who were killed while writing a traffic ticket or trying to settle a family squabble. The message is clear: even minor offenses can escalate into extreme danger. Constantly pressured to recognize signs of crime and be alert to potential violence, officers may become suspicious of everyone, everywhere. Thus, police officers remain in a constant state of "high alert," always on the lookout and never letting down their guard.

Being surrounded by risks creates tension in officers' lives. They may feel constantly on edge and worried about possible attack. This concern with danger may affect their interactions with citizens and suspects. Citizens who come into contact with them may see their caution and suspicion as hostile, and such suspicion may generate hostile reactions in turn from suspects. As a result, many on-the-street interrogations and arrests can lead to confrontations.

Authority The second aspect of the working personality is the need to exert authority. Unlike doctors, psychiatrists, lawyers, and other professionals whose clients recognize and defer to their authority, police officers must establish authority through their actions. Their uniforms, badges, guns, and nightsticks symbolize their position and power, but their demeanor and behavior are what determine whether people will defer to them.

Victims are glad to see the police when they are performing their law enforcement function, but the order maintenance function puts pressure on officers' authority. If they try too hard to exert authority in the face of hostile reactions, they may cross the line and use excessive force (C. Cooper, 2009).

Researchers have studied expressions of disrespect by officers toward members of the public and vice versa (Reisig, McCluskey, Mastrofski, & Terrill, 2004). One finding indicates that police officers' own expressions of disrespect in encounters with citizens, such as name-calling and other kinds of derogatory statements, occur most often when those citizens have already shown disrespect to the officers (Mastrofski, Reisig, & McCluskey, 2002).

In sum, working personality and occupational environment are closely linked and constantly affect the daily work of the police. Procedural rules and the structure of policing are overshadowed by the need to exert authority in the face of potential danger in many contexts in which citizens are angry, disrespectful, or uncooperative.

Police Morality

In his field observations of Los Angeles patrol officers, Steve Herbert found a high sense of morality in the law enforcement subculture. He believes that three aspects of modern policing create dilemmas that officers' morality helps to overcome. These dilemmas include (1) the contradiction between the goal of preventing crime and the officers' inability to do so, (2) the fact that officers feel that they must use their discretion to "handle" situations in ways that do not strictly follow procedures, and (3) "the fact that they invariably act against at least one citizen's interest, often with recourse to coercive force that can maim or kill" (Herbert, 1996:799).

Herbert believes that justifying their actions in moral terms, such as upholding the law, protecting society, and chasing "bad guys," helps officers lessen the dilemmas of their work. Thus, they may condone use of force as necessary for ridding "evil from otherwise peaceable streets." It is the price we pay to cleanse society of the "punks," "crazies," or "terrorists." But police morality can also be applauded: officers work long hours and are genuinely motivated to help people and improve citizens' lives, often placing themselves at risk. Yet, to the extent that police morality crudely categorizes individuals and justifies insensitive treatment of some community members, it contributes to tension between police and citizens.

Police Isolation

Police officers' suspicion of and isolation from the public may stem in part from their belief that the public is hostile to them. Many officers feel that people look on them with suspicion, in part because they have the authority to use force to gain compliance. Yet, public opinion polls have found that a majority of people have a high opinion of the police. Nevertheless, as shown in "What Americans Think," levels of confidence in police officers' honesty and integrity vary among demographic groups. Moreover, they are lower than what police executives ideally desire in order to feel certain that the public will cooperate fully and play its crucial role in reporting crimes and providing witness testimony.

Police officers' isolation from the public is made worse by the fact that many officers interact with the public mainly in moments of conflict, emotion, and crisis. Victims of crimes and accidents are often too hurt or distraught to thank the police. Citizens who are told to stop some activity when the police are trying to keep order may become angry at the police. Even something as minor as telling someone to turn down the volume on a stereo can make the police the "bad guy" in the eyes of people who believe that the officer's authority limits their personal freedom.

Ironically, these problems may be worst in poor neighborhoods, where effective policing is needed most. There, pervasive mistrust of the police may keep citizens from reporting crimes and cooperating with investigations. Because they believe that the public is hostile to them in those areas and that the nature of their work makes the situation worse, the police tend to separate themselves from the people there and to form strong in-group ties that tend to enhance that separation.

One result of the demands placed on the police is that officers often cannot separate their job from other aspects of their lives. From the time they receive badges and guns, they must always carry these symbols of the position—the "tools of the trade"—and be prepared to use them. Their obligation to remain vigilant even when off duty and to

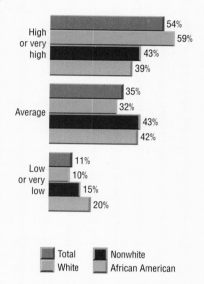

WHAT AMERICANS THINK

QUESTION: "Please tell me how you would rate the honesty and ethical standards of the police—very high, high, average, low, or very low?"

High or very high
- 54%
- 59%
- 43%
- 39%

Average
- 35%
- 32%
- 43%
- 42%

Low or very low
- 11%
- 10%
- 15%
- 20%

- Total
- White
- Nonwhite
- African American

CRITICAL THINKING: If you were a police chief and you saw these poll results in your community, what are three steps that you would take to increase public confidence in the police, especially among minority residents?

Source: Bureau of Justice Statistics, *Sourcebook of Criminal Justice Statistics, 2014.* http://www.albany.edu/sourcebook/. Table 2.21.2011.

work at odd hours reinforces the values shared with other officers. Strengthening this bond is officers' tendency to socialize mainly with their families and other officers.

Job Stress

The work environment and police subculture contribute to the stress felt by officers (Dabney, Copes, Tewsbury, & Hawk-Tourtelot, 2013; Schaible & Gecas, 2010; Noblet, Rodwell, & Allisey, 2009). This stress can affect not only the way officers treat the citizens they encounter but also the officer's health (Gershon, Barocas, Canton, Li, & Vlahov, 2009; G. Anderson, Litzenberger, & Plecas, 2002). Stress also affects how officers interact with each other (Haarr & Morash, 1999). Further, scholars have found that work environment, work–family conflict, and individual coping mechanisms are the most significant predictors of stress for individual officers (Zhao, He, Loverich, & Cancino, 2003).

Police officers are always on alert, sometimes face grave danger, and feel unappreciated by a public they perceive to be hostile. That their physical and mental health suffers at times is not surprising. Analyses of job stress place police officers among the top 10 in most stressful occupations, along with military personnel, firefighters, and taxi drivers (S. Adams, 2013). The effects of stress are compounded by the long hours many officers work, including double shifts that deprive them of sleep and make them work under conditions of severe fatigue (Vila & Kenney, 2002). The stress of police work may help explain why officer suicide poses a problem for some law enforcement agencies (Hackett & Violanti, 2003).

Only since the late 1970s have law enforcement officials become fully aware of the stress-related harms experienced by officers (Lumb & Breazeale, 2003). Psychologists have identified four kinds of stress that officers face and the factors that cause each (J. Shane, 2010; Cullen, Leming, et al., 1985):

1. *External stress.* This is produced by real threats and dangers, such as the need to enter a dark and unfamiliar building, respond to "man-with-a-gun" alarms, and chase lawbreakers at high speeds.
2. *Organizational stress.* This is produced by the nature of work in a paramilitary structure: constant adjustment to changing schedules, irregular work hours, and detailed rules and procedures.
3. *Personal stress.* This can be caused by an officer's racial or gender status among peers, which can create problems in getting along with other officers and

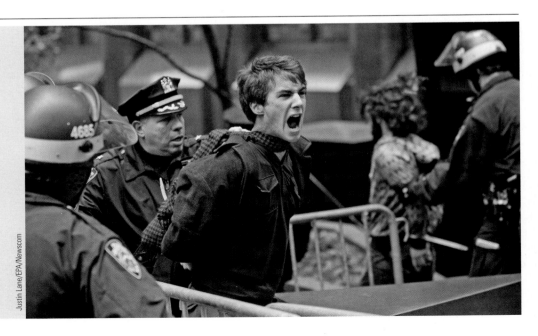

Police officers often encounter citizens in moments of fear, anger, and trauma. As a result, people can lash out at the officer or otherwise become emotionally out of control. Do the danger and stress police officers face create a risk that they will overreact when citizens fail to cooperate with their requests and instructions?

Justin Lane/EPA/Newscom

Police Officers' Well-Being

Evidence-based practices in policing are frequently discussed as if crime control is the primary goal from utilizing research to improve police training and practices. In other words, much of the attention to evidence-based policing concerns the effective use of police resources to prevent crime or apprehend criminal suspects. However, in fact, research can contribute to evidence-based practices that advance other goals, such as protecting the well-being of police officers. Jim Bueermann, the president of the Police Foundation in 2012 and an experienced former police chief, points to a number of aspects of officers' well-being that can be enhanced through the development and utilization of research and associated evidence-based practices. With respect to domestic violence, for example, research-based training on how to handle situations of conflict may both prevent crime and enhance officer safety.

For example, evidence indicates that police officers' safety can be enhanced through the use of protective vests. There are many examples of officers whose lives were saved when they were wearing a protective vest and they were shot or stabbed in the chest by an assailant. Many officers resisted wearing vests while on duty, especially in hot weather regions of the country, because the vests felt heavy and bulky. However, the practical value of the vests became so clear that the U.S. Department of Justice began to insist that departments require their officers to wear protective vests as one of the requirements for receiving certain law enforcement-assistance funds from the federal government.

Other aspects of physical safety that can be guided by research and evidence-based practices include issues related to fatigue from working night shifts; proper techniques during traffic stops on roadways; and factors affecting officers' decisions to use force, especially the discharge of a firearm at a suspect or perceived assailant. Research studies can provide a basis for improving training and supervision for contexts in which officers' lives are at risk.

In regard to officers' well-being, evidence-based practices may help departments identify and obtain appropriate treatment for officers with substance abuse problems, anger management issues, or domestic violence incidents.

Such behaviors may be related to the high-stress nature of police work, particularly if there are post-traumatic stress reactions from being involved in a shooting, seeing firsthand the horrific injuries of child abuse victims, or being the first responder to gruesome traffic collisions or crime scenes.

Researching the Internet

You can read online about George Mason University's Research Program on Evidence-Based Policing by going to http://gemini.gmu.edu/cebcp/policing.html.

Implementing New Practices

In an era of budget cuts, law enforcement executives must make difficult decisions about how to spend their limited budget allocations. Where should officer well-being stand in the priority list for spending resources? Imagine that you had to cut a police department's budget and that the cut had to come from one of four areas: crime prevention programs, officer training, equipment, or employment assistance programs (detection and treatment of officers' personal problems). Give two reasons for your choice. What impact could your choice have on the effectiveness of the police department?

Sources: James F. Ballenger et al., "Patterns and Predictors of Alcohol Use in Male and Female Urban Police Officers," *The American Journal on Addictions* 20 (2011): 21–29; Henrik Belfrage et al., "Assessment and Management of Risk for Intimate Partner Violence by Police Officers Using the Spousal Assault Risk Assessment Guide," *Law and Human Behavior* 36 (2012): 60–67; Jim Bueermann, "Evidence-Based Policing," Police Foundation Powerpoint Presentation to State of Oregon Officials, September 12, 2012 (http://www.oregon.gov/CJC/Documents/Publications/Evidence_Based_Bueermann_9.12.12.pdf); Kevin Johnson, "More Law Enforcement Agencies Require Body Armor," *USA Today*, November 16, 2012 (www.usatoday.com); Heather M. Kleider et al., "Shooting Behaviour: How Working Memory and Negative Emotionality Influence Police Officer Shoot Decisions," *Applied Cognitive Psychology* 24 (2010): 707–717; Kasey A. Tucker-Gail et al., "Felonious Line-of-Duty Officer Deaths (1995–1999): The Impact of Tenure and Age," *International Journal of Police Science and Management* 12 (2010): 119–133.

adjusting to group-held values that differ from one's own. Social isolation and perceptions of bias also contribute to personal stress.

4. *Operational stress.* This reflects the total effect of dealing with thieves, derelicts, and the mentally ill; being lied to so often that all citizens become suspect; being required to face danger to protect a public that seems hostile; and always knowing that one may be held legally liable for one's actions.

Some departments now have programs centering on stress prevention, group counseling, liability insurance, and family involvement. Although evidence-based practices in policing are generally discussed with respect to police strategies to prevent crime and catch lawbreakers, evidence-based practices could also be used to enhance the well-being of officers. Read the "Evidence-Based Practice and Policy" feature to consider how research may contribute to a wide array of policies affecting the police.

As we have seen, police officers face special pressures that can affect their interactions with the public and even harm their physical and mental health. How would you react to the prospect of facing danger and being on the lookout for crime at every moment, even when you were not actually working? It seems understandable that police officers become a close-knit group, yet their isolation from society may decrease their understanding of other people. It may also strengthen their belief that the public is ungrateful and hostile. As a result, officers' actions toward members of the public may be gruff or even violent.

☑ CHECK POINT

10. **What are the two key aspects of the police officer's working personality?**
   Danger, authority.

11. **What are the four types of stress felt by the police?**
   External stress, organizational stress, personal stress, operational stress.

STOP&ANALYZE

If you were a police chief, could you take steps to either reduce the stress experienced by officers or increase support for officers so that the effects of stress would be less harmful? List two approaches that you might use to counteract the causes or effects of stress on police officers.

Police Functions

The police are expected to maintain order, enforce the law, and prevent crime. However, they perform other tasks as well, many of them having little to do with crime and justice and more to do with community service. They direct traffic, handle accidents and illnesses, stop noisy parties, find missing persons, enforce licensing regulations, provide ambulance services, take disturbed people into protective custody, and so on. The list is long and varies from place to place. Some researchers have suggested that the police have more in common with social service agencies than with the criminal justice system.

How did the police gain such broad responsibilities? In many places, the police are the only public agency that is available seven days a week, 24 hours a day to respond to calls for help. They are also best able to investigate many kinds of problems. Moreover, the power to use force when necessary allows them to intervene in problematic situations.

The functions of the police can be classified into three groups: (1) order maintenance, (2) law enforcement, and (3) service. Police agencies divide their resources among these functions on the basis of community need, citizen requests, and departmental policy.

Order Maintenance

order maintenance The police function of preventing behavior that disturbs or threatens to disturb the public peace or that involves face-to-face conflict between two or more people. In such situations, the police exercise discretion in deciding whether a law has been broken.

The **order maintenance** function is a broad mandate to prevent behavior that either disturbs or threatens to disturb the peace or involves face-to-face conflict between two or more people. A domestic quarrel, a noisy person who drank too much alcohol, loud music in the night, a panhandler on the street, a tavern brawl—all are forms of disorder that may require action by the police.

Unlike most laws that define specific acts as illegal, laws regulating disorderly conduct deal with ambiguous situations, which different police officers could view in different ways. For many crimes, determining when the law has been broken is easy. On the other hand, order maintenance requires officers to decide not only whether a law has been broken but also whether any action should be taken and, if so, who should be blamed. In a bar fight, for example, the officer must decide who started the fight, whether an arrest should be made for assault, and whether to arrest other people besides those who started the conflict.

Officers often must make judgments in order maintenance situations. They may be required to help people in trouble, manage crowds, supervise various kinds of services, and help people who are not fully accountable for what they do. The officers have a high degree of discretion and control over how such situations will develop. Patrol officers are not subject to direct control. They have the power to arrest, but they may also decide not to make an arrest. The order maintenance function is made more complex by the fact that patrol officers are normally expected to "handle" a situation rather than to enforce the law, and this usually takes place in an emotionally charged atmosphere. In controlling a crowd outside a rock concert, for example, the arrest of an unruly person may restore order by removing a troublemaker and also serve as a warning to others that they could be arrested if they do not cooperate. However, an arrest may cause the crowd to become hostile toward the officers, making things worse. Officers cannot always predict precisely how their discretionary decisions will promote or hinder order maintenance (Gau & Brunson, 2010).

Law Enforcement

The **law enforcement** function applies to situations in which the law has been violated and the offender needs to be identified or located and then apprehended. Police officers who focus on law enforcement serve in specialized branches such as the vice squad and the burglary detail. Although the patrol officer may be the first officer at the scene of a crime, for serious offenses, a detective usually prepares the case for prosecution by bringing together all the evidence for the prosecuting attorney. When the offender is identified but not located, the detective conducts the search. If the offender is not identified, the detective must analyze clues to determine who committed the crime.

The police often portray themselves as enforcers of the law, but many factors interfere with how effectively they can do so. For example, when a property crime is committed, the perpetrator usually has some time to get away. This limits the ability of the police to identify, locate, and arrest the suspect. Burglaries, for instance, usually occur when people are away from home. The crime may not be discovered

law enforcement The police function of controlling crime by intervening in situations in which the law has clearly been violated and the police need to identify and apprehend the guilty person.

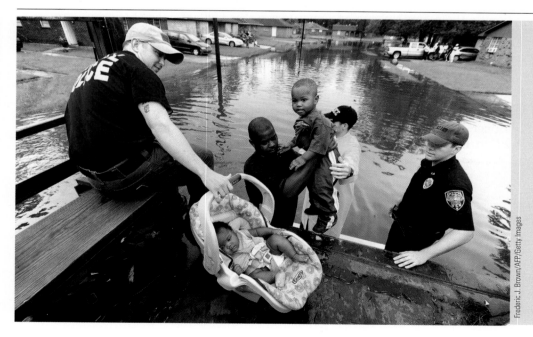

The crime fighter image of police affects both the public's view of officers' primary job and the image that may attract some new recruits to the job. In reality, police spend much of their time performing services for the public, including searching for lost children and rendering first aid. Which function—order maintenance, law enforcement, or service—do you believe officers can fulfill more effectively?

Frederic J. Brown/AFP/Getty Images

until hours or days have passed. The effectiveness of the police is also reduced when assault or robbery victims cannot identify the offender. Victims often delay in calling the police, reducing the chances that a suspect will be apprehended.

Service

service The police function of providing assistance to the public for many matters unrelated to crime as well as for crime prevention education.

Police perform a broad range of services, especially for lower-income citizens, that are not related to crime. This kind of **service**—providing first aid, rescuing animals, helping the disoriented, and so on—has become a major police function. Crime prevention has also become a major component of police services to the community. Through education and community organizing, the police can help the public take steps to prevent crime.

It may appear that valuable resources are being inappropriately diverted from law enforcement to services. However, performing service functions can help police control crime. Through the service function, officers gain knowledge about the community, and citizens come to trust the police. Checking the security of buildings clearly helps prevent crime, but other activities—dealing with runaways, people under the influence of drugs and alcohol, and public quarrels—may help solve problems before they lead to criminal behavior.

Implementing the Mandate

Although citizens depend most heavily on the order maintenance and service functions of the police, the citizenry acts as though law enforcement—the catching of lawbreakers—is the most important function of police. According to public opinion polls, the crime fighter image of the police is firmly rooted in citizens' minds and is the main function that attracts most recruits to policing careers.

Public support for police budgets is greatest when the crime-fighting function is stressed. This emphasis can be seen in the organization of big-city departments. The officers who perform this function, such as detectives, enjoy high status. The focus on crime leads to the creation of special units to deal with homicide, burglary, and auto theft. All other tasks fall to the patrol division. In some departments, this pattern creates morale problems, because extra resources are allocated and prestige is devoted to a function that is concerned with a small percentage of the problems brought to the police. In essence, police are public servants who keep the peace, but their organization reinforces its own law enforcement image and the public's focus on crime fighting.

The severe budget cuts affecting many police agencies since the 2008 downturn in the nation's economy sometimes forces law enforcement administrators to make difficult choices about which functions will receive attention and resources (M. Wilson, 2010). When police agencies must reduce the number of officers and the number of patrols, there may not be personnel available to respond to nonemergency calls for service. For example, in one Michigan county that saw its patrol force cut in half, a sheriff's department spokesman noted the harsh reality that "emergency calls come first and other problems might have to wait a day" (Hayden, 2011). Thus officers' actual attention to each of the three functions is also affected by the availability of personnel and resources.

☑ CHECK POINT

12. What is the order maintenance function? What are officers expected to do in situations where they must maintain order?
Police have a broad mandate to prevent behavior that either disturbs or threatens to disturb the peace or involves face-to-face conflict between two or more people. Officers are expected to "handle" the situation.

13. How do law enforcement situations compare with order maintenance situations?
The police in order maintenance situations must first determine if a law has been broken. In law enforcement situations, that fact is already known; thus, officers must only find and apprehend the offender.

STOP&ANALYZE

Which of the police functions do you see as most difficult to carry out? Give three reasons for your answer.

Organization of the Police

Most police agencies follow a military model of organization, with a structure of ranks and responsibilities that mark a **police bureaucracy**. Police departments are bureaucracies designed to achieve objectives efficiently and, like most bureaucracies, are characterized by a division of labor, a chain of command with clear lines of authority, and rules to guide the activities of staff. Police organization differs somewhat from place to place depending on the size of jurisdiction, the characteristics of the population, and the nature of the local crime problems. However, all sizeable departments have the basic characteristics of a bureaucracy.

Bureaucratic Elements

The police department in Odessa, Texas, reveals the elements of bureaucracy in a typical urban police force. Figure 4.2 shows the Odessa Police Department's organizational chart, which we refer to in the following discussion.

Division of Labor   As indicated in Figure 4.2, the Odessa Police Department is divided into four divisions and bureaus: Administrative Division, Operations Bureau, Special Operations Bureau, and headquarters under the Chief of Police. In each of these divisions and bureaus, authority is further delegated to offices and units that have special functions for such matters as training, finance, and communications. The Operations Bureau is divided into specific **patrol units**, designated by shift, and animal control. The Special Operations Bureau is divided according to various functions, including narcotics, crime scene investigations, and property crimes. Assignment to a unit in a Special Operations Bureau may give an officer higher status and greater freedom than that enjoyed by patrol officers. See "A Question of Ethics" at the end of the chapter to consider problems that may occur if officers violate rules in order to avoid being reassigned to regular street patrol units.

The bureaucratic organization of an urban police department such as Odessa's allows the allocation of resources and the supervision of personnel, taking into account the needs and problems that require the attention of specific units.

Chain and Unity of Command   The military character of police departments is illustrated by the **chain of command** according to ranks—officer, commander, sergeant, lieutenant, captain, major, and chief. These make clear the powers and duties of officers at each level. Each officer has an immediate supervisor who holds authority over and responsibility for the actions of those below. Relationships between superiors and subordinates emphasize discipline, control, and accountability. These values help officers mobilize resources. They also help protect important legal rights; if police officers are accountable to their superiors, they are less likely to abuse their authority by needlessly interfering with the freedom and rights of citizens.

Operational Units

All but the smallest police departments assign officers to operational units that focus on specific functions: patrol, investigation, traffic, vice, and juvenile. These units perform the basic tasks of crime prevention and control. The patrol and investigation (detective) units form the core of the modern department. The patrol unit handles a wide range of functions, including preventing crime, catching suspects, mediating quarrels, helping the ill, and giving aid at accidents. The investigation unit identifies, apprehends, and collects evidence against lawbreakers who commit serious crimes. Because of their overlapping duties, the separation of patrol and investigation can cause problems. Whereas the investigation unit usually focuses on murder, rape, and major robberies, the patrol unit has joint responsibility for investigating those crimes but is also solely responsible for investigating the more numerous lesser crimes.

police bureaucracy The organizational description of police departments' design and operations that seek to achieve efficiency through division of labor, chain of command, and rules to guide staff.

patrol units The core operational units of local police departments that deploy uniformed officers to handle the full array of police functions for service, order maintenance, and law enforcement.

chain of command Organizational structure based on a military model with clear definition of ranks to indicate authority over subordinates and obligations to obey orders from superiors.

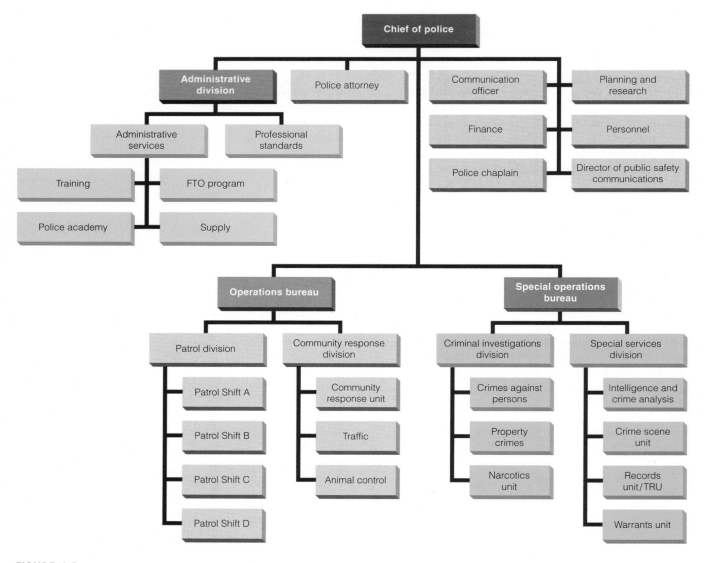

FIGURE 4.2

Organization of Odessa, Texas, Police Department This is a typical structure. Note the divisions between administrative services, operations, and special operations.

Source: Odessa, Texas, Police Department website 2013 (www.odessapd.com).

special units Units within local police departments that deploy officers, often in plain clothes if not assigned to the traffic unit, who are dedicated to a specific task, such as investigation, or type of crime, such as narcotics enforcement.

The extent to which departments create **special units** may depend on the size of the city. Many departments have traffic units, but only those in midsize to large cities also have vice and juvenile units. As a result of the war on drugs, some cities have special units working only on this problem. Large departments usually have an internal affairs section to investigate charges of corruption against officers as well as other problems associated with the staff and officers. All special units depend on the patrol officers for information and assistance.

The Police Bureaucracy and the Criminal Justice System

The police play an important role as a bureaucracy within the broader criminal justice system. Four issues arise in the organizational context within which the police operate.

First, the police are the gateway through which information and individuals enter the justice system. Police have the discretion to determine which suspects will be arrested and moved into the system. Cases that are sent to the prosecutor for charging and then to the courts for adjudication begin with an officer's decision that there is probable cause for an arrest. The ultimate success of the prosecution depends on the care taken by the officer in making the arrest and collecting evidence. To a large extent, the outcome of the case hinges on the officer's judgment and evidence-gathering activities.

Second, police administration is influenced by the fact that the outcome of a case is largely in the hands of others. The police bring suspects into the criminal justice process, but they cannot control the decisions of prosecutors and judges. In some cases, the police officers feel that their efforts have been wasted. For example, the prosecutor sometimes agrees to a plea bargain that does not, in the eyes of the officer, adequately punish the offender. The potential for conflict between police and other decision makers in the system is increased by the difference in social status between police officers, who often do not have college degrees, and lawyers and judges, who have graduate degrees.

Third, as part of a bureaucracy, police officers are expected to observe rules and follow the orders of superiors while at the same time make independent, discretionary judgments. They must stay within the chain of command yet also make choices in response to events on the streets. These factors affect police behavior on a daily basis.

Fourth, the organization and operation of police are affected by economic conditions and budgetary pressures. During the contemporary era of cutbacks in state and local budgets for law enforcement, the nature of a city's police bureaucracy can change as administrators make decisions about priorities. For example, budget cuts in 2011 led the Sacramento, California, Police Department to cut 43 patrol officers and eliminate its specialized narcotics and gang units. As a result, the police stopped responding to calls about minor traffic accidents and even burglaries, as long as the burglaries were not in progress (Maher, 2011).

☑ CHECK POINT

14. What are three characteristics of a bureaucracy?
Division of labor, chain and unity of command, rules and procedures.

15. What are four operational units of all but the smallest police departments?
Patrol, investigation, traffic, vice.

STOP&ANALYZE

In light of budget cuts affecting contemporary police departments throughout the country, if you were a police chief, what would you cut and why? Describe and explain two possible budget cuts.

Police Policy

The police cannot enforce every law and catch every lawbreaker. Legal rules limit the ways officers can investigate and pursue offenders. For example, the constitutional ban on unreasonable searches and seizures prevents police from investigating many crimes without a search warrant.

Because the police have limited resources, they cannot have officers on every street at all times of the day and night. This means that police executives must develop policies regarding how the members of their department will implement their mandate (W. Hicks, 2003). See the discussion in "The Policy Debate" to consider whether contemporary budget cuts should lead police executives to consider the use of volunteer officers as a means to carry out police functions. Policy choices by police executives guide officers as to which offenses will receive the most attention and which tactics will be used—for example, which neighborhoods to patrol and whether to patrol in cars or on foot. These policies also determine which people will be caught committing crimes and brought into the criminal justice system for prosecution and punishment. Changes in policy—such as increasing the size of the night patrol or tolerating prostitution and other public-order offenses—affect the amount of crime that gets official attention and thereby affect the system's ability to deal with offenders.

The Use of Volunteers in Law Enforcement

Budget reductions since 2008 have caused many police departments to experience significant cuts in patrol personnel. In order to minimize the impact of these cuts on the fulfillment of police functions, some departments utilize citizen volunteers as auxiliary police officers. Many cities have police auxiliary units, composed of uniformed volunteers, who assist with police functions. In 2011 the Los Angeles Police Department had 700 unpaid citizens in its Reserve Corps. When these volunteers go through police academy training, they can be deployed on the streets as armed, uniformed officers who assist regular officers in order maintenance, crime investigation, and other police functions. Is the use of volunteer officers a wise approach to increasing police resources, especially in an era of government budget cuts?

For the Use of Volunteer Officers

- The services provided by the use of volunteer officers save Los Angeles $5 million each year.
- In New York City, 4,500 volunteer auxiliary officers serve as unarmed, uniformed officers who are extra "eyes and ears" for the police department as they patrol the streets on foot, observe subway platforms, and call regular officers via police radio when their suspicions are aroused.
- Volunteer officers can handle routine tasks such as directing traffic in order to free the time of sworn officers to handle more complex and dangerous tasks.
- The use of citizen-volunteers may help create closer connections and greater understanding between police departments and the citizens that they serve.

Against the Use of Volunteer Officers

- Even routine tasks such as directing traffic may involve dangerous situations, the discovery of criminal activity, or other matters that require quick decision making by highly trained sworn officers.
- Eight auxiliary officers in New York have been killed in the line of duty in the last 50 years. In a highly publicized tragedy in 2007, two auxiliary officers were killed by a shooting suspect that they were following down the street. One victim was a 19-year-old sophomore at New York University who was intent on a career as a prosecutor, and the other was a 27-year-old aspiring novelist.
- The usefulness of such officers has been questioned, especially with respect to issues about training and judgment. In Tennessee there is a traditional elective office called "constable" through which unpaid citizens patrol, issue citations, and make arrests after only 40 hours of training. The constables' powers have been eliminated in four counties, and critics are seeking to abolish the office

statewide, in part because of the misbehavior of several constables for wrongful arrests and sexual assaults.
- In 2011 the Illinois attorney general raised questions about the legality of employing such officers in her state because some departments used such officers in ways that collided with state laws on carrying handguns and impersonating a police officer.

What Should the Policy Be?

While it may be tempting to use unpaid volunteers to handle specific police functions, there are risks involved. These risks include dangers to the volunteer officers and the community when incidents happen and someone other than a highly trained officer is making decisions. There are also risks of improper behavior by volunteer officers who may use their uniforms, badges, and inexperience in ways that violate laws, harm individual citizens, or create public relations issues for police departments. A key issue is whether departments that wish to use volunteers can adequately train and supervise those volunteers in order to avoid risks and problems. Because of the risk that police departments can be sued when someone is harmed as the result of an improper decision or action by a volunteer officer, many police chiefs and city attorneys will likely remain wary of relying on volunteers.

Researching the Internet

To learn more about the use of volunteers in policing, read the Los Angeles Police Department's website description of the qualifications and duties for volunteers in its Reserve Corps. To view the report, visit http://www.lapdonline.org/join_the_team/content_basic_view/542.

Analyzing the Issue

Imagine that a mayor has appointed you and your classmates as members of a committee responsible for recommending a policy on the use of volunteer officers by the police department. After discussing the issue with your classmates, write a memo outlining how, if at all, you would permit volunteer officers to be used if you were a police chief. Provide reasons for your decision on whether or not to use volunteers and your decisions on how they could be used.

Sources: Natalie Neysa Alund, "Value of Tennessee Constables Debated," *Knoxville News Sentinel*, December 11, 2011 (http://m.knoxnews.com); Alan Feuer and Al Baker, "Greenwich Village Gunfight Leaves Four Dead," *New York Times*, March 15, 2007 (www.nytimes.com); Gloria Hillard, "In Tight Times, L.A. Relies on Volunteer Police," National Public Radio, May 19, 2011 (http://www.npr.org); Larry Yellen, "Illinois Attorney General: Auxiliary Police Are Breaking Law," Fox Chicago News, March 1, 2011 (www.myfoxchicago.com).

Police policies may reflect the preferences and values of police executives. However, choices about policies are also influenced by politics, public pressure, and social context. American cities differ in government, economic, and racial and ethnic characteristics as well as in their degree of urbanization. These factors can affect the style of policing expected by the community. In a classic study, James Q. Wilson found that citizen expectations regarding police behavior affect departments through the political process; specifically, chiefs who run their departments in ways that antagonize the community are not likely to stay in office very long. Wilson's key finding was that a city's political culture, which reflects its socioeconomic characteristics and its government organization, had a major impact on the style of policing found there. Wilson identified three different styles of policing—the *watchman*, *legalistic*, and *service* styles (J. Q. Wilson, 1968).

Departments with a **watchman style** stress order maintenance. Patrol officers may ignore minor violations of the law, especially those involving traffic and juveniles, as long as there is order. The police exercise discretion and deal with many infractions in an informal way. Officers make arrests only for flagrant violations and when order cannot be maintained. The broad discretion exercised by officers can produce discrimination when officers do not treat members of all racial and ethnic groups in the same way.

In departments with a **legalistic style**, police work is marked by professionalism and an emphasis on law enforcement. Officers are expected to detain a high proportion of juvenile offenders, act vigorously against illicit enterprises, issue traffic tickets, and make a large number of misdemeanor arrests. They act as if there is a single standard of community conduct—that prescribed by the law—rather than different standards for juveniles, minorities, people under the influence of drugs or alcohol, and other groups. Thus, although officers do not discriminate in making arrests and issuing citations, the strict enforcement of laws, including traffic laws, can seem overly harsh to some groups in the community.

Suburban middle-class communities often experience a **service style**. Residents feel that they deserve individual treatment and expect the police to provide such service. Burglaries and assaults are taken seriously, whereas minor infractions tend to be dealt with by informal means such as stern warnings. The police are expected to deal with the misdeeds of local residents in a personal, nonpublic way so as to avoid embarrassment.

In all cases, before officers investigate crimes or make arrests, each police chief decides on policies that will govern the level and type of enforcement in the community. Given that the police are the entry point to the criminal justice system, the decisions made by police officials affect all segments of the system. Just as community expectations shape decisions about enforcement goals and the allocation of police resources, they also shape the cases that will be handled by prosecutors and correctional officials.

watchman style Style of policing that emphasizes order maintenance and tolerates minor violations of law as officers use discretion to handle small infractions informally but make arrests for major violations.

legalistic style Style of policing that emphasizes strict enforcement of laws and reduces officers' authority to handle matters informally.

service style Style of policing in which officers cater to citizens' desire for favorable treatment and sensitivity to individual situations by using discretion to handle minor matters in ways that seek to avoid embarrassment or punishment.

A. Ramey/PhotoEdit

The styles of policing employed by police departments can vary according to the characteristics of a community. Do you see evidence of the any of the three classic styles—watchman, legalistic, or service—in your hometown? Does the use of specific patrol methods, such as bicycles, tell you anything about the style of policing in a community?

16. What are the characteristics of the watchman style of policing?
Emphasis on order maintenance, extensive use of discretion, and risk of differential treatment of racial and ethnic groups.

17. What is the key feature of the legalistic style of policing?
Professionalism and use of a single standard of law enforcement throughout the community.

18. Where are you likely to find the service style of policing?
Suburban middle-class communities.

If you were a police chief, which style of policing would you seek to have your officers carry out? Would your choice depend on the type of city for which you have responsibility, or is there one style that is actually the ideal approach? Give three reasons for your choice of styles.

A QUESTION OF ETHICS

Think, Discuss, Write

In October 2011 former New York Police Department narcotics detective Stephen Anderson testified in court that a fellow undercover officer was worried about being sent back to uniformed street patrol for failing to meet his quota of drug arrests. Anderson, who had just made two buy-and-bust arrests in a bar, gave the other officer drugs, knowing that the officer was going to plant the drugs on innocent people and then arrest them on drug charges. The officers referred to this practice as "flaking." Anderson said he observed on multiple occasions that officers planted drugs on innocent people. "It was something I was seeing a lot of, whether it was from supervisors or undercovers and even investigators. . . . It's almost like you have no emotion with it, that they attach the bodies to it, they're going to be out of jail tomorrow anyway." Anderson also testified that officers made extra money by planting drugs on people because supervisors rewarded them with extra overtime pay for drug busts, even if the drug busts did not involve overtime work.

Discussion/Writing Assignment

Imagine that you are the new police chief in New York City. What will you do to counteract such illegal and unethical practices that go beyond simply one bad cop and appear to be part of accepted practice? Should you modify the productivity measure of arrest quotas? Should you change supervisors' authority to approve overtime pay? What issues and problems might follow from any changes you propose? Also think about adjustments you could make in training and supervision. Write a memo detailing the actions you would propose and predicting the possible consequences of those actions.

Sources: John Marzulli, "Cops Made Money by Fabricating Drug Charges against Innocent People, Stephen Anderson Testifies," *New York Daily News*, October 14, 2011 (www.nydailynews.com); John Marzulli, "We Fabricated Drug Charges against Innocent People to Meet Arrest Quotas, Former Detective Testifies," *New York Daily News*, October 13, 2011 (www.nydailynews.com).

SUMMARY

① Describe how policing evolved in the United States.

- The police in the United States owe their roots to early nineteenth-century developments in policing in England.
- Like their English counterparts, the American police have limited authority, are under local control, and are organizationally fragmented.
- The three distinctive eras of policing after the founding of the United States are the political era (1840–1920), the professional model era (1920–1970), and the community policing era (1970–present).

② Name the main types of law enforcement agencies.

- In the U.S. federal system of government, police agencies are found at the national, state, county, and municipal levels.
- Federal agencies include the FBI, DEA, Secret Service, and sworn officers in dozens of other agencies.
- Most states have a state police force, and sheriffs' departments are the primary county-level policing agencies.

❸ Analyze the recruitment of police officers and how they learn their job.

- People seek to become police officers for a variety of reasons, including public service, a desire for varied tasks, and civil service pay and benefits.
- To meet current and future challenges, the police must recruit and train individuals who will uphold the law and receive citizen support.
- Improvements have been made during the past quarter-century in recruiting more women, racial and ethnic minorities, and well-educated people as police officers.

❹ Describe the elements of the police officer's "working personality."

- Police work in an environment greatly influenced by their subculture.
- The concept of the working personality helps us understand the influence of the police subculture on how individual officers see their world.
- Police justify their work in moral terms to deal with dilemmas, but this can also increase tension with citizens.
- The isolation of the police strengthens bonds among officers but can also add to job stress.

❺ List the functions of the police.

- The functions of the police are order maintenance, law enforcement, and service.

- Police have cultivated an image as crime fighters preoccupied with the law enforcement function.
- The service function is actually the basis for most calls to police departments.

❻ Describe the organization of the police.

- The organization of police includes bureaucratic elements such as division of labor as well as military-style elements such as chain and unity of command.
- Most police departments assign officers to operational units that focus on specific functions: patrol, investigation, traffic, vice, and juvenile.
- The police play an important role as a bureaucracy within the broader criminal justice system.

❼ Identify influences on police policy and styles of policing.

- Police executives develop policies on how they will allocate their resources according to one of three styles: the watchman, legalistic, or service styles.
- The development of differing styles can be affected by the nature of the community and political context.
- Suburban middle-class communities often have a service style, the legalistic style emphasizes law enforcement, and the watchman style emphasizes order maintenance.

Questions for Review

1. What principles borrowed from England still underlie policing in the United States?
2. What are the three eras of policing in the United States in the nineteenth century and later, and what are the characteristics of each?
3. How do recruitment and training practices affect policing?
4. What is meant by the police subculture, and how does it influence an officer's work?
5. What are the functions of the police?
6. How are the police organized?
7. How do communities influence police policy and police styles?

Key Terms and Cases

chain of command (p. 137)

community policing (p. 116)

FBI special agents (p. 119)

frankpledge (p. 110)

intelligence-led policing (p. 117)

law enforcement (p. 135)

law enforcement certification (p. 125)

legalistic style (p. 141)

order maintenance (p. 134)

patrol units (p. 137)

police bureaucracy (p. 137)

problem-oriented policing (p. 116)

service (p. 136)

service style (p. 141)

sheriff (p. 113)

slave patrols (p. 112)

socialization (p. 129)

special units (p. 138)

subculture (p. 129)

U.S. marshals (p. 113)

watch system (p. 112)

watchman style (p. 141)

working personality (p. 130)

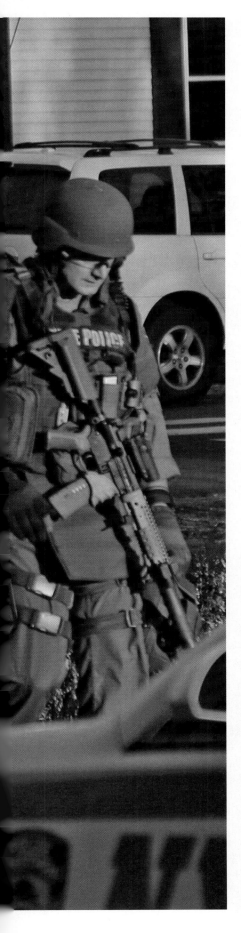

5 | Policing: Contemporary Issues and Challenges

LEARNING OBJECTIVES

1 Describe the everyday actions of police.

2 Identify the ways police can abuse their power and the challenges of controlling this abuse.

3 List the methods that can be used to make police more accountable to citizens.

4 Describe the delivery of police services.

5 Name patrol strategies that departments employ.

6 Explain the importance of connections between the police and the community.

7 Identify issues and problems that emerge from law enforcement agencies' increased attention to homeland security.

8 Describe the policing and related activities undertaken by private sector security management.

The police officers found a scene so horrific that its description captured the attention of the entire country. Amid broken glass and the smell of gunpowder inside the quiet of Sandy Hook Elementary School, the Newtown, Connecticut, officers found two women shot to death in the hallway and the bodies of teachers and 20 dead first-graders in two classrooms (Zak, 2012). On December 14, 2012, a typical quiet school day, Adam Lanza, a mentally troubled 20-year-old, had shot his way into the school carrying semiautomatic pistols and a rifle along with more than enough ammunition to kill every child and teacher in the school (Rivera, 2013). In a matter of minutes, Lanza's rapid-fire shots killed many of society's most vulnerable citizens—children too young to react and escape on their own. Lanza shot himself to death just as officers were arriving at the school. Before arriving at the school, he had murdered his mother at their family home.

The dozens of heavily armed officers who had streamed into the school within minutes of the shooting acted quickly to escort all of the building's other students and teachers into the parking lot while protecting them from seeing any blood or bodies ("Connecticut Mourns," 2012). Newspapers everywhere carried photos of crying teachers and parents clutching young children and rushing them away from the scene. Those same newspapers also carried frightening descriptions of small children's bodies hit with bullets fired at close range.

This case illustrates the range of responsibilities and challenges facing police officers. It demonstrates the diverse missions that the police must simultaneously carry out—duties ranging from emergency response to crowd control to criminal investigation. The police who first arrived at the school had to be initially concerned about possibly facing gunfire from an assailant intent on killing as many people as possible. At the same time, they needed to evacuate vulnerable children from the building as well as provide first aid to the injured. Moreover, they had to do these tasks amid a scene of indescribable horror that would likely give them haunting memories of both incomprehensible cruelty and tragic human suffering.

The 9/11 terrorist attack on the World Trade Center in New York City drew worldwide attention to courageous actions taken by hundreds of police officers and firefighters on that day. Many of these law enforcement officers and emergency responders lost their lives in the collapse of the twin towers and its aftermath. Until that event, few Americans had cause or reason to recognize the importance of law enforcement agencies at the various levels of government or to appreciate the numerous ways these officers serve society. Now there is much wider recognition that police officers are not merely crime fighters. They are essential civil servants who can act quickly and professionally to coordinate responsive efforts in the

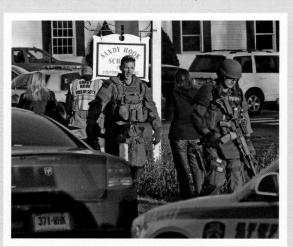

face of threats to public safety—whether the dangers be human-caused or the result of natural disasters.

In this chapter, we examine several aspects of the continuing challenges faced by American police in protecting lives and property. We focus on the actual work of the police as they pursue suspects, prevent crimes, and otherwise serve the public. The police must be organized so that patrol efforts are coordinated, investigations carried out, arrests made, evidence gathered, and violators prosecuted. Moreover, police responsibilities must be performed effectively in a variety of contexts, with an increasingly diverse society. As shown by the Newtown school example, law enforcement officials must routinely tackle issues that might not be considered in the realm of typical crime prevention, such as public-safety emergencies and natural disasters. Because each of these responsibilities must be executed while maintaining the highest principles and professional standards, we will examine the issues of police ethics, misconduct, and accountability.

This chapter also looks at the emerging challenges stemming from homeland security and antiterrorist efforts. We will conclude by discussing the role of private security officials in advancing society's interests in public safety and crime prevention. The topics explored in this chapter demonstrate the wide range of issues and problems handled by public police and private security officials in the twenty-first century as they work toward advancing society's goals of order, safety, and security.

Everyday Action of the Police

We saw in Chapter 4 how the police are organized and what three functions of policing compose their mandate: law enforcement, order maintenance, and service. We have also recognized that police officers must be guided by policies developed by their superiors as to how policing is to be implemented. Moreover, police officers' actions and effectiveness depend on the resources available to them, as illustrated by the example of computers in patrol cars that will be discussed in greater detail in Chapter 14. In this section, we look at the everyday actions of the police as they deal with citizens in often highly discretionary ways. We then discuss domestic violence to show how the police respond to serious problems.

Encounters between Police and Citizens

To carry out their mission, the police must have the public's confidence, because they depend on the public to help them identify crime and carry out investigations. Each year one in five Americans has face-to-face contact with law enforcement officers. One-fifth of the contacts occur when police respond to a call for assistance or come to the scene of an automobile collision. Another fifth involve people reporting a crime. Still another fifth involve police investigating crimes or providing service and assistance. The remaining 40 percent of these contacts involve drivers and passengers stopped by a patrol officer. Overall, 90 percent of people who had contact with the police believed that the police acted properly. However, among drivers stopped by the police, African Americans were less likely than whites or Hispanics to believe that the police had stopped them for a legitimate reason (Eith & Durose, 2011). People's contacts with the police may shape their perceptions of the police and could affect their willingness to cooperate.

Although most people are willing to help the police, factors such as fear and self-interest keep some from cooperating. Many people who avoid calling the police do so because they think it is not worth the effort and cost. They do not want to spend time filling out forms at the station, appearing as a witness, or confronting a neighbor or relative in court. In some low-income neighborhoods, citizens are reluctant to assist the police because their past experience has shown that contact with law enforcement "only brings trouble." Without information about a crime, the police may decide not to pursue an investigation. Clearly citizens have influence over the work of the police through their decisions to call or not to call them. As a result, officers learn that developing and maintaining effective communication with people is essential to doing their job.

Citizens expect the police to act both effectively and fairly—in ways consistent with American values. Yet, police departments have little direct control over the actions of individual officers. Departments have policies about when to conduct searches and other matters concerning officers' interactions with members of the public. However, officers possess the discretion to decide for themselves when to stop a driver, when to frisk a pedestrian, and when to make an arrest. Sometimes these individual decisions will violate policy or even ignore the legal rights of citizens. Thus, police officers' decisions about how to use their discretion have significant impact on how people are treated and how they feel about the criminal justice system.

Police Discretion

Police officers have the power to deprive people of their liberty, to arrest them, to take them into custody, and to use force to control them. In carrying out their professional responsibilities, officers are expected to exercise *discretion*—to make wise choices in often ambiguous situations as to how and when to apply the law. Discretion can involve ignoring minor violations of the law or holding some violators to rulebook standards. It can mean arresting a disorderly person or just taking that person safely home. In the final analysis, the officer on the scene must define the situation, decide how to handle it, and determine whether and how the law should be applied. Five factors are especially important:

1. *The nature of the crime.* The less serious a crime is to the public, the more freedom officers have to ignore it.
2. *The relationship between the alleged criminal and the victim.* The closer the personal relationship, the more variable is the use of discretion. Family squabbles may not be as grave as they appear, and police are wary of making arrests, because a spouse may later decide not to press charges.
3. *The relationship between the police and the criminal or victim.* A polite complainant will be taken more seriously than a hostile one. Similarly, a suspect who shows respect to an officer is less likely to be arrested than one who does not.

Police officers use their discretion to make many decisions. Who should be stopped and questioned? When should an arrest be made? Who needs an encouraging word, and who needs a stern warning? In making decisions, officers can significantly impact the lives of people who come into contact with the criminal justice system. Are there ways that supervisors could better monitor officers' use of discretion?

4. *Race/ethnicity, age, gender, class.* Research studies show that some officers are more likely to investigate behavior (e.g., make stops and searches) and strictly enforce the law against young, minority, poor men while being more lenient to the elderly, to whites, and to affluent women.

5. *Departmental policy.* The policies of the police chief and city officials promote more or less discretion.

Violence between spouses or intimate partners, typically called **domestic violence**, provides a good example of the role of police discretion. Twenty-six percent of violent victimizations experienced by women are at the hands of spouses or boyfriends (Truman & Rand, 2010; Truman & Planty, 2012). Until the 1970s and 1980s, many male officers treated such events as private matters for couples to handle themselves rather than as crimes, even when there was clear evidence of violence and injuries. In light of lawsuits and lobbying on behalf of injured women, nearly half of the states and the District of Columbia eventually developed policies to require the arrest of suspects in violent incidents, without a warrant, even if the officer did not witness the crime (Hoctor, 1997). In addition, most large departments and police academies have programs to educate officers about domestic violence and the victimization of women.

domestic violence The term commonly used to refer to intimate partner violence or violent victimizations between spouses, boyfriends, and girlfriends or those formerly in intimate relationships. Such actions account for a significant percentage of the violent victimizations experienced by women.

Yet, even though we can point to policy changes imposed to deal with domestic violence, the fact remains that the officer in the field is the one who must handle these situations. Each context may differ, both in terms of the officer's perceptions about what occurred and with respect to the victim's desire to see the abuser arrested and punished (Hirschel & Hutchinson, 2003). As with most law enforcement situations, laws, guidelines, and training can help; however, as is often true in police work, in the end, the discretion of the officer inevitably determines what actions will be taken (R. C. Davis, O'Sullivan, Farole, & Rempel, 2008).

Police officers possess significant discretion because so much of their work is conducted independently, beyond the observation and supervision of superior officers. Officers' independence and discretion also raises risks of improper police behavior and corruption, the topics we will examine in the next section. For police to fulfill their responsibilities properly, we count on them to be ethical and professional in all of their decisions and actions. These issues affect all aspects of police functions and performance.

☑ CHECK POINT

1. **Why do patrol officers have so much discretion?**
   They deal with citizens, often in private, and are charged with maintaining order and enforcing laws. Many of these laws are ambiguous and deal with situations in which the participants' conduct is in dispute.

2. **Why have police in the past failed to make arrests in domestic violence situations?**
   Officers assumed family conflicts are private matters and were often insensitive to the victimization of women.

STOP&ANALYZE

Discretion is a necessary element of police officers' tools to handle situations that they encounter. Yet, discretion may be used inappropriately. List two actions you would take if you were a police chief to improve the discretionary decision making of your officers.

Police Abuse of Power

Police officers can break the law and disobey departmental policies through corruption, favoritism, discrimination, and the failure to carry out their duties properly. Periodically, police corruption and abuse of power become major issues on the public agenda (Skolnick & Fyfe, 1993). In particular, the illegal use of violence by law enforcement officers, violations of constitutional rights, and the criminal activities associated with police corruption can gain news media attention and anger the public. In 2014 newspapers highlighted New York City detectives sued multiple times for making false arrests, including one officer who was sued 28 times in an eight-year period at a cost of nearly $900,000 to the city for settling those lawsuits (Ryley & Gregorian, 2014). Although most officers do not engage in misconduct, these problems deserve study because they raise questions about the extent to which the public can control and trust the police.

Use of Force

Although most people cooperate with the police, officers must at times use force to make arrests, control disturbances, and deal with the drunken or mentally ill. Thus, police may use *legitimate* force to do their job. It is when they use *excessive* force that they violate the law. But which situations and actions constitute excessive use of force? Both officers and experts debate this question.

Citizens use the term *police brutality* to describe a wide range of practices from the use of profane or abusive language to physical force and violence. Stories of police brutality are not new. However, unlike the untrained officers of the early 1900s, today's officers are supposed to be professionals who know the rules and understand the need for proper conduct. Nevertheless, a 2011 report by the Los Angeles Sheriff's Department identified instances of improper conduct, such as a deputy who shot at a driver who bumped into his vehicle in a fast-food restaurant parking lot and another who sought to cover up the fact that she had fired her gun at a burglary suspect (Faturechi, 2011).

Concerns are heightened by the fact that the public cannot know how often police engage in abusive behavior, even when it comes to light, because most violence remains hidden from public view (Weitzer, 2002). In 2008 a news helicopter filmed a dozen Philadelphia police officers beating and kicking a criminal suspect who had just been pulled from a car (Hurdle, 2008). If not for the video, how would the public know that the incident had happened? Without direct proof, will the public believe criminal suspects who claim to have been beaten by police? How can we prevent such incidents, especially when they occur without witnesses?

The concept "use of force" takes many forms in practice. We can arrange the various types of force on a continuum ranging from most severe (civilians shot and killed) to least severe (being grasped by an officer). How often must force be used? Most research has shown that in police contacts with suspects, force is used infrequently, and the type of force used is usually at the low end of the continuum— toward the less severe. Resistance by a suspect can contribute to the officers' decision to use force (R. Johnson, 2011; J. H. Garner, Maxwell, & Heraux, 2002). A report by the National Institute of Justice summarized general conclusions from research about use of force (K. Adams, 1999):

1. Police use force infrequently.
2. Police use of force typically occurs in the lower end of the force spectrum and involves grabbing, pushing, or shoving.
3. Use of force typically occurs when police are trying to make an arrest and the suspect is resisting.

Although more studies are needed, other research indicates that use of force is not necessarily linked to an officer's personal characteristics such as age, gender,

excessive use of force
Applications of force against individuals by police officers that violate either departmental policies or constitutional rights by exceeding the level of force permissible and necessary in a given situation.

Police grab a protester off his bike after he taunted them at a protest against free trade policies during a meeting of international leaders in Miami, Florida. Does this appear to be an appropriate use of force? Do police officers sometimes use force out of anger rather than out of necessity?

and ethnicity (Klahm & Tillyer, 2010). However, a small percentage of officers may be disproportionately involved in use-of-force situations. In addition, use of force occurs more frequently when police are dealing with people affected by drugs, alcohol, or mental illness (Lord & Sloop, 2010). By law, the police have the authority to use force if necessary to make an arrest, keep the peace, or maintain public order. But the questions of just how much force is necessary and under what conditions force may be used are complex and open to debate.

When police kill a suspect or bystander while trying to make an arrest, their actions may produce public outrage and hostility. Fears about the possibility of similar public disorders arose in 2005 when a police officer fired 10 shots that killed a 13-year-old boy who was driving a stolen car. The officer fired in the aftermath of a chase when the boy skidded across a sidewalk and then struck a police car while backing up (Chavez, 2005). The incident led Los Angeles police officials to revise their policies about firing at moving vehicles.

An analysis of New York City's detailed records on police shootings in 2010 showed drops in the use of firearms that coincided with the drop in crime rate over the preceding decade. Police opened fire at people fewer than 40 times in 2010, compared with 147 times in 1996 (Harris, 2011; A. Baker, 2008). Shootings increased in 2012, with 60 officers firing their weapons, and more than half of these officers fired more than one shot (Goodman, 2013). One troubling question that lingers is whether the New York City police are more inclined to use firearms against members of minority groups (Gill & Pasquale-Styles, 2009). In cities throughout the country, the use of deadly force in apprehending suspects has become a deeply emotional issue with a direct connection to race relations. Nearly 90 percent of those shot by the New York City police in the late 1990s were African American or Hispanic. Similarly, in 2010 reports show that 53 percent of those shot were African American, 26 percent were Hispanic, 15 percent were white, and 6 percent were Asian American (Harris, 2011). Data from other U.S. cities also raise questions about the use of force against minorities.

The risk of lawsuits by victims of improper police shootings and other injury-producing uses of force looms over police departments and creates an incentive for administrators to impose standards for the proper use of force (H. Lee & Vaughn, 2010). In addition to the use of firearms, police officers have caused deaths and injuries with choke holds and by striking people in the head with flashlights or batons (Klingler, 2012). Injuries can also result from seemingly routine procedures such as placing a suspect in handcuffs that are too tight.

As long as officers carry weapons, some improper uses of force, including shootings, will occur. Officers who are angry or otherwise guided by improper motives may use unnecessary force in situations beyond public view. See "A Question of Ethics" at the end of the chapter for an example of excessive force caught on video. Police administrators have limited tools available to restrain unethical officers. Training, internal review of incidents, and the disciplining or firing of quick-trigger officers may help reduce the use of unnecessary force.

As a result of lawsuits by people injured at the hands of the police, departments have sought new means of applying force in ways that will not produce injuries. Some of the new methods center on specific holds and pressure points that officers can use to incapacitate people temporarily without causing permanent harm; officers can learn these techniques through training. In addition, police departments seek new weapons that use less-than-lethal force. In Chapter 14, when we discuss the impact of technology on police practices, we shall examine new weapons that use electric shocks, projectiles, and chemical sprays. These new weapons also pose serious risks, including the possibility that officers will resort too quickly to such weapons when situations could be solved through patience and persuasion (Adang & Mensink, 2004).

Corruption

Police corruption has a long history in America. Early in the twentieth century, city officials organized liquor and gambling businesses for their personal gain. In many cities, ties between politicians and police officials ensured that favored clients would be protected and competitors harassed. Much of the Progressive movement's efforts to reform the police were aimed at combating such corrupt arrangements.

police corruption Police officers' violations of law and departmental policy for personal gain or to help their family and friends.

Although such political ties have diminished in most cities, corruption still exists. In 2011, for example, 30 Baltimore police officers were charged in an extortion scheme in which they received thousands of dollars in exchange for steering accident victims to a towing service that was not authorized to do business with the city (Fenton, 2011). In 2013 a New York City officer was the first officer fired in an ongoing scandal when an investigation of one officer's involvement in drugs and robberies inadvertently uncovered the involvement of more than 200 officers in illegally fixing parking and traffic tickets. Many of the officers involved in merely fixing tickets as favors to others admitted their responsibility in exchange for internal departmental punishment that required only forfeiting vacation days (Parascandola & Lestch, 2013). Sometimes corruption is defined so broadly that it ranges from accepting a free cup of coffee to robbing businesses or beating suspects. Obviously, corruption is not easily defined, and people disagree about what it includes. As a useful starting point, we can focus on the distinction between corrupt officers who are "grass eaters" and those who are "meat eaters."

"Grass eaters" are officers who accept payoffs that the routines of police work bring their way. These officers may accept gifts from businesses or take a $20 bribe instead of writing a traffic ticket. "Meat eaters" are officers who actively use their power for personal gain. For example, several Chicago police officers were convicted in 2011 of robbing drug dealers and conducting illegal searches in order to steal money and drugs (Meisner, 2011). Although meat eaters are few, their actions make headlines when discovered. By contrast, because grass eaters are numerous, they make corruption seem acceptable and promote a code of secrecy that brands any officer who exposes corruption as a traitor.

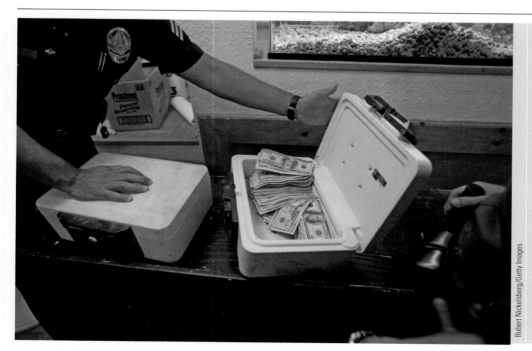

Robert Nickelsberg/Getty Images

Officers are often placed in situations where they can be tempted to enrich themselves by stealing money, property or drugs or by accepting favors, gifts, and bribes. If you were a police chief, how would you reduce the risks of police corruption?

If police administrators judge success merely by the maintenance of order on the streets and a steady flow of arrests and traffic citations, they may not have any idea what their officers actually do while on patrol. Officers therefore may learn that they can engage in improper conduct without worrying about investigations by supervisors as long as there is order on the streets and they keep their activities out of the public spotlight.

Over time, illegal activity may become accepted as normal. Ellwyn Stoddard, who studied "blue-coat crime," has said that it can become part of an "identifiable informal 'code'" (Stoddard, 1968:205). He suggests that officers are socialized to the code early in their careers. Those who "snitch" on other officers may be ostracized. Recent research shows that officers risk retaliation from peers if they break the code (Cancino & Enriquez, 2004). When corruption comes to official attention, officers protect the code by distancing themselves from the known offender rather than stopping their own improper conduct (C. Cooper, 2009; Stoddard, 1968).

New police officers need to be instilled with a sense of ethics and professionalism in both their formal and informal training. This is necessary because of the significant discretion enjoyed by police and their independence in undertaking daily tasks, which makes it impossible for administrators to detect or prevent all misconduct. The public depends on officers to take seriously the responsibilities that come with the uniform and badge. When investigations reveal improper conduct by police, we must always wonder what impact that misconduct will have on the public's trust in and cooperation with law enforcement officers.

☑ CHECK POINT

3. **What kinds of problems arise with police use of force?**
   Risks that force will be used in ways that exceed what is needed for a specific situation; risks that force will be applied disproportionately to minority group members.

4. **What is the difference between grass eaters and meat eaters?**
   Grass eaters are officers who accept payoffs that police work brings their way. Meat eaters are officers who aggressively misuse their power for personal gain.

STOP&ANALYZE

If you were a police chief, what three actions might you take to better prepare your officers to make discretionary decisions that include respect for ethical standards and adherence to proper professional standards for conduct?

Civic Accountablility

Making the police responsive to citizen complaints without burdening them with a flood of such grievances is difficult. The main challenge to improving police accountability is to use enough citizen input to force police to follow the law and departmental guidelines without restricting their ability to carry out their primary functions. At present, four less-than-perfect techniques are used in efforts to control the police: (1) internal affairs units, (2) civilian review boards, (3) standards and accreditation, and (4) civil liability lawsuits. We now look at each of these in turn.

Internal Affairs Units

The community must be confident that the department has procedures to ensure that officers will protect the rights of citizens. Yet, department complaint procedures often seem designed to discourage citizen input. People with complaints cannot always be certain that the police department will take any meaningful action.

Depending on the size of the department, a single officer or an entire section can serve as an **internal affairs unit** that receives and investigates complaints against officers. An officer charged with misconduct can face criminal prosecution

internal affairs unit A branch of a police department that receives and investigates complaints alleging violation of rules and policies on the part of officers.

or disciplinary action leading to resignation, dismissal, or suspension. Officers assigned to the internal affairs unit have duties similar to those of the inspector general's staff in the military. They must investigate complaints against other officers. Hollywood films and television series depict dramatic investigations of drug dealing and murder, but investigations of sexual harassment, alcohol or drug problems, misuse of force, and violations of departmental policies are more common.

The internal affairs unit must receive enough resources to fulfill its mission. It must also have direct access to the chief. Internal affairs investigators find the work stressful because their status prevents them from maintaining close relationships with other officers. They may face a wall of silence from fellow officers as they investigate complaints of misconduct within a department.

Civilian Review Boards

If a police department cannot show that it effectively combats corruption among officers, the public will likely demand that the department be investigated by a **civilian review board**. The Bay Area Regional Transit (BART) system in California created a citizens' board in the aftermath of a BART police officer's fatal shooting of an unarmed African American man under controversial circumstances (Melendez, 2011). Such a board allows complaints to be channeled through a committee of people who are not sworn police officers. The organization and powers of civilian review boards vary, but all oversee and review how police departments handle citizen complaints. The boards may also recommend remedial action. They do not have the power to investigate or discipline individual officers, however (S. Walker & Wright, 1995).

The main argument made by the police against civilian review boards is that people outside law enforcement do not understand the problems of policing. The police contend that civilian oversight lowers morale and hinders performance, claiming that officers will be less effective if they must worry about possible disciplinary actions. In reality, however, the boards have not been harsh.

The effectiveness of civilian review boards has not been tested, but their presence may improve police–citizen relations.

civilian review board Citizens' committee formed to investigate complaints against the police.

Standards and Accreditation

One way to increase police accountability is to require that police actions meet nationally recognized standards. The movement to accredit departments that meet these standards has gained momentum during the past decade. It has the support of the **Commission on Accreditation for Law Enforcement Agencies (CALEA)**, a private nonprofit corporation formed by four professional associations: the International Association of Chiefs of Police (IACP), the National Organization of Black Law Enforcement Executives (NOBLE), the National Sheriffs' Association (NSA), and the Police Executive Research Forum (PERF).

Police accreditation is voluntary. Departments contact CALEA, which helps them in their efforts to meet the standards. This process involves self-evaluation by departmental executives, the development of policies that meet the standards, and the training of officers. The CALEA representative acts like a military inspector general, visiting the department, examining its policies, and seeing if the standards are met in its daily operations. Departments that meet the standards receive certification. Administrators can use the standards as a management tool, training officers to know the standards and to be accountable for their actions. Obviously, the standards do not guarantee that police officers in an accredited department will not engage in misconduct. However, the guidelines serve as a major step toward providing clear guidance to officers about proper behavior. Accreditation can also show the public a department's commitment to making sure officers carry out their duties in an ethical, professional manner.

Commission on Accreditation for Law Enforcement Agencies (CALEA) Nonprofit organization formed by major law enforcement executives' associations to develop standards for police policies and practice; on request, will review police agencies and award accreditation upon meeting those standards.

Civil Liability Lawsuits

Civil lawsuits against departments for police misconduct can increase police accountability. In 1961 the U.S. Supreme Court ruled that Section 1983 of the Civil Rights Act of 1871 allows citizens to sue public officials for violations of their civil rights. The high court extended this opportunity for **Section 1983 lawsuits** in 1978 when it ruled that individual officials and local agencies may be sued when a person's civil rights are violated by an agency's "customs and usages." If an individual can show that harm was caused by employees whose wrongful acts were the result of these "customs, practices, and policies, including poor training and supervision," then he or she can sue a local agency (*Monell v. Department of Social Services of the City of New York*, 1978).

Lawsuits charging police officers with brutality, improper use of weapons, dangerous driving, and false arrest are brought in both state and federal courts. Often these lawsuits provide the basis for punishing officers who violate constitutional rights. Rights that are often subject to lawsuits are the Fourth Amendment right against unreasonable seizures, when police use excessive force or make improper arrests, and the Fourth Amendment right against unreasonable searches, when police wrongly search a house without a warrant.

In many states, people have received damage awards of millions of dollars, and police departments have settled some suits out of court. In 2013, for example, Chicago paid $4.1 million to the family of an unarmed man who was shot in the back multiple times by a police officer as he lay on the ground (St. Clair & Gorner, 2013). In the same year, five Connecticut towns agreed to pay $3.5 million to the family of an apparently innocent man who was killed by a combined SWAT team from the towns (Tepfer, 2013).

Civil liability rulings by the courts tend to be simple and severe: officials and municipalities are ordered to pay a sum of money, and the courts can enforce that judgment. The threat of significant financial awards gives police departments a strong incentive to improve the training and supervision of officers (Epp, 2009; Vaughn, 2001).

☑ CHECK POINT

5. **What are the four methods used to increase the civic accountability of the police?**
   Internal affairs units, civilian review boards, standards and accreditation, civil liability suits.

6. **What is an internal affairs unit?**
   A unit within a police department designated to receive and investigate complaints alleging violation of rules and policies on the part of officers.

7. **Why are civilian review boards criticized by police officers?**
   Police officers often fear that citizens do not understand the nature of law enforcement work and therefore will make inaccurate decisions about what constitutes improper behavior by officers.

STOP&ANALYZE

What are two arguments in favor of using only professionals in investigating and deciding whether police acted improperly? What are two arguments in favor of treating citizens as essential participants in these processes? Which set of arguments is more persuasive?

Delivery of Police Services

Law enforcement agencies attempt to structure their organization and processes to provide effective service to the public amid the reality of limited resources. In a contemporary era of significant budget cuts and reductions in personnel affecting agencies in various parts of the country, police departments must make difficult decisions about how to set priorities (Rudolph, 2012). These decisions include such matters as how to distribute officers on patrol and how to prioritize requests for assistance from the public.

Increasingly, as in other areas of the criminal justice system, police administrators look to evidence-based practices as a tool for making decisions about deployment of personnel and officers' duties on patrol (Gross-Shader, 2011). With respect to crime prevention, for example, **evidence-based policing** practices draw from research studies that guide police to proactively employ specific strategies aimed at targeted locations within a city or town (Lum, Koper, & Telep, 2011). Otherwise, officers deployed on general patrols throughout an entire city would be less effective in preventing crime than when they are engaged in specific activities at targeted trouble spots.

The effective use of evidence-based practices can be enhanced through cooperation and communication between law enforcement officials and criminal justice researchers. There are voices, however, that urge caution about an exclusive focus on evidence-based crime control research. As Jack Greene (2014:221) notes, "when we focus singularly on crime in geographic areas and [its] increase or reduction, we do not account for police-citizen interactions of a non-criminal nature, which nonetheless influence neighborhood dynamics in high and low crime areas."

Police Response

In a free society, people do not want police to stand on every street corner and ask them what they are doing. Thus, the police are mainly **reactive** (responding to citizen calls for service) rather than **proactive** (initiating actions in the absence of citizen requests). Studies of police work show that 81 percent of actions result from citizen telephone calls, 5 percent are initiated by citizens who approach an officer, and only 14 percent are initiated in the field by an officer. These facts affect the way departments are organized and the way the police respond to incidents.

Because they are mainly reactive, the police usually arrive at the scene only after the crime has been committed and the perpetrator has fled. This means that the police are hampered by the time lapse and sometimes by inaccurate information given by witnesses. For example, a mugging may happen so quickly that victims and witnesses cannot accurately describe what occurred. In about a third of cases in which police are called, no one is present when the police arrive on the scene.

Citizens have come to expect that the police will respond quickly to every call, whether it requires immediate attention or can be handled in a more routine manner. This expectation has produced **incident-driven policing**, in which calls for service are the primary instigators of action. Studies have shown, though, that less than 30 percent of calls to the police involve criminal law enforcement—most calls concern order maintenance and service (S. Walker, 1999:80). To a large extent, then, reports by victims and observers define the boundaries of policing.

Most residents in urban and suburban areas can call 911 to report a crime or obtain help or information. The 911 system has brought a flood of calls to police departments—many not directly related to police responsibilities. In Baltimore a "311 system" has been implemented to help reduce the number of nonemergency calls, estimated as 40 percent of the total calls. Residents have been urged to call 311 when they need assistance that does not require the immediate dispatch of an officer. Studies found that this innovation reduced calls to 911 and resulted in extremely high public support (Mazerolle et al., 2003).

To improve efficiency, police departments use a **differential response** system that assigns priorities to calls for service. This system assumes that it is not always necessary to rush a patrol car to the scene when a call is received. The appropriate response depends on several factors—such as whether the incident is in progress, has just occurred, or occurred some time ago, as well as whether anyone is or could be hurt.

The police do use proactive strategies such as surveillance and undercover work to combat some crimes. When addressing victimless crimes, for example, they must

evidence-based policing Police strategies and deployment of resources developed through examination of research on crime, social problems, and previously used strategies.

reactive Occurring in response, such as police activity in response to notification that a crime has been committed.

proactive Acting in anticipation, such as an active search for potential offenders that is initiated by the police without waiting for a crime to be reported. Arrests for victimless crimes are usually proactive.

incident-driven policing Policing in which calls for service are the primary instigators of action.

differential response A patrol strategy that assigns priorities to calls for service and chooses the appropriate response.

COMMON BELIEF: If more police officers actively patrolled the streets instead of having so many at headquarters sitting in offices, crime rates in a city would certainly decline.

- Crime rates are shaped by a complex variety of factors that seem unrelated to the number of officers in a city's police department.
- Some cities with the highest number of officers per capita on the streets also have the highest crime rates.
- In addition, patrols do not necessarily reduce crime. Officers cannot be everywhere at once.
- Cities that have attempted to flood neighborhoods with officers often simply see criminals move their activities to a different location.
- Research raises questions about whether more numerous patrols will necessarily impact crime rates.

CompStat Approach to crime prevention and police productivity measurement pioneered in New York City and then adopted in other cities that involves frequent meetings among police supervisors to examine detailed crime statistics for each precinct and develop immediate approaches and goals for problem solving and crime prevention.

rely on informers, stakeouts, wiretapping, stings, and raids. Because of the current focus on drug offenses, police resources in many cities have been assigned to proactive efforts to apprehend people who use or sell illegal drugs. As you read "Criminal Justice: Myth & Reality," consider whether the use of proactive strategies will reduce crime.

Productivity

Following the lead of New York City's **CompStat** program, police departments in Baltimore, New Orleans, Indianapolis, and some smaller cities emphasized precinct-level accountability for crime reduction (Bass, 2012; Rosenfeld, Fornango, & Baumer, 2005). Through twice-weekly briefings before their peers and senior executives, precinct commanders must explain the results of their efforts to reduce crime. In the CompStat approach, they are held responsible for the success of crime control efforts in their precincts as indicated by crime statistics (Weisburd, Mastrofski, McNalley, Greenspan, & Willis, 2003). Essential to this management strategy is timely, accurate information. Accordingly, computer systems have been developed to put up-to-date crime data into the hands of managers at all levels (Willis, Mastrofski, & Weisburd, 2004). This allows discussion of department-wide strategies and puts pressure on low producers (Sherman, 1998:430; Silverman, 1999). However, the CompStat approach has raised questions as to how police work should be measured. It has also raised questions about how to integrate this centralized approach for measuring performance with community policing, a decentralized strategy for crime prevention, order maintenance, and fear reduction (Willis, Mastrofski, & Kochel, 2010).

Quantifying police work is difficult in part because of the wide range of duties and day-to-day tasks of officers. In the past, the crime rate and the clearance rate have been used as measures of "good" policing. A lower crime rate might be cited as evidence of an effective department, but critics note that factors other than policing affect this measure. Like other public agencies, the police departments and the citizens in a community have trouble gauging the quantity and quality of police officers' work.

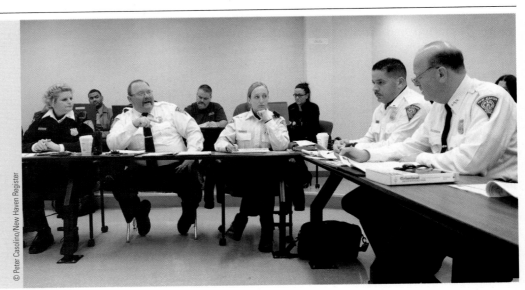

The use of crime statistics for CompStat discussions with precinct commanders is a way to measure productivity and a method of using evidence as the basis for police strategy. Should knowledge of statistics and research methods be required for officers who attain supervisory positions that involve decisions about personnel deployment and crime prevention strategies?

© Peter Casolino/New Haven Register

The **clearance rate**—the percentage of crimes known to police that they believe they have solved through an arrest—is a basic measure of police performance. The clearance rate varies by type of offense. In reactive situations, this rate can be low. For example, the police may learn about a burglary hours or even days after it has occurred; the clearance rate for such crimes is only about 13 percent. Police have much more success in handling violent crimes, in which victims often know their assailants; the clearance rate for such cases is 46 percent.

These measures of police productivity are sometimes supplemented by other data, such as the number of traffic citations issued, illegally parked cars ticketed, and suspects stopped for questioning, as well as the value of stolen goods recovered. These additional ways of counting work done reflect the fact that an officer may work hard for many hours but have no arrests to show for his or her efforts. Some of these measures, however, may have adverse consequences for police–community relations. Citizens are usually not happy with the perception that officers may be expected to issue a specific number of traffic citations each day, since it leads residents to believe that officers will make unjustified traffic stops simply to impress superiors. In New York City, during a 2013 lawsuit about racial profiling in stop-and-frisk searches of pedestrians that predominantly affected young African-American and Hispanic men, a police chief testified about criticizing officers for not making enough frisks. His description about the pressure applied by supervisory officers raised questions about whether this productivity measure contributed to discriminatory treatment of citizens (Goldstein, 2013). How do we weigh the costs and benefits of using traffic and frisk stops as productivity measures that may effectively encourage officers to employ this strategy too frequently?

Society may benefit even more when officers spend their time in activities that are hard to measure, such as calming disputes, becoming acquainted with people in the neighborhood, and providing services to those in need. Some research as well as news stories indicate that officers who engage in activities that produce higher levels of measurable productivity, such as issuing citations or making arrests, also receive higher numbers of citizen complaints about alleged misconduct (Ryley & Gregorian, 2014; Lersch, 2002).

clearance rate The percentage of crimes known to the police that they believe they have solved through an arrest; a statistic used to measure a police department's productivity.

☑ **CHECK POINT**

8. What is evidence-based policing?
Police strategies and deployment of resources developed through examination of research on crime, social problems, and previously used strategies.

9. What is differential response?
Policy that gives priority to calls according to whether an immediate or delayed response is warranted.

10. What are examples of measures of police productivity?
Crime statistics (CompStat), clearance rate, traffic citations.

STOP&ANALYZE

If you were a police chief, how would you measure your officers' productivity? Suggest two possible measures, and list the advantages and disadvantages of each.

Patrol Functions

Patrol is often called the backbone of police operations. The word *patrol* is derived from a French word, *patrouiller*, which once meant "to tramp about in the mud." This is an apt description of a function that one expert has described as "arduous, tiring, difficult, and performed in conditions other than ideal" (Chapman, 1970:ix). For most Americans, "policing" is the familiar sight of a uniformed and armed patrol officer on call 24 hours a day.

Every local police department has a patrol unit. Even in large departments, patrol officers account for up to two-thirds of all **sworn officers**—those who have taken

sworn officers Police employees who have taken an oath and been given powers by the state to make arrests and to use necessary force in accordance with their duties.

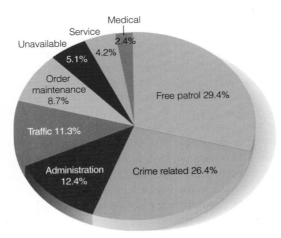

FIGURE 5.1
Time Allocated to Patrol Activities by the Police of Wilmington, Delaware
The time spent on each activity was calculated from records for each police car unit. Note the range of activities and the time spent on each.

Based on Jack R. Greene and Carl B. Klockars, "What Police Do," in *Thinking about Police*, 2nd ed., ed. Carl B. Klockars and Stephen D. Mastrofski (New York: McGraw-Hill, 1991), 279.

Medical 2.4%
Service 4.2%
Unavailable 5.1%
Order maintenance 8.7%
Traffic 11.3%
Administration 12.4%
Free patrol 29.4%
Crime related 26.4%

Free patrol: park and walk

Crime related: officer in trouble, suspicious person/vehicle, crime in progress, alarm, investigate crime not in progress, serve warrant/subpoena, assist other police

Administration: meal break, report writing, firearms training, police vehicle maintenance, at headquarters, court related

Traffic: accident investigation, parking problems, motor vehicle driving problems, traffic control, fire emergency

Order maintenance: order maintenance in progress, animal complaint, noise complaint

Service: service related

Medical: medical emergency, at local hospital

an oath and received the powers to make arrests and to use necessary force in accordance with their duties. In small communities, police operations are not specialized, and the patrol force is the department. As we have seen, the patrol officer must be prepared for any imaginable situation and must perform many duties.

Television portrays patrol officers as always on the go—rushing from one incident to another and making several arrests in a single shift. A patrol officer may indeed be called to deal with a robbery in progress or to help rescue people from a burning building. However, the patrol officer's life is not always so exciting and often involves routine and even boring tasks such as directing traffic at accident scenes and road construction sites.

Most officers on most shifts do not make even one arrest. To better understand patrol work, examine the classic study illustrated in Figure 5.1 and note how the police of Wilmington, Delaware, allocate time to various activities.

The patrol function has three parts: answering calls for help, maintaining a police presence, and probing suspicious circumstances. Patrol officers are well suited to answering calls, because they usually are near the scene and can move quickly to provide help or catch a suspect. At other times, they engage in **preventive patrol**— that is, making themselves visible and their presence known in an effort to deter crime and to make officers available to respond quickly to calls. Whether walking the streets or cruising in a car, the patrol officer is on the lookout for suspicious people and behavior. With experience, officers come to trust their own ability to spot signs of suspicious activity that merit stopping people on the street for questioning.

Patrol officers' duties sound fairly straightforward, yet these officers often find themselves in complex situations requiring sound judgments and careful actions. As the first to arrive at a crime scene, for example, the officer must comfort and give aid to victims, identify and question witnesses, control crowds, and gather evidence. These roles call for creativity and good communication skills.

Because the patrol officers have the most direct contact with the public, their actions in large part determine the image of the police and their relations with the community. Moreover, successful investigations and prosecutions often depend on patrol officers' actions in questioning witnesses and gathering evidence after a crime.

Investigation

All cities with a population of more than 250,000 and 90 percent of smaller cities have officers called **detectives** who are assigned to investigative duties. Detectives make up 15 percent of police personnel. Compared with patrol officers, they enjoy a higher status in the department: their pay is higher, their hours are more flexible, and they are supervised less closely. Detectives do not wear uniforms, and their work is considered more interesting than that of patrol officers. In addition, they engage

preventive patrol Making the police presence known to deter crime and to make officers available to respond quickly to calls.

detectives Police officers, typically working in plain clothes, who investigate crimes that have occurred by questioning witnesses and gathering evidence.

solely in law enforcement rather than in order maintenance or service work; hence, their activities conform more closely to the image of the police as crime fighters.

Within federal law enforcement agencies, the work of special agents is similar to that of detectives. In agencies such as the FBI, DEA, and Secret Service, special agents are plainclothes officers who focus on investigations. One key difference between federal special agents and detectives in local departments is that federal agents are more likely to be proactive in initiating investigations to prevent terrorism, drug trafficking, and other crimes. Local detectives are typically reactive, responding to crimes already discovered.

Detectives typically become involved after a crime has been reported and a patrol officer has done a preliminary investigation. The job of detectives is mainly to talk to people—victims, suspects, witnesses—to find out what happened. On the basis of this information, detectives develop theories about who committed the crime; they then set out to gather the evidence that will lead to arrest and prosecution.

In performing an investigation, detectives depend not only on their own experience but also on technical experts. Much of the information they need comes from criminal files, lab technicians, and forensic scientists. Many small departments turn to the state crime laboratory or the FBI for such information. Often depicted as working alone, detectives, in fact, operate as part of a team.

Apprehension   The discovery that a crime has been committed sets off a chain of events leading to the capture of a suspect and the gathering of the evidence needed to convict that person. It may also lead to several dead ends, such as a lack of clues pointing to a suspect or a lack of evidence to link the suspect to the crime.

The process of catching a suspect has three stages: detection of a crime, preliminary investigation, and follow-up investigation. Depending on the outcome of the investigation, these three steps may be followed by a fourth: clearance and arrest. As shown in Figure 5.2, these actions are designed to use criminal justice resources to arrest a suspect and assemble enough evidence to support a charge.

American police have long relied on science in gathering, identifying, and analyzing evidence. The public has become increasingly aware of the wide range of

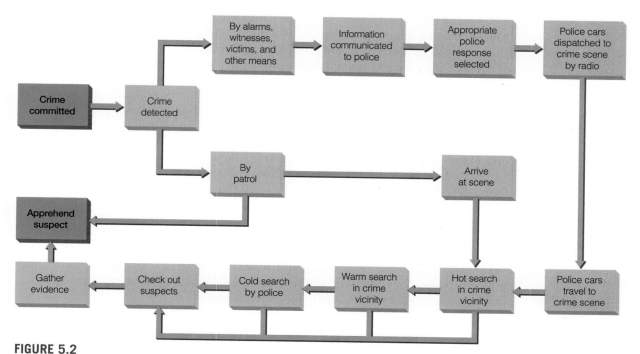

FIGURE 5.2

The Apprehension Process Apprehension of a felony suspect results from a sequence of actions by patrol officers and detectives. Coordination of these efforts is key to solving major crimes.

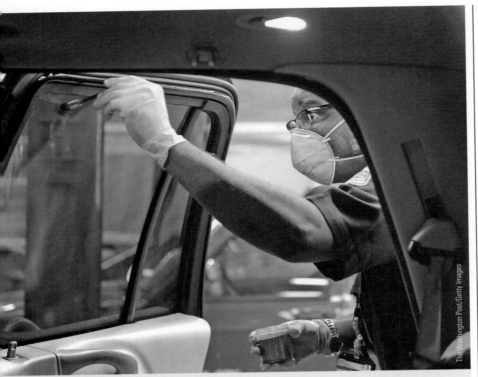

A police officer carefully dusts the window of a car in order to look for fingerprints that may identify an offender. Police departments use various forensic techniques to discover evidence. Some techniques are used at crime scenes, while others involve tests in scientific laboratories. Which techniques are likely to be most effective?

scientific testing techniques used for law enforcement purposes through the television drama *CSI: Crime Scene Investigation* and its spin-offs (S. Stephens, 2007). As we will examine in greater detail in Chapter 14, scientific analysis of fingerprints, blood, semen, hair, textiles, soil, weapons, and other materials has helped the police identify criminals.

Special Operations

Patrol and investigation are the two largest and most important units in a police department. In metropolitan areas, however, special units are set up to deal with specific types of problems. The most common of such units concern traffic, vice, juveniles, and SWAT (strategic weapons and tactics) teams. Some cities also have units to deal with organized crime and drugs. Even with such special units in place, however, regular patrol officers and investigators continue to deal individually in their daily work with the drugs, juvenile delinquency, and other problems that are targeted by special units.

It is increasingly common for police agencies to cooperate with each other in multi-agency task forces to better address specialized problems that are not confined to a specific spot in one city. Such task-force participation is especially prevalent for the largest cities. For example, more than 80 percent of cities larger than 250,000 participate in antiterrorism task forces, and more than a third of such cities participate in human-trafficking task forces (Reaves, 2010).

As we examine the special units used by many departments, bear in mind that individual officers may receive special assignments, too. A good example is the development of **school resource officers (SROs)**, police officers assigned to high schools under contractual arrangements between public schools and local police departments. More than 85 percent of police departments in cities ranging in size from 25,000 to 500,000 have officers assigned to SRO duty (Reaves, 2010). School resource officers provide a visible presence that may deter misconduct, and they have full authority to enforce laws as well as school rules. They are expected to develop relationships with students, which will permit them to provide advice and guidance. These officers are positioned to help develop positive relationships between young people and police. In addition, they frequently give formal talks in classrooms to educate students about law and the criminal justice system (Finn, Shively, McDevitt, Lassiter, & Rich, 2005). The use of SROs represents a particularly important form of individualized special assignment because it shows in one specific setting how police officers' functions and duties extend well beyond the crime-fighting image that is commonly associated with law enforcement.

Traffic   Traffic regulation is a major job of the police in which they regulate the flow of vehicles, investigate accidents, and enforce traffic laws. This work may not seem to have much to do with crime fighting or order maintenance, but in fact it does. Besides helping to maintain order, enforcement of traffic laws educates

school resource officers (SROs) Police officers assigned for duty in schools to assist in order maintenance while also developing positive relationships with students that may assist in delinquency prevention.

the public by promoting safe driving habits and provides a visible service to the community.

Traffic work is mostly proactive and permits officers to use broad discretion about whom to stop and whether to issue a citation. Traffic duty can also help the police catch criminals because in enforcing traffic laws, patrol officers can stop cars and question drivers. Stolen property and suspects linked to other criminal acts are often found this way. Most departments can now automatically check license numbers against lists of wanted vehicles and suspects.

Vice Enforcement of vice laws depends on proactive police work, which often involves the use of undercover agents and informers. Most big-city police departments have a vice unit. Strict enforcement of these laws requires that officers be given wide discretion. They often must engage in degrading and dangerous activities, such as posing as prostitutes or drug dealers, in order to catch lawbreakers. The special nature of vice work requires members of the unit to be well trained in the legal procedures required for arrests to lead to convictions.

The potential for corruption in this type of police work presents some administrative problems. Undercover officers are in a position to blackmail gamblers and drug dealers, and they may also be offered bribes. In addition, officers working undercover must be transferred when their identities become known.

Drug Law Enforcement Many large cities have a bureau to enforce drug laws. These agencies may include task forces that deal with organized crime or with gangs involved in drug dealing. Some groups may use sting operations to arrest drug sellers on the street; still others may provide drug education in the community.

Drug enforcement sometimes reflects the goal of *aggressive patrol*, or assigning resources so as to get the largest number of arrests and to stop street dealing. Police executives believe that they must show dealers and the community that drug laws are actively enforced. Streets on which drugs are dealt openly can be flooded with officers who engage in proactive stops and questionings. There are risks, however, that drug dealers will simply move their operations to new locations.

Many public officials argue that drugs should be viewed as a public health problem rather than as a crime problem. Critics of current policies believe that society would benefit more from drug-treatment programs, which can help some people to stop using drugs, than from police actions that fill prisons without doing much to reduce drug use.

☑ CHECK POINT

11. What are the three parts of the patrol function?
Answering calls for assistance, maintaining a police presence, probing suspicious circumstances.

12. What are the four steps in the apprehension process?
(1) Detection of crime, (2) preliminary investigation, (3) follow-up investigation, (4) clearance and arrest.

13. What are three kinds of special operations units that police departments often employ?
Traffic, vice, narcotics.

STOP&ANALYZE

Think about the city or town where you live. Is there a need for a special operations unit in your police department? Why or why not? Give two reasons for your answer.

Issues in Patrolling

In the last 30 years, much research has been done on police methods of assigning tasks to patrol officers, deploying them, and communicating with them. Although the conclusions have been mixed, these studies have caused experts to rethink some aspects of patrolling. Read the "Evidence-Based Practice and Policy" feature to examine examples of current research findings concerning police patrol.

Policing and Patrol

Police administrators make decisions about how to deploy their personnel. They must decide where their officers will patrol, when and how often officers will move down specific streets and sidewalks, and what officers will do at particular locations. Early research called into question the usefulness of having officers randomly patrol a city and wait for calls from citizens about crimes or other problems. Instead, research pointed to the benefits of officers devoting their attention to specific locations, typically referred to as "hot spots," where crimes or related issues of disorder repeatedly occur. Because crime and disorder are not randomly or evenly distributed around a city or town, there are benefits from targeting attention and resources to those places where trouble is known to occur. Evidence indicates that reductions in crime can occur when patrols give emphasis to known hot spots within a community (Nagin & Weisburd, 2013).

In addition, research indicates that there are benefits from officers spending time at hot spots rather than just passing through the area. By spending 15 minutes at a hot spot, officers may create deterrent effects that lead potential lawbreakers to avoid the area or to be careful about their behavior. Moreover, there may be benefits from officers actively seeking to solve problems that they see in the vicinity of hot spots. This presents a merger of *problem-oriented policing (POP)* with a hot-spot focus of patrols. As a result, police may be able to identify physical vulnerabilities to crime for businesses or residences, interact with residents to learn their concerns, and speak to individuals whose behavior troubles other residents in a neighborhood.

Another form of police intervention that shows promising results in research involves direct interactions with offenders and potential offenders to provide clear communications about the consequences of criminal activity. For example, this may involve direct contact with gang members to let them know that they are being watched and that any use of guns or other illegal activities will be dealt with harshly in the criminal justice system.

These evidence-based patrol strategies are proactive in that they lead police officers to plan and carry out a set of activities at particular locations. As such, they differ from the traditional reactive approach to policing that long characterized standard procedures by waiting for and responding to calls from the public. In addition, the evidence-based approach can lead to the removal of regular patrols from neighborhoods that seldom experience problems. However, this may cause unhappiness among citizens who had previously felt reassured by the regular presence of police patrols in their neighborhoods. Because of these and other changes that occur when moving toward a focus on evidence-based policing, there can be resistance among officers and members of the public to embrace new police patrol practices that are guided by research findings.

Researching the Internet

To read about a former police chief's assessment of evidence-based policing, read his views in a National Institute of Justice publication at http://www.nij.gov/journals/269/evidence.htm.

Implementing New Practices

If you were a police chief, how would you incorporate newer research into your plans for patrolling neighborhoods? How would you persuade your officers to adopt new approaches with enthusiasm? How would you reassure citizens who experience a reduction of patrols in their neighborhoods? Write a memo giving three reasons for your position on these questions.

Sources: Anthony A. Braga, Andrew V. Papachristos, and David M. Hureau, "The Effects of Hot Spots Policing on Crime: An Updated Systematic Review and Meta-Analysis," *Justice Quarterly* (forthcoming, 2013); Cynthia Lum, Christopher S. Koper, and Cody W. Telep, "The Evidence-Based Policing Matrix," *Journal of Experimental Criminology* 7 (2011): 3–26; Cynthia Lum, Cody W. Telep, Christopher S. Koper, and Julie Grieco, "Receptivity to Research in Policing," *Justice Research and Policy* 14 (2012): 61–95; Bruce Taylor, Christopher S. Koper, and Daniel J. Woods, "A Randomized Controlled Trial of Different Policing Strategies at Hot Spots of Violent Crime," *Journal of Experimental Criminology* 7 (2011): 149–81; Cody W. Telep and David Weiburd, "What Is Known About the Effectiveness of Police Practices in Reducing Crime and Disorder?" *Police Quarterly* 15 (2012): 331–57.

However, even when researchers agree on which patrol practices are the most effective, those practices often run counter to the desires of departmental personnel (Lum, Telep, Koper, & Grieco, 2012). For example, foot patrol may be a key component of community-policing strategies, but many officers would rather remain in squad cars than walk the pavement. Police administrators, therefore, must deal with many issues to successfully develop and implement effective patrol strategies.

Assignment of Patrol Personnel

In the past, it has been assumed that patrol officers should be assigned where and when they will be most effective in preventing crime, keeping order, and serving the public. For the police administrator, the question has been "Where should the officers be sent, when, and in what numbers?" There are no guidelines to answer this question, and most assignments seem to be based on the notion that patrols should be concentrated in "problem" neighborhoods or in areas where crime rates and calls for service are high. Thus, the assignment of officers is based on factors such as crime statistics, 911 calls, degree of urbanization, pressures from business and community groups, ethnic composition, and socioeconomic conditions. Experimentation with different strategies in various cities has led to numerous choices for police leaders. In addition, research on these strategies sheds light on the strengths and weaknesses of various options. We shall examine several options in greater detail: (1) preventive patrol, (2) hot spots, (3) foot versus motorized patrol, (4) aggressive patrol, and (5) community policing.

Preventive Patrol

Preventive patrol has long been thought to help deter crime. Many have argued that a patrol officer's moving through an area will keep criminals from carrying out illegal acts. In 1974 this assumption was tested in Kansas City, Missouri. The surprising results shook the theoretical foundations of American policing (Sherman & Weisburd, 1995).

In the Kansas City Preventive Patrol Experiment, a 15-beat area was divided into three sections, each with similar crime rates, population characteristics, income levels, and numbers of calls to the police. In one area, labeled "reactive," all preventive patrol was withdrawn, and the police entered only in response to citizens' calls for service. In another section, labeled "proactive," preventive patrol was raised to as much as four times the normal level; all other services were provided at the same levels as before. The third section was used as a control, with the usual level of services, including preventive patrol, maintained. After observing events in the three sections for a year, the researchers concluded that the changes in patrol strategies had had no major effects on the amount of crime reported, the amount of crime as measured by citizen surveys, or citizens' fear of crime (Kelling, Pate, Dieckman, & Brown, 1974). Neither a decrease nor an increase in patrol activity had any apparent effect on crime.

Despite contradictory findings of other studies using similar research methods, the Kansas City finding "remains the most influential test of the general deterrent effects of patrol on crime" (Sherman & Weisburd, 1995:626). Because of this study, many departments have shifted their focus from law enforcement to maintaining order and serving the public. Some have argued that if the police cannot prevent crime by changing their patrol tactics, they may serve society better by focusing patrol activities on other functions while fighting crime as best they can.

Hot Spots

In the past, patrols were organized by "beats." It was assumed that crime can happen anywhere, and the entire beat must be patrolled at all times. Research shows, however, that crime is not spread evenly over all times and places. Instead, direct-contact predatory crimes such as muggings and robberies occur when three elements converge: motivated offenders, suitable targets, and the absence of anyone who could prevent the violation. This means that resources should be focused on *hot spots*, places where crimes are likely to occur. The deployment of personnel in this manner can prevent crimes from occurring.

Advocates of evidence-based policing argue that "place-based policing," such as focusing on hot spots, can prevent crime and also reduce arrests and costs of processing cases (Telep & Weisburd, 2012; Aden & Koper, 2011). According to David Weisburd, "If place-based policing were to become the central focus of police crime prevention, rather than arrest and apprehension of offenders, we would likely see at the same time a reduction in prison populations and an increase in crime prevention effectiveness of the police" (2011:16).

Administrators can assign officers to **directed patrol**—a proactive strategy designed to direct resources to known high-crime areas. Research indicates that directed-patrol activities focused on suspicious activities and locations can reduce violent gun crime (McGarrell, Chermak, Weiss, & Wilson, 2001). Observers fear,

directed patrol A proactive form of patrolling that directs resources to known high-crime areas.

however, that the extra police pressure may simply cause lawbreakers to move to another area (Goldkamp & Vilcica, 2008). But one study found that increased activity in areas adjacent to the hot spots targeted by police was likely attributable to citizens in those areas increasing their willingness to call the police when they knew that police were nearby and eager to address community problems. Thus, there may have been an increase in reported crimes, but no actual increase in crime (B. Taylor, Koper, & Woods, 2010).

Foot versus Motorized Patrol   One of the most frequent citizen requests is for officers to be put back on the beat. This was the main form of police patrol until the 1930s, when motorized patrol came to be viewed as more effective. Foot patrol and bicycle patrol are used in the majority of cities larger than 10,000 residents, including approximately 90 percent of cities with 50,000 or more inhabitants (Hickman & Reaves, 2006). However, departments typically use these strategies only in selected neighborhoods or districts with a high business or population density. Most patrolling is still conducted in cars. Cars increase the amount of territory that officers can patrol; plus, with advances in communications technologies and onboard computers, patrol officers have direct links to headquarters and to criminal information databases. Now the police can be quickly sent where needed, with crucial information in their possession.

In contrast to police in vehicles, officers on foot stay close to the daily life of the neighborhood. They detect criminal activity and apprehend lawbreakers more easily than do car patrols. In addition, recent research indicates that foot patrols can be effective in reducing criminal activities at crime hot spots in neighborhoods (Ratcliffe, Taniguchi, Groff, & Wood, 2011).

aggressive patrol A patrol strategy designed to maximize the number of police interventions and observations in the community.

Aggressive Patrol   **Aggressive patrol** is a proactive strategy designed to maximize police activity in the community. It takes many forms, such as "sting" operations, firearms confiscation, raids on crack houses, programs that encourage citizens to list their valuables, and the tracking of high-risk parolees. Some have argued that the effect of the police on crime depends less on how many officers are deployed in an area than on what they do while they are there.

The zero-tolerance policing of the 1990s in New York City is an example of aggressive patrol linked to the "broken windows" theory. As you will recall, this theory asserts "that if not firmly suppressed, disorderly behavior in public will frighten citizens and attract predatory criminals, thus leading to more serious crime problems" (Greene, 1999:172). Thus, the police should focus on minor public-order crimes such as aggressive panhandling, graffiti, prostitution, and urinating in public. By putting more police on the streets, decentralizing authority to the precinct level, and instituting officer accountability, the zero-tolerance policy was claimed to be a factor in reducing New York City's crime rate (Messner, Galea, Tardiff, & Tracy, 2007; Rosenfeld, Fornango, & Rengifo, 2007). However, the surge in police stop-and-frisk searches on New York City's streets in the early twenty-first century led to widespread complaints, a major lawsuit, and findings from a federal judge that police tactics were overly intrusive and discriminatory (J. Goldstein, 2013; A Baker, 2008).

Aggressive policing has also been applied as part of the war on drugs, with police officers stopping many vehicles and frisking pedestrians on certain streets. In Detroit aggressive zero-tolerance police practices reduced gang-related crime in targeted precincts (Bynum & Varano, 2002). Police departments also use aggressive patrol strategies to track high-risk parolees and apprehend them if they commit new offenses.

Research now raises questions about whether the "broken windows" approach actually reduces crime. Several studies present new analyses of data that challenge claims that aggressive policing is what caused crime reduction during the 1990s (Harcourt & Ludwig, 2006). Moreover, the "broken windows" approach might actually lead to citizen hostility. In some urban neighborhoods, there are rumblings that aggressive patrol has gone too far and is straining police relations with young African Americans and Hispanics.

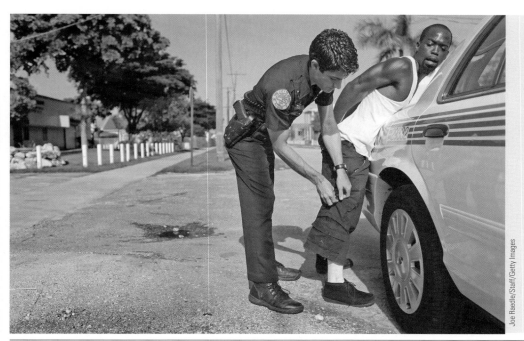

Many police chiefs credit aggressive take-back-the-streets tactics with reducing urban crime rates in the past two decades. In some cities, however, there are questions about whether such tactics have harmed police–community relations through searches and arrests that neighborhood residents view as unjustified. If you were a police chief, what patrol strategy would you choose and what specific goals would you seek to advance?

Joe Raedle/Staff/Getty Images

Community Policing   To a great extent, community policing has been seen as the solution to problems with the crime fighter stance that prevailed during the professional model era (P. V. Murphy, 1992). Community policing consists of attempts by the police to involve residents in making their own neighborhoods safer. Based on the belief that citizens are often concerned about local disorder as well as crime in general, this strategy emphasizes cooperation between the police and citizens in identifying community needs and determining the best ways to meet them (Reisig, 2010; M. Moore, 1992).

Community policing has four components (Skolnick & Bayley, 1986):

1. Focusing on community-based crime prevention
2. Changing the focus of patrol activities to nonemergency services
3. Making the police more accountable to the public
4. Decentralizing decision making to include residents

As indicated by these four components, community policing requires a major shift in the philosophy of policing. In particular, police officials must view citizens both as customers to be served and as partners in the pursuit of social goals, rather than as a population to be watched, controlled, and served reactively (Morash, Ford, White, & Boles, 2002). Although crime control may remain a priority in community policing, the change in emphasis can strengthen police effectiveness for order maintenance and service (Zhao, He, Loverich, & Cancino, 2003).

Departments that view themselves as emphasizing community policing do not necessarily share identical patrol strategies and initiatives (Thurman, Zhao, & Giacomazzi, 2001). Some departments emphasize identifying and solving problems related to disorder and crime. Other departments work mainly on strengthening local neighborhoods. A department's emphasis can affect which activities become the focus of officers' working hours. The common element in community-policing programs is a high level of interaction between officers and citizens and the involvement of citizens in identifying problems and solving them.

A central feature of community policing for many departments is **problem-oriented policing**, a strategy that seeks to find out what is causing citizens to call for help (Weisburd, Telep, Hinkle, & Eck, 2010; Goldstein, 1990). The police seek to identify, analyze, and respond to the conditions underlying the events that prompt people to call the police (Maguire, Uchida, & Hassell, 2012; Cordner & Biebel, 2005;

problem-oriented policing
An approach to policing in which officers routinely seek to identify, analyze, and respond to the circumstances underlying the incidents that prompt citizens to call the police.

DeJong, Mastrofski, & Parks, 2001). Knowing those conditions, officers can enlist community agencies and residents to help resolve them. Recent research indicates that problem-solving approaches can impact various crimes, including drug sales and homicides (Corsaro, Brunson, & McGarrell, 2012; Chermak & McGarrell, 2004). Police using this approach do not just fight crime (M. D. White, Fyfe, Campbell, & Goldkamp, 2003); they address a broad array of other problems that affect the quality of life in the community.

The Future of Patrol

Preventive patrol and reactive response to calls for help have been the hallmarks of policing in the United States for the past half century. However, research done in the past 30 years has raised many questions about which patrol strategies police should employ. For example, the rise of community policing has shifted law enforcement toward problems that affect residents' quality of life. For another example, the continuing development of evidence-based policing is producing greater attention to place-based strategies such as hot spots. Police forces need to use patrol tactics that fit the needs of the neighborhood. Neighborhoods with crime hot spots may require different strategies than do neighborhoods where residents are concerned mainly with order maintenance. Many researchers believe that traditional patrol efforts have focused too narrowly on crime control, neglecting the order maintenance and service activities for which police departments were originally formed. Critics have urged the police to become more community oriented.

The current era of budget cuts and reductions in police-force personnel will constrict many police chiefs' flexibility in their use of officers. It remains to be seen whether financial problems will reduce various forms of patrol or if they will push departments, by necessity, toward either a purely reactive or hot-spot emphasis. Some cities already face the worst-case scenario of having every patrol shift reduced to so few officers that they are unable to respond to all calls about felonies (LeDuff, 2011).

How the national effort to combat terrorism will affect local police patrol operations remains uncertain. Since the attacks of September 11, state and local police have assumed greater responsibility for investigating bank robberies and other federal crimes as the FBI and other federal agencies devote significant attention to catching people connected with terrorist organizations (Giblin, Burruss, & Schafer, 2014). In addition, even local police officers must be ready to spot suspicious activities that might relate to terrorist activity. They are the first responders in a bombing or other form of attack. Obviously, federal law enforcement officials must work closely with local police in order to be effective. The new concerns will not alter traditional police responsibilities for crime fighting, order maintenance, and service, but they will provide an additional consideration as police administrators plan how to train and deploy their personnel.

☑ CHECK POINT

14. What are the advantages of foot patrol? Of motorized patrol?
Officers on foot patrol have greater contact with residents of a neighborhood, thus gaining their confidence and assistance. Officers on motorized patrol have a greater range of activity and can respond speedily to calls.

15. What is aggressive patrol?
Aggressive patrol is a proactive strategy designed to maximize the number of police interventions and observations in a community.

16. What are the major elements of community policing?
Community policing emphasizes order maintenance and service. It attempts to involve members of the community in making their neighborhoods safe. Foot patrol and decentralization of command are usually part of community-policing efforts.

STOP&ANALYZE

If you were a police chief, what approaches to patrol would you choose to implement? Give three reasons for your answer.

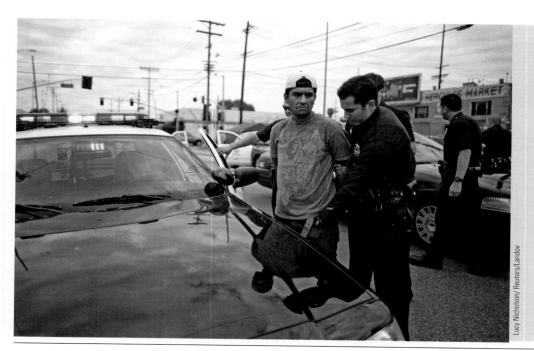

In multicultural America, police must be sensitive to the perspectives and customs of many different groups. They must enforce the law while treating people equally and upholding civil liberties. These responsibilities can be difficult when people are angry or uncooperative. Have you heard about situations in which police officers' emotions, such as anger or frustration, affected their decisions or behavior?

Police and Community

The work of a police officer in a U.S. city can be very difficult, involving hours of boring, routine work interrupted by short spurts of dangerous crime fighting. Although police work has always been frustrating and dangerous, officers today must deal with situations ranging from helping the homeless to dealing with domestic violence to confronting shootouts at drug deals gone sour. Policing actions are sometimes mishandled by officers or misinterpreted by the public, making some people critical of the police in general.

Special Populations

Urban police forces must deal with a complex population. City streets contain growing numbers of people suffering from mental illness, homelessness, alcoholism, drug addiction, or serious medical conditions such as acquired immune deficiency syndrome (AIDS) (Reuland, 2010; Hails & Borum, 2003). In addition, they may find youthful runaways and children victimized by their parents' neglect. Several factors have contributed to increasing numbers of "problem" people on the streets. These factors include overcrowded jails; cutbacks in public assistance; and the closing of many psychiatric institutions, which must then release mental health patients into society. Most of these individuals do not commit crimes, but their presence disturbs many of their fellow citizens and thus may contribute to fear of crime and disorder (T. Coleman & Cotton, 2010).

Patrol officers cooperate with social service agencies in helping individuals and responding to requests for order maintenance. Police departments have developed various techniques for dealing with special populations, such as the use of *Crisis Intervention Teams (CIT)* in conjunction with social service agencies (Morgan, 2013; Frantz & Borum, 2011). In some cities, mobile units are equipped with restraining devices and medical equipment to handle disturbed people.

Clearly, dealing with special populations is a major problem for police in most cities. Each community must develop policies so that officers will know when and how they are to intervene when a person may not have broken the law but is upsetting residents. Inevitably, police officers will make mistakes in some situations.

Living under Suspicion

One of the most invasive discretionary decisions made by police officers is the determination of when to do a warrantless search. As we will see in Chapter 6, there are specific situations in which police officers are authorized to search people and places without seeking approval from a judge in the form of a search warrant. One key situation that interferes with people's privacy and liberty is a stop-and-frisk search. This does not mean that officers are supposed to have complete discretion to simply feel the outer clothing of anyone walking down the street to see if the individual is carrying a weapon, drugs, or evidence of criminal activity. Indeed, the original Supreme Court decision in *Terry v. Ohio* (1968) was quite specific about the circumstances in which such searches could be done on the spot so as to avoid giving police officers complete freedom to do searches based on hunches or other unjustified grounds. According to the *Terry* decision, "where a police officer observes unusual conduct which leads him to reasonably conclude in light of his experience that criminal activity may be afoot and that the persons with whom he is dealing may be armed and presently dangerous," the officer may stop the individual and conduct a limited search of the outer clothing. Unfortunately, studies in a number of cities indicate that some officers may be more inclined to conclude that "criminal activity may be afoot" when they see African Americans or Latinos, while less likely to reach that conclusion when seeing whites engaging in the same behaviors.

A review of New York City police records showed that its officers conducted 575,000 stop-and-frisk searches in 2009. Whites constitute the largest racial group in the city, more than 40 percent of the city's population in the first decade of the twenty-first century, yet the number of African Americans and Latinos subjected to stop-and-frisk searches was many times more than the number of whites subjected to such searches. During 2009 there were nearly 490,000 stop-and-frisk

searches of African Americans and Latinos and only 53,000 stop-and-frisk searches of whites. Yet, whites were more likely to be found illegally carrying weapons—1.7 percent of whites versus only 1.1 percent of African Americans. Such findings raise concerns that officers are more likely to look for actual indications of potential criminal behavior before searching whites but more freely search African Americans and Latinos without the proper basis articulated in the original *Terry v. Ohio* decision. A sophisticated statistical analysis of New York City stop-and-frisk searches from the late 1990s concluded that "police were more willing to stop minority group members with less reason" (Gelman, Fagan, & Kiss, 2007:821).

Questions about racially motivated stop-and-frisk searches intensified as the number of stops in New York City increased to 685,724 in 2011 and 88 percent of those people were found to be completely innocent. A white *New York Times* reporter asked his college-age sons if they had ever been stopped by the police as they traveled all over New York City by subway and foot to visit their friends and attend social events. They both said "no." He posed the same question to eight African American students at the city's central community college, and he learned that they had been stopped and frisked collectively a total of 92 times. These disparities led to a lawsuit against the city in 2013 in which police officers testified about being instructed to stop young black males.

Indicators of racial differences in the rate of discretionary stops and searches by police officers are not limited to large cities. For example, a 2011 study of the Lansing, Michigan, police department found that although Latinos make up only 10 percent of the city's population, they were subjected to 33 percent of the discretionary searches conducted by officers in conjunction with traffic stops. A study in Kansas City found that African American drivers were five times more likely than white drivers to be searched when stopped by the police.

For instance, their interactions with troubled people sometimes lead to tragic consequences, such as using lethal force against deaf or mentally ill people whose actions are misperceived as threatening (Romney, 2012; Hubert, 2010). In 2003 a controversy erupted in Denver after police shot a legally blind, mentally handicapped teenager who was holding a knife (Felch, 2003).

Policing in a Multicultural Society

In the last half century, the racial and ethnic composition of the United States has changed. During the mid-twentieth century, many African Americans moved from rural areas of the South to northern cities. In recent years, immigrants from Central and South America have become the fastest-growing minority group in many cities. Latinos are now the largest minority population in the nation. Immigrants from Eastern Europe, Russia, the Middle East, and Asia have entered the country in greater numbers than before.

Policing requires trust, understanding, and cooperation between officers and the public. People must be willing to call for help and provide information

What do these racial disparities mean for Americans who are members of racial and ethnic minority groups? Can minority citizens avoid feeling as if they are constantly under suspicion if they see, through their own experiences or the experiences of friends and relatives, that they are much more likely than white Americans to be stopped and searched by the police?

In 2007 New York City's number of stop-and-frisk searches of African Americans was equal to more than 21 percent of the African American population of the city. By contrast, the number of such searches directed at whites was equal to less than 3 percent of the white population. How might such figures—and the thousands of experiences that they represent—affect people's views about the police? Are there risks that discretionary decisions that lead to racial disparities will ultimately harm policing by making people distrustful and unwilling to help the police?

While these disparities in the application of police discretion are cause for concern, there is also visible progress toward fair and appropriate treatment. Like many other departments, the Lansing police department pays outside researchers to study their traffic stops and searches each year because the department wants to be educated about its officers' actions in order to conduct additional training and improve supervision, if necessary. In 2010 the Arizona state legislature sought to require officers to ask people about their immigration status. The law raised fears that it would push officers to engage in racial profiling, especially with respect to Latinos. Although the law was put on hold by a court order, police departments moved forward with additional training for their officers about the proper bases for searches and about avoiding accusations of racial profiling. Some observers believe that the additional training is helping to reduce bias and errors in officers' decisions about when a stop is legally justified.

Researching the Internet

Read Bryonn Bain's provocative article "Walking While Black: The Bill of Rights for Black Men." As you read, you will understand his angry tone and use of offensive language. Bain, an African American man and former class president at Columbia University, was arrested and jailed as a second-year student at Harvard Law School as he walked down the sidewalk in New York City and was carelessly misidentified as being responsible for a minor crime. See the article at http://www.villagevoice.com/2000-04-25/news/walking-while-black/.

For Critical Analysis

Are racial and ethnic disparities in the number of stop-and-frisk searches a cause for concern, or is there no real reason to be bothered because the rate of arrests for whites from such searches is actually higher than that for African Americans and Latinos—at least in New York City? Should we worry about a brief frisk of the external clothing when such actions may help to reduce crime by deterring criminals from carrying guns and giving us greater ability to catch terrorists and other dangerous individuals? List two arguments supporting the position that this is a small intrusion that helps to make society safer. List two opposing arguments that portray these disparities as a matter of serious concern. Where do you stand?

Sources: Al Baker, "Minorities Frisked More but Arrested at Same Rate," *New York Times*, May 12, 2010 (www.nytimes.com); Charles Epp and Steven Maynard-Moody, "Driving While Black," *Washington Monthly*, January/February 2014 (www.washingtonmonthly.com); Andrew Gelman, Jeffrey Fagan, and Alex Kiss, "An Analysis of the New York City Police Department's 'Stop-and-Frisk' Policy in the Context of Claims of Racial Bias," *Journal of the American Statistical Association*, 102:813–23 (2007); Joseph Goldstein, "Stop-and-Frisk Trial Turns to Claim of Arrest Quotas," *New York Times*, March 20, 2013 (www.nytimes.com); Kevin Grasha, "Reported Finds LPD Searched Minorities' Cars More Than Whites," *Lansing State Journal*, May 5, 2011 (www.lsj.com); J. J. Hensley, "Arizona Immigration Law: Police Profiling Training Paid Off, Some Say," *Arizona Republic*, April 23, 2011 (www.azcentral.com); Michael Powell, "Former Skeptic Now Embraces Divisive Tactic," *New York Times*, April 9, 2012 (www.nytimes.com).

about wrongdoing. But in a multicultural society, relations between the police and minorities are complicated by stereotypes, cultural variations, and language differences. Most of these immigrants come from countries with cultural traditions and laws that differ from those in the United States. These traditions may be unfamiliar to American police officers. Further, some immigrants cannot communicate easily in English. Lack of familiarity, difficulties in communicating, and excessive suspicion can increase the risk that officers will violate the American principle of equal treatment of all people (C. E. Smith, McCall, Perez, & McCluskey, 2005).

Like other Americans who have limited personal experience or familiarity with people from different backgrounds, officers may attribute undesirable traits to members of minority groups (Miller, Zielaskowski, & Plant, 2012). Treating people according to stereotypes, rather than as individuals, creates tensions that harden negative attitudes. As you read the Close Up feature, consider how officers' decisions to intrude upon people's liberty by stopping and searching them may affect attitudes toward the police.

Public opinion surveys have shown that race and ethnicity play a key role in determining people's attitudes toward the police. As seen in the "What Americans

QUESTION: "Just your impression, are African Americans in your community treated less fairly than whites in the following situations? How about in dealing with the police, such as traffic incidents?"

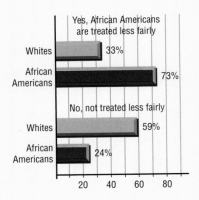

CRITICAL THINKING: Can individual police officers take actions that will improve the perceptions and relationship between police and residents in a community? If so, what can officers do?

Based on Gallup Poll, June 2–24, 2007 (http://www.gallup.com).

Think" feature, questions of fair treatment by the police differ among racial groups (Stewart, Baumer, Brunson, & Simons, 2009; Gabbidon & Higgins, 2009). Young, low-income, racial-minority men carry the most negative attitudes toward the police (Gabbidon, Higgins, & Potter, 2011; S. Walker, Spohn, & DeLeone, 2011). Inner-city neighborhoods—the areas that need and want effective policing—often significantly distrust the police; citizens may therefore fail to report crimes and refuse to cooperate with the police (Carr, Napolitano, & Keating, 2007). Encounters between officers and members of these communities are often hostile and sometimes lead to large-scale disorders. In January 2008, hundreds of protestors marched in Lima, Ohio, to express their outrage that police officers, when entering a home to look for a male drug suspect, had shot and killed a young African American woman and wounded her toddler. Twenty-seven percent of Lima's 38,000 residents are African American, yet only two of the city's 77 police officers are African American (Maag, 2008). All aspects of officers' responsibilities, including service, order maintenance, and crime control, can suffer when police officers and the communities they serve lack cooperation and trust.

Why do some residents in predominantly minority neighborhoods resent the police? One likely factor is the differential treatment of Americans by police officers that leads Hispanics and African Americans to be disproportionately chosen for searches and other unwanted encounters with police (Rojek, Rosenfeld, & Decker, 2012). Many African Americans perceive themselves as targeted for suspicion when they are engaging in routine activities such as driving their cars or shopping. One recent study found that African American drivers were three times more likely than whites to be subject to investigatory traffic stops that were not based on actual traffic violations and five times more likely than whites to be searched in such stops. Such treatment led 64 percent of African Americans in the study but only 23 percent of the whites to say that you cannot always trust the police to do the right thing (Epp & Maynard-Moody, 2014). If both police and citizens view each other with suspicion or hostility, then their encounters will be strained and the potential for conflict will increase.

Community Crime Prevention

There is a growing awareness that the police cannot control crime and disorder on their own. Social control requires involvement by all members of the community. **Community crime prevention** can be enhanced if government agencies and neighborhood organizations cooperate. Across the country, community programs to help the police have proliferated (Wehrman & DeAngelis, 2011; Arthur et al., 2010; Zhao, Gibson, Lovrich, & Gaffney, 2002). The federal government has funded and facilitated intergovernmental cooperation and citizen involvement through a variety of programs, including Project Safe Neighborhoods, an anticrime program with a significant focus on anti-gang efforts and the reduction in illegal firearms.

More than 6 million Americans belong to citizen crime-watch groups, which often have direct ties to police departments. Many communities also use the Crime Stoppers Program to enlist public help in solving crimes. Television and radio stations present the "unsolved crime of the week," sometimes with cash rewards given

community crime prevention Programs through which criminal justice officials cultivate relationships with and rely on assistance from citizens in preventing crime and apprehending offenders within neighborhoods.

for information that leads to the conviction of the offender. Although these programs help solve some crimes, the number solved remains small compared with the total number of crimes committed.

Homeland Security

The aftermath of 9/11 has brought expansion, redirection, and reorganization among law enforcement agencies, especially those at the federal level. For instance, the emphasis on counterterrorism has led to an increase in intelligence analysts in the FBI, from 1,023 holding that position in September 2001 to more than 3,118 in September 2011. Over that same time period, the number of FBI special agents assigned to national security duties increased from 2,514 to 4,815 (Mueller, 2011b). The creation of the Department of Homeland Security, the reordering of crime control policies away from street crime and drugs to international and domestic terrorism, and the great increase in federal money directed against the war against terrorism are greatly affecting law enforcement at all levels of government.

This new thrust in policy has shifted the focus of the FBI from the investigation of local street crimes to cases of international and domestic terrorism. Former FBI Director Robert Mueller has acknowledged that following 9/11 many criminal investigations had to be set aside as many agents directed their attention toward al-Qaeda and related threats. Further, the bureau has come to rely on state and local law enforcement to fill the gaps that the FBI could not respond to, such as bank robberies, which are crimes under both federal and state laws.

To meet the challenges of terrorist threats and the increasingly international nature of criminal organizations, U.S. agencies have dramatically boosted the number of officers stationed in foreign countries. The FBI has 70 overseas offices known as Legal Attaches or Legats. These offices focus on coordination with law enforcement personnel in other countries. Their activities are limited by the formal agreements negotiated between the United States and each host country. In many other countries, American agents are authorized only to gather information and facilitate communications between countries. American agencies are especially active in working with other countries on counterterrorism, drug trafficking, and cyber crime (Mueller, 2011b).

Another vehicle for international antiterrorist and anticrime efforts is **Interpol**— the International Criminal Police Organization—created in 1946 to foster cooperation among the world's police forces. Based today in Lyon, France, Interpol maintains an intelligence database and serves as a clearinghouse for information gathered by agencies of its 186 member nations, including the United States. Interpol's six priority crime areas are (1) drugs and criminal organizations, (2) public safety and terrorism, (3) financial and high-tech crime, (4) trafficking in human beings, (5) fugitive apprehension, and (6) corruption (http://www.interpol.int).

Interpol The International Criminal Police Organization formed in 1946 and based in France with the mission of facilitating international cooperation in investigating transnational criminal activities and security threats.

Preparing for Threats

The events of September 11 altered the priorities of government agencies and pushed law enforcement agencies at the federal, state, and local levels to make plans for the possibility of future significant threats to homeland security. The FBI and DHS make concerted efforts to identify and combat risks in order to reduce the threat of additional attacks. The FBI switched a significant portion of its personnel away from traditional crime control activities in order to gather intelligence on people within the United States who may pose a threat to the nation. At the same time, the creation of the DHS reflected a desire to have better coordination between agencies that were previously scattered through the federal government. The DHS also instituted new security procedures at airports and borders as a means of identifying individuals and contraband that pose threats. Many critics believe that the federal government has not done enough to protect ports and critical infrastructure, including nuclear power plants, information systems, subway systems, and other elements essential for the functioning of U.S. society. Attacks with devastating consequences could range from computer hackers disabling key military information systems or computerized controls at energy companies to a suicide airline hijacker hitting a nuclear power or chemical plant. If an attack should target and disable any of these entities, it would fall to local police to maintain order and rescue victims.

Security at borders is an important component of homeland security. **U.S. Border Patrol** agents do not merely look for illegal immigrants and drug traffickers; they must also be aware that terrorists might try to sneak across the border, bringing with them weapons, explosives, and other dangerous materials.

Police agencies have traditionally gathered **law enforcement intelligence** about criminal activities and organizations, especially in their efforts to monitor motorcycle gangs, hate groups, drug traffickers, and organized crime. The new emphasis on homeland security broadens the scope of information that agencies need to gather (Kris, 2011). According to Jonathan White (2004), police must be trained to look for and gather information about such things as

- Emergence of radical groups, including religious groups
- Suspicious subjects observing infrastructure facilities
- Growth of phony charities that may steer money to terrorists

U.S. Border Patrol Federal law enforcement agency with responsibility for border security by patrolling national land borders and coastal waters to prevent smuggling, drug trafficking, and illegal entry, including entry by potential terrorists.

law enforcement intelligence Information, collected and analyzed by law enforcement officials, concerning criminal activities and organizations such as gangs, drug traffickers, and organized crime.

Police officers throughout the nation have increased their training in emergency response procedures in light of threats concerning terrorism and homeland security. In an environment of shrinking budgets, do local police have the time and resources to effectively add homeland security responsibilities to their traditional duties of law enforcement, service, and order maintenance?

Kevin Steele/Aurora/Getty Images

CAREERS IN CRIMINAL JUSTICE

Intelligence Analyst

Erin Goff, Intelligence Analyst, Ohio Department of Public Safety, Division of Homeland Security

Assigned duties for intelligence analysts vary according to the specific mission of the federal or state agency in which they work. Intelligence analysts collect and analyze information about financial transactions, communication patterns, informants' tips, individuals' and organizations' actions, and other activities that might reveal threats to public safety. By continuously sifting through available information, they produce intelligence products such as reports, statistical analyses, and suspicious-activities notices concerning potential criminal events and threats to homeland security. They also conduct specific research projects; present briefings to law enforcement and other officials; and write reports and other materials that can be used to warn, inform, and train officials.

Qualifications for the position vary according to an agency's specific needs. In general, candidates need experience and skill in research and writing. Critical-thinking skills are especially important, as is the ability to communicate effectively, both orally and in writing. Intelligence analysts must also have an understanding of the criminal justice system and the functions and relationships of various agencies in all levels of governments.

Photo provided by Erin Goff

Because training and experience in such areas as research, computers, intelligence software programs, and statistics can be important, intelligence analysts typically are college graduates who have studied criminal justice and other relevant subjects.

In preparing for her career as an intelligence analyst, Erin Goff earned both undergraduate and graduate degrees in criminal justice. In addition, she gained experience in the field as a graduate student by working on federally funded projects through which university professors and other experts provided training for police departments concerning homeland security issues.

The biggest challenge I face on a daily basis is the constantly changing picture of terrorism. There are always new threat streams using tactics we've never seen, and we are forced to adapt our information analysis. As with other areas of criminal justice, it is essential to stay one step ahead, so I regularly seek additional education to enhance my formal knowledge. In addition, I continuously discuss emerging information and issues with other intelligence analysts.

- Groups with links to foreign countries
- Unexpected terrorist information found during criminal searches
- Discovery of bomb-making operations

Local police agencies need training that focuses on what to look for and whom to contact if any suspicious activities or materials are discovered. One effort to share information emerged in the form of **fusion centers** (Perrine, Speirs, & Horwitz, 2010). These are state and local intelligence operations that use law enforcement analysts and sophisticated computer systems to compile and analyze clues and then pass along refined information to various agencies (O'Harrow, 2008). The federal government has provided nearly $250 million for the development and operation of these centers. Read about the job of an Intelligence Analyst in "Careers in Criminal Justice," the growing occupational category that describes the professionals who are central to the operation of fusion centers.

The emphasis on information analysis and coordination among agencies at all levels of U.S. government, as well as coordination with foreign governments, also impacts law enforcement operations concerning other major problems, such as drug trafficking, money laundering, gun smuggling, and border security. For example, homeland security efforts overlap with initiatives to combat transnational street gangs. In one such case, the MS-13 gang from Central America has spread from Los Angeles to such places as Washington, D.C., and Charlotte, North Carolina, bringing with it various criminal activities, including a series of gang-related homicides (Lineberger, 2011).

Within local police departments, the emphasis on homeland security has led to changes in training, equipment, and operations to prepare first responders

fusion centers Centers run by states and large cities that analyze and facilitate sharing of information to assist law enforcement and homeland security agencies in preventing and responding to crime and terrorism threats.

to deal with the possibility of weapons of mass destruction and terrorist attacks (Magda, Canton, & Gershon, 2010). The police must also develop regional coordination with neighboring communities and state governments, because large-scale emergencies require the resources and assistance of multiple agencies. Communities need plans for conducting evacuations of buildings and neighborhoods. Police officials must work more closely with firefighters, public health officials, and emergency medical services to prepare for anything from a bomb to a bioterrorist attack using anthrax, smallpox, or other harmful agents. Some of these threats require the acquisition of new equipment, such as protective suits for suspected biological or chemical hazards, or communications equipment that can be used to contact multiple agencies. Many police departments are giving renewed attention to training specialized teams, such as bomb squads and SWAT teams, that will intervene in emergency situations. In addition, they must give all officers additional training on coordination with outside agencies, evacuation procedures for malls and hospitals, and containment of hazardous materials (Perin, 2009).

☑**CHECK POINT**

20. **What have law enforcement officials done to enhance the protection of homeland security?**
Planning and coordinating with other agencies, gathering intelligence, acquiring new equipment, and providing training.

STOP&ANALYZE

In light of the budget cuts affecting state and local government, imagine that you are a governor who must recommend choices about how to allocate shrinking resources. If faced with the following choices—reduce money for homeland security and law enforcement intelligence, reduce money for state police patrols and criminal investigation, or raise taxes—which would you choose and why? Give three reasons for your answer.

New Laws and Controversies

The hijackers' devastating attacks on September 11, 2001, spurred a variety of government actions intended to protect homeland security and combat terrorism. The Bush administration asserted new presidential powers to arrest and detain indefinitely without trial Americans whom it accused of terrorist activities. In 2004, however, the U.S. Supreme Court ruled that the president does not possess unlimited authority and that American detainees are entitled to challenge their confinement through court procedures (*Hamdi v. Rumsfeld*, 2004). The Supreme Court's decision illustrates one aspect of the challenge facing the United States: how to provide government with sufficient power to fight terrorism while also protecting individuals' constitutional rights.

In 2011 the National Defense Authorization Act, which provides annual funding for the military, included provisions permitting terrorism suspects to be arrested and detained indefinitely and permitting the military to detain and question terrorism suspects on American soil. These provisions generated harsh criticism from civil libertarians who feared the expansion of governmental powers and the potential for Americans to be denied their rights. However, members of Congress claimed that the wording was carefully designed to balance individuals' rights with national security. President Obama expressed misgivings about the language but signed the bill into law in December 2011 (Klain, 2012; Nakamura, 2012).

Other controversies arose concerning new state and federal statutes created after September 11. Both Congress and state legislatures enacted new laws aimed at addressing various aspects of homeland security. More than 30 states added new terrorism-related laws. These laws ranged from narrow to broad—from statutes addressing specific problems to authorizations of new powers for law enforcement officials and the definition of new crimes. At the narrow end of the spectrum, for example, Virginia passed a law to make it more difficult for foreign nationals to obtain a driver's license without possession of specific legal documents. This was in direct response to the discovery that several of the September 11 hijackers had obtained Virginia driver's licenses.

Because new laws provide tools for justice system officials, controversies can arise when those officials apparently stretch their authority beyond the intentions of the relevant statutes. For example, prosecutors in several cases have used new terrorism laws as a means to prosecute people for criminal acts that are not commonly understood to be related to terrorism. Thus, in New York, one of the first prosecutions under the state's antiterrorism laws enacted after September 11 arose when the Bronx district attorney charged street gang members for various crimes. There was no allegation that the gang members had connections to any foreign terrorist networks. Instead, the prosecutor used the state's antiterrorism law to charge gang members with shootings committed with the intent to intimidate or coerce a civilian population (Garcia, 2005). In another example, a North Carolina prosecutor charged the operator of a small meth lab under a terrorism statute for manufacturing a nuclear or chemical weapon ("Charging Common Criminals," 2003). In 2014 a Michigan man who was diagnosed by psychiatrists with a delusional disorder was sentenced to fewer than 10 years on felonious assault charges for driving down the highway firing a gun at other cars. However, he received a sentence of 16 to 40 years for terrorism charges pursued by prosecutors for these actions (Abdilla & Kranz, 2014). These cases generated criticism in newspaper editorials and raised concerns that government officials would exploit terrorism laws for improper purposes.

The most controversial legislation came from Congress in the form of the "Uniting and Strengthening America by Providing Appropriate Tools Required to Intercept and Obstruct Terrorism Act." It is best known by its shorthand name, the **USA PATRIOT Act**. The PATRIOT Act moved quickly through Congress after the September 11 attacks and covered a wide range of topics, including the expansion of government authority for searches and surveillance and the expansion of definitions and penalties for crimes related to terrorism.

Critics have raised concerns about many provisions because of fears that the government's assertions of excessive power will violate individuals' rights (Ahmadi, 2011; Lichtblau, 2008; Dority, 2005). The PATRIOT Act makes it easier for law enforcement officials to monitor email and obtain "sneak-and-peek" warrants in which they secretly conduct searches and do not inform the home or business owner that the premises have been searched until much later (K. M. Sullivan, 2003). The PATRIOT Act also authorizes warrantless searches of third-party records such as those at libraries, financial institutions, phone companies, and medical facilities. This provision has sparked an outcry from librarians and booksellers and was cited by many of the 150 communities across the country that passed resolutions protesting the excessive authority granted to government by the Act (J. Gordon, 2005). Despite the outcry, Congress approved an extension of the PATRIOT Act's key provisions in 2011 (Mascaro, 2011).

The PATRIOT Act defines domestic terrorism as criminal acts dangerous to human life that appear intended to intimidate civilians or influence public policy by intimidation. It also makes it a crime to provide material support for terrorism. Conservatives fear the law could be used against antiabortion protestors who block entrances at abortion clinics as well as their financial supporters. Liberals fear that it could be used against environmental activists and their financial supporters (Zerwas, 2011; Lithwick & Turner, 2003).

In 2013 new controversies arose when Edward Snowden, whom some view as a traitor and others view as a heroic whistleblower, revealed that the National Security Agency collected phone call information on virtually all Americans as well as calls involving foreign governments. One federal judge ruled that the agency's actions likely violated the U.S. Constitution. Yet, even this judge acknowledged

USA PATRIOT Act A federal statute passed in the aftermath of the terrorist attacks of September 11, 2001, that broadens government authority to conduct searches and wiretaps and expands the definitions of crimes involving terrorism.

Should Law Enforcement Agencies Use Drones within the United States?

Unmanned aircraft called "drones" were developed for use by the military. They can carry cameras to follow and record the movement of enemy forces or to spy on areas that are too dangerous to view from helicopters or planes. In addition, drones can carry missiles and be used to kill enemies by remote command. The Obama administration has drawn sharp criticism for using drones overseas to eliminate suspected terrorists, including Americans. Drone strikes in such places as Pakistan and Yemen are alleged to have killed people other than the intended targets. Moreover, there are questions about the proof that should be required before someone is assassinated by drone.

In 2011 the first use of a drone by local American law enforcement officials occurred in North Dakota. Drones had already been used for specific investigations by federal agencies such as the FBI and the Drug Enforcement Administration. A North Dakota county sheriff who was chased off a ranch by armed men asked for assistance from drones stationed at a nearby Air Force base. U.S. Customs and Border Protection had begun using drones in 2005 to monitor the North Dakota–Canada border to prevent illegal immigrants and smuggling. An unarmed drone flew over the ranch and helped local officials determine when the men had set down their guns so that they could be arrested by sheriff's deputies. These and other limited missions in support of local law enforcement were done without detailed consideration of important legal and ethical questions. For example, does the use of drones operated by military officers violate the legal and traditional limitations on activity within the United States by American armed forces? Does the use of drones threaten the privacy of individuals since a drone can fly over a house or business for many hours while

transmitting high-quality photos and video to those monitoring the activity on computer screens?

By 2013 two developments contributed to major debates about the use of drones. First, the price of drones decreased and their availability from manufacturers increased so that it became possible for police departments to acquire these devices. A small drone can cost as little as $3,000. Thus, businesses and non–law enforcement government agencies also sought to use drones to inspect pipelines and monitor highway traffic. Second, there were intensified debates about the use of drones to kill suspected terrorists and the fear that the federal government might claim the authority to make such assassination strikes within the United States. Eventually, the Obama administration provided reassurances about not using drones for lethal domestic missions, yet controversy remained about the legality, ethics, and effects of raining death from the sky.

In response to the growing debates, states and cities began to take action to define and limit the possibilities for the use of drones within the United States. No one denied that drones would be useful for such uses as ensuring port security, conducting search and rescue, and finding missing persons. However, there were grave concerns about privacy and other aspects of overhead surveillance. For example, Virginia initially enacted legislation to ban unmanned aircraft in the state for two years but later sought to change the law to permit specific uses by law enforcement agencies. Idaho's law required police to obtain warrants for most uses of drones. Proposals in North Carolina followed Idaho's approach. The Seattle City Council required that any use of drones have prior approval by the Council, but created a controversial exception for police investigations and circumstances approved by a search warrant.

the difficulty in striking a proper balance between national security interests and individuals' privacy interests (Nakashima & Marimow, 2013).

The debates about new laws and policies as part of homeland security and counterterrorist efforts illustrate the struggle to maintain American values of personal liberty, privacy, and individual rights while simultaneously ensuring that law enforcement personnel have sufficient power to protect the nation from catastrophic harm. Read the "Policy Debate" feature about one more major controversy: the potential use of drones by law enforcement officials within the United States.

Now that we have considered the government's role in homeland security, we turn our attention to the private sector. Corporations and other entities must safeguard their assets, personnel, and facilities. They, too, have heightened concerns about terrorism and other homeland security issues. For example, nuclear power plants, chemical factories, energy companies, and other private facilities make up part of the nation's critical infrastructure. Because terrorists might target such facilities, private sector officials must address these concerns, just as they have long needed to address other security issues such as employee theft, fires, and trade secrets.

For the Use of Drones

- Drones can film or take photos of locations that are too difficult for law enforcement officials to reach (e.g., mountains) or too dangerous to enter (e.g., a ranch with armed people behind barricades)
- The use of drones reduces the risk of injury and death by law enforcement officers who would otherwise personally enter specific places
- Drones are now inexpensive enough for local law enforcement agencies to purchase
- Drones can cover a broad area quickly to follow a criminal suspect or search for a lost child

Against the Use of Drones

- Drones can be armed to shoot and kill people, thereby creating risks that operators of police drones will either intentionally or accidently shoot people without proper justification or authorization
- Photographs and films taken from flying drones can invade the privacy of individual citizens, including innocent citizens
- Drones could eventually be used for perpetual surveillance by the law enforcement officials of many public places; thus, Americans will always feel that they are being watched
- Police reliance on drones clash with Americans' expectations about person-to-person contact with police officers who are visible, engaged participants in the community

What Should U.S. Policy Be?

Clearly, inexpensive unmanned aircraft carrying cameras can have useful purposes for law enforcement agencies. However, the publicity and debates surrounding the military uses of drones overseas heightened sensitivity to the risks that might be posed if use of such aircraft in the United States is not carefully defined and controlled. It remains to be seen how law enforcement agencies will, under the watchful eye of state legislatures, develop proposals for clearly defining the uses of this new technology.

Researching the Internet

To see the concerns about police use of drones raised by civil liberties groups, see the American Civil Liberties Union's website https://www.aclu.org/blog/tag/domestic-drones.

Analyzing the Issue

Should local law enforcement agencies be able to use drones? For what purposes? Should prior approval by a judge or city council be required for each use? Are there any situations in which police could use an armed drone capable of firing at targets on the ground? Imagine that you and your classmates are divided into groups that will represent each side in a public debate. One group should make a list of arguments that might be presented by a police chief. The other group should present arguments from the perspective of a civil liberties group.

Sources: Brian Bennett, "Police Employ Predator Drone Spy Planes on Home Front," *Los Angeles Times*, December 10, 2011 (www.latimes.com); John Hinton, "Legislation Would Restrict Use of Drones by Police and Deputies," *Winston-Salem Journal*, March 24, 2013 (www.journalnow.com); Jason Koebler, "Virginia Governor on Drone Ban: Police Use OK," *U.S. News and World Report*, March 26, 2013 (www.usnews.com); Lynn Thompson, "Except for Police, Use of Drones Would Need City's OK," *Seattle Times*, March 18, 2013 (www.seattletimes.com); Laura Zuckerman, "Idaho Restricts Drone Use by Police Agencies Amid Privacy Concerns," Reuters news service, April 11, 2013 (www.reuters.com).

☑CHECK POINT

21. **What are the criticisms directed at the USA PATRIOT Act?**
    Permits too much government authority for searches and wiretaps; defines domestic terrorism in ways that might include legitimate protest groups.

STOP&ANALYZE

Are you willing to give up any of your rights and liberties in order to grant the government more power to take actions to strengthen homeland security? If so, which rights and liberties? If not, why not?

Security Management and Private Policing

Only a few years ago, the term *private security* called to mind the image of security guards, people with marginal qualifications for other occupations who ended up accepting minimal wages to stand guard outside factories

Contemporary security managers are well-educated professionals with administrative experience and backgrounds in management and law. They are responsible for evaluating security needs, acquiring technology, training personnel, complying with relevant laws and regulations, and cooperating with law enforcement officials. Are there any businesses or industries that do not need the services of security personnel in today's fast-changing world?

Bloomberg/Getty Images

and businesses. This image reflected a long history of private employment of individuals who served limited police patrol functions. In recent years, by contrast, private sector activities related to policing functions have become more complex and important.

Many threats have spurred an expansion in security management and private policing; these include (1) an increase in crime in the workplace; (2) an increase in fear (real or perceived) of crime; (3) the fiscal crises of the states, which have limited public police protection; and (4) increased public and business awareness and use of more cost-effective private security services (Steden & Sarre, 2007; Cunningham, Strauchs, & Van Meter, 1990). Today if one speaks of people employed in private security, it would be more accurate to envision a variety of occupations ranging from traditional security guards to computer security experts to high-ranking corporate vice presidents responsible for planning and overseeing safety and security at a company's industrial plants and office complexes around the world.

Retail and industrial firms spend nearly as much for private protection as all localities spend for police protection. Many government entities hire private companies to provide security at specific office buildings or other facilities. In addition, private groups, such as residents of wealthy suburbs, have hired private police to patrol their neighborhoods. There are now more officers hired by private security companies than there are public police (Strom et al., 2010).

Functions of Security Management and Private Policing

Top-level security managers have a range of responsibilities that require them to fulfill multiple roles that separate individuals would handle in the public sector. For their corporations, they simultaneously function as police chiefs, fire chiefs, emergency-management administrators, and computer security experts. They hire, train, and supervise expert personnel to protect corporate computer systems that may contain credit card numbers, trade secrets, confidential corporate information, and other data sought by hackers intent on causing destruction or stealing money.

Frequently they combat cyber criminals who are attacking their computer resources from overseas and are therefore beyond the reach of U.S. law enforcement officials. They also plan security systems and emergency-response plans for fires and other disasters. Such plans include provisions for evacuating large buildings and coordinating their efforts with local police and fire departments in a variety of locales. In addition, they develop security systems to prevent employee theft that may involve sophisticated schemes to use company computer systems to transfer financial assets for illegal purposes. Because so many American companies own manufacturing plants and office buildings overseas, security companies must often implement their services in diverse countries around the globe.

At lower levels, specific occupations in private security compare more closely with those of police officers. Many security personnel are the equivalent of private sector detectives. They must investigate attacks on company computer systems or activities that threaten company assets. Thus, for example, credit card companies have large security departments that use computers to monitor unusual activity on individual customers' credit cards, which may signal that a thief is using the card. Private sector detectives must also investigate employee theft. Because this criminal activity extends beyond simple crimes such as stealing money from a store's cash register, investigations might examine whether people are making false reports on expense accounts, using company computers to run private businesses, or misspending company money.

Other activities compare more directly to those of police patrol officers, especially those of security officers who must guard specific buildings, apartments, or stores. The activities of these private security personnel vary greatly: some act merely as guards and call the police at the first sign of trouble, others have the power to carry out patrol and investigative duties similar to those of police officers, and still others rely on their own presence and the ability to make a citizen's arrest to deter lawbreakers.

Private Police and Homeland Security

Private sector corporations control security for vital facilities in the United States, including nuclear power plants, oil refineries, military manufacturing facilities, and other important sites (Nalla, 2002). Fires, tornadoes, or earthquakes at such sites could release toxic materials into the air and water. Thus, emergency planning is essential for public safety (Simonoff, Restropo, Zimmerman, Naphtali, & Willis, 2011). Moreover, because these sites are now recognized as potential targets of terrorist attacks, the role and effectiveness of security managers matter more than ever to society. They must work closely with law enforcement executives and other government officials to institute procedures that reduce known risks and to participate in emergency preparedness planning.

Private Employment of Public Police

The officials responsible for asset protection, safety, and security at the top levels of major corporations are often retired police administrators or former military personnel. For example, recently retired New York City Police Commissioner Raymond Kelly served as senior managing director of Global Corporate Security for a Wall Street financial firm after he left his position as director of the U.S. Customs Service and before he was appointed to serve as police commissioner.

The reliance on people with public sector experience for important positions in private security management reflects the fact that asset protection and security management have only recently become emphasized as topics in college and university programs. Consequently, relatively few professionals have yet gained specific educational credentials in this important area. As a result, the placement of retired law enforcement officials in high-level positions has often created opportunities for strategic communication and coordination between top-level security managers and public sector police administrators.

At operational levels of security management, private security and local police often make frequent contact. Private firms are usually eager to hire public police officers on a part-time basis. Although police departments may forbid moonlighting by their officers, some departments simultaneously facilitate and control the hiring of their officers by creating specific rules and procedures for off-duty employment. For example, the New York City Police Department coordinates a program called the Paid Detail Unit. Event planners, corporations, and organizations can hire uniformed, off-duty officers for $33 per hour. The police department must approve all events at which the officers will work, and the department imposes an additional 10 percent administrative fee for the hiring of its officers. Thus, the department can safeguard against officers working for organizations and events that will cause legal, public relations, or other problems for the police department. The department can also monitor and control how many hours its officers work so that private, part-time employment does not lead them to be exhausted and ineffective during their regular shifts.

Several models have been designed to manage off-duty employment of officers. Some approaches can lead to controversy, as in New Orleans in 2011 when several high-ranking police officials were revealed to be earning six-figure incomes beyond their police salaries by imposing "coordination fees" as part of their authority over choosing which officers would perform security work at movie sets, football games, and other private settings (McCarthy, 2012).

The *department contract model* permits close control of off-duty work, because firms must apply to the department to have officers assigned to them. New York City's system fits this model. Officers chosen for off-duty work are paid by the police department, which is reimbursed by the private firm, along with an overhead fee. Departments usually screen employers to make sure that the proposed use of officers will not conflict with the department's needs.

The *officer contract model* allows each officer to find off-duty employment and to enter into a direct relationship with the private firm. Officers must apply to the department for permission, which is granted if the employment standards listed earlier are met. Problems can arise when an officer acts as an employment agent for other officers. This can lead to charges of favoritism and nepotism, with serious effects on discipline and morale.

In the *union brokerage model*, the police union or association finds off-duty employment for its members. The union sets the standards for the work and bargains with the department over the pay, status, and conditions of the off-duty employment.

The Public–Private Interface

The relationship between public and private law enforcement is a concern for police officials. Because private agents work for the people who employ them, their goals might not always serve the public interest. Questions have arisen about the power of private security agents to make arrests, conduct searches, and take part in undercover investigations. A key issue is the boundary between the work of the police and that of private agencies.

One such area is criminal activity within a company. Many security managers in private firms tend to treat crimes by employees as internal matters that do not concern the police. They report UCR index crimes to the police, but employee theft, insurance fraud, industrial espionage, commercial bribery, and computer crime tend not to be reported to public authorities. In such cases, the chief concern of private firms is to prevent losses and protect assets. Most of these incidents are resolved through internal procedures (private justice). When such crimes are discovered, the offender may be convicted and punished within the firm by forced restitution, loss of the job, and the spreading of information about the incident throughout the industry. Private firms often bypass the criminal justice system so they do not have to deal with prosecution policies, administrative delays, rules that would open the firms' internal affairs to public scrutiny, and bad publicity. Thus, the question arises: to what extent does a parallel system of private justice exist with regard to some offenders and some crimes (M. Davis, Lundman, & Martinez, Jr., 1991)?

Recruitment and Training

Higher-level security managers are increasingly drawn from college graduates with degrees in criminal justice who have taken additional coursework in such subjects as business management and computer science. These graduates are attracted to the growing private sector employment market for security-related occupations, because the jobs often involve varied, complex tasks in a white-collar work environment. In addition, they often gain corporate benefits such as quick promotion, stock options, and other perks unavailable in public sector policing.

By contrast, the recruitment and training of lower-level private security personnel present a major concern to law enforcement officials and civil libertarians (Enion, 2009; Strickland, 2011). These personnel carry the important responsibility of guarding factories, stores, apartments, and other buildings. Often on the scene when criminal activity occurs, they are the private security personnel most likely to interact with the public in emergency situations. Moreover, any failure to perform their duties could lead to a significant and damaging event, such as a robbery or a fire. Lack of coordination and communication between public and private agencies has led to botched investigations, destruction of evidence, and overzealousness.

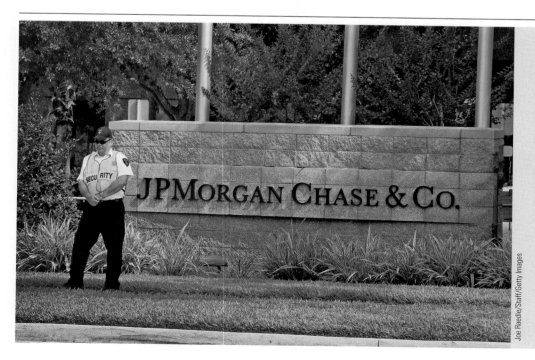

Today's security personnel must be aware of numerous potential threats and have the necessary training and equipment to communicate with law enforcement officials. If security guards are minimum-wage employees, are they likely to have the qualifications and commitment to provide adequate security at important private enterprises such as chemical factories and nuclear power plants?

Joe Raedle/Staff/Getty Images

Growing awareness of this problem has led to efforts to have private security agents work more closely with the police. Current efforts to enhance coordination involve emergency planning, building security, and general crime prevention. However, effective coordination may be hampered if private firms lack standards for hiring and conduct little training for their employees.

In spite of these important responsibilities, which parallel those of police patrol officers, studies have shown that such personnel often have little education and training. A national study in 2008 found that 46 percent of private security officers had only a high school diploma or even less education and just 12 percent had bachelor's degrees. In addition, the median annual pay for private security officers is less than half that of police officers. Many private security officers are paid only minimum wage (Strom et al., 2010). Because the pay is low, the work often attracts people who cannot find other jobs or who seek temporary work. For example, private security firms in San Francisco reported annual staff turnover rates as high as 300 percent because their low pay and benefits led employees continually to seek higher-paying jobs, especially when better-paid public sector security work opened up, such as jobs as airport screeners (Lynem, 2002).

The growth of private policing has brought calls for the screening and licensing of its personnel. However, there has been no systematic national effort to standardize training and licensing for private security personnel. As indicated in Figure 5.3, only eight states require all private security officers to be licensed. Other states require licensing only for contractual security officers or those carrying firearms. Remarkably, 16 states require no licensing at all (Strom et al., 2010).

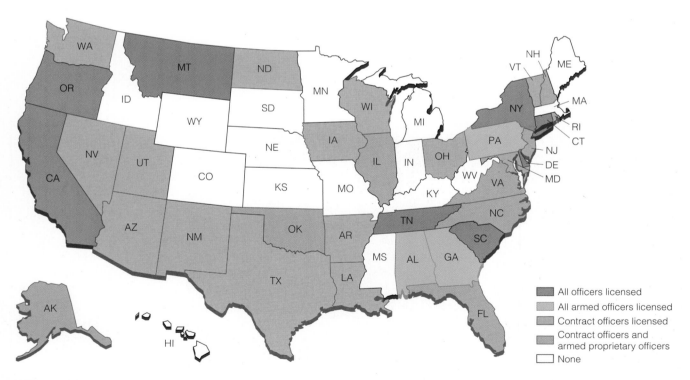

FIGURE 5.3
Licensing Requirements for Security Officers by State, 2009

Source: K. Strom, M. Berzofsky, B. Shook-Sa, K. Barrick, C. Daye, N. Horstmann, and S. Kinsey. *The Private Security Industry: A Review of the Definitions, Available Data Sources, and Paths Moving Forward.* Report prepared for Bureau of Justice Statistics, December 2010 (https://www.ncjrs .gov/pdffiles1/bjs/grants/232781.pdf).

The regulations that do exist tend to focus on contractual, as opposed to proprietary, private policing. Contractual security services are provided for a fee by locksmiths; alarm specialists; polygraph examiners; and firms such as Brink's, Burns, and Wackenhut, which provide guards and detectives. States and cities often require contract personnel to be licensed and bonded. Similar services are sometimes provided by proprietary security personnel, who are employed directly by the organizations they protect—retail stores, industrial plants, hospitals, and so forth. Except for those who carry weapons, proprietary security personnel are not usually regulated by the state or city. Certainly the importance of private security and its relation to public policing demands further exploration of these and related issues in the years to come.

☑ CHECK POINT

22. What has caused the growth of security management and private policing?

Companies' recognition of the need to protect assets and to plan for emergencies, as well as problems with employee theft, computer crime, and other issues that require active prevention and investigation.

23. What are the three models for private employment of police officers?

Department contract model, officer contract model, and union brokerage model.

STOP&ANALYZE

To what extent can private security replace public police when police personnel and services are reduced due to state and city budget cuts? Give two examples of situations or places where private security can fill the gap and two situations where private security cannot effectively provide replacement services.

A QUESTION OF ETHICS

Think, Discuss, Write

Go online to watch a one-minute video from a patrol car camera that shows three police officers dealing with an uncooperative suspect when they responded to a complaint about a domestic dispute. To link to the website, visit https://www.youtube.com/watch?v=JNX6MDktrRo.

The suspect swore at the officers and resisted while they placed him in handcuffs. When the suspect was handcuffed and standing still, an officer attempted to shoot him with a conductive energy weapon. The weapon misfired, and the officer stopped to reload. As the suspect continued to remain standing still, the officer then fired the weapon again. The suspect fell face-first into the street, breaking his jaw.

Discussion/Writing Assignment

Imagine that you are a police supervisor reviewing patrol car videos a few days later. Bear in mind that the video does not show the interactions between the suspect and officers prior to this moment. What, if anything, do you do after seeing the video? Did the officer use the conductive energy weapon in an appropriate situation? Write a memo analyzing whether the treatment of the suspect was appropriate and what actions, if any, you would take as a supervisor. Within the memo, provide rules for the circumstances in which officers can properly use this form of force.

Note: The audio from a longer four-minute video recorded on a different patrol car's camera and microphone appears to show that the suspect may have been shot with the electrical charge for a second time while lying on the ground.

Source: "Officer Tased Handcuffed Man," NBC 25 News, November 13, 2009 (http://www.minbcnews.com/news/story.aspx?id=376774).

SUMMARY

① Describe the everyday actions of police.

- To carry out their mission, the police must have the public's cooperation and assistance because they depend on the public to help them identify crime and carry out investigations.
- Factors affect how police exercise discretion and make choices about actions, especially in ambiguous situations when it is not clear how to apply the law.

② Identify the ways police can abuse their power and the challenges of controlling this abuse.

- Police corruption and excessive use of force erode community support.
- Studies of excessive use of force, especially the use of lethal force, raise questions about whether it is used in a biased manner.
- Police corruption includes officers who actively seek personal gain and others who simply accept the gifts and payoffs that come their way.

③ List the methods that can be used to make police more accountable to citizens.

- Internal affairs units, civil review boards, standards and accreditation, and civil liability lawsuits increase police accountability to citizens.

④ Describe the delivery of police services.

- The police are mainly reactive rather than proactive, which often leads to incident-driven policing.
- The productivity of a force can be measured in various ways, including clearance rate; however, measuring proactive approaches is more difficult.
- Police services are delivered through the work of the patrol, investigation, and specialized operations units.
- The patrol function has three components: answering calls for assistance, maintaining a police presence, and probing suspicious circumstances.
- The investigative function is the responsibility of detectives, who work in close cooperation with patrol officers.
- The felony apprehension process is a sequence of actions that includes crime detection, preliminary investigation, follow-up investigation, and clearance and arrest.
- Large departments usually have specialized units dealing with traffic, drugs, and vice.

⑤ Name patrol strategies that departments employ.

- Police administrators make choices about possible patrol strategies, which include preventive patrol, hot spots, foot versus motorized patrol, aggressive patrol, and community policing.
- Community policing seeks to involve citizens in identifying problems and working with police officers to prevent disorder and crime.

⑥ Explain the importance of connections between the police and the community.

- Police face challenges in dealing with special populations, such as the mentally ill and homeless, who need social services yet often disturb or offend other citizens as they walk the streets.
- Policing in a multicultural society requires an appreciation of the attitudes, customs, and languages of minority group members.
- To be effective, the police must maintain their connection with the community.

⑦ Identify issues and problems that emerge from law enforcement agencies' increased attention to homeland security.

- Homeland security has become an important priority for law enforcement agencies at all levels of government since September 11, 2001.
- Agencies need planning and coordination in order to gather intelligence and prepare for possible threats and public emergencies.
- The federal government provides funding for state and local fusion centers and emergency preparedness equipment.
- New laws such as the USA PATRIOT Act have caused controversy about the proper balance between government authority and citizens' rights.

⑧ Describe the policing and related activities undertaken by private sector security management.

- The expansion of security management and private policing reflects greater recognition of the need to protect private assets and to plan for emergencies.
- Security management produces new issues and problems, including concerns about the recruitment, training, and activities of lower-level private security personnel.
- Public–private interaction affects security through such means as joint planning for emergencies, hiring of private firms to guard government facilities, and hiring of police officers for off-duty private security work.

Questions for Review

1. What problems are posed by police corruption and excessive use of force?
2. What is the purpose of patrol? How is it carried out?
3. What responsibilities in large cities are handled by special operations units?
4. What problems do officers face in policing a diverse, multicultural society?
5. What have law enforcement agencies done to enhance homeland security?
6. What problems are associated with private policing?

Key Terms and Cases

aggressive patrol (p. 164)

civilian review board (p. 153)

clearance rate (p. 157)

Commission on Accreditation for Law Enforcement Agencies (CALEA) (p. 153)

community crime prevention (p. 170)

CompStat (p. 156)

detectives (p. 158)

differential response (p. 155)

directed patrol (p. 163)

domestic violence (p. 148)

evidence-based policing (p. 155)

excessive use of force (p. 149)

fusion centers (p. 173)

incident-driven policing (p. 155)

internal affairs units (p. 152)

Interpol (p. 171)

law enforcement intelligence (p. 172)

police corruption (p. 151)

preventive patrol (p. 158)

proactive (p. 155)

problem-oriented policing (p. 165)

reactive (p. 155)

school resource officers (SROs) (p. 160)

Section 1983 lawsuits (p. 154)

sworn officers (p. 157)

U.S. Border Patrol (p. 172)

USA PATRIOT Act (p. 175)

Bryan Mitchell/Stringer/Getty Images

6 | Police and Law

LEARNING OBJECTIVES

1 Describe the extent of police officers' authority to stop people and to conduct searches of people, their vehicles, and other property.

2 Explain how police officers seek warrants in order to conduct searches and make arrests.

3 Describe situations in which police officers can examine property and conduct searches without obtaining a warrant.

4 Explain the purpose of the privilege against compelled self-incrimination.

5 Define the exclusionary rule, and identify the situations in which it applies.

Miami, Florida, police had received a tip that marijuana was being grown inside the home of Joelis Jardines. Officers observed the home but did not see any suspicious activity. Detective Douglas Bartelt took a trained drug-sniffing dog to the front porch of the house. The dog was trained to sniff around an area, and if there was the scent of marijuana or cocaine, the dog was supposed to stop and sit at the place where the scent was strongest. After sniffing around the base of the front door to the house, the dog sat as he was trained to do and thereby indicated that he smelled an illegal drug that he was trained to detect. Based on the dog's actions, the police went to a judge and obtained a search warrant. When they searched the home, they found marijuana plants that provided the basis to charge Jardines with a crime.

The lawyer for Jardines sought to have the marijuana plants excluded from evidence for being the product of an illegal search. The defense attorney argued that police officers cannot legally bring a drug-sniffing dog to the front door of someone's home without a warrant. The attorney claimed that the Fourth Amendment protection against "unreasonable searches" should be interpreted to prohibit such investigatory actions by police that invade an individual's residential property.

In contrast, the prosecutor argued that no search took place and therefore there was nothing wrong with bringing the dog to the front porch of the home. If no search took place, then there would be no requirement for the police to justify their actions or seek a search warrant prior to bringing the dog to the front door. It was claimed that front porches and the outside of front doors, while being private property, are actually places to which the public has access. If the porch provides enough public access to permit Girl Scouts without prior permission to enter and ring the doorbell in order to sell cookies, then what is wrong with a police coming to the porch with a trained dog? In effect, it was argued that homeowners should expect strangers, whether salespeople, political candidates, or police officers, to appear at their front doors for brief visits.

What do you think? Did the officer undertake a "search" by bringing the dog to the door? Was there anything improper about the officer's action? Would your view be different if an officer took a drug-sniffing dog down a street and stopped at everyone's front door to see if there was the scent of drugs? Do you agree that homeowners should expect strangers to appear at their front doors, and thus a police officer with a dog is no greater intrusion on their property than a Girl Scout selling cookies?

As you think about the Jardines case, remember that the words of the Fourth Amendment do not provide an answer to the question of what counts as a "search" or when searches are "unreasonable." Indeed, the eighteenth-century men who wrote "unreasonable searches and seizures" as key words in the Fourth Amendment could not anticipate that drugs would be a significant social problem. Thus, today's judges must make their own decisions about how each situation falls within the intended purposes of the Fourth Amendment.

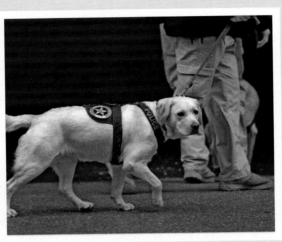

In March 2013, the U.S. Supreme Court reviewed the case and provided its answer to the question raised in *Florida v. Jardines* (Braverman, 2013). The justices were deeply divided about the issue. A narrow majority of five justices decided that the use of the dog constituted a "search" under the Fourth Amendment and was improper.

The majority concluded that bringing a trained dog to a front door in an effort to look for incriminating evidence was very different from a salesperson arriving to ring the doorbell. Unlike the salesperson, the police officer's intention is to conduct a search for criminal evidence on private property without the homeowner's consent.

Are you surprised by the U.S. Supreme Court's decision? The ruling demonstrates that we sometimes choose to protect constitutional rights even when a guilty criminal may benefit by his conviction being overturned. Do you agree with the decision? Does it place excessive or unnecessary limits on police officers' authority to search for drugs? As we examine other Supreme Court decisions, think about the challenge presented by the necessity of applying brief phrases from the Bill of Rights to actual situations, thereby determining which people can be searched and questioned and, more importantly, whether certain individuals will spend many years in prison.

In this chapter, we examine individual rights and how those legal protections define the limits of police officers' powers of investigation and arrest. In particular, we look closely at two rights that were introduced in Chapter 3: the Fourth Amendment protection against unreasonable searches and seizures and the Fifth Amendment privilege against compelled self-incrimination.

Legal Limitations on Police Investigations

The provisions of the Bill of Rights embody very important American values regarding individual rights in society. They reflect the belief that we do not want to give government officials absolute power to pursue investigations and prosecutions, because that approach to crime control would impose excessive costs on the values of individual liberty, privacy, and due process. If police could do whatever they wanted to do, then people would lack protections against arbitrary searches and arrests. On the other hand, crime control is an important policy goal; we do not want individuals' expectations about legal protections to restrict law enforcement officers' ability to protect citizens from crime or to punish wrongdoers. Judges must therefore seek to interpret the Constitution in ways that properly balance crime control and the protection of individual rights.

How does an officer know when her or his actions might violate laws protecting an individual's rights? Individual police officers do not have time to follow the details of the latest court decisions. That responsibility rests with those who train and supervise law enforcement officers. Officers depend on the information provided at the police academy and subsequent updates from city and state attorneys who monitor court decisions. Thus, police officers' compliance with the law depends on their own knowledge and decisions as well as those of their supervisors.

Search and Seizure Concepts

The Fourth Amendment prohibits police officers from undertaking "unreasonable searches and seizures." The Supreme Court defines a **search** as an action by law enforcement officials that intrudes on people's **reasonable expectation of privacy**. For example, someone who places a personal diary in a locked drawer within a bedroom of her home has demonstrated a reasonable expectation of privacy. Police officers cannot simply decide to enter her home in order to open the locked drawer and read the diary. But many situations raise questions about people's reasonable expectations. Should people reasonably expect a police officer to reach into their pockets in order to see if they have guns? Should people reasonably expect an officer not to walk up to their houses and attempt to peer through small cracks in the window blinds? Should people expect that the text messages on their phones will not be examined by employers or police officers? (Wells & Keasler, 2011). Although judges do not always answer these questions in clear, consistent ways, people's reasonable expectations about their privacy play a key role in judges' determinations about legal guidelines for police investigations.

What if a police officer is walking down the public sidewalk and sees a marijuana plant growing quite visibly in the large front window of a home? When police officers examine people's property without violating reasonable expectations of privacy, then no search occurred. In *Coolidge v. New Hampshire* (1971), the Court discussed the **plain view doctrine**, which permits officers to notice and use as evidence items that are visible to them when they are in a location where they are permitted to be, such as a public sidewalk. Similarly, police can see what is in open areas, including private property, either by walking through open fields or by flying a helicopter over people's houses and yards. Officers may not break into a home and then claim that the drugs found inside were in plain view on a table. However, if a homeowner invited officers into his home to file a report about a burglary, the officers do not need to obtain a warrant in order to seize drugs that they see lying on the kitchen table. Because the drugs were in plain view and the officers had a legal basis for their presence in the house, the owner lost any reasonable expectation of privacy that would otherwise require officers to demonstrate probable cause for a search warrant.

If no search has occurred as a result of police actions, then the Fourth Amendment's protections do not apply and police are free to take those actions. Thus, the Supreme Court is regularly faced with the challenge of deciding whether or not a specific action by police constitutes a "search" in order to trigger the Fourth Amendment. In the case of *Florida v. Jardines* (2013), described in the chapter opener, the Court faced just such a situation and the majority decided that bringing a drug-sniffing dog to the front door of a house is, indeed, a search. Thus, the officers should have had a warrant or their actions should have fit with one of the warrantless search categories that we will discuss later in this chapter. Similarly, when police officers attached a Global Positioning System (GPS) tracking device on the outside of a suspected drug dealer's car in order to monitor his movements without a warrant, the Supreme Court decided that this action constituted a search and that the Fourth Amendment's protections applied to the situation (*United States v. Jones*, 2012).

In defining **seizures**, the Supreme Court focuses on the nature and extent of officers' interference with people's liberty and freedom of movement. If an officer who is leaning against the wall of a building says to a passing pedestrian, "Where are

search Government officials' examination of and hunt for evidence on a person or in a place in a manner that intrudes on reasonable expectations of privacy.

reasonable expectation of privacy The objective standard developed by courts for determining whether a government intrusion into an individual's person or property constitutes a search because it interferes with the individual's interests that are normally protected from government examination.

plain view doctrine Officers may examine and use as evidence, without a warrant, contraband or evidence that is in open view at a location where they are legally permitted to be.

seizures Situations in which police officers use their authority to deprive people of their liberty or property and that must not be "unreasonable" according to the Fourth Amendment.

you going?" and the person replies, "To the sandwich shop down the street," as she continues to walk without interference by the officer, there is virtually no intrusion on her liberty and freedom of movement. Thus, officers are free to speak to people on the street. If people voluntarily stop in order to speak with the officer, they have not been "seized," because they are free to move along their way whenever they choose. However, if a person is not free to leave when officers assert their authority to halt that individual's movement, then a seizure has occurred and the Fourth Amendment requires that the seizure be reasonable.

One form of seizure is an arrest. This involves taking a suspect into custody. Property can also be subject to seizure, especially if it is evidence in a criminal case.

A **stop** is a brief interference with a person's freedom of movement for a duration that can be measured in minutes, usually under an hour. An interference with freedom of movement that lasts several hours risks being viewed as exceeding the proper duration of a stop and requires greater justification. When police require a driver to pull over in order to receive a traffic citation, that is a stop. Such stops can affect the rights of both drivers and passengers, especially if the stop leads to a search of the individuals or the vehicle (*Brendlin v. California*, 2007; V. Amar, 2008). In order to be permissible under the Fourth Amendment, stops must be justified by **reasonable suspicion**—a situation in which specific articulable facts lead officers to conclude that the person may be engaging in criminal activity. Officers cannot legally make stops based on hunches; they must be able to describe specific aspects of the person's appearance, behavior, and circumstances that led them to conclude that the person should be stopped in order to investigate the occurrence of a crime. As we shall see, however, the courts permit police officers to make many kinds of stops without reasonable suspicion. Such stops can occur, for example, at border crossing points where preventing illegal activities such as smuggling and drug trafficking is especially important. Thus, everyone can be stopped in certain situations even if there is no specific basis to suspect them of wrongdoing.

Use of Force and the Fourth Amendment

In Chapter 5, we examined problems stemming from excessive use of force by police officers. Such actions reflect on the application of discretion, ethics, professionalism, and training of officers. When people sue police officers for violating constitutional rights through the excessive use of force, they claim their Fourth Amendment right against "unreasonable seizures" has been violated. Although many people assume that an improper shooting or beating inflicted by a police officer might violate the Eighth Amendment prohibition on cruel and unusual punishments, the Supreme Court has interpreted this Eighth Amendment right to protect only individuals who are being "punished" by the justice system, namely people who have been convicted of crimes. For people who have not been convicted of a crime, such as those encountered by the police in free society, the use of excessive force by government officials falls under the coverage of the Fourth Amendment. According to the Supreme Court, when police officers victimize individuals through the use of excessive force, those individuals have suffered an "unreasonable seizure."

Until the 1980s, the police had broad authority to use deadly force in pursuing suspected felons. Police in about half the states were guided by the common-law principle that allowed the use of whatever force was necessary to arrest a fleeing felon. In 1985, the Supreme Court set a new standard in *Tennessee v. Garner*, ruling that the police may not use deadly force in apprehending fleeing felons "unless it is necessary to prevent the escape and the officer has probable cause to believe that the suspect poses a significant threat of death or serious physical injury to the officer or others."

The standard set by *Tennessee v. Garner* presents problems, because it can be difficult to judge how dangerous a suspect may be. Officers must make quick decisions in stressful situations, and for this reason, the Supreme Court and other courts cannot create clear rules that will guide police in every context that arises.

Arrest is the physical taking of a person into custody. What legal requirements must be met to make this a valid arrest? What limits are placed on the officers?

Bill Pugliano/Getty Images

However, to clarify the rules for police, the Supreme Court justices also established the standard of "objective reasonableness," saying that the officer's use of deadly force should be judged in terms of its reasonableness for the specific situation that confronts the officer and requires the officer to make a quick decision about appropriate actions to take (*Graham v. Connor*, 1989). This means that the use of the deadly force—or any form of force—should be judged from the point of view of the officer on the scene. The Court's decision recognized that "officers are often forced to make split-second judgments—in circumstances that are tense, uncertain, and rapidly evolving—about the amount of force that is necessary in a particular situation" (Georgiady, 2008).

The Concept of Arrest

An arrest is a significant deprivation of liberty. In an arrest, a person is taken into police custody, transported to the police station or jail, and processed into the criminal justice system. Because arrests involve a more significant intrusion on liberty, they require a higher level of justification than stops. Unlike stops, which require only reasonable suspicion, all arrests must be supported by **probable cause**. Probable cause exists when sufficient evidence is available to support the reasonable conclusion that a person has committed a crime. To obtain an arrest warrant, the police must provide a judicial officer with sufficient evidence to support a finding of probable cause. Alternatively, police officers' on-the-street determinations of probable cause can produce discretionary warrantless arrests. A judge subsequently examines such arrests for probable cause in a hearing that must occur shortly after the arrest, typically within 48 hours. If the judge determines that the police officer was wrong in concluding that probable cause existed to justify the arrest, the suspect is released from custody. Read "A Question of Ethics" at the end of the chapter to consider whether a police department's policies might increase the risk that officers will make improper arrests without the existence of probable cause.

probable cause An amount of reliable information indicating that it is more likely than not that evidence will be found in a specific location or that a specific person is guilty of a crime.

Warrants and Probable Cause

Imagine that you are a judge. Two police officers come to your chambers to ask you to authorize a search warrant. They swear that they observed frequent foot traffic of suspicious people going in and out of a house. Moreover, they swear that a reliable informant told them that he was inside the house two days earlier and saw crack cocaine being sold. Does this information rise to the level of probable cause, justifying issuance of a search warrant? Can you grant a warrant based purely on the word of police officers, or do you need more-concrete evidence?

These questions are important not only for judges but for prosecutors as well. Police and prosecutors must work closely together. If the police have made errors in seeking warrants or conducting searches, evidence could be excluded from use at trial, and as a result, prosecutors could lose their cases through no fault of their own.

The Fourth Amendment requires that "no Warrants shall issue, but upon probable cause, supported by Oath or affirmation, and particularly describing the place to be searched, and the persons or things to be seized." These particular elements of the Fourth Amendment must be fulfilled in order to issue a warrant. If they are not, then a defendant may later challenge the validity of the warrant.

The important elements are, first, the existence of probable cause. Second, evidence must be presented to the judicial officer and be supported by "oath or affirmation," which typically means that police officers must say "yes" when the judicial officer asks them if they swear or affirm that all information presented is true to the best of their knowledge. This requirement may be fulfilled by presenting an **affidavit** from the police officers, which is a written statement confirmed by oath or affirmation. Third, the warrant must describe the specific place to be searched. A "general warrant" for searching many locations cannot be issued. Fourth, the warrant must describe the person or items to be seized. Thus, if the warrant authorizes a search for a person suspected of robbery, the officers should not open small dresser drawers or other places a person could not be hiding.

The U.S. Supreme Court has attempted to guide judicial officers in identifying the existence of *probable cause*. Mere suspicion cannot constitute probable cause, yet the level of evidence to establish probable cause need not fulfill the high level of proof "beyond a reasonable doubt" needed to justify a criminal conviction. In essence, probable cause is a level of evidence sufficient to provide a reasonable conclusion that the proposed objects of a search will be found in a location that law enforcement officers request to search. For an arrest warrant, the essential issue is whether sufficient evidence is presented to lead to the reasonable conclusion that a specific person should be prosecuted for a criminal offense. There is no hard-and-fast definition of *probable cause* that can be applied to every situation. It is a flexible concept that various judicial officers apply differently. In *Illinois v. Gates* (1983), the Supreme Court announced a flexible **totality of circumstances** test for determining the existence of probable cause. Judges are permitted to make a generalized determination about whether the evidence is both sufficient and reliable enough to justify a warrant.

Cases continue to arise concerning officers' use of search warrants. In *Florida v. Jardines* (2013), described in the opening of the chapter, the Supreme Court said that police could not bring a drug-sniffing dog to the door of a house without the resident's permission for the purpose of seeking evidence that could be used to obtain a search warrant. When conducting a search with a warrant, officers may detain people found on the premises in order to protect the safety of the officers and prevent any interference in the search. However, according to the Court's decision in *Bailey v. United States* (2013), officers may not follow people that they observe leaving a residence that police are about to search and then detain those individuals a mile away, since there is no risk at that point that these people will interfere with the search.

This section's foregoing descriptions of the basic concepts of searches, arrests, and warrants generally apply to criminal justice cases. However, advancements in technology and the heightened concerns about terrorism threats have created contexts for new debates about the application of constitutional rights and proper balance between protecting individuals' liberty and safeguarding American society.

affidavit Written statement of fact, supported by oath or affirmation, submitted to judicial officers to fulfill the requirements of probable cause for obtaining a warrant.

***Illinois v. Gates* (1983)** U.S. Supreme Court decision that established the flexible totality of circumstances test for determining the existence of the probable cause needed for obtaining a search warrant.

totality of circumstances Flexible test established by the Supreme Court for identifying whether probable cause exists that permits the judge to determine whether the available evidence is both sufficient and reliable enough to issue a warrant.

As you read "The Policy Debate" feature concerning whether or how constitutional rights should apply to terrorism suspects, think about the role of an eighteenth-century document, the Bill of Rights (1791), in the twenty-first-century effort to prevent catastrophic, politically motivated attacks on innocent civilians.

☑CHECK POINT

1. **What is a search?**
   A government intrusion into an individual's reasonable expectation of privacy.

2. **What is the plain view doctrine?**
   The plain view doctrine permits officers to observe and seize illegal items that are visible to them when they are in a location in which they are legally permitted to be.

3. **What is the difference between an arrest and a stop?**
   An arrest requires probable cause and involves taking someone into custody for prosecution, whereas a stop is a brief deprivation of freedom of movement based on reasonable suspicion.

4. **What do police officers need to demonstrate in order to obtain a warrant?**
   The existence of probable cause by the totality of circumstances in the case.

STOP&ANALYZE

What are two examples of situations that you believe should be considered "unreasonable searches" in violation of the Fourth Amendment? What is it about those searches that makes them "unreasonable"?

Warrantless Searches

In day-to-day police work, the majority of searches take place without a warrant. It is in this area that the courts have been most active in defining the term *unreasonable*. Six kinds of searches may be legally conducted without a warrant and still uphold the Fourth Amendment: (1) special needs beyond the normal purposes of law enforcement, (2) stop-and-frisk on the streets, (3) search incident to a lawful arrest, (4) exigent circumstances, (5) consent, and (6) automobile searches. We examine these forms of warrantless searches in this section.

Special Needs beyond the Normal Purposes of Law Enforcement

In certain specific contexts, law enforcement officials have a justified need to conduct warrantless searches of every individual passing through. The use of metal detectors to examine airline passengers, for example, occurs in a specific context in which the need to prevent hijacking justifies a limited search of every passenger (Israelsen, 2013). Here the Supreme Court does not require officers to have any suspicions, reasonable or otherwise, about the illegal activities of any individual (Loewy, 2011).

Similarly, warrantless searches take place at the entry points into the United States—border crossings, ports, and airports (Chacon, 2010). The government's interests in guarding against the entry of people and items (weapons, drugs, toxic chemicals, and so forth) that are harmful to national interests outweigh the individuals' expectations of privacy. Typically, these border stops involve only a few moments as customs officers check any required documents such as passports and visas, ask where the person traveled, and ask what the person is bringing into the United States. The customs officers may have a trained dog sniff around people and their luggage, checking for drugs or large amounts of cash. At the Mexican and Canadian borders and at international airports, people may be chosen at random to have their cars and luggage searched. They may also be chosen for such searches because their behavior or their answers to questions arouse the suspicions of customs officers.

Should Terrorism Suspects in the United States Enjoy the Protections of the Bill of Rights?

In the aftermath of the al-Qaeda organization's September 11, 2011, attacks on New York City's World Trade Center and the Pentagon in Washington, D.C., the United States intervened militarily in Afghanistan. The administration of President George W. Bush decided to send captured terrorism suspects to the U.S. Naval base at Guantanamo Bay, Cuba, with the specific intention of avoiding the application of rights contained in the Bill of Rights. The U.S. Supreme Court had previously said that American officials are not obligated to adhere to the Bill of Rights in searching, seizing, and questioning foreign citizens overseas. This action generated debates about which aspects of international law and treaty obligations apply in such circumstances.

When the Bush administration asserted that American terrorism suspects detained on American soil could also be denied all constitutional rights, a divided Supreme Court rejected that argument. However, the Supreme Court justices did not agree on whether or how the Bill of Rights applied in such circumstances (*Hamdi v. Rumsfeld*, 2004). At one extreme within the Supreme Court, Justice Clarence Thomas argued that the president, as commander in chief, had absolute authority to hold American suspects indefinitely without providing any access to court proceedings, without providing any Fourth or Fifth Amendment rights, and without providing any evidence to prove that the individual engaged in wrongdoing. At the other extreme, Justices Antonin Scalia and John Paul Stevens insisted that the Bill of Rights applies in its entirety to all Americans held by the government on American soil. Thus, they asserted that the government must either charge such individuals with crimes and provide them with the complete constitutional rights available to all criminal suspects or set the individuals free.

This debate spurred Congress and the president to develop rules and practices for terrorism investigations, detentions, and case processing that provided limited protections without granting the full rights promised by the Bill of Rights.

As discussed in Chapter 5, there have been several incidents that produced significant debates about the role of constitutional rights. The USA PATRIOT Act expanded government authority to undertake searches and engage in wiretapping without the knowledge of people suspected of supporting terrorist activities or organizations. These practices were initiated by the Bush administration and were continued by the administration of President Barack Obama. In 2011 President Obama signed into law a controversial provision that authorized indefinite detention of terrorism suspects in the United States (Hirshkorn, 2011). In another important event, many members of Congress criticized the FBI for reportedly informing the "underwear bomber" of his Fifth Amendment right against compelled self-incrimination after he attempted to ignite an explosive device in his clothing while a passenger on an airliner approaching the Detroit airport (Hunt, 2010). Some lawmakers argued that terrorism suspects should not be entitled to benefit from constitutional rights.

For Granting Bill of Rights Protections to Domestic Terrorism Suspects in the United States

Supporters of applying the Bill of Rights in all domestic cases focus on constitutional rights as a fundamental component of the American democracy. By failing to follow this country's laws of basic constitutional rights, the government violates America's most fundamental principles and, in effect, does just what the terrorists want—it surrenders these rights to the fear of terrorism.

The Supreme Court has expanded the checkpoint concept by approving systematic stops to look for drunken drivers along highways. Michigan's state police implemented a sobriety checkpoint program. They set up a checkpoint at which they stopped every vehicle and briefly questioned each driver (*Michigan Department of State Police v. Sitz*, 1990). A group of citizens filed lawsuits alleging that checkpoints violated drivers' rights. However, the Court said that police can systematically stop drivers in order to seek information. The Court more recently approved checkpoints to ask drivers whether they had witnessed an accident (*Illinois v. Lidster*, 2004).

The U.S. Supreme Court has not given blanket approval for every kind of checkpoint or traffic stop that police might wish to use. For example, the Court forbids random stops of vehicles by officers on patrol (*Delaware v. Prouse*, 1979). Officers must have a basis for a vehicle stop, such as an observed violation of traffic laws. The Court also ruled that a city cannot set up a checkpoint in order to check drivers and passengers for possible involvement in drugs or other crimes. The Court declared that a general search for criminal evidence does not justify the use of a checkpoint. Again, such stops must be narrowly focused on a specific objective, such as checking for drunken drivers (*City of Indianapolis v. Edmond*, 2000).

As you reflect on the importance and challenges of conducting warrantless stops and searches in the protection of national borders (MacCormack, 2011),

The arguments for applying the protections of the Bill of Rights are these:

- The Bill of Rights embodies the fundamental values, principles, and rules of law for the nation.
- The country harms itself if it permits the threat of terrorism to scare it into rejecting its own most important principles.
- The nation's image in the world is harmed when its own rules and rights are ignored, thereby creating risks that other countries will be less willing to assist in antiterrorism efforts and that the nation forfeits its standing to argue that Americans should be granted rights when accused of wrongdoing in other countries.
- Without constitutional rights, there are risks that suspects will be mistreated or that errors will be made that lead to innocent people being held in jail.
- Since 9/11 the U.S. government has successfully used regular criminal trials to convict more than 300 people for terrorism-related crimes while granting them the full rights under the Bill of Rights. These trials demonstrate that constitutional rights do not prevent the United States from protecting itself against terrorism.

Against Granting Bill of Rights Protections to Domestic Terrorism Suspects in the United States

- Rights contained in the Bill of Rights, especially those concerning searches, arrests, and questioning suspects, may delay or impede terrorism investigations and hinder the acquisition of critical information. Thus, attacks may occur that otherwise would have been stopped, thereby leading to the needless, preventable deaths of innocent people.
- People engaged in terrorism plots reject and seek to destroy the principles and institutions of American democracy. Therefore, they forfeit any claim to the benefits of American law.

- Law enforcement officials need broad authority to protect American society from terrorist threats.
- Terrorist organizations may endanger the American public by seeking to attack jails and courthouses in an effort to free their associates who are processed through regular criminal trials and the rules of the legal system rather than held secretly in isolation at military facilities.

What Should U.S. Policy Be?

Do Americans even notice if the government's investigatory and detention powers grow? But what if we learned, hypothetically, that the government was intercepting email messages from all Americans—is that something that would arouse public opposition? On the other hand, how would Americans react if there is another major attack within the borders of the country?

Researching the Internet

To read about the issues and arguments identified by a civil liberties organization concerning governmental violations of the Bill of Rights in the name of national security, see https://www.aclu.org/national-security.

Analyzing the Issue

What are the risks and benefits of permitting terrorism suspects in the United States to enjoy the protections of the Bill of Rights? Are there specific rights that pose fewer risks and other rights that pose greater risks? If you and your classmates were government department heads who are members of the president's cabinet, what would you say about the issue if the president sought your advice? After discussing the issue with your classmates, write a memo summarizing and explaining your conclusions.

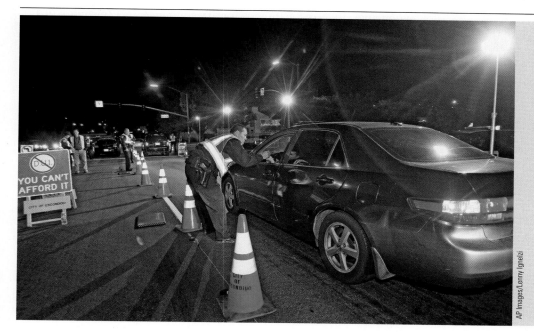

Police officers conduct a sobriety checkpoint in Escondido, California. All vehicles were stopped to detect whether any drivers had been drinking too much alcohol. Do you think such roadblocks interfere with the rights of drivers who have done nothing to raise suspicions about improper behavior?

AP Images/Lenny Ignelzi

Border Patrol Agent

Karl Huether, U.S. Border Patrol Agent, U.S. Border Patrol, Arizona

The United States Border Patrol is the mobile, uniformed law enforcement arm of the U.S. Customs and Border Protection (CBP) within the Department of Homeland Security. Since the terrorist attacks of September 11, 2001, the focus of the Border Patrol has shifted to include emphasis on the detection, apprehension, and/or deterrence of terrorists and terrorist weapons. Its overall mission remains unchanged: to detect and prevent the illegal entry of undocumented immigrants and contraband into the United States. Together with other law enforcement officers, the Border Patrol helps maintain borders that facilitate the flow of legal immigration and goods while preventing the illegal trafficking of people and contraband.

The Border Patrol is specifically responsible for patrolling the 6,000 miles of Mexican and Canadian international land borders and 2,000 miles of coastal waters surrounding Florida and Puerto Rico. Agents work around the clock on assignments on all types of terrain and in all types of weather conditions. Agents also work in many isolated communities throughout the United States.

Photo provided by Karl Huether

To become a U.S. Border Patrol Agent, one must be a U.S. citizen, possess a valid automobile driver's license, and pass the CBP Border Patrol entrance exam. Candidates must also have substantial work experience. A four-year college degree may substitute for the required work experience, or candidates may qualify through a combination of education and work experience.

Karl Huether earned an undergraduate degree in criminal justice, as well as a certificate in homeland security studies. In addition, he gained experience in the field of criminal justice through participation in internships with state police and state probation offices.

As a Border Patrol Agent, I face different challenges every day when I go out into the field. Line watch is one of the most crucial activities that a Border Patrol Agent will conduct. While conducting line watch, agents detect, prevent, and apprehend terrorists, undocumented aliens, and smugglers of aliens at or near the land border. To make line watch successful, agents must keep up with daily intelligence reports, training, and the laws which are enforced by the U.S. Border Patrol.

consider whether you would be interested in a career with the U.S. Border Patrol, as described in the "Careers in Criminal Justice" feature.

Stop-and-Frisk on the Streets

Police officers possess the authority to make stops and limited searches of individuals on the streets when specific circumstances justify such actions (Zeidman, 2012). In the landmark case of ***Terry v. Ohio*** (1968), the Court upheld the stop-and-frisk procedure when a police officer had good reasons to conclude that a person endangered the public by being involved in criminal activity. In the *Terry* case, a plainclothes detective in downtown Cleveland observed men walking back and forth to look in the window of a store and then conferring with each other. He suspected that they might be preparing to rob the store. He approached the men, identified himself as a police officer, patted down their clothing, and found unlicensed handguns on two individuals. Those individuals challenged the legality of the search.

Although the justices supported the detective's authority to conduct the pat-down search based on his observations of the men's suspicious behavior, they struck a careful balance between police authority and individuals' rights by specifying the circumstances in which such a pat-down search—more commonly known as a **stop-and-frisk search**—can occur. In the *Terry* decision, the Court specifies the following criteria, all of which must be present, to define a legal stop-and-frisk:

We merely hold today that

1. where a police officer observes unusual conduct
2. which leads him reasonably to conclude in light of his experience
3. that criminal activity may be afoot and
4. that the persons with whom he is dealing may be armed and presently dangerous,

---

Terry v. Ohio (1968) Supreme Court decision endorsing police officers' authority to stop and frisk suspects on the streets when there is reasonable suspicion that they are armed and involved in criminal activity.

stop-and-frisk search Limited search approved by the Supreme Court in *Terry v. Ohio*, that permits police officers to pat down the clothing of people on the street if there is reasonable suspicion of dangerous criminal activity.

5. where in the course of investigating this behavior
6. he identifies himself as a policeman and makes reasonable inquiries,
7. and where nothing in the initial stages of the encounter serves to dispel his reasonable fear for his own or others' safety,
8. he is entitled for the protection of himself and others in the area to conduct a carefully limited search of the outer clothing of such persons in an attempt to discover weapons which might be used to assault him.

These factors impose an obligation on police officers to make observations, draw reasonable conclusions, identify themselves, and make inquiries before conducting the stop-and-frisk search. In addition, the reasonableness of the search must be justified by a reasonable conclusion that a person is armed, thereby requiring the officer to act in order to protect him- or herself and the public.

As we discuss later with respect to the *exclusionary rule*, a suspect who, during a frisk search, is found to be carrying drugs or a weapon can seek to have the evidence excluded from use in court if the stop-and-frisk was not justified by proper observations and reasonable suspicion. Typically, a judge will believe the police officer's version of events rather than accept the claims of a person found to be carrying illegal items. Sometimes, however, the officer's version of events may not be persuasive. When an officer claims to have seen a lump under a suspect's jacket while the officer was standing 20 yards away on a busy street, judges may doubt whether an officer can reasonably draw such conclusions from such a distance. In New York City, for example, concerns arose in 2008 that police officers were regularly searching anyone they saw on the streets, even though the officers did not have the proper justifications established in *Terry v. Ohio* and later cases. In response, federal judges closely examined officers' versions of events. In nearly two dozen cases, the judges concluded that the police officers either were not being truthful or were not carefully following the *Terry* rules (Weiser, 2008).

Court decisions have given officers significant discretion to decide when factors that justify a stop-and-frisk search exist. For example, if officers see someone running at the sight of police in a high-crime neighborhood, their observation can be one consideration in determining whether a stop-and-frisk search is justified (*Illinois v. Wardlow*, 2000). Thus, officers need not actually see evidence of a weapon or interact with the suspect prior to making the stop.

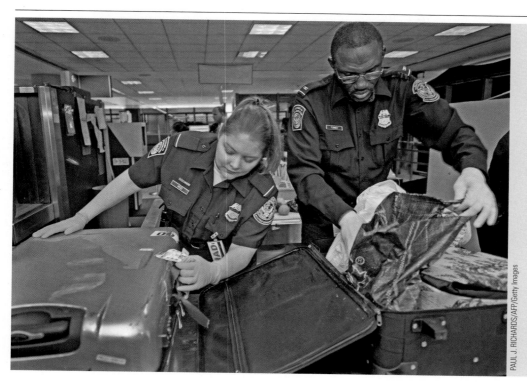

The special needs of law enforcement at borders and airports provide authority for warrantless searches based on decisions of the officers looking for suspicious behavior. The need to protect public safety and national security justifies these searches. When you go to an airport, do you feel as if your privacy and rights are being violated when you are subjected to searches?

PAUL J. RICHARDS/AFP/Getty Images

The Supreme Court also expanded police authority by permitting officers to rely on reports from reliable witnesses as the basis for conducting the stop and frisk (*Adams v. Williams*, 1972). However, an unverified anonymous tip does not serve as an adequate reason for a stop-and-frisk search (*Florida v. J. L.*, 2000).

Search Incident to a Lawful Arrest

The authority to undertake a warrantless search incident to a lawful arrest is not limited by the crime for which the arrestee has been taken into custody (Foley, 2013). Even someone arrested for a traffic offense can be searched. Although there is no reason to suspect the person has a weapon or to believe that evidence related to the offense will be found in the person's pockets (*United States v. Robinson*, 1973), the arrestee is subject to the same arrest-scene search as someone taken into custody for murder.

The justification for searches of arrestees emerged in the Supreme Court's decision in ***Chimel v. California* (1969)**. This ruling stated that searches are lawful when the officers need to be sure that the arrestee does not have a weapon that could endanger the officers or others in the vicinity. They must also look for evidence that might be destroyed or damaged by the arrestee before or during the process of transporting the individual to jail. Hence, officers are permitted to search the arrestee and the immediate area around the arrestee.

Officers can also make a protective sweep through other rooms where the suspect may recently have been. However, the arrest would not justify opening drawers and conducting a thorough search of an entire house. If, after the arrest, officers have probable cause to conduct a more thorough search, they must obtain a warrant that specifies the items that they seek and the places where they will search.

In a traffic stop, because officers possess the authority to make arrests for minor offenses, including acts that would normally only be subject to traffic citations, officers have opportunities to use arrests of drivers as a basis for conducting warrantless searches of automobiles (*Virginia v. Moore*, 2008). However, the search of the passenger compartment must be limited to areas within reach of the arrestee (May, Duke, & Gueco, 2013). In *Arizona v. Gant* (2009), a majority of justices barred the search of an automobile after an arrest when the handcuffed driver posed no danger to the officers and could not reach into the car to destroy evidence.

Recent Supreme Court decisions have clarified additional search implications that flow from arrests. In *Maryland v. King* (2013), the Supreme Court approved a state law that required taking a DNA sample using a cheek swab from those arrested for serious felonies in order to check databases to see if they might be guilty of other unsolved violent crimes, such as rape or murder, for which DNA evidence had been collected. According to the majority opinion, "When officers make an arrest supported by probable cause to hold for a serious offense and they bring the suspect to the station to be detained in custody, taking and analyzing a cheek swab of the arrestee's DNA is, like fingerprinting and photographing, a legitimate police booking procedure that is reasonable under the Fourth Amendment." Arrests, even for minor offenses, also lead those arrested to be subjected to intrusive strip searches and body cavity inspections when they are placed in jail (*Florence v. Board of Chosen Freeholders*, 2012).

Exigent Circumstances

Officers can make an arrest without a warrant when there are **exigent circumstances**. This means that officers are in the middle of an urgent situation in which they must act swiftly and do not have time to go to court to seek a warrant. With respect to arrests, for example, when officers are in hot pursuit of a fleeing suspected felon, they need not stop to seek a warrant and thereby risk permitting the suspect to get away (*Warden v. Hayden*, 1967). Similarly, exigent circumstances can justify the warrantless entry into a home or other building and an accompanying search that flows from the officers' response to the urgent situation. For example, the Supreme Court approved police officers' warrantless entry into a home when, on being called to the

Chimel v. California (1969) Supreme Court decision that endorsed warrantless searches for weapons and evidence in the immediate vicinity of people who are lawfully arrested.

exigent circumstances When there is an immediate threat to public safety or the risk that evidence will be destroyed, officers may search, arrest, or question suspects without obtaining a warrant or following other usual rules of criminal procedure.

scene of a loud party, they observed through the home's window a violent altercation between a teenager and an adult (*Brigham City, Utah v. Stuart*, 2006). The unanimous decision by Chief Justice John Roberts said that "law enforcement officers may enter a home without a warrant to render emergency assistance to an injured occupant or to protect an occupant from imminent injury." After the officers make the warrantless entry, the plain view doctrine permits them to examine and seize any criminal evidence that they can see in the course of actions taken to address the exigent circumstances.

In *Cupp v. Murphy* (1973), a man voluntarily complied with police officers' request that he come to the police station to answer questions concerning his wife's murder. At the station, officers noticed a substance on the man's fingernails that they thought might be dried blood. Over his objections, they took a sample of scrapings from his fingernails and ultimately used that tissue as evidence against him when he was convicted of murdering his wife. The Supreme Court said the search was properly undertaken under exigent circumstances. If officers had taken the time to seek a warrant, the suspect could have washed his hands and the evidence would have been lost.

Police officers can use the exigent circumstances justification for warrantless searches for the purpose of seeking evidence. To justify such searches, they do not need to show that there was a potential threat to public safety. As a practical matter, police officers make quick judgments about undertaking certain searches. If incriminating evidence is discovered, courts may be asked after the fact to determine whether the urgency of the situation justified a warrantless search and whether the nature and purpose of the search were reasonable. Judges are usually reluctant to second-guess a police officer's on-the-spot decision that the urgency of a situation required an immediate warrantless search. For example, in 2011 the Supreme Court decided a case concerning police officers who followed a drug suspect into an apartment building and then smelled marijuana outside one apartment while hearing sounds that they believed could be the destruction of evidence. The Court ruled that the officers could legally kick in the door and enter the apartment, based on exigent circumstances, even though it turned out that it was not the apartment that their drug suspect had entered (*Kentucky v. King*). The Court does not, however, automatically accept police officers' claims about exigent circumstances. Read the excerpt from the Supreme Court's opinion on *Missouri v. McNeely* (2013), a case concerning an involuntary blood alcohol test of a suspected drunk driver.

Consent

If people consent to a search, officers do not need probable cause or even any level of suspicion to justify the search. Consent effectively absolves law enforcement officers of any risk that evidence will be excluded from use at trial or that they will be found liable in a civil lawsuit alleging a violation of Fourth Amendment rights.

A **consent search** provides a valuable investigatory tool for officers who wish to conduct warrantless searches. Officers in many police departments are trained to ask people if they will consent to a search. Thus, some officers ask every motorist during a traffic stop, "May I search your car?" Or if called to the scene of a domestic dispute or a citizen complaint about noise, the officers may say, "Do you mind if I look around the downstairs area of your house?" Criminal evidence is often uncovered in such consent searches—a fact that may indicate that many citizens do not know they have the option to say "no" when officers ask for permission to search. Moreover, some citizens may fear that they will look more suspicious to the officer if they say "no," so they agree to searches in order to act as if they have nothing to hide. In addition, in **United States v. Drayton** (2002), the Supreme Court said that police officers do not have to inform people of their right to say "no" when asked if they wish to consent to a search.

In deciding if a permissible consent search has occurred, one must address two key issues. First, the consent must voluntary. Police officers may not use coercion or threats to obtain consent. Even subtler tricks, such as dishonestly telling someone

consent search A permissible warrantless search of a person, vehicle, home, or other location based on a person with proper authority or the reasonable appearance of proper authority voluntarily granting permission for the search to take place.

United States v. Drayton (2002) Judicial decision declaring that police officers are not required to inform people of their right to decline to be searched when police ask for consent to search.

Missouri v. McNeely, 133 S.Ct. 1552 (2013)

Justice Sonia Sotomayor announced the judgment of the Court and delivered the opinion of the Court [on behalf of Justices Antonin Scalia, Ruth Bader Ginsburg, and Elena Kagan. Justice Anthony Kennedy issued a separate concurring opinion that endorsed the outcome described by Justice Sotomayor].

Facts: Police officers stopped Tyler McNeely at 2 a.m. for speeding and crossing the centerline of the road. They observed his slurred speech and smelled alcohol on his breath. When he refused to submit to a blood alcohol breath test, they took him to a hospital where he similarly refused to consent to a blood test. The officers instructed a lab technician to draw a sample of McNeely's blood anyway. Test results showed his blood alcohol level as 0.154 percent, which was well above the legal limit of 0.08 percent. McNeely claimed that the officers should have obtained a search warrant before having his blood drawn without his permission. The police claimed that the warrantless blood test was permissible under the exigent circumstances exception because blood alcohol levels will decline naturally over time and waiting to get a warrant would prevent them from knowing the true level of alcohol in his blood when he was driving his vehicle.

The question presented here is whether the natural metabolization of alcohol in the bloodstream presents a *per se* [automatic] exigency that justifies an exception to the Fourth Amendment's warrant requirement for nonconsensual blood testing in all drunk-driving cases. We conclude that it does not, and we hold, consistent with general Fourth Amendment principles, that exigency in this context must be determined case by case based on the totality of the circumstances.

***

To determine whether a law enforcement officer faced an emergency that justified acting without a warrant, this Court looks to the totality of circumstances.

***

It is true that as a result of the human body's natural metabolic processes, the alcohol level in a person's blood begins to dissipate once the alcohol is fully absorbed and continues to decline until the alcohol is eliminated. . . . Testimony before the trial court in this case indicated that the percentage of alcohol in an individual's blood typically decreases by approximately 0.015 percent to 0.02 percent per hour once the alcohol has been fully absorbed. . . . More precise calculations of the rate at which alcohol dissipates depend on various individual characteristics (such as weight, gender, and alcohol tolerance) and the circumstances in which the alcohol was consumed. . . . Regardless of the exact elimination rate, it is sufficient for our purposes to note that because an individual's alcohol level gradually declines soon after he stops drinking, a significant

delay in testing will negatively affect the probative value of the results.

***

But it does not follow that we should depart from careful case-by-case assessment of exigency and adopt the categorical rule proposed by the State and its *amici*. In those drunk-driving investigations where police officers can reasonably obtain a warrant before a blood sample can be drawn without significantly undermining the efficacy of the search, the Fourth Amendment mandates that they do so. . . . We do not doubt that some circumstances will make obtaining a warrant impractical such that the dissipation of alcohol from the bloodstream will support an exigency justifying a properly conducted warrantless blood test. That, however, is a reason to decide each case on its facts, . . .

The context of blood testing is different in critical respects from other destruction-of-evidence cases in which the police are truly confronted with a "'now or never'" situation. . . . Consider, for example, a situation in which the warrant process will not significantly increase the delay before the blood test is conducted because an officer can take steps to secure a warrant while the suspect is being transported to a medical facility by another officer. In such a circumstance, there would be no plausible justification for an exception to the warrant requirement. . . .

The Federal Rules of Criminal Procedure were amended in 1977 to permit federal magistrate judges to issue a warrant based on sworn testimony communicated by telephone . . . As amended, the law now allows a federal magistrate judge to consider "information communicated by telephone or other reliable electronic means." Fed. Rule Crim. Proc. 4.1. States have also innovated. Well over a majority of States allow police officers or prosecutors to apply for search warrants remotely through various means, including telephonic or radio communication, electronic communication such as e-mail, and video conferencing. And in addition to technology-based developments, jurisdictions have found other ways to streamline the warrant process, such as by using standard-form warrant applications for drunk-driving investigations.

We by no means claim that telecommunications innovations have, will, or should eliminate all delay from the warrant-application process. Warrants inevitably take some time for police officers or prosecutors to complete and for magistrate judges to review. Telephonic and electronic warrants may still require officers to follow time-consuming formalities designed to create an adequate record, such as preparing a duplicate warrant before calling the magistrate judge. . . .

For that reason, exigent circumstances justifying a warrantless blood sample may arise in the regular course of law enforcement due to delays from the warrant application process. But adopting the State's *per se* [automatic] approach would improperly ignore the current and future technological

that there is a search warrant and thereby implying that the person has no choice but to consent, will result in the search being declared improper (*Bumper v. North Carolina*, 1968). Second, the consent must be given by someone who possesses authority to give consent and thereby waive the right. Someone cannot, for example, developments in warrant procedures, and might well diminish the incentive for jurisdictions "to pursue progressive approaches to warrant acquisition that preserve the protections afforded by the warrant while meeting the legitimate interests of law enforcement." . . .

In short, while the natural dissipation of alcohol in the blood may support a finding of exigency in a specific case, as it did in *Schmerber*, it does not do so categorically. Whether a warrantless blood test of a drunk-driving suspect is reasonable must be determined case by case based on the totality of the circumstances.

***

[Justice John Roberts, joined by Justices Stephen Breyer and Samuel Alito, issued an opinion concurring in part and dissenting in part. They agreed with the rule in Sotomayor's opinion but not with all of her analysis]

***

Justice Clarence Thomas, Dissenting

This case requires the Court to decide whether the Fourth Amendment prohibits an officer from obtaining a blood sample without a warrant when there is probable cause to believe that a suspect has been driving under the influence of alcohol. Because the body's natural metabolization of alcohol inevitably destroys evidence of the crime, it constitutes an exigent circumstance. As a result, I would hold that a warrantless blood draw does not violate the Fourth Amendment.

***

Once police arrest a suspect for drunk driving, each passing minute eliminates probative evidence of the crime. The human liver eliminates alcohol from the bloodstream at a rate of approximately 0.015 percent to 0.020 percent per hour, . . . with some heavy drinkers as high as 0.022 percent per hour, Brief for Petitioner 21 (citing medical studies), depending on, among other things, a person's sex, weight, body type, and drinking history. . . . The Court has acknowledged this fact since *Schmerber v. California*, (1966) ("We are told that the percentage of alcohol in the blood begins to diminish shortly after drinking stops, as the body functions to eliminate it from the system"). In that case, the Court recognized that destruction of evidence is inherent in drunk-driving cases and held that an officer investigating a drunk-driving crime "might reasonably [believe] that he [is] confronted with an emergency, in which the delay necessary to obtain a warrant, under the circumstances, threaten[s] 'the destruction of evidence.'" . . . The Court explained that drawing a person's blood is "a highly effective means of determining the degree to which [he] is under the influence of alcohol" and is a reasonable procedure because blood tests are "commonplace" and "involv[e] virtually no risk, trauma, or pain." . . . The Court, therefore, held that dissipation of alcohol in the blood constitutes an exigency that allows a blood draw without a warrant.

The rapid destruction of evidence acknowledged by the parties, the majority, and *Schmerber's* exigency determination occurs in *every* situation where police have probable cause to arrest a drunk driver. In turn, that destruction of evidence implicates the exigent-circumstances doctrine.

***

In today's decision, the Court elides the certainty of evidence destruction in drunk-driving cases and focuses primarily on the time necessary for destruction. In doing so, it turns the exigency inquiry into a question about the amount of evidentiary destruction police must permit before they may act without a warrant. That inquiry is inconsistent with the actual exigency at issue: the uncontested destruction of evidence due to metabolization of alcohol. . . . Moreover, the Court's facts-and-circumstances analysis will be difficult to administer, a particularly important concern in the Fourth Amendment context.

The Court's judgment reflects nothing more than a vague notion that everything will come out right most of the time so long as the delay is not too lengthy.

***

This case demonstrates the uncertainty officers face with regard to the delay caused by obtaining a warrant. The arresting officer clearly had probable cause to believe respondent was drunk, but there was no way for the officer to quantify the level of intoxication to determine how quickly he needed to act in order to obtain probative evidence. Another officer testified at respondent's trial that it typically took 1½ to 2 hours to obtain a drunk-driving warrant at night in Cape Girardeau County, Missouri. . . . Respondent submitted an exhibit summarizing six late afternoon and nighttime drunk-driving search warrants that suggests the time may be shorter. Brief for Respondent 56; App. 70. Ultimately this factual tiff is beside the point; the spotty evidence regarding timing itself illustrates the fact that delays in obtaining warrants are unpredictable and potentially lengthy. A rule that requires officers (and ultimately courts) to balance transportation delays, hospital availability, and access to magistrates is not a workable rule for cases where natural processes inevitably destroy the evidence with every passing minute.

***

Researching the Internet

The Center for Problem-Oriented Policing provides online guides for police officers on how to address specific problems, including drunk driving. http://www.popcenter.org/problems/drunk_driving/3.

For Critical Analysis

As you read the two perspectives in the opinion concerning the application of the exigent circumstances exception to the situation of drunk drivers, which viewpoint was more persuasive? Give three reasons why one opinion was more convincing than the other.

consent to have a neighbor's house searched. The resident in a dwelling must be the one to consent to a search of that dwelling. A controversial Supreme Court decision said that the police may not search when one resident of a dwelling is present and objects even if another resident consents to the search (*Georgia v. Randolph*, 2006).

In some circumstances, a permissible search may occur if the officers reasonably believe that they have been given permission to search by someone who possesses such authority even if, for example, it later turns out that the person is a former rather than a current resident of the apartment searched (*Illinois v. Rodriguez*, 1990).

Automobile Searches

The U.S. Supreme Court first addressed automobile searches in *Carroll v. United States* (1925), a case in which federal agents searched a car for illegal alcohol. The *Carroll* case, in which the warrantless search was approved, provided an underlying justification for permitting such searches of automobiles: in essence, because cars are mobile, they differ greatly from houses and other buildings. Automobiles can be driven away and disappear in the time that it would take for police to ask a judicial officer for a search warrant.

Police officers have significant authority to search automobiles and to issue commands to people riding in vehicles. For example, during a traffic stop, officers can order passengers as well as the driver to exit the vehicle even if there is no basis for suspicion that the passengers engaged in any wrongdoing (*Maryland v. Wilson*, 1997).

Two key questions arise in automobile searches: (1) when can officers stop a car? and (2) how extensively can they search the vehicle? Many automobile searches arise as a result of traffic stops. A stop can occur when an officer observes a traffic violation, including defective safety equipment, or when there is a basis for reasonable suspicion concerning the involvement of the car, its driver, or its passengers in a crime. Police officers are free to make a visible inspection of a car's interior by shining a flashlight inside and looking through the window. They can also look at the vehicle identification number on the dashboard and inside the door of a validly stopped vehicle (*New York v. Class*, 1986).

All sworn officers can make traffic stops, even if they are in unmarked vehicles and serving in special vice or detective bureaus that do not normally handle traffic offenses (*Whren v. United States*, 1996). A traffic violation by itself, however, does not provide an officer with the authority to search an entire vehicle (*Knowles v. Iowa*, 1998). Only specific factors creating reasonable suspicion or probable cause will justify officers doing anything more than looking inside the vehicle.

For example, the arrest of a driver justifies the search of a passenger's property or other locations in the vehicle if there is reason to believe that those locations could contain criminal evidence or weapons (*Wyoming v. Houghton*, 1999). In addition, the Court has expanded officers' authority to search automobiles even when no formal arrest has yet occurred. In *Michigan v. Long* (1983), the Court approved a search of the car's interior around the driver's seat after officers found the car in a ditch and the apparently intoxicated driver standing outside the car. The Supreme Court justified the search as an expansion of the *Terry* doctrine. In effect, the officers were permitted to "frisk" the car in order to protect themselves and others by making sure no weapon was available to the not-yet-arrested driver. Such a search requires that the officers have reasonable suspicion that the person stopped may be armed and may pose a threat to the officers. As described in "Criminal Justice: Myth & Reality," there are also opportunities for officers to search closed containers within a vehicle.

The Court permits thorough searches of vehicles without regard to probable cause when police officers inventory the contents of impounded vehicles

TABLE 6.1 Warrantless Searches

The Supreme Court has ruled that there are circumstances when a warrant is not required.

Case	Decision
Special needs	
Michigan Department of State Police v. Sitz (1990)	Stopping motorists systematically at roadblocks designed for specific purposes, such as detecting drunken drivers, is permissible.
City of Indianapolis v. Edmond (2000)	Police traffic checkpoints cannot be justified as a generalized search for criminal evidence; they must be narrowly focused on a specific objective.
Stop and frisk	
Terry v. Ohio (1968)	Officers may stop and frisk suspects on the street when there is reasonable suspicion that they are armed and involved in criminal activity.
Adams v. Williams (1972)	Officers may rely on reports from reliable witnesses as the basis for conducting a stop-and-frisk.
Illinois v. Wardlow (2000)	When a person runs at the sight of police in a high-crime area, officers are justified in using the person's flight as a basis for forming reasonable suspicion to justify a stop-and-frisk.
Incident to an arrest	
Chimel v. California (1969)	To preserve evidence and protect the safety of the officer and the public after a lawful arrest, the arrestee and the immediate area around the arrestee may be searched for weapons and criminal evidence.
United States v. Robinson (1973)	A warrantless search incident to an arrest is not limited by the seriousness of the crime for which the arrestee has been taken into custody.
Exigent circumstances	
Warden v. Hayden (1967)	When officers are in hot pursuit of a fleeing suspect, they need not stop to seek a warrant and thereby risk permitting the suspect to get away.
Cupp v. Murphy (1973)	Officers may seize evidence to protect it if taking time to seek a warrant creates a risk of its destruction.
Consent	
Bumper v. North Carolina (1968)	Officers may not tell falsehoods as a means of getting a suspect to consent to a search.
United States v. Drayton (2002)	An officer does not have to inform people of their right to refuse when he or she asks if they wish to consent to a search.
Automobiles	
Carroll v. United States (1925)	Because by their nature automobiles can be easily moved, warrantless searches are permissible when reasonable suspicion of illegal activity exists.
New York v. Class (1986)	An officer may enter a vehicle to see the vehicle identification number when a car has been validly stopped pursuant to a traffic violation or other permissible justification.
California v. Acevedo (1991)	Officers may search throughout a vehicle when they believe they have probable cause to do so.
Maryland v. Wilson (1997)	During traffic stops, officers may order passengers as well as the driver to exit the vehicle, even if there is no basis for suspicion that the passengers engaged in any wrongdoing.
Knowles v. Iowa (1998)	A traffic violation by itself does not provide an officer with the authority to search an entire vehicle. There must be reasonable suspicion or probable cause before officers can extend their search beyond merely looking inside the vehicle's passenger compartment.

(*South Dakota v. Opperman*, 1976). This means that containers found within the course of the **inventory search** may also be opened and searched when the examination of such containers is consistent with a police department's inventory policies.

Table 6.1 reviews selected Supreme Court cases concerning those circumstances in which the police do not need a warrant to conduct a search or to seize evidence.

inventory search Permissible warrantless search of a vehicle that has been "impounded"—meaning that it is in police custody—so that police can make a record of the items contained in the vehicle.

5. **In what situations do law enforcement's special needs justify stopping an automobile without reasonable suspicion?**

Warrantless stops of automobiles are permitted at international borders and sobriety checkpoints (unless barred within a specific state by its own supreme court) or when there is reasonable suspicion of a traffic violation or other wrongdoing.

6. **What is an exigent circumstance?**

An urgent situation in which evidence might be destroyed, a suspect might escape, or the public would be endangered if police took the time to seek a warrant for a search or an arrest.

7. **What two elements must be present for a valid consent to permit a warrantless search?**

Voluntary consent by a person with proper authority to consent.

Imagine that you were stopped for speeding while driving down a highway. If the officer gives you a warning rather than a ticket, how would you answer if the police officer then said to you, "Do you mind if I look in the trunk of your car?" What reasons would motivate your decision about how to answer? What concerns might someone have about what the officer could do upon hearing the answer "no"?

Questioning Suspects

The Fifth Amendment contains various rights, including the one most relevant to police officers' actions in questioning suspects: "No person shall . . . be compelled in any criminal case to be a witness against himself." The privilege against compelled self-incrimination should not be viewed as simply a legal protection that seeks to assist individuals who may be guilty of crimes. By protecting individuals in this way, the Fifth Amendment discourages police officers from using violent or otherwise coercive means to push suspects to confess.

In addition to discouraging the physical abuse of suspects, the privilege against compelled self-incrimination can also diminish the risk of erroneous convictions. When police officers use coercive pressure to seek confessions, they create a significant risk that innocent people will confess to crimes they did not commit. The worst-case scenario took place in the film *In the Name of the Father* (1993), based on a true story in England, in which police officers gain a confession from a bombing suspect whom they know to be innocent by placing a gun in the suspect's mouth and threatening to pull the trigger. This example from England took place at a time when people there were afraid of terrorist acts by militants who sought to use violence to force Great Britain to remove its soldiers and governing institutions from Northern Ireland. Since 9/11, many Americans feel similar fears about their own country's vulnerability to terrorists. See "What Americans Think" to assess how the threat of terrorism may have influenced the public's views on coercive questioning of terrorism suspects.

Miranda Rules

Miranda v. Arizona (1966)
U.S. Supreme Court decision declaring that suspects in custody must be informed of their rights to remain silent and be represented during questioning.

The decision by the Supreme Court in *Miranda v. Arizona* (1966) said that as soon as the investigation of a crime begins to focus on a particular suspect and that person is taken into custody, the so-called *Miranda* warnings must be read aloud before questioning can begin.

Suspects must be told that (1) they have the right to remain silent; (2) if they decide to make a statement, it can and will be used against them in court; (3) they have the right to have an attorney present during interrogation and to have an opportunity to consult with an attorney; and (4) if they cannot afford an attorney, the state will provide one.

Prior to the *Miranda* decision, police officers in some places solved crimes by picking up a poor person or an African American and torturing him or her until a confession was produced. In *Brown v. Mississippi* (1936), the Supreme Court ruled that statements produced after police beat suspects were inadmissible, but it did not insist that counsel be available at the early stages of the criminal process.

Two rulings in 1964 laid the foundation for the *Miranda* decision. In *Escobedo v. Illinois*, the Court made the link between the Fifth Amendment right against self-incrimination and the Sixth Amendment right to counsel. Danny Escobedo was questioned at the police station for 14 hours without counsel, even though he asked to see his attorney. He finally made incriminating statements that the police said were voluntary. The Court's ruling specified that defendants have a right to counsel

> when the investigation is no longer a general inquiry into an unsolved crime, but has begun to focus on a particular suspect, the suspect has been taken into police custody, [and] the police carry out a process of interrogations that lends itself to eliciting incriminating statements.

The Court effectively expanded the right to counsel to apply at an early point in the criminal justice process as a means to guard against law enforcement officers' actions that might violate the Fifth Amendment privilege against compelled self-incrimination. In *Massiah v. United States* (1964), the Supreme Court declared that the questioning of the defendant by a police agent outside of the presence of defense counsel violated the defendant's rights.

The *Miranda* warnings apply only to what are called custodial interrogations. If police officers walk up to someone on the streets and begin asking questions, there is no need to inform the person of her or his rights. The justices say that people know they can walk away when an officer asks them questions in a public place. When police have taken someone into custody, however, the Supreme Court sees risks of excessive pressure. The loss of liberty and isolation experienced by detained suspects can make them vulnerable to abusive interrogation techniques, especially when interrogations take place out of view of anyone other than police officers. When a suspect is alone in a room with the police, will anyone believe the suspect if he or she claims to have been beaten? If the police say that the suspect confessed, will anyone believe the suspect if she or he denies this? The *Miranda* warnings and presence of counsel during questioning are supposed to prevent such abuses (C. E. Smith, 2010b).

The Court has permitted police officers to forgo *Miranda* warnings when a threat to public safety would result if they took the time to provide the warnings (Wright, 2013). This exception is similar to the exigent circumstance justification for warrantless searches. The underlying premise is that some urgent, socially significant situation outweighs the necessity of respecting individuals' rights. In the case that created this **"public safety" exception**, police officers chased an armed man into a supermarket after a reported assault. When they found him with an empty shoulder holster, they asked, "Where's the gun?" after he was handcuffed but before he had been informed of his *Miranda* rights (*New York v. Quarles*, 1984). His statement in response to the question could nevertheless be used against him in court because the public's safety might have been threatened if the police had taken the time to read him his rights before asking any questions.

The Supreme Court continues to refine and clarify the requirements of *Miranda* warnings (Kinports, 2011; Dery, 2011). Most recently, in *Berghuis v.*

WHAT AMERICANS THINK

QUESTION: "How do you feel about the use of torture against suspected terrorists to obtain information about terrorism activities? Can that often be justified, sometimes be justified, rarely be justified, or never be justified?"

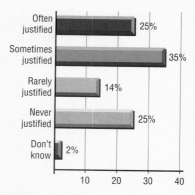

CRITICAL THINKING: Those respondents to the poll who believe that torture is justified in certain circumstances presumably also believe that torture is an effective way to obtain desired information. Alternatively, it is possible that the infliction of severe fear, pain, and discomfort will lead a tortured suspect to provide a false confession or inaccurate information out of sheer desperation—especially if the person really does not possess any pertinent information. How would you write a law that specifies when torture or coercive methods are allowed but that also ensures protection from excessive abuse or the infliction of pain? Is it possible to draft such a law in a workable manner?

Source: AP-GfK Poll conducted by GfK Roper Public Affairs and Corporate Communications, May 5–9, 2011 (www.pollingreport.com/terror.htm).

"public safety" exception
Exception to *Miranda* requirements that permits police to immediately question a suspect in custody without providing any warnings when public safety would be jeopardized by their taking the time to supply the warnings.

A police officer questions a suspect in custody. In such a confined setting, are you confident that suspects will truly understand the nature of their rights before consenting to be questioned without an attorney present?

Marmaduke St. John/Alamy

Thompkins (2010), the Court concluded that a suspect being questioned cannot assert his right to remain silent by remaining silent in the face of continued questioning by an officer. Instead, he must actually tell the officer that he is asserting his right to remain silent in order to seek an end to the officer's questioning (Weisselberg, 2011). The Court permitted police to vary the precise words used to provide the warnings in *Florida v. Powell* (2010). The Court approved the officers' delivery of the warnings even though they failed to make clear that the suspect has a right to consult with an attorney throughout the entire questioning process and not just, as they stated it to the suspect, "before answering questions." And in *J. D. B. v. North Carolina* (2011), a case concerning police officers' questioning of a seventh-grader at school, the Court declared that juveniles may be entitled to *Miranda* warnings even in some situations in which an adult could freely walk away from the police and thus not be considered a detained suspect entitled to warnings.

Although some legal commentators and police officials have criticized the *Miranda* warnings and urged the Court to eliminate the rule, the Supreme Court strongly repeated its endorsement of the *Miranda* requirement in 2000 (*Dickerson v. United States*). In declaring that *Miranda* warnings are required by the Constitution, Chief Justice William Rehnquist's majority opinion stated that "*Miranda* has become embedded in routine police practice to the point where the warnings have become part of our national culture." Rehnquist's conclusion was reinforced by a national survey of police chiefs in which more than three-quarters of respondents supported the Supreme Court's decision to keep the *Miranda* rule in place (Zalman & Smith, 2007).

The Consequences of *Miranda*

Miranda rights must be provided before questions are asked during custodial interrogations. However, police officers have adapted their techniques in various ways that enable them to question suspects without any impediment from the warnings. For example, officers may ask questions while standing on the suspect's doorstep before making an arrest. Even after arrest, the courts do not require that police inform suspects of their rights immediately. Thus, after taking a suspect into custody, some officers may delay providing *Miranda* warnings in case the suspect talks on his or her own. The suspect may be kept in the backseat of a car as officers drive around town, or the suspect may be left alone in a room at the police station. Some suspects will take the initiative to talk to officers because of feelings of guilt. Other suspects may start conversations with officers because they are so eager to convince the officers that they have an alibi or that they want to cooperate. This may lead the suspect to provide contradictory statements that will help build the case for the prosecution.

Officers are also trained in interrogation techniques that are intended to encourage suspects to talk despite *Miranda* warnings (Weisselberg, 2008). The words of the warnings are so familiar from their use in television police shows that many suspects never stop to think about the message being conveyed. In addition, officers may pretend to sympathize with the suspect (Leo, 1996). For example, they may say such things as, "We know that you had a good reason to go after that guy with a knife. Tell us how it happened." Police officers are not required to be truthful in speaking to suspects. They are permitted to use deception to induce suspects to talk. It is not uncommon for officers to say, untruthfully, "We have five witnesses that saw you do it. If you tell us everything right now, we may be able to get you a good deal." In reality, there were no witnesses and there will be no deal. Do such statements constitute improper pressure in violation of *Miranda*? Probably not—as long as the officers do not threaten suspects in ways that make them fear for their physical safety or the safety of their loved ones.

Many suspects talk to the police despite being informed of their right to remain silent and their right to have an attorney present during questioning. Some suspects do not fully understand their rights even after being read the *Miranda* warnings (Rogers, Rogstad, Steadham, & Drogin, 2011). They may believe that they will look guilty by remaining silent or asking for an attorney. They therefore feel that they must talk to officers if they are to have any hope of claiming innocence. More importantly, many suspects believe (often accurately) that they will gain a more favorable charge or plea bargain if they cooperate with officers as fully and as early as possible.

In 2004 the Supreme Court warned police officers not to try to get around *Miranda* warnings by questioning unwarned suspects and obtaining incriminating statements and then giving the warnings and asking the suspects to repeat their statements again. In *Missouri v. Seibert* (2004), Justice Souter's majority opinion concluded,

> upon hearing warnings only in the aftermath of interrogation and just after making a confession, a suspect would hardly think he had a genuine right to remain silent, let alone persist in so believing once the police began to lead him over the same ground again. . . . Thus, when *Miranda* warnings are inserted in the midst of coordinated and continuing interrogation, they are likely to mislead and "depriv[e] a defendant of knowledge essential to his ability to understand the nature of his rights and the consequences of abandoning them."

Some commentators have argued that officers' efforts to get around the *Miranda* requirement could be prevented by requiring that all police interrogations be video recorded, to provide proof that suspects' statements are voluntary. Several states have introduced video-recording requirements, but they are often limited to certain categories of cases, such as murders or serious felonies (L. Lewis, 2007). It remains to be seen whether such requirements will become more universal.

One of the issues underlying Miranda warnings is the risk that innocent people, especially vulnerable people with little education or developmental disabilities, will be pressured into making incriminating statements. This is one cause of erroneous convictions. However, the leading cause of erroneous convictions is misidentifications made by witnesses and victims (Walsh, 2013). The "Evidence-Based Practice and Policy" feature discusses the use of research to reduce the risk of misidentifications.

Identification Procedures

One of the consequences of the development of DNA testing has been the discovery that many innocent people were convicted of crimes based on misidentifications by eyewitnesses. Men convicted of rape based on the victims' certain claims that they were the perpetrators have gained release, often after spending many years in prison, thanks to newly developed scientific tests of blood or semen from the crime scene that definitely exclude them as contributors of the biological material. These disappointing revelations about flaws and mistakes in the criminal investigation process helped to encourage research by psychologists and other social scientists about how and why eyewitnesses misidentify suspects.

Research studies indicate that risks of misidentification by eyewitnesses can be reduced simply by changing identification procedures. As portrayed in many movies and television dramas, lineups with people standing in a row as a victim or witness attempts to pick out the criminal offender have been very common in police work. However, research studies have identified a number of risks in lineups and other similar procedures as follows:

- *Showups*, in which a single suspect is brought before a victim or witness, create risks that the police will be regarded as signaling that this is indeed the guilty individual. Moreover, the victim or witness has no other individuals to consider or compare in a showup.
- In any procedure, victims or witnesses should be told that the guilty individual is not necessarily present in the lineup or array of photos. Otherwise there is a risk that an individual will be chosen, even if not well-remembered, simply because of an assumption that one of these people must be the guilty individual.
- Some research indicates that fewer errors occur when victims or witnesses are shown individuals one at a time, either in person or in photos. In this way, they are pushed to compare each individual with their own memories. Otherwise, they may believe that they are supposed to choose the individual who looks most like the perpetrator from among a lineup group or simultaneously viewed photos. Looking in sequences may increase the likelihood that they will honestly say, "I don't see the individual here," rather than make an inaccurate selection from among the choices.
- Errors may be reduced if the identification procedure is supervised by a police official who has nothing to do with the case and has no idea which individual the other police officers suspect of committing the crime. When active investigators run lineups or present photo arrays, there are risks that they will subtly or unconsciously signal through statements or body language that a specific individual is the actual person whom they believe to be the perpetrator. Such actions, even if subtle, can influence the identifications made by victims and witnesses.
- Many reformers also argue that identification procedures should be videotaped so that there are opportunities to

see if the individuals supervising the procedures either intentionally or unintentionally provided cues about which individual to select. In addition, videotaping can help to show whether the victim or witness made a tentative, uncertain identification or if the identification was certain and confident.

In 2013 the Houston police department was criticized for continuing to use a photo lineup procedure in which a victim or witness is shown photos of all possible suspects at one time. By contrast, many other Texas police departments, including Austin, Dallas, and San Antonio, had switched to showing photos one at a time in order to reduce the risks of misidentification discussed in the research studies. These examples show that many police departments have adjusted their practices in light of evidence produced by research studies. However, other departments have yet to adopt evidence-based practices to reduce the risk of misidentifications.

Researching the Internet

Bearing in mind risks illuminated by research, read the identification procedure policy of the Greenbelt, Maryland, Police Department. Do you see any issues or problems with the specified procedures? http://www.greenbeltmd.gov/police /Eyewitness_identification.pdf.

Implementing New Practices

Officers may prefer to continue practices with which they are familiar. There may be resistance to change, especially if officers are distrustful of the underlying research or they believe that the new procedures needlessly permit guilty people to go free. Should the courts order police departments to conduct identification procedures in one specific way? Alternatively, would such an approach create risks that police could not adapt as new research is produced that refines understandings about the risks and benefits of different approaches? Write a memo that lists two reasons why you support either a specific, mandated set of procedures or opportunities for departments to develop their own methods? In addition, address the following question: If you were a police chief, how would you instruct your officers to conduct identification procedures, and how do you think you could convince them to cooperate in using the new methods?

Sources: Beth Schuster, "Police Lineups: Making Eyewitness Identification More Reliable," *NIJ Journal,* 258 (October 2007): 2–9; Gary L. Wells and Deah S. Quinlivan, "Suggestive Eyewitness Identification Procedures and the Supreme Court's Reliability Test in Light of Eyewitness Science: 30 Years Later," *Law and Human Behavior* 33 (2009): 1–24; Michael D. Cicchini and Joseph G. Easton, "Reforming the Law on Show-Up Identifications," *The Journal of Criminal Law and Criminology* 100 (2010): 381–413; *United States v. Ford,* 11-2034, U.S. Court of Appeals, 7th Circuit, June 6, 2012; James Pinkerton, "HPD, Sheriff Using Questioned Photo Lineups," *Houston Chronicle,* January 14, 2013 (www .houstonchronicle.com).

8. What are *Miranda* rights?

Officers must inform suspects, *before* custodial interrogation, of their right to remain silent, the prosecution's authority to use any of the suspect's statements, the right to the presence of an attorney during questioning, and the right to have an attorney appointed if the suspect is too poor to hire one.

9. What is the "public safety" exception?

Officers can ask questions of suspects in custody without first providing *Miranda* warnings when public safety would be threatened by their taking the time to supply the warnings.

10. How have police officers adapted their practices in light of Miranda?

Officers ask questions before suspects are in custody, use techniques to pretend to befriend or empathize with suspects being questioned, and misinform suspects about the existence of evidence demonstrating their guilt.

Should police officers be permitted to lie to suspects during questioning, such as falsely claiming that they have eyewitnesses or other evidence of a suspect's guilt? Do such strategies create any risks, such as innocent people feeling hopelessly doomed and admitting guilt in order to seek a plea to a lesser charge? Write an argument in favor of giving police flexibility to use such strategies as well as an argument against permitting dishonest statements. Which argument do you support? Why?

The Exclusionary Rule

What happens when police commit rights violations? One primary remedy is the exclusion of evidence from court (Gray, 2013). In 1914 the U.S. Supreme Court declared in *Weeks v. United States* that federal courts must exclude any evidence that was obtained through an improper search by federal law enforcement agents. In *Weeks*, U.S. marshals searched a home without a warrant and found incriminating evidence. According to the Court,

> if letters and private documents can thus be seized and held and used in evidence against a citizen accused of an offense, the protection of the Fourth Amendment, declaring his right to be secure against such searches and seizures, is of no value, and, so far as those thus placed are concerned, might as well be stricken from the Constitution.

Thus, the Court required that the improperly obtained evidence be excluded from use in court, even if it meant that a guilty person might go free because of a lack of enough evidence to gain a conviction. As a result of this **exclusionary rule** created by the Court, it was assumed that law enforcement officers would obey the Fourth Amendment to avoid the loss of incriminating evidence. Later, the exclusionary rule was also applied to Fifth Amendment violations caused by improper questioning, such as a failure to inform arrested individuals of their *Miranda* rights. Read the "Comparative Perspective" feature to consider whether the United States should draw from practices in other countries to refine the exclusionary rule and its impact on criminal cases.

exclusionary rule The principle that illegally obtained evidence must be excluded from trial.

The exclusionary rule does not necessarily require that cases against defendants be dismissed when constitutional rights have been violated. The prosecution can continue, but improperly obtained evidence may not be used. In some cases, other valid evidence of guilt may exist in the form of witness testimony or confessions. As described by one scholar with experience as a prosecutor,

> during my seven years as a federal prosecutor, . . . I could see that the rule's mandatory nature forced police and federal agents to think about the rules before they acted. It caused both federal and local law-enforcement authorities to train their agents in the constitutional rules in order to [avoid] evidentiary exclusion. . . . Nor was it my impression that any significant number of cases were lost as a result of the rule, especially prosecutions of violent felonies (Bradley, 2010:212).

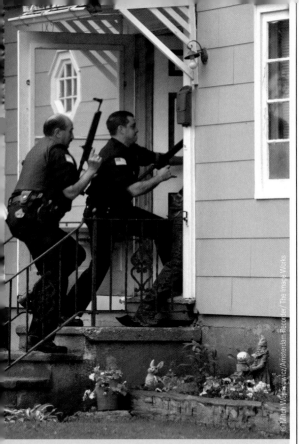

Police officers must take care to follow the rules for conducting proper searches that obey court rulings defining the Fourth Amendment protection against "unreasonable searches and seizures." Evidence will be excluded when the Fourth Amendment is violated unless the police officers' actions fall within a specific exception to the exclusionary rule.

Wolf v. Colorado (1949) Supreme Court decision in which the Fourth Amendment was applied against searches by state and local police officers, but the exclusionary rule was not imposed as the remedy for violations of the Fourth Amendment by these officials.

Mapp v. Ohio (1961) Supreme Court decision that applied the exclusionary rule as the remedy for improper searches by state and local officials.

Weeks v. United States (1914) Supreme Court decision applying the exclusionary rule as the remedy for improper searches by federal law enforcement officials.

The Application of the Exclusionary Rule to the States

In *Wolf v. Colorado* (1949), the Supreme Court incorporated the Fourth Amendment. However, the justices declined to apply the exclusionary rule to the states because they believed states could develop their own remedies to handle improper searches by police. The situation changed during the Supreme Court tenure of Chief Justice Earl Warren (1953–1969), when the Court incorporated most of the criminal justice–related rights in a way that required state law enforcement officials to adhere to the same rules federal law enforcement officials had to follow. Not until *Mapp v. Ohio* (1961) did the Court apply the exclusionary rule to the states.

Why did the Supreme Court see the exclusionary rule as necessary? Several reasons emerge in *Weeks v. United States* (1914) and *Mapp*. First, *Weeks* declared that the exclusionary rule is essential to make the Fourth Amendment meaningful. In essence, the justices believed that constitutional rights are nullified if government officials are permitted to benefit by violating those rights. Second, *Mapp* indicated that the exclusionary rule is required by the Constitution. Third, the majority opinion in *Mapp* concluded that alternatives to the exclusionary rule do not work. The opinion noted that many states had found that nothing short of exclusion of evidence would work to correct constitutional rights violations and limit the number of violations that occur. Fourth, the *Mapp* opinion argued that the use of improperly obtained evidence by officials who are responsible for upholding the law only serves to diminish respect for the law. Fifth, the *Mapp* decision indicates that the absence of an exclusionary rule would diminish the protection of all rights because it would permit all constitutional rights "to be revocable at the whim of any police officer who, in the name of law enforcement itself, chooses to suspend . . . [the] enjoyment [of rights]." Sixth, the exclusionary rule is justified in *Mapp* as an effective means of deterring police and prosecutors from violating constitutional rights (Kainen, 2013).

The existence of the exclusionary rule demonstrates the Supreme Court's conclusion that it is sometimes necessary to risk setting a guilty criminal free to ensure that constitutional rights are protected.

Exceptions to the Exclusionary Rule

The exclusionary rule has many critics who claim that the Court's decision hampers police investigations and allows guilty criminals to go free. However, research has not clearly supported claims about the negative consequences of the exclusionary rule. Studies of the impact of the exclusionary rule have produced two consistent findings. First, only a small minority of defendants file a "motion to suppress," which is used to ask a judge to exclude evidence that has allegedly been obtained in violation of the defendant's rights. Second, only a very small fraction of motions to suppress evidence are granted (Uchida & Bynum, 1991; S. Walker, 2001). Despite continuing debates about the rule's impact and effectiveness (Dripps, 2010), the Supreme Court began creating exceptions to the exclusionary rule after Warren Burger became chief justice in 1969.

The Exclusionary Rule in Canada and Europe

The exclusionary rule in the United States is mandatory when evidence is obtained in violation of the Fourth and Fifth Amendments unless the circumstances fit certain exceptions, such as the "good faith" and "inevitable discovery" situations discussed in this section of the chapter. By contrast, other countries' legal systems often consider the issue of exclusion on a case-by-case basis for searches, whereas exclusion is more consistently enforced when improper questioning of suspects occurs.

In the Canadian case of *R. v. Grant* (2009), a pedestrian was stopped and surrounded by police officers without any reasonable suspicion of wrongdoing. When asked, the pedestrian admitted that he was illegally carrying a gun. After he was convicted of the crime, the Canadian Supreme Court examined whether the gun should have been excluded from evidence since it was obtained through an improper stop. The Court applied a three-part test to consider whether the evidence should have been excluded. It considered

1. the seriousness of the violation of the Canadian Charter of Rights by the police officers' conduct;
2. the impact of the violation on the rights of the accused; and
3. society's interests in having the evidence examined at trial as part of the merits of the case.

In applying these factors to the case, the Court held that the gun was properly admitted into evidence. Presumably, if the evidence had been obtained through an involuntary search, a forceful home invasion, or other more flagrant invasion of rights, the Court's test would have weighed more heavily in favor of the accused. In cases where the exclusionary rule has been applied in Canada, the emphasis has been on maintaining the image of the judicial system for upholding rights and laws rather than an emphasis on deterring improper behavior by the police.

In Germany, there is also a case-by-case consideration of circumstances when improper searches are challenged and defendants seek to have evidence excluded. In each case, the judge must balance the protection of the suspect's rights against the interests of society in having useful evidence fully examined and lawbreakers punished for their crimes. German courts frequently admit evidence from improper searches; exclusion is more likely to occur for flagrant violations of citizens' privacy, such as improperly gaining access to medical records or improper electronic surveillance.

With respect to improper questioning of suspects in custody, however, Canada, Germany, England, and France all impose the exclusionary rule more consistently than in other situations. Scholars believe that the stronger application of the exclusionary rule for questioning reflects serious concerns about the risk of false confessions if people feel trapped, pressured, and denied their rights during questioning. By contrast, controversies about searches arise in a wider variety of circumstances, many of which involve relatively modest intrusions on rights and, moreover, produce reliable evidence of guilt (e.g., weapons, drugs, stolen goods, etc).

For Critical Analysis

Should the United States consider a two-track approach to the exclusionary rule with greater emphasis on exclusion for violations of *Miranda* rights but more case-by-case decisions for improper searches? Give three reasons to support your answer to this question. What would be the impact and effect of the approach that you advocate?

Sources: Craig M. Bradley, "Interrogation and Silence: A Comparative Study," *Wisconsin International Law Journal* 27:271–97 (2009); Craig M. Bradley, "Reconceiving the Fourth Amendment and the Exclusionary Rule," *Law and Contemporary Problems* 73:211–38 (2010); Tracey Tyler, "Should Evidence Be Allowed If Police Break the Law?" *Toronto Star,* August 8, 2009 (www.thestar.com).

"Good Faith" Exception   The Supreme Court created a **"good faith" exception** to the exclusionary rule when officers use search warrants (***United States v. Leon,*** 1984). *Good faith* means that the officers acted with the honest belief that they were following the proper rules, but the judge issued the warrant improperly. In addition, the reliance and honest belief must be reasonable. If officers knew that a judge issued a warrant based on no evidence whatsoever, the officers could not claim that they reasonably and honestly relied on the warrant. But when officers present evidence of probable cause to the judge and the judge issues a warrant based on information that actually falls below the standard of probable cause, the officers may use evidence found in the resulting search, because it was the judge who made the error, not the police (Cammack, 2010). However, evidence can still be excluded if officers undertake a warrantless search based on their own discretionary decision, even if they honestly (but wrongly) believe that such a search is permitted in such circumstances.

"good faith" exception
Exception to the exclusionary rule that permits the use of improperly obtained evidence when police officers acted in honest reliance on a defective statute, a warrant improperly issued by a magistrate, or a consent to search by someone who lacked authority to give such permission.

United States v. Leon (1984)
Supreme Court decision announcing the "good faith" exception to the exclusionary rule.

TABLE 6.2 Exclusionary Rule

The Supreme Court has created the exclusionary rule as a means of ensuring that Fourth and Fifth Amendment rights are protected. It has also provided exceptions to this rule.

Case	Decision
Exclusionary rule	
Mapp v. Ohio (1961)	Because the Fourth Amendment protects people from unreasonable searches and seizures by all law enforcement officials, evidence found through improper searches or seizures must be excluded from use at state and federal trials.
"Good faith" exception	
United States v. Leon (1984)	When officers act in good faith reliance on a warrant, the evidence will not be excluded even if the warrant was issued improperly.
"Inevitable discovery" exception	
Nix v. Williams (1984)	Improperly obtained evidence can be used when it would later have inevitably been discovered without improper actions by the police.

"inevitable discovery" rule
Supreme Court ruling that improperly obtained evidence can be used when it would later have been inevitably discovered by the police.

Nix v. Williams (1984) Legal decision in which the Supreme Court created the "inevitable discovery" exception to the exclusionary rule.

"Inevitable Discovery" Rule   Another important exception to the exclusionary rule is the **"inevitable discovery" rule** (Grubman, 2011). This rule arose from a case involving the tragic abduction and murder of a young girl. The police sought an escapee from a psychiatric hospital who was seen carrying a large bundle. The man being sought contacted an attorney and arranged to surrender to police in a town 160 miles away from the scene of the abduction. The Supreme Court subsequently found that the police improperly questioned the suspect outside of the presence of his attorney while driving him back to the city where the abduction occurred (*Brewer v. Williams*, 1977). The Court declared that the girl's body and the suspect's statements had to be excluded from evidence because they were obtained in violation of his rights. Thus, his murder conviction was overturned and he was given a new trial. At the second trial, he was convicted again. However, at the second trial, the prosecution used the body in evidence against him based on the claim that search parties would have found the body eventually even without his confession. There was a search team within two and one-half miles of the body at the time that it was found. In *Nix v. Williams* **(1984)**, the Supreme Court agreed that the improperly obtained evidence can be used when it would later have been inevitably discovered, without improper actions by the police. Table 6.2 summarizes selected Supreme Court decisions regarding the exclusionary rule as it applies to the Fourth and Fifth Amendments.

When the Court issued its decisions in *Weeks* and *Mapp*, it appeared that the exclusion of evidence would be guided by a trial judge's answer to the question, "Did police violate the suspect's rights?" By contrast, through the development of exceptions to the rule, the Court shifted its focus to the question, "Did the police make an error that was so serious that the exclusion of evidence is required?" For example, the "good faith" exception established in *United States v. Leon* (1984) emphasizes the fact that officers did what they thought they were supposed to do. The decision did not rest on the fact that the suspect's Fourth Amendment rights were violated by a search conducted with an improper warrant. Thus, the Supreme Court's creation of exceptions to the exclusionary rule has given police officers the flexibility to make specific kinds of errors in an increasing variety of situations without jeopardizing the admissibility of evidence that may help establish a defendant's guilt (Nolasco, del Carmen, & Vaughn, 2011).

In 2009 some commentators speculated that the Supreme Court was deeply divided on the issue of whether to eliminate the exclusionary rule (Liptak, 2009). Five justices declined to apply the exclusionary rule to the case of an improper search, when a man was wrongly arrested because of sloppy record keeping in a police database that erroneously informed the officers that there was an arrest warrant (*Herring v. United States*, 2009).

Critics of the exclusionary rule hope that this decision moved the Court one step closer to abolishing the rule. In reality, the fate of the rule will be determined by new justices, who could go either way (C. E. Smith, McCall, & McCall, 2009). In the immediate future, it seems unlikely that President Barack Obama would appoint new justices who would favor the elimination of the exclusionary rule, but presidents cannot always predict accurately how their nominees will decide specific issues.

☑CHECK POINT

11. Why was the exclusionary rule created and eventually applied to the states?

The exclusionary rule was created to deter officers from violating people's rights, and the Supreme Court considers it an essential component of the Fourth and Fifth Amendments.

12. What are the criticisms of the exclusionary rule?

The rule is criticized for hampering police investigations and permitting some guilty people to go free.

13. What are the main exceptions to the exclusionary rule?

A "good faith" exception in warrant situations; cases in which evidence would have been discovered by the police inevitably anyway ("inevitable discovery" rule).

STOP&ANALYZE

When you add up the pros and cons, does the exclusionary rule provide a needed benefit for our society and justice system? Describe three situations in which the exclusionary rule should definitely apply—*or* list three reasons why the exclusionary rule should be abolished. Give two reasons why you would treat *Miranda* cases differently from search cases *or* why you would treat them in the same manner with respect to the issue of excluding improperly obtained evidence.

A QUESTION OF ETHICS

Think, Discuss, Write

A newspaper's investigation of the New York City Police Department published in 2014 raised concerns about whether overtime and pension incentives could lead officers to make groundless arrests. Such arrests would violate people's Fourth Amendment rights against "unreasonable seizures." The investigation found that several of the officers most frequently sued by aggrieved citizens for rights violations were also the officers who made the most money from overtime pay. For example, an officer who had been sued 28 times over an eight-year period, leading to $884,000 being paid by the city to settle these lawsuits, made over $38,000 in overtime pay in 2012 and again in 2013, making him among the top 1 percent of officers in overtime pay.

One lawyer complained that drug arrests lead to hours of overtime pay for officers who must fill out paperwork to process the arrestees. In one case, officers were accused of arresting four men and driving them around for hours in a police vehicle before delivering them to the police station that was only two blocks away from the place of the arrest. It appeared to critics that the officers' efforts to waste time by the delay were for the purpose of gaining more overtime pay. Moreover, the city paid the arrested individuals more than $20,000 each to settle the lawsuits that they filed for false arrest.

In addition, because an officer's annual pension in New York City is set at one-half of her or his pay in the final year before retirement, there is an incentive for officers to gain as much overtime pay as possible in the year prior to retirement. In 2013 one retirement-age officer earned more than $59,000 in overtime pay on top of his base salary of $112,000.

Discussion/Writing Assignments

If you were the mayor of New York City, what proposals would you make to avoid the risk that financial incentives might lead officers to violate people's rights with groundless arrests? Write a memo that provides and explains five suggestions concerning such matters as the pay system, training, and supervision of officers.

Sources: Corrine Lestch and Jennifer Fermino, "Top 20 NYPD Overtime Earners May Be Padding Their Pensions: Report," *New York Daily News,* February 1, 2014 (www.nydailynews.com); Sarah Ryley and Dareh Gregorian, "NYPD's Most-Sued Cop Also Among Top Overtime Earners for Past Two Years," *New York Daily News,* February 17, 2014 (www.nydailynews.com).

SUMMARY

❶ Describe the extent of police officers' authority to stop people and to conduct searches of people, their vehicles, and other property.

- The Supreme Court has defined rules for the circumstances and justifications for stops, searches, and arrests in light of the Fourth Amendment's prohibition on unreasonable searches and seizures.
- The plain view doctrine permits officers to visually examine and use as evidence, without a warrant, any contraband or criminal evidence that is in open sight when the officers are in a place where they are legally permitted to be.
- Most stops must be supported by reasonable suspicion; an arrest or a search warrant must be supported by enough information to constitute probable cause.
- Police use of deadly force occurs infrequently and can no longer be applied to unarmed fleeing felons.

❷ Explain how police officers seek warrants in order to conduct searches and make arrests.

- To obtain a warrant, police officers present an affidavit (sworn statement) verifying the accuracy of the information that they present to the judge and that they hope the judge will regard as constituting probable cause to search or make an arrest.

❸ Describe situations in which police officers can examine property and conduct searches without obtaining a warrant.

- Searches are considered "reasonable" and may be conducted without warrants in specific circumstances that present special needs beyond the normal purposes of law enforcement. For example,

borders and airports always allow searches without warrants.
- Limited searches may be conducted without warrants when officers have reasonable suspicions to justify a stop-and-frisk for weapons on the streets, when officers make a lawful arrest, under exigent circumstances, when people voluntarily consent to searches of their persons or property, and in certain situations involving automobiles.

❹ Explain the purpose of the privilege against compelled self-incrimination.

- The Fifth Amendment privilege against compelled self-incrimination helps protect citizens against violence and coercion by police and helps to maintain the legitimacy and integrity of the legal system.
- The Supreme Court's decision in *Miranda v. Arizona* requires officers to inform suspects of specific rights before custodial questioning, although officers have adapted their practices to accommodate this rule so that they can question people without any impediment from the warning. Several exceptions to the warning have been created by the Supreme Court.

❺ Define the exclusionary rule, and identify the situations in which it applies.

- By barring the use of illegally obtained evidence in court, the exclusionary rule is designed to deter police from violating citizens' rights during criminal investigations.
- The Supreme Court has created several exceptions to the exclusionary rule, including the "inevitable discovery" rule and the "good faith" exception in defective warrant situations.

Questions for Review

1. What are the requirements for police officers with respect to stops, searches, arrests, and warrants?
2. Under what circumstances are warrantless searches permissible?
3. How have police officers adapted to the requirements of *Miranda v. Arizona*?
4. What are the main exceptions to the exclusionary rule?

Key Terms and Cases

affidavit (p. 192)

consent search (p. 199)

exclusionary rule (p. 209)

exigent circumstances (p. 198)

"good faith" exception (p. 211)

"inevitable discovery" rule (p. 212)

inventory search (p. 203)

plain view doctrine (p. 189)

probable cause (p. 191)

"public safety" exception (p. 205)

reasonable expectation of privacy (p. 189)

reasonable suspicion (p. 190)

search (p. 189)

seizures (p. 189)

stop (p. 190)

stop-and-frisk search (p. 196)

totality of circumstances (p. 192)

Chimel v. California (1969) (p. 198)

Illinois v. Gates (1983) (p. 192)

Mapp v. Ohio (1961) (p. 210)

Miranda v. Arizona (1966) (p. 204)

Nix v. Williams (1984) (p. 212)

Tennessee v. Garner (1985) (p. 190)

Terry v. Ohio (1968) (p. 196)

United States v. Drayton (2002) (p. 199)

United States v. Leon (1984) (p. 211)

Weeks v. United States (1914) (p. 210)

Wolf v. Colorado (1949) (p. 210)

7 | Courts and Adjudication

LEARNING OBJECTIVES

1. Describe the structure of the American court system.
2. Name the qualities that the public desires in a judge.
3. Describe the process by which American judges are selected.
4. Identify some of the roles of the prosecuting attorney.
5. Describe the role that the prosecutor's discretion plays in the process for filing criminal charges.
6. Identify those with whom the prosecutor interacts in decision making.
7. Describe the day-to-day reality of criminal defense work in the United States.
8. List the methods for providing counsel for defendants who cannot afford a private attorney.
9. Describe the courtroom work group, and explain how it functions.

On May 6, 2013, the entire nation was shocked by news reports about three women in Cleveland who had been held as sexually abused prisoners for more than a decade by a man named Ariel Castro. When Castro was away from the home where he kept the women chained in captivity, one of the women managed to break open a door and yell for help. Neighbors called the police while two nearby men pushed in a door to help free the women whose kidnappings had occurred so long ago that most people presumed that they were dead (Muskal & Pearce, 2013). Castro was quickly arrested. When he appeared in court, he entered a plea of "not guilty."

The initial plea did not mean that Castro was actually going to claim to be innocent. The evidence against him seemed overwhelming. He faced the prospect of having his three victims testify against him about the years of violent abuse that they suffered at his hands, including forced miscarriages when beatings he administered terminated pregnancies caused by his rapes. Instead, the initial plea was part of the pretrial process through which most convictions are obtained in the criminal justice system. As Castro's defense attorney Craig Weintraub openly admitted to news reporters, the goal was to engage in a negotiation process that would lead to a plea agreement (Ford, Martinez, & Sterling, 2013). Each side had something to gain from a plea agreement. Castro was seeking to avoid the death penalty, and prosecutors hoped to spare the victims from reliving their trauma during a trial by testifying and answering questions about the horrors of their violent confinement. The prosecutor would also benefit in saving substantial time and money if a lengthy death penalty trial could be avoided.

In July 2013, the two sides reached an agreement. Castro entered a guilty plea to 937 criminal charges, including multiple kidnappings and rapes. In exchange for admitting guilt and avoiding an expensive trial, Cuyahoga County Prosecutor Timothy McGinty recommended a sentence of life in prison without possibility of parole plus 1,000 additional years of imprisonment. Judge Michael Russo made sure that Castro understood the severity of the impending sentence and the fact that he was giving up his right to a trial by jury in entering the guilty plea. Castro indicated that he understood. Then Judge Russo read many individual charges, and Castro said, "Guilty" over and over again when asked for his plea on each charge (Fantz, 2013). Afterward, Judge Russo imposed the sentence recommended by the prosecutor (McLaughlin & Brown, 2013). Ultimately, Castro served only one month in prison before committing suicide by hanging himself with a bedsheet in his prison cell (Muskal & Pearce, 2013).

Because of the high stakes and uncertainty that surround criminal trials, most defendants plead guilty as they get closer to the prospect of being judged by a random group of citizens drawn from the community. Court organization and processes serve to structure the interactions of the attorneys and judges who ultimately produce the outcomes

in criminal cases. Prosecutors create incentives for guilty pleas by offering reductions in charges and sentences in exchange for admissions of guilt. Defense attorneys advise their clients by predicting the likelihood that a jury might issue a guilty verdict, weighing it against the advantages of taking a plea deal. Even if specific incentives are not offered, defendants may plead guilty if only to demonstrate to the judge that they are taking responsibility for their actions. They may hope that such honesty will lead the judge to soften the sentence. Meanwhile, judges oversee court processes, bear responsibility for ensuring that rules are followed and defendants' rights are protected, and make decisions about punishments.

Ariel Castro's case demonstrates the power and importance of prosecutors and defense attorneys. Defense attorneys must advise their clients and make strategic decisions about whether to plead guilty and, if a case goes to trial, what tactics to use during proceedings. Prosecutors determine who will be charged with a crime and what charges they will face. They communicate with victims and their families and may seek their approval for plea-negotiation offers. An attorney for the three women held captive by Castro told reporters that the women wanted a negotiated plea because they did not want to testify about their victimization in a lengthy trial (Fantz, 2013). The victims' wishes may have influenced the prosecutor to forgo his original intention to seek the death penalty, a punishment that would likely have pushed Castro to seek a trial rather than a plea.

The American criminal justice system places great power and responsibility in the hands of attorneys for each side in a criminal case. The prosecutor and defense attorney are the most influential figures in determining the outcomes of criminal cases. Their discretionary decisions and negotiations determine people's fates. As we shall see in this chapter, the justice system's ability to handle cases and produce fair results depends on the dedication, skill, and enthusiasm of these lawyers. In addition, the lawyers who become judges assume important duties for overseeing court proceedings that decide whether accused defendants will be found guilty and punished. When you read the job requirements and overview of what it takes to be a prosecutor in "Careers in Criminal Justice" later in the chapter, imagine the impact of your decisions on people's lives if you pursued such a career.

The Functions and Structure of American Courts

The United States has a dual court system. Separate federal and state court systems handle matters throughout the nation. Other countries have a single national court system, but American rules and traditions permit states to create their own court systems to handle most legal matters, including most crimes.

In the United States, both state and federal courts use the **adversarial process** to protect the rights of defendants and examine evidence to determine whether a defendant is guilty. In the adversarial process, a professional attorney, trained in the rules of evidence and the strategies of advocacy, represents each side—the prosecution (government) and defense (defendant). These attorneys challenge each other's evidence and arguments while trying to persuade the judge or jury about the defendant's guilt or lack thereof. Even when the attorneys negotiate a guilty plea without going to trial, they are supposed to adopt an adversarial stance that represents the interests of their side. Although they may hold friendly and cooperative discussions, the content of these discussions often reflects probing, bluffing, compromising, and disagreeing.

In the adversarial context of American courts, judges often act like referees at a sporting event. They oversee the interactions and enforce the rules without imposing their will on the presentation of evidence by attorneys. The adversarial process is derived from British law and exists in the criminal justice systems of other former British colonies besides the United States. By contrast, other countries typically use an **inquisitorial process**, in which the judge takes an active role in questioning witnesses and asserts herself into the investigation of the case and the examination of evidence.

The federal courts oversee a limited range of criminal cases. For example, they deal with people accused of violating the criminal laws of the national government. Federal crimes include counterfeiting, kidnapping, smuggling, and drug trafficking, among others. But such cases account for only a small portion of the criminal cases that pass through U.S. courts each year. For every offender sentenced to incarceration by federal courts, more than 10 offenders are sent to prisons and jails by state courts, because most crimes are defined by state laws (BJS, 2011b). This disparity may grow wider as federal law enforcement agencies increasingly emphasize antiterrorism activities rather than traditional crime control investigations. The gap is even greater for misdemeanors, because state courts bear the primary responsibility for processing the lesser offenses, such as disorderly conduct, that arise on a daily basis.

State supreme courts monitor the decisions of lower courts within their own states by interpreting state constitutions and statutes. Although most are named the "Supreme Court" of the state (for example, "Minnesota Supreme Court"), in a few states, they have different names. In New York, the top court is called the New York Court of Appeals, and "supreme courts" in that state are trial courts. The U.S. Supreme Court oversees both court systems by interpreting the U.S. Constitution, which protects the rights of defendants in federal and state criminal cases (Smith, DeJong, & McCall, 2011).

A third court system operates in several states; this adds to the issues of complexity and coordination that the country's decentralized courts face. Native Americans have tribal courts, whose authority is endorsed by congressional statutes and Supreme Court decisions, with **jurisdiction** over their own people on tribal land. The existence of tribal courts permits Native American judges to apply their people's cultural values in resolving civil lawsuits and processing certain criminal offenses (Florey, 2013).

The Functions of Courts

Courts serve many important functions for society. We often picture courts as the settings for criminal trials, much like those portrayed on television shows such as *Law and Order*. When courts focus on criminal matters, through bail hearings, preliminary hearings, plea bargaining, and trials, they are serving a *norm enforcement* function for society. A *norm* is a value, standard, or expectation concerning people's behavior. In other words, courts play a central role in enforcing society's rules and standards for behavior—a function that contributes to peace and stability in society. In addition, courts handle a wide variety of matters beyond criminal justice, matters that benefit society in ways that extend beyond merely determining the guilt of and punishments for criminal defendants.

adversarial process Court process, employed in the United States and other former British colonies, in which lawyers for each side represent their clients' best interests in presenting evidence and formulating arguments as a means to discover the truth and protect the rights of defendants.

inquisitorial process Court process, employed in most countries of the world, in which the judge takes an active role in investigating the case and examining evidence by, for example, questioning witnesses.

jurisdiction The geographic territory or legal boundaries within which control may be exercised; the range of a court's authority.

Courts also handle *dispute processing* for society. When people disagree about contracts, money, property, and personal injuries in ways that they cannot resolve on their own, they file lawsuits seeking government intervention on their behalf. Presumably the availability of courts for dispute processing helps avoid the possibility that people will resort to violence when they become angry about disagreements with business partners, neighbors, and others. In criminal justice, the dispute-processing function plays a significant role when people file lawsuits against police officers or correctional officials for violating constitutional rights. As a result of such lawsuits, judges may order prisons to change their procedures or order police officers or their departments to pay thousands of dollars to compensate a citizen for an erroneous arrest, excessive use of force, or the improper search of a home.

Courts also engage in *policy making*, especially the highest courts, such as state supreme courts and the U.S. Supreme Court. When judges interpret the U.S. Constitution or other forms of law and thereby define the rights of individuals, they are simultaneously telling police officers, correctional officers, and other officials what they can and cannot do. Such judicial decisions determine how searches will be conducted, how suspects will be questioned, and how prisons will be managed. This function makes courts in the United States especially important and powerful, because judges in other countries usually do not have the authority to tell officials throughout all levels of government how to carry out their jobs.

The Structure of Courts

Both the federal and state court systems have trial and appellate courts. There are three levels of courts: trial courts of limited jurisdiction, trial courts of general jurisdiction, and appellate courts.

Cases begin in a trial court, which handles determinations of guilt and sentencing. **Trial courts of limited jurisdiction** handle only misdemeanors, lawsuits for small amounts of money, and other specific kinds of cases. The full range of felony cases and all other civil lawsuits are heard in **trial courts of general jurisdiction**. Trial courts are the arenas in which evidence is presented, witnesses give testimony and are questioned by attorneys, and lawyers make arguments about the guilt (or lack thereof) of criminal defendants. These are the courts in which jury trials take place and judges impose prison sentences. The federal system has no limited jurisdiction trial courts. All federal cases begin in the general jurisdiction trial courts, the U.S. district courts.

Cases move to intermediate **appellate courts** if defendants claim that errors by police or the trial court contributed to their convictions. Further appeals may be filed with a state supreme court or the U.S. Supreme Court, depending on which court system the case is in and what kind of legal argument is being made. Unlike trial courts, appellate courts do not have juries, nor do lawyers present evidence. Instead, lawyers for each side make arguments about specific alleged errors of law or procedure that the trial judge failed to correct during the proceeding that determined the defendant's guilt. Thus, the written and oral arguments presented in an entire appellate case may focus on a single question such as, "Should the trial judge have excluded the defendant's confession because the police did not adequately inform her or him about *Miranda* rights?" Appellate judges often decide cases by issuing elaborate written opinions to explain why they answered the question at issue in a certain way (C. Jacobs & Smith, 2011).

All states have *courts of last resort* (usually called *state supreme courts*), and all but a few have an intermediate-level appellate court (usually called *courts of appeals*). In the federal system, the U.S. Supreme Court is the court of last resort, and the U.S. circuit courts of appeals are the intermediate appellate courts. The U.S. Supreme Court, with its nine justices, controls its own caseload by choosing 75 to 85 cases to hear from among the 7,000 cases submitted annually. It takes the votes of four justices for the Supreme Court to decide to grant a request to hear a case. After the justices consider the written and oral arguments in the cases selected for

trial courts of limited jurisdiction Criminal courts with trial jurisdiction over misdemeanor cases and preliminary matters in felony cases. Sometimes these courts hold felony trials that may result in penalties below a specific limit.

trial courts of general jurisdiction Criminal courts with jurisdiction over all offenses, including felonies. In some states, these courts also hear appeals.

appellate courts Courts that do not try criminal cases but hear appeals of decisions of lower courts.

The Supreme Court of the United States has the final word on questions concerning interpretations of the U.S. Constitution. Should a small group of appointed judges possess such power in a democracy?

The justices of the U.S. Supreme Court in 2012 (and year of appointment): front row (left to right): Clarence Thomas (1991); Antonin Scalia (1986); John Roberts (Chief Justice-2005); Anthony Kennedy (1988); Ruth Bader Ginsburg (1993); back row: Sonia Sotomayor (2009); Stephen Breyer (1994); Samuel Alito (2006); Elena Kagan (2010).

hearing, a majority vote will determine the outcome and the rule of law to be expressed in the Court's majority opinion.

Many decisions are unanimous, but other cases are decided by a narrow five-to-four vote when the justices are deeply divided. For example, when the Court decided in 2010 that the Second Amendment's "right to bear arms" that gives law-abiding adults the constitutional right to own and keep handguns in their homes applies against city and state laws as well as federal law, the justices split five-to-four in reaching the decision (*McDonald v. City of Chicago*, 2010). Close decisions can be overturned in later years if the new justices appointed to replace retiring justices bring viewpoints to the Court that differ from those of their predecessors.

Although the basic three-tiered structure is found throughout the United States, the number of courts, their names, and their specific functions vary widely. For example, in state systems, 13,000 trial courts of limited jurisdiction typically handle traffic cases, small claims, misdemeanors, and other less serious matters. These courts handle 90 percent of all criminal matters. Some limited jurisdiction courts bear responsibility for a specific category of cases, sometimes including serious offenses. These courts were developed as part of a movement to create **problem-solving courts** that would directly address recurring problems or troubled individuals who appeared in court repeatedly. Drug courts, for example, attempt to combine rehabilitation, close supervision, and the threat of punishment to push drug offenders to shake free from substance-abuse problems (Rempel et al., 2012; Rockwell, 2008). Mental health courts, which are expanding across the country, seek to handle cases of nonviolent offenders with mental disorders and to develop appropriate treatment, supervision, and assistance instead of incarceration (Dirks-Linhorst, Kondrat, Linhorst, & Morani, 2013; Heaphy, 2010; Kimber, 2008). Some cities have developed domestic violence courts to give focused attention to recurring problems of violence within families and among those with intimate relationships (Boyd, 2011; Gover, MacDonald, & Alpert, 2003). Other cities have dedicated judges' time to addressing problems of veterans or the homeless (S. Burns, 2010).

The federal system begins with the U.S. district courts, its trial courts of general jurisdiction. In the states, these courts have a variety of names (circuit, district, superior, and others) and are reserved for felony cases or substantial lawsuits. These are the courts in which trials take place, judges rule on evidence, and juries issue verdicts. Figure 7.1 shows the basic structure of the dual court system.

American trial courts are highly decentralized. Local political influences and community values affect the courts: local officials determine their budgets, residents make up the staff, and operations are managed so as to fit community needs. Only a few small states have a court system organized on a statewide basis, with

problem-solving courts Lower-level local courts dedicated to addressing particular social problems or troubled populations. Examples of such courts include drug courts, domestic violence courts, and mental health courts.

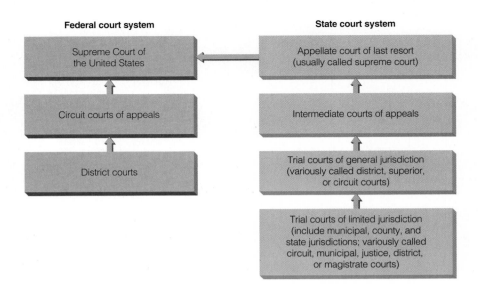

FIGURE 7.1

The Dual Court System of the United States and Routes of Appeal Whether a case enters through the federal or state court system depends on which law has been broken. The right of appeal to a higher court exists in either system.

a central administration and state funding. In most of the country, the criminal courts operate under the state penal code but are staffed, managed, and financed by county or city governments. Many of these courts have been significantly burdened by budget cuts since the onset of the nation's economic crisis in 2008. State courts in 42 states experienced budget cuts in 2011, and the New York state courts alone experienced a budget reduction of $170 million (Favate, 2012). The federal courts faced similar cancellation of trials and reduced staffing that disrupted operations during the budget deadlock between Republicans and Democrats in Congress during 2013 ("For Federal Courts, Shutdown Caused Broad Disruptions," 2013).

Lower courts, especially at the state level, do not always display the dignity and formal procedures of general jurisdiction trial courts and appellate courts. Instead, they may function informally. Decisions and processes in one judge's courtroom may differ from those in another courtroom. In most urban areas, local courts process seemingly endless numbers of people through the crime control model (see Chapter 1), and each defendant's "day in court" usually lasts only a few minutes. People expect their local courts to adhere to the standards that reflect American values of justice, and many are critical when the courts do not meet these ideals (Dyer, 2012).

☑ CHECK POINT

1. **What is the dual court system?**
   Separate federal and state court systems handling cases in the United States.

2. **What different categories of courts exist within each court system?**
   The federal system is made up of the Supreme Court of the United States, circuit courts of appeals, and district courts. State court systems are made up of an appellate court of last resort, intermediate appellate courts (in most states), trial courts of general jurisdiction, and trial courts of limited jurisdiction.

3. **What does it mean for courts to be decentralized?**
   Operated, controlled, and funded by local communities, not a statewide administration; most state and county courts are decentralized.

STOP&ANALYZE

Will contemporary budget crises lead to greater centralization in state court systems? What actors might resist moves toward centralization?

To Be a Judge

People tend to see judges as the most powerful actors in the criminal justice process. Their rulings and sentencing decisions influence the actions of police, defense attorneys, and prosecutors. For example, if judges treat certain crimes lightly, police and prosecutors may be less inclined to arrest and prosecute people who commit those offenses. Although judges are thought of primarily in connection with trials, some of their work—signing warrants, setting bail, arraigning defendants, accepting guilty pleas, and scheduling cases—takes place outside the formal trial process.

More than any other person in the system, the judge is expected to embody justice, ensuring that the right to due process is upheld and that the defendant receives fair treatment. The prosecutor and the defense attorney each represent a "side" in a criminal case. By contrast, the judge's black robe and gavel symbolize impartiality. Both within and outside the courthouse, the judge is supposed to act according to a well-defined role. Judges are expected to make careful, consistent decisions that uphold the ideal of equal justice for all citizens (McKee, 2007; Dyer, 2012).

Who Becomes a Judge?

In U.S. society, the position of judge, even at the lowest level of the judicial hierarchy, brings high status. Public service, political power, and prestige in the community may matter more than a high-paying job to those who aspire to the judiciary. Indeed, many judges take a significant cut in pay to assume a position on the bench (Tillman, 2012). Private practice attorneys often work over 50 hours or more each week preparing cases and counseling clients. By contrast, judges can typically assert control over their own working hours and schedules. For example, although judges carry heavy caseloads, they frequently decide for themselves when to go home at the end of the workday. The ability to control one's own work schedule is therefore an additional attraction for lawyers interested in becoming judges.

Historically, the vast majority of judges have been white men with strong political connections. Women and members of minority groups had few opportunities to enter the legal profession prior to the 1960s and thus were seldom considered for judgeships. In 2013 women comprised 29 percent of state judiciaries, including 34 percent of judges on state appellate courts, 27 percent on general jurisdiction trial courts, and 32 percent on limited jurisdiction courts (National Association of Women Judges, 2014).

Contemporary political factors in many cities dictate that a portion of judges be drawn from specific demographic groups as political party leaders seek to gain the support of various segments of the voting public. Thus, overall 7 percent of state trial judges are African American, 4 percent are Latino, 2 percent are Asian or Pacific Islander in ancestry, and less than one-half of 1 percent are Native American

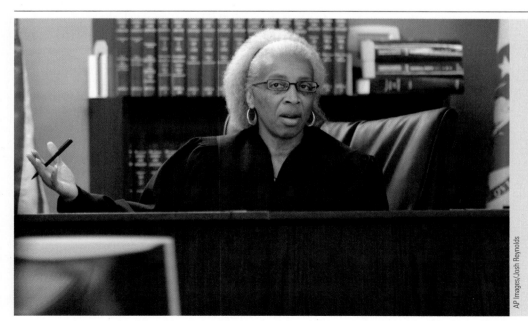

Judges bear important responsibilities for ensuring that both prosecutors and defense attorneys follow proper law and procedure. They must ensure that the rights of defendants are protected during court proceedings. Here Judge Geraldine Hines of Massachusetts Superior Court presides over her courtroom. What qualifications do you think someone should have in order to become a judge?

AP Images/Josh Reynolds

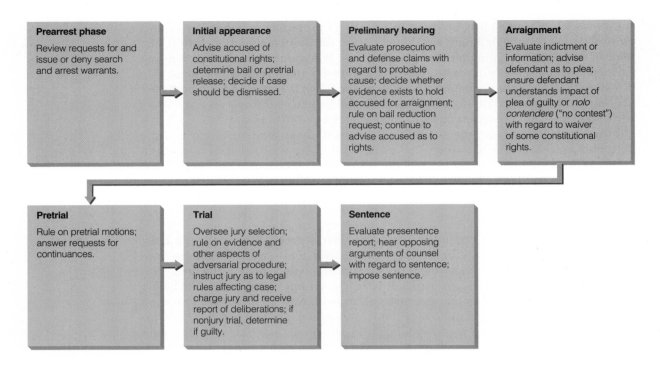

FIGURE 7.2

Actions of a Trial Court Judge in Processing a Felony Case Throughout pretrial and trial processes, the judge ensures that legal standards are upheld; he or she maintains courtroom decorum, protects the rights of the accused, meets the requirement of a speedy trial, and makes certain that case records are maintained properly.

(American Bar Association, 2010). These figures reflect great progress in advancing equal opportunity since the 1960s, but still demonstrate significant underrepresentation of every demographic group except white males. A majority of Americans are female, but women hold only one-quarter of judgeships. In addition, 2010 U.S. Census figures show the country's population to be 12.6 percent African American, 16.3 percent Latino, 5.7 percent Asian or Pacific Islander, and 1 percent Native American (Humes, Jones, & Ramirez, 2011) whereas the percentages for diversity among judges are markedly lower.

Comparing the racial and ethnic makeup of the judiciary with that of the defendants in courts raises important questions (Nava, 2008). If middle-aged white men hold nearly all the power to make judgments about people from other segments of society, will people suspect that decisions about guilt and punishment are being made in an unfair manner? Will people think that punishment is being imposed on behalf of a privileged segment of society rather than on behalf of the entire, diverse U.S. society? Moreover, the political connections necessary to gain judgeships continue to disadvantage women and members of racial minority groups in many communities. Because judges both symbolize the law and make important decisions about law, the lack of diversity in the judiciary provides a visible contrast with American values related to equal opportunity.

Functions of the Judge

Although people usually think that a judge's job is to preside at trials, in reality the work of most judges extends to all aspects of the judicial process. Defendants see a judge whenever decisions about their future are being made: when bail is set, pretrial motions are made, guilty pleas are accepted, a trial is conducted, a sentence is pronounced, and appeals are filed (see Figure 7.2). However, judges' duties are not limited to making such decisions about criminal defendants within the courtroom;

judges also perform administrative tasks outside the courtroom. Judges have three major roles: adjudicator, negotiator, and administrator.

Adjudicator Judges must assume a neutral stance in overseeing the contest between the prosecution and the defense. They must apply the law in ways that uphold the rights of the accused in decisions about detention, plea, trial, and sentence. Judges receive a certain amount of discretion in performing these tasks—for example, in setting bail—but they must do so according to the law. They must avoid any conduct that could appear biased (Geyh, 2012).

Negotiator Many decisions that determine the fates of defendants take place outside of public view, in the judge's private chambers. These decisions come about through negotiations between prosecutors and defense attorneys about plea bargains, sentencing, and bail conditions. Judges spend much of their time in their chambers talking with prosecutors and defense attorneys. They often encourage the parties to work out a guilty plea or agree to proceed in a certain way. The judge may act as a referee, keeping both sides on track in accordance with the law. Sometimes the judge takes an even more active part in the negotiations, suggesting terms for an agreement or even pressuring one side to accept an agreement (Carodine, 2010).

Administrator A seldom recognized function of most judges is managing the courthouse. In urban areas, a professional court administrator may direct the people who keep records, schedule cases, and do the many other jobs that keep a system functioning. But even in cities, judges are in charge of their own courtroom and staff. In rural areas, which do not usually employ professional court administrators, the judges' administrative tasks may expand to include managing labor relations, budgeting, as well as maintenance of the courthouse building. As administrator, the judge must deal with political actors such as county commissioners, legislators, and members of the state executive bureaucracy. Chief judges in large courts may also use their administrative powers to push other judges to cooperate in advancing the court's goals of processing cases in a timely manner (Jacob, 1973). For judges whose training as lawyers focused on learning law and courtroom advocacy skills, managing a complex organization with a sizeable budget and many employees can pose a major challenge (Levy, 2011; C. E. Smith & Feldman, 2001).

Many observers argue that a fourth role of judges is emerging in some court systems. They see judges acting as "problem solvers" in newly developed problem-solving courts discussed earlier in this chapter that seek to address the problems related to drugs, mental health, struggling veterans, and domestic violence (Melendez, 2014; S. Burns, 2010). These innovative courts steer people to treatment programs rather than jail. Because judges typically have no training in psychology or social work, critics worry that the development of the problem-solver role will lead judges to make decisions about matters in which they lack expertise. Read the Close Up feature on problem-solving courts to consider whether and how they can be effective.

How to Become a Judge

The quality of justice depends to a great extent on the quality of those who make decisions about guilt and punishment. Because judges have the power to deprive a citizen of his or her liberty through a prison sentence, judges should be thoughtful, fair, and impartial. When a judge is rude or hasty or allows the courtroom to become noisy and crowded, the public may lose confidence in the fairness and effectiveness of the criminal justice process.

Five methods are used to select state trial-court judges: **partisan election**, **nonpartisan election**, gubernatorial appointment, legislative selection, and merit selection. Some states use a combination of methods from among these approaches.

partisan election An election in which candidates openly affiliated with political parties are presented to voters for selection.

nonpartisan election An election in which candidates' party affiliations are not listed on the ballot.

Problem-Solving Courts

In 1989, a judge in Miami began to emphasize treatment and intensive monitoring of low-level substance abusers as an alternative to incarceration. From these beginnings emerged drug courts and other specialized courts aimed at diverting troubled offenders from traditional criminal sanctions while also seeking to help them with their problems. As these courts spread to other jurisdictions, the federal government provided funding to encourage new developments and to evaluate the success of such programs. In addition, several other countries have begun to copy the problem-solving courts that originated in the United States and adapt them to their own issues and objectives.

Similar efforts began to surface in regard to other problems. In the first years of the twenty-first century, many cities developed mental health courts (Redlich et al., 2012). In these courts, judges placed mentally ill people arrested for minor offenses into treatment programs and employment training. Anchorage, Alaska, experimented with a court dedicated to the problems of veterans, some of whom were arrested regularly for drunkenness, substance abuse, and disorderly conduct. In addition to these courts that address minor criminal offenses, New York City developed a parallel court for civil matters that focuses on homelessness and attempts to prevent evictions, encourage employment opportunities, and solve disputes between tenants and landlords. As described by two observers, in these courts, "judges are cheerleaders and social workers as much as jurists" (Eaton & Kaufman, 2005). Despite the positive intentions of such court programs, they raise questions about whether judges have sufficient training, knowledge, and resources to address individuals' significant personal problems.

Research shows that drug courts can have positive results in helping substance abusers and keeping them from going to jail. However, these programs do not always save money for the justice system, because they require funds to monitor, test, and provide services for troubled people. In addition, many substance abusers throughout society who could benefit from such programs do not gain access to the services and supervision that are available only to a small number of offenders in certain communities due to the limited resources and availability of drug courts (Sevigny et al., 2013). Some other kinds of courts are too new to have been fully evaluated.

As discussed elsewhere in this chapter, critics wonder whether specialized courts place judges in a role of problem solver, a position for which they are not fully prepared. In addition, questions have arisen about whether these courts advance the interests of justice. Domestic violence courts, in particular, cause controversy. Some critics believe that they are too lenient on batterers by trying to solve their problems rather than punishing them for committing acts of violence. Other critics contend that these courts favor alleged victims of domestic violence by pressuring the accused to accept anger-management treatment rather than letting the judicial processes take their course to determine whether the individual is actually guilty.

Veterans' courts, which first started in Buffalo, New York, in 2008 and subsequently are spreading across the nation, pose additional challenges about how to handle issues of violence. These courts can help facilitate the provision of mentors and treatment for those veterans who commit minor offenses while often struggling with issues of substance abuse, homelessness, unemployment, or psychological problems. There are debates, however, about whether such courts are appropriate settings to address issues of violence, such as intimate partner violence or other assaults that are regarded as connected to post-traumatic stress or substance abuse. If such problems are related to reentering society after combat experience in a war zone, then many people feel reluctant to see veterans incarcerated rather than helped with their problems. On the other hand, does diversion into treatment programs under veterans' court supervision leave family members and others in society inadequately protected against the risk of subsequent episodes of violence if treatment is not effective for a particular troubled veteran?

As these new courts develop, research is needed to determine precisely how they impact the roles of judges, the resources of the justice system, and the lives of both accused offenders and victims.

Researching the Internet

You can find more information about drug courts at the combined website of the National Association of Drug Court Professionals and the National Drug Court Institute: http://www.ndci.org.

For Critical Analysis

In a time of budget reductions for courts, should problem-solving courts be preserved and strengthened, or are they limited-purpose activities that draw needed resources away from the general court system? How do you view the value, importance, and potential of problem-solving courts? Write a memo that presents three reasons why you would either preserve them or subject them to budget cuts.

Sources: J. L. Burns, "The Future of Problem-Solving Courts: Inside the Courts and Beyond, "*University of Maryland Journal of Race, Religion, Gender, and Class* 10 (2010): 73–87; L. Eaton and L. Kaufman, "In Problem-Solving Courts, Judges Turn Therapist," *New York Times,* April 26, 2005 (www.nytimes.com); D. C. Gottfredson, S. S. Najaka, and B. Kearley, "Effectiveness of Drug Treatment Courts: Evidence from a Randomized Trial." *Criminology & Public Policy* 2 (2003): 171–96; A. R. Gover, J. M. MacDonald, and G. P. Alpert, "Combating Domestic Violence: Findings from an Evaluation of a Local Domestic Violence Court," *Criminology and Public Policy* 3 (2003): 109–31; P. Kravetz, "Way Off Base: An Argument Against Intimate Partner Violence Cases in Veterans Treatment Courts," *Veterans Law Review* 4 (2012): 162–205; A.J. Lurigio, "The First 20 Years of Drug Treatment Courts," *Federal Probation* 2008 (June): 13–17; E. C. Moore, "A Mentor in Combat Veterans Court: Observations and Challenges," in *Future Trends in State Courts 2012*, Williamsburg, VA: National Center for State Courts, 2012, pp. 39–43; J. L. Nolan, "Redefining Criminal Courts: Problem-Solving and the Meaning of Justice," *American Criminal Law Review.*

TABLE 7.1 Methods Used by States to Select Judges

States use different methods to select judges. Note that many judges are initially appointed to fill a vacancy, giving them an advantage if they must run for election at a later date.

Partisan Election	Nonpartisan Election	Gubernatorial Appointment	Legislative Selection	Merit Selection
Alabama	Arizona (some trial courts)	California (appellate)	South Carolina	Alaska
Illinois	Arkansas	Maine	Virginia	Arizona (appellate)
Indiana (trial)	California (trial)	Massachusetts (court of last resort)		Colorado
Louisiana	Florida (trial)	New Jersey		Connecticut
New Mexico	Georgia			Delaware
New York (trial)	Idaho			Florida (appellate)
Pennsylvania (initial)	Kentucky			Hawaii
Tennessee (trial)	Michigan			Indiana (appellate)
Texas	Minnesota			Iowa
West Virginia	Mississippi			Kansas
	Montana			Maryland
	Nevada			Massachusetts (trial, intermediate appellate)
	North Carolina			Missouri
	North Dakota			Nebraska
	Ohio			New Hampshire
	Oklahoma (trial)			New York (appellate)
	Oregon			Oklahoma (appellate)
	Pennsylvania (retention)			Rhode Island
	South Dakota (trial)			South Dakota (appellate)
	Washington			Tennessee (appellate)
	Wisconsin			Utah
				Vermont
				Wyoming

Source: American Judicature Society, 2012, "Judicial Selection in the States" (http://www.ajs.org).

Table 7.1 shows the method used in each of the states. All the methods bring up persistent concerns about the desired qualities of judges. By contrast, federal judges are nominated by the president and confirmed by a majority vote of the U.S. Senate. Federal judgeships also involve politics and questions about nominees' qualifications because presidents typically choose judges who are members of their own political party (Geyh, 2012). In addition, a judgeship can be a reward for loyal service to a political party's campaigns and fund-raising efforts.

Selection by public voting occurs in more than half the states and has long been part of this nation's tradition. This method of judicial selection embodies the underlying American value of democracy because it permits the citizens to control the choice of individuals who will receive the power to make decisions in civil and criminal cases. The fulfillment of this American value also helps ensure that judges will remain connected to the community and demonstrate sensitivity to the community's priorities and concerns (Griffen, 2011). The American value of democracy may, however, have detrimental consequences if it pressures judges to follow a community's prejudices rather than make independent decisions using their best judgment in each case (Canes-Wrone, Clark, & Park, 2012; Pratt, 2011). Retired U.S. Supreme Court Justice Sandra Day O'Connor mounted a public campaign against selecting judges through elections because of her concerns about the impact on the appearance of justice, especially as judicial candidates must solicit campaign contributions and subsequently may make decisions affecting their contributors (Geyh, 2012).

When lawyers are first elected to serve as judges, they obviously have no prior experience in deciding cases or supervising courthouse operations. As a result, judges must learn on the job. This fact clashes with the belief that judges are trained to "find the law" and to apply neutral judgments. In Europe, by contrast, prospective judges are given special training in law school to become professional judges. These trained judges must serve as assistant judges and lower-court judges before they can become judges in general trial and appellate courts (Provine, 1996).

Election campaigns for lower-court judgeships tend to be low-key contests marked by little controversy. Usually only a small portion of the voters participate, judgeships are not prominent on the ballot, and candidates do not discuss controversial issues because of ethical considerations. Most candidates run on the same two claims that reveal relatively little to the voters about how they will make specific decisions as judges: "I have the best prior experience" and "I'll be tough on crime." Studies indicate, however, that even lower-level judicial races have become more competitive as candidates raise money and seek connections with interest groups (Brandenburg & Berg, 2012; Abbe & Herrnson, 2002). Political parties typically want local judgeships to be elected posts, because they can use courthouse staff positions to reward party loyalists. When a party member wins a judgeship, courthouse jobs may become available for campaign workers, because the judge often chooses clerks, bailiffs, and secretaries.

In contrast, elections for seats on state supreme courts frequently receive statewide media attention (M. Hall & Bonneau, 2013). Because of the importance of state supreme courts as policy-making institutions, political parties and interest groups may devote substantial energy to organizing and funding the election campaigns of their preferred candidates. When organized interests contribute tens of thousands of dollars to judicial campaigns, questions sometimes arise about whether the successful candidates who received those contributions will favor the interests of their donors when they begin to decide court cases (Geyh, 2012).

Some states have tried to reduce the influence of political parties in the selection of judges while still allowing voters to select judges (Chertoff & Robinson, 2012). These states hold nonpartisan elections in which only the names of candidates, not their party affiliations, appear on the ballot. However, political parties are often strongly involved in such elections. In Ohio, for example, the Republican and Democratic political parties hold their own primary elections to choose the judicial candidates whose names will go on the nonpartisan ballot for the general election. In other states, party organizations raise and spend money on behalf of candidates in nonpartisan elections.

Public opinion data show that Americans express concern about the influence of politics on judges, especially with respect to elected judges. If so many Americans are concerned about judges' involvement in political campaigns, why do so many states still rely on elections to select judges?

Merit selection, which combines appointment and election, was first used in Missouri in 1940 and has since spread to other states. When a judgeship becomes vacant, a nominating committee made up of citizens and attorneys evaluates potential appointees and sends the governor the names of three candidates, from which the replacement is chosen. After one year, a referendum is held to decide whether the judge will stay on the bench. The ballot asks, "Shall Judge X remain in office?" A judge who wins support from voters serves out the full term, often eight years, before facing another retention election (Cady & Phelps, 2008).

merit selection A reform plan by which judges are nominated by a committee and appointed by the governor for a given period. When the term expires, the voters approve or disapprove the judge for a succeeding term. If the judge is disapproved, the committee nominates a successor for the governor's appointment.

Public opinion polls indicate that Americans are divided in their views about judges' honesty and ethics, and these divisions are based, in part, on race and income. It is unclear whether judges' image would improve if merit selection were more widespread (see "What Americans Think" for specific data).

Merit selection attempts to diminish the influence of politics on the selection of judges and supposedly allows the voters to unseat judges. However, interest groups sometimes mount publicity campaigns during retention elections in order to turn out judges with whom they disagree on a single issue or to open an important court seat so that a like-minded governor can appoint a sympathetic replacement. It may be difficult for judges to counteract a barrage of one-sided inflammatory television commercials focusing on a single issue such as capital punishment (T. V. Reid, 2000). If merit-selected judges feel intimidated by interest groups that might threaten their jobs at the next retention election, the independence of the judiciary will diminish (Breslin, 2010).

☑CHECK POINT

4. What are judges' main functions?
Adjudicator, negotiator, administrator.

5. Why do political parties often prefer that judges be elected?
To ensure that courthouse positions are allocated to party workers.

6. What are the steps in the merit-selection process?
When a vacancy occurs, a nominating committee is appointed that sends the governor the names of approved candidates. The governor must fill the vacancy from the list. After a year's term, a referendum is held to ask the voters whether the judge should be retained.

STOP&ANALYZE

What is the best way to select judges? List three arguments for the method that you favor. List three arguments against a method that you do not prefer.

The Prosecutorial System

Prosecuting attorneys make discretionary decisions about whether to pursue criminal charges, which charges to make, and what sentence to recommend. They represent the government in pursuing criminal charges against the accused. Except in a few states, no higher authority second-guesses or changes these decisions. Thus, prosecutors are more independent than most other public officials. As with other aspects of American government, prosecution is mainly a task of state and local governments because most crimes violate state laws. The vast majority of state criminal cases are handled in the 2,341 county-level offices of the prosecuting attorney—known in various states as the district attorney, state's attorney, commonwealth attorney, or county attorney—who pursues cases that violate state law. Prosecutors have the power to make independent decisions about which cases to pursue and what charges to file. They can also drop charges and negotiate arrangements for guilty pleas. Since 2008, budget cuts have forced many prosecutors' offices to cut staff and, as a result, reduce defendants' charges and offer attractive plea deals more frequently in order to process cases efficiently (Damron, Anderson, & Wisely, 2013; Singer, 2008).

Federal cases are prosecuted by **United States attorneys**. One U.S. attorney and a staff of assistant U.S. attorneys prosecute cases in each of the 94 U.S. district courts. Each state has an elected **state attorney general**, who usually has the power to bring prosecutions in certain cases. A state attorney general may, for example, handle a statewide consumer fraud case if a chain of auto repair shops is suspected of overcharging customers. In Alaska, Delaware, and Rhode Island, the state attorney general also directs all local prosecutions.

prosecuting attorney A legal representative of the state with sole responsibility for bringing criminal charges. In some states, this person is referred to as the district attorney, state's attorney, commonwealth attorney, or county attorney.

United States attorneys Officials responsible for the prosecution of crimes that violate the laws of the United States. Appointed by the president and assigned to a U.S. district court jurisdiction.

state attorney general Chief legal officer of a state, responsible for both civil and criminal matters.

QUESTION: "Please tell me how you would rate the honesty and ethical standards of judges—very high, high, average, low, or very low."

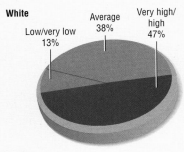

White

Low/very low 13%

Average 38%

Very high/high 47%

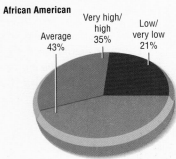

African American

Average 43%

Very high/high 35%

Low/very low 21%

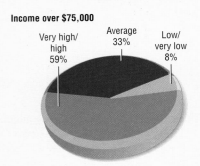

Income over $75,000

Very high/high 59%

Average 33%

Low/very low 8%

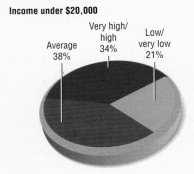

Income under $20,000

Average 38%

Very high/high 34%

Low/very low 21%

CRITICAL THINKING: What might explain the divergent perceptions by race and income? Should these differing perceptions cause concern for judges who are worried about the image of the judicial branch of government?

Source: Bureau of Justice Statistics, *Sourcebook of Criminal Justice Statistics, 2014* (http://bjs.ojp.usdoj.gov/), Table 2.0017.2010.

Read "Careers in Criminal Justice" to see the responsibilities and career path of an elected prosecutor in a major county.

Politics and Prosecution

Except in a few states, such as Alaska, Connecticut, and New Jersey, prosecutors are elected, usually for a four-year term; local politics thus heavily influence the office. By seeking to please voters, many prosecutors have tried to use their local office as a springboard to a higher office—such as state legislator, governor, or member of Congress.

Prosecutors may choose certain cases for prosecution in order to gain the favor of voters or investigate charges against political opponents and public officials to get the public's attention. Political factors may also cause prosecutors to apply their powers unevenly within a community. Prosecutors' discretionary power can create the impression that some groups or individuals receive harsh treatment while others receive protection (Podgor, 2010).

Discretion in decision making also creates the risk of discrimination. For example, some scholars see prosecutors' decisions as reflecting biases based on race, social class, and gender (Frohmann, 1997), but other researchers believe that studies have not yet documented the full extent of discrimination by prosecutors (S. Walker, Spohn, & DeLeone, 2011). Several studies raise questions about discrimination in specific situations, such as prosecutors' decisions to seek the death penalty (Unah, 2010; Sorensen & Wallace, 1999). For the criminal justice system to fulfill American values concerning equality and fairness, prosecutors must use their decision-making authority carefully to avoid inequality and injustice (Butler, 2010; Kotch & Mosteller, 2010).

The Prosecutor's Influence

Most decision makers in the criminal justice system are involved in only one part of the process. However, prosecutors are involved at multiple stages and can therefore exert great influence through the use of their broad discretion in decision making (Krischke, 2010). From arrest to final disposition of a case, prosecutors can make choices that largely determine the defendant's fate. The prosecutor decides which cases to prosecute, selects the charges to be brought, recommends the bail amount, approves agreements with the defendant, and urges the judge to impose a particular sentence (Kenny, 2009).

Throughout the justice process, prosecutors' links with the other actors in the system—police, defense attorneys, judges—shape the prosecutors' decisions. Prosecutors may, for example, recommend bail amounts and sentences that match the preferences of particular judges.

Prosecuting Attorney

Kym Worthy, Prosecuting Attorney, Wayne County, Michigan

A county's elected prosecutor oversees a staff of assistant prosecutors and support personnel in directing the investigation and prosecution of cases within the county. Wayne County, Michigan, which includes the city of Detroit, is one of the ten largest counties in the United States. The Wayne County prosecutor's office handles tens of thousands of cases each year. The prosecutor's office works with law enforcement agencies to investigate crimes, apply for search and arrest warrants, and gather evidence concerning criminal suspects. The prosecutor and his or her assistant prosecutors make decisions about which suspects to charge with crimes and what charges to pursue against each suspect. Prosecutors decide whether to offer opportunities for defendants to plead guilty in exchange for dropping specific charges for suspects accused of multiple crimes, reducing the severity of charges, or recommending specific sentences. They must discuss and negotiate with defense attorneys in defining these plea agreements. Prosecutors also present evidence in trials when defendants decline to plead guilty. They try to present enough evidence to prove a defendant's guilt "beyond a reasonable doubt." Prosecutors in many states may also be involved in appeals if they must fight against defense attorneys' claims that convictions should be thrown out because of errors by the trial judge. In some states, the state attorney general's office may

have primary responsibility for representing the prosecution in appeals.

Kym Worthy completed her undergraduate degree at the University of Michigan and earned her law degree at the University of Notre Dame Law School. She spent ten years as an assistant prosecuting attorney in Wayne County before being elected to a trial court judgeship. After nearly a decade as a trial court judge, she resigned from the bench in order to seek the position of Wayne County Prosecuting Attorney when the previous elected prosecutor resigned. With her significant experience as both an assistant prosecutor and a trial judge, she was elected as prosecutor in 2004 and overwhelmingly reelected in 2008.

When you let the facts and evidence guide you, then you just do the right thing. And the minute I feel that I'm letting any outside pressures dictate what I do, that's the day I no longer should have this position. Any prosecutors that let outside forces dictate how they handle a case or how they dispose of a case other than the facts and the law really shouldn't be doing the job.

Source: Sven Gustafson, "Wayne County Prosecutor Kym Worthy: No One Is above the Law," *Michigan Business Review*, March 4, 2009 (http://www.mlive.com /businessreview).

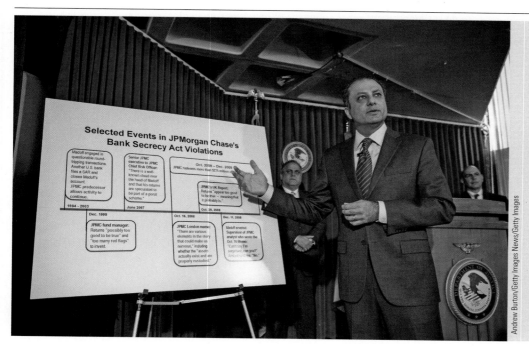

The U.S. Attorney in New York City, Preet Bharara, has handled a wide range of prosecutions, from financial crimes on Wall Street to international weapons trafficking to cyber crimes to political corruption in government. What kinds of political pressures can confront prosecutors?

The Accountability of Prosecutors

How can prosecutors be held accountable if they violate their responsibilities and the principles of justice? In theory, if the public hears about prosecutorial misconduct, the democratic selection process will enable voters to elect a new prosecutor in most states. However, as mentioned earlier, because so many of prosecutors' discretionary decisions are not visible to the news media and public, voters may lack the information necessary to provide the accountability mechanism for improper conduct.

People can file lawsuits against police officers and corrections officers to hold them accountable for violating citizens' rights or improperly causing injuries and property damage. By contrast, the American legal system generally shields prosecutors and judges from the risk of lawsuits by granting them immunity, in much the same manner that the president and governors enjoy immunity in most circumstances. These are the officials who need to use their best judgment in making tough decisions, and the law is designed to protect them from being guided by fear of liability in making those decisions. However, this immunity from lawsuits effectively removes an important and useful accountability mechanism that might otherwise deter misconduct and provide remedies for citizens who are victimized by such misconduct.

In 2011 the U.S. Supreme Court decided the case of *Connick v. Thompson*, concerning a man who spent 18 years in prison and came within one month of being executed for a murder that he did not commit. Only a stroke of luck resulting from a private detective's discovery of a crime lab report in the New Orleans Police Crime Lab files saved Thompson from execution.

Prosecutors have a legal obligation to provide defense attorneys with all evidence that might indicate a defendant's innocence. In *Brady v. Maryland* (1963), the Supreme Court declared that in their efforts to get a conviction, prosecutors cannot hide evidence that is helpful to the defense. To do so, prosecutors

would greatly increase the likelihood of innocent people being erroneously found guilty. In the *Thompson* case, New Orleans prosecutors hid evidence from the defendant's counsel. One prosecutor went so far as to remove a blood-stained piece of cloth from the evidence room, which, if tested by the defense and compared to the defendant's blood type could have proved the defendant's innocence in one of the crimes for which he was convicted. Indeed, the prosecutor possessed a lab report indicating that the blood did not match Thompson's blood type, but that information did not become available to Thompson's attorneys until the investigator discovered it in the crime lab files 18 years later. When the prosecutor in question was dying of cancer, he confessed to another prosecutor that he had intentionally hidden evidence that would have been helpful to the defendant. In addition, there were other issues raised concerning the failure of the prosecutors to accurately reveal the nature of witness statements taken during the investigation of the crime.

After he was found to be innocent and released from prison, Thompson sued the prosecutor's office for violating his rights by failing to train assistant prosecutors regarding their obligation to share relevant evidence. A jury awarded him $14 million dollars in the lawsuit. Despite evidence that the assistant prosecutors—as well as the chief prosecutor—were not fully aware of the legal requirements of the *Brady* rule, a narrow five-member majority on the Supreme Court threw out the jury award and found that Thompson had not proved his case. Indeed, their ruling made clear that prosecutors seldom, if ever, should be subject to lawsuits, even when prosecutors acknowledge the intentional violation of a suspect's rights and when a wrongly convicted man spent many years on death row as a result.

Should we make prosecutors more susceptible to lawsuits as a means to hold them accountable and control the risk that they

They may make "tough" recommendations in front of "tough" judges but tone down their arguments before judges who favor leniency or rehabilitation. Similarly, the other actors in the system may adjust their decisions and actions to match the preferences of the prosecutor. For example, police officers' investigation and arrest practices tend to reflect the prosecutor's priorities. Thus, prosecutors influence the decisions of others while also shaping their own actions in ways that reinforce their relationships with police, defense attorneys, and judges.

Prosecutors gain additional power from the fact that their decisions and actions take place away from public view. For example, a prosecutor and a defense attorney may strike a bargain whereby the prosecutor reduces a charge in exchange for a guilty plea or drops a charge if the defendant agrees to seek psychiatric help. In such instances, they reach a decision on a case in a way that is nearly invisible to the public.

The Prosecutor's Roles

As "lawyers for the state," prosecutors face conflicting pressures to press charges vigorously against lawbreakers while also upholding justice and the rights of the accused (O'Brien, 2009). These pressures are often called "the prosecutor's dilemma."

will engage in improper conduct? Here is a summary of key arguments in the debate:

For Permitting Lawsuits against Prosecutors

- Voters do not know enough about prosecutors' errors to hold prosecutors accountable by using those errors as a basis for voting them out at the next election.
- Lawsuits have proven a very effective means to pressure police executives and corrections administrators to obey rules, supervise personnel, and develop effective training programs.
- Without the threat of lawsuits, prosecutors have little to fear other than having charges against a defendant dismissed if they violate rules, either intentionally or mistakenly. Thus, they feel little pressure, other than the pressure that they put on themselves, to be careful about following rules.
- People whose lives were ruined by prosecutors' misconduct, such as Thompson, the wrongly convicted man in the Supreme Court case, lack mechanisms to seek remedies for prosecutors' misdeed.

Opposing Lawsuits against Prosecutors

- If lawsuits were permitted, prosecutors would be flooded with groundless lawsuits from many people in prison who have little else to do with their time than read books in the prison law library in order to plan how to seek revenge against prosecutors.
- Society needs prosecutors to freely use their judgment to make the best possible decision in each criminal case without worrying about whether they will be sued for trying to do the right thing.
- Prosecutors have limited time, funds, and staff. Any time that is diverted to defending against lawsuits from unhappy defendants will come at the expense of the prosecutors' important responsibility for protecting the public against crime and criminals.
- Qualified lawyers may avoid becoming prosecutors if they know that they will face a steady stream of lawsuits from unhappy defendants seeking revenge.

What Should U.S. Policy Be?

The U.S. Supreme Court's decision in *Connick v. Thompson* sent a clear message that the nation's highest court will not push changes in current policy. However, state legislatures and Congress have the authority to craft laws that could define the circumstances under which prosecutors would be subject to lawsuits. Those statutes would present an opportunity to find the right balance between the competing sets of arguments by permitting more lawsuits than currently allowed but for fewer types of actions than those directed at police and corrections officials. For example, the statutes could define limited categories such as intentional misconduct by prosecutors or inadvertent errors that result in innocent people being wrongly convicted of crimes. Should legislatures examine the issue and consider creating changes that would permit more lawsuits?

Researching the Internet

Read the Supreme Court's opinion in the *Thompson* case, including the strong objections voiced by the four dissenting justices who concluded that Thompson was entitled to the money that he was awarded by the jury in his lawsuit. http://scholar.google.com/scholar_case?case=16887528200611439212&hl=en&as_sdt=6&as_vis=1&oi=scholarr.

Analyzing the Issue

Should citizens have the opportunity to sue prosecutors for violations of legal rights? If such lawsuits are not permitted, how will society make sure that prosecutors do their jobs properly? What would be the consequences if prosecutors could be sued for rights violations or wrongful convictions? Are there alternative mechanisms that could more effectively keep prosecutors accountable? Imagine that you and your classmates are legislators discussing the accountability of prosecutors as you consider whether to propose new laws. Do a majority in your class support more opportunities to file lawsuits? If so, would such lawsuits be limited to only certain kinds of cases? If not, are you relying on other mechanisms to reduce the risk of prosecutors' errors and misconduct?

In the adversarial system, prosecutors must do everything they can to win a conviction, but as members of the legal profession, they must see that justice is done even if it means that the accused is not convicted. Even so, they always face the risk of "prosecutor's bias," sometimes called a "prosecution complex." Although they are supposed to represent all the people, including the accused, prosecutors may view themselves as instruments of law enforcement. Thus, as advocates on behalf of the state, their strong desire to close each case with a conviction may keep them from recognizing unfair procedures or evidence of innocence. As discussed in the Close Up box, it can be very difficult to hold prosecutors accountable if they ignore the interests of justice in their single-minded pursuit of a criminal conviction.

Although all prosecutors must uphold the law and pursue charges against lawbreakers, they may perform these tasks in different ways. Their personal values and professional goals, along with the political climate of their city or county, may cause them to define the prosecutor's role differently than do prosecutors in other places. For example, a prosecutor who believes that young offenders can be rehabilitated may take different actions than one who believes that young offenders should receive the same punishments as adults. One might send juveniles to counseling programs whereas the other would seek to process them though the adult system of courts and corrections. A prosecutor with no assistants and few resources for conducting jury trials may be forced to embrace effective plea bargaining whereas a prosecutor in a wealthier county may have more options when deciding whether to take cases to trial.

When prosecutors are asked about their roles in the criminal justice process, the following four functions are often mentioned:

1. *Trial counsel for the police.* Prosecutors who see their main function in this light believe that they should reflect the views of law enforcement in the courtroom and take a crime-fighter stance in public.
2. *House counsel for the police.* These prosecutors believe that their main function is to give legal advice so that arrests will stand up in court.
3. *Representative of the court.* Such prosecutors believe that their main function is to enforce the rules of due process to ensure that the police act according to the law and uphold the rights of defendants.
4. *Elected official.* These prosecutors may be most responsive to public opinion. The political impact of their decisions is one of their main concerns.

Each of these roles involves a different view of the prosecutor's "clients" as well as his or her own responsibilities. In the first two roles, prosecutors appear to believe that the police are the clients of their legal practice. Take a moment to think about who might be the clients of prosecutors who view themselves as representatives of the court or as elected officials.

Discretion of the Prosecutor

Because they have such broad discretion, prosecutors can shape their decisions to fit different interests (K. Griffin, 2009). They might base their decisions on a desire to impress voters through tough "throw-the-book-at-them" charges in a highly publicized case (Maschke, 1995). Decisions may also be driven by changing events in society. For example, when American opinion held that the greed of businesspeople had helped to create the economic crisis of 2008, certain prosecutors placed new emphasis on pursuing criminal charges for fraudulent business transactions and mortgage loans (Segal, 2009). Decisions by prosecutors might also stem from their personal values and policy priorities, such as an emphasis on leniency and rehabilitation for young offenders or a desire to work with domestic violence victims to seek a specific result (Finn, 2013; Buzawa & Buzawa, 2013; Ferguson, 2009). They may also shape their decisions to please local judges by, for example, accepting plea agreements that will keep the judges from being burdened by too many time-consuming trials. Prosecutors who have doubts about whether available evidence actually proves the defendant's guilt may just shrug their shoulders and say, "I'll just let the jury decide" rather than face public criticism for dropping charges. Any or all of these motives may shape prosecutors' decisions, because there is generally no higher authority to tell prosecutors how they must do their jobs. From the time the police turn a case over to the prosecutor, the prosecutor has almost complete control over decisions about charges and plea agreements (M. Stephens, 2008).

Research has also shown that the staffing levels of individual prosecutor's offices may affect decisions to pursue felony charges. If offices lack sufficient resources to pursue all possible cases, prosecutors may establish priorities and then reduce or dismiss charges in cases deemed less important. This situation has increasingly affected decisions in many prosecutors' offices in light of budget cuts in state and local government (Stensland, 2011).

If you were a prosecutor, what would you consider to be the most important factors in deciding whether to pursue a case? Would you have any concerns about the possibility of prosecuting an innocent person? If a prosecutor pursues a case against someone she or he does not really believe is guilty of a crime, does this pose an ethical problem?

After deciding that a case should be prosecuted, the prosecutor has great freedom in deciding what charges to file. Criminal incidents may involve several laws, so the prosecutor can often bring a single charge or more than one. Suppose that Smith, who is armed, breaks into a grocery store, assaults the proprietor, and robs the cash drawer. What charges can the prosecutor file? By virtue of having committed the robbery, the accused can be charged with at least four crimes: breaking and entering, assault, armed robbery, and carrying a dangerous weapon. Other charges, or **counts**, may be added, depending on the nature of the incident. A forger, for instance, may be charged with one count for each act of forgery committed. By filing as many charges as possible, the prosecutor strengthens his or her position in plea negotiations. In effect, the prosecutor can use discretion in deciding the number of charges and thus increase the prosecution's supply of "bargaining chips" (M. Simons, 2010).

The discretionary power to set charges does not give the prosecutor complete control over plea bargaining, however. Defense attorneys strengthen their position in the **discovery** process, in which information from the prosecutor's case file must be made available to the defense. For example, the defense has the right to see any statements made by the accused during interrogation by the police, as well as the results of any physical or psychological tests. This information tells the defense attorney about the strengths and weaknesses of the prosecution's case. The defense attorney may use it to decide whether a case is hopeless or whether engaging in tough negotiations is worthwhile.

The prosecutor's discretion does not end with the decision to file a certain charge. After the charge has been made, the prosecutor may reduce it in exchange for a guilty plea or enter a notation of *nolle prosequi* (*nol. pros.*). The latter is a freely made decision to drop the charge, either as a whole or as to one or more counts (Bowers, 2010). When a prosecutor decides to drop charges, no higher authorities can force her or him to reinstate them. When guilty pleas are entered, the prosecutor uses discretion in recommending a sentence.

Key Relationships of the Prosecutor

Prosecutors do not base their decisions solely on formal policies and role conceptions (Fridell, 1990). Relationships with other actors in the justice system also influence their choices. Despite their independent authority, prosecutors must consider how police, judges, and others will react. They depend on these other officials in order to prosecute cases successfully. In turn, the success of police, judges, and correctional officials depends on prosecutors' effectiveness in identifying and convicting lawbreakers. Thus, these officials build exchange relationships in which they cooperate with each other.

Police   Prosecutors depend on the police to provide both the suspects and the evidence needed to convict lawbreakers. Because they cannot investigate crimes on their own, prosecutors are not in command of the types of cases brought to them. Thus, the police control the initiation of the criminal justice process by investigating crimes and arresting suspects. These actions may be influenced by various factors, such as pressure on police to establish an impressive crime-clearance record. As a result, police actions may create problems for prosecutors if, for example, the police make many arrests without gathering enough evidence to ensure conviction.

Victims and Witnesses   Prosecutors depend on the cooperation of victims and witnesses (Rhodes, Dichter, Kothari, Marcus, & Cerulli, 2011). Although prosecutors can pursue a case whether or not a victim wishes to press charges, many prosecutors will not do so when the key testimony and other necessary evidence must come from a victim who is unwilling to cooperate (Dawson & Dinovitzer, 2001). In some cases, the decision to prosecute may be influenced by the victim's assertiveness in persuading the prosecutor to file charges (Stickels, Michelsen, & Del Carmen, 2007).

The decision to prosecute is often based on an assessment of the victim's role in his or her own victimization and the victim's credibility as a witness. If a victim

count Each separate offense of which a person is accused in an indictment or an information.

discovery A prosecutor's pretrial disclosure to the defense of facts and evidence to be introduced at trial.

nolle prosequi An entry, made by a prosecutor on the record of a case and announced in court, indicating that the charges specified will not be prosecuted. In effect, the charges are thereby dismissed.

has a criminal record, the prosecutor may choose not to pursue the case in the belief that a jury would not consider the victim a credible witness—despite the fact that the jury will never learn that the victim has a criminal record. If a victim is poorly dressed, uneducated, or somewhat inarticulate, the prosecutor may be inclined to dismiss charges out of fear that a jury would find the victim unpersuasive (Stanko, 1988). Research indicates that victim characteristics, such as moral character, behavior at the time of the incident, and age, influence decisions to prosecute sexual assault cases more than does the actual strength of the evidence against the suspect (Spears & Spohn, 1997). Studies have shown that prosecutions succeed most when aimed at defendants accused of committing crimes against strangers (Boland, Brady, Tyson, & Bassler, 1983). When the victim is an acquaintance, a friend, or even a relative of the defendant, she or he may refuse to act as a witness, and prosecutors and juries may consequently view the offense as less serious (Beichner & Spohn, 2012).

Judges and Courts   The sentencing history of each judge gives prosecutors an idea of how a case might be treated in the courtroom. Prosecutors may decide to drop a case if they believe that the judge assigned to it will not impose a serious punishment. Because prosecutors' offices have limited resources, they cannot afford to waste time pursuing charges in front of a specific judge who shows a pattern of dismissing those types of charges. Interactions with defense attorneys also affect prosecutors' decisions, as in the case of plea bargains.

The Community   Public opinion and the media can play a crucial role in creating an environment that either supports or scrutinizes the prosecutor. Like police chiefs and school superintendents, county prosecutors will not remain in office long if they fall out of step with community values. They will likely lose the next election to an opponent who has a better sense of the community's priorities.

Many cities are experimenting with innovations designed to enhance communication and understanding between prosecutors and the community. One innovation called *community prosecution* gives specific assistant prosecutors continuing responsibilities for particular neighborhoods. These prosecutors may become known to people in the neighborhood, attend community meetings and social functions, and learn about residents' specific concerns. In so doing, they can build relationships that will help them gather information and identify witnesses when crimes occur (Porter, 2011).

Prosecutors' relationships and interactions with police, victims, defense attorneys, judges, and the community form the core of the exchange relations that shape decision making in criminal cases. Other relationships, such as those with news media, federal and state officials, legislators, and political-party officials, also influence prosecutors' decisions. This long list of actors illustrates that prosecutors do not base their decisions solely on whether a law has been broken. The occurrence of a crime is only the first step in a decision-making process that may vary from one case to the next. Sometimes charges are dropped or reduced. Sometimes plea bargains are negotiated quickly. Sometimes cases move through the system to a complete jury trial. In every instance, relationships and interactions with a variety of actors both within and outside the justice system shape prosecutors' discretionary decisions.

Decision-Making Policies

Despite the many factors that potentially affect prosecutors' decisions, we can draw some general conclusions about how they approach their office. Prosecutors develop their own policies on how cases will be handled. These policies shape the decisions made by the assistant prosecutors and thus greatly affect the administration of justice (Holleran, Beichner, & Spohn, 2010). Within the same state, prosecutors may pursue different goals in forming policies on which cases to pursue, which ones to drop, and which ones to plea bargain. For example, prosecutors who wish to maintain a high conviction rate will drop cases with weak evidence. Others, concerned

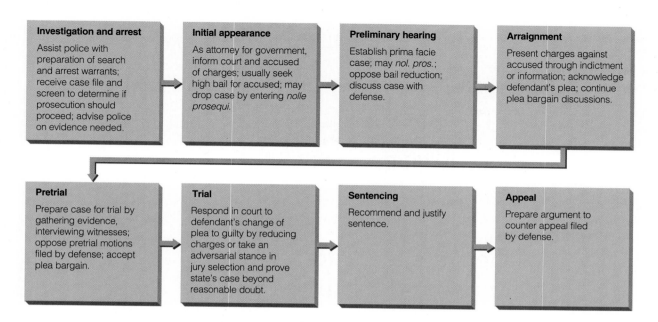

FIGURE 7.3

Typical Actions of a Prosecuting Attorney in Processing a Felony Case The prosecutor has certain responsibilities at various points in the process. At each point, the prosecutor is an advocate for the state's case against the accused.

about using limited resources effectively, will focus most of their time and energy on the most serious cases.

Some prosecutors' offices make extensive use of screening and tend not to press charges—guilty pleas are typically their main method of processing cases. Because pleas of not guilty strain the prosecutors' and courts' trial resources, there are strong reasons to offer incentives to defendants to plead guilty. Some offices process cases soon after the police bring them to the prosecutor's attention, sometimes diverting or referring them to other agencies; others have disposition occurring as late as the first day of trial. The period from the receipt of the police report to the start of the trial is thus a time of review in which the prosecutor uses her or his discretion to decide what actions should be taken.

The **accusatory process** is the series of activities that take place from the moment a suspect is arrested and booked by the police to the moment the formal charge—in the form of an indictment or information—is filed with the court. In an indictment, evidence is presented to a grand jury composed of citizens who determine whether to issue a formal charge. Grand juries are used in the federal system and in states where legislatures have mandated their use for serious charges. In jurisdictions that do not use grand juries, the prosecutor has full control of the charging decision when the filing of an information initiates prosecution. In other words, when an information is used to present formal charges, no body of citizens can protect a suspect from wrongful prosecution until the case goes to trial and a trial jury hears the case. However, earlier in the process, judges may decide at preliminary hearings that there is insufficient evidence to support the pursuit of the charges; in such circumstances, a judge can order that the charges be dismissed.

accusatory process The series of events from the arrest of a suspect to the filing of a formal charge (through an indictment or information) with the court.

Clearly the prosecutor's established policies and decisions play a key role in determining whether charges will be filed against a defendant. Keep in mind, though, that the prosecutor's decision-making power is not limited to decisions about charges. As shown in Figure 7.3, the prosecutor makes important decisions at each stage, both before and after a defendant's guilt is determined. Because the prosecutor's involvement and influence span the justice process, from seeking search warrants during early investigations to arguing against post-conviction appeals, the prosecutor is a highly influential actor in criminal cases. No other participant in the system is involved in so many different stages of the criminal process.

7. What are the roles of the prosecutor?

Trial counsel for the police, house counsel for the police, representative of the court, elected official.

8. How does the prosecutor use discretion to decide how to treat each defendant?

The prosecutor can determine the type and number of charges, reduce the charges in exchange for a guilty plea, or enter a *nolle prosequi* (thereby dropping some or all of the charges).

9. What are the prosecutor's key exchange relationships?

Police, victims and witnesses, defense attorneys, judges, the community.

Do prosecutors' exchange relationships contribute to or distract from the goal of achieving justice in each case? List two arguments in favor of exchange relationships, recognizing their benefits, and two arguments against them, citing negative consequences.

The Defense Attorney: Image and Reality

defense attorney The lawyer who represents accused offenders and convicted offenders in their dealings with criminal justice.

In an adversarial process, the **defense attorney** is the lawyer who represents accused and convicted persons in their dealings with the criminal justice system. Most Americans have seen defense attorneys in action on television dramas such as *The Good Wife* and *Law and Order*. In these dramas, defense attorneys vigorously battle the prosecution, and the jury often finds their clients innocent. These images gain strength from news stories about prominent defense attorneys, such as Chicago's Ed Genson, who represented Illinois governor Rod Blagojevich during initial impeachment proceedings, and who won an acquittal from child pornography charges for singer R. Kelly in 2008 (St. Clair, 2008). Although these images are drawn from reality, they do not give a true picture of the typical defense attorney, focusing as they do on the few highly publicized cases that result in jury trials. By contrast, most cases find resolution through plea bargaining, discretionary dismissals, and similar decisions by actors in the justice system. In these cases, the defense attorney may seem less like the prosecutor's adversary and more like a partner in the effort to dispose of cases as quickly and efficiently as possible through negotiation (Edkins, 2011).

All the key courtroom actors discussed in this chapter—judges, prosecutors, and defense attorneys—are lawyers who met the same educational requirements. After becoming lawyers, however, they made different decisions about what career to pursue. Some people cannot understand why anyone would want to be a defense attorney and work on behalf of criminals. However, defense attorneys work for people who are *accused* of crimes. Under the American system of criminal justice, defendants are supposedly presumed to be innocent. Indeed, many of them will have charges reduced or dismissed. Others will be found not guilty.

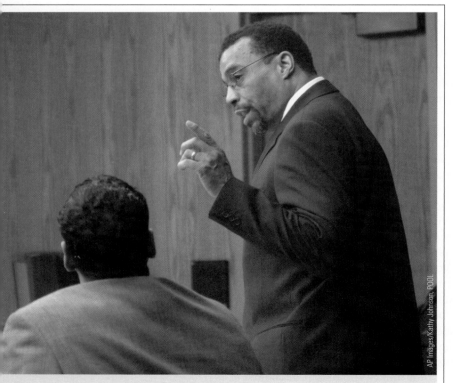

Billy Martin, a prominent defense attorney, has represented such clients as NFL star Michael Vick and U.S. Senator Larry Craig. The defense attorney must be persuasive and knowledgeable as well as creative in identifying flaws in the prosecutor's evidence. Could you use your skills to enthusiastically represent criminal defendants?

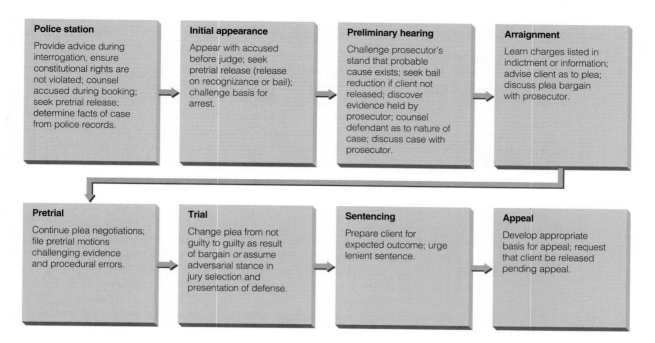

FIGURE 7.4

Typical Actions of a Defense Attorney Processing a Felony Case Defense attorneys are advocates for the accused. They have an obligation to challenge points made by the prosecution and to advise clients of their constitutional rights.

Thus, characterizing defense attorneys as representing only criminals is simply not accurate. Moreover, many lawyers who choose to work as defense attorneys see themselves as defending the Bill of Rights by ensuring that prosecutors actually respect the Constitution and provide proof beyond a reasonable doubt before defendants are convicted and punished.

The Role of the Defense Attorney

To be effective, defense attorneys must have knowledge of law and procedure, skill in investigation, experience in advocacy, and, in many cases, relationships with prosecutors and judges that will help a defendant obtain the best possible outcome. In the American legal system, the defense attorney performs the key function of ensuring that the prosecution proves its case in court or possesses substantial evidence of guilt before a guilty plea leads to conviction and punishment.

As shown in Figure 7.4, the defense attorney advises the defendant and protects his or her constitutional rights at each stage of the criminal justice process. The defense attorney advises the defendant during questioning by the police, represents her or him at each arraignment and hearing, and serves as advocate for the defendant during the appeal process. Without understanding the technical details of law and court procedures, defendants have little ability to effectively represent themselves in court. The defense attorney therefore ensures that prosecutors and judges understand and respect the defendant's rights.

While filling their roles in the criminal justice system, defense attorneys also psychologically support defendants and their families. Relatives are often bewildered, frightened, and confused. The defense attorney is the only legal actor available to answer the question, "What will happen next?" In short, the attorney's relationship with the client matters a great deal. An effective defense requires respect, openness, and trust between attorney and client. If the defendant refuses to follow the attorney's advice, the lawyer may feel obliged to withdraw from the case in order to protect his or her own professional reputation.

Realities of the Defense Attorney's Job

How well do defense attorneys represent their clients? Attorneys who are inexperienced, uncaring, or overburdened have trouble representing their clients effectively. They may quickly agree to a plea bargain and then work to persuade the defendant to accept the agreement. Their self-interest in disposing of cases quickly, receiving payment, and moving on to other cases may cause them to, in effect, work with the prosecutor to pressure the defendant to plead guilty. Skilled defense attorneys also consider plea bargaining in the earliest stages of a case; however, unlike their unskilled counterparts, these lawyers would be guided by their role as advocate for the defendant, not by outside pressures. In many cases, a negotiated plea with a predictable sentence serves the defendant better than does a trial spent fending off more serious charges. An effective defense attorney does not try to take every case all the way to trial.

The defense attorney's job is all the more difficult because neither the public nor defendants fully understand a defense attorney's duties and goals. The public often views defense attorneys as protectors of criminals when, in fact, their basic duty is not to save criminals from punishment but to protect constitutional rights, keep the prosecution honest in preparing and presenting cases, and prevent innocent people from being convicted (Flowers, 2010). Surveys indicate that lawyers place much greater emphasis on the importance of right to counsel than does the public.

Three groups of private practice lawyers can be called specialists in criminal defense because they handle criminal cases on a regular basis. The first group is composed of nationally known attorneys who charge large fees in highly publicized cases. The second group, found in every large city, is composed of the lawyers of choice for defendants who can afford to pay high fees. These attorneys make handsome incomes by representing white-collar criminals, drug dealers, and affluent people charged with crimes. The third and largest group of attorneys in full-time criminal practice is composed of courthouse regulars who accept many cases for small fees and who participate daily in the criminal justice system as either retained or assigned counsel. These attorneys handle a large volume of cases quickly. They negotiate guilty pleas and try to convince their clients that these agreements are beneficial. They depend on the cooperation of prosecutors, judges, and other courtroom actors, with whom they form exchange relationships in order to reach plea bargains quickly.

In addition to these defense specialists, many private attorneys sometimes take criminal cases. These attorneys often have little trial experience and lack well-developed relationships with other actors in the criminal justice system. In fact, their clients might be better served by a courthouse regular who has little interest in each case but whose relationships with prosecutors and judges will produce better plea bargains.

Government-salaried attorneys called *public defenders* handle criminal cases for defendants who are too poor to hire their own attorneys. These attorneys focus exclusively on criminal cases and usually develop significant expertise. They cannot always devote as much time as they want to each case, because they often have heavy caseloads.

The Environment of Criminal Practice

Defense attorneys have a difficult job. Much of their work involves preparing clients and their relatives for the likelihood of conviction and punishment. Even when they know that their clients are guilty, they may become emotionally involved because they are the only judicial actors who know the defendants as human beings and see them in the context of their family and social environment.

Most defense lawyers constantly interact with lower-income clients whose lives and problems are depressing. These attorneys might also visit the local jail at all hours of the day and night. Clearly, their work setting is far removed from the fancy offices and expensive restaurants of the world of corporate attorneys. As described by one defense attorney, "The days are long and stressful. I spend a good deal of time in jail, which reeks of stale food and body odor. My clients often think that because I'm court-appointed, I must be incompetent" (Lave, 1998:14).

Defense lawyers must also struggle with the fact that criminal practice does not pay well. Public defenders garner fairly low salaries, and attorneys appointed to represent poor defendants receive small sums. If private attorneys do not demand payment from their clients at the start of the case, they may find that they must persuade the defendants' relatives to pay—because many convicted offenders have no incentive to pay for legal services while sitting in a prison cell. To perform their jobs well and gain satisfaction from their careers, defense attorneys must focus on goals other than money, such as their key role in protecting people's constitutional rights. However, that they are usually on the losing side can make it hard for them to feel like professionals and enjoy the high self-esteem and satisfying work that is characteristic of the careers of other highly educated people. Because they work on behalf of criminal defendants, they may also face suspicion from the public.

Counsel for Indigents

Since the 1960s, the Supreme Court has interpreted the "right to counsel" in the Sixth Amendment to the Constitution as requiring that the government provide attorneys for indigent defendants who face the possibility of going to prison or jail. *Indigent defendants* are those who are too poor to afford their own lawyers. The Court has also required that attorneys be provided early in the criminal justice process, to protect suspects' rights during questioning and pretrial proceedings. See Table 7.2 for a summary of key rulings on the right to counsel.

Research on felony defendants indicates that 78 percent of those prosecuted in the 75 largest counties and 66 percent of those prosecuted in federal courts received publicly provided legal counsel (Harlow, 2000). The portion of defendants who are

TABLE 7.2 The Right to Counsel: Major Supreme Court Rulings

Case	Year	Ruling
Powell v. Alabama	1932	Indigents facing the death penalty who are not capable of representing themselves must be given attorneys.
Johnson v. Zerbst	1938	Indigent defendants must be provided with attorneys when facing serious charges in federal court.
Gideon v. Wainwright	1963	Indigent defendants must be provided with attorneys when facing serious charges in state court.
Douglas v. California	1963	Indigent defendants must be provided with attorneys for their first appeal.
Miranda v. Arizona	1966	Criminal suspects must be informed about their right to counsel before being questioned in custody.
United States v. Wade	1967	Defendants are entitled to counsel at "critical stages" in the process, including postindictment lineups.
Argersinger v. Hamlin	1972	Indigent defendants must be provided with attorneys when facing misdemeanor and petty charges that may result in incarceration.
Ross v. Moffitt	1974	Indigent defendants are not entitled to attorneys for discretionary appeals after their first appeal is unsuccessful.
Strickland v. Washington	1984	To show that ineffective assistance of counsel violated the right to counsel, defendants must prove that the attorney committed specific errors that affected the outcome of the case.
Rothgery v. Gillespie County, Texas	2008	The right to counsel attaches at the initial hearing before a magistrate when the defendant is informed of the charges and restrictions on liberty are imposed.
Missouri v. Frye	2012	Defense attorneys are obligated to inform their clients about plea agreement offers made by the prosecutor.

A public defender represents indigent clients and carries a heavy caseload under difficult conditions. The quality of representation for poor defendants may vary from courthouse to courthouse, depending on the knowledge and efforts of the attorneys, caseloads, and administrative pressures to resolve cases quickly. How can we improve the quality of defense in criminal cases?

AP Images/Paul Sakuma

provided with counsel because they are indigent has increased greatly in the past three decades. For example, in the 22 states with public defender offices funded by state government rather than county or city governments, criminal caseloads increased by 20 percent from 1999 to 2007 (Langton & Farole, 2010). Government-salaried public defenders alone received 5.5 million cases of indigent criminal defendants in 2007, a figure that does not include thousands of indigents represented by private attorneys who are paid by government on a case-by-case basis (Farole & Langton, 2010).

The quality of counsel given to indigent defendants has spurred debate. Ideally, experienced lawyers would be appointed soon after arrest to represent the defendant in each stage of the criminal justice process. Ideal conditions do not always exist, however. As we have seen, inexperienced and uncaring attorneys may be appointed. Some attorneys have little time to prepare the case. Even conscientious attorneys may be unable to provide top-quality counsel if they have heavy caseloads or do not receive enough money to enable them to spend the time required to handle the case well. For example, in 15 of 22 states with state-funded public defender offices and three-quarters of the county-funded public defender offices in 27 other states, the defense attorneys had caseloads that exceeded the U.S. Department of Justice's recommended guidelines (Farole & Langton, 2010; Langton & Farole, 2010). If attorneys lack either the time or the desire to interview the client and prepare the case, they may simply persuade defendants to plead guilty right there in the courtroom during their first and only conversation. Of course, not all publicly financed lawyers who represent poor defendants ignore their clients' best interests. Even so, the quality of counsel received by the poor may vary from courthouse to courthouse, depending on the quality of the attorneys, conditions of defense practice, and administrative pressure to reduce the caseload.

Ways of Providing Indigents with Counsel   There are three main ways of providing counsel to indigent defendants: (1) the **assigned counsel** system, in which a court appoints a private attorney to represent the accused; (2) the **contract counsel** system, in which an attorney, a nonprofit organization, or a private law firm contracts with a local government to provide legal services to indigent defendants for a specified dollar amount; and (3) **public defender** programs, which are public or private nonprofit

assigned counsel An attorney in private practice assigned by a court to represent an indigent. The attorney's fee is paid by the government with jurisdiction over the case.

contract counsel An attorney in private practice who contracts with the government to represent all indigent defendants in a county during a set period of time and for a specified dollar amount.

public defender An attorney employed on a full-time, salaried basis by a public or private nonprofit organization to represent indigents.

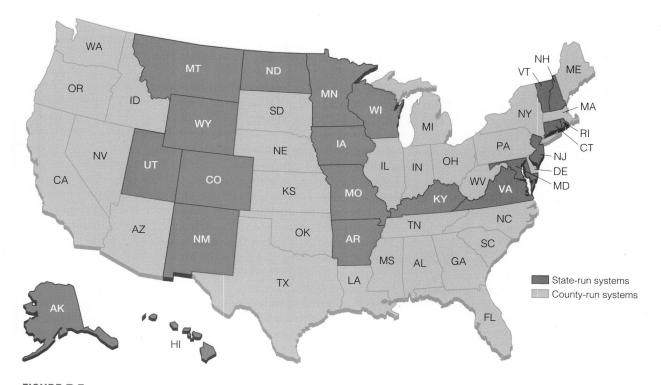

FIGURE 7.5

State-Run Public Defender Offices and County-Run Indigent Defense Systems Note that county-run systems, in particular, may use different representation models (appointed, contract, or public defender) in counties within a given state or use more than one method within a county.

Source: Lynn Langton and Donald Farole Jr., "State Public Defender Programs, 2007," *Bureau of Justice Statistics Special Report,* September 2010, NCJ 228229.

organizations with full-time or part-time salaried staff. Figure 7.5 shows the states that have statewide, centrally administered public defender systems and the other states that have county-based systems for indigent defense that may include the use of public defenders, appointed counsel, or contract counsel.

The methods for providing defense attorneys and the quality of defense services may depend on the money available to pay attorneys. In the states where counties must fund their own defense services, resources—and the quality of indigent defense—may vary from county to county within a single state. As the chief state public defender in Ohio said with respect to the 88 counties in his state's county-run system, "When you have the state of Ohio law being enforced and defended in 88 different ways . . . you end up with huge disparities in cost, quality and efficiency," (A. Manning, 2012).

Issues of resources and quality are complicated by budget cuts in the current era of economic recovery. In 2013 across-the-board cuts throughout the federal government forced public defenders who work in federal courts to take unpaid furloughs for several weeks. Such cuts affect the preparation of cases and timely representation of clients. They can also cause experienced public defenders to look for other jobs rather than deal with personal financial difficulties by being unable to pay rent or house payments because of uncertainties affecting their future working hours and paychecks (C. Johnson, 2013).

Many states were affected by budget problems earlier than the federal government. For example, in 2010 Gwinnett County, Georgia, cut the compensation for court-appointed defense attorneys from $75 to $65 per hour for serious felony cases, with even lower pay rates for misdemeanors and out-of-court activities (Simmons & Rankin, 2010). In Oklahoma the indigent defense system suffered a $1.5 million budget cut resulting in its attorneys being assigned 400 to 500 cases per year (Bisbee, 2010).

Bear in mind that these discussions of dollar amounts do not merely impact the working lives of attorneys; they also impact the quality of representation for indigent defendants who are facing punishment if convicted of a crime.

Assigned Counsel   In the assigned counsel system, the court appoints a lawyer in private practice to represent an indigent defendant. This system is widely used in small cities and in rural areas, but even some city public defender systems assign counsel in some cases, such as a case with multiple defendants, where a conflict of interest might result if a public lawyer represented all of them.

Assigned counsel systems are organized on either an ad hoc or a coordinated basis. In ad hoc assignment systems, private attorneys tell the judge that they are willing to take the cases of indigent defendants. When an indigent requires counsel, the judge either assigns lawyers in rotation from a prepared list or chooses one of the attorneys who are known and present in the courtroom. In coordinated assignment systems, a court administrator oversees the appointment of counsel.

Use of the ad hoc system raises questions about the loyalties of the assigned counsel. Are they trying to vigorously defend their clients, or are they trying to please the judges to ensure future appointments? In states where judges run for election, there are concerns about lawyers donating to judges' political campaigns. Judges could return the favor by supplying their contributors with criminal defense assignments.

The fees paid to assigned defenders are often low compared with what a lawyer might otherwise charge. As described by one attorney, "The level of compensation impacts the level of representation. . . . If an attorney takes [an appointed criminal case], it means they lose the opportunity to take other cases at higher rates" (*Third Branch*, 2008a). Whereas a private practice attorney might charge clients at rates that exceed $200 per hour, hourly rates for appointed counsel in Cook County (Chicago), Illinois, are merely $40 per hour for in-court tasks and $30 per hour for out-of-court tasks. These same rates have been in place for more than 30 years. Defense attorneys receive the low rate of $40 per hour for out-of-court work in Oklahoma, Oregon, Alabama, South Carolina, and Tennessee. Many other states pay only $50 to $75 per hour (Spangenberg Group, 2007). The average hourly overhead cost for attorneys—the amount they must make just to pay their secretaries, office rent, and telephone bills—is $64 ("Economics of CJA Representations," 2008). If their hourly fees fall short of their overhead costs, then attorneys actually lose money when spending time on these cases. Look at Table 7.3 to see examples of fees paid to assigned defense counsel.

TABLE 7.3	Fees Paid to Assigned Counsel in Noncapital Felony Cases		
State	**Out-of-Court Hourly Rate**	**In-Court Hourly Rate**	**Per-Case Maximum**
Alaska	$50	$60	$4,000 trial; $2,000 plea
Hawaii	$90	$90	$6,000
Illinois (Chicago)	$30	$40	$1,250
Maryland	$50	$50	$3,000
New York	$75	$75	$4,400
North Carolina	$65	$65	None
Ohio	$50	$60	$3,000
Wisconsin	$40	$40	None

Sources: John P. Gross, "Rationing Justice: The Underfunding of Assigned Counsel Systems," Part 1: Gideon at 50—A Three-Part Examination of Indigent Defense in America (Washington, DC: National Association of Criminal Defense Lawyers), 2013, 20–32.

Contract System A few counties, mainly in Western states that do not have large populations, use the contract system. The government contracts with an attorney, a nonprofit association, or a private law firm to handle all indigent cases. Some jurisdictions use public defenders for most cases but contract for services in multiple-defendant cases that might present conflicts of interest in extraordinarily complex cases or in cases that require more time than the government's salaried lawyers can provide.

This system has its problems (Clark, 2011). According to Robert Spangenberg and Marea Beeman (1995:49), "There are serious potential dangers with the contract model, such as expecting contract defenders to handle an unlimited caseload or awarding contracts on a low-bid basis only, with no regard to the qualifications of contracting attorneys."

Public Defenders The position of public defender developed as a response to the legal needs of indigent defendants. The most recent national survey of the 100 most populous counties found that public defender systems handled 82 percent of the 4.2 million indigent criminal cases whereas appointed counsel handled 15 percent and contract counsel represented only 3 percent of defendants (DeFrances & Litras, 2000). The public defender system, which is growing fast, is used in 43 of the 50 most populous counties and in most large cities. There are about 22 statewide, state-funded systems; in other states, the counties organize and pay for indigent defense, and some counties choose to use full-time public defenders.

Experts and others often view the public defender system as better than the assigned counsel system, because public defenders are specialists in criminal law. As full-time government employees, public defenders, unlike appointed counsel and contract attorneys, do not sacrifice their clients' cases to protect their own financial interests. Public defenders do face certain special problems, however. They may have trouble gaining the trust and cooperation of their clients. Criminal defendants may assume that attorneys on the state payroll, even with the title "public defender," have no reason to protect the defendants' rights and interests. Lack of cooperation from the defendant may make it harder for the attorney to prepare the best possible arguments for use during hearings, plea bargaining, and trials.

Public defenders may also face heavy caseloads. These burdens increase when government budget cuts affect the money devoted to indigent defense. In 2008, for example, a lawsuit in Miami sought to limit public defenders' caseloads after the average number of felony cases handled annually by each attorney grew from 367 to nearly 500. In Missouri there was no increase in the number of public defenders hired even though these attorneys were required to handle 12,000 more total cases than in previous years (Eckholm, 2008a). Public defender programs are most effective when they have enough money to keep caseloads manageable. However, these programs do not control their own budgets, and state and local legislators usually do not see them as high priorities (Jaksic, 2007). Thus, these programs are increasingly underfunded, understaffed, and less able to give adequate attention to each defendant's case. For example, 40 percent of county-based public defender offices have no staff investigators at all, so the defense attorneys must handle all aspects of their own cases (Farole & Langton, 2010). By contrast, the prosecutors, whose presentations of evidence the public defenders must counteract, can rely on the police department to handle investigation.

Attorney Effectiveness and Competence Do defendants who can afford their own counsel receive better legal services than those who cannot? Many convicted offenders say, "You get what you pay for," meaning that they believe they would have received better counsel if they had been able to pay for their own attorneys. At one time, researchers thought public defenders entered more guilty pleas than did lawyers who had been either privately retained or assigned to cases.

However, studies show little variation in case outcomes by various types of defense (Hanson & Chapper, 1991).

The right to counsel is of little value when the counsel is not competent and effective. Even in death penalty cases, attorneys with almost no knowledge of criminal law have made blunders that have needlessly sent their clients to death row (C. E. Smith, 1997). For example, lawyers have fallen asleep during their clients' death penalty trials, yet one Texas judge found no problem with such behavior. He wrote that everyone has a constitutional right to have a lawyer, but "the Constitution does not say that the lawyer has to be awake" (Shapiro, 1997:27). An appellate court later disagreed with this conclusion.

The U.S. Supreme Court has examined the question of what requirements must be met if defendants are to receive effective counsel. To prevail in claims that their counsel has been ineffective, defendants must identify specific errors made by their attorneys that affected the result of their case and made the proceedings unfair. By focusing on whether errors by an attorney were bad enough to make the trial result unreliable, thereby denying a fair trial, the Court has made it difficult for defendants to prove that they were denied effective counsel, even when defense attorneys perform very poorly. As a result, innocent people who were poorly represented have been convicted, even of the most serious crimes.

☑CHECK POINT

10. **What special pressures do defense attorneys face?**
    Carrying heavy caseloads, receiving poor pay, enduring difficult working conditions, persuading clients to accept pleas, accepting the fact that they will lose most cases.

11. **What are the three main methods of providing attorneys for indigent defendants?**
    Assigned counsel, contract counsel, public defender.

STOP&ANALYZE

Which of the three methods of providing attorneys for indigent defendants works best? List the three strongest arguments in favor of each approach as well as two arguments against each approach. Which set of arguments is most persuasive?

The Courtroom: How It Functions

Criminal cases throughout the nation follow similar rules and procedures. However, courts differ in the precise ways they apply them. Social scientists are aware that the culture of a community greatly influences how its members behave. *Culture* implies shared beliefs about proper behavior. These beliefs can span entire nations or exist in smaller communities, including organizations such as corporations, churches, or neighborhoods. In any community, large or small, the culture can strongly affect people's decisions and behaviors.

local legal culture Norms shared by members of a court community as to how cases should be handled and how a participant should behave in the judicial process.

Researchers have identified a **local legal culture** of values and norms shared by members of a particular court community (judges, attorneys, clerks, bailiffs, and others) about how cases should be handled and the way court officials should behave (Church, 1985). The local legal culture influences court operations in three ways:

1. Norms (shared values and expectations) help participants distinguish between "our" court and other courts. Often a judge or prosecutor will proudly describe how "we" do the job differently and better than officials in a nearby county or city.

2. Norms tell members of a court community how they should treat one another. For example, mounting a strong adversarial defense may be viewed as not in keeping with the norms of one court, but it may be expected in another.

3. Norms describe how cases should be processed. The best example of such a norm is the **going rate**, the local view of the proper sentence, which considers

going rate Local court officials' shared view of the appropriate sentence for the offense, the defendant's prior record, and other case characteristics.

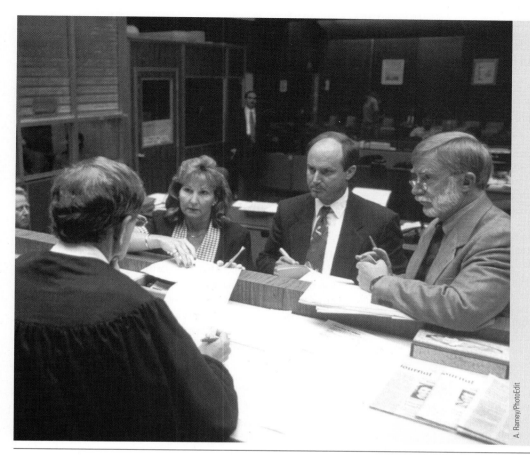

Criminal cases move through court processes as a result of discussions, interactions, and decisions involving judges, prosecutors, and defense attorneys. Even when the attorneys adopt strongly adversarial positions, courtroom participants interact, cooperate, and negotiate as they fulfill the responsibilities of their positions in the courtroom work group. How is the judge a key actor in this process?

A. Ramey/PhotoEdit

the offense, the defendant's prior record, and other factors. The local legal culture also includes attitudes on such issues as whether a judge should take part in plea negotiations, when **continuances**—lawyers' requests for delays in court proceedings—should be granted, and which defendants qualify for a public defender.

Differences among local legal cultures help explain why court decisions may differ even though the formal rules of criminal procedure are basically the same. For example, although judges play a key role in sentencing, sentences also stem from understandings of the going rate shared by the prosecutor, defense attorney, and judge. In one court, shared understandings may mean that a court imposes probation on a first-time thief; in other courts, different shared values may send first offenders to jail or prison for the same offense.

Decision making in criminal cases is influenced by the fact that participants are organized in **work groups**. The judge, prosecutor, and defense attorney, along with the support staff (clerk, reporter, and bailiff), interact in the workplace on a continuing basis, share goals, develop norms regarding how activities should be carried out, and eventually establish a network of roles that differentiates the group from others and that facilitates cooperation. These relationships are necessary if the group is to carry out its task of disposing of cases. The work-group concept is especially important for analyzing urban courts, which have many courtrooms; large numbers of lawyers, judges, and other court personnel; and a heavy caseload.

Work groups in various courthouses differ depending on the strength of the factors that define each of them in each setting. For example, a rotation system that moves judges among courtrooms in a large courthouse may limit the development of work-group norms and roles. Although the same prosecutors and defense attorneys may be present every day, the arrival of a new judge every week or month will

continuance An adjournment of a scheduled case until a later date.

work group A collection of individuals who interact in the workplace on a continuing basis, share goals, develop norms regarding how activities should be carried out, and eventually establish a network of roles, all of which differentiate the group from others and facilitate cooperation.

CRIMINAL JUSTICE
MYTH&REALITY

require them to learn and adapt to new ideas about how cases should be negotiated or tried. When shared norms cannot develop, cases will tend to proceed in a more formal manner. The actors in such a courtroom have fewer chances to follow agreed-upon routines than would a work group with a well-developed pattern of interactions.

By contrast, when there are shared expectations and consistent relationships, the business of the courtroom proceeds in a regular but informal manner, with many shared understandings among members easing much of the work (Worden, 1995). Through cooperation, each member can achieve his or her goals as well as those of the group. The prosecutor wants to gain quick convictions, the defense attorney wants fair and prompt resolution of the defendant's case, and the judge wants cooperative agreements on guilt and sentencing. All of these actors want efficient processing of the steady flow of cases that burden their working lives. Through cooperative decision making, the courtroom work group can resist outside efforts to change case processing and sentencing through new laws and policies and thereby retain control of case outcomes (Gebo, Stracuzzi, & Hurst, 2006; Harris & Jesilow, 2000). Read "Criminal Justice: Myth & Reality" to see how an understanding of the courtroom work group can provide insight into the plea bargaining process.

Judges are the leaders of the courtroom team. They ensure that procedures are followed correctly. Even if prosecutors and defense attorneys appear to make the key decisions, the judge must approve them. Judges coordinate the processing of cases. Further, each judge may perform this role somewhat differently than another judge. For example, judges who run a loose administrative ship see themselves as somewhat above the battle. They give other members of the team a great deal of freedom in carrying out their duties and will usually approve group decisions, especially when the members of the group have shared beliefs about the court's goals and the community's values. Judges who exert tighter control over the process play a more active role. They anticipate problems; provide cues for other actors; and threaten, cajole, and move the group toward the efficient achievement of its goals. Such judges command respect and participate fully in the ongoing courtroom drama. Some judges' actions can, therefore, push defense attorneys to encourage their clients to plead guilty instead of insisting on a trial.

☑CHECK POINT

12. How does the local legal culture affect criminal cases?
The local legal culture consists of norms that distinguish a given court from other jurisdictions, that stipulate how members should treat one another, and that describe how cases should be processed.

13. What is the courtroom work group?
The courtroom work group is made up of the judge, prosecutor, defense counsel, and support staff assigned regularly to a specific courtroom. Through the interaction of these members, goals and norms are shared and a set of roles becomes stabilized.

STOP&ANALYZE

Should the fates of defendants be influenced by the relationships between judges and attorneys? Are case outcomes determined by the facts of the case and law when the courtroom work group operates? Does the courtroom work group advance or hinder the attainment of justice? List three arguments that either endorse the courtroom work group or criticize it.

Think, Discuss, Write

The ethical rules for judges require them to speak and behave in ways that uphold the integrity, impartiality, and image of the courts. Unfortunately, these rules are broken with unfortunate regularity in ways that attract public attention through newspaper articles about judges' improper statements and behavior. In the first few months of 2013 alone, a variety of examples emerged around the country in which judges were reprimanded for improper actions:

- Georgia: During a court proceeding, a judge told an attorney, "Don't come back to this court" because the attorney had donated money to the election campaign of the judge's election opponent.
- Tennessee: A judge expressed the belief in court that one attorney was having a sexual relationship with another attorney.
- Minnesota: A judge joked about "women sleeping together" during jury selection after one juror noted that she had shared a hotel room with a defense attorney when they served as chaperones on a school trip for their children.
- Indiana: A judge said that it was inappropriate for taxpayers to pay for a sign language interpreter during a hearing concerning the custody of a deaf teenager because one of the adults involved in the case had not paid taxes for several years.

- Oregon: A judge called a defendant a "piece of shit" who had no soul when sentencing the defendant for sexually abusing children.

Discussion/Writing Assignment

Do the statements reportedly made by these judges harm the image of the courts? If so, how? If these statements are improper, what should happen to judges who say such things? If the judges apologize, should they be forgiven and receive another opportunity to behave in a proper manner? Is there any way to make sure that judges will always act according to the proper image of their judicial office? Write a memo analyzing whether any of these statements should lead a judge to be punished? If so, explain why and how they should be punished?

Sources: Madeline Buckley, "Nemeth Reaches Pact," *South Bend Tribune,* January 8, 2013 (articles.southbendtribune.com); Lisa Coston, "Georgia State Judge Reprimanded and Suspended," *Courthouse News Service,* March 7, 2013 (www.courthousenews .com); Pat Pheifer, "Dakota County Judge Reprimanded for Inappropriate Jokes to Jurors," *Minneapolis Star Tribune,* March 29, 2013 (www.startibune.com); "Rhea County Judge Reprimanded for Comment, Language," *Times Free Press,* April 16, 2013 (www .timesfreepress.com); Sanne Specht, "Judge Sanctioned for Comments During Sentencing," *Ashland Daily Tidings,* February 9, 2013 (www.dailytidings.com).

SUMMARY

❶ Describe the structure of the American court system.
- The United States has a dual court system consisting of state and federal courts that are organized into separate hierarchies.
- Trial courts and appellate courts have different jurisdictions and functions.

❷ Name the qualities that the public desires in a judge.
- The judge is a key figure in the criminal justice process who assumes the roles of adjudicator, negotiator, and administrator. Effective performance in these roles requires knowledge of law, fairness, communication skills, and thoughtful decision making.
- The recent development of specialized courts, such as drug courts and mental health

courts, places judges in the role of a problem solver.

❸ Describe the process by which American judges are selected.
- State judges are selected through various methods, including partisan elections, nonpartisan elections, gubernatorial appointment, legislative selection, and merit selection.
- Merit-selection methods for choosing judges have gradually spread to many states. Such methods typically use a screening committee to recommend potential appointees, who will, if placed on the bench by the governor, later go before the voters for approval or disapproval, based on their performance in office.

❹ Identify some of the roles of the prosecuting attorney.

- American prosecutors, both state and federal, have significant discretion to determine how to handle criminal cases.
- The prosecutor can play various roles, including trial counsel for the police, house counsel for the police, representative of the court, and elected official.

❺ Describe the role that the prosecutor's discretion plays in the process for filing criminal charges.

- Prosecutors possess significant authority to decide whether to pursue charges and which charges to pursue. Because most local prosecutors are elected officials who seek to please the voters, there are risks that political considerations may affect prosecutorial decisions.
- There is no higher authority over most prosecutors that can overrule a decision to pursue multiple counts against a defendant or to decline to prosecute (*nolle prosequi*).

❻ Identify those with whom the prosecutor interacts in decision making.

- Prosecutors' decisions and actions are affected by their exchange relationships with many other important actors and groups, including police, judges, defense attorneys, victims and witnesses, and the public.

❼ Describe the day-to-day reality of criminal defense work in the United States.

- The image of defense attorneys as courtroom advocates often differs from the reality of pressured, busy negotiators constantly involved in bargaining with the prosecutor over plea agreements.

- Relatively few private defense attorneys make significant incomes from criminal work, but larger numbers of private attorneys accept court appointments to handle indigent defendants' cases quickly for relatively low fees.

❽ List the methods for providing counsel for defendants who cannot afford a private attorney.

- Three primary methods for providing attorneys to represent indigent defendants are assigned counsel, contract counsel, and public defenders.
- Overall, private and public attorneys appear to provide similar quality of counsel with respect to case outcomes.
- Indigent defense systems often face limited budgets, so that appointed counsel are paid small amounts and public defenders are burdened by significant caseloads.
- The quality of representation provided to criminal defendants is a matter of significant concern, but U.S. Supreme Court rulings have made it difficult for convicted offenders to prove that their attorneys did not provide competent counsel.

❾ Describe the courtroom work group, and explain and how it functions.

- The outcomes in criminal cases depend significantly on a court's local legal culture, which defines the going rates of punishment for various offenses.
- Courtroom work groups made up of judges, prosecutors, defense attorneys, and staff who work together can smoothly and efficiently handle cases through cooperative plea bargaining processes.

Questions for Review

1. The judge plays several roles. What are they? Do they conflict with one another?
2. What is the best method for selecting judges? Why? What are the flaws or risks of alternative selection methods?
3. What are the formal powers of the prosecuting attorney?
4. What considerations influence the prosecutor's decision about whether to bring charges and what to charge?
5. Why is the prosecuting attorney often cited as the most powerful office in the criminal justice system?

6. What are some of the problems faced by attorneys who engage in private defense practice?
7. What are the methods by which defense services are provided to indigents?
8. Why might it be argued that publicly financed counsel serves defendants better than does privately retained counsel?
9. What is the courtroom work group, and what does it do?

Key Terms and Cases

accusatory process (p. 237)

adversarial process (p. 219)

appellate courts (p. 220)

assigned counsel (p. 242)

continuance (p. 247)

contract counsel (p. 242)

count (p. 235)

defense attorney (p. 238)

discovery (p. 235)

going rate (p. 246)

inquisitorial process (p. 219)

jurisdiction (p. 219)

local legal culture (p. 246)

merit selection (p. 228)

nolle prosequi (p. 235)

nonpartisan election (p. 225)

partisan election (p. 225)

problem-solving courts (p. 221)

prosecuting attorney (p. 229)

public defender (p. 242)

state attorney general (p. 229)

trial courts of general jurisdiction (p. 220)

trial courts of limited jurisdiction (p. 220)

United States attorneys (p. 229)

work group (p. 247)

8 Pretrial Procedures, Plea Bargaining, and the Criminal Trial

LEARNING OBJECTIVES

1 Identify the elements in the pretrial process in criminal cases.

2 Explain how the bail system operates.

3 Describe the experience of pretrial detention.

4 Explain how and why plea bargaining occurs.

5 Give the reasons why cases go to trial, and describe the benefits of jurors' participation in trials.

6 Describe the stages of a criminal trial.

7 Explain the basis for an appeal of a conviction.

The star quarterback of the University of Montana football team remained calm as he testified in the courtroom in February 2013, despite the fact that he faced a possible sentence of 100 years in prison if the jury were to convict him of the rape charge he faced (Florio, 2013). Defendants are not required to testify at their trials due to the Fifth Amendment protection against compelled self-incrimination. Yet, Jordan Johnson's testimony was essential because the verdict hinged on whether his claim that the woman consented to sex undercut the alleged victim's testimony that he had forced himself on her after she said "no." No one else witnessed the event. No one denied that the sexual encounter occurred. Thus, Johnson's fate rested on the jury's assessment of the contradictory he-said-she-said testimony. The 13-day trial captured the attention of the entire community of Missoula, Montana, and received coverage in the national news.

The alleged victim testified that she and Johnson were kissing while watching a movie DVD at her house and then they both removed their shirts. At that point, she claimed that she said "no" to further sexual activity while he claimed that she consented to continuing and she even joked about not having a condom at her house (Florio & Szpaller, 2013). By contrast, the woman testified that even though other people were elsewhere in the house, she did not scream because she was terrified. There was evidence that she sent a text message to a friend later saying that she had been raped (Florio & Szpaller, 2013).

When Johnson testified, defense attorney Kristin Pabst walked him through the disputed events through her questions in the direct examination process. Throughout the case, the defense tried to convey the impression that the alleged victim's charges emerged when she became angry at the defendant as she realized that he did not want a continuing relationship with her. The prosecutor Adam Durek pressed Johnson on his version of events through questioning in the cross-examination process (Florio, 2013). The prosecutor portrayed the woman as courageous for bringing forward charges despite the attacks on her motives from the defendant's attorneys (Florio & Szpaller, 2013).

Based on competing versions of an event, can jurors really know who is telling the truth? Yet, the American justice system traditionally relies on citizens drawn from the community to make important judgments about people's fates, even when there is limited evidence available. The seven women and five men on the jury faced a difficult task in determining the truth based on limited evidence. In other trials, there is often other evidence, such as testimony from eyewitnesses, that can add strength to one side's version. In Johnson's case, there was little else upon which to rely other than the jurors' perceptions of the consistency and honesty of the alleged victim and the defendant.

At the end of the attorneys' closing arguments, the jury deliberated for two and a half hours before returning a verdict: not guilty. Johnson stood between his two attorneys as the verdict was read. When he heard the announcement, he hugged his attorneys with tears on his face. The alleged victim was not in the courtroom for the verdict, thus shielding her reaction from public view.

The American system regards the trial as the best method for determining a defendant's guilt. This is especially true when the defendant can afford to pay for an attorney to mount a vigorous defense. This case occupies the top layer of Samuel Walker's criminal justice wedding cake (see Chapter 1) as one of those relatively few cases that go to trial and command great public attention because a minor celebrity with the resources to hire an attorney was facing severe punishment.

However, a trial is not a scientific process. Instead of calm, consistent evaluations of evidence, trials involve unpredictable human perceptions and reactions. Attorneys know that a mix of citizens drawn from society may react in different ways and reach different conclusions in reacting to the attorneys' presentations of evidence and the testimony of witnesses. According to an alternate juror who heard all of the evidence while standing by in case a jury member needed to be replaced, the Missoula jurors ultimately demonstrated that they were uncertain about which version of events to believe. Because the prosecutor bore the burden of proving the defendant guilty beyond a reasonable doubt, they felt that guilt had not been proven adequately to fulfill the requirements of the law (Loewen, 2013).

Because of the high stakes and uncertainty that surround criminal trials, most defendants plead guilty as they get closer to the prospect of being judged by a random group of citizens drawn from the community. Even the cases of prominent defendants, who can afford to pay top-notch attorneys, are often determined by plea bargaining. For example, multimillionaire movie star Mel Gibson entered a plea in March 2011 to misdemeanor battery charges after he allegedly punched his girlfriend in 2010 (Cieply, 2011). In his plea deal, Gibson agreed to a sentence of 36 months of probation and 52 weeks of domestic violence counseling (McCartney, 2011). Gibson gained a specific sentence and spared his children from the embarrassment of a lengthy proceeding covered by newspapers and television. The prosecutor gained a quick conviction without expending time and other resources.

In this chapter, we examine the steps in the criminal justice process from arrest to dismissal or conviction. We give particular attention to bail, plea bargaining, and trials—the processes and decisions that most influence whether people will lose their liberty or otherwise receive punishment. As we shall see, interactions and decisions involving judges, prosecutors, and defense attorneys guide the outcomes from these important processes.

From Arrest to Trial or Plea

At each stage of the pretrial process, key decisions are made that move some defendants to the next stage of the process and filter others out of the system. An innocent person could be arrested on the basis of mistaken identification or misinterpreted evidence (Streib, 2010; Huff, 2002). However, pretrial processes ideally force prosecutors and judges to review the available evidence and dismiss unnecessary charges against people who should not face trial and punishment. These processes stem from the American value of due process. Americans believe that people should be entitled to a series of hearings and other procedural steps in which their guilt is proved before they are subjected to punishments such as the loss of liberty through incarceration.

After arrest, the accused is booked at the police station. This process includes taking photographs and fingerprints, which form the basis of the case record. Within 48 hours of a warrantless arrest, the defendant is usually taken to court for the initial appearance to hear which charges are being pursued, to be advised of her or his rights, and to receive the opportunity to post bail. At the initial appearance, the judge also must confirm that evidence exists to establish probable cause that the accused committed a crime and thereby is eligible to be prosecuted. If the police used an arrest warrant to take the suspect into custody, evidence has already been presented to a judge who believed that it was strong enough to support a finding of probable cause to proceed against the defendant.

Often the first formal meeting between the prosecutor and the defendant's attorney is the **arraignment**: the formal court appearance in which the charges against the defendant are read and the defendant, advised by her or his lawyer, enters a plea of either guilty or not guilty. Most defendants will initially plead not guilty, even if they are likely to plead guilty at a later point. This is because, thus far, the prosecutor and defense attorney usually have had little chance to discuss a potential plea bargain. The more serious the charges, the more likely the prosecutor and defense attorney will need time to assess the strength of the other side's case. Only then can plea bargaining begin.

At the time of arraignment, prosecutors begin to evaluate the evidence. This screening process greatly affects the lives of accused persons, whose fate rests largely on the prosecutor's discretion (Covey, 2011). If the prosecutor believes the

arraignment The court appearance of an accused person in which the charges are read and the accused, advised by a lawyer, pleads guilty or not guilty.

Criminal defendants typically make several court appearances as the judge makes decisions about evidence and the protection of each defendant's rights. Does the American system reduce the risk of errors by using a multistep process to examine evidence, protect rights, and determine guilt?

AP Images/Todd Davis, Pool

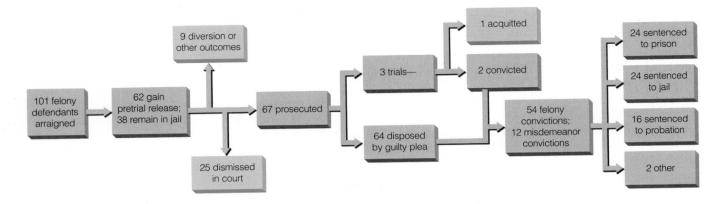

FIGURE 8.1

Typical Outcomes of 100 Urban Felony Cases Prosecutors and judges make crucial decisions during the period before trial or plea. Once cases are bound over for disposition, guilty pleas are many, trials are few, and acquittals are rare.

Sources: Brian A. Reaves, "Felony Defendants in Large Urban Counties, 2009—Statistical Tables," *Bureau of Justice Statistics Statistical Tables*, December 2013, NCJ 228944.

case against the defendant is weak, the charges may be dropped. Prosecutors do not wish to waste their limited time and resources on cases that will not stand up in court. A prosecutor may also drop charges if the alleged crime is minor, if the defendant is a first offender, or if the prosecutor believes that the few days spent in jail before arraignment have provided enough punishment for the alleged offense. Jail overcrowding or the need to work on more serious cases may also influence the decision to drop charges. In making these decisions, prosecutors at times may discriminate against the accused because of race, wealth, or some other factor, or they may discriminate against certain victims, such as women who have been sexually assaulted by an intimate partner or other acquaintance (Schlesinger, 2013; A. Davis, 2008; Spohn & Holleran, 2001).

motion An application to a court requesting that an order be issued to bring about a specific action.

Defense attorneys use pretrial proceedings to challenge the prosecution's evidence. They make **motions** to the court requesting that an order be issued to bring about a specific action. For example, the defense may seek an order for the prosecution to share certain evidence or for the exclusion of evidence that was allegedly obtained through improper questioning of the suspect or an improper search.

As Figure 8.1 shows, prosecutors use their decision-making power to filter many cases out of the system. The 100 cases illustrated are typical felony cases. The percentage of cases varies from city to city, depending on such factors as the effectiveness of police investigations and prosecutors' policies about which cases to pursue. In the figure, nearly half of those arrested did not ultimately face felony prosecutions. A small number of defendants were steered toward diversion programs (Alarid & Montemayor, 2010). A larger number had their cases dismissed for various reasons, including lack of evidence, the minor nature of the charges, or first-time offender status. Some of the 16 sentenced to probation may actually be imprisoned if the offenders commit a crime after release into the community. In these cases, the prosecutor simply chooses to pursue revocation of probation or parole, typically an easier and quicker process than proving guilt for a new crime (Weisberg, 2010; Kingsnorth, MacIntosh, & Sutherland, 2002).

During the pretrial process, defendants are exposed to the informal, "assembly-line" atmosphere of the lower criminal courts. Often decisions are quickly made about bail, arraignment, pleas, and the disposition of cases. Moving cases through court quickly seems to be the main goal of many judges and attorneys during the pretrial process. Courts throughout the nation face pressure to limit the number of cases going to trial. This pressure may affect the decisions of both judges and prosecutors, as well as the defense attorneys who seek to maintain good relationships with them. American courts often have too little funding, too few staff members, and too little time to give detailed attention to each case, let alone to the time and resources needed for a full trial. Resource scarcity is a growing problem due to the budget cuts experienced by many state and local court systems (Bluestein, 2011).

☑ **CHECK POINT**

1. **What are the purposes of the initial appearance, arraignment, and motions?**
   The initial appearance determines if there is probable cause to support the arrest. Arraignments involve the formal reading of charges and the entry of a plea. Motions seek information and the vindication of defendants' rights.

2. **Why and how are cases filtered out of the system?**
   Cases are filtered out through the discretionary decisions of prosecutors and judges when they believe that there is inadequate evidence to proceed or when prosecutors believe that their scarce resources are best directed at other cases.

STOP & ANALYZE

Do prosecutors hold too much power in the pretrial process in light of their discretionary decisions about charging and plea bargaining? List two risks and two benefits from giving prosecutors significant authority over pretrial decisions.

Bail: Pretrial Release

It is often stated that defendants are presumed innocent until proved guilty or until they enter a guilty plea. However, people who are arrested are taken to jail. They are deprived of their freedom and, in many cases, subjected to miserable living conditions while they await the processing of their cases. The fact that people who are presumed innocent can lose their freedom—sometimes for many months—as their cases work their way toward trial is one that clashes with the American values of freedom and liberty. It is not clear how committed Americans are to preserving the ideal of freedom for people who have not yet been convicted of crimes. Such concerns may have further diminished in the aftermath of September 11 as the federal government began to hold persons suspected of terrorism, labeled "enemy combatants," without providing any bail hearing, evidence of guilt, or access to defense attorneys. The outcry against such deprivations of liberty has come from civil rights groups and attorneys rather than from the general public (Tashima, 2008).

A conflict is bound to occur between the American value of individual liberty and the need to keep some criminal suspects in jail in order to protect society from violent people or from those who may try to escape prosecution. However, not every person charged with a criminal offense need be detained. Thus, bail and other release methods are used on the condition that the defendants will appear in court as required.

Bail is a sum of money or property, specified by the judge, that defendants present to the court as a condition of pretrial release. They forfeit the bail if they do not appear in court as scheduled. Although people are generally entitled to a bail hearing as part of their right to due process, there is no constitutional right to release on bail or even a right to have the court set an amount as the condition of release. The Eighth Amendment to the U.S. Constitution forbids excessive bail, and state bail laws are usually designed to prevent discrimination in setting bail. They do not guarantee, however, that all defendants will have a realistic chance of being released before trial. A study in New York City found that among 19,137 cases for which bail was set at $1,000 or less, 87 percent of those defendants could not post bail and they remained in jail for an average of 16 days while their cases were processed (Secret, 2010). Such statistics about the risk of pretrial detention for large numbers of poor people raise the possibility that such defendants may feel pressured to plead guilty, whether or not they are in fact guilty, simply to obtain a sentence of probation for minor offenses and thereby more quickly gain their freedom from custody.

Because the accused is presumed to be innocent, bail should not be used as punishment. The amount of bail should therefore be high enough to ensure that

bail An amount of money, specified by a judge, to be paid as a condition of pretrial release to ensure that the accused will appear in court as required.

the defendant appears in court for trial—but no higher. As we have seen, however, this is not the only purpose of bail. The community must be protected from the crimes that some defendants would likely commit while out on bail (Karnow, 2008). Congress and some of the states have passed laws that permit *preventive detention* of defendants when the judge concludes that they pose a threat to the community while awaiting trial (Wiseman, 2009).

The Reality of the Bail System

The reality of the bail system is far from the ideal. The question of bail may arise at the police station, at the initial court appearance in a misdemeanor case, or at the arraignment in most felony cases. For minor offenses, police officers may have a standard list of bail amounts. For serious offenses, a judge will set bail in court. In both cases, those setting bail may have discretion to set differing bail amounts for various suspects depending on the circumstances of each case. The speed of decision making and lack of information available at the moment of setting bail can enhance differential treatment. As described by the prosecutor in Staten Island, one of the boroughs of New York City, "We have an assistant prosecutor who in about 30 seconds has to come up with a dollar figure that that young person believes is adequate [an amount for bail] . . . We don't get to interview the defendant; we have to make a determination without substantiating any of the information before us" (Secret, 2010).

In almost all courts, the amount of bail is based mainly on the judge's view of the seriousness of the crime and of the defendant's record. As indicated by the foregoing statement from the New York prosecutor, this emphasis results, in part, from a lack of information about the accused. Because bail is typically determined 24 to 48 hours after an arrest, there is little time to conduct a more thorough assessment. As a result, judges in many communities have developed standard rates: so many dollars for such-and-such an offense. In some cases, a judge may set a high bail if the police or prosecutor wants a certain person to be kept off the streets.

Critics of the bail system argue that it operates to facilitate discrimination, especially against poor people (Wooldredge, 2012). Moreover, the overlap of racial minority status and poverty in American society can produce definite disparities in regard to who is actually subjected to pretrial detention. Imagine that you have been arrested and have no money. Should you be denied a chance for freedom before trial just because you are poor? What if you have a little money, but if you use it to post bail, you will not have any funds left to hire an attorney? Professional criminals and the affluent have no trouble making bail; many drug dealers, for instance, can readily make bail and go on dealing while awaiting trial. In contrast, a poor person arrested for a minor violation may spend the pretrial period in jail (Secret, 2010). Should dangerous, wealthy offenders be allowed out on bail while nonviolent, poor suspects are locked up?

According to a study of felony defendants in the nation's most populous counties, 62 percent were released before disposition of their cases, 34 percent were unable to make bail, and 4 percent were detained without bail (Reaves, 2013). Figure 8.2 shows the amounts of bail set for various types of felony offenses. Those who cannot make bail must remain in jail awaiting trial, unless they can obtain enough money to pay a bail bondsman's fee. Given the length of time between arraignment and trial in most courts and the hardships of pretrial detention, bail agents are important to defendants in many cities. In 2009 there were 17,198 felony suspects in the 75 largest counties who could not make bail or use the services of a bail bondsman to gain release (Reaves, 2013). As indicated by the previously mentioned study in New York City, far larger numbers of people lose their liberty in the bail system when one adds the people detained for failing to produce small bail amounts after being arrested for misdemeanors.

Bail Agents

The bail agent, also known as a bail bondsman, is a key figure in the bail process. Bail bondsmen (or women) are private businesspeople who are paid fees by defendants

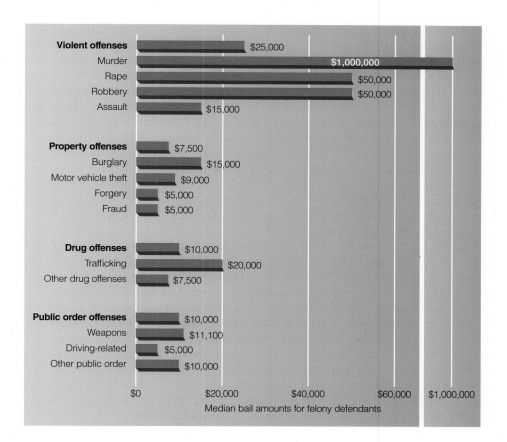

FIGURE 8.2
Median Bail Amounts for Felony Defendants by Offense Type The amount of bail varies according to the offense.

Source: Brian A. Reaves, "Felony Defendants in Large Urban Counties, 2009—Statistical Tables," *Bureau of Justice Statistics Statistical Tables,* December 2013, NCJ 228944.

who lack the money to make bail. They are licensed by the state and can choose their own clients. In exchange for a fee, which may be 5 to 10 percent of the bail amount, the bail agent will put up the money (or property) to gain the defendant's release. Bondsmen are not obliged to provide bail money for every defendant who seeks to use their services. Instead, they decide which defendants are likely to return for court appearances. If the defendant skips town, the bail agent's money is forfeited, and the bondsman therefore has a strong incentive to try to locate the missing defendant. Sometimes bondsmen and their employees have used violence or otherwise gone outside the boundaries of the law in their efforts to capture missing defendants.

Bondsmen may build relationships with police officers and jailers to obtain referrals. Many defendants may not know whom to call for help in making bail, and officers can steer them to a particular bail agent. This can lead to corruption if a bail agent pays a jailer or police officer to make such referrals. Moreover, these relationships may lead to improper cooperation, such as a bail agent refusing to help a particular defendant if the police would like to see that defendant remain in jail. Thus, the bail agent can pose ethical and practical problems for the system (Clisura, 2010).

The potential problems of using profit-seeking bail agents are widely recognized (M. Phillips, 2011). Only two countries in the world use commercial bail bond systems, the United States and the Philippines. Posting bail for a fee is illegal in many countries. In addition, four states—Illinois, Kentucky, Oregon, and Wisconsin—have abolished private bail bond systems and instead rely on deposits to courts instead of payments to private businesses (Liptak, 2008b).

There can be functional benefits from the activities of bail agents. One such benefit is that they can contribute to the smooth processing of cases. A major reason that defendants fail to appear for scheduled court appearances is forgetfulness and confusion about when and where they must appear. Courthouses in large cities are huge bureaucracies that do not always clearly communicate to a defendant a change in the time and location of a hearing. Bail agents can help by reminding defendants about court dates, calling defendants' relatives to make sure that the defendant will arrive on time, and warning defendants about the penalties for failing to appear. Such contributions, however, do not necessarily outweigh the risks and problems caused by bail agents. A bail bondsman in Brownsville, Texas, for example, was sentenced to serve time in federal prison in 2012 after bribing a state judge to reduce an accused drug trafficker's bail (Brezosky, 2012). Similarly, a bail bondsman in Portsmouth, Virginia, went to prison in 2012 for paying bribes to a judge and an employee of the sheriff's department for referring defendants to him as bail bond clients (FBI Press Release, 2012). In 2011 a bail bondsman in California went to jail for one year after admitting that he referred clients to specific defense attorneys in exchange for having those defense attorneys refer their clients to him. These actions were in direct violation of a specific state law to limit the soliciting of bail bond business from attorneys (P. Austin, 2011). These examples show the continuing risks that exist from the use of bail bondsmen in the criminal justice system.

Although the justice system benefits from the activities of bail agents, court and law enforcement officials could handle the same functions as well or better if they had the resources, time, and interest to make sure that released defendants return to court. If all courts had pretrial services offices, such as those in the federal courts, defendants could be monitored and reminded to return to court but avoid the risks of discrimination and corruption associated with the use of bail agents (Cadigan, 2009).

Further, the problems caused by bail agents and bounty hunters in using their own means to find and capture fugitives could be avoided if pretrial services offices reduced the role of bail bondsmen (M. Hirsch, 2007). The hunt for fugitives, such as defendants who skip bail, could remain the exclusive responsibility of trained law enforcement personnel. In the federal system, U.S. marshals are the main law enforcement officials in the court system and are responsible for handling court security, transporting prisoners, and tracking down fugitives.

Setting Bail

When the police set bail at the station house for minor offenses, they usually apply a standard amount for a particular charge. By contrast, when a judge sets bail, the amount of bail and conditions of release result from interactions among the judge, prosecutor, and defense attorney. These actors discuss the defendant's personal qualities and prior record. The prosecutor may stress the seriousness of the crime, the

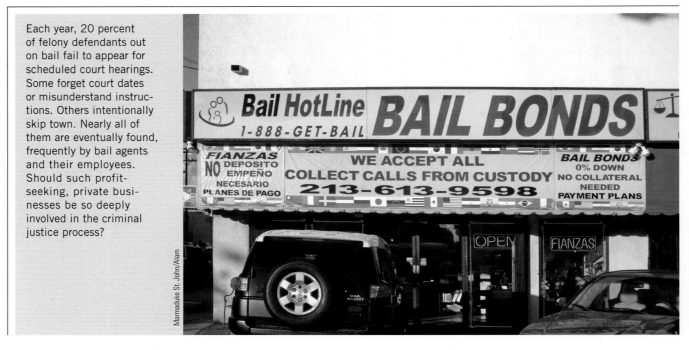

Each year, 20 percent of felony defendants out on bail fail to appear for scheduled court hearings. Some forget court dates or misunderstand instructions. Others intentionally skip town. Nearly all of them are eventually found, frequently by bail agents and their employees. Should such profit-seeking, private businesses be so deeply involved in the criminal justice process?

Marmaduke St. John/Alam

defendant's record, and negative personal characteristics. The defense attorney, if one has been hired or appointed at this point in the process, may stress the defendant's good job, family responsibilities, and place in the community. Like other aspects of bail, these factors may favor affluent defendants over the poor, the unemployed, and people with unstable families. Yet, many of these factors provide no clear information about how dangerous a defendant is or whether he or she will appear in court. The amount of bail may also reflect the defendant's social class or even racial or ethnic discrimination by criminal justice officials (M. Johnson & Johnson, 2012).

Reforming the Bail System

Studies of pretrial detention in such cities as Philadelphia and New York have raised questions about the need to hold defendants in jail. Criticisms of the bail system focus on judges' discretion in setting bail amounts, the fact that the poor are deprived of their freedom while the affluent can afford bail, the negative aspects of bail agents, and jail conditions for those detained while awaiting trial.

In response to such criticisms, efforts to reform the bail system have arisen. Such efforts often focus on reducing the number of defendants held in jail. As a result, the percentage of defendants released on bail has increased in recent decades, in part because of the use of certain pretrial release methods, which we now discuss.

Citation   A **citation**, or summons, to appear in court—a "ticket"—is often issued to a person accused of committing a traffic offense or some other minor violation. By issuing the citation, the officer avoids taking the accused person to the station house for booking and to court for arraignment and setting of bail. Citations are now being used for more serious offenses, in part because the police want to reduce the amount of time they spend booking minor offenders and waiting in arraignment court for their cases to come up.

citation A written order or summons, issued by a law enforcement officer, directing an alleged offender to appear in court at a specific time to answer a criminal charge.

Release on Recognizance   Pioneered in the 1960s by the Vera Institute of Justice in New York City, the **release on recognizance (ROR)** approach is based on the assumption that judges will grant releases if the defendant is reliable and has roots in the community. Soon after the arrest, court personnel talk to defendants about their job, family, prior record, and associations (Kim & Denver, 2011). They then decide whether to recommend release. In the first three years of the New York project, more than 10,000 defendants were interviewed, and about 3,500 were released. Only 1.5 percent failed to appear in court at the scheduled time, a rate almost three times better than the rate for those released on bail (Goldfarb, 1965). Programs in other cities have had similar results, although Sheila Royo Maxwell's research (1999) raises questions about whether women and property-crime defendants on ROR are less likely than other defendants to appear in court.

release on recognizance (ROR) Pretrial release granted on the defendant's promise to appear in court because the judge believes that the defendant's ties to the community guarantee that she or he will appear.

Ten Percent Cash Bail   Although ROR is a useful alternative to money bail, judges are unwilling to release some defendants on their own recognizance. Illinois, Kentucky, Nebraska, Oregon, and Pennsylvania have **percentage bail** programs in which the defendants deposit with the court an amount of cash equal to 10 percent of their bail. When they appear in court as required, this amount is returned minus a 1 percent fee for administrative costs. Begun in Illinois in 1964, this plan is designed to release as many defendants as possible without using bail agents.

percentage bail Defendants may deposit a percentage (usually 10 percent) of the full bail with the court. The full amount of the bail is required if the defendant fails to appear. The percentage of bail is returned after disposition of the case, although the court often retains 1 percent for administrative costs.

Bail Fund   An innovative program developed in New York City in 2009 is called the Bronx Freedom Fund. Poor people who are represented by the Bronx Defenders, a nonprofit organization that handles defense for indigent defendants, can receive loans from the fund in order to post bail and gain pretrial release (Clisura, 2010). The fund was created to prevent poor defendants from languishing in jail merely because they cannot pay a relatively small amount of money. Those freed on bail are monitored and assisted through the relationship between the fund and the defense attorneys. The organization's website claims that 93 percent of defendants assisted by the fund returned for their court appearances.

In other locations, churches and other organizations have sometimes engaged in parallel activities by loaning money for bail. However, such programs are probably most effective when the loans are tied to contact, assistance, and supervision with people, such as counselors or defense attorneys, who remind defendants about court dates and otherwise help them to avoid violating conditions of bail.

Bail Guidelines   To deal with the problem of unequal treatment, reformers have written guidelines for setting bail. The guidelines specify the standards judges should use in setting bail and also list appropriate bail amounts. Judges are expected to follow the guidelines but may deviate from them in special situations. The guidelines take into account the seriousness of the offense and the defendant's prior record in an effort to protect the community and ensure that released suspects will likely return for court appearances.

Preventive Detention   Reforms have been suggested by those concerned with unfairness in the bail system as well as by those concerned with stopping crime. Critics of the bail system point to a link between release on bail and the commission of crimes, arguing that the accused can commit other crimes while awaiting trial. A study of the nation's most populous counties found that 16 percent of felony defendants released on bail were rearrested for another crime (Reaves, 2013). To address this problem, legislatures have passed laws permitting detention of defendants without bail.

For federal criminal cases, Congress enacted the Bail Reform Act of 1984, which authorizes **preventive detention**. Under the act, if prosecutors recommend that defendants be kept in jail, a federal judge holds a hearing to determine (1) if there is a serious risk that the person will flee; (2) if the person will obstruct justice or threaten, injure, or intimidate a prospective witness or juror; or (3) if the offense is one of violence or one punishable by life imprisonment or death. On finding that any of these factors makes setting bail impossible without endangering the community, the judge can order the defendant be held in jail until the case is completed (C. E. Smith, 1990).

Critics of preventive detention argue that it violates the Constitution's due process clause because the accused is held in custody until a verdict is rendered (Wiseman, 2009). However, the Supreme Court has ruled that it is constitutional. The preventive detention provisions of the Bail Reform Act of 1984 were upheld in *United States v. Salerno and Cafero* (1987). The justices said that preventive detention was a legitimate use of government power because it was not designed to punish the accused. Instead, it deals with the problem of people who commit crimes while on bail. By upholding the federal law, the Court also upheld state laws dealing with preventive detention (M. Johnson & Johnson, 2012).

Supporters of preventive detention claim that it ensures that drug dealers, who often treat bail as a business expense, cannot flee before trial. Research has shown that the nature and seriousness of the charge, a history of prior arrests, and drug use all have a strong bearing on the likelihood that a defendant will commit a crime while on bail.

preventive detention Holding a defendant for trial, based on a judge's finding that if the defendant were released on bail, he or she would endanger the safety of any other person and the community or would flee.

United States v. Salerno and Cafero (1987) Preventive detention provisions of the Bail Reform Act of 1984 are upheld as a legitimate use of government power designed to prevent people from committing crimes while on bail.

☑ **CHECK POINT**

3. **What factors affect whether bail is set and how much money or property a defendant must provide to gain pretrial release?**
Bail decisions are based primarily on the judge's evaluation of the seriousness of the offense and the defendant's prior record. The decisions are influenced by the prosecutor's recommendations and the defense attorney's counterarguments about the defendant's personal qualities and ties to the community.

4. **What methods are used to facilitate pretrial release for certain defendants?**
Police citations, release on own recognizance (ROR), 10 percent cash bail, and bail fund.

STOP&ANALYZE

If you were the governor of a state that had never introduced reforms to reduce pretrial detention, which approach would you propose—10 percent cash bail, bail fund, release on own recognizance, bail guidelines, or citation? Make two arguments in favor of the approach that you would choose.

Pretrial Detention

People who are not released before trial must remain in jail. Often called the "ultimate ghetto," American jails hold almost 600,000 people on any one day. Most of the people in jail are poor, half are in pretrial detention, and the rest are serving sentences (normally of less than one year) or are waiting to be moved to state prison or to another jurisdiction (Clear, Cole, & Reisig, 2012).

Urban jails also contain troubled people, many with mental health and drug abuse problems, whom police have swept off the streets. Michael Welch calls this process, in which the police remove socially offensive people from certain areas, "social sanitation" (Welch, 1994:262). Conditions in jails are often much harsher than those in prisons. People awaiting trial are often held in barracks-like cells along with sentenced offenders. Thus, a "presumed innocent" pretrial detainee might spend weeks in the same confined space with troubled people or sentenced felons (Beck, Karberg, & Harrison, 2002). The problems of pretrial detention may be even worse in other countries where suspects languish in jail during the slow-moving processing of criminal cases. Read the "Comparative Perspective" on pretrial detention in the Philippines for a different perspective on the experience of pretrial detainees. What factors help keep detainees in American jails from experiencing the hardships endured by those in jails in the Philippines?

The period just after arrest is the most frightening and difficult time for suspects. Imagine freely walking the streets one minute and being locked in a small space with a large number of troubled and potentially dangerous cell mates the next. Suddenly, you have no privacy and must share an open toilet with hostile strangers. You have been fingerprinted, photographed, searched, and questioned—treated like the "criminal" that the police and the criminal justice system consider you to be (Schlanger, 2008). You are alone with people whose behavior you cannot predict and left to worry about what might happen. If you are female, you may be placed in a cell by yourself. Given the stressful nature of arrest and jailing, it is little wonder that most jail suicides and psychotic episodes occur during the first hours of detention.

Other factors can make the shock of arrest and detention even worse. Many people are arrested for offenses they committed while under the influence of drugs

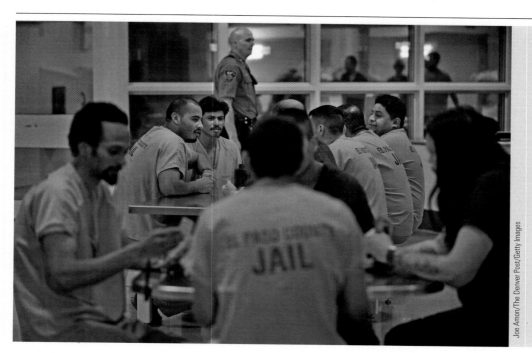

Jails holding pretrial detainees may be crowded and lack education and counseling programs. Spending time in close quarters with strangers for weeks or months can be frightening and difficult as people worry about what will happen to them. What thoughts and feelings would you experience if you were arrested and detained in jail?

Joe Amon/The Denver Post/Getty Images

Pretrial Detention in the Philippines

Raymund E. Narag

Despite legal principles that say an accused suspect has a right to a speedy trial, pretrial detainees in the Philippines can spend years in jail while undergoing processing of their cases to trial. Because jails are so overcrowded and unhealthy, time spent in pretrial detention can actually be a death sentence, as many detainees die from tuberculosis and other communicable diseases. In the Quezon City Jail, where I was held for seven years while wrongly accused of a crime, five detainees typically die every month.

Jail overcrowding combines with a lack of basic services to make life in jail nearly unbearable. The Quezon City Jail was built to hold 700 people, yet it is used to detain 3,500 suspects. I lived with more than 100 men crammed into a room that was actually only large enough to accommodate 10 residents. The money spent on food for detainees is the equivalent of 50 cents per day per detainee. Authorities do not provide clothing, sleeping mats, blankets—or even forks and spoons. Detainees must rely on friends and relatives, if they have any nearby, to provide basic provisions. Diseases spread among detainees who are crowded together and must share eating utensils.

Detainees also face dangers from their fellow inmates, including those who are organized into gangs. They may be beaten or killed if they violate the expected inmate code of behavior. The bleak, overcrowded conditions create both physical and psychological harms. Some detainees fight over scarce resources. Others risk their lives trying to escape. Others suffer from psychological problems from the pressure, illness, and boredom.

The average stay of detainees in jail is 3.2 years, but some unlucky defendants may be detained as long as 11 years while undergoing case processing to trial. The conditions create pressure on detainees to plead guilty in order to be transferred to the national penitentiary to serve a prison sentence. Ironically, among those who wait in jail for their day in court, only 18 percent will be found "guilty," as the police are frequently ineffective and disorganized in actually discovering and presenting evidence to prove an individual's guilt. Yet, many of the detainees who are found to be "not guilty" will already have had their lives destroyed, as their health has been ruined or their stay in jail has filled them with hate and led them to commit crimes that will bring them back to jail again. The people in jail who must endure these conditions are nearly all poor and uneducated. In light of how few detainees are proved to be guilty of crimes, one must ask whether jails are really holding the powerless people of society rather than the real criminals.

Source: This description of pretrial detention in the Philippines was written specifically for this book by Raymund E. Narag. He was held in jail for seven years for a crime that he did not commit and was eventually declared to be innocent by the Regional Trial Court. While in jail, he organized a literacy program and earned a diploma from the University of the Philippines through correspondence courses. After his release, he advised his country's Supreme Court on criminal justice issues, wrote a book entitled *Freedom and Death inside the City Jail*, and was awarded a Fulbright Fellowship to study in the United States. He is currently an assistant professor of criminal justice at Southern Illinois University.

or alcohol. They may be less able than others to cope with their new situation. Young arrestees who face the risk of being victimized by older, stronger cell mates may sink into depression. Detainees also worry about losing their jobs while in jail, because they do not know if or when they will be released.

Although most Americans arrested for felonies have their cases adjudicated within six months, 15 percent of felony defendants wait more than a year (Reaves, 2013). Imagine the hardships for the arrestees who cannot gain pretrial release if they are among those who must wait months before the courts complete the processing of their cases. The median time for case processing for rape suspects who are detained in jail is nearly 250 days, and for robbery suspects, it is nearly 150 days (Reaves, 2013). For the detained suspects who eventually have their charges dropped or are acquitted of the crime, this is an especially harsh deprivation of liberty. The psychological and economic hardships faced by pretrial detainees and their families can be significant and prolonged.

Pretrial detention not only imposes stresses and hardships that may reach a crisis level but also affects the outcomes of cases (McCoy, 2007). People in jail can give little help to their attorneys. They cannot help find witnesses and perform other useful tasks on their own behalf. In addition, they may feel pressured to plead guilty in order to end their indefinite stay in jail. Even if they believe that they should not be convicted of the crime charged, they may prefer to start serving a prison or jail sentence with a definite end point. Some may even gain quicker release on probation or in a community corrections program by pleading guilty, whereas they might stay in jail for a longer period by insisting on their innocence and awaiting a trial.

☑CHECK POINT

5. **What categories of people are found in jails?**
Pretrial detainees for whom bail was not set or those who are too poor to pay the bail amount required, people serving short sentences for misdemeanors, people convicted of felonies awaiting transfer to prison, and people with psychological or substance abuse problems who have been swept off the streets.

6. **What are the sources of stress for people in jail awaiting trial?**
Living with difficult and potentially dangerous cell mates; feeling uncertain about what will happen to their case, family, and job; and not being able to contribute to the preparation of a defense.

STOP&ANALYZE

Some people in jail have been convicted of crimes and are serving short sentences or awaiting transfer to prison. Others are presumptively innocent pretrial detainees awaiting the processing of their cases. Make two arguments in favor of treating pretrial detainees differently and better than convicted offenders inside jails. Now make two arguments about why such differential treatment is either undesirable or too difficult to implement.

Plea Bargaining

For the vast majority of cases, plea bargaining—also known as negotiating a settlement, copping a plea, or copping out—is the most important step in the criminal justice process. Very few cases go to trial; instead, a negotiated guilty plea arrived at through the interactions of prosecutors, defense lawyers, and judges determines what will happen to most defendants. The courtroom work group, as discussed in Chapter 7, uses plea bargaining to determine the outcomes of cases quickly and efficiently in those courthouses where the same actors work together repeatedly in processing cases.

Quick resolution of cases through negotiated guilty pleas became common and was upheld by the Supreme Court in the 1971 case of *Santobello v. New York*. In the decision, Chief Justice Warren Burger described plea bargaining in favorable terms in ruling that prosecutors were obliged to fulfill promises made during plea negotiations. According to Burger, "'Plea bargaining' is an essential component of the administration of justice. Properly administered, it is to be encouraged" because it saves time and criminal justice resources while also protecting the community.

In 1976 Justice Potter Stewart revealed the heart and soul of plea bargaining when he wrote in *Blackledge v. Allison* that plea bargaining "can benefit all concerned" in a criminal case. There are advantages for defendants, prosecutors, defense attorneys, and judges. Defendants can have their cases completed more quickly and know what the punishment will be, instead of facing the uncertainty of a judge's sentencing decision. Moreover, the defendant is likely to receive less than the maximum punishment that might have been imposed after a trial. Prosecutors are not being "soft on crime" when they plea bargain. Instead, they gain an easy conviction, even in cases in which enough evidence may not have been gathered to convince a jury to find the defendant guilty; they also save time and resources by disposing of cases without having to prepare for a trial. Plea bargaining also saves private defense attorneys the time that would be necessary to prepare for a trial. They earn their fee quickly and can move on to the next case. Similarly, plea bargaining helps public defenders cope with large caseloads. Judges, too, avoid time-consuming trials and the prospect of having to decide what sentence to impose on the defendant. Instead, they often adopt the sentence recommended by the prosecutor in consultation with the defense attorney, provided that it is within the range of sentences that they deem appropriate for a given crime and offender.

Because the public often believes that plea bargaining permits offenders to avoid appropriate punishment for their crime, some jurisdictions, including Memphis,

Santobello v. New York **(1971)** When a guilty plea rests on a promise of a prosecutor, the promise must be fulfilled.

COMMON BELIEF: Bans on plea bargaining for the most serious cases, such as murder, rape, and armed robbery, can ensure that society's most harmful offenders do not avoid the severe punishments that they deserve.

- At different times in recent decades, there have been efforts—in such places as the states of Alaska and California and the cities of Memphis and Detroit—to abolish plea bargaining either completely or for serious offenses.
- Bans on plea bargaining do not end negotiated guilty pleas; they merely alter the form and timing of the negotiations.
- When California banned plea bargaining in the general-jurisdiction Superior Courts, guilty plea negotiations simply moved to a point earlier in the process, such as the pretrial stages in the limited-jurisdiction trial courts.
- In order to respect the ban on plea bargaining, some assistant prosecutors instead engage in "charge bargaining" (negotiating over charges rather than sentences), or judges get involved in discussing with defense attorneys what sentencing expectations might produce a quick guilty plea instead of a trial.
- The ban on plea bargaining in Memphis included a provision to make an exception for certain situations, and then significant numbers of serious cases were treated as if they fit the exceptions for which plea agreements were permitted.
- It appears that the shared sense of self-interest and mutual benefit in the plea bargaining process is so powerful that actors in the system will seek ways to control and settle outcomes rather than face the risk, time, and expense of trials in most cases.

Tennessee, have attempted to prohibit it. Such prohibitions are usually aimed at preventing plea bargaining only in cases involving the most serious felony charges (McCoy, 1993). As discussed in "Criminal Justice: Myth & Reality," such bans on plea bargaining for serious crimes do not actually end negotiated case outcomes because actors in the system find ways to influence cases in a manner that advances their interests in efficient case processing.

Exchange Relationships in Plea Bargaining

As we have seen, plea bargaining is a set of exchange relationships in which the prosecutor, the defense attorney, the defendant, and sometimes the judge participate. All have specific goals, all try to use the situation to their own advantage, and all are likely to see the exchange as a success.

Plea bargaining does not always occur in a single meeting between the prosecutor and defense attorney. One study showed that plea bargaining is a process in which prosecutors and defense attorneys interact again and again as they move further along in the judicial process. As time passes, the discovery of more evidence or new information about the defendant's background may strengthen the prosecutor's hand (Emmelman, 1996). Often the prosecution rather than the defense is in the best position to obtain new evidence (Cooney, 1994). However, the defense attorney's position may gain strength if the prosecutor does not wish to spend time preparing for a trial.

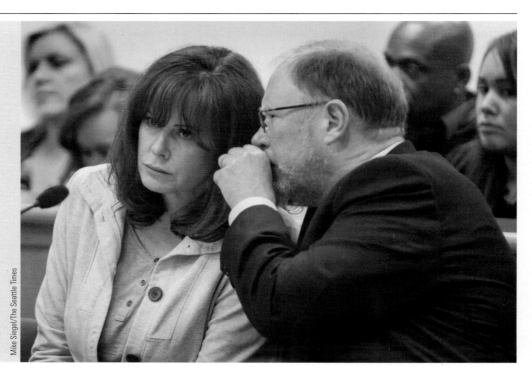

In 2013 Peggy Sue Thomas, a former beauty queen who won the Miss Washington pageant in 2000, entered a guilty plea to the charge of rendering criminal assistance—namely, assisting in the commission of a crime. Her plea came one week before she was scheduled to stand trial for first-degree murder in the killing of a former coworker's husband, a crime for which Thomas's boyfriend was sentenced to 80 years in prison. Instead of facing a life sentence for murder, she received a sentence of four years in prison. Do such reductions in charges and punishments hurt the public's confidence in the justice system?

Mike Siegel/The Seattle Times

Tactics of Prosecutor and Defense

Plea bargaining between defense counsel and prosecutor is a serious game in which friendliness and joking can mask efforts to advance each side's cause. Both sides use various strategies and tactics (D. M. Brown, 2009). Each tries to impress the other with its confidence in its own case while pointing out weaknesses in the other side's case. An unspoken rule of openness and candor usually keeps the relationship on good terms. Little effort is made to conceal information that could later be useful to the other side in the courtroom. Studies show that the outcomes of plea bargaining may depend on the relationships between prosecutors and individual attorneys, as well as the defense counsel's willingness to fight for the client (Champion, 1989).

A tactic that many prosecutors bring to plea bargaining sessions is the multiple-offense indictment. Multiple-offense charges are especially important to prosecutors in handling difficult cases—for instance, those in which the victim is reluctant to provide information, the value of the stolen item is unclear, or the evidence may not be reliable. Prosecutors often file charges of selling a drug when they know they can probably convict only for possession. Because the accused persons know that the penalty for selling is much greater, they are tempted to plead guilty to the lesser charge rather than risk a longer sentence, even if the probability of conviction on the more serious charge is uncertain. Such tactics can be especially powerful when the potential punishment upon conviction at trial would be severe (Erhard, 2008).

Defense attorneys may threaten to ask for a jury trial if concessions are not made (D. M. Bowen, 2009). To strengthen their hand further, they may also file pretrial motions that require a formal response by the prosecutor. Another tactic is to seek to reschedule pretrial activities in the hope that, with delay, witnesses will become unavailable, media attention will die down, and memories of the crime will grow weaker by the time of the trial. Rather than resort to such legal tactics, however, some attorneys prefer to bargain on the basis of friendship. Read "A Question of Ethics" at the end of the chapter to consider the risks that prosecutors and defense attorneys may include in plea agreements that advance their own interests at the expense of the defendant's.

Pleas without Bargaining

Studies have shown that in many courts give-and-take plea bargaining does not occur for certain types of cases, yet they have as many guilty pleas as do other courts (Eisenstein, Flemming, & Nardulli, 1988). The term *bargaining* may be misleading in that it implies haggling. Many scholars argue that guilty pleas emerge after the prosecutor, the defense attorney, and sometimes the judge have reached an agreement to "settle the facts" (Utz, 1978). In this view, the parties first study the facts of a case. What were the circumstances of the event? Was it really an assault, or was it more of a shoving match? Did the victim antagonize the accused? Each side may hope to persuade the other that its view of the defendant's actions is backed up by provable facts. The prosecution wants the defense to believe that strong evidence proves its version of the event. The defense attorney wants to convince the prosecution that the evidence is not solid and that there is a risk of acquittal if the case is heard by a jury.

In some cases, the evidence is strong and the defense attorney has little hope of persuading the prosecutor otherwise. Through their discussions, the prosecutor and defense attorney seek to reach a shared view of the provable facts in the case. Once they agree on the facts, they will both know the appropriate charge, and they can agree on a sentence according to the locally defined going rate. At that point, a guilty plea can be entered without any formal bargaining, because both sides agree on what the case is worth in terms of the seriousness of the charge and the usual punishment. This process may be thought of as *implicit plea bargaining*, because shared understandings create the expectation that a guilty plea will lead to a less than maximum sentence, even without any exchange or bargaining.

As we saw in Chapter 7, the going rates for sentences for particular crimes and offenders depend on local values and sentencing patterns. Often both the prosecutor and the defense attorney belong to a particular local legal culture and thus share an understanding about how cases should be handled. Thus, they may both know right away what the sentence will be for a first-time burglar or second-time robber. The sentence may differ in another courthouse, because the local legal culture and going rates vary.

Legal Issues in Plea Bargaining

In *Boykin v. Alabama* (1969), the U.S. Supreme Court ruled that before a judge may accept a plea of guilty, defendants must state that the plea was made voluntarily. Judges have created standard forms with questions for the defendant to affirm in open court before the plea is accepted. Trial judges also must learn whether the defendant understands the consequences of pleading guilty and ensure that the plea was not obtained through pressure.

In 2012 the Supreme Court issued a pair of potentially far-reaching decisions confirming that defendants are entitled to effective assistance of counsel during the plea bargaining process. In *Missouri v. Frye* (2012), a lawyer failed to inform his client about a favorable plea bargain offer from the prosecutor. In *Lafler v. Cooper* (2012), the defense attorney gave the defendant bad advice about a potential plea agreement by being mistaken about the actual seriousness of the offense for which the defendant could be charged and convicted at trial (Liptak, 2012). It remains to be seen how these decisions will impact plea bargaining, but many observers predict that more plea offers will be placed in writing and that trial judges will provide closer supervision over the plea bargaining process to guard against attorney mistakes that disadvantage defendants (Covey, 2013; Goode, 2012).

Can a trial court accept a guilty plea if the defendant claims to be innocent? In *North Carolina v. Alford* (1970), the Court allowed a defendant to enter a guilty plea for the purpose of gaining a lesser sentence, even though he maintained that he was innocent. However, the Supreme Court also stated that trial judges should not accept such a plea unless a factual basis exists for believing that the defendant is in fact guilty.

Another issue is whether the plea agreement will be fulfilled (J. Cook, 2013). If the prosecutor has promised to recommend a lenient sentence, the promise must be kept (*Santobello v. New York*, 1971). As ruled in *Ricketts v. Adamson* (1987), defendants must also keep their side of the bargain, such as testifying against a codefendant. However, in *Bordenkircher v. Hayes* (1978), the justices ruled that prosecutors may threaten to seek more serious charges, as long as such charges are supported by evidence, if defendants refuse to plead guilty. Some scholars criticize this decision as imposing pressures on a defendant that are not permitted elsewhere in the justice process (O'Hear, 2006).

Criticisms of Plea Bargaining

Critics express many concerns about plea bargaining (Sands, 2013). Two primary criticisms stand out. The first argues that plea bargaining is unfair because defendants give up some of their constitutional rights, especially the right to trial by jury (O'Keefe, 2010). The second stresses sentencing policy and points out that plea bargaining reduces society's interest in appropriate punishments for crimes. In urban areas with high caseloads, for example, harried judges and prosecutors are said to make concessions based on administrative needs, resulting in lighter sentences than those required by the penal code.

Plea bargaining also comes under fire because it is hidden from judicial scrutiny—as the agreement is most often made at an early stage when the judge has little information about the crime or the defendant and thus cannot adequately evaluate the case. Other critics believe that overuse of plea bargaining breeds disrespect

---

***Boykin v. Alabama* (1969)**
Before a judge may accept a plea of guilty, defendants must state that they are making the plea voluntarily.

***Missouri v. Frye* (2012)**
Criminal defendants' Sixth Amendment right to counsel includes protection against ineffective assistance of counsel in the plea bargaining process, such as defense attorneys' failures to inform their clients about plea bargain offers.

***North Carolina v. Alford* (1970)** A plea of guilty by a defendant who maintains his or her innocence may be accepted for the purpose of a lesser sentence.

***Ricketts v. Adamson* (1987)** Defendants must uphold the plea agreement or suffer the consequences.

***Bordenkircher v. Hayes* (1978)** A defendant's rights were not violated by a prosecutor who warned that refusing to enter a guilty plea would result in a harsher sentence.

and even contempt for the law. They say criminals look at the judicial process as a game or a sham, much like other "deals" made in life.

Critics further contend that it is unjust to penalize people who assert their right to a trial by giving them stiffer sentences than they would have received if they had pleaded guilty. Indeed, the threat of severe sentences is so great in the federal court system that the number of federal trials has dropped by two-thirds in the past 25 years—even as the number of defendants has nearly tripled (Fields & Emshwiller, 2012; "Thumb on the Scale," 2013). Research provides evidence that an extra penalty is imposed on defendants who take up the court's time by asserting their right to trial (Devers, 2011; Ulmer, Eisenstein, & Johnson, 2010).

Finally, another concern about plea bargaining is that innocent people will plead guilty to acts that they did not commit. Although it is hard to know how often this happens, it is known that certainly some defendants have entered guilty pleas when they have not committed the offense (J. Bowen, 2008). It may be hard for middle-class people to understand how anyone could possibly plead guilty when innocent. However, people with little education and low social status may lack the confidence to say "no" to an attorney who strongly encourages them to plead guilty.

People may also lack confidence in court processes. What if you feared that a jury might convict you and send you to prison for 20 years based on circumstantial evidence (such as being in the vicinity of the crime and wearing the same color shirt as the robber that day)? Might you plead guilty and take a five-year sentence, even if you knew that you were innocent? How much confidence do you have that juries and judges will always reach the correct result? Poor people, in particular, may feel helpless in the stressful climate of the courthouse and jail. If they lack faith in the system's ability to protect their rights and find them not guilty, they may accept a lighter punishment rather than risk being convicted for a serious offense.

☑CHECK POINT

7. **Why does plea bargaining occur?**
   It serves the self-interest of all relevant actors: defendants gain certain, less than maximum sentences; prosecutors gain swift, sure convictions; defense attorneys get prompt resolution of cases; judges preside over fewer time-consuming trials.

8. **What are the criticisms of plea bargaining?**
   Defendants might be pressured to surrender their rights; society's mandated criminal punishments are improperly reduced.

STOP&ANALYZE

The U.S. Supreme Court's decision in *North Carolina v. Alford* (1970) says that a judge can accept a guilty plea from someone who claims to be actually innocent. Does the acceptance of such pleas diminish the justice system's goal of punishing only those who are guilty of crimes? If you were a judge, would you accept such pleas? Write a brief statement explaining your position.

Trial: The Exceptional Case

If cases are not dismissed or terminated through plea bargaining, they move forward for trial. The seriousness of the charge is probably the most important factor influencing the decision to go to trial. Murder, felonious assault, or rape—all charges that bring long prison terms—may require judge and jury, unless the defendant fears a certain conviction and therefore seeks a negotiated plea deal. When the penalty is harsh, however, many defendants seem willing to risk the possibility of conviction at trial. Table 8.1 shows the differences in the percentages of defendants going to trial for offenses of varying severity. Notice that homicide offenses, which carry the most significant punishments, produce a higher percentage of trials than do other crimes.

Trials determine the fates of very few defendants. Although the right to trial by jury is ingrained in American ideology—it is mentioned in the Declaration of Independence, the U.S. Constitution and three of its amendments, and myriad

In 2013 a Utah jury convicted Dr. Martin MacNeill of murder in the death of his wife, Michelle. Mrs. MacNeill died shortly after being found unconscious in the bathtub with a variety of powerful prescription drugs in her system. The prosecution presented evidence the Dr. MacNeill had an extramarital affair with a woman that he hired to be his children's nanny. What other kinds of cases are likely to be processed through jury trials?

bench trials Trials conducted by a judge who acts as fact finder and determines issues of law. No jury participates.

jury A panel of citizens selected according to law and sworn to determine matters of fact in a criminal case and to deliver a verdict of guilty or not guilty.

| TABLE 8.1 | Percentage of Indicted Cases That Went to Trial, by Offense |

The percentages of cases that went to trial differ both by offense and by jurisdiction. Typically, it seems that the stiffer the possible penalty, the greater the likelihood of a trial. However, a prosecutor may be able to gain guilty pleas even in the most serious cases.

Jurisdiction	Homicide	Rape/Sexual Assault	Robbery	Assault	Drug Offenses
State courts, 75 largest counties	30%	10%	3%	4%	1%
Federal courts	15	—	4	8	3
Mercer County, NJ (Trenton)	10	0	1	1	1

Sources: Adapted from Brian A. Reaves, "Felony Defendants in Large Urban Counties, 2009—Statistical Tables," *Bureau of Justice Statistics Statistical Tables*, December 2013, NCJ 228944; "Mercer County Prosecutor's Annual Report 2012" (2013); *Sourcebook of Criminal Justice Statistics 2014*, Table 5.24.2010.

opinions of the U.S. Supreme Court—year in and year out fewer than 9 percent of felony cases go to trial. Of these, only about half are jury trials; the rest are **bench trials**, presided over by a judge without a **jury**. In 2009 trials produced only 3 percent of felony case outcomes in the nation's 75 most populous counties (Reaves, 2010). Defendants may choose a bench trial if they believe a judge will be more capable of making an objective decision, especially if the charges or evidence are likely to arouse emotional reactions in jurors.

The rates of trials also vary from city to city. This difference stems, in part, from the local legal culture. Think about how prosecutors' policies or sentencing practices in different cities may increase or decrease the incentives for a defendant to plead guilty. In addition, defense attorneys and prosecutors in different courthouses may have their own understandings about which cases should produce a plea bargain because of agreements (or disagreements) about the provable facts and the going rate of sentences for an offense.

Trials take considerable time and resources. Attorneys frequently spend weeks or months preparing for them—gathering evidence, responding to their opponents' motions, planning trial strategy, and setting aside a day to several weeks to present the case in court. From the perspective of judges, prosecutors, and defense attorneys, plea bargaining presents an attractive alternative for purposes of completing cases quickly.

Jury Trial

Trials are based on the idea that the prosecution and defense will compete as adversaries before a judge and jury so that the truth will emerge. As such, the rules of criminal law, procedure, and evidence govern the conduct of the trial. Above the battle, the judge ensures that the rules are followed and that the jury impartially evaluates the evidence and reflects the community's interests. In a jury trial, the jury alone evaluates the facts in a case. The adversarial process and inclusion of jurors in decision making often make trial outcomes difficult to predict. The verdict hinges not only on the nature of the evidence but also on the effectiveness of the prosecution and defense and on the jurors' attitudes. Does this adversarial and citizen-based process provide the best mechanism for finding the truth and doing justice in our most serious criminal cases?

However one assesses their effectiveness, juries perform six vital functions in the criminal justice system:

1. Prevent government oppression by safeguarding citizens against arbitrary law enforcement

2. Determine whether the accused is guilty on the basis of the evidence presented
3. Represent diverse community interests so that no one set of values or biases dominates decision making
4. Serve as a buffer between the accused and the accuser
5. Promote knowledge about the criminal justice system by learning about it through the jury-duty process
6. Symbolize the rule of law and the community foundation that supports the criminal justice system

As a symbol of law, juries demonstrate to the public, as well as to defendants, that decisions about depriving individuals of their liberty will be made carefully by a group of citizens who represent the community's values. In addition, juries provide the primary element of direct democracy in the judicial branch of government. Citizens have the opportunity to participate directly in decision making within the judicial branch of government. However, as indicated in "What Americans Think," even though most Americans have positive experiences with the jury process, they are not eager to serve.

In the United States, a jury in a criminal trial traditionally comprises 12 citizens, but some states now allow as few as 6 citizens to make up a jury. This reform was recommended to modernize court procedures and reduce expenses. It costs less for the court to contact, process, and pay a smaller number of jurors. The use of small juries was upheld by the Supreme Court in *Williams v. Florida* (1970). Six states use juries with fewer than 12 members in noncapital felony cases, and a larger number of states use small juries for misdemeanors. In *Burch v. Louisiana* (1979), the Supreme Court ruled that six-member juries must vote unanimously to convict a defendant, but unanimity is not required for larger juries. Some states permit juries to convict defendants by votes of ten to two or nine to three. The change to six-person juries has its critics, who charge that the smaller group is less representative of the conflicting views in the community and too quick to bring in a verdict (Diamond, Peery, Dolan, & Dolan, 2009; A. R. Amar, 1997).

WHAT AMERICANS THINK

QUESTION: "If called for jury duty in the next year, [I] would . . ."

Question: "If called for jury duty in the next year, [I] would…

Try to get excused	24%
Accept result but hope to be excused	31%
Hope to be selected	27%

QUESTION: "How would you describe your experience serving on a jury?"

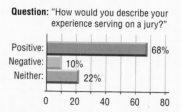

Question: "How would you describe your experience serving on a jury?"

Positive:	68%
Negative:	10%
Neither:	22%

CRITICAL THINKING: Why might people seek to avoid jury duty? If people who have served on juries have such a positive view of the experience, how can this information be conveyed to other people in order to encourage more active willingness to serve when called?

Source: Peter Moore, "Jury Duty: Hoping to Avoid It, But Still a Good Thing." YouGov.com, September 16, 2013 (https://today.yougov.com/news/2013/09/16/jury-duty/).

Williams v. Florida (1970) Juries of fewer than 12 members are constitutional.

The Trial Process

The trial process generally follows eight steps: (1) selection of the jury, (2) opening statements by prosecution and defense, (3) presentation of the prosecution's evidence and witnesses, (4) presentation of the defense's evidence and witnesses, (5) presentation of rebuttal witnesses, (6) closing arguments by each side, (7) instruction of the jury by the judge, and (8) decision by the jury. The details of each step may vary according to each state's rules. Although the proportion of trials may be small, understanding each step in the process and considering the broader impact of this institution are both important.

Jury Selection The selection of the jury, outlined in Figure 8.3, is a crucial first step in the trial process. Because people always apply their experiences, values, and biases in their decision making, prosecutors and defense attorneys actively seek to

FIGURE 8.3

Jury Selection Process for a 12-Member Jury Potential jurors are drawn at random from a source list. From this pool, a panel is selected and presented for duty. The voir dire examination may remove some, whereas others will be seated. The 14 jurors selected include two alternates.

identify potential jurors who may be automatically sympathetic or hostile to their side. When they believe they have identified such potential jurors, they try to find ways to exclude those who may sympathize with the other side, while striving to keep those who may favor their side. Lawyers do not necessarily achieve these goals, because the selection of jurors involves the decisions and interactions of prosecutors, defense attorneys, and judges, each of whom has different objectives in the selection process.

Jurors are selected from among the citizens whose names have been placed in the jury pool. The composition of the jury pool tremendously affects the ultimate composition of the trial jury. In most states, the jury pool is drawn from lists of registered voters, but research has shown that nonwhites, the poor, and young people register to vote at much lower rates than does the rest of the population. As a result, members of these groups are underrepresented on juries (Ali, 2013; Sommers, 2009).

In many cases, the presence or absence of these groups may make no difference in the ultimate verdict. In some situations, however, members of these groups may assert themselves in discussion and interpret evidence differently than do their older, white, middle-class counterparts who dominate the composition of juries (Cornwell & Hans, 2011). For example, the poor, nonwhites, and young people may be more likely to have had unpleasant experiences with police officers and therefore be less willing to believe automatically that police officers always tell the truth. Today, courts may supplement the lists of registered voters with other lists, such as those for driver's licenses, hunting licenses, and utility bills, in an effort to diversify the jury pool (Hannaford-Agor, 2011).

Several states are also considering increases in jurors' daily pay; Texas, for example, has gone from $6 per day to $40 per day in trials lasting more than one day. It is hoped that such efforts will make jury service more attractive for poor people who might otherwise avoid participating because they cannot afford to lose pay by missing work (Axtman, 2005). In addition, judges have increasing concerns about small-business owners as well as people worried about losing their jobs who seek to avoid jury duty for financial reasons (Weiss, 2009b; C. J. Williams, 2010). Unfortunately, the current era of budget cuts has hampered efforts to increase financial incentives for participation. Many jurisdictions, including Cleveland, Ohio, and Topeka, Kansas, reduced jurors' pay to save money (Dubail, 2009; KTKA-TV, 2011).

Retired people and homemakers with grown children tend to be over-represented on juries because they are less inconvenienced by serving and are often less likely to ask to be excused because of job responsibilities or child care problems. To make jury duty less onerous, many states have moved to a system called "one-day-one-trial," in which jurors serve for either one day or for the duration of one trial.

The courtroom process of **voir dire** (which means "to speak the truth") is used to question prospective jurors in order to screen out those who might be biased or otherwise incapable of making a fair decision (C. Harrison, 2011). Attorneys for each side, as well as the judge, may question jurors about their background, knowledge of the case, and acquaintance with any participants in the case (Natoli, 2013). Jurors will also be asked whether they or their immediate family members have been crime victims or otherwise involved in a criminal case in a manner that may prevent them from making open-minded decisions about the evidence and the defendant. If a juror's responses indicate that she or he will not be able to make fair decisions, the juror may be **challenged for cause**. The judge must rule on the challenge, but if the judge agrees with the attorney, then the juror is excused from that specific case (Arterton, 2008). There is usually no limit on the number of jurors that the attorneys may challenge for cause.

Although challenges for cause ultimately fall under the judge's control, the prosecution and defense can exert their own control over the jury's composition through the use of **peremptory challenges**. With these, the prosecution and defense can exclude prospective jurors without giving specific reasons. Attorneys use peremptory challenges to exclude jurors who they think will be unsympathetic to their arguments (Hoffman, 1999). Attorneys usually use hunches about which jurors to challenge; little evidence suggests that they can accurately identify which jurors will sympathize with their side or not (M. S. White, 1995). Normally, the defense is allowed eight to ten peremptory challenges and the prosecution six to eight.

The use of peremptory challenges has raised concerns that attorneys can use them to exclude, for example, African American jurors when an African American is on trial or Latino jurors when there is a Latino defendant (Bagnato, 2010; Price 2009; Enriquez & Clark, 2007). In a series of decisions in the late 1980s and early 1990s (such as *Batson v. Kentucky*, 1986), the Supreme Court prohibited using peremptory challenges to systematically exclude potential jurors because of their race or gender. In practice, however, the enforcement of this prohibition is up to the trial judge (C. E. Smith & Ochoa, 1996). If a trial judge is willing to accept flimsy excuses for race-based and gender-based exclusions, then the attorneys can ignore the ban on discrimination (Bray, 1992). Read "The Policy Debate" and consider whether you believe peremptory challenges should be eliminated.

Some lawyers believe that trials are won or lost in jury selection. If they succeed in seating a favorable jury, they may have a receptive audience that will readily support their arguments and evidence.

Opening Statements After the jury has been selected, the trial begins. The clerk reads the complaint (indictment or information) detailing the charges, and the prosecutor and the defense attorney may, if they desire, make opening statements to the jury to summarize the position that each side intends to take. The statements are not evidence. The jury is not supposed to regard the attorneys' statements as proving or disproving anything about the case.

Presentation of the Prosecution's Evidence One of the basic protections of the American criminal justice system is the presumption that the defendant is innocent until proved guilty. The prosecution carries the burden of proving beyond a reasonable doubt, within the demands of the court procedures and rules of evidence, that the individual named in the indictment committed the crime. This does not mean

voir dire A questioning of prospective jurors to screen out people the attorneys think might be biased or otherwise incapable of delivering a fair verdict.

challenge for cause Removal of a prospective juror by showing that he or she has some bias or some other legal disability. The number of such challenges available to attorneys is unlimited.

peremptory challenge Removal of a prospective juror without giving a reason. Attorneys are allowed a limited number of such challenges.

Should the Peremptory Challenge Be Abolished?

Jimmy Elem faced trial on robbery charges in a Missouri state court. During jury selection, the prosecutor used peremptory challenges to exclude two African American men from the jury. Elem's attorney objected, claiming that the prosecutor appeared to be excluding potential jurors because of their race. Under the U.S. Supreme Court's decision in *Batson v. Kentucky* (1986), a trial judge is obligated to ask the prosecutor to provide a nonracial reason for removing jurors when a prosecutor's use of peremptory challenges seems based on racial exclusion. In response to the judge's question, the prosecutor replied,

> I struck [juror] number twenty-two because of his long hair. He had long curly hair. He had the longest hair of anybody on the panel by far. He appeared to me to not be a good juror for that fact, the fact that he had long hair hanging down shoulder length, curly unkempt hair. Also he had a mustache and a goatee type beard. And juror number twenty-four also has a mustache and goatee type beard. Those are the only two people on the jury . . . with the facial hair. . . . And I don't like the way they looked, with the way the hair is cut, both of them. And the mustaches and the beards look suspicious to me.

The trial judge accepted the prosecutor's explanation and the trial moved forward. Elem subsequently filed a habeas corpus action in the federal courts claiming that the prosecutor had used a flimsy, nonsensical excuse to cover the fact that the exclusions were really based on race. The U.S. court of appeals agreed with Elem and declared that peremptory challenges that appear to be based on race are valid only if actually based on reasons related to the individuals' qualifications to be a good juror.

The court of appeals did not believe that having curly or long hair affected one's ability to be a good juror.

Missouri carried the case forward to the U.S. Supreme Court. In a seven-to-two decision, the Supreme Court reversed and said that prosecutors can put forward silly, superstitious, and implausible reasons as long as the trial judge accepts the exclusion as being based on something other than race or gender.

By contrast, the Supreme Court has looked more closely at other cases. For example, in *Snyder v. Louisiana* (2008), seven justices, including conservatives Chief Justice John Roberts and Justice Samuel Alito, called into question an African American man's conviction when prosecutors eliminated all of the African Americans from the jury pool. Unlike in *Purkett v. Elem*, the majority was not willing to automatically accept the prosecutor's and trial judge's reasons for excluding these jurors.

The use of peremptory challenges permits the attorneys in a case to influence the composition of a jury by permitting them to use their discretion to exclude potential jurors. The Supreme Court has declared that such challenges cannot be used to discriminate by race or sex, but it has not strictly enforced this rule. Trial judges continue to possess the authority to accept reasons for race- and sex-based exclusions that may merely cover up the actual discriminatory intent of the attorney.

Here is a summary of key arguments concerning the issue:

For Keeping the Peremptory Challenge

- Lawyers can use their discretion to exclude jurors who possess biases but whose biases are not obvious enough to convince a judge to exclude them for cause.

---

real evidence Physical evidence—such as a weapon, records, fingerprints, and stolen property—involved in the crime.

demonstrative evidence Evidence that is not based on witness testimony but that demonstrates information relevant to the crime, such as maps, X-rays, and photographs; includes real evidence involved in the crime.

testimony Oral evidence provided by a legally competent witness.

direct evidence Eyewitness accounts.

circumstantial evidence Evidence provided by a witness from which a jury must infer a fact.

that absolute certainty is required, only that the evidence sufficiently excludes all reasonable doubt.

In presenting evidence to the jury, the prosecution must establish a case showing that the defendant is guilty. Evidence is classified as real evidence, demonstrative evidence, testimony, direct evidence, and circumstantial evidence. **Real evidence** might include such objects as a weapon, business records, fingerprints, or stolen property. These are real objects involved in the crime. **Demonstrative evidence** is presented for jurors to see and understand without testimony. Real evidence is one form of demonstrative evidence; other forms include maps, X-rays, photographs, models, and diagrams. Most evidence in a criminal trial, however, consists of the **testimony** of witnesses. Witnesses at a trial must be legally competent. Thus, the judge may be required to determine whether the witness whose testimony is challenged has the intelligence to tell the truth and the ability to recall what was seen. Witnesses with inadequate intelligence or mental problems might not be regarded as qualified to present testimony. **Direct evidence** refers to eyewitness accounts such as, "I saw John Smith fire the gun." **Circumstantial evidence** requires that the jury infer a fact from what the witness observed: "I saw John Smith walk behind his house with a gun. A few minutes later I heard a gun go off, and then Mr. Smith walked toward me holding a gun." The witness's observation that Smith had a gun and that the witness then heard a gun go off does not provide direct evidence that Smith fired his gun; however, the jury may link the described facts and infer that

- Defendants will better accept the legitimacy of the jury and its ultimate verdict because their lawyers were able to play a role in shaping the jury's composition through the use of peremptory challenges.
- The peremptory challenge is a one of the long-standing traditions of trial practices in the American justice system.
- Because both sides in a case can use peremptory challenges, the exclusion of potential jurors by each side helps to create a fair jury with less doubt for either side that a biased juror will actually be one of the decision makers.

For Abolishing the Peremptory Challenge
- There is a long history of peremptory challenges being used by attorneys, especially prosecutors, to engage in racial discrimination and eliminate minority representation on the jury. The Supreme Court's decisions prohibiting this practice do not actually stop it from happening in individual cases.
- Lawyers merely act on hunches in excluding potential jurors through peremptory challenges. They do not actually know if they are excluding potential jurors with hidden biases.
- Lawyers use peremptory challenges in an attempt to slant the jury's composition in their own favor, not to create a fairer jury.
- Peremptory challenges are used to deny individuals the opportunity to participate in an important democratic element of the judicial process without any documentable reason for denying the chance to be jurors.

What Should U.S. Policy Be?
Although the U.S. Constitution does not say anything about peremptory challenges, Supreme Court Justice Antonin Scalia claims that peremptory challenges should be retained because they are part of a long tradition in the jury-selection process. Others argue that peremptory challenges enhance the legitimacy of the trial process by letting defendants feel they have some influence over the composition of the jury. By contrast, the late Supreme Court Justice Thurgood Marshall indicated that peremptory challenges should be abolished because they were frequently used to discriminate or add bias to the jury. For Marshall, if there is not enough evidence of bias to justify a challenge for cause, then the person should be allowed to serve on the jury. People should not be denied the opportunity to participate in this important aspect of judicial decision making just because one lawyer does not like the expression on their face or the color of their skin. How would jury trials be different if peremptory challenges were no longer allowed? Would there be positive, negative, or unclear effects from such a change?

Researching the Internet
Go online to read about recent legal cases and research findings concerning the peremptory challenge at the American Psychological Association's website. http://www.apa.org/monitor/2009/01/jn.aspx.

Analyzing the Issue
Imagine that you and your classmates are state legislators considering a proposed bill to abolish peremptory challenges in jury selection for trials in your state's courts. In your discussions of the issue, can you persuade each other to see which side's arguments are strongest? How would you vote on the bill? Do you think peremptory challenges are helpful, harmful, or irrelevant in the trial process?

Smith fired his gun. After a witness has given testimony, counsel for the other side may cross-examine him or her.

Because many cases rely on scientific evidence, especially in the form of experts' testimony about DNA, blood spatters, bullet fragments and trajectories, and the nature of physical injuries, there are concerns that judges and juries might not fully understand the information presented (Cheng, 2005). Determinations of guilt may hinge on the effectiveness of the presentation of such evidence rather than the accuracy and verifiability of the scientific conclusions (McAuliff & Duckworth, 2010). Some prosecutors fear that the prevalence of definitive scientific evidence in television crime dramas may cause jurors to expect scientific evidence in each case, such as DNA, in order to issue a guilty verdict. As discussed in the Close Up, there are debates about whether a *"CSI* effect" [*Crime Scene Investigation*] has affected jurors' expectations and made it more difficult for prosecutors to gain convictions in cases for which there is only witness testimony and no scientific evidence.

The attorney for each side challenges the other side's presentation of evidence. If evidence violates the rules, reflects untrustworthy hearsay, is a statement of opinion, or is not relevant to the issues in the case, an attorney will object to its presentation. In effect, the attorney is asking the judge to rule that the jury cannot consider the opponent's questionable evidence.

After the prosecution has presented all of the state's evidence against the defendant, the court is informed that the people's case rests. It is common for the defense

Prosecutors and defense attorneys present various forms of evidence during trials, including physical objects ("real evidence") as well as witness testimony. Do you think that the communication skills and persuasiveness of the attorneys could distract the jurors' attention from the actual evidence presented in the case?

AP Images/Andy Morrison, Pool

then to ask the court to direct the jury to bring forth a verdict of not guilty. Such a motion is based on the defense argument that the state has not presented enough evidence to prove its case. If the motion is sustained by the judge (it rarely is), the trial ends; if it is overruled, the defense presents its evidence.

Presentation of the Defense's Evidence   The defense is not required to answer the case presented by the prosecution. As it is the state's responsibility to prove the case beyond a reasonable doubt, it is theoretically possible—and in fact sometimes happens—that the defense rests its case immediately, as we have seen. Usually, however, the accused's attorney employs one strategy or a combination of three strategies: (1) contrary evidence is introduced to rebut or cast doubt on the state's case, (2) an alibi is offered, or (3) an affirmative defense is presented. As discussed in Chapter 3, defenses include self-defense, insanity, duress, and necessity.

A key issue for the defense is whether the accused will take the stand. The Fifth Amendment protection against self-incrimination means that the defendant does not have to testify. The Supreme Court has ruled that the prosecutor may not comment on, nor can the jury draw inferences from, the defendant's decision not to appear in his or her own defense. The decision is not made lightly, because if the defendant does testify, the prosecution may cross-examine. *Cross-examination*, which is questioning by the opposing attorney, is broader than direct examination. The prosecutor may question the defendant not only about the crime but also about her or his past, including past criminal convictions. On the other hand, if the defendant does not testify, jurors might make assumptions about the defendant's guilt, even though they have been instructed not to do so.

When singer R. Kelly was acquitted of child pornography charges by a Chicago jury in 2008, the defense attorneys used every argument that they could, including arguments that were not consistent with each other (Streitfeld, 2008). Their objective was to cast doubt on the prosecution's case. The case hinged on whether a VHS tape showed Kelly having sex with a specific underage girl. The defense suggested that the tape showed another man who looked like Kelly, that computer manipulation had made the tape look like Kelly, or that the tape was made with

The "*CSI* Effect" and Jurors' Expectations about Scientific Evidence

The CBS television network enjoys great success with three popular crime dramas, each entitled *CSI: Crime Scene Investigation* but distinguished by being set in Las Vegas, Miami, and New York. Other networks have emulated the success of CBS by creating their own similar shows, including *Bones* (Fox network) and *Body of Proof* (ABC), based on the scientific techniques for the investigation of crimes and the development of criminal evidence. The public's fascination with the forensic science portrayed in these television shows has led some prosecutors to complain about an escalation in jurors' unrealistic expectations about the necessity of presenting DNA analysis or other scientific evidence in order to establish guilt in each criminal trial. In reality, many criminal investigations and prosecutions are not based on DNA, fingerprints, or other scientific evidence. Instead, prosecutors present witness testimony and circumstantial evidence about a suspect's presence in a certain location and relationship with the victim. However, some prosecutors have come to fear that jurors will not render a guilty verdict without the presentation of scientific evidence. Even if the purported "*CSI* effect" is a myth, if prosecutors are fearful of jurors' expectations, this might make them more reluctant to take cases to trial and thereby pressure them to offer more favorable plea agreements to defendants.

Research on the so-called "*CSI* effect" raises questions about whether jurors are actually less inclined to convict defendants in the absence of scientific evidence. Surveys indicate that jurors may indeed expect to see specific kinds of scientific evidence, but this expectation may be related to a more general "tech effect" of Americans using technology in their daily lives rather than watching specific television shows. Moreover, the increased expectation for scientific evidence does not necessarily mean that jurors will not vote to convict a defendant without it.

While the existence of a "*CSI* effect" continues to be debated by lawyers, judges, and scholars, prosecutors face a very real issue of deciding how, if at all, they will address the issue, just in case it affects jurors in a specific trial. One problem may be a lack of resources to actually gather and evaluate all potential scientific evidence for every case. For example, many crime labs have delays of several months due to backlogs for DNA evidence and other materials requiring scientific analysis. Although it may be necessary for a prosecutor to wait for definitive DNA testing on evidence in a murder case, should the same resources and time be devoted to analyzing all evidence in a burglary case? Prosecutors' options include educating jurors very directly about scientific evidence and why it may not exist in certain cases.

Researching the Internet

Read about the controversy of the "*CSI* effect" on the National Institute of Justice's website. http://ww w.nij.gov /journals/259/Pages/csi-effect.aspx.

For Critical Analysis

Should society devote substantial additional resources to the collection, analysis, and storage of scientific evidence for all criminal cases? In times of budget cuts at all levels of government, what other departments and programs should be cut in order to devote more resources to criminal justice investigations? List two arguments about what ought to be done or, alternatively, whether attempting to educate jurors about these issues will adequately address the matter.

Sources: Simon Cole and Rachel Dioso-Villa, "Investigating the '*CSI* Effect': Media and Litigation Crisis in Criminal Law," *Stanford Law Review* 61: 1335–73 (2009); Laura Huey, "'I've Seen This On *CSI*': Criminal Investigators' Perceptions about the Management of Public Expectations in the Field," *Crime, Media, Culture* 6 (1): 49–68 (April 2010); Donald E. Shelton, "The '*CSI* Effect': Does It Really Exist?" *National Institute of Justice Journal* 259: March 2008 (www.nij.gov).

---

models and prostitutes who looked like Kelly and the alleged victim. The defense attorneys did not need to prove Kelly's innocence; they just needed to raise questions in the jurors' minds about the accuracy of the prosecution's claims. R. Kelly never testified in court and thereby avoided cross-examination about any aspects of his private life and past behavior (St. Clair & Ataiyero, 2008).

Presentation of Rebuttal Witnesses   When the defense's case is complete, the prosecution may present witnesses whose testimony is designed to discredit or counteract testimony presented on behalf of the defendant. If the prosecution brings rebuttal witnesses, the defense has the opportunity to question them and to present new witnesses in rebuttal.

Closing Arguments by Each Side   When each side has completed its presentation of the evidence, the prosecution and defense make closing arguments to the jury. The attorneys review the evidence of the case for the jury, presenting interpretations of the evidence that favor their own side. The prosecutor may use the summation to connect the individual pieces of evidence in a way that forms a basis for concluding that the defendant is guilty. The defense may set forth the applicable law and try to show that the prosecution has not proved its case beyond a reasonable doubt. Each side may remind the jury of its duty to evaluate the evidence impartially and not to be swayed by emotion. Yet, some attorneys may hope that the jurors react emotionally, especially if they think that those emotions will benefit their side.

Judge's Instructions to the Jury   The jury decides the facts of the case, but the judge determines the law. Before the jurors depart for the jury room to decide the defendant's fate, the judge instructs them on how the law should guide their decision. The judge may discuss basic legal principles such as proof beyond a reasonable doubt, the legal requirements necessary to show that all the elements have been proved by the prosecution, or the rights of the defendant. More specific aspects of the law bearing on the decision—such as complicated court rulings on the nature of the insanity defense or the ways certain types of evidence have been gathered—may be included in the judge's instructions. In complicated trials, the judge may spend an entire day instructing the jury.

The concept of **reasonable doubt** forms the heart of the jury system. As we have seen, the prosecution is not required to prove the guilt of the defendant beyond all doubt. Instead, if a juror is

> satisfied to a moral certainty that this defendant . . . is guilty of any one of the crimes charged here, you may safely say that you have been convinced beyond a reasonable doubt. If your mind is wavering, or if you are uncertain . . . you have not been convinced beyond a reasonable doubt and must render a verdict of not guilty. (S. Phillips, 1977:214)

Listening to the judge may become an ordeal for the jurors, who must hear and understand perhaps two or three hours of instruction on the law and the evidence (Bradley, 1992). It is assumed that somehow jurors will fully absorb these details on first hearing them, so that they will thoroughly understand how they are supposed to decide the case in the jury room (Kramer & Koenig, 1990). In fact, the length, complexity, and legalistic content of jury instructions make them difficult for many jurors to comprehend (Gordon, 2013; Daftary-Kapur, Dumas, & Penrod, 2010). The jurors may be confused by the instructions and reach a decision through an inaccurate understanding of the law that applies to the case, such as the legal definitions of intent, premeditation, and other elements of the crime that must be proved in order to justify a conviction (Bornstein & Green, 2011; Armour, 2008). Read the "Evidence-Based Practice and Policy" feature to consider how research findings might help to improve jury instructions.

Decision by the Jury   After they have heard the case and received the judge's instructions, the jurors retire to a room where they have complete privacy. They elect a foreperson to run the meeting, and deliberations begin. Until now, the jurors have been passive observers of the trial, unable to question witnesses or to discuss the case among themselves; now they can discuss the facts that have been presented. The jury may request that the judge reread to them portions of the instructions, ask for additional instructions, or hear portions of the transcript detailing what was said by specific witnesses.

Throughout their deliberations, the jurors may be *sequestered*—kept together day and night, away from the influences of newspapers and conversations with family and friends. If jurors are allowed to spend nights at home, they are ordered not to discuss the case with anyone. The proliferation of cell phones, personal computers, and social media presents new problems for judges seeking to focus the jury's attention solely on information presented in court (K. Brown, 2013).

If the jury becomes deadlocked and cannot reach a verdict, the trial ends with a hung jury and the prosecutor must decide whether to try the case over again in front of a new jury. When a verdict is reached, the judge, prosecution, and defense

reasonable doubt The standard used by a jury to decide if the prosecution has provided enough evidence for conviction.

The Jury and Evidence-Based Practices

Within criminal justice, most of the attention to evidence-based practices has been directed at police efforts to reduce and prevent crime as well as programs to reduce repeat offending by prisoners, juveniles, and substance abusers. These are not, however, the only topics for which research by scholars has helped to shape policy and practice. For many years, a variety of scholars, especially in the field of psychology, have studied juries and jury processes. By gaining an understanding of how jurors receive and understand information, it is hoped that court procedures could be adjusted in ways that will increase jurors' understanding of evidence and legal concepts. As a result, it is presumed that the quality of juries' decision making will improve and thereby reduce the risk of error in jury verdicts.

Jurors face challenges in remembering and understanding information presented as evidence, especially when it is a long trial that lasts for many days. In addition, studies show that jurors have difficulty understanding the jury instructions read to them at the end of the trial by the judge. As a result, many states have put effort into designing jury instructions that use plain language instead of confusing legal terms. Moreover, there is greater recognition that the length of jury instructions can exceed the attention span of jurors. Thus, the extensive work on revising and delivering jury instructions seeks to address multiple concerns.

Although there is not universal agreement on exactly what jury practices to implement based on research evidence, specific states have moved forward with reforms that seek to address the problems identified by research. Not all of the reforms have been verified by research, and, indeed, some of the jury reform efforts are considered by the states to be experiments to see if they improve jury processes.

For example, in 2011 Michigan's Supreme Court issued an order concerning jury reforms for courts to try during a three-year evaluation period. The reforms included

- Providing pretrial jury instructions to jurors so that they could begin understanding their role and the relevant law before hearing evidence
- Providing a copy of the jury instructions for each juror rather than the traditional method of giving only one copy to the entire jury

- Permitting jurors to write down questions during the trial and then request that the judge consider posing these questions to specific witnesses, thus perhaps filling information gaps if the attorneys do not realize what else the jurors would like to know
- Permitting jurors to ask questions about the final jury instructions delivered by the judge at the end of the trial

Jury trials serve an important function for determining the fates of individuals, especially in serious cases such as murder that are likely to draw the most significant punishments. Thus, any evidence-based practices produced through research studies have the potential to reduce errors and improve the quality of jury decisions.

Researching the Internet

The American Judicature Society's National Jury Center provides online information about proposed reforms for the jury system on its website. https://www.ajs.org/judicial-administration/jury-center/jury-system-overview/jury-improvement-efforts/improving-trials/plain-english-jury-instructions/.

Implementing New Practices

If you were a trial judge, would you resent having the state supreme court or other authority impose new rules on your courtroom? Would it be preferable for a trial judge to simply use those methods that the judge believes from experience will be most effective? In the role of a trial judge, write a memo describing two things you would do to improve jurors' understanding of trials. Explain your reasons for each one.

Sources: David Aaronson and Sydney Patterson, "Modernizing Jury Instructions in the Age of Social Media," *Criminal Justice* (American Bar Association), 27 (Winter 2013): 4–10; Ellen Chilton and Patricia Henley, *Improving the Jury System—Jury Instructions: Helping Jurors Understand the Evidence and the Law*, San Francisco: Public Law Research Institute (1996): Sara Gordon, "Through the Eyes of Jurors: The Use of Schemas in the Application of 'Plain-Language' Jury Instructions," *Hastings Law Journal* 64 (2013): 643–77; Philip Thomas, "Mississippi Should Consider Jury Reforms Similar to Those Adopted in Michigan," *MS Litigation Review and Commentary*, July 21, 2011 (www.mslitigationreview.com).

reassemble in the courtroom to hear it. The prosecution or the defense may request that the jury be polled: each member individually tells her or his vote in open court. This procedure presumably ensures that no juror has felt pressured to agree with the other jurors.

Evaluating the Jury System

Individual jurors differ in their processing of information and interactions with others (Gunnell & Ceci, 2010). A classic study at the University of Chicago Law School found that, consistent with theories of group behavior, participation and influence in the jury process are related to social status. Men were found to be more active participants than were women, whites more active than minority members, and the better educated more active than those less educated. Much of the discussion in the jury room was not directly concerned with the testimony but rather with trial procedures, opinions about the witnesses, and personal reminiscences (Strodtbeck, James, & Hawkins, 1957). Recent research has reinforced these results (Cornwell & Hans, 2011). Because of group pressure, only rarely did a single juror produce a hung jury (Sundby, 2010). Some jurors may doubt their own views or go along with the others if everyone else disagrees with them. Additional studies have upheld the importance of group pressure on decision making (Hastie, Penrod, & Pennington, 1983).

An examination of trials in the 75 largest counties found that 76 percent of jury trials ended in convictions, compared with 82 percent of bench trials (Kyckelhahn & Cohen, 2008). These numbers alone do not reveal whether judges and juries decide cases differently. However, research on trials provides clues about differences between these two decision makers.

Juries tend to take a more liberal view of such issues as self-defense than do judges and are likely to minimize the seriousness of an offense if they dislike some characteristic of the victim (S. J. Adler, 1994). For example, if the victim of an assault is a prostitute, the jury may minimize the assault. Perceived characteristics of the defendant may also influence jurors' assessments of guilt (Abwender & Hough, 2001). Judges have more experience with the justice process. They are more likely than juries to convict defendants based on evidence that researchers characterize as moderately strong (Eisenberg et al., 2005). As explained by the premier jury researchers Valerie Hans and Neil Vidmar (2008:227):

> [T]he jury's distinctive approach of common sense justice, and the judges' greater willingness to convict based on the same evidence, best explain why juries and judges sometimes reach different conclusions. These juror values affect the verdicts primarily in trials in which the evidence is relatively evenly balanced and a verdict for either side could be justified.

In recent years, the American Bar Association and other groups have worked to introduce reforms that might improve the quality of juries' decision making (Post, 2004). For example, some courts now permit jurors to take notes during trials and submit questions that they would like to see asked of witnesses (Bornstein & Greene, 2011). Other courts permit jurors to submit questions to the judge during the trial (Mardar, 2010). There are also efforts to make judges' instructions to the jury more understandable through less reliance on legal terminology. It is hoped that jurors can make better decisions if they have more information and a better understanding of the law and the issues in a case.

☑ CHECK POINT

9. What functions do juries serve in the criminal justice system?
Safeguard citizens against arbitrary law enforcement, determine the guilt of the accused, represent diverse community interests and values, serve as buffer between accused and accuser, become educated about the justice system, and symbolize the law.

10. What is voir dire?
The jury selection process in which lawyers and/or judges ask questions of prospective jurors and make decisions about using peremptory challenges and challenges for cause to shape the jury's composition.

11. What are the stages in the trial process?
Jury selection, attorneys' opening statements, presentation of prosecution's evidence, presentation of defense's evidence, presentation of rebuttal witnesses, closing arguments by each side, judge's instructions to the jury, and jury's decision.

STOP&ANALYZE

If you were charged with tax evasion, would you prefer a trial in front of a judge or jury? Why? Would you make a different choice if you were charged with injuring a small child when texting while driving?

Appeals

Imposition of a sentence does not mean that the case is necessarily over; the defendant typically has the right to appeal the verdict to a higher court, and the right to counsel continues through the first appeal (Heise, 2009). Some states have limited the right to appeal when defendants plead guilty. An **appeal** is based on a claim that one or more errors of law or procedure were made during the investigation, arrest, or trial process (C. E. Smith, 2000b). Such claims usually assert that the trial judge made errors in courtroom rulings or by improperly admitting evidence that the police gathered in violation of some constitutional right. A defendant might base an appeal, for example, on the claim that the judge did not instruct the jury correctly or that a guilty plea was not made voluntarily.

In appellate courts, several judges sit as a group to hear and decide cases. The appeals process provides an opportunity to correct errors that occurred in trial court proceedings. What are the advantages and disadvantages of having a group of appeals court judges decide a case together?

Appeals are based on questions of procedure, not on issues of the defendant's guilt or innocence (Place, 2013). The appellate court will not normally second-guess a jury. Instead, it will check to make sure that the trial followed proper procedures (Shay, 2009). If there were significant errors in the trial, then the conviction is set aside. The defendant may be tried again if the prosecutor decides to pursue the case again. Thus, a successful appeal may merely lead to reconviction on the charges in a second trial.

Most criminal defendants must file an appeal shortly after trial to have an appellate court review the case. By contrast, many states provide for an automatic appeal in death penalty cases (Alarcon, 2007). The quality of defense representation is important, because the appeal must usually meet short deadlines and carefully identify appropriate issues (Wasserman, 1990).

A case originating in a state court is first appealed through that state's judicial system. When a state case involves a federal constitutional question, however, a later appeal can go to the U.S. Supreme Court. State courts decide almost four-fifths of all appeals.

Most appeals do not succeed in gaining a new trial, a new sentence, or an outright acquittal. In almost 80 percent of the cases examined in one study (Chapper & Hanson, 1989), the decision of the trial courts was affirmed. Most of the other decisions produced new trials or resentencing; very few decisions (1.9 percent) produced acquittals on appeal.

appeal A request to a higher court that it review actions taken in a trial court.

Habeas Corpus

After people use their avenues of appeal, they may pursue a writ of habeas corpus if they claim that their federal constitutional rights were violated during the lower-court processes (King & Hoffmann, 2011). Known as "the great writ" from its traditional role in English law and its enshrinement in the U.S. Constitution, **habeas corpus** is a judicial order requesting that a judge examine whether an individual is being properly detained in a jail, prison, or mental hospital (Wert, 2011). If there is no legal basis for the person to be held, then the judge may grant

habeas corpus A writ or judicial order requesting the release of a person being detained in a jail, prison, or mental hospital. If a judge finds the person is being held improperly, the writ may be granted and the person released.

the writ and order the person to be released. In the context of criminal justice, convicted offenders may claim that their imprisonment is improper because one of their constitutional rights was violated during the investigation or adjudication of their case. Statutes permit offenders convicted in both state and federal courts to pursue habeas corpus actions in the federal courts. After first seeking favorable decisions by state appellate courts, convicted offenders can start their constitutional claims anew in the federal district courts and subsequently pursue their habeas cases in the federal circuit courts of appeal and the U.S. Supreme Court.

Overall, only about 1 percent of habeas petitions succeed (Flango, 1994). In one study, less than one-half of one percent of noncapital habeas petitioners gained a favorable judicial decision, but more than 12 percent of habeas petitioners in death penalty cases demonstrated a rights violation (King, Cheesman, & Ostrom, 2007). One reason may be that an individual has no right to be represented by counsel when pursuing a habeas corpus petition. Few offenders have sufficient knowledge of law and legal procedures to identify and present constitutional claims effectively in the federal courts (Shay, 2013).

In 1996, the Antiterrorism and Effective Death Penalty Act placed additional restrictions on habeas corpus petitions. The statute was quickly approved by the U.S. Supreme Court. These reforms were based, in part, on a belief that prisoners' cases were clogging the federal courts (C. E. Smith, 1995). Ironically, habeas corpus petitions in the federal courts increased by 50 percent after the passage of the restrictive legislation (Scalia, 2002). By imposing strict filing deadlines for petitions, the legislation may have inadvertently focused more prisoners' attention on the existence of habeas corpus and thereby encouraged them to move forward with petitions in order to meet the deadlines.

Evaluating the Appellate Process

The public seems to believe that many offenders are being "let off" through the appellate process. Some critics have argued that opportunities for appeal should be limited. They claim that too many offenders delay imposition of their sentences and that others completely evade punishment by filing appeals endlessly. This practice not only increases the workload of the courts but also jeopardizes the concept of the finality of the justice process. However, given that 90 percent of accused persons plead guilty, the number of cases that might be appealed is relatively small.

The appeals process performs the important function of righting wrongs. It also helps ensure consistency in the application of law by judges in different courts. Beyond that, its presence constantly influences the daily operations of the criminal justice system, as prosecutors and trial judges must consider how a higher court might later evaluate their decisions and actions.

☑ CHECK POINT

12. How does the appellate court's job differ from that of the trial court?
Unlike trial courts, which have juries, hear evidence, and decide if the defendant is guilty or not guilty, appellate courts focus only on claimed errors of law or procedure in trial court proceedings. Victory for a defendant in a trial court means an acquittal and instant freedom. Victory in an appellate court may mean only a chance at a new trial—which often leads to a new conviction.

13. What is a habeas corpus petition?
The habeas corpus process may be started after all appeals have been filed and lost. Convicted offenders ask a federal court to review whether any constitutional rights were violated during the course of a case investigation and trial. If rights were violated, the person's continued detention in prison or jail may be improper.

STOP&ANALYZE

Do criminal offenders have too many opportunities to challenge convictions? List two benefits and two costs of having an appeals process and a habeas corpus process.

Think, Discuss, Write

In the plea bargaining practices used by federal prosecutors in Florida and elsewhere, elements are included in the plea agreement that prohibit defendants from later raising claims of prosecutorial misconduct or ineffective assistance counsel. Prosecutors want to prevent harassment of attorneys with false claims when the offenders later feel unhappy and bored while sitting in prison. This plea bargaining practice received public attention in 2013 when the Florida lawyers' organizations discussed ethical rules for plea bargaining. Prosecutors argue that defendants pleading guilty are clearly admitting responsibility for the crime, and therefore any issue of the prosecutors' prior conduct is not relevant after the guilty plea is entered. By contrast, critics worry that prosecutors might engage in improper practices that helped to pressure a defendant to agree to a guilty plea rather than take the risk of going to trial. Moreover, defendants may not learn until later that prosecutors hid evidence, lied about existing evidence, or otherwise engaged in unethical or illegal practices that pressured the defendant to accept punishment for the crime.

With respect to defense attorneys, the prohibition on ineffective assistance of counsel claims could similarly shield lawyers from responsibility for serious errors or misconduct. Thus, there could be a risk that an attorney who wishes to cover up his own grave errors may pressure or persuade the defendant to plead guilty, in part, to protect the defense attorney from scrutiny and reprimand after the plea has been entered.

The Florida ethics committee that was developing rules for lawyers professional behavior voted unanimously to endorse an advisory opinion that labeled such practices as unethical. The members concluded that defense attorneys should not be able to use this mechanism to protect themselves from malpractice claims. With respect to prosecutors, the committee concluded that "it is prejudicial to the administration of justice for a prosecutor to require the criminal defendant to waive claims of prosecutorial misconduct," especially at a moment in the process when the prosecutor is likely to be the only individual who knows whether such misconduct has occurred.

Discussion/Writing Assignment

If a defendant is admitting responsibility for a crime and is willing to waive any future claims against the prosecutor and defense attorney, then what is wrong with including such provisions in plea agreements? Is your view affected by the power relationships and differences in knowledge and information possessed by participants in the plea bargaining process? If you were in charge of developing ethics rules for lawyers, would you permit these practices, or would you endorse the action of the Florida committee? Write a memo that gives three reasons for your answer to this final question.

Source: Gary Blankenship, "Board Adopts Hotly Debated Plea Bargain Ethics Opinion," *The Florida Bar News*, January 1, 2013 (www.floridabar.org).

SUMMARY

❶ Identify the elements in the pretrial process in criminal cases.

- Pretrial processes determine the fates of nearly all defendants through case dismissals, decisions defining charges, and plea bargains, all of which affect more than 90 percent of cases.
- Defense attorneys use motions to their advantage to gain information and delay proceedings to benefit their clients.

❷ Explain how the bail system operates.

- The bail process provides opportunities for many defendants to gain pretrial release, but poor defendants may be disadvantaged by their inability to come up with the money or property needed to secure release. Some preventive detention statutes permit judges to hold defendants considered dangerous or likely to flee.
- Bail agents, also known as bail bondsmen, are private businesspeople who charge a fee to provide money for defendants' pretrial release. Their activities create risks of corruption and discrimination in the bail process, but bail agents may also help the system by reminding defendants about court dates.
- Although judges bear the primary responsibility for setting bail, prosecutors are especially influential in recommending amounts and conditions for pretrial release.
- Initiatives to reform the bail process include police-issued citations, release on own recognizance (ROR), percentage bail, bail guidelines, and preventive detention.

③ Describe the experience of pretrial detention.

- Despite the presumption of innocence, pretrial detainees endure difficult conditions in jails that often contain mixed populations of convicted offenders, detainees, and troubled people. The shock of being jailed creates risks of suicide and depression.

④ Explain how and why plea bargaining occurs.

- Most convictions are obtained through plea bargaining, a process that exists because it fulfills the self-interest of prosecutors, judges, defense attorneys, and defendants.
- Plea bargaining is facilitated by exchange relations between prosecutors and defense attorneys. In many courthouses, there is little actual bargaining, as outcomes are determined through the implicit bargaining process of settling the facts and assessing the going rate of punishment according to the standards of the local legal culture.
- Plea bargaining has been criticized for pressuring defendants to surrender their rights and for reducing the sentences imposed on offenders.

⑤ Give the reasons why cases go to trial, and describe the benefits of jurors' participation in trials.

- Americans tend to presume that, through the dramatic courtroom battle of prosecutors and defense attorneys, trials are the best way to discover the truth about a criminal case.
- Less than 9 percent of cases go to trial, and half of those are typically bench trials in front of a judge, not jury trials.
- Typically, cases go to trial because they involve defendants who are wealthy enough to pay attorneys to fight to the very end or because they involve charges that are too serious to create incentives for plea bargaining.
- Juries serve vital functions for society by preventing arbitrary action by prosecutors and judges, educating citizens about the justice system, symbolizing the rule of law, and involving citizens

from diverse segments of the community in judicial decision making.

- The U.S. Supreme Court has ruled that juries need not be made up of 12 members, and 12-member juries can, if permitted by state law, convict defendants by a less than unanimous super-majority vote.

⑥ Describe the stages of a criminal trial.

- The trial process consists of a series of steps: jury selection, opening statements, presentation of prosecution's evidence, presentation of defense's evidence, presentation of rebuttal witnesses, closing arguments, judge's jury instructions, and jury's decision.
- The jury selection process, especially in the formation of the jury pool and the exercise of peremptory challenges, often creates juries that do not fully represent all segments of a community.
- Rules of evidence dictate what kinds of information may be presented in court for consideration by the jury. Types of evidence are real evidence, demonstrative evidence, testimony, direct evidence, and circumstantial evidence.

⑦ Explain the basis for an appeal of a conviction.

- Convicted offenders have the opportunity to appeal, although defendants who plead guilty, unlike those convicted through a trial, often have few grounds for an appeal.
- Appeals focus on claimed errors of law or procedure in the investigation by police and prosecutors or in the decisions by trial judges. Relatively few offenders win their appeals, and most who do simply gain an opportunity for a new trial, not release from jail or prison.
- After convicted offenders have used all of their appeals, they may file a habeas corpus petition to seek federal judicial review of claimed constitutional rights violations in their cases. Very few of such petitions succeed.

Questions for Review

1. What is bail, and how has it been reformed to limit its traditionally harsh impact on poor defendants?
2. Why are some defendants held in pretrial detention?

3. Why does plea bargaining exist?
4. Given that there are so few jury trials, what types of cases would you expect to find adjudicated in this manner? Why?
5. What is the purpose of the appeals process?

Key Terms and Cases

appeal (p. 281)

arraignment (p. 255)

bail (p. 257)

bench trials (p. 270)

challenge for cause (p. 273)

circumstantial evidence (p. 274)

citation (p. 261)

demonstrative evidence (p. 274)

direct evidence (p. 274)

habeas corpus (p. 281)

jury (p. 270)

motion (p. 256)

percentage bail (p. 261)

peremptory challenge (p. 273)

preventive detention (p. 262)

real evidence (p. 274)

reasonable doubt (p. 278)

release on recognizance (ROR) (p. 261)

testimony (p. 274)

voir dire (p. 273)

Bordenkircher v. Hayes (1978) (p. 268)

Boykin v. Alabama (1969) (p. 268)

Missouri v. Frye (2012) (p. 268)

North Carolina v. Alford (1970) (p. 268)

Ricketts v. Adamson (1987) (p. 268)

Santobello v. New York (1971) (p. 265)

United States v. Salerno and Cafero (1987) (p. 262)

Williams v. Florida (1970) (p. 271)

9 | Punishment and Sentencing

LEARNING OBJECTIVES

1 Name the goals of punishment.

2 Describe the types of sentences judges can impose.

3 Identify the influences on sentencing.

4 Explain how the system may treat wrongdoers unequally.

Wearing dark glasses and walking with her head down, Grammy-winning singer Lauryn Hill went to the Newark, New Jersey, federal courthouse in May 2013 to learn what punishment she would receive after pleading guilty for the crime of failing to file tax returns for three years. She faced the possibility of 24 to 36 months in prison for failing to pay taxes on $1.8 million in income (Wood, 2013). Her attorney had argued that she should be sentenced to probation because she paid all of her back taxes and penalties prior to the sentencing hearing. However, U.S. Magistrate Judge Madeline Cox Arleo sentenced Hill to three months in prison to be followed by three months of house arrest (McKinley, 2013). Did she receive an appropriate sentence for her crime? Was it too harsh? Alternatively, was it too lenient because she is an affluent celebrity who could afford to pay what she owed quickly after admitting guilt? Would others facing the same charges be treated the same way?

The questions about Lauryn Hill's sentence are important, but not always easily answered. People can disagree about what constitutes an appropriate sentence for specific crimes. Indeed, state legislatures frequently enact laws defining punishments that differ from the punishment statutes for the same crimes in other states. Most strikingly, most states have the possibility of imposing the death penalty for intentional murders, but more than a dozen states do not have the death penalty and therefore impose imprisonment for the same crime. Lengths of prison sentences also vary by state for specific crimes such as robbery, drug offenses, and assault.

One way to evaluate Hill's sentence is to compare it with sentences received by offenders convicted of the same crimes. For example, also in 2013, actor Stephen Baldwin pleaded guilty to failing to pay taxes for three years. However, Baldwin admitted to violating New York state laws rather than federal tax laws as Hill had done. Although Baldwin only paid $100,000 of the $400,000 that he owed to New York prior to his sentencing hearing, he received a sentence of probation with the promise that his criminal record would be erased if he paid the entire amount within one year (Martinez, 2013). However, failure to pay within one year would extend his period of probation to five years and keep his criminal record intact (D'Zurilla, 2013a). His crime was virtually the same as Hill's, yet Baldwin would face no time behind bars and could get his record erased as he was convicted under a different set of laws—state instead of federal—and he also was sentenced in a different court by a different judge.

By contrast, in the same spring months in which Hill and Baldwin faced their sentencing hearings in 2013, movie actor Wesley Snipes was released to a supervised residential facility after spending three years in prison for the very same charge: failure to file tax returns for three years (D'Zurilla, 2013b; Wood, 2013). Why did Snipes receive such a severe sentence? Many observers believe that there is a trial penalty in the form of harsher sentences for defendants who insist on going to trial rather than entering a guilty plea. Unlike Hill and Baldwin, who entered guilty pleas, Snipes was convicted after a highly publicized jury trial. He claimed that he was not guilty because he had relied on bad advice from financial advisors. In addition, Snipes failed to file a tax return and pay federal taxes during a period in which he earned an estimated $40 million, an amount far larger than the incomes of Hill and Baldwin during their periods of nonpayment (D'Zurilla, 2013b). Criminal behavior may produce a wide variety of punishments, which depend on the goals being pursued by officials who make laws and determine sentences. Are the three celebrity tax offenders' differing sentences understandable, appropriate, and fair? Such questions are often the subject of debate.

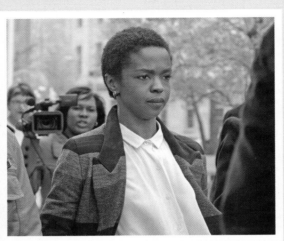

The criminal justice system aims to solve three basic issues: (1) What conduct is criminal? (2) What determines guilt? and (3) What should be done with the guilty? Earlier chapters emphasized the first two questions. The answers given by the legal system to the first question compose the basic rules of society: do not murder, rob, sell drugs, commit treason, and so forth. The law also spells out the process for determining guilt or innocence; however, the administrative and interpersonal considerations of the actors in the criminal justice system greatly affect this process. In this chapter, we begin to examine the third problem: sanction and punishment. First, we consider the four goals of punishment: retribution, deterrence, incapacitation, and rehabilitation. We then explore the forms punishment takes to achieve its goals. These are incarceration, intermediate sanctions, probation, and death. Finally, we look at the sentencing process and how it affects punishment.

The Goals of Punishment

Criminal sanctions in the United States have four main goals: retribution (deserved punishment), deterrence, incapacitation, and rehabilitation. Ultimately, all criminal punishment aims at maintaining the social order, but the justifications for sentencing proceed from the American values of justice and fairness. There is no universal agreement, however, on how to make the severity of punishment just and fair. Further, the justice sought by crime victims often conflicts with fairness to offenders.

Punishments reflect the dominant values of a particular moment in history. By the end of the 1960s, for example, the number of Americans who were sentenced to imprisonment decreased because of a widespread commitment to rehabilitating offenders. By contrast, since the mid-1970s, an emphasis on imposing strong punishments for the purposes of retribution, deterrence, and incapacitation has resulted in record numbers of offenders being sentenced to prison. At the beginning of the twenty-first century, voices are calling for the addition of *restorative justice* as a fifth goal of the criminal sanction.

Retribution—Deserved Punishment

Retribution is punishment inflicted on a person who has harmed other people and so deserves to be penalized (Cahill, 2007b). The biblical expression "an eye for an eye, a tooth for a tooth" illustrates the philosophy underlying this kind of punishment. Retribution means that those who commit a particular crime should be punished alike, in proportion to the gravity of the offense or to the suffering their crime has caused others. Retribution is deserved punishment; offenders must "pay their debts."

Some scholars claim that the desire for retribution is a basic human emotion. They maintain, therefore, that if the state does not provide retributive sanctions to reflect community revulsion at offensive acts, citizens will take the law into their own hands to punish offenders. Under this view, the failure of government to satisfy the people's desire for retribution could produce social chaos.

This argument may not be valid for all crimes, however. If a rapist is inadequately punished, then the victim's family and other members of the community may be tempted to exact their own retribution. But what about a young adult smoking marijuana? If the government failed to impose retribution for this offense, would the community care? The same apathy may hold true for offenders who commit other nonviolent crimes that modestly impact society. Even in these seemingly trivial situations, however, retribution may serve as a necessary public reminder of the general rules of law and the important values they protect.

Since the late 1970s, retribution as a justification for the criminal sanction has aroused new interest, largely because of dissatisfaction with the philosophical basis and practical results of rehabilitation. Using the concept of "just deserts" or "deserved punishment" to define retribution, some theorists argue that one who infringes on the rights of others deserves to be punished. This approach rests on the philosophical view that punishment is a moral response to harm inflicted on society (Bronsteen, 2010). In effect, these theorists believe that basic morality demands that wrongdoers be punished (von Hirsch, 1976). According to this view, punishment should be applied only for the wrong inflicted and not primarily to achieve other goals such as deterrence, incapacitation, or rehabilitation.

retribution Punishment inflicted on a person who has harmed others and so deserves to be penalized.

Deterrence

Many people see criminal punishment as a basis for affecting the future choices and behavior of individuals. Politicians frequently talk about being "tough on crime" to send a message to would-be criminals. The roots of this approach, called *deterrence*, lie in eighteenth-century England among the followers of social philosopher Jeremy Bentham.

Bentham was struck by what seemed to be the pointlessness of retribution. His fellow reformers adopted Bentham's theory of *utilitarianism*, which holds that human behavior is governed by the individual's calculation of the benefits versus the costs of his or her acts. Before stealing money or property, for example, potential offenders would consider the punishment that others have received for similar acts and would thereby be deterred.

There are two types of deterrence. **General deterrence** presumes that members of the general public, on observing the punishments of others, will conclude that the costs of crime outweigh the benefits. For general deterrence to be effective, the public must receive constant reminders of the likelihood and severity of punishment for various acts. They must believe that they will be caught, prosecuted, and given a specific punishment if they commit a particular crime. Moreover, the punishment must be severe enough to instill fear of the consequences of committing crimes.

For example, Jim Cramer, a close observer of Wall Street executives and the host of the CNBC show *Mad Money* commented on the reaction of corporate executives to the sentence of Wall Street business multimillionaire Raj Rajaratnam in 2011. For using illegal inside information from tipsters within a corporation as a

general deterrence Punishment of criminals that is intended to be an example to the general public and to discourage the commission of offenses.

Tim Boyle/Bloomberg via Getty Images

The fourteen-year sentence imposed on former Illinois Governor Rod Blagojevich for corrupt activities while in office was considered by many observers to be a surprisingly long sentence. Some people believe such stiff sentences will have a general deterrent effect and prevent misconduct by other elected officials. Other people believe that greed is such a powerful motive that many people violate the law despite the risks involved. Are there any particular types of crimes that are likely to be prevented when people hear about harsh prison sentences for those offenses?

basis for investment decisions, Rajaratnam was sentenced to 11 years in federal prison, a $10 million fine, and the forfeiture of $53.8 million (Lattman, 2011). According to Cramer, "It took their collective breaths away. . . . They are still reeling from the Raj sentence. . . . Nothing scares these guys more than jail time" (J. Warren, 2011). Whether or not Cramer is correct, there are some judges who believe that there is a general-deterrence benefit from stiff sentences for high-profile offenders. Yet, not all judges share that view, as one news reporter noted when he asked two judges about whether high-profile sentences can deter people seeking to advance their own greed for money and power. According to the reporter, both judges laughed and one said, "Deter greed, eh? . . . Good luck!" (J. Warren, 2011).

By contrast, **specific deterrence** targets the decisions and behavior of offenders who have already been convicted. Under this approach, the amount and kind of punishment are calculated to discourage that criminal from repeating the offense. The punishment must be severe enough to cause the criminal to say, "The consequences of my crime were too painful. I will not commit another crime, because I do not want to risk being punished again."

The concept of deterrence presents obvious difficulties (Stafford & Warr, 1993). Deterrence assumes that all people think before they act. As such, deterrence does not account for the many people who commit crimes while under the influence of drugs or alcohol or those whose harmful behavior stems from psychological problems or mental illness. Deterrence also does not account for people who act impulsively when stealing or damaging property. In other cases, the low probability of being caught defeats both general and specific deterrence. To be generally deterrent, punishment must be perceived as relatively fast, certain, and severe (Mannheimer, 2011). See "Criminal Justice: Myth & Reality" to explore the problems underlying fulfillment of the deterrence goal.

Knowledge of the effectiveness of deterrence is limited as well (Kleck, Sever, Li, & Gertz, 2005). For example, social science cannot measure the effects of general deterrence, because only those who are not deterred come to the attention of researchers. A study of the deterrent effects of punishment

specific deterrence Punishment inflicted on criminals to discourage them from committing future crimes.

would have to examine the impact of different forms of the criminal sanction on various potential lawbreakers. How can we truly determine how many people—or even if any people—stopped themselves from committing a crime for any reason, let alone because they were deterred by the prospect of prosecution and punishment? Therefore, although legislators often cite deterrence as a rationale for certain sanctions, no one really knows the extent to which sentencing policies based on deterrence achieve their objectives. Because contemporary U.S. society has shown little ability to reduce crime by imposing increasingly severe sanctions, the effectiveness of deterrence for many crimes and criminals should be questioned (Tonry, 2008).

Incapacitation

incapacitation Depriving an offender of the ability to commit crimes against society, usually by detaining the offender in prison.

Incapacitation assumes that society can use detention in prison or execution to keep offenders from committing further crimes. Many people express such sentiments, urging officials to "lock 'em up and throw away the key!" In primitive societies, banishment from the community was the usual method of incapacitation. In earlier periods of American history, offenders often agreed to move away or to join the army as an alternative to some other form of punishment. In the United States today, imprisonment serves as the usual method of incapacitation. Offenders can be confined within secure institutions and thereby effectively prevented from committing additional harm against society for the duration of their sentence. Capital punishment is the ultimate method of incapacitation. Any sentence that physically restricts an offender may incapacitate the person, even when the underlying purpose of the sentence is retribution, deterrence, or rehabilitation.

Sentences based on incapacitation are future oriented. Whereas retribution requires focusing on the harmful act of the offender, incapacitation looks at the offender's potential actions. If the offender is likely to commit future crimes, then the judge may impose a severe sentence—even for a relatively minor crime.

For example, under the incapacitation theory, a woman who kills her abusive husband as an emotional reaction to his verbal insults and physical assaults could receive a light sentence. As a one-time impulse killer who felt driven to kill by unique circumstances, she is not likely to commit additional crimes. By contrast, a woman who shoplifts merchandise and has been convicted of the offense on 10 previous occasions may receive a severe sentence. In a case like this, the criminal record and type of crime indicate that she will commit additional crimes if released. Thus, incapacitation focuses on characteristics of the offenders instead of aspects of their offenses.

Does it offend your sense of justice that a person could receive a severer sentence for shoplifting than for manslaughter? This question embodies one of the criticisms of incapacitation. Questions also arise about how to determine the length of sentence. Presumably, offenders will not be released until the state is reasonably sure that they will no longer commit crimes. However, can we accurately predict any person's behavior? Moreover, on what grounds can we punish people for anticipated behavior that we cannot accurately predict? In addition, there are questions about whether incapacitative policies will lead to an overall reduction in crime rates if there are other social forces that continue to foster criminal behavior among people living in various contexts in American society (Stahlkopf, Males, & Macallair, 2010).

In recent years, greater attention has been paid to the concept of **selective incapacitation**, whereby offenders who repeat certain kinds of crimes receive long prison terms. Research has suggested that a relatively small number of offenders commit a large number of violent and property crimes (Clear, 1994). Burglars, for example, tend to commit many offenses before they are caught. Thus, the reasoning goes, these "career criminals" should be locked up for long periods (Auerhahn, 1999). Such policies could be costly, however. Not only would correctional facilities have to be expanded, but the number of expensive, time-consuming trials also might increase if severer sentences caused more repeat offenders to plead not guilty. Another difficulty with this policy is that we cannot accurately predict which offenders will commit more crimes upon release (Vitiello, 2008).

Rehabilitation

Rehabilitation refers to the goal of restoring a convicted offender to a constructive place in society through some form of training or therapy. Americans want to believe

CRIMINAL JUSTICE
MYTH&REALITY

COMMON BELIEF: Long sentences will deter people from committing crimes because they will stop themselves from causing harm to society out of fear of the severe punishments that await them.

- Effective deterrence requires two elements: (1) potential offenders must think rationally, weighing the costs and benefits of crimes before committing criminal acts, and (2) potential offenders must fear that they will be caught.
- In fact, many offenders do not think rationally. They act impulsively in deciding to rob someone or steal an item from a store. They may also be driven by substance abuse problems that cloud their ability to think rationally and/or create an immediate need for money in order to obtain drugs and alcohol.
- In addition, many offenders do not believe that they will be caught. They erroneously believe that they are smarter than the police or that they are committing their crime in a manner that will let them escape without being apprehended.
- When offenders are overconfident about their ability to get away with crimes, then deterrence is unlikely to prevent them from committing illegal acts.
- Moreover, some offenders do not fear the prospect of prison. They regard stretches in prison as merely an inevitable part of their lives.
- All of the foregoing factors mean that legislators should not assume that severe sentences will have a deterrent effect, even if they themselves think, "I would never commit crimes if sentences were long and mandatory."

selective incapacitation
Making the best use of expensive and limited prison space by targeting for incarceration those individuals whose incapacity will do the most to reduce crime in society.

rehabilitation The goal of restoring a convicted offender to a constructive place in society through some form of vocational or educational training or therapy.

Restorative justice seeks to repair the damage done to the victim and community by an offender's criminal act. Here, Susanna Kay Cooper sits next to David Lee Myers as she looks at the photo of his dead wife. Cooper pled guilty to vehicular homicide in the death of Elaine Myers, received a 34-month prison sentence, and agreed to enter into talks with the victim's family.

that offenders can be treated and resocialized in ways that allow them to lead a crime-free, productive life upon release. Over the last hundred years, rehabilitation advocates have argued for techniques that they claim identify and treat the causes of criminal behavior. If the offender's criminal behavior is assumed to result from some social, psychological, or biological imperfection, the treatment of the disorder becomes the primary goal of corrections.

Rehabilitation focuses on the offender. Its objective does not imply any consistent relationship between the severity of the punishment and the gravity of the crime. People who commit lesser offenses can receive long prison sentences if experts believe effective rehabilitation requires it. By contrast, a murderer might win early release by showing signs that the psychological or emotional problems that led to the killing have been corrected.

According to the concept of rehabilitation, offenders are treated, not punished, and they will return to society when they are "cured." Consequently, adhering to this philosophy, judges would not set fixed sentences but rather ones with maximum and minimum terms so that parole boards can release inmates when they have been rehabilitated.

From the 1940s until the 1970s, the goal of rehabilitation was so widely accepted that treatment and reform of the offender were generally regarded as the only issues worth serious attention. Crime was assumed to be caused by problems affecting individuals, and modern social sciences were assumed to have the tools to address those problems. During the past 30 years, however, researchers and others have questioned the assumptions of the rehabilitation model. Studies of the results of rehabilitation programs have challenged the idea that criminal offenders can be cured (Martinson, 1974). Moreover, scholars no longer take for granted that crime is caused by identifiable, curable problems such as poverty, lack of job skills, low self-esteem, and hostility toward authority. Instead, some argue that we cannot identify the cause of criminal behavior for individual offenders.

During the first decade of the twenty-first century, rehabilitation reemerged as a goal of corrections. As we shall see in Chapter 13, it came to be discussed and applied through the concept of "reentry" rather than through a declaration that rehabilitation is a primary goal of the justice system (Butterfield, 2004a). States and the federal government endured significant financial costs through the expansion of prison systems and the growth of prison populations, caused by the imposition of severer prison sentences during the preceding two decades. Eventually, they confronted the reality that hundreds of thousands of prisoners were returning to society each year after serving long sentences. In addition, as governments at all levels experienced budget crises, officials sought ways to reduce prison populations. Thus, policies and programs emerged that were intended to prepare offenders for successful integration into society (Eckholm, 2008b). These programs are rehabilitative in nature, by providing education, counseling, skill training, and other services to help change offenders' behavior and prospects for success in society. Public opinion generally supports efforts to reform offenders through such rehabilitative efforts (Pew Charitable Trusts, 2012).

A New Approach to Punishment: Restorative Justice

restorative justice
Punishment designed to repair the damage done to the victim and community by an offender's criminal act.

In keeping with the focus on community justice for police, courts, and corrections, many people are calling for **restorative justice** to be added to the goals of the criminal sanction (Abid, 2012; J. Braithwaite, 2007). The restorative justice perspective

TABLE 9.1   The Goals of Punishment

At sentencing, the judge usually gives reasons for the punishments imposed. Here are statements that Magistrate Judge Arleo might have given singer Lauryn Hill, each promoting a different goal for the sanction.

Goal	Judge's Possible Statement
Retribution	I am imposing this sentence because you deserve to be punished for the harm caused to society by failing to make your fair, required contribution to support government programs that benefit people, including you and your family. Your criminal behavior is the basis of the punishment. Justice requires that I impose a sanction at a level that illustrates the importance that the community places on respecting the law and contributing as a member of society.
Deterrence	I am imposing this sentence so that your punishment for failing to fulfill your legal duty to pay taxes will serve as an example and deter others who may contemplate similar actions. In addition, I hope that this sentence will deter you from ever again committing an illegal act.
Incapacitation	I am imposing this sentence so that you will be incapacitated and hence unable to make the decision to fail to fulfill your legal duty as a taxpayer.
Rehabilitation	The pretrial record and information contained in the presentence report make me believe that there are aspects of your personality that led to the failure to fulfill your legal duty. I am therefore imposing this short sentence so that you can reflect on your decisions, receive counseling, and correct your behavior in the future.

views crime as more than a violation of penal law. The criminal act practically and symbolically denies community. It breaks trust among citizens and requires community members to determine how "to contradict the moral message of the crime that the offender is above the law and the victim beneath its reach" (Clear & Karp, 1999:85). Crime victims suffer losses involving damage to property and self. The primary aim of criminal justice should be to repair these losses (Waldman, 2007). Crime also challenges the heart of community, to the extent that community life depends on a shared sense of trust, fairness, and interdependence.

Shifting the focus to restorative justice requires a three-way approach that involves the offender, the victim, and the community. This approach may include mediation in which the three actors devise a punishment that all agree is fair and just, by which the offender can try to repair the harm done to victims and community. Communities in Vermont have well-established restorative justice programs through which alternative punishments, public apologies, restitution, and interaction between offenders and victims seek to advance both accountability and restoration (Dzur, 2011). This new approach to criminal justice means that losses suffered by the crime victim are restored, the threat to local safety is removed, and the offender again becomes a fully participating member of the community.

As yet, restorative justice represents a small minority of sanctions. To see how the four main punishment goals might be enacted in real life, consider again the sentencing of Lauryn Hill. Table 9.1 shows various hypothetical sentencing statements that the judge might have given, depending on prevailing correctional goals.

As we next consider how such goals are expressed though the various forms of punishment, keep in mind the underlying goal—or mix of goals—that justifies each form of sanction.

☑CHECK POINT

1. **What are the four primary goals of the criminal sanction?**
Retribution, deterrence, incapacitation, rehabilitation.

2. **What are the difficulties in showing that a punishment acts as a deterrent?**
It is impossible to show who has been deterred from committing crimes, punishment isn't always certain, people act impulsively rather than rationally, people commit crimes while on drugs.

STOP&ANALYZE

What do you think should be the primary goal of the criminal sanction? List two problems or challenges to the achievement of that goal.

Forms of the Criminal Sanction

Incarceration, intermediate sanctions, probation, and death are the basic ways that the criminal sanction, or punishment, is applied. The United States does not have a single, uniform set of sentencing laws. The criminal codes of each of the states and of the federal government specify the punishments. Each code differs to some extent in the severity of the punishment for specific crimes and in the amount of discretion given judges to tailor the sanction to the individual offender.

As we examine the various forms of criminal sanction, bear in mind that applying these legally authorized punishments gives rise to complex problems. Judges often receive wide discretion in determining the appropriate sentence within the parameters of the penal code.

Incarceration

Imprisonment is the most visible penalty imposed by U.S. courts. Although less than 30 percent of people under correctional supervision are in prisons and jails, incarceration remains the standard for punishing those who commit serious crimes. Imprisonment is thought to contribute significantly to deterring potential offenders. However, incarceration is expensive. It also creates the problem of reintegrating offenders into society upon release.

In penal codes, legislatures stipulate the types of sentences and the amount of prison time that can be imposed for each crime. Three basic sentencing structures are used: (1) indeterminate sentences (36 states), (2) determinate sentences (14 states), and (3) mandatory sentences (all states). Each type of sentence makes certain assumptions about the goals of the criminal sanction, and each provides judges with varying degrees of discretion.

indeterminate sentence
A period set by a judge that specifies a minimum and a maximum time to be served in prison. Sometime after the minimum, the offender may be eligible for parole.

Indeterminate Sentences   When the goal of rehabilitation dominated corrections, legislatures enacted **indeterminate sentences** (often called *indefinite sentences*) (Fisher, 2007). In keeping with the goal of treatment, indeterminate sentencing gives correctional officials and parole boards significant control over the amount of time a prisoner serves. Penal codes with indeterminate sentences stipulate a minimum and a maximum amount of time to be served in prison (for example, one to five years,

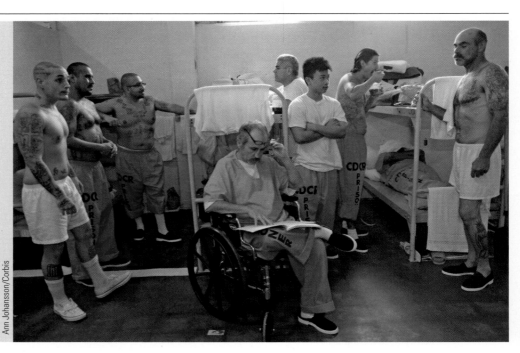

Of all correctional measures, incarceration represents the greatest restriction on freedom. These inmates are part of America's huge incarcerated population. Since 1980, the number of Americans held in prisons and jails has quadrupled. What are the costs to society from having such a large population of prisoners?

Ann Johansson/Corbis

ten to fifteen years, or one year to life). At the time of sentencing, the judge informs the offender about the range of the sentence. The offender also learns that she or he will probably be eligible for parole at some point after the minimum term has been served. The parole board determines the actual release date. Because it is based on the idea that the time necessary for treatment cannot be set, the indeterminate sentence is closely associated with rehabilitation.

Determinate Sentences
Dissatisfaction with the rehabilitation goal and support for the concept of deserved punishment led many legislatures in the 1970s to shift to **determinate sentences** (Dansky, 2008). With a determinate sentence, a convicted offender is imprisoned for a specific period (for example, two years, five years, fifteen years). At the end of the term, minus credited *good time* (to be discussed shortly), the prisoner is automatically freed. The time of release depends neither on participation in treatment programs nor on a parole board's judgment concerning the offender's likelihood of returning to criminal activities.

Some determinate-sentencing states have adopted penal codes that stipulate a specific term for each crime category. Others allow the judge to choose a range of time to be served. Some states emphasize a determinate **presumptive sentence**: the legislature, or often a commission, specifies a term based on a time range (for example, 14 to 20 months) into which most cases should fall. Only in special circumstances are judges to deviate from the presumptive sentence. Whichever variation is used, however, the offender theoretically knows at sentencing the amount of time to be served. One objective of determinate sentencing is that by reducing the judge's discretion, legislatures can limit sentencing disparities and ensure that sentences correspond to those the elected lawmakers believe are appropriate (Engen, 2009).

Mandatory Sentences
Reflecting the public's fear and anger about crime, politicians and the public periodically complain that offenders are released before serving sufficiently long terms, and legislatures have responded (Zimring, 2007). All states and the federal government now have some form of **mandatory sentences** (often called *mandatory minimum sentences*), stipulating some minimum period of incarceration that people convicted of selected crimes must serve. The judge is not permitted to consider either the circumstances of the offense or the background of the offender, and she or he cannot impose nonincarcerative sentences. Mandatory prison terms are most often specified for violent crimes, drug violations, habitual offenders, or crimes in which a firearm was used. However, opinion polls indicate that the public has become less supportive of this approach to criminal punishment (Pew Charitable Trusts, 2012).

The "three strikes and you're out" laws adopted by 26 states and the federal government provide an example of mandatory sentencing (Schultz, 2000). These laws require that judges sentence offenders with three felony convictions (in some states two or four convictions) to long prison terms, sometimes to life without parole. In some states, these laws have inadvertently clogged the courts, lowered the rates of plea bargaining, and caused desperate offenders to violently resist arrest. Mandatory minimum sentences resulted in a great increase in the number of drug offenders serving very long terms in America's prisons, mostly for nonviolent offenses (Gezari, 2008).

In recent years, state governments have been forced to cut their budgets as the nation's economic woes caused a decline in tax revenues; consequently, there has been increased attention to the high cost of long, mandatory sentences (Pew Center on the States, 2012). Some states initiated changes in sentencing in an effort to alleviate prison overcrowding and reduce their corrections budgets (Riccardi, 2009). Voters in California approved a ballot issue in 2012 to reduce the applicability of that state's three-strikes law by no longer applying life sentences to offenders whose third offense was nonviolent (Staples, 2012). The change in the law will save the state a significant amount of money as fewer offenders will receive life sentences and nearly 3,000 offenders imprisoned under the older version of the three-strikes law could seek eventual release.

determinate sentence
A sentence that fixes the term of imprisonment at a specific period.

presumptive sentence
A sentence for which the legislature or a commission sets a minimum and maximum range of months or years. Judges are to fix the length of the sentence within that range, allowing for special circumstances.

mandatory sentence
A sentence determined by statutes and requiring that a certain penalty be imposed and carried out for convicted offenders who meet certain criteria.

In addition, mandatory sentences faced reexamination because of concerns that certain sentences are unfair. For example, in 2010 Congress reformed mandatory cocaine sentencing laws that, due to differential treatment of crack cocaine and powder cocaine, had led to lengthier sentences for many African American offenders who had been the primary users and sellers of crack cocaine. The change in the law still does not treat crack cocaine offenses identically with powder cocaine offenses, for which white offenders were heavily represented, but it did reduce the number of crack offenders subjected to the mandatory five-year sentence that previously applied (P. Baker, 2010).

The Sentence versus Actual Time Served Regardless of how much discretion judges have to fine-tune the sentences they give, the prison sentences that are imposed may bear little resemblance to the actual amount of time served. In reality, parole boards in indeterminate-sentencing states have broad discretion in release decisions once the offender has served a minimum portion of the sentence. In addition, offenders can have their prison sentence reduced by earning **good time** for good behavior, at the discretion of the prison administrator.

Most states have good-time policies. Days are subtracted from prisoners' minimum or maximum term for good behavior or for participation in various types of vocational, educational, or treatment programs. Correctional officials consider these policies necessary for maintaining institutional order and for reducing crowding. Good-time credit serves as an incentive for prisoners to follow institutional rules, because recently earned credits can be taken away for misbehavior (King & Sherry, 2008). Prosecutors and defense attorneys also take good time into consideration during plea bargaining. In other words, they think about the actual amount of time a particular offender will likely serve.

The amount of good time one can earn varies among the states, usually from 5 to 10 days a month. In some states, once 90 days of good time are earned, they are vested; that is, the credits cannot be taken away as a punishment for misbehavior. Prisoners who then violate the rules risk losing only days not vested.

Contemporary budget crises have led several states to increase good-time credits as a means to reduce prison populations through quicker release from custody (Homan, 2010). In 2010, for example, Louisiana made well-behaved prisoners eligible to receive a 35-day credit for every 30 days served. The change was expected to reduce the state's prison population by 2,386 prisoners in the first year and save the state $7 million in the first year alone (KATC-TV, 2010).

More than 30 states also grant **earned time** that may be offered in addition to good time. Unlike good time, which is based on good behavior, earned time is awarded for participation in education, vocational, substance abuse, and other rehabilitation programs. Earned time may also be awarded for work assignments, such as when low-security prisoners work on disaster relief or conservation projects or fight wildfires (Lawrence, 2009). Several states have expanded the use of earned time as part of their budget-reduction strategies for shrinking expensive prison populations.

Judges in the United States often prescribe long periods of incarceration for serious crimes, but good time, earned time, and parole reduce the amount of time spent in prison. Figure 9.1 shows the estimated time actually served by offenders in state prisons versus the average (mean) sentence.

This type of national data often hides the impact of variations in sentencing and releasing laws in individual states. In many states, because of prison crowding and release policies, offenders serve less than 20 percent of their sentences. In other states, where three-strikes and truth-in-sentencing laws are employed, the average time served is longer than the national average.

Truth in Sentencing *Truth in sentencing* refers to laws that require offenders to serve a substantial proportion (usually 85 percent for violent crimes) of their prison sentence before being released on parole (Mayrack, 2008). Truth in sentencing became such a politically attractive idea that the federal government allocated

good time A reduction of an inmate's prison sentence, at the discretion of the prison administrator, for good behavior or participation in vocational, educational, or treatment programs.

earned time Reduction in a prisoner's sentence as a reward for participation in educational or other rehabilitation programs and for work assignments such as disaster relief and conservation projects.

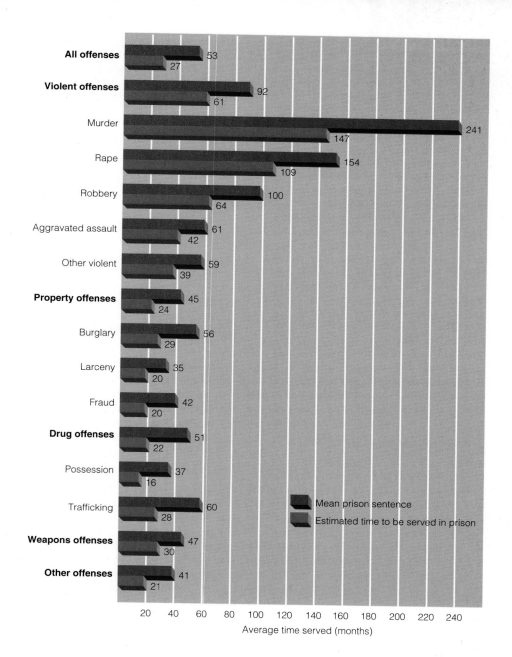

FIGURE 9.1
Estimated Time Served in State Prison Compared with Mean Length of Sentence
Most offenders serve a third or less of their mean sentences. Why is there such a difference between the sentence and actual time served?

Sources: Matthew R. Durose and Patrick A. Langan, "Felony Sentences in State Courts, 2004," Bureau of Justice Statistics *Bulletin*, July 2007; "State Court Sentencing of Convicted Felons, 2004—Statistical Tables," Table 1.5 (http://www.ojp.usdoj.gov /bjs/abstract/scscfst.htm).

Chart data — Mean prison sentence / Estimated time to be served in prison (months):

- All offenses: 53 / 27
- Violent offenses: 92 / 61
- Murder: 241 / 147
- Rape: 154 / 109
- Robbery: 100 / 64
- Aggravated assault: 61 / 42
- Other violent: 59 / 39
- Property offenses: 45 / 24
- Burglary: 56 / 29
- Larceny: 35 / 20
- Fraud: 42 / 20
- Drug offenses: 51 / 22
- Possession: 37 / 16
- Trafficking: 60 / 28
- Weapons offenses: 47 / 30
- Other offenses: 41 / 21

Legend: ■ Mean prison sentence ■ Estimated time to be served in prison

Average time served (months)

almost $10 billion for prison construction to those states adopting truth in sentencing (Donziger, 1996). Critics maintain, however, that truth in sentencing increases prison populations at a tremendous cost. The concept is less attractive today to many states beset by budget problems as they try to reduce their prison populations through greater flexibility in sentencing and early release (Riccardi, 2009).

Intermediate Sanctions

Prison crowding and the low levels of probation supervision have spurred interest in the development of **intermediate sanctions**, punishments that are less severe and less costly than prison but more restrictive than traditional probation (R. Warren, 2007). Intermediate sanctions provide a variety of restrictions on freedom, such as fines, home confinement, intensive probation supervision, restitution to victims, community service, boot camp, and forfeiture of possessions or stolen property. In 2010 Florida's Office of Program Policy Analysis and Government Accountability noted that more than 24,000 of the state's prison inmates were convicted of nonviolent

intermediate sanction
A variety of punishments that are more restrictive than traditional probation but less severe and less costly than incarceration.

TABLE 9.2 Estimated Cost Savings for Florida from Increased Use of Intermediate Sanctions (based on 2009 costs)

Sanction	First–Year Cost per Offender	Total First-Year Cost for 100 Offenders*	Potential Savings per 100 Offenders
Prison	$20,272	$2,027,200	—
Supervision with GPS monitoring	$5,121	$806,954	$1,220,246
Probation and restitution centers	$9,492	$1,639,211	$387,989
Day reporting	$4,191	$917,823	$1,109,377
Residential drug treatment	$10,539	$1,419,529	$607,671

Source: Florida Office of Program Policy Analysis and Government Accountability, *Intermediate Sanctions for Non-Violent Offenders Could Produce Savings*, Report No. 10-27, March 2010, p. 3.

*Includes additional costs for those who fail program and are imprisoned during first year.

offenses and had no prior convictions for violent offenses (Florida Office of Program Policy, 2010). As indicated in Table 9.2, the agency estimated that the state could enjoy substantial financial savings through the increased use of intermediate sanctions rather than imprisonment.

In advocating intermediate punishments, Norval Morris and Michael Tonry (1990) stipulate that these sanctions should not be used in isolation but rather in combination to reflect (1) the severity of the offense, (2) the characteristics of the offender, and (3) the needs of the community. In addition, intermediate punishments must be supported and enforced by mechanisms that take seriously any breach of the conditions of the sentence. If the law does not fulfill its promises, offenders may feel that they have "beaten" the system, which makes the punishment meaningless. Citizens who perceive any ineffectiveness in the system may develop the attitude that nothing but stiffer prison sentences will actually impose punishment.

Probation

probation A sentence that the offender is allowed to serve under supervision in the community.

The most frequently applied criminal sanction is **probation**, a sentence that an offender serves in the community under supervision. Nearly 60 percent of adults under correctional supervision are on probation. Ideally, under probation, offenders attempt to straighten out their lives. Probation is a judicial act granted by the grace of the state, not extended as a right. Conditions are imposed specifying how an offender will behave through the length of the sentence. Probationers may have to undergo regular drug tests, abide by curfews, enroll in educational programs or remain employed, stay away from certain people or parts of town, and meet regularly with probation officers. If probationers do not meet the required conditions, the supervising officer recommends to the court that the probation be revoked and that the remainder of the sentence be served in prison. Probation may also be revoked for commission of a new crime.

Although probationers serve their sentences in the community, the sanction is often tied to incarceration. In some jurisdictions, the court is authorized to modify an offender's prison sentence, after a portion is served, by changing it to probation. This is often referred to as **shock probation** (or *split probation*): an offender is released after a period of incarceration (the "shock") and resentenced to probation. An offender on probation may be required to spend intermittent periods, such as weekends or nights, in jail. Whatever its specific terms, a probationary sentence will emphasize and require guidance and supervision in the community.

shock probation A sentence in which the offender is released after a short incarceration and resentenced to probation.

Probation is generally advocated as a way of rehabilitating offenders whose crimes are not serious or whose past records are clean. It is viewed as less expensive yet more effective than imprisonment. For example, imprisonment may embitter youthful or first-time offenders and mix them with hardened criminals so that they learn more sophisticated criminal techniques.

Death

Although other Western democracies abolished the death penalty years ago, the United States continues to use it (C. E. Smith, 2010a). Capital punishment was imposed and carried out regularly prior to the late 1960s. Amid debates about the constitutionality of the death penalty and with public opinion polls showing opposition to it, the U.S. Supreme Court suspended its use from 1968 to 1976. Eventually, however, the Court decided that capital punishment does not violate the Eighth Amendment's prohibition of cruel and unusual punishments. Executions resumed in 1977 as a majority of states began, once again, to sentence murderers to death.

During the 1980s, the number of people facing the death penalty increased steadily, with the number of people sentenced to death exceeding the number of actual executions, so that from the early 1990s onward, there have been more than 3,000 offenders on death rows awaiting execution. As of July 2013, there were 3,095 people awaiting execution in 32 death-penalty states, three states (New Mexico, Maryland, and Connecticut) that had offenders awaiting execution prior to their abolition of capital punishment in the years since 2009, federal prisons (59 offenders), and U.S. military prisons (5 offenders) (Death Penalty Information Center, 2014). Two-thirds of those on death row are in the South. The greatest number of death row inmates are in California, Florida, Texas, and Pennsylvania (see Figure 9.2).

One of the most striking contemporary developments affecting the death penalty is the decline both in the number of offenders sentenced to death each year and the number of executions actually carried out. The imposition of death sentences peaked during the period from 1994 through 1996, when 312 to 315 offenders were sentenced to death during each of those years. By contrast, since 2006 fewer than 126 offenders have been sentenced to death annually, with the largest drop occurring most recently as 80 or fewer offenders were sentenced to death row each year since 2010. Executions peaked at 98 in 1999 and declined so that there were only 39 in 2013 and not more than 53 in any year since 2005 (Death Penalty Information Center, 2014).

Many scholars attribute this trend to the heavy news media attention to the discovery and release of innocent people who had been sentenced to death (Baumgartner, Linn, & Boydstun, 2010). In March 2014, Glen Ford was released after spending more than 30 years on death row in Louisiana after courts determined that prosecutors had hidden evidence and had excluded African Americans from the jury, plus local officials had testified falsely about evidence, and defense attorneys had failed to present expert witnesses to rebut the prosecution's case. The current prosecutor admitted that Ford had been victimized by an erroneous conviction (Cohen, 2014). Ford was the 144th person released from death row since 1973 as a result of later being determined to be not guilty of the murder for which he was sentenced to death.

Public opinion polls indicate less support across American society for the death penalty in recent years. These statistics presumably include those Americans called for jury duty who are asked to decide whether to impose death sentences, as opposed to prison sentences, in murder cases. As you examine Figure 9.3 showing the decline in death sentences and executions since the Supreme Court's reactivation of capital punishment in 1977, bear in mind that there were more than 3,000 offenders on death row for most of this period since the early 1990s. The data merely show the trends in new sentences and executions.

Over this time period, 7,736 convicted murderers were sent to death row, but only 1,371 executions occurred nationally. This gap reflects both the lengthy appeals process that lasts many years for death penalty cases and individual states' varying commitments to actually carrying out executions. As indicated in Figure 9.2, for example, California leads the nation with 733 offenders sentenced to death, but the state has carried out only 13 executions since the resumption of the death penalty in 1977 (Death Penalty Information Center, 2014). Thus, the death penalty in California, as well as in a number of other states, is largely symbolic as these states' governors and prosecutors have not uniformly pushed forward to see executions occur.

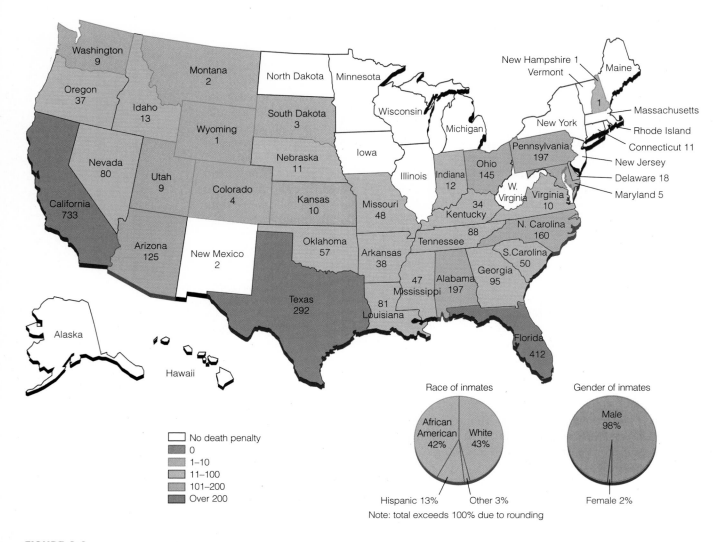

FIGURE 9.2

Death Row Census, 2013 Many of the inmates on death row are concentrated in certain states. African Americans make up about 13 percent of the U.S. population but 42 percent of the death row population. How might you explain the higher percentage of death sentences in proportion to the population?

Note: The death penalty was abolished for future crimes in New Mexico (2009), Connecticut (2012), and Maryland (2013), yet a small number of offenders remain on death row in those states for murder convictions prior to the elimination of capital punishment.

Source: Death Penalty Information Center, *Facts about the Death Penalty*, March 21, 2014, p. 2.

By contrast, the states that carry out most executions are few in number. Five states—Texas, Virginia, Oklahoma, Florida, and Missouri—together account for nearly two-thirds of the total executions carried out in the United States since 1977 (Death Penalty Information Center, 2014). Texas has carried out 511 executions in that time period, thereby demonstrating greater commitment by its public officials to put the punishment into practice. Indeed, in several cases, Texas has been accused of showing insufficient concern with careful reviews of cases, and there are accusations that the state may have executed one or more innocent people by failing to be careful about guarding against errors and by being unwilling to admit the possibility of errors (Mann, 2011). Thus, it appears that the political values and culture of a specific state affect not only whether the state's laws permit capital punishment but also the practical decisions that determine how frequently executions are carried out.

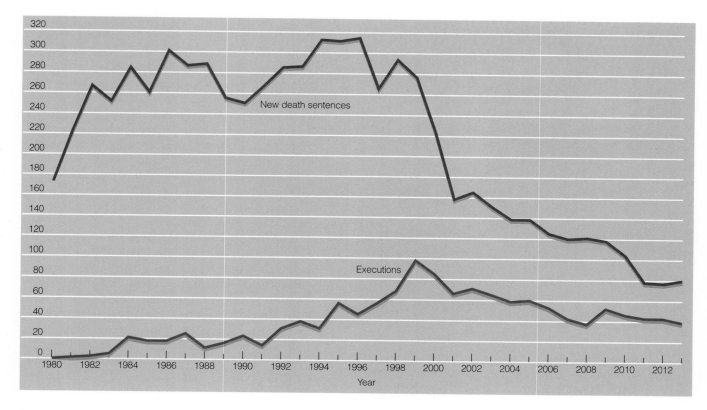

FIGURE 9.3

New Death Sentences and Executions, 1980–2013 The decline in death sentences and executions is attributed to shifts in public opinion affected by highly publicized cases of innocent people wrongly sent to death row. Does this trend indicate that the United States will eventually abolish the death penalty as the countries of Western Europe have done?

Sources: Bureau of Justice Statistics, *Sourcebook of Criminal Justice Statistics* (2014); Death Penalty Information Center, *The Death Penalty in 2013: Year End Report*, December 2013 (www.deathpenaltyinfo.org).

The Death Penalty and the Constitution Death differs from other punishments in that it is final and irreversible. The Supreme Court has therefore examined the decision-making process in capital cases to ensure that it fulfills the Constitution's requirements regarding due process, equal protection, and cruel and unusual punishments. Because life is in the balance, capital cases must be conducted according to higher standards of fairness and more careful procedures than are other kinds of cases. Several important Supreme Court cases illustrate this concern.

In *Furman v. Georgia* (1972), the Supreme Court ruled that the death penalty, as administered, constituted cruel and unusual punishment. The decision invalidated the death penalty laws of 39 states and the District of Columbia. A majority of justices found that the procedures used to impose death sentences were arbitrary and unfair. Over the next several years, more than three dozen states eventually enacted new capital punishment statutes that provided for different procedures in death penalty cases.

The new laws were tested before the Supreme Court in *Gregg v. Georgia* (1976). The Court upheld those laws that required the sentencing judge or jury to take into account specific aggravating and mitigating factors in deciding which convicted murderers should be sentenced to death. Further, the Court decided that, rather than having a single proceeding determine the defendant's guilt and whether the death sentence would be applied, states should use "bifurcated proceedings." In this two-part process, the defendant has a trial that finds her or him guilty or not guilty and then a separate hearing that focuses exclusively on the issues of punishment. It seeks to ensure a thorough deliberation before someone receives the ultimate punishment.

Furman v. Georgia (1972)
The death penalty, as administered, constitutes cruel and unusual punishment.

Gregg v. Georgia (1976)
Death penalty laws are constitutional if they require the judge and jury to consider certain mitigating and aggravating circumstances in deciding which convicted murderers should be sentenced to death. Proceedings must also be divided into a trial phase and a punishment phase, and there must be opportunities for appeal.

Prisoners sentenced to death typically must wait several years as their cases move through the appeals process. Randy Halprin was among a group of Texas prison escapees who killed a police officer during a robbery in 2000. His final unsuccessful appeal in the Texas Court of Criminal Appeals was decided in 2013. Should appeals in death penalty cases be accelerated in order to speed up executions, or would speedy appeals increase the risk of executing an innocent person?

Under the *Gregg* decision, the prosecution uses the punishment-phase hearing to focus attention on the existence of aggravating factors such as excessive cruelty or a defendant's prior record of violent crimes. The defense may focus on mitigating factors, such as the offender's youthfulness, mental condition, or lack of a criminal record. Before the judge or jury can decide to impose a death sentence, they must weigh these aggravating and mitigating factors. Because of the Court's emphasis on fair procedures and individualized decisions, state appellate courts review trial court procedures in virtually every capital case.

After *McCleskey v. Kemp* (1987), opponents of the death penalty felt disappointed that the U.S. Supreme Court failed to accept strong statistical evidence showing racial discrimination in the administration of the death penalty. In this case, the Court rejected an equal protection clause challenge to Georgia's death penalty law. Warren McCleskey, an African American, was sentenced to death for killing a white police officer. Before the U.S. Supreme Court, McCleskey's attorney cited an elaborate research study that showed a disparity in the imposition of the death penalty in Georgia based on the race of the victim and, to a lesser

McCleskey v. Kemp (1987)
The Supreme Court rejects a challenge of Georgia's death penalty on grounds of racial discrimination.

extent, the race of the defendant (Baldus, Woodworth, & Pulaski, 1994). In particular, when African American men were murdered, there was little likelihood that the death penalty would be pursued. When an African American man was convicted of killing a white person, the likelihood of the death penalty increased dramatically (M. R. Williams, Demuth, & Holcomb, 2007).

By a five-to-four vote, the justices rejected McCleskey's assertion that Georgia's capital-sentencing practices produced racial discrimination that violated the equal protection clause of the Constitution. The slim majority of justices declared that McCleskey would have to prove that the decision makers acted with a discriminatory purpose in deciding his particular case. The Court also concluded that statistical evidence showing discrimination throughout the Georgia courts did not provide adequate proof. McCleskey was executed in 1991. The decision made it very difficult to prove the existence of racial discrimination in capital cases because prosecutors and judges rarely make statements that openly indicate a discriminatory motive. Yet, when analyzed through the methods of social science, the patterns of decisions that determine which murderers receive the death penalty instead of imprisonment indicate that racial disparities are often present when looking at a state court system as whole. Thus, there are continuing concerns that death penalty cases can be infected with racial bias (R. N. Walker, 2006).

In June 2002, the Supreme Court broke new ground in a way that heartened opponents of the death penalty. First, in *Atkins v. Virginia* (2002), it ruled that execution of developmentally disabled individuals was unconstitutional. In the case, the Court used the older term "mentally retarded" to describe these individuals. Daryl Atkins, who has an IQ of 59, was sentenced to death for killing Eric Nesbitt in a 7-Eleven store parking lot. As the majority opinion noted, the characteristics of developmentally disabled offenders, people with IQs of less than 70, "undermine the strength of the procedural protections." This point is in keeping with the argument of mental health experts who say their suggestibility and willingness to please leads developmentally disabled people to confess. At trial, they

Atkins v. Virginia (2002)
Execution of developmentally disabled offenders is unconstitutional.

have problems remembering details, locating witnesses, and testifying credibly in their own behalf.

The Supreme Court further reduced the scope of capital punishment in *Roper v. Simmons* (2005). A slim majority of justices decided that offenders cannot be sentenced to death for crimes that they committed before they reached the age of 18. Prior to that decision, the United States was among only a half-dozen countries in the entire world with laws that permitted death sentences for juveniles. The same five-member majority also ruled that the death penalty cannot be imposed as a punishment for the crime of child rape (*Kennedy v. Louisiana*, 2008). Because the Court was deeply divided on these issues, some observers wonder if further changes in the Court's composition may lead to a reversal of these decisions.

All states use lethal injection as the means to conduct executions, although a few states permit the condemned prisoners to choose the electric chair or another means that was in existence at the time of their conviction (Liptak, 2008a). Lethal injection remains a controversial method because of botched executions. In these cases, prolonged and painful deaths resulted from improperly inserted needles or malfunctioning tubes that carry the chemicals (Radelet, 2004). The constitutionality of lethal injection as a means of execution was examined by the U.S. Supreme Court in *Baze v. Rees* (2008). All of the justices concluded that the attorneys for the death row inmates had not proved that the use of lethal injection violates the Eighth Amendment.

New issues will arise concerning lethal injection because the drugs used by most states for such executions are difficult to obtain and few companies manufacture them. In 2011, the federal Drug Enforcement Administration seized an execution drug purchased by the state of Georgia from a supplier in Great Britain because Georgia did not hold a proper license to import that drug (Sack, 2011). European countries that produce a key drug and oppose the death penalty have threatened to prohibit sales of the drug in the United States. This development would have harmful effects on the American medical system because the drug is used as anesthesia for many kinds of surgery. It remains to be seen if these drug shortages will affect the number of executions or whether states will simply change the combination of drugs used for their executions in order to use those that are more easily available. In 2014, for example, Oklahoma was forced to delay scheduled executions because it could not obtain the drugs needed for lethal injections (Bever, 2014). Other states are exploring the option of bringing back other execution methods such as the electric chair and hanging (Salter, 2014).

The future of the death penalty's treatment by the Supreme Court will depend on such factors as who is elected president of the United States in 2016 and thereafter appoints new justices to the nation's highest court. The newest justices appointed by President Obama, Justice Sonia Sotomayor (confirmed in 2009) and Justice Elena Kagan (confirmed in 2010), had not yet addressed the issue of capital punishment directly by mid-2014. Thus, their impact on the issue, like that of future appointees, remains to be seen.

Continuing Legal Issues   The case law since *Furman* indicates that capital punishment is legal so long as it is imposed fairly. However, opponents continue to raise several issues in litigation and in arguments presented to legislatures and the public (Acker, 2007). Just as developmentally disabled and juvenile offenders have been excluded from eligibility for the death penalty, some people argue that mentally ill offenders should also be excluded. Issues have arisen about the effectiveness of representation provided for capital defendants by defense attorneys.

Many critics are concerned about the impact of using death-qualified juries from selection processes that exclude as jurors those citizens who are strongly opposed to capital punishment. Research raises questions about whether such juries are more inclined to find defendants guilty and impose capital punishment (Summers, Hayward, & Miller, 2010). Other cases continue to raise issues about methods of execution and the lengthy periods that condemned offenders spend on

Roper v. Simmons (2005) Execution of offenders for crimes committed while under the age of 18 is unconstitutional.

QUESTION: "Generally speaking, do you believe the death penalty is applied fairly or unfairly in this country today?"

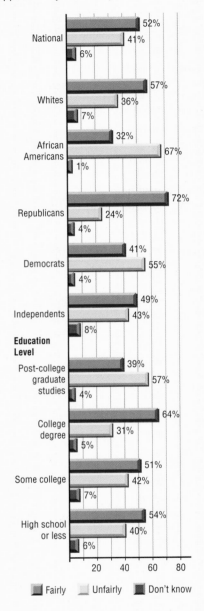

CRITICAL THINKING: What aspects of the death penalty could lead people to believe that it is applied unfairly?

Source: Constructed from Gallup Poll data for 2011 by *Sourcebook of Criminal Justice Statistics, 2014.* Table 2.54.2011.

death row because of appeals. We now look at several contemporary issues.

Execution of the Mentally Ill As we saw in Chapter 3, insanity is a recognized defense for commission of a crime. Moreover, the Supreme Court has said that people who become insane after entering prison cannot be executed (*Ford v. Wainwright*, 1986). But many people with mental illnesses do not meet the legal tests for insanity. They can be convicted of crimes and punished, and there is no guarantee that they will receive psychiatric treatment in prison. What happens if these people commit capital crimes? Is it appropriate to execute people whose mental illnesses may have affected their behavior? Opponents of the death penalty will undoubtedly seek to persuade the Supreme Court that mentally ill offenders should be excluded from capital punishment, following the rulings regarding developmentally disabled offenders and juveniles convicted of murder.

Effective Counsel In *Strickland v. Washington* (1984), the Supreme Court ruled that defendants in capital cases had the right to representation that meets an "objective standard of reasonableness." As noted by Justice Sandra Day O'Connor, the appellant must show "that there is a reasonable probability that, but for the counsel's unprofessional errors, the result of the proceeding would be different." Although it is possible to identify errors made by an attorney, it can be difficult to persuade judges that anything less than truly major errors actually affected the outcome of the case.

In recent decades, the public has learned of cases placing the defense attorney's competency in doubt, such as the case of a defense attorney sleeping during a murder trial. In 1999, the *Chicago Tribune* conducted an extensive investigation of capital punishment in Illinois. Reporters found that 33 defendants sentenced to death since 1977 were represented by attorneys who had been, or were later, disbarred or suspended for conduct that was "incompetent, unethical or even criminal." These attorneys included David Landau, who was disbarred one year after representing a Will County defendant sentenced to death, and Robert McDonnell, a convicted felon and the only lawyer in Illinois to be disbarred twice. McDonnell represented four men who landed on death row (Armstrong & Mills, 1999). Such cases may affect the public's view on fairness as indicated in "What Americans Think."

These highly publicized cases may have caught the attention of the Supreme Court. In 2003, the Court issued a decision that seemed designed to remind lawyers and judges about the need for competent defense attorneys in capital cases. In *Wiggins v. Smith* (2003), the Court found that the Sixth Amendment right to counsel was violated when a defense attorney failed to present mitigating evidence concerning the severe physical and sexual abuse suffered by the defendant during childhood. Whether the justices create clearer or stricter standards for defense attorneys remains to be seen.

Death-Qualified Juries   Should people who are opposed to the death penalty be excluded from juries in capital cases? In **Witherspoon v. Illinois (1968)**, the Supreme Court held that potential jurors who have general objections to the death penalty or whose religious convictions oppose its use cannot be automatically excluded from jury service in capital cases. However, it upheld the practice of removing, during voir dire (preliminary examination), those people whose opposition is so strong as to "prevent or substantially impair the performance of their duties." Such jurors have become known as *"Witherspoon excludables."* The decision was later reaffirmed in *Lockhart v. McCree* (1986).

Witherspoon v. Illinois (1968)
Potential jurors who object to the death penalty cannot be automatically excluded from service; however, during voir dire, those who feel so strongly about capital punishment that they could not give an impartial verdict may be excluded.

Because society is divided on capital punishment, opponents argue that death-qualified juries do not represent a cross section of the community (Summers, Hayward, & Miller, 2010). Researchers have also found that "juries are likely to be nudged toward believing the defendant is guilty and toward an imposition of the death sentence by the very process of undergoing death qualification" (Luginbuhl & Burkhead, 1994:107).

Mark Costanzo (1997) points to research indicating that death qualification has several impacts. First, those who are selected for jury duty are more conviction prone and more receptive to aggravating factors presented during the penalty phase. A second, subtler impact is that jurors answering the questions about their willingness to vote for a death sentence often conclude that both defenders and prosecutors anticipate a conviction and a death sentence.

The Death Penalty: A Continuing Controversy   Various developments in the twenty-first century appear to indicate a weakening of support for capital punishment in the United States. New York's capital punishment law was declared unconstitutional by its own state courts in 2004. The New Jersey state legislature and governor eliminated the death penalty in that state in 2007. Subsequently, the legislature of New Mexico voted to abolish capital punishment (Urbina, 2009). In March 2011, the governor of Illinois signed a law that eliminated capital punishment. He also commuted the sentences of the 15 offenders on death row so that they will now serve sentences of life without parole (Schwartz & Fitzsimmons, 2011). Illinois had not executed an offender since 2000, when it was discovered that a number of innocent people had been sentenced to death due to flaws in the justice system, including the use of dishonest jailhouse informants and incompetent defense attorneys.

In 2012, Connecticut's legislature and governor abolished capital punishment for future crimes. Unlike Illinois, Connecticut took New Mexico's approach by leaving its 11 currently condemned murderers on death row to face eventual execution (Applebome, 2012). Maryland's legislature and governor took the same step in 2013 (Witte, 2013). In March 2014, the New Hampshire House of Representatives voted to abolish capital punishment as the first step toward the possible end of the death penalty in that state, but the repeal of capital punishment narrowly failed to gain approval in the Senate (Tuohy, 2014).

Concerns about the conviction of innocent people may lead some other states to reconsider the use of capital punishment. Simultaneously, the extraordinary costs of capital trials and appeals are likely to deter many states from seeking to use the punishment widely in murder cases. Because the costs of trials are typically placed on county government, small counties frequently cannot afford to seek the death penalty in murder cases as these trials can last for weeks and require the services of expensive scientific testing and expert witnesses. On the other hand, a future terrorism attack on the United States may intensify public support for capital punishment and spur efforts to expand the penalty. Thus, it remains to be seen whether the nation will continue to see diminishing use of the death penalty.

Although public opinion polls still reflect significant support for the death penalty, the number of executions remains low. A Gallup Poll in October 2013 found that support for sentencing convicted murderers to death had dropped from a high of 80 percent of Americans in the mid-1990s to only 60 percent in 2013 (J. Jones, 2013). Recent surveys show that the public is split when asked to choose between

Should the Death Penalty Be Abolished?

The applicability of the death penalty has diminished in the twenty-first century. The execution moratorium imposed by Illinois Governor George Ryan in January 2000 reinvigorated debate on the death penalty. His announcement was soon followed by a national poll that found support for the penalty to be the lowest in 19 years, the release of a national study of appeals that found two-thirds of death penalty cases are flawed and overturned by higher courts, and research questioning the quality of counsel given to many defendants. Subsequently, the U.S. Supreme Court reduced the applicability of capital punishment by excluding the developmentally disabled and juveniles from executions. In 2011, the Illinois legislature and Governor Pat Quinn approved legislation to end capital punishment in that state, just as New Jersey did in 2007 and New Mexico in 2009. Connecticut did the same in 2012, as did Maryland in 2013, and New Hampshire's House of Representatives was moving in that direction in 2014.

Opponents of capital punishment continue the fight to abolish it. They argue that poor people and minorities receive a disproportionate number of death sentences. They also believe that executing people who are teenage, insane, or developmentally disabled is barbaric.

Even the proponents of capital punishment remain dissatisfied with how it is applied. They point to the fact that although more than 3,200 convicted murderers wait on death row, the number of executions since 1976 has never exceeded 98 per year and has declined through the first years of the twenty-first century. The appeals process is a major factor halting this pace, given that it can delay executions for years.

For the Death Penalty

Supporters argue that society should apply swift, severe punishments to killers to address the continuing problems of crime and violence. Execution should occur quite soon after conviction so that the greatest deterrent value will result. They say that justice requires that a person who murders another must be executed. To do less is to denigrate the value of human life.

The arguments for the death penalty include the following:

- The death penalty deters criminals from committing violent acts.
- The death penalty achieves justice by paying killers back for their horrible crimes.

- The death penalty prevents criminals from doing further harm while on parole.
- The death penalty is less expensive than holding murderers in prison for life.

Against the Death Penalty

Opponents believe that the death penalty lingers as a barbaric practice from a less civilized age. They point out that most other developed democracies in the world have ceased to execute criminals. Opponents challenge the death penalty's claims for effectiveness in reducing crime. They also raise concerns about whether the punishment can be applied without errors and discrimination.

The arguments against the death penalty include the following:

- No hard evidence proves that the death penalty is a deterrent.
- It is wrong for a government to participate in the intentional killing of citizens.
- The death penalty is applied in a discriminatory fashion.
- Innocent people have been sentenced to death.
- Some methods of execution are inhumane, causing painful, lingering deaths.

What Should U.S. Policy Be?

With more and more people now being sentenced to death row but fewer than 60 individuals executed each year, death penalty policy is at a significant crossroads. Will the United States increase the pace of executions; allow the number of capital offenders in prison to keep growing; or take a middle ground that satisfies neither side completely, such as life imprisonment without parole for convicted murderers?

Researching the Internet

Compare the perspectives presented at the websites of Pro-Death Penalty and the Death Penalty Information Center. You can access them both by going to http://www.prodeathpenalty.com/ and http://www.deathpenaltyinfo.org/.

For Critical Analysis

Evaluate the pros and cons of the death penalty debate. What political factors might influence your state's legislators to abolish, modify, or retain the death penalty?

life imprisonment (without parole) and death. When poll respondents know that a sentence of life without parole is available to apply to convicted murderers, then only 49 percent support death penalty sentences (Newport, 2010). Does this mean that Americans are ambivalent about carrying out the punishment? What might it say about capital punishment in the next decade? Debate on this important public policy issue has gone on for more than two hundred years, yet there is still no consensus (see "The Policy Debate" for more).

TABLE 9.3 The Punishment of Offenders

The goals of the criminal sanction are carried out in a variety of ways, depending upon the provisions of the law, the characteristics of the offender, and the discretion of the judge. Judges may impose sentences that combine several forms to achieve punishment objectives.

Form of Sanction	Description	Purposes
Incarceration	Imprisonment	
Indeterminate sentence	Specifies a maximum and minimum length of time to be served	Incapacitation, deterrence, rehabilitation
Determinate sentence	Specifies a certain length of time to be served	Retribution, deterrence, incapacitation
Mandatory sentence	Specifies a minimum amount of time that must be served for given crimes	Incapacitation, deterrence
Good time	Subtracts days from an inmate's sentence because of good behavior or participation in prison programs	Rewards behavior, relieves prison crowding, helps maintain prison discipline
Intermediate sanctions	Punishment for those requiring sanctions more restrictive than probation but less restrictive than prison	Retribution, deterrence
Administered by the judiciary		
Fine	Money paid to state by offender	Retribution, deterrence
Restitution	Money paid to victim by offender	Retribution, deterrence
Forfeiture	Seizure by the state of property illegally obtained or acquired with resources illegally obtained	Retribution, deterrence
Administered in the community		
Community service	Requires offender to perform work for the community	Retribution, deterrence
Home confinement	Requires offender to stay in home during certain times	Retribution, deterrence, incapacitation
Intensive probation supervision	Requires strict and frequent reporting to probation officer	Retribution, deterrence, incapacitation
Administered institutionally		
Boot camp/shock incarceration	Short-term institutional sentence emphasizing physical development and discipline, followed by probation	Retribution, deterrence, rehabilitation
Probation	Allows offender to serve a sentence in the community under supervision	Retribution, incapacitation, rehabilitation
Death	Execution	Incapacitation, deterrence, retribution

The criminal sanction takes many forms, with offenders punished in various ways to serve various purposes. Table 9.3 summarizes how these sanctions operate and how they reflect the underlying philosophies of punishment.

3. **What are the three types of sentences used in the United States?**
   Determinate, indeterminate, and mandatory sentences.

4. **What are thought to be the advantages of intermediate sanctions?**
   Intermediate sanctions give judges a greater range of sentencing alternatives, reduce prison populations, cost less than prison, and increase community security.

5. **What requirements specified in *Gregg v. Georgia* must exist before a death sentence can be imposed?**
   Judge and jury must be able to consider mitigating and aggravating circumstances, proceedings must be divided into a trial phase and a punishment phase, and there must be opportunities for appeal.

Which goals of punishment are advanced by intermediate sanctions? Do intermediate sanctions adequately advance those goals? Imagine that you are a state legislator. For which crimes would you vote to authorize the use of intermediate sanctions? Which goals would you be seeking to advance with those punishments?

The Sentencing Process

Regardless of how and where guilt has been determined—misdemeanor court or felony court, plea bargain or adversarial context, bench or jury trial—judges hold the responsibility for imposing sentences. Often difficult, sentencing usually involves more than applying clear-cut principles to individual cases. In one case, a judge may decide to sentence a forger to prison as an example to others, even though the offender poses no threat to community safety and probably does not need rehabilitative treatment. In another case, the judge may impose a light sentence on a youthful offender who has committed a serious crime but may be a candidate for rehabilitation if moved quickly back into society.

Legislatures establish the penal codes that set forth the sentences judges can impose. These laws generally give judges discretion in sentencing. However, there may be specific requirements that can tie the hands of judges for specific crimes or offenders. As mentioned previously concerning mandatory minimums, legislatures may specify required sentences for certain crimes. In particular, some legislatures, including Congress, have mandated specific added time periods in prison for crimes committed with firearms (P. J. Cook, 2013). In effect, these sentencing laws appear to have both deterrent and incapacitative objectives with respect to the use of guns for criminal purposes. Read the "Evidence-Based Practice and Policy" feature to consider how debates about gun policy extended beyond sentencing laws as many legislatures considered gun control proposals during 2013 in the aftermath of the Newtown, Connecticut, school shootings (McGreevy & Megerian, 2013).

Judges may combine various forms of punishment in order to tailor the sanction to the offender. The judge may specify, for example, that the prison terms for two charges are to run either concurrently (at the same time) or consecutively (one after the other) or that all or part of the period of imprisonment may be suspended. In other situations, the offender may receive a combination of a suspended prison term, a fine, and probation. Judges may suspend a sentence as long as the offender stays out of trouble, makes restitution, or seeks medical treatment. They may also delay imposing any sentence but retain the power to set penalties at a later date if the offender misbehaves.

Within the discretion allowed by the code, various elements influence the decisions of judges (B. D. Johnson, 2006). Social scientists believe that several factors influence the sentencing process: (1) the administrative context of the courts, (2) the attitudes and values of judges, (3) the presentence report, and (4) sentencing guidelines.

Gun Control Policy

In 2012, the entire country was rocked by the news of mass shootings by a lone gunman. In particular, the Aurora, Colorado, movie theater shooting in July 2012 that killed 12 audience members and wounded 58 others and the December 2012 Sandy Hook Elementary School shooting in Newtown, Connecticut, that killed 27 children and school staff led to legislative proposals aimed at reducing the risk of gun violence.

There are many impediments to analyzing and discussing gun policy in the United States. Many Americans use the Second Amendment's phrase "the right of the people to keep and bear arms shall not be infringed" to claim that most government regulation of firearms is unconstitutional. In reality, the Supreme Court has thus far interpreted the Second Amendment to mean only that law-abiding citizens enjoy a right to keep handguns in their homes for self-protection. The Supreme Court's decisions explicitly endorse the idea that federal and state government possess the authority to impose a variety of regulations on the sale, ownership, and possession of firearms.

Other opponents of gun control claim that policies such as background checks do not guarantee that ex-felons or mentally ill people will not obtain weapons and therefore background checks should not be imposed. The real question from a policy perspective is not whether a policy will be perfect, but whether it will have desired benefits that outweigh its costs. Thus, a policy analyst would not ask whether background checks will stop all improper individuals from obtaining firearms. Instead, the question would be whether this policy would either deter or apprehend *some* improper persons and whether or not these benefits are outweighed by the costs of the background-check process on law-abiding individuals and government agencies. This is how other policy issues are approached. For example, policy analysts do not advocate eliminating various criminal laws simply because they do not prevent all such crimes from occurring.

In January 2013, Johns Hopkins University in Baltimore hosted a conference at which leading researchers on firearms issues shared the findings of their studies in an effort to develop a set of evidence-based proposals for gun regulation in the aftermath of the Newtown school shootings. For example, studies showed a reduction in intimate partner homicides (i.e., murders of spouses, girlfriends, etc.) in those jurisdictions that regulated gun ownership and conducted background checks regarding individuals subject to restraining orders related to domestic violence incidents. Comparative studies of Australia, which banned various weapons and instituted a government buy-back program in the aftermath of a mass shooting, showed a significant reduction in firearms suicides as well as an impact on firearms homicides.

One of the impediments for developing evidence-based regulation proposals in the United States stems from political pressure that led Congress to restrict the ability of federal government research agencies to conduct or fund studies of gun violence. Other aspects of criminal justice are studied by researchers with assistance from government funding, but firearms issues are singled out for restrictions on government funding and data sharing. In effect, a policy was put into place that makes it difficult to examine an important policy issue and thereby blocks the government's ability to consider whether there would be benefits from recommending changes based on evidence-based research findings.

The researchers who met at the Johns Hopkins University conference compiled a list of proposals based on their research findings, including universal background checks, broader exclusions of would-be purchasers who had records of misdemeanor or juvenile violent offenses as well as those with drug offenses, and restrictions on the types of weapons that could be legally bought and sold. As debates about gun regulation continue at the national and state levels, it remains to be seen whether evidence-based policies will be adopted and implemented.

Researching the Internet

Read about the research and proposals presented by the Center for Gun Policy and Research at the Johns Hopkins University School of Public Health. http://www.jhsph.edu/research/centers-and-institutes/johns-hopkins-center-for-gun-policy-and-research/.

Implementing New Practices

Many Americans, including public officials, enter the gun control debate with firmly fixed views and an unwillingness to listen to opposing evidence and arguments. In addition, it appears that elected officials in many states may be afraid to consider proposals to regulate firearms, even in modest ways, because of the political influence of firearms manufacturers and gun-rights interest groups. The existence of firm beliefs as well as the strength of political pressure make it difficult to conduct and discuss research, let alone consider employing that research to develop effective policies. Are there any views about gun control policy that you hold which you would be willing to consider changing if research evidence could demonstrate that you have relied on faulty assumptions? Are you willing to consider evidence that contradicts your current views? Challenge yourself to step back from your current views by taking the role of a legislator and writing down the five strongest arguments that contradict your current viewpoint. Describe one or more laws that would follow from these arguments.

Sources: Daniel W. Webster and Jon S. Vernick, editors, *Reducing Gun Violence in America: Informing Policy with Evidence and Analysis*, Baltimore: Johns Hopkins University Press, 2013, including specific articles such as April M. Zeoli and Shannon Frattaroli, "Evidence for Optimism: Policies to Limit Batterers' Access to Guns," pp. 53–63; and Philip Alpers, "The Big Melt: How One Democracy Changed After Scrapping a Third of Its Firearms," pp. 205–11.

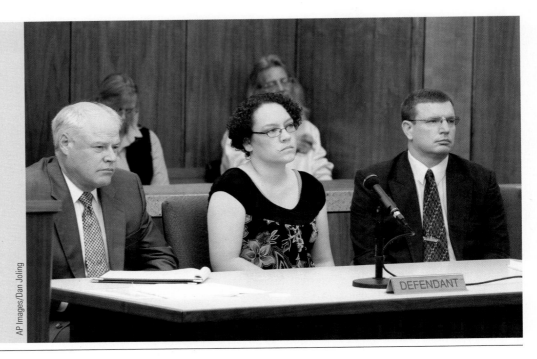

In misdemeanor cases, judges' sentencing decisions may be influenced by many factors, including the defendant's remorse, the availability of space for new offenders in the county jail, and the defendant's prior record. Is it important for judges to impose comparable sentences on offenders who are convicted of similar crimes?

AP Images/Dan Joling

The Administrative Context of the Courts

Judges are strongly influenced by the administrative context within which they impose sentences. As a result, differences are found, for example, between the assembly-line style of justice in misdemeanor courts and the more formal proceedings in felony courts.

Misdemeanor Courts: Assembly-Line Justice Misdemeanor or lower courts have limited jurisdiction because typically they can impose no greater punishment than jail sentences of less than one year. These courts hear about 90 percent of criminal cases. Whereas felony cases are processed in lower courts only for arraignments and preliminary hearings, misdemeanor cases are processed completely in the lower courts. Only a minority of cases adjudicated in lower courts end in jail sentences. Most cases result in fines, probation, community service, restitution, or a combination of these.

Most lower courts are overloaded and therefore allot minimal time to each case. Judicial decisions are mass produced because actors in the system share three assumptions: First, any person appearing before the court is guilty, because the police and prosecution have presumably filtered out doubtful cases. Second, the vast majority of defendants will plead guilty. Third, those charged with minor offenses will be processed in volume, with dozens of cases being decided in rapid succession within a single hour. The citation will be read by the clerk, a guilty plea entered, and the sentence pronounced by the judge for one defendant after another.

Defendants whose cases are processed through the lower court's assembly line may appear to receive little or no punishment. However, people who get caught in the criminal justice system experience other punishments, whether or not they are ultimately convicted. A person who is arrested but eventually released still incurs various tangible and intangible costs. Time spent in jail awaiting trial, the cost of a bail bond, and days of work lost create an immediate and concrete impact. Poor people may lose their jobs or be evicted from their homes if they fail to work and pay their bills for even a few days. For most people, simply being arrested is a devastating experience. It is impossible to measure the

TABLE 9.4 | Types of Felony Sentences Imposed by State Courts

Although a felony conviction is often equated with a prison sentence, almost a third of felony offenders receive probation.

Most Serious Conviction Offense	Percentage of Felons Sentenced to		
	Prison	Jail	Probation
All offenses	41	28	27
Murder	93	2	3
Rape	72	15	10
Robbery	71	14	13
Burglary	49	24	24
Larceny	34	34	28
Drug possession	33	31	30
Drug trafficking	41	26	29
Weapons offenses	45	28	25

Note: For persons receiving a combination of sanctions, the sentence designation came from the most severe penalty imposed—prison being the most severe, followed by jail and then probation. Rows do not add up to 100% because a small percentage of offenders for each crime were sentenced to other nonincarceration sanctions.

Source: Sean Rosenmerkel, Matthew R. Durose, and Donald Farole Jr., "Felony Sentences in State Courts, 2006—Statistical Tables," *Bureau of Justice Statistics Statistical Tables*, December 2009, p. 4.

psychological and social price of being stigmatized, separated from family, and deprived of freedom.

Felony Courts   Felony cases are processed and felony offenders are sentenced in courts of general jurisdiction. Because of the seriousness of the crimes, the atmosphere is more formal and generally lacks the chaotic, assembly-line environment of misdemeanor courts. Caseload burdens can affect how much time individual cases receive. Exchange relationships among courtroom actors can facilitate plea bargains and shape the content of prosecutors' sentencing recommendations. Sentencing decisions are ultimately shaped, in part, by the relationships, negotiations, and agreements among the prosecutor, defense attorney, and judge. Table 9.4 shows the types of felony sentences imposed for conviction on different charges.

Attitudes and Values of Judges

All lawyers recognize that judges differ from one another in their sentencing decisions. Administrative pressures, the conflicting goals of criminal justice, and the influence of community values partly explain these differences. Sentencing decisions also depend on judges' attitudes concerning the offender's blameworthiness, the protection of the community, and the practical implications of the sentence (Steffensmeier & Demuth, 2001).

Blameworthiness concerns such factors as offense severity (such as violent crime or property crime), the offender's criminal history (such as recidivist or first timer), and role in commission of the crime (such as leader or follower). For example, a judge might impose a harsh sentence on a repeat offender who organized others to commit a serious crime.

Protection of the community hinges on similar factors, such as dangerousness, recidivism, and offense severity. However, it centers mostly on the need to incapacitate the offender or to deter would-be offenders.

Judges and Sentencing

In March 2011, Andrew Stein, the former president of the New York City Council and a former candidate for Congress, stood before U.S. Magistrate Judge Ronald Ellis to hear his sentence for entering a guilty plea to one misdemeanor charge of failing to pay federal income taxes. Stein had created a phony company to hide money and avoid paying taxes on that money. He was originally charged with a felony for lying to federal investigators, but his attorney negotiated a plea agreement for him to accept responsibility for one misdemeanor for failing to pay taxes on $1 million of income in 2008. Stein also agreed to pay taxes for the years 2003 to 2008, although his plea permitted him to avoid criminal charges for failing to pay taxes in all but one year (2008) within that time period.

Stein delivered an emotional plea for leniency. In his five-minute statement, he choked up as he admitted to making a "terrible, terrible mistake." He suggested that his long career in public service should be considered as a factor in granting leniency.

Judge Ellis remarked that he had entered the courtroom expecting to sentence Stein to serve time behind bars, but he changed his mind as he listened to Stein and as he considered the 14 letters written on Stein's behalf by prominent lawyers, journalists, and entertainment figures. He ultimately sentenced Stein to three years' probation and 500 hours of community service.

In a different federal income tax case in 2008, movie star Wesley Snipes was charged with failing to pay taxes on $58 million in income over the course of a decade. Instead of negotiating a plea agreement, Snipes went to trial and a jury acquitted him of serious conspiracy and tax fraud charges. The jury apparently believed that he relied on misguided advice from an accountant who told him that he was not required to pay taxes. However, the jury convicted him of three separate misdemeanor counts of failing to file tax returns for the three years after he had been informed by the federal government that he was, indeed, required to file a return.

At his sentencing, Snipes apologized for making mistakes and offered checks totaling $5 million to begin payment on his back taxes. Snipes was not emotional, and the federal prosecutor complained that Snipes never mentioned the word "taxes," never directly admitted that he should have paid his taxes, and did not show any remorse. U.S. District Judge William Terrell Hodge gave Snipes the maximum sentence of three years in prison, one year for each misdemeanor count.

Were these two sentences fair? Are they comparable? Snipes was convicted of failing to file his tax return, while Stein pled guilty to tax evasion—yet Snipes received the much more significant sentence. Did Snipes receive extra punishment for failing to fully apologize and accept responsibility? Did he receive extra punishment because the government accused him of owing additional money—even though the jury acquitted him of the charge of tax evasion? Did he receive extra punishment for refusing to plead guilty and for ultimately taking his case to a time-consuming, expensive jury trial? By contrast, did Stein receive leniency for having so many prominent friends willing to write letters to the judge?

Researching the Internet

Look at the website of the U.S. Sentencing Commission to see what percentage of convicted tax offenders are sentenced to probation and the average sentence for tax offenders sentenced to prison. http://www.ussc.gov/.

For Critical Analysis

Consider the precise charges for which Stein and Snipes were convicted. Which one was convicted of the more serious acts? Write down the sentence that you would have given to each of these defendants in order to achieve justice. What punishment goals are advanced by the sentences that you designed?

Finally, the practical implications of a sentence can affect judges' decisions. For example, judges may take into account the offender's diminished ability to "do time," as in the case of an elderly person. They may also consider the impact on the offender's family; a mother with children may receive a different sentence than a single woman would. Finally, costs to the corrections system may play a role in sentencing, as judges consider probation officers' caseloads or prison crowding (Steffensmeier, Kramer, & Streifel, 1993). The Close Up gives examples of judges' sentencing decisions in prominent cases.

Presentence Report

presentence report A report, prepared by a probation officer, that presents a convicted offender's background and is used by the judge in selecting an appropriate sentence.

Even though sentencing is the judge's responsibility, the **presentence report** has become an important ingredient in the judicial mix. Usually a probation officer investigates the convicted person's background, criminal record, job status, and mental condition to suggest a sentence that is in the interests of both the offender and society. Although the presentence report serves primarily to help the judge select the sentence, it also assists in the classification of probationers, prisoners, and parolees for treatment planning and risk assessment. In the report, the probation officer makes judgments about what information to include and what conclusions to draw from that information. In some states, however, probation officers present only factual material to the judge and make no sentencing recommendation. Because the probation officers do not necessarily follow evidentiary rules, they may include hearsay statements as well as firsthand information.

In the federal court system, the presentence report is supplemented by an additional report written by a *pretrial services officer (PSO)*. This report focuses on the defendant's behavior and compliance with conditions while out on bail—prior to trial or plea or between the date of conviction and the date of sentencing.

The presentence report is one means by which judges ease the strain of decision making. The report lets judges shift partial responsibility to the probation department. Because a substantial number of sentencing alternatives are open to judges, they often rely on the report for guidance.

Sentencing Guidelines

Since the 1980s, **sentencing guidelines** have been established in the federal courts and in more than two dozen states. Such guidelines indicate to judges the expected sanction for particular types of offenses. They are intended to limit the sentencing discretion of judges and to reduce disparity among sentences given for similar offenses. Although statutes provide a variety of sentencing options for particular crimes, guidelines attempt to direct the judge to more specific actions that should be taken. The range of sentencing options provided for most offenses centers on the seriousness of the crime and on the criminal history of an offender.

Legislatures— and in some states and in the federal government, commissions— construct sentencing guidelines as a grid of two scores (Tonry, 1993). As shown in the Minnesota Guidelines portrayed in Table 9.5, one dimension relates to the seriousness of the offense, the other to the likelihood of offender recidivism. The offender score is obtained by totaling the points allocated to such factors as the number of juvenile offenses, adult misdemeanors, and adult felony convictions; the number of times incarcerated; the status of the accused at the time of the last offense, whether on probation or parole or escaped from confinement; and employment status or educational achievement. Judges look at the grid to see what sentence should be imposed on a particular offender who has committed a specific offense. Judges may go outside the guidelines if aggravating or mitigating circumstances exist; however, they must provide a written explanation of their reasons for doing so (Fischman & Schanzenbach, 2011).

Sentencing guidelines are to be reviewed and modified periodically so that recent decisions will be included. Given that guidelines are constructed on the basis of past sentences, some critics argue that because the guidelines reflect only what has happened, they do not reform sentencing. Others question the choice of characteristics included in the offender scale and charge that some are used to mask racial criteria. Paula Krautt (2002) found differences in drug-trafficking sentences among federal district and circuit courts. However, Lisa Stolzenberg and Stewart J. D'Alessio (1994) studied the Minnesota guidelines and found, compared with pre-guideline decisions, an 18 percent reduction in disparity for the prison/no-prison outcome and a 60 percent reduction in disparity of length of prison sentences.

Although guidelines make sentences more uniform, many judges object to having their discretion limited in this manner (Zimmerman, 2011). However, Peter Rossi and Richard Berk (1997) found a fair amount of agreement between the

sentencing guideline
A mechanism to indicate to judges the expected sanction for certain offenses, in order to reduce disparities in sentencing.

The italicized numbers in the grid are the range within which a judge may sentence without the sentence being considered a departure. The criminal-history score is computed by adding one point for each prior felony conviction, one-half point for each prior gross-misdemeanor conviction, and one-quarter point for each prior misdemeanor conviction.

Severity of Offense (Illustrative Offenses)		Criminal-History Score Less Serious ←————————————————→ More Serious						
		0	1	2	3	4	5	6 or more
Murder, second degree (intentional murder, drive-by shootings)	XI	306 *261–367*	326 *278–391*	346 *295–415*	366 *312–439*	386 *329–463*	406 *346–480*	426 *363–480*
Murder, third degree Murder, second degree (unintentional murder)	X	150 *128–180*	165 *141–198*	180 *153–216*	195 *166–234*	210 *179–252*	225 *192–270*	240 *204–288*
Assault, first degree Controlled substance crime, first degree	IX	86 *74–103*	98 *84–117*	110 *94–132*	122 *104–146*	134 *114–160*	146 *125–175*	158 *135–189*
Aggravated robbery, first degree Controlled substance crime, second degree	VIII	48 *41–57*	58 *50–69*	68 *58–81*	78 *67–93*	88 *75–105*	98 *84–117*	108 *92–129*
Felony DWI	VII	36	42	48	54 *46–64*	60 *51–72*	66 *57–79*	72 *62–84*
Controlled substance crime, third degree	VI	21	27	33	39 *34–46*	45 *39–54*	51 *44–61*	57 *49–68*
Residential burglary Simple robbery	V	18	23	28	33 *29–39*	38 *33–45*	43 *37–51*	48 *41–57*
Nonresidential burglary	IV	12	15	18	21	24 *21–28*	27 *23–32*	30 *26–36*
Theft crimes (over $5,000)	III	12	13	15	17	19 *17–22*	21 *18–25*	23 *20–27*
Theft crimes ($5,000 or less) Check forgery ($251–$2,500)	II	12	12	13	15	17	19	21 *18–25*
Sale of simulated controlled substance	I	12	12	12	13	15	17	19 *17–22*

☐ At the discretion of the judge, up to a year in jail and/or other nonjail sanctions can be imposed instead of prison sentences as conditions of probation for most of these offenses. If prison is imposed, the presumptive sentence is the number of months shown.

☐ Presumptive commitment to state prison for all offenses.

Note: First-degree murder has a mandatory life sentence and is excluded from the guidelines by law.

Source: Minnesota Sentencing Guidelines Commission, *Minnesota Sentencing Guidelines and Commentary*, effective August 1, 2013.

sentences prescribed in the federal guidelines and those desired by the general public.

The future of sentencing guidelines is uncertain. In 2004, the U.S. Supreme Court decided that aspects of Washington State sentencing guidelines violated the Sixth Amendment right to trial by jury by giving judges too much authority to enhance sentences based on unproved factual determinations (*Blakely v. Washington*). One year later the Supreme Court applied the *Blakely* precedent to the federal sentencing guidelines and found a similar violation of the Sixth Amendment when judges enhance sentences based on their own determinations (*United States v. Booker*, 2005). In effect, federal judges are expected to consult the guidelines, but they are not mandatory and federal judges can make reasonable deviations

District Associate Judge

Kirk Daily, District Associate Judge Ottumwa, Iowa

Under Iowa law, district associate judges have the authority to hear Class D felonies as well as serious and aggravated misdemeanors. Substance abuse crimes can form a significant component of the court's docket. Such crimes include operating a motor vehicle while intoxicated and possession of controlled substances. The penalties for crimes handled by this limited jurisdiction court can range from probation and other community-based sanctions to one year in county jail and up to five years in state prison. Thus, these judges' decisions significantly impact the lives of people charged with such crimes.

Judges in such courts make determinations of probable cause and decide whether to issue search warrants. They also conduct preliminary hearings in criminal cases. District associate judges also have jurisdiction over civil suits when the amount in controversy is $10,000 or less. Finally, these judges handle appeals for both criminal and civil matters that have been decided in the limited-jurisdiction magistrate court.

After graduating from college and law school, Kirk Daily entered private law practice as an attorney in his hometown of Ottumwa, Iowa. The career path to a judgeship, whether in a system of elected judges or appointed judges, typically depends on building a solid reputation for wisdom,

Photo provided by Kirk Daily

intelligence, ethics, and industriousness. Daily gained significant knowledge and experience in many areas of law through a broad, general law practice that ranged from representing criminal defendants for serious crimes, including murder, to civil cases such as medical malpractice and divorce. The breadth of his experience as a lawyer provided exceptionally good training for his later role as judge. As a judge, he must use his knowledge of law to make decisions concerning a wide variety of cases, both criminal and civil. Iowa uses a merit-selection process for choosing judges, and Daily's solid experience and impressive performance as an attorney led to his selection for a judgeship.

Substance abuse crimes, such as the use and manufacture of methamphetamine and drunk driving, take up a great deal of my time. There are high recidivism rates among substance abusers, and their cases require a high level of follow-up supervision to assist these individuals to deal with their addictions. In sentencing substance abusers, judges must often weigh public safety against treatment. Creating a sentence that aims to treat a person's addiction, rather than simply imposing prison, increases a judge's options.

(Wu & Spohn, 2010). In 2008, however, the Supreme Court ruled that federal judges are not required to give advance notice to defendants prior to imposing a sentence that varies from the guidelines (*Irizarry v. United States*, 2008). Yet, most sentences in federal courts remain in conformity with the guidelines (U.S. Sentencing Commission, 2006). Observers anticipate that the U.S. Supreme Court will need to revisit this issue in order to provide guidance about how sentencing guidelines can be properly designed and applied. For example, in 2011 the Court determined that federal judges can consider evidence of an offender's rehabilitation in imposing a sentence that is below those specified in sentencing guidelines (*Pepper v. United States*, 2011).

Judges' decisions have profound impacts on the lives of people drawn into the criminal justice system. Would you want to make sentencing decisions that determine the fates of people convicted of crimes? Consider how you would perform as a judge when you read "Careers in Criminal Justice." In addition, bear these considerations in mind as you assume the role of a judge and design a sentence for a controversial 2014 case as described at the end of the chapter in "A Question of Ethics."

Who Gets the Harshest Punishment?

Harsh, unjust punishments can occur because of sentencing disparities and wrongful convictions. The prison population in most states contains a higher proportion of African American and Hispanic men than occurs in the general population. Are these disparities caused by racial prejudices and discrimination, or are other factors at work? Wrongful conviction takes place when people who are in fact innocent are nonetheless found guilty by plea or verdict. It also occurs in those cases in which the conviction of a truly guilty person is overturned on appeal because of due process errors.

Racial Disparities Studies of racial disparities in sentencing are inconclusive. Because some studies show disparities in specific states or cities, though, there are grave concerns about the possibility of racial discrimination. Studies of sentencing in Pennsylvania, for example, found that there is a "high cost of being black, young (21–29 years), and male." Sentences given these offenders resulted in a higher proportion going to prison and incurring longer terms (Steffensmeier, Ulmer, & Kramer, 1998). While supporting the Pennsylvania results, research in Chicago, Kansas City, Missouri, and Miami found variation among the jurisdictions as to sentence length (Spohn & Holleran, 2000). Other research shows disproportionate effects on African American men being sent to prison through mandatory punishments and sentence enhancements (Schlesinger, 2011).

Do these disparities stem from the prejudicial attitudes of judges, police officers, and prosecutors? Are African Americans and Hispanics viewed as a "racial threat" when they commit crimes of violence and drug selling, which are thought to be spreading from the urban ghetto to the "previously safe places of the suburbs" (Crawford, Chiricos, & Kleck, 1998:484)? Are enforcement resources distributed so that certain groups are subject to closer scrutiny than are other groups?

Scholars have pointed out that the relationship between race and sentencing is complex. For example, recent research on federal court sentencing found racial disparities largely caused by prosecutors' decisions to charge minority defendants with more serious crimes rather than by the sentencing decisions of judges (Starr & Rehavi, 2013). These findings cannot be applied to state courts because the sentencing laws and courthouse contexts vary greatly from city to city and state to state. Judges as well as prosecutors are important decision makers in the process.

The analysis of these issues is complex because judges consider many defendant and case characteristics. According to this view, judges assess not only the legally relevant factors of blameworthiness, dangerousness, and recidivism risk but also race, gender, and age characteristics (Steen, Engen, & Gainey, 2005). The interconnectedness of these variables, not judges' negative attitudes, is what culminates in the disproportionately severe sentences given young black men.

Federal sentencing guidelines were adjusted in 2007 and 2008 to reduce the impact of a highly criticized source of racial disparities in prison sentences for offenders convicted of cocaine-related offenses. The federal sentencing guidelines for crack cocaine offenses—which disproportionately affected African American defendants—were adjusted to be more closely aligned with shorter sentences for possessing and selling similar amounts of powder cocaine, crimes more commonly associated with white offenders. The U.S. Sentencing Commission voted to apply these new guidelines retroactively, meaning that offenders currently serving long sentences for crack cocaine offenses were eligible to be resentenced to shorter terms in prison. In many cases, this adjustment led to the release in 2008 of offenders who had already served longer periods than those required under the new sentencing guidelines (Gezari, 2008; *Third Branch*, 2008b). As mentioned earlier, President Obama signed into law a new federal statute that reduced, but did not eliminate, the disparities in mandatory sentences for crack and powder cocaine offenders (Eckholm, 2010).

In recent years, the development of DNA evidence has contributed to the reinvestigation of cases and the release of people sent to prison for crimes that they did not commit. Here Gerard Richardson gained release in 2013 after spending 19 years in prison for murder. His innocence was discovered when DNA tests were performed on preserved evidence from a bite mark on the victim. How could criminal justice processes be changed to reduce the risks of erroneous convictions?

Wrongful Convictions   A serious dilemma for the criminal justice system concerns people who are wrongly convicted and sentenced. Whereas the public expresses much concern over those who "beat the system" and go free, they pay comparatively little attention to those who are innocent yet convicted. Many of these people are wrongly convicted because victims and witnesses make mistakes in identifying alleged criminals from photographs and lineups.

The development of DNA technology has increased the number of people exonerated after being convicted. However, many cases do not have DNA evidence available. C. Ronald Huff notes that "because the great majority of cases do not produce biological material to be tested, one can only speculate about the error rate in those cases" (2002:2). Even when DNA evidence is available, the U.S. Supreme Court has ruled that convicted offenders do not have a constitutional right to have the stored evidence tested. According to a five-member majority on the Court, state legislatures and Congress should develop their own rules concerning opportunities to have old evidence tested (*District Attorney's Office v. Osborne*, 2009). Every year national attention focuses on several cases in which innocent people have been erroneously convicted, yet there is no way to know how many more innocent people may be wrongly confined in prisons today.

Whether from racial discrimination or wrongful convictions, unjust punishments do not serve the ideals of justice. Such punishments raise fundamental questions about the criminal justice system and its links to the society it serves.

☑ **CHECK POINT**

6. **What are the four factors thought to influence the sentencing behavior of judges?**
   The administrative context of the courts, the attitudes and values of judges, the presentence report, and sentencing guidelines.

STOP&ANALYZE

If your son were arrested for a crime and you believed his claim that he was innocent, are there any steps you could take to reduce the likelihood that he would be subject to an erroneous conviction? Make a list of what you might do to help your son.

Think, Discuss, Write

In February 2014, a national controversy arose when Judge Jean Boyd, a state court judge in Texas, imposed a sentence of 10 years of probation on teenager Eric Couch, who as a 16-year-old, killed four people and seriously injured two others when driving while drunk. Couch pleaded guilty to charges of intoxication manslaughter. Prosecutors said Couch drove 70 miles per hour in a zone with a speed limit of 40. His blood alcohol level was three times the state limit of 0.08 when he lost control of his speeding truck and hit people changing a flat tire on a vehicle on the side of the road. One passenger in Couch's truck suffered severe brain injuries and can longer move or talk.

In addition to the long probation sentence, Couch's family committed to paying for him to go to an in-patient facility for treatment and counseling. National news reporters focused on the case because a psychologist for the defense supported the case for a lenient sentence by saying that Couch suffered from "affluenza," a shorthand term for someone who is so wealthy and spoiled that he does not connect his actions with the likelihood of bad consequences. The victims' families were outraged at the sentence, which was, in their view, too light by not requiring the youth to serve time in prison.

By contrast, two years earlier Judge Boyd imposed a 10-year sentence on a 14-year-old boy who killed another youth with one punch when the victim fell and hit his head on the pavement. In that case, the defendant could be paroled after five years or be sent to an adult prison at age 19 to serve the final five years. Critics expressed concern that Boyd had imposed a more severe sentence on the 14-year-old, an African American youth who killed one person, than she did on a wealthy white teen who killed four people and seriously injured others.

Does this provide evidence of racial discrimination? Some observers noted that Boyd had sought to emphasize rehabilitation for both boys, but no treatment program would accept the boy who threw the punch. Thus, he ended up in juvenile prison. By contrast, Couch's parents were so wealthy that they could afford to send him to a treatment facility in California that cost $450,000 per year per patient.

Wealth discrimination? Racial discrimination? Excessive leniency? Excessive emphasis on rehabilitation without proper concern for other objectives of punishment? These cases raise challenging questions about a judge's responsibilities in sentencing.

Discussion/Writing Assignment

Imagine that you were the judge in these two cases. Write a memo describing the sentence that you would impose in each case and the punishment objectives that you would pursue with these sentences. To what extent do your sentences reflect a concern or prediction about the teenagers' future lives after they complete their periods of confinement or probation?

Sources: Molly Hennessey-Fiske, "Judge in 'Affluenza' Case Rules Out Jail Time for Teen Driver," *Los Angeles Times*, February 5, 2014 (www.latimes.com); Clare Kim, "Families of 'Affluenza' Teen's Victims Reach Settlements," MSNBC online, March 18, 2014 (www.msnbc.com); Christina Sterbenz, "Judge in 'Affluenza' Case Sentenced Black Teen to 10 Years for Killing a Guy with a Single Punch," *Business Insider*, December 20, 2013 (www.businessinsider .com); Gary Strauss, "No Jail for 'Affluenza' Teen in Fatal Crash Draws Outrage," *USA Today*, February 6, 2014 (www.usatoday.com).

SUMMARY

1 Name the goals of punishment.
- In the United States, the four main goals of the criminal sanction are retribution, deterrence, incapacitation, and rehabilitation.
- Restoration, a new approach to punishment, has not become mainstream yet.
- The goals of the criminal sanction are carried out through incarceration, intermediate sanctions, probation, and death.

2 Describe the types of sentences judges can impose.
- Penal codes vary as to whether the permitted sentences are indeterminate, determinate, or mandatory. Each type of sentence makes certain

assumptions about the goals of the criminal sanction.
- "Good time" allows correctional administrators to reduce the sentence of prisoners who live according to the rules and participate in various vocational, educational, and treatment programs.
- The U.S. Supreme Court allows capital punishment only when the judge and jury are allowed to take into account mitigating and aggravating circumstances.
- Judges often have considerable discretion in fashioning sentences to account for factors such as the seriousness of the crime, the offender's prior record, and mitigating and aggravating circumstances.

③ Identify the influences on sentencing.
- The sentencing process is influenced by the administrative context of the courts, the attitudes and values of the judges, the presentence report, and sentencing guidelines.

④ Explain how the system may treat wrongdoers unequally.
- Many states have formulated sentencing guidelines as a way of reducing disparity among the sentences given offenders in similar situations.
- Harsh, unjust punishments may result from racial discrimination or wrongful convictions.

Questions for Review

1. What are the major differences between retribution, deterrence, incapacitation, and rehabilitation?
2. What is the main purpose of restoration (restorative justice)?
3. What are the forms of the criminal sanction?
4. What purposes do intermediate sanctions serve?
5. What has been the Supreme Court's position on the constitutionality of the death penalty?
6. Is there a link between sentences and race?

Key Terms and Cases

determinate sentence (p. 295)

earned time (p. 296)

general deterrence (p. 289)

good time (p. 296)

incapacitation (p. 290)

indeterminate sentence (p. 294)

intermediate sanctions (p. 297)

mandatory sentence (p. 295)

presentence report (p. 312)

presumptive sentence (p. 295)

probation (p. 298)

rehabilitation (p. 291)

restorative justice (p. 292)

retribution (p. 289)

selective incapacitation (p. 291)

sentencing guidelines (p. 313)

shock probation (p. 298)

specific deterrence (p. 290)

Atkins v. Virginia (2002) (p. 302)

Furman v. Georgia (1972) (p. 301)

Gregg v. Georgia (1976) (p. 301)

McCleskey v. Kemp (1987) (p. 302)

Roper v. Simmons (2005) (p. 303)

Witherspoon v. Illinois (1968) (p. 305)

10 Corrections

LEARNING OBJECTIVES

1 Describe how the American system of corrections has developed.

2 Describe the roles that the federal, state, and local governments play in corrections.

3 Explain the law of corrections and how it is applied to offenders and correctional professionals.

4 Explain why the prison population has nearly quadrupled in the past 30 years.

A report issued in March 2013 revealed an important development in American corrections: the prison population declined for two years in a row (Pew Center, 2013). This was extraordinary news because prison populations had increased steadily in dramatic fashion for the preceding 30 years. This new development was especially significant because the size and expense of corrections systems had reached levels few people had imagined possible. Just a few years earlier, a report released by the Pew Center on the States in February 2008 showed that for the first time in history, 1 in 100 American adults were behind bars in prisons (1,596,127) and jails (723,000). The "1 in 100" report brought home the fact of the country's tremendously large and at that time expanding prison population. The 2008 report also noted that the United States incarcerates more of its residents than any other country. China is second with 1.5 million behind bars (J. Warren, 2008). The United States has less than 5 percent of the world's population, but almost a quarter of the world's prisoners. Even with the recent decrease in prison population, the United States has approximately 35 times more prisoners than Canada while having only 10 times its population.

The foregoing developments raise two important questions. First, why does this gap exist between American justice and that of the rest of the world? Second, will the recent decrease in the American population produce a significant reduction that makes the incarceration rate less striking compared with rates elsewhere in the rest of the world? With respect to the first question, we know certain things. Over the past 30 years, the incarceration rate has quadrupled, even though crime in the United States has been declining for two decades (Liptak, 2008c). The prison populations increased due to the imposition of longer sentences on offenders, including nonviolent drug offenders who were imprisoned in large numbers. Some states imposed decades-long sentences on repeat offenders, even if they did not commit the most serious crimes.

The increase in prison populations had significant financial consequences. The larger number of offenders incarcerated in prisons and jails increased the need for new prisons, resulting in a construction boom and increased employment of correctional officers. Correctional budgets climbed an average of 10 percent annually, and many states diverted money from education, welfare, and health programs to meet the soaring needs of corrections.

With respect to the second question, we do not yet know the extent to which future trends may reduce prison populations. This historic moment may indicate that imprisonment trends will continue to move in a new direction, especially as many states take specific actions to change sentencing practices in ways that would send fewer people to prison (A. Johnson, 2011; "Indiana's Answer," 2011). A significant factor in states' reconsideration of the use of lengthy prison sentences for drug offenders and other non-homicide offenses is the high financial cost of imprisonment at a time when states face serious budget crises. Thus, states are increasingly investing their corrections funds in programs that provide alternatives to incarceration, such as community programs, as well as programs to help offenders succeed in society after they are released from prison (Pew Center, 2013).

The public usually thinks of prisons when it thinks of corrections; however, about 70 percent of persons under supervision are not in prisons or jails, but living in the community on probation or parole. The percentage of offenders in these less expensive correctional settings is likely to increase as states adjust their sentencing and release practices in their efforts to save money.

Corrections refers to the great number of programs, services, facilities, and organizations responsible for the management of people accused or convicted of criminal offenses. In addition to prisons and jails, corrections includes probation, halfway houses, education and work release programs, parole supervision, counseling, and community service. Correctional programs operate in Salvation Army hostels, forest camps, medical clinics, and urban storefronts.

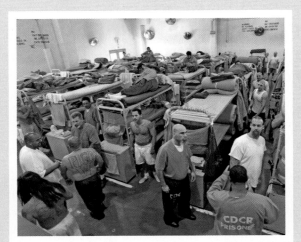

Corrections is authorized by all levels of government, is administered by both public and private organizations, and costs more than $60 billion a year. A total of 7.1 million adults and juveniles receive correctional supervision by 750,000 administrators, psychologists, officers, counselors, social workers, and other professionals (BJS, 2011b). This chapter will examine (1) the history of corrections, (2) the organization of corrections, (3) the law of corrections, and (4) the policy trends in community corrections and incarceration.

---

corrections The variety of programs, services, facilities, and organizations responsible for the management of people who have been accused or convicted of criminal offenses.

Development of Corrections

How did corrections get to where it is today? Why are offenders now placed on probation or incarcerated instead of whipped or burned as in colonial times? Over the past 200 years, ideas about punishment have moved like a pendulum from one far position to another (see Table 10.1). As we review the development of present-day policies, think about how future changes in society may lead to new forms of corrections.

Invention of the Penitentiary

Enlightenment A movement during the eighteenth century in England and France in which concepts of liberalism, rationalism, equality, and individualism dominated social and political thinking.

The late eighteenth century stands out as a remarkable period. At that time, scholars and social reformers in Europe and America were rethinking the nature of society and the place of the individual in it. During the **Enlightenment**, as this period is known, philosophers and reformers challenged tradition with new ideas about the individual, about limitations on government, and about rationalism. Such thinking was the main intellectual force behind the American Revolution and laid the foundation of American values. The Enlightenment also affected the new nation's views on law and criminal justice. Reformers began to raise questions about the nature of criminal behavior and the methods of punishment.

TABLE 10.1　**History of Corrections in America**

Note the extent to which correctional policies have shifted from one era to the next and are influenced by societal factors.

Correctional Era						
Colonial (1600s–1790s)	**Penitentiary (1790s–1860s)**	**Reformatory (1870s–1890s)**	**Progressive (1890s–1930s)**	**Medical (1930s–1960s)**	**Community (1960s–1970s)**	**Crime Control (1970s–2000s)**
Features						
Anglican Code	Separate confinement	Indeterminate sentences	Individual case approach	Rehabilitation as primary focus of incarceration	Reintegration into community	Determinate sentences
Capital and corporal punishment, fines	Reform of individual	Parole	Administrative discretion	Psychological testing and classification	Avoidance of incarceration	Mandatory sentences
	Power of isolation and labor	Classification by degree of individual reform	Broader probation and parole	Various types of treatment programs and institutions	Vocational and educational program	Sentencing guidelines
	Penance	Rehabilitative programs	Juvenile courts			Risk management
	Disciplined routine	Separate treatment for juveniles				
	Punishment according to severity of crime					
Philosophical Basis						
Religious law	Enlightenment	National Prison Association Declaration of Principles	The Age of Reform	Biomedical science	Civil rights movement	Crime control
Doctrine of predestination	Declaration of Independence	Crime as moral disease	Positivist school	Psychiatry and psychology	Critique of prisons	Rising crime rates
	Human perfectibility and powers of reason	Criminals as "victims of social disorder"	Punishment according to needs of offender	Social work practice	Small is better	Political shift to the right
	Religious penitence		Focus on the offender	Crime as signal of personal" distress" or "failure"		New punitive agenda
	Power of reformation		Crime as an urban, immigrant ghetto problem			
	Focus on the act					
	Healing power of suffering					

Prior to 1800, Americans copied Europeans in using physical punishment such as flogging, branding, and maiming as the main criminal sanction, and criminals were regularly sentenced to death for pickpocketing, burglary, robbery, and horse stealing (Rothman, 1971). Jails existed throughout the country, but they served only to hold people awaiting trial or to punish people unable to pay their debts. As in England, the American colonies maintained houses of correction, where offenders were sentenced to terms of "hard labor" as a means of turning them from crime (A. J. Hirsch, 1992).

With the spread of Enlightenment ideas during the late eighteenth century, physical punishments began to wane. Gradually, "modern" penal systems emerged that emphasized fitting the punishment to the individual offender. The new goal was not to inflict pain on the offender's body (corporal punishment) but to change the individual and set him or her on the right path.

Many people promoted the reform of corrections, but John Howard (1726–1790), sheriff of Bedfordshire, England, was especially influential. His book *The State of Prisons in England and Wales*, published in 1777, described the horrible conditions he observed in the prisons he visited (Howard, 1777/1929). Public response to the book resulted in Parliament's passing the Penitentiary Act of 1779, which called for the creation of a house of hard labor where offenders would be imprisoned for up to two years. The institution would be based on four principles:

1. A secure and sanitary building
2. Inspection to ensure that offenders followed the rules
3. Abolition of the fees charged offenders for their food
4. A reformatory regime

At night, prisoners were to be confined to individual cells. During the day, they were to work silently in common rooms. Prison life was to be strict and ordered. Influenced by his Quaker friends, Howard believed that the new institution should be a place of industry. More important, it should be a place that offered criminals opportunities for penitence (sorrow and shame for their wrongs) and repentance (willingness to change their ways). In short, the **penitentiary** served to punish and to reform.

Howard's idea of the penitentiary was not implemented in England until 1842, some 50 years after his death. Although England was slow to act, the United States applied Howard's ideas much more quickly.

Reform in the United States

From 1776 to around 1830, a new revolution occurred in the American idea of criminal punishment. Although based on the work of English reformers, the new correctional philosophy reflected many ideas expressed in the Declaration of Independence, including an optimistic view of human nature and of individual perfectibility. Emphasis shifted from the assumption that deviance was part of human nature to a belief that crime resulted from environmental forces. The new nation's humane and optimistic ideas focused on reforming the criminal.

In the first decades of the nineteenth century, the creation of penitentiaries in Pennsylvania and New York attracted the attention of legislators in other states, as well as investigators from Europe. By the mid-1800s, the U.S. penitentiary had become world famous.

The Pennsylvania System
Several groups in the United States dedicated themselves to reforming the institutions and practices of criminal punishment. One of these groups was the Philadelphia Society for Alleviating the Miseries of Public Prisons, formed in 1787. This group, which included many Quakers, was inspired by Howard's ideas. They argued that criminals could best be reformed if they were placed in penitentiaries—isolated from one another and from society to consider their crimes, repent, and reform.

In 1790 the Pennsylvania legislature authorized the construction of two penitentiaries for the solitary confinement of "hardened and atrocious offenders." The first, created out of an existing three-story stone structure in Philadelphia, was the Walnut Street Jail. This 25-by-40-foot building had eight dark cells, each measuring 6 by 8 by 9 feet, on each floor. A yard was attached to the building. Only one inmate occupied each cell, and no communications of any kind were allowed. From a small, grated window high on the outside wall, prisoners "could perceive neither heaven nor earth."

From this limited beginning, the Pennsylvania system of **separate confinement** evolved. It was based on five principles:

1. Prisoners would not be treated vengefully but should be convinced, through hard and selective forms of suffering, that they could change their lives.

Until the early 1800s, Americans followed the European practice of relying on punishment that was physically painful, such as death, flogging, and branding. Would such punishments be appropriate today?

penitentiary An institution intended to punish criminals by isolating them from society and from one another so they can reflect on their past misdeeds, repent, and reform.

separate confinement
A penitentiary system, developed in Pennsylvania, in which each inmate was held in isolation from other inmates. All activities, including craft work, took place in the cells.

Eastern State Penitentiary, located outside Philadelphia, became the model for the Pennsylvania system of separate confinement. The building was designed to ensure that each offender was separated from all human contact so that he could reflect on his misdeeds. If you designed a prison, what details would it contain?

© The Library Company of Philadelphia

2. Solitary confinement would prevent further corruption inside prison.
3. In isolation, offenders would reflect on their transgressions and repent.
4. Solitary confinement would be punishment, because humans are by nature social animals.
5. Solitary confinement would be economical, because prisoners would not need a long time to repent, and so fewer keepers would be needed and the cost of clothing would be lower.

The opening of the Eastern Penitentiary near Philadelphia in 1829 culminated 42 years of reform activity by the Philadelphia Society. On October 25, 1829, the first prisoner, Charles Williams, arrived. He was an 18-year-old African American sentenced to two years for larceny. He was assigned to a 12-by-8-by-10-foot cell with an individual exercise yard 18 feet long. In the cell was a fold-up steel bed, a simple toilet, a wooden stool, a workbench, and eating utensils. Light came from an 8-inch window in the ceiling. Solitary labor, Bible reading, and reflection were the keys to the moral rehabilitation that was supposed to occur within the penitentiary. Although the cell was larger than most in use today, it was the only world the prisoner would see throughout the entire sentence. The only other human voice heard would be that of a clergyman who would visit on Sundays. Nothing was to distract the penitent prisoner from the path toward reform.

Within five years of its opening, Eastern endured the first of several outside investigations. The reports detailed the extent to which the goal of separate confinement was not fully observed, physical punishments were used to maintain discipline, and prisoners suffered mental breakdowns from isolation. Separate confinement had declined at Eastern by the 1860s, when crowding required doubling up in each cell, yet it was not abolished in Pennsylvania until 1913 (Teeters & Shearer, 1957:ch. 4).

The New York System   In 1819 New York opened a penitentiary in Auburn that evolved as a rival to Pennsylvania's concept of separate confinement. Under New York's **congregate system**, prisoners were held in isolation at night but worked with other prisoners in shops during the day. Working under a rule of silence, they were forbidden even to exchange glances while on the job or at meals.

Auburn's warden, Elam Lynds, was convinced that convicts were incorrigible and that industrial efficiency should be the overriding purpose of the prison.

congregate system
A penitentiary system, developed in Auburn, New York, in which each inmate was held in isolation during the night but worked and ate with other prisoners during the day under a rule of silence.

TABLE 10.2 Comparison of Pennsylvania and New York (Auburn) Penitentiary Systems

	Goal	Implementation	Method	Activity
Pennsylvania (separate system)	Redemption of the offender through the well-ordered routine of the prison	Isolation, penance, contemplation, labor, silence	Inmates kept in their cells for eating, sleeping, and working	Bible reading, work on crafts in cell
New York (Auburn) (congregate system)	Redemption of the offender through the well-ordered routine of the prison	Strict discipline, obedience, labor, silence	Inmates sleep in their cells but come together to eat and work	Work together in shops making goods to be sold by the state

contract labor system
A system under which inmates' labor was sold on a contractual basis to private employers who provided the machinery and raw materials with which inmates made salable products in the institution.

He instituted a reign of discipline and obedience that included the lockstep and the wearing of prison stripes. He also started a **contract labor system**. By the 1840s, Auburn was producing footwear, barrels, carpets, harnesses, furniture, and clothing. American reformers, seeing the New York approach as a great advance, copied it throughout the Northeast. Because the inmates produced goods for sale, advocates said operating costs would be covered.

During this period, advocates of the Pennsylvania and New York plans debated on public platforms and in the nation's periodicals. Advocates of both systems agreed that the prisoner must stay isolated from society and follow a disciplined routine. In their view, criminality resulted from pervasive corruption that the family and the church did not sufficiently counterbalance. Only when offenders were removed from the temptations and influences of society and kept in a silent, disciplined environment could they reflect on their sins and offenses and become useful citizens. The convicts were not inherently depraved; rather, they were victims of a society that had not protected them from vice. While offenders were being punished, they would become penitent and motivated to place themselves on the right path. See Table 10.2 for a comparison of the Pennsylvania and New York systems.

Prisons in the South and West   Scholars tend to emphasize the nineteenth-century reforms in the populous Northeast, neglecting penal developments in the South and the West. Before 1817 four Southern states—Georgia, Kentucky, Maryland, and Virginia—had built prisons, some following the penitentiary model. Later prisons, such as the ones in Jackson, Mississippi (1842), and Huntsville, Texas (1848), followed the Auburn model. Further expansion ended with the advent of the Civil War, however. With the exception of San Quentin (1852), the sparse population of the West did not lend itself to the construction of many prisons until the latter part of the nineteenth century.

After the Civil War, southerners began to rebuild their communities and largely agricultural-based economy. They lacked funds to build prisons and instead developed a "plantation model" of corrections that exploited prisoners as slave labor (Feeley & Rubin, 1998). This approach to corrections was used as a tool of oppression by falsely convicting innocent African Americans in order to maintain the supply of convict laborers (Friedman, 1993). To address their governments' need for revenue, Southern states developed the **lease system**. Businesses in need of workers negotiated with the state for the custody of prisoners and exploitation of their labor (logging, agriculture, mining, railroad construction). Because these entrepreneurs had no ownership interest in the prisoners, they subjected the prisoners to worse abuses than they had inflicted on slaves prior to the Civil War (Rotman, 1995). The prisoner death rate soared. For example, among the 285 prisoners sent to work on the Greenwood and Augusta Railroad between 1877 and 1880, 45 percent lost their lives under the brutal working conditions (Friedman, 1993). As described by historian Lawrence Friedman, "these were young black men in the prime of their lives. You can imagine what it would take, what cruelty, what conditions of work, to kill off almost half of them" (Friedman, 1993:95). In characterizing

lease system A system under which inmates were leased to contractors who provided prisoners with food and clothing in exchange for their labor.

the racial injustice and brutality of this long era in American corrections history, the subtitle of Douglas Blackmon's Pulitzer Prize winning book *Slavery by Another Name* (2008) called it "the re-enslavement of Black Americans from the Civil War to World War II."

Settlement in the West did not take off until the California gold rush of 1849. The prison ideologies of the East did not greatly influence corrections in the West, except in California. Prior to statehood, western prisoners were held in territorial facilities or federal military posts and prisons. Until Congress passed the Anticontract Law of 1887, restricting the employment of federal prisoners, leasing programs existed in California, Montana, Oregon, and Wyoming. In 1852, a lessee chose Point San Quentin and, using convict labor, built two prison buildings. In 1858, after reports of deaths, escapes, and brutal discipline, the state of California took over the facility. The Oregon territory had erected a log prison in the 1850s but soon leased it to a private company. On joining the Union in 1859, however, the state discontinued the lease system. In 1877, Oregon built a state prison on the Auburn plan, but with labor difficulties and an economic depression in the 1890s, the state turned it over to a lessee in 1895 (McKelvey, 1977:228).

Reformatory Movement

By the middle of the nineteenth century, reformers had become disillusioned with the penitentiary. Within 40 years of being built, penitentiaries had become overcrowded, understaffed, and minimally financed. Discipline was lax, brutality was common, and administrators were viewed as corrupt.

Cincinnati, 1870   The National Prison Association (the predecessor of today's American Correctional Association), at its 1870 meeting in Cincinnati, embodied a new spirit of reform. In its famous Declaration of Principles, the association advocated a new design for penology: that prisons should operate according to a philosophy of inmate change, with reformation rewarded by release. Sentences of indeterminate length would replace fixed sentences, and proof of reformation—rather than mere lapse of time—would be required for a prisoner's release. Classification of prisoners on the basis of character and improvement would encourage the reformation program.

Elmira Reformatory   The first **reformatory** took shape in 1876 at Elmira, New York, when Zebulon Brockway was appointed superintendent. Brockway believed that diagnosis and treatment were the keys to reform and rehabilitation. An interview with each new inmate resulted in an individualized work and education treatment program. Inmates followed a rigid schedule of work during the day, followed by courses in academic, vocational, and moral subjects during the evening. Inmates who did well achieved early release.

Designed for first-time felons aged 16–30, the approach at Elmira incorporated a **mark system** of classification, indeterminate sentences, and parole. Each offender entered the institution at grade 2, and if he earned nine marks a month for six months by working hard, completing school assignments, and causing no problems, he could be moved up to grade 1—necessary for release. If he failed to cooperate and violated the rules, he would be demoted to grade 3. Only after three months of satisfactory behavior could he re-embark on the path toward eventual release. In sum, this system placed "the prisoner's fate, as far as possible, in his own hands" (Pisciotta, 1994:20).

By 1900 the reformatory movement had spread throughout the nation, yet by the outbreak of World War I in 1914, it was already in decline. In most institutions, the architecture, the attitudes of the guards, and the emphasis on discipline differed little from those of the past. Too often the educational and rehabilitative efforts took a backseat to the traditional emphasis on punishment. Yet, the reformatory movement contributed the indeterminate sentence, rehabilitative programs, and parole.

reformatory An institution that emphasizes training, a mark system of classification, indeterminate sentences, and parole.

mark system A point system in which prisoners can reduce their term of imprisonment and gain release by earning "marks," or points, through labor, good behavior, and educational achievement.

The Cincinnati Declaration of Principles and the reformatory movement set goals that inspired prison activists well into the twentieth century.

Improving Prison Conditions for Women

Until the beginning of the nineteenth century, female offenders in Europe and North America were treated no differently than men and were not separated from men when they were incarcerated. Only with John Howard's 1777 exposé of prison conditions in England and the development of the penitentiary in Philadelphia did attention begin to focus on the plight of the female offender. Among the English reformers, Elizabeth Gurney Fry, a middle-class Quaker, was the first person to press for changes. When she and other Quakers visited London's Newgate Prison in 1813, they were shocked by the conditions in which the female prisoners and their children were living (Zedner, 1995).

News of Fry's efforts spread to the United States. The Women's Prison Association was formed in New York in 1844 with the goal of improving the treatment of female prisoners and separating them from men. Elizabeth Farnham, head matron of the women's wing at Sing Sing from 1844 to 1848, implemented Fry's ideas until male overseers and legislators thwarted her, forcing her to resign.

The Cincinnati Declaration of Principles did not address the problems of female offenders. It only endorsed the creation of separate treatment-oriented prisons for women. Although the House of Shelter, a reformatory for women, was created in Detroit following the Civil War, not until 1873 did the first independent female-run prison open in Indiana. Within 50 years, 13 other states had followed this lead.

Three principles guided female prison reform during this period: (1) the separation of female prisoners from men, (2) the provision of care in keeping with the needs of women, and (3) the management of women's prisons by female staff. "Operated by and for women, female reformatories were decidedly 'feminine' institutions" (Rafter, 1983:147).

As time passed, the original ideas of the reformers faltered. In 1927, the first federal prison for women opened in Alderson, West Virginia, with Mary Belle Harris as warden. Yet, by 1935 the women's reformatory movement had "run its course, having largely achieved its objective (establishment of separate prisons run by women)" (Heffernan, 1972; Rafter, 1983:165).

Rehabilitation Model

In the first two decades of the twentieth century, reformers known as the Progressives attacked the excesses of big business and urban society and advocated government actions against the problems of slums, vice, and crime. The Progressives urged that knowledge from the social and behavioral sciences should replace religious and traditional moral wisdom as the guiding ideas of criminal rehabilitation. They pursued two main strategies: (1) improving conditions in social environments that seemed to be the breeding grounds of crime and (2) rehabilitating individual offenders. By the 1920s, probation, indeterminate sentences, presentence reports, parole, and treatment programs were being promoted as a more scientific approach to criminality.

Although the Progressives were instrumental in advancing the new penal ideas, not until the 1930s did reformers attempt to implement fully what became known as the **rehabilitation model** of corrections. Taking advantage of the new prestige of the social sciences, penologists helped shift the emphasis of corrections. The new approach saw the social, intellectual, or biological deficiencies of criminals as causing their crimes. Because the essential elements of parole, probation, and the indeterminate sentence were already in place in most states, incorporating the rehabilitation model meant adding classification systems to diagnose offenders and treatment programs to rehabilitate them.

Because penologists likened the new correctional methods to those used by physicians in hospitals, this approach was often referred to as the **medical model**.

rehabilitation model A model of corrections that emphasizes the need to restore a convicted offender to a constructive place in society through some form of vocational or educational training or therapy.

medical model A model of corrections based on the assumption that criminal behavior is caused by biological or psychological conditions that require treatment.

Correctional institutions were to be staffed with people who could diagnose the causes of an individual's criminal behavior, prescribe a treatment program, and determine when the offender was cured and could be safely released to the community.

Following World War II, rehabilitation won new followers. Group therapy, behavior modification, counseling, and several other approaches became part of the "new penology." Yet even during the 1950s, when the medical model reached its height, only a small proportion of state correctional budgets went to rehabilitation. What frustrated many reformers was that even though states adopted the rhetoric of the rehabilitation model, the institutions were still run with custody as the overriding goal.

Because the rehabilitation model failed to achieve its goals, it became discredited in the 1970s. According to critics of rehabilitation, its reportedly high recidivism rates proved its ineffectiveness. Robert Martinson undertook probably the most thorough analysis of research data from treatment programs. Using rigorous standards, he surveyed 231 studies of rehabilitation programs. Martinson summarized his findings by saying, "With few and isolated exceptions, the rehabilitative efforts that have been reported so far have had no appreciable effect on recidivism" (Martinson, 1974:25). The report had an immediate impact on legislators and policy makers, who took up the cry, "Nothing works!" As a result of dissatisfaction with the rehabilitation model, new reforms emerged.

Community Model

The social and political values of particular periods have long influenced correctional goals. During the 1960s and early 1970s, U.S. society experienced the civil rights movement, the war on poverty, and resistance to the war in Vietnam. People challenged the conventional ways of government. In 1967, the U.S. President's Commission on Law Enforcement and Administration of Justice (1967:7) argued for a model of **community corrections**, which claimed that the purpose of corrections should be to reintegrate the offender into the community.

Proponents of this model viewed prisons as artificial institutions that hindered offenders from finding a crime-free lifestyle. They argued that corrections should focus on providing psychological treatment and on increasing opportunities for offenders to succeed as citizens. Programs were supposed to help offenders find jobs and remain connected to their families and the community. Imprisonment was to be avoided, if possible, in favor of probation, so that offenders could seek education and vocational training that would help their adjustment. The small proportion of offenders who had to be incarcerated would spend a minimal amount of time in prison before release on parole. To promote reintegration, correctional workers were to serve as advocates for offenders in dealing with government agencies providing employment counseling, medical treatment, and financial assistance.

The community model dominated corrections until the late 1970s, when it gave way to a new punitiveness in criminal justice, in conjunction with the rebirth of the determinate sentence. Advocates of reintegration claimed, as did advocates of previous reforms, that the idea was never adequately tested. Nevertheless, community corrections remains one of the significant ideas and practices in the recent history of corrections.

Crime Control Model

As the political climate changed in the 1970s and 1980s, legislators, judges, and officials responded with an emphasis on crime control through incarceration and risk containment. The critique of rehabilitation led to changes in the sentencing structures in more than half of the states and the abolition of parole release in many. Compared with the community model, this **crime control model of corrections** is more punitive and makes greater use of incarceration (especially for violent offenders and career criminals), longer sentences, mandatory sentences, and strict supervision of probationers and parolees.

community corrections
A model of corrections based on the goal of reintegrating the offender into the community.

crime control model of corrections A model of corrections based on the assumption that criminal behavior can be controlled by more use of incarceration and other forms of strict supervision.

The effect of these get-tough policies shows in the record number of people incarcerated, the long terms being served, the great number of parolees returned to prison, and the huge size of the probation population. In some states, the political fervor to be tough on criminals has resulted in the reinstitution of chain gangs and the removal of television sets, body-building equipment, and college courses from prisons. Some advocates point to the crime control policies as the reason for the fall of the crime rate. Others ask whether the crime control policies are in fact the reason for the difference, considering the smaller number of men in the crime-prone age group and other changes in U.S. society.

The history of corrections in the United States reflects a series of swings from one model to another. The time may now be ripe for another look at correctional policy. The rhetoric used in criminal justice journals today differs markedly from that found in their pages 40 years ago. For example, the optimism that once suffused corrections has waned. Researchers are now scrutinizing the financial and human costs of the harsh crime control policies of recent decades. Are the costs of incarceration and surveillance justified? Has crime been reduced? Is society safer today than it was 25 years ago? Many researchers think not. Will corrections, then, find a new direction? If so, what will it be?

☑ CHECK POINT

1. **What was the Enlightenment, and how did it influence corrections?**
A period in the late eighteenth century when philosophers rethought the nature of society and the place of the individual in the world. The Enlightenment affected views on law and criminal justice; reformers began to raise questions about the nature of criminal behavior and the methods of punishment.

2. **How did the Pennsylvania and New York systems differ?**
The Pennsylvania system of separate confinement held inmates in isolation from one another. The New York congregate system kept inmates in their cells at night, but they worked together in shops during the day.

3. **What are the underlying assumptions of the rehabilitation, community, and crime control models of corrections?**
Rehabilitation model: Criminal behavior is the result of a biological, psychological, or social deficiency; clinicians should diagnose the problem and prescribe treatment; when cured, the offender may be released. *Community model:* The goal of corrections is to reintegrate the offender into the community, so rehabilitation should be carried out in the community rather than in prison if possible; correctional workers should serve as advocates for offenders in their dealings with government agencies. *Crime control model:* Criminal behavior can be controlled by greater use of incarceration and other forms of strict supervision.

STOP&ANALYZE

Do you foresee the current state budget crises affecting the states' future approach to corrections? Which approach is most likely to be emphasized in the future? Give two reasons for your answer.

Organization of Corrections in the United States

The organization of corrections in the United States is fragmented, with each level of government holding some responsibility. The federal government, the 50 states, the District of Columbia, the 3,047 counties, and most cities all have at least one correctional facility and many correctional programs. State and local governments pay about 95 percent of the cost of all correctional activities in the nation (BJS, 2014).

Federal Corrections System

The correctional responsibilities of the federal government are divided between the Department of Justice, which operates prisons through the Federal Bureau of Prisons, and the Administrative Office of the United States Courts, which covers probation and parole supervision.

Federal Bureau of Prisons   The Federal Bureau of Prisons, created by Congress in 1930, now operates a system of prisons located throughout the nation and housing over 216,000 inmates, supervised by a staff of more than 38,000. Approximately 80 percent of federal offenders are in facilities run by the Bureau of Prisons, but others are in privately run or community-based facilities (U.S. Bureau of Prisons, 2014). Facilities and inmates are classified by security level, ranging from Level 1 (the least secure, camp-type settings such as the Federal Prison Camp in Pensacola, Florida) through Level 5 (the most secure, such as the "supermax" penitentiary in Florence, Colorado). Between these extremes are Levels 2 through 4 federal correctional institutions—other U.S. penitentiaries, administrative institutions, medical facilities, and specialized institutions for women and juveniles. The Bureau of Prisons enters into contractual agreements with states, cities, and private agencies to provide community services such as halfway houses, prerelease programs, and electronic monitoring.

Federal Probation and Parole Supervision   Probation and parole supervision for federal offenders are provided by the Federal Probation and Pretrial Services System, a branch of the Administrative Office of the U.S. Courts. The federal judiciary appoints probation officers, who serve the court. The first full-time federal probation officer was appointed in 1927; today nearly 4,000 are assigned to the judicial districts across the country. They assist with presentence investigations but focus primarily on supervising offenders on probation and those released either on parole or by mandatory release.

State Corrections Systems

Although states vary considerably in how they organize corrections, in all states, the administration of prisons falls under the executive branch of state government. However, the judiciary often controls probation, parole may be separate from corrections, and in most states the county governments run the jails.

Community Corrections   States vary in how they carry out the community punishments of probation, intermediate sanctions, and parole. In many states, probation and intermediate sanctions are administered by the judiciary, often by county and municipal governments. By contrast, parole is a function of state government. The decision to release an offender from prison is made by the state parole board in those states with discretionary release. Parole boards are a part of either the department of corrections or an independent agency. In states with a mandatory system, the department of corrections makes the release. In all states, a state agency supervises the parolees.

State Prison Systems   A wide range of state correctional institutions, facilities, and programs exists for adult felons; these include prisons, reformatories, prison farms, forestry camps, and halfway houses. Because of the smaller female prisoner population, this variety does not exist for women.

States vary considerably in the number, size, type, and location of correctional facilities they have. Louisiana's state prison at Angola, for example, can hold 5,100 prisoners, whereas specialized institutions hold one hundred or fewer inmates. Some states (such as New Hampshire) have centralized incarceration in a few institutions, and other states (such as California, New York, and Texas) have a wide mix of sizes and styles—secure institutions, diagnostic units, work camps, forestry centers, and prerelease centers. For example, the website of the Pennsylvania Department of Corrections (2014) describes the state corrections system as follows:

> [T]he department—with a budget of $1.9 billion—oversees 25 state correctional institutions, one motivational boot camp, 14 community corrections centers, nearly 40 contract facilities, a training academy, approximately 15,000 employees and more than 51,300 inmates.

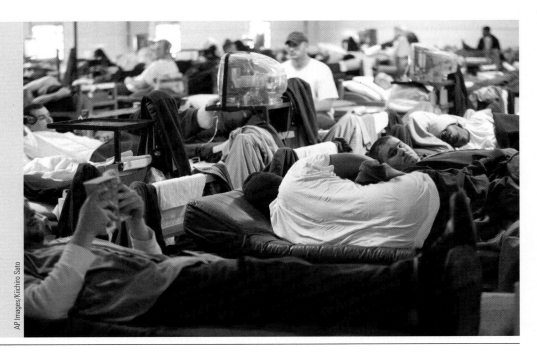

Prisoners in Ohio live under crowded conditions. Offenders in other states' prisons live under similarly crowded conditions. How should society address the issue of prison overcrowding?

AP Images/Kiichiro Sato

State correctional institutions for men are usually classified by level of security: maximum, medium, and minimum. For example, the website of the Minnesota Department of Corrections (2014) characterizes its prisons' security levels as "Level 2-Minimum," "Level-3 Medium," "Level-4 Close," and "Level 5-Maximum." Only one Minnesota prison is classified as Level 5. Each of the other security levels has three institutions, three of those have facilities designed to hold prisoners assigned to more than one security level. For example, the Minnesota prisons at Faribault and Lino Lakes have both Level 2 and Level 3 sections while Stillwater has Level 2 and Level 4 facilities.

Forty states have created prisons that exceed maximum security. An estimated 20,000 inmates are currently kept in these supermax prisons. These institutions, such as California's Pelican Bay and Connecticut's Northern Correctional Facility, hold the most disruptive, violent, and incorrigible offenders—the "toughest of the tough." In such institutions, inmates spend up to 23 hours a day in their cells. They are shackled whenever they are out of their cells—during recreation, showers, and telephone calls. All of these measures are designed to send a message to other inmates (Reiter, 2012).

The maximum-security prison (holding about 21 percent of state inmates) is built like a fortress, usually surrounded by stone walls with guard towers. It is designed to prevent escape. New facilities are surrounded by double rows of chain-link fences with rolls of razor wire in between and along the tops of the fences. Inmates live in cells that include plumbing and sanitary facilities. Some facilities' barred doors operate electronically so that an officer can confine all prisoners to their cells with the flick of a switch. The purposes of the maximum-security facility are custody and discipline. It maintains a military-style approach to order, with prisoners following a strict routine. Some of the most famous prisons, such as Attica (New York), Folsom (California), Stateville (Illinois), and Yuma (Arizona), are maximum-security facilities.

The medium-security prison (holding 40 percent of state inmates) externally resembles the maximum-security prison, but it is organized somewhat differently and its atmosphere is less rigid. Prisoners have more privileges and contact with the outside world through visitors, mail, and access to radio and television. The medium-security prison usually places greater emphasis than maximum-security prisons do on work and rehabilitative programs. Although the inmates may have committed serious crimes, they are not perceived as hardened criminals.

The minimum-security prison (with 33 percent of state inmates) houses the least violent offenders, long-term felons with clean disciplinary records, and inmates who have nearly completed their term. The minimum-security prison lacks the guard towers and stone walls associated with correctional institutions. Often chain-link fencing surrounds the buildings. Prisoners usually live in dormitories or even in small private rooms rather than in barred cells. There is more personal freedom: inmates may have television sets, choose their own clothes, and move about casually within the buildings. The system relies on rehabilitation programs and offers opportunities for education and work release. It also provides reintegration programs and support to inmates preparing for release.

In addition to the three types of institutions just described, a small percentage of state inmates are held in other settings such as work camps and county jails. Sentenced offenders may remain in local jails while they await transfer to a state prison or when there are agreements between state correctional officials and county sheriffs in response to overcrowding in state prisons. For example, beginning in October 2011, newly sentenced California offenders serving time for nonviolent, nonserious, nonsexual crimes will be sentenced to three years or less in county jails; this is a change from the previous practice of sending all offenders serving more than one year to state prison (Santos, 2013; "California's Prison Realignment," 2011).

Correctional officers face different challenges, depending on the security level of the institution in which they work. As you read about the job of a correctional officer in "Careers in Criminal Justice," ask yourself about the rewards, accomplishments, and other sources of job satisfaction that are available to those who work directly with prisoners.

State Institutions for Women   Only 7 percent of incarcerated people are women (Carson & Golinelli, 2013a). Although the ratio of arrests is approximately six men to one woman, the ratio in state and federal prisons is fourteen men to one woman. A higher proportion of female defendants are sentenced to probation and intermediate punishments, partly as a result of male offenders' tendency to commit most of the violent crimes. However, the growth rate in the number of incarcerated women has exceeded that for men in recent decades. From 2002 to 2012, the male population in state and federal prisons increased 9 percent, whereas that of women increased by nearly 12 percent (Carson & Golinelli, 2013a).

The increase in the number of women prisoners seems driven by the war on drugs. The growth also varies by state as, for example, Oklahoma incarcerates 10 times as many women per capita as Massachusetts and Rhode Island, largely due to punitive sentencing policies in drug cases (B. Palmer, 2011). This increase has significantly affected program delivery, housing conditions, medical care, staffing, and security (A. Wolf, Bloom, & Krisberg, 2008).

Conditions in correctional facilities for women are often more pleasant than those of similar institutions for men. Usually the buildings have no gun towers and barbed wire. Because of the small population, however, most states have only one facility, which is often located in a rural setting far removed from urban centers. Thus, women prisoners may be more isolated from their families and communities than male prisoners are.

Private Prisons

Corrections is a multibillion-dollar government-funded enterprise that purchases supplies and services from the private sector. Many jurisdictions have long contracted with private vendors to furnish food and medical services, educational and vocational training, maintenance, security, and the operation of aftercare facilities

Resident Unit Supervisor

Scott Yokum, Assistant Resident Unit Supervisor,
Michigan Reformatory Prison, Ionia, Michigan

The Michigan Reformatory is a multilevel facility that houses prisoners at both the Level 2 security status and the more restrictive Level 4 status. In addition, the Michigan Reformatory has a segregation unit that houses temporarily segregated prisoners and those on detention status.

Careers in most state departments of corrections typically begin with the position of corrections officer. In Michigan, job candidates are required to have taken college-level courses in corrections. When hired as corrections officers, they spend eight weeks in the state's corrections training academy, where they learn policy and procedures as well as weapons training and physical methods for controlling prisoners who threaten safety and security. They must pass a physical fitness test, written exams, and eventually a weapons qualification test. They subsequently spend eight weeks in on-the-job training while paired with a senior corrections officer. During the remainder of their first year on the job, they are probationary employees who are subject to dismissal for violating policies and procedures. Corrections officers oversee prisoners in common areas such as the yard and dining hall; conduct searches of prisoners and cells; write "tickets" when prisoners engage in misconduct; supervise prisoners' work assignments; and respond to calls for assistance when there are fights, assaults on staff, or medical emergencies.

Some corrections officers become resident unit officers who supervise prisoners within housing units, called "cell blocks" in some prisons. They share the same responsibilities as other corrections officers but have additional duties for controlling the movement of prisoners, conducting counseling sessions, and inspecting cells. The resident unit officers report to the Assistant Resident Unit Supervisor, who has oversight responsibilities for solving problems and ensuring the enforcement of policies and procedures in multiple housing units.

Scott Yokom earned an undergraduate degree in sociology with concentrations in criminal justice and social work and a minor in psychology—all fields that are relevant to his work in corrections. Currently working on a graduate degree in criminal justice, he began his career as a corrections officer. As he gained experience, he demonstrated the knowledge of policies and procedures, leadership abilities, decision-making skill in responding to problems, and communication skills that are necessary for promotion to supervisory positions. As Assistant Resident Unit Supervisor, he must identify and address problems caused by corrections officers' mistakes as well as issues that arise from prisoners' misbehavior or failure to understand institutional rules.

Photo provided by Scott Yokom

Most prisoners return to society. Our duty is not only to protect society by incapacitating the prisoner, but also to prepare them for their release so that they do not reoffend. We must deal every day with many prisoners who are hostile, manipulative, and violent. Working within corrections will change you, and it is up to you to decide if that change will be positive or negative. Thus, I often share with new employees a quote from an unknown source: "For those who fight evil and monsters must take care, that in the process, they themselves do not become evil and monstrous."

(Antonuccio, 2008). All of this has been referred to as the "prison-commercial complex," which we discuss later in the chapter.

One response to prison and jail crowding and rising staff costs has come from private entrepreneurs who argue that they can build and run prisons at least as effectively, safely, and humanely as any level of government can—and at a profit and a lower cost to taxpayers. The management of entire institutions for adult felons under private contract is a relatively new approach in corrections that was launched in the 1980s. Such privately run entities pose serious challenges for supervision and accountability as the government seeks to make sure that they are being run properly (Fathi, 2010).

By the end of 2009, the federal system and 32 states reported a total of 129,336 prisoners held in privately operated facilities. This figure reflected a slight decline in the total number of prisoners in private facilities after steady growth in the populations of such prisons from 2000 through 2008. States' budget cuts reduced opportunities for private prisons to make money by filling their cells with prisoners paid for by the government. Instead, the Corrections Corporation of America, for example, had 11,600 unoccupied beds in its facilities (N. Cook, 2010).

In 2010 private facilities held 8 percent of all state prisoners and 16 percent of all federal prisoners. Among the states, Texas, with 19,155 inmates housed in private facilities, plus Florida, with 11,796, and Oklahoma, with 6,019, reported the largest number. Seven states had nearly 25 percent or more of their prison population housed in private prisons, led by New Mexico (43.6 percent), Montana (40.4 percent), Alaska (33.5 percent), Hawaii (32.7 percent), Idaho (30.1 percent), Vermont (27.0 percent), and Mississippi (24.9). Other than Vermont, the only states outside the South and West that used private facilities for more than 10 percent of their prisoners were New Jersey (11.4 percent) and Indiana (10.1 percent) (BJS, 2014). In light of the American experience, interest in the private prison business has spread overseas to Australia, Great Britain, Brazil, and Denmark ("Private Jails," 2007).

In addition to inmates held for criminal offenses, 17 percent of the estimated 30,000 individuals detained by the Immigration and Customs Enforcement (ICE) agency of the U.S. Department of Homeland Security are held in private facilities. The increased pressure to enforce immigration laws has been a financial boon to the private prison industry (Berestein, 2008).

The $1 billion-a-year private prison business is dominated by two companies—Corrections Corporation of America (CCA) and the GEO Group (formerly known as the Wackenhut Corrections Corporation). CCA now operates the fifth largest correctional system in the United States. It currently manages 72,000 beds in 65 facilities in 19 states and the District of Columbia. This makes up half of all beds under contract. Today, because prison population reductions left many states with excess capacity in their own prisons, the growth of the private prison industry has leveled off. However, the federal government will continue to rely on private facilities to detain people who entered the country in violation of immigration laws and are awaiting hearings and deportation.

Advocates of privately operated prisons claim that they provide the same level of care as the states but do it more cheaply and flexibly (Antonuccio, 2008). Research on private prison, however, points to the difficulties of measuring the costs and quality of these institutions (Oppel, 2011). Many of the "true costs" (fringe benefits, contracting supervision, federal grants) are often not taken into consideration. A recent study of 48 juvenile correctional facilities found little difference between private and public institutions in terms of environmental quality (G. S. Armstrong & MacKenzie, 2003). The Bureau of Justice Statistics found that, compared with private prisons, a greater proportion of state facilities provide access to work, educational, and counseling programs (BJS, 2003). More recent studies continue to raise questions about whether private prisons actually provide the benefits that supporters claim (Kish & Lipton, 2013; Genter, Hooks, & Mosher, 2013).

Before corrections becomes too heavily committed to the private ownership and operation of prisons, it is hoped that researchers will examine many political, fiscal, ethical, and administrative issues. The political issues, including questions concerning the delegation of social-control functions to people other than state employees, may be the most difficult to overcome. Some people believe that the administration of justice is a basic function of government that should not be delegated. They fear that private operations would skew correctional policy, because contractors would use their political influence to continue programs not in the public interest. For example, in 2013 a newspaper's analysis of campaign contributions in Oklahoma found that private prison interests had contributed a total of nearly $200,000 in campaign dollars and gifts to 79 of the 149 members of the state legislature (Killman & Hoberock, 2013).

Some experts also fear that the private corporations will press to maintain high occupancy and will be interested only in skimming off the best inmates, leaving the most troublesome ones to the public corrections system. The profit incentive may also lead to corruption. In 2009, for example, two Pennsylvania juvenile court judges pleaded guilty to federal wire fraud and income tax fraud for taking more than $2.6 million in kickbacks to send teenagers to privately run youth detention centers (Urbina & Hamill, 2009). See the "Question of Ethics" feature at the end of the chapter to consider ethical issues that can arise when judges' sentences may be connected to their own interests.

Although some states have shown evidence of cost savings (J. F. Blumstein, Cohen, & Seth, 2008), the fiscal value of private corrections has not yet been fully demonstrated. However, labor unions have opposed these incursions into the public sector, pointing out that the salaries, benefits, and pensions of workers in spheres such as private security are lower than in their public counterparts. Finally, questions have arisen about quality of services, accountability of service providers to correctional officials, and problems related to contract supervision. Opponents cite the many instances in which privately contracted services in group homes, daycare centers, hospitals, and schools have been terminated because of reports of corruption, brutality, or substandard services. Research shows that staff turnover, escapes, and drug use are problems in many private prisons (S. D. Camp & Gales, 2002). Similar issues can also arise when prisons privatize certain aspects of their operations, such as hiring private companies to provide food services (Egan, 2014).

The idea of privately run correctional facilities has stimulated much interest among the general public and within the criminal justice community, but the future of this approach is quite uncertain. Ironically, despite the questions about the true costs and consequences of private prisons, budget-cutting governors who have a strong belief in the benefits of privatization continue to push for private prisons even without clear evidence of savings (Oppel, 2011).

Jails: Detention and Short-Term Incarceration

prison An institution for the incarceration of people convicted of serious crimes, usually felonies.

jail An institution authorized to hold pretrial detainees and sentenced misdemeanants for periods longer than 48 hours.

Most Americans do not distinguish between jails and prisons. A **prison** is a federal or state correctional institution that holds offenders who are sentenced to terms of more than one year. A **jail** is a local facility for the detention of people awaiting trial (about 50 percent of inmates) and sentenced misdemeanants. Jail also serves as a holding facility for social misfits—derelicts, drug addicts, prostitutes, the mentally ill, and disturbers of public order.

Of the 3,283 jails in the United States, 2,700 operate at the county level, with most administered by an elected sheriff. About 600 fall under municipal jurisdiction. Only in six states—Alaska, Connecticut, Delaware, Hawaii, Rhode Island, and Vermont—does the state administer jails for adults. There are also 13,500 police lockups and similar holding facilities authorized to detain people for up to 48 hours. The Federal Bureau of Prisons operates 12 jails that hold 14,000 inmates. More than 15,000 pretrial detainees and offenders are held in 37 private jails that operate under contract to state or local governments (BJS, 2014). On any given day during 2012, nearly 745,000 people were held in jails throughout the United States (Minton, 2013).

Increasingly, jails are being used to detain undocumented immigrants prior to the processing of charges or prior to deportation by U.S. Immigration and Customs Enforcement (ICE) of the Department of Homeland Security. In recent years, the federal crackdown on undocumented immigrants has escalated sharply. Holding ICE detainees not only adds to the overcrowding problems of some jails but is also costly to local governments, even with partial reimbursement by the federal government (Miroff, 2008).

Who Is in Jail? With an estimated 13 million jail admissions per year, more people directly experience jails than experience prisons, mental hospitals, and halfway houses combined. Even if we consider that some of the people represented in this total are admitted more than once, probably at least 6 to 7 million people are detained at some time during the year. Nationally, nearly 745,000 people, both the convicted and the unconvicted, sit in jail on any one day (Minton, 2013). However, the number of people held at any one time in jail does not tell the complete story.

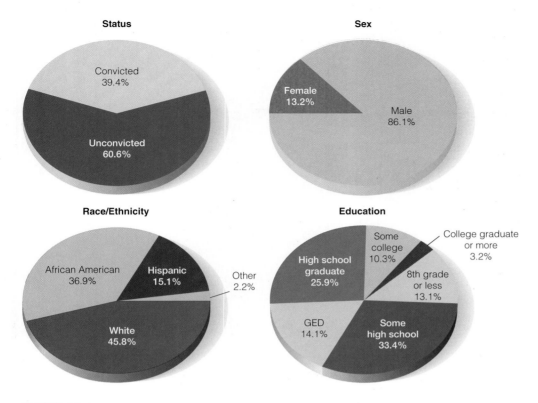

Status

Convicted 39.4%

Unconvicted 60.6%

Sex

Female 13.2%

Male 86.1%

Race/Ethnicity

African American 36.9%

Hispanic 15.1%

Other 2.2%

White 45.8%

Education

Some college 10.3%

College graduate or more 3.2%

High school graduate 25.9%

8th grade or less 13.1%

GED 14.1%

Some high school 33.4%

FIGURE 10.1

Characteristics of Adult Jail Inmates in U.S. Jails Compared with the American population as a whole, jails are disproportionately inhabited by men, minorities, the poorly educated, and those with low income.

Sources: Todd Minton, *Jail Inmates at Midyear 2012—Statistical Tables*, Washington, D.C.: Bureau of Justice Statistics, May 2013; C.W. Harlow, "Education and Correctional Populations," *Bureau of Justice Statistics Bulletin Special Report*, January 2003, p. 2. Percentages may not equal 100 due to incomplete data and rounding.

Many are held for less than 24 hours. A few may await their trial for more than a year. Others may reside in jail as sentenced offenders, typically for up to one year, but some states are now using jails to hold convicted offenders for as long as five years.

The most recent National Jail Census shows that about 87 percent of inmates are men, most are younger than 30 years old, less than half are white, and most have limited education and low incomes (Minton, 2011). A significant percentage of jail inmates have mental health problems (Petteruti & Walsh, 2008). During the last decade, as the country has become more anxious about immigrants, the jailing of people for immigration violations grew by 100 percent (Minton, 2011). The demographic characteristics of the jail population differ greatly from those of the national population (Figure 10.1).

Managing Jails Jail administrators face several problems that good management practices cannot always overcome. These problems include (1) the perceived role of the jail in the local criminal justice system, (2) the characteristics of the inmate population, and (3) fiscal problems. Read the feature on "Evidence-Based Practice and Policy" in jails to gain a greater understanding of the challenges facing administrators.

Role of the Jail As facilities to detain accused people awaiting trial, jails customarily have been run by law enforcement agencies. Most of the 150,000 correctional officers in the jail system work under the direction of the county sheriff. We might reasonably expect that the agency that arrests and transports

Jails contain both pre-trial detainees, who are presumptively innocent until proved guilty, and convicted offenders awaiting transfer to prison or serving short sentences. Should as-yet-unconvicted detainees, some of whom may eventually be found not guilty, experience the same conditions and deprivations as convicted offenders inside jails? Or should pretrial detainees be kept in separate areas and given more-extensive privileges? What if the jail lacks the space and resources to treat the groups differently?

Erica Brough/Gainesville Sun/Landov

defendants to court should also administer the facility that holds them. Typically, however, neither sheriffs nor deputies have much interest in corrections. Further, almost half the jail inmates are sentenced offenders under correctional authority. Thus, many experts argue that jails have outgrown police administration.

Inmate Characteristics

The mixture of offenders of widely diverse ages and criminal histories in U.S. jails is an often cited problem. Because criminal justice professionals view most inmates as temporary residents, they make little attempt to classify them for either security or treatment purposes. Horror stories of the mistreatment of young offenders by older, stronger, and more violent inmates occasionally come to public attention. The physical condition of most jails aggravates this situation, because most are old, overcrowded, and lacking in basic facilities. Many sentenced felons prefer to move on to state prison, where the conditions tend to be better.

Because inmate turnover is high and because local control provides an incentive to keep costs down, jails usually lack correctional services. They do not usually offer recreational facilities or treatment programs, and medical services are generally minimal. Such conditions add to the idleness and tensions of the inmates. Suicides and high levels of violence are hallmarks of many jails. In any one year, almost half the people who die while in jail have committed suicide.

Fiscal Problems

Jails help control crime but also drain local revenues. The tension between these two public interests often surfaces in debates over expenditures for jail construction and operation. Because revenues often fall short, many jails are overcrowded, lack programs, and do not have enough officers for effective supervision. In some areas, multicounty jails serve an entire region as a means of operating facilities in a cost-efficient way.

As criminal justice policy has become more punitive, jails, like prisons, have become crowded. Even with new construction and with alternatives such as release on recognizance (ROR) programs, diversion, intensive probation supervision, and house arrest with electronic monitoring, the jail population continues to rise.

Jail Management

In many areas of criminal justice, research aimed at developing evidence-based practices can focus on one or more specific goals. Thus, for policing, research has focused on such topics as how to deploy officers on patrol in order to reduce and prevent crime as well as methods for using force safely to incapacitate threatening people while minimizing the risk of injuries. In community corrections, research looks at specific programs for substance abuse treatment and reentry into society. By contrast, jails house a wide and changing array of detainees in a context of limited resources. As a result, numerous challenges face jail administrators that pose problems for identifying evidence-based practices, especially as the contexts of various jails can differ significantly.

One movement in jail design is the *direct supervision jail*. Twelve to 25 individual cells are organized into a unit (a "pod") that serves the function of a self-contained mini-jail. The cell doors open into a common living area, and a correctional officer is present at all times to supervise the small number of detainees. The small size and contained, completely visible area add to a sense of safety, familiarity, and comfort. Unfortunately, however, such ideal contexts typically are produced only through expensive new construction. Most jail administrators must handle existing facilities, including some jails that may be over a century old. Thus, jail administrators cannot easily control their own context in order to make it fit with the ideals of evidence-based practices for supervision and safety.

For certain matters, however, jail administrators may have control provided that they have sufficient resources. Thus, evidence-based practices can be useful for various aspects of jail management. One example is the classification procedures for arrestees to facilitate assignment within the jail according to security or medical needs. In addition, software systems for record keeping, training of officers, and security technology, such as cameras and fingerprint scanners, can help jails run more smoothly. They can also help to avoid the gravest risks, such as releasing the wrong detainee, failing to monitor detainees at risk for suicide, and providing insufficient supervision and security when detainees interact or move within the jail.

The other key area for evidence-based practices is programs. Because jails hold sentenced offenders as well as pretrial detainees, there is a need for effective substance abuse counseling, mental health treatment, and other programs. A variety of specific programs addressing social problems have been evaluated. Jails often adopt a course curriculum that has been effective in other institutions or has been promoted through materials and training from the federal government's National Institute of Corrections. Unfortunately, because of shrinking budgets and rapid turnover among jail inmates, this can be an especially difficult context for adopting and effectively implementing evidence-based practices. As a result, many jails may have trouble doing more than simply serving as holding facilities, even if their administrators aspire to adopt evidence-based practices in order to have a more positive impact on detainees and sentenced offenders.

Researching the Internet

Look at the wealth of materials and training programs at the National Institute of Corrections as it attempts to develop and share evidence-based practices for jails and prisons on its website http://nicic.gov/.

Implementing New Practices

If you were a sheriff who had just received a substantial grant from a private foundation for the purpose of adopting evidence-based practices, what would be your priorities? Would you invest in changes in the physical design of the facility, the management of the facility, or programs for detainees and offenders? What priority is most important for society? Write a memo describing your priorities, and give at least two reasons for your conclusions.

Sources: David Bogard, Virginia A. Hutchinson, and Vicci Persons, *Direct Supervision Jails: The Role of the Administrator.* Washington, D.C.: U.S. National Institute of Corrections, 2011; Jennifer Fratello, Tarika Daftary Kapur, and Alice Chasan, *Measuring Success: A Guide to Becoming an Evidence-Based Practice.* New York: Vera Institute of Justice, 2013; William Vetter, *Evidence-Based Practices: Substance Abuse Treatment and Jail Population Management.* Report to Pierce County (WA) Performance Audit Committee, February 27, 2008 (http://www.co.pierce.wa.us).

The annual cost of operating jails heavily burdens local governments, and this burden has become more difficult in an era of budget cuts and layoffs of sheriff's deputies and other jail officers. In New Jersey, for example, the Camden County Jail was forced to lay off 60 corrections officers in 2011—one-quarter of the workforce—due to severe budget difficulties, even though the facility handles a high volume of detainees in one of the most crime-plagued places in the state (Osborne, 2011).

4. **What agencies of the U.S. government are responsible for prisons and probation?**
   The Federal Bureau of Prisons, which handles prisons, and the Administrative Office of the U.S. Courts, which handles probation.

5. **What agencies of state government are responsible for prisons, probation, intermediate sanctions, and parole?**
   Prisons: department of corrections (executive branch); *probation:* judiciary or executive department; *intermediate sanctions:* judiciary, probation department, department of corrections; *parole:* executive agency.

6. **What are the functions of jails?**
   Holding of offenders before trial and incarceration of offenders sentenced to short terms.

Does a philosophical problem arise when convicted offenders are sent to privately run prisons and jails? In criminal law, the government imposes punishment on people for breaking the laws made by the government. Does this mean that only the government should administer the punishment? List two arguments either supporting or opposing the idea that all criminal punishment should be administered by government.

The Law of Corrections

hands-off policy Judges should not interfere with the administration of correctional institutions.

Prior to the 1960s, most courts maintained a **hands-off policy** with respect to corrections. Only a few state courts had recognized rights for offenders. Most judges felt that prisoners and probationers did not have protected rights and that courts should not interfere with the operational agencies dealing with probation, prisons, and parole.

Since the 1960s, however, offenders have gained access to the courts to contest correctional officers' decisions and challenge aspects of their punishment that they believe violate basic rights. Judicial decisions have defined and recognized the constitutional rights of probationers, prisoners, and parolees, as well as the need for policies and procedures that respect those rights. As you read "Criminal Justice: Myth & Reality," consider your own views about the recognition of constitutional rights for convicted criminal offenders.

Constitutional Rights of Prisoners

Cooper v. Pate (1964) Prisoners are entitled to the protection of the Civil Rights Act of 1871 and may challenge in federal courts the conditions of their confinement.

The U.S. Supreme Court decision in ***Cooper v. Pate*** (1964) signaled the end of the hands-off policy. The court said that through the Civil Rights Act of 1871 (referred to here as Section 1983), state prisoners were *persons* whose rights are protected by the Constitution. The act imposes *civil liability* on any official who violates someone's constitutional rights. It allows suits against state officials to be heard in the federal courts. Because of *Cooper v. Pate*, the federal courts now recognize that prisoners may sue state officials over such things as brutality by guards, inadequate nutrition and medical care, theft of personal property, and the denial of basic rights.

The first successful prisoners' rights cases involved the most excessive of prison abuses: brutality and inhumane physical conditions. Gradually, however, prison litigation has focused more directly on the daily activities of the institution, especially on the administrative rules that regulate inmates' conduct (C. E. Smith, 2007). This focus has resulted in a series of court decisions concerning the First, Fourth, Eighth, and Fourteenth Amendments to the Constitution. (See Chapter 3 for the full text of these amendments.)

First Amendment The First Amendment guarantees freedom of speech, press, assembly, petition, and religion. In the courts, prisoners have successfully challenged many of the restrictions of prison life—access to reading materials, censorship of mail, and rules affecting some religious practices (A. C. Burns, 2007). However, the Supreme Court has also approved restrictions on access to written materials, including Pennsylvania's denial of access to newspapers and magazines for prisoners housed in a disciplinary segregation unit (*Beard v. Banks*, 2006).

Since 1970 courts have extended the rights of freedom of speech and expression to prisoners. They have required correctional administrators to show why restrictions on these rights must be imposed. For example, in 1974 the Supreme Court ruled that censorship of mail was permissible only when officials could demonstrate a compelling government interest in maintaining security (*Procunier v. Martinez*). Communication between inmates and the outside world has since increased markedly. However, in *Turner v. Safley* (1987), the Court upheld a Missouri ban on correspondence between inmates in different institutions, as a means of combating gang violence and the communication of escape plans.

The First Amendment prevents Congress from making laws respecting the establishment of religion or prohibiting its free exercise. Cases concerning the free exercise of religion have caused the judiciary some problems, especially when the religious practice may interfere with prison routine and the maintenance of order.

The growth of the Black Muslim religion in prisons set the stage for suits demanding that this group be granted the same privileges as other faiths (special diets, access to clergy and religious publications, opportunities for group worship). Attorneys for the Muslims succeeded in winning several important cases that helped establish for prisoners the First Amendment right to free exercise of religion. These decisions also helped Native Americans, Orthodox Jews, and other prisoners to practice their religions. Court decisions have upheld prisoners' rights to be served meals consistent with religious dietary laws, to correspond with religious leaders, to possess religious literature, to wear a beard if their belief requires it, and to assemble for services. In sum, members of religious minorities have broken new legal ground on First Amendment issues.

Issues concerning freedom of religion continue to be raised with regularity by contemporary prisoners. For example, in 2013 John Walker Lindh, widely labeled by the news media as "the American Taliban," won a court order permitting him to join with other Muslim prisoners in daily group prayers within a federal prison in Indiana (*Lindh v. Warden*, 2013). Lindh was a middle-class American from California who converted to Islam as a teenager and moved to the Middle and Near East to study languages and religion. He ended up joining an al Qaeda group defending the Taliban government of Afghanistan in 2001 and was captured by American-backed military forces when the Taliban government was overthrown after 9/11. Lindh is serving a 20-year sentence after pleading guilty to providing services for the Taliban government and carrying weapons in opposition to U.S.-backed forces. Although Lindh was labeled as a "traitor" by many Americans, our legal system recognizes that he is entitled to rights under the Constitution.

Fourth Amendment The Fourth Amendment prohibits *unreasonable* searches and seizures, but courts have extended only very limited protections to prisoners.

CRIMINAL JUSTICE
MYTH&REALITY

COMMON BELIEF: People convicted of crimes should forfeit all constitutional rights, because they have violated laws and harmed people. They have broken their "social contract" with our country, through which they receive the benefits of rights and the opportunity for economic success in exchange for their commitment to follow the country's rules.

- The U.S. Constitution does not make the possession of rights contingent on specific behavior. In fact, many provisions of the Bill of Rights are clearly written as specific limitations on what the government can do to people, including people who commit crimes.
- The Eighth Amendment's prohibition on "cruel and unusual punishments" implies that there are limits on what the government may do to criminal offenders. If offenders literally had no rights, they could be tortured, starved, and killed without any legal intervention to save them.
- Is the American value of justice upheld if an 18-year-old who is sentenced to two years in prison for stealing cars can be beaten, starved, deprived of medical care, and even killed because he has no rights whatsoever? In other words, should a short prison sentence actually be a potential death sentence, even for nonviolent offenders?
- As you shall see, prisoners have very limited rights that are defined in light of the institution's needs to maintain safety and security. These rights establish a basis for humane treatment from institutions that carry out the punishments announced by the court.
- Punishment for incarcerated offenders is the loss of their liberty for a period of time under strict conditions. Such punishment is not supposed to include a potentially deadly environment in which they have no entitlement to food, shelter, protection from violence, or treatment for serious illnesses.
- Is there widespread agreement about exactly which rights prisoners should possess? No. However, American history itself demonstrates that an absence of rights creates risks of abuses that are contrary to our country's conceptions of justice.

Hudson v. Palmer (1984)
Prison officials have the
authority to search cells and
confiscate any materials
found.

Thus, prison regulations viewed as reasonable to maintain security and order in an institution may justify searches that would not be permitted in other contexts. For example, *Hudson v. Palmer* (1984) upheld the authority of officials to search cells and confiscate any materials found without any suspicion of wrongdoing by the prisoner or other justification for the search.

The Supreme Court's opinions with regard to the Fourth Amendment reveal the balance between institutional need and the right to privacy. Body searches have been harder for administrators to justify than cell searches, for example. But body searches have been upheld when they advance policies clearly related to identifiable and legitimate institutional needs and when they are not intended to humiliate or degrade (*Bell v. Wolfish*, 1979). In a recent decision, the U.S. Supreme Court cleared up disagreements in lower courts by declaring that people who are arrested can be strip-searched upon entering a jail, even if they are only charged with very minor offenses and there is no specific reason to believe that they are hiding drugs or weapons on their bodies (*Florence v. Board of Chosen Freeholders*, 2012). The Supreme Court declared that jails' security needs outweighed the intrusion on the privacy of people arrested for minor offenses.

Eighth Amendment   The Constitution's prohibition of cruel and unusual punishments has been tied to prisoners' needs for decent treatment and minimum health standards. The courts have traditionally applied three principal tests under the Eighth Amendment to determine whether conditions are unconstitutional: (1) whether the punishment shocks the conscience of a civilized society, (2) whether the punishment is unnecessarily cruel, and (3) whether the punishment goes beyond legitimate penal aims. In the past two decades, however, courts have coupled their concerns about these issues with a focus on the intentions of correctional administrators, especially the question of whether officials intentionally ignored problems within their institutions.

Federal courts have ruled that although some aspects of prison life may be acceptable, the combination of various factors—the *totality of conditions*—may be such that life in the institution constitutes cruel and unusual punishment. When courts have found brutality, unsanitary facilities, overcrowding, and inadequate food, judges have used the Eighth Amendment to order sweeping changes and even, in some cases, to take over administration of entire prisons or corrections systems. In these cases, judges have ordered wardens to follow specific internal procedures and to spend money on certain improvements. The U.S. Supreme Court has instructed lower court judges to focus findings of Eighth Amendment violations on those situations in which correctional officials showed "deliberate indifference" to substandard living conditions (*Wilson v. Seiter*, 1991).

In 2011, a closely divided U.S. Supreme Court upheld lower court decisions ordering California to reduce its prison population because overcrowded conditions had overwhelmed the prison system's ability to provide proper health care and mental health treatment for prisoners (*Brown v. Plata*, 2011). The competing opinions issued in the case illustrated continuing divisions among the justices about forcing prisons to uphold certain standards for living conditions as opposed to permitting states to handle their own issues and avoid the risk that public safety would be threatened by early releases (C. E. Smith, 2013. In actuality, rather than use the mass releases that some justices feared, the state reduced prison populations by shifting nonviolent, nonserious, and nonsex offenders to serve shorter sentences in county jails rather than in state prisons (Carson & Golinelli, 2013b). Read the Close Up feature on the Supreme Court opinions in *Brown v. Plata* to consider for yourself if the majority of justices went too far in ordering changes in California's prisons.

Fourteenth Amendment   One word and two clauses of the Fourteenth Amendment are key to the question of prisoners' rights. The relevant word is *state*, which is found in several clauses of the Fourteenth Amendment. It was not until the 1960s that the Supreme Court ruled that through the Fourteenth Amendment, the Bill of Rights restricts state government actions affecting criminal justice.

The first important clause concerns procedural due process, which requires that government officials treat all people fairly and justly and that official decisions be made according to procedures prescribed by law. The second important clause is the equal protection clause. Assertions that prisoners have been denied equal protection of the law are based on claims of racial, gender, or religious discrimination.

Due Process in Prison Discipline   In *Wolff v. McDonnell* (1974), the Supreme Court ruled that basic procedural rights must be present when decisions are made about the disciplining of inmates for serious infractions of prison rules. Specifically, prisoners have the right to receive notice of the complaint, to have a fair hearing, to confront witnesses, to get help in preparing for the hearing, and to be given a written statement of the decision. However, the Court also recognized special conditions of incarceration in that prisoners do not have the right to cross-examine witnesses and that the evidence presented by the offender shall not be unduly hazardous to institutional safety or correctional goals.

As a result of these Supreme Court decisions, prison officials have established rules that provide elements of due process in disciplinary and other proceedings. In many institutions, a disciplinary committee receives the charges, conducts hearings, and decides guilt and punishment. Even with these protections, prisoners remain powerless and may risk further punishment if they challenge the warden's decisions too vigorously.

Equal Protection   In 1968 the Supreme Court firmly established that racial discrimination cannot be official policy within prison walls (*Lee v. Washington*). Segregation can be justified only in rare instances by compelling circumstances, such as a temporary expedient during periods when violence between races is demonstrably imminent (*Johnson v. California*, 2005). In recent decades, some cases have concerned equal protection issues affecting female offenders. Judges in state courts and lower federal courts have addressed these issues. For example, in a series of decisions spanning nearly two decades, female inmates in Michigan successfully argued that their equal protection rights were violated because programs and services for them were not as good as those provided to male inmates (*Glover v. Johnson*, 1991). Critics who believe that prisons neglect the needs of women prisoners argue that judges have generally permitted too many differences in facilities and programs for women without providing sufficient attention to issues of equality (Carroll-Ferrary, 2006).

Impact of the Prisoners' Rights Movement   The Supreme Court in recent years has reduced its support of the expansion of prisoners' rights (C. E. Smith, 2011). Nonetheless, the prisoners' rights movement has spurred some positive changes in American corrections since the late 1970s. The most obvious are improvements in institutional living conditions and administrative practices. Law libraries and legal assistance are now generally available, communication with the outside is easier, religious practices are protected, inmate complaint procedures have been developed,

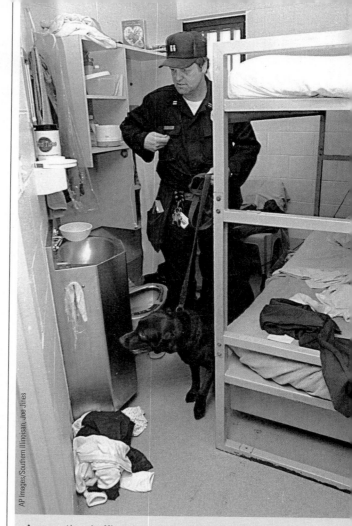

AP Images/Southern Illinoisan, Joe Jines

A correctional officer leads a "sniffer" dog through a cell at Big Muddy Correctional Center in Ina, Illinois. A 150-member tactical team conducted this search without giving the prisoners any prior warning. Is there anything that officers might do during such a search that would violate a prisoner's Fourth Amendment right against unreasonable searches and seizures?

Wolff v. McDonnell (1974)
Basic elements of procedural due process must be present when decisions are made about imposing significant punishments on prisoners for violating institutional rules.

The U.S. Supreme Court's Decision in *Brown v. Plata* (2011)

Justice Anthony Kennedy wrote the majority opinion on behalf of a narrow five-justice majority. Justice Antonin Scalia wrote a dissenting opinion joined by Justice Clarence Thomas. Justice Samuel Alito wrote a separate dissenting opinion joined by Chief Justice John Roberts. Justice Kennedy focused on the constitutional rights violations that the majority viewed as in need of remedy. By contrast, Justice Scalia argued that the courts had gone too far in telling California how to run its prisons. Justice Alito expressed his fears that public safety would be harmed by a reduction in prison populations.

JUSTICE KENNEDY delivered the opinion of the Court.

This case arises from serious constitutional violations in California's prison system. The violations have persisted for years. They remain uncorrected. . . .

After years of litigation, it became apparent that a remedy for constitutional violations would not be effective absent a reduction in the prison system population. . . . The order leaves the choice of means to reduce overcrowding to the discretion of state officials. But absent compliance through new construction, out-of-state transfers, or other means—or modification of the order upon a further showing by the State—the State will be required to release some number of prisoners before their full sentences have been served. High recidivism rates must serve as a warning that mistaken or premature release of even one prisoner can cause injury and harm. The release of prisoners in large numbers—assuming the State finds no other way to comply with the order—is a matter of undoubted, grave concern.

At the time of trial, California's correctional facilities held some 156,000 persons. This is nearly double the number that California's prisons were designed to hold, and California has been ordered to reduce its prison population to 137.5% of design capacity. By the three-judge court's own estimate, the required population reduction could be as high as 46,000 persons. Although the State has reduced the population by at least 9,000 persons during the pendency of this appeal, this means a further reduction of 37,000 persons could be required. As will be noted, the reduction need not be accomplished in an indiscriminate manner or in these substantial numbers if satisfactory, alternate remedies or means for compliance are devised. The State may employ measures, including good-time credits and diversion of low-risk offenders and technical parole violators to community-based programs, that will mitigate the order's impact. The population reduction potentially required is nevertheless of unprecedented sweep and extent.

Yet so too is the continuing injury and harm resulting from these serious constitutional violations. For years the medical and mental health care provided by California's prisons has fallen short of minimum constitutional requirements and has failed to meet prisoners' basic health needs. Needless suffering and death have been the well-documented result. Over the whole course of years during which this litigation has been pending, no other remedies have been found to be sufficient. Efforts to remedy the violation have been frustrated by severe overcrowding in California's prison system. Short term gains in the provision of care have been eroded by the long-term effects of severe and pervasive overcrowding.

Overcrowding has overtaken the limited resources of prison staff; imposed demands well beyond the capacity of medical and mental health facilities; and created unsanitary and unsafe conditions that make progress in the provision of care difficult or impossible to achieve. . . .

The degree of overcrowding in California's prisons is exceptional. California's prisons are designed to house a population just under 80,000, but at the time of the three-judge court's decision the population was almost double that. The State's prisons had operated at around 200% of design capacity for at least 11 years. Prisoners are crammed into spaces neither designed nor intended to house inmates. As many as 200 prisoners may live in a gymnasium, monitored by as few as two or three correctional officers. . . . As many as 54 prisoners may share a single toilet. . . .

The Corrections Independent Review Panel, a body appointed by the Governor and composed of correctional consultants and representatives from state agencies, concluded that California's prisons are "'severely overcrowded, imperiling the safety of both correctional employees and inmates.'" . . .

Prisoners in California with serious mental illness do not receive minimal, adequate care. Because of a shortage of treatment beds, suicidal inmates may be held for prolonged periods in telephone-booth sized cages without toilets. . . . A psychiatric expert reported observing an inmate who had been held in such a cage for nearly 24 hours, standing in a pool of his own urine, unresponsive and nearly catatonic. Prison officials explained they had "'no place to put him.'" . . . Other inmates awaiting care may be held for months in administrative segregation, where they endure harsh and isolated conditions and receive only limited mental health services. Wait times for mental health care range as high as. . . . In 2006, the suicide rate in California's prisons was nearly 80% higher than the national average for prison populations; and a court appointed Special Master found that 72.1% of suicides involved "some measure of inadequate assessment, treatment, or intervention, and were therefore most probably foreseeable and/or preventable." . . .

Prisoners suffering from physical illness also receive severely deficient care. California's prisons were designed to meet the medical needs of a population at 100% of design capacity and so have only half the clinical space needed to treat the current population. . . . A correctional officer testified that, in one prison, up to 50 sick inmates may be held together in a 12-by 20-foot

and due process requirements are emphasized. Prisoners in solitary confinement undoubtedly suffer less neglect than they did in the past. Although overcrowding remains a major problem, many conditions have greatly improved, and the most brutalizing elements of prison life have diminished.

cage for up to five hours awaiting treatment. . . . The number of staff is inadequate, and prisoners face significant delays in access to care. A prisoner with severe abdominal pain died after a 5-week delay in referral to a specialist; a prisoner with "constant and extreme" chest pain died after an 8-hour delay in evaluation by a doctor; and a prisoner died of testicular cancer after a "failure of MDs to work up for cancer in a young man with 17 months of testicular pain." . . . Doctor Ronald Shansky, former medical director of the Illinois state prison system, surveyed death reviews for California prisoners. He concluded that extreme departures from the standard of care were "widespread," . . . and that the proportion of "possibly preventable or preventable" deaths was "extremely high." . . . Many more prisoners, suffering from severe but not life-threatening conditions, experience prolonged illness and unnecessary pain. . . .

. . .The medical and mental health care provided by California's prisons falls below the standard of decency that inheres in the Eighth Amendment. This extensive and ongoing constitutional violation requires a remedy, and a remedy will not be achieved without a reduction in overcrowding. The relief ordered by the three-judge court is required by the Constitution and was authorized by Congress in the [Prison Litigation Reform Act]. The State shall implement the order without further delay.

Justice SCALIA, with whom Justice THOMAS joins, dissenting.

Today the Court affirms what is perhaps the most radical injunction issued by a court in our Nation's history: an order requiring California to release the staggering number of 46,000 convicted criminals.

There comes before us, now and then, a case whose proper outcome is so clearly indicated by tradition and common sense, that its decision ought to shape the law, rather than vice versa. One would think that, before allowing the decree of a federal district court to release 46,000 convicted felons, this Court would bend every effort to read the law in such a way as to avoid that outrageous result. Today, quite to the contrary, the Court disregards stringently drawn provisions of the governing statute, and traditional constitutional limitations upon the power of a federal judge, in order to uphold the absurd.

The proceedings that led to this result were a judicial travesty. I dissent because the institutional reform the District Court has undertaken violates the terms of the governing statute, ignores bedrock limitations on the power of Article III judges, and takes federal courts wildly beyond their institutional capacity. . . .

Justice ALITO, with whom THE CHIEF JUSTICE joins, dissenting.

The decree in this case is a perfect example of what the Prison Litigation Reform Act of 1995 . . . was enacted to prevent.

The Constitution does not give federal judges the authority to run state penal systems. Decisions regarding state prisons have profound public safety and financial implications, and the States are generally free to make these decisions as they choose. . . .

The three-judge court ordered the premature release of approximately *46,000 criminals—the equivalent of three Army divisions. . . .*

. . . The three-judge court would have us believe that the early release of 46,000 inmates will not imperil—and will actually improve—public safety. . . . Common sense and experience counsel greater caution.

I would reverse the decision below for three interrelated reasons. First, the three-judge court improperly refused to consider evidence concerning present conditions in the California prison system. Second, the court erred in holding that no remedy short of a massive prisoner release can bring the California system into compliance with the Eighth Amendment. Third, the court gave inadequate weight to the impact of its decree on public safety. . . .

. . . The prisoner release program carried out a few years earlier in Philadelphia is illustrative. In the early 1990's, federal courts enforced a cap on the number of inmates in the Philadelphia prison system, and thousands of inmates were set free. Although efforts were made to release only those prisoners who were least likely to commit violent crimes, that attempt was spectacularly unsuccessful. During an 18-month period, the Philadelphia police rearrested thousands of these prisoners for committing 9,732 new crimes. Those defendants were charged with 79 murders, 90 rapes, 1,113 assaults, 959 robberies, 701 burglaries, and 2,748 thefts, not to mention thousands of drug offenses. . . .

The prisoner release ordered in this case is unprecedented, improvident, and contrary to the PLRA. In largely sustaining the decision below, the majority is gambling with the safety of the people of California. Before putting public safety at risk, every reasonable precaution should be taken. The decision below should be reversed, and the case should be remanded for this to be done.

I fear that today's decision, like prior prisoner release orders, will lead to a grim roster of victims. I hope that I am wrong.

In a few years, we will see.

Researching the Internet
To read the Supreme Court's complete opinion, visit http://www.supremecourt.gov/opinions/10pdf/09-1233.pdf.

For Critical Analysis
Which justice was most persuasive? If you agree with one of the dissenters, can you identify a different way to correct the problems in the prisons? Write a memo explaining what you would say if you wrote an opinion for the Supreme Court in this case.

These changes did not entirely result from court orders, however. They also coincided with the growing influence of college-educated correctional professionals who sought on their own to improve prisons (C. E. Smith, 2000a). There are, however, lingering debates about whether judges have intruded improperly.

Should Judges Defer to Decisions of Prison Officials?

As you saw in the Close Up example of the Supreme Court justices' competing opinions in *Brown v. Plata* (2011), there are significant disagreements about whether and when it is proper for judges to order changes in prison policies and practices. Everyone agrees that judges bear responsibility for identifying constitutional rights violations in prisons. However, judges and commentators express strong disagreements about the rights to which convicted offenders are entitled and how broadly those rights should be defined.

Moreover, heated controversies arise when judges do not merely identify rights violations, but actually issue detailed orders about needed changes in prisons in order to remedy rights violations. Some of these remedies, such as constructing new facilities or hiring more staff, could impose significant financial expenses. Other orders were viewed by critics as threatening order and security in prisons. Prison officials argue that judges should leave it to them to figure out how to fix problems while also maintaining safety and security. After all, it is prison officials rather than judges who have training and experience in prison administration. Thus, state officials resisted court orders to reduce prison populations in *Brown v. Plata* (2011). In *Johnson v. California* (2005) concerning Fourteenth Amendment equal protection issues, prison officials argued unsuccessfully that they needed to separate prisoners by race and ethnicity during initial processing in order to avoid violence between race-based gangs.

Governors whose prisons were affected by court orders lobbied Congress to enact laws that would limit the authority of judges. Congress passed the Prison Litigation Reform Act in 1996 that limited the authority of individual federal judges to order reductions in prison populations. It also required that judges' orders expire after two years unless new hearings took place to prove that there were continuing rights violations. In addition, the law limited the ability of prisoners to file repeated lawsuits over rights violations if they could not pay their own court fees. Three unsuccessful lawsuits that were deemed to be "frivolous" forfeited future opportunities for individual prisoners to ask the courts to waive filing fees for subsequent rights-violation lawsuits, even for matters related to such issues as sexual assaults or violations of religious rights.

For Judges' Deference to Prison Officials

- Prison officials rather than judges are the actual experts on what policies and procedures need to be imposed to maintain safety and security in prisons.
- Judges, who lack training and experience in corrections, may impose orders that cause difficult problems in prisons.
- Judges' orders may impose needless expenses whereas prison officials, if left to handle their own problems, could develop effective, less costly solutions.
- Judges' orders that include expensive remedies, such as the construction of new facilities or the hiring of staff, improperly affect state government budgets and taxes by forcing money to be shifted away from other priorities such as schools and road construction.
- Judges' orders can make prisoners bolder in filing additional lawsuits, resisting prison rules and regulations, and

Read "The Policy Debate" to consider the long-running dispute about whether judges should avoid telling prison officials how corrections institutions should be run.

Law and Community Corrections

Although most correctional law concerns prisons and jails, two-thirds of adults under supervision live in the community on probation and parole. However, as with prisoners, offenders in the community have certain rights, and courts have addressed issues concerning due process and searches and seizures.

Probationers and parolees must live according to conditions specified at the time of their sentencing or parole release. These conditions may interfere with their constitutional rights in that they typically limit the right of free association by restricting offenders from contact with their crime partners or victims. However, courts have struck down conditions that prevented parolees from exercising their First Amendment rights to give public speeches and receive publications.

The case of *Griffin v. Wisconsin* (1987) presents a good example of the clash between the Fourth Amendment and community corrections. Learning that Griffin might have a gun, probation officers searched his apartment without a warrant. Noting the practical problems of obtaining a search warrant while a probationer was under supervision, the Supreme Court said that the probation agency must be able to act before the offender damages himself or society. In Griffin's case, the Court felt that the agency had satisfied the Fourth Amendment's reasonableness requirement.

assuming that they can use the courts to force changes in aspects of prison operations that they do not like.

For Judges' Independence in Upholding Constitutional Rights

- Judges swear an oath to uphold the Constitution, which includes the responsibility to make absolutely sure that constitutional rights are respected in prison.
- There is a long history in the United States of officials in many prisons failing to respect the constitutional rights of prisoners.
- Without strong orders from judges, prison officials will not receive needed money from state legislatures in order to genuinely fix problems related to certain constitutional-rights problems, such as inadequate medical care.
- Prison officials often use the claim of safety and security issues too broadly as a means to deny access to non-threatening elements of constitutional rights, such as First Amendment access to reading materials or opportunities for certain kinds of religious worship.
- Because prisons are closed institutions that cannot be scrutinized by the news media or the public, judges must have the authority to look closely at what happens inside in order to identify and fix problems as well as ensure that relevant laws are being followed.

What Should U.S. Policy Be?

The debates about judges' roles illustrate the risks and benefits of strong court actions to supervise and correct problems in prisons. Perspectives on this debate are often driven by very different viewpoints about whether prisoners have too many rights or, alternatively, inadequate protection under the Constitution. Where do you stand on this latter issue of adequacy and extensiveness of constitutional rights for prisoners? Too many rights or too few? Does your perspective on this issue affect how you evaluate the proper role of judges in prison litigation?

Researching the Internet

To read about criticisms of the Prison Litigation Reform Act and its limitations on opportunities to protect convicted offenders' rights, visit https://www.acslaw.org/files/Schlanger%20Shay%20PLRA%20Paper%203-28-07.pdf.

Analyzing the Issue

Imagine that you and your classmates are on a panel of federal appellate court judges considering a claim that convicted offenders in a women's prisons have been denied equal protection of the law under the Fourteenth Amendment. Assume that you all agree that rights violations have occurred under the Fourteenth Amendment because, unlike in men's prisons, there is no gymnasium for prisoners to have indoor exercise during bad weather and there is no vocational program to teach women prisoners job skills in electronics and computer repair. In addition, no one on the medical staff specializes in women's issues, an issue that is not relevant in men's prisons. What do you say in your decision about the case? Do you order specific remedies for these problems? Do you leave it to prison officials to come up with solutions, even though they say that they will have to develop solutions without spending any additional money due to budget cuts? Can you and your fellow "judges" agree on what the court's decision should say?

Similarly, in *Samson v. California* (2006), the Supreme Court approved a California statute that requires every parolee to agree to be subject to warrantless searches, even in the absence of any suspicion of wrongdoing.

When parole is revoked, prisoners are returned to prison to complete their sentences. Before that happens, a revocation hearing takes place. In a 1998 case, *Pennsylvania Board of Pardons and Parole v. Scott*, a closely divided Court ruled that evidence that would be barred from use in a criminal trial can be used in parole revocation hearings. Operating without a search warrant, officers found guns in the home of a paroled murderer who was barred from owning weapons. Although the Pennsylvania courts decided that an improper search had been conducted, the U.S. Supreme Court concluded that the weapons could be used as evidence at a parole revocation hearing despite any Fourth Amendment violations that may have occurred. The exclusionary rule does not apply to parole revocation proceedings.

The Supreme Court has also addressed the question of due process when revocation is being considered. In *Morrissey v. Brewer* (1972), the court ruled that parolees facing revocation must be given a two-stage hearing process. In the first stage, a hearing officer determines whether there is probable cause that a violation has occurred. Parolees have the right to be notified of the charges against them, to know the evidence against them, to be allowed to speak on their own behalf, to present witnesses, and to confront the witnesses against them. In the second stage, the revocation hearing, the parolee must receive a notice of charges, the evidence of a violation is disclosed, and he or she may cross-examine witnesses. The hearing body determines

Morrissey v. Brewer (1972)
Due process rights require a prompt, informal, two-stage inquiry before an impartial hearing officer before parole may be revoked. The parolee may present relevant information and confront witnesses.

if the violation is sufficiently severe to warrant revocation. It must give the parolee a written statement outlining the evidence, with reasons for the decision.

In the following year, the Supreme Court applied the *Morrissey* procedures to probation revocation proceedings in *Gagnon v. Scarpelli* (1973). In this case, however, the Court also looked at the question of the right to counsel. It ruled that there was no absolute requirement but that in some cases probationers and parolees might request counsel, to be allowed on a case-by-case basis depending on the complexity of the issues, mitigating circumstances, and the competence of the offender.

Law and Correctional Personnel

Just as law governs relationships among inmates, probationers, and parolees, laws and regulations also define the relationships between correctional administrators and their staff. With the exception of those working for private, nonprofit organizations, correctional personnel are public employees. Here we consider two important aspects of correctional work. First, as public employees, all correctional employees are governed by civil service rules and regulations. Second, correctional clients may sue state employees using Section 1983 of the United States Code.

Civil Service Laws   Civil service laws set the procedures for hiring, promoting, assigning, disciplining, and firing public employees. These laws protect public employees from arbitrary actions by their supervisors. Workplace rules also come to be developed through collective-bargaining agreements between correctional-employee unions and the government. These agreements have the force of law and contain rules concerning assignments, working conditions, and grievance procedures.

Like their counterparts in the private sector, government employees are protected from discrimination. With the Civil Rights Act of 1964, Congress prohibited employment discrimination based on race, gender, national origin, and religion. Subsequent federal legislation prohibits some forms of age discrimination (Age Discrimination in Employment Act) and discrimination against people with disabilities (Americans with Disabilities Act). States have their own antidiscrimination laws. All these laws have increased the number of minorities and women who work in corrections.

Unlike many public employees, those who work in corrections operate from a difficult position. They must assert authority over persons who have shown that they lack self-control or have little regard for society's rules. Whether in prison, in a probationer's home, or on the street, this responsibility creates pressures and difficult—sometimes dangerous—situations.

Liability of Correctional Personnel   In *Cooper v. Pate* (1964), the Supreme Court said that Section 1983 provides a means for prisoners, but also probationers and parolees, to bring lawsuits against correctional officials. *Monell v. Department of Social Services of the City of New York* (1978) clarified the meaning of Section 1983. Individual public employees and their agency may be sued when a person's civil rights are violated by the agency's "customs and usages." Specifically, if an individual can show that harm was caused by employees whose wrongful acts were the result of these "customs, practices, and policies, including poor training and supervision," then the employees may be sued.

The Supreme Court has identified other kinds of legal actions that may be filed against corrections officials. For example, the Supreme Court has said that federal corrections officials can be sued under the Federal Tort Claims Act for intentional harms inflicted on prisoners (*Millbrook v. United States*, 2013). In the case decided by the high court, the prisoner claimed that he had been sexually assaulted by corrections officials. The Court's decision permitted him to proceed with his opportunity to prove the case after corrections officials had sought to have the case dismissed for using the wrong kind of legal action.

Although huge financial settlements make headlines and the number of Section 1983 filings is large, few cases come to trial and very few correctional employees

Gagnon v. Scarpelli (1973)
Before probation can be revoked, a two-stage hearing must be held and the offender provided with specific elements of due process. Requested counsel will be allowed on a case-by-case basis.

must personally pay financial awards to plaintiffs. However, no correctional employee wants to be involved in such legal situations.

Correctional Policy Trends

The United States has a large and expanding population under correctional supervision. Since the middle of the 1970s, the United States has fought a war on crime mainly by increasing the severity of sanctions against offenders. This has led to a 500 percent increase in correctional budgets, more than 4 million people on probation, over 2 million incarcerated in prisons and jails, and more than 800,000 under parole supervision. These are staggering figures, especially considering that crime has been decreasing for the past decade. Figure 10.2 shows the tremendous growth in the correctional population since 1985. As you read the "Comparative Perspective," note how incarceration rates in the United States exceed those elsewhere in the world.

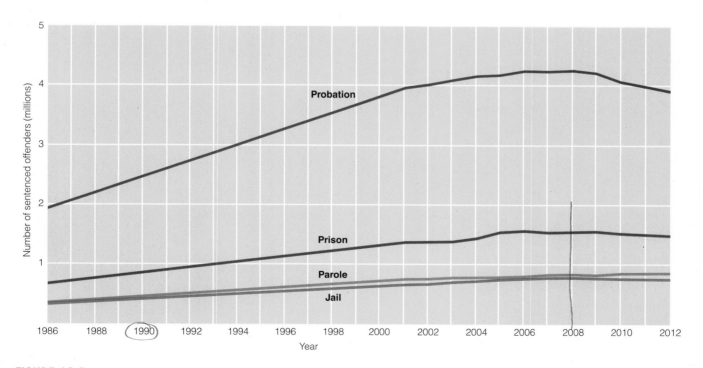

FIGURE 10.2
Correctional Populations in the United States 1992–December 2012 Although the increase in prison populations receives the most publicity, a greater proportion of correctional growth has occurred in probation and parole.

Source: Lauren E. Glaze and Erinn J. Herberman, "Correctional Populations in the United States, 2012," *Bureau of Justice Statistics Bulletin,* December 2013, NCJ 243936.

Behind Bars in North America and Europe

Most Western countries have put increasing numbers of people behind bars in recent years, but in none has the incarceration rate risen higher than in the United States. The cause of the extraordinary American figure is not higher levels of crime, for the crime rate in the United States is about the same as in Western Europe (except for the rate of homicide, which is two to eight times greater in the United States, mostly because of the ready availability of guns).

The high U.S. rate—which rivals those of former Soviet nations—can be traced primarily to a shift in public attitudes toward crime that began more than 30 years ago as apprehension about violence and drugs escalated. Politicians were soon exploiting the new attitudes with promises to get criminals off the streets. Congress and state legislatures, often at the prodding of presidents and governors, promoted "tough on crime" measures, including mandatory sentencing, three-strikes laws, longer sentences, and increased budgets for prison construction.

As a result, the length of sentences, already severe by Western European standards, became even more punitive. Consequently, the number of those locked up rose more than fivefold between 1972 and 2008 to more than 2 million. Most of those sentenced in recent years are perpetrators of nonviolent crimes, such as drug possession, offenses that would not ordinarily be punished by long prison terms in other Western countries.

Researching the Internet

Access the article by Marc Mauer of *The Sentencing Project*, "Comparative International Rates of Incarceration," online at http://www.sentencingproject.org/doc/publications /inc_comparative_intl.pdf. What are his major findings?

For Critical Analysis

Do these incarceration rates reflect differences in the nature of crime problems, differences in philosophies about punishment, or other factors? Do higher incarceration rates indicate that a country's citizens are safer than those in other countries? List three reasons why you believe the United States has such a relatively high incarceration rate compared with those of other countries. Can any of these reasons be changed to achieve a lower extent and expense of imprisonment in the United States?

Sources: Adapted from Roger Doyle, "By the Numbers," *Scientific American*, August 1999, p. 25; Bureau of Justice Statistics, *Sourcebook of Criminal Justice Statistics* (2014) Table 6.1.2011; One in 100: *Behind Bars in America, 2008* (Washington, DC: Pew Center on the States, 2008), p. 35; *World Prison Brief—2008*, London: King's College; E. Ann Carson and William J. Sabol, "Prisoners in 2011," *Bureau of Justice Statistics Bulletin*, December 2012, NCJ 239808.

Inmates in Prisons and Jails per 100,000 Residents

Prisoner population (per 100,000)
- Under 100
- 100 to 199
- 200 or more
- No data

Source: Bureau of Justice Statistics, *Sourcebook of Criminal Justice Statistics 2011* (http://www.albany.edu/sourcebook/).

Correctional costs are mainly borne by the states and are now outpacing budget growth in education, transportation, and public assistance. Only Medicaid spending grew faster than that of corrections in recent years. Correctional costs have quadrupled during the past two decades. Even as states face huge budget shortfalls, prison costs are driving spending increases. Some states spend more than 10 percent of all tax dollars on corrections, and nearly 90 percent of correction's allocations are for prisons. A survey of states found that they spent an average of $31,000 a year on each prisoner (Henrichson & Delaney, 2012). By contrast, costs for probationers and parolees were much lower, only $1,250 per probationer and $2,750 per parolee (S. Moore, 2009). California represents one of the most difficult budgetary situations because of the size of the prison population and the relatively high compensation paid to its corrections officers. In 2011, the state spent $9.6 billion on prisons but only $5.7 billion on state colleges and universities. As critics have noted, California has built only one university since 1980 yet has built 20 new prisons in that time period (Flock, 2012).

Some observers believe that the drop in crime has resulted from harsher arrest and sentencing policies. Critics, however, say that the "lock 'em up" policies have had little impact as drops in crime rates have been seen in states with different imprisonment rates. Moreover, critics claim that the financial and human costs of current policies severely damage families and communities. In the rest of the chapter, we examine community corrections and incarceration policies in order to understand current practices and future trends.

Community Corrections

Although escalating prison growth has captured the public's attention, the number of people on probation and parole has actually risen at a faster rate than the number of people incarcerated. Many factors may explain this growth, including more arrests and successful prosecutions, the lower costs of probation compared with incarceration, prison and jail crowding, and the large numbers of felons now being released from prison.

Probation People on probation now make up 60 percent of the correctional population, yet budgets and staffing have not risen accordingly. In many urban areas, probation caseloads are growing well beyond reasonable management levels: 200- and even 300-person caseloads are no longer unusual for individual probation officers. This has led to a deterioration in the quality of supervision. Yet, the importance of probation for public safety has never been greater. As a result, a renewed emphasis on public safety has arisen. Many agencies have seen a resurgence of intensive and structured supervision for selected offenders.

In many respects, then, probation finds itself at a crossroads. Although its credibility is probably as low as it has ever been, its workload is growing dramatically and, in view of the crowding in prison and jails, will probably continue to do so. Under the strain of this workload and on-again, off-again public support, probation faces a serious challenge. Can its methods of supervision and service be adapted successfully to high-risk offenders?

Parole With the incarcerated population nearly quadrupling during the past 30 years, the number of parolees has, not surprisingly, also grown. Currently, over 635,000 felons gain release from prison each year (Carson & Golinelli, 2013b). In 2012, 851,200 parolees under supervision, a threefold increase since 1980 (Glaze & Herberman, 2013). With the prison population growth of recent decades, the number on parole will likely reach 1 million in the next few years because several states gave renewed emphasis to increasing parole releases as a way to cut expensive prison budgets (Lambert, 2011).

Compared with parolees in 1990, today's parolees are older, are more likely to have been sentenced for drug violations, have served longer prison sentences, and have higher levels of substance abuse and mental illness. These characteristics increase reentry problems related to renewing family ties, obtaining a job, and living according to parole rules. Most parolees cannot obtain the assistance necessary to reenter the community successfully. (The reentry problem is extensively discussed in Chapter 13.)

Further, increased numbers of offenders are being returned to prison as parole violators. Studies show that within three years of their release, 68 percent are arrested and 47 percent convicted for a new felony; 25 percent are returned to prison for their new crime. Taking revocations for new convictions and "technical violations" together, 52 percent of released prisoners are back in prison within three years (Langan & Levin, 2002). The return of parolees accounts for much of the growth in total admissions to state prisons.

Incarceration

From 1940 until 1973, the number of people incarcerated in the United States remained fairly stable, ranging from 250,000 to 330,000. However, since 1973, when the overall crime rate started to fall, the incarceration rate has quadrupled so that nearly 2.3 million were in prisons and jails by 2010. As we saw in the chapter opener and in the "Comparative Perspective" feature, the United States has the highest incarceration rate in the developed world. With subsequent budget cuts at the state and federal level as well as changes in sentencing policies, there were nearly 40,000 fewer people in prison by end of 2012, a point at which 1 out of 108 adult residents of the United States were behind bars (Glaze & Herberman, 2013). The ongoing influence of budget issues and new approaches to sentencing are projected to produce continued decreases in prison populations in various states.

Keep in mind that the size and growth of the prison population varies across the country. Some states have had recent declines in prison populations as others have continued to see their corrections populations grow. As Figure 10.3 shows, 8 of the 10 states with the highest incarceration rates are in the South.

Crime rates dropped throughout the country in recent years, even in states that did not have high incarceration rates. If little relationship exists between the crime rate and the incarceration rate, what factors explain the growth in imprisonment since 1980? Five reasons are often cited for the rise: (1) increased arrests and more likely incarceration, (2) tougher sentencing, (3) prison construction, (4) the war on drugs, and (5) state politics. None of these reasons should be viewed as being the only explanation or as having more demonstrated impact than the others.

Increased Arrests and More Likely Incarceration Some analysts argue that the billions of dollars spent on the crime problem may be paying off. Not only have arrest rates increased, particularly for some offenses such as drug violations, aggravated assaults, and sexual assaults, but the probability of being sent to prison has also dramatically increased. In 2009, the U.S. Sentencing Guidelines Commission reported that the percentage of federal offenders sent to prison increased over the past 10 years from 75.4 percent to 85.3 percent, while the use of alternatives to incarceration such as probation and intermediate sanctions decreased over the same period (Coyle, 2009).

In addition, the number of offenders returned to prison for parole violations has also increased. In 2012, one-quarter of the 609,000 people admitted into American prisons were parolees who either had committed new crimes or violated the conditions of parole. Of the 153,000 parolees sent back to prison in 2012, only one-third returned because of a conviction on a new felony; most returned to prison for violating parole conditions (Maruschak & Bonczar, 2013; Carson & Golinelli, 2013b).

Tougher Sentencing Practices Some observers think that a hardening of public attitudes toward criminals resulted in longer sentences, in a smaller proportion of those convicted getting probation, and in fewer being released at the time of the first parole hearing. Yet, in the past few years, budget pressures have led some states to emphasize probation and parole to reduce the costs of prisons.

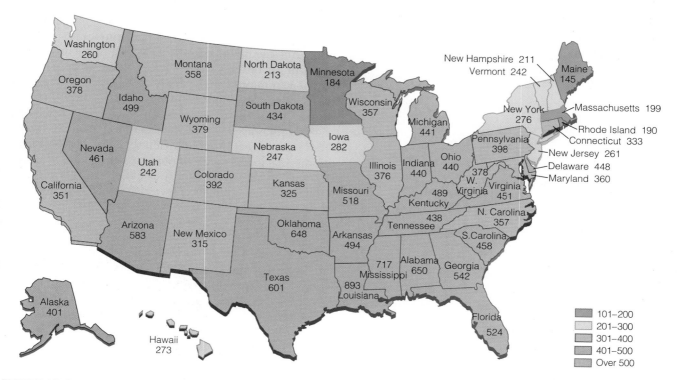

FIGURE 10.3

Sentenced Prisoners in State Institutions per 100,000 Population, December 31, 2012 What can be said about the differences in incarceration rates among the states? There are not only regional differences but also differences between adjacent states that seem to have similar socioeconomic and crime characteristics.

Note: For Illinois, Nevada, and Washington, data were available only for 2011. All other states' rates are for 2012.

Source: E. Ann Carson and Daniela Golinelli, "Prisoners in 2012—Advance Counts," *Bureau of Justice Statistics Bulletin*, July 2013. NCJ 242467.

Between 1980 and the early twenty-first century, the states and the federal government have passed laws that increase sentences for most crimes. However, the tougher sentences themselves do not seem to be the main factor keeping offenders in prison for longer periods. The key factor is not merely the sentenced announced by judge, but rather the actual sentence served after consideration of reductions in time for good behavior and parole grants prior to the end of the sentence. Thus, the 13 percent increase in the actual amount of time served is largely the aspect of sentencing that affected the total number of inmates. Recent budget-driven developments may diminish the prior effects of tougher sentencing and contribute to further declines in prison growth.

Prison Construction As the public in the 1970s began to favor harsher sentencing policies, the rate of incarceration grew. Prison crowding eventually reached crisis proportions, creating health and security issues. Many states attempted to build their way out of this problem—literally.

Large state budget surpluses during the booming economy of the 1990s made many legislatures willing to advance the huge sums required for prison expansion. Between 1975 and 2000, more than 400 prisons were built across the country, at least doubling the

During the 1990s, many new, expensive correctional facilities were built throughout the country by both state governments and private corporations. As economic problems affected state budgets in the first decade of the twenty-first century, many states found it difficult to justify additional construction. Instead, states began to rethink their sentencing policies and look for ways to assist increasing numbers of parolees to reenter society successfully. Will shorter sentences and the faster release of offenders pose any problems for society?

QUESTION: "Do you think the use of marijuana should be made legal or not?"

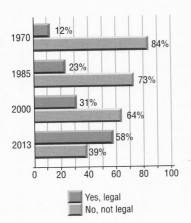

	Yes, legal	No, not legal
1970	12%	84%
1985	23%	73%
2000	31%	64%
2013	58%	39%

CRITICAL THINKING: How can changing public attitudes toward the permissibility of using certain drugs affect laws and policies in the criminal justice system? Make a prediction about what laws and policies will exist 25 years from now concerning drug use in the United States.

Source: Art Swift, "For First Time, Americans Favor Legalizing Marijuana," Gallup Poll website, October 22, 2013 (www.gallup.com).

number of facilities in each state. The new facilities increased the capacity of state prisons by 81 percent. Pressures from contractors, building material providers, and correctional-officer unions also spurred expansion in many states. Often states that tried to build their way out of their crowded facilities found that as soon as a new prison came on line it was quickly filled.

The increased rate of incarceration may thus be related to the creation of additional space in the nation's prisons. As Joseph Davey notes, "The presence of empty state-of-the-art prison facilities can encourage a criminal court judge to incarcerate a defendant who may otherwise get probation" (J. D. Davey, 1998:84).

The War on Drugs Crusades against the use of drugs have recurred in U.S. politics since the late 1800s. The latest manifestation began in 1982, when President Ronald Reagan declared another "war on drugs" and asked Congress to set aside more money for drug enforcement personnel and for prison space. This came at a time when the country faced the frightening advent of crack cocaine, which ravaged many communities and increased the murder rate. In 1987, Congress imposed stiff mandatory minimum sentences for federal drug law violations, and many states copied these sentencing laws. The war continues today, with recent presidents urging Congress to appropriate billions more for an all-out law enforcement campaign against drugs.

The war on drugs succeeded on one front by packing the nation's prisons with drug law offenders, but many scholars think this is about all it has achieved. With additional resources and pressures for enforcement, the number of people sentenced to prison for drug offenses increased steadily. In 1980, only 19,000, or about 6 percent of state prisoners, had been convicted of drug offenses; by 2003, the number had risen to 250,000. More than 18 percent of state prisoners were incarcerated for drug offenses in 2010, and the percentage in federal prisons was even higher at 51 percent (Guerino, Harrison, & Sabol, 2011). Furthermore, the average state drug sentence increased during the 1980s and 1990s.

Changes in the public opinion about drugs may help to lessen the steady increase in prison populations attributable to stiff sentences for drug offenses in recent decades. As illustrated by "What Americans Think," for the first time, a national public opinion poll found in 2011 that half of Americans favor the legalization of marijuana, and the support increased to 58 percent in favor of legalization in 2013. The convergence of the budget crisis affecting the criminal justice system with a softening of punitive attitudes toward certain drugs is likely to affect future sentencing policies.

State Politics Incarceration rates vary among the regions and states, but why do states with similar characteristics differ in their use of prisons? How much do local political factors influence correctional policies?

One might think that each state would show an association between crime rates and incarceration rates—the more crime, the more prisoners. However, even when states have similar socioeconomic and demographic characteristics—poverty, unemployment, racial composition, drug arrests—unaccountable variations among their incarceration rates exist. For example, North Dakota and South Dakota share similar social characteristics and crime rates, yet the incarceration rate in South Dakota is 434 per 100,000 adult population; North Dakota's rate is 213 per 100,000 adult population in 2012 (Carson & Golinelli, 2013a). One can even find similar and contiguous states such as Connecticut and Massachusetts, Arizona and New

Mexico, or Minnesota and Wisconsin, where the state which at times has the *higher* crime rate also has the *lower* incarceration rate.

In recent years, scholars have shown that local officials often promote the siting of prisons in their towns as a means of economic development. A good example of the impact of prison siting is found in the state of New York, which in the 1970s passed tough drug-sentencing laws. New prisons had to be built to handle the resulting increase in the incarcerated population. Most of the new prisons were located in the northern, rural, economically impoverished region of the state. The influx of prisoners brought jobs to the region. Legislative districts with local employment rates tied to prison payrolls soon found their politics dominated by the union representing correctional officers (F. Santos, 2008). Across the nation, 221 counties have been found in which at least 21 percent of the residents were inmates (Butterfield, 2004a).

No one factor stands alone as the primary cause of the doubling of the incarceration rate in recent decades. Several plausible hypotheses exist. However, now that the costs of this form of punishment impinge more on the pockets of taxpayers and affect funding for other priorities, such as education, we are seeing a shift to greater consideration of alternatives to incarceration in many states. As described in the chapter opener, several states have taken steps to reduce prison populations. Yet, serious challenges remain because of the monumental growth in prison populations that preceded the very recent slight declines. Prison systems across the United States still remain very large and very expensive.

☑ CHECK POINT

9. **What are five explanations for the great increase in the incarcerated population?**

   Increased arrests and more likely incarceration, tougher sentencing, prison construction, the war on drugs, state politics.

STOP&ANALYZE

In light of what you have read about the factors that led to the increase in incarceration, if you were hired as a governor's consultant and were tasked with finding ways to reduce the cost of a state's prison system, what would you recommend? List three recommendations that you would make, and state your reasons for each one.

A QUESTION OF ETHICS

Think, Discuss, Write

One of the concerns about the existence of private, profit-seeking organizations handling corrections functions is the political influence private companies may exert to convince public officials to send them offenders to treat or hold. A newspaper investigation in 2014 revealed that a Detroit area judge regularly subjected misdemeanor offenders to months of daily drug and alcohol testing as well as the use of interlock devices that prevent cars from starting if the driver has alcohol on her or his breath. At the same time, the judge's son was employed for 16 months as a case manager for the largest Detroit-area private drug- and alcohol-testing company where many of the offenders ended up. These offenders must each pay $9 per day to the company for many months of daily testing. In addition, the judge's wife worked from home in a part-time position paying $40,000 per year plus overtime bonuses as the executive director of the Michigan Association of Drug Court Professionals—an organization that receives thousands of dollars annually in contributions from private drug- and alcohol-testing companies. Judicial ethics rules forbid judges from having any financial interests that could affect their

decisions. The judge in question claims that there is no conflict of interests because he receives no benefits from these private companies.

Discussion/Writing Assignment

Imagine that you are a member of Michigan's Judicial Tenure Commission that examines allegations of misconduct by judges. Would you regard this situation as violating ethical rules against judges having any self-interest in decisions? Is there actual self-interest here, or if not, should the activity be prohibited anyway because of the possible appearance of self-interest in the eyes of the public? Write a memo describing your analysis of the case and any recommendations you would make, including any sanctions against the judge if you believe they would be appropriate.

Sources: L.L. Braiser and John Wisely, "Oakland Prosecutor Says Novi District Judge Brian MacKenzie Continues to Mishandle Cases," *Detroit Free Press*, January 16, 2014 (www.freep.com); John Wisely and L.L. Brasier, "Novi Judge Denies Conflict Over Ties to Testing Firms," *Detroit Free Press*, February 13, 2014 (www.freep.com).

❶ Describe how the American system of corrections has developed.

- From colonial days to the present, the methods of criminal sanctions that are considered appropriate have varied.
- The development of the penitentiary brought a shift away from corporal punishment.
- The Declaration of Principles of 1870 contained the key elements for the reformatory and rehabilitation models of corrections.
- Although based on the social sciences, the rehabilitation/medical model failed to reduce recidivism.
- The community model of corrections tried to increase opportunities for offenders to be successful citizens and receive psychological treatment.
- The crime control model emphasized incarceration, long and mandatory sentencing, and strict supervision.

❷ Describe the roles that the federal, state, and local governments play in corrections.

- The administration of corrections in the United States is fragmented, in that various levels of government are involved.
- The correctional responsibilities of the federal government are divided between the Federal Bureau of Prisons (of the U.S. Department of Justice) and the Administrative Office of the U.S. Courts.
- In all states, the administration of prisons falls under the executive branch of state government.

Jails, which are administered by local government, hold people waiting trial and hold sentenced offenders.

❸ Explain the law of corrections and how it is applied to offenders and correctional professionals.

- Until the 1960, the courts held a hands-off policy with respect to corrections.
- The rights of offenders are found in the First, Fourth, Eighth, and Fourteenth Amendments to the U.S. Constitution.
- Through lawsuits in the federal courts, the prisoners' rights movement has brought many changes to the administration and conditions of U.S. prisons.
- Decisions of the Supreme Court have affected community corrections through rules governing probation and parole revocation.
- Civil service laws set the procedures for hiring, promoting, and firing correctional professionals. Individual public employees and their agency may be sued when a person's civil rights are violated.

❹ Explain why the prison population has nearly quadrupled in the past 30 years.

- Scholars trying to explain the great increase in the prison population have advanced the following explanations: increased arrests and more likely incarceration, tougher sentencing practices, prison construction, the war on drugs, state politics. No factor stands alone as the primary cause of the increase.

Questions for Review

1. What were the major differences between the New York and Pennsylvania systems in the nineteenth century?
2. What pressures do administrators of local jails face?
3. What types of correctional programs does your state support? What government agencies run them?
4. Why do some state officials see private prisons as an attractive correctional option?
5. What Supreme Court decisions are the most significant to corrections today? What effect has each had on correctional institutions? On probation and parole?
6. What explanations might be given for the increased use of incarceration during the past few decades?

Key Terms and Cases

community corrections (p. 329)

congregate system (p. 325)

contract labor system (p. 326)

corrections (p. 322)

crime control model of corrections (p. 329)

Enlightenment (p. 322)

hands-off policy (p. 340)

jail (p. 336)

lease system (p. 326)

mark system (p. 327)

medical model (p. 328)

penitentiary (p. 324)

prison (p. 336)

reformatory (p. 327)

rehabilitation model (p. 328)

separate confinement (p. 324)

Cooper v. Pate (1964) (p. 340)

Gagnon v. Scarpelli (1973) (p. 348)

Hudson v. Palmer (1984) (p. 342)

Morrissey v. Brewer (1972) (p. 347)

Wolff v. McDonnell (1974) (p. 343)

11 | Incarceration and Prison Society

LEARNING OBJECTIVES

1. Describe how contemporary institutions differ from the old-style "big-house" prisons.
2. Identify the three models of incarceration that have predominated since the 1940s.
3. Describe the organization of prisons and their staffs.
4. Explain how a prison is governed.
5. Summarize the roles of correctional officers in a prison.
6. List the characteristics of the incarcerated population.
7. Describe the world of the convict.
8. Discuss what prison is like for men and for women.
9. List some of the programs and services available to prisoners.
10. Describe the nature of prison violence.

It's 6:30 a.m. The morning whistle blows, and inmates wake and clean their cells. At 7:00 a.m., another whistle tells inmates that it is time for breakfast. They are escorted to the mess hall to eat, where they have 25 minutes to finish their meals before reporting to work duty. Some inmates work in the laundry; others work in the kitchen or library; others take on janitorial duties to keep the prison clean. After eating lunch at noon, inmates continue working in the afternoon with recreation time at 4:10 p.m. and dinner served at 4:40 p.m. Prisoners spend the evening in their cells, perhaps reading or playing cards. "Lights out" occurs at 9:30 p.m., with the prisoners to be awakened the next morning at 6:30 a.m., to start the process again.

In the prison's "Rules and Regulations" handbook, inmates are told that they are entitled to "food, clothing, shelter, and medical attention. Anything else that you get is a privilege." Recreational activities include baseball, handball, and table games. Movies are shown two times per month.

This description is pretty typical of most prisons in the United States. Inmates arise, eat breakfast, work, eat lunch, work or study, eat dinner, and then go to sleep. The day described above, however, is an account of the daily activities at Alcatraz prison, circa 1956. In some ways, prison life has not changed in the past 60 years. Compare this historical example with the very similar daily schedule in a contemporary high-security state prison (North Carolina Department of Public Safety, 2014):

6 a.m. Wake up

7 a.m. Breakfast

8 a.m. Work at prison job

Noon Lunch (30 minutes)

Lunch to 3 p.m. Work at prison job

3 p.m. Recreation/prison yard time

4 p.m. Return to cell

5 p.m. Supper (30 minutes)

Supper to 8 p.m. Evening programs—religious services, anger management, addiction group counseling, etc.

8 p.m. In cell

11 p.m. Lights out

The continuing similarities in daily routines do not mean that prisons have remained unchanged. The mix of offenders serving in prisons has changed, especially with greater numbers of drug offenders in recent decades. In addition, as American society and culture change, those changes can be reflected in the knowledge and expectations of prisoners. For example, the civil rights movement for racial equality was just gathering momentum in 1956, and racial segregation was accepted in certain states' prisons. Today, however, expectations about constitutional rights and freedom from racial discrimination are widely shared among prison officials and prisoners. In addition, technological advancements, social science research on behavior, and formalization of training, policies, and procedures have all changed aspects of contemporary prisons.

What goes on inside U.S. prisons? What does incarceration mean to the inmates, the guards, the administrators, and the public? Are the officers in charge, or do the prisoners "rule the joint"? In the Close Up feature on page 362, Michael Santos describes his anxiety as a 24-year-old first-time offender entering the U.S. Federal Penitentiary in Atlanta.

In this chapter, we focus on the goals of incarceration, the challenges of management, and the inmates' experience. Discussion also centers on violence in prison and the policies and programs intended to keep that violence from boiling over.

The Modern Prison: Legacy of the Past

American correctional institutions have always been more varied than the way movies or novels portray them. Fictional depictions of prison life are typically set in a fortress, the "big house"—the maximum-security prisons where the inmates are tough and the guards are just as tough or tougher. Although so-called big houses predominated in much of the country during the first half of the twentieth century, many prisons were based on other models. In the South, for instance, prisoners worked outside at farm labor, and the massive walled structures were not so common.

The typical big house of the 1940s and 1950s was a walled prison with large, tiered cell blocks, a yard, shops, and industrial workshops. About 2,500 prisoners served their time in such an institution. They came from both urban and rural areas; were usually poor; and outside the South, were predominantly white. The prison society was essentially isolated, with restricted access to visitors, mail, and other communication. Prisoners' days were strictly structured, with rules enforced by the guards. A basic division stood between inmates and staff; rank was observed and discipline maintained. In the big house, few treatment programs existed; custody stood as the primary goal.

During the 1960s and early 1970s, when the rehabilitation model prevailed, many states built new prisons and converted others into "correctional institutions." Treatment programs administered by counselors and teachers became a major part of prison life, although the institutions continued to give priority to the custody goals of security, discipline, and order.

During the past 40 years, as the population of the United States has changed, so has the prison population. The number of African American and Hispanic inmates has greatly increased. More inmates come from urban areas, and more have been convicted of drug-related and violent offenses. Former street gangs, often organized along racial lines, today regroup inside prisons; such gangs have raised the level of violence in many institutions.

Further, the focus of corrections has shifted to crime control, which emphasizes the importance of incarceration. Not only has the number of people in prison greatly increased, but many states have removed educational and recreational amenities from institutions.

Today prisoners are less isolated from the outside world than before. As we have seen, the Supreme Court has ruled on issues of communication and access to information for prisoners, weighing their constitutional rights against the need for order and safety within the prison walls. Another difference from the past is that correctional officers have used collective bargaining to improve their working conditions.

Although today's correctional administrators seek to provide humane incarceration, they must struggle with limited resources and shortages of cell space. Thus, the modern prison faces many of the difficult problems that confront other parts of the criminal justice system: racial conflicts, legal issues, limited resources, and growing populations. Despite these challenges, can prisons still achieve their objectives? The answer to this question depends, in part, on how we define the goals of incarceration.

☑ CHECK POINT

1. **How does today's prison differ from the big house of the past?**
The characteristics of the inmate population have changed, more inmates are from urban areas and have been convicted for drug-related or violent offenses, the inmate population is fragmented along racial and ethnic lines, prisoners are less isolated from the outside world, and correctional officers have used collective bargaining to improve their working conditions.

STOP&ANALYZE

With access to television, telephones, and, in an increasing number of prison systems, email communications (F. Green, 2011), prisoners are not as isolated from the outside world as they once were. What are some possible negative and positive consequences of this increased contact? How might this affect life inside prisons?

Goals of Incarceration

Citing the nature of inmates and the need to protect staff and the community, most people consider security the dominant purpose of a prison. High walls, barbed-wire fences, searches, checkpoints, and regular counts of inmates serve the security function: few inmates escape. More importantly, the features set the tone for the daily operations. Prisons stand as impersonal, quasi-military places where strict discipline, minimal amenities, and restrictions on freedom serve to punish criminals.

Three models of incarceration have predominated since the early 1940s: the custodial, rehabilitation, and reintegration models. Each is associated with one style of institutional organization.

1. The **custodial model** assumes that prisoners have been incarcerated for the purpose of incapacitation, deterrence, or retribution. It emphasizes security, discipline, and order in subordinating the prisoner to the authority of the warden. Discipline is strict, and most aspects of behavior are regulated. Having prevailed in corrections before World War II, this model dominates most maximum-security institutions today.

custodial model A model of incarceration that emphasizes security, discipline, and order.

One Man's Walk through Atlanta's Jungle

Michael G. Santos

I was not expecting to receive the southern hospitality for which Atlanta is famous when the bus turned into the penitentiary's large, circular drive, but neither did I expect to see a dozen uniformed prison guards—all carrying machine guns—surround the bus when it stopped. A month in transit already had passed by the time we made it to the U.S. Penitentiary (USP) in Atlanta, the institution that would hold me (along with over 2,000 other felons) until we were transferred to other prisons, we were released, or we were dead.

I left the jail in Tacoma, Washington, on the first of August, but I didn't see the huge gray walls that surround USP Atlanta until the first of September. That month was spent in a bus operated by the U.S. Marshal Service as it moved across the country, picking up federal prisoners in local jails and dropping them off at various Bureau of Prison facilities.

As I crossed the country, I listened to tales from numerous prisoners who sat beside me on the bus. There wasn't much to discuss except what was to come. Each of us was chained at the hands and feet. There were neither magazines to read nor music playing. Mostly people spoke about a riot that had taken place behind USP Atlanta's walls a few months earlier. A lot of the men had been to prison before, and Atlanta would be nothing new. Those prisoners only talked about reuniting with old friends, explaining prison routine, or sat like stone-cold statues waiting for what was to come. I'd never been confined before, so it was hard to tune out the stories that others were telling. While I was listening, though, I remember telling myself that I would survive this sentence. No matter what it took, I would survive.

I was in my early 20s, younger than perhaps every other prisoner on the bus. Pimples spotted my face as I began my term, but I was certain my black hair would be white by the time I finished. I had been sentenced to 45 years by a U.S. district court judge in Tacoma on charges related to cocaine trafficking. I was expected to serve close to 30 years before release. It was hard then—just as it is hard now—to believe the sentence was real. The best thing I could do, I reasoned, was to stay to myself. I'd heard the same rumors that every suburban kid hears about prison. I was anxious about what was to come, but I was determined to make it out alive and with my mind intact. Now it was all to begin!

After the bus stopped, the guards began calling us off by last name and prison number. It is not easy to walk with a twelve-inch chain connected to each ankle, and wrists bound to a chain that runs around the waist, but when my name was called, I managed to wobble through the bus's aisle, hop down the steps, and then begin the long march up the stairs leading to the fortress. As I was moving to the prison's doors, I remember glancing over my shoulder, knowing it would be the last time I'd see the world from the outside of prison walls for a long time.

Once I was inside the institution, the guards began unlocking my chains. About 50 other prisoners arrived with me that day, so the guards had plenty of chains to unlock, but their work didn't stop there. They also had to squeeze us through the dehumanizing admissions machine. The machine begins with photographs, fingerprints, and interrogations. Then comes the worst part, the strip search, where each prisoner stands before a prison official, naked, and responds to the scream: "Lift up your arms in the air! Let me see the back of your hands! Run your fingers through your hair! Open your mouth! Stick your tongue out! Lift your balls! Turn around! Bend over! Spread your ass! Wider! Lift the bottom of your feet! Move on!" The strip search, I later learned, is a ritual Atlanta's officers inflict on prisoners every time they have contact with anyone from

rehabilitation model A model of incarceration that emphasizes treatment programs to help prisoners address the personal problems and issues that led them to commit crimes.

reintegration model A model of a correctional institution that emphasizes maintaining the offender's ties to family and community as a method of reform, recognizing that the offender will be returning to society.

2. The **rehabilitation model**, developed during the 1950s, emphasizes treatment programs designed to reform the offender. According to this model, security and housekeeping activities are viewed primarily as preconditions for rehabilitative efforts. Because all aspects of the organization should center on rehabilitation, professional treatment specialists carry a higher status than do other employees. Since the rethinking of the rehabilitation goal in the 1970s, treatment programs still exist in most institutions, but few prisons conform to this model today.

3. The **reintegration model** is linked to the structures and goals of community corrections. Recognizing that prisoners will be returning to society, this model emphasizes maintaining the offenders' ties to family and community as a method of reform. Prisons following this model gradually give inmates greater freedom and responsibility during their confinement, moving them to halfway houses or work release programs before giving them community supervision.

Although one can find correctional institutions that conform to each of these models, most prisons are mainly custodial. Nevertheless, treatment programs do exist, and because almost all inmates return to society at some point, even the most custodial institutions must prepare them for reintegration. See "What Americans Think" for a look at how the public views the goals of incarceration.

outside the walls, and sometimes randomly as prisoners walk down the corridor.

There was a lot of hatred behind those walls. Walking through the prison must be something like walking through a jungle, I imagined, not knowing whether others perceive you as predator or prey, knowing that you must remain always alert, watching every step, knowing that the wrong step may be the one that sucks you into the quicksand. The tension is ever present; I felt it wrapped all over, under and around me. I remember it bothering me that I didn't have enough hatred, because not hating in the jungle is a weakness. As the serpents slither, they spot that lack of hatred and salivate over a potential target.

Every prisoner despises confinement, but each must decide how he or she is going to do the time. Most of the men run in packs. They want the other prisoners either to run with them or run away from them. I wasn't interested in doing either. Instead of scheming on how I could become king of the jungle, I thought about ways that I could advance my release date. Earning academic credentials, keeping a clean record, and initiating projects that would benefit the communities both inside and outside of prison walls seemed the most promising goals for me to achieve. Yet working toward such goals was more dangerous than running with the pack; it didn't take me long to learn that prisoners running in herds will put forth more energy to cause others to lose than they will to win themselves. Prison is a twisted world, a menagerie.

I found that a highly structured schedule would not only move me closer to my goals, but also would limit potential conflicts inside the prison. There is a pecking order in every prison, and prisoners vying for attention don't want to see others who are cutting their own path. I saw that bullies generally look for weaker targets, so I began an exercise routine that would keep me physically strong. If I were strong, I figured, others would be more reluctant to try me. Through discipline, I found, I could develop physical strength. Yet I've never figured

out how to develop the look of a killer, or the hatred off which that look feeds.

I don't know whether the strategies I have developed for doing time are right for everyone. But they are working for me. Still, I know that I may spend many more years in prison. The only fear I have—and as I'm working on my eighth year, it's still here—is that someone will try me and drag me into an altercation that may jeopardize my spotless disciplinary record. I've been successful in avoiding the ever-present quicksand on my walk through the jungle so far, but I know that on any given day, something may throw me off balance, or I may take a wrong step. And one wrong step in this jungle can drown me in quicksand, sucking me into the abysmal world of prison forever. That wrong step also could mean the loss of life, mine or someone else's.

In prison, more than anywhere else I know, understanding that some things are beyond an individual's sphere of control is vital. No matter how much preparation is made, the steel and concrete jungle is a dangerous place in which to live.

Researching the Internet

Michael Santos was incarcerated at the Federal Prison Camp in Taft, California. While in prison, he completed bachelor's and master's degrees. He is the author of *About Prison* (Belmont, CA: Wadsworth, 2004) and *Inside: Life behind Bars in America* (New York: St. Martin's Press, 2006), and four other books. He was released from prison on August 12, 2013, after serving 26 years. He now works as a life coach and teaches a course at San Francisco State University entitled "The Architecture of Imprisonment." He married his wife in 2003 (while still incarcerated), and they now live in Northern California. You can contact Santos through his website at http://michaelsantos.com/.

Source: Written for this book by Michael G. Santos. In 1987, he was sentenced to 45 years in prison for drug trafficking.

Much is asked of prisons. As Charles Logan notes, "We ask them to correct the incorrigible, rehabilitate the wretched, deter the determined, restrain the dangerous, and punish the wicked" (Logan, 1993:19). Because prisons are expected to pursue many different and often incompatible goals, they are almost doomed to fail as institutions. Logan believes that the mission of prisons is confinement. He argues that imprisonment serves primarily to punish offenders fairly and justly through lengths of confinement proportionate to the seriousness of their crimes. He summarizes the mission of prison as follows: "to keep prisoners—to keep them in, keep them safe, keep them in line, keep them healthy, and keep them busy—and to do it with fairness, without undue suffering, and as efficiently as possible" (Logan, 1993:21). If the purpose of prisons is punishment through confinement under fair and just conditions, what are the implications of this purpose for correctional managers?

☑ CHECK POINT

2. **What three models of prison have predominated since the 1940s?**

The custodial, rehabilitation, and reintegration models.

STOP&ANALYZE

Given the complex challenges facing today's prisons—including increased racial diversity within prisons, the greater likelihood of gang membership, and states' need to reduce corrections budgets—which model of prison administration seems best suited to addressing these challenges?

Prison Organization

QUESTION: "State prison systems could offer the following four alternative prison policies for people who have committed nonviolent crime. What would you prefer the state implement?"

Policy 1: Treat prison as punishment and do not offer rehabilitation services to people either during their time in prison or after their release.

Policy 2: Make state-funded rehabilitation services available to incarcerated people while they are serving time in prison.

Policy 3: Make state-funded rehabilitation services available to incarcerated people only after they have been released from prison.

Policy 4: Make state-funded rehabilitation services available to incarcerated people both while they are in prison and after they have been released from prison.

Percentage who prefer:

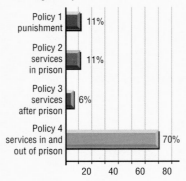

Policy 1 punishment	11%
Policy 2 services in prison	11%
Policy 3 services after prison	6%
Policy 4 services in and out of prison	70%

CRITICAL THINKING: A study of public attitudes on punishment found that women tend to be more supportive of rehabilitation than men are. List two reasons why this gender difference in attitudes might exist.

Note: May not add to 100% due to rounding and missing responses.

Source: Barry Krisberg and Susan Marchionna. "Attitudes of U.S. Voters toward Prison Rehabilitation and Reentry Policies," *Focus: Views from the National Council on Crime and Delinquency* (April) (Oakland, CA: National Council on Crime and Delinquency, 2006).

The prison's physical features and function set it apart from almost every other institution and organization in modern society. It is a place where a group of employees manage a group of captives. Prisoners must live according to the rules of their keepers, and their movements remain sharply restricted. Unlike managers of other government agencies, prison managers

- cannot select their clients.
- have little or no control over the release of their clients.
- must deal with clients who are there against their will.
- must rely on clients to do most of the work in the daily operation of the institution—work they are forced to do and for which they are not always paid.
- must depend on the maintenance of satisfactory relationships between clients and staff.

Given these unique characteristics, how should a prison be run? What rules should guide administrators? As the description just given indicates, wardens and other key personnel are asked to perform a difficult job, one that requires skilled and dedicated managers (Vickovic & Griffin, 2013).

Most prisons are expected to fulfill goals related to keeping (custody), using (working), and serving (treating) inmates. Because individual staff members are not equipped to perform all functions, separate lines of command organize the groups of employees that carry out these different tasks. One group is charged with maintaining custody over the prisoners, another group supervises them in their work activities, and a third group attempts to treat them.

The custodial employees are the most numerous. They are typically organized along military lines, from warden to captain to officer, with accompanying pay differentials down the chain of command. The professional personnel associated with the using and serving functions, such as industry supervisors, clinicians, and teachers, are not part of the custodial structure and have little in common with its staff. All employees are responsible to the warden, but the treatment personnel and the civilian supervisors of the workshops have their own salary scales and titles. Figure 11.1 presents the formal organization of staff responsibilities in a typical prison.

The multiple goals and separate lines of command often cause ambiguity and conflict in the administration of prisons. For example, the goals imposed on prisons are often contradictory and unclear. Conflict between different groups of staff (custodial versus treatment, for instance), as well as between staff and inmates, presents significant challenges for administrators.

How, then, do prisons function? How do prisoners and staff try to meet their own goals? Although the U.S. prison may not conform to the ideal goals of corrections and the formal organization may bear little resemblance to the ongoing reality of the informal relations, order *is* kept and a routine *is* followed.

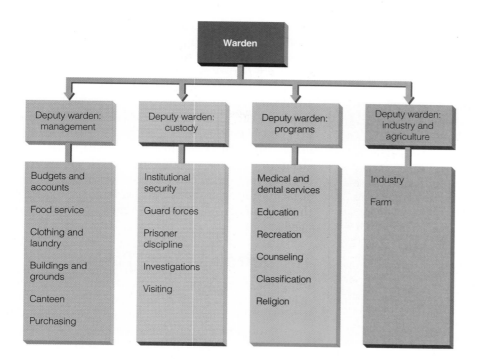

FIGURE 11.1
Formal Organization of a Prison for Adult Felons
Prison staff are divided into various sections consistent with the goals of the organization. Custodial employees are the most numerous.

Chart:

Warden
- **Deputy warden: management**
  - Budgets and accounts
  - Food service
  - Clothing and laundry
  - Buildings and grounds
  - Canteen
  - Purchasing
- **Deputy warden: custody**
  - Institutional security
  - Guard forces
  - Prisoner discipline
  - Investigations
  - Visiting
- **Deputy warden: programs**
  - Medical and dental services
  - Education
  - Recreation
  - Counseling
  - Classification
  - Religion
- **Deputy warden: industry and agriculture**
  - Industry
  - Farm

☑ CHECK POINT

3. How do prisons differ from other organizations in society?
Prisons are places where a group of workers manages a group of captives.

STOP&ANALYZE

How might the multiple goals of prisons collide with each other? Select two of the goals, and describe how the pursuit of one goal may make the effective attainment of the other goal more difficult.

Governing a Society of Captives

Much of the public believes that prisons are operated in an authoritarian manner. In such a society, correctional officers give orders and inmates follow orders. Strictly enforced rules specify what the captives may and may not do. Staff members have the right to grant rewards and to inflict punishment. In theory, any inmate who does not follow the rules could be placed in solitary confinement. Because the officers have a monopoly on the legal means of enforcing rules and can call in the state police and the National Guard if necessary, many people believe that no question should arise as to how the prison is run. Read "Criminal Justice: Myth & Reality" to test your perceptions about the power of correctional officials.

What quality of life should be maintained in prison? According to John DiIulio, a good prison is one that "provides as much order, amenity, and service as possible given the human and financial resources" (1987:12). *Order* is here defined as the absence of individual or group misconduct that threatens the safety of others—for example, assault, rape, and other forms of violence or threat. *Amenities* include anything that enhances the comfort of the inmates, such as good food, clean cells, and recreational opportunities. *Service* includes programs designed to improve the lives of inmates: vocational training, remedial education, and work opportunities. Here, too, we expect inmates to be engaged in activities during incarceration that will make them better people and enhance their ability to lead crime-free lives upon release.

COMMON BELIEF: Because correctional officers have access to guns, clubs, tear gas, and other weapons, they can readily control the behavior of prisoners through the threat of force or, if necessary, the use of force, including lethal force.

- Although prison officials typically have firearms locked in an accessible area for emergencies and the correctional officers standing guard in towers or walking outside the prison's perimeter carry guns, most correctional officers cannot carry weapons.
- These officers must supervise, question, and frisk prisoners close at hand and in a context in which they are heavily outnumbered by the prisoners. If they carried weapons, they might easily be overpowered and have their weapons taken by the prisoners.
- Thus, effective officers cannot rely on the threat of force to accomplish their daily tasks smoothly. Instead, they must encourage the cooperation and obedience of the prisoners by communicating effectively, establishing their own reputations for toughness and fairness, and showing some understanding and flexibility in the enforcement of minor rules.
- If a violent event or uprising occurs, prison staff members will use force to restore order. However, the use of force throughout the day is not an efficient way to keep the institution running smoothly.
- Moreover, there are now legal rules that limit when and how force may be used, and prisoners may file lawsuits for rights violations and personal injuries suffered through the improper use of force.

If we accept the premise that inmates, staff, and society need well-run prisons, what problems must correctional administrators address? The correctional literature points to four factors that make governing prisons different from administering other public institutions: (1) the defects of total power, (2) the limitation on the rewards and punishments officials can use, (3) the co-optation of correctional officers by inmates through exchange relationships, and (4) the strength of inmate leadership. After reviewing each of these research findings, we examine what kind of administrative systems and leadership styles ensure that prisons are safe and humane and serve inmates' needs.

The Defects of Total Power

Imagine a prison society in which officers could use force to rule hostile and uncooperative inmates. Prisoners could legally be isolated from one another, physically abused until they cooperate, and put under continuous surveillance. Although all of these things are possible, such practices would probably not be countenanced for long, because the public expects correctional institutions to be run humanely.

In reality, the power of officers is limited because many prisoners have little to lose by misbehaving, and unarmed officers have only limited ability to force compliance with rules. Perhaps more important is the fact that forcing people to follow commands is an inefficient way to make them carry out complex tasks; efficiency further diminishes because of the ratio of inmates to officers (typically 40 to 1) and the consequent potential danger of inmates overpowering officers.

Rewards and Punishments

Correctional officers often rely on rewards and punishments to gain cooperation. To maintain security and order among a large population in a confined space, they impose extensive rules of conduct. Instead of using force to ensure obedience, however, they reward compliance by granting privileges and punish rule violators by denying these same privileges.

To promote control, officers may follow any of several policies. One is to offer cooperative prisoners rewards such as choice job assignments, residence in the honor unit, and favorable parole reports. Inmates who do not break rules receive good time. Informers may also be rewarded, and administrators may ignore conflict among inmates on the assumption that it keeps prisoners from uniting against authorities.

The system of rewards and punishments has some deficiencies. One is that the punishments for rule breaking do not represent a great departure from the prisoners' usual circumstances. Because inmates already lack many freedoms and valued goods—heterosexual relations, money, choice of clothing, and so on—not being allowed to attend, say, a recreational period does not carry much weight. Further, inmates receive authorized privileges at the start of the sentence and lose them if rules are broken, but officials authorize few rewards for progress or exceptional behavior. However, as an inmate approaches release, opportunities for furloughs, work release, or transfer to a halfway house can serve as incentives to obey rules.

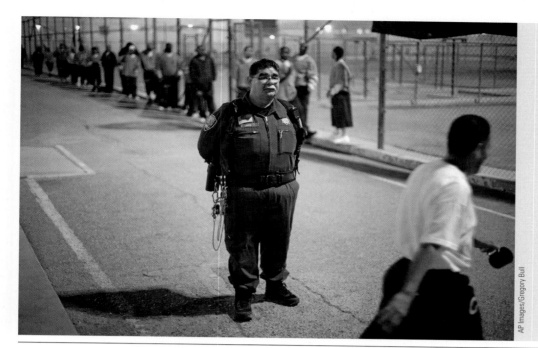

Officers face significant challenges in maintaining order and safety while outnumbered by prisoners, especially when many prisons are understaffed. What qualities and skills do correctional officers need in order to be effective?

Gaining Cooperation: Exchange Relationships

One way that correctional officers obtain inmate cooperation is by tolerating minor rule infractions in exchange for compliance with major aspects of the custodial regime. The correctional officer plays the key role in these exchange relationships. Officers and prisoners remain in close proximity both day and night—in the cell block, workshop, dining hall, recreation area, and so on. Although the formal rules require a social distance between officers and inmates, the physical closeness makes them aware that each relies on the other. The officers need the cooperation of the prisoners so that they will look good to their superiors, and the inmates count on the officers to relax the rules or occasionally look the other way. For example, officers in a Midwestern prison told researcher Stan Stojkovic that flexibility in rule enforcement especially mattered as it related to the ability of prisoners to cope with their environment. As one officer said, "Phone calls are really important to guys in this place. You cut off their calls and they get pissed. So what I do is give them a little extra and they are good to me." Yet, the officers also told Stojkovic that prison personnel would be crazy to intervene to stop illicit sex or drug use (Stojkovic, 1990:214).

Correctional officers must take care not to pay too high a price for the cooperation of their charges. Under pressure to work effectively with prisoners, officers may be blackmailed into doing illegitimate favors in return for cooperation. Officers who establish *sub-rosa*, or secret, relationships can be manipulated by prisoners into smuggling contraband or committing other illegal acts. Corrections officers are caught each year smuggling drugs and cell phones to prisoners. In addition, bans on cigarettes inside some prisons have created a lucrative and tempting market for corrections officers to smuggle tobacco into institutions and receive payments from the prisoners' relatives. Because scarce tobacco can be worth hundreds of dollars per bag, unethical officers can significantly enhance their incomes through such smuggling—at the same time that they risk being arrested and sent to prison themselves for such illegal activity (Goldschmidt & Shoichet, 2013; Ingold, 2011). At the end of the chapter, "A Question of Ethics" presents a recent example of such risks of co-optation for corrections officers.

Inmate Leadership

In the traditional prison of the big-house era, administrators enlisted the inmate leaders to help maintain order. Inmate leaders had been "tested" over time so that they were neither pushed around by other inmates nor distrusted as stool pigeons. Because the staff could rely on them, they served as the essential communications link between staff and inmates. Their ability to acquire inside information and gain access to higher officials brought inmate leaders the respect of other prisoners and special privileges from officials. In turn, they distributed these benefits to other prisoners, thus bolstering their own influence within the prison society.

Prisons seem to function more effectively now than they did in the recent past. Although prisons are more crowded, riots and reports of violence have declined. In many prisons, the inmate social system may have reorganized, so that correctional officers again can work through prisoners respected by fellow inmates. Yet, some observers contend that when wardens maintain order in this way, they enhance the positions of some prisoners at the expense of others. The leaders profit by receiving illicit privileges and favors, and they influence other prisoners by distributing benefits.

Further, descriptions of the contemporary maximum-security prison raise questions about administrators' ability to run these institutions using inmate leadership. In most of today's prisons, inmates are divided by race, ethnicity, age, and gang affiliation, so that no single leadership structure exists.

The Challenge of Governing Prisons

The factors of total power, rewards and punishments, exchange relationships, and inmate leadership exist in every prison and must be managed. How they are managed greatly influences the quality of prison life (Griffin & Hepburn, 2013). John DiIulio's research (1987) challenged the common assumption of many correctional administrators that "the cons run the joint." Instead, successful wardens have made their prisons function well by applying management principles within the context of their own style of leadership. Prisons can be governed, violence minimized, and services provided to the inmates if correctional executives and wardens exhibit leadership. Although governing prisons poses an extraordinary challenge, it can be and has been effectively accomplished.

☑**CHECK POINT**

4. **What four factors make governing prisons different from administering other public institutions?**
   The defects of total power, a limited system of rewards and punishments, exchange relations between correctional officers and inmates, and the strength of inmate leadership.

STOP&ANALYZE

Think about the type of rewards that correctional officers can use to recognize and encourage good behavior among prisoners. What types of rewards would you expect to be most effective, and why?

Correctional Officers: The Linchpins of Management

A prison is simultaneously supposed to keep, use, and serve its inmates. The achievement of these goals depends heavily on the performance of its correctional officers. Their job is not easy. Not only do they work long and difficult hours with a hostile client population, but their superiors expect them to do so with few resources or punishments at their disposal. Most of what they are expected to do must be accomplished by gaining and keeping the cooperation of the prisoners.

The Officer's Role

Over the past 30 years, the correctional officer's role has changed greatly. No longer responsible merely for "guarding," the correctional officer now stands as a crucial professional who has the closest contact with the prisoners and performs a variety of tasks. Officers are expected to counsel, supervise, protect, and process the inmates under their care. But the officer also works as a member of a complex bureaucratic organization and is expected to deal with clients impersonally and to follow formal procedures. Fulfilling these contradictory role expectations is difficult in itself, and the physical closeness of the officer and inmate over long periods exacerbates this difficulty.

Recruitment of Officers

Employment as a correctional officer is neither glamorous nor popular. The work is thought to be boring, the pay is low,

Much of the work of correctional officers involves searches and counting. Officers have a saying: "We're all doing time together, except guards are doing it in eight-hour shifts." What are the professional rewards—if any—of working as a correctional officer?

and career advancement is minimal. Studies have shown that one of the primary incentives for becoming involved in correctional work is the financial security that civil service status provides (Schlosser, Safran, & Sbaratta, 2010). In addition, because most correctional facilities are located in rural areas, prison work often is better than other available employment. Because correctional officers are recruited locally, many of them are rural and white (see Figure 11.2), in contrast to the majority of prisoners who come from urban areas and are often either African American or Hispanic (see Figure 11.3 page 372). Yet, some correctional officers see their work as a way of helping people, often the people most in need in U.S. society.

Today, because they need well-qualified, effective correctional officers, states seek to recruit quality personnel. Salaries have been raised so that the average annual pay nationally is $39,000 although states vary in their pay rates for corrections personnel. Thus, the lowest paid 10 percent of corrections officers nationally have salaries below $27,000 while the highest paid 10 percent earns more than $69,000 (Bureau of Labor Statistics, 2014). For example, the starting salary for corrections officers in Texas is $29,000, and after step increases over time, Texas officers reach a top salary of $39,000 after seven years of service (Texas Department of Criminal Justice, 2014). By contrast, after graduating from the state training academy, corrections officers in California begin their careers making $45,000 with the prospect of earning nearly $74,000 when they reach the top pay grade (California Department of Corrections and Rehabilitation, 2014). Because of attractive pay and retirement benefits, California can receive as many as 120,000 applications for 900 places in a training academy class (Finley, 2011). In other states, however, factors such as low salaries, crowded prisons, and a more violent class of prisoners have all probably contributed to a shortage of correctional officers when other job opportunities are available in the local area.

Correctional administrators have made special efforts to recruit women and minorities. Today approximately 30 percent of correctional officers belong to minority groups, and 25 percent of officers are women (see Figure 11.2). Female officers are no longer restricted to working with female offenders. For example, in Maryland, approximately 60 percent of correctional officers are women (Goldman, 2013).

FIGURE 11.2
Characteristics of Correctional Officers Compare these pie charts with the data found in Figure 11.3. How do correctional officers differ from those incarcerated in terms of sex and race/ethnicity?

Source: J. J. Stephan and J. C. Karberg, *Census of State and Federal Correctional Facilities, 2000* (Washington, DC: U.S. Department of Justice, 2003); J. J. Stephan, *Census of State and Federal Correctional Facilities, 2005.* Washington, DC: U.S. Department of Justice, 2008).

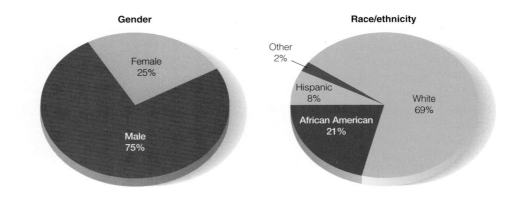

In the Federal Bureau of Prisons, only 27 percent of staff were women in 2012 (Bureau of Prisons, 2014; C. G. Camp, 2003; Stephan, 2008).

The diversification of the corrections workforce can create issues for corrections administrators who must be concerned about performance, effectiveness, job satisfaction, and stress among corrections officers (Cheeseman & Downey, 2012). For example, female officers often have greater perceptions of the risk of victimization on the job than do their male counterparts (J.A. Gordon, Proulx, & Grant, 2013). There are also issues about corrections officers' attitudes toward prisoners and whether prisoners' attitudes and behavior with respect to officers varies according to the demographic composition of the workforce.

States generally require cadets, or new recruits, to complete a preservice training program. The length of preservice training varies from state to state. For example, cadets in California receive 640 hours of training (California Department of Corrections and Rehabilitation, 2014). In contrast, new recruits in Kentucky receive only 120 hours of classroom and firearms training prior to supervised work (Kentucky Department of Corrections, 2014). These new recruits remain on probation while working for the first eight months of their tenure as corrections officers (Kleymeyer, 2010). In most states, new cadets receive at least a rudimentary knowledge of the job and correctional rules. Classroom work includes learning about report writing, communicable diseases, inmate classification, self-defense, and use of force. The classroom work, however, often bears little resemblance to problems confronted on the cell block or in the yard. On completing the course, the new officer is placed under the supervision of an experienced officer. On the job, the new officer experiences real-life situations and learns the necessary techniques and procedures. Through encounters with inmates and officers, the recruit becomes socialized to life behind the walls and gradually becomes part of that subculture.

For most correctional workers, being a custodial officer is a dead-end job. Although officers who perform well may be promoted to higher ranks, such as correctional counselor, few ever move into administrative positions. However, in some states and in the Federal Bureau of Prisons, people with college degrees can move up the career ladder to management positions without having to rise through the ranks of the custodial force.

Use of Force

The use of force by correctional officers, like that by the police, generates much controversy. Although corporal punishment and the excessive use of force are not permitted, correctional officers use force in many situations. They often confront inmates who challenge their authority or are attacking other inmates. Though unarmed and outnumbered, officers must maintain order and uphold institutional rules. Under these conditions, they feel justified in using force.

All correctional agencies now have policies regarding the legitimate use of force. Officers violating these policies may face an inmate lawsuit and dismissal

(M. Miller, 2014). There are five situations in which the use of force is legally acceptable:

1. *Self-defense.* If officers are threatened with physical attack, they may use a level of force that is reasonable to protect themselves from harm.
2. *Defense of third persons.* As in self-defense, an officer may use force to protect an inmate or another officer. Again, only reasonably necessary force may be used.
3. *Upholding prison rules.* If prisoners refuse to obey prison rules, officers may need to use force to maintain safety and security. For example, if an inmate refuses to return to his or her cell, using handcuffs and forcefully transferring the prisoner may be necessary.
4. *Prevention of a crime.* Force may be used to stop a crime, such as theft or destruction of property, from being committed.
5. *Prevention of escapes.* Officers may use force to prevent escapes, because they threaten the well-being of society and order within correctional institutions. Some agencies limit the use of deadly force to prisoners thought to be dangerous, whereas others require warning shots.

Correctional officers face challenges to self-control and professional decision making. Inmates often "push" officers in subtle ways such as moving slowly, or they use verbal abuse to provoke officers. Correctional officers are expected to run a "tight ship" and maintain order, often in situations where they are outnumbered and dealing with troubled people. In confrontational situations, they must defuse hostility yet uphold the rules—a difficult task at best.

☑ CHECK POINT

5. **Name three of the five legally acceptable reasons for the use of force.**
   Self-defense, defense of third persons, upholding prison rules, prevention of crime, prevention of escapes.

STOP&ANALYZE

What should happen when a corrections officer uses force in an inappropriate situation or uses too much force in an approved situation? If you were a warden, what procedures would you put in place to hear excessive-force complaints from prisoners? What would you do if you were persuaded that excessive force had been used by one of your officers?

Who Is in Prison?

The age, education, and criminal history of the inmate population influence how correctional institutions function. What are the characteristics of inmates in our nation's prisons? Do most offenders have long records of serious offenses, or are many of them first-time offenders who have committed minor crimes? Do some inmates have special needs that dictate their place in prison? These questions are crucial to understanding the work of wardens and correctional officers.

The federal government routinely collects information on all people incarcerated in the United States. The Bureau of Justice Statistics reports that a majority of prisoners are men aged 25 to 44 and members of minority groups. Approximately 40 percent of state prisoners have not completed high school (see Figure 11.3).

Recidivists and those convicted of violent crimes make up an overwhelming portion of the prison population. It is time-consuming to collect data on recidivism, because sufficient time has to lapse (usually several years) in order to collect reliable data on re-offending. In 2012, for example, out of 610,000 admissions to prison, 153,000 were parole violators being returned to prison for committing new crimes or violating parole conditions while living under supervision in the community (Carson & Golinelli, 2013b). The rate of return for parolees varies by region, with lower rates

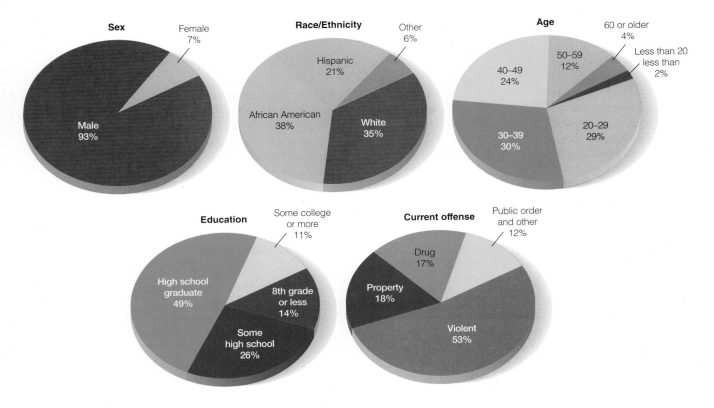

FIGURE 11.3

Characteristics of Male and Female Inmates in State Prisons These data reflect the types of people held in state prisons. Are any of the percentages surprising? Do these numbers provide any clues about whether too many people are held in prison or the specific challenges faced by corrections administrators?

Note: Totals may not equal 100% due to rounding.

Sources: E. A. Carson and W. J. Sabol, "Prisoners in 2011," *Bureau of Justice Statistics Bulletin* (Washington, DC: U.S. Department of Justice, 2012); E. A. Carson and D. Golinelli, "Prisoners in 2012—Advance Counts," *Bureau of Justice Statistics Bulletin* (Washington, DC: U.S. Department of Justice, 2013); E. A. Carson and D. Golinelli, "Prisoners in 2012: Trends in Admissions and Releases, 1991–2012," *Bureau of Justice Statistics Bulletin* (Washington, DC: U.S. Department of Justice, 2013); C. W. Harlow, "Education and Correctional Populations," *Bureau of Justice Statistics Special Report* (Washington, DC: U.S. Department of Justice, 2003).

of return in southern states and the highest rates in western states (Glaze & Bonczar, 2007). Many of today's prisoners have a history of persistent criminality. Four additional factors affect correctional operations: the increased number of elderly prisoners, the many prisoners with HIV/AIDS, the thousands of prisoners who are mentally ill, and the increase in long-term prisoners.

Elderly Prisoners

Correctional officials face difficult and costly problems from the growing number of inmates over age 55. In 2000, approximately 42,300 inmates in U.S. prisons were 55 years or older (A. J. Beck & Harrison, 2001). By 2011, this number had increased to over 121,000 (Carson & Sabol, 2012). In Florida, where the government defines *elderly* as over age 50, the oldest male inmate in 2010 was 90, and the oldest female inmate was 91. Prisoners over the age of 50 accounted for more than *twice* the number of sick calls as for younger inmates (State of Florida Correctional Medical Authority, 2010). A number of states have created "geriatric prisons" designed to hold older inmates classified according to need: wheelchair users and prisoners needing long-term (nursing home) care. Programs like the "True Grit" Senior Structured Living Program in Nevada is one example of a program created specifically for elderly prisoners. In this program, inmates benefit from programs designed to enhance their physical, mental, and spiritual health (M. T. Harrison, 2006).

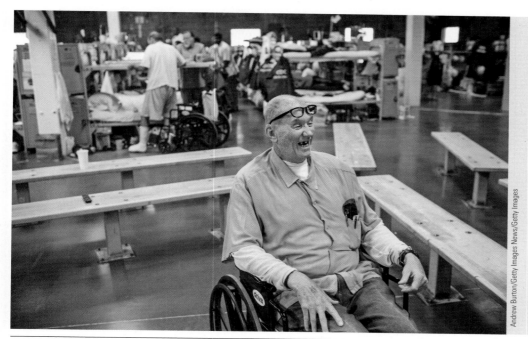

The imposition of long mandatory sentences increased the population of elderly prisoners and also prolonged the confinement of many prisoners who need medical care. These prisoners create extra financial burdens on correctional budgets. Are there less expensive ways to punish elderly and chronically ill prisoners?

To some extent, the prison population is growing older because it reflects the aging of the overall citizenry, but more so because sentencing practices have changed. Consecutive lengthy sentences for heinous crimes, long mandatory minimum sentences, and life sentences without parole mean that more people who enter prison will spend most or all of the rest of their lives behind bars.

Elderly prisoners have medical and security needs that differ from those of the average inmate (Habes, 2011). For example, they cannot climb into top bunks. In many states, special sections of the institution have been designated for this older population so they will not have to mix with the younger, tougher inmates. Elderly prisoners are more likely to develop chronic illnesses such as heart disease, stroke, and cancer; thus, the cost for maintaining an elderly inmate averages about $69,000 per year, triple the average cost for a younger inmate. Ironically, while in prison, the offender will benefit from much better medical care and live a longer life than if she or he were discharged and living in poverty in free society.

Prisoners with HIV/AIDS

For several decades, AIDS was found to be a leading cause of death for inmates aged 35 and younger. With 52 percent of the adult inmate population under age 35, correctional officials must cope with the problem of HIV as well as AIDS and related health issues. By the end of 2008, there were more than 20,000 HIV-positive inmates in state facilities (1.6 percent of the prison population) and 1,538 federal inmates (0.8 percent of the federal population) with AIDS or HIV-positive status (Maruschak, 2009). The number of HIV-positive inmates is undoubtedly low because not all states conduct mandatory testing of inmates. Further, the rate of confirmed AIDS cases in state and federal prisons is two and a half times higher than in the total U.S. population. Because many inmates who are HIV infected remain undiagnosed, these numbers underestimate the scope of the problem. However, advances in treatment and improved reporting have reduced the number of AIDS-related deaths in prison significantly, from over 1,000 deaths in 1995 to 79 in 2010 (Maruschak, 2012).

To deal with offenders who have AIDS symptoms or who test positive for the virus, prison officials can develop policies on methods to prevent transmission of the disease, including the housing arrangements of those infected and medical care for inmates with the full range of symptoms. However, administrators face a host of competing pressures as they decide what actions the institution should take (Westergaard, Spaulding, & Flanigan, 2013).

Mentally Ill Prisoners

Mass closings of public hospitals for the mentally ill began in the 1960s. At the time, new antipsychotic drugs made treating patients in the community seem a more humane and less expensive alternative to long-term hospitalization. It soon became apparent, however, that community treatment works only if the drugs are taken and if clinics and halfway houses actually exist to help the mentally ill. Mentally ill inmates tend to follow a revolving door from homelessness to incarceration and then back to the streets, with little treatment. In Miami, for example, 97 people diagnosed with a mental illness were arrested 2,200 times and spent a combined 27,000 days in jail over a five-year period, costing taxpayers $13 million (National Public Radio [NPR], 2011). Other people with mental illness commit crimes that lead them to serve sentences in prison. Thus, there are an estimated 350,000 mentally ill offenders currently in custody in corrections institutions and the three largest inpatient psychiatric facilities in the country are inside jails in Los Angeles, New York City, and Chicago (NPR, 2011).

Correctional workers are usually unprepared to deal with the mentally ill (Galanek, 2013). Cell-block officers, for instance, often do not know how to respond to disturbed inmates. Although most corrections systems have mental health units that segregate the ill, many inmates with psychiatric disorders live among other prisoners in the general population where they are teased and otherwise exploited. Mentally ill prisoners often suffer as the stress of confinement deepens their depression, intensifies delusions, or leads to mental breakdown. Some commit suicide.

Long-Term Prisoners

More prisoners in the United States serve longer sentences than do prisoners in other Western nations. A recent survey shows that nearly 310,000 prisoners are currently serving at least 20-year sentences. Of all inmates, about 10 percent are serving "natural life," which means there is no possibility that they will be paroled, a tripling since 1992. These long-term prisoners are often the same people who will become elderly offenders, with all their attendant problems. Each life sentence costs the taxpayers over $1 million.

Severe depression, feelings of hopelessness, and other health problems are common among long-termers. Such emotional stress tends to take place earlier in the sentence as these inmates lose contact with their families. Addressing the mental health needs of this special population is critical to preventing suicide attempts.

Long-term prisoners are generally not seen as control problems. They receive disciplinary infractions about half as often as do short-term inmates. Rather, administrators must find ways to make long terms bearable. Experts suggest that administrators follow three main principles: (1) maximize opportunities for inmates to exercise choice in their living circumstances, (2) create opportunities for meaningful living, and (3) help inmates maintain contact with the outside world (Flanagan, 1995). Many long-term inmates will eventually be released after spending their prime years incarcerated. Will offenders be able to support themselves when they return to the community at age 50, 60, or 70?

The contemporary inmate population presents several challenges to correctional workers. Resources may not be available to provide rehabilitative programs for most inmates. Even if the resources exist, the goal of maintaining a safe and healthy environment may tax the staff's abilities. These difficulties are multiplied still further by AIDS and the increasing numbers of elderly and long-term prisoners.

☑ **CHECK POINT**

6. **What are the major characteristics of today's prisoners?**
Today's prisoners are largely men in their late twenties to early thirties with less than a high school education. They are disproportionately members of minority groups.

STOP&ANALYZE

Draft a solution to alleviate one of the four problems discussed above: elderly prisoners, prisoners with HIV/AIDS, mental illness in prisons, or prisoners serving long sentences. In light of the budget difficulties faced by states, are there any solutions that can save money?

The Convict World

Inmates of a maximum-security prison do not serve their time in isolation. Rather, prisoners form a society with its own traditions, norms, and leadership structure. Some choose to associate with only a few close friends; others form cliques along racial or "professional" lines. Still others serve as the politicians of the convict society; they attempt to represent convict interests and distribute valued goods in return for support. Just as the free world has a social culture, the "inside" has a prisoner subculture. Membership in a group provides mutual protection from theft and physical assault, the basis of wheeling and dealing, and a source of cultural identity.

As in any society, the convict world has certain norms and values. Often described as the **inmate code**, these norms and values develop within the prison social system and help define the inmate's image of the model prisoner. As Robert Johnson notes, "The public culture of the prison has norms that dictate behavior 'on the yard' and in other public areas of the prison such as mess halls, gyms, and the larger program and work sites" (2002:100). Prison is an ultramasculine world. The culture breathes masculine toughness and insensitivity, impugning softness, and emphasizes the use of hostility and manipulation in one's relations with fellow inmates and staff. It makes caring and friendly behavior, especially with respect to the staff, look servile and silly (Sabo, Kupers, & London, 2001:7).

The code also emphasizes the solidarity of all inmates against the staff. For example, according to the code, inmates should never inform on one another, pry into one another's affairs, "run off at the mouth," or put another inmate on the spot. They must be tough and trust neither the officers nor the principles for which they stand. Guards, who are called "hacks" or "screws," are to be considered always wrong and the prisoners always right.

Some sociologists believe that the code emerges within the institution as a way to lessen the pain of imprisonment (Sykes, 1958); others believe that it is part of the criminal subculture that prisoners bring with them (Irwin & Cressey, 1962). The inmate who follows the code enjoys a certain amount of admiration from other inmates as a "right guy" or a "real man." Those who break the code are labeled "rat" or "punk" and will probably spend their prison life at the bottom of the convict social structure, alienated from the rest of the population and targeted for abuse (Sykes, 1958:84).

A single, overriding inmate code probably no longer exists in American prisons. Instead, convict society has divided itself along racial lines (Carroll, 1974; Irwin, 1980). The level of adherence to the inmate code also differs among institutions, with greater modifications to local situations found in maximum-security prisons. Still, the core code described by Sykes over 50 years ago remains.

In a changing society that has no single code of behavior accepted by the entire population, the tasks of administrators become much more difficult. They must be aware of the different groups, recognize the norms and rules that members hold in each, and deal with the leaders of many cliques rather than with a few inmates who

inmate code The values and norms of the prison social system that define the inmates' idea of the model prisoner.

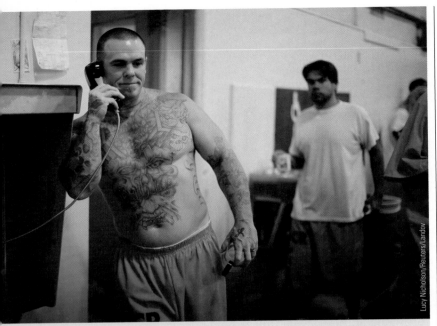

Contemporary prison society is divided along social, ethnic, and gang subgroups. There is no longer a single inmate code to which all prisoners subscribe. As a correctional officer, how would you deal with white supremacists and other gangs based on racial and ethnic divisions within the prison population?

have risen to top positions in the inmate society. In the Close Up feature, TJ Granack provides "Survival Tips for Beginners."

Adaptive Roles

On entering prison, a newcomer ("fish") is confronted by the question "How am I going to do my time?" Some decide to withdraw and isolate themselves. Others decide to become full participants in the convict social system. The choice, influenced by prisoners' values and experiences, helps determine strategies for survival and success.

Most male inmates use one of four basic role orientations to adapt to prison: "doing time," "gleaning," "jailing," and functioning as a "disorganized criminal" (Irwin, 1970:67).

Doing Time   Men "doing time" view their prison term as a brief, inevitable break in their criminal careers, a cost of doing business. They try to serve their terms with the least amount of suffering and the greatest amount of comfort. They avoid trouble by living by the inmate code, finding activities to fill their days, forming friendships with a few other convicts, and generally doing what they think is necessary to survive and to get out as soon as possible.

Gleaning   Inmates who are "gleaning" try to take advantage of prison programs to better themselves and improve their prospects for success after release. They use the resources at hand: libraries, correspondence courses, vocational training, schools. Some make a radical conversion away from a life of crime.

Jailing   "Jailing" is the choice of those who cut themselves off from the outside and try to construct a life within the prison. These are often "state-raised" youths who have spent much of their lives in institutional settings and who identify little with the values of free society. These are the inmates who seek power and influence in the prison society, often becoming key figures in the politics and economy of prison life.

Disorganized Criminal   A fourth role orientation—the "disorganized criminal"— describes inmates who cannot develop any of the other three orientations. They may be of low intelligence or afflicted with psychological or physical disabilities, and they find functioning in prison society difficult. They are "human putty" to be manipulated by others. These are also the inmates who cannot adjust to prison life and who develop emotional disorders, attempt suicide, and violate prison rules (K. Adams, 1992).

As these roles suggest, prisoners are not members of an undifferentiated mass. Individual convicts choose to play specific roles in prison society. The roles they choose reflect the physical and social environment they have experienced and also influence their relationships and interactions in prison. How do most prisoners serve their time? Although the media generally portray prisons as violent, chaotic places, research shows that most inmates want to get through their sentence without trouble. As journalist Pete Earley found in his study of Leavenworth, roughly 80 percent of inmates try to avoid trouble and do their time as easily as possible (1992:44).

CLOSE UP

Survival Tips for Beginners

TJ Granack

Okay, so you just lost your case. Maybe you took a plea bargain. Whatever. The point is you've been sentenced. You've turned yourself over to the authorities and you're in the county jail waiting to catch the next chain to the R Unit (receiving) where you'll be stripped and shaved and photographed and processed and sent to one of the various prisons in your state.

So what's a felon to do? Here are some survival tips that may make your stay less hellish:

1. *Commit an Honorable Crime.* Commit a crime that's considered, among convicts, to be worthy of respect. I was lucky. I went down for first-degree attempted murder, so my crime fell in the "honorable" category. Oh, goodie. So I just had to endure the everyday sort of danger and abuse that comes with prison life.
2. *Don't Gamble.* Not cards, not chess, not the Super Bowl, and if you do, don't bet too much. If you lose too much and pay up (don't even think of doing otherwise), then you'll be known as a rich guy who'll be very popular with the vultures. . . .
3. *Never Loan Anyone Anything.* Because if you do, you'll be expected to collect one way or another. If you don't collect you will be known as a mark, as someone without enough heart to take back his own. . . .
4. *Make No Eye Contact.* Don't look anyone in the eye. Ever. Locking eyes with another man, be he a convict or a guard, is considered a challenge, a threat, and should therefore be avoided.
5. *Pick Your Friends Carefully.* When you choose a friend, you've got to be prepared to deal with anything that person may have done. Their reputation is yours, and the consequences can be enormous.

6. *Fight and Fight Dirty.* You have to fight, and not according to the Marquis of Queensbury Rules, either. If you do it right, you'll only have to do it once or twice. If you don't, expect regular whooping and loss of possessions. . . .
7. *Mind Your Own Business.* Never get in the middle of anyone else's discussion/argument/confrontation/fight. Never offer unsolicited knowledge or advice.
8. *Keep a Good Porn Collection.* If you don't have one, the boys will think you're funny. . . .
9. *Don't Talk to Staff, Especially Guards.* Any prolonged discussion or associations with staff make you susceptible to rumor and suspicion of being a snitch.
10. *Never Snitch.* Or even appear to snitch. And above all, avoid the real thing. And if you do, you'd better not get caught.

Researching the Internet

Compare this set of rules with the official information given to North Carolina prisoners to convey the rules and regulations of prison. To link to this document, go to http://www.doc.state.nc.us/Publications/inmate%20rule%20book.pdf.

For Critical Analysis

If you were sent to prison, how would you seek to learn the code that prisoners enforce among themselves?

Source: From TJ Granack "Welcome To The Steel Hotel: Survival Tips for Beginners" in The Funhouse Mirror (pp. 6–10), edited by Robert Gordon Ellis. Copyright © 2000 by Washington State University Press. Reprinted by permission of Washington State University Press. http://wsupress.wsu.edu/recenttitles/.

The Prison Economy

In prison, as outside, individuals want goods and services. Although the state feeds, clothes, and houses all prisoners, amenities are sparse. Prisoners lack everything but bare necessities. Their diet and routine are monotonous and their recreational opportunities scarce. They experience a loss of identity (due to uniformity of treatment) and a lack of responsibility. In short, prison is relatively unique in having been deliberately designed as "an island of poverty in the midst of a society of relative abundance" (V. Williams & Fish, 1974:40).

The number of items that a prisoner can purchase or receive through legitimate channels differs from state to state and from facility to facility. For example, prisoners in some state institutions may have televisions, civilian clothing, and hot plates. Not all prisoners enjoy these luxuries, nor do these amenities satisfy the lingering desire for a variety of other goods. Some state legislatures have decreed that amenities will be prohibited and that prisoners should return to the spartan living conditions that existed before amenities were introduced.

Recognizing that prisoners do have some basic needs that are not met, prisons have a commissary, or "store," from which inmates may, on a scheduled basis, purchase a limited number of items—toilet articles, tobacco, snacks, and other food products—in exchange for credits drawn on their "bank accounts." The size of a bank account depends on the amount of money deposited at the time of the inmate's entrance, gifts sent by relatives, and amounts earned in the low-paying prison industries.

However, the peanut butter, soap, and cigarettes of the typical prison store in no way satisfy the consumer needs and desires of most prisoners. Consequently, an informal, underground economy acts as a major element in prison society. Many items taken for granted on the outside are inordinately valued on the inside. For example, talcum powder and deodorant become more important because of the limited bathing facilities. Goods and services that a prisoner would not have consumed at all outside prison can take on an exaggerated importance inside prison. For example, unable to get alcohol, offenders may seek a similar effect by sniffing glue. Or, to distinguish themselves from others, offenders may pay laundry workers to iron a shirt in a particular way, a modest version of conspicuous consumption.

Many studies point to the pervasiveness of this economy. The research shows that a market economy provides the goods (contraband) and services not available or not allowed by prison authorities. In many prisons, inmates run private "stores." Food stolen from the kitchen for late-night snacks, homemade wine, and drugs such as marijuana are available in these stores.

As a principal feature of prison culture, this informal economy reinforces the norms and roles of the social system and influences the nature of interpersonal relationships. The extent of the underground economy and its ability to produce desired goods and services—food, drugs, alcohol, sex, preferred living conditions—vary according to the scope of official surveillance, the demands of the consumers, and the opportunities for entrepreneurship. Inmates' success as "hustlers" determines the luxuries and power they can enjoy.

Because real money is always prohibited, a traditional currency of the prison economy is cigarettes—even when prison officials try to ban smoking. Cigarettes are easily transferable, have a stable and well-known standard of value, and come in "denominations" of singles, packs, and cartons. Furthermore, they are in demand by smokers. Even those who do not smoke keep cigarettes for prison currency. As more prisons become smoke free, however, institutions that ban cigarettes have seen new forms of currency emerge, such as cans of tuna fish, postage stamps, and soap (M. Santos, 2004). At the same time, tobacco becomes more valuable because of its scarcity in the smoke-free facilities, with prisoners making efforts to persuade corrections officers to smuggle in tobacco. This issue is described in "A Question of Ethics" at the end of the chapter.

Certain positions in the prison society enhance opportunities for entrepreneurs. For example, inmates assigned to work in the kitchen, warehouse, and administrative office steal food, clothing, building materials, and even information to sell or trade to other prisoners. The goods may then become part of other market transactions. Thus, the exchange of a dozen eggs for two packs of cigarettes may result in the reselling of the eggs in the form of egg sandwiches made on a hot plate for five cigarettes each. Meanwhile, the kitchen worker who stole the eggs may use the income to get a laundry worker to starch his shirts, to get drugs from a hospital orderly, or to pay another prisoner for sex.

Participation in the prison economy can put inmates at greater risk for victimization while incarcerated (Copes, Higgins, Tewksbury, & Dabney, 2010). Economic transactions can lead to violence when goods are stolen, debts are not paid, or agreements are violated. Disruptions of the economy can occur when officials conduct periodic "lockdowns" and inspections. Confiscation of contraband can result in temporary shortages and price readjustments, but gradually, profits result. The prison economy, like that of the outside world, allocates goods and services, rewards and sanctions, and it is closely linked to the society it serves.

7. Why is it unlikely that a single, overriding inmate code exists in today's prisons?
The prison society is fragmented by racial and ethnic divisions.

8. What are the four role orientations found in adult male prisons?
Doing time, gleaning, jailing, and functioning as a disorganized criminal.

9. Why does an underground economy exist in prison?
To provide goods and services not available through regular channels.

Is it possible to stop the underground economy in prisons? If you were a warden, what are two steps you would take to reduce the problems associated with the underground economy? (For this discussion, disregard whether you believe that you—or anyone—can completely stop it.)

Women in Prison

Most studies of prisons have focused on institutions for men. How do prisons for women differ, and what special problems do female inmates face?

Women constitute only 7 percent (about 101,000) of the entire U.S. prison population (Carson & Golinelli, 2013b). However, the growth rate in the number of incarcerated women has exceeded that of men since 1981. In fact, from 2000 to 2010, the male population increased by 16 percent, whereas that of women increased by 25 percent (Guerino, Harrison, & Sabol, 2011). The increased number of women in prison has significantly affected the delivery of programs, housing conditions, medical care, staffing, and security.

Female offenders are incarcerated in 98 confinement facilities for women and 93 facilities that house men and women separately. Life in these facilities both differs from and resembles life in institutions for men alone. Women's prisons are smaller, with looser security and less structured relationships; the underground economy is not as well developed; and female prisoners seem less committed to the inmate code. Women also serve shorter sentences than do men, so their prison society is more fluid as new members join and others leave.

Many women's prisons have the outward appearance of a college campus, often seen as a group of "cottages" around a central administration/dining/program building.

Women's experiences in prison can differ markedly from those of men. Although there is less violence between prisoners in women's institutions, women often have fewer options for educational and vocational programs. In addition, many prisons have discovered problems with male correctional officers sexually abusing women prisoners. How would you organize the selection of staff, staff training, and the development of programs to properly run a prison for women?

Generally these facilities lack the high walls, guard towers, and cyclone fences found at most prisons for men. In recent years, however, the trend has been to upgrade security for women's prisons by adding barbed wire, higher fences, and other devices to prevent escapes.

The characteristics of correctional facilities for women also include geographic remoteness and inmate heterogeneity. Few states operate more than one institution for women, so inmates generally live far from children, families, friends, and attorneys. In many institutions, the small numbers of inmates limit the extent to which the needs of individual offenders can be recognized and treated. Housing classifications are often so broad that dangerous or mentally ill inmates are mixed with women who have committed minor offenses and have no psychological problems. Similarly, available rehabilitative programs are often not used to their full extent, because correctional departments fail to recognize women's problems and needs.

In most respects, we can see incarcerated women, like male prisoners, as disadvantaged losers in this complex and competitive society. However, the two groups differ with regard to types of offenses and length of sentences, patterns of drug use, and criminal history. Thirty-seven percent of female prisoners are sentenced for violent offenses, compared with 54 percent of male prisoners, and 25 percent for drug-related offenses, versus 16 percent of the men (Carson & Golinelli, 2013a). Overall, women receive shorter maximum sentences than do men. Half of the women have a maximum sentence of 5 years or less, whereas half of the men have a sentence of 10 years or less.

The Subculture of Women's Prisons

Studies of the subculture of women's prisons have been less extensive than those of male convict society. Further, just as few ethnographic studies of men's prisons have taken place during the past two decades, very few of women's prisons exist.

Much early investigation of women's prisons focused on types of social relationships among female offenders. As in all types of penal institutions, same-sex relationships were found, but unlike in male prisons, such relationships among women appeared more voluntary than coerced. Perhaps more importantly, scholars reported that female inmates tended to form pseudo-families in which they adopted various roles—father, mother, daughter, sister—and interacted as a unit, rather than identifying with the larger prisoner subculture (Girshick, 1999; Propper, 1982). Esther Heffernan views these "play" families as a "direct, conscious substitution for the family relationships broken by imprisonment, or . . . the development of roles that perhaps were not fulfilled in the actual home environment" (1972:41–42). She also notes the economic aspect of the play families and the extent to which they are formed to provide for their members. Such cooperative relationships help relieve the tensions of prison life, assist the socialization of new inmates, and permit individuals to act according to clearly defined roles and rules.

In discussing the available research on women in prison, we need to consider the most recent shifts in prison life. Just as the subculture of male prisons has changed since the pioneering research of the 1950s, the climate of female prisons has undoubtedly changed. Kimberly Greer (2000) found support for the idea that, compared with male prisons, prisons for women are less violent, involve less gang activity, and lack racial tension; however, the respondents indicated that their interpersonal relationships may be less stable and less familial than in the past. They reported higher levels of mistrust among women and greater economic manipulation.

In one notable study of women's prison culture, Barbara Owen (1998) found that the inmates at the Central California Women's Facility developed various styles of doing time. She observed that the vast majority wanted to avoid "the mix"—"behavior that can bring trouble and conflict with staff and other prisoners." A primary feature of "the mix" is anything for which one can lose "good time" or can result in being sent to administrative segregation. Being in "the mix" was related to "'homo-secting,' involvement in drugs, fights, and 'being messy,' that is, being involved in conflict and trouble." Owen found that most women want to do their time and go home, but some "are more at home in prison and do not seem to care if they 'lost time'" (Owen, 1998:179).

Male versus Female Subcultures

Comparisons of male and female prisons are complicated by the nature of the research: most studies have been conducted in single-sex institutions, and most follow theories and concepts first developed in male prisons. However, it is important to recognize the differences between men and women who are incarcerated. Figure 11.3 contains descriptive information on the characteristics of incarcerated men and women in the United States. Based on what we know about women's prisons, the following facts may explain the differences in subculture:

- Over half of male inmates but only a third of female inmates are serving time for violent offenses.
- There is less violence in prisons for women than in prisons for men.
- Women show greater responsiveness to prison programs.
- Men's prison populations are divided by security level, but most women serve time in facilities where the entire population is mixed.
- Men tend to segregate themselves by race; this is less true of women.
- Men rarely become intimate with their keepers, but many women share their lives with officers.

A major difference between the two types of prisons relates to interpersonal relationships. Male prisoners act for themselves and are evaluated by others according to how they adhere to subcultural norms. An early comparative study of one women's prison and four men's prisons found that men believe they must demonstrate physical strength and consciously avoid any mannerisms that might imply homosexuality (Fox, 1982). To gain recognition and status within the convict community, the male prisoner must strictly adhere to these values. Men form cliques, but not the family networks found in prisons for women. Male norms stress autonomy, self-sufficiency, and the ability to cope with one's own problems, and men are expected to "do their own time." Fox found little sharing in the men's prisons.

Women, on the other hand, place less emphasis on achieving status or recognition within the prisoner community. Women are also less likely "to impose severe restrictions on the sexual (or emotional) conduct of other members" (Fox, 1982:100). As noted previously, in prisons for women, close ties seem to exist among small groups akin to extended families. These family groups provide emotional support and share resources.

The differences between male and female prisoner subcultures have been ascribed to the nurturing, maternal qualities of women. Some critics charge that such an analysis stereotypes female behavior and imputes a biological basis to personality where none exists. Of importance as well is the issue of inmate–inmate violence in male and female institutions. Physical violence between female inmates occurs less often than between male inmates, but it is important to note that the violence that does exist is shaped by the different culture in women's prisons (Owen, Wells, Pollock, Muscat, & Torres, 2008).

Issues in the Incarceration of Women

Under pressures for equal opportunity, states seem to believe that they should run women's prisons as they do prisons for men, with the same policies and procedures. However, advocates for female prisoners have urged governments to keep in mind that women inmates have different needs than men (Bartels & Gaffney, 2011). Understanding the pathways by which women end up incarcerated can also help prison and jail administrators manage their facilities. Many incarcerated women have been victims of physical and sexual abuse, and that history can affect their behavior while incarcerated (McCampbell, 2005).

Although correctional departments have been playing "catch up" to meet the unique needs of women offenders, sexual misconduct by officers persists, along with women prisoners' demands for education and training, medical services, and methods for dealing with the problems of mothers and their children. We next examine each of these issues and the policy implications they pose for the future.

Sexual Misconduct   When the number of female prisoners increased in the late 1990s, cases of sexual misconduct by male correctional officers escalated. After an investigation of sexual misconduct of officers in the women's prisons of five states—California, Georgia, Illinois, Michigan, and New York—Human Rights Watch reported that male officers had raped, sexually assaulted, and abused female inmates. In 2009, the state of Michigan paid over $100 million to 500 female prisoners who were raped in Michigan prisons (McFarlane, 2009).

Congress approved the federal Prison Rape Elimination act as a national law in 2003 (Struckman-Johnson & Struckman-Johnson, 2013). This law requires that all state correctional systems develop standards in an effort to collect data on rape in prisons and reduce its incidence; the act also provides funding to state agencies to meet these national standards (Prison Rape Elimination Act, 117 STAT. 972). Research funded by this initiative has determined that prison inmates do not view rape in the same way that people outside prisons do. Even with protections against rape, women in prison frequently report their knowledge of "consensual" sexual relationships between inmates and guards (Fleischer & Krienert, 2006). However, because prison guards exert power and control over inmates in prisons, it is difficult to argue that sex between the two can be considered consensual. In fact, guards who have sex with inmates under their care can be charged criminally for such behavior.

Educational and Vocational Training Programs   A major criticism of women's prisons is that they lack the variety of vocational and educational programs available in male institutions. Critics also charge that programs tend to conform to sexual stereotypes of "female" occupations—cosmetology, food service, housekeeping, sewing (Morash, Haarr, & Rucker, 1994). Such training does not correspond to the wider employment opportunities available to women in today's world. However, both men's and women's facilities usually offer educational programs so inmates can become literate and earn general equivalency diplomas (GEDs).

Such programs matter a great deal, considering that, upon release, most women must support themselves, and many must support their children as well (Kruttschnitt, 2010). In addition, vocational training programs have been shown to reduce the likelihood that inmates will return to prison after being released. Female offenders in prison have different needs than male offenders, and vocational training should be designed around the specific needs of women (Holtfreter & Morash, 2003).

Medical Services   Women's prisons lack proper medical services. Yet, because of their socioeconomic status and limited access to preventive medical care, women usually have more serious health problems than do men. Compared with men, they have a higher incidence of asthma, drug abuse, diabetes, and heart disorders (T. L. Anderson, 2003). In addition, prison officials often dismiss the gynecological needs of female inmates as "unimportant" (L. Braithwaite, Treadwell, & Arriola, 2005). Although a higher percentage of women than men report receiving medical services in prison, women's institutions are less likely than men's to have a full-time medical staff or hospital facilities.

Saying that corrections must "defuse the time bomb," Leslie Acoca argues that failure to provide female inmates with basic preventive and medical treatments such as immunizations, breast cancer screenings, and management of chronic diseases "is resulting in the development of more serious health problems that are exponentially more expensive to treat" (1997:67). She says that poor medical care for the incarcerated merely shifts costs to overburdened community health care systems after release.

Mothers and Their Children   Of greatest concern to incarcerated women is the fate of their children. Over 60 percent of women inmates are mothers, with 25 percent having children aged four or younger. Especially troubling is the increase in the number of children younger than 18 with an incarcerated parent—the number of children with a mother in prison more than doubled between 1991 and 2007 (Glaze & Maruschak, 2008).

Because about 65 percent of incarcerated mothers were single caretakers of minor children before they entered prison, they do not always have partners to take care of their children. In about one-third of these cases, children are cared for by their fathers. In most cases, though, they live with grandparents or other relatives. If neither the father nor other relatives take them, they live with friends of the family or are placed in foster care (Glaze & Maruschak, 2008). Due to high incarceration rates in black communities, locking up parents differentially affects black children and harms communities (Roberts, 2004). Children with incarcerated mothers are more likely to have contact with the criminal justice system as adults and are more likely to be convicted of crimes as adults (Huebner & Gustafson, 2007).

Imprisoned mothers have difficulty maintaining contact with their children. Because most states have only one or two prisons for women, mothers may be incarcerated 150 miles or more away. This makes transportation difficult, visits short and infrequent, and phone calls uncertain and irregular. When the children do visit the prison, they face strange and intimidating surroundings. In some institutions, children must conform to the rules governing adult visitations: strict time limits and no physical contact.

Other correctional facilities, however, seek ways to help mothers maintain links to their children. For example, at Logan Correctional Center, the prison to which all women prisoners in Illinois were moved in 2013, there are a variety of programs (Fak, 2013). The "Mom and Me" Camp brings children ages 7 through 12 together with their imprisoned mothers for three days of activities in the summer. Through the "Family Connections Visitation" program, an outside social services agency transports 30 children and their caregivers, usually their grandmothers, to visit imprisoned mothers each month. The assistance of the outside agency with transportation and arrangements creates visitation opportunities that would otherwise not occur. In the prison's "Operation Storybook" program, incarcerated mothers and grandmothers have the opportunity to read children's books aloud that are recorded and copied on CDs to be sent to their children and grandchildren. The Illinois prison also cooperates with the national Angel Tree program through which volunteers provide Christmas gifts, summer camp experiences, and mentors for the children of incarcerated mothers.

In some states, children can meet with their mothers at almost any time, for extended periods, and in playrooms or nurseries where contact is possible. Some states even transport children to visit their mothers; some institutions let children stay overnight with their mothers. A few prisons have family visitation programs that let the inmate, her legal husband, and her children be together, often in a mobile home or apartment, for up to 72 hours (D'Alessio, Flexon, & Stolzenberg, 2013).

The future of women's correctional institutions is hard to predict. More women are being sent to prison now, and more have committed the violent crimes and drug offenses that used to be more typical of male offenders. Will these changes continue to affect the adaptive roles and social relationships that differentiate women's prisons from men's? Will women's prisons need to become more security conscious

☑ CHECK POINT

10. **What accounts for the neglect of facilities and programs in women's prisons?**
The small number of female inmates compared with the number of male inmates.

11. **How do the social relationships among female prisoners differ from those among their male counterparts?**
Men are more individualistic, and their norms stress autonomy, self-sufficiency, and the ability to cope with one's own problems. Women are more sharing with one another.

12. **What problems do female prisoners face in maintaining contact with their children?**
The distance of prisons from homes, intermittent telephone privileges, and unnatural visiting environment.

STOP&ANALYZE

To what extent should society worry about, pay attention to, and spend money on programs for children whose parents are in prison? Give two arguments supporting each side of this debate.

Prison Programs

Modern correctional institutions differ from those of the past in the number and variety of programs provided for inmates. Early penitentiaries included prison industries, but educational, vocational, and treatment programs were added when rehabilitation goals became prevalent. During the last 35 years, as the public called for harsher punishment of criminals, legislators have gutted prison educational and treatment programs as "frills" that only "coddled" inmates. In addition, the great increase in the number of prisoners has limited access to those programs that are still available.

Administrators argue that programs help them deal with the problem of time on the prisoners' hands. They know that the more programs prisons offer, the less likely that inmate idleness will turn into hostility; less cell time means fewer tensions. Evidence suggests that inmate education and jobs may positively affect the running of prisons, as well as reduce recidivism. However, in an era of government budget cuts, prison vocational training and education programs are often targeted for reduction because they are less essential than preserving resources for safety and security. In 2010, California cut its prisoner vocational training programs in half and reduced the number of instructional hours for literacy classes and other education programs ("California to Redesign Prison Education," 2011). In other examples, Indiana cut millions of dollars from a program that permitted prisoners to earn college credits, and advocates in North Carolina worry that prison programs will be targeted for reductions (Slabaugh, 2011; Freskos, 2011).

There is also the first indication of a potential countertrend in support of prison programs. As governors and legislators become more aware of the need to prepare convicted offenders for reentry into society, they may become more willing to devote resources to vocational and educational programs. In 2014, for example, New York Governor Andrew Cuomo proposed spending state money to provide college classes for incarcerated offenders, a practice that had ended 2 years earlier. However, many people oppose providing free programs for criminal offenders that law-abiding citizens must struggle to pay for on their own. Thus, it remains to be seen whether Cuomo's proposal will become a reality or if other states might make similar moves (Rivard, 2014). The New York proposal reflects the idea that programs can be used to cut recidivism. There are also other research-based programs and treatments that can be used to cut recidivism, as discussed in the "Evidence-Based Practice and Policy" feature.

Prison Practices to Reduce Recidivism

The National Institute of Corrections promotes evidence-based practices in prisons by holding training sessions and distributing research-based materials on effective practices, procedures, and programs. A central element of evidence-based programming to reduce recidivism is the assessment and classification of prisoners to identify their individual problems and needs. Effective classification requires the use of an assessment instrument that asks appropriate and necessary questions to determine prisoners' needs. One prominent assessment tool is the Level of Service Inventory-Revised instrument that is used in structured interviews with individual prisoners to gather information about 54 items, including criminal history, educational background, family relationships, substance abuse problems, emotional and personal issues, and social attitudes. According to the evidence-practice approach, programs and treatments cannot produce effective results unless the needs and problems of prisoners have been accurately assessed.

Other principles of evidence-based practices in prisons include focusing resources on prisoners with the greatest needs and ensuring that programs and treatments are of sufficient duration and appropriate timing to help with successful reentry and avoidance of recidivism. Thus, studies indicate that high-risk offenders should spend 40 to 70 percent of their time in highly structured activities and programs in the months preceding their release from prison into community supervision. In addition, there should be extended continuity of treatment during community supervision for those with specific, difficult problems, such as drug addicts and sex offenders. As one state's description of evidence-based practices described the approach and goal, "treatment should be delivered as a life-long plan for changing entrenched negative lifestyle behaviors."

Evidence-based practices also rely on positive reinforcement approaches to helping offenders change their attitudes and behavior and learn new ways to think about values, choice of friends, intoxicating substances, and interactions with others. Obviously, the use of effective evidence-based practices does not merely require devoting time and resources to teaching and counseling offenders, but also extensive training for staff members who are responsible for such efforts.

Researching the Internet

Learn more about classification of prisoners through the many publications available online from the National Institute of Corrections. To link to this website, go to http://nicic.gov/library/topic/440-prison-classification.

Implementing New Practices

Prisons face challenges in considering whether and how to implement evidence-based practices aimed at reducing recidivism. They must always place a priority on safety and security. In addition, they may not have staff members with appropriate expertise and training to implement evidence-based programs. How much time, money, and staff should be devoted to programs for offenders in prison? In an era of budget cuts, can states afford to present extensive programs when they must reduce prison populations and staffing in order to save money? If you were a governor, would you see the greatest benefit to society from cutting budgets for corrections programs in order to reduce burdens on taxpayers or increasing corrections program budgets in order to reduce recidivism? Write a memo that explains two reasons that support your position.

Source: "Evidence Based Correctional Practices," report prepared by the Colorado Division of Criminal Justice based on materials from the National Institute of Corrections, August 2007.

Classification of Prisoners

Determining the appropriate program for an individual prisoner usually involves a process called **classification**. A committee—often comprising the heads of the security, treatment, education, and industry departments—evaluates the inmate's security level, treatment and educational needs, work assignment, and eventually readiness for release.

Classification decisions are often based on the institution's needs rather than on those of the inmates. For example, inmates from the city may be assigned to farm work because that is where they are needed. Further, certain programs may remain limited even though the demand for them is great. Thus, inmates may find that the few open seats in, for example, a computer course are filled and that there is a long waiting list. Prisoners often become angered and frustrated by the classification process and the limited availability of programs. Although release on parole can depend on a good record of participation in these programs, entrance for some inmates is blocked.

classification The process of assigning an inmate to a category specifying his or her needs for security, treatment, education, work assignment, and readiness for release.

Companies are finding that prison labor can be more efficient than outsourcing to low-wage countries elsewhere in the world. Prisoners at Wabash Valley Correctional Facility assemble yo-yos as part of a joint venture between the Indiana Department of Corrections' prison industry program and the Flambeau Products Corporation. Are these prisoners doing jobs that would otherwise provide wages for law-abiding citizens?

AP Images/Tribune-Star, Jim Avelis

Educational Programs

Offenders constitute one of the most undereducated groups in the U.S. population. In many systems, all inmates who have not completed eighth grade are assigned full-time to prison school. Many programs provide remedial help in reading, English, and math. Nearly 80 percent of prisons offer courses to enable prisoners to earn their GED, but only 35 percent offer courses in cooperation with a college or university (Stephan, 2008). Funds have been reduced for college courses available to prisoners. The Comprehensive Crime Control Act of 1994 bans federal funding (Pell Grants) to prisoners for postsecondary education (Buruma, 2005). Studies have shown that prisoners assigned to education programs tend to avoid committing crimes after release (Skorton & Altschuler, 2013; Andrews & Bonta, 1994). However, it remains unclear whether education helps rehabilitate these offenders or whether the types of prisoners ("gleaners") assigned to education programs tend to be those motivated to avoid further crimes.

Vocational Education

Vocational education programs attempt to teach offenders a marketable job skill. Unfortunately, too many programs train inmates for trades that already have an adequate labor supply or in which new methods have made the skills taught obsolete.

Inmates often lack the attributes necessary to obtain and keep a job—punctuality, accountability, deference to supervisors, cordiality to coworkers. Therefore, most prisoners need to learn not only a skill but also how to act in the work world. For example, Minnesota's "Affordable Homes Program" teaches prisoners construction skills as they build or remodel homes for low-income families. An evaluation of this program determined that prisoners who participated were more likely to be hired in construction jobs after release, and the state saved over $13 million by using inmate labor; however, graduates of this program did not have reduced rates of criminal behavior after release (Bohmert & Duwe, 2012).

Yet another problem is perhaps the toughest of all. In one state or another, the law bars ex-felons from practicing certain occupations, including nurse, beautician, barber, real estate salesperson, chauffeur, worker where alcoholic beverages are sold, cashier, and insurance salesperson. Unfortunately, some prison vocational programs actually train inmates for jobs they can never hold.

Prison Industries

Prison industries, which trace their roots to the early workshops of New York's Auburn Penitentiary, are intended to teach work habits and skills that will assist prisoners' reentry into the outside workforce. In practice, institutions rely on prison labor to provide basic food, maintenance, clerical, and other services it requires. In addition, many prisons contain manufacturing facilities that produce goods, such as office furniture and clothing, used in correctional and other state institutions.

The prison industries system has a checkered career. During the nineteenth century, factories were established in many prisons, and inmates manufactured items that were sold on the open market. With the rise of the labor movement, however, state legislatures and Congress passed laws restricting the sale of prison-made goods so that they would not compete with those made by free workers. In 1979, Congress lifted restrictions on the interstate sale of prison-made products and urged correctional administrators to explore with the private sector possible improvements for prison industry programs. Industrial programs would relieve idleness, allow inmates to earn wages that they could save until release, and reduce the costs of incarceration. The Federal Bureau of Prisons and some states have developed industries, but generally their products are not sold on the free market, and the percentage of prisoners employed varies greatly. Nonetheless, about 3.5 percent of the prisoners in the United States produced goods and services worth $1.5 billion (Swarz, 2004).

Although the idea of employing inmates sounds attractive, the inefficiencies of prison work may offset its economic value. Turnover is great, because many inmates are transferred among several institutions or released over a two-year period. Many prisoners have little education and lack steady work habits, making it difficult for them to perform many of the tasks of modern production. An additional cost to efficiency is the need to stop production periodically to count heads and to check that tools and materials have not been stolen. Also, participation in prison industry programs does not reduce recidivism post-release for many inmates (Richmond, 2012).

Rehabilitative Programs

Rehabilitative programs seek to treat the personal defects thought to have brought about the inmate's criminality. Most people agree that rehabilitating offenders is a desirable goal, but they disagree a great deal on the amount of emphasis that these programs should receive. Counseling and special programs are offered in 97 percent of public prisons but in only 74 percent of private institutions (Stephan, 2008).

Reports in the 1970s cast doubt on the ability of treatment programs to stem recidivism. They also questioned the ethics of requiring inmates to participate in rehabilitative programs in exchange for the promise of parole (Martinson, 1974). Supporters of treatment programs argue that certain programs, if properly run, work well for certain types of offenders (Andrews et al., 1990; T. Palmer, 1992). Others argue that the idea of "rehabilitation" has changed from in-prison programming to a greater focus on reentry and transitioning inmates back into communities (Phelps, 2011).

Most corrections systems still offer a range of psychological, behavioral, and social services programs. How much they are used seems to vary according to the goals of the institution and the attitudes of the administrators. Researcher Michelle Phelps (2011) argues that while public opinion supported the "nothing works" perspective that decried rehabilitative efforts, there was no significant change in prison programming until the 1990s. At that point, efforts to rehabilitate inmates focused more on preparing inmates to reenter society (to be discussed in Chapter 13) than on providing them with educational programming. Incarceration's current goal of humane custody implies no effort to change inmates.

Can you imagine yourself working closely with criminal offenders to help them improve themselves? Consider the challenges of such jobs as you read "Careers in Criminal Justice."

Medical Services

Most prisons offer medical services through a full-time staff of nurses, augmented by part-time physicians under contract to the corrections system. Nurses take care of routine health care and dispense medicines from a secure in-prison pharmacy; regularly scheduled visits to the prison by doctors can enable prisoners to obtain checkups and diagnoses. For cases needing a specialist, surgery, or emergency medical assistance, prisoners must be transported to local hospitals, under close supervision by correctional staff. The aim is for the prison system to provide a range of medical assistance to meet the various needs of the population as a whole. In 2008 most states spent about $5,000 annually per inmate for health care, but some spend up to $12,000 (California) and a few under $3,000 (Louisiana, South Carolina, Illinois) (Pew Charitable Trusts, 2013). Costs are also dependent on inmate age—health care costs in Oregon prisons range from $299 per inmate for those under age 30, up to $6,527 per inmate for those older than 70 (Zaitz, 2011).

Medical services in some states have not kept up with the increase in the incarcerated population. In 1976, the U.S. Supreme Court ruled that prisoners have a constitutional right to health care. In 2011, the Supreme Court's decision in *Brown v. Plata* ordered California to reduce its incarcerated population significantly to reduce overcrowding and create a healthier prison environment. The decision supported earlier findings by lower court judges that the state's failure to provide medical and mental health care was needlessly causing the death of at least one inmate every month and was subjecting prisoners to cruel and unusual punishment, which is prohibited by the Constitution (Liptak, 2011).

Should Prisons Use Private Companies to Provide Health Care?

Incarcerated criminal offenders have a limited constitutional right to health care under the Eighth Amendment's cruel and unusual punishments clause. In *Estelle v. Gamble* (1976), the Supreme Court declared that prisoners' rights are violated if corrections officials are "deliberately indifferent" to their "serious medical needs."

Prisoners have health care needs that are frequently different from the non-incarcerated population. The most important issues in health care for prisoners are mental health, substance abuse, and communicable diseases. Prisons sometimes struggle to provide adequate health care to all of their inmates. Medical care can be expensive. Thus, many states have considered ways to reduce the cost of providing needed medical examinations and treatments for prisoners. Several states have sought to save money by contracting with private providers to handle medical care in the belief that private companies can handle the job less expensively than if the state government hired its own doctors, nurses, and other medical personnel to work in prisons. Here is a summary of key arguments for each side in the debate.

For Privatization of Health Care

- Supporters of privatization claim that private businesses are more efficient than the government and can provide medical care at lower cost.
- Under privatization, costs related to providing benefits and pensions for health care employees would no longer be the responsibility of the state but would become the responsibility of the corporation providing services.
- Prison administrators are not experts on how to administer medical programs; therefore, they should seek the services of companies with expertise in medical care.
- As prison populations are beginning to decline, it is less costly to contract for fewer services from a private company than it is to have an excessive number of doctors and nurses on the state payroll.

Against Privatization of Health Care

- Businesses are primarily interested in making a profit rather than providing good medical care.
- Private companies will seek to gain extra profit by providing fewer services, such as denying prisoners' opportunities to be examined by specialists or claiming that they do not need certain procedures despite their symptoms.

- Published accounts provide examples of prisoners who needlessly suffered deprivation of treatment when private businesses handled medical care at various correctional institutions.
- Private businesses are more difficult to supervise and hold accountable by prison officials.

What Should U.S. Policy Be?

Health care is always an important issue in prisons because many convicted offenders, having lacked access to doctors and dentists prior to arriving in prison, may arrive in prison with increased needs for medical treatment. This is true even for younger prisoners. In addition, as long-term prisoners continue to age (particularly as the baby boomer generation ages in prison), health issues will become increasingly costly and difficult for state governments to manage. Many politicians and policymakers are divided by philosophical disagreements about whether businesses are always more efficient than government or whether businesses' profit motives are especially inappropriate for the issue of people's health care needs. Do you have a viewpoint on the issue? Could your view be changed if research indicated that businesses are, indeed, more efficient or, alternatively, public employees provide better care?

Researching the Internet

To read a critical report about privatization of health care, go to http://seanc.org/files/4913/3961/6270/Privatizing _state_prison_report.pdf.

Analyzing the Issue

Imagine that you and your classmates are state legislators considering a proposal to privatize health care for all of your state's prisons. What information would you ideally want to have before making a decision? What arguments can be made on each side of the proposal? Take a vote, and justify your position.

Sources: Bob Egelko, "CA Request to Take over Inmate Health Care Denied," SFGate, May 31, 2012 (http://www.sfgate.com); *Estelle v. Gamble* (429 U.S. 97, 1976); Kimberly Leonard, "Privatized Prison Health Care Scrutinized," *The Washington Post*, July 21, 2012 (http://www.washingtonpost.com); Roger Watson, Anne Stimpson, and Tony Hostick, "Prison Health Care: A Review of the Literature," *International Journal of Nursing Studies*, 41(2):119–28.

Although inmates' medical needs often echo those of the general population, prisoners pose two special needs, one due to poverty and the other to aging. Because prisoners as a group are very poor, they often bring to the prison years of neglect of their general health. Other consequences of being poor, such as an inadequate diet and poor hygiene, also affect the general health of the prison population. Read "The Policy Debate" to consider the question of whether states should seek to save money by hiring private businesses to provide medical care in prisons.

☑ **CHECK POINT**

13. **Why are prison programs important from the standpoint of prison administrators?**
    Programs keep prisoners busy and reduce security problems.

14. **Why have legislators and the general public been so critical of educational and rehabilitative programs in prisons?**
    Such programs are thought to"coddle" prisoners and may not reduce future criminal behavior.

STOP&ANALYZE

If budget cuts led to the elimination of all vocational training and education programs in prisons, how would that impact daily life for prisoners and corrections officers? List three possible effects from the elimination of programs.

Violence in Prison

Prisons provide a perfect recipe for violence. They confine in cramped quarters a thousand men, some with histories of violent behavior. While incarcerated, these men are not allowed contact with women and live under highly restrictive conditions. Sometimes these conditions spark collective violence, as in the riots at Attica, New York (1971); Santa Fe, New Mexico (1980); Atlanta, Georgia (1987); Lucasville, Ohio (1993); Folsom, California (2012); and Florence, Colorado (2008).

Although prison riots are widely reported in the news, few people have witnessed the level of everyday interpersonal violence that takes place in U.S. prisons. For example, each year about 34,000 inmates are physically attacked by other inmates. In 2002, 48 assault victims died. An additional 168 prisoners committed suicide (Mumola, 2005). Great numbers of prisoners live in a state of constant uneasiness, always on the lookout for people who might demand sex, steal their few possessions, or otherwise hurt them. Some researchers suggest that the level of violence varies by offender age, institutional security designation, and administrative effectiveness (Maitland & Sluder, 1998). Others point out that inmates' own behavior affects their likelihood of victimization, with those who have violent prior offenses and those who participate in the prison economy more likely to be victimized in prison (Copes et al., 2010; Kerley, Hochstetler, & Copes, 2009).

Assaultive Behavior and Inmate Characteristics

For the person entering prison for the first time, the anxiety level and fear of violence run especially high. Gary, an inmate at Leavenworth, told Pete Earley, "Every convict has three choices, but only three. He can fight (kill someone), he can hit the fence (escape), or he can fuck (submit)" (1992:55). Even if a prisoner is not assaulted, the potential for violence permeates the environments of many prisons, adding to the stress and pains of incarceration.

Violence in correctional institutions raises serious questions for administrators, criminal justice specialists, and the general public. What causes prison violence? What can be done about it? We consider these questions by examining three main categories of prison violence: prisoner–prisoner, prisoner–officer, and officer–prisoner. First, we discuss three characteristics of prisoners that underlie these behavioral factors: age, race, and mental illness.

Age Studies have shown that young men aged 16 to 24, both inside and outside prison, are more prone to violence than are older men. Not surprisingly, 96 percent of adult prisoners are men, with an average age of 27 at time of admission.

Besides having greater physical strength than their elders, young men lack the commitments to career and family that can restrict antisocial behavior. In addition, many have difficulty defining their position in society. Thus, they interpret many things as challenges to their status. Studies also show that younger prisoners face a greater risk of being victimized than do older inmates.

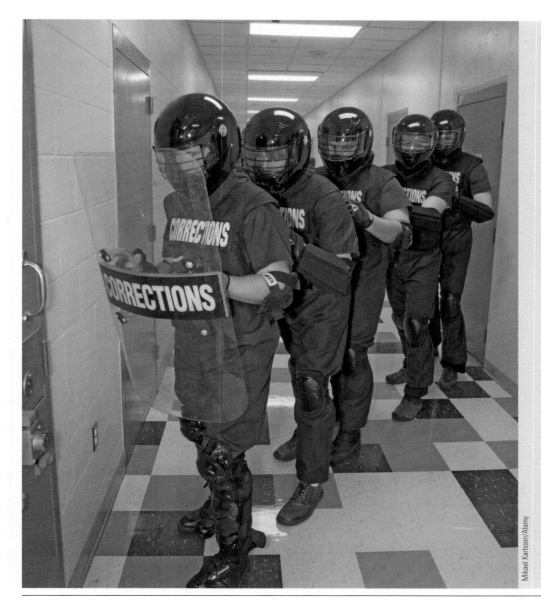

When officers must remove an uncooperative or violent prisoner from a cell, trained cell extraction teams must overwhelm the prisoner through the use of force while also limiting the risk of injury to themselves. Such events are often filmed to prevent false claims by prisoners that officers used excessive force. Are there additional precautions that these officers should take in order to avoid injuries to themselves and to the prisoner?

Mikael Karlsson/Alamy

Machismo, the concept of male honor and the sacredness of one's reputation as a man, requires physical retaliation against those who insult one's honor. Some inmates adopt a preventive strategy of trying to impress others with their bravado, which may result in counterchallenges and violence. The potential for violence among such prisoners is clear.

Race Race has become a major divisive factor in today's prisons. Racist attitudes, common in the larger society, have become part of the convict code. Forced association—having to live with people one would not likely associate with on the outside—exaggerates and amplifies racial conflict. Violence against members of another race may be how some inmates deal with the frustrations of their lives. The presence of gangs organized along racial lines contributes to violence in prison.

Mental Illness Inmates with diagnosed mental illnesses are significantly more likely to be victims of violence in prison than those not mentally ill (Blitz, Wolff, & Shi, 2008), including being more likely to be abused sexually during incarceration (Cristanti & Frueh, 2011). Prison is a traumatic experience and can cause mental illness to develop in individuals who were not suffering from illness when they arrived. Incarceration can also exacerbate preexisting mental conditions, leaving more inmates in need of psychological treatment (Rich, Wakeman, & Dickman, 2011). If these inmates are more likely to be victimized, their mental condition can worsen, causing even greater problems for them during their incarceration (Listwan, Colvin, Hanley, & Flannery, 2010).

Prisoner–Prisoner Violence

Although prison folklore may attribute violence to sadistic guards, most prison violence occurs between inmates. As Hans Toch has observed, the climate of violence in prisons has no free-world counterpart: "Inmates are terrorized by other inmates, and spend years in fear of harm. Some inmates request protective custody segregation, others lock themselves in, and some are hermits by choice" (1976:47–48). The Bureau of Justice Statistics reports that the rate of prisoner–prisoner assaults between inmates is 26 attacks per 1,000 inmates (Stephan & Karberg, 2003). But official statistics likely do not reflect the true amount of prisoner–prisoner violence, because many inmates who are assaulted do not make their victimization known to prison officials.

Prison Gangs Racial or ethnic gangs (also referred to as "security threat groups") are now linked to acts of violence in most prison systems. Gangs make it difficult for wardens to maintain control. By continuing their street wars inside prison, gangs make some prisons more dangerous than even the worst American neighborhoods. Gangs are organized primarily to control an institution's drug, gambling, loan-sharking, prostitution, extortion, and debt-collection rackets. In addition, gangs protect their members from other gangs and instill a sense of macho camaraderie.

Prison gangs exist in the institutions of most states and the federal system, but it is sometimes difficult for management to determine the percentage of their inmates with gang affiliations. A survey of prisons in the United States found that wardens reported between 2 percent and 50 percent of their inmates were gang members, with a mean of 19 percent (Winterdyk & Ruddell, 2010). In Illinois, as much as 60 percent of the population are gang members (Hallinan, 2001:95), and the Florida Department of Corrections has identified 240 street gangs operating in their prisons (Davitz, 1998).

Many facilities segregate rival gangs by housing them in separate units of the same prison or by moving members to other prisons (sometimes even in different states), which wardens believe is an effective means of reducing gang-related violence (Winterdyk & Ruddell, 2010). Administrators have also set up intelligence units to gather information on gangs, particularly about illegal acts both inside and outside the prison. In some prisons, however, these policies create a power vacuum within the convict society that newer groups with new codes of behavior soon fill.

Prison Rape Much of the mythology of prison life revolves around sexual assaults. Perpetrators are typically strong, experienced cons, either African American or white, who are serving sentences for violent offenses. Victims are portrayed as young, white, physically weak, mentally challenged, effeminate first-time nonviolent offenders.

Prison rape is a crime hidden by a curtain of silence. Inmate–inmate and inmate–staff sexual contact is prohibited in all prisons, yet it exists, and much of it remains hidden from authorities. Sexual violence ranges from unwanted touching to nonconsensual sex. When incidents are reported, correctional officers say that it is difficult to distinguish between rapes and consensual sex. Most officers do not catch the inmates in the act; when they do observe sexual activity, only a few officers report that they ignored the inmates' violations of prison rules (Eigenberg, 2000).

The 2004 Prison Rape Elimination Act (PREA) established a zero-tolerance standard for the incidence of rape in prison. This law requires the Bureau of Justice Statistics to conduct annual surveys in the nation's prisons and jails to measure the incidence of rape. The law also requires the attorney general to provide a list of the incidence of prison rape in each institution.

Data collected as part of PREA indicate that 7,744 allegations of inmate–inmate sexual assaults among state prisoners were reported in 2008, which is a rate of 3.1 attacks per 1,000 inmates. Perpetrators of substantial incidents of inmate-on-inmate assault tend to be male (82 percent), aged 25 to 39, acting alone (88 percent). Victims were most likely to be male (77 percent), aged 25 to 39 (45 percent). Most incidents were found to take place between 6 PM and midnight, with few victims reporting physical injuries (18 percent). Offenders are most frequently punished by time in solitary or isolation (72 percent), arrest/prosecution (32 percent), transfer to a higher-security area of the prison (27 percent), or some combination of those sanctions (Guerino & Beck, 2011).

Guerino and Beck (2011) also assessed the characteristics of victims and offenders in incidents of staff-on-inmate sexual violence. Unlike inmate-on-inmate violence, a greater percentage of staff-on-inmate violence was directed at female prisoners (37 percent), and female guards committed a majority of substantiated sexual assaults (56 percent of such assaults were by female corrections officers, compared with only 44 percent by male guards). Most of these types of incidents were committed in program service areas, such as the commissary, kitchen, storage areas, laundry, cafeteria, workshop, and hallways between the hours of noon and 6 PM.

Victims of prisoner–prisoner sexual victimization have few options. According to the inmate code, prisoners should "stand and fight" their own battles. For many, this is not feasible. Alternatively, some may seek the protection of a gang or a stronger inmate to whom the victim is then indebted. Others may try to fade into the shadows. Still others may seek protective custody. Each option has its pluses and minuses, but none provides victims with the ability to serve their time without constantly looking over their shoulder.

Protective Custody   For many victims of prison violence, protective custody offers the only way to escape further abuse. About 5,000 state prisoners are in protective custody. Life is not pleasant for these inmates (Browne, Cambier, & Agha, 2011). Often they are let out of their cells only briefly to exercise and shower. Inmates who ask for "lock up" have little chance of returning to the general prison population without being viewed as a weakling—a "snitch" or a "punk"—to be preyed on. Even when they are transferred to another institution, their reputations follow them through the grapevine.

Prisoner–Officer Violence

The mass media have focused on riots in which guards are taken hostage, injured, and killed. However, violence against officers typically occurs in specific situations and against certain individuals. Yearly, inmates assault approximately 18,000 staff members (Stephan & Karberg, 2003). Correctional officers do not carry weapons within the institution, because a prisoner might seize them. However, prisoners do manage to obtain lethal weapons and can use the element of surprise to injure an officer. In the course of a workday, an officer may encounter situations that require the use of physical force against an inmate—for instance, breaking up a fight or moving a prisoner to segregation. Because such situations are especially dangerous, officers may enlist others to help them minimize the risk of violence. The officer's greatest fear is an unexpected attack, such as a "missile" thrown from an upper tier or an officer's "accidental" fall down a flight of stairs. The need to watch constantly against personal attacks adds stress and keeps many officers at a distance from the inmates.

Officer–Prisoner Violence

A fact of life in many institutions is unauthorized physical violence by officers against inmates. Stories abound of guards giving individual prisoners "the treatment" when supervisors are not looking. Many guards view physical force as an everyday, legitimate procedure. In some institutions, authorized "goon squads" composed of physically powerful officers use their muscle to maintain order.

Correctional officers are expected to follow departmental rules in their dealings with prisoners, yet supervisors generally cannot observe staff–prisoner confrontations directly. Further, prisoner complaints about officer brutality are often not believed until the officer involved gains a reputation for harshness. Even in this case, wardens may feel they must support their officers in order to retain their support in return. Research indicates that officers are more likely to victimize inmates who are male and nonwhite and who are confined in maximum-security institutions. Inmates with a paid work assignment are less likely to be victimized by staff (Perez, Gover, Tennyson, & Santos, 2009).

Decreasing Prison Violence

Five factors contribute to prison violence: (1) inadequate supervision by staff members, (2) architectural design that promotes rather than inhibits victimization, (3) the easy availability of deadly weapons, (4) the housing of violence-prone prisoners near relatively defenseless people, and (5) a general high level of tension produced by close quarters (Bowker, 1982:64). The physical size and condition of the prison and the relations between inmates and staff also affect violence.

The Effect of Architecture and Size The fortress-like prison certainly does not create an atmosphere for normal interpersonal relationships, and the size of the larger institutions can create management problems. The massive scale of the megaprison, which may hold up to 3,000 inmates, provides opportunities for aggressive inmates to hide weapons, dispense private "justice," and engage more or less freely in other illicit activities. The size of the population in a large prison may also result in some inmates "falling through the cracks"—being misclassified and, though not violent themselves, forced to live among violent offenders.

Much of the emphasis on "new generation prisons"—small housing units, clear sight lines, security corridors linking housing units—is designed to limit such opportunities and thus prevent violence. However, a study of rape in Texas prisons found that cell blocks with solid doors may contribute to sexual assault (Austin et al., 2006).

The Role of Management The degree to which inmate leaders are allowed to take matters into their own hands can affect the level of violence among inmates. When administrators run a tight ship, security measures prevent sexual attacks in dark corners, the making of "shivs" and "shanks" (knives) in the metal shop, and open conflict among inmate groups. A prison must afford each inmate defensible space, and administrators should ensure that every inmate remains secure from physical attack.

Effective management can decrease the level of assaultive behavior by limiting opportunities for attacks. Wardens and correctional officers must therefore recognize the types of people with whom they are dealing, the role of prison gangs, and the structure of institutions. John DiIulio argues that no group of inmates is "unmanageable [and] no combination of political, social, budgetary, architectural, or other factors makes good management impossible" (1991:12). He points to such varied institutions as the California Men's Colony, New York City's Tombs and Rikers Island, the Federal Bureau of Prisons, and the Texas Department of Corrections under the leadership of George Beto. According to DiIulio, good management practices have resulted in prisons and jails where inmates can "do time" without fearing for their personal safety. Wardens who exert leadership can manage their prisons effectively, so that problems do not fester and erupt into violent confrontations. Prisons must also be managed transparently—that is, incidents of violence in prisons must be dealt with openly and investigated by management. In addition, the public should be made aware of the nature of prison violence to better understand the challenges faced by inmates during incarceration and upon release (Byrne & Hummer, 2007).

Budget cuts in the area of corrections increasingly affect the management and organization of prisons. Reductions in the crime rate mean that fewer prisons are needed, but states are also looking to solutions that are both economical and successful in rehabilitating prisoners (Pew Center on the States, 2008). In addition, there has been increasing public concern that most states spend more on corrections than on public education. For example, in 2007 Michigan spent $1.19 on corrections for every $1.00 spent on education. Compare this to Minnesota, which spent $.17 on corrections for every $1.00 spent on education (Pew Center on the States, 2008). Which of these institutions is more important in terms of state funding? How can states balance public safety with public education?

In sum, prisons must be made safe. Because the state uses its authority to incarcerate inmates, it has a responsibility to prevent violence and maintain order. To exclude violence from prisons, officials may have to limit movement within institutions, contacts with the outside, and the right of inmates to choose their associates. Yet, these measures may run counter to the goal of producing men and women who will be accountable when they return to society.

☑CHECK POINT

15. **What five factors are thought to contribute to prison violence?**
Inadequate supervision, architectural design, availability of weapons, housing of violence-prone inmates with the defenseless, and the high level of tension among people living in close quarters.

STOP&ANALYZE

Think about the role of architectural design in facilitating or preventing prison violence. Draw a design of a prison that would reduce the risks of and opportunities for violence. List three aspects of your design that are intended to reduce opportunities for violence.

A QUESTION OF ETHICS

Think, Discuss, Write

A significant problem for corrections officials in many states is the smuggling of cell phones into prisons for use by prisoners. In 2013, Florida seized more than 4,000 cell phones from prisoners. The use of secret phones by prisoners creates many difficult problems, including harassment of crime victims, planning of crimes and escapes, and communication between prisoners in different prisons. In 2014, a prisoner in North Carolina used a smuggled cell phone to arrange the kidnapping of the father of the prosecutor who had put the prisoner behind bars. Prisoners in Indiana used cell phones smuggled by guards to run a drug trafficking operation while sitting behind bars.

How do prisoners obtain cell phones, an item that they are not allowed to have? Sadly, one primary source of cell phones is corrections officers who smuggle them into prisons and sell them to convicted offenders. A prisoner on death row in Texas told a state legislator that he obtained a cell phone and charger after paying $2,100. In November 2013, for example, a dozen former employees of a Texas prison were convicted and given prison sentences for smuggling cell phones and other contraband into the institution for use by prison gang members in coordinating continued criminal activities outside the walls.

Discussion/Writing Assignment

If you were the warden of a prison, what steps would you take to prevent unethical activity by corrections officers, monitor the actions of officers, and create an environment in which you could stop improper conduct from taking place? Create a list of actions that you would take, and explain your reasoning for each.

Sources: "Final 4 of 29 Inmates and Guards Convicted in Operation Prison Cell in Southeast Texas," U.S. Immigration and Customs Enforcement News Release, November 26, 2013 (www.ice.gov); B. Farrington, "Smuggled Cellphones in Prisons Run Rampant," *Huffington Post*, February 17, 2014 (www.huffingtonpost.com); M. Biesecker and A. G. Breed, "FBI: Inmate Orchestrates Kidnapping of Lawyer's Father Using Smuggled Cellphone," Associated Press, April 11, 2014 (www.thespec.com).

SUMMARY

1 Describe how contemporary institutions differ from the old-style "big house" prisons.

- The typical "big house" was a walled prison with large, tiered cell blocks, a yard, and workshops.
- Prisoners came from both rural and urban areas, were poor, and outside of the South were mainly white.
- The prison society in the past was isolated, with restrictions on visitors, mail, and other communications. The inmates' days were highly structured, with rules enforced by the guards.

2 Identify the three models of incarceration that have predominated since the 1940s.

- The custodial model emphasizes the maintenance of security.
- The rehabilitation model views security and housekeeping activities as mainly a framework for treatment efforts.
- The reintegration model recognizes that prisoners must be prepared for their return to society.

3 Describe the organization of prisons and their staffs.

- Most prisons are expected to fulfill goals related to keeping (custody), using (working), and serving (treating) inmates. They are organized to fulfill these goals.

4 Explain how a prison is governed.

- The public's belief that the warden and officers have total power over the inmates is outdated.
- Good management through effective leadership can maintain the quality of prison life as measured by levels of order, amenities, and services.
- Four factors make managing prisons different from administering other public institutions: defects of total power, limited use of rewards and punishments, exchange relationships, and strength of inmate leadership.

5 Summarize the roles of correctional officers in a prison.

- Because they remain in close contact with the prisoners, correctional officers are the linchpins of the prison system. The effectiveness of the institution rests on their shoulders.

6 List the characteristics of the incarcerated population.

- Most prisoners are male, young, members of minority groups, with low education levels.
- Prison administrators must deal with the special needs of some groups, including elderly prisoners, prisoners with HIV/AIDS, mentally ill prisoners, and long-term prisoners.

7 Describe the world of the convict.

- Inmates do not serve their time in isolation but are members of a subculture with its own traditions, norms, and leadership structure. Such norms are often described as the inmate code.
- Today's prisons, unlike those of the past, do not have a uniform inmate code but several, in part because of the influence of gangs.
- Inmates deal with the pain of incarceration by assuming an adaptive role and lifestyle.

8 Discuss what prison is like for men and for women.

- Male inmates are individualistic, and their norms stress autonomy, self-sufficiency, and the ability to cope with one's own problems. Female inmates share with one another and place less emphasis on achieving status or recognition within the prisoner community. There is less violence in female prisons than in male ones.

9 List some of the programs and services available to prisoners.

- Educational, vocational, industrial, and rehabilitative programs are available in prisons. Administrators believe that these programs are important for maintaining order.
- Medical services are provided to all inmates.

10 Describe the nature of prison violence.

- Violence occurs between prisoners and between prisoners and guards.
- Violence in prison depends on such things as administrative effectiveness; the architecture and size of prisons; and inmate characteristics such as age, attitudes, and race. Prison gangs play an increasing role in causing prison violence.

Questions for Review

1. How do modern prisons differ from those in the past?
2. What characteristics of prisons distinguish them from other institutions?
3. What must a prison administrator do to ensure successful management?
4. What is meant by an adaptive role? Which roles are found in male prison society? In female prison society?
5. How does the convict society in institutions for women differ from that in institutions for men?
6. What are the main forms of prison programs, and what purposes do they serve?
7. What are forms and causes of prison violence?

Key Terms and Cases

classification (p. 385)
custodial model (p. 361)

inmate code (p. 375)
rehabilitation model (p. 362)

reintegration model (p. 362)

12 Probation and Intermediate Sanctions

LEARNING OBJECTIVES

1. Name the philosophical assumptions that underlie community corrections.

2. Describe how probation evolved and how probation sentences are implemented today.

3. Describe intermediate sanctions, and give examples of how they are administered.

4. Identify the key issues faced by community corrections at the beginning of the twenty-first century.

In April 2014, R & B singer Chris Brown was transported from California to Virginia by criminal justice officials. He was placed in jail in Los Angeles for violating conditions of probation and then transported to the East Coast to face assault charges in Washington, D.C. Originally, he had been sentenced to five years of probation and 1,400 hours of community service after his conviction for the February 2009 assault on his then-girlfriend, singer Rihanna. During an argument in Brown's car, he attempted to force Rihanna out of the car while it was moving. After she called her assistant for help, he punched and bit her. Tabloid photos of Rihanna after the assault revealed extensive bruising and bleeding on her face (Duke & Rowlands, 2009). Unfortunately for Brown, during his years on probation, he was repeatedly brought back to court for violating the conditions that permitted him to serve his sentence in the community instead of serving time in jail or prison (Sung, 2014).

Much like many other offenders serving sentences in the community, Brown seemed to struggle with personal issues and choices that clashed with his obligation to behave properly in order to avoid jail. In October 2013, Brown was arrested on an assault charge in Washington, D.C., for allegedly punching a man. Avoiding arrest on new charges is always a condition of probation. In November, a judge revoked Brown's probation and placed him in a mandatory 90-day anger management and drug rehabilitation program after Brown broke the window of his mother's car with a rock after participating in a family counseling session with her. His probation was revoked again in March 2014 after he was kicked out of a rehabilitation program for violating its rules. This time the judge sent him to jail in Los Angeles for a few weeks before having him transported to his scheduled trial on the East Coast (Sung, 2014).

Normally, the public has little reason to notice community corrections and probation unless the news media publicizes events in a celebrity's case. Not only was

Brown a celebrity, but his case was one that generated news stories about how troubled people on probation flirt with the risk of jail as they struggle with personal issues such as substance abuse. Another case of behavior choices that led to rearrest while on probation was that of the actress Lindsay Lohan, who in 2013 was jailed briefly for violating the terms of her probation for reckless driving and providing false information to a police officer. While on probation, Lohan was charged with shoplifting and struggled with fulfilling requirements for substance abuse treatment and community service (Duke, 2013).

Since the early nineteenth century, supervision in the community has been recognized as an appropriate punishment for some offenders. Probation was developed in the 1840s, and parole followed in the 1870s. By the 1930s, every state and the federal government used these forms of community corrections either to punish offenders without incarceration (probation) or to supervise offenders in the community after leaving prison (parole). Intermediate sanctions were developed in the 1980s when people saw the need for punishments that were less restrictive than prison but more restrictive than probation.

Two-thirds of offenders who are under correctional supervision are in the community, not behind bars (see Figure 12.1). In 2012, 1 in 50 adults was on probation or parole, while 1 in 108 was in prison or jail (Glaze & Herberman, 2013). In 2009 the Pew Center on the States released a major report emphasizing the major role played by community corrections in the criminal justice system. A key finding was that strong community supervision programs for lower-risk, nonviolent offenders not only cost significantly less than incarceration but, when appropriately resourced and managed, could cut recidivism by as much as 30 percent. Diverting these offenders to community supervision programs also frees up prison beds needed to house violent offenders and can offer budget makers additional resources for other pressing public priorities (Pew Center on the States, 2009).

FIGURE 12.1
Percentage of People in Each Category of Correctional Supervision

Source: L. E. Glaze and E. J. Herberman, "Correctional Populations in the United States, 2012," *Bureau of Justice Statistics Bulletin*, December 2013. NCJ 243936.

In years to come, community corrections can be expected to play a much greater role in the criminal justice system. This role will likely increase as states try to reduce the high costs of imprisoning large populations of offenders. Formal programs are emerging across the nation to give increased emphasis to community options. For example, the Justice Reinvestment Initiative, funded by the federal government's U.S. Bureau of Justice Assistance, provides financial incentives and technical assistance for states to find ways to reduce their prison populations and then reinvest those savings in community-oriented alternatives to imprisonment (Keller, 2014). One of the biggest drivers of increased costs in corrections stems from the number of people sent from community supervision into expensive prisons and jails as a result of violating conditions of probation and parole. Thus, a major emphasis of the Justice Reinvestment Initiative is to develop evidence-based approaches to community supervision as well as effective diversion programs, such as drug courts, to efficiently encourage and monitor appropriate behavior through incentives and sanctions other than incarceration (LaVigne et al., 2014).

Community Corrections: Assumptions

Probation and intermediate sanctions are important components of community corrections. As discussed in Chapter 10, community corrections seeks to keep offenders in the community by building ties to family, employment, and other normal sources of stability and success. This model of corrections assumes that the offender must change, but it also recognizes that factors within the community that might encourage criminal behavior (unemployment, for example) must also change. Probation and intermediate sanctions are sentences imposed for lesser offenses in an effort to avoid the expense and consequences of imprisonment.

Parole, another component of community corrections, to be discussed in Chapter 13, involves completing a sentence in the community after serving a term in prison. Parolees, who often served time in prison for violent offenses or a lengthy list of other crimes, face especially significant challenges in seeking to reintegrate into the community.

Proponents usually cite four factors in support of community corrections:

1. Many offenders' criminal records and current offenses are not serious enough to warrant incarceration.
2. Community supervision is cheaper than incarceration.
3. Rates of **recidivism**, or returning to crime, for those under community supervision are no higher than for those who go to prison.
4. Ex-inmates require both support and supervision as they try to remake their lives in the community.

Community corrections is based on the goal of finding the "least restrictive alternative"—punishing the offender only as severely as needed to protect the community and to satisfy the public. Advocates call for programs to assist offenders in the community so they will have opportunities to succeed in law-abiding activities and to reduce their contact with the criminal world. Surveys have found that the public supports community placement for some offenders currently in prison. The increasing severity of prison sentences for drug offenders was a significant driver of expensive increases in prison populations. Thus, new trends in opinions by the public, as well as by politicians from both political parties, seem to indicate that community corrections will continue to receive significant emphasis in the immediate future (See "What Americans Think.")

recidivism A return to criminal behavior.

QUESTION: "On drug policy, government should focus more on . . .

Don't know 7%

Prosecuting drug users 26%

Providing treatment 67%

QUESTION: "Some states have moved away from mandatory prison sentences for nonviolent drug crimes. Is this a . . .

Don't know 5%

Bad thing 32%

Good thing 63%

CRITICAL THINKING: If a governor directed you to be in charge of developing alternatives to imprisonment for nonviolent drug users, what approaches to treatment and/or punishment would you suggest? What factors or considerations would guide your thinking?

Note: Survey conducted February 14–23, 2014.

Source: Pew Research Center for the People and the Press, "America's New Drug Policy Landscape," Pew Center website, April 2, 2014, http://www.people-press.org/2014/04/02/americas-new-drug-policy-landscape/.

Probation: Correction without Incarceration

As we have seen, probation is the conditional release of the offender into the community under the supervision of correctional officials. Although probationers live at home and have regular jobs, they must report regularly to their probation officers.

FIGURE 12.2

Most Serious Offenses Committed by Offenders Sentenced to Probation Most probationers are serving their sentence because they committed property or drug offenses, but almost 20 percent of probationers have been convicted of violent offenses. Sex offenders comprise only a small portion of people sentenced to probation.

Source: L. M. Maruschak and T. P. Bonczar, "Probation and Parole in the United States, 2012," *Bureau of Justice Statistics Bulletin*, December 2013 NCJ 243826.

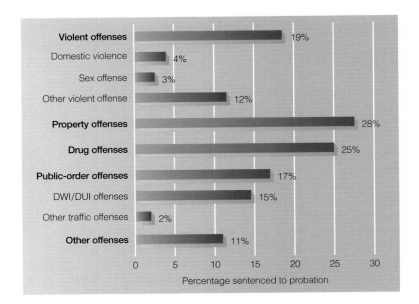

They must also abide by specific conditions, such as submitting to drug tests, obeying curfews, and staying away from certain people or parts of town. Although probation is used mainly for lesser offenses, states are increasingly using probation for more serious felonies, as shown in Figure 12.2.

Probation is significantly less expensive than imprisonment, a fact that has become increasingly important as state budget cuts force justice system officials to consider how to expand the use of lower-cost punishments for criminal offenders. Pennsylvania officials calculated that it costs the state more than $32,000 per year for each offender held in prison but less than $3,000 per year for each offender supervised in the community on probation (Couglin, 2012). When one multiplies the amount saved by the hundreds or thousands of offenders placed on probation rather than sent to prison, it represents a significant reduction in the corrections system's burden on the state budget. Thus, there is consideration for using probation for a larger number of offenders, including even those who have committed crimes that led to imprisonment in the past.

Probation can be combined with other sanctions, such as fines, restitution, and community service. Fulfillment of these other sanctions may, in effect, become a condition for successful completion of probation. The sentencing court retains authority over the probationer, and if she or he violates the conditions or commits another crime, the judge can order the entire sentence to be served in prison. Although probation offers many benefits over incarceration, the public often sees it as merely a "slap on the wrist" for offenders (Public Opinion Strategies, 2010).

Today, although nearly 4 million offenders are on probation, probation budgets in many states have been cut and caseloads increased as lawmakers struggle with shrinking resources. In 2012, for example, the Florida Department of Corrections attempted to address a $79 million budget deficit in part by cutting funds for probation (Campbell, 2012). Given that caseloads in some urban areas reach 300 offenders per officer, probation officers often cannot provide the level of supervision necessary (Edgemon, 2013).

Origins and Evolution of Probation

Probation first developed in the United States when John Augustus, a Boston boot maker, persuaded a judge in the Boston Police Court in 1841 to give him custody of a convicted offender for a brief period and then helped the man appear rehabilitated by the time of sentencing.

Massachusetts developed the first statewide probation system in 1880; by 1920 another 21 states had followed suit. The federal courts were authorized to hire probation officers in 1925. By the beginning of World War II, probation systems had been established in 44 states.

Probation began as a humanitarian effort to allow first-time and minor offenders a second chance. Early probationers were expected not only to obey the law but also to behave in a morally acceptable fashion. Officers sought to provide moral leadership to help shape probationers' attitudes and behavior with respect to family, religion, employment, and free time.

By the 1940s, the development of psychology as a field of social science research led probation officers to shift their emphasis from moral leadership to therapeutic counseling. This shift brought three important changes. First, the officer no longer acted primarily as a community supervisor charged with enforcing a particular morality. Second, the officer became more of a clinical social worker who aimed at helping the offender solve psychological and social problems. Third, the offender was expected to become actively involved in the treatment. The pursuit of rehabilitation as the primary goal of probation gave the officer extensive discretion in defining and treating the offender's problems. Officers used their judgment to evaluate each offender and develop a treatment approach to the personal problems that presumably had led to crime.

During the 1960s, probation moved in another direction. Rather than counseling offenders, probation officers provided them with concrete social services such as assistance with employment, housing, finances, and education. This emphasis on reintegrating offenders and remedying the social problems they faced fit with federal efforts to wage a war on poverty. Instead of being a counselor or therapist, the probation officer served as an advocate, dealing with private and public institutions on the offender's behalf.

In the late 1970s, the orientation of probation changed again as the goals of rehabilitation and reintegration gave way to "risk management." This approach, still dominant today, seeks to minimize the probability that an offender will commit a new offense (Cadigan, Johnson, & Lowenkamp, 2012). Risk management reflects two basic goals. First, in accord with the deserved-punishment ideal, the punishment should fit the offense, and correctional intervention should neither raise nor lower the level of punishment. Second, according to the community-protection criterion, the degree of risk that the probationer will return to crime determines the amount and type of supervision.

Today there is a growing interest in probation's role as part of **community justice**, a philosophy that emphasizes restorative justice (see Chapter 9), reparation to the victim and the community, problem-solving strategies instead of adversarial procedures, and increased citizen involvement in crime prevention. By breaking away from traditional bureaucratic practices, community justice advocates hope to develop a more flexible and responsive form of local justice initiatives—and many see probation leading the way (Hudson, 2012).

community justice A model of justice that emphasizes reparation to the victim and the community, a problem-solving perspective with regard to crime, and citizen involvement in crime prevention.

Organization of Probation

As a form of corrections, probation falls under the executive branch, and people usually see it as a concern of state government. However, in about 25 percent of the states, probation falls to county and local governments. Further, in many states, the judiciary administers it locally. The state sets the standards and provides financial support and training courses, but locally administered programs handle about two-thirds of all people under probation supervision.

In many jurisdictions, although the state is formally responsible for all probation services, the locally elected county judges are in charge. This seemingly odd arrangement produces benefits as well as problems. On the positive side, having probationers under the supervision of the court permits judges to keep closer tabs

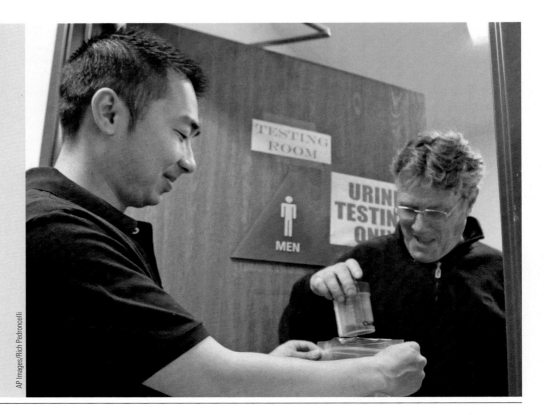

Frequent alcohol and drug testing are a condition of probation for many offenders. Administering these tests has become part of the officer's supervisory role. How difficult is it to monitor the behavior of offenders in the community?

AP Images/Rich Pedroncelli

on them and to order incarceration if the conditions of probation are violated. On the negative side, some judges know little about the goals and methods of corrections, and the probation responsibility adds to the administrative duties of already overworked courts.

Judicially enforced probation seems to work best when the judges and the supervising officers have close relationships. Proponents of this system say that judges need to work with probation officers whom they can trust, whose presentence reports they can accurately evaluate, and on whom they can rely to report the success or failure of individual cases.

For the sake of their clients and the goals of the system, probation officers need direct access to corrections and other human services agencies. However, these agencies are located within the executive branch of government. Several states have combined probation and parole services in the same agency to coordinate resources and services better. Others point out, however, that probationers differ from parolees. Parolees already have served prison terms, frequently have been involved in more serious crimes, and often have been disconnected from mainstream society. By contrast, most probationers have not developed criminal lifestyles to the same degree and do not have the same problems of reintegration into the community.

Probation Services

Probation officers play roles similar to both the police and social workers. In addition to assisting the judiciary with presentence investigations (see Chapter 9), probation officers supervise clients to keep them out of trouble and enforce the conditions of the sentence. This law enforcement role involves discretionary decisions about whether to report violations of probation conditions. Probation officers are also expected to act like social workers by helping clients obtain the housing, employment, and treatment services they need (Bourgon, Gutierrez, & Ashton, 2012). The potential conflict between the roles is great. Not surprisingly, individual officers sometimes emphasize one role over the other. Advocates of

Probation Officer Assistant

Scott Lopofsky, U.S. Probation Officer Assistant, U.S. Probation Office, Northern District of Illinois

The duties of a U.S. probation officer assistant vary by district and by the need or mission of each office. In the Northern District of Illinois, officer assistants are responsible for conducting collateral criminal-history investigations and home visits; they also monitor Immigration and Naturalization Service cases and perform various tasks in the offender urinalysis lab. Collateral criminal-history investigations consist of analyzing a defendant's criminal-history report and collecting all necessary documents for disposition information. When the complete past criminal history is collected, the officer writes a report to present her or his findings. The report is used in presentence investigation reports as a tool for judges and probation officers to determine the number of criminal-history points a defendant will receive when sentencing guidelines are applied by the judge. Home visits require face-to-face contact with the defendant, or with a family member of the defendant, for residential verification. A probation officer assistant also has the task of conducting presentence interviews when the defendant resides within the district but is being sentenced in a different district.

Photo provided by Scott Lopofsky

The qualifications for this position vary for each district. The majority of districts require a bachelor's degree, as well as strong writing skills and effective case-management abilities. An applicant must also pass a full government background investigation. The majority of probation officer assistants have criminal justice or social work backgrounds.

In preparing for his career as a probation officer assistant, Scott Lopofsky earned a bachelor's degree in criminal justice. He then worked for one year as an investigator conducting background investigations for a government contractor that developed reports on applicants for federal law enforcement positions. He is currently enrolled part-time in a criminal justice graduate program.

The biggest challenge I face as a probation officer assistant is producing accurate and thorough reports while adhering to strict deadlines. Criminal-history reports can be complex and require numerous follow-ups with different law enforcement agencies. This is a challenging task because my caseload is high and the turnaround time to complete the investigation is short.

evidence-based practices argue that probation officers must find "balanced roles" in which they are "neither indulgent of anti-social attitudes and noncompliance nor authoritative and heavy-handed" (Whetzel, Paparozzi, Alexander, & Lowenkamp, 2011). As you read about the job of a probation officer in "Careers in Criminal Justice," consider whether you would be interested in supervising offenders in the community.

During the past decade, probation officials have developed methods of classifying clients according to their service needs, the element of risk they pose to the community, and the chance that they will commit another offense (Cadigan, Johnson, & Lowenkamp, 2012). Risk classification fits the deserved-punishment model of the criminal sanction in that the most serious cases receive the greatest restrictions and supervision. If probationers live according to the conditions of their sentence, the level of supervision is gradually reduced.

A continuing issue for probation officers is the size of their caseloads. How many clients can one officer effectively handle? In the 1930s, the National Probation Association recommended a 50-unit caseload; in 1967, the U.S. President's Commission on Law Enforcement and Administration of Justice reduced it to 35. However, today the national average for adult supervision is about 150, with some urban caseloads exceeding 300. The oversized caseload is usually cited as one of the main obstacles to successful probation. In Sacramento, California, $12 million in budget cuts over five years left over 90 percent of the county's 22,000 probationers without any supervision, drug testing, or services because probation officers simply could not handle the average caseload of 124 that resulted from staff reductions (Branan, 2013). In such situations, it is difficult to see how any goal of punishment is being advanced.

In some cities, budget cuts have led to the expanded use of volunteers to assist in probation functions. These programs operate according to at least two different models. In one model, the volunteers actually act as unpaid probation officers. After receiving training, they carry out the duties of professionals, enabling their cities and counties to administer probation programs less expensively. For example, the website of the city of Westminster, Colorado, insists that "volunteers do not do 'social' type activities with the clients" and describes the responsibilities carried out by volunteers: enforce court orders, provide mentoring, monitor compliance with probation terms, write monthly reports on each offender, attend probation court hearings, and attend monthly training sessions (City of Westminster website, 2014). In the second model, volunteers conduct a wider array of activities in support of the probation office. For example, in San Diego, the Volunteers in Probation program carries out fund-raising activities and clothing drives to provide clothing, eye exams, scholarships, emergency funds, and bus passes for probationers who are fulfilling the conditions of probation. (www.volunteersinprobation .org, 2014).

Revocation and Termination of Probation

Probation ends in one of two ways: (1) the person successfully completes the period of probation, or (2) the probationary status is revoked because of misbehavior. Revocation of probation typically occurs for either a **technical violation** or a new arrest.

technical violation The probationer's failure to abide by the rules and conditions of probation (specified by the judge), resulting in revocation of probation.

Technical violations occur when a probationer fails to meet the conditions of a sentence by, for instance, violating curfew, failing a drug test, or using alcohol. Officers have discretion as to whether or not they bring this fact to the attention of the judge. In making these discretionary decisions, they must be professional, ethical, and fair. Read "A Question of Ethics" at the end of the chapter to consider ethical issues, including the problem of probation officers who improperly accept gifts and bribes.

As indicated by Table 12.1, probation revocations in New York counties outside New York City were triggered by technical violations in 54 percent of cases and by arrests in 23 percent of cases (New York State Division of Criminal Justice Services, 2008). The table also shows the kinds of sanctions imposed after probation was revoked.

Probation officers and judges have widely varying notions of what constitutes grounds for revoking probation. When encountering technical violations, probation officers may first try to impose stricter rules, sternly lecture the probationer, and increase the frequency of contacts with the probationer. Yet, the probation officer may face special challenges if the probationer does not take seriously the likelihood of consequences for technical violations. Indeed, a study in Wisconsin found that 68 percent of probationers failed on at least one occasion to report as required to the probation officer, in contrast to only 42 percent of parolees committing the same technical violation (Van Stelle & Goodrich, 2009). Unlike parolees, who, as we will see in Chapter 13, have already been to prison and therefore may be more likely to fear being sent back, many probationers are young and less experienced with the system. This failure to fulfill probation conditions may demonstrate their greater immaturity as well as their failure to recognize that technical violations could actually lead to incarceration if their probation officer seeks revocation. Nationally, among offenders who exited from probation supervision in 2012, 68 percent completed their probation sentence successfully and only 15 percent were incarcerated. The remainder left probation supervision for a variety of other reasons, including absconding, gaining early release from probation, and being deported from the country for immigration law violations (Maruschak & Bonczar, 2013).

Once the officer calls a violation to the attention of the court, the probationer may be arrested or summoned for a revocation hearing. The Legislative Analyst's Office for the State of California calculates that it costs taxpayers an extra $50,000,

TABLE 12.1   Probation Revocation Hearings: Justifications and Outcomes

This is a snapshot of the reasons for outstate New York probation officers' recommendations for revocation and the outcomes when probationers were resentenced as a result of revocation.*

Violation Reasons	
Technical violations	54%
Arrest	23
New conviction	13
Abscond (go missing)	11
Total†	100%

Resentence after Probation Revocation	
Local jail	74%
State prison	15
Probation	4
Intermittent imprisonment	4
Unconditional discharge	2
Fine	1
Total	100%

Note: Two additional offenders were sent to juvenile detention facilities.

*The data present reasons and outcomes for the 57 counties outside New York City. New York City's probation population is much more heavily composed of convicted felons. The outstate counties' mix of misdemeanants and felons on probation may be more similar to the probation populations throughout the country.

†Total does not equal 100% due to rounding.

Source: New York State Probation Population: 2007 Profile, Albany: New York State Division of Criminal Justice Services, June 2008.

on average, each time an offender is sent to prison for a probation revocation. That amount includes not only the marginal cost of sending an offender to prison but also the average length of the probationer's sentence (17 months), the subsequent cost of parole supervision, and the likelihood that some percentage of these offenders will be sent to prison again for parole violations (Taylor, 2009). Because of the contemporary emphasis on avoiding the expense of incarceration except for flagrant and continual violations of the conditions of probation, revocations increasingly rest on a new arrest or multiple violations of rules rather than on a small number of technical violations.

As discussed in Chapter 10, the U.S. Supreme Court extended due process rights to probationers by ruling that before probation can be revoked, the offender is entitled to both a preliminary and a final hearing, and a right to counsel in some cases. When a probationer is taken into custody for violating the conditions of probation, a preliminary hearing must be held to determine whether probable cause exists to believe that the incident occurred. If there is a finding of probable cause, a final hearing, where the revocation decision is made, is mandatory. At these hearings, the probationer has the right to cross-examine witnesses and to receive notice of the alleged violations and receive a written report of the proceedings. The Court ruled, though, that the probationer does not have an automatic right to counsel; this decision is to be made on a case-by-case basis. At the final hearing, the judge decides whether to continue probation or to impose tougher restrictions, such as incarceration.

For those who successfully complete probation, the sentence ends. Ordinarily, the probationer is then a free citizen again, with obligation neither to the court nor to the probation department.

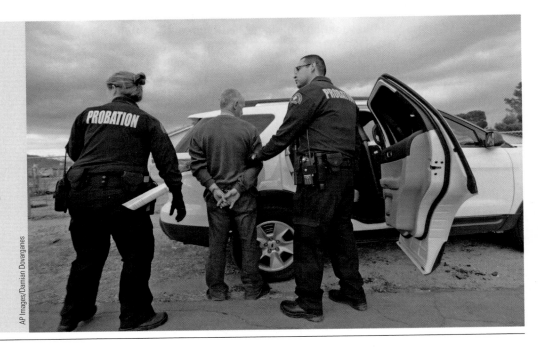

Probation officers make decisions about whether probationers should be taken into custody for violating the terms of probation. After the decision is made, they often require police assistance for this task. Do probation officers need the same training as police officers, or should they receive a different kind of training in order to do their jobs effectively?

AP Images/Damian Dovarganes

Assessing Probation

As states deal with continuing budget difficulties, the use of probation is certain to expand. Yet, critics see probation as nothing more than a slap on the wrist, an absence of punishment. Nevertheless, the importance of probation for public safety has never been greater: studies indicate that 53 percent of those sentenced to probation were assigned that punishment upon conviction for a felony (Maruschak & Bonczar, 2013). This statistic is striking because many people assume that probationers have typically committed only misdemeanors.

Despite the fact that many probationers have been convicted of serious crimes, caseload burdens and limited resources lead many probation officers to meet with individual offenders little more than once a month. Such limited contact raises questions about whether convicted felons receive adequate supervision and monitoring in the community. Yet, as budget cuts aimed at the expense of imprisonment increase the number of offenders assigned to community sanctions, contact between officers and probationers may be further reduced in many jurisdictions that cannot afford to simultaneously increase the number of probation officers.

Although the recidivism rate for probationers is lower than the rate for those who have been incarcerated, researchers question whether this is a direct result of supervision or an indirect result of the maturing of the offenders. Most offenders placed on probation do not become career criminals—their criminal activity is short-lived, and they become stable citizens as they obtain jobs and get married. Most of those who are arrested a second time do not repeat their mistake.

To offer a viable alternative to incarceration, probation services need the resources to supervise and assist their clients appropriately. The new demands on probation have brought calls for increased electronic monitoring and for risk-management systems that provide different levels of supervision for different kinds of offenders. Because of the growing importance of probation and other forms of community corrections, it is important for criminal justice officials to use evidence-based practices in order to enhance the effectiveness of these approaches to punishment and treatment. Read the "Evidence-Based Practice and Policy" feature concerning community corrections, and consider whether there are any impediments to the implementation of these practices.

Probation and Community Corrections

Significant efforts are being undertaken to identify and verify the effectiveness of programs and then publicize and provide training about effective programs for agencies interested in implementing reforms. In 2009, the Administrative Office of the U.S. Courts formed the Evidence-Based Practice Working Group, chaired by experienced federal probation officers, to advise the federal Office of Probation and Pretrial Services about evidence-based principles and effective approaches. This Working Group identified important priorities, including the nationwide use of proven, evidence-based risk assessment tools to determine the supervisory and programmatic needs of offenders. In addition, the Working Group emphasized the need to train probation personnel in evidence-based practices as well as particular skills that have proven to have the greatest effect on reducing recidivism.

One important approach for advancing the use of evidence-based practices is the STARR program—"Staff Training Aimed at Reducing Rearrest." The training program is provided for federal probation officers, but its principles are also useful for community corrections officials at the state and local levels of government. The program teaches active listening, effective use of reinforcement and punishment, and techniques for addressing offenders' thought processes that may not appropriately connect their thinking to their behavior.

The program recognizes that high-risk offenders need more intensive services. It also is based on the idea that counseling and other services should target those factors that are actually associated with criminal behavior, such as substance abuse, contact with those who commit criminal acts, and attitudes that endorse criminal behavior, rather than such matters as self-esteem or emotional distress. Research indicates that these elements, as well as others, such as involving families in the treatment process and providing treatment for at least 90 days, can be effective in reducing the number of offenders in community corrections who commit subsequent crimes.

The 2009 report of the Pew Center on the States presents research-based recommendations designed to strengthen community corrections systems, saving money and reducing crime. These recommendations include the following:

- Sort offenders by risk to public safety to determine appropriate levels of supervision.
- Base intervention programs on sound research about what works reduce recidivism.
- Harness advances in supervision technology such as electronic monitoring and rapid-result alcohol and drug tests.
- Impose swift and certain sanctions for offenders who break the rules of their release but who do not commit new crimes.
- Create incentives for offenders and supervision agencies to succeed, and monitor their performance.

The literature on evidence-based practices in community corrections makes clear that important challenges extend beyond identifying effective practices and providing training to justice system officials who have face-to-face contact and supervisory responsibility with offenders. There is also an issue of convincing individual officers and agencies to actually incorporate evidence-based practices into their standard routines. When people have been doing their jobs and operating their offices in a certain way over a long period of time, it can be difficult to get them to change their customary practices, even when there is evidence that new approaches will be more effective. In addition, budget cuts can complicate the implementation of new practices as there may be insufficient time or personnel to carry out evidence-based practices in the manner that is most effective.

Researching the Internet

Read a brief report by the Evidence-Based Practices Working Group addressed to the federal Office of Probation and Pretrial Services. http://www.uscourts.gov/uscourts/FederalCourts/PPS/Fedprob/2011-09/development.html.

Implementing New Practices

Are you optimistic that probation officers and other community corrections officials can be trained to effectively help offenders become less likely to commit new crimes? Given the number of people on probation and other community corrections programs and the limited number of officials who must supervise these offenders, the available time and resources may make the actual implementation of evidence-based practices an impossible dream. If you are optimistic about the possibility of progress, describe what you see as the two biggest priorities for those seeking to implement evidence-based practices. If you are not optimistic, would you steer time, attention, and resources to other aspects of probation and community corrections? Briefly describe what you would do if you were the head of a local probation office.

Sources: Pew Center on the States, *One in 31: The Long Reach of American Corrections*, Washington, DC: Pew Charitable Trusts, 2009; Jonathan Hurtig and Lisa Marie Lenart, "The Development of the Evidence-Based Practice Blue Print and Where We Are Now," *Federal Probation* 75 (2011): 35–36; "Program Profile: Staff Training Aimed at Reducing Rearrest (STARR)," U.S. Office of Justice Programs website, 2013 (http://www.crimesolutions.gov); Charles R. Robinson, Scott VanBenschoten, Melissa Alexander, and Christopher T. Lowenkamp, "A Random (Almost) Study of Staff Training Aimed at Reducing Re-arrest (STARR): Reducing Recidivism through Intentional Design," *Federal Probation* 75 (2011): 57–63; Faye S. Taxman and Steven Belenko, *Implementing Evidence-Based Practices in Community Corrections and Addiction Treatment*, New York: Springer, 2013.

1. What are the four main assumptions underlying community corrections?
Many offenders' crimes and records do not warrant incarceration; community supervision is cheaper; recidivism rates for those supervised in the community are no higher than for those who serve prison time; incarceration is more destructive to the offender and society.

2. What are the main tasks of the probation officer?
To assist judges by preparing presentence reports and to provide assistance and supervision to offenders in the community.

3. What are the grounds for revocation of probation?
An arrest for a new offense or a technical violation of the conditions of probation that were set by the judge.

Why would a probation officer decline to seek revocation for every technical violation? Does the criminal justice system benefit from such decisions? Give two arguments for each side of this question.

Intermediate Sanctions in the Community

Dissatisfaction with the traditional means of probation supervision, coupled with the crowding and high cost of prisons, has resulted in the expansion of intermediate sanctions. These sanctions are more restricting than simple probation and therefore constitute a greater degree of actual punishment, especially for those who have committed more serious offenses.

Many experts support the case for intermediate sanctions. For example, Norval Morris and Michael Tonry say, "Prison is used excessively; probation is used even more excessively; between the two is a near vacuum of purposive and enforced punishments" (1990:3). Sixty-nine percent of convicted felons are incarcerated, incarceration being the severest sentence, whereas 27 percent receive probation, the least severe. Hence, nearly all convicted felons receive either the severest or the most lenient of possible penalties (Rosenmerkel, Durose, & Farole, 2009). Morris and Tonry have urged that punishments be created that are more restrictive than probation yet match the severity of the offense and the characteristics of the offender and that can be carried out while still protecting the community. In addition, they emphasize that intermediate punishments must be supported and enforced by mechanisms that take any breach of the conditions of the sentence seriously.

We can view intermediate sanctions as a continuum—a range of punishments that vary in levels of intrusiveness and control, as shown in Figure 12.3. Corrections employs many types of intermediate sanctions. They can be divided into (1) those administered primarily by the judiciary (fines, restitution, and forfeiture), (2) those administered primarily in the community with a supervision component (home confinement, community service, day reporting centers, and intensive probation supervision), and (3) those administered inside institutions and followed by community supervision. Furthermore, sanctions may be imposed in combination—for example, a fine and probation, or boot camp with community service and probation.

Intermediate Sanctions Administered Primarily by the Judiciary

The judiciary administers many kinds of intermediate sanctions. Here we discuss three of them—fines, restitution, and forfeiture. Because all three involve the transfer of money or property from the offender to the government or crime victim, the judiciary is considered the proper body not only to impose the sanction but also to collect what is due.

Fines

Fines are routinely imposed for offenses ranging from traffic violations to felonies. Studies have shown that the fine is used widely as a criminal sanction and that nationally well over $1 billion in fines has been collected annually. Yet, judges in the United States make little use of fines as the *sole* punishment for crimes more serious than motor vehicle violations. Instead, they typically use fines in conjunction with other sanctions, such as probation and incarceration: for example, two years of probation and a $500 fine.

Many judges cite the difficulty of collecting fines as the reason that they do not make greater use of this punishment. They note that offenders tend to be poor, and many judges fear that fines will be paid from the proceeds of additional illegal acts. Other judges are concerned that relying on fines as an alternative to incarceration will let affluent offenders "buy" their way out of jail while forcing the poor to serve time.

Fines are used extensively in Europe. There they are enforced and are normally the sole sanction for a wide range of crimes. To deal with the concern that fines exact a heavier toll on the poor than on the wealthy, Finland, Sweden, and Germany have developed the "day fine," which bases the penalty on offenders' daily income and the gravity of the offense. The day fine has been tested in Arizona, Connecticut, Iowa, New York, and Washington (Zedlewski, 2010). As you read the "Comparative Perspective," consider the philosophical and practical difficulties involved in the use of the day fine as a sanction.

Restitution

Restitution is repayment by an offender to a victim who has suffered some form of financial loss from the crime. It is *reparative* in that it seeks to repair the harm done. In the Middle Ages, restitution was a common way to settle a criminal case (Karmen, 2001). The offender was ordered to pay the victim or do the victim's work. The growth of the modern state saw the decline of such punishments based on "private" arrangements between offender and victim. Instead, the state prosecuted offenders, and punishments focused on the wrong the offender had done to society.

Though largely unpublicized, victim restitution has remained a part of the U.S. criminal justice system. In many instances, restitution derives from informal agreements between the police and offenders at the station, during plea bargaining, or in the prosecutor's sentence recommendation. Only since the late 1970s has restitution been institutionalized, usually as one of the conditions of probation.

As with fines, convicted offenders differ in their ability to pay restitution, and the conditions inevitably fall more harshly on less affluent offenders. Someone who has the "good fortune" to be victimized by an affluent criminal might receive full compensation, whereas someone victimized by a poor offender might never receive a penny.

fine A sum of money to be paid to the state by a convicted person as punishment for an offense.

restitution Repayment—in the form of money or service—by an offender to a victim who has suffered some loss from the offense.

The Day Fine: Questions and Challenges from a European Punishment

Northern European countries began to develop the day fine as a criminal punishment in the 1920s. Now it is a primary form of punishment for various offenses in countries such as Sweden, Finland, and Germany. In Germany 80 percent of criminal sentences are day fines. Such fines are intended to reduce the use of expensive imprisonment and make more affluent offenders feel the punitive effects of fines to the same degree as less affluent offenders who would have difficulty paying any fine.

The formulation of the day fine depends on the seriousness of the offense and the income of the offender. The fine is stated as a number of days' worth of income for the particular offender, with allowances for offenders' need to retain money for their families' daily living expenses. As a result, wealthy people can receive eye-popping fines for relatively minor offenses. Periodically, news reports will note, for example, that a multimillionaire in Finland or elsewhere received a fine of $200,000 for driving 25 miles per hour over the speed limit. An individual with a modest income would have received a much lower fine for the same offense.

The unequal results of day fines are intended to advance the goal of equity by making offenders experience comparable severity. Otherwise, wealthy people might just pay fines and continue to break the same laws with impunity because their checkbooks would permit them to pay standardized fines without feeling any "pain." Yet, important philosophical and practical challenges lurk within the day-fine system—challenges that Americans would need to confront before widely adopting this form of punishment that is currently used in relatively few American jurisdictions.

Is it fair to impose a harsher punishment on offenders who are more wealthy? The underlying purpose is to make punishments equitable and impactful, but the effect is to make punishments unequal. Would this form of inequality be less acceptable to Americans than it is to Europeans?

Should the formulation of the day fine take account of an individual's monthly debts—credit cards, car payments, and student loans? In addition, should the formulation take account of assets? If not, wealthy people with large bank accounts might be able to easily pay substantial fines without noticing any meaningful effect on their incomes.

What should happen to people who cannot or do not pay their mandated day fines? Should people be jailed, or should courts use community service or another intermediate sanction as an alternative?

Day fines have been used in many European countries for decades. The United States can consider expanded use of this punishment as a means to reduce the costs of jail and other sanctions. However, as with other punishments, the choice to use this sanction brings with it complications and potential problems.

For Critical Analysis

Would you support the use of day fines in the United States? If not, why not? If so, for which offenses should it apply, and how many days' worth of fines should be imposed for each offense?

Sources: Hans-Joerg Albrecht, "Sentencing in Germany—Explaining Long Term Stability in the Structure of Criminal Sanctions and Sentencing," unpublished paper presented at University of Haifa, 2011; Lina Eriksson and Robert E. Goodin, "The Measuring Rod of Time: The Example of the Swedish Day-fines," *Journal of Applied Philosophy* 24 (2007): 125–36; Craig Howie, "The World's Highest Speeding Fines," AOL Autos News, January 7, 2011 (http://autos.aol.com); Justice Policy Institute, "Fact Sheet: Sentencing," *Finding Direction: Expanding Criminal Justice Options by Considering Policies of Other Nations,* April 2011; Edwin Zedlewski, "Alternatives to Custodial Supervision: The Day Fine," National Institute of Justice Discussion Paper, April 2010.

In Colorado, a corps of investigators work with probation officers to monitor cases, collecting restitution and working out payment plans if necessary. As a result, collections in Colorado counties have increased by 25 to 50 percent since the late 1980s. However, even in a well-organized system, it can be difficult to collect from many offenders. In 2009 offenders in Colorado still owed an uncollected $563 million in restitution and $215 million in court fines and costs. Pennsylvania, which was less active and organized in collecting from offenders, was owed $1.5 billion by criminal offenders (Crummy, 2009).

Restitution is more easily imposed when the "damage" inflicted can be easily measured—value of property destroyed or stolen or medical costs, for instance. Thus, restitution is most frequently ordered for property crimes.

Forfeiture   With the passage of two laws in 1970—the Racketeer Influenced and Corrupt Organizations Act (RICO) and the Continuing Criminal Enterprise Act (CCE)—Congress resurrected forfeiture, a criminal sanction that had lain dormant since the American Revolution. Through amendments in 1984 and 1986, Congress improved ways to implement the law. Most states now have similar laws, particularly to deal with organized crime and with trafficking in controlled substances.

Forfeiture is government seizure of property and other assets derived from or used in criminal activity. Assets seized by federal and state agencies through forfeiture can be quite considerable and have increased significantly in the past 30 years. For example, in 1989, U.S. attorneys seized $285 million in assets—by 2010, that amount had increased to $1.8 billion (BJS, 2014).

Forfeiture is controversial. Critics argue that confiscating property without a court hearing violates citizens' constitutional rights. They have also raised concerns about the excessive use of this sanction, because forfeited assets often go into the budget of the law enforcement agency taking the action (Witt, 2009).

A potential buyer examines property seized by federal officials from Congressman Randy "Duke" Cunningham after his conviction for taking bribes. Presumably obtained through illegal funds, the property items were to be sold at auction. Should law enforcement agencies be permitted to keep or sell the property that they seize from criminal offenders?

Those in opposition further argue that ownership of the seized property is often unclear. For example, in Hartford, Connecticut, a woman's home was seized because her grandson, unbeknownst to her, was using it as a base for selling drugs. Under a law passed by Congress in 2000, owners' property cannot be seized if they can demonstrate their innocence by a preponderance of evidence.

forfeiture Government seizure of property and other assets derived from or used in criminal activity.

Intermediate Sanctions Administered in the Community

One argument for intermediate sanctions is that probation, as traditionally practiced, cannot accommodate the large numbers of offenders whom probation officers must supervise today. Probation leaders have responded to this criticism by developing new intermediate sanction programs and expanding old ones. Four of these are home confinement, community service, day reporting centers, and intensive supervision probation.

Home Confinement With technological innovations that provide for electronic monitoring, **home confinement**, in which offenders must remain at home during specific periods, has gained attention. Offenders under home confinement (often called "house arrest") may face other restrictions, such as the usual probation rules against the use of alcohol and drugs, as well as strictly monitored curfews and check-in times. As you read the "Close Up," consider whether home confinement is either too soft as a punishment or, alternatively, is too frequently violated to serve as an appropriate intermediate sanction.

Some offenders are allowed to go to a place of employment, education, or treatment during the day but must return to their homes by a specified hour. Those supervising home confinement may telephone offenders' homes at various times of the day or night to speak personally with offenders to make sure they are complying.

Home confinement offers a great deal of flexibility for judges and corrections officials. It can be used as a sole sanction or in combination with other penalties. It can be imposed at almost any point in the criminal justice process: during the pretrial period, after a short term in jail or prison, or as a condition of probation or parole. In addition, home confinement relieves the government of the responsibility

home confinement A sentence requiring the offender to remain inside his or her home during specified periods.

Life under Home Confinement

As government officials struggle to deal with budget cuts, cost-saving measures such as electronic monitoring and home confinement become more attractive. In Rock County, Wisconsin, it costs $64 per day to hold an offender in jail. By contrast, it costs only $9 per day for an electronic monitoring device that is used in conjunction with home confinement. The offenders and their families handle their own living expenses during home confinement. Moreover, many counties charge the offenders a fee to cover the costs of electronic monitoring. Sheriffs can save their jail space and resources for offenders with records of violence. Low-risk offenders can be punished in their homes without expending scarce resources.

For many offenders, home confinement is a desirable alternative to jail. They are in familiar surroundings with control over their own indoor activities and meals. They are also removed from the changing array of threatening characters with whom they may end up sharing cells at jail. From the perspective of a sheriff, police chief, or judge, home confinement also can create an incentive for good behavior by those low-risk offenders who wish to avoid jail. Thus, society can benefit from using this form of community corrections.

Critics believe that home confinement is not really punishment because offenders enjoy too much freedom. Yet, offenders often discover that home confinement actually creates more pressure and control than they anticipated. They are kept on rigid schedules that define when they can go to work, when they can go grocery shopping, and when they must be at home. They may live in fear that if they open the front door to get the newspaper, their device will record a violation. In 2011, when actress Lindsay Lohan served 35 days of electronic monitoring and home confinement after conviction for shoplifting from a jewelry store, her ankle monitor notified police that she had left the house without authorization. Authorities found her at home reading scripts, and she claimed that her monitor experienced a mechanical malfunction. Her example illustrates another source of worry for offenders who are concerned about being wrongly blamed for violating the requirements of home confinement.

Another source of pressure is the experience of being so close to people in free society—watching them pass by the window every day—but not being able to enjoy freedom. Johnnie Whichard, a man who served home confinement in Montgomery Country, Maryland, was permitted to leave home at certain times in order to go to his job. He noted, however, that he gave up on using his six allotted hours to leave home

each week for other purposes because there was so much planning involved as well as a two-day wait for approval of the detailed itineraries that were required. Kerry Wehrwein, a Wisconsin woman sentenced to home confinement for multiple drunk-driving convictions, was not allowed to have visitors and was tested regularly by a deputy sheriff who arrived to give her breathalyzer tests. Because she also wore an alcohol monitor, she had to avoid cosmetics and cleaning products for fear that exposure to chemicals would make the monitor register a false reading for consumption of alcohol.

There are some offenders who will repeatedly violate home confinement rules when, for example, they know that the jail is full and that the police really cannot take them into custody. Such offenders are obviously not good candidates for electronic monitoring and eventually they will be carted off to jail. For low-risk offenders who are fearful of jail, however, home confinement can be an inexpensive means of control and punishment.

Researching the Internet

Michigan's system of electronically monitoring offenders in the community is described online. To link to the website, see http://www.michigan.gov/corrections/0,4551,7-119-1435_1498-5032–,00.html.

For Critical Analysis

Electronic monitoring makes the lives of Johnnie Whichard and Kerry Wehrwein different than they would like, yet they are allowed to live at home and move about the community at approved times. Thus, their loss of liberty is not nearly as severe as it would have been in prison or jail. In fact, some observers may believe that this isn't much of a punishment. List three crimes for which electronic monitoring would be appropriate. What is the most serious offense for which you would consider a sentence of home confinement? If you believe that electronic monitoring is not appropriate for any offenses, give three reasons for your conclusion.

Sources: Paul Duggan, "Long Arm of the Law Has Man by the Ankle," *Washington Post*, March 28, 2005, p. B1; Lauren Kravets, "Electronic Monitoring Reducing Recidivism in Rock County," WIFR.com, February 17, 2011 (www.wifr.com); Tracy Pepey, "Lindsay Lohan's Electronic Monitoring Device Goes Off," iVillage.com, June 3, 2011 (www.ivillage.com); Ted Sullivan, "Life Under Surveillance," *Janesville Gazette*, January 4, 2009 (http://gazettextra.com).

of providing the offender with food, clothing, and housing, as it must do in prisons. For these reasons, home confinement programs have grown and proliferated.

The development of electronic monitoring equipment has made home confinement an enforceable sentencing option. Two basic types of electronic monitoring devices exist. Passive monitors respond only to inquiries; most commonly, the offender receives an automated telephone call from the probation office and is told to place the device on a receiver attached to the phone. Active monitors send continuous signals that a receiver picks up; a computer notes any break in the signal.

Despite favorable publicity, home confinement with electronic monitoring poses certain legal, technical, and correctional issues that must be addressed before it can become a standard punishment. First, some criminal justice scholars question its constitutionality. Monitoring may violate the Fourth Amendment's protection against unreasonable searches and seizures. At issue is a clash between the constitutionally protected reasonable expectation of privacy and the invasion of one's home by surveillance devices. Second, the monitoring devices still have extensive technical problems, such as frequently giving erroneous reports that the offender is home. Third, offender failure rates may prove to be high. There is little evidence that electronic monitoring reduces recidivism rates (Renzema & Mayo-Wilson, 2005). Being one's own warden is difficult, and visits by former criminal associates and other negative enticements may become problematic for many offenders. Anecdotal evidence suggests that four months of full-time monitoring is about the limit before a violation will occur. Fourth, an additional issue is that some crimes—such as child abuse, drug sales, and assaults—can be committed while the offender is at home. Finally, observers point out that the only offenders eligible for this type of program are those who own telephones and can afford the weekly rental rates of $35–$120 for the electronic system and components.

Clark County, Washington, informs offenders that they must meet three specific conditions in order to be eligible for home confinement: "[1] A stable and approved residence; [2] A dedicated phone line for the EHC equipment (no options like call-waiting or call forwarding); [3] Ability to pay $15.00 per EHC day plus a $40.00 hookup fee" (www.clark.wa.gov, 2010). As indicated by these requirements, home confinement seems best suited to low-risk offenders who have relatively stable residences.

Whatever the potential benefits of home confinement, they cannot be achieved unless monitoring programs operate appropriately. Newspaper investigations in 2013 found that Florida judges were ordering home confinement for some people who were supposed to be ineligible for such sanctions due to the violent crimes for which they had been convicted. In one county, more than 50 people on home confinement disappeared. Nearly all were eventually caught, but not before some committed crimes and used drugs. In the worst instance, a defendant on home confinement—as part of conditions of bail prior to trial—murdered one of the witnesses against him in his upcoming home invasion trial. County officials noted that the escapees represented only 6 percent of the 900 people assigned to home confinement in Orange County, Florida. However, that small percentage still represented a large number of people who caused harm in the community and raised questions about the effectiveness of the entire home confinement program (Weiner, 2013a; Weiner, 2013b). These problems highlighted the need for judges to be careful about which individuals are assigned to home confinement and the need for equipment to work properly and officials to respond quickly and effectively when people violate their assignment to home confinement.

Probation officers are responsible for offenders who are subject to home confinement and other forms of electronic monitoring, such as GPS (global positioning systems) to keep track of a probationer's movements. Does home confinement and monitoring actually impose punishment on offenders?

Community Service

A **community service** sentence requires the offender to perform a certain amount of unpaid labor in the community. As indicated in the chapter opening, singer Chris Brown was required to perform community labor as part of his sentence. Community service can take a variety of forms, including assisting in social-service agencies, cleaning parks and roadsides, or helping the poor. The sentence specifies the number of hours to be worked and usually requires supervision by a probation officer. Judges can tailor community service to the skills and abilities of offenders. For example, less educated offenders might pick up litter along the highway, whereas those with schooling might teach reading in evening literacy classes.

community service A sentence requiring the offender to perform a certain amount of unpaid labor in the community.

COMMON BELIEF: Community service does not punish those who receive the sanction.

- There are elements of punishment in the community service sanction.
- Individuals suffer a partial loss of liberty as they must report to specific locations, surrender their time and freedom of movement, and obey authorities' orders to complete tasks that they would otherwise not do.
- They also risk feeling the shame and embarrassment of being seen doing tasks, such as collecting trash along a highway, that indicate to other people that they have gotten into trouble with the law.
- Does this mean that community service is sufficiently severe to serve as a punishment for all kinds of nonviolent offenses? No. Society may legitimately conclude that greater restrictions on liberty and behavior, such as those associated with home confinement, may be appropriate for some offenses and repeat offenders.
- We should recognize, however, that community service carries sanctioning elements while simultaneously avoiding the high costs of more expensive sanctions and permitting minor offenders to stay connected to their families and communities by retaining their jobs or continuing in school.

Many judges order community service when an offender cannot pay a fine. The offender's effort to make reparation to the community harmed by the crime also serves a symbolic function.

Although community service has many supporters, some labor unions and workers criticize it for possibly taking jobs away from law-abiding citizens. In addition, some experts believe that if community service is the only sanction, it may be too mild a punishment, especially for upper-class and white-collar criminals. Examine your own views about community service as a punishment when you read "Criminal Justice: Myth & Reality."

Day Reporting Centers   Another intermediate sanction is the **day reporting center**—a community correctional center to which the offender must report each day to carry out elements of the sentence. Designed to ensure that probationers follow the employment and treatment stipulations attached to their sentence, day reporting centers also increase the likelihood that offenders and the general public will consider probation supervision to be credible.

Most day reporting centers incorporate multiple correctional methods. For example, in some centers, offenders must remain in the facility for eight hours or report for drug-related urine checks before going to work. Centers with a rehabilitation component carry

day reporting center A community correctional center where an offender reports each day to comply with elements of a sentence.

out drug and alcohol treatment, literacy programs, and job searches. Others provide staff–offender contact levels equal to or greater than those in intensive supervision programs.

So far, there are few evaluations of these programs. As with many newly established criminal justice programs, strict eligibility requirements result in small numbers of cases actually entering the program; but even with the limited number of participants under day reporting center supervision, there is evidence that recidivism rates can be reduced (Ostermann, 2009). Evaluations of jail-run day reporting centers find that the participants have lower levels of drug use and absconding. However, because participants were carefully screened for acceptance, applicability may be limited to low-risk cases (Porter, Lee, & Lutz, 2002).

One additional problem often faces day reporting centers and other community corrections facilities: opposition from citizens about the placement of such facilities in or near their neighborhoods. Even when people recognize the value of community corrections facilities, they may be very nervous about the thought of convicted offenders congregating each day near their homes or their children's schools. Read "The Policy Debate" to consider the controversy about deciding where to place community corrections facilities.

intensive supervision probation (ISP) Probation granted under conditions of strict reporting to a probation officer with a limited caseload.

Intensive Supervision Probation (ISP)   Intensive supervision probation (ISP) is a means of dealing with offenders who need greater restrictions than traditional community-based programs can provide. Jurisdictions in every state have programs to intensively supervise such offenders. ISP uses probation as an intermediate form of punishment by imposing conditions of strict reporting to a probation officer who has a limited caseload.

There are two general types of ISP programs. *Probation diversion* puts under intensive surveillance those offenders thought to be too risky for routine supervision. *Institutional diversion* selects low-risk offenders already sentenced to prison and provides supervision for them in the community. Daily contact between the

Should Community Corrections Facilities Be Dispersed Throughout a City?

Newspapers regularly report about citizens' efforts to prevent the placement of community corrections facilities near their neighborhoods. People sign petitions and gather groups to attend city council or local zoning commission meetings. The attitude that many people have about the siting of community corrections is referred to as "NIMBY"—Not In My Back Yard. Similar citizen activism can arise when cities discuss the placement of waste disposal facilities, power plants, and other needed public facilities that are feared as being noisy, being unpleasant, or posing risks to housing values and quality of life for people who live nearby. In efforts to influence where facilities are placed, middle-class and affluent people typically possess more political power. As a result, there can be risks that community corrections facilities will be concentrated in poor neighborhoods or commercial areas, even if the buildings available at those locations are less suitable for providing needed space and services than other buildings located closer to middle-class neighborhoods.

For Dispersing Community Corrections Facilities

- Community corrections programs should be housed in the most suitable building without regard to the opposition and political influence of middle-class and affluent people.
- Everyone benefits from effective programs to reduce crime; therefore, everyone in a city should bear equal risks and burdens in the placement of facilities, which means they should not be concentrated in poor neighborhoods.
- Placement of community corrections centers in poor neighborhoods or commercial areas may place offenders, especially those with substance abuse issues, closer to the associates and locations that may tempt them to relapse and reoffend.

Against Dispersing Community Corrections Facilities

- Placing offenders in residential neighborhoods creates needless risks for citizens and their homes, especially as offenders travel to the area every day at the same time that many homes are empty because the homeowners are at work.
- Many offenders under community supervision are drug users who relapse during their period of supervision, thus creating risks that drug transactions will begin occurring near homes and schools.
- Many offenders live in poor neighborhoods. Thus, it is easier for them to travel to nearby locations or take public transportation to commercial areas rather than try to find their way to far-flung residential areas that are not necessarily served by frequent public bus service.

What Should U.S. Policy Be?

The siting of community corrections facilities is controversial because there is no escaping the fact that the administrators of such facilities cannot guarantee that the offender-clients will never misbehave. The opposition to facilities becomes even more intense when it is a residential facility for substance abuse treatment or transitional reentry into society by parolees just released from prison. In such cases, local residents are very aware that offenders will be nearby 24 hours a day, including the nighttime hours. It is difficult for those who would be neighbors to proposed facilities to be reassured by the fact that many offenders in community corrections programs have a strong motivation to obey rules in order to avoid jail or a return to prison.

At the heart of the controversy is the question of who should decide where community corrections facilities will be located. Should state officials have the authority to place such facilities in the most appropriate building, wherever it happens to be located? Should city councils and local zoning commissions, comprised of and influenced by local residents, make such decisions about their own communities?

Researching the Internet

To read the policy position of the International Community Corrections Association on siting facilities, visit http://iccalive.org/icca/index.php?option=com_content&view=article&id=95&Itemid=554.

Analyzing the Issue

Imagine that you and your classmates are staff members of the community corrections unit of your state department of corrections. You must select the best site for the state to build a new day reporting center in the town where your college is located (or in your hometown). What factors would you consider in deciding where to place the building? In anticipation of public opposition, provide the arguments that you would use to educate the public about the necessity and desirability of placing a day reporting center in the community? Can you and your classmates agree on the best location for the center?

probationer and the probation officer may cut rearrest rates. Such contact also gives the probationer greater access to the resources the officer can provide, such as treatment services in the community. Offenders have incentives to obey rules, knowing that they must meet with their probation officers daily and, in some cases, must speak with them even more frequently. Offenders often face additional restrictions as well, such as electronic monitoring, alcohol and drug testing, community service, and restitution.

ISP programs have been called "old style" probation because each officer has only 20 clients and requires frequent face-to-face contact (Jalbert & Rhodes, 2012).

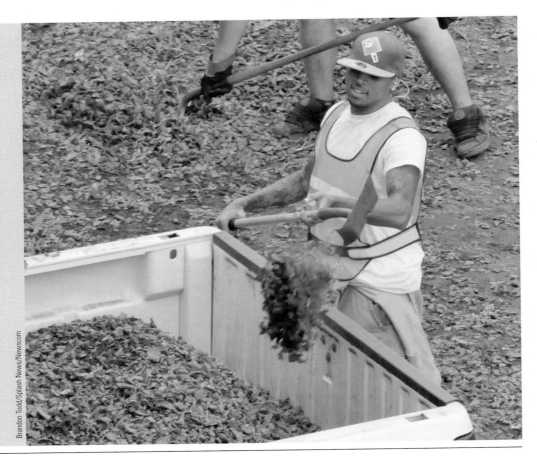

Singer Chris Brown did physical labor outdoors at a police horse stable and elsewhere along roads in fulfillment of his community service sentence. Such sanctions can provide benefits to the community. There may also be a "shaming" effect if offenders are embarrassed to be seen in public fulfilling a criminal punishment. Can you think of creative and effective ways to expand the use of community services sanctions?

Brandon Todd/Splash News/Newscom

Nonetheless, some people question how much of a difference constant surveillance can make to probationers with numerous problems. Such offenders frequently need help to get a job, counseling to deal with emotional and family situations, and a variety of supports to avoid drug or alcohol problems that may have contributed to their criminality. Yet, ISP may be a way of getting the large number of drug-addicted felons into treatment.

Because it presents a "tough" image of community supervision and addresses the problem of prison crowding, ISP has become popular among probation administrators, judges, and prosecutors. Most ISP programs require a specific number of monthly contacts with officers; performance of community service; curfews; drug and alcohol testing; and referral to appropriate job-training, education, or treatment programs.

Some observers warn that ISP is not a "cure" for the rising costs and other problems facing corrections systems. Ironically, ISP can increase the number of probationers sent to prison. All evaluations of ISP find that probably because of the closer contact with clients, probation officers uncover more violations of rules than they do in regular probation. Therefore, ISP programs often have higher failure rates than do regular probation, even though their clients produce fewer arrests. But recent analyses of recidivism post-ISP indicate that it can be successful, particularly if combined with rewards for noncriminal behavior (Wodahl, Garland, Culhane, & McCarty, 2011).

One surprising finding is that when given the option of serving prison terms or participating in ISP, many offenders choose prison. In New Jersey, 15 percent of offenders withdrew their applications for ISP once they learned the conditions and requirements. Similarly, when offenders in Marion County, Oregon, were asked if they would participate in ISP, one-third chose prison instead (Petersilia, 1990). Apparently, some offenders would rather spend a short time in prison, where tough conditions may differ little from their accustomed life, than a longer period under demanding conditions in the community. To these offenders, ISP does not represent freedom, because it is so intrusive and the risk of revocation seems high.

Despite problems and continuing questions about its effectiveness, ISP has rejuvenated probation. Many of these programs have demonstrated especially effective supervision of offenders. As with regular probation, the size of a probation officer's caseload, within reasonable limits, often matters less in preventing recidivism than does the quality of supervision and assistance provided to probationers. If properly implemented, ISP may improve the quality of supervision and services that foster success for more kinds of offenders.

Military-type drills and physical workouts are part of the regimen at most boot camps, such as this one in Massachusetts. Evaluations of boot camps have reduced the initial optimism about this approach. Boot camps have been closed in many states. What are the potential shortcomings of using boot camps as punishment?

Intermediate Sanctions Administered in Institutions and the Community

Among the most publicized intermediate sanctions are **boot camps**. Often referred to as *shock incarceration*, these programs vary; however, all stem from the belief that young offenders (usually 14- to 21-year-olds) can be "shocked" out of their criminal ways. Boot camps put offenders through a 30- to 90-day physical regimen designed to develop discipline and respect for authority. Like the Marine Corps, most programs emphasize a spit-and-polish environment and restrict the offenders to a disciplined and demanding routine that seeks ultimately to build self-esteem. Most camps also include education, job-training programs, and other rehabilitation services. On successful completion of the program, offenders are released to the community. At this point, probation officers take over, and the conditions of the sentence are imposed.

Boot camps proliferated in the 1980s. By 1995, some states and the Federal Bureau of Prisons operated 93 camps for adults and 30 for juveniles. At their peak, boot camps held more than 7,000 offenders. By 2000, however, about one-third of the camps had closed, and the decline in boot camp operations has continued. Further, the public uproar following the death of teenager Martin Anderson caused Florida to scrap its system of juvenile boot camps. Anderson died after being pummeled by a group of guards at a Panama City boot camp. He had been sent to the camp for joyriding in his grandmother's automobile (Caputo & Miller, 2006).

Evaluations of boot camp programs have reduced the initial optimism about such approaches. Critics suggest that the emphasis on physical training ignores young offenders' real problems. Other critics point out that, like the military, boot camp builds esprit de corps and solidarity, characteristics that can improve the leadership qualities of the young offender and therefore enhance a criminal career. In fact, follow-up studies of boot camp graduates do show evidence of changes in attitudes (Kurlychek, 2010), but not necessarily changed behavior in avoiding subsequent criminal acts (Meade & Steiner, 2010).

Research has also found that, like intensive supervision probation, boot camps do not automatically reduce prison crowding. A National Institute of Justice summary of the boot-camp experiment notes that they fail to reduce recidivism or prison populations (Parent, 2003). Yet, because boot camps have been popular with the public, which imagines that strict discipline and harsh conditions will instill positive attitudes in young offenders, such camps will probably continue operating whether or not they are more effective than probation or prison.

boot camp A short-term institutional sentence, usually followed by probation, that puts the offender through a physical regimen designed to develop discipline and respect for authority. Also referred to as *shock incarceration*.

Although there are fewer boot camps run by the criminal justice agencies, the concept has spread as a means of instilling discipline in troubled youths who have not yet entered the criminal justice system. With federal funding, the National Guard runs three dozen ChalleNGe programs throughout the United States, including the Michigan Youth ChalleNGe Academy. At no cost to teens and their families, high school dropouts can enroll in military-style programs that include tough discipline, uniforms, marching, full days of academic classes, and rigorous physical exercise. As with the use of boot camps as punishment, these programs are intended to instill discipline in troubled teens while helping them to earn high school diplomas (Estep, 2009; National Guard Youth Foundation, 2014).

Implementing Intermediate Sanctions

Although the use of intermediate sanctions has spread rapidly, three major questions have emerged about their implementation: (1) Which agencies should implement the sanctions? (2) Which offenders should be admitted to these programs? (3) Will the "community corrections net" widen as a result of these policies so that more people will come under correctional supervision?

As in any public-service organization, administrative politics play an ongoing role in corrections. In many states, agencies compete for the additional funding needed to run the programs. The traditional agencies of community corrections, such as probation offices, could receive the funding, or the new programs could be contracted out to nonprofit organizations. Probation organizations argue that they know the field, have the experienced staff, and—given the additional resources—could do an excellent job. They correctly point out that a great many offenders sentenced to intermediate sanctions are also on probation. Those critical of giving this role to probation services argue that the established agencies are not receptive to innovation. They say that probation agencies place a high priority on the traditional supervision function and would not actively help clients solve their problems.

The different types of offenders who receive intermediate sanctions prompt a second issue in the implementation debate. One school of thought emphasizes the seriousness of the offense; the other focuses on the problems of the offender.

If categorized by the seriousness of their offense, offenders may receive such close supervision that they will not be able to abide by the sentence. Sanctions for serious offenders may accumulate to include, for example, probation, drug testing, addiction treatment, and home confinement. As the number of sentencing conditions increases, even the most willing probationers find fulfilling every one of them difficult.

Some agencies want to accept into their intermediate sanctions program only those offenders who *will* succeed. These agencies are concerned about their success rate, especially because of threats to future funding if the program does not reduce recidivism. Critics point out that this strategy leads to "creaming," taking the most promising offenders and leaving those with worse problems to traditional sanctions.

net widening Process in which new sentencing options increase rather than reduce control over offenders' lives.

The third issue concerns **net widening**, a process in which the new sanction increases the control over offenders' lives, rather than reducing it. This can occur when a judge imposes a more intrusive sentence than is usual. For example, rather than merely giving an offender probation, the judge might also require that he or she perform community service. Critics of intermediate sanctions in this regard argue that they have created the following:

- *Wider nets.* Reforms increase the proportion of individuals in society whose behavior is regulated or controlled by the state.
- *Stronger nets.* By intensifying the state's intervention powers, reforms augment the state's capacity to control individuals.
- *Different nets.* Reforms transfer jurisdictional authority from one agency or control system to another.

Some have advocated intermediate sanctions as a less costly alternative to incarceration and a more effective alternative to probation. But how have such sanctions been working in that regard? Significant questions still remain to be answered about whether such programs reduce recidivism, especially as states vary in enforcement of rule violations (Tonry & Lynch, 1996; Pew Center on the States, 2011). With incarceration rates still at record highs and probation caseloads increasing, intermediate sanctions will probably play a major role in corrections through the next decade of this century. However, correctional reform has always had its limitations, and intermediate sanctions may not achieve the goals of their advocates.

☑ **CHECK POINT**

4. What is the main argument for intermediate sanctions?
Judges need a range of sentencing options that are less restrictive than prison and more restrictive than simple probation.

5. How does intensive supervision probation differ from traditional probation?
In ISP, the offender is required to make stricter and more frequent reporting to an officer who carries a much smaller caseload than is typical.

6. What are three problems in the implementation of intermediate sanctions?
Deciding which agencies should implement the sanctions, deciding which offenders should be admitted to these programs, and possibly widening the "community corrections net."

STOP&ANALYZE

If the contemporary government budget crisis leads states and counties to make a genuine commitment to expanding intermediate sanctions, what will be the consequences for society? List three likely outcomes.

The Future of Community Corrections

In 1995, there were 3.7 million Americans under community supervision; by 2010, this figure stood at 4.8 million (Maruschak & Bonczar, 2013). Despite this growth, community corrections still lacks firm public support. Community corrections suffers from the image of being "soft on crime." Moreover, news stories about probationers and offenders on home confinement committing serious crimes can reduce public support when community corrections is perceived to threaten public safety (Weiner, 2013a).

Community corrections also faces the challenge that offenders today require closer supervision. The crimes, criminal records, and drug problems of many offenders are worse than those of lawbreakers of earlier eras. Fifty-three percent of the offenders on probation in 2012 had been convicted of felonies, and 19 percent were guilty of violent felonies (Maruschak & Bonczar, 2013). Those people are supervised by probation officers whose caseloads can number in the hundreds. Such officers, and their counterparts in parole who will be discussed in Chapter 13, cannot readily provide effective supervision and services to all their clients.

Community corrections is burdened by even greater caseload pressures than in the past. With responsibility for about three-fourths of all offenders under correctional supervision, community corrections needs an infusion of resources. For community corrections to succeed, the public must support it. However, such support will come only if citizens believe that offenders are receiving appropriate punishments.

Citizens must realize that policies designed to punish offenders in the community yield not mere "slaps on the wrists" but meaningful sanctions, even while these policies allow offenders to retain and reforge their ties to their families and society. Joan Petersilia argues that long-term investments in community corrections will pay off for the offender and the community. While acknowledging the need for prisons to house violent offenders with no inclination to change, she says, "we need to invest heavily in helping offenders who are not yet steeped in criminal behavior and wish to chart a different path. Sending someone to prison should be our last resort—it is expensive, it is stigmatizing, and it can increase risk for future criminal behavior" (Pew Center on the States, 2007).

Think, Discuss, Write

Like other officials in the criminal justice system, probation officers work independently on a wide range of tasks. They use their discretion to make decisions, including those that can have significant impact on others' lives, such as recommending the revocation of probation. Thus, probation officers, like police officers and corrections officers, need to be professional, ethical, and educated as they make discretionary decisions and perform important tasks without anyone directly supervising each moment of their day. Obviously, probation officers need to act professionally and treat probationers fairly, taking care to avoid any improper discrimination when making decisions.

Probation officers also must avoid temptations to abuse their power or enrich themselves. Unfortunately, cases arise occasionally that reveal probation officers falling short of proper behavior. In March 2012, a probation officer in Georgia was arrested for stealing money that probationers had given him for fines and fees that they were obligated to pay to the court. A probation officer in Tennessee was charged in November 2011 with accepting bribes from probationers seeking favorable treatment. A federal probation officer in Texas was sentenced to 14 years in prison in September 2011 for accepting money to provide confidential information to drug traffickers. In 2010, a probation officer in New Mexico was arrested for receiving payment to supply clean urinalysis reports to cover for probationers who were actually flunking drug tests.

Discussion/Writing Assignment

Even if we cannot prevent unlawful behavior by all probation officers, what can be done to reduce the problems illustrated by the foregoing cases? Selection of better candidates for probation officer positions? Better training? Better supervision? Develop four recommendations to help guard against unethical behavior by probation officers.

SUMMARY

❶ Name the philosophical assumptions that underlie community corrections.

- Community corrections is based on four assumptions: (1) Many offenders' crimes do not warrant incarceration. (2) Community supervision is cheaper than incarceration. (3) Recidivism is no greater for those under community supervision than for those who go to prison. (4) Ex-inmates require both support and supervision when they return to the community.
- Community supervision through probation, intermediate sanctions, and parole is a growing part of the criminal justice system.

❷ Describe how probation evolved and how probation sentences are implemented today.

- Probation evolved as a humanitarian effort to allow first-time and minor offenders a second chance.
- Probation is imposed on more than half of offenders. People with this sentence live in the community according to conditions set by the judge and under the supervision of a probation officer.

❸ Describe intermediate sanctions, and give examples of how they are administered.

- Intermediate sanctions are designed as punishments that are more restrictive than probation and less restrictive than prison.
- The range of intermediate sanctions allows judges to design sentences that incorporate one or more of these punishments.
- Some intermediate sanctions are implemented by courts (fines, restitution, forfeiture), others in the community (home confinement, community service, day reporting centers, intensive supervision probation), and others in institutions and the community (boot camps).

❹ Identify the key issues faced by community corrections at the beginning of the twenty-first century.

- Despite its growth and the necessity amid budget cuts and efforts to reduce the high costs of imprisonment, community sanctions often lack public support.
- Many offenders today require closer supervision with attendant higher costs.
- The use of community corrections is expected to grow in the twenty-first century in spite of the problems of implementing these sanctions.

Questions for Review

1. What is the aim of community corrections?
2. What is the nature of probation, and how is it organized?
3. What is the purpose of intermediate sanctions?
4. What are the primary forms of intermediate sanctions?
5. Why is net widening a concern?

Key Terms and Cases

boot camp (p. 419)

community justice (p. 403)

community service (p. 415)

day reporting center (p. 416)

fine (p. 411)

forfeiture (p. 413)

home confinement (p. 413)

intensive supervision probation (ISP) (p. 416)

net widening (p. 420)

recidivism (p. 401)

restitution (p. 411)

technical violation (p. 406)

13 | Reentry into the Community

LEARNING OBJECTIVES

1 Describe the nature of the "reentry problem."

2 Explain the origins of parole and how it operates today.

3 Name and define the mechanisms for the release of felons to the community.

4 Describe how ex-offenders are supervised in the community.

5 Identify the problems that parolees face during their reentry.

The excited looks on the men's faces highlighted the special quality of the occasion. As a group, with their tattoos, scars, and lined faces, they did not call to mind the image of a graduating class. However, with hugs from family members and congratulatory handshakes from corrections officials, they had reason to bask in a moment of accomplishment and optimism—despite the harsh and uncertain reality of the difficulties they would face in finding jobs and reentering society. Through an initiative at the Orleans Parish Prison in New Orleans, these offenders had completed a ten-week course on job skills, self-development, and behavior intended to help them succeed as they neared release from incarceration. Fifty-two-year-old J. C. Alford, who had been in and out of prison since 1977, noted that it was the first time that anyone cared about whether or not he would succeed in society after being released (Chang, 2012).

The New Orleans program is just one example of the rapidly expanding effort to address the fact that many offenders released from prison will simply end up right back in the criminal justice system if they do not have any preparation and support in their effort to reenter society successfully. Reentry initiatives do not simply involve prerelease education programs. They can also involve community corrections centers where released offenders can go to seek clothing, assistance in finding jobs and housing, and access to counseling, as at the Partners Reentry Center in Anchorage, Alaska. The Anchorage center is a joint project of several nonprofit organizations that receive government grants and private contributions (Boots, 2013).

Newspaper headlines regularly remind us about the risks posed by offenders who are released from prison: "Parolee Arrested in Drug Bust" (Handy, 2012); "Parolee Arrested after Attacking Former Girlfriend" (Valenzuela, 2012); "Parolee Arrested in Pimping of 15-Year-Old Girl" (Emery, 2012).

With more than 600,000 people released from state and federal prisons each year, such events can make people understandably fearful about the return of convicted offenders to society. Yet, society must become ready for the return of these offenders and, more importantly, have developed programs to prepare these offenders for successful reentry into the community. Only a small percentage of imprisoned offenders are serving life sentences, as illustrated by a description of the Montana

Women's Prison: "Only one inmate . . . is currently serving a life sentence. That means at some point roughly 265 offenders will be released back into society" (Wooley, 2011). Reentry issues are important as an inevitable component of the corrections process, and they have become even more important as budget crises push states to reduce prison populations by moving offenders back into society more quickly.

Offenders who leave prison, either under parole supervision or after the completion of their sentences, face serious difficulties. Many of them were never successful in mainstream society prior to incarceration, so they are in greater need than average Americans for education, job training, and a reorientation to values and proper behavior. Moreover, many offenders will be returning to the community environment in which their problems with drugs and alcohol may be renewed. These newly released individuals will seek jobs in a sluggish economy that makes finding jobs difficult even for those who do not have criminal records. If a criminal record does not stop an employer from considering a former prisoner as a potential employee, many of

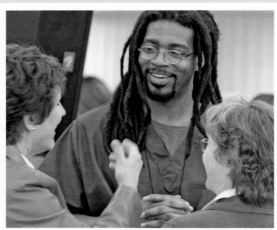

those leaving prison are further hindered by their limited education and lack of legitimate employment experience and weak skills that do not match up to those of other job applicants.

Many offenders stumble when they initially reenter society by failing to obey their conditions of parole, returning to drug use, or quitting education and job-training programs. Some of these offenders will overcome their stumbles, perhaps after a stint in jail awakens them to the looming prospect of a return to prison. Although numerous offenders will fail and be returned to prison for parole violations or the commission of new crimes, given the expense of incarceration—$32,000 per year for each imprisoned offender in Pennsylvania, for example—it is in society's interest to find ways to reduce the number returned to prison. Yet, reentry programs are not available for all offenders as they near their release date.

In this chapter, we examine the mechanisms by which prisoners are released from incarceration; we also look at their supervision in the community. Finally, we discuss the many problems facing parolees as they reenter society.

Prisoner Reentry

Reentry has been described as a "transient state between liberty and recommitment" (A. Blumstein & Beck, 2005:50). It is a limited period of supervision whereby an inmate either moves to full liberty in the community or returns to prison for committing a new crime or for violating the terms of parole. Prisoner reentry has become an important public issue. As indicated in "What Americans Think," many Americans believe there are too many people in prison.

In response to the increasing recognition of the importance of the issue, U.S. Attorney General Eric Holder established the Federal Interagency Reentry Council in 2011 to bring together the leaders of 20 federal agencies in order to think and plan comprehensively about the full range of issues and problems related to prisoner reentry. In the words of Attorney General Holder (2013),

> After all, we know reentry is not just a matter of public safety—it's also an issue of housing and health care policy; a question of education and employment; and a fatherhood and family challenge that affects millions across the country every year.

Holder described the work of the Federal Interagency Reentry Council by saying, "We're calling attention to successful programs, striving to dispel myths about reentry, strengthening our policies, and engaging with an expanding group of allies to advance this comprehensive work." As indicated by the attorney general's statements, there are now increased efforts to address a wide range of issues that may affect successful reentry and to coordinate efforts among agencies at different levels of government.

The sudden flood of offenders leaving prison and the fact that more than 40 percent may return to prison, because of either a new crime or a parole violation, raise serious questions as to how the criminal justice system should deal with the reentry of ex-felons (Carson & Golinelli, 2013b). Moreover, the ones who avoid a return to prison need significant initial help with respect to housing, employment, and other factors that affect their ability to support themselves and live successfully in a free society. What is the crux of the problem?

Jeremy Travis and Joan Petersilia (2001) point to several factors contributing to the reentry problem. They argue that, beginning in the 1970s, the power of parole boards to make release decisions was abolished in mandatory release states and severely restricted in discretionary release states. This means that more inmates are automatically leaving prison, ready or not, when they meet the requirements of their sentence. It also means that there has been little or no prerelease planning to ensure that the new parolee has a job, housing, and a supportive family when he or she hits the streets.

WHAT AMERICANS THINK

QUESTION: "Do you believe there are too many people in prison in the United States, not enough people in prison, or is the number of people in prison about right?"

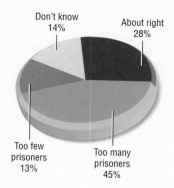

Don't know
14%

About right
28%

Too few prisoners
13%

Too many prisoners
45%

CRITICAL THINKING: Can government officials use these opinions to convince voters to invest more money in reentry programs? What factors might hinder the ability of officials to persuade the public to spend more government funds on reentry?

Source: Pew Center on the States, "Public Opinion on Sentencing and Corrections Policy in America." National poll conducted by Public Opinion Strategies and The Mellman Group, January 2012.

A second factor they believe contributes to the reentry problem is the uneven commitment of resources for prison education, job training, and other rehabilitation programs designed to prepare inmates for their return to the community. States developed programs in an effort to reduce expensive prison populations, but across-the-board budget cuts since the national financial crisis of 2008 often created pressure to cut funding for all aspects of corrections, including reentry programs (Bousequet, 2012a).

Finally, Travis and Petersilia note that the profile of returning prisoners has changed in ways that pose new challenges to successful reentry. In particular, the conviction offense and time served differ from what they were 20 years ago. Now, more than a third of prisoners released to parole are incarcerated for a drug offense—up from 12 percent in 1985. The average time served has also increased by almost a half year since 1990. Further, some drug and violent offenders are exiting prison after very long terms, perhaps 20 or more years. The longer time in prison means a longer period the prisoner has lived apart from family and friends.

Many have expressed concern regarding how the corrections system prepares prisoners to live as law-abiding citizens. Successful prisoner reentry requires that parole and post-release services focus on linking offenders with community institutions—churches, families, self-help groups, and nonprofit programs. Research indicates that the prisoners most likely to succeed in the job market are those who had work experience prior to prison, connected to employers prior to release, and had conventional family relationships (Visher, Debus-Sherill, & Yahner, 2011). Many prisoners do not have these assets as they exit prison. Thus, efforts must be made to improve their chances for success in free society. According to Joan Petersilia (2003), because public safety and neighborhood stability depend on successful reentry, communities must share with corrections officials the responsibility for transitioning offenders to the community.

Contemporary Budget Cuts and Prisoner Release

The economic recession of 2008 and its lingering aftermath produced a drop in employment rates and created difficulties for many American businesses and families. When the incomes of families fall and businesses are less profitable, the government receives less tax revenue to fund needed programs, including corrections. Because incarceration is such an expensive form of punishment, with states and counties paying $25,000 or more annually to cover the costs of holding each prisoner in a secure facility, government officials began to rethink sentencing policies that caused prison populations to skyrocket since the 1980s. In particular, they gave consideration to greater utilization of probation and community corrections for nonviolent and drug offenders. In addition, many states sought ways to reduce their prison populations by accelerating the release into the community of nondangerous offenders and those nearing the completion of their sentences. For example, Michigan, a state with budget problems stemming from one of the nation's highest unemployment rates, reduced its prison population from a peak of 51,554 in March 2007 to 43,636 in December 2012 (Carson & Golinelli, 2013b; Deng, 2012). The reductions enabled the state to save money by closing several prisons. These developments were facilitated in part by Michigan's effort to develop reentry programs that would help prisoners become prepared to move back into the community (Pew Center, 2011).

Such efforts to reduce prison populations can be affected by continuing budget difficulties that lead to cuts in reentry programs, thereby diminishing the state's ability to prepare offenders for effective reentry. In 2014, Michigan cut its budget for reentry programs by 37 percent (Ruiter, 2014). Kansas cut funding for its reentry programs by nearly 50 percent from 2009 to 2013, raising concerns from officials at the state's department of corrections that short-sighted cuts would increase overall expenses as released offenders ended up back in prison (Marso, 2014). Thus, in the second decade of the twenty-first century, states face problems from cutting corrections budgets by reducing prison populations. Those state budget cuts also often terminate programs and reduce services that help to prepare early release prisoners for reentry into society.

Institutional Reentry Preparation Programs

Most of this chapter discusses post-release community corrections, especially issues involving parole. As you read "Careers in Criminal Justice," about the job of a reentry specialist in the Indiana corrections system, you will see that states are increasingly developing programs within prisons as the first step to begin offenders' preparation for reentry. The career description illustrates the effort to create an institution dedicated to preparing offenders for reentering society so that they can spend the last portion of their sentences in a special prison among other prisoners who are also focused on taking classes to prepare for release. Some correctional officials argue that preparation for reentry should begin at an even earlier point in the prison sentence. As one prison warden said,

> Instead of waiting until the last few months, or when we know they had parole, to start this re-entry, we're trying to start the day they come in [to the prison]. I want you to start looking at what do you need to do here to prepare yourself when you go. We try to get that into their minds immediately. (Wooley, 2011)

In 2011, the Pew Center on the States issued a report entitled *State of Recidivism: The Revolving Door of America's Prisons*, which noted that nationwide a consistent percentage of offenders—40 percent—was re-imprisoned within three years of release. This percentage remained steady throughout the study period of 1999–2007 (Pew Center, 2011). The Pew Center report pointed out that the recidivism rate actually varied by state and that some individual states had seen declines in recidivism even as the national rate hovered at the same level. After examining approaches taken by different states, one of the Pew Center report's recommendations was "begin preparation for release at time of prison admission" (Pew Center, 2011).

Reentry Specialist

Richard Rosales, Reentry Specialist, Indiana Department of Correction, Indianapolis Re-Entry Educational Facility

The position of reentry specialist is unique in the field of corrections because it exists only at the Indianapolis Re-Entry Educational Facility (IREF), which is, in turn, the only "application facility" in the United States. Offenders must apply from another facility in Indiana; if they meet the criteria for admittance, they are then transferred to IREF. At IREF, offenders are called "residents" to facilitate a different atmosphere. Residents dress in civilian clothes, live in dormitory-style housing, and manage their own daily schedule. IREF has numerous programs designed to assist successful reentry; these include educational, vocational, substance abuse, and spiritual programs.

A reentry specialist is responsible for fulfilling three different roles: case manager, counselor, and custody officer. Specialists manage a caseload of residents, including every aspect of their reentry preparation. Their reentry accountability plan, for instance, details everything—the programs and plans for self-improvement and preparation—that will facilitate a successful reentry into society. Residents who need counseling for personal problems and other matters rely on their specialist for assistance. Specialists also handle the custody functions that are necessary for safety and security in any correctional institution. Among other duties, they conduct counts and shakedowns and monitor residents' compliance with rules.

Reentry specialists must have thorough knowledge of the criminal justice system in order to understand the documents and procedures. They must have thorough knowledge of the processes that lead an offender to incarceration and also of the challenges that confront parolees on their return to the community. Superior communication skills are essential to working with both offenders and staff. Anyone in corrections can expect to be manipulated and tested and therefore must maintain constant vigilance regarding their surroundings and interactions. A reentry specialist is also expected to prepare numerous reports, both in-house and for outside criminal justice agencies such as the courts and those dealing with probation and parole.

Photo provided by Lindsey Murray

Richard Rosales prepared for this position by obtaining undergraduate and graduate degrees in criminal justice. During college and graduate school, he completed internships with a state police agency. He first worked with the Indiana Department of Correction through the AmeriCorps*VISTA program, a public service program funded by the federal government. At the conclusion of his year of service, he applied and was accepted for his current position.

The best part of my position in the field of corrections is that every day I have the chance to make a difference in the lives of my residents. The work I do today can prevent someone from returning to prison tomorrow and, in turn, make the community safer for the citizens of Indiana. We are seeing the direction of corrections shift to reentry, and IREF is at the forefront of this exciting movement.

The report highlighted the need to see the period of imprisonment as a time in which efforts can be made to address offenders' problems and needs. This is contrary to the traditional practice of using prisons for custody, a practice that typically gives little attention to preparing inmates for reentry into the community at the time of release. The perspective presented in the report is not advocating treating offenders as "victims of society" who deserve attention and care. Instead, it reflects merely the practical recognition that society benefits from thinking in advance about the reality that most offenders will eventually be released back into the community. Critics of the prison system have raised this question: if we treat offenders as "monsters" while they are in prison, shouldn't we expect that they will inevitably affect society by acting as "monsters" when they again live among us?

South Carolina, Florida, Indiana, and other states have developed reentry preparation programs within prisons to assist offenders with the transition back to society. These programs are often in special facilities and involve individuals spending a specific period of months in the programs just prior to release. Indiana developed an innovation by creating the nation's first prison dedicated to preparation for reentry. The Indianapolis Re-entry Education Facility (IREF), discussed in the "Careers in Criminal Justice" feature, houses only 350 prisoners who are nearing their release date. It focuses on providing a range of programs that cover job readiness, business ownership, fatherhood, conflict resolution, financial knowledge, and other concrete subjects (Indiana Department of Corrections, 2009). By establishing these programs, criminal justice officials are acknowledging that successful reentry depends not only on gaining employment but also on having sufficient knowledge about finances and asset management to use money wisely for expenses and family responsibilities (Martin, 2011).

The concept of prerelease facilities and programs has gained the support of those people, including legislators, who recognize that society benefits in many ways, including cost savings, by helping offenders avoid a return to the expensive environment of prison. In 2012, the Florida Department of Corrections announced that it would close two reentry facilities as part of an effort to solve a $79 million budget deficit. Closing the centers would result in cutting 300 prisoners from job-training and life-skills courses and returning them to the general inmate population at other prisons. State legislators and newspaper editorial writers complained that it was shortsighted to target reentry programs for cuts. They argued that in closing the two centers, the short-term budget savings would amount to only $1 million, which would barely affect the overall corrections budget deficit. Ultimately, the political pressure and public outcry led Florida's corrections officials to decide to keep the reentry facilities in operation (Bousquet, 2012a, 2012b). In other states, however, budget pressures have led to a reduction in reentry programs.

☑ CHECK POINT

1. **How have government budget problems contributed to challenges in prisoner reentry?**
   States seek to reduce expensive prison populations, yet continuing budget difficulties can hamper efforts to develop and sustain programs to facilitate offenders' successful return to society.

STOP&ANALYZE

Take note of Professor Petersilia's argument that communities must share with corrections officials the responsibility for transitioning offenders into society. What are two things that community members can do to help parolees stay away from criminal activities and succeed in reentry?

Release and Supervision

Except for the less than 7 percent of inmates who die in prison, all will eventually be released to live in the community. Currently about 77 percent of felons will be released on parole and will remain under correctional supervision for a specific period. About 19 percent will be released at the expiration of their sentence, having "maxed out" and earned the freedom to live in the community without supervision.

Parole is the *conditional* release of an offender from incarceration but not from the legal custody of the state. Thus, offenders who comply with parole conditions and do not have further conflict with the law receive an absolute discharge from supervision at the end of their sentences. If a parolee breaks a rule, parole can be revoked and the person can be returned to a correctional facility. Parole rests on three concepts:

parole The conditional release of an inmate from incarceration, under supervision, after part of the prison sentence has been served.

1. *Grace*. The prisoner could be kept incarcerated, but the government extends the privilege of release.
2. *Contract*. The government enters into an agreement with the prisoner whereby the prisoner promises to abide by certain conditions in exchange for being released.
3. *Custody*. Even though the offender is released from prison, she or he remains a responsibility of the government. Parole is an extension of correctional programs into the community.

Only felons are released on parole; adult misdemeanants are usually released immediately after they have finished serving their sentences. Today about 850,000 people are under parole supervision, a fourfold increase since 1980 (Glaze & Herberman, 2013).

The Origins of Parole

Parole in the United States evolved during the nineteenth century from the English, Australian, and Irish practices of conditional pardon, apprenticeship by indenture, transportation of criminals from one country to another, and issuance of "tickets of leave." These were all methods of moving criminals out of prison as a response to overcrowding, unemployment, and the cost of incarceration.

A key figure in developing the concept of parole in the nineteenth century was Captain Alexander Maconochie, an administrator of British penal colonies in Tasmania and elsewhere in the South Pacific. A critic of definite prison terms, Maconochie devised a system of rewards for good conduct, labor, and study. Under his classification procedure, prisoners could pass through stages of increasing responsibility and freedom: (1) strict imprisonment, (2) labor on government chain gangs, (3) freedom within a limited area, (4) a ticket of leave or parole resulting in a conditional pardon, and (5) full restoration of liberty. Like modern correctional practices, this procedure assumed that prisoners should be prepared gradually for release. The roots of the American system of parole lie in the transition from imprisonment to conditional release to full freedom.

Maconochie's idea of requiring prisoners to earn their early release caught on first in Ireland. There Sir Walter Crofton built on Maconochie's idea to link an offender's progress in prison to a "ticket of leave." Prisoners who graduated through Crofton's three successive levels of treatment were released on parole under a series of conditions. Most significant was the requirement that parolees submit monthly reports to the police. In Dublin, a special civilian inspector helped releasees find jobs, visited them periodically, and supervised their activities.

The Development of Parole in the United States

In the United States, parole developed during the prison reform movement of the latter half of the nineteenth century. Relying on the ideas of Maconochie and Crofton, American reformers such as Zebulon Brockway of the Elmira State Reformatory in New York began to experiment with the concept of parole. After New York adopted indeterminate sentences in 1876, Brockway started to release prisoners on parole. Under the new sentencing law, prisoners could be released when their conduct showed they were ready to return to society. This idea spread, so that 20 states had parole systems by 1900, and 44 states and the federal government had them by 1932 (Friedman, 1993). Today every state has some procedure for the release of offenders before the end of their sentences.

Although it has been used in the United States for more than a century, parole remains controversial. To many people, parole allows convicted offenders to avoid serving the full sentence they deserve. The public hue and cry following commission of a particularly heinous act by a parolee creates pressure for authorities to limit release. For example, when two parolees in Michigan were accused of committing home invasions and murdering a senior citizen, media attention and public outcry contributed to an audit of prisoner release programs, a report criticizing aspects of parole supervision, and the suspensions of two parole officials (Martindale, 2012). On the other hand, public officials are obligated to balance shrinking corrections budgets, so they feel countervailing pressures to find ways to reduce the number of offenders in prison through increased parole releases.

☑CHECK POINT

2. In what countries did the concept of parole first develop?
England, Australia, Ireland.

STOP&ANALYZE

If you were placed in charge of a state's parole system, what are three steps that you would take to diminish the likelihood that parolees would commit crimes?

Release Mechanisms

From 1920 to 1973, there was a nationwide sentencing and release policy. During this period, all states and the federal government used indeterminate sentencing, authorized discretionary release by parole boards, and supervised prisoners after release—and they did this all in the interest of the rehabilitation of offenders.

With the 1970s came critiques of rehabilitation along with a move to determinate sentencing and the public's view that the system was "soft" on criminals. By 2002, 16 states and the federal government had abolished discretionary release by parole boards. Another 5 states had abolished discretionary parole for certain offenses (Petersilia, 2003:65). Further, in some of the states that kept discretionary release, parole boards were reluctant to grant it.

There are now four basic mechanisms for people to be released from prison: (1) expiration release, (2) mandatory release, (3) other conditional release, and (4) discretionary release. Figure 13.1 shows the percentage of felons released by the various mechanisms.

Expiration Release

expiration release The release of an inmate from incarceration, without further correctional supervision; the inmate cannot be returned to prison for any remaining portion of the sentence for the current offense.

An increasing percentage of prisoners receive an **expiration release**. As noted earlier, such offenders have served the maximum court sentence, minus good time—in other words, they have "maxed out." These inmates are released from any further correctional supervision and cannot be returned to prison for their current offense because they are not on parole and therefore not subject to parole restrictions.

Mandatory Release

mandatory release The required release of an inmate from incarceration to community supervision upon the expiration of a certain period, as specified by a determinate-sentencing law or parole guidelines.

Mandatory release occurs after an inmate has served time equal to the total sentence minus good time, if any, or to a certain percentage of the total sentence as specified by law. Mandatory release is found in federal jurisdictions and states with determinate sentences and good-time provisions (see Chapter 9). Without a parole board to make discretionary decisions, mandatory release is a matter of bookkeeping to check the correct amount of good time and other credits and make sure the sentence has been accurately interpreted. The prisoner is conditionally released to parole supervision for the rest of the sentence.

Other Conditional Release

other conditional release A term used in some states to avoid the rigidity of mandatory release by placing convicts in various community settings, under supervision.

Because of the growth of prison populations, many states have devised ways to get around the rigidity of mandatory release by placing inmates in the community through furloughs, home supervision, halfway houses, emergency release, and other programs (Linke & Ritchie, 2004). These types of **other conditional release** also avoid the appearance of the politically sensitive label "discretionary parole."

Circumstances may also arise in which prison officials use their discretion to release offenders early instead of going through the usual parole process. In order to close a budget deficit in 2002, Montana corrections officials released nonviolent

FIGURE 13.1

Methods of Release from State Prison Felons are released from prison to the community, usually under parole supervision, through various means depending on the law.

Source: Bureau of Justice Statistics *Bulletin*, November 2006, p. 8.

offenders early from prison and placed them under the supervision of community corrections authorities. An important study of the results of that release showed that those offenders who received this conditional release from prison, instead of going through the usual parole decision process, had higher levels of recidivism (Wright & Rosky, 2011). As in other states, a significant portion of admissions to prison in Montana are composed of offenders returning to prison for violating conditions of release or for committing new crimes while under the supervision of community corrections. According to Wright and Rosky (2011:901), "Montana, in particular, experienced a significant increase in the annual 3-year recidivism rate as a result of the early release program."

Thus, when undertaking conditional releases, states need to be aware of preparing prisoners for release and of the supervision capabilities of community corrections officials. Inadequate preparation and oversight may result in returning many offenders to the expensive environment of imprisonment, thereby undercutting the intended financial benefits of reducing prison populations through this mechanism.

The situation faced by Montana is reflected in larger debates about the proper course of action, just as it reflected specific debates within Montana itself. As the authors of the study observed, "Not surprisingly, a public battle among the [Montana Department of Corrections] and legislators, judges, and prosecutors ensued over the appropriateness of the early release program in Montana" (Wright & Rosky, 2011:887). Although there has been a growing consensus among liberal and conservative politicians alike about rethinking the costs of using incarceration to punish nonviolent offenders (Savage, 2011b), there are debates about the wisdom of releasing prisoners as opposed to a more gradual approach of simply changing sentencing policies as they affect certain offenders ("Our View," 2011; Mauer, 2011). As you read "The Policy Debate" on this issue, consider which side has the more compelling argument.

Litigation can also create pressure to reduce prison populations through releases outside the usual parole process if overcrowding causes constitutional violations. In the provisions of the Prison Litigation Reform Act of 1996, Congress attempted to limit the ability of judges to order the release of prisoners by mandating that any such decisions be made by three-judge panels rather than by a single judge. However, as the Supreme Court decided with respect to overcrowding and the lack of medical services in California's prisons in *Brown v. Plata* (2011), circumstances can arise in which states may be forced to quickly and creatively find ways to reduce prison populations. Because most states are currently seeking ways to save money by reducing prison populations, the prospect for more litigation affecting releases seems unlikely during the current era.

Discretionary Release

States retaining indeterminate sentences allow **discretionary release** by the parole board within the boundaries set by the sentence and the penal law. This is a conditional release to parole supervision. This approach, as discussed in the next section, lets the board members assess the prisoner's readiness for release within the minimum and maximum terms of the sentence. In reviewing the prisoner's file and asking questions, the parole board focuses on the nature of the offense, the inmate's behavior, and his or her participation in rehabilitative programs. This process places great faith in the ability of parole board members to predict the future behavior of offenders.

discretionary release The release of an inmate from prison to conditional supervision at the discretion of the parole board within the boundaries set by the sentence and the penal law.

The Parole Board Process

State parole boards are typically composed of citizens who are appointed for fixed terms in office by the governor. For example, the Vermont Parole Board consists of five regular members and two alternates who are appointed for three-year terms by the governor. The Texas Board of Pardons and Paroles consists of seven members who receive appointments by the governor for renewable six-year terms. The people on the Texas board include a former government official, a former probation and

Should Prison Populations Be Reduced through the Accelerated Release of Offenders?

States throughout the country currently face budget pressures as their tax revenues remain uncertain during a period when the national economy is slowly recovering from the recession of 2008. Because incarceration is an especially expensive form of punishment, with each imprisoned offender costing the state tens of thousands of dollars each year, many state governments have sought to reduce their prison populations through accelerated releases.

For Accelerated Release of Offenders

Those who support the accelerated release of offenders find fault in the overuse of expensive incarceration during the past three decades. They point to the many nonviolent and drug offenders who, through needlessly long prison sentences, have had no hope of being rehabilitated or of regaining a productive place in the community. As a result of these long incarcerations, families and specific neighborhoods suffered financial declines and devastation that affected children, as well as the quality of life in those communities. Moreover, taxpayers paid needlessly high bills for expensive punishments when cheaper approaches within the community would have been a more effective mechanism to simultaneously punish offenders as well as to support and guide their reentry into the community.

The arguments for accelerating the release of offenders from prison include these:

- Imprisonment has been overused through application to thousands of nonviolent offenders.
- State budget difficulties require the immediate reduction of prison populations in favor of less expensive approaches to punishment within the community.
- Moving offenders from prison to community settings or early release will assist in their successful reentry into the community and permit them to reestablish relationships with family members, thereby providing support to children and needed contributions to families' financial support.
- Community-based programs are more effective in rehabilitating offenders.

Against Accelerated Release of Offenders

Opponents of accelerated release worry that offenders released early from prison are likely to commit new crimes or otherwise violate the conditions of their release. They also worry that the focus on saving money through releases often outweighs careful examination of which offenders should be released. This focus also ignores the inadequate resources and unproven effectiveness of many community-based programs, thus leading to troubling recidivism rates in many states. They further worry that shortened prison sentences will mean that some offenders do not receive appropriately severe punishment.

The arguments against accelerated release of offenders include these:

- Excessive focus on saving money through accelerated prison releases can lead to inadequate evaluation of early release candidates and insufficient supervision of these offenders once they are in the community.
- Because studies present evidence of troubling recidivism rates in many states, the release of offenders places citizens under unnecessary risk of crime victimization from these offenders who would otherwise be behind bars.
- Early releases mean that some offenders do not receive appropriately severe punishments for their crimes.
- Community-based programs have not proven their effectiveness in lowering the recidivism rates of those offenders released early from prison.

What Should U.S. Policy Be?

The massive increase in incarceration since the 1980s has been very costly in both financial and human terms. Because of budget pressures, states have accelerated efforts to reduce their prison populations, including the use of early release for many offenders. Have enough resources been devoted to community programs for us to feel confident that society is prepared to assist in the reentry of increasing numbers of released offenders? Do persistent recidivism rates in many states indicate that the releases pose risks to society? Alternatively, do recidivism rates merely show that some states have not prepared adequate programs for education and supervision of offenders released from prison? Does the weight of budget pressures lead policymakers to engage in wishful thinking about the effectiveness of less expensive community corrections?

Researching the Internet

To see the 2011 report *State of Recidivism: The Revolving Door of America's Prisons* issued by the Pew Center on the States, visit the Criminal Justice CourseMate at cengagebrain.com, then access the weblinks for this chapter. http://www.pewtrusts.org/uploadedFiles /wwwpewtrustsorg/Reports/sentencing_and_corrections/State _Recidivism_Revolving_Door_America_Prisons%20.pdf.

Analyzing the Issue

Imagine that you and your classmates are advisors to the governor of a state who wishes to reduce costs associated with a large prison population. You must develop recommendations in order to advise the governor on the following questions: What are the consequences of choosing not to accelerate the release of offenders? What steps could be taken to reduce the concerns expressed by the opponents of accelerated release? Provide a list of recommendations for the governor.

parole official, a former county sheriff, two former police officers, a former member of a victims' services board, and an individual with experience in education and criminal justice—who is also the spouse of a former top official in the Texas corrections system (Texas Board of Pardons and Parole website, 2014).

Obviously, the members bring with them values, perspectives, and experiences that inform their judgments about whether offenders should be released on parole. It is possible that the governor's decision to appoint board members with prior connections to the criminal justice system may be an effort to ensure there is caution and skepticism about prisoners' claims of self-improvement during incarceration. The Texas structure also includes 11 commissioners, all of whom are experienced criminal justice professionals, who join with the parole board members in making decisions about parole.

Parole boards are often described as if the governors' appointees sit together as they question and listen to the parole-eligible prisoner and also hear arguments from the prisoner's attorney. In fact, there are differences in the parole processes in various states. For example, parole-eligible prisoners in California, all of whom are serving life sentences, have attorneys at parole hearings, either one that they hire or one that is appointed for them. In other states, parole board members simply interview the prisoner. Elsewhere, the parole board may simply review the written file on the prisoner's progress in prison. There is no single model for what "the parole board process" looks like.

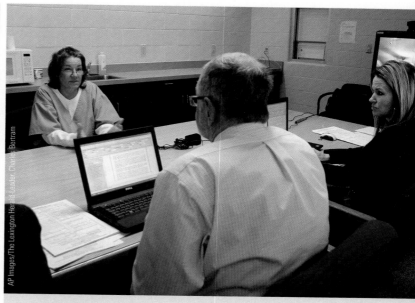

Parole hearings are often brief proceedings in which board members ask questions of the prisoner who is eligible for parole. In many places, the crime victim or the victim's family are permitted to communicate with the board, in writing or in person, to express their views about the prospect of the offender's early release from prison. How much influence should crime victims have over parole decisions?

As indicated by the great increase in prison populations in the last few decades, large numbers of prisoners become parole eligible each year—too many to have hearings in front of a state's full parole board. Thus, parole processes involve hearings or interviews conducted by only a portion of a parole board, often with other members of the board making decisions based on the report written by their colleague. In some circumstances, if a panel of a board is divided on a decision, the full board may examine the records in the case and make a decision.

In California, for example, each parole hearing is conducted by a two-member panel. At least one of the two members is a "commissioner," the title used in that state for the 12 parole board members appointed by the governor. The other member is either a second commissioner or a "deputy commissioner," which is a state employee who works in the parole process. Immediately after the hearing, the two decision makers leave the hearing room and finalize their decision. If they disagree about whether to recommend parole, then there will be a second hearing in front of the full 12-member California Board of Parole Hearings. After a unanimous decision by the two-member panel or a vote by the full board, the decision goes to the staff of the board to make sure that there were no errors of law or fact in the process. The decision is then submitted to the governor, who can approve the parole, add a condition to the parole release, refer a panel decision to the full board, or reverse the decision to grant parole in cases of convicted murderers (California Department of Corrections and Rehabilitation, 2014).

By using only a portion of the parole board for interviews and hearings, states can conduct many interviews and hearings simultaneously. This is the only way that they can handle the large volume of cases. Texas uses a different procedure to process the 77,540 prisoners who were considered for parole in 2010. The Texas Board of Pardons and Paroles operates out of six different offices around the state, each with three-member panels composed of one board member and two "commissioners." For each parole-eligible prisoner, a parole official interviews the prisoner and writes a report before panel members review that report and the written file. If two of the three members approve, then the prisoner gains release under parole supervision (Texas Board of Pardons and Paroles, 2014).

A Personal Encounter with the Parole Process in Michigan

Note: *Dr. Christopher Smith, one of the coauthors of this textbook, served as the "representative" for Christopher Jones (whose story of arrest and imprisonment appears in Chapter 1) at the parole board interview that ultimately led to Jones's release on parole. This is a first-person account of that process.*

I agreed to serve as the "representative" for Christopher Jones at the parole interview because I had known him and his family since he was a teenager. As an outside observer, I had seen his self-destruction through drugs and theft crimes as well as his gradual self-rehabilitation, as I corresponded with him and occasionally visited him during his 10 years behind bars. Moreover, I was grateful for his eagerness to present his story in this book so that college students could learn about the justice process through his mistakes and experiences. In Michigan, a parole interview representative is typically a family member or someone else who can vouch for the prisoner's progress and good qualities. In speaking with a former parole board member prior to the interview, I knew that prisoners often had their mothers appear as their representatives. However, this was often counterproductive because mothers too often made excuses for their children or displayed emotion rather than providing information that would be useful in the parole decision. Although I am trained as a lawyer, prisoners are not represented by lawyers to make arguments on their behalf (unlike in California parole hearings). In Michigan, they each have only one representative present to provide personal endorsement and information.

After spending nearly an hour in the prison's visitor waiting room, I was searched and led through several sets of locked doors to a small office. Outside of the office, I came upon a dozen or more prisoners fidgeting nervously in a long line of chairs as they waited to be called one-by-one into the interview room. Mr. Jones was in the first chair. He rose to greet me, and we were immediately ushered into the office together.

I had driven nearly 250 miles from Lansing, in the middle of Michigan's Lower Peninsula, to a low-security prison in the Upper Peninsula to be present for the interview. Ironically, the interview was conducted via video conference by one of the 10 members of the Michigan parole board who was physically back in Lansing—the very place I had left the day before and to which I would return later that day. We saw him live on a television screen in the prison up north while he saw us on a screen in his office in Lansing. Video technology permits Michigan to save a substantial amount of money that previously would have been spent for the parole board members to travel to prisons throughout the state to conduct interviews.

After Mr. Jones introduced me as his representative, the parole board member introduced himself and informed me that he had many questions for Mr. Jones and that I should refrain from speaking until questions were directed to me. The parole board member noted that Mr. Jones had participated in many prison programs and that the file contained an impressive number of letters of support from family members and a minister.

Even small states divide their parole boards for hearings. In Wyoming, the least populous state in the country, a seven-member board sits in three-member hearing panels and conducts some hearings by telephone and video conference (Wyoming Board of Parole website, 2014). In Vermont, another of the least-populous states, hearings and interviews are conducted by a minimum of three of the parole board's five members and two alternates (Vermont Parole Board, 2013).

Parole board hearings and interviews are much less formal than court proceedings. Board members want the opportunity to ask prisoners about their crimes, their remorse, their attitudes, their disciplinary records and their participation in programs in prison, and their concrete plans for where they will live and work if they are granted parole. Prisoners are typically nervous because they do not know exactly what will be asked. They may quickly discover that the board members seem very skeptical about what they say. They may also find that board members lecture them about what they have done wrong in life and issue stern warnings to them about what will happen if they are released and then violate conditions of parole. Because board panels must necessarily schedule back-to-back-to-back interviews or hearings with numerous parole-eligible prisoners on any given day, each prisoner may leave the brief encounter feeling very dissatisfied and disappointed—as if she or he did not have a full opportunity to explain how much change has occurred in attitude and behavior since entering prison. When a prisoner feels as if there was no complete opportunity to make a good, persuasive presentation about being reformed, there is likely to be great anxiety about whether the long-awaited opportunity to speak to a parole board member or panel will actually lead to release.

Crime victims have become much more important participants in the parole decision process in recent decades. Many states have victims' rights laws that

The board member asked Mr. Jones about his plan to live with his parents and work for his father's home inspection business. Mr. Jones was asked about how he had changed from when he committed his crimes. The board member pressed Mr. Jones about how he would respond to the availability of drugs and alcohol if he was on parole back in his hometown. Predictably, Mr. Jones, who had spent years looking forward to the chance to have a parole interview, provided reassuring responses and pledged to stay away from the people, places, and substances that had been his downfall in the past. The board member spoke sternly to him about the consequences of violating the conditions of parole or committing new crimes. During this lecture, Mr. Jones nodded his head and repeatedly said, "yes, sir, yes, sir."

Throughout the interview with Mr. Jones, I restrained myself from speaking as I thought of many helpful things to say. I kept quiet, however, and then the board member turned to me to ask what I had to add as information for the board's consideration. I gave a brief endorsement of the changes that I had observed over the years Mr. Jones had been in prison and described his participation in education and substance abuse recovery programs. And then the interview was over. It was obvious that the board member had many other interviews that he needed to do, so he could not spend more than 15 minutes or so on any individual interview.

I came away from the brief experience without any strong sense about what the decision would be. The interview seemed to go as well as it could have gone, but it was so short that there was not much information exchanged. Moreover, I wondered whether a parole board member could really trust reassurances from a parole-eligible prisoner, especially a former drug user, when the board member obviously knew that a notable percentage of such offenders return to drugs, violate parole conditions, or commit new crimes once back in the community. Obviously, the most significant information for the decision came from the reports and prison disciplinary records in the file. The quick interview gave the board member an opportunity to gain a brief impression of the prisoner's attitude and demeanor. Moreover, it was an opportunity to issue stern warnings to the prisoner about returning to prison for any failure to behave properly on parole. The release decision hinged on this board member's recommendation and report that would be significant factors in determining whether at least two of the three board members (including himself) assigned to the case would vote to grant parole.

Ultimately, the parole decision is shaped by impressions and judgments, not just those of the board members, but also those of the prison counselors who wrote evaluative reports for the file and thereby shaped the impressions of the board members. No one can make an absolutely certain prediction about whether a specific prisoner will commit future violations or crimes on parole—not even the prisoner himself. The prisoner may feel determined to succeed, but he does not yet know the practical challenges of parole that await in being offered drugs, feeling frustrated by unemployment, or having conflicts with friends and family who have become, in some sense, strangers after years of separation.

For Critical Analysis

Does this parole interview process, as described, provide enough information to make a decision about whether or not to grant parole? Should the process be changed in any way? Provide three arguments either supporting the interview process as adequate or supporting specific changes in the process.

require officials to keep victims informed of offenders' upcoming parole consideration and to invite victims to provide input in the process. In California, crime victims and their families are invited to parole hearings where they are permitted to speak or they can bring a representative to speak for them about the impact of the crime and their concerns about the offender being granted parole. Alternatively, they can submit written statements or audio or video statements for consideration by the board members. At the hearing, the victim is accompanied by a victim services representative from the state's Office of Victim and Survivor Rights and Services. A prosecutor also attends the hearing and may speak about the offender who is being considered for parole. In addition, news reporters may be permitted to attend California parole hearings (California Department of Corrections and Rehabilitation, 2014).

In Wyoming, crime victims are invited to meet with the board separately from the prisoner's hearing. Similarly, in Vermont the victim can testify prior to the scheduled appearance of the prisoner before the board. In both of these states, the interviews or hearings are held in private, and the policies about victims' participation are designed to prevent the victim from having a face-to-face encounter with the offender. By contrast, Connecticut is more like California in that the victim is invited to speak at hearings that, while not open to the public, are more available to the public in the sense that they can be recorded and broadcast on public television, just as California's hearings may be covered by the news media in some cases. In all of these states, victims have the option of submitting written statements to be added to the file that is reviewed by the board members. Read the "Close Up" for a personal account of the parole process in Michigan.

FIGURE 13.2

Estimated Time to be Served by Adults Convicted of Selected Crimes The data indicate that the average felony offender going to prison for the first time spends about two years in prison. How would you expect the public to react to that fact?

Source: Thomas P. Bonczar, *National Corrections Reporting Program—Statistical Tables*, May 5, 2011, Table 9 (http://bjs.ojp .usdoj.gov /index.cfm?ty=pbdetail&iid =2174).

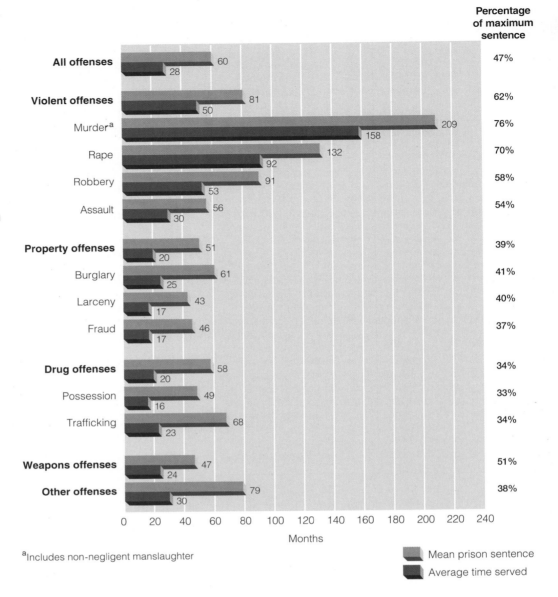

	Percentage of maximum sentence
All offenses (60 / 28)	47%
Violent offenses (81 / 50)	62%
Murder[a] (209 / 158)	76%
Rape (132 / 92)	70%
Robbery (91 / 53)	58%
Assault (56 / 30)	54%
Property offenses (51 / 20)	39%
Burglary (61 / 25)	41%
Larceny (43 / 17)	40%
Fraud (46 / 17)	37%
Drug offenses (58 / 20)	34%
Possession (49 / 16)	33%
Trafficking (68 / 23)	34%
Weapons offenses (47 / 24)	51%
Other offenses (79 / 30)	38%

Months

[a]Includes non-negligent manslaughter

Mean prison sentence
Average time served

Impact of Release Mechanisms

Parole release mechanisms do more than simply determine the date at which a particular prisoner will be sent back into the community. Parole release also greatly affects other parts of the system, including sentencing, plea bargaining, and the size of prison populations.

One important effect of discretionary release is that an administrative body—the parole board—can shorten a sentence imposed by a judge. Even in states that have mandatory release, various potential reductions built into the sentence mean that the full sentence is rarely served. Good time, for example, can reduce punishment even if there is no eligibility for parole.

To understand the impact of release mechanisms on criminal punishment, we must compare the amount of time actually served in prison with the sentence specified by the judge. In most states, good time and jail time are the main factors that reduce the time actually served. On a national basis, felony inmates serve an average of two and a half years before release. Figure 13.2 shows the average time served for selected offenses.

Supporters of discretion for the paroling authority argue that parole benefits the overall system. Discretionary release mitigates the harshness of the penal code. If the legislature must establish exceptionally strict punishments as a means of conveying a "tough on crime" image to frustrated and angry voters, parole can effectively permit sentence adjustments that make the punishment fit the crime. Not everyone convicted of larceny, for example, has done equivalent harm, yet some legislatively mandated sentencing schemes impose equally strict sentences. Early release on parole can be granted to an offender who is less deserving of strict punishment, such as someone who voluntarily makes restitution, cooperates with the police, or shows genuine regret.

A major criticism of discretionary release is that it shifts responsibility for many primary criminal justice decisions from a judge, who holds legal procedures uppermost, to an administrative board, where discretion rules. Judges know a great deal about constitutional rights and basic legal protections, but parole board members may not have such knowledge. Moreover, in most states with discretionary release, parole hearings are secret, with only board members, the inmate, and correctional officers present. Often, no published criteria guide decisions, and prisoners receive no reason for denial or granting of parole. However, an increasing number of states permit oral or written testimony by victims and by members of the offender's family.

☑CHECK POINT

3. **What are the four release mechanisms for prisoners?**
   Discretionary release, mandatory release, other conditional release, and expiration release.

STOP&ANALYZE

In light of the differences in parole processes used in different states, how do you see the importance (or lack thereof) of involvement by defense attorneys and crime victims in parole hearings? Do they provide helpful information about whether an offender is reformed enough for release? Provide two advantages and two risks in permitting attorneys to represent prisoners at parole hearings. Provide two advantages and two risks in allowing victims to provide input.

Parole Supervision in the Community

Parolees are released from prison on condition that they abide by laws and follow rules, known as **conditions of release**, designed to aid their readjustment to society and control their movement. As in probation, the parolee may be required to abstain from alcohol, keep away from undesirable associates, maintain good work habits, and not leave the state without permission. If they violate any of these conditions, they could be returned to prison to serve out the rest of their sentence. Nearly 80 percent of released prisoners are subject to some form of community supervision. Only those who have served their full sentence minus good time ("maxed out") are free from supervision.

conditions of release
Conduct restrictions that parolees must follow as a legally binding requirement of being released.

The restrictions are justified on the ground that people who have been incarcerated must readjust to the community so that they will not fall back into preconviction habits and associations. The strict enforcement of these rules may create problems for parolees who cannot fulfill all the demands placed on them. For example, a parolee may find it impossible to be tested for drugs, attend an Alcoholics Anonymous meeting, and work full-time while also meeting family obligations.

The day they come out of prison, parolees face a staggering array of problems. In most states, they receive only clothes, a token amount of money, a list of rules governing their conditional release, and the name and address of the parole officer to whom they must report within 24 hours. Although a promised job is often required for release, an actual job may be another matter. Most former convicts are unskilled or semiskilled, and the conditions of release may prevent them from moving to areas

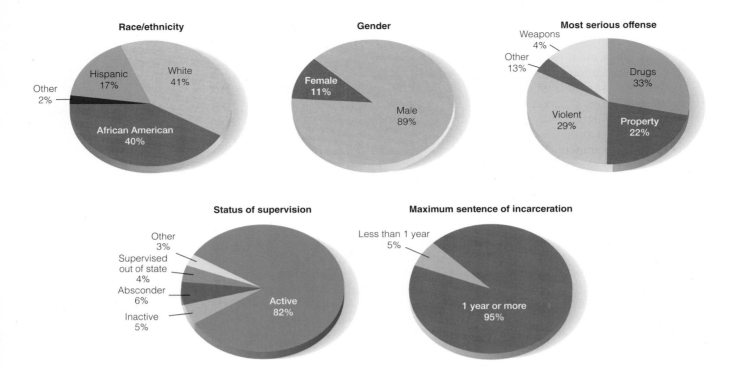

FIGURE 13.3

Personal Characteristics of Parolees Prison releasees tend to be men in their thirties who have an inadequate education and were incarcerated for a nonviolent offense.

Source: L. M. Maruschak, and T. P. Bonczar. 2013. "Probation and Parole in the United States, 2012." *Bureau of Justice Statistics Bulletin*, December. NCJ 243826.

where they could find work. If the parolee is African American, male, and under 30, he joins the largest demographic group of unemployed people in the country. Figure 13.3 shows the personal characteristics of parolees.

Parolees bear the added handicap of former-convict status. In most states, laws prevent former prisoners from working in certain types of establishments—where alcohol is sold, for example—thus ruling out many jobs. In some states, those who have served time are assumed to have "a lack of good moral character and trustworthiness," a condition required to acquire a license to be a barber, for example. Finally, ex-convicts face a significant dilemma. If they are truthful about their backgrounds, many employers will not hire them. If they are not truthful, they can be fired for lying if the employer ever learns about their conviction.

Other reentry problems plague parolees. For many, the transition from the highly structured life in prison to open society is too difficult to manage. Many just do not have the social, psychological, and material resources to cope with the temptations and complications of modern life. For these parolees, freedom may be short-lived as they fall back into forbidden activities such as drinking, using drugs, and stealing.

Community Programs Following Release

There are various programs to assist parolees. Some help prepare offenders for release while they are still in prison; others provide employment and housing assistance after release. Together, the programs are intended to help the offender progress steadily toward reintegration into the community. Almost all penologists agree that there should be pre- and post-release programs to assist reentry, yet many prisoners do not now participate in such programs. Although all states offer reentry programs, relatively few prisoners have access to them.

Among the many programs developed to help offenders return to the community, three are especially important: work and educational release, furloughs, and

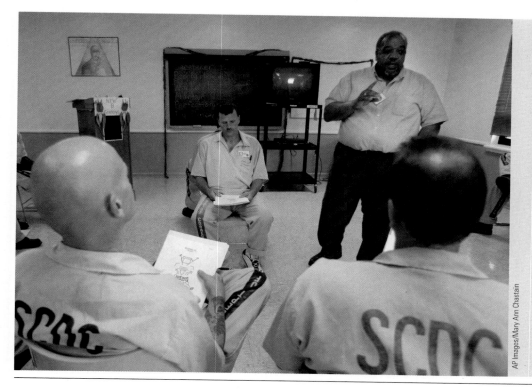

William Harrington instructs a class at the Watkins Pre-Release Center in South Carolina. Prisoners with substance abuse problems spend their final 60 days of imprisonment in the center's programs. What do prisoners need to be taught in order to prepare them for release into the community?

halfway houses. Although similar in many ways, each offers a specific approach to helping formerly incarcerated individuals reenter the community.

Work and Educational Release

Programs of **work and educational release**, in which inmates are released from correctional institutions during the day to work or attend school, were first established in Vermont in 1906. However, the Huber Act, passed by the Wisconsin legislature in 1913, is usually cited as the model on which such programs are based. By 1972, most states and the federal government had instituted these programs. Nonetheless, by 2002, only about one-third of prisons operated them, for fewer than 3 percent of U.S. inmates (Petersilia, 2009).

Although most work and educational release programs are justifiable in terms of rehabilitation, many correctional administrators and legislators also like them because they cost relatively little. In some states, a portion of the inmate's earnings from work outside may be deducted for room and board. One problem with these programs is that they allegedly take jobs from free citizens, a complaint often made by organized labor.

Furloughs

Isolation from loved ones is one of the pains of imprisonment. Although correctional programs in many countries include conjugal visits, only a few U.S. corrections systems have used them. Many penologists view the **furlough**—the temporary release of an inmate from a correctional institution for a visit home—as a meaningful approach to inmate reintegration.

Furloughs are thought to offer an excellent means of testing an inmate's ability to cope with the larger society. Through home visits, the inmate can renew family ties and relieve the tensions of confinement. Most administrators also feel that furloughs increase prisoners' morale. The general public, however, does not always support the concept. Public outrage is inevitable if an offender on furlough commits another crime or fails to return. Correctional authorities are often nervous about using furloughs, because they fear being blamed for such incidents.

Halfway Houses

As its name implies, the **halfway house** is a transitional facility for soon-to-be-released inmates that connects them to community services, resources,

work and educational release The daytime release of inmates from correctional institutions so they can work or attend school.

furlough The temporary release of an inmate from a correctional institution for a brief period, usually one to three days, for a visit home. Such programs help maintain family ties and prepare inmates for release on parole.

halfway house A correctional facility housing convicted felons who spend a portion of their day at work in the community but reside in the halfway house during nonworking hours.

Many states have programs that permit offenders to participate in work release. They work at jobs in the community while living in a lower-security correctional setting, such as a halfway house. These programs ease reentry into the community. Should the government assist offenders in finding jobs?

and support. Usually, felons work in the community but reside in the halfway house during nonworking hours. Halfway houses range from secure institutions in the community, with programs designed to assist inmates who are preparing for release on parole, to group homes where parolees, probationers, or others diverted from the system live with minimal supervision and direction. Some halfway houses deliver special treatment services, such as programs designed to deal with alcohol, drug, or mental problems.

Residential programs face specific problems. Few neighborhoods want to host halfway houses or treatment centers for convicts. Community resistance has significantly impeded the development of community-based correctional facilities and has even forced some successful facilities to close. Many communities, often wealthier ones, have blocked the placement of halfway houses or treatment centers within their boundaries. For example, a suburban city council near Grand Rapids, Michigan, considered a new ordinance in 2012 that would limit future housing facilities for parolees to locations in the industrial area of the city (L. Smith, 2012). As you recall from "The "Policy Debate" in Chapter 12, one result of the NIMBY ("not in my backyard") attitude is that many centers are established in deteriorating neighborhoods inhabited by poor people, who lack the political power and resources to block unpopular programs.

Nonetheless, a survey found a striking increase in the number of community-based residential corrections facilities. Such facilities were defined as those in which 50 percent or more of residents regularly leave unaccompanied for work or study in the community, thus including halfway houses and similar programs that provide substance abuse treatment. What was most striking about the survey was the decrease in the number of public facilities from 297 to 221 between 2000 and 2005 at the same time that private facilities increased from 163 to 308 (Stephan, 2008). These private facilities undoubtedly rely on contracts from state governments to provide services that the state believes are less expensive in the private sector. The interesting question for contemporary times is whether, in an atmosphere of budget cuts, state governments will find money for the use of such facilities to assist in the reentry of prisoners. Budget reductions can eliminate the availability of funds for outside contracts but, alternatively, such cuts can also lead to increased reliance on private facilities if their use is viewed as means of saving money (S. Davis, 2012).

Parole Officer: Cop or Social Worker?

After release, a parolee's principal contact with the criminal justice system is the parole officer, who must provide both surveillance and assistance. Thus, parole officers are asked to play two different, some might say incompatible, roles: cop and social worker. Whereas parole was originally designed to help offenders make the transition from prison to the community, supervision has shifted ever more toward conducting surveillance, testing for drugs, monitoring curfews, and collecting restitution. Safety and security have become major issues in parole services.

The Parole Officer as Cop In their role as cop, parole officers have the power to restrict many aspects of the parolee's life, to enforce the conditions of release, and to initiate revocation proceedings if parole conditions are violated. Like other officials in the criminal justice system, the parole officer has extensive discretion in low-visibility situations. In many states, parole officers have the authority to search the parolee's house without warning; to arrest him or her, without the possibility of bail, for suspected violations; and to suspend parole pending a hearing before the board. This authoritarian component of the parole officer's role can give the ex-offender a sense of insecurity and hamper the development of mutual trust.

The parole officer is responsible for seeing that the parolee follows the conditions imposed by the parole board or department of corrections. Typically, the conditions require the parolee to follow the parole officer's instructions; to permit the officer to visit the home and place of employment; to maintain employment; not to leave the state without permission; not to marry without permission; not to own a firearm; not to possess, use, or traffic in narcotics; not to consume alcohol to excess; and to comply with all laws and be a good citizen.

Parole officers are granted law enforcement powers in order to protect the community from offenders coming out of prison. However, because these powers diminish the possibility for the officer to develop a close relationship with the client, they can weaken the officer's ability to help the parolee adjust to the community. Read "A Question of Ethics" at the end of the chapter to consider how training might be developed to avoid the risk that parole officers will exceed their authority in carrying out law enforcement functions.

The Parole Officer as Social Worker Parole officers must act as social workers by helping the parolee to find a job and to restore family ties. Officers channel parolees to social agencies, such as psychiatric, drug, and alcohol clinics, where they can obtain help. As caseworkers, officers try to develop a relationship that allows parolees to confide their frustrations and concerns.

Because parolees may not talk honestly if they are constantly aware of the parole officer's ability to send them back to prison, some researchers have suggested that parole officers' conflicting responsibilities of cop and social worker should be separated. Parole officers could maintain the supervisory aspects of the position, and other personnel—perhaps a separate parole counselor—could perform the casework functions. Another option would be for parole officers to be charged solely with social work duties, while local police check for violations.

Because of the new emphasis on decreasing prison populations and strengthening efforts to help parolees succeed with reentry, some states have shifted the focus of their parole officers' priorities. While protection of public safety will always be a concern, there is a renewed emphasis in some places to focus on assisting parolees with reentry rather than just monitoring them to watch for parole violations. This emphasis can result in hiring different kinds of people, such as actual trained social workers, to be parole officers as well as shifting the emphasis of training and evaluation for parole officers (Justice Policy Institute, 2010; Eckholm, 2008). The attitude of parole and law enforcement officials toward the desirability of assisting with reentry can make a big difference in the prospects for success of individual parolees (Valley, 2012).

The Parole Bureaucracy

Although parole officers have smaller caseloads than do probation officers, parolees require more extensive services. One reason is that parolees, by the very fact of their incarceration, generally have committed more serious crimes than those perpetrated by probationers. Another reason is that parolees must make a difficult transition from the highly structured prison environment to a society in which they have previously failed to live as law-abiding citizens. It is exceptionally difficult for a parole officer to monitor, control, and assist clients who may have little knowledge of or experience with living successfully within society's rules.

The parole officer works within a bureaucratic environment. Like most other human services organizations, parole agencies are short on resources and expertise. Because the difficulties faced by many parolees are so complex, the officer's job is almost impossible. As a result, parole officers frequently must classify parolees and give priority to those most in need. For example, most parole officers spend extra time with the newly released. As the officers gain greater confidence in the parolees, they can adjust their level of supervision to "active" or even "reduced" surveillance. Depending on how the parolees have functioned in the community, they may eventually be allowed to check in with their officers periodically instead of submitting to regular home visits, searches, and other intrusive monitoring.

Adjustment to Life Outside Prison

With little preparation, the ex-offender moves from the highly structured, authoritarian life of the institution into a world filled with temptations and complicated problems. Suddenly, ex-convicts who are unaccustomed to undertaking even simple tasks such as going to the store for groceries are expected to assume pressing, complex responsibilities. Finding a job and a place to live are not the only problems the newly released person faces (Arditti & Parkman, 2011). Parolees no longer receive medical care from the department of corrections (Sung, Mahoney, & Mellow, 2011). Also, the parolee must make significant social and psychological role adjustments. A male ex-convict, for example, must suddenly become not only a parolee but also an employee, a neighbor, and possibly a father, husband, and son. The expectations, norms, and social relations in the free world differ greatly from those learned in prison. The relatively predictable inmate code gives way to society's often unclear rules of behavior—rules that the offender had failed to cope with during his or her previous life in free society.

In terms of living a crime-free life, today's parolees face even greater obstacles than did those released prior to 1990. Since that time, Congress and many state legislatures have imposed new restrictions on ex-felons. These include denial of many things, including welfare benefits such as food stamps, for those convicted of even minor drug crimes; access to public housing; receipt of student loans; and in some states voting rights. Studies have found that returning inmates often face so many restrictions after long periods of incarceration that the conditions amount to years of "invisible punishment" (Mauer & Chesney-Lind, 2002:1). The effects of these policies impact not only individual parolees but also their families and communities (Travis, 2002).

News accounts of brutal crimes committed by ex-offenders on parole fuel a public perception that parolees pose a threat to the community. The murder of 12-year-old Polly Klaas by a parolee and the rape and murder of 7-year-old Megan Kanka by a paroled sex offender spurred legislators across the nation to enact "sexual offender notification" laws. These laws require that the public be notified of the whereabouts of "potentially dangerous" sex offenders. In some states, paroled sex offenders must register with the police, whereas in others, the immediate neighbors must be informed. Many states now have publicly accessible sex offender websites listing the names and addresses of those registered. The state of Washington created a statewide online database that not only lets you see which sex predators are in your midst but also can alert you by email if an offender moves close by (J. Sullivan, 2009).

These laws have generated several unintended consequences. For example, parolees have been "hounded" from communities, the media have televised the parolees' homecomings, homes have been burned, parolees have been killed, and neighbors have assaulted parolees they erroneously thought were sex offenders. In some states, legislators wrote laws so broadly that consensual sex between teenagers and third-degree assault that might constitute inappropriate touching or sexual contact are included in the notification mandate. In 2006, two Maine parolees were shot by a man intent on killing registered sex offenders. One of those killed was on the list because, at age 19, he had been convicted of having consensual sex with his underage girlfriend. His murder heightened national debate as to whether the online registries put those who are listed at risk (G. Adams, 2006).

The fact of repeat violence fuels a public perception that parolees represent a continuing threat to the community. Although the new laws primarily focus on people who have committed sex offenses against children, some fear that the community will eventually target all parolees. This preoccupation with potential parolee criminality makes successful reentry even more difficult for ex-offenders. Read "Criminal Justice: Myth & Reality," and consider your views on the policies adopted by some states to control the offenders whom they fear most.

Revocation of Parole

The potential revocation of parole, for committing a new crime or violating the conditions of release, hangs constantly over the ex-inmate's head. The public tends to view the high number of revocations as a failure of parole. Correctional officials point to the great number of parolees who are required to be drug free, be employed, and pay restitution—conditions that many find difficult to fulfill.

As discussed in Chapter 10, the Supreme Court ruled in *Morrissey v. Brewer* (1972) that if the parole officer alleges a technical violation, a two-step revocation proceeding is required. In the first stage, a hearing determines whether there is probable cause to believe the conditions have been violated. The parolee has the right to be notified of the charges, to be informed of the evidence, to present witnesses, and to confront the witnesses. In the second stage, the parole authority decides if the violation is severe enough to warrant the return to prison.

Because of the effort to reduce prison populations, a recent trend in many states is to increase the number of prisoners released on parole and avoid revoking parole unless there is serious misconduct. The emphasis on successful reentry can lead to using alternative incentives and sanctions regarding compliance with conditions of parole. Thus, there is decreased emphasis on technical violations of parole conditions. On the other hand, arrest and conviction for a new crime are still likely to lead to a return to prison.

In Texas, for example, the Board of Pardons and Paroles approved only 25 percent of parole applications in 2001. By contrast, the board approved 37 percent of the 80,644 parole applications in 2012 (Battson, 2012; Texas Board of Pardons and Paroles, 2013). An additional factor in the increase in parole approval is a recognition that keeping offenders in prison until they have served their complete sentences means that they will be freed without parole supervision. Thus, a greater awareness of the importance of reentry preparation may lead to more approvals of parole releases late in a sentence for those who might have previously served their complete terms (Ward, 2012).

At the same time that the number of parolees is growing in Texas, there has also been a reduction in the number parole revocations. In 2003, the board revoked parole for 10,554 parolees out of the 30,598 called before hearings to face the possibility of revocation. By contrast, in 2012, the board revoked parole for only 5,935 parolees out of 33,032 called before hearings (Texas Board of Pardons and Paroles, 2013).

CRIMINAL JUSTICE
MYTH&REALITY

COMMON BELIEF: Offenders who never qualify for parole will still inevitably be returned to society upon completion of their sentences.

- The foregoing statement is generally true for those offenders who are not serving life sentences. However, some states, such as Kansas and Washington, enacted laws to prolong the detention of offenders whom officials regard as especially dangerous: predatory sex offenders.
- Under these laws, offenders who are diagnosed with mental conditions that make them highly likely to commit further sex crimes are transported to secure mental facilities upon the completion of their prison sentences. In other words, even after serving their full prison sentences, they remain locked up in state facilities.
- The U.S. Supreme Court ruled that such indefinite detention statutes are permissible as long as the purpose of the laws is treatment rather than punishment (*Kansas v. Hendricks, 1997*).
- In theory, these individuals will be released when psychiatrists conclude that they can safely reenter society. In practice, they may never receive such approval.
- One of the most significant risks of such laws is that they will be applied to people who actually do not pose a significant risk of re-offending. This is especially true because the psychiatric conditions that justify post-sentence detentions are vaguely defined and difficult to diagnose accurately.

4. What are three programs designed to ease the reentry of offenders into the community?
Work and educational release programs, furlough programs, and halfway houses.

5. What are the main tasks of parole officers?
Surveillance and assistance.

6. What two conditions can result in the revocation of parole?
Arrest for a new crime or a technical violation of one or more of the conditions of parole.

Should criminal justice officials be able to revoke parole without a hearing? Alternatively, should parolees be entitled to a full trial and representation by counsel before parole is revoked, since the revocation decision has such a huge impact on their personal liberty? Give three reasons for your responses to these two questions.

The Future of Prisoner Reentry

The rising number of offenders returning to the community has new importance to policymakers. Large numbers of offenders are gaining release each year as a natural consequence of the nation's significant expansion of its prison population in the past few decades. Moreover, many states are attempting to increase the number of offenders released from prison as a means to cut costs amid the contemporary budget crisis affecting all levels of government. These factors increase the necessity of looking closely at ways to make reentry effective for offenders and society.

The likelihood of rules violations by released offenders is affected not only by the kinds of crimes for which they were convicted but also by the intensity and duration of their supervision (Grattet, Lin, & Petersilia, 2011). The longer the period of time under a strict set of rules, the greater is the likelihood that some rules will be broken, and then states are faced with the question of whether to send an offender back to prison, even if the offender has not committed a new crime.

The 2011 report by the Pew Center on the States highlighted Oregon as a place where great efforts are made to respond to violations by parolees without sending them back to the expensive and unproductive environment of prison. For example, research has shown that using community-based sanctions for parole violations can be an effective and less costly approach to combatting recidivism (Steiner, Makarios, Travis, & Meade, 2012). States can also benefit from proactively reaching out to employers and, in cooperation with employers, developing transitional job programs that provide financial and personal support as well as the necessary training and supervision for parolees and ex-offenders (Rosenberg, 2012). Successful entry into the workforce can have substantial beneficial effects for offenders, although this important step can contain numerous obstacles for the many offenders who lack meaningful prior work experience or the commitment to fulfill the responsibilities of a job.

An additional challenge facing reentry is the maintenance of budgets for programs that facilitate reintegration into the community even as states are cutting funds elsewhere in corrections. For example, some cities have used reentry courts with judges dedicated to overseeing the progress of parolees (Hamilton, 2010). Yet, in San Francisco in 2011, budget cuts eliminated the Parole Reentry Court

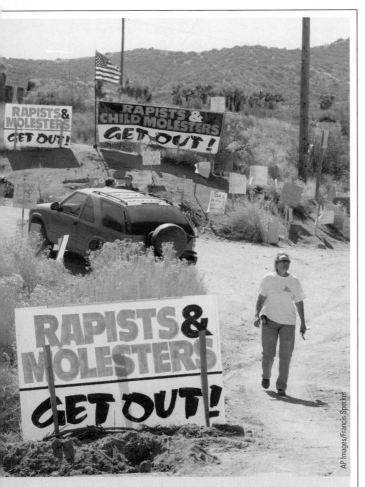

Sex offender registration laws have made adjustment to the community difficult for many parolees. Residents of some neighborhoods, such as these in Placentia, California, have protested the renting or sale of property to paroled sex offenders. To what extent have these laws resulted in all parolees being labeled as "dangerous"?

AP Images/Francis Specker

Parole and Reentry

The Justice Policy Institute has highlighted a number of approaches to help states reduce prison populations and increase success rates for parolees reentering society. Although many of these recommendations require creation of programs and the expenditure of money, evidence that these strategies can work may serve to convince legislators and corrections officials that these approaches are worthwhile endeavors for spending limited financial resources. Examine the list of recommendations, and ask yourself if any can be followed without significant commitments of new funds.

- *Utilize risk assessments.* By analyzing specific characteristics of offenders (mental health, education level, criminal record, support from family, etc.) in light of prior research, states can predict more effectively which offenders are likely to succeed on parole and which may need special services or extra supervision.
- *Reduce administrative delays in parole hearings and decisions.* Efficiency can help reduce the costs associated with time spent in prison awaiting parole processing.
- *Increase access to in-prison programming.* Prerelease education can help begin the process of eventual transition to society.
- *Use medical parole and parole for aging prisoners.* Elderly prisoners and those with chronic medical conditions are especially expensive to house in prisons and often pose much lower risks of reoffending.
- *Allow offenders to earn "good time" credits while on parole and not just while in prison.* The opportunity to shorten the sentence and period of supervision can be an effective incentive to encourage proper behavior and compliance with parole conditions.
- *Expand work release and community corrections.* These programs can provide important mechanisms to assist offenders in reestablishing connections with society.
- *Match the intensity of parole supervision with the level of risk posed by the offender's record and characteristics.* Resources are wasted when all parolees receive the same level of supervision despite presenting differing levels of risk.

- *Increase access to treatment in the community.* Many offenders have substance abuse or mental health problems for which they need treatment in order to assist with their transition to society.

Researching the Internet

To read about Kentucky's efforts to reduce prison populations and enhance reentry, including strengthening the effectiveness of parole, go to the Criminal Justice CourseMate at cengagebrain.com, then access the web links for this chapter. http://www.pewstates.org/uploadedFiles/2011 _Kentucky_Reforms_Cut_Recidivism.pdf.

Implementing New Practices

Legislators and corrections officials face difficult choices. They are responsible for protecting public safety and, indeed, can lose their positions if they are blamed for an unfortunate incident such as a parolee committing a horrific crime. Although they are likely to be cautious about new initiatives that place offenders in the community, they also increasingly recognize that states are spending more money than they need to spend on prisons in order to keep the public safe. Thus, more and more decision makers in criminal justice recognize that they must devote more attention and resources to parole and reentry.

As you look through the list of recommendations, which ones do you think are likely to encounter resistance? Are there recommendations that actually will not cost much extra money but simply require more effectiveness in organizing how the criminal justice system carries out its responsibilities? Which recommendations do you see as most important and beneficial to society? Write a memo that addresses these three questions.

Source: Justice Policy Institute. 2010. "How to Safely Reduce Prison Populations and Support People Returning to Their Communities." June (Press Release). http://www.justicepolicy.org /images/upload/10-06_fac_forimmediaterelease_ps-ac.pdf.

despite its record of helping parolees avoid recidivism, leading Judge Jeffrey Tauber to apologize to parolees in the courtroom by saying, "I'm truly apologizing that I've not been able to fulfill my commitment and promise to you" (Bundy, 2011). Elsewhere in the country, other parole and reentry programs have shared the burden of budget cuts. The need to facilitate the successful reentry of a large number of parolees and ex-offenders will lead to hard questions and difficult choices about how to allocate resources in the justice system.

The recognition of the important need to reduce prison populations and facilitate successful reentry at the same time that states are dealing with budget problems makes a focus on evidence-based practices especially important. When there are limited resources to devote to parole and reentry, then they should be used efficiently with great awareness of approaches that have been proven to enhance success. Read the "Evidence-Based Practice and Policy" feature to consider recommended approaches for reducing prison populations and facilitating reentry.

Legislators and correctional officials increasingly recognize that government lacks the money and facilities to incarcerate all offenders for the sentence lengths that had been imposed in recent decades. Alternative approaches will affect not only sentencing decisions for nonviolent and drug offenders but also efforts to increasingly reduce prison populations through various release mechanisms. Parole and other community programs represent an effort to address the inevitability of prison reentry. Even if such programs do not prevent all offenders from returning to crime, they do help some to turn their lives around.

A QUESTION OF ETHICS

Think, Discuss, Write

For parole officers, as well as for other criminal justice officials, it is important to behave professionally in all circumstances and avoid any temptation to abuse authority based on feelings of anger or contempt for parolees and their families. A U.S. Court of Appeals decision described the behavior of a parole officer and several police officers who were instructed to conduct searches of parolees' homes, including parolees not under the supervision of this particular parole officer. The manner in which they conducted the search raises troubling questions about their attitudes and behavior.

The officers who searched Motley's residence for purported parolee Janae Jamerson conducted the search in a harassing manner. When [the parolee's girlfriend] Motley came to the door in her pajamas, the officers told her several falsehoods. Kading said that he was there with Jamerson's [actual supervising] parole officer and that they had a warrant to search the apartment, neither of which was true. Motley told the searching officers that [the parolee] Jamerson did not live there and was in custody. One of the officers then told her that Jamerson had been released three days earlier, another lie. When the officers then asked Motley who else was inside the house with her, she said that only she and her five-week-old son were there. Kading told Motley that if she did not let them in, they would arrest her and put her son in foster care. Faced with Kading's threat to take her son away, Motley unlocked the security gate. Kading pushed her out of the way and against the wall

with his forearm as he went into the house. The officers all entered the apartment with their guns drawn. During the search, the officers were "going through things," including closets and a file box, a search that was completely unauthorized.

Kading knew that the baby was in the back bedroom, and as soon as he entered that room he pointed his gun directly at the five-week-old infant. The baby was on his back on the bed looking toward the bedroom door. The baby began screaming as soon as Kading entered, and so Motley ran to the room, where Kading was still pointing the gun at the baby. Kading did not move his gun when Motley entered, and he kept it pointed at Motley's tiny son while he searched the room.

The officers searched for over twenty minutes when it could have been ascertained much more quickly that [the parolee] Jamerson was not present.

[*Motley v. Parks*, 383 F.3d 1058 (2004) (U.S. Court of Appeals for the 9th Circuit)]

Discussion/Writing Assignment

Describe four recommendations for lecture topics, discussion topics, experiences, guest lecturers, or other elements that you would incorporate into the training of parole officers to help instill professionalism and ethical behavior so that abusive conduct would be less likely to occur.

SUMMARY

1 Describe the nature of the "reentry problem."

- Prisoner reentry to the community has become an important public issue because of the large number of offenders who gain parole eligibility or complete their sentences each year.
- Preventing recidivism by assisting parolees to become law-abiding citizens requires government

resources and the development of helpful programs to prepare offenders for release.

- During the contemporary period of state government budget problems, there is an effort to reduce prison populations, yet funding cuts for reentry programs can hamper efforts to prepare offenders to rejoin society.

② Explain the origins of parole and how it operates today.

- Parole is the conditional release from prison and is the primary method by which inmates return to society. While on parole, they remain under correctional supervision.
- Parole in the United States evolved during the nineteenth century from the English, Australian, and Irish practices of conditional pardon, apprenticeship by indenture, transportation to distant colonies, and issuance of "tickets of leave."
- Today most felons leave prison and are supervised by parole officers for a period of time. They may be returned to prison if they commit another crime or violate the conditions (rules) of their release.

③ Name and define the mechanisms for the release of felons to the community.

- There are four types of release: expiration release, mandatory release, other conditional release, and discretionary release.
- Expiration release occurs when inmates have completed their full sentence. They have "maxed out" and leave the prison without community supervision.
- Mandatory release is the required release of an inmate to the community upon the expiration of a certain period, as specified by a determinate-sentencing law or parole guidelines.
- Other conditional release is the placement of convicts in various community settings while under

supervision; some states use this to avoid the rigidity of mandatory release.
- Discretionary release is based on a decision by the parole board within the boundaries set by the sentence and the penal law.
- Describe differences in the parole board process in different states.

④ Describe how ex-offenders are supervised in the community.

- Parole officers are assigned to supervise and assist ex-inmates making the transition to society and to ensure that they follow the conditions of their release.
- Parole officers' functions include roles as cops and as social workers.
- Parole may be revoked for commission of a crime or for violating the rules governing behavior while on parole (failing to appear for meetings with parole officers, using drugs or alcohol, and so forth).

⑤ Identify the problems that parolees face during their reentry.

- Upon release, offenders face many problems. For instance, they must find housing and employment and reestablish relationships with family and friends.
- Adjustment to life outside the prison is often difficult in that those released must move from the highly structured environment of an institution into a world with temptations and complicated problems.

Questions for Review

1. What are the basic assumptions of parole?
2. How do mandatory release, discretionary release, and unconditional release differ?
3. What roles does the parole officer play?
4. What problems confront parolees upon their release?

Key Terms and Cases

conditions of release (p. 439)

discretionary release (p. 433)

expiration release (p. 432)

furlough (p. 441)

halfway house (p. 441)

mandatory release (p. 432)

other conditional release (p. 432)

parole (p. 430)

work and educational release (p. 441)

14 Technology and Criminal Justice

LEARNING OBJECTIVES

1 Describe how adaptation and belief in science can affect the use of technology.

2 Identify the various aspects of cyber crime and counterfeiting.

3 Explain the role of communications, computers, and databases in policing.

4 Describe developments and problems in DNA testing and new weapons technologies.

5 Name the uses of technology in courts and corrections.

6 List some continuing questions about the effects of technology on civil liberties.

Dwindling crowds of people lined the sidewalks in downtown Boston on April 15, 2013. They cheered as the late arriving finishers of the Boston Marathon came across the finish line. Suddenly two loud explosions and clouds of smoke shattered the celebratory atmosphere. Amid screams and chaos, medical personnel on the scene to help marathoners found themselves suddenly providing first aid to spectators suffering catastrophic leg injuries from two crude bombs placed in backpacks and left among the crowds on the sidewalk. Police officers and bystanders rushed to assist with moving the wounded to arriving ambulances. The unexpected and incomprehensible act of violence killed three people and wounded 170 others (Seelye et al., 2013). In the immediate aftermath, the police did not have any specific suspects.

Reports on the bombing dominated news broadcasts throughout the day. For most Americans, the bombing at the Boston Marathon raised disturbing questions about the protection of homeland security. Government intelligence officials reported that there was no forewarning or specific threat about Boston as a target for suspected terrorist groups. As with the 2001 attacks on the World Trade Center and the Pentagon on 9/11, people were forced to wonder whether this was the act of a small group based in the United States or an organized terrorist group directed and trained by enemies overseas. People could not avoid fearing that this might signal the beginning of new random attacks designed to kill Americans and instill fear throughout society.

Four days later, the entire nation sat transfixed watching live coverage of the substantial force of police from multiple local, state, and federal agencies moving door-to-door through Watertown, Massachusetts, to check each house for 19-year-old bombing suspect Dzhokhar Tsarnaev. His brother Tamarlan, the other bombing suspect, had been killed in a shootout with police the previous evening. Eventually, the police found the young bombing suspect, bleeding heavily from wounds, in his hiding place in a boat stored at the back of a driveway on a quiet street. He was arrested and taken to the hospital.

Modern technology served as the crucial element in solving this important criminal case affecting homeland security. Throughout much of history, it was nearly impossible to identify or apprehend criminals unless there were eyewitnesses to the crime, the criminal was caught at the crime scene, or the criminal was found later to be in possession of stolen items or other incriminating evidence. In the case of a disguised assailant whose motive was murder rather than robbery, it was exceptionally difficult to solve the case unless someone was caught with the murder weapon. This problem was even more challenging in the case of people who left bombs at a big public event and then disappeared anonymously into the crowd. The development of technology, however, has improved the capabilities of law enforcement officers to identify and apprehend lawbreakers.

In little more than a day after the bombing, law enforcement authorities were able to isolate and enhance video from store security cameras at the bombing site in order to post photos of the two suspects carrying the bomb backpacks. Posting the photos nationwide through news media and social media led to the identification of the two brothers. Police also used cell phone records to hunt for the bombers. In addition, forensic scientists analyzed bomb fragments to determine the contents of the explosive device and whether it seemed to be built by professionals or amateurs. When the younger brother escaped from a later shootout with police, helicopters with thermal imaging devices and bomb squad robots were brought to Watertown in anticipation of searching for the perpetrator and dismantling any bombs that he might have been carrying (Walsh, 2013).

Contemporary Americans take for granted the availability and usefulness of technology. American television viewers are fascinated by the *CSI: Crime Scene Investigation* television shows and other programs that show the impressive ability of scientists to identify criminal suspects by examining microscopic bits of evidence. Because the United States is a relatively wealthy and technologically sophisticated country, it can fund and benefit from the development of new technologies that provide crucial assistance in various operations of the criminal justice system. As we learn about the role and impact of technology in criminal justice, we must also remember that existing technological resources are not necessarily available for use in all state and county criminal justice systems. Agencies must have enough money to acquire new technology, and their personnel must have expertise and resources for training in order to make effective use of it.

In this chapter, we examine the role of technology in criminal justice. Each year brings new inventions—as well as improvements to existing technologies—that affect crime and justice. As we shall see, technological change affects the nature of crime even as it boosts the capacity of law enforcement officials to prevent criminal acts and apprehend criminal offenders. Technology also impacts the processing of criminal cases in courts and the monitoring and control of convicted offenders in correctional settings. The use of technology increases the capability of criminal justice officials to perform their vital functions effectively. Simultaneously, however, technology creates its own issues and problems, including concerns about the ways in which it may collide with citizens' expectations about their privacy and other constitutional rights.

Technological Development and Criminal Justice

Throughout history, humans have sought to invent tools to advance their goals. The invention of early tools and wheels, for example, promoted agriculture and transport. Over time, simple farming tools gave way to gigantic tractors and other farm machinery. The wheel has similarly been updated through advancing transportation mechanisms—from horse-drawn wagons to steam trains to jet planes. The appreciation for the advantages of technology naturally leads to inventive developments affecting all areas of human experience, including criminal justice.

However, the use of technology in criminal justice differs from its use in many other areas of human activity. Technology in this case is not merely an effort to overcome the natural environment by increasing productivity, easing daily life, and expanding the range of travel. In criminal justice, as in military affairs, technology becomes an element in the interaction, competition, and conflict among human beings who have opposing objectives. In this case, the clash is between those who would seek to profit or cause harm by breaking society's laws (as in theft or murder) and those who seek to stop, identify, apprehend, process, and punish criminals. This observation highlights two important points about technological development in criminal justice. First, new developments that benefit one side in this competition, whether lawbreaker or law enforcer, will lead to adjustments and adaptations by the other. Second, the pressure to find new and better devices to combat crime can lead to excessive faith in the effectiveness of technology; this can lead to problems when people do not stop to examine all the consequences of new technology. After we briefly examine each of these points, keep them in mind to see how they relate to the topics discussed in the rest of this chapter.

Competition and Adaptation

Throughout history, the development of both weapons and protective devices has affected the preservation of persons and property, which is one of the fundamental goals of criminal justice. As weaponry advanced from daggers and swords to firearms and then later to multishot pistols that could be concealed inside pockets, the threats posed by robbers increased. Thus, when American policing expanded in the nineteenth century, law enforcement officers in the western frontier, and later throughout the country, armed themselves in a way that would help them deal with pistol-toting criminals. These developments continue. News reports have made contemporary Americans well aware that many police departments now struggle to match the firepower of the automatic weapons possessed by some criminal offenders and organized crime groups (A. Klein, 2008).

Similarly, the development of fortified walls, door locks, and safes led to criminals' adaptive strategies for overcoming these barriers. For example, the creation of locks spawned devices and techniques for picking locks. So, too, the creation of safes led to the birth of professional safecrackers. Later, the introduction of police radar to detect speeders led to a profitable industry selling radar detectors to motorists who wanted to drive at excessive speeds without paying fines. Today criminals' efforts to overcome residential burglar alarms, as well as cyber criminals' creativity in overcoming security software, illustrate the interactions among technological development, criminals' adaptive behavior, and society's efforts to counteract new forms of criminality.

Fundamentally, these examples should remind us that technological developments do not always help criminal justice officials. New technologies can be developed and used by those who seek to violate criminal laws. Moreover, new devices designed specifically to protect property or to assist police officers will generate adaptive behavior by would-be lawbreakers who adjust their behavior, invent their own devices, or otherwise develop strategies to overcome new barriers to the attainment of their goals. James Byrne summarizes the overall impact of technology:

> Advances . . . in technology have resulted in new opportunities for crime (through the Internet), new forms of criminality (e.g., Internet scams . . .), new techniques for committing crimes (e.g., computer software programs, . . . the use of [T]asers as weapons in robberies), and new categories of offenders and victims (such as online predators and identity theft victims) (2008:10–11).

Many people presumed that the electric chair provided a quicker, more humane way to execute criminals because the use of electricity was developed through experimentation and other methods of science. In fact, many such executions seemed to be far more painful and prolonged than the traditional use of hanging. Are there any new technologies in criminal justice that are likely to have unexpected and undesirable consequences?

Science and the Presumption of Progress

From the mid-nineteenth century through today, Americans have benefited from industrialization, the development of electricity, the rise of the scientific method, and advances in various scientific fields, such as medicine and engineering. In light of the extraordinary advancements in human knowledge and the new inventions that have dramatically altered the nature of American society, it is not surprising that many people equate technological advancements with "progress." However, contemporary Americans are regularly reminded that new developments can produce consequences, such as side effects from new medicines, that are unexpected and undesirable. Thus, in the field of criminal justice, as in other fields, we need to guard against the assumption that new technologies will always be better than older techniques and devices. Similarly, even when the benefits of new technologies are clear, we need to consider the possibility of undesirable risks and consequences that have not yet been discovered.

In the late nineteenth century, the development of electricity brought with it efforts to apply this "miracle" resource to various societal needs. One idea applied to criminal justice was the invention of the electric chair as a modern method to produce an instantaneous and presumably humane execution for criminals sentenced to death. At that time, most executions were carried out through hanging. This "old-fashioned" execution method had been used for centuries, with little change in its use of rope and a means to drop the condemned person's body so that the neck would break or the person would be strangled.

The first man condemned to execution by electric chair was William Kemmler, a convicted murderer in New York. Kemmler challenged his sentence through the court system, eventually presenting to the U.S. Supreme Court a claim that execution by electricity constituted "cruel and unusual punishment" in violation of Kemmler's constitutional rights. After all, what could be more "unusual" than to be the first person executed through the use of a newfangled invention?

In rejecting Kemmler's claim in 1890, the U.S. Supreme Court noted that the New York statute permitting execution by electric chair "was passed in the effort to devise a more humane method of reaching the result [of extinguishing life and] that courts were bound to presume that the legislature was possessed of the facts upon which it took action" (*In re Kemmler*, 1890). Thus, there was acceptance of the idea that this new scientific method would be more effective and humane than hanging. When Kemmler was actually executed, however, the first jolt of 1,000 volts did not kill him, and witnesses saw that he was still breathing despite the attending physician's initial declaration that he was dead (Moran, 2002). The wires were reattached to his head, and the chair was revved up to 2,000 volts for an extended period.

Froth oozed out of Kemmler's strapped mouth. The small blood vessels under his skin began to rupture. Blood trickled down his face and arms. . . . The awful smell of burning flesh filled the death chamber. Kemmler's body first smoldered and then caught fire. . . . From the moment he first sat down on the chair until the electricity was shut off the second time, eight minutes had elapsed. (Moran, 2002:15–19)

Did the electric chair fulfill its presumed function of using science to provide instantaneous, humane executions? Although it was used in 2,000 executions in the century after Kemmler's death, highly publicized instances of other gruesome death-chamber scenes eventually led to a complete reconsideration of its use. In 2001, Georgia's Supreme Court declared that this method of execution imposed unconstitutional "cruel and unusual punishment" on condemned offenders in its state criminal justice system (H. Weinstein, 2001). By the time that the Nebraska Supreme Court made an identical ruling in 2008, all states had moved toward the use of lethal injection as the method of execution for new capital murder convictions. Clearly, the original presumptions about the humane scientific "progress" represented by the electric chair had been rejected nationwide (Mears, 2008). Interestingly, however, new issues later arose with the use of lethal injections, especially the availability of specific drugs used in the process that European countries refused to sell to American states for use in executions. Thus, several states in 2014 began to discuss the possibility of returning to "old-fashioned methods" such as hanging and the gas chamber (Salter, 2014).

The story of the electric chair provides a graphic example of slow reconsideration of the effects of particular technological and scientific developments. Today we see similar examples concerning the actual risks and consequences of certain technologies. For example, in 2009, the National Academy of Sciences (2009) produced a report that questioned the validity and accuracy of many forensic science methods used by police and prosecutors. In one section, the report

CRIMINAL JUSTICE
MYTH&REALITY

COMMON BELIEF: As long as forensic scientists do not mishandle evidence, modern scientific methods ensure that reliable conclusions can be drawn after the laboratory testing of various forms of evidence, including fingerprints, hair, soil, handwriting, and bite marks.

- In reality, the National Academy of Sciences concluded that "many forensic disciplines—including analysis of fingerprints, bite marks, and the striations and indentations left by a pry bar or a gun's firing mechanism—were not grounded in the kind of rigorous, peer-reviewed research that is the hallmark of classic science" (Fountain, 2009).
- Major scandals have emerged when experts purported to state definitive conclusions about bite marks, handwriting analysis, and other forms of evidence after scientific testing, only to discover later that these conclusions were incorrect and had led to the conviction of innocent people (F. Santos, 2007).
- DNA analysis is the only form of scientific evidence that has been subjected to rigorous testing through the methods of science.
- Although courts admit into evidence other forms of scientific testing, as well as conclusions drawn about such evidence by scientists, many of these other tests have not been validated through rigorous research. Thus, judges and attorneys should display caution in examining and accepting such evidence.

said that forensic science "analyses are often handled by poorly trained technicians who then exaggerate the accuracy of their methods in court" (S. Moore, 2009). Obviously, the effectiveness of technology is limited by the errors made by the human beings who use that technology, despite the seeming infallibility of forensic techniques dramatized in *CSI: Crime Scene Investigation* and other popular shows. Indeed, even the use of a simple photo from a surveillance camera can cause problems when people make mistakes. This point was experienced by Cornell University sociology professor Stephen Morgan in New York when he saw that his old driver's license photo was being mistakenly circulated on the Internet—instead of a photo of the actual Stephen Morgan being sought for a fatal shooting in Connecticut at Wesleyan University's student bookstore in 2009—as officials asked for the public's help in finding the shooter (M. Spencer, 2009). In addition, the technology itself, even when properly used, may also produce unanticipated risks and consequences. An accurate understanding of the role of technology in criminal justice requires recognition of the potential for undesirable results. Think about your own perceptions of the scientific testing of criminal evidence as you read "Criminal Justice: Myth & Reality."

☑CHECK POINT

1. **What are two reasons to be cautious about assuming that new technological developments automatically provide benefits for the criminal justice system?**
   Lawbreakers can develop and use technology for the purpose of committing crimes; new technologies produce the risks of unanticipated, undesirable risks and consequences.

STOP&ANALYZE

What steps do you take to avoid victimization by technology-based crimes? Which technology-based crimes do you fear most?

Crime and Technology

As new technologies emerge, so do people who take advantage of them for their own gain. One has only to think of how the invention of the automobile enhanced criminals' mobility to realize the extent to which computers and other new technologies will enhance existing criminal enterprises. For example, the acquisition of automatic weapons can make drug traffickers more dangerous in battling their rivals and threatening witnesses. Instantaneous transfers of funds between banks via computer networks can make it easier for criminals to move money in order to purchase weapons, drugs, and other contraband, as well as to hide assets from government agencies responsible for law enforcement and tax collection. Computers and other technologies also create opportunities to commit new kinds of crimes, such as cyber crime and counterfeiting. We should note as well that individual citizens can respond by using technology themselves to thwart crime through improved lighting and alarm systems in their homes, security software on their computers, and pepper-spray canisters and other weapons for personal protection.

Cyber Crime

As we saw in Chapter 2, cyber crimes involve the use of computers and the Internet to commit acts against people, property, public order, or morality. Cyber criminals use computers to steal information, resources, or funds. These thefts can be aimed at simply stealing money, or they can involve the theft of companies' trade secrets, chemical formulas, and other valuable information. The scope of these thefts can be shocking when discovered and revealed to the public. In 2014, for example, the Target chain of stores revealed that hackers had obtained credit and debit card information on as many as 70 million of the stores' customers, putting those individuals at risk of identity theft (Yang & Jayakumar, 2014). Other criminals use computers for malicious, destructive acts, such as releasing Internet viruses and "worms" to harm computer systems. They may also use innocent victims' computers, via remote commands, to assist in crimes such as the dissemination of child pornography (Kravets, 2011). In 2012, the countries in the European Union announced that they would open a new anticrime center in the Netherlands dedicated to combatting cyber crimes, many of which are increasingly perpetrated by organized crime groups. The European Union has estimated that organized crime groups gained $388 billion annually from cyber crime, an amount greater than the total profits produced through global trade in marijuana, cocaine, and heroin (H. Morris, 2012).

In addition, the illegal downloading of software, music, videos, and other copyrighted materials is widespread (Hinduja, 2007). Doing so is a federal crime. However, although millions of Americans perform illegal downloads every day, they are seldom prosecuted unless the government identifies individuals or organizations with substantial involvement in such activities. The government has acted to shut down large operations engaged in illegally disseminating movies and other copyrighted entertainment media. In 2012, for example, the FBI, in cooperation with officials in nearly a dozen countries, gained the arrests of three individuals in New Zealand and sought three other suspects abroad for gaining more than $175 million in illegal profits from posting movies and other copyrighted works online (U.S. Department of Justice, 2012).

New issues continually arise that produce suggestions about criminalizing new forms of cyber behavior, such as cyber bullying among teens that may lead to psychological harms and behavioral problems (Patchin & Hinduja, 2012).

Identity theft has become a huge problem affecting many middle-class and affluent Americans who would otherwise seldom find themselves victimized by criminals (J. Collins, 2005). Perpetrators of identity theft use other people's credit card numbers and social security numbers to secure fraudulent loans and steal money and merchandise. In December 2011, for example, 55 people in New York City were

identity theft The theft of social security numbers, credit card numbers, and other information in order to secure loans, withdraw bank funds, and purchase merchandise while posing as someone else: the unsuspecting victim who will eventually lose money in these transactions.

TABLE 14.1 Type of Identity Theft Experienced by Households and Total Financial Loss Attributed to Each Type of Identity Theft in 2012

Types of Identity Theft	Number of Victimizations	Percent of Victimizations	Average Total Out-of-Pocket Loss
All types	16.6 million	100%	$4,804
Existing credit card	6.7 million	40%	$1,991
Existing bank account	6.2 million	37%	$1,444
Other existing account	1.15 million	7%	$1,264
Personal information	622,900	3%	$34,352
New account	683,400	4%	$863
Multiple types	1.25 million	8%	$9,001

Source: E. Harrell and L. Langton, "Victims of Identity Theft, 2012," *Bureau of Justice Statistics Bulletin*, December 2013, p. 19.

charged with being part of a cyber-crime ring in which one person stole financial information from donors to a philanthropic foundation and then supplied that information to crime partners who opened bank accounts and created counterfeit checks in the names of the donors (Nir, 2011). According to the National Crime Victimization Survey, millions of American households were victimized by identity theft in 2012, with losses totaling $24.7 billion (Harrell & Langton, 2013).

For many Americans, identity theft can occur without any financial loss if, for example, they are reimbursed by a bank or credit card company for their losses. Yet, they still suffer victimization from computer crime since they may have to go through lengthy hassles in changing online financial records, getting new credit cards, or straightening out government records (Florencio & Herley, 2012).

As indicated by Table 14.1, the theft of existing credit card information is the most common form of identity theft, although other thefts involve existing bank accounts, PayPal accounts, and personal information used by thieves to set up fraudulent new accounts or file for fraudulent tax refunds. Credit card numbers can be stolen by dishonest restaurant servers and retail clerks who use electronic "skimmer" devices to quickly record the magnetic strip on the back of the card so that the information can be sold to organized crime gangs or used to purchase items and manufacture counterfeit credit cards (Conte, 2012).

Other offenders use the Internet to disseminate child pornography, to advertise sexual services, or to stalk the unsuspecting. Police departments have given special emphasis to stopping computer predators who establish online relationships with juveniles in order to manipulate those children into sexual victimization. Thus, officers often pose as juveniles in "chat rooms" to see if sexual predators will attempt to cultivate a relationship and set up a personal meeting (Bai, 2012; Eichenwald, 2006). However, local police departments face challenges in training and equipping officers to investigate online child pornography and other cyber crimes (Holt & Bossler, 2012).

The various forms of cyber crime present a serious concern to Americans. See "What Americans Think," and compare your own concerns and awareness with those of the rest of the country.

In attacking these problems, the FBI's National Computer Crime Squad lists its responsibilities as covering the following:

- Intrusions of the public switched network (the telephone company)
- Major computer network intrusions
- Network integrity violations
- Privacy violations

QUESTION: "What do you know and believe about cyber crime?"

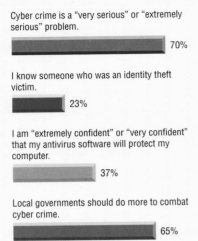

Cyber crime is a "very serious" or "extremely serious" problem.
70%

I know someone who was an identity theft victim.
23%

I am "extremely confident" or "very confident" that my antivirus software will protect my computer.
37%

Local governments should do more to combat cyber crime.
65%

CRITICAL THINKING: In the current era of government budget cuts, do you believe that Americans' expressed concern about the growing problem of cyber crime will lead to increased funding for efforts to catch and punish cyber criminals? Why or why not?

Source: Kelly Jackson Higgins, "Poll: 65% of Consumers Want Local Government to Do More about Cybercrime," April 23, 2009, national poll by Competitive Edge Research and Communication (http://cerc.net).

- Industrial espionage
- Pirated computer software
- Other crimes where the computer is a major factor in committing the criminal offense

The global nature of the Internet presents new challenges to the criminal justice system. For example, in 2014, with the cooperation of foreign law enforcement officials, the U.S. Justice Department announced the arrest of individuals in Romania, India, and China, as well as several of their American customers, related to the sale of passwords in order to hack into thousands of email accounts (U.S. Department of Justice, 2014). In 2011, the FBI, in cooperation with other countries' law enforcement agencies, announced criminal charges against two individuals in Latvia for leading an international cyber-crime operation that stole more than $70 million. The operation sent hundreds of thousands of computer "scareware" messages that warned people of serious virus infections and then offered to sell them fake software to remedy the nonexistent virus infections. In disrupting this operation, law enforcement officials also shut down computers and servers in seven European countries (U.S. Department of Justice, 2011).

Nigerian thieves have become well known for their "419 scams," named after a section of their country's criminal code, in which they send email messages to Americans and people in other countries offering large sums of money in exchange for payments from these targeted fraud victims that will enable the thieves to unfreeze these actually nonexistent assets in banks and trust funds. For example, they falsely claim that if the individual would simply send $5,000 to cover an overdue fee owed to a bank, then the bank will unfreeze an account containing a multimillion-dollar inheritance that will be split with the investor-scam victim (Bjelopera & Finklea, 2012). In another example, stolen credit card numbers are sold on the Internet, primarily by dealers based in states that were formerly part of the Soviet Union. Computer hackers steal thousands of credit card numbers from the computer systems of legitimate businesses and sell them in bulk to dealers who market them throughout the world via members-only websites. Credit card fraud costs online merchants more than $1 billion each year (Richtel, 2002; Segal, Ngugi, & Mana, 2011).

It is extremely difficult to know how many cyber crimes occur and how much money is lost through identity theft, auction fraud, investment fraud, and other forms of financial computer crime. Unfortunately for businesses, many harmful attacks and thefts carried out by computer are done by people inside a company. Moreover, many of these events are not reported to the police.

Efforts to create and enforce effective laws that will address such activities have been hampered by the international nature of cyber crime. Agencies in various countries are seeking to improve their ability to cooperate and share information. However, not all law enforcement officials throughout the world are equally committed to, nor capable of, catching cyber thieves and hackers. Criminals in some countries may have better computer equipment and expertise than do the officials trying to catch them. However, the FBI and other law enforcement agencies have made a concerted effort to improve their equipment, hire computer experts, and train their officers to investigate cyber crime. The FBI uses Cyber Action Teams, or CATs, to act quickly in addressing large-scale or

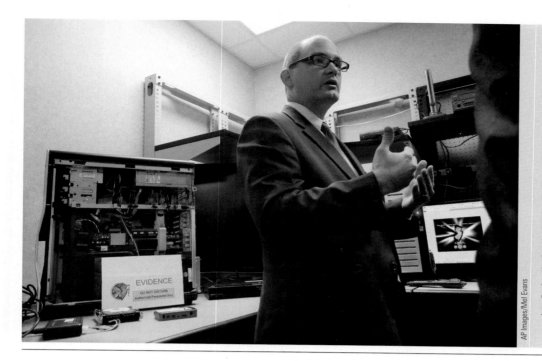

Law enforcement officers need up-to-date knowledge and equipment to have any hope of pursuing cyber criminals on the Internet. Local police officers often successfully pretend to be teenagers in chat rooms, drawing out people who would sexually abuse children. Local officials cannot usually maintain the expertise to counteract international cyber crime operations, so the FBI takes the lead in those efforts. Should computer science courses become a required component of every college criminal justice program?

AP Images/Mel Evans

very damaging cyber crimes. The FBI describes CATs as "small, highly trained teams of FBI agents, analysts, and computer forensics and malicious code experts who travel around the world on a moment's notice to respond to cyber intrusions" (FBI, 2006).

Since the events of September 11, many countries' law enforcement agencies have increased their communication and cooperation in order to thwart terrorist activities. As these countries cooperate in investigating and monitoring the financial transactions of groups that employ terror tactics, it seems likely that they will also improve their capacity to discover and pursue cyber criminals. For example, the FBI has also joined forces with the national police agencies of Australia, Canada, New Zealand, and the United Kingdom to form the Strategic Alliance Cyber Crime Working Group, an international organization for sharing information and cooperating in cyber crime investigations (FBI, 2008).

Law enforcement agencies cannot prevent cyber crimes from occurring. Generally, they react to such harmful activities in order to limit theft and damage. People cannot rely on law enforcement efforts to protect them from such harms. The first defense against some forms of cyber crime is citizen awareness and caution. Do you think most people know enough about cyber crime to protect themselves from becoming victims?

Counterfeiting

Traditional counterfeiting involves the creation of fake currency that can be used for illegal profit. Counterfeiting not only constitutes theft by permitting criminals to exchange fake bills for actual products and services but also harms the economy by placing into circulation bills that have no monetary value. Additional victims may receive the worthless paper as change in a purchase transaction or in payment for products and services. Historically, currency counterfeiters in the United States had difficulty matching the paper, ink, and intricate designs of real currency. While they could produce counterfeit bills that might fool individual clerks in stores, restaurants, and banks, criminals rarely avoided the eventual discovery that the bills were fakes. As image-reproduction technology developed, however, especially photocopiers and scanners, criminals found new ways of counterfeiting. Among the reasons that it is a crime to make any reproduction of U.S. currency

Counterfeiting poses serious problems for the American economy through the production of phony currency and bogus consumer products. What should the United States government do to stop the importation of counterfeit currency, such as high-quality fake bills produced by North Korea to harm the American economy?

AP Images/Lee Jin-man

is that counterfeiters initially found ways to photocopy currency images and feed those images into change machines. In went the fake paper currency and out came an equal amount of coins with real monetary value that the counterfeiters could then take to a bank and exchange for real paper money.

Continued improvements in computer and printing technology permitted counterfeiters to produce fake currency of increasing quality (Lazarus, 2010). Thus, in 1996, the United States began to redesign American currency and employ new technological techniques in order to make imitation more difficult. Unfortunately, North Korea purchased the same currency-printing technology that a Swiss company had sold to the U.S. Department of Treasury. As a result, American officials have seized shipments of counterfeit currency that North Korea reportedly produced specifically to harm the American economy and gain income for itself (Mihm, 2006; Rose, 2009). The U.S. government began circulating a newly designed $100 bill in 2013 as an additional counter measure against actions by the North Korean government and other counterfeiters (Eckel, 2013).

Currency is not the only product susceptible to counterfeiting through the use of available reproduction technologies. For example, legitimate businesses lose billions of dollars in potential sales each year when consumers purchase illegally copied, or "pirated," Hollywood DVDs, as well as counterfeit luxury products that purport to have authentic name brands. The pirated American movies, music, and computer software produced in China alone cost legitimate businesses more than $2 billion in sales each year at last reckoning (LaFraniere, 2009). In 2014, for example, a man in Springfield, Massachusetts, was convicted of selling counterfeit products bearing the brand names of Gucci, Nike, Coach, Chanel, and Oakley (U.S. Department of Justice, 204b). Although American law enforcement agencies can attempt—with limited success—to prevent the importation of counterfeit and pirated products, they can do little to prevent the manufacture of such products without the cooperation of authorities in the countries where the counterfeiters are located.

Although counterfeit consumer products impose significant costs on American businesses, far worse human costs result from the counterfeiting of another product: prescription drugs (Toscano, 2011). Technological advancements produced a sharp increase in counterfeit medications during the first decade of the twenty-first century. The discovery of counterfeit versions of specific medications increased from 5 different prescription and over-the-counter drugs per year in the late 1990s to more than 20 new counterfeit drugs per year beginning in 2000 (Grady, 2003). The dangers of counterfeit drugs are obvious: they can cause the deaths of patients who believe that they are taking genuine drugs or prevent patients from recovering appropriately from nonfatal illnesses. In 2008, a counterfeit version of the blood-thinning drug heparin came to the United States from China and led to the deaths of 19 Americans as well as causing hundreds of serious allergic reactions (Bogdanich, 2008). The serious risks from counterfeit drugs include the following:

> Counterfeit drugs are worthless fakes passed off as genuine. They may contain inactive substances like tap water or chalk, wrong ingredients, incorrect dosages or contaminants. Expensive drugs for severe cases of cancer and AIDS have been among the targets. In one case, aspirin tablets were substituted for the schizophrenia drug, Zyprexa. (Grady, 2003)

Imagine needing immediate medications to fight a dangerous illness but unknowingly receiving counterfeit drugs that will have no effect on the illness. This kind of illegal activity can easily kill vulnerable people. In 2012, a warning was issued that counterfeit vials of the best-selling cancer drug Avastin were turning up in hospital pharmacies (Associated Press, 2012b). These drugs represented exactly the type of worst-case situation in which a counterfeit product could lead to the deaths of people receiving medical treatments.

Because counterfeiting prescription drugs can be quite profitable, it has attracted organized crime groups. In one case, criminals in Florida copied the packaging and labels of the anemia drug Procrit, which is used to treat people with cancer and AIDS. They diluted the dosages in some bottles and filled other bottles with water. Because Procrit sells for $500 per dosage bottle, the criminals gained an estimated $46 million in profit before the scheme was discovered (Grady, 2003).

The U.S. Food and Drug Administration (FDA) and other government agencies face significant challenges in finding and seizing counterfeit drugs. New efforts to inspect and supervise pharmaceutical production facilities in the United States and abroad and to track individual medications as they move from factory to pharmacy have sought to reduce the risks for the American public (Harris, 2014). Unfortunately, profit-seeking criminals are working just as hard to defeat any new monitoring systems that are developed to intercept counterfeits. The proliferation of Internet pharmacies, which sell prescription medications online, has presented new challenges. Such enterprises may be located outside the borders of the United States. FDA officials have worked to warn Americans against purchasing medications from online sources other than the websites of established pharmacy retail chains.

☑ CHECK POINT

2. **What actions have been taken to combat counterfeit currency in the United States?**
Redesign of U.S. currency; seizure of counterfeit currency.

3. **What types of harm are caused by counterfeit products in the United States?**
Billions of dollars in losses for American businesses because of counterfeit and pirated products; deaths and other harmful health consequences from counterfeit medications.

STOP&ANALYZE

If you were the director of the U.S. Food and Drug Administration, what steps would you recommend to diminish the likelihood that counterfeit prescription drugs would reach American patients?

Policing and New Technology

Policing has long made use of technological developments. Twentieth-century police departments adopted the use of automobiles and radios in order to increase the effectiveness of their patrols, including better response time to criminal events and emergencies. Over time, technological advances also helped to provide better protection for police officers, including stronger, lighter bulletproof vests and protective features of patrol cars. Technology has affected the investigation of crime as well. As early as 1911, fingerprint evidence was used to convict an offender. Police officers have collected fingerprints, blood, fibers, and other crime-scene materials to be analyzed through scientific methods in order to identify and convict criminal offenders.

Police officers also use polygraphs, the technical name for lie detectors, that measure people's heart rates and other physical responses as they answer questions. Although polygraph results are typically not admissible as evidence, police officers have often used these examinations on willing suspects and witnesses as a basis for excluding some suspects or for pressuring others to confess.

Several issues arise as police adopt new technologies. First, questions about the accuracy and effectiveness of technological developments persist, even though the developments were originally embraced with great confidence. For example, despite the long and confident use of fingerprint evidence by police and prosecutors, its accuracy has been questioned. In 2002, a federal judge ruled that expert witnesses could compare crime-scene fingerprints with those of a defendant, but they could not testify that the prints definitely matched. The judge pointed out that fingerprint evidence processes have not been scientifically verified, the error rate for such identifications has never been measured, and there are no scientific standards for determining when fingerprint samples match (Loviglio, 2002). Prosecutors later persuaded the judge to reverse his original decision and admit the expert testimony about a fingerprint match, but the judge's first decision raises the possibility that other judges will scrutinize fingerprint evidence more closely.

Second, some worry that innovative technologies will create new collisions with citizens' constitutional rights. As police gain greater opportunities for sophisticated electronic surveillance, for example, new questions arise about what constitutes a search that violates citizens' reasonable expectations of privacy. As another example, a technology that allows law enforcement agencies to intercept email messages raises questions about privacy that were not foreseeable in prior decades. Similarly, in several cities, police officers with DNA evidence from a rape have asked all the men in a particular community to submit a DNA sample from inside the cheek in order to find a match with DNA of the perpetrator. Many critics believe that innocent citizens who have done nothing suspicious should not be pressured to provide the government with a sample of their DNA. Yet, in *Maryland v. King* (2013), the Supreme Court approved a state law mandating taking DNA samples from everyone arrested for certain serious crimes despite these suspects' legal status as "presumptively innocent" prior to being actually convicted of any crime.

Communications and Computer Technology

Communications and the exchange of information serve as central elements in effective law enforcement. Dispatchers receive calls for service and bear responsibility for communicating citizens' immediate needs to patrol officers. In addition, police officers have traditionally relied on communication with dispatchers to obtain essential information, such as whether a particular car was stolen or whether a particular individual is being sought under an arrest warrant. New computer technology has altered both citizens' communications with dispatchers and police officers' reliance on their central headquarters. In addition, the use of computers and databases has enhanced the ability of law enforcement officers to investigate many kinds of crimes (E. Sullivan, 2013).

Communications   In many places, the number of calls to 911 emergency operators increased significantly as the spread of cell phones made it easier for people to call as incidents arose. In 1997, the Federal Communications Commission (FCC) set aside "311" as an option for cities to use as a nonemergency number. First Baltimore, then Detroit and New York, implemented the 311 call system, but many cities have not done so. The FCC later set aside "211" for social services information and "511" for traffic information, but relatively few cities have implemented call centers to use these numbers (McMahon, 2002). Although 911 systems can automatically trace the location of calls made from landlines, many cities are struggling to upgrade their 911 systems so that they can trace wireless calls to the vicinity of the nearest cell-phone tower (Reaves, 2010; Dewan, 2007). Such efforts to upgrade equipment, procedures, and training become more visible in the aftermath of tragedies. One such example is the murder of a University of Wisconsin student in 2008 who dialed 911 from her cell phone, apparently when confronted by an intruder in her apartment; the operator did not know her precise location or the nature of the emergency (Arnold, 2008). The 911 system remains the primary means for callers to reach their local government, but there are always concerns that those lines may become too tied up with emergency calls and thereby disrupt the ability of police and other emergency responders to receive quick reports about urgent situations.

Computers   The use of computers inside patrol cars has improved police efficiency and reduced officers' demands on central office dispatchers. Computers enable instant electronic communication that permits the radio airwaves to be reserved for emergency calls rather than being used for requests to check license numbers and other routine matters. Computer programs also permit officers to type information about traffic violations, crime suspects, and investigations directly into central computers without filling out numerous separate forms by hand. For example, new computers in the Lansing, Michigan, police department patrol cars permit officers to swipe the bar code on Michigan drivers' licenses to call up a driver's record instantly (M. Miller, 2009). Increasingly police vehicles are equipped with automated license plate readers. These readers use high-speed cameras to scan, record, and send to a central computer the license plate numbers of passing vehicles and parked cars so that officials can identify stolen vehicles as well as those associated with unpaid tickets and expired insurance (Musgrave, 2013).

Officers can also gain quick access to information about automobile license plates and pending warrants because of computers (J. Fields & Peveto, 2008). This technology can reduce the time required for an officer to process a drunken-driving arrest from four hours to less than one hour and enable officers to ticket twice as many speeders. The computer-connected officers have been shown to make more felony and misdemeanor arrests, presumably because paperwork absorbs less of their time. In a recent example, the Wyoming Highway Patrol upgraded its in-car computer systems in 2014 to give troopers new nationwide access to drivers' license checks and vehicle registrations as well as to facilitate the elimination of verbal radio traffic by enabling two-way computer messaging with dispatchers (Wyoming Highway Patrol, 2014).

The increase in efficiency gained through the use of computers may give police administrators greater flexibility in deciding how to deploy officers on patrol. However, the new technology has its costs and consequences. Patrol-car computers can require increased time and money for training officers. They also raise safety issues in that the computers become dangerous projectiles within the vehicles during high-speed pursuits or collisions. In addition, because local police departments are under the control of local governments that do not possess equal resources, some departments cannot afford to purchase computers for patrol cars.

By 2007, more than 90 percent of departments in cities with 25,000 or more inhabitants used in-vehicle computers. A survey by the U.S. Bureau of Justice Statistics reported, "From 2003 to 2007, there was an increase in the percentage of local police officers employed by a department with in-field computer access to vehicle

FIGURE 14.1
**Local Police Departments
Using Video Cameras in Patrol
Cars, 2000 and 2007**

Source: Brian A. Reaves, Local Police
Departments, 2007 (Washington,
DC: Bureau of Justice Statistics,
December 2010), 21.

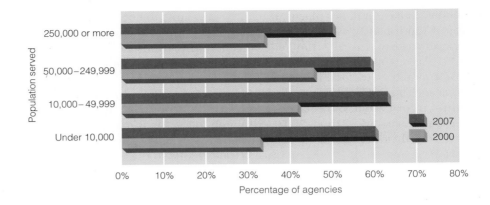

records (78% to 86%), driving records (71% to 80%), calls-for-service histories (39% to 65%), and criminal histories (39% to 56%)" (Reaves, 2010:7). From these figures, we can see that the availability of communications and information technology is expanding, yet it still varies depending on departmental resources.

As mentioned, patrol-car computers enhance police officers' investigative capabilities through quick access to databases and other sources of information that help identify suspects. Depending on the software used and the organization of databases, many officers can make quick checks of individuals' criminal histories, driving records, and outstanding warrants (Reaves, 2010). With more advanced computers and software, some officers can even receive mug shots and fingerprint records on their computer screens. Advances in technology provide a variety of possibilities for improving officers' ability to evaluate evidence at the scene of an event. With mobile scanners, officers can potentially run a quick check of an individual's fingerprints against the millions of fingerprint records stored in the FBI's database (Pochna, 2002).

Most people are familiar with the presence of dashboard cameras in many police vehicles. New developments with these systems include automatic downloads to a central computer server to avoid prior problems of running out of recording tape or filling the car's hard drive. There can be a second camera pointed at the backseat so that, without turning around, the officer can see on a screen what any arrested suspects are doing. In addition, these systems use Global Positioning Systems (GPS) to automatically record the vehicle's location, speed, and use of sirens and other emergency equipment. Thus, the technology helps to keep officers safer and provides a basis for supervisors to evaluate aspects of the officers' performance on patrol ("UTC Police," 2014). One snapshot of the speed with which the use of patrol-car technology is expanding is represented in Figure 14.1. In this available data from the U.S. Bureau of Justice Statistics, note how rapidly video cameras came into use in more and more patrol cars when this study was conducted a few years ago. Just imagine how much more technology has been put into use today.

Computers have become very important for investigating specific types of crimes, especially cyber crimes. Many police departments have begun to train and use personnel to investigate people who use computers to meet children online with the intention of luring them into exploitative relationships (Bundy, 2012). As we have seen, computer investigations also involve pursuing people who commit identity theft, steal credit card numbers, and engage in fraudulent financial transactions using computers. At the national level, federal officials must use computers to detect and prevent sophisticated efforts to hack into government and corporate computer systems in order to steal secrets or harm critical infrastructures, such as regional electrical systems and emergency warning systems (Edwards, 2014).

Computers are also essential for crime analysis and crime mapping, methods used with increasing frequency by local police departments. Through the use of **Geographic Information System (GIS)** technology and software, police departments can analyze hot spots, crime trends, and other crime patterns with a level of

Geographic Information System (GIS) Computer technology and software that permit law enforcement officials to map problem locations in order to understand calls for service and the nature and frequency of crimes and other issues within specific neighborhoods.

sophistication and precision that was previously unavailable (Ratcliffe, 2010). By analyzing the locations and frequency of specific crimes, such as burglary, or the nature of calls for service in various neighborhoods, police are better able to deploy their personnel effectively and plan targeted crime-prevention programs (Stroshine, 2005).

The use of GIS is one component of the rapidly expanding development of computer software programs that process various kinds of information in order to guide decisions about where to deploy police resources. In 2013, police officials in Tempe, Arizona, credited information analysis and data sharing for significant decreases in crime. New software helped officers to analyze crime trends and update records databases immediately. Thus, information on reported crimes, suspects, and other aspects of investigations can be accessed immediately by officers in the field. In addition, information is instantly added to national databases so that departments can share information about suspects and crime trends. Information sharing has led to greater cooperation with neighboring police departments as well as state and federal officials and contributed to solving a number of crimes (Coe, 2013).

Police officials in Santa Cruz, California, contacted researchers who had developed software to predict earthquakes and asked them to develop prediction software to anticipate when and where crimes such as burglary, bicycle thefts, and assaults were likely to take place. Based on existing crime data, officers were given reports at the start of each shift about the likeliest times and locations for specific crimes to occur. The city saw nearly a 20 percent reduction in burglaries over the course of a year even as a decrease in police personnel occurred due to budget cuts (Kelly, 2012). Based on the example of California cities following the lead of Santa Cruz, the Seattle police department began to use prediction software to address its own crime problems (deLeon, 2013).

Microsoft computer company worked with New York City to develop software called the Domain Awareness System. The system incorporates information from public surveillance cameras, license-plate readers at the city's entry bridges and tunnels, radiation detection devices around the city, and other information such as emergency calls within the city. The system proved very useful to the city in solving several highly publicized crimes. Other cities began inquiring about purchasing the system so as to employ it to address their own issues (Roberts, 2013).

Although these advances in the analysis of data place cities in the position to employ evidence-based practices, certain risks can arise from the acquisition of new technology. An audit of the Oakland, California, police department in 2012 found that the department purchased several expensive anticrime technology systems yet did not end up using them. One system did not work as expected, and then the company that sold it went out of business, so no refund or repair was possible. The use of other systems can be affected by the need to periodically upgrade software or upgrade equipment at moments when budget cuts limit resources available for new technology purchases (Kanaracus, 2012).

Another promising computerized tool for police is a system for detecting gunshots, quickly analyzing their location, and instantly communicating the information to police without reliance on human witnesses to dial the phone and guess where a shooting took place. Read the "Close Up" feature to learn about this technological advancement that assists with public safety and crime investigation.

Databases Computer technology permits law enforcement officials to gather, store, and analyze data. In minutes, or even seconds, computers can sort through data with the effectiveness that spares a user from spending hours combing through papers stored in a filing cabinet. For example, New York City detectives solved an armed robbery case in 2005 by taking a witness's description of the robber's tattoo and running it through the police department's computerized tattoo database. Very quickly, the detectives identified a suspect, showed his mug shot to the robbery victim, and tracked him down to make the arrest. The New York Police Department's database contains records on criminal complaints, warrants, 911 calls,

Gunshot Detection Technology

In January 2013, the U.S. Secret Service, the agency assigned to protect the president's safety, announced that it was interested in information about gunshot detection systems. Commentators presumed that the agency was interested in acquiring the technology for use in protecting the White House. The request called attention to a promising computerized tool that analyzes the location of gunshots and instantly communicates that information to police without reliance on human witnesses to dial the phone and guess where a shooting took place. These systems were originally developed for the military as a means to identify sniper locations. For police use, once the system is installed, it is supposed to electronically distinguish gunshots from other sounds and detect the location of the gunshots through the interaction between a series of sound sensors placed in a specific neighborhood. As a result, the system can enable police officers to drive straight to the spot of the shooting and avoid driving around a neighborhood trying to figure where a shooting occurred. The precision in pinpointing the location of the shooting can help to save the lives of shooting victims by allowing them to receive first aid more quickly as well as assist in catching whoever fired the shots.

The systems are expensive and thus difficult to acquire for many cities that are struggling with budget cuts. More than 70 cities, however, have decided that such systems are important enough for the expenditure of funds and the allocation of personnel to monitor technology. Many cities have systems that rely on technicians at a corporate headquarters far away who use satellite maps to quickly communicate the location of gunfire to the police department in the affected city. Obviously, it would be prohibitively expensive for most cities to install such systems in a way to provide coverage throughout an entire municipality. Typically, the systems are placed only in areas that have recurring crime problems involving gun violence.

Police officials generally express enthusiasm about the usefulness of the gunshot detection technology. It can provide a huge advantage over the prior practice of waiting to respond to a 911 call about gunshots without always knowing the exact location of the shooting. In addition, there is often a delay of five minutes or longer as residents decide whether or not to call the police at the sound of a gunshot. Indeed, use of gunshot detection systems has demonstrated that in certain neighborhoods, gunshots are so routine that residents do not even bother to call 911 when they hear shooting. The new technology can call police to the location even if no citizens are willing to report the gunfire. Enthusiasm for the systems is such that in Springfield, Massachusetts, a neighborhood group

raised money to acquire a system for its residential area as a way to assist police at a moment of tight budgets.

As with any technology, there are questions about the accuracy of the system, particularly with respect to distinguishing gunshots from other sounds, such as fire crackers or car horns. In addition, there has been controversy when the systems pick up and record yelling or loud conversations, troubling many privacy experts about the prospect of this technology inadvertently becoming a government surveillance system that records the private verbal communications of citizens on the streets. In 2014, Wilmington, Delaware, concluded that the particular gunshot detection system the city purchased with the assistance of $250,000 federal grant had failed to perform as expected. During a period in which 600 people called police about shootings and 175 people were shot, the system detected the sounds of gunshots only a half dozen times. This raised concerns that the range of the system's sensors was too limited to fulfill the city's purposes.

Researching the Internet

To read a government summary of research on gunshot detection technology, find the link to the website at Criminal Justice CourseMate at cengagebrain.com, then access the web links for this chapter. http://www.crimesolutions.gov /ProgramDetails.aspx?ID=273.

For Critical Analysis

If you were a mayor or police chief, how much would you be willing to spend to acquire a gunshot detection system? The systems can have annual costs of $40,000 to $60,000 per square mile of coverage. Would your answer depend on how many shootings your city typically experienced each year within a particular neighborhood? If you had to reduce any part of the police department's budget in order to acquire this technology, what cuts would you make? Describe how you would address these issues.

Sources: Erica Goode, "Shots Fired, Pinpointed and Argued Over," *New York Times*, May 28, 2012. (http://www.nytimes.com); Michelle McGuinness, "Secret Service Seeks Gunshot Detection Technology," MSN.com, January 22, 2013 (http://news.msn.com /science-technology/secret-service-seeks-gunshot-detection -technology); Paul Tuthill, "Springfield Police Expand Use of Gunshot Detection Technology," WAMC.com, March 14, 2013 (http://www.wamc.org/post/springfield-police-expand-use-gunshot -detection-technology); Greg Toppo, "Gunshot Detection System in Delaware Comes Up Blank," *USA Today*, February 7 (http://www .usatoday.com).

individuals' criminal and parole records, and other kinds of property and public records (Hays, 2006).

In the discussion that follows, keep in mind that the accuracy and usefulness of any database, including that of New York, depend on the accurate input of correct information and methods to permit the information to be accessed efficiently

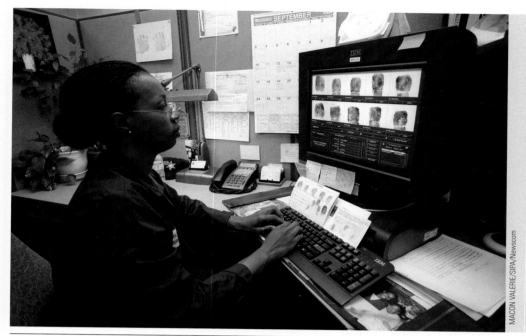

The development of databases and improvements in nationwide computer access to them help investigators identify suspects through DNA samples, fingerprints, tattoos, and other markers. Is there any information about Americans that should not be recorded in a centralized database?

by police officers. Human errors in database development and management can not only limit the usefulness of this technology but also wreak havoc in the lives of people whose information is misclassified. For example, since 9/11 many innocent people, including small children, have faced problems trying to board airplanes because their names were among the thousands on the Transportation Safety Agency's overly broad terrorist watch list. Even the late Senator Edward Kennedy of Massachusetts found himself denied plane tickets when the name "Edward Kennedy" appeared on the list (Sharkey, 2008; Swarns, 2004).

One of the largest and historically most important criminal justice databases is the fingerprint database. Police departments throughout the country can submit fingerprints from a crime scene in the hope of finding the criminal's identity from among the more than 47 million sets of fingerprints stored in the FBI computers. Local and federal law enforcement officials routinely submit the fingerprints of everyone arrested for a serious charge so that the prints can be added to the database. If a suspect is found not guilty, the prints are supposed to be removed from the system. These databases may also be used for background checks on people who work in regulated industries such as casinos and banks (Engber, 2005).

Matching fingerprints was initially time-consuming because fingerprints had to be sent to the FBI on cards. Since 1999, however, the Integrated Automated Fingerprint Identification System (IAFIS) has enabled police to send fingerprints electronically and then have those prints matched against the millions of prints in the database. The FBI can also provide electronic images of individuals' fingerprints to local law enforcement agencies upon request. Finally, the FBI provides training for state and local police on taking fingerprints and transmitting those prints to the IAFIS for evaluation.

The Department of Homeland Security has developed its own fingerprint database from two primary sources. New post-9/11 rules require the collection of fingerprints from every noncitizen entering the United States. This has created a database of more than 64 million fingerprints, which can be linked to the FBI database containing an additional 40 million sets. Military and intelligence officials are also collecting unidentified **latent fingerprints** from cups, glasses, firearms, ammunition, doorknobs, and any other objects that they find overseas in abandoned al-Qaeda training camps, safe houses, and battle sites. These prints are the patterned residue of natural skin secretions or contaminating materials such as ink, blood, or dirt that

latent fingerprints
Impressions of the unique pattern of ridges on the fingertip that are left behind on objects; these impressions are the residue of natural skin secretions or contaminating materials such as ink, blood, or dirt that were present on the fingertips at the time of their contact with the objects.

were present on the fingertips at the time of their contact with the objects. The hope is that terrorists will be identified if their fingerprints match those of visitors to the United States (Richey, 2006). As we shall see later in this chapter, DNA databases present similar hopes for identifying perpetrators, especially in domestic criminal cases (Eligon & Kaplan, 2012).

New debates have emerged about whether there should be a national database of ballistic evidence. Advocates argue that every gun sold should undergo a firing test so that its ballistic fingerprint can be stored in the database, just in case the weapon is later used in a crime. Opponents claim that this is an undesirable step toward national gun registration and that such a database would be useless because the ballistic characteristics of a gun's fired bullets change as the gun is used over time (Chaddock, 2002). The usefulness of these databases depends on the accuracy of technology to match evidence with stored information and the accessibility of database information to police departments and individual officers (M. A. Johnson, 2010). In addition, as indicated by the debate about ballistic evidence, the nature and use of evidence databases rely in part on public policy debates about what information can be gathered and how it will be used.

☑CHECK POINT

4. **How do computers in patrol cars aid officers in communication issues?**
   Officers do not need to tie up the radio airwaves and the attention of dispatchers to check on stolen cars, drivers' records, and other important information that can be accessed via computer.

5. **How can the use of Geographic Information Systems (GIS) assist criminal justice officials?**
   They can create sophisticated maps for the analyses of crime patterns and other problems in neighborhoods.

6. **What kinds of information can be collected in law enforcement databases?**
   Fingerprints, tattoos, DNA samples, gun/ballistics records.

STOP&ANALYZE

Are there other kinds of information that could be usefully stored in databases to help solve crimes? Are there any kinds of information that pose risks of error or risks to people's rights if kept in databases and used by the police?

DNA Analysis

DNA analysis A scientific technique that identifies people through their distinctive gene patterns (also called *genotypic features*). DNA, or deoxyribonucleic acid, is the basic component of all chromosomes; all the cells in an individual's body, including those in skin, blood, organs, and semen, contain the same unique DNA.

In recent years, scientific advances have enabled police and prosecutors to place greater reliance on **DNA analysis**. This technique identifies people through their distinctive gene patterns (also called *genotypic features*). DNA, or deoxyribonucleic acid, is the basic component of all chromosomes; all the cells in an individual's body, including those in skin, blood, organs, and semen, contain the same unique DNA. The characteristics of certain segments of DNA vary from person to person and thus form a genetic fingerprint. Forensic labs can analyze DNA from, for example, samples of hair, and compare them with those of suspects. As described by several law enforcement officials, the increasing effectiveness of DNA testing as an investigative tool has stemmed from "improved technology, better sharing of DNA databases among states and a drop in crime . . . that allowed detectives more time to work on unsolved cases" (Yardley, 2006). Although fingerprint evidence is still used, advances in DNA technology have greatly reduced reliance on the less precise testing of blood and hair evidence as the sole means of identifying suspects.

Forensic science laboratories perform many kinds of scientific tests. As indicated in Table 14.2, many of these labs examine narcotics, firearms, and fingerprints as well as DNA. The information in Table 14.2 is from 2009, the last year for which the Bureau of Justice Statistics has data, so one might presume that the capacity of crime labs to do additional tests has expanded over time. However, the impact of government budget cuts has affected crime labs and led to reduced capability and longer delays in processing evidence for testing (M. A. Johnson, 2010). Alabama, for example, cut the annual funding for crime labs from $15 million to $9 million

TABLE 14.2 Percentage of Labs Performing Each Function, by Jurisdiction Type

Forensic Function	Total[a]	State	County	Municipal
Controlled substances	82%	86%	85%	75%
Firearms/toolmarks	55	55	63	62
Biology screening/DNA	59	64	66	49
Latent prints	60	54	63	78
Trace evidence	50	50	55	44
Toxicology	42	50	43	35
Impressions	44	44	53	43
Crime scene	52	44	62	71
Questioned documents	16	13	13	24
Digital/computer evidence	19	10	21	32
Number of labs reporting	397	211	88	63

[a]Includes federal labs, not shown separately.

Source: M. R. Durose, K. A. Walsh, and A. M. Burch, "Census of Publicly Funded Forensic Crime Laboratories, 2009," *Bureau of Justice Statistics Bulletin*, August 2012, p. 2.

over the period of 2009 to 2012. Several crime labs were closed, and toxicology tests statewide were directed to a single lab, leading to 90-day waiting periods for police departments to obtain results (Malone, 2012).

Although many publicly funded labs are not equipped to do DNA testing, DNA analysis has become especially important in criminal justice. It is revolutionizing the use of science for the investigation of crimes. Because scientists are increasing their capacity to extract testable DNA samples from tiny samples of biological material, law enforcement officials are increasingly able to tie specific individuals to a location or piece of evidence. When the local government lab is not able to conduct DNA tests, agencies hire private labs to do the analysis.

DNA Databases   In spite of questions about which offenders should be required to submit DNA samples, many states and the federal government are building a national database of DNA records that is maintained by the FBI. Known as CODIS, which stands for Combined DNA Index System, the project began in 1990 as a pilot project serving a few state and local laboratories. CODIS has now grown to include 137 laboratories in 47 states and the District of Columbia. The federal Justice for All Act, enacted in October 2004, greatly expanded the number of offenders in the federal justice system who must submit DNA samples. Previously, samples were taken only from those who had committed specific violent crimes. Later, collection expanded to federal offenders convicted of any felony, violent act, or conspiracy. In 2009, collection of DNA samples expanded further to all people arrested for federal crimes and all noncitizens who are detained (Weiss, 2008).

The Federal Bureau of Prisons obtains DNA through blood samples from *all* incoming offenders. In addition, federal probation offices must now obtain samples under the newer law. Federal probation offices are scrambling to find qualified phlebotomists (people trained to draw blood samples), as well as to acquire enough test kits for thousands of additional offenders. Moreover, Congress mandated that the samples be collected but did not provide any funds for the probation offices within federal courts to collect these samples (Administrative Office of the U.S. Courts, 2005). Thus, the new requirement is causing budget problems in the justice system.

States throughout the country have their own laws governing DNA and which people are required to submit a sample. Depending on a particular state's law, samples are taken from either convicted offenders or those arrested for specific crimes. In 2012, for example, New York officials began to collect samples from all convicted offenders; previously the state's law mandated collection only for those convicted of specific offenses (Eligon & Kaplan, 2012). In 2008, Maryland joined a dozen other states in collecting samples from people arrested but not yet convicted for murder, rape, and assault (Arena & Bohn, 2008). California began taking samples from everyone arrested on felony charges in 2009, whether or not they are ultimately convicted of a crime (Felch & Dolan, 2008). Georgia instituted a new law in 2008 to permit investigators to compare DNA evidence with samples collected from suspects when a search warrant is obtained to require a subject to provide a sample. Previously, DNA evidence in Georgia could only be compared with samples taken from convicted felons (Armstrong, 2008). One southern California prosecutor regards DNA databases as such a useful resource for solving serious crimes that he began to dismiss some misdemeanor and drug charges against defendants if they would agree to provide a DNA sample. Skeptics questioned whether the so-called "spit and acquit" program was appropriate, because it permitted drug offenders to go free without any treatment (Weiss, 2009a).

Another proposal to expand the use of DNA testing and evidence concerns searches that look for relatives rather than the exact person whose DNA was left at the crime scene. Although only exact matches of crime-scene evidence and an individual's DNA are supposed to be used in court, it is possible to identify other suspects through wider comparisons. For example, DNA comparisons may indicate that a convicted felon whose sample is in the database is not the perpetrator of a rape, but that he is a relative of the rapist. Thus, police would have reason to undertake further investigations of the convicted felon's close male relatives. So-called "kinship-based DNA searching" is already used in Great Britain but is not used as widely in the United States (Wade, 2006).

By taking samples from people convicted of specific crimes in the state and federal systems, officials hope that CODIS will enable them to close unsolved crimes that involve DNA evidence. Unfortunately, problems and delays in collecting and processing the samples persist. Nonetheless, the use of DNA testing and databases has led to arrests in a growing number of unsolved cases.

Many examples illustrate the use of DNA identification to close cold cases. In March 2011, DNA tests on a discarded cigarette butt led to the arrest of a Connecticut man who was tied through DNA testing to 17 rapes in various eastern states from 1997 through 2009 (T. Moore, 2011). In April 2005, DNA tests linked a man in Georgia with 25 unsolved rapes in three states, including a rape committed in New York in 1973. The man had fled New York nearly 20 years earlier when facing different rape charges. He was eventually located when Georgia conducted a routine background check when the man attempted to purchase a gun. At the time, officials did not know he was linked to the other unsolved rapes, but the matches emerged when his sample was run through the national database (Preston, 2005). The successful use of the DNA database to close an old case raised officials' optimism about solving other cold cases by testing evidence that had been saved from many years ago. Such was the case, for example, of an imprisoned man in Georgia whose DNA analysis in 2006 indicated that he was responsible for four unsolved murders in Connecticut in the late 1980s and early 1990s (Yardley, 2006) and a serial murderer-rapist in Buffalo, New York, whose unsolved crimes spanned two decades (Staba, 2007).

Issues and Problems with DNA Analysis Such examples illustrate the benefit of using DNA testing and databases, but other cases demonstrate problems that need to be addressed. In Truro, Massachusetts, a writer was raped and murdered in her home in 2002. Her bloody body was found on the floor with her two-year-old daughter, who was clinging to it when a friend came to check on her whereabouts. The police sought DNA samples from all men in the small community. Their efforts to obtain these samples led to protests by civil liberties advocates who believed the rights of innocent men were threatened, especially when police said that they would look closely at men who refused to provide a sample. In April 2005, police arrested a man after his sample matched DNA from the crime scene. The suspect was the trash collector who went to the victim's house each week. Unfortunately, although the suspect had volunteered to provide a sample in April 2002, the police did not collect the sample until March 2004. Further, because of a backlog of DNA samples to be tested at the state crime lab, the sample was not evaluated until April 2005 (Belluck, 2005). This means that suspect could have committed additional crimes during the long delay.

In another example, it took police only five days to learn that a man's DNA sample in Vermont identified him as a murder suspect. Unfortunately, however, five years had already passed from the time when the man provided the DNA sample to the time when Vermont crime lab officials could put the sample in the state's database (Ring, 2005). Thus, the long delay prevented quick identification and arrest. The lack of resources for prompt tests always raises the possibility that additional crimes could have been prevented if a suspect had been identified and arrested earlier in the process.

The problem of too few laboratories and inadequate staff and equipment plagues many states and the federal government. These issues can be compounded by contemporary budget cuts. A report from the Bureau of Justice Statistics estimates that we would need 1,900 additional laboratory staff members at a cost of more than $70 million to reduce backlogs in DNA labs throughout the nation (Peterson & Hickman, 2005). These backlogs are compounded when government officials expand the categories of individuals from whom samples are taken. The move from collecting samples of convicted felons to also testing arrestees in many states, as well as detained illegal immigrants, greatly expanded the number of samples to be processed and tested. Technological advances may eventually reduce this problem. For example, the FBI laboratory now has robotic systems for processing DNA samples. The FBI's new system was designed to process 90,000 samples per month in 2010, a stark contrast to the 5,000 sample per year processed by the lab in 2002 (S. Moore, 2009).

Another potential problem with DNA testing, along with other aspects of forensic science, concerns the ethics and competence of scientists and technicians. Such problems have emerged in the FBI crime labs as well as in various states (M. A. Johnson, 2010). For example, crime laboratories in Houston and Fort Worth, Texas, were investigated and shut down after improper handling and analyzing of DNA evidence led to the convictions of people who were actually innocent. Scandals involving improper lab procedures and erroneous testimony by forensic scientists have led states such as Oklahoma and Texas to enact laws requiring crime labs to meet national accreditation standards (Kimberly, 2003).

The federal government now requires crime labs to meet these standards to qualify for federal funds, but many labs have not yet gone through the credential process. Moreover, critics contend that accreditation will not prevent mistakes and erroneous testimony by scientists and technicians with questionable ethics, skills, or knowledge. This is especially true in the worst cases, such as that of a West Virginia forensic scientist who falsified test results and provided false testimony in order to help prosecutors gain convictions (Roane & Morrison, 2005). Scientists have an obligation to present truthful and impartial analyses, so they must avoid seeing themselves as part of the law enforcement team that seeks to convict people of crimes.

The expansion of DNA databases is raising a new issue that ultimately may be viewed as related to ethics. Sometimes genetic material from an unsolved case deteriorates over the years. By the time it is tested against a database, forensic scientists may not be able to identify all 13 markers that are usually used to match individuals. However, using fewer markers creates risks that the person matched to the sample really is not guilty. In one case in Britain, a man's DNA sample matched six markers from criminal evidence, but when officials identified and tested four more markers, his DNA no longer matched (Felch & Dolan, 2008). The use of this approach and its misplaced reliance on incomplete marker comparisons can lead DNA testing to produce erroneous results.

For example, when evidence from an unsolved 1972 rape-murder in California was tested in 2004, the degraded sample provided only 5.5 markers to use in seeking to identify the perpetrator. The scientists used material from other markers, which were too faint to be conclusive evidence, as a means to produce the total of seven markers necessary for the computer search. These markers matched a man who had been convicted of rape in the late 1970s and were the basis for his prosecution and conviction for the 1972 crime. The prosecution told the jury that the odds were remote that the match was merely a coincidence. However, the defense was barred from telling the jury that there was also a one in three risk that the match was in error because of the small number of genetic markers used and the hundreds of thousands of people in the database whose samples were compared. A juror later said that the verdict would likely have been different if the jury had been given complete information about how this DNA match differed from those that match a complete set of 13 markers (Felch & Dolan, 2008).

DNA is an investigative tool for law enforcement, but it can also be used to correct grave errors by exonerating wrongly convicted people when old evidence is tested with new scientific techniques or when newly discovered evidence is tested. As of June 2014, there had been 316 post-conviction DNA exonerations, including two in 2014 in which men in New York had spent 20 years in prison for murders that they did not commit (Innocence Project, 2014). However, it can only serve this aspect of justice when evidence is properly preserved and available for later testing as DNA technology steadily improves. In the 1990s, states belatedly began to create laws concerning the preservation of evidence and opportunities for convicted offenders to obtain tests on old and on newly discovered evidence. However, errors by court clerks and lab technicians have led to the disposal of relevant evidence, even in states with laws that require preservation. In addition, many such laws impose strict time limits and other restrictions on opportunities for convicted offenders to have evidence tested. Most troubling to many critics is the tendency of prosecutors to fight against having tests conducted even when those tests might prove that an innocent person has wrongly spent many years in prison (Dewan, 2009). A more uniform and structured system of evidence preservation is necessary for DNA to benefit the justice system fully.

The increasing importance of DNA and other forensic evidence is reflected in the issues arising in the Supreme Court. In 2009, the Supreme Court decided two important cases about forensic evidence. In narrow five-to-four decisions, the justices decided that convicted offenders have no constitutional right to have available DNA evidence tested (*District Attorney's Office v. Osborne*, 2009) and that laboratory technicians who test evidence must be available for cross-examination by defense attorneys during trials (*Melendez-Diaz v. Massachusetts*, 2009). In 2013, the Court approved a state statute requiring the submission of DNA samples by people arrested for certain serious offenses (*Maryland v. King*, 2013). The Supreme Court will undoubtedly consider additional issues as technological advancements affect the nature of evidence presented in criminal cases.

Consider whether you would like to become a laboratory scientist who conducts DNA testing when you read "Careers in Criminal Justice."

☑ CHECK POINT

7. From whom is DNA collected for submission to the national database?
Federal officials and some states collect samples from all arrestees. Other states collect samples from convicted felons. Very few states do not have laws mandating collection of DNA samples from offenders.

8. What problems exist in the effective use of DNA analysis?
Inadequate resources to test the backlog of DNA samples, careless testing or unethical testimony from some labs, prosecutors' opposition to permitting convicted offenders to have DNA tests performed on old or new evidence.

STOP&ANALYZE

Should state governments increase funding for crime labs? Why or why not? If necessary, what aspects of criminal justice should receive reduced funding to allow for increased resources for crime labs?

Forensic DNA Analyst

Lindsey Murray, Forensic DNA Analyst, Bode Technology

A forensic DNA analyst, also called a forensic biologist or criminalist, is responsible for analyzing evidentiary items for biological material. This can include blood, saliva, semen, bone, or "touch DNA": samples of skin cells left behind when someone touches objects at a crime scene. The job of a DNA analyst requires meticulous laboratory skills, a desire to solve crime, and the ability to remain unbiased. The forensic DNA analyst determines whether biological material is in fact present on the evidence and, if so, who contributed that biological material.

Although some state and local laboratories require that a DNA analyst attend the crime scene to collect the evidence, most labs, including private labs, do not have this option. Rather, the evidence is collected by a crime-scene technician and sent to the agency for analysis. DNA obtained from the evidence item is then compared with a known sample, and a conclusion is made in a formal report. In addition to laboratory work, a forensic DNA analyst may be required to testify in court about his or her findings.

In order to become a forensic DNA analyst, an individual must have a bachelor of science degree in biology, chemistry, or a related field and complete four core courses: biochemistry, genetics, molecular biology, and population genetics

Photo provided by Lindsey Murray

(or statistics). Many labs recommend that an analyst obtain a master's degree in forensic science, biology, chemistry, or a related field, as this is required for higher positions such as laboratory technical leader.

In preparing for a career as forensic DNA scientist, Lindsey Murray earned an undergraduate degree in biological sciences and a graduate degree in forensic science, with a concentration in forensic biology. In addition, she gained experience in the field by taking on a thesis research project in biology and anthropology involving DNA analysis of skeletal remains. She now works for Bode Technology, a private laboratory that does scientific testing for law enforcement agencies.

One of the widespread challenges that DNA analysts face today is what's known as the "CSI effect." This is the result of popular television shows portraying a forensic DNA analyst as the primary investigator on the case. Often, these shows suggest DNA results can be obtained in just seconds from any source. This misconception may influence jurors, heighten the expectations of law enforcement agencies, and, worst of all, may show potential criminals how to cover up a crime.

Surveillance and Identification

Police have begun using surveillance cameras in many ways. Recall "The Policy Debate" presented in Chapter 5 concerning police agencies' use of camera-equipped aerial drones within the United States for search and surveillance purposes. American cities increasingly use surveillance cameras at intersections to monitor and ticket people who run red lights or exceed speed limits, although quality problems affecting the video and photographs can limit the effectiveness of these efforts (Hensley & Wynn, 2009). In Scotland, England, and Australia, law enforcement officials have adopted the use of surveillance cameras that permit police to monitor activities that occur in downtown commercial areas or other selected locations. Officials in a control room can watch everyone who passes within the cameras' fields. Advances in camera technology enable these officials to see clearly the license plate numbers of cars and other specific information. American cities, such as New York and Washington, have made moves toward experimenting with this approach to combat crime in specific areas.

Chicago has moved forward with plans for the widespread use of surveillance cameras in public places. Using a $5 million grant from the U.S. Department of Homeland Security, Chicago's 2,000 cameras will rotate 360 degrees, possess night-vision capability, and use software designed to detect suspicious activity such as someone leaving a suitcase or other potential bomb container in a busy public place (Howlett, 2004). City officials hope that surveillance will help them fight crime as well as improve their ability to identify and prevent potential acts of terrorism. Thus, the increased use of surveillance cameras in cities may become one element of local police departments' increased emphasis on homeland security. Surveillance cameras frequently help local police solve crimes such as robberies and burglaries.

Critics complain that constant surveillance by the government intrudes on the privacy of innocent, unsuspecting citizens and that there is insufficient evidence that this surveillance leads to reduced crime rates (Peralta, 2011; Taifa, 2002). There may be other problems with surveillance as well. For example, there are allegations in some British cities that bored officers in the control booth spend their time engaged in close-up monitoring of attractive women and ignore or hide evidence of police misconduct that is caught on camera. Training, supervision, and the establishment of clear procedures will be necessary to avoid such problems. Despite these allegations, the 500,000 surveillance cameras in London proved especially valuable in the aftermath of the July 2005 subway and bus terrorist bombings when officials used recorded images to identify the bombing suspects (Stecklow, Singer, & Patrick, 2005).

Cameras can also help protect rights and hold police accountable when used in different surveillance contexts. For example, some states now mandate the video recording of police interrogations for murder cases and other serious crimes. When police know that their actions are being recorded, they are less likely to engage in questionable behavior that may violate suspects' rights (Taslitz, 2012). Similarly, video cameras in police cars and surveillance cameras on buildings have caught officers engaged in crimes or using excessive force. For example, a surveillance camera showed two police officers entering and exiting an apartment building multiples times—and trying to avoid the camera in the process—on a night that led a woman to file a rape complaint against an officer who had escorted her back to her building when she was drunk (Lee, 2009). In California, a camera in 2009 recorded an officer kicking a suspect in the head after a chase (Vives & Blankstein, 2009).

An important new technology in policing is the use of personal body cameras on individual officers to record what they see. However, some officers have resisted the use of these cameras because they, in effect, are a form of surveillance on officers. Read "The Policy Debate" to consider your views.

American law enforcement officials have experimented with other surveillance and detection technologies. The National Institute of Justice provides funding to help scientists develop devices that will assist the police. For example, scanners have been developed to permit officers to detect whether individuals are carrying weapons, bombs, or drugs. Some of these devices detect foreign masses hidden on the human body, while others detect trace particles and vapors that are differentiated from those associated with human bodies and clothing (Business Wire, 2001b; PR Newswire, 2001). There are public debates about the use of backscatter X-rays at airports, both because of fears about radiation exposure for flyers every time they pass through airport security and because of privacy concerns about the near-naked image of each individual seen by the TSA officer on the monitor (Ravitz, 2009). There are also mobile versions of these scanners in vans and trucks. These models were originally designed for use by the military to detect car bombs, but they are available for broader use in border security to detect contraband in vehicles (Greenberg, 2010). They could also have applications for detection of weapons and contraband by police on America's streets.

In another example, acting under a search warrant, the FBI installed a keystroke-logging device on the computer of a suspected organized crime figure named Nicodemo Scarfo, Jr. The device detects the exact keystrokes typed, and the agents hoped to use it to discover the suspect's passwords. If police can monitor the exact keystrokes on a computer, they can learn the content of documents, outgoing Internet messages, and passwords to enable them to overcome encryption software. With such monitoring devices in place, little remains private on an individual's computer.

The use of such technology is likely to expand as part of the government's efforts to identify suspected terrorists. The USA PATRIOT Act enhances federal law enforcement officials' authority to monitor electronic communications, including the use of "roving" surveillance aimed at particular individuals without identifying

Should Police Officers Wear Individual Body Cameras?

During 2013, a highly publicized trial took place in New York City concerning allegations that police officers improperly performed hundreds of thousands of stop-and-frisk searches and that they engaged in racial discrimination in targeting young African American and Latino men. The trial judge's decision finding that the police engaged in improper actions brought attention to an emerging technology. The judge ordered a one-year pilot program for a limited number of precincts spread throughout the city in which officers would wear individual body cameras that would record their interactions with citizens. Many observers see this technology as beneficial to both police officers and citizens. The cameras can help police refute false claims that they used excessive force or engaged in improper searches. At the same time, the cameras can provide evidence if police officers violate citizens' rights. However, other observers fear that the cameras may fail to fulfill expectations and even create risks of new problems (Bruinius, 2013). In the cities that have begun using the cameras, many police officers initially resist the requirement of using the cameras because, in effect, the devices put them under constant surveillance when the recording device in operating.

For Using Individual Body Cameras

- Cameras can provide evidence of police errors and wrongdoing in conducting searches and using force on people.
- The presence of the camera will force officers to be very conscious of following proper rules of police procedure and thereby reduce the risks of mistakes and misbehavior by police.
- The cameras can help protect police officers against false claims of improper searches and excessive use of force.
- The cameras will provide a basis for supervisors to review officers' actions in order to identify errors, hold officers accountable, and identify needs for additional policies and training.
- The city of Rialto, California, experienced an 89 percent drop in complaints against officers during the first year of using the cameras (Associated Press, 2014b).

Against Using Individual Body Cameras

- Equipping entire police departments with individual cameras is expensive and not necessarily the best use of scarce resources during a time of budget shortfalls.
- The limited field in the camera's view may not record a complete and accurate picture of the circumstances facing an officer at the moment when decisions are made to use force or conduct searches.
- Camera breakdowns or limited camera views may lead to assumptions that police have intentionally failed to use

the equipment properly and then any dispute about events will weigh against the officer, even when the officer is telling the truth about what happened.

- A significant increase in the number of cameras used by a police department, in addition to the already-in-use patrol car cameras, will lead to enormous expenditures of time and money when reviewing footage in order to respond to requests for evidence or public information.
- There are risks to officers' privacy if they forget to turn the cameras off as the device will be running when they are on bathroom breaks and when they engage in private phone conversations with their own family members (Associated Press, 2014a).

What Should the Policy Be?

By 2014, roughly 3,000 law enforcement agencies had begun using the cameras with at least some of their officers. In some departments, the use of the technology has gone smoothly and officers come to view the device as protecting them against false allegations. In other departments, concerns have arisen about the development of appropriate policies and practices. If there is an allegation against the officer, should the officer be able to view the footage before answering questions about the incident? If the officer is not allowed to view the footage, will inconsistencies between the footage from the camera and the officer's statement be viewed with sensitivity to the fact that the officer's honest perceptions and memories of the entire context are not fully captured in the recording? In the New York City case, the judge's order was presented in order to consider how to address a specific problem. In such situations, the cameras have a very specific purpose: ensure that officers properly follow the law in a city where evidence has shown that improper behavior occurred. In places that have not been proven to have problems with police behavior, is there enough reason to undertake the expense and risks of using the cameras?

Researching the Internet

To read a study on the Police Foundation's website about the effects of police body cameras, visit the Criminal Justice CourseMate at cengagebrain.com, then access the links for http://www.policefoundation.org/content/body-worn-camera.

Analyzing the Issue

Imagine that you and your classmates are advisors to a city's mayor and police chief. Discuss the competing arguments and issues surrounding the use of body cameras by police. Prepare a recommendation that includes the three most significant arguments and concerns on each side of the issue.

or limiting specific facilities and devices to be monitored (Savage, 2011). In 2012, controversies emerged about cell phone companies providing information to local police agencies that sought to monitor individuals without obtaining a court order (Lichtblau, 2012).

The U.S. Supreme Court has already given a sign that it will look critically at some new police technologies. In *United States v. Jones* (2012), the justices decided that placing a GPS device on a car to follow a suspected drug trafficker's movements constituted a "search" and therefore required a warrant or a sufficient justification. Officers cannot freely place electronic monitoring devices on vehicles.

In *Kyllo v. United States* (2001), law enforcement officials pointed a thermal-imaging device at a house to detect unusual heat sources that might indicate marijuana being cultivated under grow lights. Their efforts led to a search of the home and the discovery of 100 marijuana plants. In the majority opinion, Justice Antonin Scalia declared the use of the device in this manner to be an illegal search. According to Scalia, "Obtaining by sense-enhancing technology any information regarding the interior of the home that could not otherwise have been obtained without physical intrusion into a constitutionally protected area constitutes a search" and is therefore covered by the limitations of the Fourth Amendment, especially the warrant requirement (*Kyllo v. United States*, 2001:2043). Thus, it is not clear how judges may evaluate the constitutionally permissible uses of new technologies.

Kyllo v. United States (2001) Law enforcement officials cannot examine a home with a thermal-imaging device unless they obtain a warrant.

☑ CHECK POINT

9. **What issues have been raised concerning police surveillance technology, including scanners used to examine people boarding planes at airports?**
   There are concerns about government intrusions on people's privacy as well as concerns about other impacts of specific technologies, such as radiation exposure from X-ray devices.

STOP&ANALYZE

What government surveillance activities, if directed at you, your computer, and your communications, would you consider to be going "too far" if officials did not have a basis to suspect you of any wrongdoing? Should police be required to seek a search warrant from a judge before monitoring any activities on computers and cell phones?

Weapons Technology

Police officers have been sued in many cases when they injured or killed people without proper justification. Some of these lawsuits have resulted in cities and counties paying millions of dollars to people who were injured when police used guns or nightsticks improperly or in an inappropriate situation. To avoid future lawsuits, departments have given greater attention to the training of officers. They have also sought nonlethal weapons that could be used to incapacitate or control people without causing serious injuries or deaths. Traditional **less-lethal weapons**, such as nightsticks and pepper spray, can be used only when officers are in close contact with suspects, and they are not suitable for all situations that officers face.

Police officers need to have the ability to incapacitate agitated people who are threatening to harm themselves or others. This need arises when they confront someone suspected of committing a serious crime as well as when they are attempting to control a crowd causing civil disorder. They also seek to enhance their ability to stop criminal suspects from fleeing. A variety of less-lethal weapons have been developed to accomplish these goals. Police use some of them widely, while others are still undergoing testing and refinement.

Projectile weapons shoot objects at people whom the police wish to subdue. Some projectiles, such as rubber bullets, can travel a long distance. Others are employed only when suspects are within a few yards of the officers. Rubber bullets have been used for many years. Although they are generally nonlethal, they can cause serious injuries or death if they hit someone in the eye or elsewhere in the head. Many departments have turned to the use of beanbags, small canvas bags containing tiny lead beads, fired from a shotgun (C. Spencer, 2000). They are intended to stun people on impact without causing lasting injury. Several police departments in the Los Angeles area, however, abandoned the use of beanbags because of concerns about injuries and a few deaths caused by these projectiles as well as dissatisfaction with their accuracy when fired at a target (Leonard, 2002).

less-lethal weapons Weapons such as pepper spray and air-fired beanbags or nets that are meant to incapacitate a suspect without inflicting serious injuries.

Other departments have used air guns that shoot PepperBalls, small plastic pellets filled with a peppery powder that causes coughing and sneezing on release after the suspect is stunned by the impact of the pellet. This weapon drew increased scrutiny after an Emerson College student died when she was hit in the eye by such a pellet as police officers attempted to disperse a crowd of revelers who were celebrating a Boston Red Sox victory (CNN, 2004a). Officers can also fill the pellets with green dye in order to mark and later arrest individuals in an out-of-control crowd (Randolph, 2001).

Other weapons under development include one that shoots nets that wrap around individual suspects and another that sprays a fountain of foam that envelops the suspect in layers of paralyzing ooze. Law enforcement agencies may also eventually have versions of new weapons being developed for the military, such as devices that send out incapacitating blasts of heat or blinding flash explosions (Hambling, 2005). For example, a new military weapon called "Silent Guardian" shoots a focused beam of radiation that is tuned precisely to stimulate human pain nerves. It inflicts unbearable, incapacitating pain but, according to the inventors, does not cause injuries (Hanlon, 2007). A law enforcement version, if it worked as intended, could be an alternative to using lethal firearms in some situations.

Conducted-energy devices, such as Tasers, now give police officers the opportunity to subdue threatening people by using less-than-lethal force, when in prior years they might have used firearms. Because some people have died after being subjected to these alternative weapons, controversies exist about whether their use should be strictly limited to truly dangerous situations. Are there risks that new weapons technology will be used in the field without fully understanding the harm that may be inflicted on people with specific medical conditions or other vulnerabilities?

For suspects who are close at hand, many police departments use CEDs—conducted energy devices—the most well-known of which is the Taser, a weapon with prongs that sends an incapacitating electric jolt of 50,000 volts into people on contact (Ith, 2001). Recent research found a rise in citizen injuries from the use of CEDs and urged greater attention to their use and their consequences (Terrill & Paoline, 2012). More than 12,000 law enforcement agencies in the United States use these devices. As a result, there is great potential for the devices to be used frequently. However, a study by Amnesty International found that more than 330 people died in the United States between 2001 and 2008 after being shocked by Tasers (Ferretti & Feighan, 2009). Nearly all of them were unarmed. Some of those who received shocks for failing to obey police commands reportedly suffered from mental or physical disabilities that impeded their ability to cooperate. The manufacturer of Tasers as well as some researchers dispute whether the device actually caused the deaths.

Issues have also arisen about whether officers are too quick to use Tasers when they could use persuasion or other means to calm agitated or uncooperative people. The controversy reached a high point when Miami police officers used a Taser on a six-year-old child who was threatening to harm himself (CNN, 2004b). In late 2012 and early 2013, there were news reports of cities in Utah, Ohio, and North Carolina paying large sums to settle significant lawsuits based on deaths and permanent injuries that occurred after police officers' use of CED weapons (Callahan, 2013; Adams, 2012; T. Reaves, 2012). One man's death in Utah led that state's legislature to enact a resolution encouraging police departments to participate in specific training on how to handle uncooperative mentally ill people without resorting quickly to the use of force (Rogers, 2011).

The development of less-lethal weapons has undoubtedly saved officers from firing bullets in many situations in which they previously would have felt required to shoot threatening suspects. The use of CEDs may reduce overall injuries to officers and citizens (Bulman, 2010). However, as with all technologies, these weapons do not magically solve the problem of incapacitating suspects safely. Mechanical problems or misuse by the officer may make the new weapons ineffectual. In addition, officers may act too quickly in firing a less-lethal weapon during inappropriate situations. In such circumstances, needless minor injuries may be inflicted, or the targeted person may become more enraged and thus more threatening to the officers who later must transport the person to jail. Moreover, an officer can carry only so many weapons in her or his arms. The existence of less-lethal weapons will not ensure that such weapons are actually handy when officers must make difficult, on-the-spot decisions about how to handle a threatening situation.

☑ **CHECK POINT**

10. What kinds of new weaponry have police employed?
Less-lethal weapons, including beanbag projectiles, CEDs, and PepperBall projectiles.

STOP&ANALYZE

Should all police officers submit themselves during training to receive the application of any less-than-lethal weapons that they might be called upon to use? Why or why not?

Technology in Courts and Corrections

Much of the investment in new technology has been directed toward surveillance equipment and investigation techniques, including DNA analysis, that will assist law enforcement officers in identifying and convicting criminal offenders. Although fewer resources have been directed toward technology in other segments of the criminal justice system, courts and corrections both face new issues and opportunities stemming from the use of technology.

Courts

Many local courthouses struggle to keep up with the processing of cases and the attendant consequences of case backlogs. One of the central issues for many busy courthouses is simply the matter of having case files up-to-date and readily available for judges, prosecutors, and defense attorneys. The volume of files in many courthouses can create storage and accessibility problems. There are only so many rooms and filing cabinets available for storing files in any building. Thus, older files may be moved to remote locations where they are not easily accessible and must be retrieved if a case is reexamined on appeal or through later motions concerning the discovery of new evidence and other matters.

electronic file management
Computerization of court records done to reduce reliance on paper documents and make documents easily accessible to the judge and attorneys via computer.

Technology provides a mechanism for reducing the problems of "too much paper" in courthouse files. Many courts have moved toward **electronic file management** systems in which records are digitized and made available as computer files. Such systems typically also use electronic filing systems in which attorneys file motions and other documents via email rather than as traditional paper documents.

One example of a court moving toward a reduction in paper used for case processing is the state circuit court in Eaton County, Michigan. The prosecutors carry into the courtroom laptops that can wirelessly access police reports, 911 calls, court orders, and crime-scene photos. As noted by the county prosecutor, "We go to court with much more information than a prosecutor carrying a stack of files" (Grasha, 2009a). Gradually, other courts throughout the country are purchasing equipment and software to enable efficient access to information and to reduce the costs of producing and storing paper documents (Richter & Humke, 2011).

Computers, projection screens, and other technologies permit attorneys to present evidence more effectively in the courtroom. Do these high-tech presentations necessarily advance the search for truth?

Don Hogan Charles/The New York Times/Redux Pictures

Computers can also help increase efficiency in judges' calculation of possible sentencing options. The development of sentencing guidelines has reduced judges' discretion for determining appropriate sentences. Instead, judges add up points, based on the offense and the prior record, to determine the sentence range mandated by the legislature. Private computer companies have developed software that will do sentencing calculations quickly for judges and for the probation officers who write presentence reports.

Does relying on computer calculations pose any risks? Obviously, if incorrect numbers are included in the calculations, an improper sentence will be produced. For defendants with complex records, such as numerous arrests and probation violations, the person inputting the data could easily miscount arrests and reported probation violations in the score, even though the sentence is supposed to be based on the number of actual criminal convictions. More importantly, does the software program diminish the image of justice, giving the impression that sentencing occurs by machine? State judges are supposed to represent the community, delivering messages about justice on the community's behalf as they make rulings.

The presentation of evidence in court is changing through the introduction of new technology. Previously, lawyers presenting documents and objects as evidence often needed to carry them in front of jurors or have jurors pass them through the jury box. This meant that jurors often got only a fleeting glimpse of specific pieces of evidence. Now, many courthouses are developing electronic courtrooms, using presentation technologies that have long been used in business meetings. These mechanisms include projection screens or multiple monitors that permit jurors to study documents and photographs simultaneously. Websites of U.S. district courts often list the equipment available in each courtroom and instruct attorneys on how to use the equipment. For example, a partial list of equipment presented on one district court's website includes the following:

- *Evidence presentation cart*, containing
  Evidence camera
  Annotation monitor
  Microphone
  VCR
  Auxiliary connections

- *Counsel table*, containing
  PC connection
  Internet access
  Real-time court reporting connection
- *Jury box/plasma screen.* A 50-inch retractable plasma screen over the jury box can be lowered when needed.
- *Gallery. Two* monitors are located on the sides of the gallery to allow spectators to see evidence being presented during a court proceeding.
- *Side camera.* A side camera is located near the ceiling above the jury box. It is used to display demonstrative exhibits that may be placed on a tripod easel in front of the jury box or by the witness stand. Use of the side camera allows the judge, the witness, the jury, all counsel, and those seated in the gallery to view the exhibit with ease.
- *Hearing assistance system.* Wireless headphones are available for use by the hearing impaired or for language interpretation.
- *Color video printer.* The printer is available should counsel wish to print a displayed image for admission into evidence.

Such technologies are obviously useful in communicating more effectively to everyone in the courtroom. There are risks, however, that some uses of technology may distort rather than clarify an accurate understanding of the evidence. For example, the use of computer simulations raises issues about the accurate presentation of evidence.

Attorneys have traditionally attempted to use their words to "paint a picture" for the jurors. In a criminal case, the prosecutor and defense each presents its own version of a chain of events or the circumstances under which a crime allegedly occurred. It is entirely possible that after hearing the same presentations, individual jurors will leave the courtroom with very different perceptions about what happened at the crime scene (McCormick, 2000). Contemporary attorneys have attempted to use computer technology to advance an image of their version of events. Much like realistic video games, similar realism has now been developed in computer-generated re-creations of crime scenes (McCormick, 2000). The jury may see, for example, a computer-generated film of a person being struck from behind or falling in a manner consistent with the victim's injuries. Yet, this film will be prepared in accordance with a particular version of events, the prosecutor's or the defendant's. There are risks that the realism of the re-created events on the screen will stick in the minds of jurors, even if the presentation is not an objective interpretation of the facts in the case (Schofield, 2011). Judges and attorneys must be wary about the use of such technologies if they distort perceptions rather than contribute to accurate fact-finding.

Problems also arise through jurors' use of technology. Typically, a judge will tell jurors that they cannot investigate the facts of a case on their own. They are sometimes instructed not to read any articles in a newspaper about the case being presented before them. The widespread use of the Internet, however, makes seeking information about a case not only easy but also quite tempting for some jurors. Whereas a judge may hear if a juror attempted to visit a crime scene and thereby exclude the juror from the trial for misconduct, it is much more difficult to know whether jurors have sought information about a case through an Internet search. The use of such devices as iPhones and BlackBerrys has even enabled disobedient jurors to do their own research on a case during a lunch break in the middle of the attorneys' arguments. In one case in Florida, 8 out of 12 jurors eventually admitted that they had done their own Internet research on the case, including finding information that was excluded from presentation at trial through the rules of evidence. Thus, the judge had to declare a mistrial, and eight weeks of work by prosecutors and defense attorneys went to waste; the long, complex trial had to begin again after the selection of a new jury (Schwartz, 2009).

Problems have also arisen as jurors use blogs and social media sites to post announcements about the progress of a case or about jury deliberations. There is evidence that some jurors even send out messages by cell phone during breaks in the

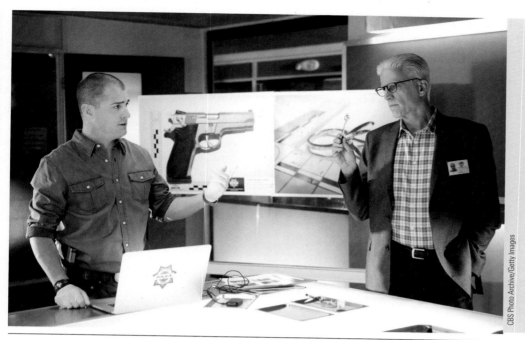

Many prosecutors and judges worry that the "*CSI* effect" may help guilty defendants go free if there is no DNA or other scientific evidence to use against them. Critics claim that the "*CSI* effect" is a myth that is perpetuated by prosecutors and the media. What evidence would you want to see in order to conclude whether or not the "*CSI* effect" exists?

trial (Schwartz, 2009). Thus, judges have become more keenly aware of the need to bar jurors from bringing cell phones to court as well as the need to give thorough and stern warnings about the rule against jurors conducting their own investigations. Under the adversarial system, evidence is presented by the opposing attorneys who have been trained to respect the rules of evidence. Independent examinations of evidence by jurors acting as amateur detectives can enhance risks of inaccurate conclusions about facts. Because of media attention directed at the misbehavior of jurors in San Francisco, starting in 2012, California implemented a new law that authorized judges to impose jail sentences on jurors who used cell phones or other devices to either research a case or provide information to others about a case (Ward, 2011).

Another potential impact of technology on jury trials is embodied in fears of a so-called **CSI effect** that makes jurors unwilling to render "guilty" verdicts unless there is scientific evidence to link the defendant to the crime. Americans are fascinated by dramatized television programs that show the use of science for solving crimes and medical mysteries. According to a 2009 Harris Poll, the television show *CSI: Crime Scene Investigation* set in Las Vegas is Americans' all-time favorite television series (Harris Poll, 2009). The show was so popular that the CBS network created two *CSI* spin-off shows, set in Miami and New York, respectively. The fourth most popular show is *NCIS*, a parallel drama about the U.S. Navy's Criminal Investigative Service, which also portrays the use of forensic science. The third most-popular program, *House*, shows the use of science to solve medical mysteries (Harris Poll, 2009).

Because these popular programs portray specialists using science to make definitive conclusions, many judges and prosecutors believe jurors now erroneously think there should be DNA evidence, soil sample testing, and other scientific evidence in every criminal case (Toobin, 2007). In fact, the evidence in many cases consists of witness testimony, circumstantial evidence, and objects with no fingerprints or DNA on them. Moreover, the television programs show fictional situations in which experts instantly make accurate and definitive conclusions about a "match" between hair samples, fiber samples, handwriting samples, or other materials for which real forensic scientists have grave doubts about anyone's ability to make definitive identifications of suspects.

Students of criminal justice should regard claims about the *CSI* effect with caution. The claims emerge from individual prosecutors' and judges' feelings of surprise or disappointment with the decisions and questions of juries in particular cases.

CSI effect A widely discussed but unproved belief that television dramas revolving around forensic science raise jurors' expectations about the use of scientific evidence in criminal cases and thereby reduce the likelihood of "guilty" verdicts in trials that rely solely on witness testimony and other forms of nonscientific evidence.

Moreover, because news stories have presented the *CSI* effect as if it were a real phenomenon, prosecutors and judges may merely assume that it has an impact when, in fact, it may not even exist.

In reality, the existence of any actual *CSI* effect remains the subject of debate (S. Stephens, 2007). Actual research on the *CSI* effect calls its existence into question (Podlas, 2006). Surveys indicate that jurors may expect to see specific kinds of scientific evidence, but this expectation may be related to a more general "tech effect" of American using technology in their daily lives rather than watching specific television shows. Moreover, the increased expectation for scientific evidence does not necessarily mean that jurors will not vote to convict a defendant without it (Huey, 2010). The debate about the *CSI* effect illustrates the possibility that decision making within the criminal justice system can be affected by popular perceptions and assumptions about the role of technology and science in the investigation of criminal cases.

☑ CHECK POINT

11. **How is technology employed in courthouses?**
    Electronic file management for records and presentation technology in courtrooms for displaying evidence.

12. **How can technology disrupt jury trials?**
    Jurors using the Internet to investigate cases or using blogs and social media sites to reveal information about jury deliberations; risks of the so-called *CSI* effect.

STOP&ANALYZE

Should one side in a case be permitted to present computer simulations in the courtroom if the other side—such as a poor defendant represented by a public defender—cannot afford to hire consultants who are experts in using technology?

Corrections

Many of the technologies previously discussed for policing and courts also have applications in corrections. Computerized record keeping and statewide databases can reduce the burden of maintaining, storing, and transporting paper files on each prisoner. Instead, officials throughout the state can access records instantly via computer. In fact, many states have set up online records-retrieval systems that are accessible to the public. Often called OTIS (Offender Tracking Information Systems), these accessible databases permit crime victims to keep track of when specific offenders gain release on parole. They can also help employers to do background checks on job applicants. Separate public-access information systems often provide specific information on the residences of convicted sex offenders. Typically, members of the public can use the state correctional department's website to discover the identities and home addresses of sex offenders within a specific zip code. These databases are intended to warn people about the presence of a specific category of ex-convicts in their neighborhoods.

Public access to information about ex-offenders can cause serious problems. In Maine, Washington, and New Hampshire, individuals looked up the names and addresses of released sex offenders on a state database, then hunted them down and shot them. As we saw in Chapter 13, one of the murder victims in Maine was on the sex offender registry for the "sex crime" of misdemeanor sexual abuse because, as a 19-year-old youth, he had consensual sex with his girlfriend, who was two weeks shy of making their sexual contact legal by reaching her sixteenth birthday (Ellement & Smalley, 2006). These crimes led to debates about which offenders should actually be listed in databases and whether such databases should be open to the public.

In correctional institutions, technology enhances safety and security through the use of such developments as electronically controlled cell doors and locks, motion sensors, surveillance cameras, and small radios attached to the shirts of correctional officers. Note that surveillance cameras are not always popular with correctional officers, because cameras also reveal whether officers are doing their jobs conscientiously and properly. There is also a big push in many prisons to provide body armor for correctional officers. Although the stiff vests may be uncomfortable and make upper-body movements less free and easy, they can save lives by protecting officers against being stabbed by inmates' homemade knives (U.S. Government Accountability Office, 2011).

Because security is the top priority for correctional institutions, most technology resources are devoted to this goal rather than on prisoners' vocational training and rehabilitation. In a fast-changing world, prisoners who face the challenges of reentry are often like Rip Van Winkle, the character in the Washington Irving short story who awakens after sleeping for 20 years and discovers many changes in the world. For a contemporary inmate emerging from prison after serving a long sentence, basic facts of modern life, such as email and cell phones, may be completely unknown or baffling. Released prisoners may also lack basic skills for modern employment, such as the rudimentary use of computers, word processing, and spreadsheet programs. Although new technologies change modern life, limited resources cause correctional officials to focus on improvements in security rather than on a fuller range of goals serving prisoners.

As in policing, technological developments increase the variety of less-lethal weapons that are available for correctional officers to use in subduing and controlling offenders who pose a threat to institutional safety or who attempt to escape. Corrections officers typically do not have weapons when they are working within the prison population because they can have weapons taken away from them as they are so outnumbered by the prisoners. In 2012, however, Michigan began issuing Tasers for corrections officers to improve safety by enabling officers to break up fights without putting themselves at risk by becoming physically involved in the conflict (Kloepfer, 2012). It remains to be seen if there are adverse consequences from the presence of the CED less-lethal weapons within the yard and cell blocks that are numerically dominated by prisoners.

The transportation of prisoners presents a daily challenge for officials at courts, jails, and prisons. People in custody must be moved from jails and prisons to courts for hearings. They must be transferred from jails to prisons and moved between different prisons when they begin to serve their sentences. New technologies have been developed to prevent prisoners from attempting to escape or otherwise misbehaving while being transported. The most controversial device is the remote-controlled stun belt that prisoners may be required to wear while being transported. The deputy or bailiff in control of the belt can deliver an excruciating eight-second, 50,000-volt jolt of electricity to prisoners. Americans became aware of the belts when a California prisoner, who was zapped in a courtroom at the order of a judge, filed a $50 million lawsuit. The prisoner had not attempted to escape or threaten anyone; he had merely talked too much when the judge had told him to be silent (Canto, 1998). The international human rights organization Amnesty International mounted a campaign to have the devices banned as torture (Amnesty International, 1999). Although the New York Corrections Department canceled an order for the devices, 25 state correctional departments and 100 county jails reportedly still use them.

Such devices may reduce the number of officers required to escort a prisoner, and they deter prisoners from misbehaving. However, such a jolt of electricity may kill some people if their heart rhythm is susceptible to disruption or if they hit their heads when they fall during the electric shock. There are also issues about whether officers will limit their use to appropriate circumstances.

One particularly important and expanding use of technology is the electronic monitoring of offenders within the community. Offenders in home confinement or "on tether" in the community wear various electronic devices that help monitor whether they obey curfews, remain at home, or otherwise fulfill restrictions about where they are permitted to be. Increasingly, local jails save money by charging fees to nonviolent offenders who choose to pay for electronic monitoring and home confinement rather than imposing expenses on the county for food and supervision by serving their misdemeanor sentences in jail (Grasha, 2009b). There is also expanded use of monitors with GPS capability to track the movements of criminal stalkers and perpetrators of domestic violence. Thus, law enforcement officials can be warned if individuals under restraining orders attempt to approach the homes of their victims (A. Green, 2009).

☑ **CHECK POINT**

13. **Corrections has several goals. Which of these goals is advanced by the use of technology?**
   Technology is used for security, control surveillance, and record keeping, but technology resources are less likely to be devoted to rehabilitation.

STOP&ANALYZE

If you were a prison warden, would you require corrections officers to wear body armor? How would you respond to their complaints that the vests are too hot in the summer and interfere with their mobility if they need to run to another part of the prison to respond to an urgent situation?

Current Questions and Challenges for the Future

As we have just seen, technological changes have affected nearly every agency and process within the criminal justice system. Most of this chapter's discussion has focused on new technological devices designed to assist officials with specific tasks. James Byrne (2008) classifies these devices as "hard technology" and contrasts them with the development of "soft technology," such as computer software for crime mapping and sentencing calculations. Both categories of technology are important for criminal justice. In some respects, the soft technology may present especially significant possibilities for affecting the performance of criminal justice officials, as computer experts invent new ways to gather and evaluate information that can be used for training, classification of offenders, risk assessment, and other important purposes. Table 14.3 shows examples of various hard and soft technological innovations that have affected each institutional segment of the criminal justice system.

There is no doubt that the desire for efficiency and effectiveness will lead to continued efforts to create new technologies and refine existing technologies to assist the police in their tasks. One can easily envision increased access to information through computers, better surveillance cameras and body scanners, and expanded use of GPS devices. In addition, there will be continued development and experimentation with less-lethal weapons, some of which are likely to be borrowed from those being developed by the U.S. military, including devices that rely on heat or light or sound to incapacitate threatening individuals.

In light of financial problems affecting state and local correctional budgets, there will inevitably be efforts to refine and expand the use of surveillance and monitoring technology to reduce the costs associated with confining lesser offenders. For example, the future will likely see the expanded use of ignition interlock systems for convicted drunken drivers. In this system, drivers blow into a tube set up in their car, and the engine starts only if they have not consumed alcohol. This can help prevent drunken driving without relying so heavily on incarceration for first offenders. New and expanded use of surveillance and control mechanisms may also improve officials' ability to monitor probationers, parolees, and other offenders under correctional supervision in the community.

As noted, technological developments produce risks, questions, and consequences beyond increased efficiency in carrying out tasks. Technological devices are operated by human beings who can make errors that affect the lives of others. What happens when a forensic scientist makes an error in conducting a test? What happens when incorrect information about an individual is entered into a database? With a perception that new weapons will not cause serious injury or death, are police officers more inclined to use CEDs, PepperBalls, and other less-lethal weapons in situations that might otherwise have been resolved through determined use of verbal warnings and other communications? These are important questions that arise with increasing frequency as we analyze events in which technology produced unintended and undesirable results.

TABLE 14.3 The Application of Hard and Soft Technology to Crime Prevention and Control

	Hard Technology	Soft Technology
Crime prevention	• CCTV • Street lighting • Citizen-protection devices (e.g., Mace, Tasers) • Metal detectors • Ignition interlock systems (drunk drivers)	• Threat assessment instruments • Risk assessment instruments • Bullying ID protocol • Sex offender registration • Risk assessment prior to involuntary civil commitment • Profiling
Police	• Improved police protection devices (helmets, vests, cars, buildings) • Improved/new weapons • Less-than-lethal force (mobile/riot control) • Computers in squad cars • Hands-free patrol car control (Project 54) • Offender and citizen IDs via biometrics/fingerprints • Gunshot-location devices	• Crime mapping (hot spots) • Crime analysis (e.g., COMPSTAT) • Criminal-history data systems enhancement • Info sharing within CJS and private sector • New technologies to monitor communications (phone, mail, Internet) to/from targeted individuals • Amber alerts
Court	• The high-tech courtroom (computers, video, cameras, design features of buildings) • Weapon-detection devices • Video conferencing • Electronic court documents • Drug testing at pretrial stage	• Case-flow management systems • Radio frequency identification technology • Data warehousing • Automation of court records • Problem-oriented courts
Institutional corrections	• Contraband detection devices • Duress alarm systems • Language-translation devices • Remote monitoring • Perimeter screening • Less-than-lethal force in prison • Prison design (supermax) • Expanded use of segregation units	• Use of simulations as training tools (mock prison riots) • Facial-recognition software • New inmate classification systems (external/internal) • Within-prison crime analysis (hot spots; high-rate offenders) • Information sharing with police, community, victims, and community-based corrections (reentry)
Community corrections	• GPS for offender monitoring and location-restriction enforcement • New devices (breathalyzers, instant drug tests, language translators, plethysmographs) • Polygraph tests (improved) • Laptops/GPS for line staff • Reporting kiosks	• New classification devices for sex, drugs, and MI [mentally ill] offenders • New workload software • New computer monitoring programs for sex offenders • Information with community police, treatment providers (for active offender supervision and for absconder location)

Source: James M. Byrne, "The Best Laid Plans: An Assessment of the Varied Consequences of New Technologies for Crime and Social Control," *Federal Probation* 72 (no. 3, 2008): 11.

Equally important are concerns about the impact of technology on the civil rights and liberties of individual Americans. In the post-9/11 era, there are already indications that some government officials will react to perceived threats by making use of available technology without necessarily planning for the protection of civil liberties or adherence to existing law. The administration of President George W. Bush, for example, secretly intercepted Americans' phone calls and emails without the court authorizations required under federal law (Sanger & Lichtblau, 2006). When Congress later granted limited authority to undertake such electronic surveillance of communications, the National Security Agency (NSA) violated the law by intercepting calls that did not fall within the scope of the law (Lichtblau & Risen, 2009).

Similar complaints arose concerning actions in the Obama administration as information became public about the NSA keeping records of Americans' phone calls (Gellman & Soltani, 2014). As with other technologies, the means available could be misused in ways that violate Fourth Amendment restrictions on unreasonable searches and other rights under the Constitution. Read "A Question of Ethics" below to consider what policies you would develop to address these issues.

Another large question looms. Have new technologies been effective in preventing crime and catching criminals? We know that certain technologies, such as DNA testing, have been highly effective in identifying individuals whose biological matter, such as blood or tissue, is found at a crime scene or on a weapon. It is less clear, however, that all of the surveillance, communications, and search technologies have produced entirely desirable benefits. For example, in pointing to declining clearance rates for homicide crimes, James Byrne concludes, "I would be hard pressed to offer an assessment of the positive effect of new technological innovations during this period given these data on police performance" (2008:14). The underlying point is that we know many new technologies expand the scope of social control by government through collecting information, watching and searching the citizenry, and providing new tools for police to use in coercing compliant behavior (as in CEDs). Are the costs of this social control justified? Can we use the benefits of technology without reducing the extent of Americans' freedom and privacy? These are questions that future criminal justice officials and policymakers must continually reexamine. They can do this by systematically studying the performance of police, courts, and corrections as well as by evaluating the consequences for Americans' civil liberties.

☑CHECK POINT

14. What questions about technology will bear watching in the future?

How will government budget problems affect the use of technology? How will the risk of human errors affect the use of technology? How will technology impact civil rights and liberties? Are new technologies actually effective in preventing crime and catching criminals?

STOP&ANALYZE

If you were a governor or mayor struggling with difficult budget choices as tax revenues decline, what decisions would you make about technology affecting criminal justice? Would increasing the use of technology be a high priority for you? If so, what other aspects of the government budget would you cut to advance this priority? Among the various technologies currently available, which ones would you regard as especially worthy of additional expenditures from your budget? Why?

A QUESTION OF ETHICS

Think, Discuss, Write

In 2011, newspaper stories described a dispute between the Michigan State Police and the American Civil Liberties Union (ACLU) over state troopers' reported use of forensic cell-phone analysis devices that can extract information from cell phones. The ACLU became aware that troopers used the devices to obtain information from drivers' cell phones at traffic stops, and the organization complained that such actions could constitute a violation of drivers' Fourth Amendment right against unreasonable seizures. Many members of the public did not know that such devices existed, let alone that the police could use them to quickly copy phone numbers, text messages, photos, and other information stored in people's cell phones and smartphones.

The Michigan State Police initially refused to provide information to the ACLU about its use of the devices. Amid growing public attention, the agency issued a statement saying that the devices are only used when the police have a search warrant or when the cell-phone owner consents to the search of the phone.

Discussion/Writing Assignment

Cell phones and smartphones may contain evidence of crimes, such as messages about drug trafficking or child pornography; thus, law enforcement officials may be tempted to find out what information people have in their phones. However, the phones may also contain very personal messages and photos owned by innocent people who have no connection to crime. If you were the commander of the Michigan State Police, what policies would you put in place to ensure that your officers were not tempted to use the devices merely to undertake "fishing expeditions" on drivers' phones during traffic stops or other encounters with the public. Describe at least four policies and practices that you would recommend, and explain your reasons for each one.

Source: "ACLU Concerned over Michigan State Police Extracting Data from Cellphones," *Los Angeles Times*, April 21, 2011 (www.latimes.com).

SUMMARY

❶ Describe how adaptation and belief in science can affect the use of technology.

- New technology can be employed by criminals as well as by criminal justice officials.
- Criminal justice officials and the public must be wary of automatically assuming that new scientific developments will achieve their intended goals or will produce only desirable consequences.

❷ Identify the various aspects of cyber crime and counterfeiting.

- Cyber crime includes identity theft, Internet child pornography, hackers' theft of trade secrets, and destruction of computer networks.
- Counterfeiting extends beyond currency and consumer goods to include dangerous and worthless fake prescription drugs.

❸ Explain the role of communications, computers, and databases in policing.

- Calls for service to police have expanded from 911 numbers to 311 and 211 for nonemergency purposes.
- Computers in patrol cars have expanded police officers' access to information.
- Police also use computers in crime mapping, gunshot detection systems, and investigation of cyber crimes.
- Databases permit the collection and matching of information concerning fingerprints, DNA, tattoos, criminal records, and other useful data.

❹ Describe developments and problems in DNA testing and new weapons technologies.

- DNA testing permits scientists to identify the source of biological material with a high degree of certainty.
- Some crime labs have been careless and unethical in testifying about DNA results, and some prosecutors have opposed DNA testing that might benefit criminal defendants.
- New less-lethal weapons such as CEDs (e.g., Tasers), PepperBalls, and other projectiles are used by police.
- Less-lethal weapons have been involved in incidents that led to the deaths of individuals against whom the police used these weapons.

❺ Name the uses of technology in courts and corrections.

- Courts use technology in computerized record keeping and presentation of evidence.
- Jurors' perceptions about forensic science and use of technology during trials may cause problems.
- Correctional officials use technology for security purposes and for monitoring offenders in the community.

❻ List some continuing questions about the effects of technology on civil liberties.

- The expanded use of technology by government raises questions about the protection of Americans' rights.
- There are questions about the extent to which many new technologies advance criminal justice goals and do not merely expand mechanisms for societal surveillance and control.

Questions for Review

1. How have criminals adapted to changes in technology?
2. How are computers used to investigate crimes?
3. What questions and problems arise from the development of new weapons for police?
4. What undesirable effects can science and technology have on jury trials?
5. How can GPS devices assist correctional officials?
6. How can the use of technology clash with Americans' expectations about rights, liberty, and privacy?

Key Terms and Cases

CSI effect (p. 481)

DNA analysis (p. 468)

electronic file management (p. 478)

Geographic Information System (GIS) (p. 464)

identity theft (p. 456)

latent fingerprints (p. 467)

less-lethal weapons (p. 476)

Kyllo v. United States (2001) (p. 476)

15 | Juvenile Justice

LEARNING OBJECTIVES

1. Describe the extent of youth crime in the United States.
2. Explain how the juvenile justice system developed and the assumptions on which it was based.
3. Identify what determines the jurisdiction of the juvenile justice system.
4. Describe how the juvenile justice system operates.
5. Name some of the issues facing the American system of juvenile justice.

The Steubenville High School football team had been extremely successful since the 2006 season, winning three Ohio state championships in six years (Dissell, 2012). On August 12, 2012, local teens were celebrating the end of summer and the beginning of a new football season. Several Steubenville football players were in attendance, as well as some local kids getting ready to return to college over the next weeks. At three different parties, the young men and women had access to alcohol and several became visibly drunk over the course of the evening (Abad-Santos, 2013). Two days later, the parents of a teenage girl who attended the party contacted the police, reporting that she had been sexually assaulted that evening (Gossett & Law, 2012). After she became unconscious after drinking to excess, partygoers removed her clothes, penetrated her with their fingers, and might have even urinated on her unconscious body (Macur & Schweber, 2012). Almost as shocking as the assault itself was the lack of concern displayed by witnesses at the party. Not only did none of them intervene, several posted images and videos of the victim on social media outlets (Dissell, 2012).

In May 2013, two members of the team were found guilty and incarcerated. Ma'Lik Richmond (age 16) and Trent Mays (age 17) were convicted of sexual assault and kidnapping in juvenile court, with an added charge for Mays of "distributing nude images of a minor." They were sentenced to a juvenile detention facility for at least one year and will be required to register as juvenile sex offenders with the state of Ohio (Kelley, 2013). Richmond's attorney has appealed the conviction, arguing that his client's "brain wasn't fully developed" when he assaulted the victim (McDonough, 2013).

Shortly after Richmond and Mays were arrested, two teenage girls threatened and harassed the victim via social media. Charges for harassment, menacing, and witness intimidation were brought against the girls, who ended up with reduced charges of "telecommunications harassment" and were sentenced to probation (Welsh-Huggins, 2013b). Several school officials were charged with crimes, including the volunteer assistant coach of the football team. His home was used as the party location and the crime scene. He was sentenced to ten days in jail, one year of probation,

40 hours of community service, and a monetary fine (WKYC, 2014).

How many people in this case should be punished? Should the two 16-year-old offenders have been charged as adults rather than juveniles? In Ohio, serious juvenile offenders can be sentenced to a juvenile detention center with the possibility of the sentence carrying over to an adult facility if there is a low chance for rehabilitation (Gossett & Law, 2012). In addition, a grand jury in Ohio was convened to determine if the football coach was aware of the assault but did not report it to the police (Welsh-Huggins, 2013a).

The two boys found guilty of sexual assault were sentenced to incarceration, but what about the bystanders who failed to act to protect the young woman?

What about partygoers who posted pictures of the victim to social media? Is it true that juveniles have brain development that differs from adults and this difference should excuse their actions (at least in part)?

Although the juvenile justice system is separate from the adult criminal justice system, the key values of freedom, fairness, and justice undergird both systems. The formal processes of each differ mainly in emphasis, not in values. Although different, the systems are interrelated. One cannot separate the activities and concerns of policing, courts, and corrections from the problems of youth. With juveniles committing a significant portion of criminal offenses, officials in the adult system must pay serious attention to the juvenile system as well.

Youth Crime in the United States

In Detroit, a group of people, including two teenagers, brutally beat a motorist who accidentally hit a child with his car. Fourteen-year-old Kathon Anderson shot a man on a Brooklyn bus while attempting to shoot a rival gang member. Police in Northport, Alabama, arrested five young people, aged 15 to 25, for running a methamphetamine lab. Such dramatic criminal acts make headlines. Are these only isolated incidents, or is the United States facing a major increase in youth crime?

The juvenile crime incidents just described are rare. In a nation with 74 million people under age 18, about 1 million arrests of juveniles occur each year, 47,000 of which (just over 4.5 percent) are for violent crimes (FBI, 2013: Table 41). Murders committed by juveniles have decreased dramatically since 1993, when juveniles were responsible for 16 percent of all murder arrests; in 2010 this fell to 9 percent of all arrests for murder, which represents a record low for juvenile homicide (Snyder, 2012).

Youth crimes range from UCR Index Crimes (for example, murder, rape, robbery, assault) to "youthful crimes" such as violating curfew, loitering, and being a runaway (see Figure 15.1). Consistent with the trends discussed above, although about 1.5 million delinquency cases were handled in the juvenile court in 2009, the decline in caseloads since the mid-1990s is the largest since 1960. Most juvenile crimes are committed by young men, but young women make up an increasing percentage of juveniles appearing in court. Between 1985 and 2009, the percentage of young women appearing in juvenile courts increased from 19 percent to 28 percent of all cases heard (Knoll & Sickmund, 2012).

Criminologists have tried to explain the rise of the "epidemic" of violent youth crime that erupted in the mid-1980s, reaching its peak in 1993. One of the first explanations used a "cohort" approach, arguing that during the 1980s, the increase

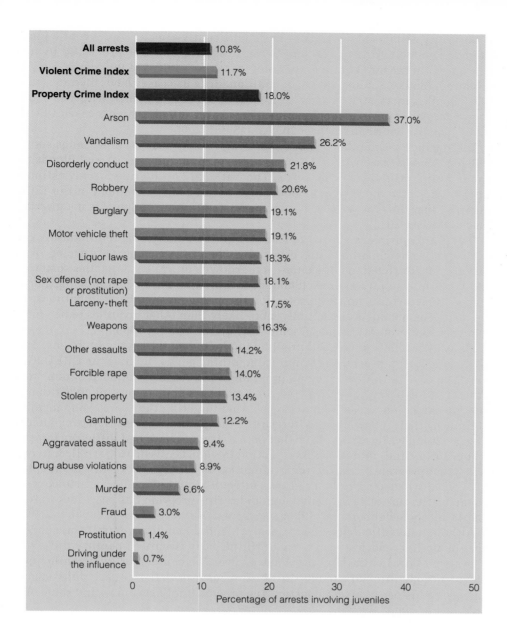

FIGURE 15.1
Percentage of Arrests of People under 18 Years Old (rounded) Juveniles are arrested for a wide range of offenses. For some offenses—such as arson, vandalism, motor-vehicle theft, and burglary—juveniles account for a larger proportion of arrests than the percentage of juveniles in the general population would suggest.

Source: Federal Bureau of Investigation, *Crime in the United States, 2012* (Washington, DC: U.S. Government Printing Office, 2013), Table 41.

Figure data (Percentage of arrests involving juveniles):

Category	Percentage
All arrests	10.8%
Violent Crime Index	11.7%
Property Crime Index	18.0%
Arson	37.0%
Vandalism	26.2%
Disorderly conduct	21.8%
Robbery	20.6%
Burglary	19.1%
Motor vehicle theft	19.1%
Liquor laws	18.3%
Sex offense (not rape or prostitution)	18.1%
Larceny-theft	17.5%
Weapons	16.3%
Other assaults	14.2%
Forcible rape	14.0%
Stolen property	13.4%
Gambling	12.2%
Aggravated assault	9.4%
Drug abuse violations	8.9%
Murder	6.6%
Fraud	3.0%
Prostitution	1.4%
Driving under the influence	0.7%

in violence was due to an increase in the prevalence of exceptionally violent individuals—so-called "super predators." Critics of this approach, however, say that the birth cohort that peaked during the early 1990s was not at all exceptional with respect to involvement in violence in their younger years (P. J. Cook & Laub, 2002). In addition, there was little evidence that "super predators" even existed, and much of the attention given to this explanation was blamed on media hype (Haberman, 2014).

A different explanation focuses on environmental factors that influenced the rise in violent youth crime. Scholars holding this position point to the impact of the drug trade, especially crack cocaine, and the related increase in gun use and possession by youths. Alfred Blumstein (2002) suggests that as more juveniles, particularly inner-city minorities, were recruited into the drug trade, they armed themselves with guns and used those firearms in battles over market turf. Other factors may have also played a role—violent crime by youth was most prevalent in neighborhoods with deteriorating social and economic conditions. These changes led to increases in family instability and reductions in shared social expectations about behavior, particularly in minority neighborhoods (Strom & MacDonald, 2007).

Certainly drug use by juveniles has significantly affected the juvenile justice system. From 1985 to 2010, the number of drug offense cases processed by juvenile courts increased from about 75,000 cases to about 164,000 cases per year (Sickmund, Sladky, & Kang, 2013). In addition, drug use cases have skyrocketed for white juveniles, increasing 341 percent from 1984 to 2004 (compared with a 32 percent increase for African American juveniles). This has resulted in higher caseloads handled by juvenile courts in the past 20 years (Stahl, 2008).

Youth gangs are another factor explaining violent youth crime. Gangs such as the Black P Stone Nation, CRIPS (Common Revolution in Progress), and Bloods first came to police attention in the 1970s. The National Youth Gang Survey estimates that there are now more than 29,900 gangs with 756,000 members in the United States and that the most significant factor related to gang violence is drug activity (Egley & Howell, 2013).

Gangs are a primary source of fear and peril in many neighborhoods. A gang can destabilize neighborhood life, especially when gang members are armed. Youth gangs are not restricted to large cities—crackdowns on violence in cities sometimes force gangs into suburban areas (Sanchez & Giordano, 2008). Fear of being a crime victim can lead youths to seek protection through gang membership without realizing that gang members are actually more likely than other juveniles to be victims of violence and property crimes (Melde, Taylor, & Esbensen, 2009).

Many cities have developed programs to help deal with gang problems. Some programs focus on preventing youth from joining gangs, such as the GRYD (Gang Reduction and Youth Development) program in Los Angeles. Other programs focus on intervention—that is, identifying gang members and attempting to get them to leave the gang. Some researchers suggest that targeting the "core" gang members and limiting their involvement will result in the greatest decreases in gang violence (Maxson, 2011), while others argue that police agencies have had difficulty targeting the appropriate individuals for intervention (Melde, Gavassi, McGarrell, & Bynum, 2011). Other programs focus on the community. In Chicago, "violence interrupters" get involved when gang violence erupts, attempting to reduce further violence and decreasing the risk of gang-related homicide. This program has been successful in several Chicago neighborhoods (Skogan, Hartnet, Bump, & Dubois, 2008).

Although juvenile delinquency, neglect, and dependency have been concerns since the nation's earliest years, not until the early twentieth century did a separate system to deal with these problems evolve. The contemporary juvenile justice system has gone through a major shift of emphasis as well. The rest of this chapter explores the history of juvenile justice, the process it follows today, and some of the problems associated with it.

☑ CHECK POINT

1. **How have criminologists attempted to explain the epidemic of violent crime committed by juveniles in the 1990s?**
   Large youth cohorts, gun use related to drug sales, and gangs.

STOP&ANALYZE

There appears to be a strong link between drug use and delinquency rates. What might you recommend to lawmakers to help reduce juvenile drug use so that delinquency rates can be decreased?

The Development of Juvenile Justice

The system and philosophy of juvenile justice that began in the United States during the social reform period of the late nineteenth century was based on the idea that the state should act as a parent would in the interest of the child. This view remained unchallenged until the 1960s, when the Supreme Court ushered in the juvenile rights period. With the rise in juvenile crime in the 1980s, the juvenile justice system shifted again to one focusing on the problem of controlling youth crime.

TABLE 15.1 | Juvenile Justice Developments in the United States

Period	Major Developments	Causes and Influences	Juvenile Justice System
Puritan 1646–1824	Massachusetts Stubborn Child Law (1646)	A. Puritan view of child as evil B. Economically marginal agrarian society	Law provides A. Symbolic standard of maturity B. Support for family as economic unit
Refuge 1824–1899	Institutionalization of deviants; House of Refuge in New York established (1825) for delinquent and dependent children	A. Enlightenment B. Immigration and industrialization	Child seen as helpless, in need of state intervention
Juvenile court 1899–1960	Establishment of separate legal system for juveniles; Illinois Juvenile Court Act (1899)	A. Reformism and rehabilitative ideology B. Increased immigration; urbanization; large-scale industrialization	Juvenile court institutionalized legal irresponsibility of child
Juvenile rights 1960–1980	Increased "legalization" of juvenile law; *Gault* decision (1967); Juvenile Justice and Delinquency Prevention Act (1974) calls for deinstitutional-ization of status offenders	A. Criticism of juvenile justice system on humane grounds B. Civil rights movement by disadvantaged groups	Movement to define and protect rights as well as to provide services to children
Crime control 1980–2005	Concern for victims; punishment for serious offenders; transfer to adult court of serious offenders; protection of children from physical and sexual abuse	A. More-conservative public attitudes and policies B. Focus on serious crimes by repeat offenders	System more formal, restrictive, punitive; increased percentage of police referrals to court; incarcerated youths stay longer periods
"Kids are different" 2005–present	Elimination of death penalty for juveniles, focus on rehabilitation, states increasing age of transfer to adult court	A. *Roper v. Simmons* (2005) B. Scientific evidence on youth's biological, emotional, and psychological development	Recognition that juveniles are less culpable than adults

Sources: Portions adapted from Barry Krisberg, Ira M. Schwartz, Paul Litsky, and James Austin, "The Watershed of Juvenile Justice Reform," *Crime and Delinquency* 32 (January 1985): 5–38; U.S. Department of Justice, *A Preliminary National Assessment of the Status Offender and the Juvenile Justice System* (Washington, DC: U.S. Government Printing Office, 1980), 29.

Today people are again reexamining the philosophy and processes of the juvenile justice system.

The idea that children should be treated differently from adults originated in the common law and in the chancery courts of England. The common law had long prescribed that children under seven years of age were incapable of felonious intent and were therefore not criminally responsible. Children aged 7 to 14 could be held accountable only if it could be shown that they understood the consequences of their actions.

The English chancery courts, established during the Middle Ages, heard only civil cases, mainly concerning property. However, under the doctrine of **parens patriae**, which held the king to be the father of the realm, the chancery courts exercised protective jurisdiction over all children, particularly those involved in questions of dependency, neglect, and property. At this time, the criminal courts, not a separate juvenile court, dealt with juvenile offenders. In legitimizing the actions of the state on behalf of the child, however, the concept of *parens patriae* laid the groundwork for the development of juvenile justice.

Table 15.1 outlines the shifts in how the United States has dealt with the problems of youth. These shifts fall into six periods of American juvenile justice history. Each was characterized by changes in juvenile justice that reflected the social,

parens patriae The state as parent; the state as guardian and protector of all citizens (such as juveniles) who cannot protect themselves.

intellectual, and political currents of the time. During the past 200 years, population shifts from rural to urban areas, immigration, developments in the social sciences, political reform movements, and the continuing problem of youth crime have all influenced how Americans have treated juveniles.

The Puritan Period (1646–1824)

The English procedures were maintained in the American colonies and continued into the nineteenth century. The earliest attempt by a colony to deal with problem children was passage of the Massachusetts Stubborn Child Law in 1646. With this law, the Puritans of the Massachusetts Bay Colony imposed the view that the child was evil, and they emphasized the need of the family to discipline and raise youths. Those who would not obey their parents were dealt with by the law.

The Refuge Period (1824–1899)

As the population of American cities began to grow during the early 1800s, the problem of youth crime and neglect became a concern for reformers. Just as the Quakers of Philadelphia had been instrumental during the same period in reforming correctional practices, other groups supported changes concerning the education and protection of youths. These reformers focused their efforts primarily on the urban immigrant poor, seeking to have parents declared "unfit" if their children roamed the streets and were apparently "out of control." Not all such children were engaged in criminal acts, but the reformers believed that children whose parents did not discipline and train them to abide by the rules of society would end up in prison. The state would therefore use its power to prevent delinquency. The solution was to create institutions where these children could learn good work and study habits, live in a disciplined and healthy environment, and develop "character."

During the nineteenth century, reformers were alarmed by the living conditions of inner-city youths. Reformers in Chicago ushered in the juvenile justice system. Why should juveniles be treated differently from adults when they commit the same criminal acts?

The first of these institutions was the House of Refuge of New York, which opened in 1825. This half-prison, half-school housed destitute and orphaned children as well as those convicted of crime (Friedman, 1993:164). Similar facilities followed in Boston, Philadelphia, and Baltimore. Children were placed in these homes by court order usually because of neglect or vagrancy. They often stayed until they were old enough to be legally regarded as adults. The houses were run according to a strict program of work, study, and discipline.

Some states created "reform schools" to provide the discipline and education needed by wayward youth in a "homelike" atmosphere, usually in rural areas. The first, the Lyman School for Boys, opened in Westboro, Massachusetts, in 1848. A similar Massachusetts reform school for girls opened in 1855 for "the instruction . . . and reformation, of exposed, helpless, evil disposed and vicious girls" (Friedman, 1993:164). Institutional programs began in New York in 1849; Ohio in 1850; and Maine, Rhode Island, and Michigan in 1906.

Despite these reforms, children could still be arrested, detained, tried, and imprisoned. Even in states that had institutions for juveniles, the criminal justice process for children was the same as that for adults.

The Juvenile Court Period (1899–1960)

With most states providing services to neglected youth by the end of the nineteenth century, the problem of juvenile criminality became the focus of attention.

Progressive reformers pushed for the state to provide individualized care and treatment to deviants of all kinds—adult criminals, the mentally ill, juvenile delinquents. They urged adoption of probation, treatment, indeterminate sentences, and parole for adult offenders and succeeded in establishing similar programs for juveniles.

Referred to as the "child savers," these upper-middle-class reformers sought to use the power of the state to save children from a life of crime (Platt, 1977). They shared a concern about the effect of environmental factors on behavior and a belief that benevolent state action could solve social problems. They also believed the claim of the new social sciences that they could treat the problems underlying deviance.

Reformers wanted a separate juvenile court system that could address the problems of individual youths by using flexible procedures that, as one reformer said, "banish entirely all thought of crime and punishment" (Rothman, 1980:213). They put their idea into action with the creation of the juvenile court.

Passage of the Juvenile Court Act by Illinois in 1899 established the first comprehensive system of juvenile justice. The act placed cases of dependency, neglect, and delinquency ("incorrigibles and children threatened by immoral associations as well as criminal lawbreakers") under one jurisdiction for children under 16. The act had four major elements:

1. A separate court for delinquent, dependent, and neglected children
2. Special legal procedures that were less adversarial than those in the adult system
3. Separation of children from adults in all portions of the justice system
4. Programs of probation to assist the courts in deciding what the best interest of the state and the child would entail

Activists such as Jane Addams, Lucy Flower, and Julia Lathrop, of the settlement-house movement; Henry Thurston, a social work educator; and the National Congress of Mothers successfully promoted the juvenile court concept. By 1904, ten states had implemented procedures similar to those of Illinois. By 1917, all but three states provided for a juvenile court.

The philosophy of the juvenile court derived from the idea that the state should deal with a child who broke the law much as a wise parent would deal with a wayward child. The doctrine of *parens patriae* again helped legitimize the system. Procedures were informal, and private, and records would be confidential. Children would be detained apart from adults, and probation and social workers would be appointed. Even the vocabulary and physical setting of the juvenile system were changed to emphasize diagnosis and treatment instead of findings of guilt. The term *criminal behavior* was replaced with *delinquent behavior* when referring to the acts of children. The terminology reflected the underlying belief that these children could be "cured" and returned to society as law-abiding citizens.

Because procedures were not to be adversarial, lawyers were unnecessary. The main professionals attached to the system were psychologists and social workers, who could determine the juvenile's underlying behavioral problem. These reforms, however, took place in a system in which children lacked the due process rights held by adults.

While the creation of the juvenile court was a positive development for juveniles in general, some contemporary researchers criticize the tendency for these reformers to hold different standards for girls and boys. For example, girls found guilty of the status offense of "promiscuity" were frequently incarcerated until adulthood (age 18) for their own protection. Boys were rarely charged with this type of offense.

The Juvenile Rights Period (1960–1980)

Until the early 1960s, few questioned the sweeping powers of juvenile justice officials. When the U.S. Supreme Court expanded the rights of adult defendants,

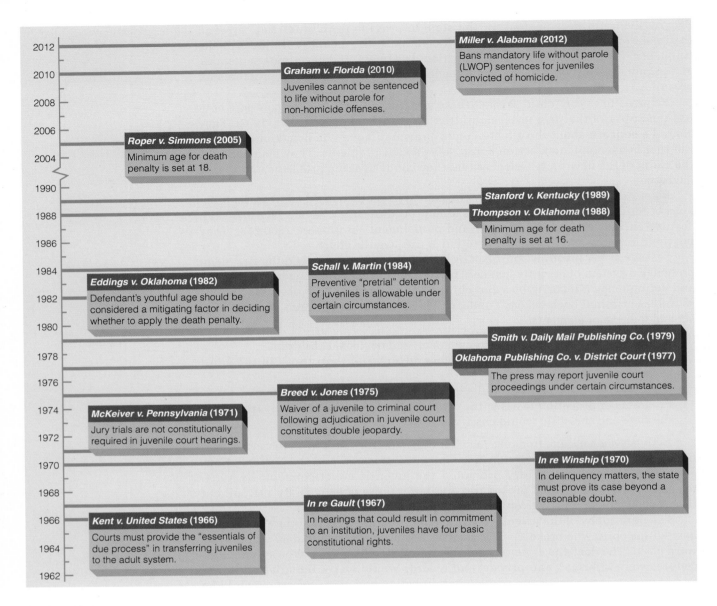

FIGURE 15.2

Major Decisions by the U.S. Supreme Court Regarding the Rights of Juveniles Since the mid-1960s, the Supreme Court has gradually expanded the rights of juveniles but has continued to recognize that the logic of the separate system for juvenile offenders justifies differences from some adult rights.

Note: For discussion of death penalty cases, see Chapter 9.

Sources: Office of Juvenile Justice and Delinquency Prevention, *1999 National Report* (Washington, DC: U.S. Government Printing Office, 1999), 90–91; *Roper v. Simmons,* 543 U.S. 551 (2005); *Graham v. Florida,* 130 S. Ct. 2011 (2010); *Miller v. Alabama,* 132 S. Ct. 2455 (2012).

however, lawyers and scholars began to criticize the extensive discretion given to juvenile justice officials. In a series of decisions (see Figure 15.2), the U.S. Supreme Court expanded the rights of juveniles.

In the first of these cases, *Kent v. United States* (1966), the Supreme Court ruled that juveniles had the right to counsel at a hearing at which a juvenile judge could waive jurisdiction and pass the case to the adult court.

In re Gault (1967) extended due process rights to juveniles. Fifteen-year-old Gerald Gault had been sentenced to six years in a state training school for making a prank phone call. Had he been an adult, the maximum punishment for making such a call would have been a fine of $5 to $50 or imprisonment for two months at most. Gault was convicted and sentenced in an informal proceeding without being

In re Gault (1967) Juveniles have the right to counsel, to confront and examine accusers, and to have adequate notice of charges when confinement is a possible punishment.

represented by counsel. The justices held that a child in a delinquency hearing must be given certain procedural rights, including notice of the charges, right to counsel, right to confront and cross-examine witnesses, and protection against self-incrimination. Writing for the majority, Justice Abe Fortas emphasized that due process rights and procedures have a place in juvenile justice: "Under our Constitution the condition of being a boy does not justify a kangaroo court."

The precedent-setting *Gault* decision was followed by a series of cases further defining the rights of juveniles. In the case of ***In re Winship*** (1970), the Court held that proof must be established "beyond a reasonable doubt" and not on "a preponderance of the evidence" before a juvenile could be classified as a delinquent for committing an act that would be a crime if it were committed by an adult. The Court was not willing to give juveniles every due process right, however: it held in ***McKeiver v. Pennsylvania*** (1971) that "trial by jury in the juvenile court's adjudicative stage is not a constitutional requirement." But in ***Breed v. Jones*** (1975), the Court extended the protection against double jeopardy to juveniles by requiring that before a case is adjudicated in juvenile court, a hearing must be held to determine if it should be transferred to the adult court.

Another area of change concerned **status offenses**— acts that are not illegal if committed by an adult; these include skipping school, running away from home, and living a "wayward, idle or dissolute life" (Feld, 1993:203). In 1974, Congress passed the Juvenile Justice and Delinquency Prevention Act, which included provisions for taking status offenders out of correctional institutions. Since then, people have worked on diverting such children out of the system, reducing the possibility of incarceration, and rewriting status offense laws.

As juvenile crime rates continued to rise during the 1970s, the public began calling for tougher approaches in dealing with delinquents. In the 1980s, at the same time that stricter sanctions were imposed on adult offenders, juvenile justice policies shifted to crime control.

Although the courts expanded the definition of rights for juveniles, consider the state of teenagers' rights today as you read "Criminal Justice: Myth & Reality."

The Crime Control Period (1980–2005)

The public demand to "crack down on crime" began in 1980. Legislators responded in part by changing the juvenile system. Greater attention began to be focused on repeat offenders, with policymakers calling for harsher punishment for juveniles who commit crimes.

In ***Schall v. Martin*** (1984), the Supreme Court significantly departed from the trend toward increased juvenile rights. The Court confirmed that the general notion of *parens patriae* was a primary basis for the juvenile court, equal in importance to the Court's desire to protect the community from crime. Thus, juveniles may be held in preventive detention before trial if they are deemed a "risk" to the community.

The *Schall* decision reflects the ambivalence permeating the juvenile justice system. On one side are the liberal reformers, who call for increased procedural and substantive legal protections for juveniles accused of crime. On the other side are

CRIMINAL JUSTICE
MYTH&REALITY

COMMON BELIEF: With the exception of convicted criminal offenders, who have limited constitutional rights, all other Americans receive identical protections from the rights contained in the Constitution.

- The recognition and expansion of rights for youths in the justice system did not lead to equal application of rights for juveniles and adults.
- Some of the most obvious differences concern protections against unreasonable searches and seizures, especially in the context of public schools.
- The U.S. Supreme Court has approved school policies that mandate random drug testing for student athletes (*Vernonia School District v. Acton*, 1995) and for all other students participating in extracurricular activities (*Board of Education v. Earls*, 2002).
- Schools can mandate drug tests, which are considered searches under the Fourth Amendment, even if there is no reason to suspect wrongdoing by a student. By contrast, the Supreme Court forbade the state of Georgia from requiring drug testing of adult candidates for political office (*Chandler v. Miller*, 1997).
- Students possess some protections in schools. In 2009, the Supreme Court declared constitutional rights were violated when school officials strip-searched a teenage girl based on the false claim by another student that the student was carrying prescription-strength painkillers (*Safford Unified School District #1 v. Redding*, 2009).

In re Winship (1970) The standard of proof beyond a reasonable doubt applies to juvenile delinquency proceedings.

McKeiver v. Pennsylvania (1971) Juveniles do not have a constitutional right to a trial by jury.

Breed v. Jones (1975) Juveniles cannot be found delinquent in juvenile court and then transferred to adult court without a hearing on the transfer; to do so violates the protection against double jeopardy.

status offense Any act committed by a juvenile that is considered unacceptable for a child, such as truancy or running away from home, but that would not be a crime if it were committed by an adult.

conservatives, who are devoted to crime control policies and alarmed by the rise in juvenile crime.

Crime control policies resulted in many more juveniles being tried in adult courts. As noted by Alex Kotlowitz during this period, "the crackdown on children has gone well beyond those accused of violent crimes" (1994:40). Data from the National Juvenile Court Data Archive show that delinquency cases waived to the adult criminal courts increased 121 percent from 1985 to 1994, demonstrating the "get tough" attitude during this period (Puzzanchera & Addie, 2014). In addition, some claim that increased penalties on juvenile offenders affect minority youth more than they do those who are white (Feld, 1999, 2003).

The "Kids Are Different" Period (2005–Present)

Some observers believe that a new period in juvenile justice may be developing. In *Roper v. Simmons* (2005), discussed in Chapter 9, the U.S. Supreme Court ruled that executions were unconstitutional for crimes committed by those younger than 18 years of age. This important ruling shepherded in a new era of juvenile justice. In *Roper*, the Court focused on the issue of culpability. The justices ruled that juveniles were less culpable than adults because of factors related to physical and emotional development that result from the growth and maturation process of the human brain (MacArthur Foundation, 2007c). Additional research indicates that intellectual maturity occurs at age 16, but other factors (such as control over impulsiveness) are not fully developed until age 24 to 26. This growing recognition of teenage development provides a basis for new programs and proposed laws designed to treat juveniles differently from adults for purposes of treatment and punishment.

Emotional and intellectual development also play a role in how juveniles understand (or fail to understand) their rights according to the Constitution, particularly with regard to their rights during questioning by police. In 2011, a divided Court decided (*J. D. B. v. North Carolina*) that police must take age into account when explaining *Miranda* rights to juveniles. As stated by Justice Sotomayor, "[t]he law has historically reflected the same assumption that children characteristically lack the capacity to exercise mature judgment and possess only an incomplete ability to understand the world around them."

Current program trends aim at helping juvenile offenders through rehabilitation and the prevention of delinquency. Such programs are not yet widespread or fully developed. For example, there are few free substance abuse programs for juveniles outside correctional institutions. This means that a juvenile must be incarcerated to receive such assistance. Reducing drug use before it increases delinquency is important for limiting criminal behavior, so there is increasing interest in developing more programs that are accessible to youths in the community. Research is also focusing on the relationship between parents and children and how parenting programs may help to keep kids out of juvenile court (MacArthur Foundation, 2007b).

Once popular, the use of judicial **waiver**, the process to waive juvenile court jurisdiction in order to move juveniles into adult court for prosecution and punishment, declined dramatically from 1994 to 2001 and remained stable through 2008. Waiver decreased 27 percent between 2008 and 2010, returning to 1985 levels (Puzzanchera & Addie, 2014). This decrease in waiver mirrors the decrease in violent juvenile crime during that period (Adams & Addie, 2011). Recent changes in a few states indicate that waiver is becoming less popular. Several states are considering the abolition of juvenile waiver by increasing their minimum age for adult trial to 18. Research on public attitudes also indicates that U.S. citizens are becoming less supportive of waiver and believe it should be used "sparingly and selectively" and only when the adult justice system is able to provide a rehabilitative component to punishment for juveniles (Applegate, Davis, & Cullen, 2009). However, the state of Florida has recently been criticized for its "direct file" law, which allows prosecutors to send juveniles directly to adult court without input from a judge (Human Rights Watch, 2014). In addition, Florida transfers more youth to adult courts than any other state and uses transfer disproportionately for black youth (Clark, 2014).

Courts are beginning to focus on the use of *Life Without Parole*, or *LWOP*, for juvenile offenders. In 2010, the Supreme Court decided in *Graham v. Florida* that the use of LWOP was unconstitutional for juveniles convicted of *non-homicide* offenses; however, only a small percentage of juveniles were then serving life sentences for non-homicide crimes (Graham himself was convicted of armed burglary and later violated the terms of his probation). Some legal scholars have argued that the "Kids Are Different" philosophy should apply to all juveniles, even those convicted of serious crimes (Berkheiser, 2011). In 2012, the Court placed another limitation on sentences. In *Miller v. Alabama*, the majority ruled that juveniles cannot be subject to a mandatory LWOP sentence for *homicide* offenses.

In spite of the increasingly tough policies directed at juvenile offenders in the late twentieth century, changes that occurred during the juvenile rights period continue to affect the system profoundly. Lawyers are now routinely present at court hearings and other stages of the process, adding a note of formality that was not present 30 years ago. Status offenders seldom end up in secure, punitive environments such as training schools. The juvenile justice system looks more like the adult justice system than it did, but it remains less formal. Its stated intention is also less harsh: to keep juveniles in the community whenever possible. The rulings in *Roper v. Simmons* and *Graham v. Florida* may indicate further changes away from tough policies.

AP Images/The Dominion-Post/Ron Rittenhouse

During the final decades of the twentieth century, the police and courts followed crime control policies in reacting to juvenile crime. Many legislators favor severe sentences for juveniles who commit serious crimes. Can the threat of long prison sentences deter juveniles from committing crimes?

☑ CHECK POINT

2. What were the major elements of the Illinois Juvenile Court Act of 1899?
A separate court for delinquent, dependent, and neglected children; special legal procedures that were less adversarial than in the adult system; separation of children from adults throughout the system; programs of probation to assist judges in deciding what is in the best interests of the child.

3. What scientific evidence has been used to argue that "Kids Are Different"?
Research indicating that brain development in juveniles is still occurring into adulthood and that juveniles have lower levels of emotional/intellectual development, implying that they may not understand the outcomes of their actions or their rights under questioning.

STOP&ANALYZE

The Supreme Court has been deeply divided over the issue of whether sentences of death for murder and life without parole for non-homicide offenses are out of step with the values of contemporary society. Do you think modern society's values would reject such sentences for juveniles? If you were a lawyer, what evidence could you use to attempt to demonstrate that current values either reject or accept such harsh sentences for juveniles?

The Juvenile Justice System

Juvenile justice operates through a variety of procedures in different states; even different counties within the same states vary. Because the offenses committed by juveniles are mostly violations of state laws, there is little federal involvement in the juvenile justice system. Despite internal differences, the juvenile justice system is characterized by two key factors: (1) the age of clients and (2) the categories of cases under juvenile instead of adult court jurisdiction.

Age of Clients

Age normally determines whether a person is processed through the juvenile or adult justice system. The upper age limit for original juvenile court jurisdiction varies from 15 to 17. In 39 states and the District of Columbia, offenders can no longer be tried in juvenile court after their 18th birthday; in ten states, the 17th; and in the remaining two states, the 16th (OJJDP, 2012). In 45 states, judges have the discretion to transfer juveniles to adult courts through a waiver hearing (Puzzanchera & Addie, 2014). Figure 15.3 shows the age at which juveniles can be transferred to adult court.

Categories of Cases under Juvenile Court Jurisdiction

Four types of cases fall under the jurisdiction of the juvenile justice system: delinquency, status offenses, neglect, and dependency. Mixing together young criminals and children who suffer from their parents' inadequacies dates from the earliest years of juvenile justice.

Delinquent children have committed acts that if committed by an adult would be criminal—for example, auto theft, robbery, or assault. Juvenile courts handle about 1.6 million delinquency cases each year. Males are most frequently in court,

delinquent A child who has committed an act that if committed by an adult would be a criminal act.

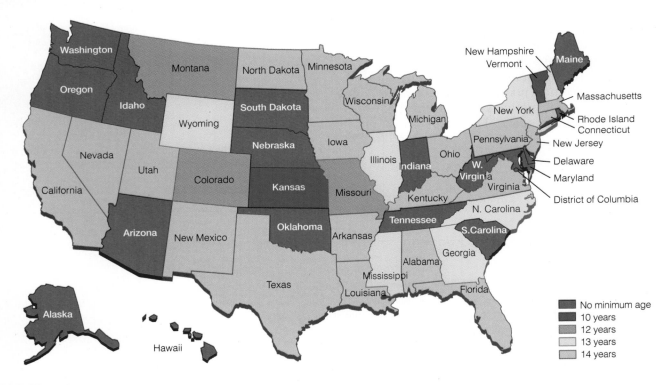

FIGURE 15.3

The Youngest Age at Which Juveniles May Be Transferred to Adult Criminal Court by Discretionary Waiver of Juvenile Jurisdiction
The waiver provisions of states vary greatly, and no clear regional or other factor explains the differences.

Source: Patrick Griffin, "Transfer Provisions," *State Juvenile Justice Profiles* (Pittsburgh: National Center for Juvenile Justice, 2010).

representing 72 percent of delinquency cases. Among the criminal charges brought before the juvenile court, 25 percent are for crimes against the person, 37 percent for property offenses, 12 percent for drug law violations, and 26 percent for public-order offenses (Puzzanchera & Robson, 2014).

Recall that certain acts are illegal only if they are committed by a juvenile. Status offenders have not violated a penal code; instead, they are charged with being ungovernable or incorrigible: as runaways, truants, or **PINS** (persons in need of supervision). Status offenders make up about 10 percent of the juvenile court caseload. Although female offenders account for only 27 percent of delinquency cases, they make up 43 percent of the status offense cases. In addition, females are more likely than males to be referred for runaway and truancy status offenses than males are (Puzzanchera, Adams, & Hockenberry, 2012).

PINS Acronym for *person(s) in need of supervision*, a term that designates juveniles who are either status offenders or thought to be on the verge of trouble.

Some states do not distinguish between delinquent offenders and status offenders; they label both as juvenile delinquents. Thus, those judged to be ungovernable and those judged to be robbers may be sent to the same correctional institution. Beginning in the early 1960s, many state legislatures attempted to distinguish status offenders and to exempt them from a criminal record. In states that have decriminalized status offenses, juveniles who participate in these activities may now be classified as dependent children and placed in the care of child-protective agencies.

Juvenile justice also deals with problems of neglect and dependency. Some children are hurt through no fault of their own because their parents have failed to provide a proper environment for them. People see the state's proper role as acting as a parent to a child whose own parents are unable or unwilling to provide proper care. Illinois, for example, defines a **neglected child** as one who is receiving inadequate care because of some action or inaction of his or her parents. This may include not being sent to school, not receiving medical care, being abandoned, living in an injurious environment, or not receiving some other care necessary for the child's well-being. A **dependent child** either has no parent or guardian or is receiving inadequate care because of the physical or mental disability of the parent. The law governing neglected and dependent children is broad and includes situations in which the child is viewed as a victim of adult behavior.

neglected child A child who is receiving inadequate care because of some action or inaction of his or her parents.

dependent child A child who has no parent or guardian or whose parents cannot give proper care.

Juvenile courts hear cases related to delinquency, status offenses, and dependency cases. The system, then, deals with both criminal and noncriminal cases. Often juveniles who have done nothing wrong are categorized, either officially or in the public mind, as delinquents. In some states, little effort is made in pre-judicial detention facilities or in social service agencies to separate the classes of juveniles.

☑ **CHECK POINT**

4. What are the jurisdictional criteria for the juvenile court?
The age of the youth, usually under 16 or 18, and the type of case—delinquency, status offense, neglect, or dependency.

STOP&ANALYZE

Why do most state laws use 18 as the age of majority? Is there something special that occurs at age 18 that indicates a shift from "juvenile" to "adult"? Would you use a specific age or instead design some tests of knowledge and maturity or some other basis for deciding whether to try an older teen as a juvenile or adult? Why?

The Juvenile Justice Process

Underlying the juvenile justice system is the philosophy that police, judges, and correctional officials should focus primarily on the interests of the child. Prevention of delinquency is the system's justification for intervening in the lives of juveniles who are involved in either status or criminal offenses.

In theory at least, juvenile proceedings are to be conducted in a nonadversarial environment. The juvenile court is to be a place where the judge, social workers, clinicians, and probation officers work together to diagnose the child's problem and select a treatment program to attack that problem.

Juvenile justice is a bureaucracy based on an ideology of social work. It is staffed primarily by people who think of themselves as members of the helping professions. Not even the recent emphasis on crime control and punishment has removed the treatment philosophy from most juvenile justice arenas. However, political pressures and limits on resources may stymie the implementation of this philosophy by focusing on the punishment of offenders rather than the prevention of delinquency. Politicians may view increased spending for rehabilitative programs as being "soft on crime," even though the public supports rehabilitation and believes that juvenile offenders can be reformed (Piquero et al., 2010).

Like the adult system, juvenile justice functions within a context of exchange relationships between officials of various government and private agencies that influence decisions. The juvenile court must deal not only with children and their parents but also with patrol officers, probation officers, welfare officials, social workers, psychologists, and the heads of treatment institutions, all of whom have their own goals, perceptions of delinquency, and concepts of treatment.

Figure 15.4 outlines the sequence of steps that are taken from police investigation to correctional disposition. As you examine this figure, compare the procedures with those of the criminal justice system for adults. Note the various options available to decision makers and the extensive discretion that they can exercise.

Police Interface

Many police departments, especially in cities, have special juvenile units. The juvenile officer is often selected and trained to relate to youths, knows much about relevant legal issues, and is sensitive to the special needs of young offenders. This officer also serves as an important link between the police and other community institutions, such as schools and other organizations serving young people. As discussed in Chapter 5, some communities hire *school resource officers* (SROs), who provide counseling and a security presence in school buildings. There is debate about whether SROs actually reduce crime in schools (Na & Gottfredson, 2011), but some studies report that SROs provide students with a positive image of police and increase student likelihood of reporting problems (Finn & McDevitt, 2005). There are also concerns that the presence of SROs leads to larger numbers of youths being sent into the juvenile court system for misbehavior that could otherwise be handled through a school's internal disciplinary procedures (Petteruti, 2011).

Most complaints against juveniles are brought by the police, although an injured party, school officials, and even the parents can initiate them as well. The police must make three major decisions with regard to the processing of juveniles:

1. Whether to take the child into custody
2. Whether to request that the child be detained following apprehension
3. Whether to refer the child to court

The police exercise enormous discretion in these decisions. They do extensive screening and make informal adjustments in the street and at the station house. In communities and neighborhoods where the police have developed close relationships with the residents or where policy dictates, the police may deal with violations by giving warnings to the juveniles and notifying their parents. Figure 15.5 shows the disposition of juveniles taken into police custody.

Initial decisions about what to do with a suspected offender are influenced by such factors as the predominant attitude of the community; the officer's attitude toward the juvenile, the juvenile's family, the offense, and the court; and the officer's conception of her or his own role. The disposition of juvenile cases at the arrest stage also relies on the seriousness of the offense, the child's prior record, and his or

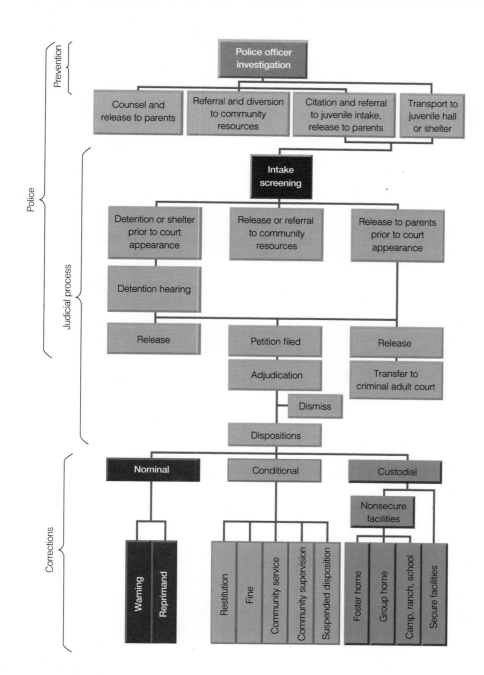

FIGURE 15.4
**The Juvenile Justice
System** Decision makers have
more options for the disposition of juvenile offenders,
compared with options in the
criminal justice system for
adults.

Source: National Advisory Commission on Criminal Justice Standards
and Goals, *Report of the Task Force
on Juvenile Justice and Delinquency
Prevention* (Washington, DC: Law
Enforcement Assistance Administration, 1976).

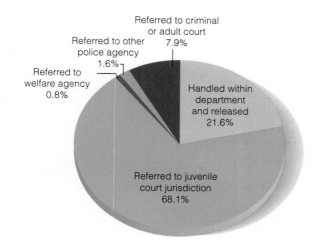

FIGURE 15.5
**Disposition of Juveniles Taken
into Police Custody** The police
have discretion in the disposition of juvenile arrest cases.
What factors can influence
how a case is disposed?

Source: Federal Bureau of Investigation, *Uniform Crime Reports, 2012,*
Table 68 (www.fbi.gov).

her demeanor. To summarize, several key factors influence how the police dispose of a case of juvenile delinquency:

1. The seriousness of the offense
2. The willingness of the parents to cooperate and to discipline the child
3. The child's behavioral history as reflected in school and police records
4. The extent to which the child and the parents insist on a formal court hearing
5. The local political and social norms concerning dispositions in such cases
6. The officer's beliefs and attitudes

Although young people commit many serious crimes, the juvenile function of police work is concerned largely with order maintenance. In most incidents of this sort, the law is ambiguous, and blame cannot easily be assigned. Many offenses committed by juveniles that involve physical or monetary damage are minor infractions: breaking windows, hanging around the business district, disturbing the peace, public sexual behavior, and shoplifting. Here the function of the investigating officer is not so much to solve crimes as to handle the often legally uncertain complaints involving juveniles. The officer seeks both to satisfy the complainant and to keep the youth from future trouble. Given this emphasis on settling cases within the community instead of strictly enforcing the law, the threat of arrest can be used as a weapon to deter juveniles from criminal activity and to encourage them to conform to the law.

Intake Screening at the Court

The juvenile court processing of delinquency cases begins with a referral in the form of a petition, not an arrest warrant as in the adult system. When a petition is filed, an intake hearing is held, over which a hearing officer presides. During this stage, the officer determines whether the alleged facts are sufficient for the juvenile court to take jurisdiction or whether some other action would be in the child's best interest.

Nationally, 45 percent of all referrals are disposed of at this stage, without formal processing by a judge (Puzzanchera, Adams, & Hockenberry, 2012). **Diversion** is the process of screening children out of the system without a decision by the court, thereby limiting their involvement in the formal juvenile justice system. In 42 percent of these cases, the charges are dismissed; another 24 percent are diverted to an informal probation, and 33 percent are dealt with through some agreed-on alternative sanction (Puzzanchera & Robson, 2014).

diversion The process of screening children out of the juvenile justice system without a decision by the court.

The concept of restorative justice is applied to juveniles in some settings. Teen courts, for example, deal with less serious offenses, often before formal charges have been brought. Teens are judged by their peers, and typically the sentences include restitution, letters of apology, and community service. Is this an effective way to deal with youthful offenders?

The Washington Post/Getty Images

Intake Referee

Kia Loggins, Intake Referee, Circuit Court—Family Division, Lansing, Michigan

An intake referee conducts preliminary inquiries and preliminary hearings regarding juvenile delinquency petitions, traffic violations (such as "minor in possession of alcohol" or "no operator's license"), and abuse and neglect matters. Also, an intake referee takes testimony, investigates family situations, determines probable cause, and decides appropriate legal action. In a hearing, a referee might have to determine the custody of minors, prepare preliminary orders, or assign the case to a juvenile court officer for further investigative work or supervision. When a case is resolved informally, the intake referee must recommend appropriate community-based services such as counseling, community service, behavioral groups, or other diversion programs.

Kia Loggins studied criminal justice as an undergraduate and counseling as a graduate student. In college she sought a wide range of volunteer and internship opportunities to gain experience in juvenile justice.

Photo provided by Kia Loggins

For example, she served as a juvenile court tutor and as an intern in a residential program for troubled boys. After college she worked in a juvenile detention facility before becoming a juvenile probation officer. She subsequently spent several years working for a nonprofit organization that provides training and consulting services for staff members at juvenile detention facilities throughout the country. By the time she had the opportunity to become an intake referee, Loggins had gained professional experience in many aspects of the juvenile justice system.

The most challenging aspect of my job is working with parents or teens who are not willing to improve themselves but are quick to blame the system. In that situation, I must make the best decision possible while hoping that some positive seeds of change will be planted in the process.

Would you want to undertake the important and difficult responsibility of determining what should be done with juveniles taken into custody by the police? Consider this question as you read "Careers in Criminal Justice."

Pretrial Procedures

When a decision is made to refer the case to the court, the court holds an initial hearing. Here the juveniles are informed of their rights and told that if a plea is given, it must be voluntary.

If the juvenile is to be detained pending trial, most states require a **detention hearing**, which determines if the youth is to be released to a parent or guardian or to be held in a detention facility until adjudication. Some children are detained to keep them from committing other crimes while awaiting trial. Others are held to protect them from the possibility of harm from gang members or parents. Still others are held because, if released, they will likely not appear in court as required. Nationally, about 20 percent of all delinquency cases involve detention between referral to the juvenile court and disposition of the case (Sickmund, Sladky, & Kang, 2012).

The conditions in many detention facilities are poor; abuse is often reported. In some rural areas, juveniles continue to be detained in adult jails even though the federal government has pressed states to hold youths in separate facilities. In 2003, the city of Baltimore unveiled a new juvenile detention facility meant to expedite juvenile cases and centralize services to delinquent youth. After its opening, the facility was called a "monstrosity," with poor lines of sight (officers cannot easily observe and supervise the juvenile detainees), overcrowding, and increasing rates of violence within its walls (Bykowicz, 2008). A 2010 evaluation has determined that the high rates of violence in the facility had begun to decrease (Dedel, 2010), with greater reductions in violence from 2010 to 2012 (Moroney, 2014). Baltimore currently holds juveniles charged as adults in the same facility as adult offenders, which has been a source of controversy as well. In 2013, officials determined that

detention hearing A hearing by the juvenile court to determine if a juvenile is to be detained or released prior to adjudication.

The juvenile waiver process permits juveniles to be sent to adult court and receive the same punishments as adults for serious crimes—except for the death penalty and life without parole for non-homicide offenses. Here a juvenile suspect makes a court appearance after being charged with murder. What is the appropriate sentence for a juvenile who commits violent crimes such as murder or rape?

AP Images/The Salt Lake Tribune/Al Hartmann

this facility was controlled by gang members and that guards had been sneaking in contraband (Toobin, 2014). While some recommended that a separate jail be constructed for juveniles being tried as adults, the state of Maryland decided that the low numbers of these juveniles did not warrant new construction and therefore it will build a facility for juvenile offenders as part of the Baltimore City Detention Center reconstruction (Duncan, 2013).

Believing that detaining youths accelerates their delinquent behaviors, some jurisdictions have attempted to stem the tide of rising numbers of juveniles in detention. In Durham, North Carolina, a new program is being implemented to keep 16- and 17-year-olds who commit minor crimes out of the juvenile justice system. Their "Misdemeanor Diversion Program" allows juvenile offenders to complete community service requirements and avoid being charged as adults, which would otherwise occur under state law (Oleniacz, 2014).

Transfer (Waiver) to Adult Court

One of the first decisions to be made after a juvenile is referred is whether a case should be transferred to the criminal (adult) justice system. In 45 states, juvenile court judges may waive their jurisdiction. This means that after considering the seriousness of the charge, the age of the juvenile, and the prospects of rehabilitation, the judge can transfer the case to adult court. In 29 states, certain violent crimes such as murder, rape, and armed robbery are excluded by law from the jurisdiction of the juvenile courts. In 1970, only three states allowed prosecutors the authority to decide whether to file in adult or juvenile court. Today 15 states give prosecutors the authority to do so (P. Griffin, 2011). Critics question whether prosecutors will "make better informed and more appropriate 'criminal adulthood' decisions than would judges in an adversarial waiver hearing" (Feld, 2004:599).

After a "tougher" approach to juvenile crime took hold in the 1970s, the number of cases transferred increased dramatically. Several states expanded their ability to transfer juveniles by excluding certain crimes from juvenile court jurisdiction or lowering the minimum age for transfer to adult court. The likelihood of waiver varies by seriousness of offense, offender age, and offender race. This disparity can be affected by offending patterns (that is, which offenses are more frequently committed by which youths) as well as by the risk of biased decision making. Even after controlling for seriousness of arrest and prior criminal record, African American and Hispanic juveniles are more likely to be waived than white juveniles, and boys are more likely to be waived than girls (Brown & Sorensen, 2013).

One result of the increased use of the waiver was that more juveniles were being sent to adult state prisons. Between 1985 and 1997, the number doubled from 3,400 to 7,400 (Austin, Johnson, & Gregoriou, 2000). As the use of waiver subsequently

Should Juvenile Offenders Be Tried as Adults?

Arrests of juveniles for violent crimes more than doubled between 1988 and 1994. Since their peak in 1994, juvenile arrests for violent crime have declined, yet cases still come up that are so serious that the public demands severe punishment. On the other hand, youths are also the primary victims of violent crime. Experts cite the availability of guns, the prevalence of urban youth gangs, and the problem of drugs as the causes of violent youth crimes.

For Trying Juveniles as Adults

Those who want to make it easier to try juveniles as adults point to the heinous nature of some crimes committed by youths. They see the juvenile courts as "coddling" these serious offenders. Often only when a youth is transferred to the adult system is his or her long record of felonies revealed—felonies for which the juvenile court ordered little punishment. They say that criminal acts of violence by juveniles require that offenders be dealt with swiftly and quickly so as to deter the upcoming generation from following in the footsteps of their older siblings.

The arguments for trying serious juvenile offenders in the adult criminal justice system include

- Violence by juveniles is a serious problem and must be dealt with in a swift and certain manner.
- Juvenile courts have not been effective in stemming the tide of violence by young people.
- Procedures for waiving juvenile jurisdiction are cumbersome in many states.
- Justice demands that heinous crimes, regardless of the age of the accused, be dealt with to the full extent the law provides.

Against Trying Juveniles as Adults

Although they recognize that serious youth crime is a problem, many experts believe that trying juveniles as adults only makes things worse. They point out that treating adolescents as adults ignores the fact that they are at a different stage of social and emotional development. They argue that children should not be held to the same standards as adults. In an increasingly violent world, children need help to navigate the temptations and threats of adolescence.

The arguments against trying serious juvenile offenders in the adult criminal justice system include

- The juvenile justice system is better able to deal with the social and emotional problems of young offenders.
- The basic foundations of criminal law recognize that children carry diminished responsibility for their acts.
- Punishing juveniles in adult institutions robs them of their childhood and threatens their future.
- The problem of violent crime by juveniles must be dealt with by changing the environment within which they live.

What Should U.S. Policy Be?

During the peak of juvenile offending, legislators proposed that the age of adulthood be lowered and that the cases of serious offenders be tried in the adult criminal justice system; however, rates of juvenile delinquency have decreased. Can we still justify waiving juveniles to adult court given changes in offending patterns? Is the juvenile corrections system equipped to treat serious juvenile offenders in a way that will return them to their communities as productive people?

Researching the Internet

You can read the article "Delinquents or Criminals: Policy Options for Young Offenders" by visiting http://www.urban.org/publications/307452.html.

For Critical Analysis

What are the likely consequences—for both the individual offender and society—of trying juveniles as adults? What are the likely consequences of trying these offenders in the juvenile courts?

---

declined, so, too, did the number of juveniles sent to prison. From 1997 to 2002, there was a 45 percent decline in the number of new admissions of offenders under age 18 into state prisons (Snyder & Sickmund, 2006). Critics of the policies claim that waiver subverts the intent of the juvenile justice system and exposes juvenile offenders to harsh conditions in adult prisons—where they are susceptible to physical and sexual victimization (DeJong & Merrill, 2000). In addition, those juveniles tried in adult courts are more likely to reoffend after release (Johnson, Lanza-Kaduce, & Woolard, 2011). There is also evidence that increased use of waiver has had no effect on juvenile crime rates (Steiner, Hemmens, & Bell, 2006; Steiner & Wright, 2006). Transferring juveniles to be tried in the adult courts remains controversial, as outlined in "The Policy Debate."

Adjudication

Juvenile courts deal with almost 1.5 million delinquency cases a year (Knoll & Sickmund, 2012). *Adjudication* is the trial stage of the juvenile justice process. If the child has not admitted to the charges and the case has not been transferred to the adult court, an adjudication hearing is held to determine the facts in the case and, if appropriate, label the juvenile as a "delinquent."

The Supreme Court's decision in *Gault* and other due process rulings mandated changes that have altered the philosophy and actions of the juvenile court. Contemporary juvenile proceedings are more formal than those of the past, although still more informal than adult courts. The parents and child must receive copies of petitions with specific charges; counsel may be present, and free counsel can be appointed if the juvenile cannot pay; witnesses can be cross-examined; and a transcript of the proceedings must be kept.

As with other Supreme Court decisions, local practice may differ sharply from the procedures spelled out in the high court's rulings. Juveniles and their parents often waive their rights in response to suggestions from the judge or probation officer. The lower social status of the offender's parents, the intimidating atmosphere of the court, and judicial hints that the outcome will be more favorable if a lawyer is not present are reasons the procedures outlined in *Gault* might not be followed. The litany of "getting treatment," "doing what's right for the child," and "working out a just solution" may sound enticing, especially to people who are unfamiliar with the intricacies of formal legal procedures. In practice, then, juveniles still lack many of the protections given to adult offenders. Some of the differences between the juvenile and adult criminal justice systems are listed in Table 15.2.

The increased concern about crime has given prosecuting attorneys a more prominent part in the system. In keeping with the traditional child-saver philosophy, prosecuting attorneys rarely appeared in juvenile court prior to the *Gault* decision. Now that a defense attorney is present, the state often uses legal counsel as well. In many jurisdictions, prosecutors are assigned to deal specifically with juvenile cases. Their functions are to advise the intake officer, administer diversion programs, negotiate pleas, and act as an advocate during judicial proceedings.

Juvenile proceedings and court records have traditionally remained closed to the public to protect the child's privacy and potential for rehabilitation. As such, judges in the adult courts usually do not have access to juvenile records. This means that people who have already served time on juvenile probation or in institutions are erroneously perceived to be first offenders when they are processed for crimes as adults. Some people argue that adult courts should have access to juvenile records and that young criminals should be treated more severely than adults to deter them from future illegal activity.

Disposition

If the court makes a finding of delinquency, the judge will schedule a dispositional hearing to decide what action should be taken. Typically, before passing sentence, the judge receives a *predispositional report* prepared by a probation officer. Similar to a presentence report, it serves to assist the judge in deciding on a disposition that is in the best interests of the child and is consistent with the treatment plan developed by the probation officer.

The court finds most juveniles to be delinquent at trial, because the intake and pretrial processes normally filter out cases in which a law violation cannot be proved. Besides dismissal, four other choices are available: (1) probation, (2) intermediate sanctions, (3) custodial care, and (4) community treatment. Intermediate sanctions might include assigning the juvenile to a specific treatment program or suspending the judgment while monitoring the youth's behavior and performance in school with the possibility of later dismissing the charge.

Juvenile court advocates have traditionally believed that rehabilitation is the only goal of the sanction imposed on young people. For most of the twentieth century, judges sentenced juveniles to indeterminate sentences so that correctional administrators could decide when release was appropriate. As in the adult criminal justice system, indeterminate sentences and unbridled discretion in juvenile justice

TABLE 15.2   The Adult and Juvenile Criminal Justice Systems

Compare the basic elements of the adult and juvenile systems. To what extent does a juvenile have the same rights as an adult? Are the different decision-making processes necessary because a juvenile is involved?

	Adult System	Juvenile System	
Philosophical assumptions	Decisions made as a result of adversarial system in context of due process rights	Decisions made as a result of inquiry into needs of juvenile within context of some due process elements	
Jurisdiction	Violations of criminal law	Violations of criminal law, status offenses, neglect, dependency	
Primary sanctioning goals	Retribution, deterrence, rehabilitation	Retribution, rehabilitation	
Official discretion	Widespread	Widespread	
Entrance	Official action of arrest, summons, or citation	Official action, plus referral by school, parents, other sources	
Role of prosecuting and defense attorneys	Required and formalized	Sometimes required; less structured; poor role definition	
Adjudication	Procedural rules of evidence in public jury trial required	Less formal structure to rules of evidence and conduct of trial; no right to public trial or jury in most states	
Treatment programs	Run primarily by public agencies	Broad use of private and public agencies	
Terminology	Arrest Preliminary hearing Prosecution Sentencing Parole	Referral Intake Adjudication Disposition Aftercare	
Application of Bill of Rights amendments			
Fourth	Unreasonable searches and seizures	Applicable	Applicable
Fifth	Double jeopardy	Applicable	Applicable (re: waiver to adult court)
	Self-incrimination	Applicable (*Miranda* warnings)	Applicable
Sixth	Right to counsel	Applicable	Applicable
	Public trial	Applicable	Applicable in less than half of states
	Trial by jury	Applicable	Applicable in less than half of states
Fourteenth	Right to treatment	Not applicable	Applicable

have faced attack during the last three decades. Several states have tightened the sentencing discretion of judges, especially with regard to serious offenses.

Corrections

Many aspects of juvenile corrections resemble those of adult corrections. Both systems, for example, mix rehabilitative and retributive sanctions. However, juvenile corrections differs in many respects from the adult system. Some of the differences flow from the *parens patriae* concept and the youthful, seemingly innocent people with whom the system deals. At times, the differences show up in formal operational policies, such as contracting for residential treatment. At other times, the differences appear only in the style and culture of an operation, as they do in juvenile probation.

One predominant aim of juvenile corrections is to avoid unnecessary incarceration. When children are removed from their homes, they are inevitably damaged emotionally, even when the home life is harsh and abusive, for they are forced to abandon the only environment they know. Further, placing children in institutions

Teen Court

A 15-year-old boy was caught with marijuana on school property. Rather than being referred to juvenile court, his case is heard by a jury of his peers—a group of teens—who decide on the appropriate outcome of the case. During questioning, the defendant indicated an interested in studying culinary arts, so one jury member suggested he spend time volunteering somewhere that involved cooking. The final disposition involved writing a code of ethics, apologizing to his school, and paying court fees.

In Ingham County, Michigan, the Lansing Teen Court Program has provided diversion services to over 200 juvenile offenders since its creation in 2000. Rather than face an adult judge, Lansing Teen Court uses teenagers from around the county to serve as a jury of peers for juveniles referred for low-level offenses. The teen jury works together to decide how offenders can repair the harm done by their delinquency and decide on the most appropriate social services to assist offenders in maintaining delinquency-free lifestyles. Since the creation of the Lansing Teen Court, over 4,500 youths have been recruited and trained to serve as peer jurors, bailiffs, and clerks.

The defendants must be first offenders who agree to plead guilty and who are referred to the Teen Court where a jury of teenage volunteers, who have been trained in the Teen Court's processes and goals, will determine their punishments. Punishments often emphasize restorative justice by requiring community service and restitution. Defendants may also be required to write letters of apology to victims and write honor codes that will force them to think about and learn from their experiences. A faculty member from Cooley Law School in Lansing serves as the "judge" who ensures that the proceedings remain serious and that fair procedures are followed.

In many Teen Courts, teenagers who have gained experience as jurors later serve as "attorneys" in these cases, either arguing for specific punishments as "prosecutors" or serving as "defense attorneys" who support the defendant's explanation for why the offenses occurred. The jury carefully questions the defendant and then reaches a unanimous decision about punishment. These courts are relatively informal in the sense that they do not follow formal trial rules, but they are serious affairs in which the defendant and other participants are expected to be well dressed and respectful of the process.

Researching the Internet

The Teen Court program in San Diego, California, provides detailed information about its operations on its website. To link to this website, go to http://www.saysandiego.org/programs/programdetails.asp?id=18.

For Critical Analysis

Will teen offenders take seriously the sanctions imposed by a Teen Court? Will decision makers in Teen Court produce appropriate and fair decisions? What might be the weaknesses or risks that could reduce the effectiveness of the Teen Court process? What might be done to counteract or prevent these risks? Identify two weaknesses or risks, and make two suggestions for strengthening the Teen Court process.

Sources: Drawn from Larry O'Connor, "Lansing Teen Court," *Capital Gains,* May 11, 2011 (www.capitalgains.com); Thomas M. Cooley Law School, "Teen Court Celebrates 10th Anniversary at Cooley Law School," October 22, 2010 (www.cooley.edu).

has labeling effects; the children may perceive themselves as bad because they have received punitive treatment, and children who see themselves as "bad" may actually behave that way. Finally, treatment is believed to be more effective when the child is living in a normal, supportive home environment. For these reasons, noninstitutional forms of corrections are seen as highly desirable in juvenile justice and have proliferated in recent years. See the "Close Up" for an example of an experimental "Teen Court" program in Lansing, Michigan, that attempts to divert juvenile offenders from the formal juvenile court system.

Probation In 60 percent of cases, the juvenile delinquent is placed on probation and released to the custody of a parent or guardian (Livsey, 2012). Often the judge orders that the delinquent undergo some form of education or counseling. The delinquent can also be required to pay a fine or make restitution while on probation.

Juvenile probation operates in much the same way that adult probation does, and sometimes the same agency carries it out. In two respects, however, juvenile probation can differ markedly from adult probation. First, juvenile probation officers have smaller caseloads. Second, the juvenile probation officer is often infused with the sense that the offender is worthwhile and can change and that the job is valuable and enjoyable. Such attitudes make for greater creativity than adult probation officers usually express. For example, a young offender can be paired with a "big brother" or "big sister" from the community.

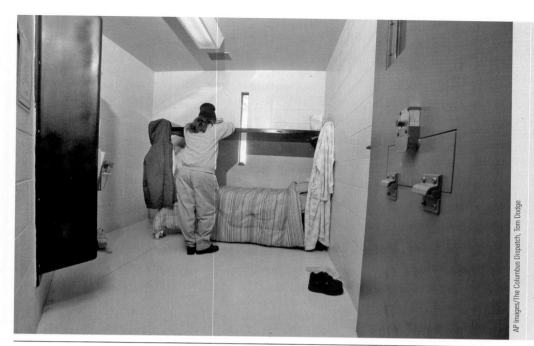

Detention inside a juvenile facility can be an intimidating experience for many youths. They may be threatened, bullied, or assaulted by older or larger teens. The physical condition of the facilities and the limited number of educational and training programs may contribute to the difficult experience of living there. Are taxpayers willing to pay for the personnel and facilities necessary to provide a good environment for implementing effective treatment programs for juvenile offenders?

AP Images/The Columbus Dispatch, Tom Dodge

Intermediate Sanctions   Although probation and commitment to an institution are the system's two main dispositional options, intermediate sanctions served in the community now account for 13 percent of adjudicated juvenile cases (Puzzanchera, Adams, & Hockenberry, 2012). Judges have wide discretion to warn, to fine, to arrange for restitution, to order community service, to refer a juvenile for treatment at either a public or a private community agency, or to withhold judgment.

Judges sometimes suspend judgment—that is, they continue a case without a finding when they wish to put a youth under supervision but are reluctant to apply the label "delinquent." The judge holds off on a definitive judgment but can give one should a youth misbehave while under the informal supervision of a probation officer or parents.

Custodial Care   Of those juveniles declared delinquent, 28 percent are placed in public or private facilities, with girls less likely to be placed (22 percent) than boys (30 percent). The placement rate of juveniles over time has decreased from about one in three adjudicated juveniles in 1985, to about one in four juveniles in 2010 (Sickmund, Sladky, & Kang, 2013). The national incarceration rate per 100,000 juveniles aged 10 to 18 was 225 in 2010—this includes juveniles held both prior to trial and as a sentence of incarceration. Like the adult incarceration rate, these rates vary widely among the states, with the highest rate in South Dakota (575) and the lowest in Vermont (53).

The number of juveniles incarcerated in public and private facilities decreased steadily from 1997 through 2010, with only a few states exhibiting increased rates of incarceration of juvenile delinquents during that period (Arkansas, Idaho, Nebraska, North Dakota, Pennsylvania, South Dakota, and West Virginia) (Hockenberry, 2013). See "What Americans Think" for a picture of attitudes toward punishment for juveniles.

Policymakers are concerned about the overrepresentation of incarcerated African American juveniles. Research has found that the disproportionate confinement of minority juveniles often stems from disparity at the early stages of case processing. Thus, if more African Americans are detained than others, more of them will likely be adjudicated in juvenile court and more placed in residential facilities. Some research suggests that juvenile court actors have biased perceptions of minority juveniles, and thus, these youths receive more severe treatment at all levels of the juvenile justice system (Leiber & Mack, 2003). Other studies indicate the importance of examining both race and gender when analyzing court outcomes, as girls are generally treated more leniently than boys in the justice system (Guevara, Herz, & Spohn, 2006).

QUESTION: "Tell me which of the following punishments you think an adolescent convicted of committing a homicide should receive as punishment, offering three options—(a) the adolescent should be sentenced to a juvenile facility and should be released after 21 years of age, (b) the adolescent should be sentenced to a juvenile facility with the possibility of parole after 21 years of age, or (c) the adolescent should be sentenced to adult prison and no possibility of parole at the age of 21."

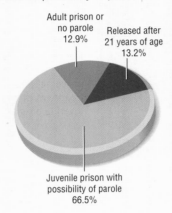

Adult prison or
no parole
12.9%

Released after
21 years of age
13.2%

Juvenile prison with
possibility of parole
66.5%

CRITICAL THINKING: Do the responses to this question indicate that most Americans disagree with the Supreme Court's decisions that treat juveniles differently from adults by prohibiting death sentences for juveniles and life without parole sentences for non-homicide offenses? Do you believe that the results would be different if the question asked specifically about applying the death penalty to juveniles? Why or why not?

Source: Terrence T. Allen, Eileen Trzcinski, and Sheryl Pimlott Kubiak. 2012. Public Attitudes toward Juveniles Who Commit Crimes: The Relationship between Assessments of Adolescent Development and Attitudes toward Severity of Punishment. *Crime & Delinquency*, 58(1): 8–102.

Institutions for juvenile offenders are classified as either nonsecure or secure. *Nonsecure* placements (foster homes, group homes, camps, ranches, or schools) include a significant number of nonoffenders—youths referred for abuse, neglect, or emotional disturbance. *Secure* facilities, such as reform schools and training schools, deal with juveniles who have committed crimes and have significant personal problems. Most secure juvenile facilities are small, designed to hold 40 or fewer residents. However, many states have at least one facility holding 200 or more hard-core delinquents who are allowed limited freedom. Because the residents are younger and somewhat more volatile than adults, behavioral control is often an everyday issue, and fights and aggression are common. Poor management practices can lead to difficult situations.

Boot camps for juvenile offenders saw a growth spurt in the early 1990s. By 1997, more than 27,000 teenagers were passing through 54 camps in 34 states annually. However, as with boot camps for adults, the results have not been promising. A national study shows that recidivism among boot camp attendees ranges from 64 percent to 75 percent, slightly higher than for youths sentenced to adult prisons (Blair, 2000). Additionally, reports of mistreatment of inmates at juvenile boot camps prompted the U.S. House of Representatives to develop standards of care for such inmates (J. Abrams, 2008). States are rethinking their policies, with many closing their programs.

The Survey of Youth in Residential Placement (SYRP), conducted in 2003, showed that 43 percent of juveniles were incarcerated for violent offenses, 44 percent were under the influence of alcohol or drugs at the time of their arrest, and 45 percent were living with only one parent when they were taken into custody. Also, 85 percent of the residents were male, the percentages of African Americans (32 percent) and Hispanics (24 percent) were greater than the percentages of those groups in the general population, and the majority (57 percent) had been suspended from school in the same year of their entry into the juvenile justice system (Snyder & Sickmund, 2006). Figure 15.6 shows the types of offenses of juveniles in public correctional facilities.

The 2008–2010 recession led to major funding cuts for state juvenile justice agencies around the United States. For example, the state of New York cut 371 juvenile justice workers from its payroll in 2011 (J. Campbell, 2011); New Hampshire cut the majority of funding for its CHINS (Children in Need of Services) program (Fahey, 2011); and Fresno County, California, considered the partial closure of a juvenile facility that was built in 2006 (K. Alexander, 2011). It is unclear how these cuts will impact the rate of juvenile delinquency in these areas, but the lack of treatment options for juveniles does not bode well for their ability to avoid criminal behavior as adults.

Institutional Programs Because of the emphasis on rehabilitation that has dominated juvenile justice for much of the past 50 years, a wide variety of treatment programs have been used. Counseling, education, vocational training, and an assortment of psychotherapeutic methods have been incorporated into the juvenile correctional programs of most states. Unfortunately, research has raised many questions about the effectiveness of rehabilitation programs in juvenile corrections. For example, incarceration in a juvenile training institution primarily seems to prepare

FIGURE 15.6
Juveniles in Public Facilities: Types of Offenses and Non-delinquent Reasons for Placement

Source: H. N. Snyder and M. Sickmund, *Juvenile Offenders and Victims: 2006 National Report* (Washington, DC: U.S. Office of Juvenile Justice and Delinquency Prevention, 2006), 198.

many offenders for entry into adult corrections. John Irwin's (1970) concept of the state-raised youth is a useful way of looking at children who come in contact with institutional life at an early age, lack family relationships and structure, become accustomed to living in a correctional facility, and cannot function in other environments. Current recommendations focus on the importance of prevention and keeping first-time juvenile offenders out of placement and in their homes, with family (Ryan, Abrams, & Huang, 2014).

Aftercare   The juvenile equivalent of parole is known as **aftercare**. Upon release, the offender is placed under the supervision of a juvenile parole officer who assists with educational, counseling, and treatment services. Quality aftercare is associated with lower rates of recidivism after release from incarceration, and many have blamed the failure of boot camps on poor aftercare (Kurlychek & Kempinen, 2006). As with the adult system, juveniles can be returned to custodial care should they violate the conditions of their parole.

aftercare Juvenile justice equivalent of parole, in which a delinquent is released from a custodial sentence and supervised in the community.

Community Treatment   In the past decade, treatment in community-based facilities has become much more common. Today many private, nonprofit agencies contract with states to provide services for troubled youths. Community-based options include foster homes, in which juvenile offenders live with families, usually for a short period, and group homes, which are often privately run facilities for groups of 12 to 20 juvenile offenders. Each group home has several staff personnel who work as counselors or house parents during 8- or 24-hour shifts. Group-home placements provide individual and group counseling, allow juveniles to attend local schools, and offer a more structured life than most of the residents have received in their own homes. These programs must be adequately funded and staffed with trained professionals in order to be effective. However, critics suggest that group homes often are mismanaged and may do little more than "warehouse" youths.

Reforms developed to increase the use of community treatment can also have unintended effects elsewhere in the system. For example, a 2012 report on the Texas juvenile corrections system found that as more offenders were

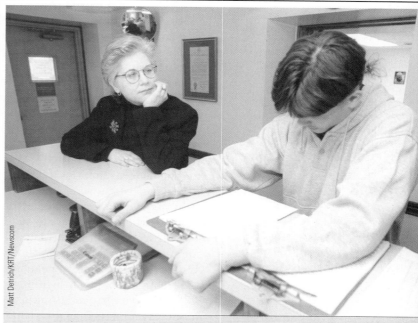

Many courts develop community programs in an effort to avoid confining youthful offenders in juvenile institutions. Here a juvenile offender meets with his attorney for monitoring, guidance, and support. What are the potential advantages and benefits of emphasizing community-based programs?

diverted to community programs, the secure institutional settings were left with higher concentrations of the most difficult offenders. In the wake of these changes, youth-on-youth assaults increased from 17 assaults per 100 detained youths in 2007 to 54 assaults per 100 youths in 2011. The institutions also experienced a similar rise in assaults against staff by youths (Grissom, 2012). Criminal justice planners think very carefully about the impacts of new policies, yet it can be very difficult to anticipate what issues may arise. Read "A Question of Ethics" at the end of the chapter to consider what recommendations you would make to address problems in correctional settings for juveniles.

☑ CHECK POINT

5. **What three discretionary decisions do the police make with regard to processing juveniles?**
   Whether to take the child into custody, whether to request that the child be detained, whether to refer the child to court.

6. **What is the purpose of diversion?**
   To avoid formal proceedings when the child's best interest can be served by treatment in the community.

7. **What sentencing dispositions are available to the judge?**
   Probation, intermediate sanctions, custodial care, community treatment.

STOP&ANALYZE

Juvenile records are sealed and generally cannot be used against adult offenders. Why would such a policy exist? Would it make more sense to allow juvenile records to be used routinely in adult criminal proceedings? State your view, and give two reasons to support your position.

Problems and Perspectives

Much of the criticism of juvenile justice has emphasized the disparity between the treatment ideal and the institutionalized practices of an ongoing bureaucratic system. Commentators have focused on how the language of social reformers has disguised the day-to-day operations that lack the elements of due process and in which custodial incarceration is all too frequent. Other criticisms claim that the juvenile justice system does not control juvenile crime.

The juvenile court, in both theory and practice, is a remarkably complex institution that must perform a wide variety of functions. The juvenile justice system must play such a range of roles that goals and values will inevitably collide.

In many states, the same judges, probation officers, and social workers are asked to deal with both neglected children and young criminals. Although departments of social services usually deal primarily with cases of neglect, the distinction between the criminal and the neglected child is often not maintained.

In addition to recognizing that the juvenile system has organizational problems, society must acknowledge that little is known about the causes of delinquency and its prevention or treatment. Over the years, people have advanced various social and behavioral theories to explain delinquency. One generation looked to slum conditions as the cause of juvenile crime, and another pointed to the affluence of the suburbs. Psychologists sometimes point to masculine insecurity in a matriarchal family structure, and some sociologists note the peer-group pressures of the gang. This array of theories has led to a variety of proposed and often contradictory treatments. In such confusion, those interested in the problems of youth may despair. What is clear is that we need additional research on the causes of delinquency and the treatment of juvenile offenders.

Youth gangs pose unique problems to those making decisions in the juvenile justice system. Gangs are responsible for a significant amount of delinquency in communities, and these gangs also thrive in correctional institutions (particularly in adult institutions). How does the presence and behavior of youth gangs affect juvenile justice policy? Recent research has indicated that gang members are more likely than non-gang members to carry guns, thereby also increasing the likelihood of severe or lethal violence among these groups.

Gang Behavior and the Criminal Justice Response in Europe: Eurogang

The problem of youth gangs is not unique to the United States. Researchers in the United States and Europe have been collaborating for the past 15 years to determine whether and how youth gangs differ across cultures. Called "The Eurogang Project," this group of researchers has created the following goals:

- To build a foundation of knowledge regarding the European socioeconomic conditions and institutional processes that foster or curtail the social exclusion and subsequent emergence and persistence/dissolution of youth gangs and problematic groups;
- To construct an infrastructure for comparative, multi-method, cross-national research on youth violence in group contexts; and
- To disseminate and effectively utilize knowledge to inform the development of effective local, national and international responses to emerging youth crime and violence issues.

Source: Eurogang home page: http://www.umsl.edu/ccj/eurogang /euroganghome.html.

In short, they desire to increase knowledge about gangs in the United States and Europe, conduct research in this area, and use that knowledge to generate potential solutions to gang-related problems.

Working together, this group has formulated a concise definition of the word *gang* for their purposes: "A street gang . . . is any durable, street-oriented youth group whose involvement in illegal activity is part of its group identity." This definition contains several important characteristics:

- *Number of members:* A "group" is defined as more than two people, so youth gangs (as defined here) must have more than two members.
- *Age:* The definition includes the word "youth," which means members must be young.
- *Location:* Youth gangs are defined as "street-oriented" to imply that these groups of young people are out walking the streets, not sitting home in groups. This image frequently instills fear in members of the community.
- *Stability:* Gangs are durable—members join for long periods of time and are committed to the group.
- *Group identity:* Gang members feel that they are part of a group and not simply a collection of individuals.
- *Illegal activity:* Youth gangs that do not engage in illegal activity are not generally a concern for law enforcement.

Also, to be considered a "street gang," the group must feel that illegal activity is an important part of how they define the activities of their group.

While this definition might fit with the United States version of youth gangs, some research of gangs in European countries indicates important differences. For example, in the United Kingdom, street gangs tend to be more disorganized, with no strong leadership. In fact, some gang members report that they are "simply a group of friends doing what they choose to do." In the Netherlands, problematic youth groups are referred to as *jeugdbendes*, but officials take care to distinguish these groups from the stereotypical view of violent American youth gangs.

Studying youth gangs in a non-American context helps to clarify why young people join gangs. Some researchers hypothesize that young men and women join gangs due to a shared set of circumstances or experiences. For example, young men of German ancestry living in Russia have formed youth gangs, and may have a common feeling of being "outsiders" in their country. One in-depth study of an Italian youth gang found that they all came from families in southern Italy and shared values and a language common to their ancestry.

The importance of understanding immigration issues has been underscored in research as well. In the United States, early gangs were comprised of immigrant youth whose parents had come to America in search of a better life than they had experienced in their home countries. This phenomenon is not specific to the United States—there have been extensive studies of Moroccan youth forming gangs in the Netherlands and Pakistani immigrants forming gangs in Norway.

Based on the work of Eurogang and other international researchers, the patterns found in gang membership share many common traits, even if researchers have had difficulty creating a common definition of what constitutes a "youth gang."

Sources: Information taken from Scott Decker and Frank M. Weerman, *European Street Gangs and Troublesome Youth Groups* (Lanham, MD: AltaMira, 2005); Finn-Aage Esbensen and Cheryl L. Maxson, *Youth Gangs in International Perspective* (New York: Springer, 2012); Frank van Gemert, Dana Peterson, and Inger-Lise Lien, *Street Gangs, Migration and Ethnicity* (Portland, OR: Willan, 2008). More information on the Eurogang program can be found on its web page at http://www.umsl.edu/ccj/eurogang /euroganghome.html.

Gang members are also more likely to receive longer sentences, given that gang membership and weapon ownership can increase the severity of punishment for juveniles (Melde, Esbensen, & Taylor, 2009). Youth gangs are a problem outside the United States as well. Review the "Comparative Perspective" to learn more about the Eurogang project, in which American researchers work with colleagues in Europe to study and formulate solutions to youth gang problems.

In recent years, juveniles have been engaging in delinquent behavior online. The phenomenon of "cyber bullying" involves the use of computers, cell phones, and other electronic devices by youths to mistreat and harm their peers. Approximately 24 percent of adolescents have been bullied online, while approximately 16 percent of youth admit to cyber bullying others (Cyberbullying Research Center, 2014). While additional inquiry is necessary, cyber bullying has been correlated with traditional bullying and various forms of school violence (Hinduja & Patchin, 2007).

What trends foretell the future of juvenile justice? The conservative crime control policies that hit the adult criminal justice system with their emphasis on deterrence, retribution, and getting tough have also influenced juvenile justice in the past 20 years. One can point to growing levels of overcrowding in juvenile institutions, increased litigation challenging the abuse of children in training schools and detention centers, and higher rates of minority youth incarceration. All of these problems have emerged during a period of declining youth populations and fewer arrests of juveniles. With a renewed focus on juvenile crime under the philosophy that "kids are different," the juvenile justice system may be embarking on a less severe path to dealing with juvenile offenders.

On the other hand, future developments and events might ultimately lead to a continuation of the crime control orientation in many states. We must wait to see if we are truly moving into a new era that recognizes and focuses on the vast developmental differences between juveniles and adults. For example, the Supreme Court's ban on the execution of offenders for crimes committed prior to the age of 18 is not necessarily permanent. *Roper v. Simmons* (2005) was decided on a five-to-four vote of the Supreme Court's justices. Similarly, the decision in *Miller v. Alabama* (2012) forbidding mandatory life-without-parole sentences for juvenile homicide offenders was also decided by a five-to-four vote. Thus, a change in the Court's composition may lead to the reinstatement of the death penalty or mandatory life-without-parole sentences for juveniles in some states if a newly appointed future justice replaces a supporter of the *Roper* or *Miller* majorities and votes to change the law when the issue arises in a new case.

A QUESTION OF ETHICS

Think, Discuss, Write

A newspaper's investigation in 2013 found that pepper spray was used in San Diego County juvenile detention facilities 461 times in 2011 and 414 times in 2012. By contrast, pepper spray was used only 91 times in Los Angeles County in 2011. Its use in San Diego was characterized as exceptionally high by experts who examined the detention facilities' records. Does the disparity in usage between large urban counties in the same state raise questions about whether it is used excessively in one county?

Thirty-six states do not use pepper spray in juvenile facilities, and nine of the fourteen states that do permit its use do not allow it to be carried routinely by officers. It is stored for use only in riot-type emergencies. By contrast, California permits detentions officers to carry pepper spray, and it was used 60 times in 2012 in incidents that were unrelated to fights. One former detainee said pepper spray was used on him for talking back to an officer and for failing to fall into line properly when instructed to do so.

Many experts argue that pepper spray should not be used in juvenile detention facilities. They claim that appropriate training and policies can produce an atmosphere within detention facilities that make such less-than-lethal weapons unnecessary. In addition, exposure to the spray can be dangerous to juveniles with asthma or those who take medications for psychiatric conditions. Other techniques for control can arguably avoid these serious risks.

Discussion/Writing Assignment

What ethical considerations arise when staff members of a juvenile corrections facility choose to pepper spray a teenager, especially if the application was for failing to obey an order rather than to stop acts of violence? Are there risks that staff will use such weapons too quickly without attempting to understand the nature and source of the problem? Does the use of such weapons communicate to the juvenile offenders that it is legitimate to use weapons and violence to solve conflicts? Might such weapons be used inconsistently or in discriminatory ways when deciding which juveniles to spray rather than restrain? Describe the policies and training that you would develop for instructing staff members on when to use pepper spray—if at all—and when to use physical restraint.

Source: Dave Maass, "The Sting of Juvenile Detention," *The Crime Report* online, July 29, 2013, http://www.thecrimereport.org/news/inside-criminal-justice/2013-07-the-sting-of-juvenile-detention.

SUMMARY

1 **Describe the extent of youth crime in the United States.**

- Crimes committed by juveniles remain a serious concern even though crimes of violence in general have decreased.

2 **Explain how the juvenile justice system developed and the assumptions on which it was based.**

- The history of juvenile justice comprises six periods: Puritan, refuge, juvenile court, juvenile rights, crime control, and "kids are different."
- Creation of the juvenile court in 1899 established a separate juvenile justice system.
- The *In re Gault* decision by the U.S. Supreme Court in 1967 brought due process to the juvenile justice system.

3 **Identify what determines the jurisdiction of the juvenile justice system.**

- The juvenile system handles cases based on the ages of youths.
- Juvenile cases fall into one of four categories: delinquency, status offenses, neglect, or dependency.

4 **Describe how the juvenile justice system operates.**

- Decisions by police officers and juvenile intake officers dispose of a large portion of the many cases that are never referred to the court.
- In juvenile court, most cases are settled through a plea agreement.
- After conviction or plea, a disposition hearing is held. Before passing sentence, the judge reviews the offense and the juvenile's social history.
- Possible dispositions of a juvenile case include probation, intermediate sanctions, custodial care, and community treatment.
- Juvenile court jurisdiction may be waived so that youths can be tried in the adult criminal justice system, but such waivers have decreased since the mid-1990s.

5 **Name some of the issues facing the American system of juvenile justice.**

- Juvenile justice faces issues of racial disparities in punishment; criminal activity by gangs; and new behavioral problems, such as cyber bullying, that involve computers and other electronic devices.
- It remains to be seen whether the current move toward increased rehabilitation will continue or whether crime control policies will remain a priority.

Questions for Review

1. What are the major historical periods of juvenile justice in the United States?
2. What is the jurisdiction of the juvenile court system?
3. What are the major processes in the juvenile justice system?
4. What are the sentencing and institutional alternatives for juveniles who are judged delinquent?
5. What due process rights do juveniles have?

Key Terms and Cases

aftercare (p. 513)

delinquent (p. 500)

dependent child (p. 501)

detention hearing (p. 505)

diversion (p. 504)

neglected child (p. 501)

parens patriae (p. 493)

PINS (p. 501)

status offense (p. 497)

waiver (p. 498)

Breed v. Jones (1975) (p. 497)

In re Gault (1967) (p. 496)

In re Winship (1970) (p. 497)

McKeiver v. Pennsylvania (1971) (p. 497)

Schall v. Martin (1984) (p. 498)

GLOSSARY

accusatory process The series of events from the arrest of a suspect to the filing of a formal charge (through an indictment or information) with the court.

adjudication The process of determining whether the defendant is guilty.

adversarial process Court process, employed in the United States and other former British colonies, in which lawyers for each side represent their clients' best interests in presenting evidence and formulating arguments as a means to discover the truth and protect the rights of defendants.

affidavit Written statement of fact, supported by oath or affirmation, submitted to judicial officers to fulfill the requirements of probable cause for obtaining a warrant.

aftercare Juvenile justice equivalent of parole, in which a delinquent is released from a custodial sentence and supervised in the community.

aggressive patrol A patrol strategy designed to maximize the number of police interventions and observations in the community.

anomie A breakdown or disappearance of the rules of social behavior.

appeal A request to a higher court that it review actions taken in a trial court.

appellate courts Courts that do not try criminal cases but hear appeals of decisions of lower courts.

arraignment The court appearance of an accused person in which the charges are read and the accused, advised by a lawyer, pleads guilty or not guilty.

arrest The physical taking of a person into custody on the grounds that there is reason to believe that he or she has committed a criminal offense. Police are limited to using only reasonable physical force in making an arrest. The purpose of the arrest is to hold the accused for a court proceeding.

assigned counsel An attorney in private practice assigned by a court to represent an indigent. The attorney's fee is paid by the government with jurisdiction over the case.

Atkins v. Virginia (2002) Execution of developmentally disabled offenders is unconstitutional.

bail An amount of money, specified by a judge, to be paid as a condition of pretrial release to ensure that the accused will appear in court as required.

Barron v. Baltimore (1833) Case deciding that the protections of the Bill of Rights apply only to actions of the federal government.

bench trials Trials conducted by a judge who acts as fact finder and determines issues of law. No jury participates.

Bill of Rights The first 10 amendments added to the U.S. Constitution to provide specific rights for individuals, including criminal justice rights concerning searches, trials, and punishments.

biological explanations Explanations of crime that emphasize physiological and neurological factors that may predispose a person to commit crimes.

boot camp A short-term institutional sentence, usually followed by probation, that puts the offender through a physical regimen designed to develop discipline and respect for authority. Also referred to as *shock incarceration*.

Bordenkircher v. Hayes (1978) A defendant's rights were not violated by a prosecutor who warned that refusing to enter a guilty plea would result in a harsher sentence.

Boykin v. Alabama (1969) Before a judge may accept a plea of guilty, defendants must state that they are making the plea voluntarily.

Breed v. Jones (1975) Juveniles cannot be found delinquent in juvenile court and then transferred to adult court without a hearing on the transfer; to do so violates the protection against double jeopardy.

chain of command Organizational structure based on a military model with clear definition of ranks to indicate authority over subordinates and obligations to obey orders from superiors.

challenge for cause Removal of a prospective juror by showing that he or she has some bias or some other legal disability. The number of such challenges available to attorneys is unlimited.

Chimel v. California (1969) Supreme Court decision that endorsed warrantless searches for weapons and evidence in the immediate vicinity of people who are lawfully arrested.

circumstantial evidence Evidence provided by a witness from which a jury must infer a fact.

citation A written order or summons, issued by a law enforcement officer, directing an alleged offender to appear in court at a specific time to answer a criminal charge.

civilian review board Citizens' committee formed to investigate complaints against the police.

civil infractions Minor offenses that are typically punishable by small fines and produce no criminal record for the offender.

civil law Law regulating the relationships between or among individuals, usually involving property, contracts, or business disputes.

classical criminology A school of criminology that views behavior as stemming from free will, demands responsibility and accountability of all perpetrators, and stresses the need for punishments severe enough to deter others.

classification The process of assigning an inmate to a category specifying his or her needs for security, treatment, education, work assignment, and readiness for release.

clearance rate The percentage of crimes known to the police that they believe they have solved through an arrest; a statistic used to measure a police department's productivity.

Commission on Accreditation for Law Enforcement Agencies (CALEA) Nonprofit organization formed by major law enforcement executives' associations to develop standards for police policies and practice; on request, will review police agencies and award accreditation upon meeting those standards.

community corrections A model of corrections based on the goal of reintegrating the offender into the community.

community crime prevention Programs through which criminal justice officials cultivate relationships with and rely on assistance from citizens in preventing crime and apprehending offenders within neighborhoods.

community justice A model of justice that emphasizes reparation to the victim and the community, approaching crime from a problem-solving perspective, and citizen involvement in crime prevention.

community policing Approach to policing that emphasizes close personal contact between police and citizens and the inclusion of citizens in efforts to solve problems, including vandalism, disorder, youth misbehavior, and crime.

community service A sentence requiring the offender to perform a certain amount of unpaid labor in the community.

CompStat Approach to crime prevention and police productivity measurement pioneered in New York City and then adopted in other cities that involves frequent meetings among police supervisors to examine detailed crime statistics for each precinct and develop immediate approaches and goals for problem solving and crime prevention.

conditions of release Conduct restrictions that parolees must follow as a legally binding requirement of being released.

congregate system A penitentiary system, developed in Auburn, New York, in which each inmate was held in isolation during the night but worked and ate with other prisoners during the day under a rule of silence.

consent search A permissible warrantless search of a person, vehicle, home, or other location based on a person with proper authority or the reasonable appearance of proper authority voluntarily granting permission for the search to take place.

continuance An adjournment of a scheduled case until a later date.

contract counsel An attorney in private practice who contracts with the government to represent all indigent defendants in a county during a set period of time and for a specified dollar amount.

contract labor system A system under which inmates' labor was sold on a contractual basis to private employers who provided the machinery and raw materials with which inmates made salable products in the institution.

control theories Theories holding that criminal behavior occurs when the bonds that tie an individual to society are broken or weakened.

Cooper v. Pate (1964) Prisoners are entitled to the protection of the Civil Rights Act of 1871 and may challenge in federal courts the conditions of their confinement.

corrections The variety of programs, services, facilities, and organizations responsible for the management of people who have been accused or convicted of criminal offenses.

count Each separate offense of which a person is accused in an indictment or an information.

crime control model A model of the criminal justice system that assumes freedom is so important that every effort must be made to repress crime; it emphasizes efficiency, speed, finality, and the capacity to apprehend, try, convict, and dispose of a high proportion of offenders.

crime control model of corrections A model of corrections based on the assumption that criminal behavior can be controlled by more use of incarceration and other forms of strict supervision.

crimes Actions that violate laws defining which socially harmful behaviors will be subject to the government's power to impose punishments.

criminogenic Having factors thought to bring about criminal behavior in an individual.

critical criminology Theories that assume criminal law and the criminal justice system are primarily a means of controlling the lower classes, women, and minorities.

CSI **effect** A widely discussed but unproved belief that television dramas revolving around forensic science raise jurors' expectations about the use of scientific evidence in criminal cases and thereby reduce the likelihood of "guilty" verdicts in trials that rely solely on witness testimony and other forms of nonscientific evidence.

custodial model A model of incarceration that emphasizes security, discipline, and order.

cyber crimes Offenses that involve the use of one or more computers.

dark figure of crime A metaphor that emphasizes the dangerous dimension of crimes that are never reported to the police.

day reporting center A community correctional center where an offender reports each day to comply with elements of a sentence.

defense attorney The lawyer who represents accused offenders and convicted offenders in their dealings with criminal justice.

delinquent A child who has committed an act that if committed by an adult would be a criminal act.

demonstrative evidence Evidence that is not based on witness testimony but that demonstrates information relevant to the crime, such as maps, X-rays, and photographs; includes real evidence involved in the crime.

dependent child A child who has no parent or guardian or whose parents cannot give proper care.

detectives Police officers, typically working in plain clothes, who investigate crimes that have occurred by questioning witnesses and gathering evidence.

detention hearing A hearing by the juvenile court to determine if a juvenile is to be detained or released prior to adjudication.

determinate sentence A sentence that fixes the term of imprisonment at a specific period.

differential response A patrol strategy that assigns priorities to calls for service and chooses the appropriate response.

directed patrol A proactive form of patrolling that directs resources to known high-crime areas.

direct evidence Eyewitness accounts.

discovery A prosecutor's pretrial disclosure to the defense of facts and evidence to be introduced at trial.

discretion The authority to make decisions without reference to specific rules or facts, using instead one's own judgment; allows for individualization and informality in the administration of justice.

discretionary release The release of an inmate from prison to conditional supervision at the discretion of the parole board within the boundaries set by the sentence and the penal law.

discrimination Differential treatment of individuals or groups based on race, ethnicity, gender, sexual orientation, or economic status, instead of on their behavior or qualifications.

disparity A difference between groups that may be explained either by legitimate factors or by discrimination.

diversion The process of screening children out of the juvenile justice system without a decision by the court.

DNA analysis A scientific technique that identifies people through their distinctive gene patterns (also called *genotypic features*). DNA, or deoxyribonucleic acid, is the basic component of all chromosomes; all the cells in an individual's body, including those in skin, blood, organs, and semen, contain the same unique DNA.

domestic violence The term commonly used to refer to intimate partner violence or violent victimizations between spouses, boyfriends, and girlfriends or those formerly in intimate relationships. Such actions account for a significant percentage of the violent victimizations experienced by women.

double jeopardy The subjecting of a person to prosecution more than once in the same jurisdiction for the same offense; prohibited by the Fifth Amendment.

dual court system A system consisting of a separate judicial system for each state in addition to a national system. Each case is tried in a court of the same jurisdiction as that of the law or laws broken.

due process model A model of the criminal justice system that assumes freedom is so important that every effort must be made to ensure that criminal justice decisions are based on reliable information; it emphasizes the adversarial process, the rights of defendants, and formal decision-making procedures.

earned time Reduction in a prisoner's sentence as a reward for participation in educational or other rehabilitation programs and for work assignments such as disaster relief and conservation projects.

electronic file management Computerization of court records, done to reduce reliance on paper documents and make documents easily accessible to the judge and attorneys via computer.

enlightenment A movement during the eighteenth century in England and France in which concepts of liberalism, rationalism, equality, and individualism dominated social and political thinking.

entrapment The defense that the individual was induced by the police to commit the criminal act.

evidence-based policing Police strategies and deployment of resources developed through examination of research on crime, social problems, and previously used strategies.

evidence-based practices Policies developed through guidance from research studies that demonstrate which approaches are most useful and cost-effective for advancing desired goals.

excessive use of force Applications of force against individuals by police officers that violate either departmental policies or constitutional rights by exceeding the level of force permissible and necessary in a given situation.

exchange A mutual transfer of resources: a balance of benefits and deficits that flow from behavior based on decisions about the values and costs of alternatives.

exclusionary rule The principle that illegally obtained evidence must be excluded from trial.

exigent circumstances When there is an immediate threat to public safety or the risk that evidence will be destroyed, officers may search, arrest, or question suspects without obtaining a warrant or following other usual rules of criminal procedure.

expiration release The release of an inmate from incarceration, without further correctional supervision; the inmate cannot be returned to prison for any remaining portion of the sentence for the current offense.

FBI special agents The sworn law enforcement officers in the FBI who conduct investigations and make arrests.

federalism A system of government in which power is divided between a central (national) government and regional (state) governments.

felonies Serious crimes usually carrying a penalty of death or of incarceration for more than one year.

feminist theories Theories that criticize existing theories for ignoring or undervaluing women's experiences as offenders, victims, and people subjected to decision making by criminal justice officials. These theories seek to incorporate an understanding of differences between the experiences and treatment of men and women while also integrating consideration of other factors, such as race and social class.

filtering process A screening operation; a process by which criminal justice officials screen out some cases while advancing others to the next level of decision making.

fine A sum of money to be paid to the state by a convicted person as punishment for an offense.

forfeiture Government seizure of property and other assets derived from or used in criminal activity.

frankpledge A system in old English law in which members of a tithing (a group of 10 families) pledged to be responsible for keeping order and bringing violators of the law to court.

fundamental fairness A legal doctrine supporting the idea that so long as a state's conduct maintains basic standards of fairness, the Constitution has not been violated.

furlough The temporary release of an inmate from a correctional institution for a brief period, usually one to three days, for a visit home. Such programs help maintain family ties and prepare inmates for release on parole.

***Furman v. Georgia* (1972)** The death penalty, as administered, constitutes cruel and unusual punishment.

fusion centers Centers run by states and large cities that analyze and facilitate sharing of information to assist law enforcement and homeland security agencies in preventing and responding to crime and terrorism threats.

***Gagnon v. Scarpelli* (1973)** Before probation can be revoked, a two-stage hearing must be held and the offender provided with specific elements of due process. Requested counsel will be allowed on a case-by-case basis.

general deterrence Punishment of criminals that is intended to be an example to the general public and to discourage the commission of offenses.

Geographic Information System (GIS) Computer technology and software that permits law enforcement officials to map problem locations in order to understand calls for service and the nature and frequency of crimes and other issues within specific neighborhoods.

Gideon v. Wainwright (1963) Case deciding that indigent defendants have a right to counsel when charged with serious crimes for which they could face six or more months of incarceration.

going rate Local court officials' shared view of the appropriate sentence for the offense, the defendant's prior record, and other case characteristics.

"good faith" exception Exception to the exclusionary rule that permits the use of improperly obtained evidence when police officers acted in honest reliance on a defective statute, a warrant improperly issued by a magistrate, or a consent to search by someone who lacked authority to give such permission.

good time A reduction of an inmate's prison sentence, at the discretion of the prison administrator, for good behavior or participation in vocational, educational, or treatment programs.

grand jury Body of citizens drawn from the community to hear evidence presented by the prosecutor in order to decide whether enough evidence exists to file charges against a defendant.

Gregg v. Georgia (1976) Death penalty laws are constitutional if they require the judge and jury to consider certain mitigating and aggravating circumstances in deciding which convicted murderers should be sentenced to death. Proceedings must also be divided into a trial phase and a punishment phase, and there must be opportunities for appeal.

habeas corpus A writ or judicial order requesting the release of a person being detained in a jail, prison, or mental hospital. If a judge finds the person is being held improperly, the writ may be granted and the person released.

halfway house A correctional facility housing convicted felons who spend a portion of their day at work in the community but reside in the halfway house during nonworking hours.

hands-off policy Judges should not interfere with the administration of correctional institutions.

home confinement A sentence requiring the offender to remain inside his or her home during specified periods.

Hudson v. Palmer (1984) Prison officials have the authority to search cells and confiscate any materials found.

identity theft The theft of social security numbers, credit card numbers, and other information in order to secure loans, withdraw bank funds, and purchase merchandise while posing as someone else: the unsuspecting victim who will eventually lose money in these transactions.

Illinois v. Gates (1983) U.S. Supreme Court decision that established the flexible totality of circumstances test for determining the existence of the probable cause needed for obtaining a search warrant.

incapacitation Depriving an offender of the ability to commit crimes against society, usually by detaining the offender in prison.

inchoate or incomplete offenses Conduct that is criminal even though the harm that the law seeks to prevent has not been done but merely planned or attempted.

incident-driven policing Policing in which calls for service are the primary instigators of action.

incorporation The extension of the due process clause of the Fourteenth Amendment to make binding on state governments the rights guaranteed in the first 10 amendments to the U.S. Constitution (the Bill of Rights).

indeterminate sentence A period set by a judge that specifies a minimum and a maximum time to be served in prison. Sometime after the minimum, the offender may be eligible for parole.

indictment A document returned by a grand jury as a "true bill" charging an individual with a specific crime on the basis of a determination of probable cause as presented by a prosecuting attorney.

"inevitable discovery" rule Supreme Court ruling that improperly obtained evidence can be used when it would later have been inevitably discovered by the police.

information A document charging an individual with a specific crime. It is prepared by a prosecuting attorney and presented to a court at a preliminary hearing.

inmate code The values and norms of the prison social system that define the inmates' idea of the model prisoner.

inquisitorial process Court process, employed in most countries of the world, in which the judge takes an active role in investigating the case and examining evidence by, for example, questioning witnesses.

In re Gault (1967) Juveniles have the right to counsel, to confront and examine accusers, and to have adequate notice of charges when confinement is a possible punishment.

In re Winship (1970) The standard of proof beyond a reasonable doubt applies to juvenile delinquency proceedings.

integrated theories Theories that combine differing theoretical perspectives into a larger model.

intelligence-led policing An approach to policing, in conjunction with concerns about homeland security, that emphasizes gathering and analyzing information to be shared among agencies in order to develop cooperative efforts to identify, prevent, and solve problems.

intensive supervision probation (ISP) Probation granted under conditions of strict reporting to a probation officer with a limited caseload.

intermediate sanction A variety of punishments that are more restrictive than traditional probation but less severe and less costly than incarceration.

internal affairs unit A branch of a police department that receives and investigates complaints alleging violation of rules and policies on the part of officers.

Interpol The International Criminal Police Organization formed in 1946 and based in France with the mission of facilitating international cooperation in investigating transnational criminal activities and security threats.

inventory search Permissible warrantless search of a vehicle that has been "impounded"—meaning that it is in police custody—so that police can make a record of the items contained in the vehicle.

jail An institution authorized to hold pretrial detainees and sentenced misdemeanants for periods longer than 48 hours.

jurisdiction The geographic territory or legal boundaries within which control may be exercised; the range of a court's authority.

jury A panel of citizens selected according to law and sworn to determine matters of fact in a criminal case and to deliver a verdict of guilty or not guilty.

Kyllo v. United States (2001) Law enforcement officials cannot examine a home with a thermal-imaging device unless they obtain a warrant.

labeling theories Theories emphasizing that the causes of criminal behavior are not found in the individual but in the social process that labels certain acts as deviant or criminal.

latent fingerprints Impressions of the unique pattern of ridges on the fingertip that are left behind on objects; these impressions are the residue of natural skin secretions or contaminating materials such as ink, blood, or dirt that were present on the fingertips at the time of their contact with the objects.

law enforcement The police function of controlling crime by intervening in situations in which the law has clearly been violated and the police need to identify and apprehend the guilty person.

law enforcement certification Preservice training required for sworn officers in many states, which includes coursework on law, use of weapons, psychology, and police procedures. Police departments for state and large cities often run training programs called *police academies* for their own recruits.

law enforcement intelligence Information, collected and analyzed by law enforcement officials, concerning criminal activities and organizations such as gangs, drug traffickers, and organized crime.

learning theories Theories that see criminal behavior as learned, just as legal behavior is learned.

lease system A system under which inmates were leased to contractors who provided prisoners with food and clothing in exchange for their labor.

legalistic style Style of policing that emphasizes strict enforcement of laws and reduces officers' authority to handle matters informally.

legal responsibility The accountability of an individual for a crime because of the perpetrator's characteristics and the circumstances of the illegal act.

less-lethal weapons Weapons such as pepper spray and air-fired beanbags or nets that are meant to incapacitate a suspect without inflicting serious injuries.

life course theories Theories that identify factors affecting the start, duration, nature, and end of criminal behavior over the life of an offender.

local legal culture Norms shared by members of a court community as to how cases should be handled and how a participant should behave in the judicial process.

mala in se Offenses that are wrong by their very nature.

mala prohibita Offenses prohibited by law but not necessarily wrong in themselves.

mandatory release The required release of an inmate from incarceration to community supervision upon the expiration of a certain period, as specified by a determinate-sentencing law or parole guidelines.

mandatory sentence A sentence determined by statutes and requiring that a certain penalty be imposed and carried out for convicted offenders who meet certain criteria.

Mapp v. Ohio (1961) Supreme Court decision that applied the exclusionary rule as the remedy for improper searches by state and local officials.

mark system A point system in which prisoners can reduce their term of imprisonment and gain release by earning "marks," or points, through labor, good behavior, and educational achievement.

McCleskey v. Kemp (1987) The Supreme Court rejects a challenge of Georgia's death penalty on grounds of racial discrimination.

McKeiver v. Pennsylvania (1971) Juveniles do not have a constitutional right to a trial by jury.

medical model A model of corrections based on the assumption that criminal behavior is caused by biological or psychological conditions that require treatment.

mens rea "Guilty mind," or blameworthy state of mind, necessary for legal responsibility for a criminal offense; criminal intent, as distinguished from innocent intent.

merit selection A reform plan by which judges are nominated by a committee and appointed by the governor for a given period. When the term expires, the voters approve or disapprove the judge for a succeeding term. If the judge is disapproved, the committee nominates a successor for the governor's appointment.

Miranda v. Arizona (1966) U.S. Supreme Court decision declaring that suspects in custody must be informed of their rights to remain silent and be represented during questioning.

misdemeanors Offenses less serious than felonies and usually punishable by incarceration of no more than one year in jail, probation, or intermediate sanctions.

Missouri v. Frye (2012) Criminal defendants' Sixth Amendment right to counsel includes protection against ineffective assistance of counsel in the plea bargaining process, such as defense attorneys' failures to inform their clients about plea bargain offers.

money laundering Moving the proceeds of criminal activities through a maze of businesses, banks, and brokerage accounts so as to disguise their origin.

Morrissey v. Brewer (1972) Due process rights require a prompt, informal, two-stage inquiry before an impartial hearing officer before parole may be revoked. The parolee may present relevant information and confront witnesses.

motion An application to a court requesting that an order be issued to bring about a specific action.

National Crime Victimization Surveys (NCVS) Interviews of samples of the U.S. population conducted by the Bureau of Justice Statistics to determine the number and types of criminal victimizations and thus the extent of unreported as well as reported crime.

National Incident-Based Reporting System (NIBRS) A reporting system in which the police describe each offense in a crime incident, together with data describing the offender, victim, and property.

neglected child A child who is receiving inadequate care because of some action or inaction of his or her parents.

net widening Process in which new sentencing options increase rather than reduce control over offenders' lives.

Nix v. Williams **(1984)** Legal decision in which the Supreme Court created the "inevitable discovery" exception to the exclusionary rule.

nolle prosequi An entry, made by a prosecutor on the record of a case and announced in court, indicating that the charges specified will not be prosecuted. In effect, the charges are thereby dismissed.

nonpartisan election An election in which candidates' party affiliations are not listed on the ballot.

North Carolina v. Alford **(1970)** A plea of guilty by a defendant who maintains his or her innocence may be accepted for the purpose of a lesser sentence.

occupational crimes Criminal offenses committed through opportunities created in a legal business or occupation.

order maintenance The police function of preventing behavior that disturbs or threatens to disturb the public peace or that involves face-to-face conflict between two or more people. In such situations, the police exercise discretion in deciding whether a law has been broken.

organized crime A framework for the perpetuation of criminal acts—usually in fields such as gambling, drugs, and prostitution—providing illegal services that are in great demand.

other conditional release A term used in some states to avoid the rigidity of mandatory release by placing convicts in various community settings, under supervision.

parens patriae The state as parent; the state as guardian and protector of all citizens (such as juveniles) who cannot protect themselves.

parole The conditional release of an inmate from incarceration, under supervision, after part of the prison sentence has been served.

partisan election An election in which candidates openly affiliated with political parties are presented to voters for selection.

patrol units The core operational units of local police departments that deploy uniformed officers to handle the full array of police functions for service, order maintenance, and law enforcement.

penitentiary An institution intended to punish criminals by isolating them from society and from one another so they can reflect on their past misdeeds, repent, and reform.

percentage bail Defendants may deposit a percentage (usually 10 percent) of the full bail with the court. The full amount of the bail is required if the defendant fails to appear. The percentage of bail is returned after disposition of the case, although the court often retains 1 percent for administrative costs.

peremptory challenge Removal of a prospective juror without giving a reason. Attorneys are allowed a limited number of such challenges.

PINS Acronym for *person(s) in need of supervision*, a term that designates juveniles who are either status offenders or thought to be on the verge of trouble.

plain view doctrine Officers may examine and use as evidence, without a warrant, contraband or evidence that is in open view at a location where they are legally permitted to be.

plea bargain A defendant's plea of guilty to a criminal charge with the reasonable expectation of receiving some consideration from the state for doing so, usually a reduction of the charge. The defendant's ultimate goal is a penalty lighter than the one formally warranted by the charged offense.

police bureaucracy The organizational description of police departments' design and operations that seek to achieve efficiency through division of labor, chain of command, and rules to guide staff.

police corruption Police officers' violations of law and departmental policy for personal gain or to help their family and friends.

political crime An act, usually done for ideological purposes, that constitutes a threat against the state (such as treason, sedition, or espionage); also describes a criminal act by the state.

positivist criminology A school of criminology that views behavior as stemming from social, biological, and psychological factors. It argues that punishment should be tailored to the individual needs of the offender.

Powell v. Alabama **(1932)** Case deciding that an attorney must be provided to a poor defendant facing the death penalty.

presentence report A report, prepared by a probation officer, that presents a convicted offender's background and is used by the judge in selecting an appropriate sentence.

presumptive sentence A sentence for which the legislature or a commission sets a minimum and maximum range of months or years. Judges are to fix the length of the sentence within that range, allowing for special circumstances.

preventive detention Holding a defendant for trial, based on a judge's finding that if the defendant were released on bail, he or she would endanger the safety of any other person and the community or would flee.

preventive patrol Making the police presence known to deter crime and to make officers available to respond quickly to calls.

prison An institution for the incarceration of people convicted of serious crimes, usually felonies.

proactive Acting in anticipation, such as an active search for potential offenders that is initiated by the police without waiting for a crime to be reported. Arrests for victimless crimes are usually proactive.

probable cause An amount of reliable information indicating that it is more likely than not that evidence will be found in a specific location or that a specific person is guilty of a crime.

probation A sentence that the offender is allowed to serve under supervision in the community.

problem-oriented policing An approach to policing in which officers routinely seek to identify, analyze, and respond to the circumstances underlying the incidents that prompt citizens to call the police.

problem-solving courts Lower-level local courts dedicated to addressing particular social problems or troubled populations. Examples of such courts include drug courts, domestic violence courts, and mental health courts.

procedural criminal law Law defining the procedures that criminal justice officials must follow in enforcement, adjudication, and corrections.

prosecuting attorney A legal representative of the state with sole responsibility for bringing criminal charges. In some states, this person is referred to as the district attorney, state's attorney, commonwealth attorney, or county attorney.

psychological explanations Explanations of crime that emphasize mental processes and behavior.

public defender An attorney employed on a full-time, salaried basis by a public or private nonprofit organization to represent indigents.

"public safety" exception Exception to *Miranda* requirements that permits police to immediately question a suspect in custody without providing any warnings when public safety would be jeopardized by their taking the time to supply the warnings.

reactive Occurring in response, such as police activity in response to notification that a crime has been committed.

real evidence Physical evidence—such as a weapon, records, fingerprints, and stolen property—involved in the crime.

reasonable doubt The standard used by a jury to decide if the prosecution has provided enough evidence for conviction.

reasonable expectation of privacy The objective standard developed by courts for determining whether a government intrusion into an individual's person or property constitutes a search because it interferes with the individual's interests that are normally protected from government examination.

reasonable suspicion A police officer's belief based on articulable facts that would be recognized by others in a similar situation as indicating that criminal activity is afoot and necessitates further investigation that will intrude on an individual's reasonable expectation of privacy.

recidivism A return to criminal behavior.

reformatory An institution that emphasizes training, a mark system of classification, indeterminate sentences, and parole.

rehabilitation The goal of restoring a convicted offender to a constructive place in society through some form of vocational or educational training or therapy.

rehabilitation model A model of corrections that emphasizes the need to restore a convicted offender to a constructive place in society through some form of vocational or educational training or therapy.

reintegration model A model of a correctional institution that emphasizes maintaining the offender's ties to family and community as a method of reform, recognizing that the offender will be returning to society.

release on recognizance (ROR) Pretrial release granted on the defendant's promise to appear in court because the judge believes that the defendant's ties to the community guarantee that she or he will appear.

restitution Repayment—in the form of money or service—by an offender to a victim who has suffered some loss from the offense.

restorative justice Punishment designed to repair the damage done to the victim and community by an offender's criminal act.

retribution Punishment inflicted on a person who has harmed others and so deserves to be penalized.

Ricketts v. Adamson (1987) Defendants must uphold the plea agreement or suffer the consequences.

Roper v. Simmons (2005) Execution of offenders for crimes committed while under the age of 18 is unconstitutional.

Santobello v. New York (1971) When a guilty plea rests on a promise of a prosecutor, the promise must be fulfilled.

Schall v. Martin (1984) Juveniles can be held in preventive detention if there is concern that they may commit additional crimes while awaiting court action.

school resource officers (SROs) Police officers assigned for duty in schools to assist in order maintenance while also developing positive relationships with students that may assist in delinquency prevention.

search Government officials' examination of and hunt for evidence on a person or in a place in a manner that intrudes on reasonable expectations of privacy.

Section 1983 lawsuits Civil lawsuits authorized by a federal statute against state and local officials and local agencies when citizens have evidence that these officials or agencies have violated their federal constitutional rights.

seizures Situations in which police officers use their authority to deprive people of their liberty or property and that must not be "unreasonable" according to the Fourth Amendment.

selective incapacitation Making the best use of expensive and limited prison space by targeting for incarceration those individuals whose incapacity will do the most to reduce crime in society.

self-incrimination The act of exposing oneself to prosecution by being forced to respond to questions when the answers may reveal that one has committed a crime. The Fifth Amendment protects defendants against compelled self-incrimination.

sentencing guideline A mechanism to indicate to judges the expected sanction for certain offenses, in order to reduce disparities in sentencing.

separate confinement A penitentiary system, developed in Pennsylvania, in which each inmate was held in isolation from other inmates. All activities, including craft work, took place in the cells.

service The police function of providing assistance to the public for many matters unrelated to crime as well as for crime prevention education.

service style Style of policing in which officers cater to citizens' desire for favorable treatment and sensitivity to individual situations by using discretion to handle minor matters in ways that seek to avoid embarrassment or punishment.

sheriff Top law enforcement official in county government who was an exceptionally important police official during the country's westward expansion and continues to bear primary responsibility for many local jails.

shock probation A sentence in which the offender is released after a short incarceration and resentenced to probation.

slave patrols Distinctively American form of law enforcement in southern states that sought to catch and control slaves through patrol groups that stopped and questioned African Americans on the roads and elsewhere in public places.

social conflict theories Theories that view crime as the result of conflict in society, such as conflict between economic classes caused by elites using law as a means to maintain power.

socialization The process by which the rules, symbols, and values of a group or subculture are learned by its members.

social process theories Theories that see criminality as normal behavior in the sense that everyone has the potential to become a criminal, depending on (1) the influences that impel one toward or away from crime and (2) how one is regarded by others.

social structure theories Theories that blame crime on the existence of a powerless lower class that lives with poverty and deprivation and often turns to crime in response.

sociological explanations Explanations of crime that emphasize as causes of criminal behavior the social conditions that bear on the individual.

special units Units within local police departments that deploy officers, often in plain clothes if not assigned to the traffic unit, who are dedicated to a specific task, such as investigation, or type of crime, such as narcotics enforcement.

specific deterrence Punishment inflicted on criminals to discourage them from committing future crimes.

state attorney general Chief legal officer of a state, responsible for both civil and criminal matters.

status offense Any act committed by a juvenile that is considered unacceptable for a child, such as truancy or running away from home, but that would not be a crime if it were committed by an adult.

stop Government officials' interference with an individual's freedom of movement for a duration that typically lasts less than one hour and only rarely extends for as long as several hours.

stop-and-frisk search Limited search approved by the Supreme Court in *Terry v. Ohio*, that permits police officers to pat down the clothing of people on the street if there is reasonable suspicion of dangerous criminal activity.

subculture The symbols, beliefs, values, and attitudes shared by members of a subgroup of the larger society.

substantive criminal law Law that defines acts that are subject to punishment and specifies the punishments for such offenses.

sworn officers Police employees who have taken an oath and been given powers by the state to make arrests and to use necessary force in accordance with their duties.

system A complex whole consisting of interdependent parts whose actions are directed toward goals and are influenced by the environment within which they function.

technical violation The probationer's failure to abide by the rules and conditions of probation (specified by the judge), resulting in revocation of probation.

***Tennessee v. Garner* (1985)** Deadly force may not be used against an unarmed and fleeing suspect unless necessary to prevent the escape and unless the officer has probable cause to believe that the suspect poses a significant threat of death or serious injury to the officers or others.

***Terry v. Ohio* (1968)** Supreme Court decision endorsing police officers' authority to stop and frisk suspects on the streets when there is reasonable suspicion that they are armed and involved in criminal activity.

testimony Oral evidence provided by a legally competent witness.

theory of differential association The theory that people become criminals because they encounter more influences that view criminal behavior as normal and acceptable than they do influences that are hostile to criminal behavior.

totality of circumstances Flexible test established by the Supreme Court for identifying whether probable cause exists that permits the judge to determine whether the available evidence is both sufficient and reliable enough to issue a warrant.

transnational crime Profit-seeking criminal activities that involve planning, execution, or victimization that crosses national borders.

trial courts of general jurisdiction Criminal courts with jurisdiction over all offenses, including felonies. In some states, these courts also hear appeals.

trial courts of limited jurisdiction Criminal courts with trial jurisdiction over misdemeanor cases and preliminary matters in felony cases. Sometimes these courts hold felony trials that may result in penalties below a specific limit.

U.S. Border Patrol Federal law enforcement agency with responsibility for border security by patrolling national land borders and coastal waters to prevent smuggling, drug trafficking, and illegal entry, including entry by potential terrorists.

U.S. marshals Federal law enforcement officials appointed to handle duties in western territories and today bear responsibility for providing federal court security and apprehending fugitives.

Uniform Crime Reports (UCR) An annually published statistical summary of crimes reported to the police, based on voluntary reports to the FBI by local, state, and federal law enforcement agencies.

United States attorneys Officials responsible for the prosecution of crimes that violate the laws of the United States. Appointed by the president and assigned to a U.S. district court jurisdiction.

***United States v. Drayton* (2002)** Judicial decision declaring that police officers are not required to inform people of their right to decline to be searched when police ask for consent to search.

***United States v. Leon* (1984)** Supreme Court decision announcing the "good faith" exception to the exclusionary rule.

***United States v. Salerno and Cafero* (1987)** Preventive detention provisions of the Bail Reform Act of 1984 are upheld as a legitimate use of government power designed to prevent people from committing crimes while on bail.

USA PATRIOT Act A federal statute passed in the aftermath of the terrorist attacks of September 11, 2001, that broadens government authority to conduct searches and wiretaps and expands the definitions of crimes involving terrorism.

victimless crimes Offenses involving a willing and private exchange of illegal goods or services that are in strong demand. Participants do not feel they are being harmed, but these crimes are prosecuted on the grounds that society as a whole is being injured.

victimology A field of criminology that examines the role the victim plays in precipitating a criminal incident and also examines the impact of crimes on victims.

visible crime An offense against persons or property, committed primarily by members of the lower class. Often referred to as "street crime" or "ordinary crime," this type of offense is the one most upsetting to the public.

voir dire A questioning of prospective jurors to screen out people the attorneys think might be biased or otherwise incapable of delivering a fair verdict.

waiver Procedure by which the juvenile court waives its jurisdiction and transfers a juvenile case to the adult criminal court.

warrant A court order authorizing police officers to take certain actions—for example, to arrest suspects or to search premises.

watchman style Style of policing that emphasizes order maintenance and tolerates minor violations of law as officers use discretion to handle small infractions informally but make arrests for major violations.

watch system Practice of assigning individuals to night observation duty to warn the public of fires and crime; first introduced to the American colonies in Boston and later evolved into a system of paid, uniformed police.

Weeks v. United States (1914) Supreme Court decision applying the exclusionary rule as the remedy for improper searches by federal law enforcement officials.

Williams v. Florida (1970) Juries of fewer than 12 members are constitutional.

Witherspoon v. Illinois (1968) Potential jurors who object to the death penalty cannot be automatically excluded from service; however, during voir dire, those who feel so strongly about capital punishment that they could not give an impartial verdict may be excluded.

Wolff v. McDonnell (1974) Basic elements of procedural due process must be present when decisions are made about imposing significant punishments on prisoners for violating institutional rules.

Wolf v. Colorado (1949) Supreme Court decision in which the Fourth Amendment was applied against searches by state and local police officers, but the exclusionary rule was not imposed as the remedy for violations of the Fourth Amendment by these officials.

work and educational release The daytime release of inmates from correctional institutions so they can work or attend school.

work group A collection of individuals who interact in the workplace on a continuing basis, share goals, develop norms regarding how activities should be carried out, and eventually establish a network of roles, all of which differentiate the group from others and facilitate cooperation.

working personality A set of emotional and behavioral characteristics developed by members of an occupational group in response to the work situation and environmental influences.

A. Swift. 2013. "For First Times, Americans Favor Legalizing Marijuana," Gallup Poll, October 22. www.gallup.com.

Abad-Santos, A. 2013. "The Steubenville Rape Case Is Back—Are Parents at Party Houses to Blame?" Atlantic Wire, April 8th. www.theatlanticwire.com.

Abbe, O. G., and P. S. Herrnson. 2002. "How Judicial Election Campaigns Have Changed." *Judicature* 85:286–95.

Abdilla, K., and M. Kranz. 2014. "Livingston County Judge Gives I-96 Shooter Up to 44 Years in Prison for Terrorism, Assault." *State News,* March 3. http://statenews.com/article/2014/03/casteelsentence2-web.

Abid, A. 2012. "Restorative Justice in the Gilded Age: Shard Principles Underlying Two Movements in Criminal Justice." *Criminal Law Brief* 8:29–42.

Abrams, J. 2008. "House Sets Standards for Juvenile Boot Camps." Associated Press, June 25. http://www.ap.org.

Abwender, D. A., and K. Hough. 2001. "Interactive Effects of Characteristics of Defendant and Mock Juror on U.S. Participants' Judgment and Sentencing Recommendations." *Journal of Social Psychology* 141:603–16.

Acker, J. R. 2007. "Impose an Immediate Moratorium on Executions." *Criminology & Public Policy* 6:641–50.

Acoca, L. 1997. "Hearts on the Ground: Violent Victimization and Other Themes in the Lives of Women Prisoners." *Corrections Management Quarterly* 1 (Spring):44–55.

Adams, B. 2012. "Utah's Cardall Family Settles Lawsuit Over Taser Death." *Salt Lake City Tribune*, December 29. http://www.sltrib.com.

Adams, B., and S. Addie. 2011. "Delinquency Cases Waived to Criminal Court, 2008." Office of Juvenile Justice and Delinquency Programs. Washington, DC: U.S. Government Printing Office.

Adams, G. 2006. "Sex Offenders' Killer Studied States' Lists." http://www.boston.com.

Adams, K. 1992. "Adjusting to Prison Life." In *Crime and Justice: A Review of Research*, vol. 16, ed. M. Tonry. Chicago: University of Chicago Press, 275–359.

Adams, S. 2013. "The Most Stressful Jobs of 2013." *Forbes Magazine* website, January 3. www.forbes.com.

Adang, O. M. J., and J. Mensink. 2004. "Pepper Spray: An Unreasonable Response to Suspect Verbal Resistance." *Policing* 27:206–19.

Aden, H., and C. Koper. 2011. "The Challenges of Hot Spots Policing." *Translational Criminology* (Summer):6–7.

Adler, S. J. 1994. *The Jury: Disorder in the Court*. New York: Doubleday.

Administrative Office of the U.S. Courts. 2005. "Need for DNA Testing Taxes Courts." *The Third Branch* 37 (February):3.

Ahmadi, S. 2011. "The Erosion of Civil Rights: Exploring the Effects of the Patriot Act on Muslims in America." *Rutgers Race and the Law Journal* 12:1–55.

Alarcon, A. L. 2007. "Remedies for California's Death Row Gridlock." *Southern California Law Review* 80:697–52.

Alarid, L., and C. Montemayor. 2010. "Legal and Extralegal Factors in Attorney Recommendations of Pretrial Diversion." *Criminal Justice Studies* 23:239–52.

Albanese, J. 2010. *Organized Crime in Our Times*. Burlington, MA: Elsevier.

Albanese, J. 2011. *Transnational Crime and the 21st Century*. New York: Oxford University Press.

Alexander, K. 2011. "Fresno Co. Juvenile Justice Campus Hit by Budget Woes." *Fresno Bee*, April 25. http://www.fresnobee.com.

Alexander, M. 2011. "The New Jim Crow." *Ohio State Journal of Criminal Law* 9:7–26.

Ali, F. 2013. "Multilingual Prospective Jurors: Assessing California Standards Twenty Years after Hernandez v. New York." *Northwestern Journal of Law and Social Policy* 8:236–72.

Alpert, G. 2007. "Eliminate Race as the Only Reason for Police–Citizen Encounters." *Criminology & Public Policy* 6:671–78.

Alvarez, L., and C. Buckley. 2013. "Zimmerman Is Acquitted in Trayvon Martin Killing." *New York Times*, July 13. www.nytimes.com.

Amar, A. R. 1997. *The Constitution and Criminal Procedure: First Principles*. New Haven, CT: Yale University Press.

Amar, V. 2008. "An Enigmatic Court? Examining the Roberts Court as It Begins Year Three: Criminal Justice." *Pepperdine Law Review* 35:523–31.

Amnesty International. 1999. "Annual General Meeting Highlights USA Campaign." Anglen, R. 2008. "Judge Rules for Taser in Cause-of-Death Decisions." *Arizona Republic*, May 2. http://www.azcentral.com.

Anderson, T. L. 2003. "Issues in the Availability of Healthcare for Women in Prison." In *The Incarcerated Woman:*

Rehabilitative Programming in Women's Prisons, eds. S. F. Sharp and R. Muraskin. Upper Saddle River, NJ: Prentice Hall, 49–60.

Andrews, D. A., and J. Bonta. 1994. *The Psychology of Criminal Behavior*. Cincinnati, OH: Anderson.

Andrews, D. A., I. Zinger, R. D. Hoge, J. Bonta, P. Gendreau, and F. T. Cullen. 1990. "Does Correctional Treatment Work? A Clinically Relevant and Psychologically Informed Meta-Analysis." *Criminology* 28:369–404.

Antonuccio, R. 2008. "Prisons for Profit: Do the Social and Political Problems Have a Legal Solution?" *Journal of Corporation Law* 33:577–92.

Applebome, P. 2012. "Death Penalty Repeal Goes to Connecticut Governor." *New York Times*, April 12. www.nytimes.com.

Applegate, B. K., R. K. Davis, and F. T. Cullen. 2009. "Reconsidering Child Saving: The Extent and Correlates of Public Support for Excluding Youths from the Juvenile Court." *Crime & Delinquency* 55(1):51–77.

Arditti, J. A., and T. Parkman. 2011. "Young Men's Reentry after Incarceration: A Development Paradox. *Family Relations* 60:205–20.

Arena, K., and K. Bohn. 2008. "Rape Victim Pushes for Expanded DNA Database." CNN.com, May 12. http://www.cnn.com.

Armour, M. 2008. "Dazed and Confused: The Need for a Legislative Solution to the Constitutional Problem of Juror Comprehension." *Temple Political and Civil Rights Law Review* 17:641–73.

Armstrong, G. S., and D. L. MacKenzie. 2003. "Private versus Public Juvenile Facilities: Do Differences in Environmental Quality Exist?" *Crime & Delinquency* 49 (October):542–63.

Armstrong, J. 2008. "Perdue Signs DNA Bill, Expanding Use in Crimes; It Allows Comparisons from Suspects, Not Just Those Already Convicted." *Florida Times Union*, May 8. http://jacksonville.com.

Armstrong, K., and S. Mills. 1999. "Death Row Justice Derailed." *Chicago Tribune*, November 14 and 15, p. 1.

Arterton, J.B. 2008. "Unconscious Bias and the Impartial Jury." *Connecticut Law Review* 40:1023–33.

Arthur, M., J. D. Hawkins, E. Brown, J. Briney, S. Oesterle, and R. Abbott. 2010. "Implementation of the Communities That Care Prevention System by Coalitions in the Community Youth

Development Study." *Journal of Community Psychology* 38:245–58.

———. 2012. "Roche Warns of Counterfeit Avastin in U.S." *USA Today*, February 14. www.usatoday.com.

Associated Press. 2013. "Maryland House Gives Initial Approval to Medical Marijuana Proposal With Little Discussion." *Washington Post*, March 23, www.washingtonpost.com.

———. 2014a. "Police Body Cameras Raise Privacy Concerns." *New York Daily News*, March 15.

———. 2014b. "Questions That Arise When Placing Cameras on Cops." *New York Times*, March 15. www.nytimes.com.

Auerhahn, K. 1999. "Selective Incapacitation and the Problem of Prediction." *Criminology* 37:703–34.

Austin, J., K. D. Johnson, and M. Gregoriou. 2000. Juveniles in Adult Prisons and Jails. Bureau of Justice Assistance *Monograph*. Washington, DC: U.S. Department of Justice.

Austin, J., T. Fabelo, A. Gunter, and K. McGinnis. 2006. Sexual Violence in the Texas Prison System. Washington, DC: The JFA Institute.

Austin, P. 2011. "Seal Beach Man Sentenced in Corrupt Bail Bond Scheme." *Los Alamitos–Seal Beach Patch*. January 28. http://losalamitos.patch.com/articles/seal-beach-man-sentenced-in-corrupt-bail-bond-scheme.

Axtman, K. 2005. "A New Motion to Make Jury Service More Attractive." *Christian Science Monitor*, May 23, pp. 2–3.

Bagnato, C. F. 2010. "Change Is Needed: How Latinos Are Affected by the Process of Jury Selection." *Chicana/o-Latina/o Law Review* 29:59–67.

Bai, M. 2012. "Scott Ritter's Other War." *New York Times*, October 27. www.nytimes.com.

Baker, A. 2008a. "11 Years of Police Gunfire, in Painstaking Detail." *New York Times*, May 8. www.nytimes.com.

———. 2008b. "Police Data Shows Increase in Street Stops." *New York Times*, May 6. www.nytimes.com.

Baker, P. 2010. "Obama Signs Law Narrowing Cocaine Sentencing Disparities." *New York Times*, August 3. www.nytimes.com.

Baldus, D. C., G. Woodworth, and C. A. Pulaski. 1994. *Equal Justice and the Death Penalty: A Legal and Empirical Analysis*. Boston: Northeastern University Press.

Bandy, D. 1991. "$1.2 Million to Be Paid in Stray-Bullet Death." *Akron Beacon Journal*, December 3, p. B6.

Bartels, L., and A. Gaffney. 2011. Good Practices in Women's Prisons: A Literature Review. Canberra, Australia: Australian Institute of Criminology.

Bass, P. 2012. "CompStat Ramps Up." *New Haven Independent*, January 31. www.newhavenindependent.org.

Battson, H. 2012. "Parole Granted More Often, Revoked Less" (Press Release), August 13. Texas Board of Pardons and Paroles. http://www.tdcj.state.tx.us/bpp/parole_increase.pdf.

Baumgartner, B., S. Linn, and A. Boydstun. 2010. "The Decline of the Death Penalty: How Media Framing Changed Capital Punishment in America." In *Winning with Words: The Origins and Impact of Framing*, ed. B. Schaffner and P. Sellers. New York: Routledge, 159–84.

Beck, A. J., and P. M. Harrison. 2001. "Prisoners in 2000." Bureau of Justice Statistics *Bulletin*. Washington, DC: U.S. Department of Justice.

Beck, A. J., J. C. Karberg, and P. M. Harrison. 2002. "Prison and Jail Inmates at Mid-Year 2001." Bureau of Justice Statistics *Bulletin*, April.

Beckett, K., K. Nyrop, and L. Pfingst. 2006. "Race, Drugs, and Policing: Understanding Disparities in Drug Delivery Arrests." *Criminology* 44:105–37.

Beichner, D., and C. Spohn. 2012. "Modeling the Effects of Victim Behavior and Moral Character on Prosecutors' Charging Decisions in Sexual Assault Cases." *Violence and Victims* 27:3–24.

Bell, D. 1967. *The End of Ideology*. 2nd rev. ed. New York: Collier.

Belluck, P. 2001. "Desperate for Prison Guards, Some States Even Rob Cradles." *New York Times*, April 21, p. A1.

Bennion, E. 2011. "Death Is Different No Longer: Abolishing the Insanity Defense Is Cruel and Unusual under *Graham v. Florida*." *DePaul Law Review* 61:1–56.

Berestein, L. 2008. "Lawsuits Raise Questions about Private Prisons. *San Diego Union-Tribune*, May 4. http://www.signonsandiego.com/uniontrib/20080504/news_1n4detain.html.

Berkheiser, M. 2011. "Death Is Not So Different after All: *Graham v. Florida* and the Court's 'Kids Are Different' Eighth Amendment Jurisprudence." *Vermont Law Review* 36(1):1–62.

Bersin, A. D. 2012. "Lines and Flows: The Beginning and End of Borders." *Brooklyn Journal of International Law* 37:389–406.

Bever, L. 2014. "Oklahoma Court Postpones Executions Because State Can't Get Drugs in Time." *Washington Post,* March 19. www.washingtonpost.com.

Bigler, M. 2013. "Santa Cruz Police Release Detailed Timeline of Rampage That Killed 2 Officers." KCBS News, May 23. http://sanfrancisco.cbslocal.com/2013/05/23/santa-cruz-police-release-detailed-timeline-of-rampage-that-killed-2-officers/.

Bisbee, J. 2010. "Oklahoma Indigent Defense System Struggles to Survive Cuts." *The Oklahoman*, April 14. http://newsok.com.

Bjelopera, J., and K. Finklea. 2012. *Organized Crime: An Evolving Challenge for U.S. Law Enforcement*. Congressional Research Service Report to Congress, January 6. http://www.fas.org/sgp/crs/misc/R41547.pdf.

BJS (Bureau of Justice Statistics). 2008. "Survey Methodology for Criminal Victimization in the United States." Washington, DC: U.S. Department of Justice.

———. 2011b. Sourcebook of Criminal Justice Statistics. http://www.albany.edu/sourcebook/.

———. 2014. *Sourcebook of Criminal Justice Statistics*. Washington, DC: U.S. Department of Justice.

Blackmon, D. 2008. *Slavery by Another Name: The Re-Enslavement of Black Americans from the Civil War to World War II*. New York: Anchor Books.

Blair, J. 2000. "Ideas and Trends; Boot Camps: An Idea Whose Time Came and Went." *New York Times*, January 2. http://nytimes.com.

Blitz, C. L., N. Wolff, and J. Shi. 2008. "Physical Victimization in Prison: The Role of Mental Illness." *International Journal of Law and Psychiatry* 31(5):385–93.

Bluestein, G. 2011. "State Budget Cuts Clog Criminal Justice System." *Seattle Post Intelligencer*, October 26. www.seattlepi.com.

Blumstein, A. 2002. "Youth, Guns, and Violent Crime." The Future of Children, Volume 12 (Number 2). Los Altos, CA: The David and Lucille Packard Foundation.

Blumstein, A., and A. Beck. 2005. "Reentry as a Transient State between Liberty and Recommitment" (with Allen J. Beck). In *Prisoner Reentry and Crime in America*, ed. Jeremy Travis and Christy Visher. New York: Cambridge University Press, 55–79.

Blumstein, J. F., M. A. Cohen, and S. Seth. 2008. "Do Government Agencies Respond to Market Pressures? Evidence from Private Prisons." *Virginia Journal of Social Policy and Law* 15:446–69.

Bogdanich, W. 2008. "Heparin Find May Point to Chinese Counterfeiting." *New York Times*, March 20. http://www.nytimes.com.

Bohmert, M. B., and G. Duwe. 2011. "Minnesota's Affordable Homes Program: Evaluating the Effects of a Prison Work Program on Recidivism, Employment and Cost Avoidance." Criminal Justice Policy Review (online).

Boland, B., E. Brady, H. Tyson, and J. Bassler. 1983. *The Prosecution of Felony Arrests*. Washington, DC: Bureau of Justice Statistics, U.S. Government Printing Office.

Bontrager, S., W. Bales, and T. Chiricos. 2005. "Race, Ethnicity, Threat and the Labeling of Convicted. Felons." *Criminology* 43:589–622.

Boots, M. T. 2013. "New Prisoner Re-Entry Center Takes Aim at Criminal Recidivism." *Anchorage Daily News*, October 2. www.adn.com.

Bornstein, B., and E. Green. 2011. "Jury Decision Making: Implications For and From Psychology." *Current Directions in Psychological Science* 20:63–67.

Bourgon, G., L. Guitierrez, and J. Ashton. 2012. "The Evolution of Community Supervision Practice: The Transformation from Case Manager to Change Agent." *Federal Probation* (September):27–35.

Bousquet, S. 2012a. "Plan to Close Prison Re-Entry Centers Angers Lawmakers." *Tampa Bay Times*, March 2. www.tampabay.com.

———. 2012b. "Prison System Will Keep Re-Entry Centers Open." *Tampa Bay Times*, March 7. www.tampabay.com.

Bowen, D. M. 2009. "Calling Your Bluff: How Prosecutors and Defense Attorneys Adapt Plea Bargaining Strategies to Increased Formalization." *Justice Quarterly* 26:2–29.

Bowen, J. 2008. "Punishing the Innocent." *University of Pennsylvania Law Review* 156:1117–Bowers, J. 2010. "Legal Guilt, Normative Innocence, and the Equitable Decision Not to Prosecute." *Columbia Law Review* 110:1655–726.

Bowers. J. 2010. "Legal Guilt, Normative Innocence, and the Equitable Decision Not to Prosecute." *Columbia Law Review* 110:1655–726.

Bowker, L. H. 1982. "Victimizers and Victims in American Correctional Institutions." In *Pains of Imprisonment*, ed. R. Johnson and H. Toch. Beverly Hills, CA: Sage.

Boyd, T. 2011. "Domestic Violence Court—55th District Court." *Michigan Bar Journal* 90:42–43.

Bradley, C. 1992. "Reforming the Criminal Trial." *Indiana Law Journal* 68:659–64.

Bradley, Craig M. 2010. "Reconceiving the Fourth Amendment and the Exclusionary Rule." *Law and Contemporary Problems* 73:211–38.

Braithwaite, J. 2007. "Encourage Restorative Justice." *Criminology & Public Policy* 6:689–96.

Braithwaite, L., H. M. Treadwell, K. R. J. Arriola. 2005. "Health Disparities and Incarcerated Women: A Population Ignored." *American Journal of Public Health* 95:1679–81.

Branan, B. 2013. "Sacramento County Probation Officers Have Highest Caseload in the State." *Sacramento Bee*, April 10. http://www.sacbee.com.

Brandenburg, B., and M. Berg. 2012. "The New Storm of Money and Politics Around Judicial Retention Elections," *Drake Law Review* 60:703–13.

Braverman, I. 2013. "Passing the Sniff Test: Police Dogs as Surveillance Technology." *Buffalo Law Review* 61:81–167.

Bray, K. 1992. "Reaching the Final Chapter in the Story of Peremptory Challenges." *U.C.L.A. Law Review* 40:517–55.

Breslin, D. M. 2010. "Judicial Merit-Retention Elections in Pennsylvania." *Duquesne Law Review* 48:891–907.

Brezosky, L. 2012. "Bail Bondsman Sentenced in Corrupt Judge Case." MySanAntonio.Com. February 14. http://www.mysanantonio.com/news/article/Bail-bondsman-sentenced-in-corrupt-judge-case-3323702.php.

Britt, C. 2000. "Social Context and Racial Disparities in Punishment Decisions." *Justice Quarterly* 17:707–32.

Bronsteen, J. 2010. "Retribution's Role." *Indiana Law Journal* 84:1129–56.

Brown, D. M. 2009. "Calling Your Bluff: How Prosecutors and Defense Attorney Adapt Plea Bargaining Strategies to Increased Formalization." *Justice Quarterly* 26:2–29.

Brown, J. M. 2013. "Four Officers Cleared in Shooting of Santa Cruz Cop Killer." *Santa Cruz Sentinel,* May 23. www.santacruzsentinel.com.

Brown, J.M. and J.R. Sorensen. 2013. "Race, Ethnicity, Gender, and Waiver to Adult Court." *Journal of Ethnicity in Criminal Justice* 11:181–95.

Brown, K. 2013. "Somebody Poisoned the Jury Pool: Social Media's Effect on Jury Impartiality." *Texas Wesleyan Law Review* 19:809–35.

Browne, A., A. Cambier, and S. Agha. 2011. "Prisons Within Prisons: The Use of Segregation in the United States." *Federal Sentencing Reporter* 24:46–49.

Bruce, M. 2003. "Contextual Complexity and Violent Delinquency among Black and White Males." *Journal of Black Studies* 35:65–98.

Brunson, R. 2007. " 'Police Don't Like Black People': African American Young Men's Accumulated Police Experiences." *Criminology & Public Policy* 6:71–102.

Bueerman, J. 2012. "Being Smart on Crime with Evidence-Based Policing." *National Institute of Justice Journal* 269 (March):12–15.

Bulletin. June. NCJ 238250.

Bulman, P. 2010. "Police Use of Force: The Impact of Less-Lethal Weapons and Tactics." *National Institute of Justice Journal* 267:4–10.

Bundy, T. 2011. "At Critical Time, Budget Ax Falls on Parole Courts." *The Bay Citizen*, October 8. www.baycitizen.org.

———. 2012. "Trying to Prepare for the Toughest of Jobs." *New York Times*, March 29. www.nytimes.com.

Bureau of Justice Statistics. *See* BJS (Bureau of Justice Statistics).

Bureau of Labor Statistics. 2014a. "Correctional Officers" in *Occupational.*

Bureau of Labor Statistics. 2014b. "Employment Situation Summary." *Economic News Release*, February 7. Table A-2. www.bls.gov.

Bureau of Prisons. 2014. "BOP Statistics: Staff." U.S. Bureau of Prisons website.

Burgess-Proctor. A. 2006. "Intersections of Race, Class, Gender, and Crime: Future Directions for Feminist Criminology." *Feminist Criminology* 1:27–47.

Burns, A. C. 2007. "*Beard v. Banks*: Restricted Reading, Rehabilitation, and Prisoners' First Amendment Rights." *Journal of Law and Policy* 15:1225–70.

Burns, S. 2010. "The Role of Problem-Solving Courts: Inside the Courts and Beyond." *University of Maryland Journal of Race, Religion, Gender, and Class* 10:73–87.

Buruma, I. 2005. "What Teaching a College-Level Class at a Maximum Security Correctional Facility Did for the Inmates—and for Me." *The New York Times Magazine*, February 20, pp. 36–41.

Business Wire. 2001. "WorldNet Technologies, Creators of a State of the Art Weapons Detection System, Signs Consulting Deal with NuQuest." November 27. http://findarticles.com/p/articles/mi_m0EIN/is_2001_Nov_27/ai_80345651/.

Butler, P. 2010. "One Hundred Years of Race and Crime." *Journal of Criminal Law and Criminology* 100:1043–1060.

Butterfield, F. 2004a. "Repaving the Long Road Out of Prison." *New York Times*, May 4. http://www.nytimes.com.

Buzawa, E. S., and A. D. Buzawa. 2013. "Evidence Based Prosecution: Is It Worth the Cost?" *Criminology and Public Policy* 12:491–506.

Bykowicz, J. 2008. "Juvenile Center Home to Despair.*" Baltimore Sun*, May 25. http://baltimoresun.com.

Bynum, T., and S. Varano. 2002. "The Anti-Gang Initiative in Detroit: An Aggressive Enforcement Approach to Gangs." In *Policing Gangs and Youth Violence*, ed. S. H. Decker. Belmont, CA: Wadsworth, 214–38.

Byrne, J. M. 2008. "The Best Laid Plans: An Assessment of the Varied Consequences of New Technologies for Crime and Social Control." *Federal Probation* 72 (3):10–21.

Byrne, J. M., and D. Hummer. 2007. "Myths and Realities of Prison Violence: A Review of the Evidence." *Victims and Offenders* 2:77–90.

Cadigan, T. 2009. "Implementing Evidence-Based Practices in Federal Pretrial Services." *Federal Probation* 73:30–32.

Cadigan, T. P., J. L. Johnson, and C. T. Lowenkamp. 2012. "The Re-validation of the Federal Pretrial Services Risk Assessment (PTRA)." *Federal Probation* (September):3–9.

Cady, M.S., and J. R. Phelps. 2008. "Preserving the Delicate Balance Between Judicial Accountability and Independence: Merit Selection in the Post-White World." *Cornell Journal of Law and Public Policy* 17:343–81.

Cahill, M. T. 2007a. "Attempt, Reckless Homicide, and the Design of Criminal Law." *University of Colorado Law Review* 78:879–956.

———. 2007b. "Retributive Justice in the Real World." *Washington University Law Quarterly* 85:815–70.

California Department of Corrections and Rehabilitation. 2014. "Career Opportunities." California Department of Corrections and Rehabilitation website. www.cdcr.ca.gov_opportunities/por /documents.html.

"California to Redesign Prison Education Programs." 2011. *Correctional News*, March 16. www.correctionalnews.com.

Callahan, D. G. 2013. "Oxford Settles Taser Lawsuit." *Dayton Daily News*. March 7. http://www.daytondailynews.com.

Callahan, L. A., M. A. McGreevy, C. Cirincione, and H. J. Steadman. 1992. "Measure the Effects of the Guilty but Mentally Ill (GBMI) Verdict." *Law and Human Behavior* 16:447–62.

Cammack, M. 2010. "The Exclusionary Rule: The Rise and Fall of the Constitutional Exclusionary Rule in the United States." *American Journal of Comparative Law* 58:631–58.

Camp, C. G. 2003. *Corrections Yearbook, 2002.* Middletown, CT: Criminal Justice Institute.

Camp, S. D., and G. G. Gales. 2002. "Growth and Quality of U.S. Private Prisons: Evidence from a National Survey." *Criminology & Public Policy* 1:427–50.

Campbell, J. 2011. "State Unions Brace for Impact of Layoffs." *The Press & Sun Bulletin,* May 22. http://www.pressconnects .com.

———. 2012. "Budget Cuts Could Gut Probation Officers." FOX 13 News online, March 2. www.myfoxtampabay.com.

Cancino, J. M., and R. Enriquez. 2004. "A Qualitative Analysis of Officer Peer Retaliation: Preserving the Police Culture." *Policing: International Journal of Police Strategies and Management* 27:320–40.

Canes-Wrone, B., T. Clark, and J. Park. 2012. "Judicial Independence and Retention Elections." *Journal of Law, Economics, and Organization* 28:211–34.

Canto, M. 1998. "Federal Government Investigates Use of Stun Belt." *Lansing* (MI) *State Journal*, August 7, p. 4A.

Caputo, M., and C. M. Miller. 2006. "In Wake of Death, Juvenile Boot Camp System is Scrapped." *Miami Herald*, April 27. http://www.miami.com /miamiherald/14438114.htm.

Carlon, A. 2007. "Entrapment, Punishment, and the Sadistic State." *Virginia Law Review* 93:1081–1134.

Carodine, M. 2010. "Keeping It Real: Reform of the 'Untried Conviction' Impeachment Rule." *Maryland Law Review* 69:501–86.

Carr, P. J., L. Napolitano, and J. Keating. 2007. "We Never Call the Cops and Here's Why: A Qualitative Examination of Legal Cyncism in Three Philadelphia Neighborhoods." *Criminology* 45:445–80.

Carroll-Ferrary, 2006. "Incarcerated Men and Women, the Equal Protection Clause, and the Requirement of 'Similarly Situated.'" *New York Law School Law Review* 51:594–617.

Carroll, L. 1974. *Hacks, Blacks, and Cons: Race Relations in a Maximum Security Prison.* Lexington, MA: Lexington Books.

Carson, E.A., and D. Golinelli. 2013a. "Prisoners in 2012—Advance Counts." *Bureau of Justice Statistics Bulletin*, July. NCJ 242467.

———. 2013b. "Prisoners in 2012: Trends in Admissions and Releases, 1991-2012." *Bureau of Justice Statistics Bulletin*, December. NCJ 243920.

Carson, E.A., and W.J. Sabol, "Prisoners in 2011," *Bureau of Justice Statistics Bulletin*, December. NCJ 239808.

Chacon, J. M. 2010. "Border Exceptionalism in the Era of Moving Borders." *Fordham Urban Law Journal* 38:129–52.

Chaddock, G. R. 2002. "Sniper Revives Prospects for Gun-Tracking Moves." *Christian Science Monitor*, October 17, p. 1.

Champion, D. J. 1989. "Private Counsels and Public Defenders: A Look at Weak Cases, Prior Records, and Leniency in Plea Bargaining." *Journal of Criminal Justice* 17:253–63.

Chang, C. 2012. "Behind, but Few Have Access to the Classes." *New Orleans Times-Picayune*, May 19. www.nola .com.

Chapman, S. G. 1970. *Police Patrol Readings*. 2nd ed. Springfield, IL: Thomas.

Chapper, J. A., and R. A. Hanson. 1989. *Understanding Reversible Error in Criminal Appeals.* Williamsburg, VA: National Center for State Courts.

Chavez, P. 2005. "Shooting Raises Racial Tension in L.A." *Sacramento Union*, February 21. http://www.sacunion.com.

Cheeseman, K.A., and R. A. Downey. 2012. "'Talking 'Bout My Generation': The Effect of 'Generation' on Correctional Employee Perceptions of Work Stress and Job Satisfaction." *Prison Journal* 92:24–44.

Chen, C., and D. Wilbur. 2014. "Heroin Resurgence in U.S. Sparked by Cheap Cost, Access." *Business Week*, February 4. www.businessweek.com.

Cheng, E. 2005. "Mitochondrial DNA: Emerging Legal Issues." *Journal of Law and Policy* 13:99–118.

Chermak, S., and E. McGarrell. 2004. "Problem-Solving Approaches to Homicide: An Evaluation of Indianapolis Violence Reduction Partnership." *Criminal Justice Policy Review* 15:161–92.

Chertoff, M., and D. Robinson. 2012. "Check One and the Accountability Is Done: The Harmful Impact of Straight-Ticket Voting on Judicial Elections." *Albany Law Review* 75:1773–97.

Christopher, R. L. 1994. "Mistake of Fact in the Objective Theory of Justification." *Journal of Criminal Law and Criminology* 85:295–332.

Church, T. W. 1985. "Examining Local Legal Culture." *American Bar Foundation Research Journal* 1985 (Summer): 449.

Cieply, M. 2011. "Mel Gibson to Plead Guilty in Abuse of Former Girlfriend." *New York Times*, March 10. www .nytimes.com.

City of Seattle. 2014. "Sworn Salary Schedule." Seattle.gov website. Accessed March 5. https://www.seattle.gov /police/jobs/benefits/salary.htm.

City of Westminster, CO. 2014. "Volunteers in Probation." City of Westminster website. http://www.ci.westminster.co.us /GetInvolved/VolunteerWestminster /VolunteersinProbation.aspx.

Clark, M. 2011. "States Beginning to Rethink Indigent Defense Systems.: Stateline: State Politics & Policy website (Pew Center on the States), December 1. http://stateline.org.

———. 2014. "Report: Florida Leads the National on Charging Kids as Adults." *MSNBC*, April 11th. http://www.msnbc .com.

Clear, T. R. 1994. *Harm in American Penology*. Albany: State University of New York Press.

Clear, T. R., and D. R. Karp. 1999. *Community Justice: Preventing Crime and Achieving Justice.* New York: Westview Press.

Clear, T., G. Cole, and M. Reisig. 2012. *American Corrections*, 10th ed. Belmont, CA: Cengage Wadsworth.

Clisura, A. 2010. "None of Their Business: The Need for Another Alternative to New York's Bail Bond Business." *Journal of Law and Policy* 19:307–51.

CNN. 2004a. "Boston Police Accept 'Full Responsibility' in Death of Red Sox Fan." October 22. http://www.cnn .com.

———. 2004b. "Police Review Policy after Tasers Used on Kids." November 14. http://www.cnn.com.

———. 2012. "Timeline of Events in Trayvon Martin Case." CNN.com, April 23. www.cnn.com.

Coe, J.. 2013. "Police: Technology Helped with Drop in Tempe Crime." *Arizona Republic,* March 13. www.azcentral.com.

Coffin, K. G. 2010. "Double Take: Evaluating Double Jeopardy Reform." *Notre Dame Law Review* 85:771–808.

Cohen, L .E., and M. Felson. 1979. "Social Change and Crime Rate Trends: A Routine Activity Approach." *American Sociological Review,* 44:588–608.

Cohen, T. H., and T. Kyckelhahn. 2010. "Felony Defendants in Large Urban Counties, 2006." Bureau of Justice Statistics *Bulletin,* May. NCJ 228944.

Cohen. A. 2014. "Freedom After 30 Years on Death Row." *The Atlantic,* March 11. www.theatlantic.com.

Coleman, K. 2011. "The Mob Goes Green." National Public Radio. http://www.npr.org/blogs/thetwo-way/2011/12/07/143271128/the-mob-goes-green-organizedcrime-profits-with-new-jersey-recycling.

Coleman, T., and D. Cotton. 2010. "Reducing Risk and Improving Outcomes of Police Interactions with People with Mental Illness." *Journal of Police Crisis Negotiations* 10:39–57.

Collins, J. 2005. *Preventing Identity Theft in Your Business: How to Protect Your Business, Customers, and Employees.* New York: Wiley.

Comey, J. B. 2013. "Statement Before the Senate Committee on Homeland Security and Government Affairs." Washington, DC, November 14. www.fbi.gov.

"Connecticut Mourns After Newtown Massacre; 27 Dead, Including 20 Children." *New Haven Register,* December 14. http://www.nhregister.com.

Conte, M. 2012. "Former Belleville Man Charged As Member of Credit Card Forgery Ring." *The Jersey Journal,* February 23. www.nj.com.

Cook, J. 2013. "Plea Bargaining, Sentence Modification, and the Real World." *Wake Forest Law Review* 48:65–94.

Cook, N. 2010. "How the Recession Hurts Private Prisons." *Newsweek,* June 29. http://www.thedailybeast.com/newsweek/2010/06/30/how-the-recession-hurts-private-prisons.html.

Cook, P. J. 2013. "The Great American Gun War: Notes from Four Decades in the Trenches." *Crime and Justice* 42:19–63.

Cook, P. J., and J. Laub. 2002. "After the Epidemic: Recent Trends in Youth Violence in the United States." *Crime and Justice: A Review of Research* 29:1–37.

Cooney, M. 1994. "Evidence as Partisanship." *Law & Society Review* 28:833–58.

Cooper, C. 2009. "Yes Virginia, There is a Police Code of Silence: Prosecuting Police Officers and the Police Subculture." *Criminal Law Bulletin* 45:277–82.

Copes, H., G. E. Higgins, R. Tewksbury, and D. Dabney. 2010. "Participation in the Prison Economy and Likelihood of Physical Victimization." *Victims & Offenders* 6(1):1–18.

COPS (Community Oriented Policing Services, U.S. Department of Justice). 2014. COPS website. Accessed March 3. http://www.cops.usdoj.gov/.

Cordner, G., and E. P. Biebel. 2005. "Problem-Oriented Policing in Practice." *Criminology & Public Policy* 4:155–80.

Cornwell, E., and V. Hans. 2011. "Representation through Participation: A Multilevel Analysis of Jury Deliberations." *Law & Society Review* 45:667–98.

Corsaro, N., R. Brunson, and E. McGarrell. 2012. "Problem-Oriented Policing and Open-Air Drug Markets: Examining the Rockford Pulling Levers Deterrence Strategy." *Crime and Delinquency* (forthcoming).

Costanzo, M. 1997. *Just Revenge.* New York: St. Martin's Press.

Costinett, A. H. 2011. "'In a Puff of Smoke': Drug Crime and the Perils of Subjective Entrapment." *American Criminal Law Review* 48:1757–87.

Coughlin, M. 2012. "Prison Reform Bill to Help Fund Probation and Parole." PhillyBurbs.com website, July 15. www.phillyburbs.com.

Covey, R. D. 2011. "Longitudinal Guilt: Repeat Offenders, Plea Bargaining, and the Variable Standard of Proof." *Florida Law Review* 63:431–55.

———. 2013. "Plea Bargaining After *Laflar* and *Frye.*" *Duquesne Law Review* 51:595–623.

Coyle, M. 2009. "New Report Shows Sharp Rise in Prison Time for Federal Offenders." *National Law Journal* February 12. www.law.com.

Crawford, C., T. Chiricos, and G. Kleck. 1998. "Race, Racial Threat, and Sentencing of Habitual Offenders." *Criminology* 36 (August):481–512.

Cristani, A. S., and B. C. Frueh. 2011. "Risk of Trauma Exposure among Persons with Mental Illness in Jails and Prisons: What Do We Really Know?" *Current Opinion in Psychiatry* 24(5):431–35.

Crummy, K. 2009. "Colorado Criminals Owe State's Victims Nearly $778 Million." *Denver Post,* September 24. www.denverpost.com.

Cullen, F. T., T. Leming, B. Link, and J. Wozniak. 1985. "The Impact of Social Supports in Police Stress." *Criminology* 23:503–22.

Cunningham, W. C., J. J. Strauchs, and C. W. Van Meter. 1990. *Private Security Trends, 1970 to the Year 2000.* Boston: Butterworth-Heinemann.

Cyberbullying Research Center. 2014. "Cyberbullying Facts." http://cyberbullying.us/research/facts/.

D'Alessio, S., J. Flexon, and L. Stolzenberg. 2013. "The Effect of Conjugal Visitation on Sexual Violence in Prison." *American Journal of Criminal Justice* 38:13–26.

D'Zurilla, C. 2013a. "Stephen Baldwin Avoids Jail with Guilty Plea in Tax Case." *Los Angeles Times.* March 29. http://www.latimes.com.

———. 2013b. "Wesley Snipes Released from Prison, Still Under House Arrest." *Los Angeles Times.* April 5. http://www.latimes.com.

Dabney, D. A., H. Copes, R. Tewksbury, and S. R. Hawk-Tourtelot. 2013. "A Qualitative Assessment of Stress Perceptions Among Members of a Homicide Unit." *Justice Quarterly* 30:811–36.

Daftary-Kapur, T., R. Dumas, and S. D. Penrod. 2010. "Jury Decision-Making Biases and Methods to Counter Them." *Legal and Criminological Psychology* 15:133–54.

Damron, G., E. Anderson, and J. Wisely. 2013. "Wayne County Prosecutor Kym Worth Cuts Start to Affect Suburbs." *Detroit Free Press,* April 1. www.freep.com.

Dansky, K. 2008. "Understanding California Sentencing." *University of San Francisco Law Review* 43:45–86.

Davey, J. D. 1998. *The Politics of Prison Expansion: Winning Elections by Waging War on Crime.* Westport, CT: Praeger.

Davis, A. 2008. *Arbitrary Justice: The Power of the American Prosecutor.* New York: Oxford University Press.

Davis, M., R. Lundman, and R. Martinez Jr. 1991. "Private Corporate Justice: Store Police, Shoplifters, and Civil Recovery." *Social Problems* 38:395–408.

Davis, R. C., C. S. O'Sullivan, D. J. Farole, and M. Rempel. 2008. "A Comparison of Two Prosecution Policies in Cases of Intimate Partner Violence: Mandatory Case Filing Versus Following the Victim's Lead." *Criminology & Public Policy* 7:633–62.

Davis, S. 2012. "Ionia Site Targeted in Budget Proposal." *Lansing State Journal,* April 7. www.lsj.com.

Davitz, T. 1998. "The Gangs Behind Bars." *Insight on the News,* September 28.

Dawson, M., and R. Dinovitzer. 2001. "Victim Cooperation and the Prosecution of Domestic Violence in a Specialized Court." *Justice Quarterly* 18:593–622.

De Leon, 2013. "Seattle Police Turn to Computer Software to Predict, Fight Crime." *Seattle Times,* February 27. www.seattletimes.com.

Death Penalty Information Center. 2014. *Facts About the Death Penalty*, March 21 (www.deathpenaltyinfo.org).

Dedel, K. 2010. "Fifth Monitor's Report for the Baltimore City Juvenile Justice Center (BCJJC) for the Period of July 1, 2009 through December 31, 2009." http://www.djs.state.md.us.

DeFrances, C. J., and J. Litras. 2000. "Indigent Defense Services in Large Counties, 1999." Bureau of Justice Statistics *Bulletin*, November.

DeJohn, I. 2014. "'Loud Music' Case: Jury Was Deadlocked Two Days into Trial Due to Stand Your Ground Law: Juror." *New York Daily News,* February 19. www.nydailynews.com.

DeJong, C., and E. S. Merrill, 2000. "Getting 'Tough on Crime': Juvenile Waiver and the Criminal Court." *Ohio Northern University Law Review* 27:175–96.

DeJong, C., S. Mastrofski, and R. Parks. 2001. "Patrol Officers and Problem Solving: An Application of Expectancy Theory." *Justice Quarterly* 18:31–61.

Deng, X. 2012. "Prison Population Continues to Drop." *Daily Tribune*, April 1. www.dailytribune.com.

Dery, G. 2011. "Do You Believe in *Miranda*? The Supreme Court Reveals Its Doubts in *Berghuis v. Thompkins* by Paradoxically Ruling That Suspects Can Only Invoke Their Right to Remain Silent by Speaking." *George Mason University Civil Rights Law Journal* 21:407–40.

Devers, L. 2011. *Plea and Charge Bargaining: Research Summary.* Washington, DC: U.S. Bureau of Justice Assistance.

Dewan, S. 2007. "An SOS for 911 Systems in Age of High-Tech." *New York Times*, April 6. http://www.nytimes.com.

———. 2009. "Prosecutors Block Access to DNA Testing for Inmates." *New York Times*, May 18. http://www.nytimes.com.

Diamond, S., D. Peery, F. Dolan, and E. Dolan. 2009. "Achieving Diversity on the Jury: Jury Size and the Peremptory Challenge." *Journal of Empirical Legal Studies* 6:425–49.

Dickerson, B.E. 2008. "Hard Lemonade, Hard Price." *Detroit Free Press*, April 28. http://www.freep.com.

Diedrich, J., and G. Barton. 2013. "New Milwaukee Police Procedures Address Racial Profiling, Crime Data." *Milwaukee Journal Sentinel*, February 7. www.jsonline.com.

DiIulio, J. J., Jr. 1987. *Governing Prisons.* New York: Free Press.

———. 1991. *No Escape: The Future of American Corrections.* New York: Basic Books.

———. 1993. "Rethinking the Criminal Justice System: Toward a New Paradigm." In *Performance Measures for the Criminal Justice System.* Washington,

DC: Bureau of Justice Statistics, U.S. Government Printing Office.

Dirks-Linhorst, P. A., D. Kondrat, D. M. Linhorst, and N. Morani. 2013. "Factors Associated with Mental Health Court Nonparticipation and Negative Termination." *Justice Quarterly* 30:681–710.

Dissell, R. 2012. "Rape Charges against High School Players Divide Football Town of Steubenville, Ohio." Cleveland Plain Dealer, September 2. www.cleveland.com.

Doerner, J. K., and S. Demuth. 2010. "The Independent and Joint Effects of Race/Ethnicity, Gender, and Age on Sentencing Outcomes in U.S. Federal Courts." *Justice Quarterly* 27:1–27.

Donziger, S. R., ed. 1996. *The Real War on Crime: The Report of the National Criminal Justice Commission.* New York: HarperCollins.

Dority, B. 2005. "The USA Patriot Act Has Decimated Many Civil Liberties." In *Homeland Security: Current Controversies*, ed. A. Nakaya. Detroit: Thomson/Gale, 130–36.

Dripps, D. 2010. "The 'New' Exclusionary Rule Debate: From 'Still Preoccupied with 1985' to 'Virtual Deterrence,'" *Fordham Urban Law Journal* 37:743–801.

Dubail, J. 2009. "Cuyahoga County Jury Pay Cut to Save Money." May 14. www.cleveland.com.

Duke, A. 2013. "Lindsay Lohan Goes to Jail on Probation Violation." CNN.com, September. www.cnn.com.

Duke, A., and T. Rowlands. 2009. "Chris Brown Pleads Guilty in Rihanna Assault Case." CNN.com, June 22. http://www.cnn.com.

Duncan, I. 2013. "Lawmakers Call for Replacement of Baltimore Jail." *The Baltimore Sun*, December 11th. http://baltimoresun.com.

Durose, M. R., E. L. Schmitt, and P. Langan. 2005. *Contacts between Police and Public: Findings from the 2002 National Survey.* Washington, DC: Bureau of Justice Statistics, U.S. Government Printing Office, April.

Dyer, B. 2012. "Mayors' Courts Should Be Nuked." *Akron Beacon Journal*, January 24. www.ohio.com.

Dzur, A. 2011. "Restorative Justice and Democracy: Fostering Public Accountability for Criminal Justice." *Contemporary Justice Review*, 14:367–81.

Earley, P. 1992. *The Hot House: Life inside Leavenworth Prison.* New York: Bantam Books.

Eaton, L., and L. Kaufman. 2005. "In Problem-Solving Court, Judges Turn Therapist." *New York Times*, April 26. www.nytimes.com.

Eckholm, E. 2008a. "Citing Workload, Public Lawyers Reject New Cases."

New York Times, November 9. http://www.nytimes.com.

———. 2008b. "New Tack on Straying Parolees Offers a Hand Instead of Cuffs." *New York Times*, May 17. www.nytimes.com.

———. 2008c. "U.S. Shifting Prison Focus to Re-entry Into Society." *New York Times*, April 8. http://www.nytimes.com.

———. 2010. "Congress Moves to Narrow Cocaine Sentencing Disparities." *New York Times*, July 28. www.nytimes.com.

"Economics of CJA Representations Costly to Attorneys." 2008. *The Third Branch* (April) http://www.uscourts.gov/news/TheThirdBranch/08-04-01/Economics_of_CJA_Representations_Costly_to_Attorneys.aspx.

Edgemon, E. 2013. "10 Minutes Per Month: Alabama Probation, Parole Officers Get Little Time with 67,410 They Oversee." *Birmingham News.* May 20. http://blog.al.com.

Edkins, V. 2011. "Defense Attorney Plea Recommendations and Client Race: Does Zealous Representation Apply Equally to All?" *Law and Human Behavior* 35:413–25.

Edwards, B. 2014. "Cyber-Crime Becoming Top Priority for Federal Law Enforcement." CBS Chicago online, Feburary 18. http://chicago.cbslocal.com/2014/02/18/cyber-crime-becoming-top-priority-for-federal-law-enforcement/.

Egan, P. 2014. "Michigan Urged to Reject $145M Prison Food Contract Over Safety Concerns." *Detroit Free Press*, March 19. www.freep.com.

Egley, A. and J.C. Howell. 2013. *Highlights of the 2011 National Youth Gang Survey* (NCJ 242884). Washington, DC: U.S. Department of Justice.

Eichenwald, K. 2006. "On the Web, Pedophiles Extend Their Reach." *New York Times*, August 21. http://www.nytimes.com.

Eigenberg, H. 2000. "Correctional Officers and Their Perceptions of Homosexuality, Rape, and Prostitution in Male Prisons." *Prison Journal* 80 (December): 415–33.

Eisenberg, T., P. Hannaford-Agor, V. P. Hans, N. L. Mott, G. T. Munsterman, S. J. Schwab, and M. T. Wells. 2005. "Judge-Jury Agreement in Criminal Cases: A Partial Replication of Kalven and Zeisel's *The American Jury.*" *Journal of Empirical Legal Studies* 2:171–206.

Eisenstein, J., R. B. Flemming, and P. F. Nardulli. 1988. *The Contours of Justice: Communities and Their Courts.* Boston: Little, Brown.

Eith, C., and M. R. Durose. 2011. "Contacts between Police and the Public, 2008." *BJS Special Report*. October. NCJ234599.

Eligon, J., and T. Kaplan. 2012. "New York State Set to Add All Convict DNA to Its Database." *New York Times*, March 13. www.nytimes.com.

Ellement, J. R., and S. Smalley. 2006. "Six Crime Disclosure Questioned." *Boston Globe*, April 18. http://www.boston.com.

Emery, S. 2012. "Parolee Arrested in Pimping of 15-Year-Old Girl." *Orange County Register*, February 28. www.ocregister.com.

Emmelman, D. S. 1996. "Trial by Plea Bargain: Case Settlement as a Product of Recursive Decisionmaking." *Law & Society Review* 30:335–60.

Engber, D. 2005. "Does the FBI Have Your Fingerprints?" *Slate*, April 22. http://www.slate.msn.com/id/2117226.

Engel, R. S., and J. M. Calnon. 2004. "Examining the Influence of Drivers' Characteristics during Traffic Stops with Police: Results from a National Survey." *Justice Quarterly* 21:49–90.

Engel, R. S., J. M. Calnon, and T. J. Bernard. 2002. "Theory and Racial Profiling: Shortcomings and Future Directions in Research." *Justice Quarterly* 19:249–73.

Engen, R. 2009. "Assessing Determinate and Presumptive Sentencing—Making Research Relevant." *Criminology & Public Policy* 8:323–36.

Enion, M.R. 2009. "Constitutional Limits on Private Policing and the State's Allocation of Force." *Duke Law Journal* 59:519–51.

Enriquez, R., and J. W. Clark. 2007. "The Social Psychology of Peremptory Challenges: An Examination of Latino Jurors." *Texas Hispanic Journal of Law and Policy* 13:25–38.

Epp, C., and S. Maynard-Moody. 2014. "Driving While Black." *Washington Monthly*, January/February. www.washingtonmonthly.com.

Epp, Charles R. 2009. *Making Rights Real: Activists, Bureaucrats, and the Creation of the Legalistic State*. Chicago: University of Chicago Press.

Erhard, S. 2008. "Plea Bargaining and the Death Penalty: An Exploratory Study." *Justice System Journal* 29:313–27.

Estep, D. 2009. "Wyoming Mom Says Michigan Youth Challenge Academy Pays Off, Deserves State Funding." *Grand Rapids Press*, August 29. www.mlive.com.

Fahey, T. 2011. "Tough Decisions Remain Regarding State Budget." *The Union Leader*, May 20. http://www.unionleader.com.

Fak, M. 2013. "Musical Chairs Complete with Dwight Women Transferred to Logan County Correctional Center." *Logan County Herald*, March 30. http://www.logancountyherald.com.

Fantz,, A. 2013. "Ariel Castro Agrees to Plea to Avoid Death Penalty." CNN.com, July 28. www.cnn.com.

Farole, D. J., and L. Langton. 2010. "County-Based and Local Public Defender Offices, 2007." Bureau of Justice Statistics *Special Report*, September. NCJ 231175.

Fathi, D. C. 2010. "The Challenge of Prison Oversight." *American Criminal Law Review* 47:1453–62.

Faturechi, R. 2011. "Report Details Misconduct by L.A. County Sheriff's Deputies." *Los Angeles Times*, August 5. www.latimes.com.

Favate, S. 2012. "Shrinking State Court Budgets: Not Just A New York Thing." *Wall Street Journal*, January 12. www.wsj.com.

FBI (Federal Bureau of Investigation). 2006. "FBI Cyber Action Teams: Traveling the World to Catch Cyber Criminals." March 6. http://www.fbi.gov.

———. 2008. "Cyber Solidarity: Five Nations, One Mission." March 18. http://www.fbi.gov.

———. 2011. *Hate Crime Statistics*, 2010. Washington, DC.

———. 2012. "Special Agent FAQs." FBI website. https://www.fbijobs.gov/114.asp.

———. 2013a. *Crime in the United States, 2012* (Uniform Crime Reports). www.fbi.gov.

———. 2013b. *Crime in the United States, 2013 (Preliminary Semiannual Uniform Crime Report)*. http://www.fbi.gov.

———. 2013c. "NIBRS Participation by State." *National Incident Based Reporting System, 2012* (Uniform Crime Reports). http://www.fbi.gov.

———. 2013d. *Today's FBI: Facts and Figures, 2013–14*. Washington, D.C.: U.S. Department of Justice.

———. 2014. "Special Agent Frequently Asked Questions." FBI.gov website. Accessed March 5. www.fbi.gov.

FBI Press Release. 2012. "Portsmouth Bail Bondsman Sentenced to 30 Months in Prison for Bribing Public Officials." November 2. http://www.fbi.gov.

Feeley, M., and E. Rubin. 1998. *Judicial Policy Making and the Modern State*. New York: Cambridge University Press.

Feingold, D.A. 2005. "Human Trafficking." *Foreign Policy* 150:26–30.

Felch, J. 2003. "How a 'Calm but Aggravated' Teenager Died on East Thrill Place." *Denver Post*, July 11. http://www.denverpost.com.

Felch, J., and M. Dolan. 2008. "DNA Matches Aren't Always a Lock." *Los Angeles Times*, May 4. http://www.latimes.com.

Feld, B. 1999. *Bad Kids: Race and the Transformation of the Juvenile Court*. New York: Oxford University Press.

———. 2004. "Editorial Introduction: Juvenile Transfers." *Criminology & Public Policy* 3 (November):599–603.

Feld, B. C. 1993. "Criminalizing the American Juvenile Court." In *Crime and Justice: A Review of Research*, vol. 17, ed. M. Tonry. Chicago: University of Chicago Press, 197–280.

Fenton, J. 2011. "More than 30 Baltimore Police Officers Charged, Suspended in Towing Scheme." *Baltimore Sun*, February 23. www.baltimoresun.com.

Ferguson, J. 2009. "Professional Discretion and the Use of Restorative Justice Programs in Appropriate Domestic Violence Cases: An Effective Innovation." *Criminal Law Brief* 4:3–17.

Ferretti, C. and M. Feighan. 2009. "Teen Dies after Warren Police Use Taser." *Detroit News*, April 11. http://www.detnews.com.

Feuer, A. 2006. "For Ex-F.B.I. Agent Accused in Murders, a Case of What Might Have Been." *New York Times*, April 15. http://www.nytimes.com.

Fields, G., and J. R. Emshwiller. 2012. "Federal Guilty Pleas Soar As Bargains Trump Trials." *Wall Street Journal*, September 23. http://online.wsj.com.

Fields, J., and K. Peveto. 2008. "Local Cop Cars Going Hi-Tech." *Abilene (TX) Reporter News*, December 4. http://www.reporternews.com.

Finley, A. 2011. "California Prison Academy: Better Than a Harvard Degree." *Wall Street Journal*, April 30. http://online.wsj.com.

Finn, B., M. Shively, J. McDevitt, W. Lassiter, and T. Rich. 2005. *Comparison of Activities and Lessons Learned among 19 School Resource Officer (SRO) Programs*. Boston: Abt Associates.

Finn, M. 2013. "Evidence-Based and Victim-Centered Prosecutorial Policies: Examination of Deterrent and Therapeutic Jurisprudence Effects on Domestic Violence." *Criminology and Public Policy* 12:443–72.

Finn, P., and J. McDevitt. 2005. National Assessment of School Resource Officer Programs. Report to the National Institute of Justice. Unpublished.

Fischman, J., and M. Schanzenbach. 2011. "Do Standards of Review Matter? The Case of Federal Criminal Sentencing." *Journal of Legal Studies* 40:405–37.

Fisher, B. S., L. E. Daigle, & F. T. Cullen. 2010. "What Distinguishes Single from Recurrent Sexual Victims? The Role of Lifestyle-Routine Activities and First-Incident Characteristics," *Justice Quarterly*, 27(1):102–29.

Fisher, D. M. 2007. "Striking a Balance: The Need to Temper Judicial Discretion against a Background of Legislative Interest in Federal Sentencing." *Duquesne Law Review* 46:65–97.

Flanagan, T. J., ed. 1995. *Long-Term Imprisonment*. Thousand Oaks, CA: Sage.

Flango, V. E. 1994. *Habeas Corpus in State and Federal Courts*. Williamsburg, VA: National Center for State Courts.

Fleisher, M. S., and J. L. Krienert. 2006. The Culture of Prison Sexual Violence. Unpublished.

Flock, E. 2012. "California School Protests: 5 Reasons Students Are Demonstrating." *Washington Post*, March 6. www.washingtonpost.com.

Florencio, D. and C. Herley. 2012. "The Cybercrime Wave That Wasn't." *New York Times*, April 14. www.nytimes.com.

Florey, K. 2013. "Beyond Uniqueness: Reimagining Tribal Courts' Jurisdiction." *California Law Review* 101:1499–1564.

Florida Office of Program Policy Analysis and Government Accountability. 2010. *Intermediate Sanctions for Non-Violent Offenders Could Produce Savings*, Report No. 10-27 (March).

Florio, G. 2013. "Jordan Johnson to Jurors: 'She Never Said No." *The Missoulian*. February 27. http://missoulian.com.

Florio, G., and K. Szpaller. 2013. "Final Arguments in Johnson Case Focus on Accuser." *The Missoulian*. March 1. http://missoulian.com.

Flowers, R. 2010. "The Role of the Defense Attorney: Not Just An Advocate." *Ohio State Journal of Criminal Law* 7:647–52.

Foley, S. 2013. "The Newly Murky World of Searches Incident to Lawful Arrest: Why the Gant Restrictions Should Apply to All Searches Incident to Arrest." *University of Kansas Law Review* 61:753–83.

"For Federal Courts, Shutdown Caused Broad Disruptions." 2013. *The Third Branch News*, October 25. http://news.uscourts.gov/federal-courts-shutdown-caused-broad-disruptions.

Ford, D., M. Martinez, and J. Sterling. 2013. "Not Guilty Plea for Suspect in Alleged Decade-Long Ohio Kidnapping." CNN.com, June 12. www.cnn.com.

Fountain, H. 2009. "Plugging Holes in the Science of Forensics." *New York Times*, May 12. http://www.nytimes.com.

Fox, J. G. 1982. *Organizational and Racial Conflict in Maximum Security Prisons*. Lexington, MA: Lexington Books.

Frantz, S., and R. Borum. 2011. "Crisis Intervention Teams May Prevent Arrests of People with Mental Illnesses." *Police Practice and Research: An International Journal* 12:265–72.

Freskos, B. 2011. "Education in N.C. Prisons Is Top of the Class." *Wilmington Star News,* May 20. www.starnewsonline.com.

Fridell, L. 1990. "Decision Making of the District Attorney: Diverting or Prosecuting Intrafamilial Child Sexual Abuse Offenders." *Criminal Justice Policy Review* 4:249–67.

Friedman, L. M. 1993. *Crime and Punishment in American History*. New York: Basic Books.

Friedrichs, D. O. 2010. *Trusted Criminals: White Collar Crime in Contemporary Society*. 4th ed. Belmont, CA: Cengage.

Frohmann, L. 1997. "Convictability and Discordant Locales: Reproducing Race, Class, and Gender Ideologies in Prosecutorial Decisionmaking." *Law & Society Review* 31:531–56.

Frosch, D., and K. Johnson. 2012. "Gunman Kills 12 in Colorado, Reviving Gun Law Debate." *New York Times*, July 20. www.nytimes.com.

Gabbidon, S., and G. Higgins. 2009. "The Role of Race/Ethnicity and Race Relations on Public Opinion Related to the Treatment of Blacks by the Police." *Police Quarterly* 12:102–15.

Gabbidon, S., G. Higgins, and H. Potter. 2011. "Race, Gender, and the Perception of Recently Experiencing Unfair Treatment by the Police: Exploratory Results from an All-Black Sample." *Criminal Justice Review* 36:5–21.

Galanek, J. 2013. "The Cultural Construction of Mental Illness in Prison: A Perfect Storm of Pathology." *Culture, Medicine, and Psychiatry* 37:195–225.

Garcia, M. 2005. "N.Y. Using Terrorism Law to Prosecute Street Gang." *Washington Post*, February 1, p. A3.

Gebo, E., N. Stracuzzi, and V. Hurst. 2006. "Juvenile Justice Reform and the Courtroom Workgroup: Issues of Perception and Workload." *Journal of Criminal Justice* 34:425–33.

Gelman, A., J. Fagan, and A. Kiss. 2007. "An Analysis of the New York City Police Department's 'Stop-and-Frisk' Policy in the Context of Claims of Racial Bias." *Journal of the American Statistical Society* 102:813–23.

Genter, S., G. Hooks, and C. Mosher. 2013. "Prisons, Jobs, and Privatization: The Impact of Prisons on Employment Growth in Rural U.S. Counties, 1997–2004." *Social Science Research* 42:596–610.

Georgiady, B. N. 2008. "An Exceedingly Painful Encounter: The Reasonableness of Pain and De Minimis Injuries for Fourth Amendment Excessive Force Claims." *Syracuse Law Review* 59:123–64.

Gest, T. 2013. "Juvenile Justice Programs Face Sharp New Cuts in Federal $$." *The Crime Report*, July 12. www.thecrimereport.org.

Geyh, C. 2012. "Can the Rule of Law Survive Judicial Politics?" *Cornell Law Review* 97:191–253.

Gezari, V. M. 2008. "Cracking Open." *Washington Post*, June 1. http://www.washingtonpost.com.

Giblin, M. J., G. W. Burruss, and J. A. Schafer. 2014. "A Stone's Throw from the Metropolis: Re-Examining Small-Agency Homeland Security Practices." *Justice Quarterly* 31:368–93.

Gill, J., and M. Pasquale-Styles. 2009. "Firearm Deaths by Law Enforcement." *Journal of Forensic Sciences* 54:185–88.

Girshick, L. B. 1999. *No Safe Haven: Stories of Women in Prison*. Boston: Northeastern University Press.

Glaze, L. 2011. "Correctional Population in the United States, 2010." Bureau of Justice Statistics *Bulletin*, December. NCJ236319.

Glaze, L., and E. J. Herberman. 2013. "Correctional Populations in the United States, 2012." *Bureau of Justice Statistics Bulletin*, December. NCJ 243936.

Glaze, L. E. and L. M. Maruschak. 2008. Parents in Prison and Their Minor Children. Bureau of Justice Statistics *Special Report*. Washington, DC: U.S. Department of Justice.

Glaze, L. E., and T. P. Bonczar. 2009. "Probation and Parole in the United States, 2007 Statistical Tables." *Bureau of Justice Statistics Bulletin,* August. NCJ 224707.

———. 2010. "Probation and Parole in the United States, 2009." Bureau of Justice Statistics *Bulletin*, December. NCJ 231674.

Goldfarb, R. L. 1965. *Ransom: A Critique of the American Bail System*. New York: Harper & Row.

Goldkamp, J. S., and E. R. Vilcica. 2008. "Targeted Enforcement and Adverse System Side Effects: The Generation of Fugitives in Philadelphia." *Criminology* 46:371–409.

———. 1990. *Problem-Oriented Policing*. New York: McGraw-Hill.

Goldman, R. 2013. "Gang Leader Impregnates Four Female Prison Guards." ABC News online, April 24. http://abcnews.go.com.

Goldschmidt, D., and C. E. Shoichet. 2013. "Former Guards Accused of Smuggling Cell Phones into Texas Prison." CNN.com, February 28. http://www.cnn.com.

Goldstein, J. 2013. "Judge Tells Ex-Chief of Police Not to Turn Testimony Into a Speech." *New York Times*. April 9. http://www.nytimes.com.

Goldstein, S. 2014. "Both Sides of the Michael Dunn Trial Speak Out Against Jury's Ruling." *New York Daily News*, February 17. www.nydailynews.com.

Goode, E. 2012. "Stronger Hand for Judges in the 'Barzaar' of Plea Deals." *New York Times*, March 22. www.nytimes.com.

Goodman, J. 1994. *Stories of Scottsboro*. New York: Random House.

Goodman, J. D. 2013. "Report Documents a Rise in Fatal Shootings by New York City's Police Officers." *New York Times*, November 19. www.nytimes.com.

Gordon, J. 2005. "In Patriots' Cradle, the Patriot Act Faces Scrutiny." *New York Times*, April 24. http://www.nytimes.com.

Gordon, J. A., B. Proulx, and P.H. Grant. 2013. "Trepidation Among the "Keepers": Gendered Perceptions of Fear and Risk of Victimization Among Corrections Officers." *American Journal of Criminal Justice* 38:245–65.

Gordon, S. 2013. "Through the Eyes of Jurors: The Use of Schemas in the Application of 'Plain Language' Jury Instructions." *Hastings Law Journal* 64:643–67.

Gossett, D., and M. Law. 2012. "Charges Filed against Two Juveniles." Herald Star Online (Steubenville, Ohio), August 24. Heraldstaronline.com.

Gover, A. R., J. M. MacDonald, and G. P. Alpert. 2003. "Combating Domestic Violence: Findings from an Evaluation of a Local Domestic Violence Court." *Criminology & Public Policy* 3:109–31.

Governor's Office on Drug Control Policy. 2006. *Iowa's Drug Control Strategy, 2006*. http://www.iowa.gov/odcp /images/pdf/Strategy_06.pdf.

Grady, D. 2003. "F.D.A. Outlines Plans to Counter Growing Trade in Counterfeit Pharmaceuticals." *New York Times*, October 3. http://www.nytimes.com.

Grasha, K. 2009a. "Going Paperless." *Lansing (MI) State Journal*, February 9, pp. 1A, 4A.

———. 2009b. "Ingham Co. Jail Inmates May Opt for House Arrest." *Lansing (MI) State Journal*, March 11, p. 1A–2A.

Grattet, R., J. Lin, and J. Petersilia. 2011. "Supervision Regimes, Risk, and Official Reactions to Parolees Deviance." *Criminology* 49:371–400.

Gray, D. 2013. "A Spectacular Non Sequitur: The Supreme Court's Contemporary Fourth Amendment Exclusionary Rule Jurisprudence." *American Criminal Law Review* 50:1–57.

Green, A. 2009. "More States Use GPS to Track Abusers." *New York Times*, May 9. http://www.nytimes.com.

Green, F. 2011. "System Allows Federal Prisoners to Send E-Mail." *Richmond Times-Dispatch*, September 6. www2.timesdispatch.com.

Green, R. 2011. "State Puts Gingerich in Facility for Youths." *Ft. Wayne Journal Gazette*, January 15. www.journalgazette.com.

Greenberg, A. 2010. "Full-Body Scan Technology Deployed in Street-Roving Vans." *Forbes*, August 24. www .forbes.com.

Greene, J. A. 1999. "Zero Tolerance: A Case Study of Police Policies and Practices in New York City." *Crime and Delinquency* 45 (April):171–87.

Greene, J. R. 2014. "New Directions in Policing: Balancing Prediction and Meaning in Police Research." *Justice Quarterly* 31:193–228.

Greer, K. R. 2000. "The Changing Nature of Interpersonal Relationships in a Women's Prison." *Prison Journal* 80 (December):442–68.

Griffin, K. 2009. "Criminal Lying, Prosecutorial Power, and Social Meaning." *California Law Review* 97:1515–68.

Griffin, L. 2010. "Untangling Double Jeopardy in Mixed Verdict Cases. *Southern Methodist University Law Review* 63:1033–68.

Griffin, M. L., and J. R. Hepburn. 2013. "Inmate Misconduct and the Institutional Capacity for Control." *Criminal Justice and Behavior* 40:270–88.

Griffin, P. 2011. "National Overviews." State Juvenile Justice Profiles. Pittsburgh: National Center for Juvenile Justice. http://www.ncjj.org/stateprofiles.

Grissom, B. 2011. "Proposals Could Make It Harder to Leave Prison." *New York Times*, March 12. www.nytimes.com.

Gross-Shader, C. 2011. "Partnerships in Evidence-Based Policing." *Translational Criminology* (Summer), 8–9.

Grubman, S. 2011. "Bark with No Bite: How the Inevitable Discovery Rule Is Undermining the Supreme Court's Decision in *Arizona v. Gant*." *Journal of Criminal Law and Criminology* 101:119–70.

Guerino, P., and A. J. Beck. 2011. *Sexual Victimization Reported by Adult Correctional Authorities, 2007–2008*. Bureau of Justice Statistics *Special Report*. Washington, DC: U.S. Department of Justice.

Guerino, P., P. M. Harrison, and W. J. Sabol. 2011. "Prisoners in 2010." Bureau of Justice Statistics *Bulletin*, December. NCJ 236096.

Guevara, L., D. Herz, and C. Spohn. 2006. "Gender and Juvenile Justice Decision-Making: What Role Does Race Play?" *Feminist Criminology* 1(4):258–82.

Gunnell, J. J., and S. J. Ceci. 2010. "When Emotionality Trumps Reason: A Study of Individual Processing Style and Juror Bias." *Behavioral Sciences and the Law* 28:850–77.

Haberman, C. 2014. "When Youth Violence Spurred 'Superpredator' Fear." *The New York Times*. April 6th.

Habes, H. 2011. "Paying for the Graying: How California Can More Effectively Manage Its Growing Elderly Inmate Population." *Southern California Interdisciplinary Law Journal* 20:395–424.

Hagan, F. E. 1997. *Political Crime: Ideology and Criminality*. Needham Heights, MA: Allyn & Bacon.

Hails, J., and R. Borum. 2003. "Police Training and Specialized Approaches to Respond to People with Mental Illness." *Crime and Delinquency* 49:52–61.

Hall, J. 1947. *General Principles of Criminal Law*. 2nd ed. Indianapolis: Bobbs-Merrill.

Hall, M., and C. Bonneau. 2013. "Attack Advertising, the *White* Decision, and Voter Participation in State Supreme Court Elections." *Political Research Quarterly* 66:115–26.

Hallinan, J. T. 2001. *Going Up the River: Travels in a Prison Nation*. New York: Random House.

Hambling, D. 2005. "Police Toy with 'Less Lethal' Weapons." April 30. http://www.newscientist.com.

Hamilton, Z. 2010. Do Reentry Courts Reduce Recidivism? Results from the Harlem Parole Reentry Court. New York: Center for Court Innovation. http://www.courtinnovation.org.

Handy, R. 2012. "Parolee Arrested in Drug Bust." *Colorado Springs Gazette*, March 9. www.gazette.com.

Hanlon, M. 2007. "Run Away the Ray-Gun Is Coming: We Test U.S. Army's New Secret Weapon." *Daily Mail*, September 18. http://www.dailymail.co.uk.

Hannaford-Agor, P. 2011. "Systematic Negligence in Jury Operations: Why the Definition of Systematic Exclusion in Fair Cross Section Claims Must Be Expanded." *Drake Law Review* 59:762–98.

Hans, V., and N. Vidmar. 2008. "The Verdict on Juries." *Judicature* 91:226–30.

Hanson, R. A., and J. Chapper. 1991. *Indigent Defense Systems*. Williamsburg, VA: National Center for State Courts.

Harcourt, B. E., and J. Ludwig. 2006. "Broken Windows: New Evidence from New York City and a Five-City Social Experiment." *University of Chicago Law Review* 73:271–320.

Harkin, T. 2005. "Confronting the Meth Crisis." Press release, February 7. http://www.harkin.senate.gov.

Harlow, C. 2000. "Defense Counsel in Criminal Cases." Bureau of Justice Statistics *Bulletin*, November.

Harrell, E., and L. Langton. 2013. "Victims of Identity Theft, 2012." *Bureau of Justice Statistics Bulletin*. December. NCJ 243779.

Harris Poll. 2009. "Who Are You? *CSI* Answers that Question Each Week and Is America's Favorite TV Show." *Harris Interactive*. April 21. http://www.harrisinteractive.com.

Harris, D. 2013. "Across the Hudson: Taking the Stop and Frisk Debate Beyond New York City." *NYU Journal of Legislation and Public Policy* 16:853–82.

Harris, G. 2014. "Medicines Made in India Set Off Safety Worries." *New York Times*, February 14. www.nytimes .com.

Harris, J., and P. Jesilow. 2000. "It's Not the Old Ball Game: Three Strikes and the

Courtroom Workgroup." *Justice Quarterly* 17:185–204.

Harris, R. 2011. "Shootings by Police Continue to Decline." *New York Times*, November 22. www.nytimes.com.

Harrison, C. 2011. "Ten Rules for Great Jury Selection: With Some Lessons from Texas Case Law." *Defense Counsel Journal* 78:29–54.

Harrison, M. T. 2006. "True Grit: An Innovative Program for Elderly Inmates." *Corrections Today* 68(7):46–49.

Hartley, R., S. Maddan, and C. Spohn. 2007. "Prosecutorial Discretion: An Examination of Substantial Assistance Departures in Federal Crack Cocaine and Powder Cocaine Cases." *Justice Quarterly* 24:382–407.

Hastie, R., S. Penrod, and N. Pennington. 1983. *Inside the Jury*. Cambridge, MA: Harvard University Press.

Hays, T. 2006. "NYC Real Time Crime Center Tracks Suspects." *Washington Post*, May 10. http://www.washingtonpost.com.

Healy, J. 2014. "Colorado Expects to Reap Tax Bonanza from Legal Marijuana Sales." *New York Times*, February 20. http://www.nytimes.com.

Heaphy, W. 2010. "Wayne County's Mental Health Court." *Michigan Bar Journal* 89:36–38.

Heffernan, E. 1972. *Making It in Prison*. New York: Wiley.

Heil, E. 2014. "Sen. Mark Udall's Son Charged with Trespassing, Heroin Possession." *Washington Post*, January 30. www.washingtonpost.com.

Heise, M. 2009. "Federal Criminal Appeals: A Brief Empirical Perspective." *Marquette Law Review* 93:825–43.

Hennning, K. 2013. "Criminalizing Normal Adolescent Behavior in Communities of Color: The Role of Prosecutors in Juvenile Justice Reform." *Cornell Law Review* 98:383–461.

Henrichson, C., and R. Delaney. 2012. *The Price of Prisons: What Incarceration Costs Taxpayers*. New York: Vera Institute of Justice, 2012.

Hensley, J. J., and M. Wynn. 2009. "Close to Two-Thirds of Photos Taken by Speed Cameras Tossed." *Arizona Republic*, May 15. http://www.azcentral.com.

Hermann, P. 2014. "Air Force Major Charged in Child Pornography Case." *Washington Post*, January 31. www.washingtonpost.com.

Hickman, M., and B. Reaves. 2006. *Local Police Departments, 2003* (NCJ210118). Washington, DC: U.S. Department of Justice, Bureau of Justice Statistics.

———. 2007. "Neutralization Theory and Online Software Piracy: An Empirical Analysis." *Ethics and Information Technology* 9 (3):187–204.

Hinduja, S., and J. W. Patchin. 2007. "Offline Consequences of Online Victimization: School Violence and Delinquency." *Journal of School Violence* 6(3):89–112.

Hirsch, A. J. 1992. *The Rise of the Penitentiary*. New Haven, CT: Yale University Press.

Hirsch, M. 2007. "Midnight Run Re-Run: Bail Bondsmen, Bounty Hunters, and the Uniform Criminal Extradition Act." *University of Miami Law Review* 62:59–94.

Hirschel, D., and I. Hutchinson. 2003. "The Voices of Domestic Violence Victims: Predictors of Victim Preference for Arrest and the Relationship between Preference for Arrest and Revictimization." *Crime and Delinquency* 49:313–36.

Hirschkorn, P. 2011. "WH OKs Military Detention of Terrorism Suspects." CBS News.com, December 14. www.cbsnews.com.

Hockenberry, S. 2013. *Juveniles in Residential Placement, 2010* (NCJ 241060). Washington, DC: U.S. Department of Justice.

Hoctor, M. 1997. "Domestic Violence as a Crime against the State." *California Law Review* 85 (May):643–700.

Hoffman, M. 1999. "Abolish Peremptory Challenges." *Judicature* 82:202–4.

Holder, E. 2013. Speech at National Association of Counties Legislative Conference, March 4, 2013, Washington, D.C. http://www.justice.gov.

Holleran, D., D. Beichner, and C. Spohn. 2010. "Examining Charging Agreement between Police and Prosecutors in Rape Cases." *Crime and Delinquency* 56:385–413.

Holt, T., and A. Bossler. 2012. "Predictors of Patrol Officer Interest in Cybercrime Training and Investigation in Selected United States Police Departments." *Cyberpsychology, Behavior, and Social Networking*. 15:464-72.

Holtfreter, K., and M. Morash. 2003. "The Needs of Women Offenders." *Women & Criminal Justice* 14, 137–60.

Homan, C. 2010. "Michigan Lawmakers to Debate Bringing Good Time Back for Prisoners." *Holland Sentinel,* February 15. www.hollandsentinel.com.

Horwitz, S. 2013. "New FBI Director James B. Comey Stunned Impact of Sequestration on Agents in the Field." *Washington Post*, September 27. www.washingtonpost.com.

Howlett, D. 2004. "Chicago Plans Advanced Surveillance." *USA Today*, September 9. http://www.usatoday.com .http://www.albany.edu/sourcebook/.

Hubert, C. 2010. "Placerville Shooting Fuels Debate About Use of Deadly Force Against Mentally Ill." *Sacramento Bee*, April 4. www.sacbee.com.

Hudson, J. 2012. "Contemporary Origins of Restorative Justice Programming: The Minnesota Restitution Center." *Federal Probation* (September):49–55.

Huebner, B. M., and R. Gustafson. 2007. "The Effect of Maternal Incarceration on Adult Offspring Involvement in the Criminal Justice System." *Journal of Criminal Justice* 35:283–96.

Huey, L. 2010. "'I've Seen This On CSI': Criminal Investigators Perceptions about the Management of Public Expectations in the Field." *Crime, Media, Culture* 6:49–68.

Huff, C. R. 2002. "Wrongful Conviction and Public Policy: The American Society of Criminology, 2001 Presidential Address." *Criminology* 40:1–18.

Human Rights Watch. 2014. *Branded for Life: Florida's Prosecution of Children as Adults under its "Direct File" Statute*. New York, NY: Human Rights Watch.

Humes, K. R., N. A. Jones, and R. R. Ramirez. 2011. "Overview of Race and Hispanic Origin: 2010." *2010 Census Briefs* (March). Washington, DC: U.S. Census Bureau.

Hunt, K. 2010. "GOP Rips Holder on Miranda Rights." January 27. www .politico.com.

Hurdle, J. 2008. "Police Beating of Suspects Is Taped by TV Station in Philadelphia." *New York Times*, May 8. www.nytimes.com.

Indiana Department of Corrections. 2009. "Press Release: Plainfield Educational Facility Relocates to Indianapolis." December 16. http://www.in.gov/idoc/files /PREF_Relocation_Press_Release.pdf.

"Indiana's Answer to Prison Costs." 2011. *New York Times*, January 17. www .nytimes.com.

Ingold, J. 2011. "Prison Black Market A Steal: Correctional Officers Get Drawn into Contraband Smuggling." *Denver Post*, December 18. www.denverpost .com.

Innocence Project. 2014. "Know the Cases." Innocence Project website. http://www.innocenceproject.org /know/.

Irwin, J. 1970. *The Felon*. Englewood Cliffs, NJ: Prentice-Hall.

———. 1980. *Prisons in Turmoil*. Boston: Little, Brown.

Irwin, J., and D. Cressey. 1962. "Thieves, Convicts, and the Inmate Culture." *Social Problems* 10:142–55.

Israelsen, R. G. 2013. "Applying the Fourth Amendment's National-Security Exception to Airport Security and the TSA." *Journal of Air Law and Commerce* 78:501–39.

Ith, I. 2001. "Taser Fails to Halt Man with Knife; Seattle Officer Kills 23-Year-Old." *Seattle Times*, November 28, p. A1.

Jacob, H. 1973. *Urban Justice*. Boston: Little, Brown.

Jacobs, C., and C. Smith. 2011. "The Influence of Justice John Paul Stevens: Opinion Assignments by the Senior Associate Justice." *Santa Clara Law Review* 51: 743–74.

Jaksic, V. 2007. "Public Defenders, Prosecutors Face Crisis in Funding." *National Law Journal.* March 27. http://www.law.com.

Jalbert, S. K., and W. Rhodes. 2012. "Reduced Caseloads Improve Probation Outcomes." *Journal of Crime and Justice* 35:221–38.

Johnson, A. 2011. "Sentencing Overhaul Would Save State $78 Million." *Columbus Dispatch*, May 5. www.dispatchpolitics.com.

Johnson, B. D. 2006. "The Multilevel Context of Criminal Sentencing: Integrating Judge- and County-Level Influences." *Criminology* 44:259–98.

———. 2011. "Some States Rethink Felony Property Crimes." *USA Today*, October 30. www.usatoday.com.

Johnson, C. 2013. "Some Public Defenders Warn: 'We Have Nothing Left to Cut.'" National Public Radio, April 10. www.npr.org.

Johnson, K. & R. Chebium. 2013. "Justice Dept. Won't Challenge State Marijuana Laws." USA Today, August 29. http://www.usatoday.com.

Johnson, K. 2010. "How Racial Profiling in America Became the Law of the Land." Georgetown Law Journal 98:1005–77.

Johnson, K., L. Lanza-Kaduce, and J. Woolard. 2011. "Disregarding Graduated Treatment: Why Transfer Aggravates Recidivism." *Crime & Delinquency* 57:756–77.

Johnson, M. A. 2010. "Already under Fire, Crime Labs Cut to the Bone." MSNBC.com, February 23. www.msnbc.com.

Johnson, M., and L. A. Johnson. 2012. "Bail: Reforming Policies to Address Overcrowded Jails, the Impact of Race on Detention, and Community Revival in Harris County, Texas." *Northwestern Journal of Law and Social Policy* 7:42–87.

Jones, J. 2013. "U.S. Death Penalty Support Lowest in More than 40 Years." Gallup Poll, October 29. www.gallup.com.

Justice Policy Institute. 2010. "How to Safely Reduce Prison Populations and Support People Returning to Their Communities." June (Press Release). http://www.justicepolicy.org/images/upload/10-06_fac_forimmediaterelease_ps-ac.pdf.

Kainen, J. L. 2013. "Shields, Swords, and Fulfilling the Exclusionary Rule's Deterrent Function." *American Criminal Law Review* 50:59–108.

Kanaracus, C. 2012. "Audit: Police Wasted Millions on Software, Crime-Fighting Tech They Never Used." *Computer World,* August 1. www.computerworld.com.

Karmen, A. 2001. *Crime Victims.* 4th ed. Belmont, CA: Wadsworth.

Karnow, C. E. A. 2008. "Setting Bail for Public Safety." *Berkeley Journal of Criminal Law* 13:1–30.

Karnowski, S. 2008. "City's I-35W Bridge Response Generally Praised." Associated Press, April 22. www.twincities.com.

KATC-TV. 2010. "New Prison 'Good Time' Law Frees 463." KATC.com, October 27. www.katc.com.

Keller, B. 2014. "Americans on Probation." *New York Times*, January 26. www.nytimes.com.

Kelley, M. 2013. "GUILTY: Verdict Handed Down in Steubenville High School Rape Case." Business Insider. March 17th. www.businessinsider.com.

Kelling, G. L., and M. Moore. 1988. "The Evolving Strategy of Policing." In *Perspective on Policing, no. 13.* Washington, DC: National Institute of Justice.

Kelling, G. L., T. Pate, D. Dieckman, and C. E. Brown. 1974. *The Kansas City Preventive Patrol Experiments: A Summary Report.* Washington, DC: Police Foundation.

Kelly, H. 2012. "Police Embracing Tech That Predicts Crime." CNN.com, July 9. www.cnn.com.

Kenney, D. J., and J. O. Finckenauer. 1995. *Organized Crime in America.* Belmont, CA: Wadsworth.

Kenny, K. 2009. "When Cultural Tradition and Criminal Law Collide: Prosecutorial Discretion in Cross-Cultural Cases." *Judicature* 92:216–19.

Kentucky Department of Corrections. 2014. *2014 Division of Corrections Training Program Catalog.* http://corrections.ky.gov.

Kerley, K. R., A. Hochstetler, and H. Copes. 2009. "Self-Control, Prison Victimization, and Prison Infractions." *Criminal Justice Review*, 34:553–68.

Killman, C., and B. Hoberock. 2013. "Lawmakers Benefit from Private Prison Donations." *Tulsa World.* May 19. http://www.tulsaworld.com .

Kim, K., and M. Denver. 2011. *A Case Study on the Practices of Pretrial Services and Risk Assessment in Three Cities.* Washington, DC: District of Columbia Policy Institute.

Kimber, K. 2008. "Mental Health Courts—Idaho's Best Kept Secret." *Idaho Law Review* 45:249–81.

Kimberly, J. 2003. "House Passes Crime Lab Bill." *Houston Chronicle*, May 2. http://www.houstonchronicle.com.

King, N. J., and S. Sherry. 2008. "Habeas Corpus and Sentencing Reform: A Story of Unintended Consequences." *Duke Law Journal* 58:1–67.

King, N., and J. Hoffmann. 2011. *Habeas for the 21st Century.* Chicago: University of Chicago Press.

King, N., F. Cheesman, and B. Ostrom. 2007. *Habeas Litigation in the U.S. District Courts: An Empirical Study of Habeas Corpus Cases Filed By State Prisoners under the Antiterrorism and Effective Death Penalty Act of 1996.* Williamsburg, VA: National Center for State Courts.

Kingsnorth, R., R. MacIntosh, and S. Sutherland. 2002. "Criminal Charge or Probation Violation? Prosecutorial Discretion and Implications for Research in Criminal Court Processing." *Criminology* 40:553–77.

Kinports, K. 2011. "The Supreme Court's Love-Hate Relationship with *Miranda*." *Journal of Criminal Law and Criminology* 101:375–440.

Kirby, S., A. Quinn, and S. Keay. 2010. "Intelligence-Led and Traditional Policing Approaches to Open Drug Markets—A Comparison of Offenders." *Drugs and Alcohol Today* 10:13–19.

Kish, R. J., and A. F. Lipton. 2013. "Do Private Prisons Really Offer Savings Compared with Their Public Counterparts?" *Economic Affairs* 33:93–107.

Klahm, C., and R. Tillyer. 2010. "Understanding Police Use of Force: A Review of the Evidence." *Southwest Journal of Criminal Justice* 7:214–39.

Klain, E. 2012. "President Obama Signed the National Defense Authorization Act—Now What?" *Forbes*, January 2. www.forbes.com.

Kleck, G., B. Sever, S. Li, and M. Gertz. 2005. "The Missing Link in General Deterrence Research." *Criminology* 43 (3):623–59.

Klein, A. 2008. "D.C. Police to Carry Semiautomatic Rifles on Patrol." *Washington Post*, May 17, p. B1.

Kleymeyer, C. 2010. Division of Corrections Training 2010 Annual Report. Kentucky Department of Corrections.

Klingler, D. 2012. "On the Problems and Promise of Research on Legal Police Violence." *Homicide Studies* 16:78–96.

Kloepfer, C. 2012. "Prison Guards Now Equipped with Tasers." WLNS.com. March 2. www.wlns.com.

Klofas, J., and J. Yandrasits. 1989. "'Guilty but Mentally Ill' and the Jury Trial: A Case Study." *Criminal Law Bulletin* 24:423–43.

Knoll, C. and M. Sickmund. 2012. *Delinquency Cases in Juvenile Court, 2009* (NCJ 239081). Washington, DC: U.S. Department of Justice.

Kotch, S., and R. Mosteller. 2010. "The Racial Justice Act and the Long Struggle with Race and the Death Penalty in North Carolina." *North Carolina Law Review* 88:2031–128.

Kotlowitz, A. 1994. "Their Crimes Don't Make Them Adults." *New York Times Magazine*, February 13, p. 40.

Kovaleski, S. 2014. "U.S. Issues Marijuana Guidelines for Banks," *New York Times*. February 14. www.nytimes.com.

Kramer, G. P., and D. M. Koenig. 1990. "Do Jurors Understand Criminal Justice Instructions? Analyzing the Results of the Michigan Juror Comprehension Project." *University of Michigan Journal of Law Reform* 23:401–37.

Krautt, P. 2002. "Location, Location, Location: Interdistrict and Intercircuit Variation in Sentencing Outputs for Federal Drug-Trafficking Offenses." *Justice Quarterly* 19 (December):633–71.

Kravets, D. 2011. "Wi-Fi-Hacking Neighbor from Hell Sentenced to 18 Years in Prison." WIRED.Com, July 12. http://www.wired.com/threatlevel/2011/07/hacking-neighbor-from-hell/.

Kris, D. 2011. "Law Enforcement as a Counterterrorism Tool." *Journal of National Security Law and Policy* 5:1–79.

Krischke, S. 2010. "Absent Accountability: How Prosecutorial Impunity Hinders the Fair Administration of Justice in America." *Journal of Law and Policy* 19:395–434.

Kruttschnitt, C. 2010. "The Paradox of Women's Imprisonment." *Daedelus*, 139(3):32–42.

KTKA-TV. 2011. "Shawnee Co. Looks to Cost Cuts with Early Retirement, Jury Pay Cuts." KTKA.com, February 10. www.ktka.com.

Kurlychek, M. 2010. "Transforming Attitudinal Change into Behavioral Change: The Missing link." *Criminology & Public Policy*. 9:119–26.

Kurlychek, M., and C. Kempinen. 2006. "Beyond Boot Camp: The Impact of Aftercare on Offender Re-Entry." *Criminology & Public Policy* 5:363–88.

Kuruvilla, C. 2014. "Juror Claims 'Race Was Never a Factor' Over Deliberations in Michael Dunn's Shooting of Jordan Davis." *New York Daily News*, February 21. www.nydailynews.com.

Kyckelhahn T., and T. Martin, 2013. "Justice Expenditure and Employment Extracts, 2010—Preliminary." *Bureau of Justice Statistics Bulletin*, July. NCJ 242544. www.bjs.gov.

Kyckelhahn, T., and T. Cohen. 2008. *Felony Defendants in Large Urban Counties, 2004—Statistical Tables*. Washington, DC: Bureau of Justice Statistics.

LaFraniere, S. 2009. "Facing Counterfeiting Crackdown, Beijing Vendors Fight Back." *New York Times*, March 2. http://www.nytimes.com.

Lambert, L. 2011. "States Seek to Escape Rising Prison Costs." Reuters News Service, May 20. www.reuters.com.

Langan, P., and D. Levin. 2002. "Recidivism of Released Prisoners Released in 1994. Bureau of Justice Statistics *Special Report*, June. NCJ 193427.

Langton, L., and D. Farole. 2010. "State Public Defender Programs, 2007." Bureau of Justice Statistics *Special Report*, September. NCJ 228229.

Lattman, P. 2011. "Galleon Chief Sentenced to 11-Year Term in Insider Case." *New York Times*, October 13. www.nytimes.com.

Lave, T. R. 1998. "Equal before the Law." *Newsweek*, July 13, p. 14.

LaVigne, N., S. Bieler, L. Cramer, H. Ho, C. Kontonias, D. Mayer, D. McClure, L. Pacifici, E. Parks, B. Peterson, and J. Samuels. 2014. *Justice Reinvestment Initiative State Assessment Report*, January. Washington, D.C.: Urban Institute and U.S. Bureau of Justice Assistance.

Lawrence, A. 2009. *Cutting Corrections Costs: Earned Time Policies for State Prisoners*. Denver, CO: National Conference of State Legislatures.

Lazarus, D. 2010. "Customer Stuck with Counterfeit Money from Post Office." *Los Angeles Times*, May 25. www.latimes.com.

LeDuff, C. 2011. "Riding along with the Cops in Murdertown, U.S.A." *New York Times*, April 15. www.nytimes.com.

Lee, H., and M. Vaughn. 2010. "Organizational Factors that Contribute to Police Deadly Force Liability." *Journal of Criminal Justice* 38:193–206.

Lee, J. 2009. "Study Questions Whether Cameras Cut Crime." *New York Times*, March 3. http://www.nytimes.com.

Lehti, M., and K. Aromaa. 2006. "Trafficking for Sexual Exploitation." *Crime and Justice* 34:133–227.

Leiber, M. J., and K. Y. Mack. 2003. "The Individual and Joint Effects of Race, Gender, and Family Status on Juvenile Decision-Making." *Journal of Research in Crime & Delinquency* 40(1):34–70.

Leo, R. A. 1996. "*Miranda*'s Revenge: Police Interrogation as a Confidence Game." *Law & Society Review* 30:259–88.

Leonard, J. 2002. "Dropping 'Nonlethal' Beanbags as Too Dangerous." *Los Angeles Times*, June 3, p. 1.

Levy, M. 2011. "The Mechanics of Federal Appeals: Uniformity and Case Management in Circuit Courts." *Duke Law Journal* 61:315–91.

Lewis, N. A., 2009. "Stimulus Plan Has $1 Billion to Hire More Local Police." *New York Times*, February 6. www.nytimes.com.

Lichtblau, E. 2008. "Senate Approves Bill to Broaden Wiretap Powers." *New York Times*, July 10. www.nytimes.com.

———. 2012. "Police Are Using Tracking as Routine Tool." *New York Times*, March 31. www.nytimes.com.

Lichtblau, E., and J. Risen. 2009. "Officials Say U.S. Wiretaps Exceeded Law." *New York Times*, April 16. http://www.nytimes.com.

Lineberger, K. 2011. "The United States-El Salvador Extradition Treaty: A Dated Obstacle in the Transnational War against Mara Salvatrucha (MS-13)." *Vanderbilt Journal of Transnational Law* 44:187–216.

Linke, L., and P. Ritchie. 2004. *Releasing Inmates from Prison: Profiles of State Practices*. Washington, DC.: National Institute of Corrections.

Liptak, A. 2003. "County Says It's Too Poor to Defend the Poor." *New York Times*, April 15. http://www.nytimes.com.

———. 2008a. "Electrocution Is Banned in Last State to Rely on It." *New York Times*, February 9. http://www.nytimes.com.

———. 2008c. "U.S. Prison Population Dwarfs That of Other Nations." *New York Times*, April 23. www.nytimes.com.

———. 2009. "Supreme Court Steps Closer to Repeal of Evidence Ruling." *New York Times*, January 31. www.nytimes.com.

———. 2011. "Justices, 5–4, Tell California to Cut Prisoner Population." *New York Times*, May 23. www.nytimes.com.

———. 2012. "Justices' Ruling Expands Rights of Accused in Plea Bargains." *New York Times*, March 21. www.nytimes.com.

Listwan, S. J., M. Colvin, D. Hanley, and D. Flanner. 2010. "Victimization, Social Support, and Psychological Well-Being: A Study of Recently Released Prisoners." *Criminal Justice and Behavior* 37:1140–59.

Lithwick, D., and J. Turner. 2003. "A Guide to the Patriot Act, Part 4." *Slate*, September 11. http://www.slate.msn.com.

Livsey, S. 2012. *Juvenile Delinquency Probation Caseload, 2009*. Washington, DC: Office of Juvenile Justice and Delinquency Programs.

Loewen, B. 2013. "Jordan Johnson Acquitted of Rape." *The Montana Kaimin*. March 1. http://www.montanakaimin.com.

Loewy, A. 2011. "Rethinking Search and Seizure in a Post-9/11 World." *Mississippi Law Journal* 80:1507–21.

Logan, C. 1993. "Criminal Justice Performance Measures in Prisons." In *Performance Measures for the Criminal Justice System*. Washington, DC: Bureau of Justice Statistics, U.S. Government Printing Office, 19–60.

Lord, V. B., and M. Sloop. 2010. "Suicide by Cop: Police Shooting as a Method of Self-Harming." *Journal of Criminal Justice* 38:889–95.

Luginbuhl, J., and M. Burkhead. 1994. "Sources of Bias and Arbitrariness in the Capital Trial." *Journal of Social Issues* 7:103–12.

Lum, C., C. Koper, and C. Telep. 2011. "The Evidence-Based Policing Matrix." *Journal of Experimental Criminology* 7:3–26.

Lum, C., C. Telep, C. Koper, and J. Grieco. 2012. "Receptivity to Research in Policing." *Justice Research and Policy* 14:61–95.

Lundman, R., and R. Kaufman. 2003. "Driving While Black: Effects of Race, Ethnicity, and Gender on Citizen Self-Reports of Traffic Stops and Police Actions." *Criminology* 41:195–220.

Lunney, L. A. 2009. "Has the Fourth Amendment Gone to the Dogs?: Unreasonable Expansion of Canine Sniff Doctrine to Include Sniffs of the Home." *Oregon Law Review* 88:829–903.

Lynch, J. P., and L. A. Addington. 2009. *Understanding Crime Statistics: Revisiting the Divergence of the NCVS and UCR*. New York: Cambridge University Press.

Lynem, J. N. 2002. "Guards Call for Higher Wages, More Training: Industry Faces Annual Staff Turnover Rate of up to 300%." *San Francisco Chronicle*, August 22, p. B3.

Maag, C. 2008. "Police Shooting of Mother and Infant Exposes a City's Racial Tension." *New York Times*, January 30. http://www.nytimes.com.

MacArthur Foundation. 2007b. "Creating Turning Points for Serious Adolescent Offenders: Research on Pathways to Desistance." MacArthur Foundation Research Network on Adolescent Development and Juvenile Justice, *Issue Brief 2*. http://www.aadj.org/content.

MacArthur Foundation. 2007c. "Less Guilty by Reason of Adolescence." MacArthur Foundation Research Network on Adolescent Development and Juvenile Justice, *Issue Brief 3*. http://www.aadj.org/content.

MacCormack, J. 2011. "Border Issues Not Confined to the Border." *San Antonio Express-News*, June 8. www.mysanantonio.com.

Macur, J., and N. Schweber. 2012. "Rape Case Unfolds on Web and Splits City." New York Times, December 16. www.newyorktimes.com.

Magda, L., A. Canton, and R. Gershon. 2010. "Web-Based Weapons of Mass Destruction Training for Transit Police." *Journal of Public Transportation* 13:63–78.

Maguire, E., C. Uchida, and K. Hassell. 2012. "Problem-Oriented Policing in Colorado Springs: A Content Analysis of 753 Cases." *Crime and Delinquency* (forthcoming 2012).

Maitland, A. S., and R. D. Sluder. 1998. "Victimization and Youthful Prison Inmates: An Empirical Analysis." *Prison Journal* 78:55–73.

Maki, A. 2012. "Crimes Lurk in Memphis Police Department Memos." *Memphis Commercial Appeal*, January 25. www.commercialappeal.com.

Malone, P. 2012. "Crime Labs Fear Budget Cuts." FOX 10 TV, January 12. www.fox10tv.com.

"Man Acquitted of Concealed Weapon Charge on 'Necessity' Defense." *San Francisco Examiner*, July 10. www.sfexaminer.com.

Mann, D. 2011. "Why the Willingham Case Matters." *Texas Observer*, September 8. www.texasobserver.org.

Mannheimer, M. 2011. "Not the Crime but the Cover-Up: A Deterrence-Based Rationale for the Premeditation-Deliberation Formula." *Indiana Law Journal* 86:879–37.

Manning, A. 2012. "Local Officials Look to State to Pay Indigent-Defense Bills." *Columbus Dispatch*, February 26. www.dispatch.com.

Marceau, J. F. 2008. "Un-Incorporating the Bill of Rights: The Tension between the Fourteenth Amendment and the Federalism Concerns of Modern Criminal Procedure Reforms." *Journal of Criminal Law and Criminology* 98:1231–302.

Mardar, N. 2010. Answering Jurors' Questions: Next Steps in Illinois." *Loyola University Chicago Law Journal* 41:727–52.

Marimow, A. E. 2013. "John Hinckley Case Attorneys Debate Plans for Unsupervised Visits." *Washington Post*, January 24. www.washingtonpost.com.

Marso, A. 2014. "Corrections Secretary: Funding Cuts Drive Recidivism." *Topeka Capital-Journal*, January 14. http://cjonline.com/news/2014-01-14/corrections-secretary-funding-cuts-drive-recidivism.

Martin, L. 2011. "Debt to Society: Asset Poverty and Prisoner Reentry." *Review of Black Political Economy* 38:131–43.

Martindale, M. 2012. "Audit: Michigan's Prisoner Re-Entry Initiative Harms Public Safety, Fails to Track Ex-Convicts." *Detroit News*, February 8. www.detroitnews.com.

Martinez, M. 2013. "Stephen Baldwin Pleads Guilty to Tax Charge, Will Pay $300,000." CNN.com. March 30. http://www.cnn.com.

Martinson, R. 1974. "What Works? Questions and Answers about Prison Reform." *Public Interest*, Spring, p. 25.

Maruschak, L. M. 2009. "HIV in Prisons, 2007–2008." *Bureau of Justice Statistics Bulletin*. Washington, DC: U.S. Department of Justice.

Maruschak, L., and T. Bonczar. 2013. "Probation and Parole in the United States, 2012." *Bureau of Justice Statistics Bulletin*, December. NCJ 243826.

Maruschak, L.M. 2012. "HIV in Prisons, 2001–2010." *Bureau of Justice Statistics Bulletin*, September. NCJ 238877.

Mascaro, L. 2011. "Patriot Act Provisions Extended Just In Time." *Los Angeles Times*, May 27. www.latimes.com.

Maschke, K. J. 1995. "Prosecutors as Crime Creators: The Case of Prenatal Drug Use." *Criminal Justice Review* 20:21–33.

Mauer, M. 2011. "Opposing View: Reduce Prison Populations." *USA Today*, May 24. www.usatoday.com.

Mauer, M., and M. Chesney-Lind, eds. 2002. *Invisible Punishment: The Collateral Consequences of Mass Imprisonment*. New York: New Press.

Maxson, C. 2011. *Street Gangs. In Crime and Public Policy*, ed. J. Q. Wilson and J. Petersilia. New York: Oxford University Press.

Maxwell, S. R. 1999. "Examining the Congruence between Predictors of ROR and Failures to Appear." *Journal of Criminal Justice* 27:127–41.

May, J. D., R. Duke, and S. Gueco. 2013. "Pretext Searches and Seizures: In Search of Solid Ground." *Alaska Law Review* 30:151–88.

Mayrack, B. 2008. "The Implications of *State ex rel. Thomas v. Schwarz* on Wisconsin Sentencing Policy after Truth-in-Sentencing II." *Wisconsin Law Review* 2008:181–223.

McAuliff, B., and T. Duckworth. 2010. "I Spy with My Little Eye: Jurors' Detection of Internal Validity Threats in Expert Evidence." *Law and Human Behavior* 34:489–500.

McCall, M. A., M. M. McCall, and C. E. Smith. 2008. "Criminal Justice and the U.S. Supreme Court 2007–2008 Term." *Southern University Law Review* 36:33–87.

McCall, M. M., M. A. McCall, and C. Smith. 2011. "Criminal Justice and the 2010–2011 United States Supreme Court Term." *South Texas Law Review* 53:307–43.

McCall, M. M., M. A. McCall, and C. Smith. 2013. "Criminal Justice and the 2011–2012 United States Supreme Court Term." *Florida Coastal Law Review* 14:239–84.

McCampbell, S. W. 2005. *Gender-Responsive Strategies for Women Offenders*. Washington, DC: National Institute of Corrections.

McCarthy, B. 2012. "Marlon Defillo Is Still Coordinating Police Details for Movie Sets." *New Orleans Times-Picayune*, February 6. www.nola.com.

McCartney, A. 2011. "Mel Gibson Pleads Guilty to Battery Charge of Ex-Girlfriend." *Chicago Sun Times*, March 12. www.suntimes.com.

McCormick, J. 2000. "Scene of the Crime." *Newsweek*, February 28, p. 60.

McCoy, C. 1993. *Politics and Plea Bargaining: Victims' Rights in California*. Philadelphia: University of Pennsylvania Press.

———. 2007. "Caleb Was Right: Pretrial Detention Mostly Determines Everything." *Berkeley Journal of Criminal Law* 12:135–48.

McDonough, K. 2013. "Lawyer for Steubenville Rapist to Appeal Conviction." Salon, March 20th. www.salon.com.

McFarlane, L. 2009. "Ending Prisoner Rape in Michigan." *Free Press*, July 21.

McGarrell, E., S. Chermak, A. Weiss, and J. Wilson. 2001. "Reducing Firearms Violence through Directed Patrol." *Criminology & Public Policy* 1:119–48.

McGreevy, P., and C. Megerian. 2013. "California Lawmakers OK a Dozen Gun Control Measures." *Los Angeles Times*, May 29. www.latimes.com.

McKee, T. A. 2007. "Judges as Umpires." *Hofstra Law Review* 35:1709–24.

McKelvey, B. 1977. *American Prisons.* Montclair, NJ: Patterson Smith.

McKinley, J. C. 2013. "Lauryn Hill Sentenced to 3 Months in Tax Case." *New York Times.* May 6. http://www .nytimes.com.

McLaughlin, E. C., and P. Brown. 2013. "Judge Sentences Cleveland Kidnapper Ariel Castro to Life, Plus 1,000 Years." CNN.com, August 1. www.cnn.com.

McMahon, P. 2002. "311 Lightens Load for Swamped 911 Centers." *USA Today*, March 5. http://www.usatoday.com.

McNulty, T. L., and P. E. Bellair. 2003. "Explaining Racial and Ethnic Differences in Adolescent Violence: Structural Disadvantage, Family, Well-Being, and Social Capital." *Justice Quarterly* 20:1–31.

Meade, B., and B. Steiner. 2010. "The Total Effects of Boot Camps that House Juveniles: A Systematic Review of the Evidence." *Journal of Criminal Justice* 38:841–53.

Mears, B. 2008. "Nebraska Court Bans the Electric Chair." CNN, February 8. http://www.cnn.com.

Meier, R. F., and T. D. Miethe. 1993. "Understanding Theories of Criminal Victimization." In *Crime and Justice: A Review of Research*, ed. M. Tonry. Chicago: University of Chicago Press.

Meisner, J. 2011. "What Happened to the Elite Officers Charged." *Chicago Tribune*, September 9. www.chicagotribune .com.

Melde, C. 2009. "Lifestyle, Rational Choice, and Adolescent Fear: A Test of a Risk-Assessment Framework." *Criminology* 47:781–812.

Melde, C. S. Gavassi, E. McGarrell and T. Bynum. 2011. "On the Efficacy of Targeted Gang Interventions: Can We Identify Those Most at Risk?" *Youth Violence and Juvenile Justice* 9:279–94.

Melde, C., F-A. Esbensen, and T. J. Taylor. 2009. "May Piece Be with You: A Typological Examination of the Fear and Victimization Hypothesis of Adolescent Weapon Carrying." *Justice Quarterly* 26:348–76.

Melendez, L. 2011. "BART's Citizen Review Board Questions SFPD Investigation." KGO-TV website, September 19. http://abclocal.go.com/kgo.

Melendez, L. 2014. "SF Celebrates First Year of Vet Court." KGO-TV website, March 5. http://abclocal.go.com /kgo/story?section=news/local /san_francisco&id=9456255.

Menard, S. 2000. 'The Normality' of Repeat Victimization from Adolescence through Early Adulthood." *Justice Quarterly* 17:543–74.

Messner, S. F., S. Galea, K. J. Tardiff, and M. Tracy. 2007. "Policing, Drugs, and the Homicide Decline in New York City in the 1990s." *Criminology* 45:385–413.

Mihm, S. 2006. "No Ordinary Counterfeit." *New York Times*, July 23. http://www .nytimes.com.

Milhizer, E. 2004. "Justification and Excuse: What They Were, What They Are, and What They Ought to Be." *St. Johns Law Review* 78:725–895.

Miller, M. 2009. "LPD Cars Receive $24K Upgrade." *Lansing (MI) State Journal*, May 14, p. 4B.

———. 2014. "Court Backs Firing of State Prison Guard Who Repeatedly Kicked Inmate." PennLive website, February 11. www.pennlive.com.

Miller, S. L., K. Zielaskowski, and E.A. Plant. 2012. "The Basis of Shooter Biases: Beyond Cultural Stereotypes." *Personality and Social Psychology Bulletin* 38:1358–66.

Minnesota Department of Corrections. 2014. "Adult Facilities." Department of Corrections website. www.doc.state .mn.us.

Minton, T. 2013. "Jail Inmates at Midyear 2012—Statistical Tables." *Bureau of Justice Statistics Bulletin*, May. NCJ 241264.

Minton, T. D. 2011. *Jail Inmates at Midyear 2010—Statistical Tables.* Washington, DC: U.S. Bureau of Justice Statistics.

Miroff, N. 2008. "Detainee Program Strains Va. Jail." *Washington Post*, April 8, p. A01.

Moore, M. 1992. "Problem-Solving and Community Policing." In *Modern Policing*, ed. M. Tonry and N. Morris. Chicago: University of Chicago Press, 99–158.

Moore, S. 2009. "Number of Life Terms Hits Record." *New York Times*, July 22. www.nytimes.com.

Moore, T. 2011. "'East Coast Rapist' Caught, Officials Say after Man's DNA Linked to Spree of Sex Assaults." *New York Daily News*, March 5. www.dailynews.com.

Moran, R. 2002. *Executioner's Current: Thomas Edison, George Westinghouse, and the Invention of the Electric Chair.* New York: Knopf.

Morash, M., and R. Haarr. 2012. "Doing, Redoing, and Undoing Gender: Variation in Gender Identities of Women Working as Police Officers." *Feminist Criminology* 7:3–23.

Morash, M., J. K. Ford, J. P. White, and J. G. Boles. 2002. "Directing the Future of Community-Policing Initiatives." In *The Move to Community Policing: Making Change Happen*, ed. M. Morash and J. Ford. Thousand Oaks, CA: Sage, 277–88.

Morash, M., R. N. Haarr, and L. Rucker. 1994. "A Comparison of Programming for Women and Men in the U.S. Prisons in the 1980s." *Crime and Delinquency* 40 (April):197–221.

Morgan, D. 2013. "Impressed by Fairfield Police Crisis Intervention Team." *Connecticut Post,* February 20. http://www.ctpost.com/opinion/article /Impressed-by-Fairfield-Police -Crisis-Intervention-4294457.php .

Moroney, N. 2014. *Juvenile Justice Monitoring Unit, 2013 Annual Report.* Baltimore, MD: Office of the Attorney General.

Morris, H. 2012. "Europe Cracks Down on Cybercrime." *New York Times*, March 29. www.nytimes.com.

Morris, N., and M. Tonry. 1990. *Between Prison and Probation: Intermediate Punishments in a Rational Sentencing System.* New York: Oxford University Press.

Moses, P. 2005. "Corruption? It Figures: NY Police Department's Crime Stats and the Art of Manipulation." *Village Voice*, March 29. http://www .villagevoice.com.

Mosher, C., T. Miethe, and D. Phillips. 2002. *The Mismeasure of Crime.* Thousand Oaks, CA: Sage.

———. 2011b. "Statement before Senate Committee on Homeland Security and Governmental Affairs." Washington, DC, September 13.

Mumola, C. 2005. "Suicide and Homicide in State Prisons and Local Jails." *Bureau of Justice Statistics Special Report*, August. NCJ 210036.

Murphy, P. V. 1992. "Organizing for Community Policing." In *Issues in Policing: New Perspectives*, ed. J. W. Bizzack. Lexington, KY: Autumn Press, 113–28.

Musgrave, S. 2013. "Boston Police Halt License Scanning Program." *Boston Globe*, December 14. www.boston.com.

Muskal, M., and M. Pearce. 2013. "Ariel Castro Commits Suicide, Hangs Himself with Bedsheet, Officials Say." *Los Angeles Times*, September 4. www .latimes.com.

Na, C., and D. C. Gottfredson. 2011. "Police Officers in Schools: Effects on School Crime and the Processing of Offending Behaviors." *Justice Quarterly*, 1–32.

Nagin, D., and D. Weisburd. 2013. "Evidence and Public Policy: The Example of Evaluation Research in Policing." *Criminology & Public Policy* 12:651–79.

Nakamura, D. 2012. "Obama Signs Defense Bill, Pledges to Maintain Legal Rights of U.S. Citizens." *Washington Post*, December 31. www.washingtonpost.com.

Nakashima, E., and A. Marimow. 2013. "Judge: NSA's Collecting of Phone Records Is Probably Unconstitutional." *Washington Post*, December 16. www.washingtonpost.com.

Nalla, M. 2002. "Common Practices and Functions of Corporate Security: A Comparison of Chemical, Financial, Manufacturing, Service, and Utility Industries." *Journal of Security Administration* 25:33–46.

National Academy of Sciences. 2009. *Strengthening Forensic Sciences in the United States* Washington, DC: National Academy of Sciences.

National Association of Women Judges. 2014. "2013 Representation of United States State Court Women Judges." http://www.nawj.org/us_state_court_statistics_2013.asp.

National Guard Youth Foundation. 2014. "We Support Second Chances." National Guard Youth Foundation website. www.ngyf.org/challenge.

National Public Radio (NPR). 2011. "Nation's Jails Struggle with Mentally Ill Prisoners." *All Things Considered* show website. September 4. www.npr.org.

Natoli, M. 2013. "Au Revoir, Voir Dire and Other Costly and Socioeconomically Unjust Judicial Practices." *New England Law Review* 47:605–29.

Nava, M. 2008. "The Servant of All: Humility, Humanity, and Judicial Diversity." *Golden Gate University Law Review* 38:175–94.

Nelson, S. 2013. "Marijuana Business Rules Debated in Colorado, Washington." *U.S. News and World Report*, March 22, 2013. www.usnews.com.

New York State Division of Criminal Justice Services. 2008. *New York State Probation Population: 2007 Profile*. (June).

New York Times. 2012. "The Events Leading to the Shooting of Trayvon Martin." *New York Times*, April 2. www.nytimes.com.

Newport, F. 2010. "In U.S., 64% Support Death Penalty in Cases of Murder, Gallup Poll, November 8. www.gallup.com.

Newport, F. 2012. "Americans Want Fed Gov't Out of State Marijuana Laws." Gallup Poll, December 10. www.gallup.com.

Nir, S. 2011. "Indictment of 55 in Cybercrime Ring Expected Friday." *New York Times*, December 15. www.nytimes.com.

Nolasco, C., R. delCarmen, and M. Vaughn. 2011. "What *Herring* Hath Wrought: An Analysis of Post-*Herring* Cases in the Federal Courts." *American Journal of Criminal Law* 38:221–61.

North Carolina Department of Public Safety. 2014. "24 Hours in Prison." North Carolina Department of Public Safety website. http://www.doc.state.nc.us/DOP/HOURS24.htm.

Nowlin, J. W. 2012. "The Warren Court's House Built on Sand: From Security in Persons, Houses, Papers, and Effects to Mere Reasonableness in Fourth Amendment Doctrine." *Mississippi Law Journal* 81:1017–82.

O'Brien, B. 2009. "A Recipe for Bias: An Empirical Look at the Interplay between Institutional Incentives and Bounded Reality in Prosecutorial Decision Making." *Missouri Law Review* 74:999–1048.

O'Harrow, R. 2008. "Centers Tap into Personal Databases." *Washington Post*, April 2. www.washingtonpost.com.

O'Hear, M. M. 2006. "The End of *Bordenkircher*: Extending the Logic of *Apprendi* to Plea Bargaining." *Washington University Law Review* 84:835–49.

O'Keefe, K. 2010. "Two Wrongs Make a Wrong: A Challenge to Plea Bargaining and Collateral Consequence Statutes through Their Integration." *Journal of Criminal Law and Criminology* 100:243–77.

Oberfield, Z. W. 2012. "Socialization and Self-Selection: How Police Develop Their Views about Using Force." *Administration and Society* 44:70230.

Office of Juvenile Justice and Delinquency Prevention (OJJDP). 2012. *OJJDP Statistical Briefing Book*. http://www.ojjdp.gov/ojstatbb/structure_process/qa04101.asp?qaDate=2011.

Oleniacz, L. 2014. "Durham Minor Misdemeanor Diversion Program Launches for 16, 17-Year-Olds." *The Herald Sun*. April 4th. http://www.heraldsun.com.

Oppel, R.A. 2011. "Private Prisons Found to Offer Little in Savings." *New York Times*, May 18. www.nytimes.com.

Osborne, J. 2011. "Union Faults Camden County Jail's Elevators." *Philadelphia Inquirer*, April 18. www.philly.com.

Ostermann, M. 2009. "An Analysis of New Jersey's Day Reporting Center and Halfway Back Program: Embracing the Rehabilitative Ideal through Evidence-Based Practices." *Journal of Offender Rehabilitation* 48:139–53.

"Our View: Don't Just Cut Prisoners Loose" [Editorial]. 2011. *USA Today*, May 24. www.usatoday.com.

Outlook Handbook online. www.bls.gov/ooh/protective-service/correctional-officers.htm.

Owen, B. 1998. *"In the Mix": Struggle and Survival in a Woman's Prison*. Albany: State University of New York Press.

Owen, B., J. Wells, J. Pollock, B. Muscat, and S. Torres. 2008. "Gendered Violence and Safety: A Contextual Approach to Improving Security in Women's Facilities" (Final Report). Unpublished.

Packer, H. L. 1968. *The Limits of the Criminal Sanction*. Stanford, CA: Stanford University Press.

Palmer, B. 2011. "Oklahoma's Female Inmate Population Skyrockets." *Oklahoman*, January 30. http://newsok.com.

Parascandola, R., and C. Lestch. 2013. "NYPD Sergeant First to Be Fired, Lose Pension in Massive Police Ticket-Fixing Scandal." *New York Daily News*, December 10. www.nydailynews.com.

Parent, D. 2003. *Correctional Boot Camps: Lessons from a Decade of Research*. Washington, DC: National Institute of Justice.

Patchin, J. W., and S. Hinduja. 2012. *Cyberbullying Prevention and Response: Expert Perspectives*. New York: Routledge.

Peart, N. 2011. "Why Is the N.Y.P.D. after Me?" *New York Times*, December 17. www.nytimes.com.

Pennsylvania Department of Corrections. 2014. "About Us—Department of Corrections." Department of Corrections website. www.cor.state.pa.us.

Peralta, E. 2011. "In Report, ACLU Claims Chicago's Surveillance Cameras Violate Privacy." National Public Radio, February 8. www.npr.org.

Perez, D. M., A. R. Gover, K. M. Tennyson, and S. Santos. 2009. "Individual and Institutional Characteristics Related to Inmate Victimization." *International Journal of Offender Therapy and Comparative Criminology* 54:378–94.

Perin, M. 2009. "Hazswat Changed?: Combining Hazmat and SWAT Training for Tactical Operations." *Law Enforcement Technology* 36:20–25.

Perrine, J., V. Speirs, and J. Horwitz. 2010. "Fusion Centers and the Fourth Amendment." *Capital University Law Review* 38:721–87.

Petersilia, J. 1990. "When Probation Becomes More Dreaded Than Prison." *Federal Probation*, March, p. 24.

———. 2003. *When Prisoners Come Home: Parole and Prisoner Reentry*. New York: Oxford University Press.

———. 2009. *When Prisoners Come Home: Parole and Prisoner Reentry*. New York: Oxford University Press.

Peterson, J. L., and M. J. Hickman. 2005. "Census of Publicly Funded Forensic Crime Laboratories, 2002." Bureau of Justice Statistics *Bulletin*, February, p. 1.

Peterson, M. 2005. *Intelligence-Led Policing: The Intelligence Architecture*. Washington, DC: U.S. Bureau of Justice Assistance.

Petteruti, A. 2011. *Education Under Arrest: The Case against Police in Schools*. Washington, DC: Justice Policy Institute.

Petteruti, A., and N. Walsh. 2008. *Jailing Communities: The Impact of Jail Expansion and Effective Public Safety Strategies*. Washington, DC: Justice Policy Institute.

Pew Center on the States. 2007. "What Works in Community Corrections: An Interview with Dr. Joan Petersilia." *Public Safety Performance Project*, No. 2. November.

———. 2008. One in 100: Behind Bars in America 2008. Washington, DC: Pew Center on the States.

———. 2009. *One in 31: The Long Reach of American Corrections*. Washington, DC: Pew Charitable Trusts.

———. 2011. *State of Recidivism: The Revolving Door of America's Prisons*. Washington, DC: Pew Charitable Trusts

———. 2012. *Time Served: The High Cost, Low Return of Longer Prison Terms*, June. Washington, DC: Pew Center on the States.

———. 2013. "More Than Half of States Cut Imprisonment Rates from 2006 to 2011." Press Release. March 8. http://www.pewstates.org.

Pew Charitable Trusts. 2012. Public Opinion on Sentencing and Corrections Policy in America. (March). http://www.pewstates.org/research /analysis/public-opinion-on-sentencing -and-corrections-policy-in-america -85899380361.

———. 2013. *Managing Prison Health Care Spending*. Washington, DC: The Pew Charitable Trusts. http://www .pewstates.org.

Phelps, M. S. 2011. "Rehabilitation in the Punitive Era: The Gap Between Rhetoric and Reality in U.S. Prison Programs." *Law & Society Review* 45, 33–68.

Phillips, M. 2011. *Commercial Bail Bonds in New York City: Characteristics and Implications*. New York: New York City Criminal Justice Agency.

Phillips, S. 1977. *No Heroes, No Villains*. New York: Random House.

Piquero, A.R., F.T. Cullen, J.D. Unnever, N.L. Piquero, and J.A. Gordon. 2010. "Never Too Late: Public Optimism about Juvenile Rehabilitation." *Punishment & Society* 12:187–207.

Pisciotta, A. W. 1994. *Benevolent Repression: Social Control and the American Reformatory-Prison Movement*. New York: New York University Press.

Place, T. 2013. "Closing Direct Appeal to Ineffectiveness Claims: The Supreme Court of Pennsylvania's Denial of State Constitutional Rights." *Widener Law Journal* 22:687–719.

Platt, A. 1977. *The Child Savers*. 2nd ed. Chicago: University of Chicago Press.

Pochna, P. 2002. "N.J. Police Linking with National Data Network." *Baltimore Sun*, April 2. http://articles.baltimoresun. com/2002-04-02/news/0204020041_1

_jersey-state-police-bergen-county -computer-center.

Podgor, E. 2010. "The Tainted Federal Prosecutor in an Overcriminalized Justice System." *Washington and Lee Law Review* 67:1569–85.

Podlas, K. 2006. "The 'CSI Effect' and Other Forensic Fictions." *Loyola of Los Angeles Entertainment Law Review* 27:87–125.

Porter, R. 2011. *Choosing Performance Indicators for Your Community Prosecution Initiative*. Washington, DC: Association of Prosecuting Attorneys.

Porter, R., S. Lee, and M. Lutz. 2002. *Balancing Punishment and Treatment: Alternatives to Incarceration in New York City*. New York: Vera Institute of Justice.

Post, L. 2004. "ABA Wants to Transform Way Jurors Do Their Jobs." *New Jersey Law Journal* August 16:1.

Poston, B. 2011. "Racial Gap Found in Traffic Stops in Milwaukee." *Milwaukee Journal Sentinel*, December 3. www.jsonline.com.

PR Newswire. 2001. "Ion Track Instruments Unveils New Technology to Aid in Fight against Terrorism and Drug Trafficking." March 22 (available on Lexis-Nexis).

Pratt, J. 2011. "Are We Being Fair to Our Judges and the Perception of Justice in Alabama by Having Partisan Elections for Judicial Office?" *Alabama Lawyer* 72:443–44.

Preston, J. 2005. "Rape Victims' Eyes Were Covered, but a Key Clue Survived." *New York Times*, April 28. http://www .nytimes.com.

Price, M. 2009. "Performing Discretion or Performing Discrimination: Race, Ritual, and Peremptory Challenges in Capital Jury Selection." *Michigan Journal of Race and Law* 15:57–107.

"Private Jails: Locking in the Best Price." 2007. *Economist*, January 25. http://www.economist.com/node /8599146.

Propper, A. 1982. "Make Believe Families and Homosexuality among Imprisoned Girls." *Criminology* 20:127–39.

Provine, D. M. 1996. "Courts in the Political Process in France." In *Courts, Law, and Politics in Comparative Perspective*, ed. H. Jacob, E. Blankenburg, H. Kritzer, D. M. Provine, and J. Sanders. New Haven, CT: Yale University Press, 177–248.

Public Opinion Strategies. 2010. *National Research of Public Attitudes on Crime and Punishment* (September). Washington, DC: Pew Center on the States.

Puzzanchera, C. and C. Robson. 2014. *Delinquency Cases in Juvenile Court, 2010* (NCJ 243041). Washington, DC: U.S. Department of Justice.

Puzzanchera, C., and W. Kang. 2011. "Easy Access to the FBI's

Supplementary Homicide Reports: 1980–2009." http://www.ojjdp.gov /ojstatbb/ezashr/.

Puzzanchera, C., B. Adams, and S. Hockenberry. 2012. *Juvenile Court Statistics, 2009*. Pittsburgh, PA: National Center for Juvenile Justice.

Puzzanchera, D. and S. Addie. 2014. *Delinquency Cases Waived to Criminal Court, 2010* (NCJ 243042). Washington, DC: U.S. Department of Justice.

Radelet, M. L. 2004. "Post-*Furman* Botched Executions." http://www.deathpenaltyinfor .org/article.php?scid=8&did=478.

Rafter, N. H. 1983. "Prisons for Women, 1790–1980." In *Crime and Justice*, 5th ed., ed. M. Tonry and N. Morris. Chicago: University of Chicago Press.

Raganella, A. J., and M. D. White. 2004. "Race, Gender, and Motivation for Becoming a Police Officer: Implications for Building a Representative Police Department." *Journal of Criminal Justice* 32:501–13.

Rainville, G., and S. Smith. 2003. "Juvenile Felony Defendants in Criminal Courts." Bureau of Justice Statistics *Special Report*, May. NCJ 197961.

Rand, M., and J. Robinson. 2011. "*Criminal Victimization in the United States, 2008—Statistical Tables*. Bureau of Justice Statistics. May. NCJ 231137.

Randolph, E. D. 2001. "Inland Police Like New Weaponry." *Riverside* (CA) *Press-Enterprise*, November 24, p. B4.

Ratcliffe, J. 2010. "Crime Mapping: Spatial and Temporal Challenges." *Handbook of Quantitative Criminology* 1:5–24.

Ratcliffe, J., T. Taniguchi, E. Groff, and J. Wood. 2011. "The Philadelphia Foot Patrol Experiment: A Randomized Controlled Trial of Police Patrol Effectiveness in Violent Crime Hotspots." *Criminology* 49:795–831.

Ravitz, J. 2009. "Scanners Take 'Naked' Pics, Groups Says." CNN.com, May 18. www.cnn.com.

Reaves, B. 2006. "Violent Felons in Large Urban Counties." Bureau of Justice Statistics *Special Report*, July. NCJ 205289.

———. 2010. *Local Police Departments, 2007*. Washington, DC: U.S. Bureau of Justice Statistics.

———. 2011. "Census of State and Local Law Enforcement Agencies, 2008." Bureau of Justice Statistics *Bulletin*, July. NCJ233982.

———. 2012. "Federal Law Enforcement Officers, 2008." *Bureau of Justice Statistics*.

———. 2013. "Felony Defendants in Large Urban Counties, 2009—Statistical Tables." *Bureau of Justice Statistics Bulletin*, December. NCJ 243777.

Redlich, A., S. Liu, H. Steadman, L. Callahan, and P. Robbins. "Is Diversion Swift? Comparing Mental Health Court and Traditional Criminal Justice

Processing." *Criminal Justice and Behavior* 39:420–33.

Reid, T. R. 2004. "Rape Case against Bryant Is Dropped." *Washington Post*, September 2. http://www.washingtonpost.com.

Reisig, M. D. 2010. "Community and Problem-Oriented Policing." *Crime and Justice* 39:2–53.

Reiter, K. A. 2012. "Parole, Snitch, or Die: California's Supermax Prisons and Prisoners, 1997–2007." *Punishment and Society* 14:530–63.

Rempel, M., J. Zweig, C. Lindquist, J. Roman, S. Rossman, and D. Krastein. 2012. "Multi-Site Evaluation Demonstrates Effectiveness of Adult Drug Courts." *Judicature* 95:154–57.

Renzema, M., and E. Mayo-Wilson. 2005. "Can Electronic Monitoring Reduce Crime for Moderate to High-Risk Offenders?" *Journal of Experimental Criminology* 1:215–37.

Reuland, M. 2010. "Tailoring the Police Response to People with Mental Illness to Community Characteristics in the USA." *Police Practice and Research: An International Journal* 11:315–29.

Riccardi, N. 2009. "Cash-Strapped States Revise Laws to Get Inmates Out." *Los Angeles Times*, September 5. www.latimes.com.

Rich, J., S. E. Wakeman, and S. L. Dickman. 2011. "Medicine and the Epidemic of Incarceration in the United States." *New England Journal of Medicine* 364:2081–83.

Richey, W. 2006. "US Creates Terrorist Fingerprint Database." *Christian Science Monitor*, December 27, pp. 1, 4.

Richmond, K. M. 2012. "The Impact of Federal Prison Industries Employment on the Recidivism Outcomes of Female Inmates." *Justice Quarterly* (forthcoming).

Richtel, M. 2002. "Credit Card Theft Thrives Online as Global Market." *New York Times*, May 13. http://www.nytimes.com.

Richter, E., and A. Humke. 2011. "Demonstrative Evidence: Evidence and Technology in the Courtroom." In *Handbook of Trial Consulting*, ed. Richard L. Wiener and Brian H. Bornstein. New York: Springer, 187–201.

Riddell, K. 2014. "Hoffman's Death Highlights U.S. Spike in Heroin Use." *Washington Times*, February 3. www.washingtontimes.com.

Ring, W. 2005. "Backlogs in Labs Undercut DNA's Crime-Solving Value." *Lansing* (MI) *State Journal*, April 28, p. A3.

Rivard, R. 2014. "Prison U." *Inside Higher Education*, February 28. www.inside-highereducation.com.

Rivera, R. 2013. "Reliving Horror and Faint Hope at Massacre Site." *New York Times*. January 28. http://www.nytimes.com.

Roane, K. R., and D. Morrison. 2005. "The CSI Effect." *U.S. News and World Report*, April 25. http://www.usnews.com.

Robbins, L. 2011. "A Fateful Stop for Candy for a Helper to So Many." *New York Times*, November 1. www.nytimes.com.

Roberts, C. 2012. "T.J. Holmes, Former CNN Anchor, Pulled Over in Atlanta, Tweets: 'Driving While Black Ain't No Joke.'" *New York Daily News*, July 30. www.nydailynews.com.

Roberts, D. E. 2004. "The Social and Moral Costs of Mass Incarceration in African-American Communities." *Stanford Law Review* 56 1271–1305.

Roberts, S. 2013. "Police Surveillance May Earn Money for City." *New York Times*, April 3. www.nytimes.com.

Robinson, P. H., and M. D. Dubber. 2007. "The American Model Penal Code: A Brief Overview." *New Criminal Law Review* 10:319–41.

Rockwell, F. G. 2008. "The Chesterfield/Colonial Heights Drug Court: A Partnership between the Criminal Justice System and the Treatment Community." *University of Richmond Law Review* 43:5–17.

Rogers, M. 2011. "Cardell's Taser Death Inspires Utah Police Training." *Salt Lake City Tribune*, May 12. http://www.sltrib.com.

Rogers, R., J. Rogstad, J. Steadham, and E. Drogin. 2011. "In Plain English: Avoiding Recognized Problems with *Miranda* Miscomprehension." *Psychology, Public Policy, and Law* 17:264–85.

Rojek, J., G. Alpert, and S. Decker. 2012. "The Racial Stratification of Searches in Police Traffic Stops." *Criminology* 50:993–1024.

Rojek, J., R. Rosenfeld, and S. Decker. 2012. "Policing Race: The Racial Stratification of Searches in Police Traffic Stops." *Criminologyy* 50:993–1024.

Romney, L. 2012. "Task Force Seeks to Change California's Mental Health Commitment Law." *Los Angeles Times*, April 8. http://articles.latimes.com/2012/apr/08/local/la-me-mental-health-task-force-20120409.

Rose, D. 2009. "North Korea's Dollar Store." *Vanity Fair*, August 5. www.vanityfair.com.

Rosen, L. 1995. "The Creation of the Uniform Crime Report: The Role of Social Science." *Social Science History* 19 (Summer):215–38.

Rosenberg, T. 2012. "Out of Jail, and Into a Job." *New York Times*, March 28. www.nytimes.com.

Rosenfeld, R., R. Fornango, and A. F. Rengifo. 2007. "The Impact of Order-Maintenance Policing on New York City Homicide and Robbery Rates: 1988–2001. *Criminology* 45:355–83.

Rosenfeld, R., R. Fornango, and E. Baumer. 2005. "Did *Ceasefire, Compstat,* and *Exile* Reduce Homicide?" *Criminology & Public Policy* 4:419–50.

Rosenmerkel, S., M. Durose, and D. Farole. 2009. "Felony Sentences in State Courts, 2006—Statistical Tables." Bureau of Justice Statistics *Statistical Tables* (December). http://bjs.ojp.usdoj.gov/.

Rossi, P. H., and R. A. Berk. 1997. *Just Punishments: Federal Guidelines and Public Views Compared.* New York: Aldine DeGruyter.

Rothman, D. 1980. *Conscience and Convenience: The Asylum and Its Alternatives in Progressive America.* New York: Aldine de Gruyter.

Rothman, D. J. 1971. *The Discovery of the Asylum: Social Order and Disorder in the New Republic.* Boston: Little, Brown.

Rotman, E. 1995. "The Failure of Reform." In *Oxford History of the Prison*, ed. N. Morris and D. J. Rothman. New York: Oxford University Press.

Rudolph, J. 2012. "Police Layoffs Ripple through Key Swing State of Florida." *Huffington Post*, January 31. http://www.huffingtonpost.com/2012/01/31/police-layoffs-florida_n_1244364.html.

Ruiter, G. 2014. "Prison Cuts Force Grand Rapids to Scale Back Prison Reentry Services." *Calvin College Chimes*, March 20. http://www.calvin.edu/chimes/2014/03/20/prison-cuts-force-grand-rapids-to-scale-back-prison-reentry-services/.

Ryan, J.P., L.S. Abrams, and H. Huang. 2014. "First-Time Violent Juvenile Offenders: Probation, Placement, and Recidivism." *Social Work Research* 38:7–18.

Ryley, S., and D. Gregorian. 2014. "NYPD's Most Sued Cop Also Among Top Overtime Earners for Past Two Years." *New York Daily News*, February 17. www.nydailynews.com.

Sabo, D., T. A. Kupers, and W. London. 2001. "Gender and the Politics of Punishment." In *Prison Masculinities*, ed. D. Sabo, T. A. Kupers, and W. London. Philadelphia: Temple University Press.

Sack, K. 2011. "Executions in Doubt in Fallout over Drug." *New York Times*, March 16. www.nytimes.com.

Salter, J. 2014. "States Consider Reviving Old-Fashioned Executions." *Lansing State Journal*, February 2. www.lansingstatejournal.com.

Samaha, J. 2011. *Criminal Law*, 10th ed. Belmont, CA: Cengage.

Sanchez, C. E, and M. Giordano. 2008. "Gang Activity in Suburbs

Acknowledged." *Nashville Tennessean*, April 28. http://tennessean.com.

Sands, W. L. 2013. "Plea Bargaining After *Frye* and *Lafler*: A Real Problem in Search of a Reasonable and Practical Solution." *Duquesne Law Review* 51:537–49.

Sanger, D. E., and E. Lichtblau. 2006. "Administration Starts Weeklong Blitz in Defense of Eavesdropping Program." *New York Times*, January 24. http://www.nytimes.com.

Santos, F. 2007. "'CSI Effect'; Evidence From Bite Marks, It Turns Out, Is Not So Elementary." *New York Times*, January 28. http://www.nytimes.com.

———. 2008. "Plan to Close Prisons Stirs Anxiety in Rural Towns." *New York Times*, January 27. www.nytimes.com.

Santos, M. 2004. *About Prison*. Belmont, CA: Wadsworth.

———. 2013. "California's Realignment: Real Prison Reform or Shell Game?" *Huffington Post*. March 11. http://www.huffingtonpost.com.

Sarche, J. 2005. "Kobe Case Settled." *Pasadena Star-News*, March 2. http://www.pasadenastarnews.com.

Savage, C. 2011. "Trend to Lighten Harsh Sentences Catches on in Conservative States." *New York Times*, August 12. www.nytimes.com.

Scalia, J. 2002. "Prisoners Petitions Filed in U.S. District Courts, 2000, with Trends 1980–2000." Bureau of Justice Statistics *Special Report*, January.

Schlanger, M. 2008. "Jail Strip-Search Cases: Patterns and Participants." *Law and Contemporary Problems* 71:65–88.

Schlesinger, T. 2011. "The Failure of Race Neutral Policies: How Mandatory Terms and Sentencing Enhancements Contribute to Mass Incarceration." *Crime and Delinquency* 57:56–81.

———. 2013. "Racial Disparities in Pretrial Diversion: An Analysis of Outcomes Among Men Charged with Felonies and Processed in State Courts." *Race and Justice* (print version forthcoming—published online April 5, 2013), raj.sagepub.com.

Schlosser, L. Z., D. A. Safran, and C. A. Sbaratta. 2010. "Reasons for Choosing a Correction Officer Career." *Psychological Services* 7(1):34–43.

Schofield, D. 2011. "Playing with Evidence: Using Video Games in the Courtroom." *Entertainment Computing* 2:47–58.

Schultz, D. 2000. "No Joy in Mudville Tonight: The Impact of Three Strikes' Laws on State and Federal Corrections Policy, Resources, and Crime Control." *Cornell Journal of Law and Public Policy* 9:557–83.

Schwartz, J. 2009. "Mistrial by iPhone: Juries' Web Research Upends Trials." *New York Times*, March 18. http://www.nytimes.com.

Schwartz, J., and E. G. Fitzsimmons. 2011. "Illinois Governor Signs Capital Punishment Ban." *New York Times*, March 9. www.nytimes.com.

Secret, M. 2010. "N.Y.C. Misdemeanor Defendants Lack Bail Money." *New York Times*, December 2. www.nytimes.com.

Seelye, K. Q., W. K. Rashbaum, and M. Cooper. 2013. "Boston Bomb Suspect Is Captured after Standoff." *New York Times*, April 19. www.nytimes.com.

Segal, D. 2009. "Financial Fraud Is Focus of Attack by Prosecutors." *New York Times*, March 12. http://www.nytimes.com.

Segal, L., B. Ngugi, and J. Mana. 2011. "Credit Card Fraud: A New Perspective on Tackling an Intransigent Problem." *Fordham Journal of Corporate and Financial Law* 16:743–81.

Sevigny, E. L., B. K. Fuliehan & F. V. Ferdik. 2013. "Do Drug Courts Reduce the Use of Incarceration? A Meta-Analysis." *Journal of Criminal Justice* 41:416–25.

Shamir, H. 2012. "A Labor Paradigm for Human Trafficking." *UCLA Law Review* 60:76–136.

Shane, J. 2010. "Organizational Stressors and Police Performance." *Journal of Criminal Justice* 38:807–18..

Shapiro, B. 1997. "Sleeping Lawyer Syndrome." *Nation*, April 7, pp. 27–29.

Sharkey, J. 2008. "Mistakes on Terrorist Watch List Affect Even Children." *New York Times*, September 9. http://www.nytimes.com.

Shay, G. 2009. "What We Can Learn about Appeals from Mr. Tillman's Case: More Lessons from Another DNA Exoneration." *University of Cincinnati Law Review* 77:1499–553.

———. 2013. "The New State Postconviction." *Akron Law Review* 46:473–88.

Sherman, L. W. 1998. "Police." In *Handbook of Crime and Punishment*, ed. M. Tonry. New York: Oxford University Press, 429–56.

Sherman, L. W., and D. A. Weisburd. 1995. "General Deterrent Effects of Police Patrol in Crime 'Hot Spots': A Randomized Controlled Trial." *Justice Quarterly* 12 (December):625–48.

Shermer, L., and B. D. Johnson. 2010. "Criminal Prosecutions: Examining Prosecutorial Discretion and Charging Decisions in U.S. Federal District Courts" *Justice Quarterly* 27:394–430.

Sickmund, M., A. Sladky, and W. Kang. 2012. "Easy Access to Juvenile Court Statistics: 1985–2009." http://www.ojjdp.gov/ojstatbb/ezajcs/.

Sickmund, M., A. Sladky, and W. Kang. 2013. "Easy Access to Juvenile Court Statistics: 1985–2010." Pittsburgh, PA: National Center for Juvenile Justice. www.ojjdp.gov/ojstatbb/ezajcs/.

Silverman, E. 1999. *NYPD Battles Crime*. Boston: Northeastern University Press.

Simmons, A., and B. Rankin. 2010. "Gwinnett Cuts Pay Rate for Defending Indigent." *Atlanta Journal Constitution*, February 1. www.ajc.com.

Simonoff, J., C. Restropo, R. Zimmerman, Z. Naphtali, and H. Willis. 2011. "Resource Allocation, Emergency Response Capability, and Infrastructure Concentration around Vulnerable Sites." *Journal of Risk Research* 5:597–613.

Simons, K. W. 2008. "Self-Defense: Reasonable Belief or Reasonable Self-Control?" *New Criminal Law Review* 11:51–90.

Simons, M. 2010. "Prosecutorial Discretion in the Shadow of Advisory Guidelines and Mandatory Minimums." *Temple Political and Civil Rights Law Review* 19:377–87.

Singer, N. 2008. "Budget Cuts Force King County Charging Process to Change." *Seattle Times*, September 25. http://seattletimes.nwsource.com.

Skogan, W. G. 1995. "Crime and Racial Fears of White Americans." *Annals of the American Academy of Political and Social Science* 539 (May):59–71.

Skogan, W. G., S. M. Hartnett, N. Bump, and J. Dubois. 2008. Evaluation of CeaseFire-Chicago. Unpublished Report (March 20).

Skolnick, J. H., and D. H. Bayley. 1986. *The New Blue Line*. New York: Free Press.

Skolnick, J. H., and J. J. Fyfe. 1993. *Above the Law: Police and Excessive Use of Force*. New York: Free Press.

Skorton, D., and G. Altschuler. 2013. "College Behind Bars: How Educating Prisoners Pays Off." *Forbes*. March 25. http://www.forbes.com.

Slabaugh, S. 2011. "Inmate Education Programs Facing Major Budget Cuts." *Muncie Star Press*, May 21. www.thestarpress.com.

Smith, C. E. 1990. *United States Magistrates in the Federal Courts: Subordinate Judges*. New York: Praeger.

———. 1995. "Federal Habeas Corpus Reform: The State's Perspective." *Justice System Journal* 18:1–11.

———. 1997. *Courts, Politics, and the Judicial Process*. 2nd ed. Belmont, CA: Wadsworth.

———. 1999. "Criminal Justice and the 1997–98 U.S. Supreme Court Term." *Southern Illinois University Law Review* 23:443–67.

———. 2000a. "The Governance of Corrections: Implications of the Changing Interface of Courts and Corrections." In *Boundary Changes in Criminal Justice Organizations*. Vol. 2 of *Criminal Justice 2000*. Washington, DC: National Institute of Justice, 113–66.

———. 2000b. *Law and Contemporary Corrections*. Belmont, CA: Wadsworth.

———. 2004. *Constitutional Rights: Myths and Realities*. Belmont, CA: Wadsworth.

———. 2007. "Prisoners' Rights and the Rehnquist Court Era." *Prison Journal* 87:457–76.

———. 2010a. "Justice John Paul Stevens and Capital Punishment." *Berkeley Journal of Criminal Law* 15:205–60.

———. 2010b. "Justice John Paul Stevens: Staunch Defender of *Miranda* Rights." *DePaul Law Review* 60:99–140.

———. 2011. "The Changing Supreme Court and Prisoners' Rights." *Indiana Law Review* 44:853–88.

———. 2013. "*Brown v. Plata*, the Roberts Court, and the Future of Conservative Perspectives on Rights behind Bars." *Akron Law Review* 46:519–50.

Smith, C. E., and H. Feldman. 2001. "Burdens of the Bench: State Supreme Courts' Non-Judicial Tasks." *Judicature* 84:304–9.

Smith, C. E., and R. Ochoa. 1996. "The Peremptory Challenge in the Eyes of the Trial Judge." *Judicature* 79:185–89.

Smith, C. E., C. DeJong, and M. McCall. 2011. *The Rehnquist Court and Criminal Justice*. Lanham, MD: Lexington Books.

Smith, C. E., M. A. McCall, and M. M. McCall. 2009. "The Roberts Court and Criminal Justice at the Dawn of the 2008 Term." *Charleston Law Review* 3:265–87.

Smith, C. E., M. McCall, and C. Perez McCluskey. 2005. *Law and Criminal Justice: Emerging Issues in the Twenty-First Century*. New York: Peter Lang.

Smith, L. 2012. "Wyoming City Council Adopts Zoning Limits on Where Parolees May Live." Michigan Public Radio. January 16. http://michiganradio.org.

Snyder, H. N. 2012. *Arrest in the United States, 1980–2010*. Washington, DC: U.S. Department of Justice.

Snyder, H. N., and M. Sickmund. 2006. *Juvenile Offenders and Victims: 2006 National Report*. Washington, DC: U.S. Office of Juvenile Justice and Delinquency Prevention.

Sommers, S. 2009. "On the Obstacles to Jury Diversity." *Jury Expert* 21:1–10.

Soree, N. B. 2013. "Show and Tell, Seek and Find: A Balanced Approach to Defining a Fourth Amendment Search and the Lessons of Rape Reform." *Seton Hall Law Review* 43:127–227.

Sorensen, J. R., and D. H. Wallace. 1999. "Prosecutorial Discretion in Seeking Death: An Analysis of Racial Disparity in the Pretrial Stages of Case Processing in a Midwestern County." *Justice Quarterly* 16:561–78.

Spangenberg, R. L., and M. L. Beeman. 1995. "Indigent Defense Systems in the United States." *Law and Contemporary Problems* 58:31–49.

Spears, J. W., and C. C. Spohn. 1997. "The Effect of Evidence Factors and Victim Characteristics on Prosecutors' Charging Decisions in Sexual Assault Cases." *Justice Quarterly* 14:501–24.

Spellman, J., and S. Nottingham. 2013. "Judge Accepts Theater Suspect's Insanity Plea." CNN.com, June 5. www.cnn.com.

Spencer, C. 2000. "Nonlethal Weapons Aid Lawmen: Police Turn to Beanbag Guns, Pepper Spray to Save Lives of Defiant Suspects." *Arkansas Democrat-Gazette*, November 6, p. B1.

Spencer, M. 2009. "The Wrong Stephen Morgan's Photo Posted Online in Wesleyan Student's Death." *Hartford Courant*, May 8. http://www.courant.com.

Spohn, C. 2011. "Unwarranted Disparity in the Wake of the *Booker/Fanfan* Decision: Implications for Research and Policy." *Criminology & Public Policy* 10(4):1119–27.

Spohn, C., and D. Holleran. 2001. "The Imprisonment Penalty Paid by Young, Unemployed Black and Hispanic Male Offenders." *Criminology* 38:281–306.

St. Clair, S. 2008. "R. Kelly Verdict: Not Guilty." *Chicago Tribune*, June 13. http://www.chicagotribune.com.

St. Clair, S., and J. Gorner. 2013. "City Plans $4.1 Million Settlement in Fatal Police Shooting." *Chicago Tribune*, February 8. http://articles.tribune.com.

St. Clair, S., and K. Ataiyero. 2008. "R. Kelly Defense Rests Case after 2 Days of Testimony." *Chicago Tribune*, June 10. http://articles.chicagotribune.com.

Staba, D. 2007. "Killer of 3 Women in Buffalo Area Is Given a Life Term." *New York Times*, August 15. http://www.nytimes.com.

Stafford, M. C., and M. Warr. 1993. "A Reconceptualization of General and Specific Deterrence." *Journal of Research in Crime and Delinquency* 30 (May):123–35.

Stahl, A. 2008. "Drug Offense Cases in Juvenile Courts." 1985–2004. Washington, DC: U.S. Department of Justice.

Stahlkopf, C., M. Males, and D. Macallair. 2010. "Testing Incapacitation Theory: Youth Crime and Incarceration in California." *Crime and Delinquency* 56:253–68.

Stanko, E. 1988. "The Impact of Victim Assessment on Prosecutors' Screening Decisions: The Case of the New York District Attorney's Office." In *Criminal Justice: Law and Politics*, 5th ed., ed. G. F. Cole. Pacific Grove, CA: Brooks/Cole.

Stanley, K. 2011. "Florida Crime Keeps Falling, and Experts and Law Enforcement Search for Why." *St. Petersburg Times*, November 17. http://www.tampabay.com/news/publicsafety/crime/article1203703.ece.

Staples, B. 2012. "California Horror Stories and the 3-Strikes Law." *New York Times*, November 24. www.nytimes.com.

Starr, S., and M. Rehavi. 2013. "Mandatory Sentencing and Racial Disparity: Assessing the Roles of Prosecutors and the Effects of *Booker*." *Yale Law Journal* 123:2–79.

State of Florida Correctional Medical Authority. 2010. Aging and Older Inmates in the Florida Department of Corrections. http://www.doh.state.fl.us/cma/meetings.

Stecklow, S., J. Singer, and A. O. Patrick. 2005. "Watch on the Thames." *Wall Street Journal*, July 8. http://www.wsj.com.

Steden, R., and R. Sarre. 2007. "The Growth of Private Security: Trends in the European Union." *Security Journal* 20:222–35.

Steen, S., R. Engen, and R. Gainey. 2005. "Images of Danger and Culpability: Racial Stereotyping, Case Processing, and Criminal Sentencing." *Criminology* 43:435–68.

Steffensmeier, D., and S. Demuth. 2010. "Ethnicity and Judges' Sentencing Decisions: Hispanic-Black-White Comparisons." *Criminology* 39:145–78.

Steffensmeier, D., B. Feldmeyer, C. T. Harris, and J. T. Ulmer. 2011. "Reassessing Trends in Black Violent Crime 1980–2008: Sorting out the 'Hispanic Effect' in Uniform Crime Reports Arrests, National Crime Victimization Survey Offender Estimates, and U.S. Prisoner Counts." *Criminology* 49:197–252.

Steffensmeier, D., J. Kramer, and C. Streifel. 1993. "Gender and Imprisonment Decisions." *Criminology* 31:411–46.

Steffensmeier, D., J. Ulmer, and J. Kramer. 1998. "The Interaction of Race, Gender, and Age in Criminal Sentencing: The Punishment Cost of Being Young, Black, and Male." *Criminology* 36:763–97.

Steinberg, J. 1999. "The Coming Crime Wave Is Washed Up." *New York Times*, January 3, p. 4WK.

Steiner, B., and E. Wright. 2006. "Assessing the Relative Effects of State Direct File Waiver Laws on Violent Juvenile Crime: Deterrence or Irrelevance?" *Journal of Criminal Law and Criminology* 96:1451–77.

Steiner, B., C. Hemmens, and V. Bell. 2006. "Legislative Waiver Reconsidered: General Deterrent Effects of Statutory Exclusion Laws Enacted Post-1979." *Justice Quarterly* 23(1):34–59.

Steiner, B., M. Makarios, L. Travis, and B. Meade. 2012. "Examining the Effects of Community-Based Sanctions on

Offender Recidivism." *Justice Quarterly* 29:229–55.

Stensland, J. 2011. "Island County Sheriff, Prosecutor Struggle with Cuts." *Whidbey (WA) News Times*, January 25. www.whidbeynewstimes.com.

Stephan, J. 2008. *Census of State and Federal Correctional Facilities, 2005*, October. NCJ 222182.

Stephan, J., and J. Karberg. 2003. *Census of State and Federal Correctional Facilities, 2000*. (August) Washington, DC: Bureau of Justice Statistics.

Stephens, M. 2008. "Ignoring Justice: Prosecutorial Discretion and the Ethics of Charging." *Northern Kentucky Law Review* 35:53–65.

Stephens, S. 2007. "The True Effect of Crime Scene Television on the Justice System: The "CSI Effect" on Real Crime Labs." *New England Law Review* 41:591–607.

Steward, D., and M. Totman. 2005. *Racial Profiling: Don't Mind If I Take a Look, Do Ya? An Examination of Consent Searches and Contraband Hits at Texas Traffic Stops*. Austin: Texas Justice Coalition.

Stewart, E., E. Baumer, R. Brunson, and R. Simons. 2009. "Neighborhood Racial Context and Perceptions of Police-Based Racial Discrimination Among Black Youth." *Criminology* 47:847–87.

Stickels, J. W., B. J. Michelsen, and A. Del Carmen. 2007. "Elected Texas District and County Attorneys' Perceptions of Crime Victim Involvement in Prosecution." *Texas Wesleyan Law Review* 14:1–25.

Stoddard, E. R. 1968. "The Informal 'Code' of Police Deviancy: A Group Approach to Blue-Coat Crime." *Journal of Criminal Law, Criminology, and Police Science* 59:204–11.

Stojkovic, S. 1990. "Accounts of Prison Work: Corrections Officers' Portrayals of Their Work Worlds." *Perspectives on Social Problems* 2:211–30.

Stolzenberg, L., and S. J. D'Alessio. 1994. "Sentencing and Unwarranted Disparity: An Empirical Assessment of the Long-Term Impact of Sentencing Guidelines in Minnesota." *Criminology* 32:301–10.

Streib, V. 2010. "Innocence: Intentional Wrongful Conviction of Children." *Chicago-Kent Law Review* 85:163–77.

Streitfeld, D. 2008. R. Kelly Is Acquitted in Child Pornography Case." *New York Times*, June 14. www.nytimes.com.

Strickland, C. 2011. "Regulation without Agency: A Practical Response to Private Policing in *United States v. Day*." *North Carolina Law Review* 89:1338–62.

Strodtbeck, F., R. James, and G. Hawkins. 1957. "Social Status in Jury Deliberations." *American Sociological Review* 22:713–19.

Strom, K. J., and J. M. MacDonald 2007. "The Influence of Social and Economic Disadvantage on Racial Patterns in Youth Homicide over Time." *Homicide Studies* 11(1):50–69.

Strom, K., M. Berzofsky, B. Shook-Sa, K. Barrick, C. Daye, N. Horstmann, and S. Kinsey. 2010. *The Private Security Industry: A Review of the Definitions, Available Data Sources, and Paths Moving Forward*, report prepared for U.S. Bureau of Justice Statistics (December), https://www.ncjrs.gov/pdffiles1/bjs/grants/232781.pdf.

Stroshine, M. S. 2005. "Information Technology Innovations in Policing." In *Critical Issues in Policing*, 5th ed., ed. R. G. Dunham and G. P. Alpert. Long Grove, IL: Waveland Press, 172–83.

Struckman-Johnson, C., and D. Struckman-Johnson. 2013. "Stopping Prison Rape: The Evolution of Standards Recommended PREA's National Prison Rape Elimination Commission. *Prison Journal* 93:335–54.

Sullivan, C. 2014. "Legislature Looks at Softening Illegal Drug Punishments." MyNorthwest.com, January 15. http://mynorthwest.com/11/2433407/Legislature-looks-at-softening-illegal-drug-punishments.

Sullivan, E. 2013. "Local Police Grapple with Response to Cybercrimes." *Lexington Herald Leader*. April 13. http://www.kentucky.com.

Sullivan, J. 2009. "New Statewide Database Tracks Sex Offenders." *Seattle Times*, March 10. www.seattletimes.com.

Sullivan, K. M. 2003. "Under a Watchful Eye: Incursions on Personal Privacy." In *The War on Our Freedoms: Civil Liberties in an Age of Terrorism*, ed. R. C. Leone and G. Anrig Jr. New York: Public Affairs, 128–46.

Summers, A., R. D. Hayward, and M. Miller. 2010. "Death Qualification as Systematic Exclusion of Jurors with Certain Religious and Other Characteristics." *Journal of Applied Social Psychology* 40:3218–34.

Sundby, S. 2010. "War and Peace in the Jury Room: How Capital Juries Reach Unanimity." *Hastings Law Journal* 62:103–54.

Sung, C. 2014. "Chris Brown Loses Effort to Toss D.C. Assault Charge." CNN.com, April 7. www.cnn.com.

Sung, H., A. M. Mahoney, and J. Mellow. 2011. "Substance Abuse Treatment Gap among Adult Parolees: Prevalence, Correlates, and Barriers." *Criminal Justice Review* 36:40–77.

Swanson, E. 2013. "George Zimmerman Poll Finds Divide Over Not Guilty Verdict." *Huffington Post*, July 17. www.huffingtonpost.com.

Swarns, R. L. 2004. "Senator? Terrorist? A Watch List Stops Kennedy at Airport." *New York Times*, August 20. http://www.nytimes.com.

Swarz, J. 2004. "Inmates vs. Outsourcing." *USA Today*, July 6, p. 1.

Sykes, G. M. 1958. *The Society of Captives*. Princeton, NJ: Princeton University Press.

Taifa, N. 2002. Testimony on Behalf of American Civil Liberties Union of the National Capital Area Concerning Proposed Use of Surveillance Cameras, before the Joint Public Oversight Hearing Committee on the Judiciary, Council of the District of Columbia, June 13. http://www.dcwatch.com.

Tashima, A. W. 2008. "The War on Terror and the Rule of Law." *Asian American Law Journal* 15:245–65.

Taslitz, A. E. 2010. "Fourth Amendment Federalism and the Silencing of the American Poor." *Chicago-Kent Law Review* 85:277–312.

———. 2012. "High Expectations and Some Wounded Hopes: The Policy and Politics of a Uniform Statute on Videotaping Custodial Interrogations." *Northwestern Journal of Law and Social Policy* (forthcoming).

Taxman, F. S., and S. Belenko, 2013. *Implementing Evidence-Based Practices in Community Corrections and Addiction Treatment*. New York: Springer.

Taylor, B., C. Koper, and D. J. Woods. 2010. "A Randomized Controlled Trial of Different Policing Strategies at Hot Spots of Violent Crime." *Journal of Experimental Criminology* 7:149–81.

Taylor, M. 2009. *Achieving Better Outcomes for Adult Probation*. Sacramento: Legislative Analyst's Office (May).

Teeters, N. K., and J. D. Shearer. 1957. *The Prison at Philadelphia's Cherry Hill*. New York: Columbia University Press.

Telep, C., and D. Weisburd. 2012. "What Is Known About the Effectiveness of Police Practices in Reducing Crime and Disorder?" *Police Quarterly* 15:331–57.

Tepfer, D. 2013. "Towns to Pay $3.5M in Deadly Raid." *Connecticut Post*, February 20. http://www.ctpost.com.

Terrill, W. 2005. "Police Use of Force: A Transactional Approach." *Justice Quarterly* 22:107–38.

Terrill, W., and E. Paoline. 2012. "Conducted Energy Devices (CEDs) and Citizen Injuries: The Shocking Empirical Reality." *Justice Quarterly* 29:153–82.

Texas Board of Pardons and Paroles. 2013. *Annual Statistical Report—Fiscal Year 2012*. Austin, TX: Texas Board of Pardons and Paroles.

———. 2014. "Hearing Process." Texas Board of Pardons and Paroles website. http://www.tdcj.state.tx.us/bpp/publications/Hearings.pdf.

Texas Department of Criminal Justice. 2014. "Correctional Officer Salary."

Texas Department of Criminal Justice website. www.tdcj.state.tx.us.

Third Branch. 2008a. "Economics of CJA Regulations Costly to Attorneys." Administrative Office of the U.S. Courts. Vol. 40 (4), April. http://www.uscourts.gov.

———. 2008b. "National Summits Help Federal Courts Prepare for Sentence Reduction Requests." Administrative Office of the U.S. Courts. Vol. 40 (2), February, pp. 1–3, 6. http://www.uscourts.gov.

Thompson, G. 2009. "Couple's Capital Ties Said to Veil Spying for Cuba." *New York Times*, June 18. http://www.nytimes.com.

"Thumb on the Scale." 2013. *The Economist*. January 26. http://www.economist.com.

Thurman, Q., J. Zhao, and A. Giacomazzi. 2001. *Community Policing in a Community Era*. Los Angeles: Roxbury.

Tillman, Z. 2012. "D.C. Judicial Applicants, Complaints Up in 2011." *The Blog of the Legal Times*, February 24. http://legaltimes.typepad.com/blt/2012/02/dc-judicial-applicants-complaints-up-in-2011.html.

Toch, H. 1976. *Peacekeeping: Police, Prisons, and Violence*. Lexington, MA: Lexington Books.

Tonry, M. 1993. "Sentencing Commissions and Their Guidelines." In *Crime and Justice*, vol. 17, ed. M. Tonry. Chicago: University of Chicago Press.

———. 1995. *Malign Neglect: Race, Crime, and Punishment in America*. New York: Oxford University Press.

———. 2008. "Learning from the Limitations of Deterrence Research." *Crime and Justice* 37:279–307.

Tonry, M., and M. Lynch. 1996. "Intermediate Sanctions." In *Crime and Justice*, vol. 20, ed. M. Tonry. Chicago: University of Chicago Press, 99–144.

Toobin, J. 2007. "The CSI Effect." *New Yorker*, May 7. http://www.newyorker.com.

———. 2014. "'This is My Jail': Where Gang Members and Female Guards Set the Rules." *The New Yorker*, April 14th.

Toscano, P. 2011. "The Dangerous World of Counterfeit Prescription Drugs." *USA Today*. October 7. www.usatoday.com.

Travis, J. 2002. "Invisible Punishment: An Instrument of Social Exclusion." In *Invisible Punishment: The Collateral Consequences of Mass Imprisonment*, ed. M. Bauer and M. Chesney-Lind. New York: New Press, 15–36.

Travis, J., and J. Petersilia. 2001. "Reentry Reconsidered: A New Look at an Old Question." *Crime and Delinquency* 47 (July):291–313.

Truman, J. L., and Planty, M. 2002. "Criminal Victimization, 2011." *Bureau of Justice Statistics Bulletin*. October. NCJ239437.

Truman, J., and M. Rand. 2010. "Criminal Victimization 2009." Bureau of Justice Statistics *Bulletin*, October. NCJ 231327.

Tuohy, L. 2014. "New Hampshire House Votes to Repeal Death Penalty." *Boston Globe*, March 12. www.boston.com.

Tyler, K. A., and M. R. Beal. 2010. "The High-Risk Environment of Homeless Young Adults: Consequences for Physical and Sexual Victimization." *Violence and Victims* 25:101–15.

U.S. Bureau of Prisons. 2014. "About Our Facilities." Federal Bureau of Prisons website. www.bop.gov.

U.S. Department of Health and Human Services. 2007. "Illicit Drug Use, by Race/Ethnicity, in Metropolitan and Non-Metropolitan Counties: 2004 and 2005." *NSDUH Report* (National Survey on Drug Use and Health), June 21.

———. 2013. "Information on Poverty and Income Statistics: A Summary of 2013 Current Population Survey Data." *ASPE Issue Brief*, September 17. http://aspe.hhs.gov/hsp/13/PovertyAndIncomeEst/ib_poverty2013.pdf.

U.S. Department of Justice, 2011. "Department of Justice Disrupts International Cyber Crime Rings Distributing Scareware." *FBI National Press Releases*, June 22. www.fbi.gov.

———. 2012. "Justice Department Charges Leaders of Megaupload with Widespread Online Copyright Infringement." *FBI National Press Releases*, January 19. www.fbi.gov.

———. 2014. "Springfield Man Pleads Guilty to Trafficking Counterfeit Goods." Press Release, March 6. www.justice.gov.

U.S. Government Accountability Office. 2011. Bureau *of Prisons: Evaluating the Impact of Protective Equipment Could Help Enhance Officer Safety*. April. GAO-11–410.

U.S. Marshals Service. 2013. "Facts and Figures, 2013." U.S. Marshals Service website. January 10. www.usmarshals.gov.

U.S. President's Commission on Law Enforcement and Administration of Justice. 1967. *The Challenge of Crime in a Free Society*. Washington, DC: U.S. Government Printing Office.

U.S. Sentencing Commission. 2006. *Final Report on the Impact of* United States v. Booker *On Federal Sentencing* (Washington, DC: U.S. Sentencing Commission).

Uchida, C., and T. Bynum. 1991. "Search Warrants, Motions to Suppress and 'Lost Cases': The Effects of the Exclusionary Rule in Seven Jurisdictions." *Journal of Criminal Law and Criminology* 81:1034–66.

Ullman, S. 2007. "A 10-Year Update of 'Review and Critique of Empirical Studies of Rape Avoidance.'" *Criminal Justice and Behavior* 34:411–29.

Ulmer, J. T., J. Eisenstein, and B. Johnson. 2010. "Trial Penalties in Federal Sentencing: Extra-Guidelines Factors and District Variation." *Justice Quarterly* 27:560–92.

Ulmer, J. T., M. T. Light, and J. H. Kramer. 2011. "Racial Disparity in the Wake of the *Booker/Fanfan* Decision." *Criminology & Public Policy* 10(4):1077–118.

Unah, I. 2010. "Choosing Who Will Die: The Effect of Race, Gender, and Law in Prosecutorial Decisions to Seek the Death Penalty in Durham County, North Carolina." *Michigan Journal of Race and Law* 15:135–79.

"Under the Dome: Today Is February 1, the 20th Day of 60-Day Legislative Session." *The Olympian* (Olympia, WA), February 1, 2014 www.the olympian.com/2014/02/01/2960527/news-brief-01domes.html.

United Nations Office on Drugs and Crime (UNODC). 2011. *Research Report: Estimating Illicit Financial Flows Resulting from Drug Trafficking and Other Transnational Organized Crimes*. October. Vienna: UNODC.

Unnever, J. D. 2008. "Two Worlds Far Apart: Black-White Differences in Beliefs about Why African-American Men Are Disproportionately Imprisoned." *Criminology* 46:511–38.

Urbina, I. 2009. "Citing Cost, States Consider End to Death Penalty." *New York Times*, February 25. http://www.nytimes.com.

Urbina, I., and S. D. Hamill. 2009. "Judges Plead Guilty in Scheme to Jail Youths for Profit." *New York Times*, February 13, p. A1.

Utz, P. 1978. *Settling the Facts*. Lexington, MA: Lexington Books.

Valenzuela, B. 2012. "Parolee Arrested after Attacking Former Girlfriend." *Victorville Daily Press*, March 14. www.vvdailypress.com.

Valley, J. 2012. "Re-entry Programs Give Former Prisoners Hope in the Real World." *Las Vegas Sun*, August 23. www.lasvegassun.com.

Van Stelle, K., and J. Goodrich. 2009. *The 2008/2009 Study of Probation and Parole Revocation*. Madison: University of Wisconsin Population Health Institute (June).

Vaughn, M. S. 2001. "Assessing the Legal Liabilities in Law Enforcement: Chiefs' Views." *Crime and Delinquency* 47:3–27.

Vickovic, S., and M. L. Griffin. 2013. "A Comparison of Line and Supervisory Officers and the Impact of Support on Commitment to the Prison Organization." *Criminal Justice Policy Review* online edition, October 3.

Vidmar, N., and V. P. Hans. 2007. *American Juries: The Verdict*. New York: Prometheus Books.

Viser, M. 2013. "Tensions Emerge Over Lack of Tsarnaev Information Shared Between FBI, Local Authorities." *Boston Globe*, May 9. www.boston.com.

Visher, C., S. Debus-Sherrill, and J. Yahner. 2011. "Employment after Prison: A Longitudinal Study of Former Prisoners." *Justice Quarterly* 28:698–718.

Vitiello, M. 2008. "Punishing Sex Offenders: When Good Intentions Go Bad." *Arizona State Law Journal* 40:651–90.

Vives, R., and A. Blankstein. 2009. "A Mixed Reaction to a Use of Force." *Los Angeles Times*, May 15. http://www.latimes.com.

von Hirsch, A. 1976. *Doing Justice*. New York: Hill and Wang.

Wade, N. 2006. "Wider Use of DNA Lists Is Urged in Fighting Crime." *New York Times*, May 12. http://www.nytimes.com.

Wagner, J. 2014. "Md. Gubernatorial Hopeful Mizeur Introduces Bill that Would Decriminalize Marijuana." *Washington Post*, February 7. www.washingtonpost.com.

Waldman, E. 2007. "Restorative Justice and the Pre-Condition for Grace: Taking Victims' Needs Seriously." *Cardozo Journal of Conflict Resolution* 9:91–108.

Walker, R. N. 2006. "How the Malfunctioning Death Penalty Challenges the Criminal Justice System." *Judicature* 89 (5):265–69.

———. 1999. *The Police in America*. 3rd ed. New York: McGraw-Hill.

———. 2001. *Sense and Nonsense about Crime and Drugs: A Policy Guide*. 5th ed. Belmont, CA: Wadsworth.

Walker, S., and B. Wright. 1995. "Citizen Review of the Police, 1994: A National Survey." In *Fresh Perspectives*. Washington, DC: Police Executive Research Forum.

Walker, S., C. Spohn, and M. DeLone. 2007. *The Color of Justice: Race, Ethnicity, and Crime in America*, 4th ed. Belmont, CA: Wadsworth.

———. 2011. *The Color of Justice: Race, Ethnicity and Crime in America*, 5th ed. Belmont, CA: Cengage Wadsworth.

Walsh, D. 2013. "The Dangers of Eyewitness Identification: A Call for Greater State Involvement to Ensure Fundamental Fairness." *Boston College International and Comparative Law Review* 36:1415–1453.

Ward, M. 2012. "Parole Rates Surge to Avoid Unsupervised Cases." *Austin American-Statesman,* May 15. www.statesman.com.

Ward, S. 2011. "Tweeting Jurors to Face Jail Time with New California Law." *American Bar Association Journal*, August 8. www.abajournal.com.

Warren, J. 2008. *One in 100: Behind Bars in America 2008*. Washington, DC: Pew Center on the States.

Warren, J. 2011. "What Blagojevich's Sentence Says about Corruption and Greed." *New York Times*, December 8. www.nytimes.com.

Warren, P., D. Tomaskovic-Devey, W. Smith, M. Zingraff, and M. Mason. 2006. "Driving while Black: Bias Processes and Racial Disparity in Police Stops." *Criminology* 44:709–38.

Warren, R. 2007. "Evidence-Based Practices and State Sentencing Policy: Ten Policy Initiatives to Reduce Recidivism." *Indiana Law Journal* 82:1307–17.

Washburn, K. K. 2008. "Restoring the Grand Jury." *Fordham Law Review* 76:2333–88.

Wasserman, D. T. 1990. *A Sword for the Convicted: Representing Indigent Defendants on Appeal*. New York: Greenwood Press.

Weiner, J. 2013a. "Monitoring Programs Have History of Trouble." *Orlando Sentinel*. May 25. http://www.orlandosentinel.com.

———. 2013b. "Review of Home Confinement Program Finds Lost Defendants, New Crime." *Orlando Sentinel*. March 23. http://www.orlandosentinel.com.

Weinstein, H. 2001. "Georgia High Court Relegates Electric Chair to History." *Los Angeles Times*, October 6. http://www.latimes.com.

Weisberg, R. 2010. "The Not-So-Golden State of Sentencing and Corrections: California's Lessons for the Nation." *Justice Research and Policy* 12:133–68.

Weisburd, D. 2011. "The Evidence for Place-Based Policing." *Translational Criminology* (Summer), 10–11, 16.

Weisburd, D., C. Telep, J. Hinkle, and J. Eck. 2010. "Is Problem-Oriented Policing Effective in Reducing Crime and Disorder?" *Criminology & Public Policy* 9:139–72.

Weisburd, D., C. W. Telep, J. C. Hinkle, and J. E. Eck. 2010. "Is Problem-Oriented Policing Effective in Reducing Crime and Disorder?" *Criminology & Public Policy* 9:139–72.

Weisburd, D., S. D. Mastrofski, A. M. McNally, R. Greenspan, and J. J. Willis. 2003. "Reforming to Preserve: Compstat and Strategic Problem Solving in American Policing." *Criminology & Public Policy* 2:421–56.

Weiser, B. 2008. "Police in Gun Searches Face Disbelief in Court." *New York Times*, May 12, p. 1.

———. 2011. "A New York Prosecutor with Worldwide Reach." *New York Times*, March 27. www.nytimes.com.

Weiss, D. C. 2008. "New DOJ Rule Expands FBI Database to Include Arrestee DNA." *American Bar Association Journal*, December 12. http://abajournal.com.

———. 2009a. "Calif. DA Dismisses Misdemeanor and Drug Charges in Exchange for DNA." *American Bar Association Journal*, April 15. http://abajournal.com.

———. 2009b. "Fear of Financial Ruin Has More Potential Jurors Claiming Hardship." *American Bar Association Journal*, September 2. www.abajournal.com.

Weisselberg, C. 2011. "Selected Criminal Law Cases in the United States Supreme Court and a Look Ahead." *Court Review* 47:52–62.

Weisselberg, C. D. 2008. "Mourning *Miranda*." *California Law Review* 96:1519–600.

Weitzer, R. 2002. "Incidents of Police Misconduct and Public Opinion." *Journal of Criminal Justice* 30:397–408.

Welch, M. 1994. "Jail Overcrowding: Social Sanitation and the Warehousing of the Urban Underclass." In *Critical Issues in Crime and Justice*, ed. A. Roberts. Thousand Oaks, CA: Sage, 249–74.

Wells, J., and M. Keasler. 2011. "Criminal Procedure: Confessions, Searches, and Seizures." *Southern Methodist University Law Review* 64:199–220.

Welsh-Huggins, A. 2013a. "Steubenville Rape Case Moves Forward with Search Warrants." The Huffington Post. April 25th. www.huffingtonpost.com.

———. 2013b. "Steubenville Rape: Teen Girls GUILTY of Threatening Rape Victim on Twitter." The Huffington Post. May 2nd. www.huffingtonpost.com.

Wert, J. 2011. *Habeas Corpus in America*. Lawrence, KS: University of Kansas Press.

Westergaard, R., A. Spaulding, and T. Flanigan. 2013. "HIV Among Persons Incarcerated in the U.S.: A Review of Evolving Concepts in Testing, Treatment, and Linkage to Community Care." *Current Opinion in Infectious Diseases* 26:10–16.

Whetzel, J., M. Paparozzi, M. Alexander, and C. T. Lowenkamp. 2011. "Goodbye to a Worn-Out Dichotomy: Law Enforcement, Social Work, and a Balanced Approach (A Survey of Federal Probation Officer Attitudes)." *Federal Probation* 75:7–12.

White, J. 2004. *Defending the Homeland*. Belmont, CA: Thomson/Wadsworth.

White, M. D., J. Cooper, J. Saunders, and A. J. Raganella. 2010. "Motivations for Becoming a Police Officer: Re-assessing Officer Attitudes and Job Satisfaction After Six Years on the Street. *Journal of Criminal Justice* 38:520–30.

White, M. D., J. Fyfe, S. Campbell, and J. Goldkamp. 2003. "The Police Role in Preventing Homicide: Considering the Impact of Problem-oriented Policing on the Prevalence of Murder." *Journal of Research in Crime and Delinquency* 40:194–225.

White, M. S. 1995. "The Nonverbal Behaviors in Jury Selection." *Criminal Law Bulletin* 31:414–45.

White, T., and E. Baik. 2010. "Venire Reform: Assessing the State and Federal Efforts to Attain Fair, Cross-Sectional Representation in Jury Pools." *Journal of Social Sciences* 6:113–18.

Wian, C., J. Spellman, and M. Pearson. 2013. "New Details Emerge in Hearing for Colorado Theater Shooting Suspect." CNN.com, January 8. www.cnn.com.

Williams, C. J. 2010. "Weighed Down by Recession Woes, Jurors Are Becoming Disgruntled." *Los Angeles Times*, February 15. www.latimes.com.

Williams, M. R., S. Demuth, and J. E. Holcomb. 2007. "Understanding the Influence of Victim Gender in Death Penalty Cases: The Importance of Victim Race, Sex-Related Victimization, and Jury Decision Making." *Criminology* 45:865–91.

Williams, V., and M. Fish. 1974. *Convicts, Codes, and Contraband*. Cambridge, MA: Ballinger.

Willis, J. J., S. D. Mastrofski, and D. Weisbrud. 2004. "Compstat and Bureaucracy: A Case Study of Challenges and Opportunities for Change." *Justice Quarterly* 21:463–96.

Willis, J., S. Mastrofski, and T. Kochel. 2010. "Recommendations for Integrating Compstat and Community Policing." *Policing: A Journal of Policy and Practice* 4:182–93.

Winkeljohn, M. 2002. "A Random Act of Hate: Duckett's Attack Linked to Racism." *Atlanta Journal and Constitution*, August 4, p. E1.

Winterdyk, J., and R. Ruddell. 2010. "Managing Prison Gangs: Results from a Survey of U.S. Prison Systems." *Journal of Criminal Justice* 38:730–36.

Wiseman, S. 2009. "Discrimination, Coercion, and the Bail Reform Act of 1984." *Fordham Urban Law Journal* 26:121–57.

Witt, H. 2009. "Highway Robbery? Texas Police Seize Black Motorists' Cash, Cars." *Chicago Tribune*, March 10. www.chicagotribune.com.

Witte, B. 2013. "Maryland Death Penalty Repeal Signed Into Law by Martin O'Malley." *Huffington Post*, May 2. http://www.huffingtonpost.com.

WKYC. 2014. "Steubenville Rape Case Defendant/Coach Found Guilty." WKYC News, April 22nd. http://www.wkyc.com.

Wodahl, E. J., B. Garland, S. E. Culhane, and William P. McCarty. 2011. "Utilizing Behavioral Interventions to Improve Supervision Outcomes in Community-Based Corrections." *Criminal Justice and Behavior* 38:386–405.

Wolf, A., B. E. Bloom, and B. A. Krisberg. 2008. "The Incarceration of Women in California." *University of San Francisco Law Review* 43:139–70.

Wood, R. W. 2013. "Lauryn Hill Jail Time—What's a Fair Tax Sentence?" *Forbes*. May 7. http://www.forbes.com.

Wooldredge, J. 2012. "Distinguishing Race Effects in Pre-Trial Release and Sentencing Decisions." *Justice Quarterly* 29:41–75.

Wooley, B. 2011. "Inside the Montana Women's Prison: Preparing for Reentry." KAJ18 News, November 4. www.kaj18.com.

Worden, A. P. 1993. "The Attitudes of Women and Men in Policing: Testing Conventional and Contemporary Wisdom." *Criminology* 31 (May):203–24.

———. 1995. "The Judge's Role in Plea Bargaining: An Analysis of Judges' Agreement with Prosecutors' Sentencing Recommendations." *Justice Quarterly* 12:257–78.

Worth, R. F. 2001. "73 Tied to Genovese Family Are Indicted, Officials Say." *New York Times*, December 6, p. A27.

Wright, J. 2013. "Applying *Miranda*'s Public Safety Exception to Dzhokhar Tsarnaev: Restricting Criminal Procedure Rights By Expanding Judicial Exceptions." *Columbia Law Review Sidebar* 113:136–55.

Wright, K., and J. Rosky, 2011. "Too Early Is Too Soon: Lessons from the Montana Department of Corrections Early Release Program." *Criminology & Public Policy* 10:881–908.

Wu, J., and C. Spohn. 2010. "Interdistrict Disparity in Sentencing in Three U.S. District Courts." *Crime and Delinquency* 56:290–322.

Wyoming Board of Parole. 2014. "Frequently Asked Questions." Wyoming Board of Parole website. http://boardofparole.wy.gov/faq/faq.htm.

Wyoming Highway Patrol. 2014. "WHP Advances to In-Car Computer Aided Dispatch and Reporting." Press Release, January 17. www.whp.dot.state.wy.us.

Yang, J. L, and A. Jayakumar. 2014. "Target Says Up to 70 Million More Customers Were Hit by December Data Breach." *Washington Post*, January 10, 2014. www.washingtonpost.com.

Yardley, W. 2006. "DNA Samples Link 4 Murders in Connecticut." *New York Times*, June 8. http://www.nytimes.com.

Zagaris, B. 1998. "U.S. International Cooperation against Transnational Organized Crime." *Wayne Law Review* 44 (Fall):1401–64.

Zaitz, L. 2011. "Oregon Taxpayers Pay Spiraling Cost of Prison Health Care with No Solution in Sight." June 18, 2011. http://oregonlive.com.

Zak, D. 2012. "Newtown School Shooting's First Responders Deal with Searing Memories." *Washington Post*, December 30. http://www.washingtonpost.com.

Zalman, M., and B. W. Smith. 2007. "The Attitudes of Police Executives toward *Miranda* and Interrogation Policies." *Journal of Criminal Law and Criminology* 97:873–942.

Zedlewski, E. 2010. "Alternatives to Custodial Supervision: The Day Fine." National Institute of Justice Discussion Paper, April. NCJ 230401. https://www.ncjrs.gov/pdffiles1/nij/grants/230401.pdf.

Zedner, L. 1995. "Wayward Sisters." In *The Oxford History of Prisons*, ed. N. Morris and D. J. Rothman. New York: Oxford University Press, 329–61.

Zeidman, S. 2012. "Whither the Criminal Court: Confronting Stops-and-Frisks." *Albany Law Review* 76:1187–9.

Zhao, J. S., N. P. He, N. Loverich, and J. Cancino. 2003. "Marital Status and Police Occupational Stress." *Journal of Crime & Justice* 26:23–46.

Zhao, J., C. Gibson, N. Lovrich, and M. Gaffney. 2002. "Participation in Community Crime Prevention: Are Volunteers More or Less Fearful of Crime?" *Journal of Crime & Justice* 25:41–61.

Zimmerman, E. 2011. "The Federal Sentencing Guidelines: A Misplaced Trust." *University of Michigan Journal of Law Reform* 43:841–70.

Zimring, F. E. 2007. *The Great American Crime Decline*. New York: Oxford University Press.

Greene, E., 280
Greene, J. A., 164
Greene, J. R., 155, 158
Greenspan, R., 156
Greer, K., 380
Gregorian, D., 149, 157, 213
Gregoriou, M., 506
Grieco, J., 162
Griffen, W., 227
Griffin, K., 234
Griffin, L., 99
Griffin, M. L., 364, 368
Griffin, P., 500, 506
Grissom, B., 514
Groff, E. R., 164
Gross, J. P., 244
Gross-Shader, C., 155
Grubman, S., 212
Gueco, S., 198
Guerino, P., 354, 379, 393
Guevara, L., 511
Gunnell, J. J., 279
Gustafson, R., 383
Gustafson, S., 231
Gutierrez, L., 404

Haarr, R. N., 128, 132, 382
Haba, C., 128
Habes, H., 373
Hackett, D. P., 132
Hagan, F. E., 49
Hails, J., 167
Hall, J., 83, 84
Hall, M., 228
Hallinan, J. T., 392
Halprin, R., 302
Hambling, D., 477
Hamill, S. D., 336
Hamilton, W., 50, 446
Handy, R., 425
Hanley, D., 392
Hanlon, M., 477
Hannaford-Agor, P., 272
Hans, V., 101, 272, 280
Hanson, R. A., 246, 281
Harcourt, B. E., 164
Harfield, C., 47
Harkin, T., 31
Harlow, C., 241
Harlow, C. W., 337, 372
Harrell, E., 60, 457
Harrington, W., 441
Harris, C., 99
Harris, J. C., 248
Harris, M. B., 328, 461
Harris, R., 150
Harrison, C., 273
Harrison, M. T., 372
Harrison, P. M., 263, 354, 372, 379
Hartley, R., 34
Hartnett, S. M., 492
Hassell, K., 128, 165
Hastie, R., 280
Hathaway, W., 67
Hawk-Tourtelot, S., 132
Hawkins, G., 280
Hayden, J., 136
Hays, J., 466

Hayward, R. D., 303, 305
He, N. P., 132, 165
Healy, D., 48
Heaphy, W., 221
Heffernan, E., 328
Heil, E., 31
Heimer, K., 72
Heise, M., 281
Hemmens, C., 507
Hennessey-Fiske, M., 318
Henley, P., 279
Henning, K., 89–90
Henrichson, C., 351
Henry, S., 71
Hensley, J. J., 169, 473
Hepburn, J. R., 368
Heraux, C. G., 149
Herberman, E. J., 20, 349, 351, 352, 400, 430
Herbert, S., 131
Herley, C., 457
Hernson, P. S., 228
Herrnstein, R., 66
Herz, D., 511
Hewitt, J. D., 67
Hickman, M., 164
Hickman, M. J., 471
Hickok, W. B., 113–114
Hicks, W., 139
Higgins, G., 170, 379
Higgins, K. J., 458
Hill, L., 287–288, 293
Hillard, G., 140
Hinkle, J. C., 116, 165
Hinckley, J., 92
Hinduja, S., 456, 516
Hinton, J., 177
Hirsch, A. J., 323
Hirsch, M., 260
Hirschel, D., 148
Hirschi, T., 69
Hirshkorn, P., 194
Hoberock, B., 335
Hochstetler, A., 390
Hockenberry, S., 501, 504, 511
Hoctor, M., 148
Hodge, W. T., 312
Hoffman, M., 273
Hoffman, P. S., 31
Hoffmann, J., 281
Holcomb, J. E., 302
Holder, E., 426
Holleran, D., 236, 256, 316
Holmes, J., 77–78, 85, 91
Holmes, T. J., 34
Holt, T., 58, 457
Holtfreter, K., 382
Homan, C., 296
Hooks, G., 335
Hoover, J. E., 119
Horne, P., 128
Horstmann, N., 182
Horwitz, J., 173
Hostick, T., 389
Hough, K., 280
Houston, O., 14
Howard, J., 323, 324
Howie, C., 412

Howlett, D., 473
Hsu, T., 50
Huang, H., 513
Hudson, J., 403
Huebner, B. M., 383
Huether, K., 196
Huey, L., 277, 482
Huff, C. R., 255, 317
Huguely, G., 67
Humes, K. R., 224
Humke, A., 478
Hummer, D., 395
Hunt, K., 194
Hurdle, J., 149
Hureau, D. M., 162
Hurst, V., 248
Hurtig, J., 409
Hutchinson, I., 148
Hutchinson, V. A., 339
Hutt, A. V., 85, 86

Ingold, J., 367
Iribarren, C. J., 67
Irwin, J., 375, 376, 513
Israelsen, B., 193
Ith, I., 477

Jacobs, C. , 220, 225
Jacobson, G., 43
Jaksic, V., 245
Jalbert, S. K., 418
James, R., 280
Jardines, J., 187–188
Jayakumar, A., 456
Jesilow, P., 248
Johnson, A., 322
Johnson, B., 269
Johnson, B. D., 34, 308
Johnson, C., 243
Johnson, J., 253–254
Johnson, J. L., 403, 405
Johnson, K., 32, 48, 77, 80, 133
Johnson, K. D., 506, 507
Johnson, L. A., 261, 262
Johnson, M., 261, 262
Johnson, M. A., 468, 471
Johnson, R., 149
Jones, C., 25, 38–41, 436–437
Jones, J., 305
Jones, N. A., 224
Jordan, J., 128
Jordan, W. L., 126

Kagan, E., 105, 200, 221, 303
Kainen, J., 210
Kanaracus, C., 465
Kane, R., 45
Kang, W., 57, 492, 505, 511
Kanka, M., 444
Kaplan, T., 468, 470
Kapur, T. D., 339
Karberg, J. C., 263, 370, 392, 393
Karmen, A., 57, 411
Karnow, C. E. A., 258
Karnowski, 117
Karp, D. R., 293
Kaufman, L., 226
Kaufman, R., 29

Martindale, M., 431
Martinez, M., 217, 287
Martinez, R., Jr., 181
Martinson, R., 292, 329
Maruschak, L. M., 352, 373, 383, 402, 406, 408, 421, 440
Marzulli, John, 142
Mascaro, L., 175
Maschke, K. J., 234
Mason, M., 32
Masterson, B., 113
Mastrofski, S. D., 130, 156, 158, 166
Mauer, M., 433, 444
Maxson, C. L., 492, 515
Maxwell, C., 70, 149
Maxwell, S. R., 70, 261
May, J. D., 198
Mays, T., 489
Maynard-Moody, S., 169, 170
Mayo-Wilson, E., 415
Mayrack, B., 296
Mayweather, F., Jr., 15, 35
Mazerolle, L. D., 155
McAuliff, B., 275
McCall, M., 169, 219
McCall, M. A., 100, 105, 213
McCall, M. M., 100, 105, 213
McCampbell, S. W., 382
McCarthy, B., 126, 180
McCartney, A., 254
McCarty, W. P., 418
McCleskey, W., 302
McCluskey, C. P., 169
McCluskey, J. D., 58, 130
McCollister, K. E., 62
McCormick, J., 480
McCoy, C., 264, 266
McCoy, J., 124
McDevitt, J., 502
McDonnell, R., 304
McDonough, K., 489
McFarlane, L., 382
McGarrell, E., 163, 166, 492
McGinty, T., 217
McGreevy, P., 308
McGuinness, M., 466
McKee, T. A., 223
McKelvey, B., 327
McKinley, J. C., 287
McKinley, W., 120
McLaughlin, E., 218
McMahon, P., 463
McNalley, A., 156
McNeely, T., 200
McNulty, T. L., 31
McVeigh, T., 49
Meade, B., 419, 446
Mears, B., 455
Mednick, S. A., 66
Megerian, C., 308
Meier, B., 87
Meier, R. F., 58, 60
Meisner, J., 151
Melde, C., 59, 492, 515
Melendez, L., 153, 225
Mellow, J., 444
Menard, S., 57
Mensink, J., 151

Mentzer, A., 121
Merrill, E. S., 507
Merton, R., 68
Messerschmidt, J. W., 72
Messner, S. F., 65, 68, 164
Michelsen, B. J., 235
Miethe, T., 55, 58, 60, 63
Mihm, S., 460
Milhizer, E., 85
Miller, C. M., 419
Miller, M., 303, 305, 371, 463
Miller, S., 169
Miller, T., 43–44, 64
Mills, S., 304
Minton, T. D., 336, 337
Miroff, N., 336
M'Naghten, D., 91
Monkkonen, E. H., 113
Montemayor, C., 256
Moore, E. C., 226
Moore, M., 165
Moore, M. H., 112, 116
Moore, P., 271
Moore, S., 87, 351, 455, 471
Moore, T., 470
Moran, R., 454
Morani, N., 221
Morash, M., 128, 132, 165, 382
Morgan, S., 89, 167, 455
Moroney, N., 506
Morris, H., 456
Morris, N., 91, 298, 410
Morrison, D., 471
Moses, P., 52
Mosher, C., 55, 335
Mosteller, R., 230
Mueller, R., 171
Mumola, C. J., 390
Murphy, P. V., 112, 165
Murray, L., 473
Muscat, B., 382
Musgrave, S., 463
Muskal, M., 217, 218
Myers, D. L., 292
Myers, E., 292

Na, C., 502
Najaka, S. S., 226
Nakamura, D., 174
Nakashima, E., 176
Nalla, M., 179
Napolitano, L., 170
Narag, R. E., 264
Nardulli, P. F., 267
Nava, M., 224
Nesbitt, E., 302
Newport, F., 306
Ngugi, B., 458
Nir, S., 457
Noblet, A., 132
Nolan, J. L., 226
Nolasco, C., 212
Nottingham, S., 77–78, 91
Nyrop, K., 32

Obama, B., 105, 117, 174, 176, 194, 303, 316, 485
Oberfield, Z. W., 129

O'Brien, B., 232
O'Brien, C., 50
Ochoa, R., 273
O'Connor, A., 87
O'Connor, L., 510
O'Connor, S. D., 228, 304
O'Harrow, R., 173
O'Hear, M. M., 268
O'Keefe, K., 268
Oldfather, C., 102
Oleniacz, L., 506
Oppel, R. A., 335, 336
Osborne, J., 339
Ostermann, M., 416
Ostrom, B., 282
O'Sullivan, C. S., 148
Oulson, C., 43, 64
Outlaw, M., 55
Oviatt, J., 77
Owen, B., 380, 381

Pabst, K., 253
Packer, H., 27, 28
Padgett, K., 63
Palmer, B., 333
Palmer, T., 387
Paoline, E., 129, 477
Papachristos, A. V., 162
Papparozzi, M., 405
Parascandola, R., 151
Parent, D., 419
Park, J-K., 228
Parkman, T., 444
Parks, R., 166
Pasquale-Styles, M., 150
Patchin, J. W., 58, 456, 516
Pate, T., 163
Patrick, A. O., 474
Patterson, S., 279
Pearce, M., 217, 218
Pearson, M., 77
Peart, N., 29, 30
Peel, R., 91, 111
Peery, D., 271
Pennington, N., 280
Penrod, S., 278, 280
Pepey, T., 414
Peralta, E., 474
Perez, D. M., 394
Perin, M., 174
Perrine, J., 173
Persons, V., 339
Petersilia, J., 418, 421, 427, 432, 441, 446
Peterson, D., 515
Peterson, J. L., 471
Peterson, M., 14, 117, 124
Petteruti, A., 337, 502
Peveto, K., 463
Pfingst, L., 32
Pheifer, P., 249
Phelps, J. R., 228
Phelps, M., 387
Phillips, D., 55
Phillips, M., 259
Phillips, S., 278
Pinkerton, J., 208
Piquero, A. R., 66
Piquero, N. L., 68, 502

Smith, B. W., 206
Smith, C. E., 100, 101, 105, 169, 205, 213, 219, 220, 225, 246, 262, 273, 281, 282, 299, 340, 342, 343, 345, 436
Smith, E. L., 61
Smith, J., 274
Smith, L., 442
Smith, S., 29
Smith, W., 32
Snipes, W., 288, 312
Snowden, E., 49, 175
Snyder, H. N., 490, 507, 512, 513
Soltani, A., 485
Sommers, S., 272
Sorensen, J. R., 230, 506
Sotomayor, S., 105, 200, 201, 221, 303, 498
Spangenberg, R., 245
Sparrow, M. K., 116
Spaulding, A., C., 374
Spears, J. W., 236
Specht, S., 249
Speirs, V., 173
Spellman, J., 77–78, 91
Spencer, C., 476
Spencer, M., 455
Spitzer, S., 70
Spohn, C., 29, 30, 31, 34, 170, 230, 236, 256, 315, 316, 511
St. Clair, S., 154, 238, 277
Staba, D., 470
Stafford, M. C., 290
Stahl, A., 492
Stahlkopf, C., 291
Stanko, E., 236
Stanley, K., 57
Staples, B., 295
Starr, S., 316
Steadham, J. A., 207
Stecklow, S., 474
Steden, R., 178
Steen, S., 316
Steffensmeier, D., 31, 311, 312, 316
Stein, A., 312
Steinberg, J., 57
Steinberg, L., 66
Steiner, B., 419, 446, 507
Stensland, J., 234
Stephan, J. J., 370, 386, 387, 392, 393, 442
Stephens, M., 234
Stephens, S., 160, 482
Sterbenz, C., 318
Stevens, J. P., 194
Steward, D., 32
Stewart, E., 170
Stewart, E. A., 72–73
Stewart, P., 265
Stickels, J. W., 235
Stimpson, A., 389
Stoddard, E. R., 152
Stojkovic, S., 367
Stolzenberg, L., 313, 384
Stone, C., 33
Stracuzzi, N., 248
Strauchs, J. J., 178
Strauss, G., 318
Streib, V., 255

Streifel, C., 312
Streitfeld, D., 276
Sterling, J., 217
Strickland, C., 181
Strodtbeck, F., 280
Strom, K., 178, 182, 182, 491
Stroshine, M. S., 465
Sullivan, E., 462
Sullivan, J., 444
Sullivan, K. M., 175
Sullivan, T., 414
Summers, A., 303, 305
Sundby, S, 280
Sung, D., 399
Sung, H-E., 444
Sutherland, E., 69
Sutherland, S., 256
Swarns, R. L., 467
Swarz, J., 387
Swift, A., 354
Sykes, G. M., 375
Szpaller, K., 253–254

Taifa, N., 474
Taniguchi, T., 164
Tardiff, K. J., 164
Tashima, A. W., 257
Taslitz, A. E., 98, 474
Tauber, J., 447
Taxman, F. S., 409
Taylor, B., 162, 164
Taylor, M., 407
Taylor, T. J., 492, 515
Teeters, N. K., 325
Telep, C., 116, 155, 162, 163, 165
Tepfer, D., 154
Terrill, W., 130, 477
Tewsbury, R., 132, 379
Thomas, C., 194, 201, 221, 344
Thomas, P., 279
Thompson, G., 49
Thompson, L, 177
Thurman, Q., 165
Thurston, H., 495
Tillman, Z., 223
Tillyer, R., 150
Tissinger, S., 51
Toch, H., 392
Tomaskovic-Devey, D., 32
Tonry, M., 35, 290, 298, 313, 410, 421
Toobin, J., 481, 506
Toppo, G., 466
Torres, S., 382
Toscano, P., 461
Totman, M., 32
Tracy, M., 164
Travis, J., 427, 444, 446,
Treadwell, H. M., 382
Trulson, C. R., 64
Tucker-Gail, K. A., 133
Truman, J., 18, 52, 55, 56, 59, 61, 62, 148
Trzcinski, E., 512
Tsarnaev, D., 451
Tsarnaev, T., 451
Tuohy, L., 305
Turner, J., 175

Tuthill, P., 466
Tyler, K. A., 58
Tyler, T., 211
Tyson, H., 236

Uchida, C., 112, 117, 165, 210
Ulmer, J., 29, 269, 316
Unah, I., 230
Unnever, J. D., 32
Urbina, I., 305, 336
Utz, P., 267

Valdmanis, T., 126
Valenzuela, B., 425
Valley, F., 443
VanBenschoten, S., 409
van Gemert, F., 515
Van Meter, C. W., 178
Van Stelle, K., 406
Varano, S., 164
Varano, S. P., 58
Vaughn, M., 150, 154, 212
Vernick, J. S., 309
Vetter, W., 339
Vick, M., 238
Vickovic, S., 364
Vidmar, N., 101, 280
Vila, B., 132
Vilcica, E. R., 164
Violanti, J. M., 132
Visher, C., 427
Vitiello, M., 291
Vives, R., 474
Vlahov, D., 132
Volavka, J., 66
Vollmer, A., 114–115
von Hirsch, A., 289

Wade, N., 470
Wakeman, S. E., 392
Waldman, E., 293
Walker, R. N., 302
Walker, S., 25, 30, 31, 34, 112, 117, 153, 155, 170, 210, 230, 254
Wallace, D. H., 230
Walsh, K. A., 469
Walsh, M., 452
Walsh, N., 337
Walsh, R., 207
Ward, S., 445, 481
Warr, M., 290
Warren, E., 97 103, 210
Warren, J., 290, 321
Warren, P., 32, 127
Warren, R., 297
Washburn, K. K., 99
Wasserman, D. T., 281
Watson, R., 389
Webster, D. W., 309
Weerman, F. M., 515
Wehrman, M., 170
Wehrwein, , K., 414
Weiner, J., 415, 421
Weinstein, H., 455
Weintraub, C., 217
Weisberg, R., 256
Weisburd, D., 116, 156, 162, 163, 165